Ian Hay, Collection novels

In this book:
The First Hundred Thousand
All In It K(1) Carries On
A Continuation of the
First Hundred Thousand
The Willing Horse
A Safety Match
Happy-go-lucky
The Right Stuff, Some Episodes
in the Career of a North Briton
Getting Together

Major General John Hay Beith, (1876 – 1952), was a British novelist, playwright, essayist and historian who wrote under the pen name Ian Hay. During the First World War, Beith served as an officer in the army in France. His good-humoured account of army life, The First Hundred Thousand, published in 1915, was a best-seller. He made a considerable career as a dramatist, writing light comedies, often in collaboration with other authors including P. G. Wodehouse and Guy Bolton.

In this book:

The First Hundred Thousand

BOOK ONE	7
II	8
III	10
IV	11
V	13
VI	16
VII	21
VIII	29
IX	32
X	35
XI	42
XII	46
XIII	50
BOOK TWO	55
XIV	55
XV	59
XVI	63
XVII	67
XVIII	69
XIX	77
XX	86

| XXI | 89 |

All In It K(1) Carries On A Continuation of the First Hundred Thousand 99
- AUTHOR'S NOTE 99
- I 99
- II 104
- III 110
- IV 118
- V 120
- VI 127
- VII 135
- VIII 141
- IX 150
- X 155
- XI 158
- XII 163
- XIII 166

The Willing Horse 172
A Safety Match 260
- CHAPTER ONE. 260
- CHAPTER TWO. 265
- CHAPTER THREE. 268
- CHAPTER FOUR. 272
- CHAPTER FIVE. 278
- CHAPTER SIX. 283
- CHAPTER SEVEN. 286
- CHAPTER EIGHT. 288
- BOOK TWO. 291

FLICKERINGS. 291
- CHAPTER NINE. 291
- CHAPTER TEN. 296
- CHAPTER ELEVEN. 301

- CHAPTER TWELVE. 306
- CHAPTER THIRTEEN. 309
- CHAPTER FOURTEEN. 315
- CHAPTER FIFTEEN. 318
- BOOK THREE. 320

THE LIGHTING OF THE CANDLE. 320
- CHAPTER SIXTEEN. 320
- CHAPTER SEVENTEEN. 322
- CHAPTER EIGHTEEN. 326
- CHAPTER NINETEEN. 329
- CHAPTER TWENTY. 331
- CHAPTER TWENTY-ONE. 333
- CHAPTER TWENTY-TWO. 335
- CHAPTER TWENTY-THREE. 338
- CHAPTER TWENTY-FOUR. 340

Happy-go-lucky 343

The Right Stuff, Some Episodes in the Career of a North Briton 436
- CHAPTER ONE. 436
  - OATMEAL AND THE SHORTER CATECHISM. 436
- CHAPTER TWO. 440
  - INTRODUCES A PILLAR OF STATE AND THE APPURTENANCES THEREOF. 440
- CHAPTER THREE. 444
  - "ANENT." 444
- CHAPTER FOUR. 446
  - A TRIAL TRIP. 446
- CHAPTER FIVE. 450
  - ROBIN ON DUTY. 450
- CHAPTER SIX. 453
  - ROBIN OFF DUTY. 453
- CHAPTER SEVEN. 458

- A DISSOLUTION OF PARTNERSHIP. 458
- CHAPTER EIGHT. 463
  - OF A PIT THAT WAS DIGGED, AND WHO FELL INTO IT. 463
- CHAPTER NINE. 471
  - THE POLICY OF THE CLOSED DOOR. 471
- CHAPTER TEN. 474
  - ROBIN'S WAY OF DOING IT. 474
- BOOK TWO. 478
  - THE FINISHED ARTICLE 478
- CHAPTER ELEVEN. 478
  - A MISFIRE. 478
- CHAPTER TWELVE. 487
  - THE COMPLEAT ANGLER. 487
- CHAPTER THIRTEEN. 491
  - A HOSTAGE TO FORTUNE. 491
- CHAPTER FOURTEEN. 496
  - "TO DIE—WILL BE AN *AWFULLY* BIG ADVENTURE!" — *Peter Pan*. 496
- CHAPTER FIFTEEN. 500
  - TWO BATTLES. 500
- CHAPTER SIXTEEN. 503
  - "QUI PERD, GAGNE." 503
- CHAPTER SEVENTEEN. 507
  - IN WHICH ALL'S RIGHT WITH THE WORLD. 507
- CHAPTER EIGHTEEN. 509
  - A PROPHET IN HIS OWN COUNTRY. 509

Getting Together 511
- CHAPTER ONE 511
- CHAPTER TWO 511
- CHAPTER THREE 512
- CHAPTER FOUR 514

CHAPTER FIVE	517
CHAPTER SIX	519
CHAPTER SEVEN	520

The First Hundred Thousand

BOOK ONE

BLANK CARTRIDGES

The First Hundred Thousand

I
AB OVO

"Squoad—*'Shun!* Move to the right in fours. Forrm—*fourrrs!*"

The audience addressed looks up with languid curiosity, but makes no attempt to comply with the speaker's request.

"Come away now, come away!" urges the instructor, mopping his brow. "Mind me: on the command 'form fours,' odd numbers will stand fast; even numbers tak' a shairp pace to the rear and anither to the right. Now—forrm *fourrs!*"

The squad stands fast, to a man. Apparently—nay, verily—they are all odd numbers.

The instructor addresses a gentleman in a decayed Homburg hat, who is chewing tobacco in the front rank.

"Yous, what's your number?"

The ruminant ponders.

"Seeven fower ought seeven seeven," he announces, after a prolonged mental effort.

The instructor raises clenched hands to heaven.

"Man, I'm no askin' you your regimental number! Never heed that. It's your number in the squad I'm seeking. You numbered off frae the right five minutes syne."

Ultimately it transpires that the culprit's number is ten. He is pushed into his place, in company with the other even numbers, and the squad finds itself approximately in fours.

"Forrm—two *deep!*" barks the instructor.

The fours disentangle themselves reluctantly, Number Ten being the last to forsake his post.

"Now we'll dae it jist yince more, and have it right," announces the instructor, with quite unjustifiable optimism. "Forrm—*fourrs!*"

This time the result is better, but there is confusion on the left flank.

"Yon man, oot there on the left," shouts the instructor, "what's your number?"

Private Mucklewame, whose mind is slow but tenacious, answers—not without pride at knowing—
"Nineteen!"

(Thank goodness, he reflects, odd numbers stand fast upon all occasions.)

"Weel, mind this," says the sergeant—"Left files is always even numbers, even though they are odd numbers."

This revelation naturally clouds Private Mucklewame's intellect for the afternoon; and he wonders dimly, not for the first time, why he ever abandoned his well-paid and well-fed job as a butcher's assistant in distant Wishaw ten long days ago.

And so the drill goes on. All over the drab, dusty, gritty parade-ground, under the warm September sun, similar squads are being pounded into shape. They have no uniforms yet: even their instructors wear bowler hats or cloth caps. Some of the faces under the brims of these hats are not too prosperous. The junior officers are drilling squads too. They are a little shaky in what an actor would call their "patter," and they are inclined to lay stress on the wrong syllables; but they move their squads about somehow. Their seniors are dotted about the square, vigilant and helpful—here prompting a rusty sergeant instructor, there unravelling a squad which, in a spirited but misguided endeavour to obey an impossible order from Second Lieutenant Bobby Little, has wound itself up into a formation closely resembling the third figure of the Lancers.

Over there, by the officers' mess, stands the Colonel. He is in uniform, with a streak of parti-coloured ribbon running across above his left-hand breast-pocket. He is pleased to call himself a "dug-out." A fortnight ago he was fishing in the Garry, his fighting days avowedly behind him, and only the Special Reserve between him and *embonpoint*. Now he finds himself pitchforked back into the Active List, at the head of a battalion eleven hundred strong.

He surveys the scene. Well, his officers are all right. The Second in Command has seen almost as much service as himself. Of the four company commanders, two have been commandeered while home on leave from India, and the other two have practised the art of war in company with brother Boer. Of the rest, there are three subalterns from the Second Battalion—left behind, to their unspeakable woe—and four from the O.T.C. The juniors are very junior, but keen as mustard.

But the men! Is it possible? Can that awkward, shy, self-conscious mob, with scarcely an old soldier in their ranks, be pounded, within the space of a few months, into the Seventh (Service) Battalion of the Bruce and Wallace Highlanders—one of the most famous regiments in the British Army?

The Colonel's boyish figure stiffens.

"They're a rough crowd," he murmurs, "and a tough crowd: but they're a stout crowd. By gad! we'll make them a credit to the Old Regiment yet!"

II

THE DAILY GRIND

We have been in existence for more than three weeks now, and occasionally we are conscious of a throb of real life. Squad drill is almost a thing of the past, and we work by platoons of over fifty men. To-day our platoon once marched, in perfect step, for seven complete and giddy paces, before disintegrating into its usual formation—namely, an advance in irregular *échelon*, by individuals.

Four platoons form a company, and each platoon is (or should be) led by a subaltern, acting under his company commander. But we are very short of subalterns at present. (We are equally short of N.C.O.'s; but then you can always take a man out of the ranks and christen him sergeant, whereas there is no available source of Second Lieutenants save capricious Whitehall.) Consequently, three platoons out of four in our company are at present commanded by N.C.O.'s, two of whom appear to have retired from active service about the time that bows and arrows began to yield place to the arquebus, while the third has been picked out of the ranks simply because he possesses a loud voice and a cake of soap. None of them has yet mastered the new drill—it was all changed at the beginning of this year—and the majority of the officers are in no position to correct their anachronisms.

Still, we are getting on. Number Three Platoon (which boasts a subaltern) has just marched right round the barrack square, without—

(1) Marching through another platoon.
(2) Losing any part or parts of itself.
(3) Adopting a formation which brings it face to face with a blank wall, or piles it up in a tidal wave upon the verandah, of the married quarters.

They could not have done that a week ago.

But stay, what is this disturbance on the extreme left? The command "Right form" has been given, but six files on the outside flank have ignored the suggestion, and are now advancing (in skirmishing order) straight for the ashbin outside the cookhouse door, looking piteously round over their shoulders for some responsible person to give them an order which will turn them about and bring them back to the fold. Finally they are rounded up by the platoon sergeant, and restored to the strength.

"What went wrong, Sergeant?" inquires Second Lieutenant Bobby Little. He is a fresh-faced youth, with an engaging smile. Three months ago he was keeping wicket for his school eleven.

The sergeant comes briskly to attention.

"The order was not distinctly heard by the men, sir," he explains, "owing to the corporal that passed it on wanting a tooth. Corporal Blain, three paces forward—march!"

Corporal Blain steps forward, and after remembering to slap the small of his butt with his right hand, takes up his parable—

"I was sittin' doon tae ma dinner on Sabbath, sir, when my front teeth met upon a small piece bone that was stickit' in—"

Further details of this gastronomic tragedy are cut short by the blast of a whistle. The Colonel, at the other side of the square, has given the signal for the end of parade. Simultaneously a bugle rings out cheerfully from the direction of the orderly-room. Breakfast, blessed breakfast, is in sight. It is nearly eight, and we have been as busy as bees since six.

At a quarter to nine the battalion parades for a route-march. This, strange as it may appear, is a comparative rest. Once you have got your company safely decanted from column of platoons into column of route, your labours are at an end. All you have to do is to march; and that is no great hardship when you are as hard as nails, as we are fast becoming. On the march the mental gymnastics involved by the formation of an advanced guard or the disposition of a piquet line are removed to a safe distance. There is no need to wonder guiltily whether you have sent out a connecting-file between the vanguard and the main-guard, or if you remembered to instruct your sentry groups as to the position of the enemy and the extent of their own front.

Second Lieutenant Little heaves a contented sigh, and steps out manfully along the dusty road. Behind him tramp his men. We have no pipers as yet, but melody is supplied by "Tipperary," sung in ragged chorus, varied by martial interludes upon the mouth-organ. Despise not the mouth-organ. Ours has been a constant boon. It has kept sixty men in step for miles on end.

Fortunately the weather is glorious. Day after day, after a sharp and frosty dawn, the sun swings up into a cloudless sky; and the hundred thousand troops that swarm like ants upon, the undulating plains of Hampshire can march, sit, lie, or sleep on hard, sun-baked earth. A wet autumn would have thrown our training back months. The men, as yet, possess nothing but the fatigue uniforms they stand up in, so it is imperative to keep them dry.

Tramp, tramp, tramp. "Tipperary" has died away. The owner of the mouth-organ is temporarily deflated. Here is an opportunity for individual enterprise. It is soon seized. A husky soloist breaks into one of the deathless ditties of the new Scottish Laureate; his comrades take up the air with ready response; and presently we are all swinging along to the strains of "I Love a Lassie,"—"Roaming in the Gloaming" and "It's Just Like Being at Hame" being rendered as encores.

Then presently come snatches of a humorously amorous nature—"Hallo, Hallo, Who's Your Lady Friend?"; "You're my Baby"; and the ungrammatical "Who Were You With Last Night?" Another great favourite is an involved composition which always appears to begin in the middle. It deals severely with the precocity of a youthful lover who has been detected wooing his lady in the Park. Each verse ends, with enormous gusto—

"Hold your haand *oot*, you naughty boy!"

Tramp, tramp, tramp. Now we are passing through a village. The inhabitants line the pavement and smile cheerfully upon us—they are always kindly disposed toward "Scotchies"—but the united gaze of the rank and file wanders instinctively from the pavement towards upper windows and kitchen entrances, where the domestic staff may be discerned, bunched together and giggling. Now we are out on the road again, silent and dusty. Suddenly, far in the rear, a voice of singular sweetness strikes up "The Banks of Loch Lomond." Man after man joins in, until the swelling chorus runs from end to end of the long column. Half the battalion hail from the Loch Lomond district, and of the rest there is hardly a man who has not indulged, during some Trades' Holiday or other, in "a pleesure trup" upon its historic but inexpensive waters.

"You'll tak' the high road and I'll tak' the low road—"

On we swing, full-throated. An English battalion, halted at a cross-road to let us go by, gazes curiously upon us. "Tipperary" they know, Harry Lauder they have heard of; but this song has no meaning for them. It is ours, ours, ours. So we march on. The feet of Bobby Little, as he tramps at the head of his platoon, hardly touch the ground. His head is in the air. One day, he feels instinctively, he will hear that song again, amid sterner surroundings. When that day comes, the song, please God, for all its sorrowful wording, will reflect no sorrow from the hearts of those who sing it—only courage, and the joy of battle, and the knowledge of victory.

"—And I'll be in Scotland before ye.
But me and my true love will never meet again
On the bonny, bonny *baanks*—"

A shrill whistle sounds far ahead. It means "March at Attention." "Loch Lomond" dies away with uncanny suddenness—discipline is waxing stronger every day—and tunics are buttoned and rifles unslung. Three minutes later we swing demurely on to the barrack-square, across which a pleasant aroma of stewed onions is wafting, and deploy with creditable precision into the formation known as "mass." Then comes much dressing of ranks and adjusting of distances. The Colonel is very particular about a clean finish to any piece of work.

Presently the four companies are aligned: the N.C.O.'s retire to the supernumerary ranks. The battalion stands rigid, facing a motionless figure upon horseback. The figure stirs.

"Fall out, the officers!"

They come trooping, stand fast, and salute—very smartly. We must set an example to the men. Besides, we are hungry too.

"Battalion, slope *arms!* Dis-*miss!*"

Every man, with one or two incurable exceptions, turns sharply to his right and cheerfully smacks the butt of his rifle with his disengaged hand. The Colonel gravely returns the salute; and we stream away, all the thousand of us, in the direction of the savoury smell. Two o'clock will come round all too soon, and with it company drill and tiresome musketry exercises; but by that time we shall have *dined*, and Fate cannot touch us for another twenty-four hours.

III

GROWING PAINS

We have our little worries, of course.

Last week we were all vaccinated, and we did not like it. Most of us have "taken" very severely, which is a sign that we badly needed vaccinating, but makes the discomfort no easier to endure. It is no joke handling a rifle when your left arm is swelled to the full compass of your sleeve; and the personal contact of your neighbour in the ranks is sheer agony. However, officers are considerate, and the work is made as light as possible. The faint-hearted report themselves sick; but the Medical Officer, an unsentimental man of coarse mental fibre, who was on a panel before he heard his country calling, merely recommends them to get well as soon as possible, as they are going to be inoculated for enteric next week. So we grouse—and bear it.

There are other rifts within the military lute. At home we are persons of some consequence, with very definite notions about the dignity of labour. We have employers who tremble at our frown; we have Trades Union officials who are at constant pains to impress upon us our own omnipotence in the industrial world in which we live. We have at our beck and call a Radical M.P. who, in return for our vote and suffrage, informs us that we are the backbone of the nation, and that we must on no account permit ourselves to be trampled upon by the effete and tyrannical upper classes. Finally, we are Scotsmen, with all a Scotsman's curious reserve and contempt for social airs and graces.

But in the Army we appear to be nobody. We are expected to stand stiffly at attention when addressed by an officer; even to call him "sir"—an honour to which our previous employer has been a stranger. At home, if we happened to meet the head of the firm in the street, and none of our colleagues was looking, we touched a cap, furtively. Now, we have no option in the matter. We are expected to degrade ourselves by meaningless and humiliating gestures. The N.C.O.'s are almost as bad. If you answer a sergeant as you would a foreman, you are impertinent; if you argue with him, as all good Scotsmen must, you are insubordinate; if you endeavour to drive a collective bargain with him, you are mutinous; and you are reminded that upon active service mutiny is punishable by death. It is all very unusual and upsetting.

You may not spit; neither may you smoke a cigarette in the ranks, nor keep the residue thereof behind your ear. You may not take beer to bed with you. You may not postpone your shave till Saturday: you must shave every day. You must keep your buttons, accoutrements, and rifle speckless, and have your hair cut in a style which is not becoming to your particular type of beauty. Even your feet are not your own. Every Sunday morning a young officer, whose leave has been specially stopped for the purpose, comes round the barrack-rooms after church and inspects your extremities, revelling in blackened nails and gloating over hammer-toes. For all practical purposes, decides Private Mucklewame, you might as well be in Siberia.

Still, one can get used to anything. Our lot is mitigated, too, by the knowledge that we are all in the same boat. The most olympian N.C.O. stands like a ramrod when addressing an officer, while lieutenants make obeisance to a company commander as humbly as any private. Even the Colonel was seen one day to salute an old gentleman who rode on to the parade-ground during morning drill, wearing a red band round his hat. Noting this, we realise that the Army is not, after all, as we first suspected, divided into two classes—oppressors and oppressed. We all have to "go through it."

Presently fresh air, hard training, and clean living begin to weave their spell. Incredulous at first, we find ourselves slowly recognising the fact that it is possible to treat an officer deferentially, or carry out an order smartly, without losing one's self-respect as a man and a Trades Unionist. The insidious habit of cleanliness, once acquired, takes despotic possession of its victims: we find ourselves looking askance at room-mates who have not yet yielded to such predilections. The swimming-bath, where once we flapped unwillingly and ingloriously at the shallow end, becomes quite a desirable resort, and we look forward to our weekly visit with something approaching eagerness. We begin, too, to take our profession seriously. Formerly we regarded outpost exercises, advanced guards, and the like, as a rather fatuous form of play-acting, designed to amuse those officers who carry maps and notebooks. Now we begin to consider these diversions on their merits, and seriously criticise Second Lieutenant Little for having last night posted one of his sentry groups upon the skyline. Thus is the soul of a soldier born.

We are getting less individualistic, too. We are beginning to think more of our regiment and less of ourselves. At first this loyalty takes the form of criticising other regiments, because their marching is slovenly, or their accoutrements dirty, or—most significant sign of all—their discipline is bad. We are especially critical of our own Eighth Battalion, which is fully three weeks younger than we are, and is not in the First Hundred Thousand at all. In their presence we are war-worn veterans. We express it as our opinion that the officers of some of these battalions must be a poor lot. From this it suddenly comes home to us that our officers are a good lot, and we find ourselves taking a queer pride in our company commander's homely strictures and severe sentences the morning after pay-night. Here is another step in the quickening life of the regiment. *Esprit de corps* is raising its head, class prejudice and dour "independence" notwithstanding.

Again, a timely hint dropped by the Colonel on battalion parade this morning has set us thinking. We begin to wonder how we shall compare with the first-line regiments when we find ourselves "oot there." Silently we resolve that when we, the first of the Service Battalions, take our place in trench or firing line alongside the Old Regiment, no one shall be found to draw unfavourable comparisons between parent and offspring. We intend to show ourselves chips of the old block. No one who knows the Old Regiment can ask more of a young battalion than *that*.

IV

THE CONVERSION OF PRIVATE M'SLATTERY

One evening a rumour ran round the barracks. Most barrack rumours die a natural death, but this one was confirmed by the fact that next morning the whole battalion, instead of performing the usual platoon exercises, was told off for instruction in the art of presenting arms. "A" Company discussed the portent at breakfast.

"What kin' o' a thing is a Review?" inquired Private M'Slattery.

Private Mucklewame explained. Private M'Slattery was not impressed, and said so quite frankly. In the lower walks of the industrial world Royalty is too often a mere name. Personal enthusiasm for a Sovereign whom they have never seen, and who in their minds is inextricably mixed up with the House of Lords, and capitalism, and the police, is impossible to individuals of the stamp of Private M'Slattery. To such, Royalty is simply the head and corner-stone of a legal system which officiously prevents a man from being drunk and disorderly, and the British Empire an expensive luxury for which the working man pays while the idle rich draw the profits.

If M'Slattery's opinion of the Civil Code was low, his opinion of Military Law was at zero. In his previous existence in his native Clydebank, when weary of rivet-heating and desirous of change and rest, he had been accustomed to take a day off and become pleasantly intoxicated, being comfortably able to afford the loss of pay involved by his absence. On these occasions he was accustomed to sleep off his potations in some public place—usually upon the pavement outside his last house of call—and it was his boast that so long as nobody interfered with him he interfered with nobody. To this attitude the tolerant police force of Clydebank assented, having their hands full enough, as a rule, in dealing with more militant forms of alcoholism. But Private M'Slattery, No. 3891, soon realised that he and Mr. Matthew M'Slattery, rivet-heater and respected citizen of Clydebank, had nothing in common. Only last week, feeling pleasantly fatigued after five days of arduous military training, he had followed the invariable practice of his civil life, and taken a day off. The result had fairly staggered him. In the orderly-room upon Monday morning he was charged with—

(1) Being absent from Parade at 9 A.M. on Saturday.
(2) Being absent from Parade at 2 P.M. on Saturday.
(3) Being absent from Tattoo at 9.30 P.M. on Saturday.
(4) Being drunk in High Street about 9.40 P.M. on Saturday.
(5) Striking a Non-Commissioned Officer.
(6) Attempting to escape from his escort.
(7) Destroying Government property. (Three panes of glass in the guard-room.)

Private M'Slattery, asked for an explanation, had pointed out that if he had been treated as per his working arrangement with the police at Clydebank, there would have been no trouble whatever. As for his day off, he was willing to forgo his day's pay and call the thing square. However, a hidebound C.O. had fined him five shillings and sentenced him to seven days' C.B. Consequently he was in no mood for Royal Reviews. He stated his opinions upon the subject in a loud voice and at some length. No one contradicted him, for he possessed the straightest left in the company; and no dog barked even when M'Slattery said that black was white.

"I wunner ye jined the Airmy at all, M'Slattery," observed one bold spirit, when the orator paused for breath.

"I wunner myself," said M'Slattery simply. "If I had kent all aboot this 'attention,' and 'stan'-at-ease,' and needin' tae luft your hand tae your bunnet whenever you saw yin o' they gentry-pups of officers goin' by,—dagont if I'd hae done it, Germans or no! (But I had a dram in me at the time.) I'm weel kent in Clydebank, and they'll tell you there that I'm no the man to be wastin' my time presenting airms tae kings or any other bodies."

However, at the appointed hour M'Slattery, in the front rank of A Company, stood to attention because he had to, and presented arms very creditably. He now cherished a fresh grievance, for he objected upon principle to have to present arms to a motor-car standing two hundred yards away upon his right front.

"Wull we be gettin' hame to our dinners now?" he inquired gruffly of his neighbour.

"Maybe he'll tak' a closer look at us," suggested an optimist in the rear rank. "He micht walk doon the line."

"Walk? No him!" replied Private M'Slattery. "He'll be awa' hame in the motor. Hae ony o' you billies gotten a fag?"

There was a smothered laugh. The officers of the battalion were standing rigidly at attention in front of A Company. One of these turned his head sharply.

"No talking in the ranks there!" he said. "Sergeant, take that man's name."

Private M'Slattery, rumbling mutiny, subsided, and devoted his attention to the movements of the Royal motor-car.

Then the miracle happened.

The great car rolled smoothly from the saluting-base, over the undulating turf, and came to a standstill on the extreme right of the line, half a mile away. There descended a slight figure in khaki. It was the King—the King whom Private M'Slattery had never seen. Another figure followed, and another.

"Herself iss there too!" whinnied an excited Highlander on M'Slattery's right. "And the young leddy! Pless me, they are all for walking town the line on their feet. And the sun so hot in the sky! We shall see them close!"

Private M'Slattery gave a contemptuous sniff.

The excited battalion was called to a sense of duty by the voice of authority. Once more the long lines stood stiff and rigid—waiting, waiting, for their brief glimpse. It was a long time coming, for they were posted on the extreme left.

Suddenly a strangled voice was uplifted—"In God's name, what for can they no come tae *us*? Never heed the others!"

Yet Private M'Slattery was quite unaware that he had spoken.

At last the little procession arrived. There was a handshake for the Colonel, and a word with two or three of the officers; then a quick scrutiny of the rank and file. For a moment—yea, more than a moment—keen Royal eyes rested upon Private M'Slattery, standing like a graven image, with his great chest straining the buttons of his tunic.

Then a voice said, apparently in M'Slattery's ear—

"A magnificent body of men, Colonel. I congratulate you."

A minute later M'Slattery was aroused from his trance by the sound of the Colonel's ringing voice—

"Highlanders, three cheers for His Majesty the King!"

M'Slattery led the whole Battalion, his glengarry high in the air.

Suddenly his eye fell upon Private Mucklewame, blindly and woodenly yelling himself hoarse.

In three strides M'Slattery was standing face to face with the unconscious criminal.

"Yous low, lousy puddock," he roared—"tak' off your bonnet!" He saved Mucklewame the trouble of complying, and strode back to his place in the ranks.

"Yin mair, chaps," he shouted—"for the young leddy!"

And yet there are people who tell us that the formula, O.H.M.S., is a mere relic of antiquity.

V

"CRIME"

"Bring in Private Dunshie, Sergeant-Major," says the Company Commander.

The Sergeant-Major throws open the door, and barks—"Private Dunshie's escort!"

The order is repeated *fortissimo* by some one outside. There is a clatter of ammunition boots getting into step, and a solemn procession of four files into the room. The leader thereof is a stumpy but enormously important-looking private. He is the escort. Number two is the prisoner. Numbers three and four are the accuser—counsel for the Crown, as it were—and a witness. The procession reaches the table at which the Captain is sitting. Beside him is a young officer, one Bobby Little, who is present for "instructional" purposes.

"Mark time!" commands the Sergeant-Major. "Halt! Right turn!"

This evolution brings the accused face to face with his judge. He has been deprived of his cap, and of everything else "which may be employed as, or contain, a missile." (They think of everything in the King's Regulations.)

"What is this man's crime, Sergeant-Major?" inquires the Captain.

"On this sheet, sir," replies the Sergeant-Major....

By a "crime" the ordinary civilian means something worth recording in a special edition of the evening papers—something with a meat-chopper in it. Others, more catholic in their views, will tell you that it is a crime to inflict corporal punishment on any human being; or to permit performing animals to appear upon the stage; or to subsist upon any food but nuts. Others, of still finer clay, will classify such things as Futurism, The Tango, Dickeys, and the Albert Memorial as crimes. The point to note is, that in the eyes of all these persons each of these things is a sin of the worst possible degree. That being so, they designate it a "crime." It is the strongest term they can employ.

But in the Army, "crime" is capable of infinite shades of intensity. It simply means "misdemeanour," and may range from being unshaven on parade, or making a frivolous complaint about the potatoes at dinner, to irrevocably perforating your rival in love with a bayonet. So let party politicians, when they discourse vaguely to their constituents about "the prevalence of crime in the Army under the present effete and undemocratic system," walk warily.

Every private in the Army possesses what is called a conduct-sheet, and upon this his crimes are recorded. To be precise, he has two such sheets. One is called his Company sheet, and the other his Regimental sheet. His Company sheet contains a record of every misdeed for which he has been brought before his Company Commander. His Regimental sheet is a more select document, and contains only the more noteworthy of his achievements—crimes so interesting that they have to be communicated to the Commanding Officer.

However, this morning we are concerned only with Company conduct-sheets. It is 7.30 A.M., and the Company Commander is sitting in judgment, with a little pile of yellow Army forms before him. He picks up the first of these, and reads—

"*Private Dunshie. While on active service, refusing to obey an order.* Lance-Corporal Ness!"

The figure upon the prisoner's right suddenly becomes animated. Lance-Corporal Ness, taking a deep breath, and fixing his eyes resolutely on the whitewashed wall above the Captain's head, recites—

"Sirr, at four P.M. on the fufth unst. I was in charge of a party told off for tae scrub the floor of Room Nummer Seeventeen. I ordered the prisoner tae scrub. He refused. I warned him. He again refused."

Click! Lance-Corporal Ness has run down. He has just managed the sentence in a breath.

"Corporal Mackay!"

The figure upon Lance-Corporal Ness's right stiffens, and inflates itself.

"Sirr, on the fufth unst. I was Orderly Sergeant. At aboot four-thirrty P.M., Lance-Corporal Ness reported this man tae me for refusing for tae obey an order. I confined him."

The Captain turns to the prisoner.

"What have you to say, Private Dunshie?"

Private Dunshie, it appears, has a good deal to say.

"I jined the Airmy for tae fight they Germans, and no for tae be learned tae scrub floors—"

"Sirr!" suggests the Sergeant-Major in his ear.

"Sirr," amends Private Dunshie reluctantly. "I was no in the habit of scrubbin' the floor mysel' where I stay in Glesca'; and ma wife would be affronted—"

But the Captain looks up. He has heard enough.

"Look here, Dunshie," he says. "Glad to hear you want to fight the Germans. So do I. So do we all. All the same, we've got a lot of dull jobs to do first." (Captain Blaikie has the reputation of being the most monosyllabic man in the British Army.) "Coals, and floors, and fatigues like that: they are your job. I have mine too. Kept me up till two this morning. But the point is this. You have refused to obey an order. Very serious, that. Most serious crime a soldier can commit. If you start arguing now about small things, where will you be when the big orders come along—eh? Must learn to obey. Soldier now, whatever you were a month ago. So obey all orders like a shot. Watch me next time I get one. No disgrace, you know! Ought to be a soldier's pride, and all that. See?"

"Yes—sirr," replies Private Dunshie, with less truculence.

The Captain glances down at the paper before him.

"First time you have come before me. Admonished!"

"Right turn! Quick march!" thunders the Sergeant-Major.

The procession clumps out of the room. The Captain turns to his disciple.

"That's my homely and paternal tap," he observes. "For first offenders only. That chap's all right. Soon find out it's no good fussing about your rights as a truc-born British elector in the Army. Sergeant-Major!"

"Sirr?"

"Private McNulty!"

After the usual formalities, enter Private McNulty and escort. Private McNulty is a small scared-looking man with a dirty face.

"Private McNulty, sirr!" announces the Sergeant-Major to the Company Commander, with the air of a popular lecturer on entomology placing a fresh insect under the microscope.

Captain Blaikie addresses the shivering culprit—

"*Private McNulty; charged with destroying Government property.* Corporal Mather!"

Corporal Mather clears his throat, and assuming the wooden expression and fish-like gaze common to all public speakers who have learned their oration by heart, begins—

"Sirr, on the night of the sixth inst. I was Orderly Sergeant. Going round the prisoner's room about the hour of nine-thirty I noticed that his three biscuits had been cut and slashed, appariently with a knife or other instrument."

"What did you do?"

"Sirr, I inquired of the men in the room who was it had gone for to do this. Sirr, they said it was the prisoner."

Two witnesses are called. Both, certify, casting grieved and virtuous glances at the prisoner, that this outrage upon the property of His Majesty was the work of Private McNulty.

To the unsophisticated Bobby Little this charge appears rather a frivolous one. If you may not cut or slash a biscuit, what *are* you to do with it? Swallow it whole?

"Private McNulty?" queries the Captain.

Private McNulty, in a voice which is shrill with righteous indignation, gives the somewhat unexpected answer—

"Sirr, I plead guilty!"

"Guilty—eh? You did it, then?"

"Yes, sir."

"Why?"

This is what Private McNulty is waiting for.

"The men in that room, sirr," he announces indignantly, "appear tae look on me as a sort of body that can be treated onyways. They go for tae aggravate me. I was sittin' on my bed, with my knife in my hand, cutting a piece bacca and interfering with naebody, when they all commenced tae fling biscuits at me. I was keepin' them off as weel as I could; but havin' a knife in my hand, I'll no deny but what I gave twa three of them a bit cut."

"Is this true?" asks the Captain of the first witness, curtly.

"Yes, sir."

"You saw the men throwing biscuits at the prisoner?"

"Yes, sir."

"He was daen' it himsel'!" proclaims Private McNulty.

"This true?"

"Yes, sir."

The Captain addresses the other witness.

"You doing it too?"

"Yes, sir."

The Captain turns again to the prisoner.

"Why didn't you lodge a complaint?" (The schoolboy code does not obtain in the Army.)

"I did, sir. I tellt"—indicating Corporal Mather with an elbow—"this genelman here."

Corporal Mather cannot help it. He swells perceptibly. But swift puncture awaits him.

"Corporal Mather, why didn't you mention this?"

"I didna think it affected the crime, sir."

"Not your business to think. Only to make a straightforward charge. Be very careful in future. You other two"—the witnesses come guiltily to attention—"I shall talk to your platoon sergeant about you. Not going to have Government property knocked about!"

Bobby Little's eyebrows, willy-nilly, have been steadily rising during the last five minutes. He knows the meaning of red tape now!

Then comes sentence.

"Private McNulty, you have pleaded guilty to a charge of destroying Government property, so you go before the Commanding Officer. Don't suppose you'll be punished, beyond paying for the damage."

"Right turn! Quick march!" chants the Sergeant-Major.

The downtrodden McNulty disappears, with his traducers. But Bobby Little's eyebrows have not been altogether thrown away upon his Company Commander.

"Got the biscuits here, Sergeant-Major?"

"Yes, sirr."

"Show them."

The Sergeant-Major dives into a pile of brown blankets, and presently extracts three small brown mattresses, each two feet square. These appear to have been stabbed in several places with a knife.

Captain Blaikie's eyes twinkle, and he chuckles to his now scarlet-faced junior—

"More biscuits in heaven and earth than ever came out of Huntley and Palmer's, my son! Private Robb!"

Presently Private Robb stands at the table. He is a fresh-faced, well-set-up youth, with a slightly receding chin and a most dejected manner.

"*Private Robb*," reads the Captain. "*While on active service, drunk and singing in Wellington Street about nine p.m. on Saturday, the sixth.* Sergeant Garrett!"

The proceedings follow their usual course, except that in this case some of the evidence is "documentary"—put in in the form of a report from the sergeant of the Military Police who escorted the melodious Robb home to bed.

The Captain addresses the prisoner.

"Private Robb, this is the second time. Sorry—very sorry. In all other ways you are doing well. Very keen and promising soldier. Why is it—eh?"

The contrite Robb hangs his head. His judge continues—

"I'll tell you. You haven't found out yet how much you can hold. That it?"

The prisoner nods assent.

"Well—find out! See? It's one of the first things a young man ought to learn. Very valuable piece of information. I know myself, so I'm safe. Want you to do the same. Every man has a different limit. What did you have on Saturday?"

Private Robb reflects.

"Five pints, sirr," he announces.

"Well, next time try three, and then you won't go serenading policemen. As it is, you will have to go before the Commanding Officer and get punished. Want to go to the front, don't you?"

"Yes, sirr." Private Robb's dismal features flush.

"Well, mind this. We all want to go, but we can't go till every man in the battalion is efficient. You want to be the man who kept the rest from going to the front—eh?"

"No, sirr, I do not."

"All right, then. Next Saturday night say to yourself: 'Another pint, and I keep the Battalion back!' If you do that, you'll come back to barracks sober, like a decent chap. That'll do. Don't salute with your cap off. Next man, Sergeant-Major!"

"Good boy, that," remarks the Captain to Bobby Little, as the contrite Robb is removed. "Keen as mustard. But his high-water mark for beer is somewhere in his boots. All right, now I've scared him."

"Last prisoner, sirr," announces the Sergeant-Major.

"Glad to hear it. H'm! Private M'Queen again!"

Private M'Queen is an unpleasant-looking creature, with a drooping red moustache and a cheese-coloured complexion. His misdeeds are recited. Having been punished for misconduct early in the week, he has piled Pelion on Ossa by appearing fighting drunk at defaulters' parade. From all accounts he has livened up that usually decorous assemblage considerably.

After the corroborative evidence, the Captain asks his usual question of the prisoner—

"Anything to say?"

"No," growls Private M'Queen.

The Captain takes up the prisoner's conduct-sheet, reads it through, and folds it up deliberately.

"I am going to ask the Commanding Officer to discharge you," he says; and there is nothing homely or paternal in his speech now. "Can't make out why men like you join the Army—especially *this* Army. Been a nuisance ever since you came here. Drunk—beastly drunk—four times in three weeks. Always dirty and insubordinate. Always trying to stir up trouble among the young soldiers. Been in the army before, haven't you?"

"No."

"That's not true. Can always tell an old soldier on parade. Fact is, you have either deserted or been discharged as incorrigible. Going to be discharged as incorrigible again. Keeping the regiment back, that's why: that's a real crime. Go home, and explain that you were turned out of the King's Army because you weren't worthy of the honour of staying in. When decent men see that people like you have no place in this regiment, perhaps they will see that this regiment is just the place for them. Take him away."

Private M'Queen shambles out of the room for the last time in his life. Captain Blaikie, a little exhausted by his own unusual loquacity, turns to Bobby Little with a contented sigh.

"That's the last of the shysters," he says. "Been weeding them out for six weeks. Now I have got rid of that nobleman I can look the rest of the Company in the face. Come to breakfast!"

VI

THE LAWS OF THE MEDES AND PERSIANS

One's first days as a newly-joined subaltern are very like one's first days at school. The feeling is just the same. There is the same natural shyness, the same reverence for people who afterwards turn out to be of no consequence whatsoever, and the same fear of transgressing the Laws of the Medes and Persians—regimental traditions and conventions—which alter not.

Dress, for instance. "Does one wear a sword on parade?" asks the tyro of himself his first morning. "I'll put it on, and chance it." He invests himself in a monstrous claymore and steps on to the barrack square. Not an officer in sight is carrying anything more lethal than a light cane. There is just time to scuttle back to quarters and disarm.

Again, where should one sit at meal-times? We had supposed that the C.O. would be enthroned at the head of the table, with a major sitting on his right and left, like Cherubim and Seraphim; while the rest disposed themselves in a descending scale of greatness until it came down to persons like ourselves at the very foot. But the C.O. has a disconcerting habit of sitting absolutely anywhere. He appears to be just as happy between two Second Lieutenants as between Cherubim and Seraphim. Again, we note that at breakfast each officer upon entering sits down and shouts loudly, to a being concealed behind a screen, for food, which is speedily forthcoming. Are we entitled to clamour in this peremptory fashion too? Or should we creep round behind the screen and take what we can get? Or should we sit still, and wait till we are served? We try the last expedient first, and get nothing. Then we try the second, and are speedily convinced, by the demeanour of the gentleman behind the screen, that we have committed the worst error of which we have yet been guilty.

There are other problems—saluting, for instance. On the parade ground this is a simple matter enough; for there the golden rule appears to be—When in doubt, salute! The Colonel calls up his four Company Commanders. They salute. He instructs them to carry on this morning with coal fatigues and floor-scrubbing. The Company Commanders salute, and retire to their Companies, and call up their subalterns, who salute. They instruct these to carry on this morning with coal fatigues and floor-scrubbing. The sixteen subalterns salute, and retire to their platoons. Here they call up their Platoon Sergeants, who salute. They instruct these to carry on this morning with coal fatigues and floor-scrubbing. The Platoon Sergeants salute, and issue commands to the rank and file. The rank and file, having no instructions to salute sergeants, are compelled, as a last resort, to carry on with the coal fatigues and floor-scrubbing themselves. You see, on parade saluting is simplicity itself.

But we are not always on parade; and then more subtle problems arise. Some of those were discussed one day by four junior officers, who sat upon a damp and slippery bank by a muddy roadside during a "fall-out" in a route-march. The four ("reading from left to right," as they say in high journalistic society) were Second Lieutenant Little, Second Lieutenant Waddell, Second Lieutenant Cockerell, and Lieutenant Struthers, surnamed "Highbrow." Bobby we know. Waddell was a slow-moving but pertinacious student of the science of war from the kingdom of Fife. Cockerell came straight from a crack public-school corps, where he had been a cadet officer; so nothing in the heaven above or the earth beneath was hid from him. Struthers owed his superior rank to the fact that in the far back ages, before the days of the O.T.C., he had held a commission in a University Corps. He was a scholar of his College, and was an expert in the art of accumulating masses of knowledge in quick time for examination purposes. He knew all the little red manuals by heart, was an infallible authority on buttons and badges, and would dip into the King's Regulations or the Field Service Pocket-book as another man might dip into the "Sporting Times." Strange to say, he was not very good at drilling a platoon. We all know him.

"What do you do when you are leading a party along a road and meet a Staff Officer?" asked Bobby Little.

"Make a point," replied Cockerell patronisingly, "of saluting all persons wearing red bands round their hats. They may not be entitled to it, but it tickles their ribs and gets you the reputation, of being an intelligent young officer."

"But I say," announced Waddell plaintively, "*I* saluted a man with a red hat the other day, and he turned out to be a Military Policeman!"

"As a matter of fact," announced the pundit Struthers, after the laughter had subsided, "you need not salute anybody. No compliments are paid on active service, and we are on active service now."

"Yes, but suppose some one salutes *you*?" objected the conscientious Bobby Little. "You must salute back again, and sometimes you don't know how to do it. The other day I was bringing the company back from the ranges and we met a company from another battalion—the Mid Mudshires, I think. Before I knew where I was the fellow in charge called them to attention and then gave 'Eyes right!'"

"What did you do?" asked Struthers anxiously.

"I hadn't time to do anything except grin, and say, 'Good morning!'" confessed Bobby Little.

"You were perfectly right," announced Struthers, and Cockerell murmured assent.

"Are you sure?" persisted Bobby Little. "As I passed the tail of their company one of their subs turned to another and said quite loud, 'My God, what swine!'"

"Showed his rotten ignorance," commented Cockerell.

At this moment Mr. Waddell, whose thoughts were never disturbed by conversation around him, broke in with a question.

"What does a Tommy do," he inquired, "if he meets an officer wheeling a wheelbarrow?"

"Who is wheeling the barrow," inquired the meticulous Struthers—"the officer or the Tommy?"

"The Tommy, of course!" replied Waddell in quite a shocked voice. "What is he to do? If he tries to salute he will upset the barrow, you know."

"He turns his head sharply towards the officer for six paces," explained the ever-ready Struthers. "When a soldier is not in a position to salute in the ordinary way—"

"I say," inquired Bobby Little rather shyly, "do you ever look the other way when you meet a Tommy?"

"How do you mean?" asked everybody.

"Well, the other day I met one walking out with his girl along the road, and I felt so blooming *de trop* that—"

Here the "fall-in" sounded, and this delicate problem was left unsolved. But Mr. Waddell, who liked to get to the bottom of things, continued to ponder these matters as he marched. He mistrusted the omniscience of Struthers and the superficial infallibility of the self-satisfied Cockerell. Accordingly, after consultation with that eager searcher after knowledge, Second Lieutenant Little, he took the laudable but fatal step of carrying his difficulties to one Captain Wagstaffe, the humorist of the Battalion.

Wagstaffe listened with an appearance of absorbed interest. Finally he said—

"These are very important questions, Mr. Waddell, and you acted quite rightly in laying them before me. I will consult the Deputy Assistant Instructor in Military Etiquette, and will obtain a written answer to your inquiries."

"Oh, thanks awfully, sir!" exclaimed Waddell.

The result of Captain Wagstaffe's application to the mysterious official just designated was forthcoming next day in the form of a neatly typed document. It was posted in the Ante-room (the C.O. being out at dinner), and ran as follows:—

SALUTES

YOUNG OFFICERS, HINTS FOR THE GUIDANCE OF

The following is the correct procedure for a young officer in charge of an armed party upon meeting—
(a) A Staff Officer riding a bicycle.
Correct Procedure.—If marching at attention, order your men to march at ease and to light cigarettes and eat bananas. Then, having fixed bayonets, give the order: *Across the road—straggle!*
(b) A funeral.
Correct Procedure.—Strike up *Tipperary*, and look the other way.
(c) A General Officer, who strolls across your Barrack Square precisely at the moment when you and your Platoon have got into mutual difficulties.
Correct Procedure.—Lie down flat upon your face (directing your platoon to do the same), cover your head with gravel, and pretend you are not there.

SPECIAL CASES

(a) A soldier, wheeling a wheelbarrow and balancing a swill-tub on his head, meets an officer walking out in review dress.
Correct Procedure.—The soldier will immediately cant the swill-tub to an angle of forty-five degrees at a distance of one and a half inches above his right eyebrow. (In the case of Rifle Regiments the soldier will balance the swill-tub on his nose.) He will then invite the officer, by a smart movement of the left ear, to seat himself on the wheelbarrow.
Correct Acknowledgment.—The officer will comply, placing his feet upon the right and left hubs of the wheel respectively, with the ball of the toe in each case at a distance of one inch (when serving abroad, 2-1/2 centimetres) from the centre of gravity of the wheelbarrow. (In the case of Rifle Regiments the officer

will tie his feet in a knot at the back of his neck.) The soldier will then advance six paces, after which the officer will dismount and go home and have a bath.

(b) A soldier, with his arm round a lady's waist in the gloaming, encounters an officer.

Correct Procedure.—The soldier will salute with his disengaged arm. The lady will administer a sharp tap with the end of her umbrella to the officer's tunic, at point one inch above the lowest button.

Correct Acknowledgment.—The officer will take the end of the umbrella firmly in his right hand, and will require the soldier to introduce him to the lady. He will then direct the soldier to double back to barracks.

(c) A party of soldiers, seated upon the top of a transport waggon, see an officer passing at the side of the road.

Correct Procedure.—The senior N.C.O. (or if no N.C.O. be present, the oldest soldier) will call the men to attention, and the party, taking their time from the right, will spit upon the officer's head in a soldier-like manner.

Correct Acknowledgment.—The officer will break into a smart trot.

(d) A soldier, driving an officer's motor-car without the knowledge of the officer, encounters the officer in a narrow country lane.

Correct Procedure.—The soldier will open the throttle to its full extent and run the officer over.

Correct Acknowledgment.—No acknowledgment is required.

NOTE.—*None of the above compliments will be paid upon active service.*

Unfortunately the Colonel came home from dining out sooner than was expected, and found this outrageous document still upon the notice-board. But he was a good Colonel. He merely remarked approvingly—

"H'm. Quite so! *Non semper arcum tendit Apollo.* It's just as well to keep smiling these days."

Nevertheless, Mr. Waddell made a point in future, when in need of information, of seeking the same from a less inspired source than Captain Wagstaffe.

* * * * *

There was another Law of the Medes and Persians with which our four friends soon became familiar—that which governs the relations of the various ranks to one another. Great Britain is essentially the home of the chaperon. We pride ourselves, as a nation, upon the extreme care with which we protect our young gentlewomen from contaminating influences. But the fastidious attention which we bestow upon our national maidenhood is as nothing in comparison with the protective commotion with which we surround that shrinking sensitive plant, Mr. Thomas Atkins.

Take etiquette and deportment. If a soldier wishes to speak to an officer, an introduction must be effected by a sergeant. Let us suppose that Private M'Splae, in the course of a route-march, develops a blister upon his great toe. He begins by intimating the fact to the nearest lance-corporal. The lance-corporal takes the news to the platoon sergeant, who informs the platoon commander, who may or may not decide to take the opinion of his company commander in the matter. Anyhow, when the hobbling warrior finally obtains permission to fall out and alleviate his distress, a corporal goes with him, for fear he should lose himself, or his boot—it is wonderful what Thomas *can* lose when he sets his mind to it—or, worst crime of all, his rifle.

Again, if two privates are detailed to empty the regimental ashbin, a junior N.C.O. ranges them in line, calls them to attention, and marches them off to the scene of their labours, decently and in order. If a soldier obtains leave to go home on furlough for the week-end, he is collected into a party, and, after being inspected to see that his buttons are clean, his hair properly cut, and his nose correctly blown, is marched off to the station, where a ticket is provided for him, and he and his fellow-wayfarers are safely tucked into a third-smoker labelled "Military Party." (No wonder he sometimes gets lost on arriving at Waterloo!) In short, if there is a job to be done, the senior soldier present chaperons somebody else while he does it.

This system has been attacked on the ground that it breeds loss of self-reliance and initiative. As a matter of fact, the result is almost exactly the opposite. Under its operation a soldier rapidly acquires the art of placing himself under the command of his nearest superior in rank; but at the same time he learns with equal rapidity to take command himself if no superior be present—no bad thing in times of battle and sudden death, when shrapnel is whistling, and promotion is taking place with grim and unceasing automaticity.

This principle is extended, too, to the enforcement of law and order. If Private M'Sumph is insubordinate or riotous, there is never any question of informal correction or summary justice. News of the incident wends its way upward, by a series of properly regulated channels, to the officer in command. Presently, by the same route, an order comes back, and in a twinkling the offender finds himself taken under arrest and marched off to the guard-room by two of his own immediate associates. (One of them may be his own rear-rank man.) But no officer or non-commissioned officer ever lays a finger on him. The penalty for striking a superior officer is so severe that the law decrees, very wisely, that a soldier must on no account ever be arrested by any save men of his own rank. If Private M'Sumph, while being removed in custody, strikes Private Tosh upon the nose and kicks Private Cosh upon the shin, to the effusion of blood, no great harm is done—except to the lacerated Cosh and Tosh; but if he had smitten an intruding officer in the eye, his punishment would have been dire and grim. So, though we may call military law cumbrous and grandmotherly, there is sound sense and real mercy at the root of it.

* * * * *

But there is one Law of the Medes and Persians which is sensibly relaxed these days. We, the newly joined, have always been given to understand that whatever else you do, you must never, never betray any interest in your profession—in short, talk shop—at Mess. But in our Mess no one ever talks anything else. At luncheon, we relate droll anecdotes concerning our infant platoons; at tea, we explain, to any one who will listen, exactly how we placed our sentry line in last night's operations; at dinner, we brag about our Company musketry returns, and quote untruthful extracts from our butt registers. At breakfast, every one has a newspaper, which he props before him and reads, generally aloud. We exchange observations upon the war news. We criticise von Kluck, and speak kindly of Joffre. We note, daily, that there is nothing to report on the Allies' right, and wonder regularly how the Russians are really getting on in the Eastern theatre.

Then, after observing that the only sportsman in the combined forces of the German Empire is—or was—the captain of the *Emden*, we come to the casualty lists—and there is silence.

Englishmen are fond of saying, with the satisfied air of men letting off a really excellent joke, that every one in Scotland knows every one else. As we study the morning's Roll of Honour, we realise that never was a more truthful jest uttered. There is not a name in the list of those who have died for Scotland which is not familiar to us. If we did not know the man—too often the boy—himself, we knew his people, or at least where his home was. In England, if you live in Kent, and you read that the Northumberland Fusiliers have been cut up or the Duke of Cornwall's Light Infantry badly knocked about, you merely sigh that so many more good men should have fallen. Their names are glorious names, but they are only names. But never a Scottish regiment comes under fire but the whole of Scotland feels it. Scotland is small enough to know all her sons by heart. You may live in Berwickshire, and the man who has died may have come from Skye; but his name is quite familiar to you. Big England's sorrow is national; little Scotland's is personal.

Then we pass on to our letters. Many of us—particularly the senior officers—have news direct from the trenches—scribbled scraps torn out of field-message books. We get constant tidings of the Old Regiment. They marched thirty-five miles on such a day; they captured a position after being under continuous shell fire for eight hours on another; they were personally thanked by the Field-Marshal on another. Oh, we shall have to work hard to get up to that standard!

"They want more officers," announces the Colonel. "Naturally, after the time they've been having! But they must go to the Third Battalion for them: that's the proper place. I will not have them coming here: I've told them so at Headquarters. The Service Battalions simply *must* be led by the officers who have trained them if they are to have a Chinaman's chance when we go out. I shall threaten to resign if they try any more of their tricks. That'll frighten 'em! Even dug-outs like me are rare and valuable objects at present."

The Company Commanders murmur assent—on the whole sympathetically. Anxious though they are to get upon business terms with the Kaiser, they are loath to abandon the unkempt but sturdy companies over which they have toiled so hard, and which now, though destitute of blossom, are rich in promise of fruit. But the senior subalterns look up hopefully. Their lot is hard. Some of them have been in the Service for ten years, yet they have been left behind. They command no companies. "Here," their faces say, "we are merely marking time while others learn. Send *us*!"

* * * * *

However, though they have taken no officers yet, signs are not wanting that they will take some soon. To-day each of us was presented with a small metal disc.

Bobby Little examined his curiously. Upon the face thereof was stamped, in ragged, irregular capitals—

[Illustration: LITTLE, R., 2ND LT.,
B. & W. HIGHRS.
C. OF E.]

"What is this for?" he asked.

Captain Wagstaffe answered.

"You wear it round your neck," he said.

Our four friends, once bitten, regarded the humorist suspiciously.

"Are you rotting us?" asked Waddell cautiously.

"No, my son," replied Wagstaffe, "I am not."

"What is it for, then?"

"It's called an Identity Disc. Every soldier on active service wears one."

"Why should the idiots put one's religion on the thing?" inquired Master Cockerell, scornfully regarding the letters "C. of E." upon his disc.

Wagstaffe regarded him curiously.

"Think it over," he suggested.

VII

SHOOTING STRAIGHT

"What for is the wee felly gaun' tae show us puctures?"

Second Lieutenant Bobby Little, assisted by a sergeant and two unhandy privates, is engaged in propping a large and highly-coloured work of art, mounted on a rough wooden frame and supported on two unsteady legs, against the wall of the barrack square. A half-platoon of A Company, seated upon an adjacent bank, chewing grass and enjoying the mellow autumn sunshine, regard the swaying masterpiece with frank curiosity. For the last fortnight they have been engaged in imbibing the science of musketry. They have learned to hold their rifles correctly, sitting, kneeling, standing, or lying; to bring their backsights and foresights into an undeviating straight line with the base of the bull's-eye; and to press the trigger in the manner laid down in the Musketry Regulations—without wriggling the body or "pulling-off."

They have also learned to adjust their sights, to perform the loading motions rapidly and correctly, and to obey such simple commands as—

"*At them two, weemen*"—officers' wives, probably—"*proceeding from left tae right across the square, at five hundred yairds*"

—they are really about fifteen yards away, covered with confusion—"*five roonds, fire!*"

But as yet they have discharged no shots from their rifles. It has all been make-believe, with dummy cartridges, and fictitious ranges, and snapping triggers. To be quite frank, they are getting just a little tired of musketry training—forgetting for the moment that a soldier who cannot use his rifle is merely an expense to his country and a free gift to the enemy. But the sight of Bobby Little's art gallery cheers them up. They contemplate the picture with childlike interest. It resembles nothing so much as one of those pleasing but imaginative posters by the display of which our Railway Companies seek to attract the tourist to the less remunerative portions of their systems.

"What for is the wee felly gaun' tae show us puctures?"

Thus Private Mucklewame. A pundit in the rear rank answers him.

"Yon's Gairmany."

"Gairmany ma auntie!" retorts Mucklewame. "There's no chumney-stalks in Gairmany."

"Maybe no; but there's wundmulls. See the wundmull there—on yon wee knowe!"

"There a pit-heid!" exclaims another voice. This homely spectacle is received with an affectionate sigh. Until two months ago more than half the platoon had never been out of sight of at least half a dozen.

"See the kirk, in ablow the brae!" says some one else, in a pleased voice. "It has a nock in the steeple."

"I hear they Gairmans send signals wi' their kirk-nocks," remarks Private M'Micking, who, as one of the Battalion signallers—or "buzzers," as the vernacular has it, in imitation of the buzzing of the Morse instrument—regards himself as a sort of junior Staff Officer. "They jist semaphore with the haunds of the nock—"

"I wonder," remarks the dreamy voice of Private M'Leary, the humorist of the platoon, "did ever a Gairman buzzer pit the ba' through his ain goal in a fitba' match?"

This irrelevant reference to a regrettable incident of the previous Saturday afternoon is greeted with so much laughter that Bobby Little, who has at length fixed his picture in position, whips round.

"Less talking there!" he announces severely, "or I shall have to stand you all at attention!"

There is immediate silence—there is nothing the matter with Bobby's discipline—and the outraged M'Micking has to content himself with a homicidal glare in the direction of M'Leary, who is now hanging virtuously upon his officer's lips.

"This," proceeds Bobby Little, "is what is known as a landscape target."

He indicates the picture, which, apparently overcome by so much public notice, promptly falls flat upon its face. A fatigue party under the sergeant hurries to its assistance.

"It is intended," resumes Bobby presently, "to teach you—us—to become familiar with various kinds of country, and to get into the habit of picking out conspicuous features of the landscape, and getting them by heart, and—er—so on. I want you all to study this picture for three minutes. Then I shall face you about and ask you to describe it to me."

After three minutes of puckered brows and hard breathing the squad is turned to its rear and the examination proceeds.

"Lance-Corporal Ness, what did you notice in the foreground of the picture?"

Lance-Corporal Ness gazes fiercely before him. He has noticed a good deal, but can remember nothing. Moreover, he has no very clear idea what a foreground may be.

"Private Mucklewame?"

Again silence, while the rotund Mucklewame perspires in the throes of mental exertion.

"Private Wemyss?"

No answer.

"Private M'Micking!"

The "buzzer" smiles feebly, but says nothing.

"Well,"—desperately—"Sergeant Angus! Tell them what you noticed in the foreground."

Sergeant Angus (*floruit* A.D. 1895) springs smartly to attention, and replies, with the instant obedience of the old soldier—

"The sky, sirr."

"Not in the foreground, as a rule," replies Bobby Little gently.
"About turn again, all of you, and we'll have another try."

In his next attempt Bobby abandons individual catechism.

"Now," he begins, "what conspicuous objects do we notice on this target? In the foreground I can see a low knoll. To the left I see a windmill. In the distance is a tall chimney. Half-right is a church. How would that church be marked on a map?"

No reply.

"Well," explains Bobby, anxious to parade a piece of knowledge which he only acquired himself a day or two ago, "churches are denoted in maps by a cross, mounted on a square or circle, according as the church has a square tower or a steeple. What has this church got?"

"A nock!" bellow the platoon, with stunning enthusiasm. (All but
Private M'Micking, that is.)

"A clock, sir," translates the sergeant, *sotto voce*.

"A clock? All right: but what I wanted was a steeple. Then, farther away, we can see a mine, a winding brook, and a house, with a wall in front of it. Who can see them?"

To judge by the collective expression of the audience, no one does.
Bobby ploughs on.

"Upon the skyline we notice—Squad, '*shun!*"

Captain Wagstaffe has strolled up. He is second in command of A
Company. Bobby explains to him modestly what he has been trying to do.

"Yes, I heard you," says Wagstaffe. "You take a breather, while I carry on for a bit. Squad, stand easy, and tell me what you can see on that target. Lance-Corporal Ness, show me a pit-head."

Lance-Corporal Ness steps briskly forward and lays a grubby forefinger on Bobby's "mine."

"Private Mucklewame, show me a burn."

The brook is at once identified.

"Private M'Leary, shut your eyes and tell me what there is just to the right of the windmill."

"A wee knowe, sirr," replies M'Leary at once. Bobby recognises his "low knoll"—also the fact that it is no use endeavouring to instruct the unlettered until you have learned their language.

"Very good!" says Captain Wagstaffe. "Now we will go on to what is known as Description and Recognition of Targets. Supposing I had sent one of you forward into that landscape as a scout.—By the way, what is a scout?"

Dead silence, as usual.

"Come along! Tell me, somebody! Private Mucklewame?"

"They gang oot in a procession on Setter-day efternoons, sirr, in short breeks," replies Mucklewame promptly.

"A procession is the very last thing a scout goes out in!" raps Wagstaffe. (It is plain to Mucklewame that the Captain has never been in Wishaw, but he does not argue the point.) "Private M'Micking, what is a scout?"

"A spy, sirr," replies the omniscient one.

"Well, that's better; but there's a big difference between the two. What is it?"

This is a poser. Several men know the difference, but feel quite incapable of explaining it. The question runs down the front rank. Finally it is held up and disposed of by one Mearns (from Aberdeen).

"A spy, sirr, gets mair money than a scout."

"Does he?" asks Captain Wagstaffe, smiling. "Well, I am not in a position to say. But if he does, he earns it! Why?"

"Because if he gets catched he gets shot," volunteers a rear-rank man.

"Right. Why is he shot?"

This conundrum is too deep for the squad. The Captain has to answer it himself.

"Because he is not in uniform, and cannot therefore be treated as an ordinary prisoner of war. So never go scouting in your nightshirt, Mucklewame!"

The respectable Mucklewame blushes deeply at this outrageous suggestion, but Wagstaffe proceeds—

"Now, supposing I sent you out scouting, and you discovered that over there—somewhere in the middle of this field"—he lays a finger on the field in question—"there was a fold in the ground where a machine-gun section was concealed: what would you do when you got back?"

"I would tell you, sirr," replied Private M'Micking politely.

"Tell me what?"

"That they was there, sirr."

"Where?"

"In yon place."

"How would you indicate the position of the place?"

"I would pint it oot with ma finger, sirr."

"Invisible objects half a mile away are not easily pointed out with the finger," Captain Wagstaffe mentions. "Lance-Corporal Ness, how would you describe it?"

"I would tak' you there, sirr."

"Thanks! But I doubt if either of us would come back! Private Wemyss?"

"I would say, sirr, that the place was west of the mansion-hoose."

"There's a good deal of land west of that mansion-house, you know," expostulates the Captain gently; "but we are getting on. Thompson?"

"I would say, sir," replies Thompson, puckering his brow, "that it was in ablow they trees."

"It would be hard to indicate the exact trees you meant. Trees are too common. You try, Corporal King."

But Corporal King, who earned his stripes by reason of physical rather than intellectual attributes, can only contribute a lame reference to "a bit hedge by yon dyke, where there's a kin' o' hole in the tairget." Wagstaffe breaks in—

"Now, everybody, take some conspicuous and unmistakable object about the middle of that landscape—something which no one can mistake. The mansion-house will do—the near end. Now then—*mansion-house, near end*! Got that?"

There is a general chorus of assent.

"Very well. I want you to imagine that the base of the mansion-house is the centre of a great clock-face. Where would twelve o'clock be?"

The platoon are plainly tickled by this new round-game. They reply—

"Straught up!"

"Right. Where is nine o'clock?"

"Over tae the left."

"Very good. And so on with all the other hours. Now, supposing I were to say, *End of mansion-house—six o'clock—white gate*—you would carry your eye straight *downward*, through the garden, until it encountered the gate. I would thus have enabled you to recognise a very small object in a wide landscape in the quickest possible time. See the idea?"

"Yes, sirr."

"All right. Now for our fold in the ground. *End of mansion-house—eight o'clock—*got that?"

There is an interested murmur of assent.

"That gives you the direction from the house. Now for the distance! *End of mansion-house—eight o 'clock—two finger-breadths*—what does that give you, Lance-Corporal Ness?"

"The corrner of a field, sirr."

"Right. This is *our* field. We have picked it correctly out of about twenty fields, you see. *Corner of field. In the middle of the field, a fold in the ground. At nine hundred—at the fold in the ground—five rounds—fire!* You see the idea now?"

"Yes, sirr."

"Very good. Let the platoon practise describing targets to one another, Mr. Little. Don't be too elaborate. Never employ either the clock or finger method if you can describe your target without. For instance: *Left of windmill—triangular cornfield. At the nearest corner—six hundred—rapid fire!* is all you want. Carry on, Mr. Little."

And leaving Bobby and his infant class to practise this new and amusing pastime, Captain Wagstaffe strolls away across the square to where the painstaking Waddell is contending with another squad.

They, too, have a landscape target—a different one. Before it half a dozen rifles stand, set in rests. Waddell has given the order: *Four hundred—at the road, where it passes under the viaduct—fire!* and six privates have laid the six rifles upon the point indicated. Waddell and Captain Wagstaffe walk down the line, peering along the sights of the rifles. Five are correctly aligned: the sixth points to the spacious firmament above the viaduct.

"Hallo!" observes Wagstaffe.

"This is the man's third try, sir," explains the harassed Waddell. "He doesn't seem to be able to distinguish anything at all."

"Eyesight wrong?"

"So he says, sir."

"Been a long time finding out, hasn't he?"

"The sergeant told me, sir," confides Waddell, "that in his opinion the man is 'working for his ticket.'"

"Umph!"

"I did not quite understand the expression, sir," continues the honest youth, "so I thought I would consult you."

"It means that he is trying to get his discharge. Bring him along:
I'll soon find out whether he is skrim-shanking or not."

Private M'Sweir is introduced, and led off to the lair of that hardened cynic, the Medical Officer. Here he is put through some simple visual tests. He soon finds himself out of his depth. It is extremely difficult to feign either myopia, hypermetria, or astigmatism if you are not acquainted with the necessary symptoms, and have not decided beforehand which (if any) of these diseases you are suffering from. In five minutes the afflicted M'Sweir is informed, to his unutterable indignation, that he has passed a severe ocular examination with flying colours, and is forthwith marched back to his squad, with instructions to recognise all targets in future, under pain of special instruction in the laws of optics during his leisure hours. Verily, in K (1)—that is the tabloid title of the First Hundred Thousand—the way of the malingerer is hard.

Still, the seed does not always fall upon stony ground. On his way to inspect a third platoon Captain Wagstaffe passes Bobby Little and his merry men. They are in pairs, indicating targets to one another.

Says Private Walker (oblivious of Captain Wagstaffe's proximity) to his friend, Private M'Leary—in an affected parody of his instructor's staccato utterance—

"*At yon three Gairman spies, gaun' up a close for tae despatch some wireless telegraphy—fufty roonds—fire!*"

To which Private M'Leary, not to be outdone, responds—

"*Public hoose—in the baur—back o' seeven o'clock—twa drams—fower fingers—rapid!*"

II

From this it is a mere step to—

"Butt Pairty, '*shun!* Forrm fourrs! Right! By your left, quick *marrch!*"

—on a bleak and cheerless morning in late October. It is not yet light; but a depressed party of about twenty-five are falling into line at the acrid invitation of two sergeants, who have apparently decided that the pen is mightier than the Lee-Enfield rifle; for each wears one stuck in his glengarry like an eagle's feather, and carries a rabbinical-looking inkhorn slung to his bosom. This literary pose is due to the fact that records are about to be taken of the performances of the Company on the shooting-range.

A half-awakened subaltern, who breakfasted at the grisly hour of a quarter-to-six, takes command, and the dolorous procession disappears into the gloom.

Half an hour later the Battalion parades, and sets off, to the sound of music, in pursuit. (It is perhaps needless to state that although we are deficient in rifles, possess neither belts, pouches, nor greatcoats, and are compelled to attach, our scanty accoutrements to our persons with ingenious contrivances of string, we boast a fully equipped and highly efficient pipe band, complete with pipers, big drummer, side drummers, and corybantic drum-major.)

By eight o'clock, after a muddy tramp of four miles, we are assembled at the two-hundred-yards firing point upon Number Three Range. The range itself is little more than a drive cut through, a pine-wood. It is nearly half a mile long. Across the far end runs a high sandy embankment, decorated just below the ridge with, a row of number-boards—one for each target. Of the targets themselves nothing as yet is to be seen.

"Now then, let's get a move on!" suggests the Senior Captain briskly. "Cockerell, ring up the butts, and ask Captain Wagstaffe to put up the targets."

The alert Mr. Cockerell hurries to the telephone, which lives in a small white-painted structure like a gramophone-stand. (It has been left at the firing-point by the all-providing butt-party.) He turns the call-handle smartly, takes the receiver out of the box, and begins....

There is no need to describe the performance which ensues. All telephone-users are familiar with it. It consists entirely of the word "Hallo!" repeated *crescendo* and *furioso* until exhaustion supervenes.

Presently Mr. Cockerell reports to the Captain—

"Telephone out of order, sir."

"I never knew a range telephone that wasn't," replies the Captain, inspecting the instrument. "Still, you might give this one a sporting chance, anyhow. It isn't a *wireless* telephone, you know! Corporal Kemp, connect that telephone for Mr. Cockerell."

A marble-faced N.C.O. kneels solemnly upon the turf and raises a small iron trapdoor—hitherto overlooked by the omniscient Cockerell—revealing a cavity some six inches deep, containing an electric plug-hole. Into this he thrusts the terminal of the telephone wire. Cockerell, scarlet in the face, watches him indignantly.

Telephonic communication between firing-point and butts is now established. That is to say, whenever Mr. Cockerell rings the bell some one in the butts courteously rings back. Overtures of a more intimate nature are greeted either with stony silence or another fantasia on the bell.

Meanwhile the captain is superintending firing arrangements.

"Are the first details ready to begin?" he shouts.

"Quite ready, sir," runs the reply down the firing line.

The Captain now comes to the telephone himself. He takes the receiver from Cockerell with masterful assurance.

"Hallo, there!" he calls. "I want to speak to Captain Wagstaffe."

"Honkle yang-yang?" inquires a ghostly voice.

"Captain Wagstaffe! Hurry up!"

Presently the bell rings, and the Captain gets to business.

"That you, Wagstaffe?" he inquires cheerily. "Look here, we're going to fire Practice Seven, Table B,—snap-shooting. I want you to raise all the targets for six seconds, just for sighting purposes. Do you understand?"

Here the bell rings continuously for ten seconds. Nothing daunted, the Captain tries again.

"That you, Wagstaffe? Practice Seven, Table B!"

"T'chk, t'chk!" replies Captain Wagstaffe.

"Begin by raising all the targets for six seconds. Then raise them six times for five seconds each.—no, as you were! Raise them five times for six seconds each. Got that? I say, are you *there*? What's that?"

"*Przemysl*" replies the telephone—or something to that effect. "*Czestochowa! Krsyszkowice! Plock!*"

The Captain, now on his mettle, continues:—

"I want you to signal the results on the rear targets as the front ones go down. After that we will fire—oh, *curse* the thing!"

He hastily removes the receiver, which is emitting sounds suggestive of the buckling of biscuit-tins, from his ear, and lays it on its rest. The bell promptly begins to ring again.

"Mr. Cockerell," he says resignedly, "double up to the butts and ask Captain Wagstaffe—"

"I'm here, old son," replies a gentle voice, as Captain Wagstaffe touches him upon the shoulder. "Been here some time!"

After mutual asperities, it is decided by the two Captains to dispense with the aid of the telephone proper, and communicate by bell alone. Captain Wagstaffe's tall figure strides back across the heather; the red flag on the butts flutters down; and we get to work.

Upon a long row of waterproof sheets—some thirty in all—lie the firers. Beside each is extended the form of a sergeant or officer, tickling his charge's ear with incoherent counsel, and imploring him, almost tearfully, not to get excited.

Suddenly thirty targets spring out of the earth in front of us, only to disappear again just as we have got over our surprise. They are not of the usual bull's-eye pattern, but are what is known as "figure" targets. The lower half is sea-green, the upper, white. In the centre, half on the green and half on the white, is a curious brown smudge. It might be anything, from a splash of mud to one of those mysterious brown-paper patterns which fall out of ladies' papers, but it really is intended to represent the head and shoulders of a man in khaki lying on grass and aiming at us. However, the British private, with his usual genius for misapprehension, has christened this effigy "the beggar in the boat."

With equal suddenness the targets swing up again. Crack! An uncontrolled spirit has loosed off his rifle before it has reached his shoulder. Blistering reproof follows. Then, after three or four seconds, comes a perfect salvo all down the line. The conscientious Mucklewame, slowly raising his foresight as he has been taught to do, from the base of the target to the centre, has just covered the beggar in the boat between wind and water, and is lingering lovingly over the second pull, when the inconsiderate beggar (and his boat) sink unostentatiously into the abyss, leaving the open-mouthed marksman with his finger on the trigger and an unfired cartridge still in the chamber. At the dentist's Time crawls; in snap-shooting contests he sprints.

Another set of targets slide up as the first go down, and upon these the hits are recorded by a forest of black or white discs, waving vigorously in the air. Here and there a red-and-white flag flaps derisively. Mucklewame gets one of these.

The marking-targets go down to half-mast again, and then comes another tense pause. Then, as the firing-targets reappear, there is another volley. This time Private Mucklewame leads the field, and decapitates a dandelion. The third time he has learned wisdom, and the beggar in the boat gets the bullet where all mocking foes should get it—in the neck!

Snap-shooting over, the combatants retire to the five-hundred-yards firing-point, taking with them that modern hair-shirt, the telephone.

Presently a fresh set of targets swing up—of the bull's-eye variety this time—and the markers are busy once more.

III

The interior of the butts is an unexpectedly spacious place. From the nearest firing-point you would not suspect their existence, except when the targets are up. Imagine a sort of miniature railway station—or rather, half a railway station—sunk into the ground, with a very long platform and a very low roof—eight feet high at the most. Upon the opposite side of this station, instead of the other platform, rises the sandy ridge previously mentioned—the stop-butt—crowned with its row of number-boards. Along the permanent way, in place of sleepers and metals, runs a long and narrow trough, in which, instead of railway carriages, some thirty great iron frames are standing side by side. These frames are double, and hold the targets. They are so arranged that if one is pushed up the other comes down. The markers stand along the platform, like railway porters.

There are two markers to each target. They, stand with their backs to the firers, comfortably conscious of several feet of earth and a stout brick wall, between them and low shooters. Number one squats down, paste-pot in hand, and repairs the bullet-holes in the unemployed target with patches of black or white paper. Number two, brandishing a pole to which is attached a disc, black on one side and white on the other, is acquiring a permanent crick in the neck through gaping upwards at the target in search of hits. He has to be sharp-eyed, for the bullet-hole is a small one, and springs into existence without any other intimation than a spirt of sand on the bank twenty yards behind. He must be alert, too, and signal the shots as they are made; otherwise the telephone will begin to interest itself on his behalf. The bell will ring, and a sarcastic voice will intimate—assuming that you can hear what it says—that C Company are sending a wreath and message of condolence as their contribution to the funeral of the marker at Number Seven target, who appears to have died at his post within the last ten minutes; coupled with a polite request that his successor may be appointed as rapidly as possible, as the war is not likely to last more than three years. To this the butt-officer replies that C Company had better come a bit closer to the target and try, try again.

There are practically no restrictions as to the length to which one may go in insulting butt-markers. The Geneva Convention is silent upon the subject, partly because it is almost impossible to say anything which can really hurt a marker's feelings, and partly because the butt-officer always has the last word in any unpleasantness which may arise. That is to say, when defeated over the telephone, he can always lower his targets, and with his myrmidons feign abstraction or insensibility until an overheated subaltern arrives at the double from the five-hundred-yards firing-point, conveying news of surrender.

Captain Wagstaffe was an admitted master of this game. He was a difficult subject to handle, for he was accustomed to return an eye for an eye when repartees were being exchanged; and when overborne by heavier metal—say, a peripatetic "brass-hat" from Hythe—he was accustomed to haul up the red butt-flag (which automatically brings all firing to a standstill), and stroll down the range to refute the intruder at close quarters. We must add that he was a most efficient butt-officer. When he was on duty, markers were most assiduous in their attention to theirs, which is not always the case.

Thomas Atkins rather enjoys marking. For one thing, he is permitted to remove as much clothing as he pleases, and to cover himself with stickiness and grime to his heart's content—always a highly prized privilege. He is also allowed to smoke, to exchange full-flavoured persiflage with his neighbours, and to refresh himself from time to time with mysterious items of provender wrapped in scraps of newspaper. Given an easy-going butt-officer and some timid subalterns, he can spend a very agreeable morning. Even when discipline is strict, marking is preferable to most other fatigues.

Crack! Crack! Crack! The fusilade has begun. Privates Ogg and Hogg are in charge of Number Thirteen target. They are beguiling the tedium of their task by a friendly gamble with the markers on Number Fourteen—Privates Cosh and Tosh. The rules of the game are simplicity itself. After each detail has fired, the target with the higher score receives the sum of one penny from its opponents. At the present moment, after a long run of adversity, Privates Cosh and Tosh are one penny to the good. Once again fortune smiles upon them. The first two shots go right through the bull—eight points straight away. The third is an inner; the fourth another bull; the fifth just grazes the line separating inners from outers. Private Tosh, who is scoring, promptly signals an inner. Meanwhile, target Number Thirteen is also being liberally marked—but by nothing of a remunerative nature. The gentleman at the firing-point is taking what is known as "a fine sight"—so fine, indeed, that each successive bullet either buries itself in the turf fifty yards short, or ricochets joyously from off the bank in front, hurling itself sideways through the target, accompanied by a storm of gravel, and tearing holes therein which even the biassed Ogg cannot class as clean hits.

"We hae gotten eighteen that time," announces Mr. Tosh to his rival, swinging his disc and inwardly blessing his unknown benefactor. (For obvious reasons the firer is known only to the marker by a number.) "Hoo's a' wi' you, Jock?"

"There's a [adjective] body here," replies Ogg, with gloomy sarcasm, "flingin' bricks through this yin!" He picks up the red-and-white flag for the fourth time, and unfurls it indignantly to the breeze.

"Here the officer!" says the warning voice of Hogg. "I doot he'll no allow your last yin, Peter."

He is right. The subaltern in charge of targets Thirteen to Sixteen, after a pained glance at the battered countenance of Number Thirteen, pauses before Fourteen, and jots down a figure on his butt-register.

"Fower, fower, fower, three, three, sirr," announces Tosh politely.

"Three bulls, one inner, and an ahter, sir," proclaims the Cockney sergeant simultaneously.

"Now, suppose *I* try," suggests the subaltern gently.

He examines the target, promptly disallows Tosh's last inner, and passes on.

"Seventeen *only!*" remarks Private Ogg severely. "I thocht sae!"

Private Cosh speaks—for the first time—removing a paste-brush, and some patching-paper from his mouth—

"Still, it's better nor a wash-oot! And onyway, you're due us tippence the noo!"

By way of contrast to the frivolous game of chance in the butts, the proceedings at the firing-point resolve themselves into a desperately earnest test of skill. The fortnight's range-practice is drawing to a close. Each evening registers have been made up, and firing averages adjusted, with the result that A and D Companies are found to have entirely outdistanced B and C, and to be running neck and neck for the championship of the battalion. Up till this morning D's average worked out at something under fifteen (out of a possible twenty), and A's at something over fourteen points. Both are quite amazing and incredible averages for a recruits' course; but then nearly everything about "K(1)" is amazing and incredible. Up till half an hour ago D had, if anything, increased their lead: then dire calamity overtook them.

One Pumpherston, Sergeant-Major and crack shot of the Company, solemnly blows down the barrel of his rifle and prostrates himself majestically upon his more than considerable stomach, for the purpose of firing his five rounds at five hundred yards. His average score so far has been one under "possible." Three officers and a couple of stray corporals gather behind him in eulogistic attitudes.

"How are the Company doing generally, Sergeant-Major?" inquires the Captain of D Company.

"Very well, sirr, except for some carelessness," replies the great man impressively. "That man there"—he indicates a shrinking figure hurrying rearwards—"has just spoilt his own score and another man's by putting two shots on the wrong target."

There is a horrified hum at this, for to fire upon some one else's target is the gravest crime in musketry. In the first place, it counts a miss for yourself. In the second, it may do a grievous wrong to your neighbour; for the law ordains that, in the event of more than five shots being found upon any target, only the worst five shall count. Therefore, if your unsolicited contribution takes the form of an outer, it must be counted, to the exclusion, possibly, of a bull. The culprit broke into a double.

Having delivered himself, Sergeant-Major Pumpherston graciously accepted the charger of cartridges which an obsequious acolyte was proffering, rammed it into the magazine, adjusted the sights, spread out his legs to an obtuse angle, and fired his first shot.

All eyes were turned upon target Number Seven. But there was no signal. All the other markers were busy flourishing discs or flags; only Number Seven remained cold and aloof.

The Captain of D Company laughed satirically.

"Number Seven gone to have his hair cut!" he observed.

"Third time this morning, sir," added a sycophantic subaltern.

The sergeant-major smiled indulgently,

"I can do without signals, sir," he said "I know where the shot went all right. I must get the next a *little* more to the left. That last one was a bit too near to three o'clock to be a certainty."

He fired again—with precisely the same result.

Every one was quite apologetic to the sergeant-major this time.

"This must be stopped," announced the Captain. "Mr. Simson, ring up Captain Wagstaffe on the telephone."

But the sergeant-major would not hear of this.

"The butt-registers are good enough for me, sir," he said with a paternal smile. He fired again. Once more the target stared back, blank and unresponsive.

This time the audience were too disgusted to speak. They merely shrugged their shoulders and glanced at one another with sarcastic smiles. The Captain, who had suffered a heavy reverse at the hands of Captain Wagstaffe earlier in the morning, began to rehearse the wording of his address over the telephone.

The sergeant-major fired his last two shots with impressive aplomb—only to be absolutely ignored twice more by Number Seven. Then he rose to his feet and saluted with ostentatious respectfulness.

"Four bulls and one inner, I *think*, sir. I'm afraid I pulled that last one off a bit."

The Captain is already at the telephone. For the moment this most feminine of instruments is found to be in an accommodating frame of mind. Captain Wagstaffe's voice is quickly heard.

"That you, Wagstaffe?" inquires the Captain. "I'm so sorry to bother you, but could you make inquiries and ascertain when the marker on Number Seven is likely to come out of the chloroform?"

"He has been sitting up and taking nourishment for some hours," replies the voice of Wagstaffe. "What message can I deliver to him?"

"None in particular, except that he has not signalled a single one of Sergeant-Major Pumpherston's shots!" replies the Captain of D, with crushing simplicity.

"Half a mo'!" replies Wagstaffe.... Then, presently—

"Hallo! Are you there, Whitson?"

"Yes. We are still here," Captain Whitson assures him frigidly.

"Right. Well, I have examined Number Seven target, and there are no shots on it of any kind whatever. But there are ten shots on Number Eight, if that's any help. Buck up with the next lot, will you? We are getting rather bored here. So long!"

There was nothing in it now. D Company had finished. The last two representatives of A were firing, and subalterns with note-books were performing prodigies of arithmetic. Bobby Little calculated that if these two scored eighteen points each they would pull the Company's total average up to fifteen precisely, beating D by a decimal.

The two slender threads upon which the success of this enterprise hung were named Lindsay and Budge. Lindsay was a phlegmatic youth with watery eyes. Nothing disturbed him, which was fortunate, for the commotion which surrounded him was considerable. A stout sergeant lay beside him on a waterproof sheet, whispering excited counsels of perfection, while Bobby Little danced in the rear, beseeching him to fire upon the proper target.

"Now, Lindsay," said Captain Whitson, in a trembling voice, "you are going to get into a good comfortable position, take your time, and score five bulls."

The amazing part of it all was that Lindsay very nearly did score five bulls. He actually got four, and would have had a fifth had not the stout sergeant, in excess of solicitude, tenderly wiped his watery eye for him with a grubby handkerchief just as he took the first pull for his third shot.

Altogether he scored nineteen; and the gallery, full of congratulations, moved on to inspect the performance of Private Budge, an extremely nervous subject: who, thanks to the fact that public attention had been concentrated so far upon Lindsay, and that his ministering sergeant was a matter-of-fact individual of few words, had put on two bulls—eight points. He now required to score only nine points in three shots.

Suddenly the hapless youth became aware of the breathless group in his rear. He promptly pulled his trigger, and just nicked the outside edge of the target—two points.

"I doot I'm gettin' a thing nairvous," he muttered apologetically to the sergeant.

"Havers! Shut your held and give the bull a bash!" responded that admirable person.

The twitching Budge, bracing himself, scored an inner—three points.

"A bull, and we do it!" murmured Bobby Little. Fortunately Budge did not hear.

"Ye're no daen badly," admitted the sergeant grudgingly.

Budge, a little piqued, determined to do better. He raised his foresight slowly; took the first pull; touched "six o'clock" on the distant bull—luckily the light was perfect—and took the second pull for the last time.

Next moment a white disc rose slowly out of the earth and covered the bull's-eye.

So Bobby Little was able next morning to congratulate his disciples upon being "the best-shooting platoon in the best-shooting Company in the best-shooting Battalion in the Brigade."

Not less than fifty other subalterns within a radius of five miles were saying the same thing to their platoons. It is right to foster a spirit of emulation in young troops.

VIII

BILLETS

Scene, a village street, deserted. Rain falls. (It has been falling for about three weeks.) *A tucket sounds. Enter, reluctantly, soldiery. They grouse. There appear severally, in doorways, children. They stare. And at chamber-windows, serving-maids. They make eyes. The soldiery make friendly signs.*

Such is the stage setting for our daily morning parade. We have been here for some weeks now, and the populace is getting used to us. But when we first burst upon this peaceful township I think we may say, without undue egoism, that we created a profound sensation. In this sleepy corner of Hampshire His Majesty's uniform, enclosing a casual soldier or sailor on furlough, is a common enough sight, but a whole regiment on the march is the rarest of spectacles. As for this tatterdemalion northern horde, which swept down the street a few Sundays ago, with kilts swinging, bonnets cocked, and Pipes skirling, as if they were actually returning from a triumphant campaign instead of only rehearsing for one—well, as I say, the inhabitants had never seen anything like us in the world before. We achieved a *succès fou*. In fact, we were quite embarrassed by the attention bestowed upon us. During our first few parades the audience could with difficulty be kept off the stage. It was impossible to get the children into school, or the maids to come in and make the beds. Whenever a small boy spied an officer, he stood in his way and saluted him. Dogs enlisted in large numbers, sitting down with an air of pleased expectancy in the supernumerary rank, and waiting for this new and delightful pastime to take a fresh turn. When we marched out to our training area, later in the day, infant schools were decanted on to the road under a beaming vicar, to utter what we took to be patriotic sounds and wave handkerchiefs.

Off duty, we fraternised with the inhabitants. The language was a difficulty, of course; but a great deal can be done by mutual goodwill and a few gestures. It would have warmed the heart of a philologist to note the success with which a couple of kilted heroes from the banks of Loch Lomond would sidle up to two giggling damosels of Hampshire at the corner of the High Street, by the post office, and invite them to come for a walk. Though it was obvious that neither party could understand a single word that the other was saying, they never failed to arrive at an understanding; and the quartette, having formed two-deep, would disappear into a gloaming as black as ink, to inhale the evening air and take sweet counsel together—at a temperature of about twenty-five degrees Fahrenheit.

You ought to see us change guard. A similar ceremony takes place, we believe, outside Buckingham Palace every morning, and draws a considerable crowd; but you simply cannot compare it with ours. How often does the guard at Buckingham Palace fix bayonets? Once! and the thing is over. It is hardly worth while turning out to see. *We* sometimes do it as much as seven or eight times before we get it right, and even then we only stop because the sergeant-in-charge is threatened with clergyman's sore throat. The morning Private Mucklewame fixed his bayonet for the first time, two small boys stayed away from school all day in order to see him unfix it when he came off guard in the afternoon. Has any one ever done that at Buckingham Palace?

However, as I say, they have got used to us now. We fall in for our diurnal labours in comparative solitude, usually in heavy rain and without pomp. We are fairly into the collar by this time. We have been worked desperately hard for more than four months; we are grunting doggedly away at our job, not because we like it, but because we know it is the only thing to do. To march, to dig, to extend, to close; to practise advance-guards and rear-guards, and pickets, in fair weather or foul, often with empty stomachs—that is our daily and sometimes our nightly programme. We are growing more and more efficient, and our powers of endurance are increasing. But, as already stated, we no longer go about our task like singing birds.

It is a quarter to nine in the morning. All down the street doors are opening, and men appear, tugging at their equipment. (Yes, we are partially equipped now.) Most of B Company live in this street. They are fortunate, for only two or three are billeted in each little house, where they are quite domestic pets by this time. Their billeting includes "subsistence," which means that they are catered for by an experienced female instead of a male cooking-class still in the elementary stages of its art.

"A" are not so fortunate. They are living in barns or hay-lofts, sleeping on the floor, eating on the floor, existing on the floor generally. Their food is cooked (by the earnest band of students aforementioned) in open-air camp-kitchens; and in this weather it is sometimes difficult to keep the fires alight, and not always possible to kindle them.

"D" are a shade better off. They occupy a large empty mansion at the end of the street. It does not contain a stick of furniture; but there are fireplaces (with Adam mantelpieces), and the one thing of which the War Office never seems to stint us is coal. So "D" are warm, anyhow. Thirty men live in the drawing-room. Its late tenant would probably be impressed with its new scheme of upholstery. On the floor, straw palliasses and gravy. On the walls, "cigarette phobies"—by the way, the children down here call them "fag picters." Across the room run clothes-lines, bearing steaming garments (and tell it not in Gath!) an occasional hare skin.

"C" are billeted in a village two miles away, and we see them but rarely.

The rain has ceased for a brief space—it always does about parade time—and we accordingly fall in. The men are carrying picks and shovels, and make no attempt to look pleased at the circumstance. They realise that they are in for a morning's hard digging, and very likely for an evening's field operations as well. When we began, company training a few weeks ago, entrenching was rather popular. More than half of us are miners or tillers of the soil, and the pick and shovel gave us a home-like sensation. Here was a chance, too, of showing regular soldiers how a job should be properly accomplished. So we dug with great enthusiasm.

But A Company have got over that now. They have developed into sufficiently old soldiers to have acquired the correct military attitude towards manual labour. Trench-digging is a "fatigue," to be classed with, coal-carrying, floor-scrubbing, and other civilian pursuits. The word "fatigue" is a shibboleth with, the British private. Persuade him that a task is part of his duty as a soldier, and he will perform it with tolerable cheerfulness; but once allow him to regard that task as a "fatigue," and he will shirk it whenever possible, and regard himself as a deeply injured individual when called upon to undertake it. Our battalion has now reached a sufficient state of maturity to be constantly on the *qui vive* for cunningly disguised fatigues. The other day, when kilts were issued for the first time, Private Tosh, gloomily surveying his newly unveiled extremities, was heard to remark with a sigh—

"Anither fatigue! Knees tae wash, noo!"

Presently Captain Blaikie arrives upon the scene; the senior subaltern reports all present, and we tramp off through the mud to our training area.

We are more or less in possession of our proper equipment now. That is to say, our wearing apparel and the appurtenances thereof are no longer held in position with string. The men have belts, pouches, and slings in which to carry their greatcoats. The greatcoats were the last to materialise. Since their arrival we have lost in decorative effect what we have gained in martial appearance. For a month or two each man wore over his uniform during wet weather—in other words, all day—a garment which the Army Ordnance Department described as—"Greatcoat, Civilian, one." An Old Testament writer would have termed it "a coat of many colours." A tailor would have said that it was a "superb vicuna raglan sack." You and I would have called it, quite simply, a reach-me-down. Anyhow, the combined effect was unique. As we plodded patiently along the road in our tarnished finery, with our eye-arresting checks and imitation velvet collars, caked with mud and wrinkled with rain, we looked like nothing so much on earth as a gang of weighers returning from an unsuccessful day at a suburban race-meeting.

But now the khaki-mills have ground out another million yards or so, and we have regulation greatcoats. Water-bottles, haversacks, mess-tins, and waterproof sheets have been slowly filtering into our possession; and whenever we "mobilise," which we do as a rule about once a fortnight—whether owing to invasion scares or as a test of efficiency we do not know—we fall in on our alarm-posts in something distinctly resembling 'the full "Christmas-tree" rig. Sam Browne belts have been wisely discarded by the officers in favour of web-equipment; and although Bobby Little's shoulders ache with the weight of his pack, he is comfortably conscious of two things—firstly, that even when separated from his baggage he can still subsist in fair comfort on what he carries upon his person; and secondly, that his "expectation of life," as the insurance offices say, has increased about a hundred per cent. now that the German sharpshooters will no longer be able to pick him out from his men.

Presently we approach the scene of our day's work, Area Number Fourteen. We are now far advanced in company training. The barrack square is a thing of the past. Commands are no longer preceded by cautions and explanations. A note on a whistle, followed by a brusque word or gesture, is sufficient to set us smartly on the move.

Suddenly we are called upon to give a test of our quality. A rotund figure upon horseback appears at a bend in the road. Captain Blaikie recognises General Freeman.

(We may note that the General's name is not really Freeman. We are much harried by generals at present. They roam about the country on horseback, and ask company commanders what they are doing; and no company commander has ever yet succeeded in framing an answer which sounds in the least degree credible. There are three generals; we call them Freeman, Hardy, and Willis, because we suspect that they are all—to judge from their fondness for keeping us on the run—financially interested in the consumption of shoe-leather. In other respects they differ, and a wise company commander will carefully bear their idiosyncrasies in mind and act accordingly, if he wishes to be regarded as an intelligent officer.)

Freeman is a man of action. He likes to see people running about. When he appears upon the horizon whole battalions break into a double.

Hardy is one of the old school: he likes things done decently and in order. He worships bright buttons, and exact words of command, and a perfectly wheeling line. He mistrusts unconventional movements and individual tactics. "No use trying to run," he says, "before you can walk." When we see him, we dress the company and advance in review order.

Willis gives little trouble. He seldom criticises, but when he does his criticism is always of a valuable nature; and he is particularly courteous and helpful to young officers. But, like lesser men, he has his fads. These are two—feet and cookery. He has been known to call a private out of the ranks on a route-march and request him to take his boots off for purposes of public display. "A soldier marches on two things," he announces—"his feet and his stomach." Then he calls up another man and asks him if he knows how to make a sea-pie. The man never does know, which is fortunate, for otherwise General Willis would not be able to tell him. After that he trots happily away, to ask some one else.

However, here we are face to face with General Freeman. Immediate action is called for. Captain Blaikie flings an order over his shoulder to the subaltern in command of the leading platoon—

"Pass back word that this road is under shell fire. Move!"

—and rides forward to meet the General.

In ten seconds the road behind him is absolutely clear, and the men are streaming out to right and left in half-platoons. Waddell's platoon has the hardest time, for they were passing a quickset hedge when the order came. However, they hurl themselves blasphemously through, and double on, scratched and panting.

"Good morning, sir!" says Captain Blaikie, saluting.

"Good morning!" says General Freeman. "What was that last movement?"

"The men are taking 'artillery' formation, sir. I have just passed the word down that the road is under shell fire."

"Quite so. But don't you think you ought to keep some of your company in rear, as a supporting line? I see you have got them all up on one front."

By this time A Company is advancing in its original direction, but split up into eight half-platoons in single file—four on each side of the road, at intervals of thirty yards. The movement has been quite smartly carried out. Still, a critic must criticise or go out of business. However, Captain Blaikie is an old hand.

"I was assuming that my company formed part of a battalion, sir," he explained. "There are supposed to be three other companies in rear of mine."

"I see. Still, tell two of your sections to fall back and form a supporting line."

Captain Blaikie, remembering that generals have little time for study of such works as the new drill-book, and that when General Freeman says "section" he probably means "platoon," orders Numbers Two and Four to fall back. This manoeuvre is safely accomplished.

"Now, let me see them close on the road."

Captain Blaikie blows a whistle, and slaps himself on the top of the head. In three minutes the long-suffering platoons are back on the road, extracting thorns from their flesh and assuaging the agony of their abrasions by clandestine massage.

General Freeman rides away, and the column moves on. Two minutes later Captain Wagstaffe doubles up from the rear to announce that General Hardy is only two hundred yards behind.

"Pass back word to the men," groans Captain Blaikie, "to march at attention, put their caps straight, and slope their shovels properly. And send an orderly to that hilltop to look out for General Willis. Tell him to unlace his boots when he gets there, and on no account to admit that he knows how to make a sea-pie!"

IX

MID-CHANNEL

The Great War has been terribly hard on the text-books.

When we began to dig trenches, many weeks ago, we always selected a site with a good field of fire.

"No good putting your trenches," said the text-book, "where you can't see the enemy."

This seemed only common-sense; so we dug our trenches in open plains, or on the forward slope of a hill, where we could command the enemy's movements up to two thousand yards.

Another maxim which we were urged to take to heart was—When not entrenched, always take advantage of *natural* cover of any kind; such as farm buildings, plantations, and railway embankments.

We were also given practice in describing and recognising inconspicuous targets at long range, in order to be able to harass the enemy the moment he showed himself.

Well, recently generals and staff officers have been coming home from the front and giving us lectures. We regard most lectures as a "fatigue"—but not these. We have learned more from these quiet-mannered, tired-looking men in a brief hour than from all the manuals that ever came out of Gale and Poldens'. We have heard the history of the War from the inside. We know why our Army retreated from Mons; we know what prevented the relief of Antwerp. But above all, we have learned to revise some of our most cherished theories.

Briefly, the amended version of the law and the prophets comes to this:—

Never, under any circumstances, place your trenches where you can see the enemy a long way off. If you do, he will inevitably see you too, and will shell you out of them in no time. You need not be afraid of being rushed; a field of fire of two hundred yards or so will be sufficient to wipe him off the face of the earth.

Never, under any circumstances, take cover in farm buildings, or plantations, or behind railway embankments, or in any place likely to be marked on a large-scale map. Their position and range are known to a yard. Your safest place is the middle of an open plain or ploughed field. There it will be more difficult for the enemy's range-takers to gauge your exact distance.

In musketry, concentrate all your energies on taking care of your rifle and practising "rapid." You will seldom have to fire over a greater distance than two hundred yards; and at that range British rapid fire is the most dreadful medium of destruction yet devised in warfare.

All this scraps a good deal of laboriously acquired learning, but it rings true. So we site our trenches now according to the lessons taught us by the bitter experience of others.

Having arrived at our allotted area, we get to work. The firing-trench proper is outlined on the turf a hundred yards or so down the reverse slope of a low hill. When it is finished it will be a mere crack in the ground, with no front cover to speak of; for that would make it conspicuous. Number One Platoon gets to work on this. To Number Two is assigned a more subtle task—namely, the construction of a dummy trench a comfortable distance ahead, dug out to the depth of a few inches, to delude inquisitive aeroplanes, and rendered easily visible to the enemy's observing stations by a parapet of newly-turned earth. Numbers Three and Four concentrate their energies upon the supporting trench and its approaches.

The firing-trench is our place of business—our office in the city, so to speak. The supporting trench is our suburban residence, whither the weary toiler may betake himself periodically (or, more correctly, in relays) for purposes of refreshment and repose. The firing-trench, like most business premises, is severe in design and destitute of ornament. But the suburban trench lends itself to more imaginative treatment. An auctioneer's catalogue would describe it as *A commodious bijou residence, on* (or of) *chalky soil; three feet wide and six feet deep; in the style of the best troglodyte period. Thirty seconds brisk crawl (or per stretcher) from the firing line. Gas laid on—*

But only once, in a field near Aldershot, where Private Mucklewame first laid bare, and then perforated, the town main with his pick.

—*With own water supply*—ankle-deep at times—*telephone, and the usual offices*.

We may note that the telephone communicates with the observing-station, lying well forward, in line with the dummy trench. The most important of the usual offices is the hospital—a cavern excavated at the back of the trench, and roofed over with hurdles, earth, and turf.

It is hardly necessary to add that we do not possess a real field-telephone. But when you have spent four months in firing dummy cartridges, performing bayonet exercises without bayonets, taking hasty cover from non-existent shell fire, capturing positions held by no enemy, and enacting the part of a "casualty" without having received a scratch, telephoning without a telephone is a comparatively simple operation. All you require is a ball of string and no sense of humour. Second Lieutenant Waddell manages our telephone.

Meanwhile we possess our souls in patience. We know that the factories are humming night and day on our behalf; and that if, upon a certain day in a certain month, the contractors do not deliver our equipment down to the last water-bottle cork, "K" will want to know the reason why; and we cannot imagine any contractor being so foolhardy as to provoke that terrible man into an inquiring attitude of mind.

Now we are at work. We almost wish that Freeman, Hardy, and Willis could see us. Our buttons may occasionally lack lustre; we may cherish unorthodox notions as to the correct method of presenting arms; we may not always present an unbroken front on the parade-ground—but we *can* dig! Even the fact that we do not want to, cannot altogether eradicate a truly human desire to "show off." "Each man to his art," we say. We are quite content to excel in ours, the oldest in the world. We know enough now about the conditions of the present war to be aware that when we go out on service only three things will really count—to march; to dig; and to fire, upon occasion, fifteen rounds a minute. Our rapid fire is already fair; we can march more than a little; and if men who have been excavating the bowels of the earth for eight hours a day ever since they were old enough to swing a pick cannot make short work of a Hampshire chalk down, they are no true members of their Trades Union or the First Hundred Thousand.

We have stuck to the phraseology of our old calling.

"Whaur's ma drawer?" inquires Private Hogg, a thick-set young man with bandy legs, wiping his countenance with a much-tattooed arm. He has just completed five strenuous minutes with a pick. "Come away, Geordie, wi' yon shovel!"

The shovel is preceded by an adjective. It is the only adjective that
A Company knows. (No, not that one. The second on the list!)

Mr. George Ogg steps down into the breach, and sets to work. He is a small man, strongly resembling the Emperor of China in a third-rate provincial pantomime. His weapon is the spade. In civil life he would have shovelled the broken coal into a "hutch," and "hurled" it away to the shaft. That was why Private Hogg referred to him as a "drawer." In his military capacity he now removes the chalky soil from the trench with great dexterity, and builds it up into a neat parapet behind, as a precaution against the back-blast of a "Black Maria."

There are not enough, picks and shovels to go round—*cela va sans dire*. However, Private Mucklewame and others, who are not of the delving persuasion, exhibit no resentment. Digging is not their department. If you hand them a pick and shovel and invite them to set to work, they lay the pick upon the ground beside the trench and proceed to shovel earth over it until they have lost it. At a later stage in this great war-game they will fight for these picks and shovels like wild beasts. Shrapnel is a sure solvent of professional etiquette.

However, to-day the pickless squad are lined up a short distance away by the relentless Captain Wagstaffe, and informed—

"You are under fire from that wood. Dig yourselves in!"

Digging oneself in is another highly unpopular fatigue. First of all you produce your portable entrenching-tool—it looks like a combination of a modern tack-hammer and a medieval back-scratcher—and fit it to its haft. Then you lie flat upon your face on the wet grass, and having scratched up some small lumps of turf, proceed to build these into a parapet. Into the hole formed by the excavation of the turf you then put your head, and in this ostrich-like posture await further instructions. Private Mucklewame is of opinion that it would be equally effective, and infinitely less fatiguing, simply to lie down prone and close the eyes.

After Captain Wagstaffe has criticised the preliminary parapets—most of them are condemned as not being bullet-proof—the work is continued. It is not easy, and never comfortable, to dig lying down; but we must all learn to do it; so we proceed painfully to construct a shallow trough for our bodies and an annexe for our boots. Gradually we sink out of sight, and Captain Wagstaffe, standing fifty yards to our front, is able to assure us that he can now see nothing—except Private Mucklewame's lower dorsal curve.

By this time the rain has returned for good, and the short winter day is drawing to a gloomy close. It is after three, and we have been working, with one brief interval, for nearly five hours. The signal is given to take shelter. We huddle together under the leafless trees, and get wetter.

Next comes the order to unroll greatcoats. Five minutes later comes another—to fall in. Tools are counted; there is the usual maddening wait while search is made for a missing pick. But at last the final word of command rings out, and the sodden, leaden-footed procession sets out on its four-mile tramp home.

We are not in good spirits. One's frame of mind at all times depends largely upon what the immediate future has to offer; and, frankly, we have little to inspire us in that direction at present. When we joined, four long months ago, there loomed largely and splendidly before our eyes only two alternatives—victory in battle or death with honour. We might live, or we might die; but life, while it lasted, would not lack great moments. In our haste we had overlooked the long dreary waste which lay—which always lies—between dream and fulfilment. The glorious splash of patriotic fervour which launched us on our way has subsided; we have reached mid-channel; and the haven where we would be is still afar off. The brave future of which we dreamed in our dour and uncommunicative souls seems as remote as ever, and the present has settled down into a permanency.

To-day, for instance, we have tramped a certain number of miles; we have worked for a certain number of hours; and we have got wet through for the hundredth time. We are now tramping home to a dinner which will probably not be ready, because, as yesterday, it has been cooked in the open air under weeping skies. While waiting for it, we shall clean the same old rifle. When night falls, we shall sleep uneasily upon a comfortless floor, in an atmosphere of stale food and damp humanity. In the morning we shall rise up reluctantly, and go forth, probably in heavy rain, to our labour until the evening—the same labour and the same evening. We admit that it can't be helped: the officers and the authorities do their best for us under discouraging circumstances: but there it is. Out at the front, we hear, men actually get as much as three days off at a time—three days of hot baths and abundant food and dry beds. To us, in our present frame of mind, that seems worth any number of bullets and frost-bites.

And—bitterest thought of all—New Year's Day, with all its convivial associations, is only a few weeks away. When it comes, the folk at home will celebrate it, doubtless with many a kindly toast to the lads "oot there," and the lads "doon there." But what will that profit us? In this barbarous country we understand that they take no notice of the sacred festival at all. There will probably be a route-march, to keep us out of the public-houses.

Et patiti, et patita. Are we fed up? YES!

As we swing down the village street, slightly cheered by a faint aroma of Irish stew—the cooks have got the fires alight after all—the adjutant rides up, and reins in his horse beside our company commander.

Battalion orders of some kind! Probably a full-dress parade, to trace a missing bayonet!

Presently he rides away; and Captain Blaikie, instead of halting and dismissing us in the street as usual, leads us down an alley into the backyard which serves as our apology for a parade-ground. We form close column of platoons, stand at ease, and wait resignedly.

Then Captain Blaikie's voice falls upon our ears.

"A Company, I have an announcement to make to you. His Majesty the King—"

So that is it. Another Royal Review! Well, it will be a break in the general monotony.

"—who has noted your hard work, good discipline, and steady progress with the keenest satisfaction and pride—"

We are not utterly forgotten, then.

"—has commanded that every man in the battalion is to have seven days' full leave of absence."

"A-a-ah!" We strain our tingling ears.

"We are to go by companies, a week at a time. 'C' will go first."

"C" indeed! Who are "C," to—?

"A Company's leave—*our* leave—will begin on the twenty-eighth of December, and extend to the third of January."

The staccato words sink slowly in, and then thoughts come tumbling.

"Free—free on New Year's Day! Almichty! Free to gang hame! Free tae—"

Then comes an icy chill upon our hearts. How are we to get home? Scotland is hundreds of miles away. The fare, even on a "soldier's" ticket—

But the Captain has not quite finished.

"Every man will receive a week's pay in advance; and his fare, home and back, will be paid by Government. That is all."

And quite enough too! We rock upon our squelching feet. But the Captain adds, without any suspicion of his parade-ground manner—

"If I may say so, I think that if ever men deserved a good holiday, you do. Company, slope arms! Dis-*miss*!"

* * * * *

We do not cheer: we are not built that way. But as we stream off to our Irish stew, the dourest of us says in his heart—

"God Save the King!"

X

DEEDS OF DARKNESS

A moonlit, wintry night. Four hundred men are clumping along the frost-bound road, under the pleasing illusion that because they are neither whistling nor talking they are making no noise.

At the head of the column march Captains Mackintosh and Shand, the respective commanders of C and D Companies. Occasionally Mackintosh, the senior, interpolates a remark of a casual or professional nature. To all these his colleague replies in a low and reproachful whisper. The pair represent two schools of military thought—a fact of which their respective subalterns are well aware,—and act accordingly.

"In preparing troops for active service, you must make the conditions as *real* as possible from the very outset," postulates Shand. "Perform all your exercises just as you would in war. When you dig trenches, let every man work with his weather-eye open and his rifle handy, in case of sudden attack. If you go out on night operations don't advertise your position by stopping to give your men a recitation. No talking—no smoking—no unnecessary delay or exposure! Just go straight to your point of deployment, and do what you came out to do."

To this Mackintosh replies,—

"That's all right for trained troops. But ours aren't half-trained yet; all our work just now is purely educational. It's no use expecting a gang of rivet-heaters from Clydebank to form an elaborate outpost line, just because you whispered a few sweet nothings in the dark to your leading section of fours! You simply *must* explain every step you take, at present."

But Shand shakes his head.

"It's not soldierly," he sighs.

Hence the present one-sided—or apparently one-sided—dialogue. To the men marching immediately behind, it sounds like something between a soliloquy and a chat over the telephone.

Presently Captain Mackintosh announces,—

"We might send the scouts ahead now I think."

Shand gives an inaudible assent. The column is halted, and the scouts called up. A brief command, and they disappear into the darkness, at the double. C and D Companies give them five minutes start, and move on. The road at this point runs past a low mossy wall, surmounted by a venerable yew hedge, clipped at intervals into the semblance of some heraldic monster. Beyond the hedge, in the middle distance, looms a square and stately Georgian mansion, whose lights twinkle hospitably.

"I think, Shand," suggests Mackintosh with more formality, now that he is approaching the scene of action, "that we might attack at two different points, each of us with his own company. What is your opinion?"

The officer addressed makes no immediate reply. His gaze is fixed upon the yew hedge, as if searching for gun positions or vulnerable points. Presently, however, he turns away, and coming close to Captain Mackintosh, puts his lips to his left ear. Mackintosh prepares his intellect for the reception of a pearl of strategy.

But Captain Shand merely announces, in his regulation whisper,—

"Dam pretty girl lives in that house, old man!"

II

Private Peter Dunshie, scout, groping painfully and profanely through a close-growing wood, paused to unwind a clinging tendril from his bare knees. As he bent down, his face came into sudden contact with a cold, wet, prickly bramble-bush, which promptly drew a loving but excoriating finger across his right cheek.

He started back, with a muffled exclamation. Instantly there arose at his very feet the sound as of a motor-engine being wound up, and a flustered and protesting cock-pheasant hoisted itself tumultuously clear of the undergrowth and sailed away, shrieking, over the trees.

Finally, a hare, which had sat cowering in the bracken, hare-like, when it might have loped away, selected this, the one moment when it ought to have sat still, to bolt frantically between Peter's bandy legs and speed away down a long moon-dappled avenue.

Private Dunshie, a prey to nervous shock, said what naturally rose to his lips. To be frank, he said it several times. He had spent the greater part of his life selling evening papers in the streets of Glasgow: and the profession of journalism, though it breeds many virtues in its votaries, is entirely useless as a preparation for conditions either of silence or solitude. Private Dunshie had no experience of either of these things, and consequently feared them both. He was acutely afraid. What he understood and appreciated was Argyle Street on a Saturday night. That was life! That was light! That was civilisation! As for creeping about in this uncanny wood, filled with noxious animals and adhesive vegetation—well, Dunshie was heartily sorry that he had ever volunteered for service as a scout. He had only done so, of course, because the post seemed to offer certain relaxations from the austerity of company routine—a little more freedom of movement, a little less trench-digging, and a minimum of supervision. He would have been thankful for a supervisor now!

That evening, when the scouts doubled ahead, Lieutenant Simson had halted them upon the skirts of a dark, dreich plantation, and said—

"A and B Companies represent the enemy. They are beyond that crest, finishing the trenches which were begun the 'other day. They intend to hold these against our attack. Our only chance is to take them by surprise. As they will probably have thrown out a line of outposts, you scouts will now scatter and endeavour to get through that line, or at least obtain exact knowledge of its composition. My belief is that the enemy will content themselves with placing a piquet on each of the two roads which run through their position; but it is possible that they will also post sentry-groups in the wood which lies between. However, that is what you have to find out. Don't go and get captured. Move!"

The scouts silently scattered, and each man set out to pierce his allotted section of the enemy's position. Private Dunshie, who had hoped for a road, or at least a cart-track, to follow, found himself, by the worst of luck, assigned to a portion of the thick belt of wood which stretched between the two roads. Nature had not intended him for a pioneer: he was essentially a city man. However, he toiled on, rending the undergrowth, putting up game, falling over tree-roots, and generally acting as advertising agent for the approaching attack.

By way of contrast, two hundred yards to his right, picking his way with cat-like care and rare enjoyment, was Private M'Snape. He was of the true scout breed. In the dim and distant days before the call of the blood had swept him into "K(1)," he had been a Boy Scout of no mean repute. He was clean in person and courteous in manner. He could be trusted to deliver a message promptly. He could light a fire in a high wind with two matches, and provide himself with a meal of sorts where another would have starved. He could distinguish an oak from an elm, and was sufficiently familiar with the movements of the heavenly bodies to be able to find his way across country by night. He was truthful, and amenable to discipline. In short, he was the embodiment of a system which in times of peace had served as a text for innumerable well-meaning but muddle-headed politicians of a certain type, who made a specialty of keeping the nation upon the alert against the insidious encroachments of—Heaven help us!—Militarism!

To-night all M'Snape's soul was set on getting through the enemy's outpost line, and discovering a way of ingress for the host behind him. He had no map, but he had the Plough and a fitful moon to guide him, and he held a clear notion of the disposition of the trenches in his retentive brain. On his left he could hear the distressing sounds of Dunshie's dolorous progress; but these were growing fainter. The reason was that Dunshie, like most persons who follow the line of least resistance, was walking in a circle. In fact, a few minutes later his circuitous path brought him out upon the long straight road which ran up over the hill towards the trenches.

With a sigh of relief Dunshie stepped out upon the good hard macadam, and proceeded with the merest show of stealth up the gentle gradient. But he was not yet at ease. The over-arching trees formed a tunnel in which his footsteps reverberated uncomfortably. The moon had retired behind a cloud. Dunshie, gregarious and urban, quaked anew. Reflecting longingly upon his bright and cosy billet, with the "subsistence" which was doubtless being prepared against his return, he saw no occasion to reconsider his opinion that in the country no decent body should over be called up to go out after dark unaccompanied. At that moment Dunshie would have bartered his soul for the sight of an electric tram.

The darkness grew more intense. Something stirred in the wood beside him, and his skin tingled. An owl hooted suddenly, and he jumped. Next, the gross darkness was illuminated by a pale and ghostly radiance, coming up from behind; and something brushed past him—something which squeaked and panted. His hair rose upon his scalp. A friendly "Good-night!" uttered in a strong Hampshire accent into his left ear, accentuated rather than soothed his terrors. He sat down suddenly upon a bank by the roadside, and feebly mopped his moist brow.

The bicycle, having passed him, wobbled on up the hill, shedding a fitful ray upon alternate sides of the road. Suddenly—raucous and stunning, but oh, how sweet!—rang out the voice of Dunshie's lifelong friend, Private Mucklewame.

"Halt! Wha goes there!"

The cyclist made no reply, but kept his devious course. Private Mucklewame, who liked to do things decently and in order, stepped heavily out of the hedge into the middle of the road, and repeated his question in a reproving voice. There was no answer.

This was most irregular. According to the text of the spirited little dialogue in which Mucklewame had been recently rehearsed by his piquet commander, the man on the bicycle ought to have said "Friend!" This cue received, Mucklewame was prepared to continue. Without it he was gravelled. He tried once more.

"Halt! Wha goes—"

"On His Majesty's Service, my lad!" responded a hearty voice; and the postman, supplementing this information with a friendly good-night, wobbled up the hill and disappeared from sight.

The punctilious Mucklewame was still glaring severely after this unseemly "gagger," when he became aware of footsteps upon the road. A pedestrian was plodding up the hill in the wake of the postman. He would stand no nonsense this time.

"Halt!" he commanded. "Wha goes there?"

"Hey, Jock," inquired a husky voice, "is that you?"

This was another most irregular answer. Declining to be drawn into impromptu irrelevancies, Mucklewame stuck to his text.

"Advance yin," he continued, "and give the coontersign, if any!"

Private Dunshie drew nearer.

"Jock," he inquired wistfully, "hae ye gotten a fag?"

"Aye," replied Mucklewame, friendship getting the better of conscience.

"Wull ye give a body yin?"

"Aye. But ye canna smoke on ootpost duty," explained Mucklewame sternly. "Forbye, the officer has no been roond yet," he added.

"Onyway," urged Dunshie eagerly, "let nae be your prisoner! Let me bide with the other boys in here ahint the dyke!"

The hospitable Mucklewame agreed, and Scout Dunshie, overjoyed at the prospect of human companionship, promptly climbed over the low wall and attached himself, in the *rôle* of languishing captive, to Number Two Sentry-Group of Number Three Piquet.

III

Meanwhile M'Snape had reached the forward edge of the wood, and was cautiously reconnoitring the open ground in front of him. The moon had disappeared altogether now, but M'Snape was able to calculate, by reason of the misdirected exuberance of the vigilant Mucklewame, the exact position of the sentry-group on the left-hand road. About the road on his right he was not so certain; so he set out cautiously towards it, keeping to the edge of the wood, and pausing every few yards to listen. There must be a sentry-group somewhere here, he calculated—say midway between the roads. He must walk warily.

Easier said than done. At this very moment a twig snapped beneath his foot with a noise like a pistol-shot, and a covey of partridges, lying out upon the stubble beside him, made an indignant evacuation of their bedroom. The mishap seemed fatal: M'Snape stood like a stone. But no alarm followed, and presently all was still again—so still, indeed, that presently, out on the right, two hundred yards away, M'Snape heard a man cough and then spit. Another sentry was located!

Having decided that there was no sentry-group between the two roads, M'Snape turned his back upon the wood and proceeded cautiously forward. He was not quite satisfied in his mind about things. He knew that Captain Wagstaffe was in command of this section of the defence. He cherished a wholesome respect for that efficient officer, and doubted very much if he would really leave so much of his front entirely unguarded.

Next moment the solution of the puzzle was in his very hand—in the form of a stout cord stretching from right to left. He was just in time to avoid tripping over it. It was suspended about six inches above the ground.

You cannot follow a clue in two directions at once; so after a little consideration M'Snape turned and crawled along to his right, being careful to avoid touching the cord. Presently a black mass loomed before him, acting apparently as terminus to the cord. Lying flat on his stomach, in order to get as much as possible of this obstacle between his eyes and the sky, M'Snape was presently able to descry, plainly silhouetted against the starry landscape, the profile of one Bain, a scout of A Company, leaning comfortably against a small bush, and presumably holding the end of the cord in his hand.

M'Snape wriggled silently away, and paused to reflect. Then he began to creep forward once more.

Having covered fifty yards, he turned to his right again, and presently found himself exactly between Bain and the trenches. As he expected, his hand now descended upon another cord, lying loosely on the ground, and running at right angles to the first. Plainly Bain was holding one end of this, and some one in the trenches—Captain Wagstaffe himself, as like as not—was holding the other. If an enemy stumbled over the trip-cord, Bain would warn the defence by twitching the alarm-cord.

Five minutes later M'Snape was back at the rendezvous, describing to Simson what he had seen. That wise subaltern promptly conducted him to Captain Mackintosh, who was waiting with his Company for something to go upon. Shand had departed with his own following to make an independent attack on the right flank. Seven of the twelve scouts were there. Of the missing, Dunshie, as we know, was sunning his lonely soul in the society of his foes; two had lost themselves, and the remaining two had been captured by a reconnoitring patrol. Of the seven which strayed not, four had discovered the trip-cord; so it was evident that that ingenious contrivance extended along the whole line. Only M'Snape, however, had penetrated farther. The general report was that the position was closely guarded from end to end.

"You say you found a cord running back from Bain to the trenches, M'Snape," asked Captain Mackintosh, "and a sentry holding on to it?"

"Yess, sirr," replied the scout, standing stiffly to attention in the dark.

"If we could creep out of the wood and rush *him*, we might be able to slip our attack in at that point," said the Captain. "You say there is cover to within twenty yards of where he is sitting?"

"Yes, sirr."

"Still, I'm afraid he'll pull that cord a bit too soon for us."

"He'll no, sirr," remarked M'Snape confidently.

"Why not?" asked the Captain.

M'Snape told him.

Captain Mackintosh surveyed the small wizened figure before him almost affectionately.

"M'Snape," he said, "to-morrow I shall send in your name for lance-corporal!"

IV

The defenders were ready. The trenches were finished: "A" and "B" had adjusted their elbow-rests to their liking, and blank ammunition had been served out. Orders upon the subject of firing were strict.

"We won't loose off a single shot until we actually *see* you," Captain Blaikie had said to Captain Mackintosh. "That will teach your men to crawl upon their little tummies, and ours to keep their eyes skinned."

(Captain Wagstaffe's string alarm had been an afterthought. At least, it was not mentioned to the commander of the attack.)

Orders were given that the men were to take things easily for half an hour or so, as the attack could not possibly be developed within that time. The officers established themselves in a splinter-proof shelter at the back of the supporting trench, and partook of provender from their haversacks.

"I don't suppose they'll attack much before nine," said the voice of a stout major named Kemp. "My word, it is dark in here! *And* dull! Curse the Kaiser!"

"I don't know," said Wagstaffe thoughtfully. "War is hell, and all that, but it has a good deal to recommend it. It wipes out all the small nuisances of peace-time."

"Such as—!"

"Well, Suffragettes, and Futurism, and—and—"

"Bernard Shaw," suggested another voice. "Hall Caine—"

"Yes, and the Tango, and party politics, and golf-maniacs. Life and Death, and the things that really are big, get viewed in their proper perspective for once in a way."

"And look how the War has bucked up the nation," said Bobby Little, all on fire at once. "Look at the way girls have given up fussing over clothes and things, and taken to nursing."

"My poor young friend," said the voice of the middle-aged Kemp, "tell me honestly, would you like to be attended to by some of the young women who have recently taken up the nursing profession?"

"Rather!" said Bobby, with thoughtless fervour.

"I didn't say *one*," Kemp pointed out, amid laughter, "but *some*. Of course we all know of one. Even I do. It's the rule, not the exception, that we are dealing with just now."

Bobby, realising that he had been unfairly surprised in a secret, felt glad that the darkness covered his blushes.

"Well, take my tip," continued Kemp, "and avoid amateur ministering angels, my son. I studied the species in South Africa. For twenty-four hours they nurse you to death, and after that they leave you to perish of starvation. Women in war-time are best left at home."

A youthful paladin in the gloom timidly mentioned the name of Florence Nightingale.

"One Nightingale doesn't make a base hospital," replied Kemp. "I take off my hat—we all do—to women who are willing to undergo the drudgery and discomfort which hospital training involves. But I'm not talking about Florence Nightingales. The young person whom I am referring to is just intelligent enough to understand that the only possible thing to do this season is to nurse. She qualifies herself for her new profession by dressing up like one of the chorus of 'The Quaker Girl,' and getting her portrait, thus attired, into the 'Tatler.' Having achieved this, she has graduated. She then proceeds to invade any hospital that is available, where she flirts with everything in pyjamas, and freezes you with a look if you ask her to empty a basin or change your sheets. I know her! I've had some, and I know her! She is one of the minor horrors of war. In peace-time she goes out on Alexandra Day, and stands on the steps of men's clubs and pesters the members to let her put a rose in their button-holes. What such a girl wants is a good old-fashioned mother who knows how to put a slipper to its right use!"

"I don't think," observed Wagstaffe, since Kemp had apparently concluded his philippic, "that young girls are the only people who lose their heads. Consider all the poisonous young blighters that one sees about town just now. Their uplift is enormous, and their manners in public horrid; and they hardly know enough about their new job to stand at attention when they hear 'God Save the King.' In fact, they deserve to be nursed by your little friends, Bobby!"

"They are all that you say," conceded Kemp. "But after all, they do have a fairly stiff time of it on duty, and they are going to have a much stiffer time later on. And they are not going to back out when the romance of the new uniform wears off, remember. Now these girls will play the angel-of-mercy game for a week or two, and then jack up and confine their efforts to getting hold of a wounded officer and taking him to the theatre. It is *dernier cri* to take a wounded officer about with you at present. Wounded officers have quite superseded Pekinese, I am told."

"Women certainly are the most extraordinary creatures," mused Ayling, a platoon commander of "B." "In private life I am a beak at a public school—"

"What school?" inquired several voices. Ayling gave the name, found that there were two of the school's old boys present, and continued—

"Just as I was leaving to join this battalion, the Head received a letter from a boy's mother intimating that she was obliged to withdraw her son, as he had received a commission in the army for the duration of the war. She wanted to know if the Head would keep her son's place open for him until he came back! What do you think of that?"

"Sense of proportion wasn't invented when women were made," commented Kemp. "But we are wandering from the subject, which is: what advantages are we, personally, deriving from the war? Wagger, what are you getting out of it?"

"Half-a-crown a day extra pay as Assistant Adjutant," replied Wagstaffe laconically. "Ainslie, wake up and tell us what the war has done for you, since you abandoned the Stock Exchange and took to foot-slogging."

"Certainly," replied Ainslie. "A year ago I spent my days trying to digest my food, tind my nights trying to sleep. I was not at all successful in either enterprise. I can now sit down to a supper of roast pork and bottled stout, go to bed directly afterwards, sleep all night, and wake up in the morning without thinking unkind things of anybody—not even my relations-in-law! Bless the Kaiser, say I! Borrodaile, what about you? Any complaints?"

"Thank you," replied Borrodaile's dry voice; "there are no complaints. In civil life I am what is known as a 'prospective candidate.' For several years I have been exercising this, the only, method of advertising permitted to a barrister, by nursing a constituency. That is, I go down to the country once a week, and there reduce myself to speechlessness soliciting the votes of the people who put my opponent in twenty years ago, and will keep him in by a two thousand majority as long as he cares to stand. I have been at it five years, but so far the old gentleman has never so much as betrayed any knowledge of my existence."

"That must be rather galling," said Wagstaffe.

"Ah! but listen! Of course party politics have now been merged in the common cause—see local organs, *passim*—and both sides are working shoulder to shoulder for the maintenance of our national existence."

"*Applause!*" murmured Kemp.

"That is to say," continued Borrodaile with calm relish, "my opponent, whose strong suit for the last twenty years has been to cry down the horrors of militarism, and the madness of national service, and the unwieldy size of the British Empire, is now compelled to spend his evenings taking the chair at mass meetings for the encouragement of recruiting. I believe the way in which he eats up his own previous utterances on the subject is quite superb. On these occasions I always send him a telegram, containing a kindly pat on the back for him and a sort of semi-official message for the audience. He has to read this out on the platform!"

"What sort of message?" asked a delighted voice.

"Oh—*Send along some more of our boys. Lord Kitchener says there are none to touch them. Borrodaile, Bruce and Wallace Highlanders*. Or—*All success to the meeting, and best thanks to you personally for carrying on in my absence. Borrodaile, Bruce and Wallace Highlanders*. I have a lot of quiet fun," said Borrodaile meditatively, "composing those telegrams. I rather fancy"—he examined the luminous watch on his wrist—"it's five minutes past eight: I rather fancy the old thing is reading one now!"

The prospective candidate leaned back against the damp wall of the dug-out with a happy sigh. "What have you got out of the war, Ayling?" he inquired.

"Change," said Ayling.

"For better or worse?"

"If you had spent seven years in a big public school," said Ayling, "teaching exactly the same thing, at exactly the same hour, to exactly the same kind of boy, for weeks on end, what sort of change would you welcome most?"

"Death," said several voices.

"Nothing of the kind!" said Ayling warmly. "It's a great life, if you are cut out for it. But there is no doubt that the regularity of the hours, and the absolute certainty of the future, make a man a bit groovy. Now in this life we are living we have to do lots of dull or unpleasant things, but they are never quite the same things. They are progressive, and not circular, if you know what I mean; and the immediate future is absolutely unknown, which is an untold blessing. What about you, Sketchley?"

A fat voice replied—

"War is good for adipose Special Reservists. I have decreased four inches round the waist since October. Next?"

So the talk ran on. Young Lochgair, heir to untold acres in the far north and master of unlimited pocket-money, admitted frankly that the sum of eight-and-sixpence per day, which he was now earning by the sweat of his brow and the expenditure of shoe-leather, was sweeter to him than honey in the honeycomb. Hattrick, who had recently put up a plate in Harley Street, said it was good to be earning a living wage at last. Mr. Waddell, pressed to say a few words of encouragement of the present campaign, delivered himself of a guarded but illuminating eulogy of war as a cure for indecision of mind; from which, coupled with a coy reference to "some one" in distant St. Andrews, the company were enabled to gather that Mr. Waddell had carried a position with his new sword which had proved impregnable to civilian assault.

Only Bobby Little was silent. In all this genial symposium there had been no word of the spur which was inciting him—and doubtless the others—along the present weary and monotonous path; and on the whole he was glad that it should be so. None of us care to talk, even privately, about the Dream of Honour and the Hope of Glory. The only difference between Bobby and the others was that while they could cover up their aspirations with a jest, Bobby must say all that was in his heart, or keep silent. So he held his peace.

A tall figure loomed against the starlit sky, and Captain Wagstaffe, who had been out in the trench, spoke quickly to Major Kemp:—

"I thing we had better get to our places, sir. Some criminal has cut my alarm-cord!"

V

Five minutes previously, Private Bain, lulled to a sense of false security by the stillness of the night, had opened his eyes, which had been closed for purposes of philosophic reflection, to find himself surrounded by four ghostly figures in greatcoats. With creditable presence of mind he jerked his alarm-cord. But, alas! the cord came with his hand.

He was now a prisoner, and his place in the scout-line was being used as a point of deployment for the attacking force.

"We're extended right along the line now," said Captain Mackintosh to Simson. "I can't wait any longer for Shand: he has probably lost himself. The sentries are all behind us. Pass the word along to crawl forward. Every man to keep as low as he can, and dress by the right. No one to charge unless he hears my whistle, or is fired on."

The whispered word—Captain Mackintosh knows when to whisper quite as well as Captain Shand—runs down the line, and presently we begin to creep forward, stooping low. Sometimes we halt; sometimes we swing back a little; but on the whole we progress. Once there is a sudden exclamation. A highly-strung youth, crouching in a field drain, has laid his hand upon what looks and feels like a clammy human face, lying recumbent and staring heavenward. Too late, he recognises a derelict scarecrow with a turnip head. Again, there is a pause while the extreme right of the line negotiates an unexpected barbed-wire fence. Still, we move on, with enormous caution. We are not certain where the trenches are, but they must be near. At any moment a crackling volley may leap out upon us. Pulses begin to beat.

In the trench itself eyes are strained and ears cocked. It is an eerie sensation to know that men are near you, and creeping nearer, yet remain inaudible and invisible. It is a very dark night. The moon appears to have gone to bed for good, and the stars are mostly covered. Men unconsciously endeavour to fan the darkness away with their hands, like mist. The broken ground in front, with the black woods beyond, might be concealing an army corps for all the watchers in the trenches can tell. Far away to the south a bright finger of light occasionally stabs the murky heavens. It is the searchlight of a British cruiser, keeping ceaseless vigil in the English Channel, fifteen miles away. If she were not there we should not be making-believe here with such comfortable deliberation. It would be the real thing.

Bobby Little, who by this time can almost discern spiked German helmets in the gloom, stands tingling. On either side of him are ranged the men of his platoon—some eager, some sleepy, but all silent. For the first time he notices that in the distant woods ahead of him there is a small break—a mere gap—through which one or two stars are twinkling. If only he could contrive to get a line of sight direct to that patch of sky—

He moves a few yards along the trench, and brings his eye to the ground-level. No good: a bush intervenes, fifteen yards away. He moves further and tries again.

Suddenly, for a brief moment, against the dimly illuminated scrap of horizon, he descries a human form, clad in a kilt, advancing stealthily....

"*Number one Platoon—at the enemy in front—rapid fire!*"

He is just in time. There comes an overwrought roar of musketry all down the line of trenches. Simultaneously, a solid wall of men rises out of the earth not fifty yards away, and makes for the trenches with a long-drawn battle yell.

Make-believe has its thrills as well as the genuine article.

And so home to bed. M'Snape duly became a lance-corporal, while Dunshie resigned his post as a scout and returned to duty with the company.

XI

OLYMPUS

Under this designation it is convenient to lump the whole heavenly host which at present orders our goings and shapes our ends. It includes—

(1) The War Office;
(2) The Treasury;
(3) The Army Ordnance Office;
(4) Our Divisional Office;

—and other more local and immediate homes of mystery.

The Olympus which controls the destinies of "K(1)" differs in many respects from the Olympus of antiquity, but its celestial inhabitants appear to have at least two points in common with the original body— namely, a childish delight in upsetting one another's arrangements, and an untimely sense of humour when dealing with mortals.

So far as our researches have gone, we have been able to classify Olympus, roughly, into three departments—

(1) Round Game Department (including Dockets, Indents, and all official correspondence).
(2) Fairy Godmother Department.
(3) Practical Joke Department.

The outstanding feature of the Round Game Department is its craving for irrelevant information and its passion for detail. "Open your hearts to us," say the officials of the Department; "unburden your souls; keep nothing from us—and you will find us most accommodating. But stand on your dignity; decline to particularise; hold back one irrelevant detail—and it will go hard with you! Listen, and we will explain the rules of the game. Think of something you want immediately—say the command of a brigade, or a couple of washers for the lock of a machine-gun—and apply to us. The application must be made in writing, upon the Army Form provided for the purpose, and in triplicate. *And*—you must put in all the details you can possibly think of."

For instance, in the case of the machine-gun washers—by the way, in applying for them, you must call them *Gun, Machine, Light Vickers, Washers for lock of, two*. That is the way we always talk at the Ordnance Office. An Ordnance officer refers to his wife's mother as *Law, Mother-in-, one*—you should state when the old washers were lost, and by whom; also why they were lost, and where they are now. Then write a short history of the machine-gun from which they were lost, giving date and place of birth, together with, a statement of the exact number of rounds which it has fired—a machine-gun fires about five hundred rounds a minute—adding the name and military record of the pack-animal which usually carries it. When you have filled up this document you forward it to the proper quarter and await results.

The game then proceeds on simple and automatic lines. If your application is referred back to you not more than five times, and if you get your washers within three months of the date of application, you are the winner. If you get something else instead—say an aeroplane, or a hundred wash-hand basins—it is a draw. But the chances are that you lose.

Consider. By the rules of the game, if Olympus can think of a single detail which has not been thought of by you—for instance, if you omit to mention that the lost washers were circular in shape and had holes through the middle—you are *ipso facto* disqualified, under Rule One. Rule Two, also, is liable to trip you up. Possibly you may have written the pack-mule's name in small block capitals, instead of ordinary italics underlined in red ink, or put the date in Roman figures instead of Arabic numerals. If you do this, your application is referred back to you, and you lose a life. And even if you survive Rules One and Two, Rule Three will probably get you in the end. Under its provision your application must be framed in such language and addressed in such a manner that it passes through every department and sub-department of Olympus before it reaches the right one. The rule has its origin in the principle which governs the passing of wine at well-regulated British dinner-tables. That is, if you wish to offer a glass of port to your neighbour on your right, you hand the decanter to the neighbour on your left, so that the original object of your hospitality receives it, probably empty, only after a complete circuit of the table. In the present instance, the gentleman upon your right is the President of the Washer Department, situated somewhere in the Army Ordnance Office, the remaining guests representing the other centres of Olympian activity. For every department your application misses, you lose a life, three lost lives amounting to disqualification.

When the washers are issued, however, the port-wine rule is abandoned; and the washers are despatched to you, in defiance of all the laws of superstition and tradition, "widdershins," or counter-clockwise. No wonder articles thus jeopardised often fail to reach their destination!

Your last fence comes when you receive a document from Olympus announcing that your washers are now prepared for you, and that if you will sign and return the enclosed receipt they will be sent off upon their last journey. You are now in the worst dilemma of all. Olympus will not disgorge your washers until it has your receipt. On the other hand, if you send the receipt, Olympus can always win the game by losing the washers, and saying that *you* have got them. In the face of your own receipt you cannot very well deny this. So you lose your washers, and the game, and are also made liable for the misappropriation of two washers, for which Olympus holds your receipt.

Truly, the gods play with loaded dice.

On the whole, the simplest (and almost universal) plan is to convey a couple of washers from some one else's gun.

The game just described is played chiefly by officers; but this is a democratic age, and the rank and file are now occasionally permitted to take part.

For example, boots. Private M'Splae is the possessor, we will say, of a pair of flat feet, or arched insteps, or other military incommodities, and his regulation boots do not fit him. More than that, they hurt him exceedingly, and as he is compelled to wear them through daily marches of several miles, they gradually wear a hole in his heel, or a groove in his instep, or a gathering on his great toe. So he makes the first move in the game, and reports sick—"sair feet."

The Medical Officer, a terribly efficient individual, keenly—sometimes too keenly—alert for signs of malingering, takes a cursory glance at M'Splae's feet, and directs the patient's attention to the healing properties of soap and water. M'Splae departs, grumbling, and reappears on sick parade a few days later, palpably worse. This time, the M.O. being a little less pressed with work, M'Splae is given a dressing for his feet, coupled with a recommendation to procure a new pair of boots without delay. If M'Splae is a novice in regimental diplomacy, he will thereupon address himself to his platoon sergeant, who will consign him, eloquently, to a destination where only boots with asbestos soles will be of any use. If he is an old hand, he will simply cut his next parade, and will thus, rather ingeniously, obtain access to his company commander, being brought up before him at orderly-room next morning as a defaulter. To his captain he explains, with simple dignity, that he absented himself from parade because he found himself unable to "rise up" from his bed. He then endeavours, by hurriedly unlacing his boots, to produce his feet as evidence; but is frustrated, and awarded three extra fatigues for not formally reporting himself sick to the orderly sergeant. The real point of issue, namely, the unsuitability of M'Splae's boots, again escapes attention.

There the matter rests until, a few days later, M'Splae falls out on a long regimental route-march, and hobbles home, chaperoned by a not ungrateful lance-corporal, in a state of semi-collapse. This time the M.O. reports to the captain that Private M'Splae will be unfit for further duty until he is provided with a proper pair of boots. Are there no boots in the quartermaster's store?

The captain explains that there are plenty of boots, but that under the rules of the present round game no one has any power to issue them. (This rule was put in to prevent the game from becoming too easy, like the spot-barred rule in billiards.) It is a fact well known to Olympus that no regimental officer can be trusted with boots. Not even the colonel can gain access to the regimental boot store. For all Olympus can tell, he might draw a pair of boots and wear them himself, or dress his children up in them, or bribe the brigadier with them, instead of issuing them to Private M'Splae. No, Olympus thinks it wiser not to put temptation in the way of underpaid officers. So the boots remain locked up, and the taxpayer is protected.

But to be just, there is always a solution to an Olympian enigma, if you have the patience to go on looking for it. In this case the proper proceeding is for all concerned, including the prostrate M'Splae, to wait patiently for a Board to sit. No date is assigned for this event, but it is bound to occur sooner or later, like a railway accident or an eclipse of the moon. So one day, out of a cloudless sky, a Board materialises, and sits on M'Splae's boots. If M'Splae's company commander happens to be president of the Board the boots are condemned, and the portals of the quarter-master's store swing open for a brief moment to emit a new pair.

When M'Splae comes out of hospital, the boots, provided no one has appropriated them during the term, of his indisposition, are his. He puts them on, to find that they pinch him in the same place as the old pair.

* * * * *

Then there is the Fairy Godmother Department, which supplies us with unexpected treats. It is the smallest department on Olympus, and, like most philanthropic institutions, is rather unaccountable in the manner in which it distributes its favours. It is somewhat hampered in its efforts, too, by the Practical Joke Department, which appears to exercise a sort of general right of interference all over Olympus. For instance, the Fairy Godmother Department decrees that officers from Indian regiments, who were home on leave when the War broke out and were commandeered for service with the Expeditionary Force, shall continue to draw pay on the Indian scale, which is considerably higher than that which prevails at home. So far, so good. But the Practical Joke Department hears of this, and scents an opportunity, in the form of "deductions." It promptly bleeds the beneficiaire of certain sums per day, for quarters, horse allowance, forage, and the like. It is credibly reported that one of these warriors, on emerging from a week's purgatory in a Belgian trench, found that his accommodation therein had been charged against him, under the head of "lodgings," at the rate of two shillings and threepence a night!

But sometimes the Fairy Godmother Department gets a free hand. Like a benevolent maiden aunt, she unexpectedly drops a twenty-pound note into your account at Cox's Bank, murmuring something vague about "additional outfit allowance"; and as Mr. Cox makes a point of backing her up in her little secret, you receive a delightful surprise next time you open your pass-book.

She has the family instinct for detail, too, this Fairy Godmother. Perhaps the electric light in your bedroom fails, and for three days you have to sit in the dark or purchase candles. An invisible but observant little cherub notes this fact; and long afterwards a postal order for tenpence flutters down upon you from Olympus, marked "light allowance." Once Bobby Little received a mysterious postal order for one-and-fivepence. It was in the early days of his novitiate, before he had ceased to question the workings of Providence. So he made inquiries, and after prolonged investigation discovered the source of the windfall. On field service an officer is entitled to a certain sum per day as "field allowance." In barracks, however, possessing a bedroom and other indoor comforts, he receives no such gratuity. Now Bobby had once been compelled to share his room for a few nights with a newly-joined and homeless subaltern. He was thus temporarily rendered the owner of only half a bedroom. Or, to put it another way, only half of him was able to sleep in barracks. Obviously, then, the other half was on field service, and Bobby was therefore entitled to half field allowance. Hence the one-and-fivepence. I tell you, little escapes them on Olympus. So does much, but that is another story.

* * * * *

Last of all comes the Practical Joke Department. It covers practically all of one side of Olympus—the shady side.

The jokes usually take the form of an order, followed by a counter-order. For example—

In his magisterial days Ayling, of whom we have previously heard, was detailed by his Headmaster to undertake the organisation of a school corps to serve as a unit of the Officers' Training Corps—then one of the spoilt bantlings of the War Office. Being a vigorous and efficient young man, Ayling devoted four weeks of his summer holiday to a course of training with a battalion of regulars at Aldershot. During that period, as the prospective commander of a company, he was granted the pay and provisional rank of captain, which all will admit was handsome enough treatment. Three months later, when after superhuman struggles he had pounded his youthful legionaries into something like efficiency, his appointment to a commission was duly confirmed, and he found himself gazetted—Second Lieutenant. In addition to this, he was required to refund to the Practical Joke Department the difference between second lieutenant's pay and the captain's pay which he had received during his month's training at Aldershot!

But in these strenuous days the Department has no time for baiting individuals. It has two or three millions of men to sharpen its wit upon. Its favourite pastime at present is a sort of giant's game of chess, the fair face of England serving as board, and the various units of the K. armies as pieces. The object of the players is to get each piece through as many squares as possible in a given time, it being clearly understood that no move shall count unless another piece is evicted in the process. For instance, we, the _x_th Brigade of the _y_th Division, are suddenly uprooted from billets at A and planted down in barracks at B, displacing the _p_th Brigade of the _q_th Division in the operation. We have barely cleaned tip after the _p_th—an Augean task—and officers have just concluded messing, furnishing, and laundry arrangements with the local *banditti*, when the Practical Joke Department, with its tongue in its cheek, bids us prepare to go under canvas at C. Married officers hurriedly despatch advance parties, composed of their wives, to secure houses or lodgings in the bleak and inhospitable environs of their new station; while a rapidly ageing Mess President concludes yet another demoralising bargain with a ruthless and omnipotent caterer. Then—this is the cream of the joke—the day before we expect to move, the Practical Joke Department puts out a playful hand and sweeps us all into some half-completed huts at D, somewhere at the other end of the Ordnance map, and leaves us there, with a happy chuckle, to sink or swim in an Atlantic of mud.

So far as one is able to follow the scoring of the game, some of the squares in the chessboard are of higher value than others. For instance, if you are dumped down into comparatively modern barracks at Aldershot, which, although they contain no furniture, are at least weatherproof and within reach of shops, the Practical Joke Department scores one point. Barracks condemned as unsafe and insanitary before the war, but now reckoned highly eligible, count three points; rat-ridden billets count five. But if you can manoeuvre your helpless pawns into Mudsplosh Camp, you receive ten whole points, with a bonus of two points thrown in if you can effect the move without previous notice of any kind.

We are in Mudsplosh Camp to-day. In transferring us here the Department secured full points, including bonus.

Let it not be supposed, however, that we are decrying our present quarters. Mudsplosh Camp is—or is going to be—a nobly planned and admirably equipped military centre. At present it consists of some three hundred wooden huts, in all stages of construction, covering about twenty acres of high moorland. The huts are heated with stoves, and will be delightfully warm when we get some coal. They are lit by—or rather wired for—electric light. Meanwhile a candle-end does well enough for a room only a hundred feet long. There are numerous other adjuncts to our comfort—wash-houses, for instance. These will be invaluable, when the water is laid on. For the present, there is a capital standpipe not a hundred yards away; and all you have to do, if you want an invigorating scrub, is to wait your turn for one of the two tin basins supplied to each fifty men, and then splash to your heart's content. There is a spacious dining-hall; and as soon as the roof is on, our successors, or their successors, will make merry therein. Meanwhile, there are worse places to eat one's dinner than the floor—the mud outside, for instance.

The stables are lofty and well ventilated. At least, we are sure they will be. Pending their completion the horses and mules are very comfortable, picketed on the edge of the moor.... After all, there are only sixty of them; and most of them have rugs; and it can't possibly go on snowing for ever.

The only other architectural feature of the camp is the steriliser, which has been working night and day ever since we arrived. No, it does not sterilise water or milk, or anything of that kind—only blankets. Those men standing in a *queue* at its door are carrying their bedding. (Yes, quite so. When blankets are passed from regiment to regiment for months on end, in a camp where opportunities for ablution are not lavish, these little things will happen.)

You put the blankets in at one end of the steriliser, turn the necessary handles, and wait. In due course the blankets emerge, steamed, dried, and thoroughly purged. At least, that is the idea. But listen to Privates Ogg and Hogg, in one of their celebrated cross-talk duologues.

Ogg (examining his blanket). "They're a' there yet. See!"

Hogg (an optimist). "Aye; but they must have gotten an awfu' fricht!"

But then people like Ogg are never satisfied with anything.

However, *the* feature of this camp is the mud. That is why it counts ten points. There was no mud, of course, before the camp was constructed—only dry turf, and wild yellow gorse, and fragrant heather. But the Practical Joke Department were not to be discouraged by the superficial beauties of nature. They knew that if you crowd a large number of human dwellings close together, and refrain from constructing any roads or drains as a preliminary, and fill these buildings with troops in the rainy season, you will soon have as much mud as ever you require. And they were quite right. The depth varies from a few inches to about a foot. On the outskirts of the camp, however, especially by the horse lines or going through a gate, you may find yourself up to your knees. But, after all, what is mud! Most of the officers have gum-boots, and the men will probably get used to it. Life in K(1) is largely composed of getting used to things.

In the more exclusive and fashionable districts—round about the Orderly-room, and the Canteen, and the Guard-room—elevated "duck-walks" are laid down, along which we delicately pick our way. It would warm the heart of a democrat to observe the ready—nay, hasty—courtesy with which an officer, on meeting a private carrying two overflowing buckets of kitchen refuse, steps down into the mud to let his humble brother-in-arms pass. Where there are no duck-walks, we employ planks laid across the mud. In comparatively dry weather these planks lie some two or three inches below the mud, and much innocent amusement may be derived from trying to locate them. In wet weather, however, the planks float to the surface, and then of course everything is plain sailing. When it snows, we feel for the planks with our feet. If we find them we perform an involuntary and unpremeditated ski-ing act: if we fail, we wade to our quarters through a sort of neapolitan ice—snow on the top, mud underneath.

Our parade-ground is a mud-flat in front of the huts. Here we take our stand each morning, sinking steadily deeper until the order is given to move off. Then the battalion extricates itself with one tremendous squelch, and we proceed to the labours of the day.

Seriously, though—supposing the commanding officer were to be delayed one morning at orderly-room, and were to ride on to the parade-ground twenty minutes late, what would he find? Nothing! Nothing but a great *parterre* of glengarries, perched upon the mud in long parallel rows, each glengarry flanked on the left-hand side by the muzzle of a rifle at the slope. (That detached patch over there on the left front, surrounded by air-bubbles, is the band. That cavity like the crater of an extinct volcano, in Number one Platoon of A Company, was once Private Mucklewame.)

And yet people talk about the sinking of the *Birkenhead!*

* * * * *

This morning some one in the Department has scored another ten points. Word has just been received that we are to move again to-morrow—to a precisely similar set of huts about a hundred yards away!

They are mad wags on Olympus.

XII

AND SOME FELL BY THE WAYSIDE

"*Firing parrty, revairse arrms!*"

Thus the platoon sergeant—a little anxiously; for we are new to this feat, and only rehearsed it for a few minutes this morning.

It is a sunny afternoon in late February. The winter of our discontent is past. (At least, we hope so.) Comfortless months of training are safely behind us, and lo! we have grown from a fortuitous concourse of atoms to a cohesive unit of fighting men. Spring is coming; spring is coming; our blood runs quicker; active service is within measurable distance; and the future beckons to us with both hands to step down at last into the arena, and try our fortune amid the uncertain but illimitable chances of the greatest game in the World.

To all of us, that is, save one.

The road running up the hill from the little mortuary is lined on either side by members of our company, specklessly turned out and standing to attention. At the foot of the slope a gun-carriage is waiting, drawn by two great dray horses and controlled by a private of the Royal Artillery, who looks incongruously perky and cockney amid that silent, kilted assemblage. The firing party form a short lane from the gun-carriage to the door of the mortuary. In response to the sergeant's command, each man turns over his rifle, and setting the muzzle carefully upon his right boot—after all, it argues no extra respect to the dead to get your barrel filled with mud—rests his hands upon the butt-plate and bows his head, as laid down in the King's Regulations.

The bearers move slowly down the path from the mortuary, and place the coffin upon the gun-carriage. Upon the lid lie a very dingy glengarry, a stained leather belt, and a bayonet. They are humble trophies, but we pay them as much reverence as we would to the *bâton* and cocked hat of a field-marshal, for they are the insignia of a man who has given his life for his country.

On the hill-top above us, where the great military hospital rears its clock-tower foursquare to the sky, a line of convalescents, in natty blue uniforms with white facings and red ties, lean over the railings deeply interested. Some of them are bandaged, others are in slings, and all are more or less maimed. They follow the obsequies below with critical approval. They have been present at enough hurried and promiscuous interments of late—more than one of them has only just escaped being the central figure at one of these functions—that they are capable of appreciating a properly conducted funeral at its true value.

"They're putting away a bloomin' Jock," remarks a gentleman with an empty sleeve.

"And very nice, too!" responds another on crutches, as the firing party present arms with creditable precision. "Not 'arf a bad bit of eye-wash at all for a bandy-legged lot of coal-shovellers."

"That lot's out of K(1)," explains a well-informed invalid with his head in bandages. "Pretty 'ot stuff they're gettin'. *Très moutarde!* Now we're off."

The signal is passed up the road to the band, who are waiting at the head of the procession, and the pipes break into a lament. Corporals step forward and lay four wreaths upon the coffin—one from each company. Not a man in the battalion has failed to contribute his penny to those wreaths; and pennies are not too common with us, especially on a Thursday, which comes just before payday. The British private is commonly reputed to spend all, or most of, his pocket-money upon beer. But I can tell you this, that if you give him his choice between buying himself a pint of beer and subscribing to a wreath, he will most decidedly go thirsty.

The serio-comic charioteer gives his reins a twitch, the horses wake up, and the gun-carriage begins to move slowly along the lane of mourners. As the dead private passes on his way the walls of the lane melt, and his comrades fall into their usual fours behind the gun-carriage.

So we pass up the hill towards the military cemetery, with the pipes wailing their hearts out, and the muffled drums marking the time of our regulation slow step. Each foot seems to hang in the air before the drums bid us put it down.

In the very rear of the procession you may see the company commander and three subalterns. They give no orders, and exact no attention. To employ a colloquialism, this is not their funeral.

Just behind the gun-carriage stalks a solitary figure in civilian clothes—the unmistakable "blacks" of an Elder of the Kirk. At first sight, you have a feeling that some one has strayed into the procession who has no right there. But no one has a better. The sturdy old man behind the coffin is named Adam Carmichael, and he is here, having travelled south from Dumbarton by the night train, to attend the funeral of his only son.

II

Peter Carmichael was one of the first to enlist in the regiment. There was another Carmichael in the same company, so Peter at roll-call was usually addressed by the sergeant as "Twenty-seven fufty-fower Carmichael," 2754 being his regimental number. The army does not encourage Christian names. When his attestation paper was filled up, he gave his age as nineteen; his address, vaguely, as Renfrewshire; and his trade, not without an air, as a "holder-on." To the mystified Bobby Little he entered upon a lengthy explanation of the term in a language composed almost entirely of vowels, from which that officer gathered, dimly, that holding-on had something to do with shipbuilding.

Upon the barrack square his platoon commander's attention was again drawn to Peter, owing to the passionate enthusiasm with which he performed the simplest evolutions, such as forming fours and sloping arms—military exercises which do not intrigue the average private to any great extent. Unfortunately, desire frequently outran performance. Peter was undersized, unmuscular, and extraordinarily clumsy. For a long time Bobby Little thought that Peter, like one or two of his comrades, was left-handed, so made allowances. Ultimately he discovered that his indulgence was misplaced: Peter was equally incompetent with either hand. He took longer in learning to fix bayonets or present arms than any other man in the platoon. To be fair, Nature had done little to help him. He was thirty-three inches round the chest, five feet four in height, and weighed possibly nine stone. His complexion was pasty, and, as Captain Wagstaffe remarked, you could hang your hat on any bone in his body. His eyesight was not all that the Regulations require, and on the musketry-range he was "put back," to his deep distress, "for further instruction." Altogether, if you had not known the doctor who passed him, you would have said it was a mystery how he passed the doctor.

But he possessed the one essential attribute of the soldier. He had a big heart. He was keen. He allowed nothing to come between him and his beloved duties. ("He was aye daft for to go sogerin'," his father explained to Captain Blaikie; "but his mother would never let him away. He was ower wee, and ower young.") His rifle, buttons, and boots were always without blemish. Further, he was of the opinion that a merry heart goes all the way. He never sulked when the platoon were kept on parade five minutes after the breakfast bugle had sounded. He made no bones about obeying orders and saluting officers—acts of abasement which grated sorely at times upon his colleagues, who reverenced no one except themselves and their Union. He appeared to revel in muddy route-marches, and invariably provoked and led the choruses. The men called him "Wee Pe'er," and ultimately adopted him as a sort of company mascot. Whereat Pe'er's heart glowed; for when your associates attach a diminutive to your Christian name, you possess something which millionaires would gladly give half their fortune to purchase.

And certainly he required all the social success he could win, for professionally Peter found life a rigorous affair. Sometimes, as he staggered into barracks after a long day, carrying a rifle made of lead and wearing a pair of boots weighing a hundredweight apiece, he dropped dead asleep on his bedding before he could eat his dinner. But he always hotly denied the imputation that he was "sick."

Time passed. The regiment was shaking down. Seven of Peter's particular cronies were raised to the rank of lance-corporal—but not Peter. He was "off the square" now—that is to say, he was done with recruit drill for ever. He possessed a sound knowledge of advance-guard and outpost work; his conduct-sheet was a blank page. But he was not promoted. He was "ower wee for a stripe," he told himself. For the present he must expect to be passed over. His chance would come later, when he had filled out a little and got rid of his cough.

The winter dragged on: the weather was appalling: the grousers gave tongue with no uncertain voice, each streaming field-day. But Wee Pe'er enjoyed it all. He did not care if it snowed ink. He was a "sojer."

One day, to his great delight, he was "warned for guard"—a particularly unpopular branch of a soldier's duties, for it means sitting in the guard-room for twenty-four hours at a stretch, fully dressed and accoutred, with intervals of sentry-go, usually in heavy rain, by way of exercise. When Peter's turn for sentry-go came on he splashed up and down his muddy beat—the battalion was in billets now, and the usual sentry's verandah was lacking—as proud as a peacock, saluting officers according to their rank, challenging stray civilians with great severity, and turning out the guard on the slightest provocation. He was at his post, soaked right through his greatcoat, when the orderly officer made his night round. Peter summoned his colleagues; the usual inspection of the guard took place; and the sleepy men were then dismissed to their fireside. Peter remained; the officer hesitated. He was supposed to examine the sentry in his knowledge of his duties. It was a profitless task as a rule. The tongue-tied youth merely gaped like a stranded fish, until the sergeant mercifully intervened, in some such words as these—

"This man, sirr, is liable to get over-excited when addressed by an officer."

Then, soothingly—

"Now, Jimmy, tell the officer what would ye dae in case of fire?"

"Present airrms!" announces the desperate James. Or else, almost tearfully, "I canna mind. I had it all fine just noo, but it's awa' oot o' ma heid!"

Therefore it was with no great sense of anticipation that the orderly officer said to Private Carmichael,—

"Now, sentry, can you repeat any of your duties?"

Peter saluted, took a full breath, closed both eyes, and replied rapidly,—

"For tae tak' chairge of all Government property within sicht of this guairdhoose tae turrn out the guaird for all arrmed pairties approaching also the commanding officer once a day tae salute all officers tae challenge all pairsons approaching this post tae—"

His recital was interrupted by a fit of coughing.

"Thank you," said the officer hastily; "that will do. Good night!"

Peter, not sure whether it would be correct to say "good night" too, saluted again, and returned to his cough.

"I say," said the officer, turning back, "you have a shocking cold."

"Och, never heed it, sirr," gasped Peter politely.

"Call the sergeant," said the officer.

The fat sergeant came out of the guardhouse again, buttoning his tunic.

"Sirr?"

"Take this man off sentry-duty and roast him at the guard-room fire."

"I will, sirr," replied the sergeant; and added paternally, "this man has no right for to be here at all. He should have reported sick when warned for guard; but he would not. He is very attentive to his duties, sirr."

"Good boy!" said the officer to Peter. "I wish we had more like you."

Wee Pe'er blushed, his teeth momentarily ceased chattering, his heart swelled. Appearances to the contrary, he felt warm all through. The sergeant laid a fatherly hand upon his shoulder.

"Go you your ways intil the guard-room, boy," he commanded, "and send oot Dunshie. He'll no hurt. Get close in ahint the stove, or you'll be for Cambridge!"

(The last phrase carries no academic significance. It simply means that you are likely to become an inmate of the great Cambridge Hospital at Aldershot.)

Peter, feeling thoroughly disgraced, cast an appealing look at the officer.

"In you go!" said that martinet.

Peter silently obeyed. It was the only time in his life that he ever felt mutinous.

A month later Brigade Training set in with customary severity. The life of company officers became a burden. They spent hours in thick woods with their followers, taking cover, ostensibly from the enemy, in reality from brigade-majors and staff officers. A subaltern never tied his platoon in a knot but a general came trotting round the corner. The wet weather had ceased, and a biting east wind reigned in its stead.

On one occasion an elaborate night operation was arranged. Four battalions were to assemble at a given point five miles from camp, and then advance in column across country by the light of the stars to a position indicated on the map, where they were to deploy and dig themselves in! It sounded simple enough in operation orders; but when you try to move four thousand troops—even well-trained troops—across three miles of broken country on a pitch-dark night, there is always a possibility that some one will get mislaid. On this particular occasion a whole battalion lost itself without any delay or difficulty whatsoever. The other three were compelled to wait for two hours and a half, stamping their feet and blowing on their fingers, while overheated staff officers scoured the country for the truants. They were discovered at last waiting virtuously at the wrong rendezvous, three-quarters of a mile away. The brazen-hatted strategist who drew up the operation orders had given the point of assembly for the brigade as: ... *the field* S.W. *of* WELLINGTON WOOD *and due* E.*of* HANGMAN'S COPSE, *immediately below the first* O *in* GHOSTLY BOTTOM,—but omitted to underline the O indicated. The result was that three battalion commanders assembled at the O in "ghostly," while the fourth, ignoring the adjective in favour of the noun, took up his station at the first O in "bottom."

The operations had been somewhat optimistically timed to end at 11 P.M., but by the time that the four battalions had effected a most unloverly tryst, it was close on ten, and beginning to rain. The consequence was that the men got home to bed, soaked to the skin, and asking the Powers Above rhetorical questions, at three o'clock in the morning.

Next day Brigade Orders announced that the movement would be continued at nightfall, by the occupation of the hastily-dug trenches, followed by a night attack upon the hill in front. The captured position would then be retrenched.

When the tidings went round, fourteen of the more quick-witted spirits of "A" Company hurriedly paraded before the Medical Officer and announced that they were "sick in the stomach." Seven more discovered abrasions upon their feet, and proffered their sores for inspection, after the manner of Oriental mendicants. One skrimshanker, despairing of producing any bodily ailment, rather ingeniously assaulted a comrade-in-arms, and was led away, deeply grateful, to the guard-room. Wee Peter, who in the course of last night's operations had stumbled into an old trench half-filled with ice-cold water, and whose temperature to-day, had he known it, was a hundred and two, paraded with his company at the appointed time. The company, he reflected, would get a bad name if too many men reported sick at once.

Next day he was absent from parade. He was "for Cambridge" at last.

Before he died, he sent for the officer who had befriended him, and supplemented, or rather corrected, some of the information contained in his attestation paper.

He lived in Dumbarton, not Renfrewshire. He was just sixteen. He was not—this confession cost him a great effort—a full-blown "holder-on" at all; only an apprentice. His father was "weel kent" in the town of Dumbarton, being a chief engineer, employed by a great firm of shipbuilders to extend new machinery on trial trips.

Needless to say, he made a great fight. But though his heart was big enough, his body was too frail. As they say on the sea, he was over-engined for his beam.

And so, three days later, the simple soul of Twenty-seven fifty-four Carmichael, "A" Company, was transferred, on promotion, to another company—the great Company of Happy Warriors who walk the Elysian Fields.

III

"*Firing parrty, one round blank—load*!"

There is a rattle of bolts, and a dozen barrels are pointed heavenwards. The company stands rigid, except the buglers, who are beginning to finger their instruments.

"*Fire!*"

There is a crackling volley, and the pipes break into a brief, sobbing wail. Wayfarers upon the road below look up curiously. One or two young females with perambulators come hurrying across the grass, exhorting apathetic babies to sit up and admire the pretty funeral.

Twice more the rifles ring out. The pipes cease their wailing, and there is an expectant silence.

The drum-major crooks his little finger, and eight bugles come to the "ready." Then "Last Post," the requiem of every soldier of the King, swells out, sweet and true.

The echoes lose themselves among the dripping pines. The chaplain closes his book, takes off his spectacles, and departs.

Old Carmichael permits himself one brief look into his son's grave, resumes his crape-bound tall hat, and turns heavily away. He finds Captain Blaikie's hand waiting for him. He grips it, and says—

"Weel, the laddie has had a grand sojer's funeral. His mother will be pleased to hear that."

He passes on, and shakes hands with the platoon sergeant and one or two of Peter's cronies. He declines an invitation to the Sergeants' Mess.

"I hae a trial-trup the morn," he explains. "I must be steppin'. God keep ye all, brave lads!"

The old gentleman sets off down the station road. The company falls in, and we march back to barracks, leaving Wee Pe'er—the first name on our Roll of Honour—alone in his glory beneath, the Hampshire pines.

XIII

CONCERT PITCH

We have only two topics of conversation now—the date of our departure, and our destination. Both are wrapped in mystery so profound that our range of speculation is practically unlimited.

Conjecture rages most fiercely in the Officers' Mess, which is in touch with sources of unreliable information not accessible to the rank and file. The humblest subaltern appears to be possessed of a friend at court, or a cousin in the Foreign Office, or an aunt in the Intelligence Department, from whom he can derive fresh and entirely different information each week-end leave.

Master Cockerell, for instance, has it straight from the Horse Guards that we are going out next week—as a single unit, to be brigaded with two seasoned regiments in Flanders. He has a considerable following.

Then comes Waddell, who has been informed by the Assistant sub-Editor of an evening journal widely read in his native Dundee, that The First Hundred Thousand are to sit here, eating the bread of impatience, until The First Half Million are ready. Thereupon we shall break through our foeman's line at a point hitherto unassailed and known only to the scribe of Dundee, and proceed to roll up the German Empire as if it were a carpet, into some obscure corner of the continent of Europe.

Bobby Little, not the least of whose gifts is a soaring imagination, has mapped out a sort of strategical Cook's Tour for us, beginning with the sack of Constantinople, and ending, after a glorified route-march up the Danube and down the Rhine, which shall include a pitched battle once a week and a successful siege once a month, with a "circus" entry into Potsdam.

Captain Wagstaffe offers no opinion, but darkly recommends us to order pith helmets. However, we are rather suspicious of Captain Wagstaffe these days. He suffers from an over-developed sense of humour.

The rank and file keep closer to earth in their prognostications. In fact, some of them cleave to the dust. With them it is a case of hope deferred. Quite half of them enlisted under the firm belief that they would forthwith be furnished with a rifle and ammunition and despatched to a vague place called "the front," there to take pot-shots at the Kaiser. That was in early August. It is now early April, and they are still here, performing monotonous evolutions and chafing under the bonds of discipline. Small wonder that they have begun to doubt, these simple souls, if they are ever going out at all. Private M'Slattery put the general opinion in a nutshell.

"This regiment," he announced, "is no' for the front at all. We're jist tae bide here, for tae be inspeckit by Chinese Ministers and other heathen bodies!"

This withering summary of the situation was evoked by the fact that we had once been called out, and kept on parade for two hours in a north-east wind, for the edification of a bevy of spectacled dignitaries from the Far East. For the Scottish, artisan the word "minister," however, has only one significance; so it is probable that M'Slattery's strictures were occasioned by sectarian, rather than racial, prejudice.

Still, whatever our ultimate destination and fate may be, the fact remains that we are now as fit for active service as seven months' relentless schooling, under make-believe conditions, can render us. We shall have to begin all over again, we know, when we find ourselves up against the real thing, but we have at least been thoroughly grounded in the rudiments of our profession. We can endure hail, rain, snow, and vapour; we can march and dig with the best; we have mastered the first principles of musketry; we can advance in an extended line without losing touch or bunching; and we have ceased to regard an order as an insult, or obedience as a degradation. We eat when we can and what we get, and we sleep wherever we happen to find ourselves lying. That is something. But there are certain military accomplishments which can only be taught us by the enemy. Taking cover, for instance. When the thin, intermittent crackle of blank ammunition shall have been replaced by the whistle of real bullets, we shall get over our predilection for sitting up and taking notice. The conversation of our neighbour, or the deplorable antics of B Company on the neighbouring skyline, will interest us not at all. We shall get down, and stay down.

We shall also be relieved of the necessity of respecting the property of those exalted persons who surround their estates with barbed wire, and put up notices, even now, warning off troops. At present we either crawl painfully through that wire, tearing our kilts and lacerating our legs, or go round another way. "Oot there," such unwholesome deference will be a thing of the past. Would that the wire-setters were going out with us. We would give them the place of honour in the forefront of battle!

We have fired a second musketry course, and are now undergoing Divisional Training, with the result that we take our walks abroad several thousand strong, greatly to the derangement of local traffic.

Considered all round, Divisional Training is the pleasantest form of soldiering that we have yet encountered. We parade bright and early, at full battalion strength, accompanied by our scouts, signallers, machine-guns, and transport, and march off at the appointed minute to the starting-point. Here we slip into our place in an already moving column, with three thousand troops in front of us and another two thousand behind, and tramp to our point of deployment. We feel pleasantly thrilled. We are no longer a battalion out on a route-march: we are members of a White Army, or a Brown Army, hastening to frustrate the designs of a Blue Army, or a Pink Army, which has landed (according to the General Idea issued from Headquarters) at Portsmouth, and is reported to have slept at Great Snoreham, only ten miles away, last night.

Meanwhile our Headquarters Staff is engaged in the not always easy task of "getting into touch" with the enemy—*anglicè*, finding him. It is extraordinary how elusive a force of several thousand troops can be, especially when you are picking your way across a defective half-inch map, and the commanders of the opposing forces cherish dissimilar views as to where the point of encounter is supposed to be. However, contact is at length established; and if it is not time to go home, we have a battle.

Various things may now happen to you. You may find yourself detailed for the Firing-line. In that case your battalion will take open order; and you will advance, principally upon your stomach, over hill and dale until you encounter the enemy, doing likewise. Both sides then proceed to discharge blank ammunition into one another's faces at a range, if possible, of about five yards, until the "cease fire" sounds.

Or you may find yourself in Support. In that case you are held back until the battle has progressed a stage or two, when you advance with fixed bayonets to prod your own firing line into a further display of valour and agility.

Or you may be detailed as Reserve. Membership of Brigade Reserve should be avoided. You are liable to be called upon at any moment to forsake the sheltered wood or lee of a barn under which you are huddling, and double madly up a hill or along a side road, tripping heavily over ingenious entanglements composed of the telephone wires of your own signallers, to enfilade some unwary detachment of the enemy or repel a flank attack. On the other hand, if you are ordered to act as Divisional Reserve, you may select the softest spot on the hillside behind which you are sheltering, get out your haversack ration, and prepare to spend an extremely peaceful (or extremely dull) day. Mimic warfare enjoys one enormous advantage over the genuine article: battles—provided you are not out for the night—*must always* end in time for the men to get back to their dinners at five o'clock. Under this inexorable law it follows that, by the time the General has got into touch with the enemy and brought his firing line, supports, and local reserves into action, it is time to go home. So about three o'clock the bugles sound, and the combatants, hot and grimy, fall back into close order at the point of deployment, where they are presently joined by the Divisional Reserve, blue-faced and watery-eyed with cold. This done, principals and understudies, casting envious glances at one another, form one long column of route and set out for home, in charge of the subalterns. The senior officers trot off to the "pow-wow," there, with the utmost humility and deference, to extol their own tactical dispositions, belittle the achievements of the enemy, and impugn the veracity of one another.

Thus the day's work ends. Our divisional column, with its trim, sturdy, infantry battalions, its jingling cavalry and artillery, its real live staff, and its imposing transport train, sets us thinking, by sheer force of contrast, of that dim and distant time seven months ago, when we wrestled perspiringly all through long and hot September days, on a dusty barrack square, with squad upon squad of dazed and refractory barbarians, who only ceased shuffling their feet in order to expectorate. And these are the self-same men! Never was there a more complete vindication of the policy of pegging away.

II

So much for the effect of its training upon the regiment as a whole. But when you come to individuals, certain of whom we have encountered and studied in this rambling narrative, you find it impossible to generalise. Your one unshakable conclusion is that it takes all sorts to make a type.

There are happy, careless souls like McLeary and Hogg. There are conscientious but slow-moving worthies like Mucklewame and Budge. There are drunken wasters like—well, we need name no names. We have got rid of most of these, thank heaven! There are simple-minded enthusiasts of the breed of Wee Pe'er, for whom the sheer joy of "sojering" still invests dull routine and hard work with a glamour of their own. There are the old hands, versed in every labour-saving (and duty-shirking) device. There are the feckless and muddle-headed, making heavy weather of the simplest tasks. There is another class, which divides its time between rising to the position of sergeant and being reduced to the ranks, for causes which need not be specified. There is yet another, which knows its drill-book backwards, and can grasp the details of a tactical scheme as quickly as a seasoned officer, but remains in the ruck because it has not sufficient force of character to handle so much as a sentry-group. There are men, again, with initiative but no endurance, and others with endurance but no initiative. Lastly, there are men, and a great many of them, who appear to be quite incapable of coherent thought, yet can handle machinery or any mechanical device to a marvel. Yes, we are a motley organisation.

But the great sifting and sorting machine into which we have been cast is shaking us all out into our appointed places. The efficient and authoritative rise to non-commissioned rank. The quick-witted and well-educated find employment on the Orderly Room staff, or among the scouts and signallers. The handy are absorbed into the transport, or become machine-gunners. The sedentary take post as cooks, or tailors, or officers' servants. The waster hews wood and draws water and empties swill-tubs. The great, mediocre, undistinguished majority merely go to stiffen the rank and file, and right nobly they do it. Each has his niche.

To take a few examples, we may begin with a typical member of the undistinguished majority. Such an one is that esteemed citizen of Wishaw, John Mucklewame. He is a rank-and-file man by training and instinct, but he forms a rare backbone for K(1). There are others, of more parts—Killick, for instance. Not long ago he was living softly, and driving a Rolls-Royce for a Duke. He is now a machine-gun sergeant, and a very good one. There is Dobie. He is a good mechanic, but short-legged and shorter-winded. He makes an excellent armourer.

Then there is Private Mellish. In his company roll he is described as "an actor." But his orbit in the theatrical firmament has never carried him outside his native Dunoon, where he follows the blameless but monotonous calling of a cinematograph operator. On enlistment he invited the attention of his platoon, from the start by referring to his rear-rank man as "this young gentleman"; and despite all the dissuading influences of barrack-room society, his manners never fell below this standard. In a company where practically every man is addressed either as "Jock" or "Jimmy," he created a profound and lasting sensation one day, by saying in a winning voice to Private Ogg,—

"Do not stand on ceremony with me, Mr. Ogg. Call me Cyril!"

For such an exotic there could only be one destination, and in due course Cyril became an officer's servant. He now polishes the buttons and washes the hose-tops of Captain Wagstaffe; and his elegant extracts amuse that student of human nature exceedingly.

Then comes a dour, silent, earnest specimen, whose name, incredible as it may appear, is M'Ostrich. He keeps himself to himself. He never smiles. He is not an old soldier, yet he performed like a veteran the very first day he appeared on parade. He carries out all orders with solemn thoroughness. He does not drink; he does not swear. His nearest approach to animation comes at church, where he sings the hymns—

especially *O God, our help in ages past!*—as if he were author and composer combined. His harsh, rasping accent is certainly not that of a Highlander, nor does it smack altogether of the Clydeside. As a matter of fact he is not a Scotsman at all, though five out of six of us would put him down as such. Altogether he is a man of mystery; but the regiment could do with many more such.

Once, and only once, did he give us a peep behind the scenes. Private Burke, of D Company, a cheery soul, who possesses the entirely Hibernian faculty of being able to combine a most fanatical and seditious brand of Nationalism with a genuine and ardent enthusiasm for the British Empire, one day made a contemptuous and ribald reference to the Ulster Volunteers and their leader. M'Ostrich, who was sitting on his bedding at the other side of the hut, promptly rose to his feet, crossed the floor in three strides, and silently felled the humorist to the earth. Plainly, if M'Ostrich comes safe through the war, he is prepared for another and grimmer campaign.

Lastly, that jack-of-all trades and master of none, Private Dunshie. As already recorded, Dunshie's original calling had been that of a street news-vendor. Like all literary men, he was a Bohemian at heart. Routine wearied him; discipline galled him; the sight of work made him feel faint. After a month or two in the ranks he seized the first opportunity of escaping from the toils of his company, by volunteering for service as a Scout. A single experience of night operations in a dark wood, previously described, decided him to seek some milder employment. Observing that the regimental cooks appeared to be absolved, by virtue of their office, not only from all regimental parades, but from all obligations on the subject of correct attire and personal cleanliness, he volunteered for service in the kitchen. Here for a space—clad in shirt, trousers, and canvas shoes, unutterably greasy and waxing fat—he prospered exceedingly. But one sad day he was detected by the cook-sergeant, having just finished cleaning a flue, in the act of washing his hands in ten gallons of B Company's soup. Once more our versatile hero found himself turned adrift with brutal and agonising suddenness, and bidden to exercise his talents elsewhere.

After a fortnight's uneventful dreariness with his platoon, Dunshie joined the machine-gunners, because he had heard rumours that these were conveyed to and from their labours in limbered waggons. But he had been misinformed. It was the guns that were carried; the gunners invariably walked, sometimes carrying the guns and the appurtenances thereof. His very first day Dunshie was compelled to double across half a mile of boggy heathland carrying two large stones, meant to represent ammunition-boxes, from an imaginary waggon to a dummy gun. It is true that as soon as he was out of sight of the corporal he deposited the stones upon the ground, and ultimately proffered two others, picked up on nearing his destination, to the sergeant in charge of the proceedings; but even thus the work struck him as unreasonably exacting, and he resigned, by the simple process of cutting his next parade and being ignominiously returned to his company.

After an unsuccessful application for employment as a "buzzer," or signaller, Dunshie made trial of the regimental transport, where there was a shortage of drivers. He had strong hopes that in this way he would attain to permanent carriage exercise. But he was quickly undeceived. Instead of being offered a seat upon the box of a G.S. waggon, he was bidden to walk behind the same, applying the brake when necessary, for fourteen miles. The next day he spent cleaning stables, under a particularly officious corporal. On the third, he was instructed in the art of grooming a mule. On the fourth, he was left to perform this feat unaided, and the mule, acting under extreme provocation, kicked him in the stomach. On the fifth day he was returned to his company.

But Mecca was at hand. That very morning Dunshie's company commander received the following ukase from headquarters:—

Officers commanding Companies will render to the Orderly Room without fail, by 9 A.M. to-morrow, the name of one man qualified to act as chiropodist to the Company.

Major Kemp scratched his nose in a dazed fashion, and looked over his spectacles at his Quartermaster-Sergeant.

"What in thunder will they ask for next?" he growled. "Have we got any tame chiropodists in the company, Rae?"

Quartermaster-Sergeant Rae turned over the Company roll.

"There is no—no—no man of that profession here, sirr," he reported, after scanning the document. "But," he added optimistically, "there is a machine-fitter and a glass-blower. Will I warn one of them?"

"I think we had better call for a volunteer first," said Major Kemp tactfully.

Accordingly, that afternoon upon parade, Platoon commanders were bidden to hold a witch hunt, and smell out a chiropodist. But the enterprise terminated almost immediately; for Private Dunshie, caressing his injured abdomen in Number Three Platoon, heard the invitation, and quickly stepped forward.

"So you are a chiropodist as well as everything else, Dunshie!" said Ayling incredulously.

"That's right, sirr," assented Dunshie politely.
"Are you a professional?"
"No exactly that, sirr," was the modest reply.
"You just make a hobby of it?"
"Just that, sirr."
"Have you had much experience?"
"No that much."
"But you feel capable of taking on the job?"
"I do, sirr."
"You seem quite eager about it."
"Yes, sirr," said Dunshie, with gusto.
A sudden thought occurred to Ayling.
"Do you know what a chiropodist is?" he asked.
"No, sirr," replied Dunshie, with unabated aplomb.
* * * * *

To do him justice, the revelation of the nature of his prospective labours made no difference whatever to Dunshie's willingness to undertake them. Now, upon Saturday mornings, when men stand stiffly at attention beside their beds to have their feet inspected, you may behold, sweeping majestically in the wake of the Medical Officer as he makes his rounds, the swelling figure of Private Dunshie, carrying the implements of his gruesome trade. He has found his vocation at last, and his bearing in consequence is something between that of a Court Physician and a Staff Officer.

III

So much for the rank and file. Of the officers we need only say that the old hands have been a godsend to our young regiment; while the juniors, to quote their own Colonel, have learned as much in six months as the average subaltern learns in three years; and whereas in the old days a young officer could always depend on his platoon sergeant to give him the right word of command or instruct him in company routine, the positions are now in many cases reversed. But that by the way. The outstanding feature of the relationship between officers and men during all this long, laborious, sometimes heart-breaking winter has been this—that, despite the rawness of our material and the novelty of our surroundings, in the face of difficulties which are now happily growing dim in our memory, the various ranks have never quite given up trying, never altogether lost faith, never entirely forgotten the Cause which has brought us together. And the result—the joint result—of it all is a real live regiment, with a *morale* and soul of its own.

But so far everything has been purely suppositious. We have no knowledge as to what our real strength or weakness may be. We have run our trial trips over a landlocked stretch of smooth water. To-morrow, when we steam out to face the tempest which is shaking the foundations of the world, we shall see what we shall see. Some of us, who at present are exalted for our smartness and efficiency, will indubitably be found wanting—wanting in stamina of body or soul—while others, hitherto undistinguished, will come to their own. Only War itself can discover the qualities which count in War. But we silently pray, in our dour and inarticulate hearts, that the supreme British virtue—the virtue of holding on, and holding on, and holding on, until our end is accomplished—may not be found wanting in a single one of us.

To take a last survey of the regiment which we have created—one little drop in the incredible wave which has rolled with gathering strength from, end to end of this island of ours during the past six months, and now hangs ready to crash upon the gates of our enemies—what manner of man has it produced? What is he like, this impromptu Thomas Atkins?

Well, when he joined, his outstanding feature was a sort of surly independence, the surliness being largely based upon the fear of losing the independence. He has got over that now. He is no longer morbidly sensitive about his rights as a free and independent citizen and the backbone of the British electorate. He has bigger things to think of. He no longer regards sergeants as upstart slave-drivers—frequently he is a sergeant himself—nor officers as grinding capitalists. He is undergoing the experience of the rivets in Mr. Kipling's story of "The Ship that Found Herself." He is adjusting his perspectives. He is beginning to merge himself in the Regiment.

He no longer gets drunk from habit. When he does so now, it is because there were no potatoes at dinner, or because there has been a leak in the roof of his hut for a week and no one is attending to it, or because his wife is not receiving her separation allowance. Being an inarticulate person, he finds getting drunk the simplest and most effective expedient for acquainting the powers that be with the fact that he has a grievance. Formerly, the morning list of "drunks" merely reflected the nearness or remoteness of payday. Now, it is a most reliable and invaluable barometer of the regimental atmosphere.

He has developed—quite spontaneously, for he has had few opportunities for imitation—many of the characteristics of the regular soldier. He is quick to discover himself aggrieved, but is readily appeased if he feels that his officer is really doing his best for him, and that both of them are the victims of a higher power. On the other hand, he is often amazingly cheerful under uncomfortable and depressing surroundings. He is growing quite fastidious, too, about his personal appearance when off duty. (You should see our quiffs on Saturdays!) He is quite incapable of keeping possession of his clothing, his boots, his rifle, his health, or anything that is his, without constant supervision and nurse-maiding. And that he is developing a strong bent towards the sentimental is evinced by the choruses that he sings in the gloaming and his taste in picture post-cards.

So far he may follow the professional model, but in other respects he is quite *sui generis*. No sergeant in a Highland regiment of the line would ever refer to a Cockney private, with all humility, as "a young English gentleman"; neither would an ordinary soldier salute an officer quite correctly with one hand while employing the other to light his pipe. In "K(1)" we do these things and many others, which, give us a *cachet* of our own of which we are very rightly and properly proud.

So we pin our faith to the man who has been at once our despair and our joy since the month of August. He has character; he has grit; and now that he is getting discipline as well, he is going to be an everlasting credit to the cause which roused his manhood and the land which gave him birth.

* * * * *

That is the tale of The First Hundred Thousand—Part One. Whether Part Two will be forthcoming, and how much of it there will be, depends upon two things—the course of history, and the present historian's eye for cover.

BOOK TWO

LIVE ROUNDS

XIV

THE BACK OF THE FRONT

I

The last few days have afforded us an excellent opportunity of studying the habits of that ubiquitous attendant of our movements, the Staff Officer.

He is not always a real Staff Officer—the kind that wears a red hatband. Sometimes he is an obvious "dug-out," with a pronounced *embonpoint* or a game leg. Sometimes he is a mere stripling, with a rapidly increasing size in hats. Sometimes he is an ordinary human being. But whoever he is, and whatever his age or rank, one thing is certain. He has no mean: he is either very good or very bad. When he is good he is very good indeed, and when he is bad he is horrid. He is either Jekyll or Hyde.

Thrice blessed, then, is that unit which, upon its journey to the seat of war, encounters only the good of the species. To transfer a thousand men, with secrecy and despatch, from camp to train, from train to ship, from ship to train, and from train to a spot near the battle line, is a task which calls for the finest organisation and the most skilful administration. Let it be said at once that our path to our present address has been almost universally lined with Jekylls. The few Hydes whom we have encountered are by this time merely a subject for amusing anecdote.

As for the organisation of our journey—well, it was formulated upon Olympus, and was marked by those Olympian touches of which mention has been previously made. For instance, immense pains were taken, by means of printed rules and official memoranda, to acquaint us with the procedure to be followed at each point of entrainment or embarkation. Consequently we set out upon our complicated pilgrimage primed with explicit instructions and ready for any emergency. We filled up forms with countless details of our equipment and personnel, which we knew would delight the heart of the Round Game Department. We divided our followers, as directed, into Loading Parties, and Ration Parties, and Hold Parties, and many other interesting subdivisions, as required by the rules of the game. But we had reckoned without the Practical Joke Department. The Round Game Department having furnished us with one set of rules, the Practical Joke Department prepared another, entirely different, and issued them to the officers who superintended such things as entrainment and embarkation. At least, that is the most charitable explanation of the course of action adopted by the few Mr. Hydes whom we encountered.

Two of these humorists linger in the memory. The first was of the type which is admiringly referred to in commercial circles as a hustler. His hustling took the form of beginning to shout incomprehensible orders almost before the train had drawn up at the platform. After that he passed from party to party, each of which was working strenuously under its own sergeant, and commanded them (not the sergeant) to do something else, somewhere else—a course of action naturally calculated to promote unity and celerity of action all round. A perspiring sergeant who ventured to point out that his party were working under the direct orders of their Company Commander, was promptly placed under arrest, and his flock enjoyed a welcome and protracted breathing-space until an officer of sufficient standing to cope with Mr. Hyde—unfortunately he was Major Hyde—could be discovered and informed.

The second required more tactful handling. As our train-load drew up at the platform, the officer in charge—it was Captain Blaikie, supported by Bobby Little—stepped out, saluted the somewhat rotund Colonel Hyde whom he saw before him, and proffered a sheaf of papers.

"Good-morning, sir," he said. "Here is my train statement. Shall I carry on with the unloading? I have all my parties detailed."

The great man waved away the papers magnificently. (To be just, even the Jekylls used to wave away our papers.)

"Take those things away," he commanded, in a voice which made it plain that we had encountered another hustler. "Burn them, if you like! Now listen to me. Tell off an officer and seventy men at once."

"I have all the necessary parties detailed already, sir."

"Will you listen to me?" roared the Colonel. He turned to where Captain Blaikie's detachment were drawn up on the platform, "Take the first seventy men of that lot, and tell them to stand over there, under an officer."

Captain Blaikie gave the necessary order.

"Now," continued Colonel Hyde, "tell them to get the horses out and on board that steamer at once. The rest of your party are to go by another steamer. See?"

"Yes, sir, perfectly. But—"

"Do you understand my order?" thundered the Colonel, with increasing choler.

"I do, sir," replied Blaikie politely, "but—"

"Then, for heaven's sake, carry on!"

Blaikie saluted.

"Very good, sir," he answered. "Mr. Little, come with me."

He turned upon his heel and disappeared rapidly round a corner, followed by the mystified Bobby.

Once out of the sight of the Colonel, Captain Blaikie halted, leaned against a convenient pillar, and lit a cigarette.

"And what do you think of that?" he inquired.

Bobby told him.

"Quite so," agreed Blaikie. "But what you say helps nobody, though doubtless soothing to the feelings. Now listen, Bobby, and I will give you your first lesson in the Tactical Handling of Brass Hats. Of course we might do as that dear old gentleman suggests, and send seventy horses and mules on a sea voyage in charge of a party of cooks, signallers, and machine-gunners, and let the grooms and drivers go with the bicycles and machine-guns and field kitchens. But I don't think we will. Nobody would enjoy the experiment much—except perhaps the mules. No: we will follow the golden rule, which is: When given an impossible job by a Brass Hat, salute smartly, turn about, and go and wait round a corner for five minutes. Then come back and do the job in a proper manner. Our five minutes are up: the coast should be clear. Come along, Bobby, and help me to exchange those two parties."

But we encountered surprisingly few Hydes. Nearly all were Jekylls—Jekylls of the most competent and courteous type. True, they were inclined to treat our laboriously completed returns with frivolity.

"Never mind those things, old man," they would say. "Just tell me who you are, and how many. That's right: now I know all about you. Got your working parties fixed up? Good! They ought to have everything cleared in a couple of hours. I'll see that a ration of hot tea is served out for them. Your train starts at a quarter past seven this evening—remember to call it nineteen-fifteen, by the way, in this country—and you ought to be at the station an hour before the time. I'll send you a guide. What a fine-looking lot these chaps of yours are! Best lot I've seen here for a very long time. Working like niggers, too! Now come along with me for ten minutes and I'll show you where to get a bite of breakfast. Expect you can do with a bit!"

That is Brass-Hat Jekyll—officer and gentleman; and, to the eternal credit of the British Army, be it said that he abounds in this well-conducted campaign. As an instance of his efficiency, let the case of our own regiment be quoted. The main body travelled here by one route, the transport, horses, and other details by another. The main body duly landed, and were conveyed to the rendezvous—a distant railway junction in Northern France. There they sat down to await the arrival of the train containing the other party; which had left England many hours before them, had landed at a different port, and had not been seen or heard of since.

They had to wait exactly ten minutes!

"Some Staff—what?" as the Adjutant observed, as the train lumbered into view.

II

Most of us, in our travels abroad, have observed the closed trucks which are employed upon French railways, and which bear the legend—

Hommes.... 40

Chevaux.... 8

Doubtless we have wondered, idly enough, what it must feel like to be one of the forty hommes. Well, now we know.

When we landed, we were packed into a train composed of fifty such trucks, and were drawn by a mighty engine for a day and a night across the pleasant land of France. Every six hours or so we were indulged with a *Halte Répas*. That is to say, the train drew up in a siding, where an officer with R.T.O. upon his arm made us welcome, and informed us that hot water was available for taking tea. Everybody had two days' rations in his haversack, so a large-scale picnic followed. From the horse-trucks emerged stolid individuals with canvas buckets—you require to be fairly stolid to pass the night in a closed box, moving at twenty miles an hour, in company with eight riotous and insecurely tethered mules—to draw water from the hydrant which supplied the locomotives. The infant population gathered round, and besought us for "souvenirs," the most popular taking the form of "biskeet" or "bully-boeuf." Both were given freely: with but little persuasion our open-handed warriors would have fain squandered their sacred "emergency ration" upon these rapacious infants.

After refreshment we proceeded to inspect the station. The centre of attraction was the French soldier on guard over the water-tank. Behold this same sentry confronted by Private Mucklewame, anxious to comply with Divisional Orders and "lose no opportunity of cultivating the friendliest relations with those of our Allies whom you may chance to encounter." So Mucklewame and the sentry (who is evidently burdened with similar instructions) regard one another with shy smiles, after the fashion of two children who have been introduced by their nurses at a party.

Presently the sentry, by a happy inspiration, proffers his bayonet for inspection, as it were a new doll. Mucklewame bows solemnly, and fingers the blade. Then he produces his own bayonet, and the two weapons are compared—still in constrained silence. Then Mucklewame nods approvingly.

"Verra goody!" he remarks, profoundly convinced that he is speaking the French language.

"Olrigh! Tipperaree!" replies the sentry, not to be outdone in international courtesy.

Unfortunately, the further cementing of the Entente Cordiale is frustrated by the blast of a whistle. We hurl ourselves into our trucks; the R.T.O. waves his hand in benediction; and the regiment proceeds upon its way, packed like herrings, but "all jubilant with song."

III

We have been "oot here" for a week now, and although we have had no personal encounter with the foe, our time has not been wasted. We are filling up gaps in our education, and we are tolerably busy. Some things, of course, we have not had to learn. We are fairly well inured, for instance, to hard work and irregular meals. What we have chiefly to acquire at present is the art of adaptability. When we are able to settle down into strange billets in half an hour, and pack up, ready for departure, within the same period, we shall have made a great stride in efficiency, and added enormously to our own personal comfort.

Even now we are making progress. Observe the platoon who are marching into this farmyard. They are dead tired, and the sight of the straw-filled barn is too much for some of them. They throw themselves down anywhere, and are asleep in a moment. When they wake up—or more likely, are wakened up—in an hour or two, they will be sorry. They will be stiff and sore, and their feet will be a torment. Others, more sensible, crowd round the pump, or dabble their abraded extremities in one of the countless ditches with which this country is intersected. Others again, of the more enterprising kind, repair to the house-door, and inquire politely for "the wife." (They have long given up inquiring for "the master." There is no master on this farm, or indeed on any farm throughout the length and breadth of this great-hearted land. Father and sons are all away, restoring the Bosche to his proper place in the animal kingdom. We have seen no young or middle-aged man out of uniform since we entered this district, save an occasional imbecile or cripple.)

Presently "the wife" comes to the door, with a smile. She can afford to smile now, for not so long ago her guests were Uhlans. Then begins an elaborate pantomime. Private Tosh says "Bonjourr!" in husky tones—last week he would have said "Hey, Bella!"—and proceeds to wash his hands in invisible soap and water. As a reward for his ingenuity he receives a basin of water: sometimes the water is even warm. Meanwhile Private Cosh, the linguist of the platoon, proffers twopence, and says: "Doolay—ye unnerstand?" He gets a drink of milk, which is a far, far better thing than the appalling green scum-covered water with which his less adaptable brethren are wont to refresh themselves from wayside ditches. Thomas Atkins, however mature, is quite incorrigible in this respect.

Yes, we are getting on. And when every man in the platoon, instead of merely some, can find a place to sleep, draw his blanket from the waggon, clean his rifle and himself, and get to his dinner within the half-hour already specified, we shall be able justly to call ourselves seasoned.

We have covered some distance this week, and we have learned one thing at least, and that is, not to be uppish about our sleeping quarters. We have slept in chateaux, convents, farm-houses, and under the open sky. The chateaux are usually empty. An aged retainer, the sole inhabitant, explains that M. le Comte is at Paris; M. Armand at Arras; and M. Guy in Alsace,—all doing their bit. M. Victor is in hospital, with Madame and Mademoiselle in constant attendance.

So we settle down in the chateaux, and unroll our sleeping-bags upon its dusty parquet. Occasionally we find a bed available. Then two officers take the mattress, upon the floor, and two more take what is left of the bed. French chateaux do not appear to differ much as a class. They are distinguished by great elegance of design, infinite variety in furniture, and entire absence of drains. The same rule applies to convents, except that there is no furniture.

Given fine weather, by far the most luxurious form of lodging is in the open air. Here one may slumber at ease, fanned by the wings of cockchafers and soothed by an unseen choir of frogs. There are drawbacks, of course. Mr. Waddell one evening spread his ground-sheet and bedding in the grassy meadow, beside a murmuring stream. It was an idyllic resting-place for a person of romantic or contemplative disposition. Unfortunately it is almost impossible nowadays to keep one's favourite haunts select. This was evidently the opinion of the large water-rat which Waddell found sitting upon his air-pillow when he returned from supper. Although French, the animal exhibited no disposition to fraternise, but withdrew in the most pointed fashion, taking an Abernethy biscuit with him.

Accommodation in farms is best described by the word "promiscuous." There are twelve officers and two hundred men billeted here. The farm is exactly the same as any other French farm. It consists of a hollow square of buildings—dwelling-house, barns, pigstyes, and stables—with a commodious manure-heap, occupying the whole yard except a narrow strip round the edge, in the middle, the happy hunting-ground of innumerable cocks and hens and an occasional pig. The men sleep in the barns. The senior officers sleep in a stone-floored boudoir of their own. The juniors sleep where they can, and experience little difficulty in accomplishing the feat. A hard day's marching and a truss of straw—these two combined form an irresistible inducement to slumber.

Only a few miles away big guns thunder until the building shakes. To-morrow a select party of officers is to pay a visit to the trenches. Thereafter our whole flock is to go, in its official capacity. The War is with us at last. Early this morning a Zeppelin rose into view on the skyline. Shell fire pursued it, and it sank again—rumour says in the British lines. Rumour is our only war correspondent at present. It is far easier to follow the course of events from home, where newspapers are more plentiful than here.

But the grim realities of war are coming home to us. Outside this farm stands a tall tree. Not many months ago a party of Uhlans arrived here, bringing with them a wounded British prisoner. They crucified him to that self-same tree, and stood round him till he died. He was a long time dying.

Some of us had not heard of Uhlans before. These have now noted the name, for future reference—and action.

XV

IN THE TRENCHES—AN OFF-DAY

This town is under constant shell fire. It goes on day after day: it has been going on for months. Sometimes a single shell comes: sometimes half a dozen. Sometimes whole batteries get to work. The effect is terrible. You who live at home in ease have no conception of what it is like to live in a town which is under intermittent shell fire.

I say this advisedly. You have no conception whatsoever.

We get no rest. There is a distant boom, followed by a crash overhead. Cries are heard—the cries of women and children. They are running frantically—running to observe the explosion, and if possible pick up a piece of the shell as a souvenir. Sometimes there are not enough souvenirs to go round, and then the clamour increases.

We get no rest, I say—only frightfulness. British officers, walking peaceably along the pavement, are frequently hustled and knocked aside by these persons. Only the other day, a full colonel was compelled to turn up a side-street, to avoid disturbing a ring of excited children who were dancing round a beautiful new hole in the ground in the middle of a narrow lane.

If you enter into a café or estaminet, a total stranger sidles to your table, and, having sat down beside you, produces from the recesses of his person a fragment of shrapnel. This he lays before you, and explains that if he had been standing at the spot where the shell burst, it would have killed him. You express polite regret, and pass on elsewhere, seeking peace and finding none. The whole thing is a public scandal.

Seriously, though, it is astonishing what contempt familiarity can breed, even in the case of high-explosive shells. This little town lies close behind the trenches. All day long the big guns boom. By night the rifles and machine-guns take up the tale. One is frequently aroused from slumber, especially towards dawn, by a perfect tornado of firing. The machine-guns make a noise like a giant tearing calico. Periodically, too, as already stated, we are subjected to an hour's intimidation in the shape of bombardment. Shrapnel bursts over our heads; shells explode in the streets, especially in open spaces, or where two important streets cross. (With modern artillery you can shell a town quite methodically by map and compass.)

Brother Bosche's motto appears to be: "It is a fine morning. There is nothing in the trenches doing. We abundant ammunition have. Let us a little frightfulness into the town pump!" So he pumps.

But nobody seems to mind. Of course there is a casualty now and then. Occasionally a hole is blown in a road, or the side of a house is knocked in. Yet the general attitude of the population is one of rather interested expectancy. There is always the cellar to retire to if things get really serious. The gratings are sandbagged to that end. At other times—well, there is always the pleasing possibility of witnessing the sudden removal of your neighbour's landmark.

Officers breakfasting in their billets look up from their porridge, and say,—

"That's a dud! *That's* a better one! Stick to it, Bill!"

It really is most discouraging, to a sensitive and conscientious Hun.

The same unconcern reigns in the trenches. Let us imagine that we are members of a distinguished party from Headquarters, about to make a tour of inspection.

We leave the town, and after a short walk along the inevitable poplar-lined road turn into a field. The country all round us is flat—flat as Cheshire; and, like Cheshire, has a pond in every field. But in the hazy distance stands a low ridge.

"Better keep close to the hedge," suggests the officer in charge. "There are eighty guns on that ridge. It's a misty morning; but they've got all the ranges about here to a yard; so they *might*—"

We keep close to the hedge.

Presently we find ourselves entering upon a wide but sticky path cut in the clay. At the entrance stands a neat notice-board, which announces, somewhat unexpectedly:—

OLD KENT ROAD

The field is flat, but the path runs downhill. Consequently we soon find ourselves tramping along below the ground-level, with a stout parapet of clay on either side of us. Overhead there is nothing—nothing but the blue sky, with the larks singing, quite regardless of the War.

"Communication trench," explains the guide.

We tramp along this sunken lane for the best part of a mile. It winds a good deal. Every hundred yards or so comes a great promontory of sandbags, necessitating four right-angle turns. Once we pass under the shadow of trees, and apple-blossom flutters down upon our upturned faces. We are walking through an orchard. Despite the efforts of ten million armed men, brown old Mother Earth has made it plain that seedtime and harvest shall still prevail.

Now we are crossing a stream, which cuts the trench at right angles. The stream is spanned by a structure of planks—labelled, it is hardly necessary to say, LONDON BRIDGE. The side-street, so to speak, by which the stream runs away, is called JOCK'S JOY. We ask why?

"It's the place where the Highlanders wash their knees," is the explanation.

Presently we arrive at PICCADILLY CIRCUS, a muddy excavation in the earth, from which several passages branch. These thoroughfares are not all labelled with strict regard for London geography. We note THE HAYMARKET, also PICCADILLY; but ARTILLERY LANE seems out of place, somehow. On the site, too, of the Criterion, we observe a subterranean cavern containing three recumbent figures, snoring lustily. This bears the sign CYCLISTS' REST.

We, however, take the turning marked SHAFTESBURY AVENUE, and after passing (quite wrongly, don't you think?) through TRAFALGAR SQUARE—six feet by eight—find ourselves in the actual firing trench.

It is an unexpectedly spacious place. We, who have spent the winter constructing slits in the ground two feet wide, feel quite lost in this roomy thoroughfare. For a thoroughfare it is, with little toy houses on either side. They are hewn out of the solid earth, lined with planks, painted, furnished, and decorated. These are, so to speak, permanent trenches, which have been occupied for more than six months.

Observe this eligible residence on your left. It has a little door, nearly six feet high, and a real glass window, with a little curtain. Inside, there is a bunk, six feet long, together with an ingenious folding washhand-stand, of the nautical variety, and a flap-table. The walls, which are painted pale green, are decorated with elegant extracts from the "Sketch" and "La Vie Parisienne." Outside, the name of the villa is painted up. It is in Welsh—that notorious railway station in Anglesey which runs to thirty-three syllables or so—and extends from one end of the façade to the other. A small placard announces that Hawkers, Organs, and Street-cries are prohibited.

"This is my shanty," explains a machine-gun officer standing by. "It was built by a Welsh Fusilier, who has since moved on. He was here all winter, and made everything himself, including the washhand-stand. Some carpenter—what? of course I am not here continuously. We have six days in the trenches and six out; so I take turns with a man in the Midland Mudcrushers, who take turns with us. Come in and have some tea."

It is only ten o'clock in the morning, but tea—strong and sweet, with condensed milk—is instantly forthcoming. Refreshed by this, and a slice of cake, we proceed upon our excursion.

The trench is full of men, mostly asleep; for the night cometh, when no man may sleep. They lie in low-roofed rectangular caves, like the interior of great cucumber-frames, lined with planks and supported by props. The cave is really a homogeneous affair, for it is constructed in the R.E. workshops and then brought bodily to the trenches and fitted into its appointed excavation. Each cave holds three men. They lie side by side, like three dogs in a triple kennel, with their heads outward and easily accessible to the individual who performs the functions of "knocker-up."

Others are cooking, others are cleaning their rifles. The proceedings are superintended by a contemplative tabby cat, coiled up in a niche, like a feline flower in a crannied wall.

"She used ter sit on top of the parapet," explains a friendly lance-corporal; "but became a casualty, owin' to a sniper mistakin' 'er for a Guardsman's bearskin. Show the officer your back, Christabel!"

We inspect the healed scar, and pass on. Next moment we round a traverse—and walk straight into the arms of Privates Ogg and Hogg!

No need now to remain with the distinguished party from Headquarters. For the next half-mile of trench you will find yourselves among friends. "K(1)" and Brother Bosche are face to face at last, and here you behold our own particular band of warriors taking their first spell in the trenches.

Let us open the door of this spacious dug-out—the image of an up-river bungalow, decorated with window-boxes and labelled Potsdam View—and join the party of four which sits round the table.

"How did your fellows get on last night, Wagstaffe?" inquires Major Kemp.

"Very well, on the whole. It was a really happy thought on the part of the authorities—almost human, in fact—to put us in alongside the old regiment."

"Or what's left of them."

Wagstaffe nods gravely.

"Yes. There are some changes in the Mess since I last dined there," he says. "Anyhow, the old hands took our boys to their bosoms at once, and showed them the ropes."

"The men did not altogether fancy look-out work in the dark, sir," says Bobby Little to Major Kemp.

"Neither should I, very much," said Kemp. "To take one's stand on a ledge fixed at a height which brings one's head and shoulders well above the parapet, and stand there for an hour on end, knowing that a machine-gun may start a spell of rapid traversing fire at any moment—well, it takes a bit of doing, you know, until you are used to it. How did you persuade 'em, Bobby?"

"Oh, I just climbed up on the top of the parapet and sat there for a bit," says Bobby Little modestly. "They were all right after that."

"Had you any excitement, Ayling?" asks Kemp. "I hear rumours that you had two casualties."

"Yes," says Ayling. "Four of us went out patrolling in front of the trench—"

"Who?"

"Myself, two men, and old Sergeant Carfrae."

"Carfrae?" Wagstaffe laughs. "That old fire-eater? I remember him at Paardeberg. You were lucky to get back alive. Proceed, my son!"

"We went out," continues Ayling, "and patrolled."

"How?"

"Well, there you rather have me. I have always been a bit foggy as to what a patrol really does—what risks it takes, and so on. However, Carfrae had no doubts on the subject whatever. His idea was to trot over to the German trenches and look inside."

"Quite so!" agreed Wagstaffe, and Kemp chuckled.

"Well, we were standing by the barbed wire entanglement, arguing the point, when suddenly some infernal imbecile in our own trenches—"

"Cockerell, for a dollar!" murmurs Wagstaffe. "Don't say he fired at you!"

"No, he did worse. He let off a fireball."

"Whew! And there you stood in the limelight!"

"Exactly."

"What did you do?"

"I had sufficient presence of mind to do what Carfrae did. I threw myself on my face, and shouted to the two men to do the same."

"Did they?"

"No. They started to run back towards the trenches. Half a dozen German rifles opened on them at once."

"Were they badly hit?"

"Nothing to speak of, considering. The shots mostly went high. Preston got his elbow smashed, and Burke had a bullet through his cap and another in the region of the waistband. Then they tumbled into the trench like rabbits. Carfrae and I crawled after them."

At this moment the doorway of the dugout is darkened by a massive figure, and Major Kemp's colour-sergeant announces—

"There's a parrty of Gairmans gotten oot o' their trenches, sirr. Will we open fire?"

"Go and have a look at 'em, like a good chap, Wagger," says the Major. "I want to finish this letter."

Wagstaffe and Bobby Little make their way along the trench until they come to a low opening marked MAXIM VILLA. They crawl inside, and find themselves in a semicircular recess, chiefly occupied by an earthen platform, upon which a machine-gun is mounted. The recess is roofed over, heavily protected with sandbags, and lined with iron plates; for a machine-gun emplacement is the object of frequent and pressing attention from high-explosive shells. There are loopholes to right and left, but not in front. These deadly weapons prefer diagonal or enfilade fire. It is not worth while to fire them frontally.

Wagstaffe draws back a strip of sacking which covers one loophole, and peers out. There, a hundred and fifty yards away, across a sunlit field, he beholds some twenty grey figures, engaged in the most pastoral of pursuits, in front of the German trenches.

"They are cutting the grass," he says. "Let 'em, by all means! If they don't, we must. We don't want their bomb-throwers crawling over here through a hay-field. Let us encourage them by every means in our power. It might almost be worth our while to send them a message. Walk along the trench, Bobby, and see that no excitable person looses off at them."

Bobby obeys; and peace still broods over the sleepy trench. The only sound which breaks the summer stillness is the everlasting crack, crack! of the snipers' rifles. On an off-day like this the sniper is a very necessary person. He serves to remind us that we are at war. Concealed in his own particular eyrie, with his eyes for ever laid along his telescopic sight, he keeps ceaseless vigil over the ragged outline of the enemy's trenches. Wherever a head, or anything resembling a head, shows itself, he fires. Were it not for his enthusiasm, both sides would be sitting in their shirt-sleeves upon their respective parapets, regarding one another with frank curiosity; and that would never do. So the day wears on.

Suddenly, from far in our rear, comes a boom, then another. Wagstaffe sighs resignedly.

"Why can't they let well alone?" he complains. "What's the trouble now?"

"I expect it's our Divisional Artillery having a little target practice," says Captain Blaikie. He peers into a neighbouring trench-periscope. "Yes, they are shelling that farm behind the German second-line trench. Making good shooting too, for beginners," as a column of dust and smoke rises from behind the enemy's lines. "But brother Bosche will be very peevish about it. We don't usually fire at this time of the afternoon. Yes, there is the haymaking party going home. There will be a beastly noise for the next half-hour. Pass the word along for every man to get into his dug-out."

The warning comes none too soon. In five minutes the incensed Hun is retaliating for the disturbance of his afternoon siesta. A hail of bullets passes over our trench. Shrapnel bursts overhead. High-explosive shells rain upon and around the parapet. One drops into the trench, and explodes, with surprisingly little effect. (Bobby Little found the head afterwards, and sent it home as a memento of his first encounter with reality.)

Our trench makes no reply. There is no need. This outburst heralds no grand assault. It is a mere display of "frightfulness," calculated to cow the impressionable Briton. We sit close, and make tea. Only the look-out men, crouching behind their periscopes and loopholes, keep their posts. The wind is the wrong way for gas, and in any case we all have respirators. Private M'Leary, the humorist of "A" Company, puts his on, and pretends to drink his tea through it.

Altogether, the British soldier appears sadly unappreciative either of "frightfulness" or practical chemistry. He is a hopeless case.

The firing ceases as suddenly as it began. Silence reigns again, broken only by a solitary shot from a trench-mortar—a sort of explosive postscript to a half hour's Hymn of Hate.

"And that's that!" observes Captain Blaikie cheerfully, emerging from Potsdam View. "The Hun is a harmless little creature, but noisy when roused. Now, what about getting home? It will be dark in half an hour or so. Platoon commanders, warn your men!"

It should be noted that upon this occasion we are not doing our full spell of duty—that is, six days. We have merely come in for a spell of instruction, of twenty-four hours' duration, under the chaperonage of our elder and more seasoned brethren.

Bobby Little, having given the necessary orders to his sergeant, proceeded to Trafalgar Square, there to await the mustering of his platoon.

But the first arrival took the form of a slow-moving procession—a corporal, followed by two men carrying a stretcher. On the stretcher lay something covered with a ground-sheet. At one end projected a pair of regulation boots, very still and rigid.

Bobby caught his breath. He was just nineteen, and this was his first encounter with sudden death.

"Who is it?" he asked unsteadily.

The corporal saluted.

"Private M'Leary, sirr. That last shot from the trench-mortar got him. It came in kin' o' sideways. He was sittin' at the end of his dug-oot, gettin' his tea. Stretcher party, advance!"

The procession moved off again, and disappeared round the curve of
Shaftesbury Avenue. The off-day was over.

XVI

"DIRTY WORK AT THE CROSS-ROADS TO-NIGHT"

Last week we abandoned the rural billets in which we had been remodelling some of our methods (on the experiences gained by our first visit to the trenches), and paraded at full strength for a march which we knew would bring us right into the heart of things. No more trial trips; no more chaperoning! This time, we decided, we were "for it."

During our three weeks of active service we have learned two things—the art of shaking down quickly into our habitation of the moment, as already noted; and the art of reducing our personal effects to a portable minimum.

To the private soldier the latter problem presents no difficulties. Everything is arranged for him. His outfit is provided by the Government, and he carries it himself. It consists of a rifle, bayonet, and a hundred and twenty rounds of ammunition. On one side of him hangs his water-bottle, containing a quart of water, on the other, a haversack, occupied by his "iron ration"—an emergency meal of the tinned variety, which must never on any account be opened except by order of the C.O.—and such private effects as his smoking outfit and an entirely mythical item of refreshment officially known as "the unexpended portion of the day's ration." On his back he carries a "pack," containing his greatcoat, waterproof sheet, and such changes of raiment as a paternal Government allows him. He also has to find room therein for a towel, housewife, and a modest allowance of cutlery. (He frequently wears the spoon in his stocking, as a skean-dhu.) Round his neck he wears his identity disc. In his breast-pocket he carries a respirator, to be donned in the event of his encountering the twin misfortunes of an east wind and a gaseous Hun. He also carries a bottle of liquid for damping the respirator. In the flap of his jacket is sewn a field dressing.

Slung behind him is an entrenching tool.

Any other space upon his person is at his own disposal, and he may carry what he likes, except "unsoldierly trinkets"—whatever these may be. However, if the passion for self-adornment proves too strong, he may wear "the French National Colours"—a compliment to our gallant ally which is slightly discounted by the fact that her national colours are the same as our own.

However, once he has attached this outfit to his suffering person, and has said what he thinks about its weight, the private has no more baggage worries. Except for his blanket, which is carried on a waggon, he is his own arsenal, wardrobe, and pantry.

Not so the officer. He suffers from *embarras de choix*. He is the victim of his female relatives, who are themselves the victims of those enterprising tradesmen who have adopted the most obvious method of getting rid of otherwise unsaleable goods by labelling everything *For Active Service*—a really happy thought when you are trying to sell a pipe of port or a manicure set. Have you seen Our Active Service Trouser-Press?

By the end of April Bobby Little had accumulated, with a view to facilitating the destruction of the foe—

An automatic Mauser pistol, with two thousand rounds of ammunition.
A regulation Service revolver.
A camp bed.
A camp table.
A camp chair.
A pneumatic mattress.
[This ingenious contrivance was meant to be blown up, like an air-cushion, and Bobby's servant expended most of the day and much valuable breath in performing the feat. Ultimately, in a misguided attempt to save his lungs from rupture, he employed a bicycle pump, and burst the bed.]
A sleeping (or "flea") bag.
A portable bath.
A portable washhand-stand.
A dressing-case, heavily ballasted with cut-glass bottles.
A primus stove.
A despatch case.
The "Service" Kipling (about forty volumes.)
Innumerable socks and shirts.
A box of soap.

Fifty boxes of matches.

A small medicine chest.

About a dozen first-aid outfits.

A case of pipes, and cigarettes innumerable.

[Bobby's aunts regarded cigars as not quite ascetic enough for active service. Besides, they might make him sick.]

About a cubic foot of chocolate (various).

Numerous compressed foods and concentrated drinks.

An "active service" cooking outfit.

An electric lamp, with several refills.

A pair of binoculars.

A telescope.

A prismatic compass.

A sparklet siphon.

A luminous watch.

A pair of insulated wire-cutters.

"There's only one thing you've forgotten," remarked Captain Wagstaffe, when introduced to this unique collection of curios.

"What is that?" inquired Bobby, always eager to learn.

"A pantechnicon! Do you known how much personal baggage an officer is allowed, in addition to what he carries himself?"

"Thirty-five pounds."

"Correct."

"It sounds a lot," said Bobby.

"It looks precious little!" was Wagstaffe's reply.

"I suppose they won't be particular to a pound or so," said Bobby optimistically.

"Listen," commanded Wagstaffe. "When we go abroad, your Wolseley valise, containing this"—he swept his hand round the crowded hut—"this military museum, will be handed to the Quartermaster. He is a man of singularly rigid mind, with an exasperating habit of interpreting rules and regulations quite literally. If you persist in this scheme of asking him to pass half a ton of assorted lumber as a package weighing thirty-five pounds, he will cast you forth and remain your enemy for life. And personally," concluded Wagstaffe, "I would rather keep on the right side of my Regimental Quartermaster than of the Commander-in-Chief himself. Now, send all this stuff home—you can use it on manoeuvres in peace-time—and I will give you a little list which will not break the baggage-waggon's back."

The methodical Bobby produced a notebook.

"You will require to wash occasionally. Take a canvas bucket, some carbolic soap, and a good big towel. Also your toothbrush, and—excuse the question, but do you shave?"

"Twice a week," admitted the blushing Bobby.

"Happy man! Well, take a safety-razor. That will do for cleanliness. Now for clothing. Lots of socks, but only one change of other things, unless you care to take a third shirt in your greatcoat pocket. Two good pairs of boots, and a pair of slacks. Then, as regards sleeping. Your flea-bag and your three Government blankets, with your valise underneath, will keep you (and your little bedfellows) as warm as toast. You may get separated from your valise, though, so take a ground-sheet in your pack. Then you will be ready to dine and sleep simply anywhere, at a moment's notice. As regards comforts generally, take a 'Tommy's cooker,' if you can find room for it, and scrap all the rest of your cuisine except your canteen. Take a few meat lozenges and some chocolate in one of your ammunition-pouches, in case you ever have to go without your breakfast. Rotten work, marching or fighting on a hollow tummy!"

"What about revolvers?" inquired Bobby, displaying his arsenal, a little nervously.

"If the Germans catch you with that Mauser, they will hang you. Take the Webley. Then you can always draw Service ammunition." Wagstaffe ran his eye over the rest of Bobby's outfit. "Smokes? Take your pipe and a tinder-box: you will get baccy and cigarettes to burn out there. Keep that electric torch; and your binoculars, of course. Also that small map-case: it's a good one. Also wire-cutters. You can write letters in your field-message-book. Your compass is all right. Add a pair of canvas shoes—they're a godsend after a long day,—an air-pillow, some candle-ends, a tin of vaseline, and a ball of string, and I think you will do. If you find you still have a pound or so in hand, add a few books—something to fall back on, in case supplies fail. Personally, I'm taking 'Vanity Fair' and 'Pickwick.' But then, I'm old-fashioned."

* * * * *

Bobby took Wagstaffe's advice, with the result that that genial obstructionist, the Quartermaster, smiled quite benignly upon him when he presented his valise; while his brother officers, sternly bidden to revise their equipment, were compelled at the last moment to discriminate frantically between the claims of necessity and luxury—often disastrously.

However, we had all found our feet, and developed into seasoned vagabonds when we set out for the trenches last week. A few days previously we had been inspected by Sir John French himself.

"And that," explained Major Kemp to his subalterns, "usually means dirty work at the cross-roads at no very distant period!"

* * * * *

Major Kemp was right—quite literally right.

Our march took us back to Armentières, whose sufferings under intermittent shell fire have already been described. We marched by night, and arrived at breakfast-time. The same evening two companies and a section of machine-gunners were bidden to equip themselves with picks and shovels and parade at dusk. An hour later we found ourselves proceeding cautiously along a murky road close behind the trenches.

The big guns were silent, but the snipers were busy on both sides. A German searchlight was combing out the heavens above: a constant succession of star-shells illumined the earth beneath.

"What are we going to do to-night, sir?" inquired Bobby Little, heroically resisting an inclination to duck, as a Mauser bullet spat viciously over his head.

"I believe we are going to dig a redoubt behind the trenches," replied Captain Blaikie. "I expect to meet an R.E. officer somewhere about here, and he will tell us the worst. That was a fairly close one, Bobby! Pass the word down quietly that the men are to keep in to each side of the road, and walk as low as they can. Ah, there is our sportsman, I fancy. Good evening!"

A subaltern of that wonderful corps, the Royal Engineers, loomed out of the darkness, removed a cigarette from his mouth, and saluted politely.

"Good evening, sir," he said to Blaikie. "Will you follow me, please? I have marked out each man's digging position with white tape, so they ought to find no difficulty in getting to work. Brought your machine-gun officer?"

The machine-gun officer, Ayling, was called up.

"We are digging a sort of square fort," explained the Engineer, "to hold a battalion. That will mean four guns to mount. I don't know much about machine-guns myself; so perhaps you"—to Ayling—"will walk round with me outside the position, and you can select your own emplacements."

"I shall be charmed," replied Ayling, and Blaikie chuckled.

"I'll just get your infantry to work first," continued the phlegmatic youth. "This way, sir!"

The road at this point ran through a hollow square of trees, and it was explained to the working-party that the trees, roughly, followed the outlines of the redoubt.

"The trenches are about half-finished," added the Engineer. "We had a party from the Seaforths working here last night. Your men have only to carry on where they left off. It's chiefly a matter of filling sandbags and placing them on the parapet." He pointed to a blurred heap in a corner of the wood. "There are fifty thousand there. Leave what you don't want!"

"Where do we get the earth to fill the sandbags?" asked Blaikie. "The trenches, or the middle of the redoubt?"

"Oh, pretty well anywhere," replied the Engineer. "Only, warn your men to be careful not to dig too deep!"

And with this dark saying he lounged off to take Ayling for his promised walk.

"I'll take you along the road a bit, first," he said, "and then we will turn off into the field where the corner of the redoubt is, and you can look at things from the outside."

Ayling thanked him, and stepped somewhat higher than usual, as a bullet struck the ground at his feet.

"Extraordinary how few casualties one gets," continued the Sapper chattily. "Their snipers go potting away all night, but they don't often get anybody. By the way, they have a machine-gun trained on this road, but they only loose it off every second night. Methodical beggars!"

"Did they loose it off last night?"

"No. To-night's the night. Have you finished here!"

"Yes, thanks!"

"Right-o! We'll go to the next corner. You'll get a first-class field of fire there, I should say."

The second position was duly inspected, the only incident of interest being the bursting of a star-shell directly overhead.

"Better lie down for a minute," suggested the Engineer.

Ayling, who had been struggling with a strong inclination to do so for some time, promptly complied.

"Just like the Crystal Palace on a benefit night!" observed his guide admiringly, as the landscape was lit up with a white glare. "Now you can see your position beautifully. You can fire obliquely in this direction, and then do a first-class enfilade if the trenches get rushed."

"I see," said Ayling, surveying the position with real interest. He was beginning to enjoy selecting gun-emplacements which really mattered. It was a change from nine months of "eye-wash."

When the German star-shell had spent itself they crossed the road, to the rear of the redoubt, and marked the other two emplacements—in comparative safety now.

"The only trouble about this place," said Ayling, as he surveyed the last position, "is that my fire will be masked by that house with the clump of trees beside it."

The Engineer produced a small note-book, and wrote in it by the light of a convenient star-shell.

"Right-o!" he said. "I'll have the whole caboodle pushed over for you by to-morrow night. Anything else?"

Ayling began to enjoy himself. After you have spent nine months in an unprofitable attempt to combine practical machine-gun tactics with a scrupulous respect for private property, the realisation that you may now gratify your destructive instincts to the full comes as a welcome and luxurious shock.

"Thanks," he said. "You might flatten out that haystack, too."

* * * * *

They found the others hard at work when they returned. Captain Blaikie was directing operations from the centre of the redoubt.

"I say," he said, as the Engineer sat down beside him, "I'm afraid we're doing a good deal of body-snatching. This place is absolutely full of little wooden crosses."

"Germans," replied the Engineer laconically.

"How long have they been—here?"

"Since October."

"So I should imagine," said Blaikie, with feeling.

"The crosses aren't much guide, either," continued the Engineer. "The deceased are simply all over the place. The best plan is to dig until you come to a blanket. (There are usually two or three to a blanket.) Then tell off a man to flatten down clay over the place at once, and try somewhere else. It is a rotten job, though, however you look at it."

"Have you been here long?" inquired Bobby Little, who had come across the road for a change of air.

"Long enough! But I'm not on duty continuously. I am Box. Cox takes over to-morrow." He rose to his feet and looked at his watch.

"You ought to move off by half-past one, sir," he said to Blaikie. "It begins to get light after that, and the Bosches have three shells for that cross-road over there down in their time-table at two-fifteen. They're a hide-bound lot, but punctual!"

"Thanks," said Blaikie. "I shall not neglect your advice. It is half-past eleven now. Come along, Bobby, and we'll see how old Ayling is getting on."

* * * * *

Steadily, hour by hour, in absolute silence, the work went on. There was no talking, but (under extenuating circumstances) smoking was permitted. Periodically, as the star-shells burst into brilliance overhead, the workers sank down behind a parapet, or, if there was no time, stood rigid—the one thing to avoid upon these occasions is movement of any kind—and gave the snipers a chance. It was not pleasant, but it was duty; and the word duty has become a mighty force in "K(1)" these days. No one was hit, which was remarkable, when you consider what an artist a German sniper is. Possibly the light of the star-shells was deceptive, or possibly there is some truth in the general rumour that the Saxons, who hold this part of the line, are well-disposed towards us, and conduct their offensive operations with a tactful blend of constant firing and bad shooting, which, while it satisfies the Prussians, causes no serious inconvenience to Thomas Atkins.

At a quarter-past one a subdued order ran round the trenches; the men fell in on the sheltered side of the plantation; picks and shovels were checked; rifles and equipment were resumed; and the party stole silently away to the cross-road, where the three shells were timed to arrive at two-fifteen. When they did so, with true Teutonic punctuality, an hour later, our friends were well on their way home to billets and bed—with the dawn breaking behind them, the larks getting to work overhead, and all the infected air of the German graveyard swept out of their lungs by the dew of the morning.

As for that imperturbable philosopher, Box, he sat down with a cigarette, and waited for Cox.

XVII

THE NEW WARFARE

The trench system has one thing to recommend it. It tidies things up a bit.

For the first few months after the war broke out confusion reigned supreme. Belgium and the north of France were one huge jumbled battlefield, rather like a public park on a Saturday afternoon—one of those parks where promiscuous football is permitted. Friend and foe were inextricably mingled, and the direction of the goal was uncertain. If you rode into a village, you might find it occupied by a Highland regiment or a squadron of Uhlans. If you dimly discerned troops marching side by side with you in the dawning, it was by no means certain that they would prove to be your friends. On the other hand, it was never safe to assume that a battalion which you saw hastily entrenching itself against your approach was German. It might belong to your own brigade. There was no front and no rear, so direction counted for nothing. The country swarmed with troops which had been left "in the air," owing to their own too rapid advance, or the equally rapid retirement of their supporters; with scattered details trying to rejoin their units; or with despatch riders hunting for a peripatetic Divisional Headquarters. Snipers shot both sides impartially. It was all most upsetting.

Well, as already indicated, the trench system has put all that right. The trenches now run continuously—a long, irregular, but perfectly definite line of cleavage—from the North Sea to the Vosges. Everybody has been carefully sorted out—human beings on one side, Germans on the other. ("Like the Zoo," observes Captain Wagstaffe.) Nothing could be more suitable. *You're there, and I'm here, so what do we care?* in fact.

The result is an agreeable blend of war and peace. This week, for instance, our battalion has been undergoing a sort of rest-cure a few miles from the hottest part of the firing line. (We had a fairly heavy spell of work last week.) In the morning we wash our clothes, and perform a few mild martial exercises. In the afternoon we sleep, in all degrees of *déshabille*, under the trees in an orchard. In the evening we play football, or bathe in the canal, or lie on our backs on the grass, watching our aeroplanes buzzing home to roost, attended by German shrapnel. We could not have done this in the autumn. Now, thanks to our trenches, a few miles away, we are as safe here as in the wilds of Argyllshire or West Kensington.

But there are drawbacks to everything. The fact is, a trench is that most uninteresting of human devices, a compromise. It is neither satisfactory as a domicile nor efficient as a weapon of offence. The most luxuriant dug-out; the most artistic window-box—these, in spite of all biased assertions to the contrary, compare unfavourably with a flat in Knightsbridge. On the other hand, the knowledge that you are keeping yourself tolerably immune from the assaults of your enemy is heavily discounted by the fact that the enemy is equally immune from yours. In other words, you "get no forrarder" with a trench; and the one thing which we are all anxious to do out here is to bring this war to a speedy and gory conclusion, and get home to hot baths and regular meals.

So a few days ago we were not at all surprised to be informed, officially, that trench life is to be definitely abandoned, and Hun-hustling to begin in earnest.

(To be just, this decision was made months ago: the difficulty was to put it into execution. The winter weather was dreadful. The enemy were many and we were few. In Germany, the devil's forge at Essen was roaring night and day: in Great Britain Trades Union bosses were carefully adjusting the respective claims of patriotism and personal dignity before taking their coats off. So we cannot lay our want of progress to the charge of that dogged band of Greathearts which has been holding on, and holding on, and holding on—while the people at home were making up for lost time—ever since the barbarian was hurled back from the Marne to the Aisne and confined behind his earthen barrier. We shall win this war one day, and most of the credit will go, as usual, to those who are in at the finish. But—when we assign the glory and the praise, let us not forget those who stood up to the first rush. The new armies which are pouring across the Channel this month will bring us victory in the end. Let us bare our heads, then, in all reverence, to the memory of those battered, decimated, indomitable legions which saved us from utter extinction at the beginning.)

The situation appears to be that if we get through—and no one seems to doubt that we shall: the difficulty lies in staying there when you have got through—we shall be committed at once to an endless campaign of village-fighting. This country is as flat as Cambridgeshire. Every yard of it is under cultivation. The landscape is dotted with farm-steadings. There is a group of cottages or an *estaminet* at every cross-roads. When our great invading line sweeps forward, each one of these buildings will be held by the enemy, and must be captured, house by house, room by room, and used as a base for another rush.

And how is this to be done?

Well, it will be no military secret by the time these lines appear. It is no secret now. The answer to the conundrum is—Bombs!

To-day, out here, bombs are absolutely *dernier cri*. We talk of nothing else. We speak about rifles and bayonets as if they were so many bows and arrows. It is true that the modern Lee-Enfield and Mauser claim to be the most precise and deadly weapons of destruction ever devised. But they were intended for proper, gentlemanly warfare, with the opposing sides set out in straight lines, a convenient distance apart. In the hand-to-hand butchery which calls itself war to-day, the rifle is rapidly becoming *démodé*. For long ranges you require machine-guns; for short, bombs and hand-grenades. Can you empty a cottage by firing a single rifle-shot in at the door? Can you exterminate twenty Germans in a fortified back-parlour by a single thrust with a bayonet? Never! But you can do both these things with a jam-tin stuffed with dynamite and scrap-iron.

So the bomb has come to its own, and has brought with it certain changes—tactical, organic, and domestic. To take the last first, the bomb-officer, hitherto a despised underling, popularly (but maliciously) reputed to have been appointed to his present post through inability to handle a platoon, has suddenly attained a position of dazzling eminence. From being a mere super, he has become a star. In fact, he threatens to dispute the pre-eminence of that other regimental parvenu, the Machine-Gun Officer. He is now the confidant of Colonels, and consorts upon terms of easy familiarity with Brigade Majors. He holds himself coldly aloof from the rest of us, brooding over the greatness of his responsibilities; and when he speaks, it is to refer darkly to "detonators," and "primers," and "time-fuses." And we, who once addressed him derisively as "Anarchist," crowd round him and hang upon his lips.

The reason is that in future it is to be a case of—"For every man, a bomb or two"; and it is incumbent upon us, if we desire to prevent these infernal machines from exploding while yet in our custody, to attain the necessary details as to their construction and tender spots by the humiliating process of conciliating the Bomb Officer.

So far as we have mastered the mysteries of the craft, there appear to be four types of bomb in store for us—or rather, for Brother Bosche. They are:—

(1) The hair-brush.
(2) The cricket-ball.
(3) The policeman's truncheon.
(4) The jam-tin.

The hair-brush is very like the ordinary hair-brush, except that the bristles are replaced by a solid block of high-explosive. The policeman's truncheon has gay streamers of tape tied to its tail, to ensure that it falls to the ground nose downwards. Both these bombs explode on impact, and it is unadvisable to knock them against anything—say the back of the trench—when throwing them. The cricket-ball works by a time-fuse. Its manipulation is simplicity itself. The removal of a certain pin releases a spring which lights an internal fuse, timed to explode the bomb in five seconds. You take the bomb in your right hand, remove the pin, and cast the thing madly from you. The jam-tin variety appeals more particularly to the sportsman, as the element of chance enters largely into its successful use. It is timed to explode about ten seconds after the lighting of the fuse. It is therefore unwise to throw it too soon, as there will be ample time for your opponent to pick it up and throw it back. On the other hand, it is unwise to hold on too long, as the fuse is uncertain in its action, and is given to short cuts.

Such is the tactical revolution promised by the advent of the bomb and other new engines of war. As for its effect upon regimental and company organisation, listen to the plaintive voice of Major Kemp:—

"I was once—only a few months ago—commander of a company of two hundred and fifty disciplined soldiers. I still nominally command that company, but they have developed into a heterogeneous mob of specialists. If I detail one of my subalterns to do a job of work, he reminds me that he is a bomb-expert, or a professor of sandbagging, or director of the knuckle-duster section, or Lord High Thrower of Stink-pots, and as such has no time to play about with such a common thing as a platoon. As for the men, they simply laugh in the sergeant-major's face. They are 'experts,' if you please, and are struck off all fatigues and company duty! It was bad enough when Ayling pinched fourteen of my best men for his filthy machine-guns; now, the company has practically degenerated into an academy of variety artists. The only occasion upon which I ever see them all together is payday!"

* * * * *

Meanwhile, the word has just gone forth, quietly and without fuss, that we are to uproot ourselves from our present billets, and be ready to move at 5 A.M. to-morrow morning.

Is this the Big Push at last?

II

We have been waiting for the best part of two days and nights listening to the thunder of the big guns, but as yet we have received no invitation to "butt in."

"Plenty of time yet," explains Captain Blaikie to his subalterns, in reply to Bobby Little's expressions of impatience. "It's this way. We start by 'isolating' a section of the enemy's line, and pound it with artillery for about forty-eight hours. Then the guns knock off, and the people in front rush the German first-line trenches. After that they push on to their second and third lines; and if they can capture and *hold them*—well, that's where the fun comes in. We go for all we are worth through the gaps the others have made, and carry on the big push, and keep the Bosches on the run until they drop in their tracks! That's the situation. If we are called up to-night or to-morrow, it will mean that things are going well. If not, it means that the attack has failed—or, very likely, has succeeded, but it has been found impossible to secure the position—and a lot of good chaps have been scuppered, all for nothing."

III

Next morning has arrived, and with it the news that our services will not be required. The attack, it appears, was duly launched, and succeeded beyond all expectations. The German line was broken, and report says that four Divisions poured through the gap. They captured the second-line trenches, then the third, and penetrated far into the enemy's rear.

Then—from their front and flanks, artillery and machine-guns opened fire upon them. They were terribly exposed; possibly they had been lured into a trap. At any rate, the process of "isolation" had not been carried far enough. One thing, and only one thing, could have saved them from destruction and their enterprise from disaster—the support of big guns, and big guns, and more big guns. These could have silenced the hostile tornado of shrapnel and bullets, and the position could have been made good.

But—apparently the supply of big-gun ammunition is not quite so copious as it might be. We have only been at war ten months, and people at home are still a little dazed with the novelty of their situation. Out here, we are reasonable men, and we realise that it requires some time to devise a system for supplying munitions which shall hurt the feelings of no pacifist, which shall interfere with no man's holiday or glass of beer, which shall insult no honest toiler by compelling him to work side by side with those who are not of his industrial tabernacle, and which shall imperil no statesman's seat in Parliament. Things will be all right presently.

Meanwhile, the attacking party fell back whence they came—but no longer four full Divisions.

XVIII

THE FRONT OF THE FRONT

We took over these trenches a few days ago; and as the Germans are barely two hundred yards away, this chapter seems to justify its title.

For reasons foreshadowed last month, we find that we are committed to an indefinite period of trench life, like every one else.

Certainly we are starting at the bottom of the ladder. These trenches are badly sited, badly constructed, difficult of access from the rear, and swarming with large, fat, unpleasant flies, of the bluebottle variety. They go to sleep, chiefly upon the ceiling of one's dug-out, during the short hours of darkness, but for twenty hours out of twenty-four they are very busy indeed. They divide their attentions between stray carrion—there is a good deal hereabout—and our rations. If you sit still for five minutes they also settle upon *you*, like pins in a pin-cushion. Then, when face, hands, and knees can endure no more, and the inevitable convulsive wriggle occurs, they rise in a vociferous swarm, only to settle again when the victim becomes quiescent. To these, high-explosives are a welcome relief.

The trenches themselves are no garden city, like those at Armentières. They were sited and dug in the dark, not many weeks ago, to secure two hundred yards of French territory recovered from the Bosche by bomb and bayonet. (The captured trench lies behind us now, and serves as our second line.) They are muddy—you come to water at three feet—and at one end, owing to their concave formation, are open to enfilade. The parapet in many places is too low. If you make it higher with sandbags you offer the enemy a comfortable target: if you deepen the trench you turn it into a running stream. Therefore long-legged subalterns crawl painfully past these danger-spots on all-fours, envying Little Tich.

Then there is Zacchaeus. We call him by this name because he lives up a tree. There is a row of pollarded willows standing parallel to our front, a hundred and fifty yards away. Up, or in, one of these lives Zacchaeus. We have never seen him, but we know he is there; because if you look over the top of the parapet he shoots you through the head. We do not even know which of the trees he lives in. There are nine of them, and every morning we comb them out, one by one, with a machine-gun. But all in vain. Zacchaeus merely crawls away into the standing corn behind his trees, and waits till we have finished. Then he comes back and tries to shoot the machine-gun officer. He has not succeeded yet, but he sticks to his task with gentle persistence. He is evidently of a persevering rather than vindictive disposition.

Then there is Unter den Linden. This celebrated thoroughfare is an old communication-trench. It runs, half-ruined, from the old German trench in our rear, right through our own front line, to the present German trenches. It constitutes such a bogey as the Channel Tunnel scheme once was: each side sits jealously at its own end, anticipating hostile enterprises from the other. It is also the residence of "Minnie." But we will return to Minnie later.

The artillery of both sides, too, contributes its mite. There is a dull roar far in the rear of the German trenches, followed by a whirring squeak overhead. Then comes an earth-shaking crash a mile behind us. We whip round, and there, in the failing evening light, against the sunset, there springs up the silhouette of a mighty tree in full foliage. Presently the silhouette disperses, drifts away, and—

"The coals is hame, right enough!" comments Private Tosh.

Instantly our guns reply, and we become the humble spectators of an artillery duel. Of course, if the enemy gets tired of "searching" the countryside for our guns and takes to "searching" our trenches instead, we lose all interest in the proceedings, and retire to our dug-outs, hoping that no direct hits will come our way.

But guns are notoriously erratic in their time-tables, and fickle in their attentions. It is upon Zacchaeus and Unter den Linden—including Minnie—that we mainly rely for excitement.

As already recorded, we took over these trenches a few days ago, in the small hours of the morning. In the ordinary course of events, relieving parties are usually able to march up under cover of darkness to the reserve trench, half a mile in rear of the firing line, and so proceed to their appointed place. But on this occasion the German artillery happened to be "distributing coal" among the billets behind. This made it necessary to approach our new home by tortuous ways, and to take to subterranean courses at a very early stage of the journey. For more than two hours we toiled along a trench just wide enough to permit a man to wear his equipment, sometimes bent double to avoid the bullets of snipers, sometimes knee-deep in glutinous mud.

Ayling, leading a machine-gun section who were burdened with their weapons and seven thousand rounds of ammunition, mopped his steaming brow and inquired of his guide how much farther there was to go.

"Abart two miles, sir," replied the youth with gloomy satisfaction. He was a private of the Cockney regiment whom we were relieving; and after the manner of his kind, would infinitely have preferred to conduct us down half a mile of a shell-swept road, leading straight to the heart of things, than waste time upon an uninteresting but safe *détour*.

At this Ayling's Number One, who was carrying a machine-gun tripod weighing forty-eight pounds, said something—something distressingly audible—and groaned deeply.

"If we'd come the way I wanted," continued the guide, much pleased with the effect of his words upon his audience, "we'd a' been there be now. But the Adjutant, 'e says to me—"

"If we had come the way you wanted," interrupted Ayling brutally, "we should probably have been in Kingdom Come by now. Hurry up!" Ayling, in common with the rest of those present, was not in the best of tempers, and the loquacity of the guide had been jarring upon him for some time.

The Cockney private, with the air of a deeply-wronged man, sulkily led on, followed by the dolorous procession. Another ten minutes' laboured progress brought them to a place where several ways met.

"This is the beginning of the reserve trenches, sir," announced the guide. "If we'd come the way I—"

"Lead on!" said Ayling, and his perspiring followers murmured threatening applause.

The guide, now in his own territory, selected the muddiest opening and plunged down it. For two hundred yards or so he continued serenely upon his way, with the air of one exhibiting the metropolis to a party of country cousins. He passed numerous turnings. Then, once or twice, he paused irresolutely; then moved on. Finally he halted, and proceeded to climb out of the trench.

"What are you doing?" demanded Ayling suspiciously.

"We got to cut across the open 'ere, sir," said the youth glibly. "Trench don't go no farther. Keep as low as you can."

With resigned grunts the weary pilgrims hoisted themselves and their numerous burdens out of their slimy thoroughfare, and followed their conductor through the long grass in single file, feeling painfully conspicuous against the whitening sky. Presently they discovered, and descended into, another trench—all but the man with the tripod, who descended into it before he discovered it—and proceeded upon their dolorous way. Once more the guide, who had been refreshingly but ominously silent for some time, paused irresolutely.

"Look here, my man," said Ayling, "do you, or do you not, know where you are?"

The paragon replied hesitatingly:—

"Well, sir, if we'd come by the way I—"

Ayling took a deep breath, and though conscious of the presence of formidable competitors, was about to make the best of an officer's vocabulary, when a kilted figure loomed out of the darkness.

"Hallo! Who are you?" inquired Ayling.

"This iss the Camerons' trenches, sirr," replied a polite West Highland voice. "What trenches wass you seeking?"

Ayling told him.

"They are behind you, sirr."

"I was just goin' to say, sir," chanted the guide, making one last effort to redeem his prestige, "as 'ow—"

"Party," commanded Ayling, "about turn!"

Having received details of the route from the friendly Cameron, he scrambled out of the trench and crawled along to what was now the head of the procession. A plaintive voice followed him.

"Beg pardon, sir, where shall *I* go now?"

Ayling answered the question explicitly, and moved off, feeling much better. The late conductor of the party trailed disconsolately in the rear.

"I should like to know wot I'm 'ere for," he murmured indignantly.

He got his answer, like a lightning-flash.

"For tae carry *this*," said the man with the tripod, turning round. "Here, caatch!"

II

The day's work in trenches begins about nine o'clock the night before. Darkness having fallen, various parties steal out into the no-man's-land beyond the parapet. There are numerous things to be done. The barbed wire has been broken up by shrapnel, and must be repaired. The whole position in front of the wire must be patrolled, to prevent the enemy from creeping forward in the dark. The corn has grown to an uncomfortable height in places, so a fatigue party is told off to cut it—surely the strangest species of harvesting that the annals of agriculture can record. On the left front the muffled clinking of picks and shovels announces that a "sap" is in course of construction: those incorrigible night-birds, the Royal Engineers, are making it for the machine-gunners, who in the fulness of time will convey their voluble weapon to its forward extremity, and "loose off a belt or two" in the direction of a rather dangerous hollow midway between the trenches, from which of late mysterious sounds of digging and guttural talking have been detected by the officer who lies in the listening-post, in front of our barbed-wire entanglement, drawing secrets from the bowels of the earth by means of a microphone.

Behind the firing trench even greater activity prevails. Damage done to the parapet by shell fire is being repaired. Positions and emplacements are being constantly improved, communication trenches widened or made more secure. Down these trenches fatigue parties are filing, to draw rations and water and ammunition from the limbered waggons which are waiting in the shadow of a wood, perhaps a mile back. It is at this hour, too, that the wounded, who have been lying pathetically cheerful and patient in the dressing-station in the reserve trench, are smuggled to the Field Ambulance—probably to find themselves safe in a London hospital within twenty-four hours. Lastly, under the kindly cloak of night, we bury our dead.

Meanwhile, within various stifling dug-outs, in the firing trench or support-trench, overheated company commanders are dictating reports or filling in returns. (Even now the Round Game Department is not entirely shaken off.) There is the casualty return, and a report on the doings of the enemy, and another report of one's own doings, and a report on the direction of the wind, and so on. Then there are various indents to fill up—scrawled on a wobbly writing-block with a blunt indelible pencil by the light of a guttering candle—for ammunition, and sandbags, and revetting material.

All this literature has to be sent to Battalion Headquarters by one A.M., either by orderly or telephone. There it is collated and condensed, and forwarded to the Brigade, which submits it to the same process and sends it on, to be served up piping hot and easily digestible at the breakfast-table of the Division, five miles away, at eight o'clock.

You must not imagine, however, that all this night-work is performed in gross darkness. On the contrary. There is abundance of illumination; and by a pretty thought, each side illuminates the other. We perform our nocturnal tasks, in front of and behind the firing trench, amid a perfect hail of star-shells and magnesium lights, topped up at times by a searchlight—all supplied by our obliging friend the Hun. We, on our part, do our best to return these graceful compliments.

The curious and uncanny part of it all is that there is no firing. During these brief hours there exists an informal truce, founded on the principle of live and let live. It would be an easy business to wipe out that working-party, over there by the barbed wire, with a machine-gun. It would be child's play to shell the road behind the enemy's trenches, crowded as it must be with ration-waggons and water-carts, into a blood-stained wilderness. But so long as each side confines itself to purely defensive and recuperative work, there is little or no interference. That slave of duty, Zacchaeus, keeps on pegging away; and occasionally, if a hostile patrol shows itself too boldly, there is a little exuberance from a machine-gun; but on the whole there is silence. After all, if you prevent your enemy from drawing his rations, his remedy is simple: he will prevent you from drawing yours. Then both parties will have to fight on empty stomachs, and neither of them, tactically, will be a penny the better. So, unless some elaborate scheme of attack is brewing, the early hours of the night are comparatively peaceful. But what is that sudden disturbance in the front-line trench? A British rifle rings out, then another, and another, until there is an agitated fusilade from end to end of the section. Instantly the sleepless host across the way replies, and for three minutes or so a hurricane rages. The working parties out in front lie flat on their faces, cursing patiently. Suddenly the storm dies away, and perfect silence reigns once more. It was a false alarm. Some watchman, deceived by the whispers of the night breeze, or merely a prey to nerves, has discerned a phantom army approaching through the gloom, and has opened fire thereon. This often occurs when troops are new to trench-work.

It is during these hours, too, that regiments relieve one another in the trenches. The outgoing regiment cannot leave its post until the incoming regiment has "taken over." Consequently you have, for a brief space, two thousand troops packed into a trench calculated to hold one thousand. Then it is that strong men swear themselves faint, and the Rugby football player has reason to be thankful for his previous training in the art of "getting through the scrum." However perfect your organisation may be, congestion is bound to occur here and there; and it is no little consolation to us to feel, as we surge and sway in the darkness, that over there in the German lines a Saxon and a Prussian private, irretrievably jammed together in a narrow communication trench, are consigning one another to perdition in just the same husky whisper as that employed by Private Mucklewame and his "opposite number" in the regiment which has come to relieve him.

These "reliefs" take place every four or five nights. There was a time, not so long ago, when a regiment was relieved, not when it was weary, but when another regiment could be found to replace it. Our own first battalion once remained in the trenches, unrelieved and only securing its supplies with difficulty, for five weeks and three days. During all that time they were subject to most pressing attentions on the part of the Bosches, but they never lost a yard of trench. They received word from Headquarters that to detach another regiment for their relief would seriously weaken other and most important dispositions. The Commander-in-Chief would therefore be greatly obliged if they could hold on. So they held on.

At last they came out, and staggered back to billets. Their old quarters, naturally, had long been appropriated by other troops, and the officers had some difficulty in recovering their kits.

"I don't mind being kept in trenches for several weeks," remarked their commander to the staff officer who received him when he reported, "and I can put up with losing my sleeping-bag; but I do object to having my last box of cigars looted by the blackguards who took over our billets!"

The staff officer expressed sympathy, and the subject dropped. But not many days later, while the battalion were still resting, their commander was roused in the middle of the night from the profound slumber which only the experience of many nights of anxious vigil can induce, by the ominous message:—

"An orderly to see you, from General Headquarters, sir!"

The colonel rolled stoically out of bed, and commanded that the orderly should be brought before him.

The man entered, carrying, not a despatch, but a package, which he proffered with a salute.

"With the Commander-in-Chief's compliments, sir!" he announced.

The package was a box of cigars!

But that was before the days of "K(1)."

But the night is wearing on. It is half-past one—time to knock off work. Tired men, returning from ration-drawing or sap-digging, throw themselves down and fall dead asleep in a moment. Only the sentries, with their elbows on the parapet, maintain their sleepless watch. From behind the enemy's lines comes a deep boom—then another. The big guns are waking up again, and have decided to commence their day's work by speeding our empty ration-waggons upon their homeward way. Let them! So long as they refrain from practising direct hits on our front-line parapet, and disturbing our brief and hardly-earned repose, they may fire where they please. The ration train is well able to look after itself.

"A whiff o' shrapnel will dae nae harrm to thae strawberry-jam pinchers!" observes Private Tosh bitterly, rolling into his dug-out. By this opprobrious term he designates that distinguished body of men, the Army Service Corps. A prolonged diet of plum-and-apple jam has implanted in the breasts of the men in the trenches certain dark and unworthy suspicions concerning the entire altruism of those responsible for the distribution of the Army's rations.

* * * * *

It is close on daybreak, and the customary whispered order runs down the stertorous trench:—

"Stand to arms!"

Straightway the parapets are lined with armed men; the waterproof sheets which have been protecting the machine-guns from the dews of night are cast off; and we stand straining our eyes into the whitening darkness.

This is the favourite hour for attack. At any moment the guns may open fire upon our parapet, or a solid wall of grey-clad figures rise from that strip of corn-land less than a hundred yards away, and descend upon us. Well, we are ready for them. Just by way of signalising the fact, there goes out a ragged volley of rifle fire, and a machine-gun rips off half a dozen bursts into the standing corn. But apparently there is nothing doing this morning. The day grows brighter, but there is no movement upon the part of Brother Bosche.

But—what is that light haze hanging over the enemy's trenches? It is slight, almost impalpable, but it appears to be drifting towards us. Can it be—?

Next moment every man is hurriedly pulling his gas helmet over his head, while Lieutenant Waddell beats a frenzied tocsin upon the instrument provided for the purpose—to wit, an empty eighteen-pounder shell, which, suspended from a bayonet stuck into the parados (or back wall) of the trench, makes a most efficient alarm-gong. The sound is repeated all along the trench, and in two minutes every man is in his place, cowled like a member of the Holy Inquisition, glaring through an eye-piece of mica, and firing madly into the approaching wall of vapour.

But the wall approaches very slowly—in fact, it almost stands still—and finally, as the rising sun disentangles itself from a pink horizon and climbs into the sky, it begins to disappear. In half an hour nothing is left, and we take off our helmets, sniffing the morning air dubiously. But all we smell is the old mixture—corpses and chloride of lime.

The incident, however, was duly recorded by Major Kemp in his report of the day's events, as follows:—

4.7 A.M.—*Gas alarm, false. Due either to morning mist, or the fact that enemy found breeze insufficient, and discontinued their attempt.*

"Still, I'm not sure," he continued, slapping his bald head with a bandana handkerchief, "that a whiff of chlorine or bromine wouldn't do these trenches a considerable amount of good. It would tone down some of the deceased a bit, and wipe out these infernal flies. Waddell, if I give you a shilling, will you take it over to the German trenches and ask them to drop it into the meter?"

"I do not think, sir," replied the literal Waddell, "that an English shilling would fit a German meter. Probably a mark would be required, and I have only a franc. Besides, sir, do you think that—"

"Surgical operation at seven-thirty, sharp!" intimated the major to the medical officer, who entered the dug-out at that moment. "For our friend here"—indicating the bewildered Waddell. "Sydney Smith's prescription! Now, what about breakfast?"

* * * * *

About nine o'clock the enemy indulges in what is usually described, most disrespectfully, as "a little morning hate"—in other words, a bombardment. Beginning with a *hors d'oeuvre* of shrapnel along the reserve trench—much to the discomfort of Headquarters, who are shaving—he proceeds to "search" a tract of woodland in our immediate rear, his quarry being a battery of motor machine-guns, which has wisely decamped some hours previously. Then, after scientifically "traversing" our second line, which has rashly advertised its position and range by cooking its breakfast over a smoky fire, he brings the display to a superfluous conclusion by dropping six "Black Marias" into the deserted ruins of a village not far behind us. After that comes silence; and we are able, in our hot, baking trenches, assisted by clouds of bluebottles, to get on with the day's work.

This consists almost entirely in digging. As already stated, these are bad trenches. The parapet is none too strong—at one point it has been knocked down for three days running—the communication trenches are few and narrow, and there are not nearly enough dug-outs. Yesterday three men were wounded; and owing to the impossibility of carrying a stretcher along certain parts of the trench, they had to be conveyed to the rear in their ground-sheets—bumped against projections, bent round sharp corners, and sometimes lifted, perforce, bodily into view of the enemy. So every man toils with a will, knowing full well that in a few hours' time he may prove to have been his own benefactor. Only the sentries remain at the parapets. They no longer expose themselves, as at night, but take advantage of the laws of optical reflection, as exemplified by the trench periscope. (This, in spite of its grand title, is nothing but a tiny mirror clipped on to a bayonet.)

At half-past twelve comes dinner—bully-beef, with biscuit and jam—after which each tired man, coiling himself up in the trench, or crawling underground, according to the accommodation at his disposal, drops off into instant and heavy slumber. The hours from two till five in the afternoon are usually the most uneventful of the twenty-four, and are therefore devoted to hardly-earned repose.

But there is to be little peace this afternoon. About half-past three, Bobby Little, immersed in pleasant dreams—dreams of cool shades and dainty companionship—is brought suddenly to the surface of things by—

"Whoo-oo-*oo*-oo-UMP!"

—followed by a heavy thud upon the roof of his dug-out. Earth and small stones descend in a shower upon him.

"Dirty dogs!" he comments, looking at his watch. Then he puts his head out of the dug-out.

"Lie close, you men!" he cries. "There's more of this coming. Any casualties?"

The answer to the question is obscured by another burst of shrapnel, which explodes a few yards short of the parapet, and showers bullets and fragments of shell into the trench. A third and a fourth follow. Then comes a pause. A message is passed down for the stretcher-bearers. Things are growing serious. Five minutes later Bobby, having despatched his wounded to the dressing-station, proceeds with all haste to Captain Blaikie's dug-out.

"How many, Bobby?"

"Six wounded. Two of them won't last as far as the rear, I'm afraid, sir."

Captain Blaikie looks grave.

"Better ring up the Gunners, I think. Where are the shells coming from?"

"That wood on our left front, I think."

"That's P 27. Telephone orderly, there?"

A figure appears in the doorway.

"Yes, sirr."

"Ring up Major Cavanagh, and say that H 21 is being shelled from P 27. Retaliate!"

"Verra good, sirr."

The telephone orderly disappears, to return in five minutes.

"Major Cavanagh's compliments, sirr, and he is coming up himself for tae observe from the firing trench."

"Good egg!" observes Captain Blaikie. "Now we shall see some shooting, Bobby!"

Presently the Gunner major arrives, accompanied by an orderly, who pays out wire as he goes. The major adjusts his periscope, while the orderly thrusts a metal peg into the ground and fits a telephone receiver to his head.

"Number one gun!" chants the major, peering into his periscope; "three-five-one-nothing—lyddite—fourth charge!"

These mystic observations are repeated into the telephone by the Cockney orderly, in a confidential undertone.

"Report when ready!" continues the major.

"Report when ready!" echoes the orderly. Then—"Number one gun ready, sir!"

"Fire!"

"Fire!" Then, politely—"Number one has fired, sir."

The major stiffens to his periscope, and Bobby Little, deeply interested, wonders what has become of the report of the gun. He forgets that sound does not travel much faster than a thousand feet a second, and that the guns are a mile and a half back. Presently, however, there is a distant boom. Almost simultaneously the lyddite shell passes overhead with a scream. Bobby, having no periscope, cannot see the actual result of the shot, though he tempts Providence (and Zacchaeus) by peering over the top of the parapet.

"Number one, two-nothing minutes more right," commands the major.
"Same range and charge."

Once more the orderly goes through his ritual, and presently another shell screams overhead.

Again the major observes the result.

"Repeat!" he says. "Nothing-five seconds more right."

This time he is satisfied.

"Parallel lines on number one," he commands crisply. "One round battery fire—twenty seconds!"

For the last time the order is passed down the wire, and the major hands his periscope to the ever-grateful Bobby, who has hardly got his eyes to the glass when the round of battery fire commences. One—two—three—four—the avenging shells go shrieking on their way, at intervals of twenty seconds. There are four muffled thuds, and four great columns of earth and *débris* spring up before the wood. Answer comes there none. The offending battery has prudently effaced itself.

"Cease fire!" says the major, "and register!" Then he turns to Captain
Blaikie.

"That'll settle them for a bit," he observes. "By the way, had any more trouble with Minnie?"

"We had Hades from her yesterday," replies Blaikie, in answer to this extremely personal question. "She started at a quarter-past five in the morning, and went on till about ten."

(Perhaps, at this point, it would be as well to introduce Minnie a little more formally. She is the most unpleasant of her sex, and her full name is *Minenwerfer*, or German trench-mortar. She resides, spasmodically, in Unter den Linden. Her extreme range is about two hundred yards, so she confines her attentions to front-line trenches. Her *modus operandi* is to discharge a large cylindrical bomb into the air. The bomb, which is about fifteen inches long and some eight inches in diameter, describes a leisurely parabola, performing grotesque somersaults on the way, and finally falls with a soft thud into the trench, or against the parapet. There, after an interval of ten seconds, Minnie's offspring explodes; and as she contains about thirty pounds of dynamite, no dug-out or parapet can stand against her.)

"Did she do much damage?" inquires the Gunner.

"Killed two men and buried another. They were in a dug-out."

The Gunner shakes his head.

"No good taking cover against Minnie," he says. "The only way is to come out into the open trench, and dodge her."

"So we found," replies Blaikie. "But they pulled our legs badly the first time. They started off with three 'whizz-bangs'"—a whizz-bang is a particularly offensive form of shell which bursts two or three times over, like a Chinese cracker—"so we all took cover and lay low. The consequence was that Minnie was able to send her little contribution along unobserved. The filthy thing fell short of the trench, and exploded just as we were all getting up again. It smashed up three or four yards of parapet, and scuppered the three poor chaps I mentioned."

"Have you located her?"

"Yes. Just behind that stunted willow, on our left front. I fancy they bring her along there to do her bit, and then trot her back to billets, out of harm's way. She is their two o'clock turn—two A.M. and two P.M."

"Two o'clock turn—h'm!" says the Gunner major meditatively. "What about our chipping in with a one-fifty-five turn—half a dozen H E shells into Minnie's dressing-room—eh? I must think this over."

"Do!" said Blaikie cordially. "Minnie is Willie's Worst Werfer, and the sooner she is put out of action the better for all of us. To-day, for some reason, she failed to appear, but previous to that she has not failed for five mornings in succession to batter down the same bit of our parapet."

"Where's that?" asks the major, getting out a trench-map.

"P 7—a most unhealthy spot. Minnie pushes it over about two every morning. The result is that we have to mount guard over the breach all day. We build everything up again at night, and Minnie sits there as good as gold, and never dreams of interfering. You can almost hear her cooing over us. Then, as I say, at two o'clock, just as the working party comes in and gets under cover, she lets slip one of her disgusting bombs, and undoes the work of about four hours. It was a joke at first, but we are getting fed up now. That's the worst of the Bosche. He starts by being playful; but if not suppressed at once, he gets rough; and that, of course, spoils all the harmony of the proceedings. So I cordially commend your idea of the one-fifty-five turn, sir."

"I'll see what can be done," says the major. "I think the best plan would be a couple of hours' solid frightfulness, from every battery we can switch on. To-morrow afternoon, perhaps, but I'll let you know. You'll have to clear out of this bit of trench altogether, as we shall shoot pretty low. So long!"

III

It is six o'clock next evening, and peace reigns over our trench. This is the hour at which one usually shells aeroplanes—or rather, at which the Germans shell ours, for their own seldom venture out in broad daylight. But this evening, although two or three are up in the blue, buzzing inquisitively over the enemy's lines, their attendant escort of white shrapnel puffs is entirely lacking. Far away behind the German lines a house is burning fiercely.

"The Hun is a bit *piano* to-night," observes Captain Blaikie, attacking his tea.

"The Hun has been rather firmly handled this afternoon," replies Captain Wagstaffe. "I think he has had an eye-opener. There are no flies on our Divisional Artillery."

Bobby Little heaved a contented sigh. For two hours that afternoon he had sat, half-deafened, while six-inch shells skimmed the parapet in both directions, a few feet above his head. The Gunner major had been as good as his word. Punctually at one-fifty-five "Minnie's" two o'clock turn had been anticipated by a round of high-explosive shells directed into her suspected place of residence. What the actual result had been nobody knew, but Minnie had made no attempt to raise her voice since. Thereafter the German front-line trenches had been "plastered" from end to end, while the trenches farther back were attended to with methodical thoroughness. The German guns had replied vigorously, but directing only a passing fire at the trenches, had devoted their efforts chiefly to the silencing of the British artillery. In this enterprise they had been remarkably unsuccessful.

"Any casualties?" asked Blaikie.

"None here," replied Wagstaffe. "There may be some back in the support trenches."

"We might telephone and inquire."

"No good at present. The wires are all cut to pieces. The signallers are repairing them now."

"*I* was nearly a casualty," confessed Bobby modestly.

"How?"

"That first shell of ours nearly knocked my head off! I was standing up at the time, and it rather took me by surprise. It just cleared the parados. In fact, it kicked a lot of gravel into the back of my neck."

"Most people get it in the neck here, sooner or later," remarked Captain Blaikie sententiously. "Personally, I don't much mind being killed, but I do bar being buried alive. That is why I dislike Minnie so." He rose, and stretched himself. "Heigho! I suppose it's about time we detailed patrols and working parties for to-night. What a lovely sky! A truly peaceful atmosphere—what? It gives one a sort of Sunday-evening feeling, somehow."

"May I suggest an explanation?" said Wagstaffe.

"By all means."

"It *is* Sunday evening!"

Captain Blaikie whistled gently, and said—

"By Jove, so it is." Then, after a pause: "This time last Sunday—"

Last Sunday had been an off-day—a day of cloudless summer beauty. Tired men had slept; tidy men had washed their clothes; restless men had wandered at ease about the countryside, careless of the guns which grumbled everlastingly a few miles away. There had been impromptu Church Parades for each denomination, in the corner of a wood which was part of the demesne of a shell-torn chateau.

It is a sadly transformed wood. The open space before the chateau, once a smooth expanse of tennis-lawn, is now a dusty picketing-ground for transport mules, destitute of a single blade of grass. The ornamental lake is full of broken bottles and empty jam-tins. The pagoda-like summer-house, so inevitable to French chateau gardens, is a quartermaster's store. Half the trees have been cut down for fuel. Still, the July sun streams very pleasantly through the remainder, and the Psalms of David float up from beneath their shade quite as sweetly as they usually do from the neighbourhood of the precentor's desk in the kirk at home—perhaps sweeter.

The wood itself is a *point d'appui*, or fortified post. One has to take precautions, even two or three miles behind the main firing line. A series of trenches zigzags in and out among the trees, and barbed wire is interlaced with the undergrowth. In the farthermost corner lies an improvised cemetery. Some of the inscriptions on the little wooden crosses are only three days old. Merely to read a few of these touches the imagination and stirs the blood. Here you may see the names of English Tommies and Highland Jocks, side by side with their Canadian kith and kin. A little apart lie more graves, surmounted by epitaphs written in strange characters, such as few white men can read. These are the Indian troops. There they lie, side by side—the mute wastage of war, but a living testimony, even in their last sleep, to the breadth and unity of the British Empire. The great, machine-made Empire of Germany can show no such graves: when her soldiers die, they sleep alone.

The Church of England service had come last of all. Late in the afternoon a youthful and red-faced chaplain had arrived on a bicycle, to find a party of officers and men lying in the shade of a broad oak waiting for him. (They were a small party: naturally, the great majority of the regiment are what the identity-discs call "Pres" or "R.C.")

"Sorry to be late, sir," he said to the senior officer, saluting. "This is my sixth sh—service to-day, and I have come seven miles for it."

He mopped his brow cheerfully; and having produced innumerable hymn-books from a saddle-bag and set his congregation in array, read them the service, in a particularly pleasing and well-modulated voice. After that he preached a modest and manly little sermon, containing references which carried Bobby Little, for one, back across the Channel to other scenes and other company. After the sermon came a hymn, sung with great vigour. Tommy loves singing hymns—when he happens to know and like the tune.

"I know you chaps like hymns," said the padre, when they had finished.
"Let's have another before you go. What do you want?"

A most unlikely-looking person suggested "Abide with Me." When it was over, and the party, standing as rigid as their own rifles, had sung "God Save the King," the preacher announced, awkwardly—almost apologetically—

"If any of you would like to—er—communicate, I shall be very glad. May not have another opportunity for some time, you know. I think over there"—he indicated a quiet corner of the wood, not far from the little cemetery—"would be a good place."

He pronounced the benediction, and then, after further recurrence to his saddle-bag, retired to his improvised sanctuary. Here, with a ration-box for altar, and strands of barbed wire for choir-stalls, he made his simple preparations.

Half a dozen of the men, and all the officers, followed him. That was just a week ago.

* * * * *

Captain Wagstaffe broke the silence at last.

"It's a rotten business, war," he said pensively—"when you come to think of it. Hallo, there goes the first star-shell! Come along, Bobby!"

Dusk had fallen. From the German trenches a thin luminous thread stole up into the darkening sky, leaned over, drooped, and burst into dazzling brilliance over the British parapet. Simultaneously a desultory rifle fire crackled down the lines. The night's work had begun.

XIX

THE TRIVIAL ROUND

We have been occupying trenches, off and on, for a matter of two months, and have settled down to an unexhilarating but salutary routine. Each dawn we "stand to arms," and peer morosely over the parapet, watching the grey grass turn slowly to green, while snipers' bullets buzz over our heads. Each forenoon we cleanse our dew-rusted weapons, and build up with sandbags what the persevering Teuton has thrown down. Each afternoon we creep unostentatiously into subterranean burrows, while our respective gunners, from a safe position in the rear, indulge in what they humorously describe as "an artillery duel." The humour arises from the fact that they fire, not at one another, but at us. It is as if two big boys, having declared a vendetta, were to assuage their hatred and satisfy their honour by going out every afternoon and throwing stones at one another's little brothers. Each evening we go on sentry duty; or go out with patrols, or working parties, or ration parties. Our losses in killed and wounded are not heavy, but they are regular.

We would not grudge the lives thus spent if only we could advance, even a little. But there is nothing doing. Sometimes a trench is rushed here, or recaptured there, but the net result is—stalemate.

The campaign upon which we find ourselves at present embarked offers few opportunities for brilliancy. One wonders how Napoleon would have handled it. His favourite device, we remember, was to dash rapidly about the chessboard, insert himself between two hostile armies, and defeat them severally. But how can you insert yourself between two armies when you are faced by only one army—an army stretching from Ostend to the Alps?

One of the first elements of successful strategy is surprise. In the old days, a general of genius could outflank his foe by a forced march, or lay some ingenious trap or ambush. But how can you outflank a foe who has no flanks? How can you lay an ambush for the modern Intelligence Department, with its aeroplane reconnaissance and telephonic nervous system? Do you mass half a million men at a chosen point in the enemy's line? Straightway the enemy knows all about it, and does likewise. Each morning General Headquarters of each side finds upon its breakfast-table a concise summary of the movements of all hostile troops, the disposition of railway rolling-stock—yea, even aeroplane photographs of it all. What could Napoleon himself have done under the circumstances? One is inclined to suspect that that volcanic megalomaniac would have perished of spontaneous combustion of the brain.

However, trench life has its alleviations. There is The Day's Work, for instance. Each of us has his own particular "stunt," in which he takes that personal and rather egotistical pride which only increasing proficiency can bestow.

The happiest—or at least, the busiest—people just now are the "Specialists." If you are engaged in ordinary Company work, your energies are limited to keeping watch, dodging shells, and improving trenches. But if you are what is invidiously termed an "employed" man, life is full of variety.

Do you observe that young officer sitting on a ration-box at his dug-out door, with his head tied up in a bandage? That is Second Lieutenant Lochgair, whom I hope to make better known to you in time. He is a chieftain of high renown in his own inaccessible but extensive fastness; but out here, where every man stands on his own legs, and not his grandfather's, he is known simply as "Othello." This is due to the fact that Major Kemp once likened him to the earnest young actor of tradition, who blacked himself all over to ensure proficiency in the playing of that part. For he is above all things an enthusiast in his profession. Last night he volunteered to go out and "listen" for a suspected mine some fifty yards from the German trenches. He set out as soon as darkness fell, taking with him a biscuit-tin full of water. A circular from Headquarters—one of those circulars which no one but Othello would have treated with proper reverence—had suggested this device. The idea was that, since liquids convey sound better than air, the listener should place his tin of water on the ground, lie down beside it, immerse one ear therein, and so draw secrets from the earth. Othello failed to locate the mine, but kept his head in the biscuit-tin long enough to contract a severe attack of earache.

But he is not discouraged. At present he is meditating a design for painting himself grass-green and climbing a tree—thence to take a comprehensive and unobserved survey of the enemy's dispositions. He will do it, too, if he gets a chance!

The machine-gunners, also, contrive to chase monotony by methods of their own. Listen to Ayling, concocting his diurnal scheme of frightfulness with a colleague. Unrolled upon his knee is a large-scale map.

"I think we might touch up those cross-roads to-night," he says, laying the point of his dividers upon a spot situated some hundreds of yards in rear of the German trenches.

"I expect they'll have lots of transport there about ration-time—eh?"

"Sound scheme," assents his coadjutor, a bloodthirsty stripling named Ainslie. "Got the bearings?"

"Hand me that protractor. Seventy-one, nineteen, true. That comes to"—Ayling performs a mental calculation—"almost exactly eighty-five, magnetic. We'll go out about nine, with two guns, to the corner of this dry ditch here—the range is two thousand five hundred, exactly"—

"Our lightning calculator!" murmurs his admiring colleague. "No elastic up the sleeve, or anything! All done by simple ledger-de-mang? Proceed!"

—"And loose off a belt or two. What say?"

"Application forwarded, and strongly recommended," announced Ainslie. He examined the map. "Cross-roads—eh? That means at least one estaminet. One estaminet, with Bosches inside, complete! Think of our little bullets all popping in through the open door, five hundred a minute! Think of the rush to crawl under the counter! It might be a Headquarters? We might get Von Kluck or Rupy of Bavaria, splitting a half litre together. We shall earn Military Crosses over this, my boy," concluded the imaginative youth. "Wow, wow!"

"The worst of indirect fire," mused the less gifted Ayling, "is that you never can tell whether you have hit your target or not. In fact, you can't even tell whether there was a target there to hit."

"Never mind; we'll chance it," replied Ainslie. "And if the Bosche artillery suddenly wakes up and begins retaliating on the wrong spot with whizz-bangs—well, we shall know we've tickled up *somebody*, anyhow! Nine o'clock, you say?"

* * * * *

Here, again, is a bombing party, prepared to steal out under cover of night. They are in charge of one Simson, recently promoted to Captain, supported by that hoary fire-eater, Sergeant Carfrae. The party numbers seven all told, the only other member thereof with whom we are personally acquainted being Lance-Corporal M'Snape, the ex-Boy Scout. Every man wears a broad canvas belt full of pockets: each pocket contains a bomb.

Simson briefly outlines the situation. Our fire-trench here runs round the angle of an orchard, which brings it uncomfortably close to the Germans. The Germans are quite as uncomfortable about the fact as we are—some of us are rather inclined to overlook this important feature of the case—and they have run a sap out towards the nearest point of the Orchard Trench (so our aeroplane observers report), in order to supervise our movements more closely.

"It may only be a listening-post," explains Simson to his bombers, "with one or two men in it. On the other hand, they may be collecting a party to rush us. There are some big shell-craters there, and they may be using one of them as a saphead. Anyhow, our orders are to go out to-night and see. If we find the sap, with any Germans in it, we are to bomb them out of it, and break up the sap as far as possible. Advance, and follow me."

The party steals out. The night is very still, and a young and inexperienced moon is making a somewhat premature appearance behind the Bosche trenches. The ground is covered with weedy grass—disappointed hay—which makes silent progress a fairly simple matter. The bombers move forward in extended order searching for the saphead. Simson, in the centre, pauses occasionally to listen, and his well-drilled line pauses with him. Sergeant Carfrae calls stertorously upon the left. Out on the right is young M'Snape, tingling.

They are half-way across now, and the moon is marking time behind a cloud.

Suddenly there steals to the ears of M'Snape—apparently from the recesses of the earth just in front of him—a deep, hollow sound, the sound of men talking in some cavernous space. He stops dead, and signals to his companions to do likewise. Then he listens again. Yes, he can distinctly hear guttural voices, and an occasional *clink, clink*. The saphead has been reached, and digging operations are in progress.

A whispered order comes down the line that M'Snape is to "investigate." He wriggles forward until his progress is arrested by a stunted bush. Very stealthily he rises to his knees and peers over. As he does so, a chance star-shell bursts squarely over him, and comes sizzling officiously down almost on to his back. His head drops like a stone into the bush, but not before the ghostly magnesium flare has shown him what he came out to see—a deep shell-crater. The crater is full of Germans. They look like grey beetles in a trap, and are busy with pick and shovel, apparently "improving" the crater and connecting it with their own fire-trenches. They have no sentry out. *Dormitat Homerus.*

M'Snape worms his way back, and reports. Then, in accordance with an oft-rehearsed scheme, the bombing party forms itself into an arc of a circle at a radius of some twenty yards from the stunted bush. (Not the least of the arts of bomb-throwing is to keep out of range of your own bombs.) Every man's hand steals to his pocketed belt. Next moment Simson flings the first bomb. It flies fairly into the middle of the crater.

Half a dozen more go swirling after it. There is a shattering roar; a cloud of smoke; a muffled rush, of feet; silence; some groans. Almost simultaneously the German trenches are in an uproar. A dozen star-shells leap to the sky; there is a hurried outburst of rifle fire; a machine-gun begins to patter out a stuttering malediction.

Meanwhile our friends, who have exhibited no pedantic anxiety to remain and behold the result of their labours, are lying upon their stomachs in a convenient fold in the ground, waiting patiently until such time as it shall be feasible to complete their homeward journey.

Half an hour later they do so, and roll one by one over the parapet into the trench. Casualties are slight. Private Nimmo has a bullet-wound in the calf of his leg, and Sergeant Carfrae, whom Nature does not permit to lie as flat as the others, will require some repairs to the pleats of his kilt.

"All present?" inquires Simson.

It is discovered that M'Snape has not returned. Anxious eyes peer over the parapet. The moon is stronger now, but it is barely possible to distinguish objects clearly for more than a few yards.

A star-shell bursts, and heads sink below the parapet. A German bullet passes overhead, with a sound exactly like the crack of a whip. Silence and comparative darkness return. The heads go up again.

"I'll give him five minutes more, and then go and look for him," says Simson. "Hallo!"

A small bush, growing just outside the barbed wire, rises suddenly to its feet; and, picking its way with incredible skill through the nearest opening, runs at full speed for the parapet. Next moment it tumbles over into the trench.

Willing hands extracted M'Snape from his arboreal envelope—he could probably have got home quite well without it, but once a Boy Scout, always a Boy Scout—and he made his report.

"I went back to have a look-see into the crater, sirr."

"Well?"

"It's fair blown in, sirr, and a good piece of the sap too. I tried could I find a prisoner to bring in"—our Colonel has promised a reward of fifty francs to the man who can round up a whole live Bosche—"but there were nane. They had got their wounded away, I doubt."

"Never mind," says Simson. "Sergeant, see these men get some sleep now. Stand-to at two-thirty, as usual. I must go and pitch in a report, and I shall say you all did splendidly. Good-night!"

This morning, the official Intelligence Summary of our Division—published daily and known to the unregenerate as "Comic Cuts"—announced, with solemn relish, among other items of news:—

Last night a small party bombed a suspected saphead at—here followed the exact bearings of the crater on the large-scale map. *Loud groans were heard, so it is probable that the bombs took effect.*

For the moment, life has nothing more to offer to our seven friends.

II

As already noted, our enthusiasm for our own sphere of activity is not always shared by our colleagues. For instance, we in the trenches frequently find the artillery of both sides unduly obtrusive; and we are of opinion that in trench warfare artillery practice should be limited by mutual consent to twelve rounds per gun per day, fired by the gunners *at* the gunners. "Except, of course, when the Big Push comes." The Big Push is seldom absent from our thoughts in these days.

"That," observed Captain Wagstaffe to Bobby Little, "would leave us foot-sloggers to settle our own differences. My opinion is that we should do so with much greater satisfaction to ourselves if we weren't constantly interfered with by coal-boxes and Black Marias."

"Still, you can't blame them for loosing off their big guns," contended the fair-minded Bobby. "It must be great sport."

"They tell me it's a greatly overrated amusement," replied Wagstaffe—"like posting an insulting letter to some one you dislike. You see, you aren't there when he opens it at breakfast next morning! The only man of them who gets any fun is the Forward Observing Officer. And he," concluded Wagstaffe in an unusual vein of pessimism, "does not live long enough to enjoy it!"

The grievances of the Infantry, however, are not limited to those supplied by the Royal Artillery. There are the machine-guns and the trench-mortars.

The machine-gunner is a more or less accepted nuisance by this time. He has his own emplacements in the line, but he never appears to use them. Instead, he adopts the peculiar expedient of removing his weapon from a snug and well-fortified position, and either taking it away somewhere behind the trenches and firing salvoes over your head (which is reprehensible), or planting it upon the parapet in your particular preserve, and firing it from there (which is criminal). Machine-gun fire always provokes retaliation.

"Why in thunder can't you keep your filthy tea-kettle in its own place, instead of bringing it here to draw fire?" inquired Mr. Cockerell, not altogether unreasonably, as Ayling and his satellites passed along the trench bearing the offending weapon, with water-jacket aboil, back to its official residence.

"It is all for your good, my little man," explained Ayling loftily. "It would never do to give away one's real gun positions. If we did, the Bosches would sit tight and say nothing at the time, but just make a note of the occurrence. Then, one fine morning, when they *really* meant business, they would begin by droping a

Black Maria on top of each emplacement; and where would you and your platoon be then, with an attack coming on and *us* out of action? So long!"

But the most unpopular man in the trenches is undoubtedly the Trench Mortar Officer. His apparatus consists of what looks like a section of rain-pipe, standing on legs. Upon its upturned muzzle is poised a bomb, having the appearance of a plum-pudding on a stick. This he discharges over the parapet into the German trenches, where it causes a comforting explosion. He then walks rapidly away.

For obvious reasons, it is not advisable to fire a trench-mortar too often—at any rate from the same place. But the whole weight of public opinion in our trench is directed against it being fired from anywhere at all. Behold the Trench Mortar Officer and his gang of pariahs creeping stealthily along in the lee of the parados, just as dawn breaks, in the section of trench occupied by No. 10 Platoon. For the moment they are unheeded, for the platoon are "standing-to," and the men are lined along the firing-step, with their backs to the conspirators.

On reaching a suitable spot, the mortar party proceed to erect their apparatus with as little ostentation as possible. But they are soon discovered. The platoon subaltern hurries up.

"Awfully sorry, old man," he says breathlessly, "but the C.O. gave particular orders that this part of the trench was on no account to be used for trench-mortar fire. You see, we are only about seventy yards from the Bosche trenches here—"

"I know," explains the T.M.O.; "that is why I came."

"But it is most important," continues the platoon commander, still quoting glibly from an entirely imaginary mandate of the C.O., "that no retaliatory shell fire should be attracted here. Most serious for the whole Brigade, if this bit of parapet got pushed over. Now, there's a topping place about ten traverses away. You can lob them over from there beautifully. Come along."

And with fair words and honeyed phrases he elbows the dispirited band to a position—for his platoon—of comparative inoffensiveness.

The Trench Mortar Officer drifts on, and presently, with the uneasy assurance of the proprietor of a punch-and-judy show who has inadvertently strayed into Park Lane, attempts once more to give his unpopular entertainment. This time his shrift is even shorter, for he encounters Major Kemp—never at his sunniest in the small hours of the morning.

Field officers have no need to employ the language of diplomacy when dealing with subalterns.

"No, you *don't*, my lad!" announces the Major. "Not if I can help it! Take it away! Take your darned liver-pill out of this! Burn, it! Bury it! Eat it! But not here! Creep away!"

The abashed procession complies. This time they find a section of trench in charge of a mere corporal. Here, before any one of sufficient standing can be summoned to deal with the situation, the Trench Mortar Officer seizes his opportunity, and discharges three bombs over the parapet. He then retires defiantly to his dug-out.

But it is an Ishmaelitish existence.

III

So much for the alleviations which professional enthusiasm bestows.
Now for a few alleviations proper. These are Sleep, Food, and
Literature.

Sleep is the rarest of these. We seldom get more than a few hours at a time; but it is astonishing how readily one learns to slumber in unlikely surroundings—upon damp earth, in cramped positions, amid ceaseless noise, in clothes and boots that have not been removed for days. One also acquires the priceless faculty of losing no time in dropping off.

As for food, we grumble at times, just as people at home are grumbling at the Savoy, or Lockhart's. It is the Briton's habit so to do. But in moments of repletion we are fain to confess that the organisation of our commissariat is wonderful. Of course the quality of the *menu* varies, according to the immunity of the communication-trenches from shell fire, or the benevolence of the Quartermaster and the mysterious powers behind him, or the facilities for cooking offered by the time and place in which we find ourselves. No large fires are permitted: the smoke would give too good a ranging-mark to Minnie and her relatives. Still, it is surprising how quickly you can boil a canteen over a few chips. There is also, for those who can afford half-a-crown, that invaluable contrivance, "Tommy's Cooker"; and occasionally we get a ration of coke. When times are bad, we live on bully, biscuit, cheese, and water, strongly impregnated with chloride of lime. The water is conveyed to us in petrol-tins—the old familiar friends, Shell and Pratt—hundreds of them. Motorists at home must be feeling the shortage. In normal times we can reckon on plenty of hot, strong tea; possibly some bread; probably an allowance of bacon and jam. And sometimes, when the ration parties arrive, mud-stained and weary, in the dead of night, and throw down their bursting sacks, our eyes feast upon such revelations as tinned butter, condensed milk, raisins, and a consignment of that great chieftain of the ration race, The Maconochie of Maconochie. On these occasions Private Mucklewame collects his share, retires to his kennel, and has a gala-day.

Thirdly, the blessings of literature. Our letters arrive at night, with the rations. The mail of our battalion alone amounts to eight or ten mail-bags a day; from which you may gather some faint idea of the labours of our Field Post Offices. There are letters, and parcels, and newspapers. Letters we may pass over. They are featureless things, except to their recipient. Parcels have more individuality. Ours are of all shapes and sizes, and most of them are astonishingly badly tied. It is quite heartrending to behold a kilted exile endeavouring to gather up a heterogeneous mess of socks, cigarettes, chocolate, soap, shortbread, and Edinburgh rock, from the ruins of what was once a flabby and unstable parcel, but is now a few skimpy rags of brown paper, which have long escaped the control of a most inadequate piece of string—a monument of maternal lavishness and feminine economy.

Then there are the newspapers. We read them right through, beginning at the advertisements and not skipping even the leading articles. Then, when we have finished, we frequently read them right through again. They serve three purposes. They give us information as to how the War is progressing—we get none here, the rank and file, that is; they serve to pass the time; and they afford us topics for conversation. For instance, they enable us to follow and discuss the trend of home politics. And in this connection, I think it is time you were introduced to Captain Achille Petitpois. (That is not his real name, but it is as near to it as most of us are likely to get.) He is one of that most efficient body, the French *liaison* officers, who act as connecting-link between the Allied Forces, and naturally is an accomplished linguist. He is an ardent admirer of British institutions, but is occasionally not a little puzzled by their complexity. So he very sensibly comes to people like Captain Wagstaffe for enlightenment, and they enlighten him.

Behold Achille—a guest in A Company's billet—drinking whisky-and-sparklet out of an aluminium mug, and discussing the news of the day.

"And your people at home," he said, "you think they are taking the War seriously?" (Achille is addicted to reading the English newspapers without discrimination.)

"So seriously," replied Wagstaffe instantly, "that it has become necessary for the Government to take steps to cheer them up."

"Comment?" inquired Achille politely.

For answer Wagstaffe picked up a three-day-old London newspaper, and read aloud an extract from the Parliamentary report. The report dealt faithfully with the latest antics of the troupe of eccentric comedians which appears (to us), since the formation of the Coalition Government, to have taken possession of the front Opposition Bench.

"Who are these assassins—these imbeciles—these *crétins*," inquired Petitpois, "who would endanger the ship of the State?" (Achille prides himself upon his knowledge of English idiom.)

"Nobody knows!" replied Wagstaffe solemnly. "They are children of mystery. Before the War, nobody had ever heard of them. They—"

"But they should be shot!" explained that free-born Republican, Petitpois.

"Not a bit, old son! That is where you fail to grasp the subtleties of British statesmanship. I tell you there are no flies on our Cabinet!"

"Flies?"

"Yes: *mouches*, you know. The agility of our Cabinet Ministers is such that these little insects find it impossible to alight upon them."

"Your Ministers are athletes—yes," agreed Achille comprehendingly. "But the—"

"Only intellectually. What I mean is that they are a very downy collection of old gentlemen—"

Achille, murmuring something hazy about "Downing Street," nodded his head.

"—And when they came into power, they knew as well as anything that after three weeks or so the country would begin to grouse—"

"Grouse? A sporting bird?" interpolated Achille.

"Exactly. They knew that the country would soon start giving them the bird—"

"What bird? The grouse?"

"Oh, dry up, Wagger!" interposed Blaikie. "He means, Petitpois, that the Government, knowing that the electorate would begin to grow impatient if the War did not immediately take a favourable turn—"

Achille smiled.

"I see now," he said. "Proceed, Ouagstaffe, my old!"

"In other words," continued the officer so addressed, "the Government decided that if they gave the Opposition half a chance to get together, and find leaders, and consolidate their new trenches, they might turn them out."

"Bien," assented Achille. Every one was listening now, for Wagstaffe as a politician usually had something original to say.

"Well," proceeded Wagstaffe, "they saw that the great thing to do was to prevent the Opposition from making an impression on the country—from being taken too seriously, in fact. So what did they do? They said: 'Let's arrange for a *comic* Opposition—an Opposition *pour rire*, you know. They will make the country either laugh or cry. Anyhow, the country will be much too busy deciding which to do to have any time to worry about *us*; so we shall have a splendid chance to get on with the War.' So they sent down the Strand—that's where the Variety agents foregather, I believe—what you call *entrepreneurs*, Achille—and booked this troupe, complete, for the run of the War. They did the thing in style; spared no expense; and got a comic newspaper proprietor to write the troupe up, and themselves down. The scheme worked beautifully—what you would call a *succès fou*, Achille."

"I am desolated, my good Ouagstaffe," observed Petitpois after a pregnant silence; "but I cannot believe all you say."

"I *may* be wrong," admitted Wagstaffe handsomely, "but that's my reading of the situation. At any rate, Achille, you will admit that my theory squares with the known facts of the case."

Petitpois bowed politely.

"Perhaps it is I who am wrong, my dear Ouagger. There is such a difference of point of view between your politics and ours."

The deep voice of Captain Blaikie broke in.

"If Lancashire," he said grimly, "were occupied by a German army, as the Lille district is to-day, I fancy there would be a considerable levelling up of political points of view all round. No limelight for a comic opposition then, Achille, old son!"

IV

Besides receiving letters, we write them. And this brings us to that mysterious and impalpable despot, the Censor.

There is not much mystery about him really. Like a good many other highly placed individuals, he deputes as much of his work as possible to some one else—in this case that long-suffering maid-of-all-work, the company officer. Let us track Bobby Little to his dug-out, during one of those numerous periods of enforced retirement which occur between the hours of three and six, "Pip Emma"—as our friends the "buzzers" call the afternoon. On the floor of this retreat (which looks like a dog-kennel and smells like a vault) he finds a small heap of letters, deposited there for purposes of what the platoon-sergeant calls "censure." These have to be read (which is bad); licked up (which is far worse); signed on the outside by the officer, and forwarded to Headquarters. Here they are stamped with the familiar red triangle and forwarded to the Base, where they are supposed to be scrutinised by the real Censor—i.e., the gentleman who is paid for the job—and are finally despatched to their destination.

Bobby, drawing his legs well inside the kennel, out of the way of stray shrapnel bullets, begins his task.

The heap resolves itself into three parts. First come the post-cards, which give no trouble, as their secrets are written plain for all to see. There are half a dozen or so of the British Army official issue, which are designed for the benefit of those who lack the epistolary gift—what would a woman say if you offered such things to her?—and bear upon the back the following printed statements:—

_I am quite well.
I have been admitted to hospital.
I am sick } {and am going on well. wounded} {and hope to be discharged soon.
I have received your {letter, dated … {telegram, " {parcel, "
Letter follows at first opportunity.
I have received no letter from you {lately. {for a long time._

(The gentleman who designed this postcard must have been a descendant of Sydney Smith. You remember that great man's criticism of the Books of Euclid? He preferred the Second Book, on the ground that it was more "impassioned" than the others!)

All the sender of this impassioned missive has to do is to delete such clauses as strike him as untruthful or over-demonstrative, and sign his name. He is not allowed to add any comments of his own. On this occasion, however, one indignant gentleman has pencilled the ironical phrase, "I don't think!" opposite the line which acknowledges the receipt of a parcel. Bobby lays this aside, to be returned to the sender.

Then come some French picture post-cards. Most of these present soldiers—soldiers posing, soldiers exchanging international handgrips, soldiers grouped round a massive and *décolletée* lady in flowing robes, and declaring that *La patrie sera libre!* Underneath this last, Private Ogg has written: "Dear Lizzie,—I hope this finds you well as it leaves me so. I send you a French p.c. The writing means long live the Queen of France."

The next heap consists of letters in official-looking green envelopes. These are already sealed up, and the sender has signed the following attestation, printed on the flap: *I certify on my honour that the contents of this envelope refer to nothing but private and family matters.* Setting aside a rather bulky epistle addressed to The Editor of a popular London weekly, which advertises a circulation of over a million copies—a singularly unsuitable recipient for correspondence of a private and family nature—Bobby turns to the third heap, and sets to work upon his daily task of detecting items of information, "which if intercepted or published might prove of value to the enemy."

It is not a pleasant task to pry into another person's correspondence, but Bobby's scruples are considerably abated by the consciousness that on this occasion he is doing so with the writer's full knowledge. Consequently it is a clear case of *caveat scriptor*. Not that Bobby's flock show any embarrassment at the prospect of his scrutiny. Most of them write with the utmost frankness, whether they are conducting a love affair, or are involved in a domestic broil of the most personal nature. In fact, they seem rather to enjoy having an official audience. Others cheerfully avail themselves of this opportunity of conveying advice or reproof to those above them, by means of what the Royal Artillery call "indirect fire." Private Dunshie remarks: "We have been getting no pay these three weeks, but I doubt the officer will know what has become of the money." It is the firm conviction of every private soldier in "K(1)" that all fines and deductions go straight into the pocket of the officer who levies them. Private Hogg, always an optimist, opines: "The officers should know better how to treat us now, for they all get a read of our letters."

But, as recorded above, the outstanding feature of this correspondence is an engaging frankness. For instance, Private Cosh, who under an undemonstrative, not to say wooden, exterior evidently conceals a heart as inflammable as flannelette, is conducting single-handed no less than four parallel love affairs. One lady resides in his native Coatbridge, the second is in service in South Kensington, the third serves in a shop in Kelvinside, and the fourth moth appears to have been attracted to this most unlikely candle during our sojourn in winter billets in Hampshire. Cosh writes to them all most ardently every week—sometimes oftener—and Bobby Little, as he ploughs wearily through repeated demands for photographs, and touching protestations of lifelong affection, curses the verbose and susceptible youth with all his heart.

But this mail brings him a gleam of comfort.

So you tell me, Chrissie, writes Cosh to the lady in South Kensington, *that you are engaged to be married on a milkman....*

("Thank heaven!" murmurs Bobby piously.)

No, no, Chrissie, you need not trouble yourself. It is nothing to me.

("He's as sick as muck!" comments Bobby.)

All I did before was in friendship's name.

("Liar!")

Bobby, thankfully realising that his daily labours will be materially lightened by the withdrawal of the fickle Chrissie from the postal arena, ploughs steadily through the letters. Most of them begin in accordance with some approved formula, such as—

It is with the greatest of pleasure that I take up my pen—

It is invariably a pencil, and a blunt one at that.

Crosses are ubiquitous, and the flap of the envelope usually bears the mystic formula, S.W.A.K. This apparently means "Sealed with a kiss," which, considering that the sealing is done not by the writer but by the Censor, seems to take a good deal for granted.

Most of the letters acknowledge the receipt of a "parcle"; many give a guarded summary of the military situation.

We are not allowed to tell you about the War, but I may say that we are now in the trenches. We are all in the pink, and not many of the boys has gotten a dose of lead-poisoning yet.

It is a pity that the names of places have to be left blank. Otherwise we should get some fine phonetic spelling. Our pronunciation is founded on no pedantic rules. Armentières is Armentears, Busnes is Business, Bailleul is Booloo, and Vieille Chapclle is Veal Chapel.

The chief difficulty of the writers appears to be to round off their letters gracefully. *Having no more to say, I will now draw to a close*, is the accepted formula. Private Burke, never a tactician, concludes a most ardent love-letter thus: "*Well, Kate, I will now close, as I have to write to another of the girls.*"

But to Private Mucklewame literary composition presents no difficulties. Here is a single example of his terse and masterly style:—

Dere wife, if you could make the next postal order a trifle stronger, I might get getting an egg to my tea.—Your loving husband, JAS. MUCKLEWAME, *No*. 74077.

But there are features of this multifarious correspondence over which one has no inclination to smile. There are wistful references to old days; tender inquiries after bairns and weans; assurances to anxious wives and mothers that the dangers of modern warfare are merely nominal. There is an almost entire absence of boasting or lying, and very little complaining. There is a general and obvious desire to allay anxiety. We are all "fine"; we are all "in the pink." "This is a grand life."

Listen to Lance-Corporal M'Snape: *Well, mother, I got your parcel, and the things was most welcome; but you must not send any more. I seen a shilling stamp on the parcel: that is too much for you to afford.* How many officers take the trouble to examine the stamp on their parcels?

And there is a wealth of homely sentiment and honest affection which holds up its head without shame even in the presence of the Censor. One rather pathetic screed, beginning: *Well, wife, I doubt this will be a poor letter, for I canna get one of they green envelopes to-day, but I'll try my best*—Bobby Little sealed and signed without further scrutiny.

V

One more picture, to close the record of our trivial round.

It is a dark, moist, and most unpleasant dawn. Captain Blaikie stands leaning against a traverse in the fire-trench, superintending the return of a party from picket duty. They file in, sleepy and dishevelled, through an archway in the parapet, on their way to dug-outs and repose. The last man in the procession is Bobby Little, who has been in charge all night.

Our line here makes a sharp bend round the corner of an orchard, and for security's sake a second trench has been cut behind, making, as it were, the cross-bar of a capital A. The apex of the A is no health resort. Brother Bosche, as already explained, is only fifty yards away, and his trench-mortars make excellent practice with the parapet. So the Orchard Trench is only occupied at night, and the alternative route, which is well constructed and comparatively safe, is used by all careful persons who desire to proceed from one arm of the A to the other.

The present party are the night picket, thankfully relinquishing their vigil round the apex.

Bobby Little remained to bid his company-commander good-morning at the junction of the two trenches.

"Any casualties?" An invariable question at this spot.

"No, sir. We were lucky. There was a lot of sniping."

"It's a rum profession," mused Captain Blaikic, who was in a wakeful mood.

"In what way, sir?" inquired the sleepy but respectful Bobby.

"Well"—Captain Blaikie began to fill his pipe—"who takes about nine-tenths of the risk, and does practically all the hard work in the Army? The private and the subaltern—you and your picket, in fact. Now, here is the problem which has puzzled me ever since I joined the Army, and I've had nineteen years' service. The farther away you remove the British soldier from the risk of personal injury, the higher you pay him. Out here, a private of the line gets about a shilling a day. For that he digs, saps, marches, and fights like a hero. The motor-transport driver gets six shillings a day, no danger, and lives like a fighting cock. The Army Service Corps drive about in motors, pinch our rations, and draw princely incomes. Staff Officers are compensated for their comparative security by extra cash, and first chop at the war medals. Now—why?"

"I dare say they would sooner be here, in the trenches, with us," was
Bobby's characteristic reply.

Blaikie lit his pipe—it was almost broad daylight now—and considered.

"Yes," he agreed—"perhaps. Still, my son, I can't say I have ever noticed Staff Officers crowding into the trenches (as they have a perfect right to do) at four o'clock in the morning. And I can't say I altogether blame them. In fact, if ever I do meet one performing such a feat, I shall say: 'There goes a sahib—and a soldier!' and I shall take off my hat to him."

"Well, get ready now," said Bobby. "Look!"

They were still standing at the trench junction. Two figures, in the uniform of the Staff, were visible in Orchard Trench, working their way down from the apex—picking their steps amid the tumbled sandbags, and stooping low to avoid gaps in the ruined parapet. The sun was just rising behind the German trenches. One of the officers was burly and middle-aged; he did not appear to enjoy bending double. His companion was slight, fair-haired, and looked incredibly young. Once or twice he glanced over his shoulder, and smiled encouragingly at his senior.

The pair emerged through the archway into the main trench, and straightened their backs with obvious relief. The younger officer—he was a lieutenant—noticed Captain Blaikie, saluted him gravely, and turned to follow his companion.

Captain Blaikie did not take his hat off, as he had promised. Instead, he stood suddenly to attention, and saluted in return, keeping his hand uplifted until the slim, childish figure had disappeared round the corner of a traverse.

It was the Prince of Wales.

XX

THE GATHERING OF THE EAGLES

When this war is over, and the glory and the praise are duly assigned, particularly honourable mention should be made of the inhabitants of a certain ancient French town with a Scottish name, which lies not far behind a particularly sultry stretch of the trenches. The town is subject to shell fire, as splintered walls and shattered windows testify; yet every shop stands open. The town, moreover, is the only considerable place in the district, and enjoys a monopoly of patronage from all the surrounding billeting areas; yet the keepers of the shops have heroically refrained from putting up their prices to any appreciable extent. This combination of courage and fair-dealing has had its reward. The town has become a local Mecca. British soldiers with an afternoon to spare and a few francs to spend come in from miles around. Mess presidents send in their mess-sergeants, and fearful and wonderful is the marketing which ensues.

In remote and rural billets catering is a simple matter. We take what we can get, and leave it at that. The following business-card, which Bobby Little once found attached to an outhouse door in one of his billets, puts the resources of a French hamlet into a nutshell:—

HÉRE SMOKING ROM BEER WINE {WITHE {RAID COFFE EGS

But in town the shopper has a wider range. Behold Sergeant Goffin, a true-born Londoner, with the Londoner's faculty of never being at a loss for a word, at the grocer's, purchasing comforts for our officers' mess.

"Bong jooer, Mrs. Pankhurst!" he observes breezily to the plump *épicière*. This is his invariable greeting to French ladies who display any tendency to volubility—and they are many.

"Bon jour, M'sieu le Caporal!" replies the *épicière*, smiling.
"M'sieu le Caporal désire?"

The sergeant allows his reduction in rank to pass unnoticed. He does not understand the French tongue, though he speaks it with great fluency and incredible success. He holds up a warning hand.

"Now, keep your 'and off the tap of the gas-meter for one minute *if* you please," he rejoins, "and let me get a word in edgeways. I want"—with great emphasis—"vinblank one, vinrooge two, bogeys six, Dom one. Compree?"

By some miracle the smiling lady does "compree," and produces white wine, red wine, candles, and—a bottle of Benedictine! (Sergeant Goffin always names wines after the most boldly printed word upon the label. He once handed round some champagne, which he insisted on calling "a bottle of brute.")

"Combine?" is the next observation.

The *épicière* utters the series of short sharp sibilants of which all French numerals appear to be composed. It sounds like "song-song-song." The resourceful Goffin lays down a twenty-franc note.

"Take it out of that," he says grandly.

He receives his change, and counts it with a great air of wisdom. The *épicière* breaks into a rapid recital—it sounds rather like our curate at home getting to work on *When the wicked man*—of the beauty and succulence of her other wares. Up goes Goffin's hand again.

"Na pooh!" he exclaims.. "Bong jooer!" And he stumps out to the mess-cart.

"Na pooh!" is a mysterious but invaluable expression. Possibly it is derived from "Il n'y a plus." It means, "All over!" You say "Na pooh!" when you push your plate away after dinner. It also means, "Not likely!" or "Nothing doing!" By a further development it has come to mean "done for," "finished," and in extreme cases, "dead." "Poor Bill got na-poohed by a rifle-grenade yesterday," says one mourner to another.

The Oxford Dictionary of the English Language will have to be revised and enlarged when this war is over.

* * * * *

Meanwhile, a few doors away, a host of officers is sitting in the Café de la Terre. Cafés are as plentiful as blackberries in this, as in most other French provincial towns, and they are usually filled to overflowing with privates of the British Army heroically drinking beer upon which they know it is impossible to get intoxicated. But the proprietor of the Café de la Terre is a long-headed citizen. By the simple expedient of labelling his premises "Officers Only," and making a minimum charge of one franc per drink, he has at a single stroke ensured the presence of the *élite* and increased his profits tenfold.

Many arms of the Service are grouped round the little marble-topped tables, for the district is stiff with British troops, and promises to grow stiffer. In fact, so persistently are the eagles gathering together upon this, the edge of the fighting line, that rumour is busier than ever. The Big Push holds redoubled sway in our thoughts. The First Hundred Thousand are well represented, for the whole Scottish Division is in the neighbourhood. Beside the glengarries there are countless flat caps—line regiments, territorials, gunners, and sappers. The Army Service Corps is there in force, recruiting exhausted nature from the strain of dashing about the countryside in motor-cars. The R.A.M.C. is strongly represented, doubtless to test the purity of the refreshment provided. Even the Staff has torn itself away from its arduous duties for the moment, as sundry red tabs testify. In one corner sit four stout French civilians, playing a mysterious card-game.

At the very next table we find ourselves among friends. Here are Major Kemp, also Captain Blaikie. They are accompanied by Ayling, Bobby Little, and Mr. Waddell. The battalion came out of trenches yesterday, and for the first time found itself in urban billets. For the moment haylofts and wash-houses are things of the dim past. We are living in real houses, sleeping in real beds, some with sheets.

To this group enters unexpectedly Captain Wagstaffe.

"Hallo, Wagger!" says Blaikie. "Back already?"

"Your surmise is correct," replies Wagstaffe, who has been home on leave. "I got a wire yesterday at lunch-time—in the Savoy, of all places! Every one on leave has been recalled. We were packed like herrings on the boat. Garçon, bière—the brunette kind!"

"Tell us all about London," says Ayling hungrily. "What does it look like? Tell us!"

We have been out here for the best part of five months now. Leave opened a fortnight ago, amid acclamations—only to be closed again within a few days. Wagstaffe was one of the lucky few who slipped through the blessed portals. He now sips his beer and delivers his report.

"London is much as usual. A bit rattled over Zeppelins—they have turned out even more street lamps—but nothing to signify. Country districts crawling with troops. All the officers appear to be colonels. Promotion at home is more rapid than out here. Chin, chin!" Wagstaffe buries his face in his glass mug.

"What is the general attitude," asked Mr. Waddell, "towards the war?"

"Well, one's own friends are down in the dumps. Of course it's only natural, because most of them are in mourning. Our losses are much more noticeable at home than abroad, somehow. People seemed quite surprised when I told them that things out here are as right as rain, and that our troops are simply tumbling over one another, and that we don't require any comic M.P.'s sent out to cheer us up. The fact is, some people read the papers too much. At the present moment the London press is, not to put too fine a point on it, making a holy show of itself. I suppose there's some low-down political rig at the back of it all, but the whole business must be perfect jam for the Bosches in Berlin."

"What's the trouble?" inquired Major Kemp.

"Conscription, mostly. (Though why they should worry their little heads about it, I don't know. If K. wants it we'll have it: if not, we won't; so that's that!) Both sides are trying to drag the great British Public into the scrap by the back of the neck. The Conscription crowd, with whom one would naturally side if they would play the game, seem to be out to unseat the Government as a preliminary. They support their arguments by stating that the British Army on the Western front is reduced to a few platoons, and that they are allowed to fire one shell per day. At least, that's what I gathered."

"What do the other side say?" inquired Kemp.

"Oh, theirs is a very simple line of argument. They state, quite simply, that if the personal liberty of Britain's workers—that doesn't mean you and me, as you might think: we are the Overbearing Militarist Oligarchy: a worker is a man who goes on strike,—they say that if the personal liberty of these sacred perishers is interfered with by the Overbearing Militarist Oligarchy aforesaid, there will be a Revolution. That's all! Oh, they're a sweet lot, the British newspaper bosses!"

"But what," inquired that earnest seeker after knowledge, Mr. Waddell, "is the general attitude of the country at large upon this grave question?"

Captain Wagstaffe chuckled.

"The dear old country at large," he replied, "is its dear old self, as usual. It is not worrying one jot about Conscription, or us, or anything like that. The one topic of conversation at present is—Charlie Chaplin."

"Who is Charlie Chaplin?" inquired several voices.

Wagstaffe shook his head.

"I haven't the faintest idea," he said. "All I know is that you can't go anywhere in London without running up against him. He is It. The mention of his name in a *revue* is greeted with thunders of applause. At one place I went to, twenty young men came upon the stage at once, all got up as Charlie Chaplin."

"But who *is* he?"

"That I can't tell you. I made several attempts to find out; but whenever I asked the question people simply stared at me in amazement. I felt quite ashamed: it was plain that I ought to have known. I have a vague idea that he is some tremendous new boss whom the Government have appointed to make shells, or something. Anyhow, the great British Nation is far too much engrossed with Charles to worry about a little thing like Conscription. Still, I should like to know. I feel I have been rather unpatriotic about it all."

"I can tell you," said Bobby Little. "My servant is a great admirer of his. He is the latest cinema star. Falls off roofs, and gets run over by motors—"

"And keeps the police at bay with a firehose," added Wagstaffe.

"That's him! I know the type. Thank you, Bobby!"

Major Kemp put down his glass with a gentle sigh, and rose to go.

"We are a great nation," he remarked contentedly. "I was a bit anxious about things at home, but I see now there was nothing to worry about. We shall win all right. Well, I am off to the Mess. See you later, everybody!"

"Meanwhile," inquired Wagstaffe, as the party settled down again, "what is brewing here! I haven't seen the adjutant yet."

"You'll see him soon enough," replied Blaikie grimly. He glanced over his shoulder towards the four civilian card-players. They looked bourgeois enough and patriotic enough, but it is wise to take no risks in a café, as a printed notice upon the war, signed by the Provost-Marshal, was careful to point out. "Come for a stroll," he said.

Presently the two captains found themselves in a shady boulevard leading to the outskirts of the town. Darkness was falling, and soon would be intense; for lights are taboo in the neighbourhood of the firing line.

"Have we finished that new trench in front of our wire?" asked Wagstaffe.

"Yes. It is the best thing we have done yet. Divisional Headquarters are rightly pleased about it."

Blaikie gave details. The order had gone forth that a new trench was to be constructed in front of our present line—a hundred yards in front. Accordingly, when night fell, two hundred unconcerned heroes went forth, under their subalterns, and, squatting down in line along a white tape (laid earlier in the evening by our imperturbable friends, Lieutenants Box and Cox, of the Royal Engineers), proceeded to dig the trench. Thirty yards ahead of them, facing the curious eyes of countless Bosches, lay a covering party in extended order, ready to repel a rush. Hour by hour the work went on—skilfully, silently. On these occasions it is impossible to say what will happen. The enemy knows we are there: he can see us quite plainly. But he has his own night-work to do, and if he interferes with us he knows that our machine-guns will interfere with him. So, provided that our labours are conducted in a manner which is neither ostentatious nor contemptuous—that is to say, provided we do not talk, whistle, or smoke—he leaves us more or less alone.

But this particular task was not accomplished without loss: it was too obviously important. Several times the German machine-guns sputtered into flame, and each time the stretcher-bearers were called upon to do their duty. Yet the work went on to its accomplishment, without question, without slackening. The men were nearly all experts: they had handled pick and shovel from boyhood. Soldiers of the line would have worked quite as hard, maybe, but they would have taken twice as long. But these dour sons of Scotland worked like giants—trained giants. In four nights the trench, with traverses and approaches, was complete. The men who had made it fell back to their dug-outs, and shortly afterwards to their billets—there to spend the few odd francs which their separation allotments had left them, upon extremely hard-earned glasses of extremely small beer.

At home, several thousand patriotic Welshmen, fellows of the same craft, were upholding the dignity of Labour, and the reputation of the British Nation, by going out on strike for a further increase of pay—an increase which they knew a helpless Government would grant them. It was one of the strangest contrasts that the world has ever seen. But the explanation thereof, as proffered by Private Mucklewame, was quite simple and eminently sound.

"All the decent lads," he observed briefly, "are oot here."

"Good work!" said Wagstaffe, when Blaikie's tale was told. "What is the new trench for, exactly?"

Blaikie told him.

"Tell me more!" urged Wagstaffe, deeply interested.

Blaikie's statement cannot be set down here, though the substance of it may be common property to-day. When he had finished Wagstaffe whistled softly.

"And it's to be the day after to-morrow?" he said.

"Yes, if all goes well."

It was quite dark now. The horizon was brilliantly lit by the flashes of big guns, and a continuous roar came throbbing through the soft autumn darkness.

"If this thing goes with a click, as it ought to do," said Wagstaffe, "it will be the biggest thing that ever happened—bigger even than Charlie Chaplin."

"Yes—*if*!" assented the cautious Blaikie.

"It's a tremendous opportunity for our section of 'K(1),'" continued Wagstaffe. "We shall have a chance of making history over this, old man."

"Whatever we make—history or a bloomer—we'll do our level best," replied Blaikie. "At least, I hope 'A' Company will."

Then suddenly his reserved, undemonstrative Scottish tongue found utterance.

"Scotland for Ever!" he cried softly.

XXI

THE BATTLE OF THE SLAG-HEAPS

"Half-past two, and a cold morning, sir."

Thus Bobby Little's servant, rousing his employer from uneasy slumber under the open sky, in a newly-constructed trench running parallel to and in rear of the permanent trench line.

Bobby sat up, and peering at his luminous wrist-watch, morosely acquiesced in his menial's gruesome statement. But he cheered up at the next intimation.

"Breakfast is ready, sir."

Tea and bacon are always tea and bacon, even in the gross darkness and mental tension which precede a Big Push. Presently various humped figures in greatcoats, having gathered in the open ditch which did duty for Officers' Mess, broke into spasmodic conversation—conversation rendered even more spasmodic by the almost ceaseless roar of guns. There were guns all round us—rank upon rank: to judge by the noise, you would have said tier upon tier as well. Half a mile ahead, upon the face of a gentle slope, a sequence of flames would spout from the ground, and a storm of shells go whistling on their way. No sooner had this happened than there would come a shattering roar from the ground beneath our feet, and a heavy battery, concealed in a hedge fifty yards to our front, would launch its contribution. Farther back lay heavier batteries still, and beyond that batteries so powerful and so distant that one heard the shell pass before the report arrived. One of these monsters, coming apparently from infinity and bound for the back of beyond, lumbered wearily over the heads of "A" Company, partaking of breakfast.

Private Mucklewame paused in the act of raising his canteen to his lips.

"There's Wullie awa' for a walk!" he observed.

Considering that they were upon the eve of an epoch-making combat, the regiment were disappointingly placid.

In the Officers' Mess the prevailing note was neither lust of battle nor fear of death: it was merely that ordinary snappishness which is induced by early rising and uncomfortable surroundings.

"It's going to rain, too," grumbled Major Kemp.

At this moment the Colonel arrived, with final instructions from the Brigadier.

"We move off at a quarter to four," he said, "up Fountain Alley and Scottish Trench, into Central Boyau"—"boyau" is the name which is given to a communication-trench in trenches which, like those in front of us, are of French extraction—"and so over the parapet. There we extend, as arranged, into lines of half-companies, and go at 'em, making Douvrin our objective, and keeping the Hohenzollern and Fosse Eight upon our left."

Fosse Eight is a mighty waste-heap, such as you may behold anywhere along the railway in the colliery districts between Glasgow and Edinburgh. The official map calls such an eminence a Fosse; the Royal Engineers call it a Dump; Operation Orders call it a Slag-Heap; experts like Ogg and Hogg (who ought to know if any one does) call it a Bing. From this distance, two miles away, the Fosse looks as big as North Berwick Law. It is one of the many scattered about this district, all carefully numbered by the Ordnance. There are others, again, towards Hulluch and Loos. Number Eight has been the object of pressing attentions on the part of our big guns ever since the bombardment began, three weeks ago; but it still stands up—gaunt, grim, and defiant—against the eastern sky. Whether any one is left alive upon it, or in it, is another question. We shall have cause to remember Fosse Eight before this fight is over.

The Hohenzollern Redoubt, on the other hand, is a most inconspicuous object, but a very important factor in the present situation. It has been thrust forward from the Bosche lines to within a hundred yards of our own—a great promontory, a maze of trenches, machine-gun emplacements, and barbed wire, all flush with or under the ground, and terribly difficult to cripple by shell fire. It has been a source of great exasperation to us—a starting-point for saps, mines, and bombing parties. As already stated, this mighty fortress has been christened by its constructors, the Hohenzollern. It is attached to its parent trench-line by two communicating trenches, which the British Army, not to be outdone in reverence to the most august of dynasties, have named Big and Little Willie respectively.

A struggling dawn breaks, bringing with it promise of rain, and the regiment begins to marshal in the trench called Fountain Alley, along which it is to wind, snake-like, in the wake of the preceding troops, until it debouches over the parapet, a full mile away, and extends into line.

Presently the order is given to move off, and the snake begins to writhe. Progress is steady, but not exhilarating. We have several battalions of the Division in front of us (which Bobby Little resents as a personal affront), but have been assured that we shall see all the fighting we want. The situation appears to be that owing to the terrific artillery bombardment the attacking force will meet with little or no opposition in the German front-line trenches; or second line, for that matter.

"The whole Division," explains Captain Wagstaffe to Bobby Little, "should be able to get up into some sort of formation about the Bosche third line before any real fighting begins; so it does not very much matter whether we start first or fiftieth in the procession."

Captain Wagstaffe showed himself an accurate prophet.

We move on. At one point we pass through a howitzer battery, where dishevelled gentlemen give us a friendly wave of the hand. Others, not professionally engaged for the moment, sit unconcernedly in the ditch with their backs to the proceedings, frying bacon. This is their busy hour.

Presently the pace grows even slower, and finally we stop altogether. Another battalion has cut in ahead of us, and we must perforce wait, snapping our fingers with impatience, like theatre-goers in a Piccadilly block, whose taxis have been held up by the traffic debouching from Berkeley Street.

"Luckily the curtain doesn't rise till five-fifty," observes Captain Wagstaffe.

We move on again at last, and find ourselves in Central Boyau, getting near the heart of things. Suddenly we are conscious of an overpowering sense of relief. Our guns have ceased firing. For the first time for three days and nights there is peace.

Captain Wagstaffe looks at his watch.

"That means that our first line are going over the parapet," he says. "Punctual, too! The gunners have stopped to put up their sights and lengthen their fuses. We ought to be fairly in it in half an hour."

But this proves to be an under-estimate. There are mysterious and maddening stoppages—maddening, because in communication-trench stoppages it is quite impossible to find out what is the matter. Furious messages begin to arrive from the rear. The original form of inquiry was probably something like this: "Major Kemp would like to know the cause of the delay." As transmitted sonorously from mouth to mouth by the rank and file it finally arrives (if it ever arrives at all) in some such words as: "Pass doon; what for is this (asterisk, obelus) wait?" But as no answer is ever passed back it does not much matter.

The righteous indignation of Major Kemp, who is situated somewhere about the middle of the procession, reaches its culminating point when, with much struggling and pushing and hopeless jamming, a stretcher carrying a wounded man is borne down the crowded trench on its way to the rear. The Major delivers himself.

"This is perfectly monstrous! You stretcher-bearers will kill that poor chap if you try to drag him down here. There is a specially constructed road to the dressing-station over there—Bart's Alley, it is called. We cannot have up-and-down traffic jumbled together like this. For heaven's sake, Waddell, pass up word to the C.O. that it is mistaken kindness to allow these fellows down here. He *must* send them back."

Waddell volunteers to climb out of the trench and go forward with a message. But this the Major will not allow. "Your platoon will require a leader presently," he mentions. "We'll try the effect of a note."

The note is passed up, and anon an answer comes back to the effect that no wounded have been allowed down from the head of the column. They must be getting in by a sidetrack somewhere. The Major groans, but can do nothing.

Presently there is a fresh block.

"What is it this time?" inquires the afflicted Kemp. "More wounded, or are we being photographed?"

The answer races joyously down the line—"Gairman prisoners, sirr—seeventy of them!"

This time the Major acts with promptness and decision.

"Prisoners? No, they *don't*! Pass up word from me that the whole boiling are to be hoisted on to the parapet, with their escort, and made to walk above ground."

The order goes forward. Presently our hearts are rejoiced by an exhilarating sight. Across the field through which our trench winds comes a body of men, running rapidly, encouraged to further fleetness of foot by desultory shrapnel and stray bullets. They wear grey-green uniform, and flat, muffin-shaped caps. They have no arms or equipment: some are slightly wounded. In front of this contingent, running even more rapidly, are their escort—some dozen brawny Highlanders, armed to the teeth. But the prisoners exhibit no desire to take advantage of this unusual order of things. Their one ambition in life appears to be to put as large a space as possible between themselves and their late comrades-in-arms, and, if possible, overtake their captors.

Some of them find time to grin, and wave their hands to us. One addresses the scandalised M'Slattery as "Kamarad!" "No more dis war for me!" cries another, with unfeigned satisfaction.

After this our progress is more rapid. As we near the front line, the enemy's shrapnel reaps its harvest even in our deep trench. More than once we pass a wounded man, hoisted on to the parapet to wait for first-aid. More than once we step over some poor fellow for whom no first-aid will avail.

Five minutes later we reach the parapet—that immovable rampart over which we have peeped so often and so cautiously with our periscopes—and clamber up a sandbag staircase on to the summit. We note that our barbed wire has all been cut away, and that another battalion, already extended into line, is advancing fifty yards ahead of us. Bullets are pinging through the air, but the guns are once more silent. Possibly they are altering their position. Dotted about upon the flat ground before us lie many kilted figures, strangely still, in uncomfortable attitudes.

A mile or so upon our right we can see two towers—pit-head towers—standing side by side. They mark the village of Loos, where another Scottish Division is leading the attack. To the right of Loos again, for miles and miles and miles, we know that wave upon wave of impetuous French soldiers is breaking in a tempest over the shattered German trenches. Indeed, we conjecture that down there, upon our right, is where the Biggest Push of all is taking place. Our duty is to get forward if we can, but before everything to engage as many German troops and guns as possible. Even if we fight for a week or more, and only hold our own, we shall have done the greater part of what was required of us. But we hope to do more than that.

Upon our left lies the Hohenzollern. It is silent; so we know that it has been captured. Beyond that, upon our left front, looms Fosse Eight, still surmounted by its battered shaft-tower. Right ahead, peeping over a low ridge, is a church steeple, with a clock-face in it. That is our objective.

Next moment we have deployed into extended order, and step out, to play our little part in the great Battle of the Slag-Heaps.

II

Twenty-four hours later, a little group of officers sat in a roomy dug-out. Major Kemp was there, with his head upon the plank table, fast asleep. Bobby Little, who had neither eaten nor slept since the previous dawn, was nibbling chocolate, and shaking as if with ague. He had gone through a good deal. Waddell sat opposite to him, stolidly devouring bully-beef out of a tin with his fingers. Ayling reclined upon the floor, mechanically adjusting a machine-gun lock, which he had taken from his haversack. Captain Wagstaffe was making cocoa over a Tommy's Cooker. He looked less the worse for wear than the others, but could hardly have been described as spruce in appearance. The whole party were splashed with mud and soaked to the skin, for it had rained hard during the greater part of the night. They were all sick for want of food and sleep. Moreover, all had seen unusual sights. It was Sunday morning.

Presently Wagstaffe completed his culinary arrangements, and poured out the cocoa into some aluminium cups. He touched Major Kemp on the shoulder.

"Have some of this, Major," he said.

The burly Kemp roused himself and took the proffered cup gratefully.

Then, looking round, he said—

"Hallo, Ayling! You arrived? Whereabouts in the line were you?"

"I got cut off from the Battalion in the advance up Central Boyau, sir," said Ayling. "Everybody had disappeared by the time I got the machine-guns over the parapet. However, knowing the objective, I pushed on towards the Church Tower."

"How did you enjoy yourself passing Fosse Eight?" inquired Captain Wagstaffe.

"Thank you, we got a dose of our own medicine—machine-gun fire, in enfilade. It was beastly."

"We also noticed it," Wagstaffe intimated. "That was where poor Sinclair got knocked out. What did you do?"

"I signalled to the men to lie flat for a bit, and I did the same. I did not know that it was possible for a human being to lie as flat as I lay during that quarter of an hour. But it was no good. The guns must have been high up on the Fosse: they had excellent command. The bullets simply greased all round us. I could feel them combing out my hair, and digging into the ground underneath me."

"What were your sensations, *exactly*?" asked Kemp.

"I felt just as if an invisible person were tickling me," replied Ayling, with feeling.

"So did I," said Kemp. "Go on."

"I heard one of my men cry out that he was hit," continued Ayling, "and I came to the conclusion that we would have a better chance as moving targets than as fixed; so I passed the word to get up and move forward steadily, in single file. Ultimately we struck a stray communication-trench, into which we descended with as much dignity as possible. It led us into some quarries."

"Off our line altogether."

"So I learned from two Companies of an English regiment which were there, acting as reserve to a Brigade which was scrapping somewhere in the direction of Hulluch; so I realised that we had worked too far to the right. We moved out of the quarries and struck over half-left, and ultimately found the Battalion, a very long way ahead, in what I took to be a Bosche third-line trench, facing east."

"Right! Fosse Alley," said Kemp. "You remember it on the map?"

"Yes, I do now," said Ayling. "Well, I planted myself on the right flank of the Battalion with-two guns, and sent Sergeant Killick along with the other two to the left. You know the rest."

"I'm not sure that I do," said the Major. "We were packed so tight in that blooming trench that it was quite impossible to move about, and I only saw what was going on close around me. Did you get much machine-gun practice?"

"A fair amount, sir," replied Ayling, with professional satisfaction. "There was a lot of firing from our right front, so I combed out all the bushes and house-fronts I could see; and presently the firing died down, but not before I had had one gun put out of action with a bullet through the barrel-casing. After dark things were fairly quiet, except for constant alarms, until the order came to move back to the next trench."

Major Kemp's fist came down upon the plank table.

"Move back!" he exclaimed angrily. "Just so! To capture Fosse Alley, hold it all day and half the night, and then be compelled to move back, simply because we had pushed so far ahead of any other Division that we had no support on either flank! It was tough—rotten—hellish! Excuse my exuberance. 'You all right, Wagstaffe?"

"Wonderful, considering," replied Wagstaffe. "I was mildly gassed by a lachrymous shell about two o'clock this morning, but nothing to signify."

"Did your respirator work?"

"I found that in the heat of the moment I had mislaid it."

"What did you do?"

"I climbed on to the parapet and sat there. It seemed the healthiest spot under the circumstance: anyhow, the air was pure. When I recovered I got down. What happened to 'A,' Bobby? I heard rumours, but hoped—"

He hesitated.

"Go on," he said abruptly; and Bobby, more composed now, told his tale.

"A" Company, it appeared, had found themselves clinging grimly to the section of Fosse Alley which they had captured, with their left flank entirely in the air. Presently came an order. Further forward still, half-right, another isolated trench was being held by a portion of the Highland Brigade. These were suffering cruelly, for the German artillery had the range to a nicety, and convenient sapheads gave the German bombers easy access to their flanks. It is more than likely that this very trench had been constructed expressly for the inveiglement of a too successful attacking party. Certainly no troops could live in it for long. "A" Company were to go forward and support.

Captain Blaikie, passing word to his men to be ready, turned to Bobby.

"I'm a morose, dour, monosyllabic Scot, Bobbie," he said; "but this sort of thing bucks me up."

Next moment he was over the parapet and away, followed by his Company. In that long, steadily-advancing line were many of our friends. Mucklewame was there, panting heavily, and cannily commending his soul to Providence. Messrs. Ogg and Hogg were there, shoulder to shoulder. M'Ostrich, the Ulster visionary, was there, six paces ahead of any other man, crooning some Ironside canticle to himself. Next behind him came the reformed revolutionary, M'Slattery.

Straightway the enemy observed the oncoming reinforcements, and shrapnel began to fly. The men pressed on, at a steady double now. M'Ostrich was the first to go down. Game to the last, he waved encouragement to his mates with a failing arm as they passed over his body.

"Come along, boys!" cried Captain Blaikie, suddenly eloquent. "There is the trench! The other lads are waiting for you. Come along! Charge!"

The men needed no further bidding. They came on—with a ragged cheer—and assuredly would have arrived, but for one thing. Suddenly they faltered, and stopped dead.

Captain Blaikie turned to his faithful subaltern panting behind him.

"We are done in, Bobby," he said. "Look! Wire!"

He was right. This particular trench, it was true, was occupied by our friends; but it had been constructed in the first instance for the use of our enemies. Consequently it was wired, and heavily wired, upon the side facing the British advance.

Captain Blaikie, directing operations with a walking-stick as if the whole affair were an Aldershot field-day, signalled to the Company to lie down, and began to unbutton a leather pouch in his belt.

"You too, Bobby," he said; "and don't dare to move a muscle until you get the order!"

He strolled forward, pliers in hand, and began methodically to cut a passage, strand by strand, through the forest of wire.

Then it was that invisible machine-guns opened, and a very gallant officer and Scotsman fell dead upon the field of honour.

Half an hour later, "A" Company, having expended all their ammunition and gained never a yard, fell back upon the rest of the Battalion. Including Bobby Little (who seemed to bear a charmed life), they did not represent the strength of a platoon.

"I wonder what they will do with us next," remarked Mr. Waddell, who had finished his bully.

"If they have any sense of decency," said Major Kemp, "they will send us back to rest a bit, and put another Division in. We have opened the ball and done a lot of dirty work for them, and have lost a lot of men and officers. Bed for me, please!"

"I should be more inclined to agree with you, Major," said Wagstaffe, "if only we had a bit more to show for our losses."

"We haven't done so badly," replied Kemp, who was growing more cheerful under the influence of hot cocoa. "We have got the Hohenzollern, and the Bosche first line at least, and probably Fosse Eight. On the right I hear we have taken Loos. That's not so dusty for a start. I have not the slightest doubt that there will be a heavy counter-attack, which we shall repel. After that we shall attack again, and gain more ground, or at least keep the Bosche exceedingly busy holding on. That is our allotted task in this entertainment—to go on hammering the Hun, occupying his attention and using up his reserves, regardless of whether we gain ground or lose it, while our French pals on the right are pushing him off the map. At least, that is my theory: I don't pretend to be in touch with the official mind. This battle will probably go on for a week or more, over practically the same ground. It will be dreadful for the wounded, but even if we only hold on to what we have gained already, we are the winners. Still, I wish we could have consolidated Fosse Alley before going to bed."

At this moment the Colonel, stooping low in the tiny doorway, entered the dug-out, followed by the Adjutant. He bade his supporters good-morning.

"I am glad to find that you fellows have been able to give your men a meal," he said. "It was capital work getting the ration-carts up so far last night."

"Any news, Colonel?" asked Major Kemp.

"Most decidedly. It seems that the enemy have evacuated Fosse Alley again. Nobody quite knows why: a sudden attack of cold feet, probably. Our people command their position from Fosse Eight, on their left rear, so I don't altogether blame them. Whoever holds Fosse Eight holds Fosse Alley. However, the long and short of it all is that the Brigade are to go forward again this evening, and reoccupy Fosse Alley. Meanwhile, we consolidate things here."

Major Kemp sighed.

"Bed indefinitely postponed!" he remarked resignedly.

III

By midnight on the same Sunday the Battalion, now far under its original strength, had re-entered the scene of yesterday's long struggle, filing thither under the stars, by a deserted and ghostly German *boyau* nearly ten feet deep. Fosse Alley erred in the opposite direction. It was not much more than four feet in depth; the chalky parapet could by no stretch of imagination be described as bullet-proof; dug-outs and communication-trenches were non-existent. On our left the trench-line was continued by the troops of another Division: on our right lay another battalion of our own brigade.

"If the line has been made really continuous this time," observed the Colonel, "we should be as safe as houses. Wonderful fellows, these sappers! They have wired almost our whole front already. I wish they had had time to do it on our left as well."

Within the next few hours all defensive preparations possible in the time had been completed; and our attendant angels, most effectively disguised as Royal Engineers, had flitted away, leaving us to wait for Monday morning—and Brother Bosche.

With the dawn, our eyes, which had known no sleep since Friday night, peered rheumily out over the whitening landscape.

To our front the ground stretched smooth and level for two hundred yards, then fell gently away, leaving a clearly denned skyline. Beyond the skyline rose houses, of which we could descry only the roofs and upper windows.

"That must be either Haisnes or Douvrin," said Major Kemp. "We are much farther to the left than we were yesterday. By the way, *was* it yesterday?"

"The day before yesterday, sir," the ever-ready Waddell informed him.

"Never mind; to-day's the day, anyhow. And it's going to be a busy day, too. The fact is, we are in a tight place, and all through doing too well. We have again penetrated so much farther forward than any one else in our neighbourhood that we *may* have to fall back a bit. But I hope not. We have a big stake, Waddell. If we can hold on to this position until the others make good upon our right and left, we shall have reclaimed a clear two miles of the soil of France, my son." The Major swept the horizon with his glasses. "Let me see: that is probably Hulluch away on our right front: the Loos towers must be in line with us on our extreme right, but we can't see them for those hillocks. There is our old friend Fosse Eight towering over us on our left rear. I don't know anything about the ground on our absolute left, but so long as that flathead regiment hold on to their trench, we can't go far wrong. Waddell, I don't like those cottages on our left front. They block the view, and also spell machine-guns. I see one or two very suggestive loopholes in those red-tiled roofs. Go and draw Ayling's attention to them. A little preliminary *strafing* will do them no harm."

Five minutes later one of Ayling's machine-guns spoke out, and a cascade of tiles came sliding down the roofs of the offending cottages.

"That will tickle them up, if they have any guns set up on those rafters," observed the Major, with ghoulish satisfaction. "I wonder if Brer Bosche is going to attack. I hope he does. There is only one thing I am afraid of, and that is that there may be some odd saps running out towards us, especially on our flanks. If so, we shall have some close work with bombs—a most ungentlemanly method of warfare. Let us pray for a straightforward frontal attack."

But Brer Bosche had other cards to play first. Suddenly, out of nowhere, the air was filled with "whizz-bang" shells, moving in a lightning procession which lasted nearly half an hour. Most of these plastered the already scarred countenance of Fosse Eight: others fell shorter and demolished our parapet. When the tempest ceased, as suddenly as it began, the number of casualties in the crowded trench was considerable. But there was little time to attend to the wounded. Already the word was running down, the line—

"Look out to your front!"

Sure enough, over the skyline, two hundred yards away, grey figures were appearing—not in battalions, but tentatively, in twos and threes. Next moment a storm of rapid rifle fire broke from the trench. The grey figures turned and ran. Some disappeared over the horizon, others dropped flat, others simply curled up and withered. In three minutes solitude reigned again, and the firing ceased.

"Well, that's that!" observed Captain Wagstaffe to Bobby Little, upon the right of the Battalion line. "The Bosche has 'bethought himself and went,' as the poet says. Now he knows we are here, and have brought our arquebuses with us. He will try something more ikey next time. Talking of time, what about breakfast? When was our last meal, Bobby?"

"Haven't the vaguest notion," said Bobby sleepily.

"Well, it's about breakfast-time now. Have a bit of chocolate? It is all I have."

It was eight o'clock, and perfect silence reigned. All down the line men, infinitely grubby, were producing still grubbier fragments of bully-beef and biscuits from their persons. For an hour, squatting upon the sodden floor of the trench—it was raining yet again—the unappetising, intermittent meal proceeded.

Then—

"Hallo!" exclaimed Bobby with a jerk (for he was beginning to nod), "what was that on our right?"

"I'm afraid," replied Wagstaffe, "that it was bombs. It was right in this trench, too, about a hundred yards long. There must be a sap leading up there, for the bombers certainly have not advanced overground. I've been looking out for them since stand-to. Who is this anxious gentleman?"

A subaltern of the battalion on our right was forcing his way along the trench. He addressed Wagstaffe.

"We are having a pretty bad time with Bosche bombers on our right, sir," he said. "Will you send us down all the bombs you can spare?"

Wagstaffe hoisted himself upon the parapet.

"I will see our C.O. at once," he replied, and departed at the double. It was a risky proceeding, for German bullets promptly appeared in close attendance; but he saved a good five minutes on his journey to Battalion Headquarters at the other end of the trench.

Presently the bombs began to arrive, passed from hand to hand. Wagstaffe returned, this time along the trench.

"We shall have a tough fight for it," he said. "The Bosche bombers know their business, and probably have more bombs than we have. But those boys on our right seem to be keeping their end up."

"Can't *we* do anything?" asked Bobby feverishly.

"Nothing—unless the enemy succeed in working right down here; in which case we shall take our turn of getting it in the neck—or giving it! I fancy old Ayling and his popgun will have a word to say, if he can find a nice straight bit of trench. All we can do for the present is to keep a sharp look-out in front. I have no doubt they will attack in force when the right moment comes."

For close on three hours the bomb-fight went on. Little could be seen, for the struggle was all taking place upon the extreme right; but the sounds of conflict were plain enough. More bombs were passed up, and yet more; men, some cruelly torn, were passed down.

Then a signal-sergeant doubled up across country from somewhere in rear, paying out wire, and presently the word went forth that we were in touch with the Artillery. Directly after, sure enough, came the blessed sound and sight of British shrapnel bursting over our right front.

"That won't stop the present crowd," said Wagstaffe, "but it may prevent their reinforcements from coming up. We are holding our own, Bobby. What's that, Sergeant?"

"The Commanding Officer, sirr," announced Sergeant Carfrae, "has just passed up that we are to keep a sharp look-out to our left. They've commenced for to bomb the English regiment now."

"Golly, both flanks! This is getting a trifle steep," remarked Wagstaffe.

Detonations could now be distinctly heard upon the left.

"If they succeed in getting round behind us," said Wagstaffe in a low voice to Bobby, "we shall have to fall back a bit, into line with the rest of the advance. Only a few hundred yards, but it means a lot to *us*!"

"It hasn't happened yet," said Bobby stoutly.

Captain Wagstaffe knew better. His more experienced eye and ear had detected the fact that the position of the regiment upon the left was already turned. But he said nothing.

Presently the tall figure of the Colonel was seen, advancing in leisurely fashion along the trench, stopping here and there to exchange a word with a private or a sergeant.

"The regiment on the left may have to fall back, men," he was saying. "We, of course, will stand fast, and cover their retirement."

This most characteristic announcement was received with a matter-of-fact "Varra good, sir," from its recipients, and the Colonel passed on to where the two officers were standing.

"Hallo, Wagstaffe," he said; "good-morning! We shall get some very pretty shooting presently. The enemy are massing on our left front, down behind those cottages. How are things going on our right?"

"They are holding their own, sir."

"Good! Just tell Ayling to get his guns trained. But doubtless he has done so already. I must get back to the other flank."

And back to the danger-spot our C.O. passed—an upright, gallant figure, saying little, exhorting not at all, but instilling confidence and cheerfulness by his very presence.

Half-way along the trench he encountered Major Kemp.

"How are things on the left, sir?" was the Major's *sotto voce* inquiry.

"Not too good. Our position is turned. We have been promised reinforcements, but I doubt if they can get up in time. Of course, when it comes to falling back, this regiment goes last."

"Of course, sir."

IV

Highlanders! Four hundred yards! At the enemy advancing half-left, rapid fire!

Twenty minutes had passed. The regiment still stood immovable, though its left flank was now utterly exposed. All eyes and rifles were fixed upon the cluster of cottages. Through the gaps that lay between these could be discerned the advance of the German infantry—line upon line, moving towards the trench upon our left. The ground to our front was clear. Each time one of these lines passed a gap the rifles rang out and Ayling's remaining machine-gun uttered joyous barks. Still the enemy advanced. His shrapnel was bursting overhead; bullets were whistling from nowhere, for the attack in force was now being pressed home in earnest.

The deserted trench upon our left ran right through the cottages, and this restricted our view. No hostile bombers could be seen; it was evident that they had done their bit and handed on the conduct of affairs to others. Behind the shelter of the cottages the infantry were making a safe detour, and were bound, unless something unexpected happened, to get round behind us.

"They'll be firing from our rear in a minute," said Kemp between his teeth. "Lochgair, order your platoon to face about and be ready to fire over the parados."

Young Lochgair's method of executing this command was characteristically thorough. He climbed in leisurely fashion upon the parados; and standing there, with all his six-foot-three in full view, issued his orders.

"Face this way, boys! Keep your eyes on that group of buildings just behind the empty trench, in below the Fosse. You'll get some target practice presently. Don't go and forget that you are the straightest-shooting platoon in the Company. There they are"—he pointed with his stick—"lots of them—coming through that gap in the wall! Now then, rapid fire, and let them have it! Oh, well done, boys! Good shooting! Very good! Very good ind—"

He stopped suddenly, swayed, and toppled back into the trench. Major Kemp caught him in his arms, and laid him gently upon the chalky floor. There was nothing more to be done. Young Lochgair had given his platoon their target, and the platoon were now firing steadily upon the same. He closed his eyes and sighed, like a tired child.

"Carry on, Major!" he murmured faintly. "I'm all right."

So died the simple-hearted, valiant enthusiast whom we had christened Othello.

The entire regiment—what was left of it—was now firing over the back of the trench; for the wily Teuton had risked no frontal attack, seeing that he could gain all his ends from the left flank. Despite vigorous rifle fire and the continuous maledictions of the machine-gun, the enemy were now pouring through the cottages behind the trench. Many grey figures began to climb up the face of Fosse Eight, where apparently there was none to say them nay.

"We shall have a cheery walk back, I *don't* think!" murmured Wagstaffe.

He was right. Presently a withering fire was opened from the summit of the Fosse, which soon began to take effect in the exiguous and ill-protected trench.

"The Colonel is wounded, sir," reported the Sergeant-Major to Major Kemp.

"Badly?"

"Yes, sir."

Kemp looked round him. The regiment was now alone in the trench, for the gallant company upon their right had been battered almost out of existence.

"We can do no more good by staying here any longer," said the Major. "We have done our little bit. I think it is a case of 'Home, John!' Tell off a party to bring in the C.O., Sergeant-Major."

Then he passed the order.

"Highlanders, retire to the trenches behind, by Companies, beginning from the right."

"Whatever we may think of the Bosche as a gentleman," mused that indomitable philosopher, Captain Wagstaffe, as he doubled stolidly rearward behind his Company, "there is no denying his bravery as a soldier or his skill in co-ordinating an attack. It's positively uncanny, the way his artillery supports his infantry. (Hallo, that was a near one!) This enfilade fire from the Fosse is most unpleasant. (I fancy that one went through my kilt.) Steady there, on the left: don't bunch, whatever you do! Thank heaven, there's the next line of trenches, fully manned. And thank God, there's that boy Bobby tumbling in unhurt!"

V

So ended our share in the Big Push. It was a very small episode, spread over quite a short period, in one of the biggest and longest battles in the history of the world. It would have been easy to select a more showy episode, but hard to find a better illustration of the character of the men who took part in it. The battle which began upon that grey September morning has been raging, as I write, for nearly three weeks. It still surges backwards and forwards over the same stricken mile of ground; and the end is not yet. But the Hun is being steadily beaten to earth. (Only yesterday, in one brief furious counter-attack, he lost eight thousand killed.) When the final advance comes, as come it must, and our victorious line sweeps forward, it will pass over two narrow, ill-constructed, shell-torn trenches. In and around those trenches will be found the earthly remains of men—Jocks and Jimmies, and Sandies and Andies—clad in the uniform of almost every Scottish regiment. That assemblage of mute, glorious witnesses marks the point reached, during the first few hours of the first day's fighting, by the Scottish Division of "K(1)." *Molliter ossa cubent*.

There is little more to add to the record of those three days. For yet another night we carried on—repelling counter-attacks, securing the Hohenzollern, making sorties out of Big Willie, or manning the original front line parapet against eventualities. As is inevitable in a fight of these proportions, whole brigades were mingled together, and unexpected leaders arose to take the place of those who had fallen. Many a stout piece of work was done that night by mixed bands of kilties, flat-heads, and even cyclists, marshalled in a captured German trench and shepherded by a junior subaltern.

Finally, about midnight, came the blessed order that fresh troops were coming up to continue the attack, and that we were to be extricated from the *mêlée* and sent back to rest. And so, after a participation in the battle of some seventy-two hours, our battered Division came out—to sleep the sleep of utter exhaustion in dug-outs behind the railway line, and to receive, upon waking, the thanks of its Corps Commander.

VI

And here I propose (for a time, at least) to take leave of The First Hundred Thousand. Some day, if Providence wills, the tale shall be resumed; and you shall hear how Major Kemp, Captain Wagstaffe, Ayling, and Bobby Little, assisted by such veterans as Corporal Mucklewame, built up the regiment, with copious drafts and a fresh batch of subalterns, to its former strength.

But the title of the story will have to be changed. In the hearts of those who drilled them, reasoned with them, sometimes almost wept over them, and ultimately fought shoulder to shoulder with them, the sturdy, valiant legions, whose humorously-pathetic career you have followed so patiently for fifteen months, will always be First; but alas! they are no longer The Hundred Thousand.

So we will leave them, as is most justly due, in sole possession of their proud title.

All In It K(1) Carries On
A Continuation of the First Hundred Thousand

AUTHOR'S NOTE

The First Hundred Thousand closed with the Battle of Loos. The present narrative follows certain friends of ours from the scene of that costly but valuable experience, through a winter campaign in the neighbourhood of Ypres and Ploegsteert, to profitable participation in the Battle of the Somme.

Much has happened since then. The initiative has passed once and for all into our hands; so has the command of the air. Russia has been reborn, and, like most healthy infants, is passing through an uproarious period of teething trouble; but now America has stepped in, and promises to do more than redress the balance. All along the Western Front we have begun to move forward, without haste or flurry, but in such wise that during the past twelve months no position, once fairly captured and consolidated, has ever been regained by the enemy. To-day you can stand upon certain recently won eminences—Wytchaete Ridge, Messines Ridge, Vimy Ridge, and Monchy—looking down into the enemy's lines, and looking forward to the territory which yet remains to be restored to France.

You can also look back—not merely from these ridges, but from certain moral ridges as well—over the ground which has been successfully traversed, and you can marvel for the hundredth time, not that the thing was well or badly done, but that it was ever done at all.

But while this narrative was being written, none of these things had happened. We were still struggling uphill, with inadequate resources. So, since the incidents of the story were set down, in the main, as they occurred and when they occurred, the reader will find very little perspective, a great deal of the mood of the moment, and none at all of that profound wisdom which comes after the event. For the latter he must look home—to the lower walks of journalism and the back benches of the House of Commons.

It is not proposed to carry this story to a third volume. The First Hundred Thousand, as such, are no more. Like the "Old Contemptibles," they are now merged in a greater and more victorious army—in an armed nation, in fact. And, as Sergeant Mucklewame once observed to me, "There's no that many of us left now, onyways." So with all reverence—remembering how, when they were needed most, these men did not pause to reason why or count the cost, but came at once—we bid them good-bye.

I

WINTER QUARTERS

I

We are getting into our stride again. Two months ago we trudged into Béthune, gaunt, dirty, soaked to the skin, and reduced to a comparative handful. None of us had had his clothes off for a week. Our ankle-puttees had long dropped to pieces, and our hose-tops, having worked under the soles of our boots, had been cut away and discarded. The result was a bare and mud-splashed expanse of leg from boot to kilt, except in the case of the enterprising few who had devised artistic spat-puttees out of an old sandbag. Our headgear consisted in a few cases of the regulation Balmoral bonnet, usually minus "toorie" and badge; in a few more, of the battered remains of a gas helmet; and in the great majority, of a woollen cap-comforter.

We were bearded like that incomparable fighter, the *poilu*, and we were separated by an abyss of years, so our stomachs told us, from our last square meal.

But we were wonderfully placid about it all. Our regimental pipers, who had come out to play us in, were making what the Psalmist calls "a joyful noise" in front; and behind us lay the recollection of a battle, still raging, in which we had struck the first blow, and borne our full share for three days and nights. Moreover, our particular blow had bitten deeper into the enemy's line than any other blow in the neighbourhood. And, most blessed thought of all, everything was over, and we were going back to rest. For the moment, the memory of the sights we had seen, and the tax we had levied upon our bodies and souls, together with the picture of the countless sturdy lads whom we had left lying beneath the sinister shade of Fosse Eight, were beneficently obscured by the prospect of food, sleep, and comparative cleanliness.

After restoring ourselves to our personal comforts, we should doubtless go somewhere to refit. Drafts were already waiting at the Base to fill up the great gaps in our ranks. Our companies having been brought up to strength, a spate of promotions would follow. We had no Colonel, and only our Company Commander. Subalterns—what was left of them—would come by their own. N.C.O.'s, again, would have to be created by the dozen. While all this was going on, and the old names were being wcedcd out of the muster-roll to make way for the new, the Quartermaster would be drawing fresh equipment—packs, mess-tins, water-bottles, and the hundred oddments which always go astray in times of stress. There would be a good deal of dialogue of this sort:—

"Private M'Sumph, I see you are down for a new pack. Where is your old one?"

"Blawn off ma back, sirr!"

"Where are your puttees?"

"Blawn off ma feet, sirr!"

"Where is your iron ration?"

"Blawn oot o' ma pooch, sirr!"

"Where is your head?"

"Blawn—I beg your pardon, sirr!"—followed by generous reissues all round.

After a month or so our beloved regiment, once more at full strength, with traditions and morale annealed by the fires of experience, would take its rightful place in the forefront of "K (1)."

Such was the immediate future, as it presented itself to the wearied but optimistic brain of Lieutenant Bobby Little. He communicated his theories to Captain Wagstaffe.

"I wonder!" replied that experienced officer.

II

The chief penalty of doing a job of work well is that you are promptly put on to another. This is supposed to be a compliment.

The authorities allowed us exactly two days' rest, and then packed us off by train, with the new draft, to a particularly hot sector of the trench-line in Belgium—there to carry on with the operation known in nautical circles as "executing repairs while under steam."

Well, we have been in Belgium for two months now, and, as already stated, are getting into our stride again.

There are new faces everywhere, and some of the old faces are not quite the same. They are finer-drawn; one is conscious of less chubbiness all round. War is a great maturing agent. There is, moreover, an air of seasoned authority abroad. Many who were second lieutenants or lance corporals three months ago are now commanding companies and platoons. Bobby Little is in command of "A" Company: if he can cling to this precarious eminence for thirty days—that is, if no one is sent out to supersede him—he becomes an "automatic" captain, aged twenty! Major Kemp commands the battalion; Wagstaffe is his senior major. Ayling has departed from our midst, and rumour says that he is leading a sort of Pooh Bah existence at Brigade Headquarters.

There are sad gaps among our old friends of the rank and file. Ogg and Hogg, M'Slattery and M'Ostrich, have gone to the happy hunting-grounds. Private Dunshie, the General Specialist (who, you may remember, found his true vocation, after many days, as battalion chiropodist), is reported "missing." But his comrades are positive that no harm has befallen him. Long experience has convinced them that in the art of landing on his feet their departed friend has no equal.

"I doot he'll be a prisoner," suggests the faithful Mucklewame to the
Transport Sergeant.

"Aye," assents the Transport Sergeant bitterly; "he'll be a prisoner. No doot he'll try to pass himself off as an officer, for to get better quarters!"

(The Transport Sergeant, in whose memory certain enormities of Dunshie had rankled ever since that versatile individual had abandoned the veterinary profession, owing to the most excusable intervention of a pack-mule's off hind leg, was not far out in his surmise, as subsequent history may some day reveal. But the telling of that story is still a long way off.)

Company Sergeant-Major Pumpherston is now Sergeant-Major of the Battalion. Mucklewame is a corporal in his old company. Private Tosh was "offered a stripe," too, but declined, because the invitation did not include Private Cosh, who, owing to a regrettable lapse not unconnected with the rum ration, had been omitted from the Honours' List. Consequently these two grim veterans remain undecorated, but they are objects of great veneration among the recently joined for all that.

So you see us once more in harness, falling into the collar with energy, if not fervour. We no longer regard War with the least enthusiasm: we have seen It, face to face. Our sole purpose now is to screw our sturdy followers up to the requisite pitch of efficiency, and keep them remorselessly at that standard until the dawn of triumphant and abiding peace.

We have one thing upon our side—youth.

"Most of our regular senior officers are gone, sir," remarked Colonel Kemp one day to the Brigadier— "dead, or wounded, or promoted to other commands; and I have something like twenty new subalterns. When you subtract a centenarian like myself, the average age of our Battalion Mess, including Company Commanders, works out at something under twenty-three. But I am not exchanging any of them, thanks!"

III

Trench-life in Belgium is an entirely different proposition from trench-life in France. The undulating country in which we now find ourselves offers an infinite choice of unpleasant surroundings.

Down south, Vermelles way, the trenches stretch in a comparatively straight line for miles, facing one another squarely, and giving little opportunity for tactical enterprise. The infantry blaze and sputter at one another in front; the guns roar behind; and that is all there is to be said about it. But here, the line follows the curve of each little hill. At one place you are in a salient, in a trench which runs round the face of a bulging "knowe"—a tempting target for shells of every kind. A few hundred yards farther north, or south, the ground is much lower, and the trench-line runs back into a re-entrant, seeking for a position which shall not be commanded from higher ground in front.

The line is pierced at intervals by railway-cuttings, which have to be barricaded, and canals, which require special defences. Almost every spot in either line is overlooked by some adjacent ridge, or enfiladed from some adjacent trench. It is disconcerting for a methodical young officer, after cautiously scrutinising the trench upon his front through a periscope, to find that the entire performance has been visible (and his entire person exposed) to the view of a Boche trench situated on a hill-slope upon his immediate left.

And our trench-line, with its infinity of salients and re-entrants, is itself only part of the great salient of "Wipers." You may imagine with what methodical solemnity the Boche "crumps" the interior of that constricted area. Looking round at night, when the star-shells float up over the skyline, one could almost imagine one's self inside a complete circle, instead of a horseshoe.

The machine-gunners of both sides are extremely busy. In the plains of France the pursuit of their nefarious trade was practically limited to front-line work. When they did venture to indulge in what they called "overhead" fire, their friends in the forefront used to summon them after the performance, and reproachfully point out sundry ominous rents and abrasions in the back of the front-line parapet. But here they can withdraw behind a convenient ridge, and *strafe* Boches a mile and a half away, without causing any complaints. Needless to say, Brother Boche is not backward in returning the compliment. He has one gun in particular which never tires in its efforts to rouse us from *ennui*. It must be a long way off, for we can only just hear the report. Moreover, its contribution to our liveliness, when it does arrive, falls at an extremely steep angle—so steep, indeed, that it only just clears the embankment under which we live, and falls upon the very doorsteps of the dug-outs with which that sanctuary is honeycombed.

This invigorating shower is turned on regularly for ten minutes, at three, six, nine, and twelve o'clock daily. Its area of activity includes our tiny but, alas! steadily growing cemetery. One evening a regiment which had recently "taken over" selected 6 P.M. as a suitable hour for a funeral. The result was a grimly humorous spectacle—the mourners, including the Commanding Officer and officiating clergy, taking hasty cover in a truly novel trench; while the central figure of the obsequies, sublimely indifferent to the Hun and all his frightfulness, lay on the grass outside, calm and impassive amid the whispering hail of bullets.

As for the trenches themselves—well, as the immortal costermonger observed, "there ain't no word in the blooming language" for them.

In the first place, there is no settled trench-line at all. The Salient has been a battlefield for twelve months past. No one has ever had the time, or opportunity, to construct anything in the shape of permanent defences. A shallow trench, trimmed with an untidy parapet of sandbags, and there is your stronghold! For rest and meditation, a hole in the ground, half-full of water and roofed with a sheet of galvanised iron; or possibly a glorified rabbit-burrow in a canal-bank. These things, as a modern poet has observed, are all right in the summer-time. But winter here is a disintegrating season. It rains heavily for, say, three days. Two days of sharp frost succeed, and the rain-soaked earth is reduced to the necessary degree of friability. Another day's rain, and trenches and dug-outs come sliding down like melted butter. Even if you revet the trenches, it is not easy to drain them. The only difference is that if your line is situated on the forward slope of a hill the support trench drains into the firing-trench; if they are on the reverse slope, the firing-trench drains into the support trench. Our indefatigable friends Box and Cox, of the Royal Engineers, assisted by sturdy Pioneer Battalions, labour like heroes; but the utmost they can achieve, in a low-lying country like this, is to divert as much water as possible into some other Brigade's area. Which they do, right cunningly.

In addition to the Boche, we wage continuous warfare with the elements, and the various departments of Olympus render us characteristic assistance. The Round Game Department has issued a set of rules for the correct method of massaging and greasing the feet. (Major Wagstaffe refers to this as, "Sole-slapping; or What to do in the Children's Hour; complete in Twelve Fortnightly Parts.") The Fairy Godmother Department presents us with what the Quartermaster describes as "Boots, gum, thigh"; and there has also been an issue of so-called fur jackets, in which the Practical Joke Department has plainly taken a hand. Most of these garments appear to have been contributed by animals unknown to zoology, or more probably by a syndicate thereof. Corporal Mucklewame's costume gives him the appearance of a St. Bernard dog with Astrakhan fore legs. Sergeant Carfrae is attired in what looks like the skin of Nana, the dog-nurse in "Peter Pan." Private Nigg, an undersized youth of bashful disposition, creeps forlornly about his duties disguised as an imitation leopard. As he passes by, facetious persons pull what is left of his tail. Private Tosh, on being confronted with his winter *trousseau*, observed bitterly—

"I jined the Airmy for tae be a sojer; but I doot they must have pit me doon as a mountain goat!"

Still, though our variegated pelts cause us to resemble an unsuccessful compromise between Esau and an Eskimo, they keep our bodies warm. We wish we could say the same for our feet. On good days we stand ankle-deep; on bad, we are occasionally over the knees. Thrice blessed then are our Boots, Gum, Thigh, though even these cannot altogether ward off frost-bite and chilblains.

Over the way, Brother Boche is having a bad time of it: his trenches are in a worse state than ours. Last night a plaintive voice cried out—

"Are you dere, Jock? Haf you whiskey? We haf plenty water!"

Not bad for a Boche, the platoon decided.

There is no doubt that whatever the German General Staff may think about the war and the future, the German Infantry soldier is "fed-up." His satiety takes the form of a craving for social intercourse with the foe. In the small hours, when the vigilance of the German N.C.O.'s is relaxed, and the officers are probably in their dug-outs, he makes rather pathetic overtures. We are frequently invited to come out and shake hands. "Dis war will be ober the nineteen of nex' month!" (Evidently the Kaiser has had another revelation.) The other morning a German soldier, with a wisp of something white in his hand, actually clambered out of the firing-trench and advanced towards our lines. The distance was barely seventy yards. No shot was fired, but you may be sure that safety-catches were hastily released. Suddenly, in the tense silence, the ambassador's nerve failed him. He bolted back, followed by a few desultory bullets. The reason for his sudden panic was never rightly ascertained, but the weight of public opinion inclined to the view that Mucklewame, who had momentarily exposed himself above the parapet, was responsible.

"I doot he thocht ye were a lion escapit from the Scottish Zoo!" explained a brother corporal, referring to his indignant colleague's new winter coat.

Here is another incident, with a different ending. At one point our line approaches to within fifteen yards of the Boche trenches. One wet and dismal dawn, as the battalion stood to arms in the neighbourhood of this delectable spot, there came a sudden shout from the enemy, and an outburst of rapid rifle fire. Almost simultaneously two breathless and unkempt figures tumbled over our parapet into the firing-trench. The fusillade died away.

To the extreme discomfort and shame of a respectable citizen of Bannockburn, one Private Buncle, the more hairy of the two visitors, upon recovering his feet, promptly flung his arms around his neck and kissed him on both cheeks. The outrage was repeated, by his companion, upon Private Nigg. At the same time both visitors broke into a joyous chant of "Russky! Russky!" They were escaped Russian prisoners.

When taken to Headquarters they explained that they had been brought up to perform fatigue work near the German trenches, and had seized upon a quiet moment to slip into some convenient undergrowth. Later, under cover of night, they had made their way in the direction of the firing-line, arriving just in time to make a dash before daylight discovered them. You may imagine their triumphal departure from our trenches—loaded with cigarettes, chocolate, bully beef, and other imperishable souvenirs.

We have had other visitors. One bright day a Boche aeroplane made a reconnaissance of our lines. It was a beautiful thing, white and birdlike. But as its occupants were probably taking photographs of our most secret fastnesses, artistic appreciation was dimmed by righteous wrath—wrath which turned to profound gratification when a philistine British plane appeared in the blue and engaged the glittering stranger in battle. There was some very pretty aerial manoeuvring, right over our heads, as the combatants swooped and circled for position. We could hear their machine-guns pattering away; and the volume of sound was increased by the distant contributions of "Coughing Clara"—our latest anti-aircraft gun, which appears to suffer from chronic irritation of the mucous membrane.

Suddenly the German aeroplane gave a lurch; then righted herself; then began to circle down, making desperate efforts to cross the neutral line. But the British airman headed her off. Next moment she lurched again, and then took a "nosedive" straight into the British trenches. She fell on open ground, a few hundred yards behind our second line. The place had been a wilderness a moment before; but the crowd which instantaneously sprang up round the wreck could not have been less than two hundred strong. (One observes the same uncanny phenomenon in London, when a cab-horse falls down in a deserted street.) However, it melted away at the rebuke of the first officer who hurried to the spot, the process of dissolution being accelerated by several bursts of German shrapnel.

Both pilot and observer were dead. They had made a gallant fight, and were buried the same evening, with all honour, in the little cemetery, alongside many who had once been their foes, but were now peacefully neutral.

IV

The housing question in Belgium confronts us with several novel problems. It is not so easy to billet troops here, especially in the Salient, as in France. Some of us live in huts, others in tents, others in dug-outs. Others, more fortunate, are loaded on to a fleet of motor-buses and whisked off to more civilised dwellings many miles away. These buses once plied for hire upon the streets of London. Each bus is in charge of the identical pair of cross-talk comedians who controlled its destinies in more peaceful days. Strangely attired in khaki and sheepskin, they salute officers with cheerful *bonhomie*, and bellow to one another throughout the journey the simple and primitive jests of their previous incarnation, to the huge delight of their fares.

The destination-boards and advertisements are no more, for the buses are painted a neutral green all over; but the conductor is always ready and willing to tell you what his previous route was.

"That Daimler behind you, sir," he informs you, "is one of the Number Nineteens. Set you down at the top of Sloane Street many a time, I'll be bound. Ernie"—this to the driver, along the side of the bus—"you oughter have slowed down when thet copper waved his little flag: he wasn't pleased with yer, ole son!" (The "copper" is a military mounted policeman, controlling the traffic of a little town which lies on our way to the trenches.) "This is a Number Eight, sir. No, that dent in the staircase wasn't done by no shell. The ole girl got that through a skid up against a lamp-post, one wet Saturday night in the Vauxhall Bridge Road. Dangerous place, London!"

We rattle through a brave little town, which is "carrying on" in the face of paralysed trade and periodical shelling. Soldiers abound. All are muddy, but some are muddier than others. The latter are going up to the trenches, the former are coming back. Upon the walls, here and there, we notice a gay poster advertising an entertainment organised by certain Divisional troops, which is to be given nightly throughout the week. At the foot of the bill is printed in large capitals, A HOOGE SUCCESS! We should like to send a copy of that plucky document to Brother Boche. He would not understand it, but it would annoy him greatly.

Now we leave the town behind, and quicken up along the open road—an interminable ribbon of *pavé*, absolutely straight, and bordered upon either side by what was once macadam, but is now a quagmire a foot deep. Occasionally there is a warning cry of "Wire!" and the outside fares hurriedly bow from the waist, in order to avoid having their throats cut by a telephone wire—"Gunners for a dollar!" surmises a strangled voice—tightly stretched across the road between two poplars. Occasionally, too, that indefatigable humorist, Ernie, directs his course beneath some low-spreading branches, through which the upper part of the bus crashes remorselessly, while the passengers, lying sardine-wise upon the roof uplift their voices in profane and bloodthirsty chorus.

"Nothing like a bit o' fun on the way to the trenches, boys! It may be the last you'll get!" is the only apology which Ernie offers.

* * * * *

Presently our vehicle bumps across a nubbly bridge, and enters what was once a fair city. It is a walled city, like Chester, and is separated from the surrounding country by a moat as wide as the upper Thames. In days gone by those ramparts and that moat could have held an army at bay—and probably did, more than once. They have done so yet again; but at what a cost!

We glide through the ancient gateway and along the ghostly streets, and survey the crowning achievement of the cultured Boche. The great buildings—the Cathedral, the Cloth Hall—are jagged ruins. The fronts of the houses have long disappeared, leaving the interiors exposed to view, like a doll's house. Here is a street full of shops. That heap of splintered wardrobes and legless tables was once a furniture warehouse. That snug little corner house, with the tottering zinc counter and the twisted beer engine, is an obvious estaminet. You may observe the sign, "Aux Deux Amis," in dingy lettering over the doorway. Here is an oil-and-colour shop: you can still see the red ochre and white lead splashed about among the ruins.

In almost every house the ceilings of the upper floors have fallen in. Chairs, tables, and bedsteads hang precariously into the room below. Here and there a picture still adheres to the wall. From one of the bedposts flutters a tattered and diminutive garment of blue and white check—some little girl's frock. Where is that little girl now, we wonder; and has she got another frock?

One is struck above all things with the minute detail of the damage. You would say that a party of lunatics had been let loose on the city with coal-hammers: there is hardly a square yard of any surface which is not pierced, or splintered, or dented. The whole fabric of the place lies prostrate, under a shroud of broken bricks and broken plaster. The Hun has said in his majesty: "If you will not yield me this, the last city in the last corner of Belgium, I can at least see to it that not one stone thereof remains upon another.—So yah!"

Such is the appearance presented by the venerable and historic city of Ypres, after fifteen months of personal contact with the apostles of the new civilisation. Only the methodical and painstaking Boche could have reduced a town of such a size to such a state. Imagine Chester in a similar condition, and you may realise the number of shells which have fallen, and are still falling, into the stricken city.

But—the main point to observe is this. We are inside, and the Boche is outside! Fenced by a mighty crescent of prosaic trenches, themselves manned by paladins of an almost incredible stolidity, Ypres still points her broken fingers to the sky—shattered, silent, but inviolate still; and all owing to the obstinacy of a dull and unready nation which merely keeps faith and stands by its friends. Such an attitude of mind is incomprehensible to the Boche, and we are well content that it should be so.

II

SHELL OUT!

I

This, according to our latest subaltern from home, is the title of a *revue* which is running in Town; but that is a mere coincidence. The entertainment to which I am now referring took place in Flanders, and the leading parts were assigned to distinguished members of "K (1)."

The scene was the Château de Grandbois, or some other kind of Bois; possibly Vert. Not that we called it that: we invariably referred to it afterwards as Hush Hall, for reasons which will be set forth in due course.

One morning, while sojourning in what Olympus humorously calls a rest-camp,—a collection of antiquated wigwams half submerged in a mud-flat,—we received the intelligence that we were to extricate ourselves forthwith, and take over a fresh sector of trenches. The news was doubly unwelcome, because, in the first place, it is always unpleasant to face the prospect of trenches of any kind; and secondly, to take over strange trenches in the dead of a winter night is an experience which borders upon nightmare—the hot-lobster-and-toasted-cheese variety.

The opening stages of this enterprise are almost ritualistic in their formality. First of all, the Brigade Staff which is coming in visits the Headquarters of the Brigade which is going out—usually a château or farm somewhere in rear of the trenches—and makes the preliminary arrangements. After that the Commanding Officers and Company Commanders of the incoming battalions visit their own particular section of the line. They are shown over the premises by the outgoing tenants, who make little or no attempt to conceal their satisfaction at the expiration of their lease. The Colonels and the Captains then return to camp, with depressing tales of crumbling parapets, noisome dug-outs, and positions open to enfilade.

On the day of the relief various advance parties go up, keeping under the lee of hedges and embankments, and marching in single file. (At least, that is what they are supposed to do. If not ruthlessly shepherded, they will advance in fours along the skyline.) Having arrived, they take over such positions as can be relieved by daylight in comparative safety. They also take over trench-stores, and exchange trench-gossip. The latter is a fearsome and uncanny thing. It usually begins life at the "refilling point," where the A.S.C. motor-lorries dump down next day's rations, and the regimental transport picks them up.

An A.S.C. Sergeant mentions casually to a regimental Quartermaster that he has heard it said at the Supply Dépôt that heavy firing has been going on in the Channel. The Quartermaster, on returning to the Transport Lines, observes to his Quartermaster-Sergeant that the German Fleet has come out at last. The Quartermaster-Sergeant, when he meets the ration parties behind the lines that night, announces to a platoon Sergeant that we have won a great naval victory. The platoon Sergeant, who is suffering from trench feet and is a constant reader of a certain pessimistic halfpenny journal, replies gloomily: "We'll have had heavy losses oorselves, too, I doot!" This observation is overheard by various members of the ration party. By midnight several hundred yards of the firing-line know for a fact that there has been a naval disaster of the first magnitude off the coast of a place which every one calls Gally Polly, and that the whole of our Division are to be transferred forthwith to the Near East to stem the tide of calamity.

Still, we must have *something* to chat about.

* * * * *

Meanwhile Brigade Majors and Adjutants, holding a stumpy pencil in one hand and a burning brow in the other, are composing Operation Orders which shall effect the relief, without—

(1) Leaving some detail—the bombers, or the snipers, or the sock-driers, or the pea-soup experts—unrelieved altogether.

(2) Causing relievers and relieved to meet violently together in some constricted fairway.

(3) Trespassing into some other Brigade Area. (This is far more foolhardy than to wander into the German lines.)

(4) Getting shelled.

Pitfall Number One is avoided by keeping a permanent and handy list of "all the people who do funny things on their own" (as the vulgar throng call the "specialists"), and checking it carefully before issuing Orders.

Number Two is dealt with by issuing a strict time-table, which might possibly be adhered to by a well-drilled flock of archangels, in broad daylight, upon good roads, and under peace conditions.

Number Three is provided for by copious and complicated map references.

Number Four is left to Providence—and is usually the best-conducted feature of the excursion.

Under cover of night the Battalion sets out, in comparatively small parties. They form a strange procession. The men wear their trench-costume—thigh-boots (which do not go well with a kilt), variegated coats of skins, and woollen nightcaps. Stuffed under their belts and through their packs they carry newspapers, broken staves for firewood, parcels from home, and sandbags loaded with mysterious comforts. A dilapidated parrot and a few goats are all that is required to complete the picture of Robinson Crusoe changing camp.

Progress is not easy. It is a pitch-black night. By day, this road (and all the countryside) is a wilderness: nothing more innocent ever presented itself to the eye of an inquisitive aeroplane. But after nightfall it is packed with troops and transport, and not a light is shown. If you can imagine what the Mansion House crossing would be like if called upon to sustain its midday traffic at midnight—the Mansion House crossing entirely unilluminated, paved with twelve inches of liquid mud, intersected by narrow strips of *pavé*, and liberally pitted with "crump-holes"—you may derive some faint idea of the state of things at a busy road-junction lying behind the trenches.

Until reaching what is facetiously termed "the shell area"—as if any spot in this benighted district were not a shell area—the troops plod along in fours at the right of the road. If they can achieve two miles an hour, they do well. At any moment they may be called upon to halt, and crowd into the roadside, while a transport-train passes carrying rations, and coke, and what is called "R.E. material"—this may be anything from a bag of nails to steel girders nine feet long—up to the firing-line. When this procession, consisting of a dozen limbered waggons, drawn by four mules and headed by a profane person on horseback—the Transport Officer—has rumbled past, the Company, which has been standing respectfully in the ditch, enjoying a refreshing shower-bath of mud and hoping that none of the steel girders are projecting from the limber more than a yard or two, sets out once more upon its way—only to take hasty cover again as sounds of fresh and more animated traffic are heard approaching from the opposite direction. There is no mistaking the nature of this cavalcade: the long vista of glowing cigarette-ends tells an unmistakable tale. These are artillery waggons, returning empty from replenishing the batteries; scattering homely jests like hail, and proceeding, wherever possible, at a hand-gallop. He is a cheery soul, the R.A. driver, but his interpretation of the rules of the road requires drastic revision.

Sometimes an axle breaks, or a waggon side-slips off the *pavé* into the morass reserved for infantry, and overturns. The result is a block, which promptly extends forward and back for a couple of miles. A peculiarly British chorus of inquiry and remonstrance—a blend of biting sarcasm and blasphemous humour—surges up and down the line; until plunging mules are unyoked, and the offending vehicle man-handled out of sight into the inky blackness by the roadside; or, in extreme cases, is annihilated with axes. Everything has to make way for a ration train. To crown all, it is more than likely that the calmness and smooth working of the proceedings will be assisted by a burst of shrapnel overhead. It is a most amazing scrimmage altogether. One of those members of His Majesty's Opposition who are doing so much at present to save our country from destruction, by kindly pointing out the mistakes of the British Government and the British Army, would refer to the whole scene as a pandemonium of mismanagement and ineptitude. And yet, though the scene is enacted night after night without a break, there is hardly a case on record of the transport being surprised upon these roads by the coming of daylight, and none whatever of the rations and ammunition failing to get through.

It is difficult to imagine that Brother Boche, who on the other side of that ring of star-shells is conducting a precisely similar undertaking, is able, with all his perfect organisation and cast-iron methods, to achieve a result in any way superior to that which Thomas Atkins reaches by rule of thumb and sheer force of character.

* * * * *

At length the draggled Company worms its way through the press to the fringe of the shell-area, beyond which no transport may pass. The distance of this point from the trenches varies considerably, and depends largely upon the caprice of the Boche. On this occasion, however, we still have a mile or two to go—across country now, in single file, at the heels of a guide from the battalion which we are relieving.

Guides may be divided into two classes—

(1) Guides who do not know the way, and say so at the outset.

(2) Guides who do not know the way, but leave it to you to discover the fact.

There are no other kinds of guides.

The pace is down to a mile an hour now, except in the case of men in the tail of the line, who are running rapidly. It is a curious but quite inexplicable fact that if you set a hundred men to march in single file in the dark, though the leading man may be crawling like a tortoise, the last man is compelled to proceed at a profane double if he is to avoid being left behind and lost.

Still, everybody gets there somehow, and in due course the various
Company Commanders are enabled to telephone to their respective
Battalion Headquarters the information that the Relief is completed.
For this relief, much thanks!

After that the outgoing Battalion files slowly out, and the newcomers are left gloomily contemplating their new abiding-place, and observing—

"I wonder if there is *any* Division in the whole blessed Expeditionary Force, besides ours, which ever does a single damn thing to keep its trenches in repair!"

II

All of which brings us back to Hush Hall, where the Headquarters of the outgoing Brigade are handing over to their successors.

Hush Hall, or the Château de Quelquechose, is a modern country house, and once stood up white and gleaming in all its brave finery of stucco, conservatories, and ornamental lake, amid a pleasant wood not far from a main road. It is such a house as you might find round about Guildford or Hindhead. There are many in this fair countryside, but few are inhabited now, and none by their rightful owners. They are all marked on the map, and the Boche gunners are assiduous map-readers. Hush Hall has got off comparatively lightly. It is still habitable, and well furnished. The roof is demolished upon the side most exposed to the enemy, and many of the trees in the surrounding wood are broken and splintered by shrapnel. Still, provided the weather remains passable, one can live there. Upon the danger-side the windows are closed and shuttered. Weeds grow apace in the garden. No smoke emerges from the chimneys. (If it does, the Mess Corporal hears about it from the Staff Captain.) A few strands of barbed wire obstruct the passage of those careless or adventurous persons who may desire to explore the forbidden side of the house. The front door is bolted and barred: visitors, after approaching stealthily along the lee of a hedge, like travellers of dubious *bona fides* on a Sunday afternoon, enter unobtrusively by the back door, which is situated on the blind side of the château. Their path thereto is beset by imploring notices like the following:—

THE SLIGHTEST MOVEMENT DRAWS SHELL FIRE. KEEP CLOSE TO THE HEDGE

A later hand has added the following moving postscript:—

WE LIVE HERE. YOU DON'T!

It was the Staff Captain who was responsible for the rechristening of the establishment.

"What sort of place is this new palace we are going to doss in?" inquired the Machine-Gun Officer, when the Staff Captain returned from his preliminary visit.

The Staff Captain, who was a man of a few words, replied—

"It's the sort of shanty where everybody goes about in felt slippers, saying 'Hush!'"

* * * * *

Brigade Headquarters—this means the Brigadier, the Brigade Major, the Staff Captain, the Machine-Gun Officer, the Signal Officer, mayhap a Padre and a Liaison Officer, accompanied by a mixed multitude of clerks, telegraphists, and scullions—arrived safely at their new quarters under cover of night, and were hospitably received by the outgoing tenants, who had finished their evening meal and were girded up for departure. In fact, the Machine-Gun Officer, Liaison Officer, and Padre had already gone, leaving their seniors to hold the fort till the last. The Signal Officer was down in the cellar, handing over ohms, ampères, short-circuits, and other mysterious trench-stores to his "opposite number."

Upon these occasions there is usually a good deal of time to fill in between the arrival of the new brooms and the departure of the old. This period of waiting may be likened to that somewhat anxious interval with which frequenters of race-courses are familiar, between the finish of the race and the announcement of the "All Right!" The outgoing Headquarters are waiting for the magic words—"Relief Complete!" Until that message comes over the buzzer, the period of tension endures. The main point of difference is that the gentleman who has staked his fortune on the legs of a horse has only to wait a few minutes for the confirmation of his hopes; while a Brigadier, whose bedtime (or even breakfast-time) is at the mercy of an errant platoon, may have to sit up all night.

"Sit down and make yourselves comfortable," said A Brigade to X Brigade.

X Brigade complied, and having been furnished with refreshment, led off with the inevitable question—

"Does one—er—get shelled much here?"

There was a reassuring coo from A Brigade.

"Oh, no. This is a very healthy spot. One has to be careful, of course. No movement, or fires, or anything of that kind. A sentry or two, to warn people against approaching over the open by day, and you'll be as cooshie as anything!" ("Cooshie" is the latest word here. That and "crump.")

"I ought to warn you of one thing," said the Brigadier. "Owing to the surrounding woods, sound is most deceptive here. You will hear shell-bursts which appear quite close, when in reality they are quite a distance away. That, for instance!"—as a shell exploded apparently just outside the window. "That little fellow is a couple of hundred yards away, in the corner of the wood. The Boche has been groping about there for a battery for the last two days."

"Is the battery there?" inquired a voice.

"No; it is farther east. But there is a Gunner's Mess about two hundred yards from here, in that house which you passed on the way up."

"Oh!" observed X Brigade.

Gunners are peculiar people. When professionally engaged, no men could be more retiring. They screen their operations from the public gaze with the utmost severity, shrouding batteries in screens of foliage and other rustic disguises. If a layman strays anywhere near one of these arboreal retreats, a gunner thrusts out a visage enflamed with righteous wrath, and curses him for giving the position away. But in his hours of relaxation the gunner is a different being. He billets himself in a house with plenty of windows: he illuminates all these by night, and hangs washing therefrom by day. When inclined for exercise, he goes for a promenade across an open space labelled—"Not to be used by troops by daylight." Therefore, despite his technical excellence and superb courage, he is an uncomfortable neighbour for establishments like Hush Hall.

In this respect he offers a curious contrast to the Sapper. Off duty, the Sapper is the most unobtrusive of men—a cave-man, in fact. He burrows deep into the earth, or the side of a hill, and having secured the roof of this cavern against direct hits by ingenious contrivances of his own manufacture, constructs a suite of furniture of a solid and enduring pattern, and lives the life of a comfortable recluse. But when engaged in the pursuit of his calling, the Sapper is the least retiring of men. The immemorial tradition of the great Corps to which he belongs has ordained that no fire, however fierce, must be allowed to interfere with a Sapper in the execution of his duty. This rule is usually interpreted by the Sapper to mean that you must not perform your allotted task under cover when it is possible to do so under fire. To this is added, as a rider, that in the absence of an adequate supply of fire, you must draw fire. So the Sapper walks cheerfully about on the tops of parapets, hugging large and conspicuous pieces of timber, or clashing together sheets of corrugated iron, as happy as a king.

"You will find this house quite snug," continued the Brigadier. "The eastern suite is to be avoided, because there is no roof there; and if it rains outside for a day, it rains in the best bedroom for a week. There is a big kitchen in the basement, with a capital range. That's all, I think. The chief thing to avoid is movement of any kind. The leaves are coming off the trees now—"

At this moment an orderly entered the room with a pink telegraph message.

"Relief complete, sir!" announced the Brigade Major, reading it.

"Good work!" replied both Brigadiers, looking at their watches simultaneously, "considering the state of the country." The Brigadier of "A" rose to his feet.

"Now we can pass along quietly," he said. "Good luck to you. By the way, take care of Edgar, won't you? Any little attention which you can show him will be greatly appreciated."

"Who is Edgar?"

"Oh, I thought the Staff Captain would have told you. Edgar is the swan—the last of his race, I'm afraid, so far as this place is concerned. He lives on the lake, and usually comes ashore to draw his rations about lunch-time. He is inclined to be stand-offish on one side, as he has only one eye; but he is most affable on the other. Well, now to find our horses!"

As the three officers departed down the backdoor steps, a hesitating voice followed them—"H'm! Is there any place where one can go—a cellar, or any old spot of that kind—just in case we are—"

"Bless you, you'll be all right!" was the cheery reply. (The outgoing Brigade is always excessively cheery.) "But there are dug-outs over there—in the garden. They haven't been occupied for some months, so you may find them a bit ratty. You won't require them, though. Good-night!"

III

Whizz! Boom! Bang! Crash! Wump!

"It's just as well," mused the Brigade Major, turning in his sleep about three o'clock the following morning, "that they warned us about the deceptive sound of the shelling here. One would almost imagine that it was quite close…. That last one was heavy stuff: it shook the whole place!… This is a topping mattress: it would be rotten having to take to the woods again after getting into really cooshie quarters at last…. There they go again!" as a renewed tempest of shells rent the silence of night. "That old battery must be getting it in the neck!… Hallo, I could have sworn something hit the roof that time! A loose slate, I expect! Anyhow …"

The Brigade Major, who had had a very long day, turned over and went to sleep again.

IV

The next morning, a Sunday, broke bright and clear. Contrary to his usual habit, the Brigade Major took a stroll in the garden before breakfast. The first object which caught his eye, as he came down the back-door steps, was the figure of the Staff Captain, brooding pensively over a large crater, close to the hedge. The Brigade Major joined him.

"I wonder if that was there yesterday!" he observed, referring to the crater.

"Couldn't have been," growled the Staff Captain. "We walked to the house along this very hedge. No craters then!"

"True!" agreed the Brigade Major amiably. He turned and surveyed the garden. "That lawn looks a bit of a golf course. What lovely bunkers!"

"They appear to be quite new, too," remarked the Staff Captain thoughtfully. "Come to breakfast!"

On their way back they found the Brigadier, the Machine-Gun Officer, and the Padre, gazing silently upward.

"I wonder when that corner of the house got knocked off," the M.G.O. was observing.

"Fairly recently, I should say," replied the Brigadier.

"Those marks beside your bedroom window, sir,—they look pretty fresh!" interpolated the Padre, a sincere but somewhat tactless Christian.

Brigade Headquarters regarded one another with dubious smiles.

"I *wonder*," began a tentative voice, "if those fellows last night were indulging in a leg-pull—what is called in this country a *lire-jambe*—when they assured us—"

WHOO-OO-OO-OO-UMP!

A shell came shrieking over the tree-tops, and fell with a tremendous splash into the geometrical centre of the lake, fifty yards away.

* * * * *

For the next two hours, shrapnel, "whizz-bangs," "Silent Susies," and other explosive wildfowl raged round the walls of Hush Hall. The inhabitants thereof, some twenty persons in all, were gathered in various apartments on the lee side.

"It is still possible," remarked the Brigadier, lighting his pipe, "that they are not aiming at us. However, it is just as inconvenient to be buried by accident as by design. As soon as the first direct hit is registered upon this imposing fabric, we will retire to the dug-outs. Send word to the kitchen that every one is to be ready to clear out of the house when necessary."

Next moment there came a resounding crash, easily audible above the tornado raging in the garden, followed by the sound of splintering glass. Hush Hall rocked. The Mess waiter appeared.

"A shell has just came in through the dining-room window, sirr," he informed the Mess President, "and broke three of they new cups!"

"How tiresome!" said the Brigadier. "Dug-outs, everybody!"

V

There were no casualties, which was rather miraculous. Late in the afternoon Brigade Headquarters ventured upon another stroll in the garden. The tumult had ceased, and the setting Sabbath sun glowed peacefully upon the battered countenance of Hush Hall. The damage was not very extensive, for the house was stoutly built. Still, two bedrooms, recently occupied, were a wreck of broken glass and splintered plaster, while the gravel outside was littered with lead sheeting and twisted chimney-cans. The shell which had aroused the indignation of the Mess waiter by entering the dining-room window, had in reality hit the ground directly beneath it. Six feet higher, and the Brigadier's order to clear the house would have been entirely superfluous.

The Brigade Major and the Staff Captain surveyed the unruffled surface of the lake—a haunt of ancient peace in the rays of the setting sun. Upon the bosom thereof floated a single, majestic, one-eyed swan, performing intricate toilet exercises. It was Edgar.

"He must have a darned good dug-out somewhere!" observed the Brigade Major enviously.

III

WINTER SPORTS: VARIOUS

I

Hush Hall having become an even less desirable place of residence than had hitherto been thought possible, Headquarters very sensibly sent for their invaluable friends, Box and Cox, of the Royal Engineers, and requested that they would proceed to make the place proof against shells and weather, forthwith, if not sooner.

Those phlegmatic experts made a thorough investigation of the resources of the establishment, and departed mysteriously, after the fashion of the common plumber of civilisation, into space. Three days later they returned, accompanied by a horde of acolytes, who, with characteristic contempt for the pathetic appeals upon the notice-boards, proceeded to dump down lumber, sandbags, and corrugated iron roofing in the most exposed portions of the garden.

This done, some set out to shore up the ceilings of the basement with mighty battens of wood, and to convert that region into a nest of cunningly devised bedrooms. Others reinforced the flooring above with a layer of earth and brick rubble three feet deep. On the top of all this they relaid not only the original floor, but eke the carpet.

"The only difference from before, sir," explained Box to the admiring Staff Captain, "is that people will have to walk up three steps to get into the dining-room now, instead of going in on the level."

"I wonder what the Marquise de Chilquichose will think of it all when she returns to her ancestral home," mused the Staff Captain.

"If anything," maintained the invincible Box, "we have improved it for her. For example, she can now light the chandelier without standing on a chair—without getting up from table, in fact! However, to resume. The fireplace, you will observe, has not been touched. I have left a sort of well in the floor all round it, lined with some stuff I found in Mademoiselle's room. At least," added Box coyly, "I think it must have been Mademoiselle's room! You can sit in the well every evening after supper. The walls of this room"—prodding the same—"are lined with sandbags, covered with tapestry. Pretty artistic—what?"

"Extremely," agreed the Staff Captain. "You will excuse my raising the point, I know, but can the apartment now be regarded as shell-proof?"

"Against everything but a direct hit. I wouldn't advise you to sleep on this floor much, but you could have your meals here all right. Then, if the Boche starts putting over heavy stuff, you can pop down into the basement and have your dessert in bed. You'll be absolutely safe there. In fact, the more the house tumbles down the safer you will be. It will only make your protection shell thicker. So if you hear heavy thuds overhead, don't be alarmed!"

"I won't," promised the Staff Captain. "I shall lie in bed, drinking a nice hot cup of tea, and wondering whether the last crash was the kitchen chimney, or only the drawing-room piano coming down another storey. Now show me my room."

"We have had to put you in the larder," explained Box apologetically, as he steered his guest through a forest of struts with an electric torch. "At least, I think it's the larder: it has a sort of meaty smell. The General is in the dairy—a lovely little suite, with white tiles. The Brigade Major has the scullery: it has a sink, so is practically as good as a flat in Park Place. I have run up cubicles for the others in the kitchen. Here is your little cot. It is only six feet by four, but you can dress in the garden."

"It's a *sweet* little nest, dear!" replied the Staff Captain, quite hypnotised by this time. "I'll just get my maid to put me into something loose, and then I'll run along to your room, and we'll have a nice cosy gossip together before dinner!"

* * * * *

In due course we removed our effects from the tottering and rat-ridden dug-outs in which we had taken sanctuary during the shelling, and prepared to settle down for the winter in our new quarters.

"We might be *very* much worse off!" we observed the first evening, listening to the comfortably muffled sounds of shells overhead.

And we were right. Three days later we received an intimation from the Practical Joke Department that we were to evacuate our present sector of trenches (including Hush Hall) forthwith, and occupy another part of the line.

In all Sports, Winter and Summer, the supremacy of the Practical Joke
Department is unchallenged.

II

Meanwhile, up in the trenches, the combatants are beguiling the time in their several ways.

Let us take the reserve line first—the lair of Battalion Headquarters and its appurtenances. Much of our time here, as elsewhere, is occupied in unostentatious retirement to our dug-outs, to avoid the effects of a bombardment. But a good amount—an increasing amount—of it is devoted to the contemplation of our own shells bursting over the Boche trenches. Gone are the days during which we used to sit close and "stick it out," consoling ourselves with the vague hope that by the end of the week our gunners might possibly have garnered sufficient ammunition to justify a few brief hours' retaliation. The boot is on the other leg now. For every Boche battery that opens on us, two or three of ours thunder back a reply—and that without any delays other than those incidental to the use of that maddening instrument, the field-telephone. During the past six months neither side has been able to boast much in the way of ground actually gained; but the moral ascendancy—the initiative—the offensive—call it what you will—has changed hands; and no one knows it better than the Boche. We are the attacking party now.

The trenches in this country are not arranged with such geometric precision as in France. For instance, the reserve line is not always connected with the firing-lines by a communication-trench. Those persons whose duty it is to pay daily visits to the fire-trenches—Battalion Commanders, Gunner and Sapper officers, an occasional Staff Officer, and an occasional most devoted Padre—perform the journey as best they may. Sometimes they skirt a wood or hedge, sometimes they keep under the lee of an embankment, sometimes they proceed across the open, with the stealthy caution of persons playing musical chairs, ready to sit down in the nearest shell-crater the moment the music—in the form of a visitation of "whizz-bangs"—strikes up.

It is difficult to say which kind of weather is least favourable to this enterprise. On sunny days one's movements are visible to Boche observers upon distant summits; while on foggy days the Boche gunners, being able to see nothing at all, amuse themselves by generous and unexpected contributions of shrapnel in all directions. Stormy weather is particularly unpleasant, for the noise of the wind in the trees makes it difficult to hear the shell approaching. Days of heavy rain are the most desirable on the whole, for then the gunners are too busy bailing out their gun-pits to worry their heads over adventurous pedestrians. One learns, also, to mark down and avoid particular danger-spots. For instance, the southeast corner of that wood, where a reserve company are dug in, is visited by "Silent Susans" for about five minutes each noontide: it is therefore advisable to select some other hour for one's daily visit. (Silent Susan, by the way, is not a desirable member of the sex. Owing to her intensely high velocity she arrives overhead without a sound, and then bursts with a perfectly stunning detonation and a shower of small shrapnel bullets.) There is a fixed rifle-battery, too, which fires all day long, a shot at a time, down the main street of the ruined and deserted village named Vrjoozlehem, through which one must pass on the way to the front-line trenches. Therefore in negotiating this delectable spot, one shapes a laborious course through a series of back yards and garden-plots, littered with broken furniture and brick rubble, allowing the rifle-bullets the undisputed use of the street. The mention of Vrjoozlehem—that is not its real name, but a simplified form of it—brings to our notice the wholesale and whole-hearted fashion in which the British Army has taken Belgian institutions under its wing. Nomenclature, for instance. In France we make no attempt to interfere with this: we content ourselves with devising a pronounceable variation of the existing name. For example, if a road is called La Rue de Bois, we simply call it "Roodiboys," and leave it at that. On the same principle, Etaples is modified to "Eatables," and Sailly-la-Bourse to "Sally Booze." But in Belgium more drastic procedure is required. A Scotsman is accustomed to pronouncing difficult names, but even he is unable to contend with words composed almost entirely of the letters *j, z,* and *v*. So our resourceful Ordnance Department has issued maps—admirable maps—upon which the outstanding features of the landscape are marked in plain figures. But instead of printing the original place-names, they put "Moated Grange," or "Clapham Junction," or "Dead Dog Farm," which simplifies matters beyond all possibility of error. (The system was once responsible, though, for an unjust if unintentional aspersion upon the character of a worthy man. The C.O. of a certain battalion had occasion to complain to those above him of the remissness of one of his chaplains. "He's a lazy beggar, sir," he said. "Over and over again I have told him to come up and show himself in the front-line trenches, but he never seems to be able to get past Leicester Square!")

The naming of the trenches themselves has been left largely to local enterprise. An observant person can tell, by a study of the numerous name-boards, which of his countrymen have been occupying the line during the past six months. "Grainger Street" and "Jesmond Dene" give direct evidence of "Canny N'castle." "Sherwood Avenue" and "Notts Forest" have a Midland flavour. Lastly, no great mental effort is required to decide who labelled two communication trenches "The Gorbals" and "Coocaddens" respectively!

Some names have obviously been bestowed by officers, as "Sackville Street," "The Albany," and "Burlington Arcade" denote. "Pinch-Gut" and "Crab-Crawl" speak for themselves. So does "Vermin Villa." Other localities, again, have obviously been labelled by persons endowed with a nice gift of irony. "Sanctuary Wood" is the last place on earth where any one would dream of taking sanctuary; while "Lovers' Walk," which bounds it, is the scene of almost daily expositions of the choicest brand of Boche "hate."

And so on. But one day, when the War is over, and this mighty trench-line is thrown open to the disciples of the excellent Mr. Cook—as undoubtedly it will be—care should be taken that these street-names are preserved and perpetuated. It would be impossible to select a more characteristic and fitting memorial to the brave hearts who constructed them—too many of whom are sleeping their last sleep within a few yards of their own cheerful handiwork.

III

After this digression we at length reach the firing-line. It is quite unlike anything of its kind that we have hitherto encountered. It is situated in what was once a thick wood. Two fairly well-defined trenches run through the undergrowth, from which the sentries of either side have been keeping relentless watch upon one another, night and day, for many months. The wood itself is a mere forest of poles: hardly a branch, and not a twig, has been spared by the shrapnel. In the no-man's-land between the trenches the poles have been reduced to mere stumps a few inches high.

It is behind the firing-trench that the most unconventional scene presents itself. Strictly speaking, there ought to be—and generally is—a support-line some seventy yards in rear of the first. This should be occupied by all troops not required in the firing-trench. But the trench is empty—which is not altogether surprising, considering that it is half-full of water. Its rightful occupants are scattered through the wood behind—in dug-outs, in redoubts, or *en plein air*—cooking, washing, or repairing their residences. The whole scene suggests a gipsy encampment rather than a fortified post. A hundred yards away, through the trees, you can plainly discern the Boche firing-trench, and the Boche in that trench can discern you: yet never a shot comes. It is true that bullets are humming through the air and glancing off trees, but these are mostly due to the enterprise of distant machine-guns and rifle-batteries, firing from some position well adapted for enfilade. Frontal fire there is little or none. In the front-line trenches, at least, Brother Boche has had enough of it. His motto now is, "Live and let live!" In fact, he frequently makes plaintive statements to that effect in the silence of night.

You might think, then, that life in Willow Grove would be a tranquil affair. But if you look up among the few remaining branches of that tall tree in the centre of the wood, you may notice shreds of some material flapping in the breeze. Those are sandbags—or were. Last night, within the space of one hour, seventy-three shells fell into this wood, and the first of them registered a direct hit upon the dug-out of which those sandbags formed part. There were eight men in that dug-out. The telephone-wires were broken in the first few minutes, and there was some delay before word could be transmitted back to Headquarters. Then our big guns far in rear spoke out, until the enemy's batteries (probably in response to an urgent appeal from their own front line) ceased firing. Thereupon "A" Company, who at Bobby Little's behest had taken immediate cover in the water-logged support-trench, returned stolidly to their dug-outs in Willow Grove. Death, when he makes the mistake of raiding your premises every day, loses most of his terrors and becomes a bit of a bore.

This morning the Company presents its normal appearance: its numbers have been reduced by eight—*c'est tout*! It may be some one else's turn to-morrow, but after all, that is what we are here for. Anyhow, we are keeping the Boches out of "Wipers," and a bit over. So we stretch our legs in the wood, and keep the flooded trench for the next emergency.

Let us approach a group of four which is squatting sociably round a small and inadequate fire of twigs, upon which four mess-tins are simmering. The quartette consists of Privates Cosh and Tosh, together with Privates Buncle and Nigg, preparing their midday meal.

"Tak' off your damp chup, Jimmy," suggested Tosh to Buncle, who was officiating as stoker. "Ye mind what the Captain said aboot smoke?"

"It wasna the Captain: it was the Officer," rejoined Buncle cantankerously.

(It may here be explained, at the risk of another digression, that no length of association or degree of intimacy will render the average British soldier familiar with the names of his officers. The Colonel is "The C.O."; the Second in Command is "The Major"; your Company Commander is "The Captain," and your Platoon Commander "The Officer." As for all others of commissioned rank in the regiment, some twenty-four in all, they are as nought. With the exception of the Quartermaster, in whose shoes each member of the rank and file hopes one day to stand, they simply do not exist.)

"Onyway," pursued the careful Tosh, "he said that if any smoke was shown, all fires was tae be pitten oot. So mind and see no' to get a cauld dinner for us all, Jimmy!"

"Cauld or het," retorted the gentleman addressed, "it's little dinner I'll be gettin' this day! And ye ken fine why!" he added darkly.

Private Tosh removed a cigarette from his lower lip and sighed patiently.

"For the last time," he announced, with the air of a righteous man suffering long, "I did not lay ma hand on your dirrty wee bit ham!"

"Maybe," countered the bereaved Buncle swiftly, "you did not lay your hand upon it; but you had it tae your breakfast for all that, Davie!"

"I never pit ma hand on it!" repeated Tosh doggedly.

"No? Then I doot you gave it a bit kick with your foot," replied the inflexible Buncle.

"Or got some other body tae luft it for him!" suggested Private Nigg, looking hard at Tosh's habitual accomplice, Cosh.

"I had it pitten in an auld envelope from hame, addressed with my name," continued the mourner. "It couldna hae got oot o' that by accident!"

"Weel," interposed Cosh, with forced geniality, "it's no a thing tae argie-bargie aboot. Whatever body lufted it, it's awa' by this time. It's a fine day, boys!"

This flagrant attempt to raise the conversation to a less controversial plane met with no encouragement. Private Buncle, refusing to be appeased, replied sarcastically—

"Aye, is it? And it was a fine nicht last nicht, especially when the shellin' was gaun on! Especially in number seeven dug-oot!"

There was a short silence. Number seven dug-out was no more, and five of its late occupants were now lying under their waterproof sheets, not a hundred yards away, waiting for a Padre. Presently, however, the pacific Cosh, who in his hours of leisure was addicted to mild philosophical rumination, gave a fresh turn to the conversation.

"Mphm!" he observed thoughtfully. "They say that in a war every man has a bullet waiting for him some place or other, with his name on it! Sooner or later, he gets it. Aye! Mphm!" He sucked his teeth reflectively, and glanced towards the Field Ambulance. "Sooner or later!"

"What for would he pit his name on it, Wully?" inquired Nigg, who was not very quick at grasping allusions.

"He wouldna pit on the name himself," explained the philosopher. "What I mean is, there's a bullet for each one of us somewhere over there"—he jerked his head eastward—"in a Gairman pooch."

"What way could a Gairman pit my name on a bullet?" demanded Nigg triumphantly. "He doesna ken it!"

"Man," exclaimed Cosh, shedding some of his philosophic calm, "can ye no unnerstan' that what I telled ye was jist a mainner of speakin'? When I said that a man's name was on a bullet, I didna mean that it was *written* there."

"Then what the hell *did* ye mean?" inquired the mystified disciple—not altogether unreasonably.

Private Tosh made a misguided but well-meaning attempt to straighten out the conversation.

"He means, Sandy," he explained in a soothing voice, "that the name was just stampit on the bullet. Like—like—like an identity disc!" he added brilliantly.

The philosopher clutched his temples with both hands.

"I dinna mean onything o' the kind," he roared. "What I intend tae imply is *this*, Sandy Nigg. Some place over there there is a bullet in a Gairman's pooch, and one day that bullet will find its way intil your insides as sure as if your name was written on it! *That's* what I meant. Jist a mainner of speakin'. Dae ye unnerstand me the noo?"

But it was the injured Buncle who replied—like a lightning-flash.

"Never you fear, Sandy, boy!" he proclaimed to his perturbed ally. "That bullet has no' gotten your length yet. Maybe it never wull. There's mony a thing in this worrld with one man's name on it that finds its way intil the inside of some other man." He fixed Tosh with a relentless eye. "A bit ham, for instance!"

It was a knock-out blow.

"For ony sake," muttered the now demoralised Tosh, "drop the subject, and I'll gie ye a bit ham o' ma ain! There's just time tae cook it—"

"What kin' o' a fire is this?"

A cold shadow fell upon the group as a substantial presence inserted itself between the debaters and the wintry sunshine. Corporal Mucklewame was speaking, in his new and awful official voice, pointing an accusing finger at the fire, which, neglected in the ardour of discussion, was smoking furiously.

"Did you wish the hale wood tae be shelled?" continued Mucklewame sarcastically. "Put oot the fire at once, or I'll need tae bring ye all before the Officer. It is a cauld dinner ye'll get, and ye'll deserve it!"

IV

In the fire-trench—or perhaps it would be more correct to call it the water-trench—life may be short, and is seldom merry; but it is not often dull. For one thing, we are never idle.

A Boche trench-mortar knocks down several yards of your parapet. Straightway your machine-gunners are called up, to cover the gap until darkness falls and the gaping wound can be stanched with fresh sandbags. A mine has been exploded upon your front, leaving a crater into which predatory Boches will certainly creep at night. You summon a *posse* of bombers to occupy the cavity and discourage any such enterprise. The heavens open, and there is a sudden deluge. Immediately it is a case of all hands to the trench-pump! A better plan, if you have the advantage of ground, is to cut a culvert under the parapet and pass the inundation on to a more deserving quarter. In any case you need never lack healthful exercise.

While upon the subject of mines, we may note that this branch of military industry has expanded of late to most unpleasant dimensions. The Boche began it, of course—he always initiates these undesirable pastimes,—and now we have followed his lead and caught him up.

To the ordinary mortal, to become a blind groper amid the dark places of the earth, in search of a foe whom it is almost certain death to encounter there, seems perhaps the most idiotic of all the idiotic careers open to those who are idiotic enough to engage in modern warfare. However, many of us are as much at home below ground as above it. In most peaceful times we were accustomed to spend eight hours a day there, lying up against the "face" in a tunnel perhaps four feet high, and wielding a pick in an attitude which would have convulsed any ordinary man with cramp. But there are few ordinary men in "K(1)" There is never any difficulty in obtaining volunteers for the Tunnelling Company.

So far as the amateur can penetrate its mysteries, mining, viewed under our present heading—namely, Winter Sports—offers the following advantages to its participants:—

(1) In winter it is much warmer below the earth than upon its surface, and Thomas Atkins is the most confirmed "frowster" in the world.

(2) Critics seldom descend into mines.

(3) There is extra pay.

The disadvantages are so obvious that they need not be enumerated here.

In these trenches we have been engaged upon a very pretty game of subterranean chess for some weeks past, and we are very much on our mettle. We have some small leeway to make up. When we took over these trenches, a German mine, which had been maturing (apparently unheeded) during the tenancy of our predecessors, was exploded two days after our arrival, inflicting heavy casualties upon "D" Company. Curiously enough, the damage to the trench was comparatively slight; but the tremendous shock of the explosion killed more than one man by concussion, and brought down the roofs of several dug-outs upon their sleeping occupants. Altogether it was a sad business, and the Battalion swore to be avenged.

So they called upon Lieutenant Duff-Bertram—usually called Bertie the Badger, in reference to his rodent disposition—to make the first move in the return match. So Bertie and his troglodyte assistants sank a shaft in a retired spot of their own selecting, and proceeded to burrow forward towards the Boche lines.

After certain days Bertie presented himself, covered in clay, before
Colonel Kemp, and made a report.

Colonel Kemp considered.

"You say you can hear the enemy working?" he said.

"Yes, sir."

"Near?"

"Pretty near, sir."

"How near?"

"A few yards."

"What do you propose to do?"

Bertie the Badger—in private life he was a consulting mining engineer with a beautiful office in Victoria Street and a nice taste in spats—scratched an earthy nose with a muddy forefinger.

"I think they are making a defensive gallery, sir," he announced.

"Let us have your statement in the simplest possible language, please," said Colonel Kemp. "Some of my younger officers," he added rather ingeniously, "are not very expert in these matters."

Bertie the Badger thereupon expounded the situation with solemn relish. By a defensive gallery, it appeared that he meant a lateral tunnel running parallel with the trench-line, in such a manner as to intercept any tunnel pushed out by the British miners.

"And what do you suggest doing to this Piccadilly Tube of theirs?" inquired the Colonel.

"I could dig forward and break into it, sir," suggested Bertie.

"That seems a move in the right direction," said the Colonel. "But won't the Boche try to prevent you?"

"Yes, sir."

"How?"

"He will wait until the head of my tunnel gets near enough, and then blow it in."

"That would be very tiresome of him. What other alternatives are open to you?"

"I could get as near as possible, sir," replied Bertie calmly, "and then blowup *his* gallery."

"That sounds better. Well, exercise your own discretion, and don't get blown up unless you particularly want to. And above all, be quite sure that while you are amusing yourself with the Piccadilly Tube, the wily Boche isn't burrowing past *you*, and under my parapet, by the Bakerloo! Good luck! Report any fresh development at once."

So Bertie the Badger returned once more to his native element and proceeded to exercise his discretion. This took the form of continuing his aggressive tunnel in the direction of the Boche defensive gallery. Next morning, encouraged by the absolute silence of the enemy's miners, he made a farther and final push, which actually landed him in the "Piccadilly Tube" itself.

"This is a rum go, Howie!" he observed in a low voice to his corporal. "A long, beautiful gallery, five by four, lined with wood, electrically lighted, with every modern convenience—and not a Boche in it!"

"Varra bad discipline, sir!" replied Corporal Howie severely.

"Are you sure it isn't a trap?"

"It may be, sirr; but I doot the oversman is awa' to his dinner, and the men are back in the shaft, doing naething." Corporal Howie had been an "oversman" himself, and knew something of subterranean labour problems.

"Well, if you are right, the Boche must be getting demoralised. It is not like him to present us with openings like this. However, the first thing to do is to distribute a few souvenirs along the gallery. Pass the word back for the stuff. Meanwhile I shall endeavour to test your theory about the oversman's dinner-hour. I am going to creep along and have a look at the Boche entrance to the Tube. It's down there, at the south end, I think. I can see a break in the wood lining. If you hear any shooting, you will know that the dinner-hour is over!"

At the end of half an hour the Piccadilly Tube was lined with sufficient explosive material—securely rammed and tamped—to ensure the permanent closing of the line. Still no Boche had been seen or heard.

"Now, Howie," said Bertie the Badger, fingering the fuse, "what about it?"

"About what, sirr?" inquired Howie, who was not quite *au fait* with current catch-phrases.

"Are we going to touch off all this stuff now, and clear out, or are we going to wait and see?"

"I would like fine—" began the Corporal wistfully.

"So would I," said Bertie. "Tell the men to get back and out; and you and I will hold on until the guests return from the banquet."

"Varra good, sirr."

For another half-hour the pair waited—Bertie the Badger like a dog in its kennel, with his head protruding into the hostile gallery, while his faithful henchman crouched close behind him. Deathly stillness reigned, relieved only by an occasional thud, as a shell or trench-mortar bomb exploded upon the ground above their heads.

"I'm going to have another look round the corner," said Bertie at last. "Hold on to the fuse."

He handed the end of the fuse to his subordinate, and having wormed his way out of the tunnel, proceeded cautiously on all-fours along the gallery. On his way he passed the electric light. He twisted off the bulb and crawled on in the dark.

Feeling his way by the east wall of the gallery, he came presently to the break in the woodwork. Very slowly, lying flat on his stomach now, he wriggled forward until his head came opposite the opening. A low passage ran away to his left, obviously leading back to the Boche trenches. Three yards from the entrance the passage bent sharply to the right, thus interrupting the line of sight.

"There's a light burning just round that bend," said Bertie the Badger to himself. "I wonder if it would be rash to go on and have a look at it!"

He was still straining at this gnat, when suddenly his elbow encountered a shovel which was leaning against the wall of the gallery. It tumbled down with a clatter almost stunning. Next moment a hand came round the bend of the tunnel and fired a revolver almost into the explorer's face.

Another shot rang out directly after.

The devoted Howie, hastening to the rescue, collided sharply with a solid body crawling towards him in the darkness.

"Curse you, Howie!" said the voice of Bertie the Badger, with refreshing earnestness. "Get back out of this! Where's your fuse?"

The pair scrambled back into their own tunnel, and the end of the fuse was soon recovered. Almost simultaneously three more revolver-shots rang out.

"I thought I had fixed that Boche," murmured Bertie in a disappointed voice. "I heard him grunt when my bullet hit him. Perhaps this is another one—or several. Keep back in the tunnel, Howie, confound you, and don't breathe up my sleeve! They are firing straight along the gallery now. I will return the compliment. Ouch!"

"What's the matter, sirr?" inquired the anxious voice of Howie, as his officer, who had tried to fire round the corner with his left hand, gave a sudden exclamation and rolled over upon his side.

"I must have been hit the first time," he explained. "Collar-bone, I think. I didn't know, till I rested my weight on my left elbow…. Howie, I am going to exercise my discretion again. Somebody in this gallery is going to be blown up presently, and if you and I don't get a move on, p.d.q., it will be us! Give me the fuse-lighter, and wait for me at the foot of the shaft. Quick!"

Very reluctantly the Corporal obeyed. However, he was in due course joined at the foot of the shaft by Bertie the Badger, groaning profanely; and the pair made their way to the upper regions with all possible speed. After a short interval, a sudden rumbling, followed by a heavy explosion, announced that the fuse had done its work, and that the Piccadilly Tube, the fruit of many toilsome weeks of Boche calculation and labour, had been permanently closed to traffic of all descriptions.

Bertie the Badger received a Military Cross, and his abettor the
D.C.M.

V

But the newest and most fashionable form of winter sport this season is The Flying Matinée.

This entertainment takes place during the small hours of the morning, and is strictly limited to a duration of ten minutes—quite long enough for most matinées, too. The actors are furnished by a unit of "K(1)" and the rôle of audience is assigned to the inhabitants of the Boche trenches immediately opposite. These matinées have proved an enormous success, but require most careful rehearsal.

It is two A.M., and comparative peace reigns up and down the line. The rain of star-shells, always prodigal in the early evening, has died down to a mere drizzle. Working and fatigue parties, which have been busy since darkness set in at five o'clock,—rebuilding parapets, repairing wire, carrying up rations, and patrolling debatable areas,—have ceased their labours, and are sleeping heavily until the coming of the wintry dawn shall rouse them, grimy and shivering, to another day's unpleasantness.

Private Hans Dumpkopf, on sentry duty in the Boche firing-trench, gazes mechanically over the parapet; but the night is so dark and the wind so high that it is difficult to see and quite impossible to hear anything. He shelters himself beside a traverse, and waits patiently for his relief. It begins to rain, and Hans, after cautiously reconnoitring the other side of the traverse, to guard against prowling sergeants, sidles a few yards to his right beneath the friendly cover of an improvised roof of corrugated iron sheeting, laid across the trench from parapet to parados. It is quite dry here, and comparatively warm. Hans closes his eyes for a moment, and heaves a gentle sigh.

Next moment there comes a rush of feet in the darkness, followed by a metallic clang, as of hobnailed boots on metal. Hans, lying prostrate and half-stunned beneath the galvanised iron sheeting, which, dislodged from its former position by the impact of a heavy body descending from above, now forms part of the flooring of the trench, is suddenly aware that this same trench is full of men—rough, uncultured men, clad in short petticoats and the skins of wild animals, and armed with knobkerries. The Flying Matinée has begun, and Hans Dumpkopf has got in by the early door.

Each of the performers—there are fifty of them all told—has his part to play, and plays it with commendable aplomb. One, having disarmed an unresisting prisoner, assists him over the parapet and escorts him affectionately to his new home. Another clubs a recalcitrant foeman over the head with a knobkerry, and having thus reduced him to a more amenable frame of mind, hoists him over the parapet and drags him after his "kamarad."

Other parties are told off to deal with the dug-outs. As a rule, the occupants of these are too dazed to make any resistance,—to be quite frank, the individual Boche in these days seems rather to welcome captivity than otherwise,—and presently more of the "bag" are on their way to the British lines.

But by this time the performance is drawing to a close. The alarm has been communicated to the adjacent sections of the trench, and preparations for the ejection of the intruders are being hurried forward. That is to say, German bombers are collecting upon either flank, with the intention of bombing "inwards" until the impudent foe has been destroyed or evicted. As we are not here to precipitate a general action, but merely to round up a few prisoners and do as much damage as possible in ten minutes, we hasten to the finale. As in most finales, one's actions now become less restrained—but, from a brutal point of view, more effective. A couple of hand-grenades are thrown into any dug-out which has not yet surrendered. (The Canadians, who make quite a speciality of flying matinées, are accustomed, we understand, as an artistic variant to this practice, to fasten an electric torch along the barrel of a rifle, and so illuminate their lurking targets while they shoot.) A sharp order passes along the line; every one scrambles out of the trench; and the troupe makes its way back, before the enemy in the adjacent trenches have really wakened up, to the place from which it came. The matinée, so far as the actors are concerned, is over.

Not so the audience. The avenging host is just getting busy. The bombing-parties are now marshalled and proceed with awful solemnity and Teutonic thoroughness to clear the violated trench. The procedure of a bombing-party is stereotyped. They begin by lobbing hand-grenades over the first traverse into the first bay. After the ensuing explosion, they trot round the traverse in single file and occupy the bay. This manoeuvre is then repeated until the entire trench is cleared. The whole operation requires good discipline, considerable courage, and carefully timed co-operation with the other bombing-party. In all these attributes the Boche excels. But one thing is essential to the complete success of his efforts, and that is the presence of the enemy. When, after methodically desolating each bay in turn (and incidentally killing their own wounded in the process), the two parties meet midway—practically on top of the unfortunate Hans Dumpkopf, who is still giving an imitation of a tortoise in a corrugated shell—it is discovered that the beautifully executed counter-attack has achieved nothing but the recapture of an entirely empty trench. The birds have flown, taking their prey with them. Hans is the sole survivor, and after hearing what his officer has to say to him upon the subject, bitterly regrets the fact.

Meanwhile, in the British trenches a few yards away, the box-office returns are being made up. These take the form, firstly, of some twenty-five prisoners, including one indignant officer—he had been pulled from his dug-out half asleep and frog-marched across the British lines by two private soldiers well qualified to appreciate the richness of his language—together with various souvenirs in the way of arms and accoutrements; and secondly, of the knowledge that at least as many more of the enemy had been left permanently incapacitated for further warfare in the dug-outs. A grim and grisly drama when you come to criticise it in cold blood, but not without a certain humour of its own—and most educative for Brother Boche!

But he is a slow pupil. He regards the profession of arms and the pursuit of war with such intense and solemn reverence that he *cannot* conceive how any one calling himself a soldier can be so criminally frivolous as to write a farce round the subject—much less present the farce at a Flying Matinée. That possibly explains why the following stately paragraph appeared a few days later in the periodical communiqué which keeps the German nation in touch with its Army's latest exploits:—

During the night of Jan. 4th-5th attempts were made by strong detachments of the enemy to penetrate our line near Sloozleschump, S.E. of Ypres. The attack failed utterly.

"And they don't even realise that it was only a leg-pull!" commented the Company Commander who had stage-managed the affair. "These people simply don't deserve to have entertainments arranged for them at all. Well, we must pull the limb again, that's all!"

And it was so.

IV

THE PUSH THAT FAILED

I

"I wonder if they really mean business this time," surmised that youthful Company Commander, Temporary Captain Bobby Little, to Major Wagstaffe.

"It sounds like it," said Wagstaffe, as another salvo of "whizz-bangs" broke like inflammatory surf upon the front-line trenches. "Intermittent *strafes* we are used to, but this all-day performance seems to indicate that the Boche is really getting down to it for once. The whole proceeding reminds me of nothing so much as our own 'artillery preparation' before the big push at Loos."

"Then you think the Boches are going to make a push of their own?"

"I do; and I hope it will be a good fat one. When it comes, I fancy we shall be able to put up something rather pretty in the way of a defence. The Salient is stiff with guns—I don't think the Boche quite realises *how* stiff! And we owe the swine something!" he added through his teeth.

There was a pause in the conversation. You cannot hold the Salient for three months without paying for the distinction; and the regiment had paid its full share. Not so much in numbers, perhaps, as in quality. Stray bullets, whistling up and down the trenches, coming even obliquely from the rear, had exacted most grievous toll. Shells and trench-mortar bombs, taking us in flank, had extinguished many valuable lives. At this time nothing but the best seemed to satisfy the Fates. One day it would be a trusted colour-sergeant, on another a couple of particularly promising young corporals. Only last week the Adjutant—athlete, scholar, born soldier, and very lovable schoolboy, all most perfectly blended—had fallen mortally wounded, on his morning round of the fire-trenches, by a bullet which came from nowhere. He was the subject of Wagstaffe's reference.

"Is it not possible," suggested Mr. Waddell, who habitually considered all questions from every possible point of view, "that this bombardment has been specially initiated by the German authorities, in order to impress upon their own troops a warning that there must be no Christmas truce this year?"

"If that is the Kaiser's Christmas greeting to his loving followers," observed Wagstaffe drily, "I think he might safely have left it to us to deliver it!"

"They say," interposed Bobby Little, "that the Kaiser is here himself."

"How do you know?"

"It was rumoured in 'Comic Cuts.'" ("Comic Cuts" is the stately Summary of War Intelligence issued daily from Olympus.)

"If that is true," said Wagstaffe, "they probably will attack. All this fuss and bobbery suggest something of the kind. They remind me of the commotion which used to precede Arthur Roberts's entrance in the old days of Gaiety burlesque. Before your time, I fancy, Bobby?"

"Yes," said Bobby modestly. "I first found touch with the Gaiety over 'Our Miss Gibbs.' And I was quite a kid even then," he added, with characteristic honesty. "But what about Arthur Roberts?"

"Some forty or fifty years ago," explained Wagstaffe, "when I was in the habit of frequenting places of amusement, Arthur Roberts was leading man at the establishment to which I have referred. He usually came on about half-past eight, just as the show was beginning to lose its first wind. His entrance was a most tremendous affair. First of all the entire chorus blew in from the wings—about sixty of them in ten seconds—saying "Hurrah, hurrah, girls!" or something rather subtle of that kind; after which minor characters rushed on from opposite sides and told one another that Arthur Roberts was coming. Then the band played, and everybody began to tell the audience about it in song. When everything was in full blast, the great man would appear—stepping out of a bathing-machine, or falling out of a hansom-cab, or sliding down a chute on a toboggan. He was assisted to his feet by the chorus, and then proceeded to ginger the show up. Well, that's how this present entertainment impresses me. All this noise and obstreperousness are leading up to one thing—Kaiser Bill's entrance. Preliminary bombardment—that's the chorus getting to work! Minor characters—the trench-mortars—spread the glad news! Band *and* chorus—that's the grand attack working up to boiling-point! Finally, preceded by clouds of gas, the Arch-Comedian in person, supported by spectacled coryphées in brass hats! How's that for a Christmas pantomime?"

"Rotten!" said Bobby, as a shell sang over the parapet and burst in the wood behind.

II

Kaiser or no Kaiser, Major Wagstaffe's extravagant analogy held good. As Christmas drew nearer, the band played louder and faster; the chorus swelled higher and shriller; and it became finally apparent that something (or somebody) of portentous importance was directing the storm.

Between six and seven next morning, the Battalion, which had stood to arms all night, lifted up its heavy head and sniffed the misty dawn-wind—an east wind—dubiously. Next moment gongs were clanging up and down the trench, and men were tearing open the satchels which contained their anti-gas helmets.

Major Wagstaffe, who had been sent up from Battalion Headquarters to take general charge of affairs in the firing-trench, buttoned the bottom edge of his helmet well inside his collar and clambered up on the firing-step to take stock of the position. He crouched low, for a terrific bombardment was in progress, and shells were almost grazing the parapet.

Presently he was joined by a slim young officer similarly disguised. It was the Commander of "A" Company. Wagstaffe placed his head close to Bobby's left ear, and shouted through the cloth—

"We shan't feel this gas much. They're letting it off higher up the line. Look!"

Bobby, laboriously inhaling the tainted air inside his helmet,—being preserved from a gas attack is only one degree less unpleasant than being gassed,—turned his goggles northward.

In the dim light of the breaking day he could discern a greenish-yellow cloud rolling across from the Boche trenches on his left.

"Will they attack?" he bellowed.

Wagstaffe nodded his head, and then cautiously unbuttoned his collar and rolled up the front of his helmet. Then, after delicately sampling the atmosphere by a cautious sniff, he removed his helmet altogether. Bobby followed his example. The air was not by any means so pure as might have been desired, but it was infinitely preferable to that inside a gas-helmet.

"Nothing to signify," pronounced Wagstaffe. "We're only getting the edge of it. Sergeant, pass down that men may roll up their helmets, but must keep them on their heads. Now, Bobby, things are getting interesting. Will they attack, or will they not?"

"What do you think?" asked Bobby.

"They are certainly going to attack farther north. The Boche does not waste gas as a rule—not this sort of gas! And I think he'll attack here too. The only reason why he has not switched on our anaesthetic is that the wind isn't quite right for this bit of the line. I think it is going to be a general push. Bobby, have a look through this sniper's loophole. Can you see any bayonets twinkling in the Boche trenches?"

Bobby applied an eye to the loophole.

"Yes," he said, "I can see them. Those trenches must be packed with men."

"Absolutely stiff with them," agreed Wagstaffe, getting out his revolver. "We shall be in for it presently. Are your fellows all ready, Bobby?"

The youthful Captain ran his eye along the trench, where his Company, with magazines loaded and bayonets fixed, were grimly awaiting the onset. There had been an onset similar to this, with the same green, nauseous accompaniment, in precisely the same spot eight months before, which had broken the line and penetrated for four miles. There it had been stayed by a forlorn hope of cooks, brakesmen, and officers' servants, and disaster had been most gloriously retrieved. What was going to happen this time? One thing was certain: the day of stink-pots was over.

"When do you think they'll attack?" shouted Bobby to Wagstaffe, battling against the noise of bursting shells.

"Quite soon—in a minute or two. Their guns will stop directly—to lift their sights and set up a barrage behind us. Then, perhaps the Boche will step over his parapet. Perhaps not!"

The last sentence rang out with uncanny distinctness, for the German guns with one accord had ceased firing. For a full two minutes there was absolute silence, while the bayonets in the opposite trenches twinkled with tenfold intent.

Then, from every point in the great Salient of Ypres, the British guns replied.

Possibly the Imperial General Staff at Berlin had been misinformed as to the exact strength of the British Artillery. Possibly they had been informed by their Intelligence Department that Trades Unionism, had ensured that a thoroughly inadequate supply of shells was to hand in the Salient. Or possibly they had merely decided, after the playful habit of General Staffs, to let the infantry in the trenches take their chance of any retaliation that might be forthcoming.

Whatever these great men were expecting, it is highly improbable that they expected that which arrived. Suddenly the British batteries spoke out, and they all spoke together. In the space of four minutes they deposited *thirty thousand* high-explosive shells in the Boche front-line trenches—yea, distributed the same accurately and evenly along all that crowded arc. Then they paused, as suddenly as they began, while British riflemen and machine-gunners bent to their work.

But few received the order to fire. Here and there a wave of men broke over the German parapet and rolled towards the British lines—only to be rolled back crumpled up by machine-guns. Never once was the goal reached. The great Christmas attack was over. After months of weary waiting and foolish recrimination, that exasperating race of bad starters but great stayers, the British people, had delivered "the goods," and made it possible for their soldiers to speak with the enemy in the gate upon equal—nay, superior, terms.

"Is that all?" asked Bobby Little, peering out over the parapet, a little awe-struck, at the devastation over the way.

"That is all," said Wagstaffe, "or I'm a Boche! There will be much noise and some irregular scrapping for days, but the tin lid has been placed upon the grand attack. The great Christmas Victory is off!"

Then he added, thoughtfully, referring apparently to the star performer:—

"We *have* been and spoiled his entrance for him, haven't we?"

V

UNBENDING THE BOW

I

There is a certain type of English country-house female who is said to "live in her boxes." That is to say, she appears to possess no home of her own, but flits from one indulgent roof-tree to another; and owing to the fact that she is invariably put into a bedroom whose wardrobe is full of her hostess's superannuated ball-frocks and winter furs, never knows what it is to have all her "things" unpacked at once.

Well, we out here cannot be said to live in our boxes, for we do not possess any; but we do most undoubtedly live in our haversacks and packs. And this brings us to the matter in hand—namely, so-called "Rest-Billets." The whole of the hinterland of this great trench-line is full of tired men, seeking for a place to lie down in, and living in their boxes when they find one.

At present we are indulging in such a period of repose; and we venture to think that on the whole we have earned it. Our last rest was in high summer, when we lay about under an August sun in the district round Béthune, and called down curses upon all flying and creeping insects. Since then we have undergone certain so-called "operations" in the neighbourhood of Loos, and have put in three months in the Salient of Ypres. As that devout adherent of the Roman faith, Private Reilly, of "B" Company, put it to his spiritual adviser—

"I doot we'll get excused a good slice of Purgatory for this, father!"

We came out of the Salient just before Christmas, in the midst of the mutual unpleasantness arising out of the grand attack upon the British line which was to have done so much to restore the waning confidence of the Hun. It was meant to be a big affair—a most majestic victory, in fact; but our new gas-helmets nullified the gas, and our new shells paralysed the attack; so the Third Battle of Ypres was not yet. Still, as I say, there was considerable unpleasantness all round; and we were escorted upon our homeward way, from Sanctuary Wood to Zillebeke, and from Zillebeke to Dickebusche, by a swarm of angry and disappointed shells.

Next day we found ourselves many miles behind the firing-line, once more in France, with a whole month's holiday in prospect, comfortably conscious that one could walk round a corner or look over a wall without preliminary reconnaissance or subsequent extirpation.

As for the holiday itself, unreasonable persons are not lacking to point out that it is of the busman's variety. It is true that we are no longer face to face with the foe, but we—or rather, the authorities—make believe that we are. We wage mimic warfare in full marching order; we fire rifles and machine-guns upon improvised ranges; we perform hazardous feats with bombs and a dummy trench. More galling still, we are back in the region of squad-drill, physical exercises, and handling of arms—horrors of our childhood which we thought had been left safely interned at Aldershot.

But the authorities are wise. The regiment is stiff and out of condition: it is suffering from moral and intellectual "trench-feet." Heavy drafts have introduced a large and untempered element into our composition. Many of the subalterns are obviously "new-jined"—as the shrewd old lady of Ayr once observed of the rubicund gentleman at the temperance meeting. Their men hardly know them or one another by sight. The regiment must be moulded anew, and its lustre restored by the beneficent process vulgarly known as "spit and polish." So every morning we apply ourselves with thoroughness, if not enthusiasm, to tasks which remind us of last winter's training upon the Hampshire chalk.

But the afternoon and evening are a different story altogether. If we were busy in the morning, we are busier still for the rest of the day. There is football galore, for we have to get through a complete series of Divisional cup-ties in four weeks. There is also a Brigade boxing-tournament. (No, that was not where Private Tosh got his black eye: that is a souvenir of New Year's Eve.) There are entertainments of various kinds in the recreation-tent. This whistling platoon, with towels round their necks, are on their way to the nearest convent, or asylum, or École des Jeunes Filles—have no fear; these establishments are untenanted!—for a bath. There, in addition to the pleasures of ablution, they will receive a partial change of raiment.

Other signs of regeneration are visible. That mysterious-looking vehicle, rather resembling one of the early locomotives exhibited in the South Kensington Museum, standing in the mud outside a farm-billet, its superheated interior stuffed with "C" Company's blankets, is performing an unmentionable but beneficent work.

Buttons are resuming their polish; the pattern of our kilts is emerging from its superficial crust; and Church Parade is once more becoming quite a show affair.

Away to the east the guns still thunder, and at night the star-shells float tremblingly up over the distant horizon. But not for us. Not yet, that is. In a few weeks' time we shall be back in another part of the line. Till then—Company drill and Cup-Ties! *Carpe diem!*

II

It all seemed very strange and unreal to Second-Lieutenant Angus M'Lachlan, as he alighted from the train at railhead, and supervised the efforts of his solitary N.C.O. to arrange the members of his draft in a straight line. There were some thirty of them in all. Some were old hands—men from the First and Second Battalions, who had been home wounded, and had now been sent out to leaven "K(1)." Others were Special Reservists from the Third Battalion. These had been at the Dépôt for a long time, and some of them stood badly in need of a little active service. Others, again, were new hands altogether—the product of "K to the *nth*." Among these Angus M'Lachlan numbered himself, and he made no attempt to conceal the fact. The novelty of the sights around him was almost too much for his *insouciant* dignity as a commissioned officer.

Angus M'Lachlan was a son of the Manse, and incidentally a child of Nature. The Manse was a Highland Manse; and until a few months ago Angus had never, save for a rare visit to distant Edinburgh, penetrated beyond the small town which lay four miles from his native glen, and of whose local Academy he had been "dux." When the War broke out he had been upon the point of proceeding to Edinburgh University, where he had already laid siege to a bursary, and captured the same; but all these plans, together with the plans of countless more distinguished persons, had been swept to the winds by the invasion of Belgium. On that date Angus summoned up his entire stock of physical and moral courage and informed his reverend parent of his intention to enlist for a soldier. Permission was granted with quite stunning readiness. Neil M'Lachlan believed in straight hitting both in theology and war, and was by no means displeased at the martial aspirations of his only son. If he quitted himself like a man in the forefront of battle, the boy could safely look forward to being cock of his own Kirk-Session in the years that came afterwards. One reservation the old man made. His son, as a Highland gentleman, would lead men to battle, and not merely accompany them. So the impatient Angus was bidden to apply for a Commission—his attention during the period of waiting being directed by his parent to the study of the campaigns of Joshua, and the methods employed by that singular but successful strategist in dealing with the Philistine.

Angus had a long while to wait, for all the youth of England—and Scotland too—was on fire, and others nearer the fountain of honour had to be served first. But his turn came at last; and we now behold him, as typical a product of "K to the *nth*" as Bobby Little had been of "K(1)," standing at last upon the soil of France, and inquiring in a soft Highland voice for the Headquarters of our own particular Battalion.

He had half expected, half hoped, to alight from the train amidst a shower of shells, as he knew the Old Regiment had done many months before, just after the War broke out. But all he saw upon his arrival was an untidy goods yard, littered with military stores, and peopled by British privates in the *déshabille* affected by the British Army when engaged in menial tasks.

Being quite ignorant of the whereabouts of his regiment—when last heard of they had been in trenches near Ypres—and failing to recollect the existence of that autocratic but indispensable *genius loci*, the R.T.O., Angus took uneasy stock of his surroundings and wondered what to do next.

Suddenly a friendly voice at his elbow remarked—

"There's a queer lot o' bodies hereaboot, sirr."

Angus turned, to find that he was being addressed by a short, stout private of the draft, in a kilt much too big for him.

"Indeed, that is so," he replied politely. "What is your name?"

"Peter Bogle, sirr. I am frae oot of Kirkintilloch." Evidently gratified by the success of his conversational opening, the little man continued—

"I would like fine for tae get a contrack oot here after the War. This country is in a terrible state o' disrepair." Then he added confidentially—

"I'm a hoose-painter tae a trade."

"I should not like to be that myself," replied Angus, whose early training as a minister's son was always causing him to forget the social gulf which is fixed between officers and the rank-and-file. "Climbing ladders makes me dizzy."

"Och, it's naething! A body gets used tae it," Mr. Bogle assured him.

Angus was about to proceed further with the discussion, when the cold and disapproving voice of the Draft-Sergeant announced in his ear—

"An officer wishes to speak to you, sir."

Second-Lieutenant M'Lachlan, suddenly awake to the enormity of his conduct, turned guiltily to greet the officer, while the Sergeant abruptly hunted the genial Private Bogle back into the ranks.

Angus found himself confronted by an immaculate young gentleman wearing two stars. Angus, who only wore one, saluted hurriedly.

"Morning," observed the stranger. "You in charge of this draft?"

"Yes, sir," said Angus respectfully.

"Right-o! You are to march them to 'A' Company billets. I'll show you the way. My name's Cockerell. Your train is late. What time did you leave the Base?"

"Indeed," replied Angus meekly, "I am not quite sure. We had barely landed when they told me the train would start at seventeen-forty. What time would that be—sir?"

"About a quarter to ten: more likely about midnight! Well, get your bunch on to the road, and—Hallo, what's the matter? Let go!"

The new officer was gripping him excitedly by the arm, and as the new officer stood six-foot-four and was brawny in proportion, Master Cockerell's appeal was uttered in a tone of unusual sincerity.

"Look!" cried Angus excitedly. "The dogs, the dogs!"

A small cart was passing swiftly by, towed by two sturdy hounds of unknown degree. They were pulling with the feverish enthusiasm which distinguishes the Dog in the service of Man, and were being urged to further efforts by a small hatless girl carrying the inevitable large umbrella.

"All right!" explained Cockerell curtly. "Custom of the country, and all that."

The impulsive Angus apologised; and the draft, having been safely manoeuvred on to the road, formed fours and set out upon its march.

"Are the Battalion in the trenches at present, sir?" inquired Angus.

"No. Rest-billets two miles from here. About time, too! You'll get lots of work to do, though."

"I shall welcome that," said Angus simply. "In the dépôt at home we were terribly idle. There is a windmill!"

"Yes; one sees them occasionally out here," replied Cockerell drily.

"Everything is so strange!" confessed the open-hearted Angus. "Those dogs we saw just now—the people with their sabots—the country carts, like wheelbarrows with three wheels—the little shrines at the cross-roads—the very children talking French so glibly—"

"Wonderful how they pick it up!" agreed Cockerell. But the sarcasm was lost on his companion, whose attention was now riveted upon an approaching body of infantry, about fifty strong.

"What troops are those, please?"

Cockerell knitted his brows sardonically.

"It's rather hard to tell at this distance," he said; "but I rather think they are the Grenadier Guards."

Two minutes later the procession had been met and passed. It consisted entirely of elderly gentlemen in ill-fitting khaki, clumping along upon their flat feet and smoking clay pipes. They carried shovels on their shoulders, and made not the slightest response when called upon by the soldierly old corporal who led them to give Mr. Cockerell "eyes left!" On the contrary, engaged as they were in heated controversy or amiable conversation with one another, they cut him dead.

Angus M'Lachlan said nothing for quite five minutes. Then—

"I suppose," he said almost timidly, "that those were members of a *Reserve* Regiment of the Guards?"

Cockerell, who had never outgrown certain characteristics which most of us shed upon emerging from the Lower Fourth, laughed long and loud.

"That crowd? They belong to one of the Labour Battalions. They make roads, and dig support trenches, and sling mud about generally. Wonderful old sportsmen! Pleased as Punch when a shell falls within half a mile of them. Something to write home about. What? I say, I pulled your leg that time! Here we are at Headquarters. Come and report to the C.O. Grenadier Guards! My aunt!"

* * * * *

Angus, although his Celtic enthusiasm sometimes led him into traps, was no fool. He soon settled down in his new surroundings, and found favour with Colonel Kemp, which was no light achievement.

"You won't find that the War, in its present stage, calls for any display of genius," the Colonel explained to Angus at their first interview. "I don't expect my officers to exhibit any quality but the avoidance of *sloppiness*. If I detail you to be at a certain spot, at a certain hour, with a certain number of men—a ration-party, or a working-party, or a burial-party, or anything you like,—all I ask is that you will be *there*, at the appointed hour, with the whole of your following. That may not sound a very difficult feat, but experience has taught me that if a man can achieve it, and can be *relied* upon to achieve it, say, nine times out of ten—well, he is a pearl of price; and there is not a C.O. in the British Army who wouldn't scramble to get him! That's all, M'Lachlan. Good morning!"

By punctilious attention to this sound advice Angus soon began to build up a reputation. He treated war-worn veterans like Bobby Little with immense respect, and this, too, was counted to him for righteousness. He exercised his platoon with appalling vigour. Upon Company route-marches he had to be embedded in some safe place in the middle of the column; in fact, his enormous stride and pedestrian enthusiasm would have reduced his followers to pulp. At Mess he was mute: like a wise man, he was feeling for his feet.

But being, like Moses, slow of tongue, he provided himself with an Aaron. Quite inadvertently, be it said. Bidden to obtain a servant for his personal needs, he selected the only man in the Battalion whose name he knew—Private Bogle, the *ci-devant* painter of houses. That friendly creature obeyed the call with alacrity. If his house-painting was no better than his valeting, then his prospects of a "contrack" after the War were poor indeed; but as a Mess waiter he was a joy for ever. Despite the blood-curdling whispers of the Mess Corporal, his natural urbanity of disposition could not be stemmed. Of the comfort of others he was solicitous to the point of oppressiveness. A Mess waiter's idea of efficiency as a rule is to stand woodenly at attention in an obscure corner of the room. When called upon, he starts forward with a jerk, and usually trips over something—probably his own feet. Not so Private Bogle.

"Wull you try another cup o' tea, Major?" he would suggest at breakfast to Major Wagstaffe, leaning affectionately over the back of his chair.

"No, thank you, Bogle," Major Wagstaffe would reply gravely.

"Weel, it's cauld onyway," Bogle would rejoin, anxious to endorse his superior's decision.

Or—in the same spirit—

"Wull I luft the soup now, sir?"

"*No!*"

"Varra weel: I'll jist let it bide the way it is."

* * * * *

Lastly, Angus M'Lachlan proved himself a useful acquisition—especially in rest-billets—as an athlete. He arrived just in time to take part—no mean part, either—in a Rugby Football match played between the officers of two Brigades. Thanks very largely to his masterly leading of the forwards, our Brigade were preserved from defeat at the hands of their opponents, who on paper had appeared to be irresistible.

Rugby Football "oot here" is a rarity, though Association, being essentially the game of the rank-and-file, flourishes in every green field. But an Inverleith or Queen's Club crowd would have recognised more than one old friend among the thirty who took the field that day. There were those participating whose last game had been one of the spring "Internationals" in 1914, and who had been engaged in a prolonged and strenuous version of an even greater International ever since August of that fateful year. Every public school in Scotland was represented—sometimes three or four times over—and there were numerous doughty contributions from establishments south of the Tweed.

The lookers-on were in different case. They were to a man devoted—nay, frenzied—adherents of the rival code. In less spacious days they had surged in their thousands every Saturday afternoon to Ibrox, or Tynecastle, or Parkhead, there to yell themselves into convulsions—now exhorting a friend to hit some one a kick on the nose, now recommending the foe to play the game, now hoarsely consigning the referee to perdition. To these, Rugby Football—the greatest of all manly games—was a mere name. Their attitude when the officers appeared upon the field was one of indulgent superiority—the sort of superiority that a brawny pitman exhibits when his Platoon Commander steps down into a trench to lend a hand with the digging.

But in five minutes their mouths were agape with scandalised astonishment; in ten, the heavens were rent with their protesting cries. Accustomed to see football played with the feet, and to demand with one voice the instant execution of any player (on the other side) who laid so much as a finger upon the ball or the man who was playing it, the exhibition of savage and promiscuous brutality to which their superior officers now treated them shocked the assembled spectators to the roots of their sensitive souls. Howls of virtuous indignation burst forth upon all sides.

When the three-quarter-backs brought off a brilliant passing run, there were stern cries of "Haands, there, referee!" When Bobby Little stopped an ugly rush by hurling himself on the ball, the supporters of the other Brigade greeted his heroic devotion with yells of execration. When Angus M'Lachlan saved a certain try by tackling a speedy wing three-quarter low and bringing him down with a crash, a hundred voices demanded his removal from the field. And, when Mr. Waddell, playing a stuffy but useful game at half, gained fifty yards for his side by a series of judicious little kicks into touch, the spectators groaned aloud, and remarked caustically—

"This maun be a Cup-Tie, boys! They are playin' for a draw, for tae get a second gate!"

Altogether a thoroughly enjoyable afternoon, both for players and spectators. And so home to tea, domesticity, and social intercourse. In this connection it may be noted that our relations with the inhabitants are of the friendliest. On the stroke of six—oh yes, we have our licensing restrictions out here too!—half a dozen kilted warriors stroll into the farm-kitchen, and mumble affably to Madame—

"Bone sworr! Beer?"

France boasts one enormous advantage over Scotland. At home, you have at least to walk to the corner of the street to obtain a drink: "oot here" you can purchase beer in practically every house in a village. The French licensing laws are a thing of mystery, but the system appears roughly to be this. Either you possess a license, or you do not. If you do you may sell beer, and nothing else. If you do not, you may—or at any rate do—sell anything you like, including beer.

However, we have left our friends thirsty.

Their wants are supplied with cheerful alacrity, and, having been accommodated with seats round the stove, they converse with the family. Heaven only knows what they talk about, but talk they do—in the throaty unintelligible Doric of the Clydeside, with an occasional Gallicism, like, "Allyman no bon!" or "Compree?" thrown in as a sop to foreign idiosyncracies. Madame and family respond, chattering French (or Flemish) at enormous speed. The amazing part of it all is that neither side appears to experience the slightest difficulty in understanding the other. One day Mr. Waddell, in the course of a friendly chat with his hostess of the moment—she was unable to speak a word of English—received her warm congratulations upon his contemplated union with a certain fair one of St. Andrew (to whom reference has previously been made in these pages). Mr. Waddell, a very fair linguist, replied in suitable but embarrassed terms, and asked for the source of the good lady's information.

"Mais votre ordonnance, m'sieur!" was the reply.

Tackled upon the subject, the "ordonnance" in question, Waddell's servant—a shock-headed youth from Dundee—admitted having communicated the information; and added—

"She's a decent body, sirr, the lady o' the hoose. She lost her husband, she was tellin' me, three years ago. She has twa sons in the Airmy. Her auld Auntie is up at the top o' the hoose—lyin' badly, and no expectin' tae rise."

And yet some people study Esperanto!

We also make ourselves useful. "K(1)" contains members of every craft. If the pig-sty door is broken, a carpenter is forthcoming to mend it. Somebody's elbow goes through a pane of glass in the farm-kitchen: straightway a glazier materialises from the nearest platoon, and puts in another. The ancestral eight-day clock of the household develops internal complications; and is forthwith dismembered and reassembled, "with punctuality, civility, and despatch," by a gentleman who until a few short months ago had done nothing else for fifteen years.

And it was in this connection that Corporal Mucklewame stumbled on to a rare and congenial job, and incidentally made the one joke of his life.

One afternoon a cow, the property of Madame *la fermière*, developed symptoms of some serious disorder. A period of dolorous bellowing was followed by an outburst of homicidal mania, during which "A" Company prudently barricaded itself into the barn, the sufferer having taken entire possession of the farmyard. Next, and finally—so rapidly did the malady run its course—a state of coma intervened; and finally the cow, collapsing upon the doorstep of the Officers' Mess, breathed her last before any one could be found to point out to her the liberty she was taking.

It was decided to hold a *post-mortem*—firstly, to ascertain the cause of death; secondly, because it is easier to remove a dead cow after dissection than before. Madame therefore announced her intention of sending for the butcher, and was upon the point of doing so when Corporal Mucklewame, in whose heart, at the spectacle of the stark and lifeless corpse, ancient and romantic memories were stirring—it may be remembered that before answering to the call of "K(1)" Mucklewame had followed the calling of butcher's assistant at Wishaw—volunteered for the job. His services were cordially accepted by thrifty Madame; and the Corporal, surrounded by a silent and admiring crowd, set to work.

The officers, leaving the Junior Subaltern in charge, went with one accord for a long country walk.

Half an hour later Mucklewame arrived at the seat of the deceased animal's trouble—the seat of most of the troubles of mankind—its stomach. After a brief investigation, he produced therefrom a small bag of nails, recently missed from the vicinity of a cook-house in course of construction in the corner of the yard.

Abandoning the rôle of surgical expert for that of coroner, Mucklewame held the trophy aloft, and delivered his verdict—

"There, boys! That's what comes of eating your iron ration without authority!"

III

Here is an average billet, and its personnel.

The central feature of our residence is the refuse-pit, which fills practically the whole of the rectangular farmyard, and resembles (in size and shape *only*) an open-air swimming bath. Its abundant contents are apparently the sole asset of the household; for if you proceed, in the interests of health, to spread a decent mantle of honest earth thereover, you do so to the accompaniment of a harmonised chorus of lamentation, very creditably rendered by the entire family, who are grouped *en masse* about the spot where the high diving-board ought to be.

Round this perverted place of ablution runs a stone ledge, some four feet wide, and round that again run the farm buildings—the house at the top end, a great barn down one side, and the cowhouse, together with certain darksome piggeries and fowl-houses, down the other. These latter residences are occupied only at night, their tenants preferring to spend the golden hours of day in profitable occupation upon the happy hunting ground in the middle.

Within the precincts of this already overcrowded establishment are lodged some two hundred British soldiers and their officers. The men sleep in the barn, their meals being prepared for them upon the Company cooker, which stands in the muddy road outside, and resembles the humble vehicle employed by Urban District Councils for the preparation of tar for road-mending purposes. The officers occupy any room which may be available within the farmhouse itself. The Company Commander has the best bedroom—a low-roofed, stone-floored apartment, with a very small window and a very large bed. The subalterns sleep where they can—usually in the *grenier*, a loft under the tiles, devoted to the storage of onions and the drying, during the winter months, of the family washing, which is suspended from innumerable strings stretched from wall to wall.

For a Mess, there is usually a spare apartment of some kind. If not, you put your pride in your pocket and take your meals at the kitchen table, at such hours as the family are not sitting humped round the same with their hats on, partaking of soup or coffee. (This appears to be their sole sustenance.) A farm-kitchen in northern France is a scrupulously clean place—the whole family gets up at half-past four in the morning and sees to the matter—and despite the frugality of her own home *menu*, the *fermière* can produce you a perfect omelette at any hour of the day or night.

This brings us to the kitchen-stove, which is a marvel. No massive and extravagant English ranges here! There is only one kind: we call it the Coffin and Flower-pot. The coffin—small, black, and highly polished—projects from the wall about four feet, the further end being supported by what looks like an ornamental black flower-pot standing on a pedestal. The coffin is the oven, and the flower-pot is the stove. Given a handful of small coal or charcoal, Madame appears capable of keeping it at work all day, and of boiling, baking, or roasting you innumerable dishes.

Then there is the family. Who or what they all are, and where they all sleep, is a profound mystery. The family tree is usually headed by a decrepit and ruminant old gentleman in a species of yachting-cap. He sits behind the stove—not exactly with one foot in the grave, but with both knees well up against the coffin—and occasionally offers a mumbled observation of which no one takes the slightest notice. Sometimes, too, there is an old, a very old, lady. Probably she is some one's grandmother, or great-grandmother, but she does not appear to be related to the old gentleman. At least, they never recognise one another's existence in any way.

There are also vague people who possess the power of becoming invisible at will. They fade in and out of the house like wraiths: their one object in life appears to be to efface themselves as much as possible. Madame refers to them as "*refugiés*"; this the sophisticated Mr. Cockerell translates, "German spies."

Next in order come one or two farmhands—usually addressed as "'Nri!" and "'Seph!" They are not as a rule either attractive in appearance or desirable in character. Every man in this country, who *is* a man, is away, as a matter of course, doing a man's only possible duty under the circumstances. This leaves 'Nri and 'Seph, who through physical or mental shortcomings are denied the proud privilege, and shamble about in the muck and mud of the farm, leering or grumbling, while Madame exhorts them to further activity from the kitchen door. They take their meals with the family: where they sleep no one knows. External evidence suggests the cow-house.

Then, the family. First, Angèle. She may be twenty-five, but is more probably fifteen. She acts as Adjutant to Madame, and rivals her mother as deliverer of sustained and rapid recitative. She milks the cows, feeds the pigs, and dragoons her young brothers and sisters. But though she works from morning till night, she has always time for a smiling salutation to all ranks. She also speaks English quite creditably—a fact of which Madame is justly proud. "Collège!" explains the mother, full of appreciation for an education which she herself has never known, and taps her learned daughter affectionately upon the head.

Next in order comes Émile. He must be about fourteen, but War has forced manhood on him. All day long he is at work, bullying very large horses, digging, hoeing, even ploughing. He is very much a boy, for all that. He whistles excruciatingly—usually English music-hall melodies—grins sheepishly at the officers, and is prepared at any moment to abandon the most important tasks, in order to watch a man cleaning a rifle or oiling a machine-gun. We seem to have encountered Émile in other countries than this.

After Émile, Gabrielle. Her age is probably seven. If you were to give her a wash and brush-up, dress her in a gauzy frock, and exchange her thick woollen stockings and wooden sabots for silk and dancing slippers, she would make a very smart little fairy. Even in her native state she is a most attractive young person, of an engaging coyness. If you say: "Bonjour, Gabrielle!" she whispers: "B'jour M'sieur le Capitaine"—or, "M'sieur le Caporal"; for she knows all badges of rank—and hangs her head demurely. But presently, if you stand quite still and look the other way, Gabrielle will sidle up to you and squeeze your hand. This is gratifying, but a little subversive of strict discipline if you happen to be inspecting your platoon at the moment.

Gabrielle is a firm favourite with the rank and file. Her particular crony is one Private Mackay, an amorphous youth with flaming red hair. He and Gabrielle engage in lengthy conversations, which appear to be perfectly intelligible to both, though Mackay speaks with the solemn unction of the Aberdonian, and Gabrielle prattles at express speed in a *patois* of her own. Last week some unknown humorist, evidently considering that Gabrielle was not making sufficient progress in her knowledge of English, took upon himself to give her a private lesson. Next morning Mackay, on sentry duty at the farm gate, espied his little friend peeping round a corner.

"Hey, Garibell!" he observed cheerfully. (No Scottish private ever yet mastered a French name quite completely.)

Gabrielle, anxious to exhibit her new accomplishment, drew nearer, smiled seraphically, and replied—

"'Ello, Gingeair!"

Last of the bunch comes Petit Jean, a chubby and close-cropped youth of about six. Petit Jean is not his real name, as he himself indignantly explained when so addressed by Major Wagstaffe.

"Moi, z'ne suis pas Petit Jean; z'suis Maurrrice!"

Major Wagstaffe apologised most humbly, but the name stuck.

Petit Jean is an enthusiast upon matters military. He possesses a little wooden rifle, the gift of a friendly "Écossais," tipped with a flashing bayonet cut from a biscuit-tin; and spends most of his time out upon the road, waiting for some one to salute. At one time he used to stand by the sentry, with an ancient glengarry crammed over his bullet head, and conform meticulously to his comrade's slightest movement. This procedure was soon banned, as being calculated to bring contempt and ridicule upon the King's uniform, and Petit Jean was assigned a beat of his own. Behold him upon sentry-go.

A figure upon horseback swings round the bend in the road.

"Here's an officer, Johnny!" cries a friendly voice from the farm gate.

Petit Jean, as upright as a post, brings his rifle from stand-at-ease to the order, and from the order to the slope, with the epileptic jerkiness of a marionette, and scrutinises the approaching officer for stars and crowns. If he can discern nothing but a star or two, he slaps the small of his butt with ferocious solemnity; but if a crown, or a red hatband, reveals itself, he blows out his small chest to its fullest extent and presents arms. If the salute is acknowledged—as it nearly always is—Petit Jean is crimson with gratification. Once, when a friendly subaltern called his platoon to attention, and gave the order, "Eyes right!" upon passing the motionless little figure at the side of the road, Petit Jean was so uplifted that he committed the military crime of deserting his post while on duty—in order to run home and tell his mother about it.

* * * * *

Last of all we arrive at the keystone of the whole fabric—Madame herself. She is one of the most wonderful women in the world. Consider. Her husband and her eldest son are away—fighting, she knows not where, amid dangers and privations which can only be imagined. During their absence she has to manage a considerable farm, with the help of her children and one or two hired labourers of more than doubtful use or reliability. In addition to her ordinary duties as a parent and *fermière*, she finds herself called upon, for months on end, to maintain her premises as a combination of barracks and almshouse. Yet she is seldom cross—except possibly when the *soldats* steal her apples and pelt the pigs with the cores—and no accumulations of labour can sap her energy. She is up by half-past four every morning; yet she never appears anxious to go to bed at night. The last sound which sleepy subalterns hear is Madame's voice, uplifted in steady discourse to the circle round the stove, sustained by an occasional guttural chord from 'Nri and 'Seph. She has been doing this, day in, day out, since the combatants settled down to trench-warfare. Every few weeks brings a fresh crop of tenants, with fresh peculiarities and unknown proclivities; and she assimilates them all.

The only approach to a breakdown comes when, after paying her little bill—you may be sure that not an omelette nor a broken window will be missing from the account—and wishing her "Bonne chance!" ere you depart, you venture on a reference, in a few awkward, stumbling sentences, to the absent husband and son. Then she weeps, copiously, and it seems to do her a world of good. All hail to you, Madame—the finest exponent, in all this War, of the art of Carrying On! We know now why France is such a great country.

VI

YE MERRIE BUZZERS

I

Practically all the business of an Army in the field is transacted by telephone. If the telephone breaks down, whether by the Act of God or of the King's Enemies, that business is at a standstill until the telephone is put right again.

The importance of the disaster varies with the nature of the business. For instance, if the wire leading to the Round Game Department is blown down by a March gale, and your weekly return of Men

Recommended for False Teeth is delayed in transit, nobody minds very much—except possibly the Deputy Assistant Director of Auxiliary Dental Appliances. But if you are engaged in battle, and the wires which link up the driving force in front with the directing force behind are devastated by a storm of shrapnel, the matter assumes a more—nay, a most—serious aspect. Hence the superlative importance in modern warfare of the Signal Sections of the Royal Engineers—tersely described by the rank-and-file as the "Buzzers," or the "Iddy-Umpties."

During peace-training, the Buzzer on the whole has a very pleasant time of it. Once he has mastered the mysteries of the Semaphore and Morse codes, the most laborious part of his education is over. Henceforth he spends his days upon some sheltered hillside, in company with one or two congenial spirits, flapping cryptic messages out of a blue-and-white flag at a similar party across the valley.

A year ago, for instance, you might have encountered an old friend, Private M'Micking,—one of the original "Buzzers" of "A" Company, and ultimately Battalion Signal Sergeant—under the lee of a pine wood near Hindhead, accompanied by Lance-Corporal Greig and Private Wamphray, regarding with languid interest the frenzied efforts of three of their colleagues to convey a message from a sunny hillside three quarters of a mile away.

"Here a message comin' through, boys," announces the Lance-Corporal. "They're in a sair hurry: I doot the officer will be there. Jeams, tak' it doon while Sandy reads it."

Mr. James M'Micking seats himself upon a convenient log. In order not to confuse his faculties by endeavouring to read and write simultaneously, he turns his back upon the fluttering flag, and bends low over his field message-pad. Private Wamphray stands facing him, and solemnly spells out the message over his head.

"Tae g-o-c—I dinna ken what that means—r-e-d, *reid*—a-r-m-y, *airmy*—h-a-z—"

"All richt; that'll be Haslemere," says Private M'Micking, scribbling down the word. "Go on, Sandy!"

Private Wamphray, pausing to expectorate, continues—

"R-e-c-o-n-n-o-i-t-r—Cricky, what a worrd! Let's hae it repeatit."

Wamphray flaps his flag vigorously,—he knows this particular signal only too well,—and the word comes through again. The distant signaller, slowing down a little, continues,—

"'Reconnoitring patrol reports hostile cavalry scou—'"

"That'll be 'scouts,'" says the ever-ready M'Micking. "Carry on!"

Wamphray continues obediently,—"'Country'; stop; 'Have thrown out flank guns'; stop; 'Shall I advance or re—'"

"—tire," gabbles M'Micking, writing it down.

"—'where I am'; stop; 'From O C Advance Guard'; stop; message ends."

"And aboot time, too!" observes the scribe severely. "Haw, Johnny!"

The Lance-Corporal, who has been indulging in a pleasant reverie upon a bank of bracken, wakes up and reads the proffered message.

* * * * *

"Tae G O C, Reid Airmy, Hazlemere. Reconnoitring patrol reports hostile cavalry scouts country. Have thrown oot flank guns. Shall I advance or retire where I am? From O C Advance Guard."

"This message doesna sound altogether sense," he observes mildly. "That 'shall' should be 'wull,' onyway. Would it no' be better to get it repeatit? The officer—"

"I've given the 'message-read' signal now," objects the indolent Wamphray.

"How would it be," suggests the Lance-Corporal, whose besetting sin is a *penchant* for emendation, "if we were tae transfair yon stop, and say: 'Reconnoitring patrol reports hostile cavalry scouts. Country has thrown oot flank guns'?"

"What does that mean?" inquires M'Micking scornfully.

"I dinna ken; but these messages about Generals and sic'-like bodies—"

At this moment, as ill-luck will have it, the Signal Sergeant appears breasting the hillside. He arrives puffing—he has seen twenty years' service—and scrutinises the message.

"You boys," he says reproachfully, "are an aggravate altogether. Here you are, jumping at your conclusions again! After all I have been telling you! See! That worrd in the address should no' be Haslemere at all. It's just a catch! It's Hazebroucke—a Gairman city that we'll be capturing this time next year. 'Scouts' is no 'scouts,' but 'scouring'—meaning 'sooping up.' 'Guns' should be 'guarrd,' and 'retire' should be 'remain.' Mind me, now; next time, you'll be up before the Captain for neglect of duty. Wamphray, give the 'C.I.,' and let's get hame to oor dinners!"

II

But "oot here" there is no flag-wagging. The Buzzer's first proceeding upon entering the field of active hostilities is to get underground, and stay there.

He is a seasoned vessel, the Buzzer of to-day, and a person of marked individuality. He is above all things a man of the world. Sitting day and night in a dug-out, or a cellar, with a telephone receiver clamped to his ear, he sees little; but he hears much, and overhears more. He also speaks a language of his own. His one task in life is to prevent the letter B from sounding like C, or D, or P, or T, or V, over the telephone; so he has perverted the English language to his own uses. He calls B "Beer," and D "Don," and so on. He salutes the rosy dawn as "Akk Emma," and eventide as "Pip Emma." He refers to the letter S as "Esses," in order to distinguish it from F. He has no respect for the most majestic military titles. To him the Deputy Assistant Director of the Mobile Veterinary Section is merely a lifeless formula, entitled Don Akk Don Emma Vic Esses.

He is also a man of detached mind. The tactical situation does not interest him. His business is to disseminate news, not to write leading articles about it. (*O si sic omnes!*) You may be engaged in a life-and-death struggle for the possession of your own parapet with a Boche bombing-party; but this does not render you immune from a pink slip from the Signal Section, asking you to state your reasons in writing for having mislaid fourteen pairs of "boots, gum, thigh," lately the property of Number Seven Platoon. A famous British soldier tells a story somewhere in his reminiscences of an occasion upon which, in some long-forgotten bush campaign, he had to defend a zareba against a heavy attack. For a time the situation was critical. Help was badly needed, but the telegraph wire had been cut. Ultimately the attack withered away, and the situation was saved. Almost simultaneously the victorious commander was informed that telegraphic communication with the Base had been restored. A message was already coming through.

"News of reinforcements, I hope!" he remarked to his subordinate.

But his surmise was incorrect. The message said, quite simply:—

"Your monthly return of men wishing to change their religion is twenty-four hours overdue. Please expedite."

There was a time when one laughed at that anecdote as a playful invention. But we know now that it is true, and we feel a sort of pride in the truly British imperturbability of our official machinery.

Thirdly, the Buzzer is a humourist, of the sardonic variety. The constant clash of wits over the wires, and the necessity of framing words quickly, sharpens his faculties and acidulates his tongue. Incidentally, he is an awkward person to quarrel with. One black night, Bobby Little, making his second round of the trenches about an hour before "stand-to," felt constrained to send a telephone message to Battalion Headquarters. Taking a good breath,—you always do this before entering a trench dug-out,—he plunged into the noisome cavern where his Company Signallers kept everlasting vigil. The place was in total darkness, except for the illumination supplied by a strip of rifle-rag burning in a tin of rifle-oil. The air, what there was of it, was thick with large, fat, floating particles of free carbon. The telephone was buzzing plaintively to itself, in unsuccessful competition with a well-modulated quartette for four nasal organs, contributed by Bobby's entire signalling staff, who, locked in the inextricable embrace peculiar to Thomas Atkins in search of warmth, were snoring harmoniously upon the earthen floor.

The signaller "on duty"—one M'Gurk—was extracted from the heap and put under arrest for sleeping at his post. The enormity of his crime was heightened by the fact that two undelivered messages were found upon his person.

Divers pains and penalties followed. Bobby supplemented the sentence with a homily on the importance of vigilance and despatch. M'Gurk, deeply aggrieved at forfeiting seven days' pay, said nothing, but bided his time. Two nights later the Battalion came out of trenches for a week's rest, and Bobby, weary and thankful, retired to bed in his hut at 9 P.M., in comfortable anticipation of a full night's repose.

His anticipations were doomed to disappointment. He was roused from slumber—not without difficulty—by Signaller M'Gurk, who appeared standing by his bedside with a guttering candle-end in one hand and a pink despatch-form in the other. The message said:—

"Prevailing wind for next twenty-four hours probably S.W., with some rain."

Mindful of his own recent admonitions, Bobby thanked M'Gurk politely, and went to sleep again.

M'Gurk called again at half-past two in the morning, with another message, which announced:—

"Baths will be available for your Company from 2 to 3 P.M. to-morrow."

Bobby stuffed the missive under his air-pillow, and rolled over without a word. M'Gurk withdrew, leaving the door of the hut open.

His next visit was about four o'clock. This time the message said:—

"A Zeppelin is reported to have passed over Dunkirk at 5 P.M. yesterday afternoon, proceeding in a northerly direction."

Bobby informed M'Gurk that he was a fool and a dotard, and cast him forth.

M'Gurk returned at five-thirty, bearing written evidence that the Zeppelin had been traced as far as Ostend.

This time his Company Commander promised him that if he appeared again that night he would be awarded fourteen days' Field Punishment Number One.

The result was that upon sitting down to breakfast at nine next morning, Bobby found upon his plate yet another message—from his Commanding Officer—summoning him to the Orderly-room on urgent matters at eight-thirty.

But Bobby scored the final and winning trick. Sending for M'Gurk and Sergeant M'Micking, he said:—

"This man, Sergeant, appears to be unable to decide when a message is urgent and when it is not. In future, whenever M'Gurk is on night duty, and is in doubt as to whether a message should be delivered at once or put aside till morning, he will come to you and ask for your guidance in the matter. Do you understand?"

"Perrfectly, sirr!" replied the Sergeant, outwardly calm.

"M'Gurk, do *you* understand?"

M'Gurk looked at Bobby, and then round at Sergeant M'Micking. He received a glance which shrivelled his marrow. The game was up. He grinned sheepishly, and answered,—

"Yis, sirr!"

III

Having briefly set forth the character and habits of the Buzzer, we will next proceed to visit the creature in his lair. This is an easy feat. We have only to walk up the communication-trench which leads from the reserve line to the firing-line. Upon either side of the trench, neatly tacked to the muddy wall by a device of the hairpin variety, run countless insulated wires, clad in coats of various colours and all duly ticketed. These radiate from various Headquarters in the rear to numerous signal stations in the front, and were laid by the Signallers themselves. (It is perhaps unnecessary to mention that that single wire running, in defiance of all regulations, across the top of the trench, which neatly tipped your cap off just now, was laid by those playful humourists, the Royal Artillery.) It follows that if we accompany these wires far enough we shall ultimately find ourselves in a signalling station.

Our only difficulty lies in judicious choice, for the wires soon begin to diverge up numerous byways. Some go to the fire-trench, others to the machine-guns, others again to observation posts—or O.P.'s—whence a hawk-eyed Forward Observing Officer, peering all day through a chink in a tumble-down chimney or sandbagged loophole, is sometimes enabled to flash back the intelligence that he can discern transport upon such a road in rear of the Boche trenches, and will such a battery kindly attend to the matter at once?

However, chance guides us to the Signal dug-out of "A" Company, where, by the best fortune in the world, Private M'Gurk in person is installed as officiating sprite. Let us render ourselves invisible, sit down beside him, and "tap" his wire.

In the dim and distant days before such phrases as "Boche," and "T.N.T.," and "munitions," and "economy" were invented; when we lived in houses which possessed roofs, and never dreamed of lying down motionless by the roadside when we heard a taxi-whistle blown thrice, in order to escape the notice of approaching aeroplanes,—in short, in the days immediately preceding the war,—some of us said in our haste that the London Telephone Service was The Limit! Since then we have made the acquaintance of the military field-telephone, and we feel distinctly softened towards the young woman at home who, from her dug-out in "Gerrard," or "Vic.," or "Hop.," used to goad us to impotent frenzy. She was at least terse and decided. If you rang her up and asked for a number, she merely replied,—

(a) "Number engaged";
(b) "No reply";
(c) "Out of order"—

as the case might be, and switched you off. After that you took a taxi to the place with which you wished to communicate, and there was an end of the matter. Above all, she never explained, she never wrangled, she spoke tolerably good English, and there was only one of her—or at least she was of a uniform type.

Now, if you put your ear to the receiver of a field-telephone, you find yourself, as it were, suddenly thrust into a vast subterranean cavern, filled with the wailings of the lost, the babblings of the feeble-minded, and the profanity of the exasperated. If you ask a high-caste Buzzer—say, an R.E. Signalling Officer—why this should be so, he will look intensely wise and recite some solemn gibberish about earthed wires and induced currents.

The noises are of two kinds, and one supplements the other. The human voice supplies the libretto, while the accompaniment is provided by a syncopated and tympanum-piercing *ping-ping*, suggestive of a giant mosquito singing to its young.

The instrument with which we are contending is capable (in theory) of transmitting a message either telephonically or telegraphically. In practice, this means that the signaller, having wasted ten sulphurous minutes in a useless attempt to convey information through the medium of the human voice, next proceeds, upon the urgent advice of the gentleman at the other end, and to the confusion of all other inhabitants of the cavern, to "buzz" it, employing the dots and dashes of the Morse code for the purpose.

It is believed that the wily Boche, by means of ingenious and delicate instruments, is able to "tap" a certain number of our trench telephone messages. If he does, his daily Intelligence Report must contain some surprising items of information. At the moment when we attach our invisible apparatus to Mr. M'Gurk's wire, the Divisional Telephone system appears to be fairly evenly divided between—

(1) A Regimental Headquarters endeavouring to ring up its Brigade.
(2) A glee-party of Harmonious Blacksmiths, indulging in the Anvil Chorus.
(3) A choleric Adjutant on the track of a peccant Company Commander.
(4) Two Company Signallers, engaged in a friendly chat from different ends of the trench line.
(5) An Artillery F.O.O., endeavouring to convey pressing and momentous information to his Battery, two miles in rear.
(6) The Giant Mosquito aforesaid.

The consolidated result is something like this:—

REGIMENTAL HEADQUARTERS (*affably*). Hallo, Brigade! Hallo, Brigade! HALLO, BRIGADE!

THE MOSQUITO. Ping!

THE ADJUTANT (*from somewhere in the Support Line, fiercely*). Give me B Company!

THE FORWARD OBSERVING OFFICER (*from his eyrie*). Is that C Battery? There's an enemy working-party—

FIRST CHATTY SIGNALLER (*from B Company's Station*). Is that yoursel', Jock? How's a' wi' you?

SECOND CHATTY SIGNALLER (*from D Company's Station*). I'm daen fine! How's your—

REGIMENTAL HEADQUARTERS. HALLO, BRIGADE!

THE ADJUTANT. Is that B Company?

A MYSTERIOUS AND DISTANT VOICE (*politely.*) No, sir; this is Akk and Esses Aitch.

THE ADJUTANT (*furiously*). Then for the Lord's sake get off the line!

THE MOSQUITO. Ping! Ping!

THE ADJUTANT. And stop that —— —— —— buzzing!

THE MOSQUITO. Ping! *Ping*! PING!

THE F.O.O. Is that C Battery? There's—

FIRST CHATTY SIGNALLER (*peevishly*). What's that you're sayin'?

THE F.O.O. (*perseveringly*). Is that C Battery? There's an enemy working-party in a coppice at—

FIRST CHATTY SIGNALLER. This is Beer Company, sir. Weel, Jock, did ye get a quiet nicht?

SECOND CHATTY SIGNALLER. Oh, aye. There was a wee—

THE F.O.O. Is that C Battery? There's—

SECOND CHATTY SIGNALLER. No, sir. This is Don Company. Weel, Jimmy, there was a couple whish-bangs came intil—

REGIMENTAL HEADQUARTERS. HALLO, BRIGADE!

A CHEERFUL COCKNEY VOICE. Well, my lad, what abaht it?

REGIMENTAL HEADQUARTERS (*getting to work at once*). Hold the line, Brigade. Message to Staff Captain. "Ref. your S.C. fourr stroke seeven eight six, the worrking-parrty in question—"

THE F.O.O. (*seeing a gleam of hope*). Working-party? Is that C Battery? I want to speak to—

THE ADJUTANT. }
BRIGADE HEADQUARTERS. } Get off the line!
REGIMENTAL HEADQUARTERS. }

FIRST CHATTY SIGNALLER. Haw, Jock, was ye hearin' aboot Andra?

SECOND CHATTY SIGNALLER. No. Whit was that?

FIRST CHATTY SIGNALLER. Weel—

THE F.O.O. (*doggedly*). Is that C Battery?

REGIMENTAL HEADQUARTERS (*resolutely*). "The worrking-parrty in question was duly detailed for tae proceed to the rendiss vowse at"—

THE ADJUTANT. Is that B Company, curse you?

REGIMENTAL HEADQUARTERS (*quite impervious to this sort of thing*),—"the rendiss vowse, at seeven thirrty Akk Emma, at point H two B eight nine, near the cross-roads by the Estamint Repose dee Bicyclistees, for tae"—honk! honkle! honk!

BRIGADE HEADQUARTERS (*compassionately*). You're makin' a 'orrible mess of this message, ain't you? Shake your transmitter, do!

REGIMENTAL HEADQUARTERS (*after dutifully performing this operation*). Honkle, honkle, honk. Yang!

BRIGADE HEADQUARTERS. Buzz it, my lad, buzz it!

REGIMENTAL HEADQUARTERS (*dutifully*). Ping, ping! Ping, ping! Ping, ping, ping! Ping—

GENERAL CHORUS. Stop that ——, ——, ——, —— buzzing!

FIRST CHATTY SIGNALLER. Weel, Andra says tae the Sergeant-Major of Beer Company, says he—

THE ADJUTANT. Is that B Company?

FIRST CHATTY SIGNALLER. No, sir; this is Beer Company.

THE ADJUTANT (*fortissimo*). I *said* Beer Company!

FIRST CHATTY SIGNALLER. Oh! I thocht ye meant Don Company, sir.

THE ADJUTANT. Why the blazes haven't you answered me sooner?

FIRST CHATTY SIGNALLER (*tactfully*). There was other messages comin' through, sir.

THE ADJUTANT. Well, get me the Company Commander.

FIRST CHATTY SIGNALLER. Varra good, sirr.

A pause. Regimental Headquarters being engaged in laboriously "buzzing" its message through to the Brigade, all other conversation is at a standstill. The Harmonious Blacksmiths seize the opportunity to give a short selection. Presently, as the din dies down—

THE F.O.O. (*faint, yet pursuing*). Is that C Battery?

A JOVIAL VOICE. Yes.

THE F.O.O. What a shock! I thought you were all dead. Is that you, Chumps?

THE JOVIAL VOICE. It is. What can I do for you this morning?

THE F.O.O. You can boil your signal sentry's head!

THE JOVIAL VOICE. What for?

THE F.O.O. For keeping me waiting.

THE JOVIAL VOICE. Righto! And the next article?

THE F.O.O. There's a Boche working-party in a coppice two hundred yards west of a point—

THE MOSQUITO (*with renewed vigour*). Ping, ping!

THE F.O.O. (*savagely*). Shut up!

THE JOVIAL VOICE. Working-party? I'll settle them. What's the map reference?

THE F.O.O. They are in Square number—

THE HARMONIOUS BLACKSMITHS (*suddenly and stunningly*). Whang!

THE F.O.O. Shut up! They are in Square—

FIRST CHATTY SIGNALLER. Hallo, Headquarters! Is the Adjutant there? Here's the Captain tae speak with him.

AN EAGER VOICE. Is that the Adjutant?

REGIMENTAL HEADQUARTERS. No, sirr. He's away tae his office. Hold the line while I'll—

THE EAGER VOICE. No you don't! Put me straight through to C Battery—quick! Then get off the line, and stay there! (*Much buzzing.*) Is that C Battery?

THE JOVIAL VOICE. Yes, sir.

THE EAGER VOICE. I am O.C. Beer Company. They are shelling my front parapet, at L8, with pretty heavy stuff. I want retaliation, please.

THE JOVIAL VOICE. Very good, sir. (*The voice dies away.*)

A SOUND OVER OUR HEADS (*thirty seconds later*). Whish! Whish! Whish!

SECOND CHATTY SIGNALLER. Did ye hear that, Jimmy?

FIRST CHATTY SIGNALLER (*with relish*). Mphm! That'll sorrt them!

THE F.O.O. Is that C Battery?

THE JOVIAL VOICE. Yes. What luck, old son?

THE F.O.O. You have obtained two direct hits on the Boche parapet. Will you have a cocoanut or a ci—

THE JOVIAL VOICE. A little less lip, my lad! Now tell me all about your industrious friends in the Coppice, and we will see what we can do for *them!*

* * * * *

And so on. Apropos of Adjutants and Company Commanders, Private Wamphray, whose acquaintance we made a few pages back, was ultimately relieved of his position as a Company Signaller, and returned ignominiously to duty, for tactless if justifiable interposition in one of these very dialogues.

It was a dark and cheerless night in mid-winter. Ominous noises in front of the Boche wire had raised apprehensive surmises in the breast of Brigade Headquarters. A forward sap was suspected in the region opposite the sector of trenches held by "A" Company. The trenches at this point were barely forty yards apart, and there was a very real danger that Brother Boche might creep under his own wire, and possibly under ours too, and come tumbling over our parapet.

To Bobby Little came instructions to send a specially selected patrol out to investigate the matter. Three months ago he would have led the expedition himself. Now, as a full-blown Company Commander, he was officially precluded from exposing his own most responsible person to gratuitous risks. So he chose out that recently-joined enthusiast, Angus M'Lachlan, and put him over the parapet on the dark night in question, accompanied by Corporal M'Snape and two scouts, with orders to probe the mystery to its depth and bring back a full report.

It was a ticklish enterprise. As is frequently the case upon these occasions, nervous tension manifested itself much more seriously at Headquarters than in the front-line trenches. The man on the spot is, as a rule, much too busy with the actual execution of the enterprise in hand to distress himself by speculation upon its ultimate outcome. It may as well be stated at once that Angus duly returned from his quest, with an admirable and reassuring report. But he was a long time absent. Hence this anecdote.

Bobby had strict orders to report all "developments," as they occurred, to Headquarters by telephone. At half-past eleven that night, as Angus M'Lachlan's colossal form disappeared, crawling, into the blackness of night, his superior officer dutifully rang up Battalion Headquarters, and announced that the venture was launched. It is possible that the Powers Behind were in possession of information as to the enemy's intentions unrevealed to Bobby; for as soon as his opening announcement was received, he was switched right through to a very august Headquarters indeed, and commanded to report direct.

Long-distance telephony in the field involves a considerable amount of "linking-up." Among other slaves of the Buzzer who assisted in establishing the necessary communications upon this occasion was Private Wamphray. For the next hour and a half it was his privilege in his subterranean exchange, to sit, with his receiver clamped to his ear, an unappreciative auditor of dialogues like the following:—

"Is that 'A' Company?"

"Yes, sir."

"Any news of your patrol?"

"No, sir."

Again, five minutes later:—

"Is that 'A' Company?"

"Yes, sir."

"Has your officer returned yet?"

"No, sir. I will notify you when he does."

This sort of thing went on until nearly one o'clock in the morning. Towards that hour, Bobby, who was growing really concerned over Angus's prolonged absence, cut short his august interlocutor's fifteenth inquiry and joined his Sergeant-Major on the firing-step. The two had hardly exchanged a few low-pitched sentences when Bobby was summoned back to the telephone.

"Is that Captain Little?"

"Yes, sir."

"Has your patrol come in?"

"No, sir."

Captain's Little's last answer was delivered in a distinctly insubordinate manner. Feeling slightly relieved, he returned to the firing-step. Two minutes later Angus M'Lachlan and his posse rolled over the parapet, safe and sound, and Bobby was able, to his own great content and that of the weary operators along the line, to announce,—

"The patrol has returned, sir, and reports everything quite satisfactory. I am forwarding a detailed statement."

Then he laid down the receiver with a happy sigh, and crawled out of the dug-out on to the duck-board.

"Now we'll have a look round the sentries, Sergeant-Major," he said.

But the pair had hardly rounded three traverses when Bobby was haled back to the Signal Station.

"Why did you leave the telephone just now?" inquired a cold voice.

"I was going to visit my sentries, sir."

"But *I* was speaking to you."

"I thought you had finished, sir."

"I had *not* finished. If I had finished, I should have informed you of the fact, and would have said' Good-night!'"

"How *does* one choke off a tripe-merchant of this type?" wondered the exhausted officer.

From the bowels of the earth came the answer to his unspoken question—delivered in a strong Paisley accent—

"For Goad's sake, kiss him, and say 'Good-Nicht,' and hae done with it!"

As already stated, Private Wamphray was returned to his platoon next morning.

IV

But to regard the Buzzer simply and solely as a troglodyte, of sedentary habits and caustic temperament, is not merely hopelessly wrong: it is grossly unjust. Sometimes he goes for a walk—under some such circumstances as the following.

The night is as black as Tartarus, and it is raining heavily. Brother Boche, a prey to nervous qualms, is keeping his courage up by distributing shrapnel along our communication-trenches. Signal-wires are peculiarly vulnerable to shrapnel. Consequently no one in the Battalion Signal Station is particularly surprised when the line to "Akk" Company suddenly ceases to perform its functions.

Signal-Sergeant M'Micking tests the instrument, glances over his shoulder, and observes,—

"Line BX is gone, some place or other. Away you, Duncan, and sorrt it!"

Mr. Duncan, who has been sitting hunched over a telephone, temporarily quiescent, smoking a woodbine, heaves a resigned sigh, extinguishes the woodbine and places it behind his ear; hitches his repairing-wallet nonchalantly over his shoulder, and departs into the night—there to grope in several inches of mud for the two broken ends of the wire, which may be lying fifty yards apart. Having found them, he proceeds to effect a junction, his progress being impeded from time to time by further bursts of shrapnel. This done, he tests the new connection, relights his woodbine, and splashes his way back to Headquarters. That is a Buzzer's normal method of obtaining fresh air and exercise.

More than that. He is the one man in the Army who can fairly describe himself as indispensable.

In these days, when whole nations are deployed against one another, no commander, however eminent, can ride the whirlwind single-handed. There are limits to individual capacity. There are limits to direct control. There are limits to personal magnetism. We fight upon a collective plan nowadays. If we propose to engage in battle, we begin by welding a hundred thousand men into one composite giant. We weld a hundred thousand rifles, a million bombs, a thousand machine-guns, and as many pieces of artillery, into one huge weapon of offence, with which we arm our giant. Having done this, we provide him with a brain—a blend of all the experience and wisdom and military genius at our disposal. But still there is one thing lacking—a nervous system. Unless our giant have that,—unless his brain be able to transmit its desires to his mighty limbs,—he has nothing. He is of no account; the enemy can make butcher's-meat of him. And that is why I say that the purveyor of this nervous system—our friend the Buzzer—is indispensable. You can always create a body of sorts and a brain of sorts. But unless you can produce a nervous system of the highest excellence, you are foredoomed to failure.

Take a small instance. Supposing a battalion advances to the attack, and storms an isolated, exposed position. Can they hold on, or can they not? That question can only be answered by the Artillery behind them. If the curtain of shell-fire which has preceded the advancing battalion to its objective can be "lifted" at the right moment and put down again, with precision, upon a certain vital zone beyond the captured line, counter-attacks can be broken up and the line held. But the Artillery lives a long way—sometimes miles—in rear. Without continuous and accurate information it will be more than useless; it will be dangerous. (A successful attacking party has been shelled out of its hardly won position by its own artillery before now—on both sides!) Sometimes a little visual signalling is possible: sometimes a despatch-runner may get back through the enemy's curtain of fire; but in the main your one hope of salvation hangs upon a slender thread of insulated wire. And round that wire are strung some of the purest gems of heroism that the War has produced.

At the Battle of Loos, half a battalion of "K(1)" pushed forward into a very advanced hostile position. There they hung, by their teeth. Their achievement was great; but unless Headquarters could be informed of their exact position and needs, they were all dead men. So Corporal Greig set out to find them, unreeling wire as he went. He was blown to pieces by an eight-inch shell, but another signaller was never lacking to take his place. They pressed forward, these lackadaisical non-combatants, until the position was reached and communication established. Again and again the wire was cut by shrapnel, and again and again a Buzzer crawled out to find the broken ends and piece them together. And ultimately, the tiny, exposed limb in front having been enabled to explain its exact requirements to the brain behind, the necessary help was forthcoming and the Fort was held.

Next time you pass a Signaller's Dug-out peep inside. You will find it occupied by a coke brazier, emitting large quantities of carbon monoxide, and an untidy gentleman in khaki, with a blue-and-white device upon his shoulder-straps, who is humped over a small black instrument, luxuriating in a "frowst" most indescribable. He is reading a back number of a rural Scottish newspaper which you never heard of. Occasionally, in response to a faint buzz, he takes up his transmitter and indulges in an unintelligible altercation with a person unseen. You need feel no surprise if he is wearing the ribbon of the Distinguished Conduct Medal.

VII

PASTURES NEW

I

The outstanding feature of to-day's intelligence is that spring is coming—has come, in fact.

It arrived with a bump. March entered upon its second week with seven degrees of frost and four inches of snow. We said what was natural and inevitable to the occasion, wrapped our coats of skins more firmly round us, and made a point of attending punctually when the rum ration was issued.

Forty-eight hours later winter had disappeared. The sun was blazing in a cloudless sky. Aeroplanes were battling for photographic rights overhead; the brown earth beneath our feet was putting forth its first blades of tender green. The muck-heap outside our rest-billet displayed unmistakable signs of upheaval from its winter sleep. Primroses appeared in Bunghole Wood; larks soared up into the sky above No Man's Land, making music for the just and the unjust. Snipers, smiling cheerfully over the improved atmospheric conditions, polished up their telescopic sights. The artillery on each side hailed the birth of yet another season of fruitfulness and natural increase with some more than usually enthusiastic essays in mutual extermination. Half the Mess caught colds in their heads.

Frankly, we are not sorry to see the end of winter. Caesar, when he had concluded his summer campaign, went into winter quarters. Caesar, as Colonel Kemp once huskily remarked, knew something!

Still, each man to his taste. Corporal Mucklewame, for one, greatly prefers winter to summer.

"In the winter," he points out to Sergeant M'Snape, "a body can breathe withoot swallowing a wheen bluebottles and bum-bees. A body can aye streitch himself doon under a tree for a bit sleep withoot getting wasps and wee beasties crawling up inside his kilt, and puddocks craw-crawing in his ear! A body can keep himself frae sweitin'—"

"He can that!" assents M'Snape, whose spare frame is more vulnerable to the icy breeze than that of the stout corporal.

However, the balance of public opinion is against Mucklewame. Most of us are unfeignedly glad to feel the warmth of the sun again. That working-party, filling sandbags just behind the machine-gun emplacement, are actually singing. Spring gets into the blood, even in this stricken land. The Boche over the way resents our efforts at harmony.

  Sing us a song, a song of Bonnie Scotland!
  Any old song will do.
By the old camp-fire, the rough-and-ready choir
  Join in the chorus too.
"You'll tak' the high road and I'll tak' the low road"—
  'Tis a song that we all know,
To bring back the days in Bonnie Scotland,
  Where the heather and the bluebells—

Whang!

The Boche, a Wagnerian by birth and upbringing, cannot stand any more of this, so he has fired a rifle-grenade at the glee-party—on the whole a much more honest and direct method of condemnation than that practiced by musical critics in time of peace. But he only elicits an encore. Private Nigg perches a steel helmet on the point of a bayonet, and patronisingly bobs the same up and down above the parapet.

These steel helmets have not previously been introduced to the reader's notice. They are modelled upon those worn in the French Army—and bear about as much resemblance to the original pattern as a Thames barge to a racing yacht. When first issued, they were greeted with profound suspicion. Though undoubtedly serviceable,—they saved many a crown from cracking round The Bluff the other day,—they were undeniably heavy, and they were certainly not becoming to the peculiar type of beauty rampant in "K(1)." On issue, then, their recipients elected to regard the wearing of them as a peculiarly noxious form of "fatigue." Private M'A. deposited his upon the parapet, like a foundling on a doorstep, and departed stealthily round the nearest traverse, to report his new headpiece "lost through the exigencies of military service." Private M'B. wore his insecurely perched upon the top of his tam-o'-shanter bonnet, where it looked like a very large ostrich egg in a very small khaki nest. Private M'C. set his up on a convenient post, and opened rapid fire upon it at a range of six yards, surveying the resulting holes with the gloomy satisfaction of the vindicated pessimist. Private M'D. removed the lining from his, and performed his ablutions in the inverted crown.

"This," said Colonel Kemp, "will never do. We must start wearing the dashed things ourselves."

And it was so. Next day, to the joy of the Battalion, their officers appeared in the trenches selfconsciously wearing what looked like small sky-blue wash-hand basins balanced upon their heads. But discipline was excellent. No one even smiled. In fact, there was a slight reaction in favour of the helmets. Conversations like the following were overheard:—

"I'm tellin' you, Jimmy, the C.O. is no the man for tae mak' a show of himself like that for naething. These tin bunnets must be some use. Wull we pit oors on?"

"Awa' hame, and bile your heid!" replied the unresponsive James.

"They'll no stop a whish-bang," conceded the apostle of progress, "but they would keep off splunters, and a wheen bullets, and—and—"

"And the rain!" supplied Jimmy sarcastically.

This gibe suddenly roused the temper of the other participant in the debate.

"I tell you," he exclaimed, in a voice shrill with indignation, "that these —— helmets are some —— use!"

"And I tell *you*," retorted James earnestly, "that these —— helmets are no —— —— use!"

When two reasonable persons arrive at a controversial *impasse*, they usually agree to differ and go their several ways. But in "K(1)" we prefer practical solutions. The upholder of helmets hastily thrust his upon his head.

"I'll show you, Jimmy!" he announced, and clambered up on the firing-step.

"And I'll —— well show *you*, Wullie!" screamed James, doing likewise.

Simultaneously the two zealots thrust their heads over the parapet, and awaited results. These came. The rifles of two Boche snipers rang out, and both demonstrators fell heavily backwards into the arms of their supporters.

By all rights they ought to have been killed. But they were both very much alive. Each turned to the other triumphantly, and exclaimed,—

"I tellt ye so!"

There was a hole right through the helmet of Jimmy, the unbeliever. The fact that there was not also a hole through his head was due to his forethought in having put on a tam-o'-shanter underneath. The net result was a truncated "toorie." Wullie's bullet had struck his helmet at a more obtuse angle, and had glanced off, as the designer of the smooth exterior had intended it to do.

At first glance, the contest was a draw. But subsequent investigation elicited the fact that Jimmy in his backward fall had bitten his tongue to the effusion of blood. The verdict was therefore awarded, on points, to Wullie, and the spectators dispersed in an orderly manner just as the platoon sergeant came round the traverse to change the sentry.

II

We have occupied our own present trenches since January. There was a time when this sector of the line was regarded as a Vale of Rest. Bishops were conducted round with impunity. Members of Parliament came out for the week-end, and returned to their constituents with first-hand information about the horrors of war. Foreign journalists, and sight-seeing parties of munition-workers, picnicked in Bunghole Wood. In the village behind the line, if a chance shell removed tiles from the roof of a house, the owner, greatly incensed, mounted a ladder and put in some fresh ones.

But that is all over now. "K(1)"—hard-headed men of business, bountifully endowed with munitions—have arrived upon the scene, and the sylvan peace of the surrounding district is gone. Pan has dug himself in.

The trouble began two months ago, when our Divisional Artillery arrived. Unversed in local etiquette, they commenced operations by "sending up"—to employ a vulgar but convenient catch-phrase—a strongly fortified farmhouse in the enemy's support line. The Boche, by way of gentle reproof, deposited four or five small "whizz-bangs" in our front-line trenches. The tenants thereof promptly telephoned to "Mother," and Mother came to the assistance of her offspring with a salvo of twelve-inch shells. After that. Brother Boche, realising that the golden age was past, sent north to the Salient for a couple of heavy batteries, and settled down to shell Bunghole village to pieces. Within a week he had brought down the church tower: within a fortnight the population had migrated farther back, leaving behind a few patriots, too deeply interested in the sale of small beer and picture postcards to uproot themselves. Company Headquarters in Bunghole Wood ceased to grow primroses and began to fill sandbags.

A month ago the village was practically intact. The face of the church tower was badly scarred, but the houses were undamaged. The little shops were open; children played in the streets. Now, if you stand at the cross-roads where the church rears its roofless walls, you will understand what the Abomination of Desolation means. Occasionally a body of troops, moving in small detachments at generous intervals, trudges by, on its way to or from the trenches. Occasionally a big howitzer shell swings lazily out of the blue and drops with a crash or a dull thud—according to the degree of resistance encountered—among the crumbling cottages. All is solitude.

But stay! Right on the cross-roads, in the centre of the village, just below the fingers of a sign-post which indicates the distance to four French townships, whose names you never heard of until a year ago, and now will never forget, there hangs a large, white, newly painted board, bearing a notice in black letters six inches high. Exactly underneath the board, rubbing their noses appreciatively against the sign-post, stand two mules, attached to a limbered waggon, the property of the A.S.C. Their charioteers are sitting adjacent, in a convenient shell-hole, partaking of luncheon.

"That was a rotten place we' ad to wait in yesterday, Sammy," observes Number One. "The draught was somethink cruel."

The recumbent Samuel agrees. "This little 'oiler is a bit of all right," he remarks. "When you've done strafin' that bully-beef, 'and it over, ole man!"

He leans his head back upon the lip of the shell-hole, and gazes pensively at the notice-board six feet away. It says:—

VERY DANGEROUS. DO NOT LOITER HERE.

III

Here is another cross-roads, a good mile farther forward—and less than a hundred yards behind the fire-trench. It is dawn.

The roads themselves are not so distinct as they were. They are becoming grass-grown: for more than a year—in daylight at least—no human foot has trodden them. The place is like hundreds of others that you may see scattered up and down this countryside—two straight, flat, metalled country roads, running north and south and east and west, crossing one another at a faultless right angle.

Of the four corners thus created, one is—or was—occupied by an estaminet: you can still see the sign, *Estaminet au Commerce*, over the door. Two others contain cottages,—the remains of cottages. At the fourth, facing south and east, stands what is locally known as a "Calvaire,"—bank of stone, a lofty cross, and a life-size figure of Christ, facing east, towards the German lines.

This spot is shelled every day—has been shelled every day for months. Possibly the enemy suspects a machine-gun or an observation post amid the tumble-down buildings. Hardly one brick remains upon another. And yet—the sorrowful Figure is unbroken. The Body is riddled with bullets—in the glowing dawn you may Count not five but fifty wounds—but the Face is untouched. It is the standing miracle of this most materialistic war. Throughout the length of France you will see the same thing.

Agnostics ought to come out here, for a "cure."

IV

With spring comes also the thought of the Next Push.

But we do not talk quite so glibly of pushes as we did. Neither, for that matter, does Brother Boche. He has just completed six weeks' pushing at Verdun, and is beginning to be a little uncertain as to which direction the pushing is coming from.

No; once more the military textbooks are being rewritten. We started this war under one or two rather fallacious premises. One was that Artillery was more noisy than dangerous. When Antwerp fell, we rescinded that theory. Then the Boche set out to demonstrate that an Attack, provided your Artillery preparation is sufficiently thorough, and you are prepared to set *no* limit to your expenditure of Infantry, must ultimately succeed. To do him justice, the Boche supported his assertions very plausibly. His phalanx bundled the Russians all the way from Tannenburg to Riga. The Austrians adopted similar tactics, with similar results.

We were duly impressed. The world last summer did not quite realize how far the results of the campaign were due to German efficiency and how far to Russian unpreparedness. (Russia, we realise now, found herself in the position of the historic Mrs. Partington, who endeavoured to repel the Atlantic with a mop. This year, we understand, she is in a position to discard the mop in favour of something far, far better.)

Then came—Verdun. Military science turned over yet another page, and noted that against consummate generalship, unlimited munitions, and selfless devotion on the part of the defence, the most spectacular and highly-doped phalanx can spend itself in vain. Military science also noted that, under modern conditions, the capture of this position or that signifies nothing: the only method of computing victory is to count the dead on either side. On that reckoning, the French at Verdun have already gained one of the great victories of all time.

"In fact," said Colonel Kemp, "this war will end when the Boche has lost so many men as to be unable to man his present trench-line, and not before."

"You don't think, sir, that we shall make another Push?" suggested Angus M'Lachlan eagerly. The others were silent: they had experienced a Push already.

"Not so long as the Boche continues to play our game for us, by attacking. If he tumbles to the error he is making, and digs himself in again—well, it may become necessary to draw him. In that case, M'Lachlan, you shall have first chop at the Victoria Crosses. Afraid I can't recommend you for your last exploit, though I admit it must have required some nerve!"

There was unseemly laughter at this allusion. Four nights previously Angus had been sent out in charge of a wiring-party. He had duly crawled forth with his satellites, under cover of darkness, on to No Man's Land; and, there selecting a row of "knife-rests" which struck him as being badly in need of repair, had well and truly reinforced the same with many strands of the most barbarous brand of barbed wire. This, despite more than usually fractious behaviour upon the part of the Boche.

Next morning, through a sniper's loophole, he exhibited the result of his labours to Major Wagstaffe. The Major gazed long and silently upon his subordinate's handiwork. There was no mistaking it. It stood out bright and gleaming in the rays of the rising sun, amid its dingy surroundings of rusty ironmongery. Angus M'Lachlan waited anxiously for a little praise.

"Jolly good piece of work," said Major Wagstaffe at last. "But tell me, why have you repaired the Boche wire instead of your own?"

"The only enemy we have to fear," continued Colonel Kemp, rubbing his spectacles savagely, "is the free and independent British voter—I mean, the variety of the species that we have left at home. Like the gentleman in Jack Point's song, 'He likes to get value for money'; and he is quite capable of asking us, about June or July, 'if we know that we are paid to be funny?'—before we are ready. What's your view of the situation at home, Wagstaffe? You're the last off leave."

Wagstaffe shook his head.

"The British Nation," he said, "is quite mad. That fact, of course, has been common property on the Continent of Europe ever since Cook's Tours were invented. But what irritates the orderly Boche is that there is no method in its madness. Nothing you can go upon, or take hold of, or wring any advantage from."

"As how?"

"Well, take compulsory service. For generations the electorate of our country has been trained by a certain breed of politician—the *Bandar-log* of the British Constitution—to howl down such a low and degrading business as National Defence. A nasty Continental custom, they called it. Then came the War, and the glorious Voluntary System got to work."

"Aided," the Colonel interpolated, "by a campaign of mural advertisement which a cinema star's press agent would have boggled at!"

"Quite so," agreed Wagstaffe. "Next, when the Voluntary System had done its damnedest—in other words, when the willing horse had been worked to his last ounce—we tried the Derby Scheme. The manhood of the nation was divided into groups, and a fresh method of touting for troops was adopted. Married shysters, knowing that at least twenty groups stood between them and a job of work, attested in comparatively large numbers. The single shysters were less reckless—so much less reckless, in fact, that compulsion began to materialise at last."

"But only for single shysters," said Bobby Little regretfully.

"Yes; and the married shyster rejoiced accordingly. But the single shyster is a most subtle reptile. On examination, it was found that the single members of this noble army of martyrs were all 'starred,' or 'reserved', or 'ear-marked'—or whatever it is that they do to these careful fellows. So the poor old married shyster, who had only attested to show his blooming patriotism and encourage the others, suddenly found himself confronted with the awful prospect of having to defend his country personally, instead of by letter to the halfpenny press. Then the fat was fairly in the fire! The married martyr—"

"Come, come, old man! Not all of them!" said Colonel Kemp. "I have a married brother of my own, a solicitor of thirty-eight, who is simply clamouring for active service!"

"I know that, sir," admitted Wagstaffe quickly. "Thank God, these fellows are only a minority, and a freak minority at that; but freak minorities seem to get the monopoly of the limelight in our unhappy country."

"The whole affair," mused the Colonel, "can hardly be described as a frenzied rally round the Old Flag. By God," he broke out suddenly, "it fairly makes one's blood boil! When I think of the countless good fellows, married and single, but mainly married, who left *all* and followed the call of common decency and duty the moment the War broke out—most of them now dead or crippled; and when I see this miserable handful of shirkers, holding up vital public business while the pros and cons of their wretched claims to exemption are considered—well, I almost wish I had been born a Boche!"

"I don't think you need apply for naturalisation papers yet, Colonel," said Wagstaffe. "The country is perfectly sound at heart over this question, and always was. The present agitation, as I say, is being engineered by the more verminous section of our incomparable daily Press, for its own ends. It makes our Allies lift their eyebrows a bit; but they are sensible people, and they realise that although we are a nation of lunatics, we usually deliver the goods in the end. As for the Boche, poor fellow, the whole business makes him perfectly rabid. Here he is, with all his splendid organisation and brutal efficiency, and he can't even knock a dent into our undisciplined, back-chatting, fool-ridden, self-depreciating old country! I, for one, sympathise with the Boche profoundly. On paper, we don't *deserve* to win!"

"But we shall!" remarked that single-minded paladin, Bobby Little.

"Of course we shall! And what's more, we are going to derive a national benefit out of this war which will in itself be worth the price of admission!"

"How?" asked several voices.

Wagstaffe looked round the table. The Battalion were for the moment in Divisional Reserve, and consequently out of the trenches. Some one had received a box of Coronas from home, and the mess president had achieved a bottle of port. Hence the present symposium at Headquarters Mess. Wagstaffe's eyes twinkled.

"Will each officer present," he said, "kindly name his pet aversion among his fellow-creatures?"

"A person or a type?" asked Mr. Waddell cautiously.

"A type."

Colonel Kemp led off.

"Male ballet-dancers," he said.

"Fat, shiny men," said Bobby Little, "with walrus mustaches!"

"All conscientious objectors, passive resisters, pacifists, and other cranks!" continued the orthodox Waddell.

"All people who go on strike during war-time," said the Adjutant.

There was an approving murmur—then silence.

"Your contribution, M'Lachlan?" said Wagstaffe.

Angus, who had kept silence from shyness, suddenly blazed out:—

"I think," he said, "that the most contemptible people in the world to-day are those politicians and others who, in years gone by, systematically cried down anything in the shape of national defence or national inclination to personal service, because they saw there were no *votes* in such a programme; and who *now*"—Angus's passion rose to fever-heat,—"stand up and endeavour to cultivate popular favour by reviling the Ministry and the Army for want of preparedness and initiative. Such men do not deserve to live! Oh, sirs—"

But Angus's peroration was lost in a storm of applause.

"You are adjudged to have hit the bull's-eye, M'Lachlan," said Colonel Kemp. "But tell us, Wagstaffe, your exact object in compiling this horrible catalogue."

"Certainly. It is this. Universal Service is a *fait accompli* at last, or is shortly going to be—and without anything very much in the way of exemption either. When it comes, just think of it! All these delightful people whom we have been enumerating will have to toe the line at last. For the first time in their little lives they will learn the meaning of discipline, and fresh air, and *ésprit de corps*. Isn't that worth a war? If the present scrap can only be prolonged for another year, our country will receive a tonic which will carry it on for another century. Think of it! Great Britain, populated by men who have actually been outside their own parish; men who know that the whole is greater than the part; men who are too wide awake to go on doing just what the *Bandar-log* tell them, and allow themselves to be used as stalking-horses for low-down political ramps! When *we*, going round in bath-chairs and on crutches, see that sight—well, I don't think we shall regret our missing arms and legs quite so much, Colonel. War is Hell, and all that; but there is one worse thing than a long war, and that is a long peace!"

"I wonder!" said Colonel Kemp reflectively. He was thinking of his wife and four children in distant Argyllshire.

But the rapt attitude and quickened breath of Temporary Captain Bobby Little endorsed every word that Major Wagstaffe had spoken. As he rolled into his "flea-bag" that night, Bobby requoted to himself, for the hundredth time, a passage from Shakespeare which had recently come to his notice. He was not a Shakespearian scholar, nor indeed a student of literature at all; but these lines had been sent to him, cut out of a daily almanac, by an equally unlettered and very adorable confidante at home:—

"And gentlemen in England now a-bed,
Shall think themselves accursed they were not here,
And hold their manhoods cheap whiles any speaks
That fought with us upon Saint Crispin's day!"

Bobby was the sort of person who would thoroughly have enjoyed the Battle of Agincourt.

VIII

"THE NON-COMBATANT"

I

We will call the village St. Grégoire. That is not its real name; because the one thing you must not do in war-time is to call a thing by its real name. To take a hackneyed example, you do not call a spade a spade: you refer to it, officially, as *Shovels, General Service, One*. This helps to deceive, and ultimately to surprise, the enemy; and as we all know by this time, surprise is the essence of successful warfare. On the same principle, if your troops are forced back from their front-line trenches, you call this "successfully straightening out an awkward salient."

But this by the way. Let us get back to St. Grégoire. Hither, mud-splashed, ragged, hollow-cheeked, came our battalion—they call us the Seventh Hairy Jocks nowadays—after four months' continuous employment in the firing-line. Ypres was a household word to them; Plugstreet was familiar ground; Givenchy they knew intimately; Loos was their wash-pot—or rather, a collection of wash-pots, for in winter all the shell-craters are full to overflowing. In addition to their prolonged and strenuous labours in the trenches, the Hairy Jocks had taken part in a Push—a part not altogether unattended with glory, but prolific in casualties. They had not been "pulled out" to rest and refit for over six months, for Divisions on the Western Front were not at that period too numerous, the voluntary system being at its last gasp, while the legions of Lord Derby had not yet crystallised out of the ocean of public talk which held them in solution. So the Seventh Hairy Jocks were bone tired. But they were as hard as a rigorous winter in the open could make them, and—they were going back to rest at last. Had not their beloved C.O. told them so? And he had added, in a voice not altogether free from emotion, that if ever men deserved a solid rest and a good time, "you boys do!"

So the Hairy Jocks trudged along the long, straight, nubbly French road, well content, speculating with comfortable pessimism as to the character of the billets in which they would find themselves.

Meanwhile, ten miles ahead, the advance party were going round the town in quest of the billets.

Billet-hunting on the Western Front is not quite so desperate an affair as hunting for lodgings at Margate, because in the last extremity you can always compel the inhabitants to take you in—or at least, exert pressure to that end through the *Mairie*. But at the best one's course is strewn with obstacles, and fortunate is the Adjutant who has to his hand a subaltern capable of finding lodgings for a thousand men without making a mess of it.

The billeting officer on this, as on most occasions, was our friend Cockerell,—affectionately known to the entire Battalion as "Sparrow,"—and his qualifications for the post were derived from three well-marked and invaluable characteristics, namely, an imperious disposition, a thick skin, and an attractive *bonhomie* of manner.

Behold him this morning dismounting from his horse in the *place* of St. Grégoire. Around him are grouped his satellites—the Quartermaster-Sergeant, four Company Sergeants, some odd orderlies, and a forlorn little man in a neat drab uniform with light blue facings,—the regimental interpreter. The party have descended, with the delicate care of those who essay to perform acrobatic feats in kilts, from bicycles—serviceable but appallingly heavy machines of Government manufacture, the property of the "Buzzers," but commandeered for the occasion. The Quartermaster-Sergeant, who is not accustomed to strenuous exercise, mops his brow and glances expectantly round the *place*. His eye comes gently to rest upon a small but hospitable-looking *estaminet*.

Lieutenant Cockerell examines his wrist-watch.

"Half-past ten!" he announces. "Quartermaster-Sergeant!"

"Sirr!" The Quartermaster-Sergeant unglues his longing gaze from the *estaminet* and comes woodenly to attention.

"I am going to see the Town Major about a billeting area. I will meet you and the party here in twenty minutes."

Master Cockerell trots off on his mud-splashed steed, followed by the respectful and appreciative salutes of his followers—appreciative, because a less considerate officer would have taken the whole party direct to the Town Major's office and kept them standing in the street, wasting moments which might have been better employed elsewhere, until it was time to proceed with the morning's work.

* * * * *

"How strong are you?" inquired the Town Major.

Cockerell told him. The Town Major whistled.

"That all? Been doing some job of work, haven't you?"

Cockerell nodded, and the Town Major proceeded to examine a large-scale plan of St. Grégoire, divided up into different-coloured plots.

"We are rather full up at present," he said; "but the Cemetery Area is vacant. The Seventeenth Geordies moved out yesterday. You can have that." He indicated a triangular section with his pencil.

Master Cockerell gave a deprecatory cough.

"We have come here, sir," he intimated dryly, "for a change of scene."

The stout Town Major—all Town Majors are stout—chuckled.

"Not bad for a Scot!" he conceded. "But it's quite a cheery district, really. You won't have to doss down in the cemetery itself, you know. These two streets here—" he flicked a pencil—"will hold practically all your battalion, at its present strength. There's a capital house in the Rue Jean Jacques Rousseau which will do for Battalion Headquarters. The corporal over there will give you your *billets de logement*."

"Are there any other troops in the area, sir?" asked Cockerell, who, as already indicated, was no child in these matters.

"There ought not to be, of course. But you know what the Heavy Gunners and the A.S.C. are! If you come across any of them, fire them out. If they wear too many stars and crowns for you, let me know, and I will perform the feat myself. You fellows need a good rest and no worries, I know. Good-morning."

At ten minutes to eleven Cockerell found the Quartermaster-Sergeant and party, wiping their mustaches and visibly refreshed, at the exact spot where he had left them; and the hunt for billets began.

"A" Company were easily provided for, a derelict tobacco factory being encountered at the head of the first street. Lieutenant Cockerell accordingly detached a sergeant and a corporal from his train, and passed on. The wants of "B" Company were supplied by commandeering a block of four dilapidated houses farther down the street—all in comparatively good repair except the end house, whose roof had been disarranged by a shell during the open fighting in the early days of the war.

This exhausted the possibilities of the first street, and the party debouched into the second, which was long and straggling, and composed entirely of small houses.

"Now for a bit of the retail business!" said Master Cockerell resignedly. "Sergeant M'Nab, what is the strength of 'C' Company?"

"One hunner and thairty-fower other ranks, sirr," announced Sergeant M'Nab, consulting a much-thumbed roll-book.

"We shall have to put them in twos and threes all down the street," said Cockerell. "Come on; the longer we look at it the less we shall like it. Interpreter!"

The forlorn little man, already described, trotted up, and saluted with open hand, French fashion. His name was Baptiste Bombominet ("or words to that effect," as the Adjutant put it), and may have been so inscribed upon the regimental roll; but throughout the rank and file Baptiste was affectionately known by the generic title of "Alphonso." The previous seven years had been spent by him in the congenial and blameless atmosphere of a Ladies' Tailor's in the west end of London, where he enjoyed the status and emoluments of chief cutter. Now, called back to his native land by the voice of patriotic obligation, he found himself selected, by virtue of a residence of seven years in England, to act as official interpreter between a Scottish Regiment which could not speak English, and Flemish peasants who could not speak French. No wonder that his pathetic brown eyes always appeared full of tears. However, he followed Cockerell down the street, and meekly embarked upon a contest with the lady Inhabitants thereof, in which he was hopelessly outmatched from the start.

At the first door a dame of massive proportions, but keen business instincts, announced her total inability to accommodate *soldats*, but explained that she would be pleased to entertain *officiers* to any number. This is a common gambit. Twenty British privates in your *grenier*, though extraordinarily well-behaved as a class, make a good deal of noise, buy little, and leave mud everywhere. On the other hand, two or three officers give no trouble, and can be relied upon to consume and pay for unlimited omelettes and bowls of coffee.

That seasoned vessel, Lieutenant Cockerell, turned promptly to the Sergeant and Corporal of "C" Company.

"Sergeant M'Nab," he said, "you and Corporal Downie will billet here."

He introduced hostess and guests by an expressive wave of the hand.

But shrewd Madame was not to be bluffed.

"*Pas de sergents, Monsieur le Capitaine!*" she exclaimed. "*Officiers!*"

"*Ils sont officiers—sous-officiers*," explained Cockerell, rather ingeniously, and moved off down the street.

At the next house the owner—a small, wizened lady of negligible physique but great staying power—entered upon a duet with Alphonso, which soon reduced that very moderate performer to breathlessness. He shrugged his shoulders feebly, and cast an appealing glance towards the Lieutenant.

"What does she say?" inquired Cockerell.

"She say dis' ouse no good, sair! She 'ave seven children, and one *malade*—seek."

"Let me see," commanded the practical officer.

He insinuated himself as politely as possible past his reluctant opponent, and walked down the narrow passage into the kitchen. Here he turned, and inquired—

"Er—*ou est la pauvre petite chose?*"

Madame promptly opened a door, and displayed a little girl in bed—a very flushed and feverish little girl. Cockerell grinned sympathetically at the patient, to that young lady's obvious gratification; and turned to the mother.

"*Je suis tres—triste*," he said; "*j'ai grand miséricorde. Je ne placerai pas de soldats ici. Bon jour!*"

By this time he was in the street again. He saluted politely and departed, followed by the grateful regards of Madame.

No special difficulties were encountered at the next few houses. The ladies at the house-door were all polite; many of them were most friendly; but naturally each was anxious to get as few men and as many officers as possible—except the proprietess of an *estaminel*, who offered to accommodate the entire regiment. However, with a little tact here and a little firmness there, Master Cockerell succeeded in distributing "C" Company among some dozen houses. One old gentleman, with a black alpaca cap and a six-days beard, proprietor of a lofty establishment at the corner of the street, proved not only recalcitrant, but abusive. With him Cockerell dealt promptly.

"*Ça suffit!*" he announced. "*Montres-moi votre grenier!*"

The old man, grumbling, led the way up numerous rickety staircases to the inevitable loft under the tiles. This proved to be a noble apartment thirty feet long. From wall to wall stretched innumerable strings.

"We can get a whole platoon in here," said Cockerell contentedly. "Tell him, Alphonso. These people," he explained to Sergeant M'Nab, "always dislike giving up their lofts, because they hang their laundry there in winter. However, the old boy must lump it. After all, we are in this country for his health, not ours; and he gets paid for every man who sleeps here. That fixes 'C' Company. Now for 'D'! The other side of the street this time."

Quarters were found in due course for "D" Company; after which Cockerell discovered a vacant building-site which would serve for transport lines. An empty garage was marked down for the Quartermaster's ration store, and the Quartermaster-Sergeant promptly faded into its recesses with a grateful sigh. An empty shop in the Rue Jean Jacques Rousseau, conveniently adjacent to Battalion Headquarters, was appropriated for that gregarious band, the regimental signallers and telephone section; while a suitable home for the Anarchists, or Bombers, together with their stock-in-trade, was found in the basement of a remote dwelling on the outskirts of the area.

After this, Lieutenant Cockerell, left alone with Alphonso and the orderly in charge of his horse, heaved a sigh of exhaustion and transferred his attention from his notebook to his watch.

"That finishes the rank and file," he said. "I breakfasted at four this morning, and the battalion won't arrive for a couple of hours yet. Alphonso, I am going to have an omelette somewhere. I shall want you in half an hour exactly. Don't go wandering off for the rest of the day, pinching soft billets for yourself and the Sergeant-Major and your other pals, as you usually do!"

Alphonso saluted guiltily—evidently the astute Cockerell had "touched the spot"—and was turning away, when suddenly the billeting officer's eye encountered an illegible scrawl at the very foot of his list.

"Stop a moment, Alphonso! I have forgotten those condemned machine-gunners, as usual. *Strafe* them! Come on! Once more into the breach, Alphonso! There is a little side-alley down here that we have not tried."

The indefatigable Cockerell turned down the Rue Gambetta, followed by Alphonso, faint but resigned.

"Here is the very place!" announced Cockerell almost at once. "This house, Number Five. We can put the gunners and their little guns into that stable at the back, and the officer can have a room in the house itself. *Sonnez*, for the last time before lunch!"

The door was opened by a pleasant-faced young woman of about thirty, who greeted Cockerell—tartan is always popular with French ladies—with a beaming smile, but shook her head regretfully upon seeing the *billet de logement* in his hand. The inevitable duet with Alphonso followed. Presently Alphonso turned to his superior.

"Madame is ver' sorry, sair, but an *officier* is here already."

"Show me the *officier*!" replied the prosaic Cockerell.

The duet was resumed.

"Madame say," announced Alphonso presently, "that the *officier* is not here now; but he will return."

"So will Christmas! Meanwhile I am going to put an *Emma Gee* officer in here."

Alphonso's desperate attempt to translate the foregoing idiom into French was interrupted by Madame's retirement into the house, whither she beckoned Cockerell to follow her. In the front room she produced a frayed sheet of paper, which she proffered with an apologetic smile. The paper said:—

_This billet is entirely reserved for the Supply Officer of this District. It is not to be occupied by troops passing through the town.

By Order_.

Lieutenant Cockerell whistled softly and vindictively through his teeth.

"Well," he said, "for consummate and concentrated nerve, give me the underlings of the A.S.C.! This pot-bellied blighter not only butts into an area which doesn't belong to him, but actually leaves a chit to warn people off the grass even when he isn't here! He hasn't signed the document, I observe. That means that he is a newly joined subaltern, trying to get mistaken for a Brass Hat! I'll fix *him*!"

With great stateliness Lieutenant Cockerell tore the offending screed into four portions, to the audible concern of Madame. But the Lieutenant smiled reassuringly upon her.

"*Je vous donnerai un autre, vous savez*," he assured her.

He sat down at the table, tore a leaf from his Field Service Pocket
Book, and wrote:—

_The Supply Officer of the District is at liberty to occupy this billet only at such times as it is not required by the troops of the Combatant Services.

Signed, F.J. Cockerell,
Lieut. & Asst. Adj.,
7th B. & W. Highes_.

"That's a pretty nasty one!" he observed with relish. Then, having pinned the insulting document conspicuously to the mantelpiece, he observed to the mystified lady of the house:—

"*Voilà, Madame. Si l'officier reviendra, je le verrai moi-même, avec grand plaisir. Bon jour*!"

And with this dark saying Sparrow Cockerell took his departure.

II

The Battalion, headed by their tatterdemalion pipers, stumped into the town in due course, and were met on the outskirts by the billeting party, who led the various companies to their appointed place. After inspecting their new quarters, and announcing with gloomy satisfaction that they were the worst, dirtiest, and most uncomfortable yet encountered, everybody settled down in the best place he could find, and proceeded to make himself remarkably snug.

Battalion Headquarters and the officers of "A" Company were billeted in an imposing mansion which actually boasted a bathroom. It is true that there was no water, but this deficiency was soon made good by a string of officers' servants bearing buckets. Beginning with Colonel Kemp, who was preceded by an orderly bearing a small towel and a large loofah, each officer performed a ceremonial ablution; and it was a collection of what Major Wagstaffe termed "bright and bonny young faces" which collected round the Mess table at seven o'clock.

It was in every sense a gala meal. Firstly, it was weeks since any one (except Second Lieutenant M'Corquodale, newly joined, and addressed, for painfully obvious reasons, as "Tich") had found himself at table in an apartment where it was possible to stand upright. Secondly, the Mess President had coaxed glass tumblers out of the ancient *concierge*; and only those who have drunk from enamelled ironware for weeks on end can appreciate the pure joy of escape from the indeterminate metallic flavour which such vessels impart to all beverages. Thirdly, these same tumblers were filled to the brim with inferior but exhilarating champagne—purchased, as they euphemistically put it in the Supply Column, "locally." Lastly, the battalion had several months of hard fighting behind it, probably a full month's rest before it, and the conscience of duty done and recognition earned floating like a halo above it. For the moment memories of

Nightmare Wood and the Kidney Bean Redoubt—more especially the latter—were effaced. Even the sorrowful gaps in the ring round the table seemed less noticeable.

The menu, too, was almost pretentious. First came the *hors d'oeuvres*—a tin of sardines. This was followed by what the Mess Corporal described as a savoury omelette, but which the Second-in-Command condemned as "a regrettable incident."

"It is false economy," he observed dryly to the Mess President, "to employ Mark One [1] eggs as anything but hand-grenades."

[Footnote 1: In the British army each issue of arms or equipment receives a distinctive "Mark." Mark I denotes the earliest issue.]

However, the tide of popular favour turned with the haggis, contributed by Lieutenant Angus M'Lachlan, from a parcel from home. Even the fact that the Mess cook, an inexperienced aesthete from Islington, had endeavoured to tone down the naked repulsiveness of the dainty with discreet festoons of tinned macaroni, failed to arouse the resentment of a purely Scottish Mess. The next course—the beef ration, hacked into the inevitable gobbets and thinly disguised by a sprinkling of curry powder—aroused no enthusiasm; but the unexpected production of a large tin of Devonshire cream, contributed by Captain Bobby Little, relieved the canned peaches of their customary monotony. Last of all came a savoury—usually described as *the* savoury—consisting of a raft of toast per person, each raft carrying an abundant cargo of fried potted meat, and provided with a passenger in the shape of a recumbent sausage.

A compound of grounds and dish-water, described by the optimistic Mess Corporal as coffee, next made its appearance, mitigated by a bottle of Cointreau and a box of Panatellas; and the Mess turned itself to more intellectual refreshment. A heavy and long-overdue mail had been found waiting at St. Grégoire. Letters had been devoured long ago. Now, each member of the Mess leaned back in his chair, straightened his weary legs under the table, and settled down, cigar in mouth, to the perusal of the *Spectator* or the *Tatler*, according to rank and literary taste.

Colonel Kemp, unfolding a week-old *Times*, looked over his glasses at his torpid disciples.

"Where is young Sandeman?" he inquired.

Young Sandeman was the Adjutant.

"He went out to the Orderly Room, sir, five minutes ago," replied Bobby Little.

"I only want to give him to-morrow's Orders. No doubt he'll be back presently. I may as well mention to you fellows that I propose to allow the men three clear days' rest, except for bathing and re-clothing. After that we must do Company Drill, good and hard, so as to polish up the new draft, who are due to-morrow. I am going to start a bombing-school, too: at least seventy-five per cent. of the Battalion ought to pass the test before we go back to the line. However, we need not rush things. We should be here in peace for at least a month. We must get up some sports, and I think it would be a sound scheme to have a singsong one Saturday night. I was just saying, Sandeman,"—this to the Adjutant, who reëntered the room at that moment,—"that it would be a sound—"

The Adjutant laid a pink field-telegraph slip before his superior.

"This has just come in from Brigade Headquarters, sir," he said. "I have sent for the Sergeant-Major."

The Colonel adjusted his glasses and read the despatch. A deathly, sickening silence reigned in the room. Then he looked up.

"I am afraid I was a bit previous," he said quietly. "The Royal Stickybacks have lost the Kidney Bean, and we are detailed to go up and retake it. Great compliment to the regiment, but a trifle mistimed! You young fellows had better go to bed. Parade at 4 A.M., sharp! Good-night! Come along to the Orderly Room, Sandeman."

The door closed, and the Mess, grinding the ends of their cigars into their coffee-cups, heaved themselves resignedly to their aching feet.

"There ain't," quoted Major Wagstaffe, "no word in the blooming language for it!"

III

The Kidney Bean Redoubt is the key to a very considerable sector of trenches.

It lies just behind a low ridge. The two horns of the bean are drawn back out of sight of the enemy, but the middle swells forward over the skyline and commands an extensive view of the country beyond. Direct observation of artillery fire is possible: consequently an armoured observation post has been constructed here, from which gunner officers can direct the fire of their batteries with accuracy and elegance. Lose the Kidney Bean, and the boot is on the other leg. The enemy has the upper ground now: he can bring observed artillery fire to bear upon all our tenderest spots behind the line. He can also enfilade our front-line trenches.

Well, as already stated, the Twenty-Second Royal Stickybacks had lost the Kidney Bean. They were a battalion of recent formation, stout-hearted fellows all, but new to the refinements of intensive trench warfare. When they took over the sector, they proceeded to leave undone various vital things which the Hairy Jocks had always made a point of doing, and to do various unnecessary things which the Hairy Jocks had never done. The observant Hun promptly recognised that he was faced by a fresh batch of opponents, and, having carefully studied the characteristics of the newcomers, prescribed and administered an exemplary dose of frightfulness. He began by tickling up the Stickybacks with an unpleasant engine called the *Minenwerfer*, which despatches a large sausage-shaped projectile in a series of ridiculous somersaults, high over No Man's Land into the enemy's front-line trench, where it explodes and annihilates everything in that particular bay. Upon these occasions one's only chance of salvation is to make a rapid calculation as to the bay into which the sausage is going to fall, and then double speedily round a traverse—or, if possible, two traverses—into another. It is an exhilarating pastime, but presents complications when played by a large number of persons in a restricted space, especially when the persons aforesaid are not unanimous as to the ultimate landing-place of the projectile.

After a day and a night of these aerial torpedoes the Hun proceeded to an intensive artillery bombardment. He had long coveted the Kidney Bean, and instinct told him that he would never have a better opportunity of capturing it than now. Accordingly, two hours before dawn, the Redoubt was subjected to a sudden, simultaneous, and converging fire from all the German artillery for many miles round, the whole being topped up with a rain of those crowning instruments of demoralisation, gas-shells. At the same time an elaborate curtain of shrapnel and high explosive was let down behind the Redoubt, to serve the double purpose of preventing either the sending up of reinforcements or the temporary withdrawal of the garrison.

At the first streak of dawn the bombardment was switched off, as if by a tap; the curtain fire was redoubled in volume; and a massed attack swept across the disintegrated wire into the shattered and pulverised Redoubt. Other attacks were launched on either flank; but these were obvious blinds, intended to prevent a too concentrated defence of the Kidney Bean. The Royal Stickybacks—what was left of them— put up a tough fight; but half of them were lying dead or buried, or both, before the assault was launched, and the rest were too dazed and stupefied by noise and chlorine gas to withstand—much less to repel—the overwhelming phalanx that was hurled against them. One by one they went down, until the enemy troops, having swamped the Redoubt, gathered themselves up in a fresh wave and surged towards the reserve-line trenches, four hundred yards distant. At this point, however, they met a strong counter-attack, launched from the Brigade Reserve, and after heavy fighting were bundled back into the Redoubt itself. Here the German machine-guns had staked out a defensive line, and the German retirement came to a standstill.

Meanwhile a German digging party, many hundred strong, had been working madly in No Man's Land, striving to link up the newly acquired ground with the German lines. By the afternoon the Kidney Bean was not only "reversed and consolidated," but was actually included in the enemy's front trench system. Altogether a well-planned and admirably executed little operation.

Forty-eight hours later the Kidney Bean Redoubt was recaptured, and remains in British hands to this day. Many arms of the Service took honourable part in the enterprise—heavy guns, field guns, trench-mortars, machine-guns; Sappers and Pioneers; Infantry in various capacities. But this narrative is concerned only with the part played by the Seventh Hairy Jocks.

"Sorry to pull you back from rest, Colonel," said the Brigadier, when the commander of the Hairy Jocks reported; "but the Divisional General considers that the only feasible way to hunt the Boche from the Kidney Bean is to bomb him out of it. That means trench-fighting, pure and simple. I have called you up because you fellows know the ins and outs of the Kidney Bean as no one else does. The Brigade who are in the line just now are quite new to the place. Here is an aeroplane photograph of the Redoubt, as at present constituted. Tell off your own bombing parties; make your own dispositions; send me a copy of your provisional orders; and I will fit my plan in with yours. The Corps Commander has promised to back you with every gun, trench-mortar, culverin, and arquebus in his possession."

In due course Battalion Orders were issued and approved. They dealt with operations most barbarous amid localities of the most homelike sound. Number Nine Platoon, for instance (Commander Lieutenant Cockerell), were to proceed in single file, carrying so many grenades per man, up Charing Cross Road, until stopped by the barrier which the enemy were understood to have erected in Trafalgar Square, where a bombing-post and at least one machine-gun would probably be encountered. At this point they were to wait until Trafalgar Square had been suitably dealt with by a trench-mortar. (Here followed a paragraph addressed exclusively to the Trench-Mortar Officer.) After this the bombers of Number Three Platoon would bomb their way across the Square and up the Strand. Another party would clear Northumberland Avenue, while a Lewis gun raked Whitehall. And so on. Every detail was thought out, down to the composition of the parties which were to "clean up" afterwards—that is, extract the reluctant Boche from various underground fastnesses well known to the extractors. The whole enterprise was then thoroughly rehearsed in some dummy trenches behind the line, until every one knew his exact part. Such is modern warfare.

Next day the Kidney Bean Redoubt was in British hands again. The Hun—what was left of him after an intensive bombardment of twenty-four hours—had betaken himself back over the ridge, *via* the remnants of his two new communication trenches, to his original front line. The two communication trenches themselves were blocked and sandbagged, and were being heavily supervised by a pair of British machine-guns. Fighting in the Redoubt itself had almost ceased, though a humorous sergeant, followed by acolytes bearing bombs, was still "combing out" certain residential districts in the centre of the maze. Ever and anon he would stoop down at the entrance of some deep dug-out, and bawl—

"Ony mair doon there? Come away, Fritz! I'll gie ye five seconds. Yin, Twa, Three—"

Then, with a rush like a bolt of rabbits, two or three close-cropped, grimy Huns would scuttle up from below and project themselves from one of the exits; to be taken in charge by grinning Caledonians wearing "tin hats" very much awry, and escorted back through the barrage to the "prisoners' base" in rear.

All through the day, amidst unremitting shell fire and local counter-attack, the Hairy Jocks reconsolidated the Kidney Bean; and they were so far successful that when they handed over the work to another battalion at dusk, the parapet was restored, the machine-guns were in position, and a number of "knife-rest" barbed-wire entanglements were lying just behind the trench, ready to be hoisted over the parapet and joined together in a continuous defensive line as soon as the night was sufficiently dark.

One by one the members of Number Nine Platoon squelched—for it had rained hard all day—back to the reserve line. They were utterly exhausted, and still inclined to feel a little aggrieved at having been pulled out from rest; but they were well content. They had done the State some service, and they knew it; and they knew that the higher powers knew it too. There would be some very flattering reading in Divisional Orders in a few days' time.

Meanwhile, their most pressing need was for something to eat. To be sure, every man had gone into action that morning carrying his day's rations. But the British soldier, improvident as the grasshopper, carries his day's rations in one place, and one place only—his stomach. The Hairy Jocks had eaten what they required at their extremely early breakfast: the residue thereof they had abandoned.

About midnight Master Cockerell, in obedience to a most welcome order, led the remnants of his command, faint but triumphant, back from the reserve line to a road junction two miles in rear, known as Dead Dog Corner. Here the Battalion was to *rendezvous*, and march back by easy stages to St. Grégoire. Their task was done.

But at the cross-roads Number Nine Platoon found no Battalion: only a solitary subaltern, with his orderly. This young Casabianca informed Cockerell that he, Second Lieutenant Candlish, had been left behind to "bring in stragglers."

"Stragglers?" exclaimed the infuriated Cockerell. "Do we look like stragglers?"

"No," replied the youthful Candlish frankly; "you look more like sweeps. However, you had better push on. The Battalion isn't far ahead. The order is to march straight back to St. Grégoire and re-occupy former billets."

"What about rations?"

"Rations? The Quartermaster was waiting here for us when we *rendezvoused*, and every man had a full ration and a tot of rum." (Number Nine Platoon cleared their parched throats expectantly.) "But I fancy he has gone on with the column. However, if you leg it you should catch them up. They can't be more than two miles ahead. So long!"

IV

But the task was hopeless. Number Nine Platoon had been bombing, hacking, and digging all day. Several of them were slightly wounded—the serious cases had been taken off long ago by the stretcher-bearers—and Cockerell's own head was still dizzy from the fumes of a German gas-shell.

He lined up his disreputable paladins in the darkness, and spoke—

"Sergeant M'Nab, how many men are present?"

"Eighteen, sirr." The platoon had gone into action thirty-four strong.

"How many men are deficient of an emergency ration? I can make a good guess, but you had better find out."

Five minutes later the Sergeant reported. Cockerell's guess was correct. The British private has only one point of view about the portable property of the State. To him, as an individual, the sacred emergency ration is an unnecessary encumbrance, and the carrying thereof a "fatigue." Consequently, when engaged in battle, one of the first (of many) things which he jettisons is this very ration. When all is over, he reports with unctuous solemnity that the provender in question has been blown out of his haversack by a shell. The Quartermaster-Sergeant writes it off as "lost owing to the exigencies of military service," and indents for another.

Lieutenant Cockerell's haversack contained a packet of meat-lozenges and about half a pound of chocolate. These were presented to the Sergeant.

"Hand these round as far as they will go, Sergeant," said Cockerell. "They'll make a mouthful a man, anyhow. Tell the platoon to lie down for ten minutes; then we'll push off. It's only fifteen miles. We ought to make it by breakfast-time …"

Slowly, mechanically, all through the winter night the victors hobbled along. Cockerell led the way, carrying the rifle of a man with a wounded arm. Occasionally he checked his bearings with map and electric torch. Sergeant M'Nab, who, under a hirsute and attenuated exterior, concealed a constitution of ferro-concrete and the heart of a lion, brought up the rear, uttering fallacious assurances to the faint-hearted as to the shortness of the distance now to be covered, and carrying two rifles.

The customary halts were observed. At ten minutes to four the men flung themselves down for the third time. They had covered about seven miles, and were still eight or nine from St. Grégoire. The everlasting constellation of Verey lights still rose and fell upon the eastern horizon behind them, but the guns were silent.

"There might be a Heavy Battery dug in somewhere about here," mused
Cockerell. "I wonder if we could touch them for a few tins of bully.
Hallo, what's that?"

A distant rumble came from the north, and out of the darkness loomed a British motor-lorry, lurching and swaying along the rough cobbles of the *pavé*. Some of Cockerell's men were lying dead asleep in the middle of the road, right at the junction. The lorry was going twenty miles an hour.

"Get into the side of the road, you men!" shouted Cockerell, "or they'll run over you. You know what these M.T. drivers are!"

With indignant haste, and at the last possible moment, the kilted figures scattered to either side of the narrow causeway. The usual stereotyped and vitriolic remonstrances were hurled after the great hooded vehicle as it lurched past.

And then a most unusual thing happened. The lorry slowed down, and finally stopped, a hundred yards away. An officer descended, and began to walk back. Cockerell rose to his weary feet and walked to meet him.

The officer wore a major's crown upon the shoulder-straps of his sheepskin-lined "British Warm" and the badge of the Army Service Corps upon his cap. Cockerell, indignant at the manner in which his platoon had been hustled off the road, saluted stiffly, and muttered: "Good-morning, sir!"

"Good-morning!" said the Major. He was a stout man of nearly fifty, with twinkling blue eyes and a short-clipped mustache. Cockerell judged him to be one of the few remnants of the original British Army.

"I stopped," explained the older man, "to apologise for the scandalous way that fellow drove over you. It was perfectly damnable; but you know what these converted taxi-drivers are! This swine forgot for the moment that he had an officer on board, and hogged it as usual. He goes under arrest as soon as we get back to billets."

"Thank you very much, sir," said Master Cockerell, entirely thawed. "I'm afraid my chaps were lying all over the road; but they are pretty well down and out at present."

"Where have you come from?" inquired the Major, turning a curious eye upon Cockerell's prostrate followers.

Cockerell explained When he had finished, he added wistfully—

"I suppose you have not got an odd tin or two of bully to give away, sir? My fellows are about—"

For answer, the Major took the Lieutenant by the arm and led him towards the lorry.

"You have come," he announced, "to the very man you want. I am practically Mr. Harrod. In fact, I am a Corps Supply Officer. How would a Maconochie apiece suit your boys?"

Cockerell, repressing the ecstatic phrases which crowded to his tongue, replied that that was just what the doctor had ordered.

"Where are you bound for?" continued the Major.

"St. Grégoire."

"Of course. You were pulled out from there, weren't you? I am going to St. Grégoire myself as soon as I have finished my round. Home to bed, in fact. I haven't had any sleep worth writing home about for four nights. It is no joke tearing about a country full of shell-holes, hunting for people who have shifted their ration-dump seven times in four days. However, I suppose things will settle down again, now that you fellows have fired Brother Boche out of the Kidney Bean. Pretty fine work, too! Tell me, what is your strength, here and now?"

"One officer," said Cockerell soberly, "and eighteen other ranks."

"All that's left of your platoon?"

Cockerell nodded. The stout Major began to beat upon the tailboard of the lorry with his stick.

"Sergeant Smurthwaite!" he shouted.

There came a muffled grunt from the recesses of the lorry. Then a round and ruddy face rose like a harvest moon above the tailboard, and a stertorous voice replied respectfully—

"Sir?"

"Let down this tailboard; load this officer's platoon into the lorry; issue them with a Maconochie and a tot of rum apiece; and don't forget to put Smee under arrest for dangerous driving when we get back to billets."

"Very good, sir."

Ten minutes later the survivors of Number Nine Platoon, soaked to the skin, dazed, slightly incredulous, but at peace with all the world, reclined close-packed upon the floor of the swaying lorry. Each man held an open tin of Mr. Maconochie's admirable ration between his knees. Perfect silence reigned: a pleasant aroma of rum mellowed the already vitiated atmosphere.

In front, beside the chastened Mr. Smee, sat the Major and Master Cockerell. The latter had just partaken of his share of refreshment, and was now endeavouring, with lifeless fingers, to light a cigarette.

The Major scrutinised his guest intently. Then he stripped off his British Warm coat—incidentally revealing the fact that he wore upon his tunic the ribbons of both South African Medals and the Distinguished Service Order—and threw it round Cockerell's shoulders.

"I'm sorry, boy!" he said. "I never noticed. You are chilled to the bone. Button this round you."

Cockerell made a feeble protest, but was cut short.

"Nonsense! There's no sense in taking risks after you've done your job."

Cockerell assented, a little sleepily. His allowance of rum was bringing its usual vulgar but comforting influence to bear upon an exhausted system.

"I see you have been wounded, sir," he observed, noting with a little surprise two gold stripes upon his host's left sleeve—the sleeve of a "non-combatant."

"Yes," said the Major. "I got the first one at Le Gateau. He was only a little fellow; but the second, which arrived at the Second Show at Ypres, gave me such a stiff leg that I am only an old crock now. I was second-in-command of an Infantry Battalion in those days. In these, I am only a peripatetic Lipton. However, I am lucky to be here at all: I've had twenty-seven years' service. How old are you?"

"Twenty," replied Cockerell. He was too tired to feel as ashamed as he usually did at having to confess to the tenderness of his years.

The Major nodded thoughtfully.

"Yes," he said; "I judged that would be about the figure. My son would have been twenty this month, only—he was at Neuve Chapelle. He was very like you in appearance—very. His mother would have been interested to meet you. You might as well take a nap for half an hour. I have two more calls to make, and we shan't get home till nearly seven. Lean on me, old man. I'll see you don't tumble overboard ..."

So Lieutenant Cockerell, conqueror of the Kidney Bean, fell asleep, his head resting, with scandalous disregard for military etiquette, upon the shoulder of the stout Major.

V

An hour or two later, Number Nine Platoon, distended with concentrated nourishment and painfully straightening its cramped limbs, decanted itself from the lorry into a little *cul-de-sac* opening off the Rue Jean Jacques Rousseau in St. Grégoire. The name of the *cul-de-sac* was the Rue Gambetta.

Their commander, awake and greatly refreshed, looked round him and realised, with a sudden sense of uneasiness, that he was in familiar surroundings. The lorry had stopped at the door of Number Five.

"I don't suppose your Battalion will get back for some time," said the Major. "Tell your Sergeant to put your men into the stable behind this house—there's plenty of straw there—and—"

"Their own billet is just round the corner, sir," replied Cockerell.

"They might as well go there, thank you."

"Very good. But come in with me yourself, and doss here for a few hours. You can report to your C.O. later in the day, when he arrives. This is my *pied-à-terre*,"—rapping on the door. "You won't find many billets like it. As you see, it stands in this little backwater, and is not included in any of the regular billeting areas of the town. The Town Major has allotted it to me permanently. Pretty decent of him, wasn't it? And Madame Vinot is a dear. Here she is! *Bonjour, Madame Vinot! Avez-vous un feu*—er—*inflammé pour moi dans la chambre*?" Evidently the Major's French was on a par with Cockerell's.

But Madame understood him, bless her!

"*Mais oui, M'sieur le Colonel*!" she exclaimed cheerfully—the rank of Major is not recognised by the French civilian population—and threw open the door of the sitting-room, with a glance of compassion upon the Major's mud-splashed companion, whom she failed to recognise.

A bright fire was burning in the open stove.

Immediately above, pinned to the mantelpiece and fluttering in the draught, hung Cockerell's manifesto upon the subject of non-combatants. He could recognise his own handwriting across the room. The Major saw it too.

"Hallo, what's that hanging up, I wonder?" he exclaimed. "A memorandum for me, I expect; probably from my old friend 'Dados.'[1] Let us get a little more light."

[Footnote 1: D.A.D.O.S. Deputy Assistant Director of Ordnance Stores.]

He crossed to the window and drew up the blind. Cockerell moved too. When the Major turned round, his guest was standing by the stove, his face scarlet through its grime.

"I'm awfully sorry, sir," said Cockerell, "but that notice—memorandum—of yours has dropped into the fire."

"If it came from Dados," replied the Major, "thank you very much!"

"I can't tell you, sir," added Cockerell humbly, "what a fool I feel."

But the apology referred to an entirely different matter.

IX

TUNING UP

I

It is just one year to-day since we "came oot." A year plays havoc with the "establishment" of a battalion in these days of civilised warfare. Of the original band of stout-hearted but inexperienced Crusaders who crossed the Channel in the van of The First Hundred Thousand, in May, 1915,—a regiment close on a thousand strong, with twenty-eight officers,—barely two hundred remain, and most of these are Headquarters or Transport men. Of officers there are five—Colonel Kemp, Major Wagstaffe, Master Cockerell, Bobby Little, and Mr. Waddell, who, by the way, is now Captain Waddell, having succeeded to the command of his old Company.

Of the rest, our old Colonel is in Scotland, essaying ambitious pedestrian and equestrian feats upon his new leg. Others have been drafted to the command of newer units, for every member of "K(1)" is a Nestor now. Others are home, in various stages of convalescence. Others, alas! will never go home again. But the gaps have all been filled up, and once more we are at full strength, comfortably conscious that whereas a year ago we were fighting to hold a line, and play for time, and find our feet, while the people at home behind us were making good, now we are fighting for one thing and one thing only; and that is, to administer the knock-out blow to Brother Boche.

Our last casualty was Ayling, who left us under somewhat unusual circumstances.

Towards the end of our last occupancy of trenches the local Olympus decided that what both sides required, in order to awaken them from their winter lethargy, or spring lassitude (or whatever it is that Olympus considers that we in the firing-line are suffering from for the moment), was a tonic. Accordingly orders were issued for a Flying Matinée, or trench raid. Each battalion in the Division was to submit a scheme, and the battalion whose scheme was adjudged the best was to be accorded the honour—so said the Practical Joke Department—of carrying out the scheme in person. To the modified rapture of the Seventh Hairy Jocks their plan was awarded first prize. Headquarters, after a little excusable recrimination on the subject of unnecessary zeal and misguided ambition, set to work to arrange rehearsals of our highly unpopular production.

Brother Boche has grown "wise" to Flying Matinées nowadays, and to score a real success you have to present him with something comparatively novel and unexpected. However, our scheme had been carefully thought out; and, given sufficient preparation, and an adequate cast, there seemed no reason to doubt that the piece would have a highly successful run of one night.

At one point in the enemy's trenches opposite to us his barbed-wire defences had worn very thin, and steps were taken by means of systematic machine-gun fire to prevent him repairing them. This spot was selected for the raid. A party of twenty-five was detailed. It was to be led by Angus M'Lachlan, and was to slip over the parapet on a given moonless night, crawl across No Man's Land to within striking distance of the German trench, and wait. At a given moment the signal for attack would be given, and the wire demolished by a means which need not be specified here. Thereupon the raiding party were to dash forward and—to quote the Sergeant-Major—"mix themselves up in it."

Two elements are indispensable in a successful trench-raid—surprise and despatch. That is to say, you must deliver your raid when and where it is least expected, and then get home to bed before your victims have had time to set the machinery of retaliation in motion. Steps were therefore taken, firstly, to divert the enemy's attention as far as possible from the true objective of the raid, by a sudden and furious bombardment of a sector of trenches three hundred yards away; and secondly, to ensure as far as possible, that the raid, having commenced at 2 A.M., should conclude at 2.12, sharp.

In order to cover the retirement of the excursionists, Ayling was ordered to arrange for machine-gun fire, which should sweep the enemy's parapet for some hundreds of yards upon either flank, and so encourage the enemy to keep his head down and mind his own business.

The raid itself was a brilliant success. Dug-outs were bombed, emplacements destroyed, and a respectable bag of captives brought over. But the element of surprise, upon which so much insistence was laid above, was visited upon both attackers and attacked. To the former the contribution came from that well-meaning but somewhat addlepated warrior, Private Nigg, who formed one of the raiding party.

Nigg's allotted task upon this occasion was to "comb out" certain German dug-outs. (It may be mentioned that each man had a specific duty to perform, and a specific portion of the trench opposite to perform it in; for the raid had been rehearsed several times in a dummy trench behind the lines constructed exactly to scale from an aeroplane photograph.) For this purpose he was provided with bombs. Shortly before two o'clock in the morning the party, headed by Angus M'Lachlan, crawled over the parapet during a brief lull in the activities of the Verey lights, and crept steadily, on hands and knees, across No Man's Land. Fifty yards from the enemy's wire was a collection of shell-holes, relics of a burst of misdirected energy on the part of a six-inch battery. Here the raiders disposed themselves, and waited for the signal.

Now, it is an undoubted fact, that if you curl yourself up, with two or three preliminary twirls, after the fashion of a dog going to bed, in a perfectly circular shell-hole, on a night as black as the inside of the dog in question, you are extremely likely to lose your sense of direction. This is what happened to Private Nigg. He and his infernal machines lay uneasily in their appointed shell-hole for some ten minutes, surrounded by Verey lights which shot suddenly into the sky with a disconcerting *plop*, described a graceful parabola, burst into dazzling flame, and fluttered sizzling down. One or two of these fell quite near Nigg's party, and continued to burn upon the ground, but the raiders sank closer into their shell-holes, and no alarm resulted. Once or twice a machine-gun had a scolding fit, and bullets whispered overhead. But, on the whole, the night was quiet.

Then suddenly, with a shattering roar, the feint-artillery bombardment broke forth. Simultaneously word was passed along the raiding line to stand by. Next moment Angus M'Lachlan and his followers rose to their feet in the black darkness, scrambled out of their nests, and dashed forward to the accomplishment of their mission.

When Nigg, who had paused a moment to collect his bombs, sprang out of his shell-hole, not a colleague was in sight. At least, Nigg could see no one. However, want of courage was not one of his failings. He bounded blindly forward by himself.

Try as he would he could not overtake the raiding party. However, this mattered little, for suddenly a parapet loomed before him. In this same parapet, low down, Nigg beheld a black and gaping aperture—plainly a loophole of some kind.

Without a moment's hesitation, Nigg hurled a Mills grenade straight through the loophole, and then with one wild screech of "Come away, boys!" took a flying leap over the parapet—and landed in his own trench, in the arms of Corporal Mucklewame.

As already noted, it is difficult, when lying curled up in a circular shell-hole in the dark, to maintain a true sense of direction.

So the first-fruits of the raid was Captain Ayling, of the *Emma Gees*. He had stationed himself in a concrete emplacement in the front line, the better to "observe" the fire of his guns when it should be required. Unfortunately this was the destination selected by the misguided Niggs for his first (and as it proved, last) bomb. The raiders came safely back in due course, but by that time Ayling, liberally (but by a miracle not dangerously) ballasted with assorted scrap-iron, was on his way to the First Aid Post.

II

At the present moment we are right back at rest once more, and are being treated with a consideration, amounting almost to indulgence, which convinces us that we are being "fattened up"—to employ the gruesome but expressive phraseology of the moment—for some particularly strenuous enterprise in the near future.

Well, we are ready. It is nine months since Loos, and nearly six since we scraped the nightmare mud of Ypres from our boots, *gum, thigh*, for the last time. Our recent casualties have been light—our only serious effort of late has been the recapture of the Kidney Bean—the new drafts have settled down, and the young officers have been blooded. And above all, victory is in the air. We are going into our next fight with new-born confidence in the powers behind us. Loos was an experimental affair; and though to the humble instruments with which the experiment was made the proceedings were less hilarious than we had anticipated, the results were enormously valuable to a greatly expanded and entirely untried Staff.

"We shall do better this time," said Major Wagstaffe to Bobby Little, as they stood watching the battalion assemble, in workmanlike fashion, for a route-march. "There are just one or two little points which had not occurred to us then. We have grasped them now, I think."

"Such as?"

"Well, you remember we all went into the Loos show without any very lucid idea as to how far we were to go, and where to knock off for the day, so to speak. The result was that the advance of each Division was regulated by the extent to which the German wire in front of it had been cut by our artillery. Ours was well and truly cut, so we penetrated two or three miles. The people on our left never started at all. Lord knows, they tried hard enough. But how could any troops get through thirty feet of uncut wire, enfiladed by machine-guns? The result was that after forty-eight hours' fighting, our whole attacking front, instead of forming a nice straight line, had bagged out into a series of bays and peninsulas."

"Our crowd wasn't even a peninsula," remarked Bobby with feeling. "For an hour or so it was an island!"

"I think you will find that in the next show we shall go forward, after intensive bombardment, quite a short distance; then consolidate; then wait till the *whole* line has come up to its appointed objective; then bombard again; then go forward another piece; and so on. That will make it impossible for gaps to be created. It will also give our gunners a chance to cover our advance continuously. You remember at Loos they lost us for hours, and dare not fire for fear of hitting us. In fact, I expect that in battle plans of the future, instead of the artillery trying to conform to the movements of the infantry, matters will be reversed. The guns, after preliminary bombardment, will create a continuous Niagara of exploding shells upon a given line, marked in everybody's map, and timed for an exact period, just beyond the objective; and the infantry will stroll up into position a comfortable distance behind, reading the time-table, and dig themselves in. Then the barrage will lift on to the next line, and we shall toddle forward again. That's the new plan, Bobby! Close artillery coöperation, and a series of limited objectives!"

"It sounds all right," agreed Bobby. "We shall want a good many guns, though, shan't we?"

"We shall. But don't let that worry you. It is simply raining guns at the Base now. In fact, my grandmother in the War Office"—this mythical relative was frequently quoted by Major Wagstaffe, and certainly her information had several times proved surprisingly correct—"tells me that by the beginning of next year we shall have enough guns, of various calibres, to make a continuous line, hub to hub, from one end of our front to the other."

"Golly!" observed Captain Little, with respectful relish.

"That means," continued Wagstaffe, "that we shall be able to blow Brother Boche's immediate place of business to bits, and at the same time take on his artillery with counter-battery work. Our shell-supply is practically unlimited now; so when the next push comes, we foot-sloggers ought to have a more gentlemanly time of it than we had at Loos and Wipers. And I'll tell you another thing, Bobby. We shall have command of the air too."

"That will be a pleasant change," remarked Bobby. "I'm getting tired of putting my fellows under arrest for rushing out of carefully concealed positions in order to gape up at Boche planes going over. Angus M'Lachlan is as bad as any of them. The fellow—"

"But you have not seen many Boche planes lately?"

"No. Certainly not so many."

"And the number will grow beautifully less. Our little friends in the R.F.C. are getting fairly numerous now, and their machines have been improved out of all knowledge. They are rapidly assuming the position of top dog. Moreover, the average Boche does not take kindly to flying. It is too—too individualistic a job for him. He likes to work in a bunch with other Boches, where he can keep step, and maintain dressing, and mark time if he gets confused. In the air one cannot mark time, and it worries Fritz to death. I think you will see, in the next unpleasantness, that we shall be able to maintain our aeroplane frontier somewhere over the enemy third line. That means that we shall make our own dispositions with a certain degree of privacy, and the Boche will not. Also, when our big guns get to work, they will not need to fire blindly, as in the days of our youth, but will be directed by one of our R.F.C. lads, humming about in his little bus above the target, perhaps fifteen miles from the gun. Hallo, there go the pipes! Tell your men to fall in."

"The whole business," observed Bobby, as he struggled into his equipment, "sounds so attractive that I am beginning quite to look forward to the next show!"

"Don't forget the Boche machine-guns, my lad," replied Wagstaffe.

"One seldom gets the chance," grumbled Bobby. "Is there no way of knocking them out?"

"Well—" Wagstaffe looked intensely mysterious—"of course one never knows, but—have you heard any rumours on the subject?"

"I have. About—"

"About the Hush! Hush! Brigade?"

Bobby nodded.

"Yes," he said. "Young Osborne, my best subaltern after Angus, disappeared last month to join it. Tell me, what *is* the—"

"Hush! Hush!" said Major Wagstaffe. "*Méfiez vous! Taisez vous*! and so on!"

The battalion moved off.

So much for the war-talk of veterans. Now let us listen to the novices.

"Bogle," said Angus M'Lachlan to his henchman, "I think we shall have to lighten this Wolseley valise of mine. With one thing and another it weighs far more than thirty-five pounds."

"That's a fact, sirr," agreed Mr. Bogle. "It carries ower mony books in the heid of it."

They shook out the contents of the valise upon the floor of Angus's bedroom—a loft over the kitchen in "A" Company's farm billet—and proceeded to prune Angus's personal effects. There were boots, socks, shaving-tackle, maps, packets of chocolate, and books of every size, but chiefly of the ever-blessed sevenpenny type.

"A lot of these things will have to go, Bogle," said Angus regretfully. "The colonel has warned officers about their kits, and it would never do to have mine turned back from the waggon at the last minute."

Mr. Bogle pricked up his ears. "The waggon? Are we for off again, sirr?" he inquired.

"Indeed I could not say," replied the cautious Angus; "but it is well to be ready."

"The boys was saying, sirr," observed Bogle tentatively, "that there was to be another grand battle soon."

"It is more than likely," said Angus, with an air of profound wisdom. "Here we are in June, and we must take the offensive, sooner or later, or summer will be over."

"What kind o' a battle will it be this time, sirr?" inquired Bogle respectfully.

"Oh, our artillery will pound the German trenches for a week or two, and then we shall go over the parapet and drive them back for miles," said Angus simply.

"And what then, sirr?"

"What then? We shall go on pushing them until another Division relieves us."

Bogle nodded comprehendingly. He now had firmly fixed in his mind the essential details of the projected great offensive of 1916. He was not interested to go further in the matter. And it is this very faculty—philosophic trust, coupled with absolute lack of imagination—which makes the British soldier the most invincible person in the world. The Frenchman is inspired to glorious deeds by his great spirit and passionate love of his own sacred soil; the German fights as he thinks, like a machine. But the British Tommy wins through owing to his entire indifference to the pros and cons of the tactical situation. He settles down to war like any other trade, and, as in time of peace, he is chiefly concerned with his holidays and his creature comforts. A battle is a mere incident between one set of billets and another. Consequently he does not allow the grim realities of war to obsess his mind when off duty. One might almost ascribe his success as a soldier to the fact that his domestic instincts are stronger than his military instincts.

Put the average Tommy into a trench under fire how does he comport himself? Does he begin by striking an attitude and hurling defiance at the foe? No, he begins by inquiring, in no uncertain voice, where his —— dinner is? He then examines his new quarters. Before him stands a parapet, buttressed mayhap with hurdles or balks of timber, the whole being designed to preserve his life from hostile projectiles. How does he treat this bulwark? Unless closely watched, he will begin to chop it up for firewood. His next proceeding is to construct for himself a place of shelter. This sounds a sensible proceeding, but here again it is a case of "safety second." A British Tommy regards himself as completely protected from the assaults of his enemies if he can lay a sheet of corrugated-iron roofing across his bit of trench and sit underneath it. At any rate it keeps the rain off, and that is all that his instincts demand of him. An ounce of comfort is worth a pound of security.

He looks about him. The parapet here requires fresh sandbags; there the trench needs pumping out. Does he fill sandbags, or pump, of his own volition? Not at all. Unless remorselessly supervised, he will devote the rest of the morning to inventing and chalking up a title for his new dug-out—"Jock's Lodge," or "Burns' Cottage," or "Cyclists' Rest"—supplemented by a cautionary notice, such as—*No Admittance. This Means You.* Thereafter, with shells whistling over his head, he will decorate the parapet in his immediate vicinity with picture postcards and cigarette photographs. Then he leans back with a happy sigh. His work is done. His home from home is furnished. He is now at leisure to think about "they Gairmans" again. That may sound like an exaggeration; but "Comfort First" is the motto of that lovable but imprudent grasshopper, Thomas Atkins, all the time.

A sudden and pertinent thought occurred to Mr. Bogle, who possessed a Martha-like nature.

"What way, sir, will a body get his dinner, if we are to be fighting for twa-three days on end?"

"Every man," replied Angus, "will be issued, I expect, with two days' rations. But the Colonel tells me that during hard fighting a man does not feel the desire for food—or sleep either for that matter. Perhaps, during a lull, it may occur to him that he has not eaten since yesterday, and he may pull out a bit of biscuit or chocolate from his pocket, just to nibble. Or he may remember that he has had no sleep for twenty-four hours—so he just drops down and sleeps for ten minutes while there is time. But generally, matters of ordinary routine drop out of a man's thoughts altogether."

"That's a queer-like thing, a body forgetting his dinner!" murmured Bogle.

"Of course," continued Angus, warming to his theme like his own father in his pulpit, "if Nature is expelled with a pitchfork in this manner, for too long, *tamen usque recurret.*"

"Is that a fact?" replied Bogle politely. He always adopted the line of least resistance when his master took to audible rumination. "Weel, I'll hae to be steppin', sir. I'll pit these twa blankets oot in the sun, in some place where the dooks frae the pond will no get dandering ower them. And if you'll sorrt your books, I'll hand ower the yins ye dinna require to the Y.M.C.A. hut ayont the village."

Bogle cherished a profound admiration for Lieutenant M'Lachlan both as a scholar and a strategist, and absorbed his deliverances with a care and attention which enabled him to misquote the same quite fluently to his own associates. That very evening he set forth the coming plan of campaign, as elucidated to him by his master, to a mixed assemblage at the *Estaminet au Clef des Champs*. Some of the party were duly impressed; but Mr. Spike Johnson, a resident in peaceful times of Stratford-atte-Bow, the recognised humourist of the Sappers' Field Company attached to the Brigade, was pleased to be facetious.

"It won't be no good you Jocks goin' over no parapet to attack no 'Uns," he said, "after what 'appened last week!"

This dark saying had the effect of rousing every Scottish soldier in the *estaminet* to a state of bristling attention.

"And what was it," inquired Private Cosh with heat, "that happened last week?"

"Why," replied Mr. Johnson, who had been compounding this jest for some days, and now saw his opportunity to deliver it with effect at short range, "your trenches got raided last Wednesday, when you was in' em. By the Brandyburgers, I think it was."

The entire symposium stared at the jester with undisguised amazement.

"Our—trenches," proclaimed Private Tosh with forced calm, "were never raided by no—Brandyburrrgerrs! Was they, Jimmie?"

Mr. Cosh corroborated, with three adjectives which Mr. Tosh had not thought of.

Spike Johnson merely smiled, with the easy assurance of a man who has the ace up his sleeve.

"Oh yes, they was!" he reiterated.

"They werre *not*!" shouted half a dozen voices.

The next stage of the discussion requires no description. It terminated, at the urgent request of Madame from behind the bar, and with the assistance of the Military Police, in the street outside.

"And now, Spike Johnson," inquired Private Cosh, breathing heavily but much refreshed, "can you tell me what way Gairmans could get intil the trenches of a guid Scots regiment withoot bein' *seen*?"

"I can," replied Mr. Johnson with relish, "and I will. They got in all right, but you didn't see them, because they was disguised."

Cosh and Tosh snorted disdainfully, and Private Nigg, who was present with his friend Buncle, inquired—

"What way was they disguised?"

Like lightning came the answer—

"*As a joke*! Oh, you Jocks."

Cosh and Tosh (who had already been warned by the Police sergeant) merely glared and gurgled impotently. Private Nigg, who, as already mentioned, was slightly wanting in quickness of perception, was led away by the faithful Buncle, to have the outrage explained to him at leisure. It was Private Bogle who intervened, and brought the intellectual Goliath crashing to the ground.

"Man, Johnson," he remarked, and shook his head mournfully, "youse ought to be varra careful aboot sayin' things like that to the likes of us. 'Deed aye!"

"What for, ole son?" inquired the jester indulgently.

"Naithing," replied Bogle with artistic reticence.

"Come along—aht with it!" insisted Johnson. "Cough it up, duckie!"

"Man, man," cried Bogle with passionate earnestness, "dinna gang ower far!"

"What the 'ell *for*?" inquired Johnson, impressed despite himself.

"What for?" Bogle's voice dropped to a ghostly whisper. "Has it ever occurred to you, my mannie, what would happen tae the English—if Scotland was tae make a separate peace?"

And Mr. Bogle retired, not before it was time, within the sheltering portals of the *estaminet*, where not less than seven inarticulate but appreciative fellow-countrymen offered him refreshment.

X

FULL CHORUS

I

An Observation Post—or "O Pip," in the mysterious *patois* of the Buzzers—is not exactly the spot that one would select either for spaciousness or accessibility. It may be situated up a chimney or up a tree, or down a tunnel bored through a hill. But it certainly enables you to see something of your enemy; and that, in modern warfare, is a very rare and valuable privilege.

Of late the scene-painter's art—technically known as *camouflage*—has raised the concealment of batteries and their observation posts to the realm of the uncanny. According to Major Wagstaffe, you can now disguise anybody as anything. For instance, you can make up a battery of six-inch guns to look like a flock of sheep, and herd them into action browsing. Or you can despatch a scouting party across No Man's Land dressed up as pillar-boxes, so that the deluded Hun, instead of opening fire with a machine-gun, will merely post letters in them—valuable letters, containing military secrets. Lastly, and more important still, you can disguise yourself to look like nothing at all, and in these days of intensified artillery fire it is very seldom that nothing at all is hit.

The particular O Pip with which we are concerned at present, however, is a German post—or was a fortnight ago, before the opening of the Battle of the Somme.

For nearly two years the British Armies on the Western Front have been playing for time. They have been sticking their toes in and holding their ground, with numerically inferior forces and inadequate artillery support, against a nation in arms which has set out, with forty years of preparation at its back, to sweep the earth. We have held them, and now *der Tag* has come for us. The deal has passed into our hand at last. A fortnight ago, ready for the first time to undertake the offensive on a grand and prolonged scale,—Loos was a mere reconnaissance compared with this,—the New British Army went over the parapet shoulder to shoulder with the most heroic Army in the world—the Army of France—and attacked over a sixteen-mile front in the Valley of the Somme.

It was a critical day for the Allies: certainly it was a most critical day in the history of the British Army. For on that day an answer had to be given to a very big question indeed. Hitherto we had been fighting on the defensive—unready, uphill, against odds. It would have been no particular discredit to us had we failed to hold our line. But we had held it, and more. Now, at last, we were ready—as ready as we were ever likely to be. We had the men, the guns, and the munitions. We were in a position to engage the enemy on equal, and more than equal, terms. And the question that the British Empire had to answer in that day, the First of July 1916, was this: "Are these new amateur armies of ours, raised, trained, and equipped in less than two years, with nothing in the way of military tradition to uphold them—nothing but the steady courage of their race: are they a match for, and more than a match for, that grim machine-made, iron-bound host that lies waiting for them along that line of Picardy hills? Because if they are *not*, we cannot win this war. We can only make a stalemate of it."

We, looking back now over a space of twelve months, know how our boys answered that question. In the greatest and longest battle that the world had yet seen, that Army of city clerks, Midland farm-lads, Lancashire mill-hands, Scottish miners, and Irish corner-boys, side by side with their great-hearted brethren from Overseas, stormed positions which had been held impregnable for two years, captured seventy thousand prisoners, reclaimed several hundred square miles of the sacred soil of France, and smashed once and for all the German-fostered fable of the invincibility of the German Army. It was good to have lived and suffered during those early and lean years, if only to be present at their fulfilment.

But at this moment the battle was only beginning, and the bulk of their astounding achievement was still to come. Nevertheless, in the cautious and modest estimate of their Commander-in-Chief, they had already done something.

After ten days and nights of continuous fighting, said the first official report, *our troops have completed the methodical capture of the whole of the enemy's first system of defence on a front of fourteen thousand yards. This system of defence consisted of numerous and continuous lines of fire trenches, extending to depths of from two thousand to four thousand yards, and included five strongly fortified villages, numerous heavily entrenched woods, and a large number of immensely strong redoubts. The capture of each of these trenches represented an operation of some importance, and the whole of them are now in our hands.*

Quite so. One feels, somehow, that Berlin would have got more out of such a theme.

* * * * *

Now let us get back to our O Pip. If you peep over the shoulder of Captain Leslie, the gunner observing officer, as he directs the fire of his battery, situated some thousands of yards in rear, through the medium of map, field-glass, and telephone, you will obtain an excellent view of to-morrow's field of battle. Present in the O Pip are Colonel Kemp, Wagstaffe, Bobby Little, and Angus M'Lachlan. The latter had been included in the party because, to quote his Commanding Officer, "he would have burst into tears if he had been left out."

Overhead roared British shells of every kind and degree of unpleasantness, for the ground in front was being "prepared" for the coming assault. The undulating landscape, running up to a low ridge on the skyline four miles away, was spouting smoke in all directions—sometimes black, sometimes green, and sometimes, where bursting shell and brick-dust intermingled, blood-red. Beyond the ridge all-conquering British aeroplanes occupied the firmament, observing for "mother" and "granny" and signalling encouragement or reproof to these ponderous but sprightly relatives as their shells hit or missed the target.

"Yes, sir," replied Leslie to Colonel Kemp's question, "that is Longueval, on the slope opposite, with the road running through on the way to Flers, over the skyline. That is Delville Wood on its right. As you see, the guns are concentrating on both places. That is Waterlot Farm, on this side of the wood—a sugar refinery. Regular nest of machine-guns there, I'm told."

"No doubt we shall be able to confirm the rumour to-morrow," said Colonel Kemp drily. "That is Bernafay Wood on our right, I suppose?"

"Yes, sir. We hold the whole of that. The pear-shaped wood out beyond it—it looks as if it were joined on, but the two are quite separate really—is Trones Wood. It has changed hands several times. Just at present I don't think we hold more than the near end. Further away, half-right, you can see Guillemont."

"In that case," remarked Wagstaffe, "our right flank would appear to be strongly supported by the enemy."

"Yes. We are in a sort of right-angled salient here. We have the enemy on our front and our right. In fact, we form the extreme right of the attacking front. Our left is perfectly secure, as we now hold Mametz Wood and Contalmaison. There they are." He waved his glass to the northwest. "When the attack takes place, I understand that our Division will go straight ahead, for Longueval and Delville Wood, while the next Division makes a lateral thrust out to the right, to push the Boche out of Trones Wood and cover our flank."

"I believe that is so," said the Colonel. "Bobby, take a good look at the approaches to Longueval. That is the scene of to-morrow's constitutional."

Bobby and Angus obediently scanned the village through their glasses. Probably they did not learn much. One bombarded French village is very like another bombarded French village. A cowering assemblage of battered little houses; a pitiful little main street, with its eviscerated shops and *estaminets*; a shattered church-spire. Beyond that, an enclosure of splintered stumps that was once an orchard. Below all, cellars, reinforced with props and sandbags, and filled with machine-guns. *Voilà tout*!

Presently the Gunner Captain passed word down to the telephone operator to order the battery to cease fire.

"Knocking off?" inquired Wagstaffe.

"For the present, yes. We are only registering this morning. Not all our batteries are going at once, either. We don't want Brother Boche to know our strength until we tune up for the final chorus. We calculate that—"

"There is a comfortable sense of decency and order about the way we fight nowadays," said Colonel Kemp. "It is like working out a problem in electrical resistance by a nice convenient algebraical formula. Very different from the state of things last year, when we stuck it out by employing rule of thumb and hanging on by our eyebrows."

"The only problem we can't quite formulate is the machine-gun," said Leslie. The Boche's dug-outs here are thirty feet deep. When crumped by our artillery he withdraws his infantry and leaves his machine-gunners behind, safe underground. Then, when our guns lift and the attack comes over, his machine-gunners appear on the surface, hoist their guns after them with a sort of tackle arrangement, and get to work on a prearranged band of fire. The infantry can't do them in until No Man's Land is crossed, and—well, they don't all get across, that's all! However, *I have* heard rumours—"

"So have we all," said Colonel Kemp.

"I forgot to tell you, Colonel," interposed Wagstaffe, "that I met young Osborne at Divisional Headquarters last night. You remember, he left us some time ago to join the Hush! Hush! Brigade."

"I remember," said the Colonel.

By this time the party, including the Gunner Captain, were filing along a communication trench, lately the property of some German gentlemen, on their way back to headquarters.

"Did he tell you anything, Wagstaffe?" continued Colonel Kemp.

"Not much. Apparently the time of the H.H.B. is not yet. But he made an appointment with me for this evening—in the gloaming, so to speak. He is sending a car. If all he says is true, the Boche *Emma Gee* is booked for an eye-opener in a few weeks' time."

II

That evening a select party of sight-seers were driven to a secluded spot behind the battle line. Here they were met by Master Osborne, obviously inflated with some important matter.

"I've got leave from my C.O. to show you the sights, sir," he announced to Colonel Kemp. "If you will all stand here and watch that wood on the opposite side of this clearing, you may see something. We don't show ourselves much except in late evening, so this is our parade hour."

The little group took up its appointed stand and waited in the gathering dusk. In the east the sky was already twinkling with intermittent Verey lights. All around the British guns were thundering forth their hymns of hate—full-throated now, for the hour for the next great assault was approaching.

Wagstaffe's thoughts went back to a certain soft September night last year, when he and Blaikie had stood on the eastern outskirts of Béthune listening to a similar overture—the prelude to the Battle of Loos. But this overture was ten times more awful, and, from a material British point of view, ten times more inspiring. It would have thrilled old Blaikie's fighting spirit, thought Wagstaffe. But Loos had taken his friend from him, and he, Wagstaffe, only was left. What did fate hold in store for him to-morrow? he wondered. And Bobby? They had both escaped marvellously so far. Well, better men had gone before them. Perhaps—

Fingers of steel bit into his biceps muscle, and the excited whinny of Angus M'Lachlan besought him to look!

Down in the forest something stirred. But it was not the note of a bird, as the song would have us believe. From the depths of the wood opposite came a crackling, crunching sound, as of some prehistoric beast forcing its way through tropical undergrowth. And then, suddenly, out from the thinning edge there loomed a monster—a monstrosity. It did not glide, it did not walk. It wallowed. It lurched, with now and then a laborious heave of its shoulders. It fumbled its way over a low bank matted with scrub. It crossed a ditch, by the simple expedient of rolling the ditch out flat, and waddled forward. In its path stood a young tree. The monster arrived at the tree and laid its chin lovingly against the stem. The tree leaned back, crackled, and assumed a horizontal position. In the middle of the clearing, twenty yards farther on, gaped an enormous shell-crater, a present from the Kaiser. Into this the creature plunged blindly, to emerge, panting and puffing, on the farther side. Then it stopped. A magic opening appeared in its stomach, from which emerged, grinning, a British subaltern and his grimy associates.

And that was our friends' first encounter with a "Tank." The secret—unlike most secrets in this publicity-ridden war—had been faithfully kept; so far the Hush! Hush! Brigade had been little more than a legend even to the men high up. Certainly the omniscient Hun received the surprise of his life when, in the early mist of a September morning some weeks later, a line of these selfsame tanks burst for the first time upon his incredulous vision, waddling grotesquely up the hill to the ridge which had defied the British infantry so long and so bloodily—there to squat complacently down on the top of the enemy's machine-guns, or spout destruction from her own up and down beautiful trenches which had never been intended for capture. In fact, Brother Boche was quite plaintive about the matter. He described the employment of such engines as wicked and brutal, and opposed to the recognised usages of warfare. When one of these low-comedy vehicles (named the *Crême-de-Menthe*) ambled down the main street of the hitherto impregnable village of Flers, with hysterical British Tommies slapping her on the back, he appealed to the civilised world to step in and forbid the combination of vulgarism and barbarity.

"Let us at least fight like gentlemen," said the Hun, with simple dignity. "Let us stick to legitimate military devices—the murder of women and children, and the emission of chlorine gas. But Tanks—no! One must draw the line somewhere!"

But the ill-bred *Crême-de-Menthe* took no notice. None whatever. She simply went waddling on— towards Berlin.

"An experiment, of course," commented Colonel Kemp, as they returned to headquarters—"a fantastic experiment. But I wish they were ready now. I would give something to see one of them leading the way into action to-morrow. It might mean saving the lives of a good many of my boys."

XI

THE LAST SOLO

It was dawn on Saturday morning, and the second phase of the Battle of the Somme was more than twenty-four hours old. The programme had opened with a night attack, always the most difficult and uncertain of enterprises, especially for soldiers who were civilians less than two years ago. But no undertaking is too audacious for men in whose veins the wine of success is beginning to throb. And this undertaking, this hazardous gamble, had succeeded all along the line. During the past day and night, more than three miles of the German second system of defences, from Bazentin le Petit to the edge of Delville Wood, had received their new tenants; and already long streams of not altogether reluctant Hun prisoners were being escorted to the rear by perspiring but cheerful gentlemen with fixed bayonets.

Meanwhile—in case such of the late occupants of the line as were still at large should take a fancy to revisit their previous haunts, working-parties of infantry, pioneers, and sappers were toiling at full pressure to reverse the parapets, run out barbed wire, and bestow machine-guns in such a manner as to produce a continuous lattice-work of fire along the front of the captured position.

All through the night the work had continued. As a result, positions were now tolerably secure, the intrepid "Buzzers" had included the newly grafted territory in the nervous system of the British Expeditionary Force, and Battalion Headquarters and Supply Dépôts had moved up to their new positions.

To Colonel Kemp and his Adjutant Cockerell, ensconced in a dug-out thirty feet deep, furnished with a real bed, electric-light fittings, and ornaments obviously made in Germany, entered Major Wagstaffe, encrusted with mud, but as imperturbable as ever. He saluted.

"Good-morning, sir. You seem to have struck a cushie little home time."

"Yes. The Boche officer harbours no false modesty about acknowledging his desire for creature comforts. That is where he scores off people like you and me, who pretend we like sleeping in mud. Have you been round the advanced positions?"

"Yes. There is some pretty hard fighting going on in the village itself—the Boche still holds the north-west corner—and in the wood on the right. 'A' Company are holding a line of broken-down cottages on our right front, but they can't make any further move until they get more bombs. The Boche is occupying various buildings opposite, but in no great strength at present. However, he seems to have plenty of machine-guns."

"I have sent up more bombs," said the Colonel. "What about 'B'
Company?"

"'B' have reached their objective, and consolidated. 'C' and 'D' are lying close up, ready to go forward in support when required. I think 'A' could do with a little assistance."

"I don't want to send up 'C' and 'D'," replied the Colonel, "until the Divisional Reserve arrives. The Brigade has just telephoned through that reinforcements are on the way. When they get here, we can afford to stuff in the whole battalion. Are 'A' Company capable of handling the situation at present?"

"Yes, I think so. Little is directing his platoons from a convenient cellar. He was in touch with them all when I left. But it is possible that the Boche may make a rush when it grows a bit lighter. At present he is too demoralised to attempt anything beyond intermittent machine-gun fire."

Colonel Kemp turned to Cockerell.

"Get Captain Little on the telephone," he said, "and tell him, if the enemy displays any disposition to counter-attack, to let me know at once." Then he turned to Wagstaffe, and asked the question which always lurks furtively on the tongue of a commanding officer.

"Many—casualties?"

"'A' Company have caught it rather badly crossing the open. 'B' got off lightly. Glen is commanding them now: Waddell was killed leading his men in the rush to the final objective."

Colonel Kemp sighed.

"Another good boy gone—veteran, rather. I must write to his wife.
Fairly newly married, I fancy?"

"Four months," said Wagstaffe briefly.

"What was his Christian name, do you know?"

"Walter, I think, sir," said Cockerell.

Colonel Kemp, amid the stress of battle, found time to enter a note in his pocket-diary to that effect.
* * * * *

Meanwhile, up in the line, 'A' Company were holding on grimly to what are usually described as "certain advanced elements" of the village.

Village fighting is a confused and untidy business, but it possesses certain redeeming features. The combatants are usually so inextricably mixed up that the artillery are compelled to refrain from participation. That comes later, when you have cleared the village of the enemy, and his guns are preparing the ground for the inevitable counter-attack.

So far 'A' Company had done nobly. From the moment when they had lined up before Montauban in the gross darkness preceding yesterday's dawn until the moment when Bobby Little led them in one victorious rush into the outskirts of the village, they had never encountered a setback. By sunset they had penetrated some way farther; now creeping stealthily forward under the shelter of a broken wall to hurl bombs into the windows of an occupied cottage; now climbing precariously to some commanding position in order to open fire with a Lewis gun; now making a sudden dash across an open space. Such work offered peculiar opportunities to small and well-handled parties—opportunities of which Bobby Little's veterans availed themselves right readily.

Angus M'Lachlan, for instance, accompanied by a small following of seasoned experts, had twice rounded up parties of the enemy in cellars, and had despatched the same back to Headquarters with his compliments and a promise of more. Mucklewame and four men had bombed their way along a communication trench leading to one of the side streets of the village—a likely avenue for a counter-attack—and having reached the end of the trench, had built up a sandbag barricade, and had held the same against the assaults of hostile bombers until a Vickers machine-gun had arrived in charge of an energetic subaltern of that youthful but thriving organisation, the Suicide Club, or Machine-Gun Corps, and closed the street to further Teutonic traffic.

During the night there had been periods of quiescence, devoted to consolidation, and here and there to snatches of uneasy slumber. Angus M'Lachlan, fairly in his element, had trailed his enormous length in and out of the back-yards and brick-heaps of the village, visiting every point in his irregular line, testing defences; bestowing praise; and ensuring that every man had his share of food and rest. Unutterably grimy but inexpressibly cheerful, he reported progress to Major Wagstaffe when that nocturnal rambler visited him in the small hours.

"Well, Angus, how goes it?" inquired Wagstaffe.

"We have won the match, sir," replied Angus with simple seriousness.
"We are just playing the bye now!"

And with that he crawled away, with the unnecessary stealth of a small boy playing robbers, to encourage his dour paladins to further efforts.

"We shall probably be relieved this evening," he explained to them, "and we must make everything secure. It would never do to leave our new positions untenable by other troops. They might not be so reliable"—with a paternal smile—"as you! Now, our right flank is not safe yet. We can improve the position very much if we can secure that *estaminet*, standing up like an island among those ruined houses on our right front. You see the sign, *Aux Bons Fermiers*, over the door. The trouble is that a German machine-gun is sweeping the intervening space—and we cannot see the gun! There it goes again. See the brick-dust fly! Keep down! They are firing mainly across our front, but a stray bullet may come this way."

The platoon crouched low behind their improvised rampart of brick rubble, while machine-gun bullets swept low, with misleading *claquement*, along the space in front of them, from some hidden position on their right. Presently the firing stopped. Brother Boche was merely "loosing off a belt," as a precautionary measure, at commendably regular intervals.

"I cannot locate that gun," said Angus impatiently. "Can you, Corporal M'Snape?"

"It is not in the estamint itself, sirr," replied M'Snape. ("Estamint" is as near as our rank and file ever get to *estaminet*.) "It seems to be mounted some place higher up the street. I doubt they cannot see us themselves—only the ground in front of us."

"If we could reach the *estaminet* itself," said Angus thoughtfully, "we could get a more extended view. Sergeant Mucklewame, select ten men, including three bombers, and follow me. I am going to find a jumping-off place. The Lewis gun too."

Presently the little party were crouching round their officer in a sheltered position on the right of the line—which for the moment appeared to be "in the air." Except for the intermittent streams of machine-gun fire, and an occasional shrapnel-burst overhead, all was quiet. The enemy's counter-attack was not yet ready.

"Now listen carefully," said Angus, who had just finished scribbling a despatch. "First of all, you, Bogle, take this message to the telephone, and get it sent to Company Headquarters. Now you others. We will wait till that machine-gun has fired another belt. Then, the moment it has finished, while they are getting out the next belt, I will dash across to the *estaminet* over there. M'Snape, you will come with me, but no one else—yet. If the *estaminet* seems capable of being held, I will signal to you, Sergeant Mucklewame, and you will send your party across, in driblets, not forgetting the Lewis gun. By that time I may have located the German machine-gun, so we should be able to knock it out with the Lewis."

Further speech was cut short by a punctual fantasia from the gun in question. Angus and M'Snape crouched behind the shattered wall, awaiting their chance. The firing ceased.

"*Now!*" whispered Angus.

Next moment officer and corporal were flying across the open, and before the mechanical Boche gunner could jerk the new belt into position, both had found sanctuary within the open doorway of the half-ruined *estaminet*.

Nay, more than both; for as the panting pair flung themselves into shelter, a third figure, short and stout, in an ill-fitting kilt, tumbled heavily through the doorway after them. Simultaneously a stream of machine-gun bullets went storming past.

"Just in time!" observed Angus, well pleased. "Bogle, what are you doing here?"

"I was given tae unnerstand, sirr," replied Mr. Bogle calmly, "when I jined the regiment, that in action an officer's servant stands by his officer."

"That is true," conceded Angus; "but you had no right to follow me against orders. Did you not hear me say that no one but Corporal M'Snape was to come?"

"No, sirr. I doubt I was away at the 'phone."

"Well, now you are here, wait inside this doorway, where you can see Sergeant Mucklewame's party, and look out for signals. M'Snape, let us find that machine-gun."

The pair made their way to the hitherto blind side of the building, and cautiously peeped through a much-perforated shutter in the living-room.

"Do you see it, sirr?" inquired M'Snape eagerly.

Angus chuckled.

"See it? Fine! It is right in the open, in the middle of the street. Look!"

He relinquished his peep-hole. The German machine-gun was mounted in the street itself, behind an improvised barrier of bricks and sandbags. It was less than a hundred yards away, sited in a position which, though screened from the view of Angus's platoon farther down, enabled it to sweep all the ground in front of the position. This it was now doing with great intensity, for the brief public appearance of Angus and M'Snape had effectually converted intermittent into continuous fire.

"We must get the Lewis gun over at once," muttered Angus. "It can knock that breastwork to pieces."

He crossed the house again, to see if any of Mucklewame's men had arrived.

They had not. The man with the Lewis gun was lying dead halfway across the street, with his precious weapon on the ground beside him. Two other men, both wounded, were crawling back whence they came, taking what cover they could from the storm of bullets which whizzed a few inches over their flinching bodies.

Angus hastily semaphored to Mucklewame to hold his men in check for the present. Then he returned to the other side of the house.

"How many men are serving that gun?" he said to M'Snape. "Can you see?"

"Only two, sirr, I think. I cannot see them, but that wee breastwork will not cover more than a couple of men."

"Mphm," observed Angus thoughtfully. "I expect they have been left behind to hold on. Have you a bomb about you?"

The admirable M'Snape produced from his pocket a Mills grenade, and handed it to his superior.

"Just the one, sirr," he said.

"Go you," commanded Angus, his voice rising to a more than usually Highland inflection, "and semaphore to Mucklewame that when he hears the explosion of *this*"—he pulled out the safety-pin of the grenade and gripped the grenade itself in his enormous paw—"followed, probably, by the temporary cessation of the machine-gun, he is to bring his men over here in a bunch, as hard as they can pelt. Put it as briefly as you can, but make sure he understands. He has a good signaller with him. Send Bogle to report when you have finished. Now repeat what I have said to you…. That's right. Carry on!"

M'Snape was gone. Angus, left alone, pensively restored the safety-pin to the grenade, and laid the grenade upon the ground beside him. Then he proceeded to write a brief letter in his field message-book. This he placed in an envelope which he took from his breast pocket. The envelope was already addressed—to the *Reverend Neil M'Lachlan, The Manse*, in a very remote Highland village. (Angus had no mother.) He closed the envelope, initialled it, and buttoned it up in his breast pocket again. After that he took up his grenade and proceeded to make a further examination of the premises. Presently he found what he wanted; and by the time Bogle arrived to announce that Sergeant Mucklewame had signalled "message understood," his arrangements were complete.

"Stay by this small hole in the wall, Bogle," he said, "and the moment the Lewis gun arrives tell them to mount it here and open fire on the enemy gun."

He left the room, leaving Bogle alone, to listen to the melancholy rustle of peeling wall-paper within and the steady crackling of bullets without. But when, peering through the improvised loophole, he next caught sight of his officer, Angus had emerged from the house by the cellar window, and was creeping with infinite caution behind the shelter of what had once been the wall of the *estaminet's* back-yard (but was now an uneven bank of bricks, averaging two feet high), in the direction of the German machine-gun. The gun, oblivious of the danger now threatening its right front, continued to fire steadily and hopefully down the street.

Slowly, painfully, Angus crawled on, until he found himself within the right angle formed by the corner of the yard. He could go no further without being seen. Between him and the German gun lay the cobbled surface of the street, offering no cover whatsoever except one mighty shell-crater, situated midway between Angus and the gun, and full to the brim with rainwater.

A single peep over the wall gave him his bearings. The gun was too far away to be reached by a grenade, even when thrown by Angus M'Lachlan. Still, it would create a diversion. It was a time bomb. He would—

He stretched out his long arm to its full extent behind him, gave one mighty overarm sweep, and with all the crackling strength of his mighty sinews, hurled the grenade.

It fell into the exact centre of the flooded shell-crater.

Angus said something under his breath which would have shocked a disciple of Kultur. Fortunately the two German gunners did not hear him. But they observed the splash fifty yards away, and it relieved them from *ennui*, for they were growing tired of firing at nothing. They had not seen the grenade thrown, and were a little puzzled as to the cause of the phenomenon.

Four seconds later their curiosity was more than satisfied. With a muffled roar, the shell-hole suddenly, spouted its liquid contents and other *débris* straight to the heavens, startling them considerably and entirely obscuring their vision.

A moment later, with an exultant yell, Angus M'Lachlan was upon them. He sprang into their vision out of the descending cascade—a towering, terrible, kilted figure, bare-headed and Berserk mad. He was barely forty yards away.

Initiative is not the *forte* of the Teuton. Number One of the German gun mechanically traversed his weapon four degrees to the right and continued to press the thumb-piece. Mud and splinters of brick sprang up round Angus's feet; but still he came on. He was not twenty yards away now. The gunner, beginning to boggle between waiting and bolting, fumbled at his elevating gear, but Angus was right on him before his thumbs got back to work. Then indeed the gun spoke out with no uncertain voice, for perhaps two seconds. After that it ceased fire altogether.

Almost simultaneously there came a triumphant roar lower down the street, as Mucklewame and his followers dashed obliquely across into the *estaminet*. Mucklewame himself was carrying the derelict Lewis gun. In the doorway stood the watchful M'Snape.

"This way, quick!" he shouted. "We have the Gairman gun spotted, and the officer is needing the Lewis!"

But M'Snape was wrong. The Lewis was not required.

A few moments later, in the face of brisk sniping from the houses higher up the street, James Bogle, officer's servant,—a member of that despised class which, according to the *Bandar-log* at home, spend the whole of its time pressing its master's trousers and smoking his cigarettes somewhere back in billets,—led out a stretcher party to the German gun. Number One had been killed by a shot from Angus's revolver. Number Two had adopted Hindenburg tactics, and was no more to be seen. Angus himself was lying, stone dead, a yard from the muzzle of the gun which he, single-handed, had put out of action.

His men carried him back to the *Estaminet aux Bons Fermiers*, with the German gun, which was afterwards employed to good purpose during the desperate days of attacking and counter-attacking which ensued before the village was finally secured. They laid him in the inner room, and proceeded to put the *estaminet* in a state of defence—ready to hold the same against all comers until such time as the relieving Division should take over, and they themselves be enabled, under the kindly cloak of darkness, to carry back their beloved officer to a more worthy resting-place.

In the left-hand breast pocket of Angus's tunic they found his last letter to his father. Two German machine-gun bullets had passed through it. It was forwarded with a covering letter, by Colonel Kemp. In the letter Angus's commanding officer informed Neil M'Lachlan that his son had been recommended posthumously for the highest honour that the King bestows upon his soldiers.

* * * * *

But for the moment Mucklewame's little band had other work to occupy them. Shelling had recommenced; the enemy were mustering in force behind the village; and presently a series of counter-attacks were launched. They were successfully repelled, in the first instance by the remainder of "A"

Company, led in person by Bobby Little, and, when the final struggle came, by the Battalion Reserve under Major Wagstaffe. And throughout the whole grim struggle which ensued, the *Estaminet aux Bons Fermiers*, tenanted by some of our oldest friends, proved itself the head and corner of the successful defence.

XII

RECESSIONAL

I

Two steamers lie at opposite sides of the dock. One is painted a most austere and unobtrusive grey; she is obviously a vessel with no desire to advertise her presence on the high seas. In other words, a transport. The other is dazzling white, ornamented with a good deal of green, supplemented by red. She makes an attractive picture in the early morning sun. Even by night you could not miss her, for she goes about her business with her entire hull outlined in red lights, regatta fashion, with a great luminous Red Cross blazing on either counter. Not even the Commander of a U-boat could mistake her for anything but what she is—a hospital ship.

First, let us walk round to where the grey ship is discharging her cargo. The said cargo consists of about a thousand unwounded German prisoners.

With every desire to be generous to a fallen foe, it is quite impossible to describe them as a prepossessing lot. Not one man walks like a soldier; they shamble. Naturally, they are dirty and unshaven,. So are the wounded men on the white ship: but their outstanding characteristic is an invincible humanity. Beneath the mud and blood they are men—white men. But this strange throng are grey—like their ship. With their shifty eyes and curiously shaped heads, they look like nothing human. They move like overdriven beasts. We realise now why it is that the German Army has to attack in mass.

They pass down the gangway, and are shepherded into form in the dock shed by the Embarkation Staff, with exactly the same silent briskness that characterises the R.A.M.C., over the way. Their guard, with fixed bayonets, exhibit no more or no less concern over them than over half-a-dozen Monday morning malefactors paraded for Orderly Room. Presently they will move off, possibly through the streets of the town; probably they will pass by folk against whose kith and kin they have employed every dirty trick possible in warfare. But there will be no demonstration: there never has been. As a nation we possess a certain number of faults, on which we like to dwell. But we have one virtue at least—we possess a certain sense of proportion; and we are not disposed to make subordinates suffer because we cannot, as yet, get at the principals.

They make a good haul. Fifteen German regiments are here represented—possibly more, for some have torn off their shoulder-straps to avoid identification. Some of the units are thinly represented; others more generously. One famous Prussian regiment appears to have thrown its hand in to the extent of about five hundred.

Still, as they stand there, filthy, forlorn, and dazed, one suddenly realises the extreme appropriateness of a certain reference in the Litany to All Prisoners and Captives.

II

We turn to the hospital ship.

Two great 'brows,' or covered gangways, connect her with her native land. Down these the stretchers are beginning to pass, having been raised from below decks by cunning mechanical devices which cause no jar; and are being conveyed into the cool shade of the dock-shed. Here they are laid in neat rows upon the platform, ready for transfer to the waiting hospital train. Everything is a miracle of quietness and order. The curious public are afar off, held aloof by dock-gates. (They are there in force to-day, partly to cheer the hospital trains as they pass out, partly for reasons connected with the grey-painted ship.) In the dock-shed, organisation and method reign supreme. The work has been going on without intermission for several days and nights; and still the great ships come. The *Austurias* is outside, waiting for a place at the dock. The

Lanfranc is half-way across the English Channel; and there are rumours that the mighty Britannic[1] has selected this, the busiest moment in the opening fortnight of the Somme Battle, to arrive with a miscellaneous and irrelevant cargo of sick and wounded from the Mediterranean. But there is no fuss. The R.A.M.C. Staff Officers, unruffled and cheery, control everything, apparently by a crook of the finger. The stretcher-bearers do their work with silent aplomb.

[Footnote 1: These three hospital ships were all subsequently sunk by German submarines.]

The occupants of the stretchers possess the almost universal feature of a six days' beard—always excepting those who are of an age which is not troubled by such manly accretions. They lie very still—not with the stillness of exhaustion or dejection, but with the comfortable resignation of men who have made good and have suffered in the process; but who now, with their troubles well behind them, are enduring present discomfort under the sustaining prospect of clean beds, chicken diet, and ultimate tea-parties. Such as possess them are wearing Woodbine stumps upon the lower lip.

They are quite ready to compare notes. Let us approach, and listen, to a heavily bandaged gentleman who—so the label attached to him informs us—is Private Blank, of the Manchesters, suffering from three "G.S." machine-gun bullet wounds.

"Did the Fritzes run? Yes—they run all right! The last lot saved us trouble by running towards us—with their 'ands up! But their machine-guns—they gave us fair 'Amlet till we got across No Man's Land. After that we used the baynit, and they didn't give us no more vexatiousness. Where did we go in? Oh, near Albert. Our objective was Mary's Court, or some such place." (It is evident that the Battle of the Somme is going to add some fresh household words to our war vocabulary. 'Wipers' is a veteran by this time: 'Plugstreet,' 'Booloo,' and 'Arminteers' are old friends. We must now make room for 'Monty Ban,' 'La Bustle,' 'Mucky Farm,' 'Lousy Wood,' and 'Martinpush.')

"What were your prisoners like?"

"'Alf clemmed," said the man from Manchester.

"No rations for three days," explained a Northumberland Fusilier close by. One of his arms was strapped to his side, but the other still clasped to his bosom a German helmet. A British Tommy will cheerfully shed a limb or two in the execution of his duty, but not all the might and majesty of the Royal Army Medical Corps can force him to relinquish a fairly earned 'souvenir.' In fact, owing to certain unworthy suspicions as to the true significance of the initials, "R.A.M.C.," he has been known to refuse chloroform.

"They couldn't get nothing up to them for four days, on account of our artillery fire," he added contentedly.

"'Barrage,' my lad!" amended a rather superior person with a lance-corporal's stripe and a bandaged foot.

Indeed, all are unanimous in affirming that our artillery preparation was a tremendous affair. Listen to this group of officers sunning themselves upon the upper deck. They are 'walking cases,' and must remain on board, with what patience they may, until all the 'stretcher cases' have been evacuated.

"Loos was child's play to it," says one—a member of a certain immortal, or at least irrepressible Division which has taken part in every outburst of international unpleasantness since the Marne. "The final hour was absolute pandemonium. And when our new trench-mortar batteries got to work too,—at sixteen to the dozen,—well, it was bad enough for *us*; but what it must have been like at the business end of things, Lord knows! For a few minutes I was almost a pro-Boche!"

Other items of intelligence are gleaned. The weather was 'rotten': mud-caked garments corroborate this statement. The wire, on the whole, was well and truly cut to pieces everywhere; though there were spots at which the enemy contrived to repair it. Finally, ninety per cent. of the casualties during the assault were due to machine-gun fire.

But the fact most clearly elicited by casual conversation is this—that the more closely you engage in a battle, the less you know about its progress. This ship is full of officers and men who were in the thick of things for perhaps forty-eight hours on end, but who are quite likely to be utterly ignorant of what was going on round the next traverse in the trench which they had occupied. The wounded Gunners are able to give them a good deal of information. One F.O.O. saw the French advance.

"It was wonderful to see them go in," he said. "Our Batteries were on the extreme right of the British line, so we were actually touching the French left flank. I had met hundreds of *poilus* back in billets, in *cafés*, and the like. To look at them strolling down a village street in their baggy uniforms, with their hands in their pockets, laughing and chatting to the children, you would never have thought they were such tigers. I remember one big fellow a few weeks ago, home on leave—*permission*—who used to frisk about with a big umbrella under his arm! I suppose that was to keep the rain off his tin hat. But when they went for

Maricourt the other day, there weren't many umbrellas about—only bayonets! I tell you, they were marvels!"

It would be interesting to hear the *poilu* on his Allies.

The first train moves off, and another takes its place. The long lines of stretchers are thinning out now. There are perhaps a hundred left. They contain men of all units—English, Scottish, and Irish. There are Gunners, Sappers, and Infantry. Here and there among them you may note bloodstained men in dirty grey uniforms—men with dull, expressionless faces and closely cropped heads. They are tended with exactly the same care as the others. Where wounded men are concerned, the British Medical Service is strictly neutral.

A wounded Corporal of the R.A.M.C. turns his head and gazes thoughtfully at one of those grey men.

"You understand English, Fritz?" he enquires.

Apparently not. Fritz continues to stare woodenly at the roof of the dock-shed.

"I should like to tell 'im a story, Jock," says the Corporal to his other neighbour. "My job is on a hospital train. 'Alf-a-dozen 'Un aeroplanes made a raid behind our lines; and seeing a beautiful Red Cross train—it was a new London and North Western train, chocolate and white, with red crosses as plain as could be—well, they simply couldn't resist such a target as that! One of their machines swooped low down and dropped his bombs on us. Luckily he only got the rear coach; but I happened to be in it! D' yer 'ear that, Fritz?"

"I doot he canna unnerstand onything," remarked the Highlander. "He's fair demoralised, like the rest. D' ye ken what happened tae me? I was gaun' back wounded, with *this*—" he indicates an arm strapped close to his side—"and there was six Fritzes came crawlin' oot o' a dug-oot, and gave themselves up tae me—*me*, that was gaun' back wounded, withoot so much as my jack-knife! Demorralised—that's it!"

"Did you 'ear," enquired a Cockney who came next in the line, "that all wounded are going to 'ave a nice little gold stripe to wear—a stripe for every wound?"

There was much interest at this.

"That'll be fine," observed a man of Kent, who had been out since
Mons, and been wounded three times. "Folks'll know now that I'm not a
Derby recruit."

"Where will us wear it?" enquired a gigantic Yorkshireman, from the next stretcher.

"Wherever you was 'it, lad!" replied the Cockney humourist.

"At that rate," comes the rueful reply, "I shall 'ave to stand oop to show mine!"

III

But now R.A.M.C. orderlies are at hand, and the symposium comes to an end. The stretchers are conveyed one by one into the long open coaches of the train, and each patient is slipped sideways, with gentleness and dispatch, into his appointed cot.

One saloon is entirely filled with officers—the severe cases in the cots, the rest sitting where they can. A newspaper is passed round. There are delighted exclamations, especially from a second lieutenant whose features appear to be held together entirely by strips of plaster. Such parts of the countenance as can be discerned are smiling broadly.

"I *knew* we were doing well," says the bandaged one, devouring the headlines; "but I never knew we were doing as well as this. Official, too! Somme Battle—what? Sorry! I apologise!" as a groan ran round the saloon.

"Nevermind," said an unshaven officer, with a twinkling eye, and a major's tunic wrapped loosely around him. "I expect that jest will be overworked by more people than you for the next few weeks. Does anybody happen to know where this train is going to?"

"West of England, somewhere, I believe," replied a voice.

There was an indignant groan from various north countrymen.

"I suppose it is quite impossible to sort us all out at a time like this," remarked a plaintive Caledonian in an upper cot; "but I fail to see why the R.A.M.C. authorities should go through the mockery of *asking* every man in the train where he wants to be taken, when the train can obviously only go to one place—or perhaps two. I was asked. I said 'Edinburgh'; and the medical wallah said, 'Righto! We'll send you to Bath!'"

"I think I can explain," remarked the wounded major. "These trains usually go to two places—one half to Bath, the other, say, to Exeter. Bath is nearer to Edinburgh than Exeter, so they send you there. It is kindly meant, but—"

"I say," croaked a voice from another cot,—its owner was a young officer who must just have escaped being left behind at a Base hospital as too dangerously wounded to move,—"is that a newspaper down there? Would some one have a look, and tell me if we have got Longueval all right? Longueval? Long—I got pipped, and don't quite—"

The wounded major turned his head quickly.

"Hallo, Bobby!" he observed cheerfully. "That you? I didn't notice you before."

Bobby Little's hot eyes turned slowly on Wagstaffe, and he exclaimed feverishly:—

"Hallo, Major! Cheeroh! Did we stick to Longueval all right? I've been dreaming about it a bit, and—"

"We did," replied Wagstaffe—"thanks to 'A' Company."

Bobby Little's head fell back on the pillow, and he remarked contentedly:—

"Thanks awfully. I think I can sleep a bit now. So long! See you later!"

His eyes closed, and he sighed happily, as the long train slid out from the platform.

XIII

"TWO OLD SOLDIERS, BROKEN IN THE WARS"

The smoking-room of the Britannia Club used to be exactly like the smoking-room of every other London Club. That is to say, members lounged about in deep chairs, and talked shop, or scandal—or slumbered. At any moment you might touch a convenient bell, and a waiter would appear at your elbow, like a jinnee from a jar, and accept an order with silent deference. You could do this all day, and the jinnee never failed to hear and obey.

That was before the war. Now, those idyllic days are gone. So is the waiter. So is the efficacy of the bell. You may ring, but all that will materialise is a self-righteous little girl, in brass buttons, who will shake her head reprovingly and refer you to certain passages in the Defence of the Realm Act.

Towards the hour of six-thirty, however, something of the old spirit of Liberty asserts itself. A throng of members—chiefly elderly gentlemen in expanded uniforms—assembles in the smoking-room, occupying all the chairs, and even overflowing on to the tables and window-sills. They are not the discursive, argumentative gathering of three years ago. They sit silent, restless, glancing furtively at their wrist-watches.

The clocks of London strike half-past six. Simultaneously the door of the smoking-room is thrown open, and a buxom young woman in cap and apron bounces in. She smiles maternally upon her fainting flock, and announces:—

"The half-hour's gone. Now you can *all* have a drink!"

What would have happened if the waiter of old had done this thing, it is difficult to imagine. But the elderly gentlemen greet their Hebe with a chorus of welcome, and clamour for precedence like children at a school-feast. And yet trusting wives believe that in his club, at least, a man is safe!

Major Wagstaffe, D.S.O., having been absent from London upon urgent public affairs for nearly three years, was not well versed in the newest refinements of club life. He had arrived that morning from his Convalescent Home in the west country, and had already experienced a severe reverse at the hands of the small girl with brass buttons on venturing to order a sherry and bitters at 11.45 A.M. Consequently, at the statutory hour, his voice was not uplifted with the rest; and he was served last. Not least, however; for Hebe, observing his empty sleeve, poured out his soda-water with her own fair hands, and offered to light his cigarette.

This scene of dalliance was interrupted by the arrival of Captain Bobby Little. He wore the ribbon of the Military Cross and walked with a stick—a not unusual combination in these great days. Wagstaffe made room for him upon the leather sofa, and Hebe supplied his modest wants with an indulgent smile.

An autumn and a winter had passed since the attack on Longueval. From July until the December floods, the great battle had raged. The New Armies, supplied at last with abundant munitions, a seasoned Staff, and a concerted plan of action, had answered the question propounded in a previous chapter in no uncertain fashion. Through Longueval and Delville Wood, where the graves of the Highlanders and South Africans now lie thick, through Flers and Martinpuich, through Pozieres and Courcelette, they had fought their way, till they had reached the ridge, with High Wood at its summit, which the Boche, not altogether unreasonably, had regarded as impregnable. The tide had swirled over the crest, down the reverse slope, and up at last to the top of that bloodstained knoll of chalk known as the Butte de Warlencourt. There the Hun threw in his hand. With much loud talk upon the subject of victorious retirements and Hindenburg Lines, he withdrew himself to a region far east of Bapaume; with the result that now some thousand square miles of the soil of France had been restored once and for all to their rightful owners.

But Bobby and Wagstaffe had not been there. All during the autumn and winter they had lain softly in hospital, enjoying their first rest for two years. Wagstaffe had lost his left arm and gained a decoration. Bobby, in addition to his Cross, had incurred a cracked crown and a permanently shortened leg. But both were well content. They had done their bit—and something over; and they had emerged from the din of war with their lives, their health, and their reason. A man who can achieve that feat in this war can count himself fortunate.

Now, passed by a Medical Board as fit for Home Service, they had said farewell to their Convalescent Home and come to London to learn what fate Olympus held in store for them.

"Where have you been all day, Bobby?" enquired Wagstaffe, as they sat down to dinner an hour later.

"Down in Kent," replied Bobby briefly.

"Very well: I will not probe the matter. Been to the War Office?"

"Yes. I was there this morning. I am to be Adjutant of a Cadet school, at Great Snoreham. What sort of a job is that likely to be?"

"On the whole," replied Wagstaffe, "a Fairy Godmother Department job. It might have been very much worse. You are thoroughly up to the Adjutant business, Bobby, and of course the young officers under you will be immensely impressed by your game leg and bit of ribbon. A very sound appointment."

"What are they going to do with you?" asked Bobby in his turn.

"I am to command our Reserve Battalion, with acting rank of Lieutenant-Colonel. Think of that, my lad! They have confirmed you in your rank as Captain, I suppose?"

"Yes."

"Good! The only trouble is that you will be stationed in the South of England and I in the North of Scotland; so we shall not see quite so much of one another as of late. However, we must get together occasionally, and split a tin of bully for old times' sake."

"Bully? By gum!" said Bobby thoughtfully. "I have almost forgotten what it tastes like. (Fried sole, please; then roast lamb.) Eight months in hospital do wash out certain remembrances."

"But not all," said Wagstaffe.

"No, not all. I—I wonder how our chaps are getting on, over there."

"The regiment?"

"Yes. It is so hard to get definite news."

"They were in the Arras show. Did better than ever; but—well, they required a big draft afterwards."

"The third time!" sighed Bobby. "Did any one write to you about it?"

"Yes. Who do you think?"

"Some one in the regiment?"

"Yes."

"I didn't know there were any of the old lot left. Who was it?"

"Mucklewame."

"Mucklewame? You mean to say the Boche hasn't got *him* yet? It's like missing Rheims Cathedral."

"Yes, they got him at Arras. Mucklewame is in hospital. Fortunately his chief wound is in the head, so he's doing nicely. Here is his letter."

Bobby took the pencilled screed, and read:—

_Major Wagstaffe,

Sir,—I take up my pen for to inform you that I am now in hospital in Glasgow, having become a cassuality on the 18th inst.

I was struck on the head by the nose-cap of a German shell (now in the possession of my guidwife). Unfortunately I was wearing one of they steel helmets at the time, with the result that I sustained a serious scalp-wound, also very bad concussion. I have never had a liking for they helmets anyway.

The old regiment did fine in the last attack. They were specially mentioned in Orders next day. The objective was reached under heavy fire and position consolidated before we were relieved next morning_.

"Good boys!" interpolated Bobby softly.

_Colonel Carmichael, late of the Second Battn., I think, is now in command. A very nice gentleman, but we have all been missing you and the Captain.

They tell me that I will be for home service after this. My head is doing well, but the muscles of my right leg is badly torn. I should have liked fine for to have stayed out and come home with the other boys when we are through with Berlin.

Having no more to say, sir, I will now draw to a close.

Jas. Mucklewame,

C.S.M_.

After the perusal of this characteristic *Ave atque Vale!* the two friends adjourned to the balcony, overlooking the Green Park. Here they lit their cigars in reminiscent silence, while neighbouring search-lights raked the horizon for Zeppelins which no longer came. It was a moment for confidences.

"Old Mucklewame is like the rest of us," said Wagstaffe at last.

"How?"

"Wanting to go back, and all that. I do too—just because I'm here, I suppose. A year ago, out there, my chief ambition was to get home, with a comfortable wound and a comfortable conscience."

"Same here," admitted Bobby.

"It was the same with practically every one," said Wagstaffe. "If any man asserts that he really enjoys modern warfare, after, say, six months of it, he is a liar. In the South African show I can honestly say I was perfectly happy. We were fighting in open country, against an adversary who was a gentleman; and although there was plenty of risk, the chances were that one came through all right. At any rate, there was no poison gas, and one did not see a whole platoon blown to pieces, or buried alive, by a single shell. If Brother Boer took you prisoner, he did not stick you in the stomach with a saw-edged bayonet. At the worst he pinched your trousers. But Brother Boche is a different proposition. Since he butted in, war has descended in the social scale. And modern scientific developments have turned a sporting chance of being scuppered into a mathematical certainty. And yet—and yet—old Mucklewame is right. One *hates* to be out of it—especially at the finish. When the regiment comes stumping through London on its way back to Euston—next year, or whenever it's going to be—with their ragged pipers leading the way, you would like to be at the head of 'A' Company, Bobby, and I would give something to be exercising my old function of whipper-in. Eh, boy?"

"Never mind," said practical Bobby. "Perhaps we shall be on somebody's glittering Staff. What I hate to feel at present is that the other fellows, out there, have got to go on sticking it, while we—"

"And by God," exclaimed Wagstaffe, "what stickers they are—and were! Did you ever see anything so splendid, Bobby, as those six-months-old soldiers of ours—in the early days, I mean, when we held our trenches, week by week, under continuous bombardment, and our gunners behind could only help us with four or five rounds a day?"

"I never did," said Bobby, truthfully.

"I admit to you," continued Wagstaffe, "that when I found myself pitchforked into 'K(1)' at the outbreak of the war, instead of getting back to my old line battalion, I was a pretty sick man. I hated everybody. I was one of the old school—or liked to think I was—and the ways of the new school were not my ways. I hated the new officers. Some of them bullied the men; some of them allowed themselves to be bullied by N.C.O.'s. Some never gave or returned salutes, others went about saluting everybody. Some came into Mess in fancy dress of their own design, and elbowed senior officers off the hearthrug. I used to marvel at the Colonel's patience with them. But many of them are dead now, Bobby, and they nearly all made good. Then the men! After ten years in the regular Army I hated them all—the way they lounged, the way they dressed, the way they sat, the way they spat. I wondered how I could ever go on living with them. And now—I find myself wondering how I am ever going to live without them. We shall not see their like again. The new lot—present lot—are splendid fellows. They are probably better soldiers. Certainly they are more uniformly trained. But there was a piquancy about our old scamps in 'K(1)' that was unique—priceless—something the world will never see again."

"I don't know," said Bobby thoughtfully. "That Cockney regiment which lay beside us at Albert last summer was a pretty priceless lot. Do you remember a pair of fat fellows in their leading platoon? We called them Fortnum and Mason!"

"I do—particularly Fortnum. Go on!"

"Well, their bit of trench was being shelled one day, and Fortnum, who was in number one bay with five other men, kept shouting out to Mason, who was round a traverse and out of sight, to enquire how he was getting on. 'Are you all right, Bill?' 'Are you *sure* you're all right, Bill?' 'Are you *still* all right, Bill?' and so on. At last Bill, getting fed up with this unusual solicitude, yelled back: 'What's all the anxiety abaht, eh?'

And Fortnum put his head round the traverse and explained. 'We're getting up a little sweepstake in our bay,' he said, 'abaht the first casualty, and I've drawn you, ole son!'"

Wagstaffe chuckled.

"That must have been the regiment that had the historic poker party," he said.

"What yarn was that?"

"I heard it from the Brigadier—four times, to be exact. Five men off duty were sitting in a dug-out playing poker. A gentleman named 'Erb had just gone to the limit on his hand, when a rifle-grenade came into the dug-out from somewhere and did him in. While they were waiting for the stretcher-bearers, one of the other players picked up 'Erb's hand and examined it. Then he laid it down again, and said: 'It doesn't matter, chaps. Poor 'Erb wouldn't a made it, anyway. I 'ad four queens.'"

"Tommy has his own ideas of fun, I'll admit," said Bobby. "Do you remember those first trenches of ours at Festubert? There was a dead Frenchman buried in the parapet—you know how they used to bury people in those days?"

"I did notice it. Go on."

"Well, this poor chap's hand stuck out, just about four feet from the floor of the trench. My dug-out was only a few yards away, and I never saw a member of my platoon go past that spot without shaking the hand and saying, Good-morning, Alphonse!' I had it built up with sandbags ultimately, and they were quite annoyed!"

"They have some grisly notions about life and death," agreed Wagstaffe, "but they are extraordinarily kind to people in trouble, such as wounded men, or prisoners. You can't better them."

"And now there are five millions of them. We are all in it, at last!"

"We certainly are—men and women. I'm afraid I had hardly realised what our women were doing for us. Being on service all the time, one rather overlooks what is going on at home. But stopping a bullet puts one in the way of a good deal of inside information on that score."

"You mean hospital work, and so on?"

"Yes. One meets a lot of wonderful people that way! Sisters, and ward-maids, and V.A.D.'s—"

"I love all V.A.D.'s!" said Bobby, unexpectedly.

"Why, my youthful Mormon?"

"Because they are the people who do all the hard work and get no limelight—like—like—!"

"Like Second Lieutenants—eh?"

"Yes, that is the idea. They have a pretty hard time, you know," continued Bobby confidentially: "And nothing heroic, either. Giving up all the fun that a girl is entitled to; washing dishes; answering the door-bell; running up and downstairs; eating rotten food. That's the sort of—"

"What is her name?" enquired the accusing voice of Major Wagstaffe.

Then, without waiting to extort an answer from the embarrassed
Bobby:—

"You are quite right. This war has certainly brought out the best in our women. The South African War brought out the worst. My goodness, you should have seen the Mount Nelson Hotel at Capetown in those days! But they have been wonderful this time—wonderful. I love them all—the bus-conductors, the ticket-punchers, the lift-girls—one of them nearly shot me right through the roof of Harrod's the other day—and the window-cleaners and the page-girls and the railway-portresses! I divide my elderly heart among them. And I met a bunch of munition girls the other day, Bobby, coming home from work. They were all young, and most of them were pretty. Their faces and hands were stained a bright orange-colour with picric acid, and will be, I suppose, until the Boche is booted back into his stye. In other words, they had deliberately sacrificed their good looks for the duration of the war. That takes a bit of doing, I know, innocent bachelor though I am. But bless you, they weren't worrying. They waved their orange-coloured hands to me, and pointed to their orange-coloured faces, and laughed. They were *proud* of them; they were doing their bit. They nearly made me cry, Bobby. Yes, we are all in it now; and those of us who come out of it are going to find this old island of ours a wonderfully changed place to live in."

"How? Why?" enquired Bobby. Possibly he was interested in Wagstaffe's unusual expansiveness: possibly he hoped to steer the conversation away from the topic of V.A.D.'s—possibly towards it. You never know.

"Well," said Wagstaffe, "we are all going to understand one another a great deal better after this war."

"Who? Labour and Capital, and so on?"

"'Labour and Capital' is a meaningless and misleading expression, Bobby. For instance, our men regard people like you and me as Capitalists; the ordinary Brigade Major regards us as Labourers, and pretty common Labourers at that. It is all a question of degree. But what I mean is this. You can't call your employer a tyrant and an extortioner after he has shared his rations with you and never spared himself over your welfare and comfort through weary months of trench-warfare; neither, when you have experienced a working-man's courage and cheerfulness and reliability in the day of battle, can you turn round and call him a loafer and an agitator in time of peace—can you? That is just what the *Bandar-log* overlook, when they jabber about the dreadful industrial upheaval that is coming with peace. Most of all have they overlooked the fact that with the coming of peace this country will be invaded by several million of the wisest men that she has ever produced—the New British Army. That Army will consist of men who have spent three years in getting rid of mutual misapprehensions and assimilating one another's point of view—men who went out to the war ignorant and intolerant and insular, and are coming back wise to all the things that really matter. They will flood this old country, and they will make short work of the agitator, and the alarmist, and the profiteer, and all the nasty creatures that merely make a noise instead of *doing* something, and who crab the work of the Army and Navy—more especially the Navy—because there isn't a circus victory of some kind in the paper every morning. Yes, Bobby, when our boys get back, and begin to ask the *Bandar-log* what they *did* in the Great War—well, it's going to be a rotten season for *Bandar-log* generally!"

There was silence again. Presently Bobby spoke:—

"When our boys get back! Some of them are never coming back again, worse luck!"

"Still," said Wagstaffe, "what they did was worth doing, and what they died for was worth while. I think their one regret to-day would be that they did not live to see their own fellows taking the offensive—the line going forward on the Somme; the old tanks waddling over the Boche trenches; and the Boche prisoners throwing up their hands and yowling 'Kamerad'! And the Kut unpleasantness cleaned up, and all the kinks in the old Salient straightened out! And Wytchaete and Messines! You remember how the two ridges used to look down into our lines at Wipers and Plugstreet? And now we're on top of both of them! Some of our friends out there—the friends who are not coming back—would have liked to know about that, Bobby. I wish they could, somehow."

"Perhaps they do," said Bobby simply.

It was close on midnight. Our "two old soldiers, broken in the wars," levered themselves stiffly to their feet, and prepared to depart.

"Heigho!" said Wagstaffe. "It is time for two old wrecks like us to be in bed. That's what we are, Bobby—wrecks, dodderers, has-beens! But we have had the luck to last longer than most. We have dodged the missiles of the Boche to an extent which justifies us in claiming that we have followed the progress of their war with a rather more than average degree of continuity. We were the last of the old crowd, too. Kemp has got his Brigade, young Cockerell has gone to be a Staff Captain, and—you and I are here. Some of the others dropped out far too soon. Young Lochgair, old Blaikie—"

"Waddell, too," said Bobby. "We joined the same day."

"And Angus M'Lachlan. I think he would have made the finest soldier of the lot of us," added Wagstaffe. "You remember his remark to me, that we only had the bye to play now? He was a true prophet: we are dormy, anyhow. (Only cold feet at Home can let us down now.) And he only saw three months' service! Still, he made a great exit from this world, Bobby, and that is the only thing that matters in these days. Ha! H'm! As our new Allies would say, I am beginning to 'pull heart stuff' on you. Let us go to bed. Sleeping here?"

"Yes, till to-morrow. Then off on leave."

"How much have you got?"

"A month. I say?"

"Yes?"

"Are you doing anything on the nineteenth?"

Wagstaffe regarded his young friend suspiciously.

"Is this a catch of some kind?" he enquired.

"Oh, no. Will you be my—" Bobby turned excessively pink, and completed his request.

Wagstaffe surveyed him resignedly.

"We all come to it, I suppose," he observed.

"Only some come to it sooner than others. Are you of age, my lad? Have your parents—"

"I'm twenty-two," said Bobby shortly.

"Will the bridesmaids be pretty?"

"They are all peaches," replied Bobby, with enthusiasm. "But nothing whatever," he added, in a voice of respectful rapture, "compared with the bride!"

THE END

The Willing Horse

CHAPTER I
THE VALLEYS STAND SO THICK WITH CORN

I

A Sunday at Baronrigg is a chastening experience. It is not exactly a day of wrath—though one feels that it might easily become one—but it is a time of tribulation for people who do not want to go to church—or, if the worst happens, prefer their religious exercises to be brief and dilute.

But neither brevity nor dilution makes any appeal to my friend Tom Birnie.

"I am a member," he announces, as soon as a quorum has assembled at Sunday breakfast, "of the old Kirk of Scotland; and I propose to attend service at Doctor Chirnside's at eleven o'clock. If any of you would care"—he addresses a suddenly presented perspective of immaculate partings, bald spots and permanent waves—"to accompany me, a conveyance will leave here at ten-forty."

"Well, we can't *all* get in, that's plain," chirps Miss Joan Dexter hopefully. (The table is laid for fourteen.)

"The conveyance," continues the inexorable Tom, "holds twelve inside and four out, not counting the coachman."

"It's no good, Joan, old fruit," observes Master Roy Birnie. "We keep a pantechnicon!"

"I suppose there's not a Church of England service within reach?" asks little Mrs. Pomeroy, rather ingenuously. "One's own Church makes an appeal to one which no other denomination cannot—can—adequately—doesn't it?" she concludes, a little uncertain both of her syntax and of her host. This is her first visit to Baronrigg.

"Now she's done for herself!" whispers Master Roy into my left ear.

"I agree with you. There is an Episcopal Church—Scottish Episcopal, of course—at Fiddrie, three miles from here. I shall be happy to send you over there this evening at half-past six. This morning, I know, you will put up with our barbaric Northern rites!" replies Tom, with what he imagines to be an indulgent smile. "I like to see the Baronrigg pew full."

And full it is.

The longer I know Tom Birnie, the more I marvel that Diana Carrick married him. That sentiment is shared by a good many people, but on more abstract grounds than mine. Tom is a just and considerate landlord, an adequate sportsman, and a good specimen of that class by whose voluntary service this country gets most of its local government done, admirably, for nothing. But there are certain things against Tom.

In the first place—to quote old Lady Christina Bethune, of Buckholm—"no one knows who the creature is, or where he came from." This implies nothing worse than that since Tom represents the first generation of Birnies born in this county, his forbears must have been born somewhere else. In other words—still quoting the same distinguished authority—"they never existed at all." As a matter of fact and common knowledge, Tom's grandfather was a minister of the Kirk, somewhere in Perthshire, and his father an enormously successful member of the Scottish Bar, who bought the derelict little estate of Strawick, hard by here, and settled there in the late sixties with the presumptuous, but, I think, excusable, intention of founding a family. Naturally a family which has resided in our county for only forty-seven years can hardly be expected to have drifted, as yet, within the range of Lady Christina's lorgnette.

Secondly, Tom is a Radical. We are broad-minded people in this county, and are quite indulgent to persons who disapprove of the leasehold system (which does not obtain in Scotland), or who make excuses for the late Mr. Gladstone, or who are inclined to criticise pheasant preserving. That is the kind of Radicalism which we understand, and are prepared to tolerate. That was the sort of person Tom's father was. That is how Tom began. But of late, it must be confessed, Tom has been going it. He supports the present Government; he is for reducing the Army and Navy; he has recently helped to abolish our Second Chamber. (That was no great calamity; but he and his friends have omitted to provide us with a substitute.) He has openly applauded the efforts of a person named George to break up the foundations of our well-tried Social System; while the courses which he advocates with regard to the taxation of Land Values and the treatment of loyal Ulster, surpass belief. That is what the county has against Tom.

But I am neither a laird nor a farmer, and my indictment against Tom is based on more personal and less venial grounds. Firstly, he is not human. He is a calculating machine, with about as much passion as a parish pump. Secondly, he is absolutely destitute of all sense of humour. And yet Diana married him! Her own beautiful person exhaled humanity and humour in equal proportions. In all her short life I never knew her fail to understand a fellow-creature, or miss a humorous situation. Yet she married Tom Birnie. She married Tom Birnie, and she broke off her engagement with Eric Bethune to do it. I am a humble-minded person, and I never professed to understand any woman—not even my own wife, Diana's sister—but I wonder, even now, how any girl could have resisted Eric Bethune as he was twenty years ago, or, having got him, have relinquished him in favour of Tom Birnie. There was something pretty big and tragic behind that broken-off engagement. My Eve knew what it was—I suppose Diana told her about it—but when I asked for the explanation I was tersely instructed not to be an inquisitive old busybody. As for Eric, he never mentioned the matter to me. He simply informed me that my services as best man would not be required after all, and that he would be gratified if I would refrain from asking damn silly questions. (Not that I had asked any.) Also, that he looked to me to prevent other persons from doing so.

And now Tom Birnie is a baronet and a widower, with a son eighteen years old, and Eric Bethune is still an eligible bachelor of forty-three. And how he hates Tom Birnie! However, I will introduce Eric presently. First of all, I must get our party to church.

II

The ancestral hereditary omnibus of the house of Baronrigg deposited us at the kirk door at ten fifty-five precisely, and by the time that the Reverend Doctor Chirnside's Bible and hymn-book had been set out upon the red velvet cushion of the pulpit by a bulbous old friend of mine named James Dunshie—an octogenarian of austere piety, an infallible authority on dry-fly fishing, and a methodical but impervious drinker—we were all boxed into our places in the private gallery of Baronrigg. It is less of a gallery than a balcony, and juts out curiously from the side of the little church, with the public gallery running across the end wall on its right, and the minister on its left. It recedes into a deep alcove, and at the back is a fireplace, in which a fire is always kept burning upon wintry Sundays. The Baronrigg pew—and, indeed, Baronrigg itself—came into the family from Diana's side of the house: she brought them to Tom on her marriage. The pew is rich in Carrick associations. It is reported of old Neil Carrick, the grandfather of Diana and my Eve, that whenever he found himself dissatisfied—a not infrequent occurrence—with the discourse of Doctor Chirnside's predecessor, it was his habit to rise from his red rep chair in the forefront of the gallery, retire to the back, make up the fire with much clatter of fire-irons, and slumber peacefully before the resulting blaze with his back to the rest of the congregation. But no such licence was permitted to us. We sat austerely in two rows, gazing solemnly at the blank wall opposite us, while Doctor Chirnside worked his will upon his flock. Doctor Chirnside is a tall, silver-haired, and pugnacious old gentleman of about seventy. He fears God, and exhibits considerable deference towards Tom Birnie; but he regards the rest of his congregation as dirt. (At least, that is how we feel in his presence.) This morning he entered the pulpit precisely on the stroke of eleven, in deference to the Laird's well-known prejudices on the subject of punctuality—besides, I happened to know that he was coming on to lunch at Baronrigg after service—and, having been securely locked in by James Dunshie, adjusted his spectacles and gazed fiercely at some late comers. Then he gave out the opening psalm.

In Craigfoot Parish Church we always sing the opening psalm unaccompanied. It is true that we possess a small organ, but that instrument is still regarded with such deep suspicion by some of the older members of the congregation that we only employ it to accompany hymns—which, as is well known, have little effect one way or the other upon one's ultimate salvation. But we take no risks with the Psalms of David. These are offered without meretricious trimmings of any kind, save that furnished by the tuning-fork of Andrew Kilninver, our esteemed auctioneer, estate agent, and precentor.

Accordingly, when Doctor Chirnside took up his psalter, the young lady at the organ leaned back nonchalantly; Andrew Kilninver stirred importantly in his seat, tuning-fork in hand; and the choir—highly scented shop-girls and farmers' daughters, assisted by overheated young men in Sunday "blacks" and choker collars—braced themselves with the air of people upon whose shoulders the credit, and maybe redemption, of a whole parish rests.

There is something peculiarly majestic about the manner in which Doctor Chirnside opens his morning service. I believe that, in his view, the unaccompanied psalm is the one relic of pure orthodoxy preserved by him against the modern passion for hymns, organs, printed prayers, anthems, and "brighter worship" generally. That graceless young ruffian, Roy Birnie, gives an imitation of his performance which is celebrated throughout the parish. It runs something like this:

"Ha-humm! Brethren, we will commence the public worrship of God, this Lord's Day, by singing to His praise part of the Seven Hundred and Forty-Ninth Psalm. Psalm Seven Hundred and Forty-Nine. Ha-humm! The Church is full cold. Will Mr. John Buncle, of Sandpits, kindly rise in his pew and adjust the open window west of him? (*Imitation of Mr. John Buncle, petrified with confusion, adjusting the window.*) We will commence at verrse One Hundred and Seventy-Nine:

I, like a bottle, have been

With Thy great maircy filled,
Oh, hold me up, hold Thou me up,
That I may not be spilled!

And so on until the end of the Psalm. Psalm Seven Hundred and Forty-Nine. The Seven Hundred and Forty-Ninth Psalm. *Ping! Ping! Ping!* (*The last is supposed to be Kilninver getting to work with his tuning-fork.*) Tune, Winchester, 'I, like a bottle...'"

I am a devout person, but I am afraid it does sound something like that.

However, one feels less inclined to smile when the actual singing of the psalm commences. The Metrical Psalms, sung in unison, without accompaniment, and with strong, rugged voices predominating, are Scottish history. They bring back the days when people did not sing them in churches, but on hillsides in remote fastnesses, at services conducted by a man with a price on his head, guarded by sentries lying prone upon the skyline, on the look-out for Claverhouse and his troopers. That is why I, coming of the stock I do, like to hear the opening psalm at Craigfoot.

The start, as a rule, is not all what it might be, for the Scots are a slow-moving race; and naturally it takes a little time to catch up with Andrew Kilninver and his comparatively nimble crew. But about the middle of the second verse we draw together, and the unsophisticated rhymes, firmly welded now with the grand old melody, go rolling upwards and outwards through the open door and windows, over one of the fairest and richest farming districts in the world:

They drop upon the pastures wide,
That do in deserts lie;
The little hills on every side
Rejoice right pleasantly.
With flocks the pastures clothed be,
The vales with corn are clad;
And now they shout and sing to Thee,
For Thou hast made them glad.

I am a soldier, and have been a soldier all my life, so when I encounter an assemblage of my fellow countrymen, I naturally scrutinise them from a recruiting sergeant's point of view. (At least, Eve always said I did.) And what a sight that congregation presented! I have encountered many types in the course of my duty. I know our own Highlanders; I know the French Zouave regiments; a year or two ago—in nineteen-eleven I think it was—I saw the Prussian Guard march past the Emperor during Grand Manoeuvres; I have ridden with the Canadian North-West Mounted Police; I have seen a Zulu impi on the move in South Africa. All have their own particular incomparabilities—dash, endurance, resource, initiative—but for sheer physical solidity and fighting possibilities, commend me to the peaceful yeoman-farming stock of the Lowlands of Scotland. My own regiment is mainly recruited from this district, so perhaps I am prejudiced. Still, if ever the present era of international restlessness crystallises into something definite; if ever The Day, about which we hear so much and know so little, really arrives—well, I fancy that that heavily-built, round-shouldered throng down there, with their shy, self-conscious faces and their uncomfortable Sunday clothes, will give an account of themselves of which their sonsy, red-cheeked wives and daughters will have no cause to feel ashamed.

III

After the psalm we settle down to the Doctor's first prayer. There are two of these, separated by an entire chapter of the Old Testament—a fairly heavy sandwich, sometimes. The first prayer lasts a quarter of an hour, the second, eight minutes. The first prayer takes the form of an interview between Doctor Chirnside and his Maker—an interview so confidential in character and of a theological atmosphere so rarefied that few of us are able to attain to it. So our attention occasionally drops to lower altitudes. The second prayer is more adapted to humble intellects. The Doctor refers to it as the Prayer of Intercession. In it he prays for everything and everybody, beginning with the British Empire and ending with the Dorcas Society. Under the cloak of Intercession, too, he is accustomed, very ingeniously, to introduce, and comment upon, topics of current interest. Occasionally he springs upon us a genuine and delightful surprise. The parish still remembers the Sunday morning in eighteen-ninety-four upon which the Doctor, in his customary intercession for the Royal Family, got in twenty-four hours ahead of Monday's *Scotsman* by concluding his orison: "And we invoke Thy special blessing, O Lord, upon the infant son (and ultimate heir to the Throne of this country) born, *as Thou knowest, Lord*, to Her Majesty's grandchildren, the Duke and Duchess of York, at an early hour this morning!"

But the first prayer, as already indicated, holds no surprises. I am therefore accustomed to devote this period to a detailed inspection of the congregation below—an occupation which has the special merit of being compatible with an attitude of profound devotion.

Perhaps I ought to explain how it is that I, a mere visitor, should take such a deep interest in Craigfoot and its associations. The fact is, I am no visitor. I was born here, not ten miles away, at The Heughs, a little manor among the foothills, where my brother Walter and his lusty family still flourish. As a younger son I was destined from birth for the Army; but by the time I had passed into Sandhurst, and on to the lordly exile of our Army in India, I knew every acre of the district. I had tumbled into burns and been kicked off ponies all over the county. I knew everybody who lived there, from our local overlord, the Earl of Eskerley, down to Bob Reid, the signal porter at the railway station—who, being well aware that I went fishing every Wednesday at Burling, two stations up the line, was accustomed on those occasions to refuse right of way to the morning train, palpitating for its connection with the junction ten miles distant, until my tardy bicycle swept round the curve of the road and deposited me panting on the platform.

Inevitably, the day came when I fell in love—with Eve. That was no novelty for Eve; for she and her elder sister, Diana, had most of us on a string in those days. Baronrigg was the lodestone of every young spark in the county, except during those dismal months in summer when our twin divinities were spirited away to London for the season. Some were able to follow them there; but I was not. Neither was Eric Bethune. Regimental duty forbade, though we did what we could with the generous leave available in the early nineties.

Ultimately, I was taken and Eric was left. Why Eve took me I have never known. I was only an infantry subaltern, and a younger son into the bargain. But she picked me out from the crowd, and waited for me, bless her! for seven years. My theory was, and is, that a woman only marries a man for one of two reasons—either because he gives her "a thrill," or because she thinks he requires taking care of. There was no doubting Eve's reason for marrying me. She took care of me for one rapturous year; and then she left me, and took her baby with her. To-day both lie in the private burial-ground of Baronrigg. That is why I always accept Tom's annual invitation to stay there at Easter, rather than go to my brother Walter's cheery but distracting establishment at The Heughs.

That is enough about me. Now let us get back to the congregation.

It was a representative throng, yet not entirely representative. For one thing, our chief territorial and social luminary, Lord Eskerley, is a member of the Church of England; and when he goes to church at all—which is usually just after a heart-attack, or just before a General Election—he goes to Fiddrie. For another, no Scottish assemblage can be counted truly representative which takes no account of the adherents of Holy Church—as a peep into Father Kirkpatrick's tightly-packed conventicle on the other side of the glen would tell us. But when all is said, the parish church is still the focus of Scottish rural life, and I was well content with the selection of friends who filled the pews below me.

There was old General Bothwell, of Springburn, a Mutiny and Crimean veteran—altogether quite a celebrity among a generation which knows nothing of actual warfare. (After all, the South African affair touched our civil community very lightly.) Beside the General sits his son Jack, home on leave from India. He commands a company in a Pathan regiment. The General is trying hard not to look proud of Jack.

Just behind the Bothwells sit the Graemes, of Burling—Sir Alistair, his Lady, and their three tall daughters, known and celebrated throughout the county as "The Three Grenadiers." Across the aisle sits old Couper, of Abbottrigg—the largest farmer in the district, and one of the best curlers in Scotland—with his wife. The old couple are alone now, for all their sons and daughters are married. However, a good many of them are present in other parts of the church, holding a fidgety third generation down in its seat.

Just in front of the Coupers I observe Mr. Gillespie, manager of our branch of the Bank of Scotland, a man of immense discretion and many secrets. With him, Mrs. Gillespie. Also the two Misses Gillespie, locally and affectionately renowned as "Spot" and "Plain." I notice that their son, Robert, who is studying for the Ministry in distant Edinburgh, is with them for the week-end.

Farther back, at the end of a long pew, just under the public gallery, sits Galbraith, our chemist and druggist, a small man with a heavy cavalry moustache and—the not uncommon accompaniment of a small man—a large wife and twelve children. The children fall into two groups, separated by an interval of seven years. The first group—four in number, and somewhat wizened in appearance—were born and reared upon the slender profits of a retail business in tooth-brushes, patent medicines, and dog-soap. The other eight—fat and well-liking—began to appear serially after Mr. Galbraith had amassed a sudden and unexpected fortune out of a patent sheep-dip of his own invention, which has made the name of Galbraith celebrated as far away as Australia.

Over the way from Galbraith, in a side pew, sits Shanks, the joiner. He is a poor creature, lacking in ability either to ply his trade or invent reasons for not doing so. Eve used to say that Shanks never by any chance acceded to a professional summons, and that his excuses were three in number, and were employed in monotonous rotation—firstly, that he had swallowed some tacks; secondly, that he had had to bury "a relation of the wife's"; thirdly, that one of his numerous offspring had been overtaken by a fit.

Behind Shanks sit the Misses Peabody. They are the daughters of a retired merchant of Leith, who died many years ago. They inhabit a villa on the outskirts of our little town, live on an annuity, and exist precariously in that narrow social borderland which divides town-folk from gentry.

Passing on, I note that Mr. Menzies, Lord Eskerley's factor, has at last provided himself with a wife—a stranger to me. Well, Menzies is well connected and has an excellent house; so, doubtless, the lady will be comfortable. But I wish he had not gone so far afield. There is nothing wrong with the girls in this district, Menzies! *Experto crede*!

My eye wanders on over the bowed heads. Finally it reaches the third pew from the front, and I am aware of the handsome presence of my friend Eric Bethune, of Buckholm. Beside him, bolt upright, with a critical eye fixed upon Doctor Chirnside, sits his eccentric lady mother. Eric's attitude is more devout, but I observe that his head is turned sideways, and that he is grinning sympathetically at Tommy Milroy over the way, whose little nose is being relentlessly pressed to the book-board by an iron maternal hand encased in a hot black kid glove.

Eric, although he is as old as myself, is still very much of a boy—or perhaps I ought, in strict candour, to say a child. He was a child at school—in his exuberant vitality, his sudden friendships, his petulance. He was a child at Sandhurst; he was a child as a subaltern—at times, almost a baby. But he has been my friend all my life, and I admire him more than any man I know; perhaps because he possesses all the qualities which I lack. He is tall and debonair; I am—well, neither. He is impulsive, frank, and popular; I am cautious, reticent and regarded as a little difficult. (This is not true really, only there is no Eve now to tell me what to say to people.)

But, above all, Eric is a soldier. In the South African War he was Adjutant of our Second Battalion. They were sent out rather late, and only got to work after Paardeburg. I was with the other battalion, and saw nothing of Eric, but his Colonel considered him the smartest Adjutant in the Division, and recommended him for the D.S.O. He got it, but always declared that he had had no chance to earn it, except by instructing the men very thoroughly in what is vulgarly known as the art of "Spit and Polish." Certainly they were the best turned-out crowd I have ever seen, when they marched through the streets of Edinburgh on their return.

Directly after that we both went back to India. We were anxious to go. Eve had died just before I sailed for South Africa; Diana had broken off her engagement with Eric and married Tom Birnie three years earlier. But I did not stay in India very long. I was restless for home again; and, having decided that the Regular Army could now get along without my services, I sent in my papers and settled in London. When Roy was nine years old his mother followed her sister. She had survived Eve only six years, for the same lung trouble had marked them down long ago. After that Eric felt that he could come back to Buckholm. So he came, and they gave him command of the Regimental Depot, with the rank of Major. The Depot is not far away from here, and he is able to join his mother at Buckholm for much of the time. He is quite his old self now, and he has made the Third Battalion a marvel of smartness and efficiency. But there is one house which he never visits—Baronrigg. I do not blame him. His memories there are not like mine. Moreover, besides hating Tom Birnie, he dislikes Roy. I am surprised at this, because the boy is the image of his mother. Still, I suppose a man may be forgiven for disliking a boy who should have been his own son, but is not. Anyhow, I know I shall not meet Eric during my stay at Baronrigg, so I have arranged to lunch at Buckholm after church to-day.

That covers the congregation, I think. (Doctor Chirnside is working up to his peroration, and in a few minutes we shall be erect again.) I look over them once more. Altogether, a sturdy, satisfactory assemblage, from laird to ploughman. We have not changed much in the last two hundred years, nor will during the next two hundred, so far as I can see. We are Conservatives of Conservatives, although we return a Liberal. We shall go on tilling the fat soil, and raising fat cattle, and marrying young, and having big families, and sending a few of the boys into the Army, and a few to the Colonies, and keep the rest at home to marry strapping girls and have more big families, until the end of time.

We are a little disturbed, to be sure, at the present state of the world outside. A street-bred Government, with both eyes on the industrial vote, has recently compelled us, even us, to disburse our hard-earned pennies upon stamps, to be stuck at frequent intervals upon an objectionable card. We are informed that this wasteful and uncongenial exercise is designed to bestow upon us the benefits of insurance against sickness—upon us, who are never either sick or sorry; and if ever we are, are taken care of (under an unwritten compact of immemorial antiquity) by the employers who have known us and ours for generations back. Other political upheavals are agitating the country, but they leave us cold in comparison with this superfluous imposition of benevolence.

But still, politicians are always with us, and must be endured; so what matter? Our valleys stand so thick with corn that they laugh and sing, and even with Income Tax at one and twopence in the pound, things might be worse. After all, we have our health, and perhaps it is our duty to contribute to the insurance of those sickly city folk. A few stamps are not a very high price to pay for peace and prosperity and sleepy contentment in the heart of the British Empire.

IV.

... I think I must have begun to nod a little. It was a warm morning, and the sunshine and the songs of the birds without, and the confidential rumblings of Doctor Chirnside within, had exercised a soporific effect. But I opened my eyes with a jerk, and observed that the Netherby pew was occupied.

Netherby has stood empty so long that it is quite a shock to see its pew inhabited at all. It is a conspicuous pew, in the corner of the church, to the left of the pulpit, and my unregenerate nephews and nieces call it "The Loose Box." It is built in the form of a hollow square, and is surrounded by dingy red rep curtains, which enable its occupants to gaze upon the officiating clergy without themselves being gazed upon by the congregation. However, the pew is overlooked by the Baronrigg gallery.

This morning the Netherby pew contained seven occupants, humped devoutly round the square table in the centre. Upon the table reposed a gentleman's silk hat, or topper. Now, in this part of the country, gentlemen do not wear silk hats on Sunday. They wear bowlers, or Homburg hats, or even motoring caps. Neither do they wear frock-coats, like the obvious proprietor of "The Loose Box." He was a squarely-built man, and from what I could see of his face, he wore mutton-chop whiskers. There was also a middle-aged lady in a rather unsuitable hat. There were two boys of nineteen or twenty. There were two or three small children, constrained and restless. There was an elderly man with a beard like a goat's, gazing upwards at Doctor Chirnside with an air which struck me as critical. One felt that he would have taken the Doctor's place without any pressing whatsoever. I put him down for a visitor of some kind.

And there was a girl. At least, there was a hat—a big black tulle hat—and I assumed that there was a girl underneath it. I could see her frock, which was white. So were her gloves, which extended above her elbows. Her hands were long and slim. I began to feel curious to see her face.

Suddenly I realised that I was not alone in this ambition. On my left, that young rascal Roy was hanging outward and downward at a dangerous and indecorous angle, in a characteristically thorough attempt to look under the brim of the black tulle hat. Needless to say, in romantic enterprises of this kind, competition, especially with the young, makes one feel merely foolish, so I resumed my normal position and closed my eyes with an air of severe reproof.

Almost directly afterwards the First Prayer came to a conclusion, and we all sat up. Simultaneously the girl in the hat lifted her head. The Parish Church is small and the range was comparatively short. For a moment her face was upturned in our direction. I heard Roy give a gasp of admiration.

"Let us read together," suggested the indefatigable Doctor Chirnside, "in the Fifty-Fifth Chapter of the Book of the Prophet Isaiah. Chapter Fifty-Five. The first verse. *Ho, every one that thirsteth...*"

But I am afraid I was not listening. I was watching the girl's face—as well I might, for it was the face of a flower. She leaned back in her seat against the wall, and composed herself for the Fifty-Fifth Chapter of Isaiah. Suddenly, for some reason, she lifted her head again. This time her eyes encountered Master Roy's honest and rapturous gaze. They fell immediately, but up from the open throat of her white Sunday frock, over her face, and right into the roots of her abundant fair hair, ran a vivid burning blush.

I looked at Roy. He was crimson too.

Spring! Spring! Spring!

CHAPTER II
REBELLIOUS MARJORIE
I

While Sunday at Baronrigg was a day of mild tribulation, Sunday at Netherby was a day of wrath. It was a direct survival of the darkest period of the Victorian era.

Albert Clegg—or, rather, Mr. Albert Clegg—believed in taking no risks with his immortal soul, or with those of his family. He also believed in being master in his own house. Accordingly, when he bade his household remember the Sabbath day to keep it holy, the household, as they say in the Navy, "made it so." The necessary standard of sanctity was attained, firstly, by the removal on Saturday night to locked cupboards of everything in the shape of frivolous or worldly literature; in place of which there appeared a few "Sunday" books—the latest record, mayhap, of missionary endeavour, together with one or two godly romances of a rather distressing character. Periodical literature was represented by *The Sunday at Home*, while unsecular comment on current events was furnished by that brilliantly ingenious combination of broad religion and literary entertainment, *The British Weekly*.

The necessary atmosphere having been duly created, those two powerful engines, Prayer and Fasting, were now set in motion. The latter, to be just, was of little account: its operation merely involved the omission of afternoon tea and the substitution of cold supper for ordinary dinner. But the devotional programme of the Clegg Sunday was an exacting business. It opened with family prayers at eight-thirty a.m., including an extemporary supplication by the master of the house. Catechism came at nine-thirty, Church at eleven o'clock. The household were conveyed thither in the Rolls-Royce. In the course of time, as the glory of that extremely new vehicle faded, and the task of making an impression upon the neighbourhood accomplished itself, the young Cleggs gloomily foresaw a still further extension of Sabbath observance, in the direction of pedestrian exercise. Meanwhile, they covered the three miles to church in the car, and were thankful for small mercies.

After one o'clock dinner, the family sang hymns. Marjorie accompanied—not very convincingly, owing to the presence of a surreptitious novel or volume of poetry propped upon the music-rest beside the hymn-book. You cannot engage in psalmody and mental culture simultaneously with any degree of plausibility. The younger children sang a shrill soprano; brothers Amos and Joe growled self-consciously an octave—sometimes two octaves—lower. Sister Amy—a plain but intensely pious child of fourteen—offered a windy and unmelodious contribution which she termed "seconds." Mrs. Clegg sang—as she did everything else—dutifully, and slightly apologetically. Mr. Clegg sang what he had imagined for more than thirty years to be tenor, inciting his fellow-choristers to continued effort by beating time with his hymn-book, until post-prandial drowsiness intervened, and he retired to bed, with all his clothes on, for his Sabbath nap. During this interval the family enjoyed a slight respite from Sabbath observance—all, that is, but the younger members, who received instructions in Biblical history from two small and not uninteresting manuals, entitled *Peep of Day* and *Line Upon Line*, with maternal additions and elucidations of a somewhat surprising character.

At six o'clock the chauffeur was once more called upon to observe the Sabbath by conveying the family to evening service at the parish church. The small fry, in consideration of *Peep of Day* and *Line Upon Line*, were permitted to go to bed.

After cold supper at eight-thirty, the devotional exercises of the day petered out with a second instalment of family prayers, including what brother Joe (Marjorie's accomplice and pet) was wont to describe as "a final solo from Pa." After that, the exhausted household retired to rest, leaving the master to relax himself from the spiritual tension of the day with weak whisky-and-water.

Albert Clegg had bought Netherby a year previously. He came from the North of England, and was deeply interested in Tyneside shipping. His father had been a small tradesman in Gateshead. Albert's initial opportunities had not been too great, but he possessed two priceless natural assets—superb business capacity and a sincere dislike for recreation or amusement of any kind. At twenty-one he was a clerk in a rather moribund shipping business. At twenty-five he was managing clerk. In that capacity he took it upon himself, unofficially, to investigate the books of the firm—he was the sort of young man who would joyfully devote a series of fine Saturday afternoons to such an enterprise—and was ultimately able to expose a leakage of profits which had kept the venerable and esteemed cashier of the office in considerably greater comfort than his employers for the past ten years. Needless to say, Albert was the next cashier. At thirty he was junior partner and practically dictator. A few years later his exhausted seniors gave up the struggle, and allowed themselves to be bought out. Albert promptly called in his younger brother Fred, who, up to date, had been dividing his undoubted talents fairly evenly between jerry-building and revivalist preaching—a combination of occupations which enabled him to

Compound for sins he was inclined to,
By damning those he had no mind to—

thus marking himself down as an ultimate and inevitable ornament of our National Legislature. Fred was taken into partnership. From that day the firm of Clegg Brothers went from strength to strength.

Albert Clegg's first wife was what Lady Christina would have described as "a young person of his own station in life." She had died a few years after the birth of Master Amos. The present Mrs. Clegg was a member of an aristocratic but impoverished family named Higgie, of Tynemouth, and she came to Albert just at a time when his rising fortunes called for a helpmeet possessed of the social accomplishments which he himself so entirely lacked. On his second marriage, he removed from Gateshead to a large house in the pleasant suburb of Jesmond, and lived there for twenty years, while the Clegg firm prospered and the Clegg family multiplied. As already foreshadowed, brother Fred's combined reputations as a captain of industry and a silver-tongued orator presently wafted him into Parliament, where he established a reputation for verbosity and irrelevance remarkable even in that eclectic assembly.

That is all that need be said about Mr. Albert Clegg for the present. The main purpose of this brief summary of his character and achievements is to provide the reader with some sort of key—in so far as keys are of any use at all where feminine locks are concerned—to the character of that rather unexpected young person, his daughter Marjorie. For it was from her father, most undoubtedly, that Marjorie derived her initiative and determination. From her mother she seemed to have inherited nothing, except her Christian name and her naturally waved hair. Everything else—her superb body, her absolute honesty, her lively sense of humour, her critical attitude towards certain existing things, and, above all, her warm, impulsive young heart—came from that one supreme gift of God which is entirely our own—set high out of reach of those twin busybodies, Heredity and Environment—Personality.

II

On the particular spring morning with which we are already concerned, Marjorie made a bad start. She missed prayers altogether, and was late for breakfast into the bargain. To crown her iniquity, she entered the dining-room whistling a secular air, with her arms full of daffodils.

Whistling is at all times an unladylike accomplishment, even though one whistle like a mavis. Moreover, it was Sunday. Furthermore, Uncle Fred was present on a visit, and one has to keep up appearances before relations, however despicable.

"I am not at all satisfied with Doctor Chirnside," Mr. Clegg was remarking. "But we must employ such instruments as lie to our hands."

"That is very true," remarked Uncle Fred, making a mental note of this apt expression. Uncle Fred was an industrious gleaner of other people's impromptus, with a view to parliamentary requirements.

"As you know," continued Mr. Clegg, "our own Body is not represented in this county. The nearest United Free Church—which conforms most closely to our own beliefs—is fifteen miles away. In any case, I consider that a household should, as far as possible, worship in its own district."

"Quite right," said Uncle Fred. "Like a constituency."

"Besides, we would not get to know people any other way," interposed Mrs. Clegg timidly.

"My dear," said Mr. Clegg severely, "we cannot worship God and Mammon. And I will thank you for another cup of tea. John, my boy, eat up that crust; I know of many a poor lad that would be glad of it. The only other places of worship within easy reach," he continued, "besides the parish church (Established, of course), are a Papist Chapel, Burling way, which I do not go to very often"—Mr. Clegg paused and assumed a wintry smile, to indicate that he spoke sarcastically—"and the English Episcopal Church at Fiddrie—where I would as soon see any belongings of mine trying to disport themselves as in the Church of Rome itself."

Mr. Clegg paused, and Uncle Fred laughed sardonically. Mrs. Clegg, who all her life had hankered after the comfortable consolations of Anglican ritual and the social cachet of an Anglican connection, smothered a sigh, for she knew to what address her husband's remark was directed.

At this moment, as related, Marjorie tramped in, whistling, with her daffodils.

"Hallo! am I late?" she inquired. "I am so sorry: I was out gathering these. Good morning, everybody!"

She sat down amid a deathly silence.

"What were you all talking about?" Marjorie rattled on. "Church, wasn't it? I wonder how many hours old Chirnside will preach to-day? Oh, that awful children's sermon! I don't think it's sportsmanlike to make you listen to two sermons in one morning. My idea is that during the grown-ups' sermon the children should be allowed to go out and play, and that during the children's sermon the grown-ups should have their choice of going out too, or lying right down in the pews and having a nap!" She gazed out of the window, over the sunny landscape. "I know which I should choose!"

"My girl," interposed Mr. Clegg, "if you talk in that strain I shall regret more than ever that I allowed your mother to send you to that school in Paris."

Marjorie had been "finished"—which means "begun"—at Neuilly. It is difficult to understand why her father had sent her there, except that it was expensive. Mr. Clegg had long transferred the blame for this lapse of judgment to his wife.

During those two quickening years, Marjorie, though hedged about by every preventive device known to the scholastic hierarchy, had fairly wallowed in Life—Life as opposed to Existence. She had sucked in Life through her pores; she had scrutinised Life through her shrewd blue eyes; she had masticated Life with her vigorous young teeth. Life in Paris, even as viewed from the ranks of a governess-guided "crocodile" in the Bois de Boulogne, or a processional excursion to the Tuileries, is a stimulating and disturbing compound, especially to unemancipated seventeen. At any rate, Marjorie had returned to her home possessing certain characteristics which had not been apparent when she left it. These were, roughly, three in number:

Firstly, a passionate interest in the world and its contents. She was ablaze with enthusiasm for all mankind. She wanted to do something—to be a hospital nurse, a journalist, a chorus girl, a barmaid—anything, in fact, that would bring her into contact with her fellow-creatures and, if possible, enable her to make herself uncomfortable on their behalf. She was a Giver, through and through.

Secondly, an entire lack of sentimentality. Young men made no appeal to her. She had never flirted in her life: she did not know how. She made friendships at a rush—many of them with boys of her own age—but if any young man flattered himself that he had made a tender impression, he was soon woefully undeceived. Marjorie was purely maternal. If she was kind to a young man it was because she felt sorry for him—sorry for his adorable clumsiness, his transparency, his helplessness, his lack of finesse. Young men, as a class, never gave her a thrill. She loved her own sex too, especially the self-conscious and foolish. Marjorie's main instinct at that time, and indeed through all her life, was to interpose her own beautiful and vigorous young personality between the weaker vessels of her acquaintance and the hard knocks of this world.

Thirdly, a strongly critical attitude towards the theory that children owe a debt of gratitude to their parents for the mere fact of having been brought by them into existence. Loyal she was, because it was her nature. Dutiful she was prepared to be. She was impulsively affectionate always; but her inborn sense of equity was strong. Moreover, for two years she had associated with new companions—members of another world than her own—either young girls of the English upper class, who were accustomed to regard their parents as amiable but unsophisticated accomplices in misdemeanour, or maidens from New York and Philadelphia, who appeared to entertain no opinion of their parents, as such, at all. This association had shaken to its foundation the law of her childhood—that children existed entirely for the convenience of their parents, and must expect no consideration, no indulgence, and, above all, no *camaraderie* from those aloof and exalted beings. In the spring of nineteen-fourteen Youth had not yet been called in to rescue Age from extinction.

Such was Marjorie at eighteen—a dangerous mixture, particularly liable to explode under compression.

She had risen early this Sunday morning in order to ramble through the woods and compose her turbulent spirit. The previous evening had witnessed a sleep-destroying interview between her father and herself. After prayers, while Mr. Clegg, according to his custom, was setting the markers in the great family Bible for the following morning's devotions, Marjorie had seated herself beside him at the head of the library table, with the air of one determined upon a plunge. She waited until the servants had filed out and the rest of the family were dispersed. Then she came to the attack with characteristic promptness.

"Father," she said, "may I go and be trained as a hospital nurse?"

"No," replied Mr. Clegg, without hesitation or heat; "you may not."

"May I learn shorthand and typewriting, then?"

"No."

"May I go and take training in some profession? Any kind," she added eagerly, "as long as it is useful."

"No," said Mr. Clegg for the third time. Then with the air of a just person patient under importunity: "Why?"

"For two reasons," said the girl. "I want to be useful, and I want to be independent."

For answer, Mr. Clegg reopened the Bible, and with the accuracy of long practice came almost immediately upon what he wanted—certain illuminated manuscript pages occurring between the Old and New Testaments. There were six of these pages. Two were allotted to the Births, two to the Marriages, and two to the Deaths of the house of Clegg. Albert Clegg turned to the Births, and ran his finger down the list. There were quite a number of names, for the Bible was a family inheritance.

Presently he found what he wanted. A line in red ink had been drawn right across the page under the name of his youngest brother, Uncle Fred, to indicate the end of a generation. Below this line was written, in his own neat business hand:

Children of Albert and Mary Clegg.

This title-heading had erred on the side of plurality, for beneath it came but one entry—that of the birth of Albert's eldest son, Amos, at Gateshead, upon the tenth of March, Eighteen Ninety-two. A second heading followed immediately:

Children of Albert and Marjorie Clegg.

After this came quite a satisfying list. First, Joe's name—it proved to be Joshua, in full—recorded upon the twelfth of August, Eighteen Ninety-four. Then came the entry he was seeking:

Marjorie; born at "The Laburnums," Jesmond, April twenty-fourth, Eighteen Ninety-Six.

Albert Clegg surveyed his daughter over the top of his spectacles, which had been assumed for purposes of perusal, and performed a small exercise in mental arithmetic.

"That makes you eighteen," he observed.

Marjorie nodded. At this point, to her intense annoyance, the egregious Uncle Fred re-entered the room and joined the Board.

"Girls of eighteen—" began her father.

"Young ladies of eighteen," amended the Member of Parliament.

"—have no call to be independent," continued Albert Clegg; "and if they want to be of some use they can stay at home and help their mothers, as God meant them to."

"Mother," riposted Marjorie, "has more servants than she knows what to do with, and she hates interference with her house management, anyway. I have been home now for three months, honestly trying to help, and there isn't a single thing for me to do. There are hundreds of things I can do away from here. I do not ask to go out and do them now, but I do ask to be trained in something useful, so that when the time comes—"

"When what time comes?" asked her father quickly.

"The time when it will be a living impossibility for me to stick it out any longer," said Marjorie frankly. "Do you think I can sit here for ever"—with one comprehensive gesture she summarised Netherby, with its stodgy gentility, its squirrel-cage routine, and its cast-iron piety—"twiddling my thumbs? Every girl has a *right* to make herself efficient, nowadays."

"What comes before our rights," said Albert Clegg, "is our duty—our grateful duty to the parents that brought us up."

"*Honour thy father and thy mother*," chaunted the apposite Uncle Fred, "*that thy days—*"

Marjorie sat up.

"I hope I do honour my father and mother," she said. "I am fond of them both: they have been kind to me all my life. But I do not see why I should be particularly grateful to them for bringing me up. After all"—turning to her father—"you *had* to, hadn't you? You were responsible for my being here, weren't you? It seems to me that parents owe a debt to their children—not children to their parents!"

This amazingly audacious deliverance—and one had to be familiar with the Clegg tradition to realise how audacious it was—produced a stunning silence. Uncle Fred, fumbling in his repertoire for something really commensurate, breathed alarmingly. Presently Albert Clegg's heavy voice broke in:

"A debt? You mean I owe *you* a—a debt of gratitude?"

"Not gratitude," replied Marjorie. "Something bigger—honour. I think that parents owe it to their children, having brought them into the world—and all that sort of thing," she added a little shyly, "to give them a chance to live the sort of life that appeals to them."

Uncle Fred was ready now.

"The French," he announced, "are a giddy and godless race!"

But neither Albert Clegg nor his daughter took any notice. Wide apart as their natures lay, they had one point in common—inflexible determination. Clegg surveyed Marjorie's curving lips and hot blue eyes for a moment, and asked:

"So you want to live your own life, eh?"

Marjorie nodded.

"Yes," she said. "At least, I don't want to rush off and live it right away; but I do think I ought to be given sufficient—" she hesitated for a word.

"Equipment?" suggested her father.

"Rope?" amended Uncle Fred.

Marjorie nodded to her father again.

"Yes," she said, "sufficient equipment. A girl ought to be capable of doing something. I have told you some of the things a girl might learn to do, but there are lots of others. Even if she could support herself on the Stage it would be something."

"*The Stage?*"

Marjorie had exploded a bombshell this time. Uncle Fred's goat-beard dropped upon his shirt front, and waggled helplessly. Albert Clegg gazed at his daughter long and fixedly. Then he pulled the Bible towards him again, and turned back a page or two in the family record. He twisted the great volume round, and pushed it in his daughter's direction and pointed.

"Look at that," he said.

Marjorie looked. Upon the page of births, near the bottom of the list of her father's brothers and sisters, she saw a horizontal black strip—perhaps a quarter of an inch high—extending the full width of the page, where an entry in the record had been crossed out again, and again, and again, by a thick quill pen. She had seen it before, and had asked what it meant—without success. Now apparently she was to know.

"That," said Albert Clegg, "was my youngest sister."

"Your Aunt Eliza," added Uncle Fred.

"When she was nineteen," continued Clegg, "she ran away from home—to go on the Stage."

"Hoo! Where?" asked Marjorie, intensely interested.

"London, my father thought; but he never enquired."

"He never—? You mean—?"

"He blotted her name out of the Book, and it was never mentioned in our home again."

"And not one of you ever tried to find what had become of her?"

"Certainly not."

Marjorie looked up at her father and drew a long and indignant breath.

"Well—!" she began.

"And now," explained Uncle Fred, "it's coming out in you, my girl."

What was coming out Marjorie did not trouble him to explain. It is doubtful if she heard him at all.

"You mean to say," she said hotly to her father, "that your father let his own daughter go right out of sight and mind, just like that?"

"He did. And I want to say to you, my daughter, that I think he was right. This life is a preparation for the next. As we live now, so shall we be rewarded hereafter. A few years' empty pleasure and excitement are a poor exchange for an eternity of punishment."

"That's right! Take no risks!" recommended the sage at the other end of the table. "Safety first!"

"The wisest life," concluded Mr. Clegg, "is the safe life. The safe life is the Christian life, and the sure foundation of the Christian life is family life—united, wisely controlled, family life. So you will stay at home and live that life; and some day you will be grateful. Now go to bed. I appreciate your honesty in telling me what is in your mind, but my advice to you is forget all about it. Good-night!"

"Don't forget your prayers!" added Uncle Fred.

III

Marjorie finished her breakfast without further flippancy, and in due course the family set out for church in the Rolls-Royce. That is to say, Mr. and Mrs. Clegg, Uncle Fred, Marjorie, and the younger children—Miss Amy, already mentioned, and Masters James and John, aged ten and eight—were packed into that spacious vehicle and driven into Craigfoot, with meticulous observation of the speed limit and all the windows up. Amos and Joe followed in the two-seater. The servants had the waggonette.

The parish kirk at Craigfoot has already been described in some detail, but it may be worth while to record a few observations made from a different angle.

From her seat against the wall in the high-curtained Netherby pew Marjorie could see nothing but the last few rows of the public gallery and the Baronrigg balcony. The latter fascinated her, for it was always full—usually of interesting, and always of different, people. Sir Thomas Birnie himself was a permanent figure. He sat in the left-hand corner of the balcony, at the end nearest the pulpit. Consequently, his severe gaze, concentrated upon the preacher, was averted from the other occupants of the pew—a circumstance particularly agreeable to some of the younger members of his numerous house parties. What fun they seemed to have among themselves! How they giggled and whispered! Marjorie longed and longed to be with them and of them, especially the girls of her own age. They were so pretty, so overflowing with life, and dressed so exactly right. For three months, ever since she came back from Paris to find her family at Netherby, and the comfortable hospitality of a Newcastle suburb exchanged for the frigid waiting-list of a county society where one knew either everybody or nobody, she had taken weekly notes of the ever-changing kaleidoscope in the Baronrigg pew—studying faces, studying frocks, studying characters, and weaving histories round each.

Some of the faces were quite familiar. This morning, for instance, in the right-hand corner of the front row, sat Major Laing. He was a frequent visitor at Baronrigg, and was a widower. Marjorie knew that his wife had been a twin-sister of the late Lady Birnie. Then there were Captain and Mrs. Roper. Captain Roper owned horses, and was here—in fact, the whole house-party was here—for the Castleton Races, the largest meeting on this side of the Border. They were constant visitors. Then there was a pretty little woman in a big hat—Mrs. Pomeroy, really—of which Marjorie took mental and quite unsabbatical note. There was Arthur Langley, one of the best-known gentlemen riders in England. There was a tall girl with fair hair—not unlike Marjorie herself. Marjorie decided that this girl was dressed not quite right. She would have been better placed in a fashionable West-end church in London than in this grey, prim, Presbyterian conventicle. Probably her first visit, Marjorie decided. She would know better next time.

Her shrewd gaze passed on.

And then, for the first time in her life, she saw Roy Birnie, home after four months of toil and tribulation at an army crammer's. He had been plucked out of Eton at Christmas to that end, Eton having decided that it was a case for desperate measures. Three months of intensive brain-culture had not affected his appearance, which was healthy, nor his snub nose, nor his cheerful grin, nor the slight curl in his hair, of which his mother had once been so proud and of which he was still so ashamed. He sat on the left of Major Laing, his chin resting on the pew ledge, his grey eyes devoutly closed, and his ebullient spirits throttled down until it should please Doctor Chirnside to conclude the first prayer. He was exactly like hundreds of other clean-run Public School boys of eighteen. Marjorie had observed a dozen such in that very pew during the past three months. But, as already noted, she had never seen Roy.

That usually dependable organ, her heart, missed a couple of beats, and she lowered her head quickly.

Presently, impelled by a power greater than herself (or, indeed, than any of us), she lifted her head and looked up—only to find that Roy was gazing straight down upon her.

For the moment her eyes were interlocked with his. Then suddenly she became aware of the expression upon his face. The result has already been described.

That evening, after prayers, her father motioned to her to stay behind. When they were alone, he said:

"I hope you have given up that idea of yours about going away."

"Well," replied his daughter pleasantly, "I have postponed it, anyhow, father."

"You have decided wisely for yourself," said Mr. Clegg.

Marjorie felt inclined to agree. But it is just possible that the matter had been decided for her.

CHAPTER III
DER TAG
I

I suppose I may be forgiven for having felt a trifle preoccupied upon the first of August, nineteen-fourteen. Most people did. But the European situation, desperate though it was, was not sufficiently desperate to excuse me for forgetting that the first Saturday in August is the inexorable date of Lady Christina's annual garden party at Buckholm. So I blundered right into it.

I am a methodical person, and I like to do the same things at the same seasons. When it comes to revisiting the place of my birth, marriage and, I hope, interment, I make a practice of going to Baronrigg for Easter, Buckholm for the August cricket week, and The Heughs for the woodcock. On this particular occasion I had travelled from King's Cross by the early morning express—it leaves at five o'clock, and is the best train in the day, if only people knew about it—with the result that by four o'clock in the afternoon I found myself rumbling along in the Craigfoot station fly, in lovely, summer weather, *en route* for the Buckholm cricket week. Lady Christina, whose foes—and their name is legion, for they are many—accuse her of parsimony, does not usually send the motor to the station to meet unencumbered males. She expects such guests to cover the last stage of the journey at their own charges and, in addition, to share the conveyance with such parcels and oddments as may be lying in the station office consigned to Buckholm.

On this occasion Mr. Turnbull, the station master, apologetically packed me into the fly in company with half a sheep and three bright new zinc buckets, freshly arrived from the stores in Edinburgh.

In addition to my personal luggage, I was laden with a limp, damp package, smelling to heaven of fish, which had borne me noisome company all the way from my flat in Jermyn Street, having been delivered there by an accomplice of Lady Christina's the night before my departure, with the information that her ladyship had signified my willingness to convey it to Buckholm.

But things might have been worse. Lady Christina had played this fish trick upon me last year as well. (It is one of her most cherished economies.) On that occasion the fish was delivered at my flat five minutes after I had left for Scotland. It was marked "Very Important"; so the lift boy, a conscientious but unimaginative youth, sent for the pass-key and carefully deposited the package in my hall cupboard. I found it there, quite safe, when I returned from Scotland, three weeks later.

The first warning that all was not well came to me when my equipage drew up, to a symphonic accompaniment of rattling buckets, at the lodge gates of Buckholm. These were held, like the bridge across the Tiber upon a famous occasion, by a resolute trio composed of Mackellar, the under-gardener, and Mesdames Elspeth and Maggie Mackellar, Mackellar's daughters, aged about fourteen. Horatius Codes (Mackellar) informed me that by her ladyship's orders it was "hauf-a-croon to get in," adding (quite incomprehensibly at the moment) that it was "on account of the Feet for Charity."

My contention that, as a guest, I was entitled to exemption, or, at least, abatement of entrance fee, was overruled by a dour but respectful majority of three to one. I handed Horatius Codes a reluctant half-crown; Herminius and Spurius Lartius threw open the gates, and the experienced animal between the shafts, unusually braced by the eerie combination of sounds and smells conveyed to his senses by a following breeze, delivered me at the front door, with much spurting of gravel, four minutes later.

My worst fears were realised. Dotted about the wide lawns stood bazaar-stalls, under striped awnings. The band of our Third Battalion from the Depot was making music on the terrace, and fair women and brave men drifted here and there, shying nervously at the stalls. Too late, I understood Mackellar's reference to the "Feet for Charity." I had heard from afar of the existence of this recurrent and gruesome festival for many years. No one knew why it was held, or to what charity Lady Christina devoted the proceeds. I once asked Lord Eskerley if he could tell me. He replied that so far as he was aware it was a charity which was not puffed up, and began at home. But Lord Eskerley is a cynical old gentleman, and has been at war with Lady Christina for forty years.

A sympathetic butler received me and showed me my room. The ceremony was purely formal: I knew the room almost as well as I knew him.

"It will go on until ten o'clock, sir," he announced mournfully, in reply to my anxious query. "The present company will leave about seven; but the townspeople begin to arrive then, when the admission fee is reduced to sixpence. Are we going to have a flare-up, sir?"

"No. What's the use? We shall take it lying down, Bates, as usual. You know Lady Christina!"

"I was referring, sir, to the European situation."

"Oh, sorry! Yes, it looks like it. If Germany joins Austria against Russia, France is bound to come in on the side of Russia; and if France comes in I fancy we shall all come in. And then God knows what will happen! Is there much excitement down here?"

"Very little at present, sir—less than when the South African War was imminent. But I understand that all the officers at the Depot are being recalled from leave. You will find several of them here, sir."

"Mr. Eric is here, of course?"

"For the afternoon, sir, yes. But he sleeps at the Depot now. He is very busy. You will change into flannels, I suppose?"

"Yes."

"It will fill out the time a bit, sir, before you need go outside. Her Ladyship is not aware of your arrival. Shall I bring you a whisky and soda?"

"Please."

By judicious dawdling I staved off the moment of my entrance into the "Feet" for another half-hour. Then, fortified by Bates's timely refreshment, I went downstairs to search for my hostess.

The garden was full of people—sirens in lace caps proffering useless articles of merchandise; officers from the Depot; boys and girls just home for the holidays; local dames talking scandal in deck-chairs. Upon the distant croquet lawn I beheld my hostess engaged in battle. I could hear her quite easily, shouting: "Now then—no treachery, no treachery!" to her partner, a nervous subaltern who was furtively offering advice to a pretty opponent. I remembered Bates's hint, also a maxim to the effect that what is not missed is not mourned. Perhaps it would be wiser—

"Yes, I would if I were you," remarked a raven's voice at my elbow. "She hasn't seen you yet!"

Lord Eskerley is a very remarkable old gentleman, with certain pronounced and rather alarming characteristics. In the first place, he has an uncanny knack of reading one's thoughts, which enables him to begin a conversation without wasting time over preliminaries, which he hates. Secondly, he has a peculiar habit of side-tracking a subject right in the middle of a sentence, sometimes because he is overtaken by a reverie, sometimes because another subject occurs to him—to return sooner or later, but always without warning, to the original topic—like brackets in algebra. I once met him coming out of Brooks's Club, and accompanied him down St. James's Street.

"Just been to a funeral," he announced; and forthwith subsided into a brown study.

I offered a few appropriate observations regarding the uncertainty of human life, and then proceeded to the political situation. He replied with his usual incisiveness. Ten minutes later, as we passed through the Horse Guards into Whitehall, he stopped abruptly, shook me by the hand, and said:

"Good-bye! At Woking. We cremated him. Very interesting!"—and set off at a brisk walk in the direction of the Houses of Parliament.

These conversational acrobatics call for considerable agility on the part of the listener. The strain is increased by the circumstance that, owing to his uncanny powers of memory, Lord Eskerley is able (and usually proceeds) to take up a conversation with you exactly where he left it off, sometimes after an interval of months. I was once walking in the Park on Sunday morning with Lady Christina, whom I had encountered for my sins after church. Near the Achilles statue I was aware of Lord Eskerley, plunged in profound meditation. Suddenly he looked up and saw me. He hurried forward and shook hands, utterly ignoring Lady Christina.

"Courvoisier," he said, "not Martell!"—and departed towards Stanhope Gate.

"What does the demented creature mean?" inquired Lady Christina.

I was able to explain that His Lordship had merely been unburdening himself of a name which he had been unable to recall at the time of our last conversation. Criminology is one of his numerous hobbies, and on this occasion he had been trying to tell me the name of one of the last murderers publicly hanged in England. (Thackeray went to see it.) All he could recall, however, was that the murderer had been a valet in Park Lane, and that his name had suggested liqueur brandy.

Decidedly he is a character. But he is a Pillar of State for all that, and, unlike some Pillars of State, he has done the State some service. He likes me, because I catch his references more quickly than most people.

"Well," I rejoined, "suppose you assist me to find cover?"

"Certainly!" he replied. "By the way"—extending a hand—"how do you do? Wonderful day! Now come and find a seat, and we will smoke."

We doubled a promontory of rhododendrons and sat down on a rustic bench, somewhat apart from the turmoil. The only person in sight was a girl, with very good ankles. (Eve always reproved me for beginning at that end.) She was standing fifty yards away from us, under the dappled shade of a copper-beech, surveying the scene—a little disconsolately, I thought. My companion, as usual, was ready with an appropriate but elliptic comment.

"Doesn't know he's here!" he observed.

"Why don't you tell her?" I asked.

"No need. They'll find one another all right."

"Who is she? And he?"

The question partly answered itself, for at that moment the girl turned in our direction, and I recognised her as the unexpected young beauty of the Netherby pew. Aware that two inquisitive dotards were leering at her, she withdrew out of sight. Lord Eskerley did not answer the rest of my question, because his thoughts had run ahead of the situation.

"There is something particularly cruel and brutal," he said, "about British snobbery. If this had been America, her hostess would have introduced her to every one in sight. (If she had not been prepared to do so, she would not have invited her at all.) On the Continent, young men would have led one another up, and clicked their heels together, and announced their names, with a view to a fair exchange. But here—well, she knows nobody, and every woman in the county will see to it that she continues to know nobody. Practically, that was why she was invited here. Tantalus, and so on!"

"I have often wondered," I said, "why we never go in for introducing. It would save much discomfort to rustic persons like myself."

"I'll tell you. Roughly, our attitude is this. There are only a certain number of people in this world who are anybody—Us, in fact. You are either one of Us, or you are not. If you are, obviously there is no need to introduce you. If you are not—well, an introduction would imply that you are not one of Us! So it is almost more insulting to introduce people than to ignore them. Very ingenious system: I wonder what woman invented it! Still, *she's* all right." (Apparently His Lordship had switched back to the girl again.) "She and her mother only get invited to Gather-'em-Alls and Charity Sales-of-Work, but most of the boys have managed to scrape acquaintance with her by this time. She fairly bowled them over at the Third Battalion Gymkhana a few weeks ago. Looked a picture; won first prize for the motor obstacle race; and fairly had to keep subalterns off with a stick! *And* at least one field officer!"

"You seem to have taken considerable notice of her," I observed.

"I take considerable notice of most things," replied the old gentleman complacently, "even pretty girls. By the way, we are going to fight them."

"The girls?"

"God forbid! Germany!"

"Oh!"

"Yes. I go back to town to-night. There seems little doubt now that we shall come in. We can't leave France in the lurch. For one thing, we should be skunks if we did"—Pillars of State can be surprisingly colloquial in private life—"and for another, Germany means to gobble the whole of Europe this time, including this pacific little island of ours. It would be playing Germany's game to allow her to take us on one after another, instead of all together. Of course, the peace-at-any-price crowd are yowling; but—if we don't back our friends on this occasion, we can never hold up our heads again. It is just possible that the Germans may be fools enough to invade Belgium, in which case even the Cocoa Eaters and the Intellectuals will have to stop supporting them. But I think we shall fight anyhow. It will be a short war, but it will be the bloodiest war ever fought."

"Why do you think it will be short?"

"Because it will be so expensive in money and men that no country will be able to stand the racket for longer than a few months. Modern weapons are so destructive, and modern warfare costs so much, that before we know where we are one side will all be dead and the other side bankrupt; so we shall *have* to stop! The South African affair cost us a quarter of a million a day, while it lasted. This enterprise may run us into two, or even three millions. Think of that! Twenty millions a week! A thousand millions a year! We can't do it! Neither can France! Neither can Germany! No, it will be a short war. I am bound to admit K. of K. doesn't agree with me. He puts it at three years. I lunched with him two days ago. He was getting ready to go back to Egypt then—sorely against the grain, naturally; but it did not seem to have occurred to anybody to tell him to hold back for a week or two. We can't allow him to go out of the country at present; the thing's preposterous! Let me see, where was I?"

"Lunching with K."

"Oh, yes. He said three years. I asked why, and he replied that before this war finished every single able-bodied man of the combatant nations would be fighting in a national army, and it would take three years for this country to put its full strength into the field. But of course K. doesn't understand economic conditions. He's our greatest soldier, but not an economist. Still, that's K.'s view. I don't agree with it, but it's K.'s view. And if we go to war, K. will probably lead us; so we must expect to provide for war on K.'s scale."

All this was sufficiently stunning and bewildering in its suddenness and immensity; but it aroused my professional instincts.

"How is K. going to set about creating such an army?" I asked. "Raise supplementary Regular battalions; expand the Territorial establishment; or what?"

"I don't think he knows himself. In fact, he said so, quite frankly. In the first place, he hasn't been invited to help, as yet. In the second, he has been absent from England for the best part of fourteen years, and has not been able to keep himself conversant with the recent orgy of Army reform. He knew that the old Militia had been scrapped, but I found he was not sure whether its place had been taken by the Special Reserve or the National Reserve. And, of course, like all Regulars, he regards the Territorials with the utmost distrust. I think he shares the general soldier-man's opinion that the 'Terriers' are the old Saturday afternoon crowd with a new label. His idea seems to be to take no risks with amateur organisations, but to create a *pukka* new professional army on regular lines. He's wrong. He should take the present Territorial Army as a nucleus, and expand from that. The Territorial Associations are a most capable lot, and would build up big units for him in no time. Still, whatever way he does it, he will do it well; he's our great man. And he will need all his greatness. Germany means to smash us this time. She has been calling up her reservists, on the quiet, for the last six months. Her intelligence people have told her that we are all so tied up with the Suffragettes and Ireland that we *can't* come in, and that if we do, we cannot put up anything of a fight. I am almost tempted to believe Germany is right. I don't suppose we have a thousand spare rifles in the country. As for artillery—it takes three *years* to make a gunner! How on earth—"

"Now, then, what are you two absurd creatures conspiring about?" Our hostess was upon us brandishing a croquet-mallet. We rose hurriedly. "Alan Laing, how do you do? Why didn't you come and tell me you had arrived? As for you, Eskerley, I think you are getting into your second childhood. What's all this nonsense I hear about war with Germany? Why, I have a signed photograph of the Emperor in my drawing-room! How can one make war on people like that? And yet there you sit, talking about the thing as if it were really possible, and disorganising my *fête champêtre* by mobilising all my young men! Come and play croquet!"

Croquet with Lady Christina resembles nothing so much as croquet with the Queen in "Alice in Wonderland." It is true that she does not order our heads to be chopped off, but one sometimes wishes she would, and be done with it. Her success at the game—and she is invariably successful—is due partly to the nervous paralysis of her opponents, and partly to the uncanny property possessed by her ball of removing itself, while its owner is engaged in altercation, to a position exactly opposite its hoop. I bent my steps dutifully towards the lawn, leaving Lord Eskerley, who fears no one, not even Lady Christina, to fight a spirited rearguard action with that worthy opponent.

On the way I encountered Eric Bethune, my friend. It always thrills me, even at my sober age, to encounter Eric suddenly. I have never got over my boyish tendency to hero-worship. We shook hands.

"Come along the Green Walk with me," he said. "My car is waiting at the West Lodge; I have to fly back to my orderly room."

"We seem to be fairly for it, this time," I said, as we strode along the avenue of grass.

Eric threw up his handsome head exultantly. The sloping sunlight caught his clean-cut profile and sinewy throat.

"Yes," he said; "we're for it! The Fleet has been ordered not to disperse after Manoeuvres. The Army is mobilising. We are going to have at them at last! It's 'Der Tag,' all right! You are coming back to us, I suppose, Alan?"

"If they will have me," I said.

"Have you? They'll jump at you! They'll give you a battalion! We shall all get battalions! Brigades, perhaps!" He laughed joyfully, like a schoolboy who sees his first eleven colours ahead. "There will be promotions all round—"

"In a month or two," I said soberly, "there will be a lot more."

"Oh, I don't know," replied Eric. "We may finish Fritz off in one big battle. The German soldier is a machine: so is his officer. The whole German Army is a machine."

"A damned efficient machine, too!" I observed.

"Yes, boy; but cumbrous, cumbrous! If we let it get into its swing, it will be hard to stop. But we won't. The little British Army—and mind you, as a result of its South African lessons, it is the best trained, the best led, and the finest body of men that we have ever put into the field in all our history—will get the first move on, and it will chuck itself, like a flinty little pebble, plumb in the middle of the German machinery, and put all its gadgets out of gear! After that, the German, with his entire lack of initiative, will go to pieces, and we'll eat him up!"

Eric's old Scottish nurse was accustomed to say of him that he was "aye up in the cloods or doon in the midden." There was no mistaking his whereabouts to-day. I began to feel the thrill too.

"Are you going back to the First Battalion?" I asked.

"No word of it as yet. My orders are to stay here and perfect mobilisation arrangements. The moment the word goes out from the jolly old War Office, we shall be swamped with reservists: we may have to start a recruiting station as well. Great work! Great work! So long, old son! Run home and polish your buttons!"

He leaped into his car, and disappeared in a cloud of dust—a most characteristic embodiment of the spirit that was flaming in the hearts of all the youth of England and Scotland during that hectic, unforgettable, blissfully ignorant week.

I walked slowly back down the Green Walk, prepared to serve my sentence on the croquet lawn. It was a perfect summer evening. Not a leaf stirred: not a bird chirruped. The shadow of my somewhat square and stocky person preceded me, flatteringly elongated and attenuated by the rays of the setting sun. Deep and abiding peace seemed to brood upon the land. Yet all the land, I knew, was making ready for battle. Well, for my part, I was satisfied. I was a soldier, a widow man, and a childless man. I had no farewells to make, no last embraces—

From among the trees on my right I was conscious of a flutter of white, and a murmur of voices. A man and a woman—no, no, in those days one still talked of boys and girls—were seated side by side on a fallen tree-trunk, with their backs to me. They did not appear to be concerning themselves with war, or strife, or hostilities of any kind. Their present relation, though decorous enough, appeared to be one of most cordial agreement. I recognised them both, and passed on discreetly, silently acknowledging the prescience of that aged but perspicacious student of humanity, my Lord of Eskerley.

"They appear to have found one another all right!" I said to myself.

CHAPTER IV
A TRYST
I

Marjorie lay prone among the bracken in Craigfoot Wood, with her chin resting on her hands, and her insteps drumming restlessly upon the cool earth. Below her ran the road. To her left, beyond the wooded ridge which gave its name to Baronrigg, lay Craigfoot, nestling, like most small Lowland townships, in its own private valley. To her right, out of sight a mile away, ran the branch line of the railway which served that district, and which had furnished material to local humourists for a generation.

By the roadside, on the edge of the wood, stood the two-seater car which was accustomed to carry the overflow of the Clegg family to church on Sundays, and which Marjorie liked to pretend was her own special property. She was never so happy as when her arms were up to the elbows in gear-box grease. There was a good deal of the elemental small boy about Miss Marjorie.

It was four o'clock in the afternoon, and the month was once more August. The war which was to have been over in a few furious weeks had now been in progress for twelve months. The memory of the nightmare campaign of the first winter in Flanders had crystallised into a national epic. And now Kitchener's Army, having characteristically survived that chaotic but inevitable experiment in improvisation, its preliminary training at home during one of the worst and wettest winters ever known in England, had gone abroad. Here it had graduated, with first class honours in endurance and cheerfulness, during a season of trench warfare on the Western Front; and was now bracing itself, with incorrigible optimism, for that heroic mess afterwards known as the Battle of Loos. Everywhere the war was consolidating its position. On land the Boche, in a determined effort to recoup himself for his losses on the Western swings by a profitable exploitation of the Eastern roundabouts, had just captured Warsaw; and Hindenburg and Ludendorff were gloriously smashing their way through Russian armies in which perhaps one man in ten possessed a rifle. At sea, the battles of the Falkland Islands and the Dogger Bank had confirmed the German High Seas Fleet in a policy of watchful waiting—not to be broken, save for the disconcerting experiment of Jutland, until the final abject excursion of surrender more than three years later. Submarines and Zeppelins were beginning to function. Yarmouth and Lowestoft had been bombed, with *éclat*. The *Lusitania* had gone down, with eleven hundred souls; and a certain giant in the Far West was beginning to come out of the ether administered by Teutonic anæsthetists.

At home, the country had settled into its stride; and everyone, in camp, tube, train, and tram, argued—Heavens! how they did argue!—by a simple exercise in simple proportion, that if a mere handful of British soldiers could hold back overwhelmingly superior numbers for a whole winter, what wouldn't we do to Germany when the new British Army found their feet and got busy with the big push which everybody—friend and foe, be it said—knew was coming in September? (The possibility that the enemy might have been unsportsmanlike enough to raise a few new armies of his own did not appear to have occurred to anybody in particular.) The life of the citizen was still fairly normal. Taxicabs were plentiful: theatrical business was booming. One could still buy practically all that the heart desired, provided one had the price. The days when everybody would have money, but there would be nothing to buy, were yet to come.

Marjorie's predominant emotion during the first six months of the war had been that of fierce resentment against having been born a girl. She felt helpless; and whenever Marjorie felt helpless it made her angry. (That was why she was so frequently angry with her father.) All round her the youth of her country were on fire, both boys and girls. Yet the boys were able to stream away to fight, while Marjorie, who was quite as brave, quite as vigorous, and infinitely more capable of leadership than many young men, was debarred by the accident of her sex from doing anything at all. In the year nineteen-fifteen the great conflict was still regarded as a man's war: the inevitability of mobilised womanhood had not yet been recognised. The accepted theory was that men must work and women must weep—for the duration.

The countryside was full of soldiers, in all stages of growth. Marjorie used to encounter whole columns of them, route marching—strange creatures, clothed in apparel which by no stretch of imagination could be described as uniform. But for all their fantastic blends of khaki and tweed, glengarry and billycock, Marjorie's heart warmed to them. They were so boisterous, so childlike, so absolutely certain of what was going to happen to the Boche when they got "oot there."

At their head, as often as not, rode Major Bethune. He and Marjorie had become acquainted under circumstances which will be recorded hereafter, and his punctilious salute never failed to thrill her. He was an inspiring figure, and conspicuously solitary in his present *entourage*. He alone was left of all the cheery, careless brotherhood who had pursued the unexacting peace-time existence of a regular soldier at the depot of the Royal Covenanters—the prop and mainstay of every covert-shoot and tennis-party in the county. They were all in France now. Many of them would never come back. But Eric Bethune remained, to lick recruits into shape—with astonishing speed and efficiency, be it said—and send them out, draft after draft, to stiffen the ever-thinning ranks of the First and Second Battalions. He hated being kept at home, and said so. Marjorie sympathised with him deeply, for she knew exactly how he felt. One day she told him so. After that, Eric took considerable notice of her. He had the simple vanity of a spoiled child, and reacted promptly to all those who took especially deferential notice of him.

The pair met here and there—at Buckholm, whither Marjorie was sometimes bidden with her mother to war relief committee meetings; at entertainments organised for the recruits; at crossroads, where Marjorie's two-seater was frequently hung up by columns of marching men. On these occasions they exchanged greetings—even confidences. Eric was more than twenty years Marjorie's senior—a circumstance which, if anything, heightened their attraction for one another. It gratified Eric hugely to find himself frankly admired by a young girl; while Marjorie, born hero-worshipper that she was, felt pleasantly thrilled at attracting the appreciative attention of a man so distinguished in his record and so much more important than herself. Also, Eric's great age—and to twenty, forty-three and infinity are very much the same thing—made him "safe." Fortunately for Eric's self-esteem, he did not know this.

They had small chance to become really intimate. There were few opportunities for social amenity in those days, and such as survived hardly covered Netherby at all. In that bleak household itself opinion on the war was sharply divided. Albert Clegg came of a stock which had been educated to regard war as a luxury of the upper classes. He believed that all wars were started by collusion between the "military oligarchy" and the armament firms. He maintained that no war had ever been fought which could not have been avoided. The sight of a uniform filled him with horror. He was eloquent—though not quite so fluent as Uncle Fred—upon the iniquity of placing what he called a "musket" upon the shoulder of a growing boy, and setting him for a period of three years to strengthen his body by martial exercises, when he might have been earning dividends for somebody. Finally, he said that the Germans were an industrious, peace-loving, musical nation, and that it was sinful to attack—by which it is to be presumed he meant resist—an army which was merely the involuntary instrument of despotism.

So when the British nation declined, by acclamation, to break faith with France and Belgium, Albert Clegg was sincerely depressed. Moreover, being deeply interested in shipping, he foresaw ruin for the overseas trade of the country. Even when the unforeseen happened; when, as the submarines began to take toll, the market value of tramp steamers shot up a thousand per cent., and freights soared out of sight altogether, he was not entirely comforted. According to his lights he was an honest man, and it was with a twinge of conscience that he found the war accumulating for him profits on a scale which not even a swelling income-tax could altogether moderate. But he compounded with his conscience in the end. He drew his profits, but he drew them under formal protest every time. As Pooh Bah once explained, "It revolts me, but I do it!"

Of the rest of the household, Mrs. Clegg for her part found the war almost pleasantly exhilarating. None of her kith and kin were participating in hostilities, which relieved her from such trifling cares as beset old Mrs. Couper, who was interested in the matter to the extent of five sons and fourteen grandsons; or Mrs. Gillespie, the banker's wife, who had contributed all she had, the *ci-devant* student of divinity, to the cause; or General Bothwell, whose son Jack had arrived in Flanders from India with his Pathans in early December, and had already met the almost inevitable end of a white officer who undertakes the conspicuous task of leading dusky troops into action under modern conditions; or Lord Eskerley, both of whose sons had died at Le Cateau. Bobby Laing, of The Heughs, nephew of our autobiographical Major, had been killed in the landing of the King's Own Scottish Borderers at Gallipoli. Neither of Mrs. Clegg's sons had exhibited any leaning towards what their father described as "this fashionable military nonsense," so Mrs. Clegg's mind was at rest. She left everything, quite cheerfully—like too many of her kind—to the Willing Horse.

Of course, she admitted, there was little going on socially. Still, it was gratifying to roll bandages or pack comfort-bags in company with countesses; and though there were flies in the ointment—in the shape of common persons like Mrs. Galbraith, the chemist's wife, and the Misses Peabody, included in the same gathering by the caste-destroying processes of wartime—there were consolations. Netherby itself, with its spacious accommodation for meetings and committees, was a card which only great social strongholds like Buckholm and Baronrigg could overtrump.

It has been noted that Amos and Joshua Clegg had betrayed no disposition to join up. But while Amos in this matter followed his undoubted inclinations, Joe was restrained only by the bonds of parental discipline. For one thing, Joe was a Public-School boy, and Amos was not. Joe's school had only been a small establishment in the North of England, but in nineteen-fourteen its little Officers' Training Corps had contributed its full quota of young men. To Amos, Public Schools (to quote his father) were places where boys learned "to take care of their H's and despise their parents": to his younger brother the Public-School tradition was the ark and covenant, not to be lightly profaned by parental sneers or fraternal failure to understand. So Joe kept his own counsel, and ate his dour young Northumbrian heart out for twelve sickening months.

The climax had come that very morning, with the arrival, for Joe, of a circular from his old school, requesting that he would "be so kind as to fill up the enclosed form" with certain specific information regarding his military service, for inclusion in the School Roll of Honour—his rank, his unit, mentions in dispatches, and the like. There was no alternative column to fill in; no comfortable loophole labelled "Civilian war work of national importance"—nothing of that kind at all: nothing but a stark request for poor Joe's military status and record. It had not occurred to the editors that any Old Boy could, in these days, be elsewhere than in khaki.

Consequently, Marjorie had found Joe after breakfast, with his head in his arms, crying like a child in a corner of the unfrequented and cheerless Netherby smoking-room. (Albert Clegg did not smoke.) After comforting him in the only fashion she knew—and a very acceptable fashion any young man but a brother would have considered it—she made up her mind on the spot to accept a certain sentimental invitation somewhat shyly offered by Roy Birnie, and laughingly refused by herself, two days previously. That was why she was now lying in the bracken on the edge of Craigfoot Wood, gazing up the road to Baronrigg.

II

It was Roy's last day at home. At the outbreak of war, to his own intense indignation, he had been refused a commission. Many of his young friends, common civilians no older than himself, had been endowed with what they described as 'one pip' and set to command platoons all over the country. But Roy, as a prospective regular, had been despatched—the victim of a conspiracy in which he traced the hand of every person but the right one—to Sandhurst, where he was compelled to undergo an intensive education in the science of warfare, speculating grimly meanwhile as to the kind of mess his amateur supplanters were making of the British Expeditionary Force. Sometimes he woke at night in a cold sweat, having dreamed, as he had sometimes dreamed before a house match, that the war had come to an end before he had had his innings.

Now, at last, he was emancipated. He was a second lieutenant. He could wear a Sam Browne belt and look an A.P.M. right in the face—instead of hurriedly plunging down side streets to avoid that suspicious official's eye, as he had frequently done when up in London on leave with a crony, the pair of them decked in borrowed trappings to which a cadet's rank did not entitle them. He was an officer, holding the King's Commission; and, best of all, had been gazetted to the Second Battalion of the old regiment, of which his uncle, "Leathery Laing," was now second-in-command. He had completed his draft leave, and was to report at the Depot at six o'clock this Sunday evening, to take charge of a contingent bound overseas to reënforce the battalion at a point on the Western Front as yet unrevealed.

He had made his farewells—in the offhand, jocular fashion affected by our race in cases where the probability of return is more than doubtful. His father had shaken hands with him, and shaken his own head at the same time. Tom Birnie's heart was not in the war: he persisted in his belief that it was started by the Jingoes.

His friends—and Roy had friends in every walk of life—had loaded him with messages to fathers, brothers and sweethearts who were gone before into the pillar of cloud. Mr. Gillespie, the bank manager, entrusted him with a small package (on behalf of Mesdames Spot and Plain), containing mysterious comforts for son Robert. Jamie Leslie, the organ-blower of the parish church, buttonholed him in the street.

"Mr. Roy," he said wistfully, "you'll tell the boys oot there that I have tried, and *tried*, for to get ower; but they winna hae me! It's because I'm no quite richt in the heid," he added, with a candour which might well have been imitated by others occupying more exalted official positions than his own. "You'll tell them? I wouldna like them for tae think—"

Roy supplied the necessary assurance, and passed on to receive a message from old Mrs. Rorison, whose son John, a giant of six feet four inches, had abandoned the service of the post office in order to join the Scots Guards.

"Tell oor John," said the old lady—it was universally assumed that Roy would encounter the entire Craigfoot contingent, regardless of rank or unit, immediately upon landing—"tae keep his heid doon in they trenches. I ken him! And dinna go keeking ower the top yourself, Mr. Roy!" This, on the whole, was the most practical valediction that Roy received.

Lord Eskerley's farewell was quite characteristic.

"Good-bye! Don't give away any military news when you write to her. It has done a lot of harm already."

There was no one left now to say good-bye to but Marjorie. Like the young sentimentalist that he was, Roy was reserving her for the last. He wanted to bid her farewell at the very final moment—and, if possible, clandestinely. There existed no obstacle whatever to his driving openly to Netherby and delivering his farewell speech on the hearthrug in the library, or among the raspberry-canes in the kitchen garden. But war sharpens our romantic appetites to a surprising degree. At the most ordinary times lovers are accustomed to bid one another good night with an expenditure of time and intensity which takes no account of the fact that they are going to meet again directly after breakfast to-morrow morning. How much more pardonable and ecstatic, then, must that exercise be when it really is good night—when it is more than probable that before the time for reunion comes round again, one of the participants may have blown out his little candle for good.

Roy's preference for surreptitious love-making was natural enough, for another reason. He was a member of the shyest and most self-conscious brotherhood in the world—the tribe of the less-than-twenty-one's. By rights he should not have been in love—matrimonially—at all. A healthy English Public-School boy of nineteen is not entitled to such emotions as inspired Master Roy and his friends in the year of grace nineteen-fifteen. His mind should be set—and in normal times almost invariably is set—upon his biceps muscle, or his first salmon, or his college rowing colours, or (at moments of periodic festivity) the acquisition of souvenirs, like policemen's helmets or door-knockers. Permanent association with one of the softer sex should be to him, for several years yet, a delightful unattainability. He matures late, does our young Briton, and premature responsibility as husband and father usually prevents him from ever developing into the man he was meant to be. But wise old Nature is always ready to modify her own laws in an emergency. In nineteen-fifteen people, especially young people, found their perspectives considerably foreshortened. It is no use taking long views about life at a time when life promises to be more than usually short. There is just one thing to do, and that is to reach out with both hands after such of life's gifts as are normally reserved, especially in this country of ours, for those of riper years.

So, engaged couples who in nineteen-fourteen had taken it as a matter of course that their wedding must be postponed until after the war, suddenly realised that there might be no after the war for one of them, and incontinently got married. Boys and girls whose sentimental exercises in normal times would have been limited to sitting out dances behind a screen in the Christmas holidays not only became engaged, but usually plunged into matrimony a few weeks later. They were governed by forces which they did not entirely comprehend, and which few of them would have been capable of resisting if they had. They had no idea how they were going to live after the war; but they married all the same. It was essentially a case where the morrow must take thought for itself. They capitalised all their stock, both of money and of youth, these happy young gamblers, and lived ecstatically on that capital, stoically resigned to the probability that before it was exhausted their little partnership would have been dissolved. And in too many cases, poor souls, they were justified in their expectations. But who shall say that they were wrong, or improvident, to do as they did? Prudence, perhaps; commonsense, possibly. But not nature, nor patriotism, nor romance, nor the spirit of adventure.

It is not to be supposed that our impetuous Roy had reasoned out these matters with any degree of profundity. All he knew was that he had loved that glorious girl, Marjorie Clegg, from the moment he had first seen her in Craigfoot parish church a year and a half ago; and that now he was called upon to go away and relinquish even his present scanty opportunities of seeing her. Moreover, his battalion had got through twenty-three second lieutenants in the last ten months. One, obvious, course was indicated; but it was a big step for a reserved schoolboy of nineteen. To tell Marjorie, *tout court*, that he loved her frightened him—far more than any statistics about second lieutenants. If it had been peace-time he would have followed the natural path of a boy who falls in love with a girl of his own age. He would have decided to grow up, and become an eligible *parti* at the earliest possible moment. He might, possibly, have declared himself, and invited his beloved to "wait for him." It is within the bounds of probability that the damsel would have promised to do so. The *affaire* would then have proceeded on its innocuous course—spasmodically enough, owing to the interposition of such things as University terms, regimental duties, or vulgar office hours—to its normal end. That is to say, the girl would probably have met and married some one really eligible a few years older than herself, leaving it to the hand of Time to heal the wounds of her late cavalier and unite him in due course to another really eligible girl some years younger than himself, recently the property of a shaveling of nineteen.

But this was not peace-time. The country was at war, and for reasons already indicated waiting and seeing had gone out of fashion. The watchword of the moment, whether applied to munitions or matrimony, was, "Do It Now!" No wonder that Roy felt his heart leap to his throat as the Baronrigg car, conveying him to the Depot seven miles away, surmounted the last crest on the undulating road, and revealed to him Marjorie's two-seater standing in the hollow below, under the lee of Craigfoot Wood. For all her preliminary refusal and offhand acceptance, Marjorie had kept tryst.

CHAPTER V
THE INEVITABLE

Marjorie stood on the bank above the road, knee-deep in bracken. The Baronrigg chauffeur, an elderly gentleman with that perfect repose of manner which is given only to such members of the tribe as are promoted coachmen, drew up beside the two-seater. Roy jumped out and saluted with great smartness. He was in uniform, and was hung about with that warlike paraphernalia professionally known as "the whole Christmas Tree." Having disencumbered himself of this, he threw it into the car, climbed the bank, and joined his lady. His heart bumped.

"You do look nice," said Marjorie. "But what is the matter with your buttons?"

"I have painted them with some black stuff," replied Roy. "Quite the thing—not swank! It is always done on active service: otherwise my twinkling little buttons might attract the eye of vigilant Boche." He took her arm, a little feverishly. "What about a stroll in the shades of the forest? What about it, what?"

This was not the way in which Roy had intended to begin the interview. Upon such occasions of stress no man knows what humiliating tricks self-consciousness may not play upon him. But Marjorie, of the superior sex, appeared quite unruffled.

"All right," she said cheerfully; "come along! I am so glad you are here."

"Are you, Marjorie?" exclaimed Roy, much encouraged.

"Yes. I want to consult you about something."

Roy drew back an overhanging branch.

"Step inside the consulting room!" he suggested.

Marjorie seated herself upon a ledge of rock in the snug nook which the branch had concealed. Roy lay down on the grass at her feet. There was silence. At last Marjorie said:

"When must you be at the Depot?"

"Six." Roy glanced at his new, luminous, dust-proof, non-breakable wrist-watch. "That gives me twenty minutes. What did you want to talk to me about, Marjorie?"

"About Joe."

"Oh!" There was a certain lack of enthusiasm about the interjection, but Marjorie did not notice it. Roy looked up at her. Her brow was puckered, and her eyes were troubled. She was very fond of brother Joe. Roy, resolutely disengaging his attention from the high lights in her hair, said gently:

"Tell me."

Marjorie blazed out suddenly.

"He can't stand it any longer! He has done his best to be patient, and obedient to father, and all that; but it's breaking his heart. Why, only this morning—"

She related the pitiful incident of the school circular and the Roll of Honour. There were tears in her eyes when she had finished.

"So," she concluded, "he has made up his mind to join up."

"Good egg!" observed Roy. "Is he going to apply for a commission, or what?"

"That was what I wanted to consult you about," said Marjorie. "You are so clever about these things, Roy."

"Fire away!" replied Roy, much inflated.

"Commissions," asked Marjorie—"can you get them easily?"

"Not so easily now. The authorities are beginning to sit up and take notice. The first lot of officers in the new armies were mostly all right. They didn't know much, but they were sahibs, who played the game and handled their men properly. Now they are getting used up, and some pretty strange fish have been given commissions lately. The voice of the T.G. is heard in the land. Here is a letter from my uncle, Alan Laing—our second-in-command. You know him?"

"No, but I have seen him."

Roy chuckled.

"Yes," he said, "and he has seen you; and you fairly knocked him flat! But never mind Uncle Alan now. He's a wicked old man, anyhow. About this T.G. business. Uncle Alan wrote to me the other day. He said that some of the officers lately sent out were about the stickiest crowd he had yet handled. Here's the letter."

Of course, among ourselves in the Mess, he read, we make allowances, and try to get the best out of them; for after all, most of them are plucky enough and efficient enough. Unfortunately, the rank-and-file, with the true British passion for inequality, do not share our democratic sentiments. They say, in effect: "This blankety blighter is no better than we are. Why should we salute him, or obey him, or follow him?" The T.G. too often confirms his own sentence; I caught one of my subalterns trying to stand a corporal a drink the other day. I hear they are going to start officers' schools soon. The sooner the better!

"Of course," said Marjorie, flying, woman-like, to the personal application of the subject, "Joe wouldn't behave like that."

"Good Lord, no! Of course he wouldn't," said Roy.

"Amos probably would, though," added honest Marjorie. "He has never been to a proper school, so he has had no chance to have his Clegg manners improved. But we aren't troubling about Amos: it's Joe. Would they take him into a Cadet Officers' School, do you think?"

"I am sure they would," said Roy confidently. "Only, it might require a little time, you know."

"That's a drawback," replied Marjorie. "Once father knows what Joe is trying to do, his life at home won't be worth living. It'll be a fight all day long: he will be lectured, and badgered, and prayed over. I shouldn't wonder if they sent for Uncle Fred!"

A thought struck Roy.

"I say," he enquired, "how old is Joe?"

"Twenty."

"That hangs the crape on Joseph!" announced Roy—"for a year, at any rate. They won't give a commission to a minor without his father's consent." He wriggled. "Don't I know it! If they did, I'd have been in the show a year ago."

"In that case," said Marjorie, "we must fall back on our second plan."

"We?"

"I mean Joe and I."

"Oh, sorry. I was hoping you meant you and me! What is the plan?"

"It's a secret just now," said Marjorie. "Perhaps I'll tell you about it, when I write."

Roy looked up eagerly.

"You *will* write to me?" he said. "Often?"

"Of course I will!" said the girl. "It will be wonderful!"

What she meant was that it would be wonderful to have, in future, a personal interest in the British Expeditionary Force. As already indicated, the circle in which Marjorie had been born and bred was not very heavily represented in France—nor would be until conscription came. But now Roy would be there. She would have a personal outlet for her imagination, and a peg to hang her prayers on. Women hate abstract patriotism, as they hate all abstractions. Roy would supply the human, personal element, upon which a woman's visions must always be founded. Male orators might volley and thunder about the common cause and the redemption of civilization; but to most women the Great War and its issues were usually embodied in the person of a single undistinguished individual in a tin bowler.

Roy, of course, did not understand.

"How glorious of you to say that, Marjorie!" he exclaimed.

"You do not know," continued Marjorie rapturously, "how I have longed and longed to have some one to write to, and send parcels to, and everything—some one I really knew!—instead of a bundle of things to be distributed among a whole platoon!"

"And you are going to make me that particular person?" said Roy, joyfully.

"Rather! You see," explained Marjorie with fatal frankness, "I don't know anyone else. At least, I shan't, until Joe—"

Roy's face fell. "I thought there was a catch about it!" he said woefully.

"About what?"

"About what you said. I didn't understand that all you wanted was some one to write to; and any old thing would do—even me! I did hope, for a minute—"

Marjorie was all repentance at once.

"Oh!" she cried. "How hateful of me! Roy, I didn't mean it! What must you think of me? I must seem like a common little war-flapper. But I'm not, am I? Roy, you *know* I'm not! Will you forgive me?" She extended a hand impetuously.

It fired the train. Next moment Roy had caught it in both of his, and was kissing it rapturously.

"Marjorie—dear!" he murmured. He was kneeling before her now, with his arms crossed upon her knees. He looked up into her face, and suddenly realised what he was leaving behind. A great sob shook him. Perhaps the thought of the twenty-three second lieutenants had something to do with it. After all, he was only nineteen, and love and life were very sweet. His head sank on to his arms; his shoulders heaved.

There followed a brief interval of silence—perhaps three minutes. But within that interval something happened to Marjorie.

Presently a slim hand removed Roy's glengarry bonnet, and began to stroke his obstinately curly hair. Next, Roy was conscious of a warm splash, somewhere behind his right ear—followed by another, and another. Marjorie was shaking now. Roy looked up at her again, and the sight of her wet face suddenly braced him against his own weakness. He sprang up.

"You poor, poor, poor!" he said. "Let me—"

He produced a khaki handkerchief from his sleeve, and dried her eyes, Marjorie meekly submitting. After that, inevitably, he kissed her. It was not a very successful kiss: first kisses seldom are. Then he sat down upon the grass again with his head against her knee, and her hand against his cheek. He sighed, long and rapturously. Marjorie stroked his hair with her free hand. Children both, they were living through a moment for which others, less fortunate, have sometimes waited a lifetime, and which in no case ever comes to man or maid a second time.

Presently they began to talk, employing the two inevitable topics of the newly-betrothed—"When did it begin?" and, "Do you remember?"

They recalled their first glimpse of one another—that May morning in church, more than a year ago.

"Uncle Alan was very witty on the subject," said Master Roy. "Oh, most diverting! It's my belief the old ruffian was having a good one-time-look-see at you himself, and that was why he caught me at it. Well, I can't say I blame him!"

They wandered on to the second subject. Here they had much ground to cover.

They had not actually met until three weeks after the glimpse. During those weeks Roy religiously attended dances, tea-parties, political meetings, even a church soirée, in the hope of encountering his divinity; but in vain. Once he bought three numbered and reserved seats for an amateur theatrical entertainment in the Town Hall, and sent two of these to Netherby, "With the compliments of the committee." But Mrs. Clegg, knowing that her husband did not hold with theatrical entertainments, and that under no circumstances would she or the family be permitted to attend this one, had passed the tickets on to a more emancipated quarter, with the result that Roy witnessed the performance in the giggling company of two Netherby housemaids. He told the story to Marjorie now, and was rewarded with tears and laughter.

But they had met at last—at the local Hunt Steeplechases. Marjorie was present, privily, in the two-seater, with brother Joe. Roy had spied the pair from the regimental enclosure. He was due back at his crammer's in two days' time, and was a desperate man. Summoning his entire stock of audacity—it was considerable, but he needed it all—he left the enclosure, pushed his way through the crowd, and addressed himself to the male member of the rather forlorn couple standing by the rails.

"I say, sir, aren't you Mr. Clegg, of Netherby?"

Joe, quite unequal to the situation, murmured something inarticulate; but Marjorie came to the rescue.

"How do you do?" she said. "You are Mr. Birnie, aren't you?"

"Yes. We are your next-door neighbours—your nearest little playmates, in fact," replied Master Roy. (Netherby is some four or five miles from Baronrigg; but no matter.) "My father has been meaning to shoot cards on you for a long time. Meanwhile, would you care to come into the enclosure? Bracing air! Gravel soil! Commands a distant prospect of the Cheviot Hills, and so on! Highly recommended! Do come!" He waited breathlessly for her reply, fearful of having gone too far. But the invitation was accepted.

"What a moment!" he said. "*What* a moment!" He looked up at Marjorie again. "I was afraid you would turn me down, for cheek. You hesitated a bit, didn't you?"

Marjorie laughed, joyously.

"My dear, that was for manners! I wouldn't have let you go at that moment for anything in the world!" She played a gentle arpeggio on the brown cheek under her hand.

"By gum, I wish I had known that!" observed Roy, with sincerity.

Once inside the enclosure Marjorie created a profound sensation. It is true that not many of her own sex addressed themselves to her, but this omission was more than balanced by the *empressement* of the gentlemen.

First of all, naturally, she was introduced to the senior officer present—Major Eric Bethune, who, in the secret view of his subordinates, proceeded to take an unsportsmanlike and unduly prolonged advantage of his superior rank. Duty called him at last to the side of a lady of riper years. Thereafter, Marjorie, almost invisible for second lieutenants, was escorted about the course, shown the jumps, plied with tea, and invited to back horses at other people's expense. She had driven home in a dream, with her exhausted relative slumbering beside her.

After that a few mothers and sisters, hounded thereto by clamorous menkind, had left cards at Netherby. The calls had been duly returned, with the result that some of the sisters added themselves, quite voluntarily, to the ranks of the brothers. Marjorie possessed the supreme quality in a woman of being attractive to her own sex. Mrs. Clegg and her daughter began to be seen at subscription balls and the more comprehensive garden parties; presently at more intimate entertainments. In the end, Netherby usually received a card for any function that was going, always excepting such—formal dinner parties and the like—as necessitated inviting Albert Clegg.

"The girl is a peach," was the local verdict, "and mother does her best; but the old man merely suggests eternal punishment!"

And wherever Marjorie appeared—at ball, function, fête, bazaar, gymkhana, or tea-fight, Master Roy Birnie, home for good from the crammer's, was usually visible in respectful attendance.

Not that she had not other adherents. Even Major Bethune himself, the handsomest man and the most eligible *parti* in the county, did not consider it beneath his dignity to sit out a dance or two with the daughter of Albert Clegg. But Roy's devotion was marked by its unflagging and conscientious continuity. He was a regular visitor at Netherby. It was his habit to ride over every morning—usually about eleven, when the master of the house was engaged in transacting business in the library, mostly over the telephone to Newcastle—where he would play tennis, perform tricks on the billiard table, give the children riding-lessons, pick roses for Mrs. Clegg—do anything, in fact, which afforded him a reasonable excuse for remaining on the premises. Being British, and only eighteen, his passion had not declared itself in words; nor would have for many a day, but for the quickening influences already indicated. Even when the coming of war suddenly laid a man's responsibilities upon his young shoulders, and removed most of his rivals, real and imaginary, *en masse*, to the other side of the Channel, he did not look higher, for the present, than the foot of Marjorie's pedestal. His intention was to leave his lady perched upon the summit thereof for the duration; and then, if and when he returned safe and whole from castigating the Boche, to invite her to step down to earth and start, under his escort, upon the adventure of life. To do more at present struck him as unsportsmanlike. He would be forcing her hand unfairly; he would be taking a sentimental advantage of the military situation. But the last ten minutes had entirely upset his plan of operations. He had kissed Marjorie; Marjorie had indubitably kissed him back; and now they were sitting side by side in Craigfoot Wood, in an attitude which twelve months ago would have outraged both his susceptibilities and his sense of humour, facing the prospect of indefinite separation. What was the next step? What about it, what? Pending a decision, he saluted his lady afresh.

From the road below them came a respectful toot from the horn of the Craigfoot motor, suggestive of a faithful attendant coughing a discreet reminder behind his hand. Roy glanced at his watch, and rose to his feet with a heartrending sigh.

"Time to go!" he groaned.

He held out his hands to Marjorie, and raised her up. For a moment those two young people looked one another bravely in the face—for the last time, for aught they knew. They were very much of a height; Roy had the advantage of perhaps an inch. Then that direct young maiden, Marjorie, put both arms round Roy's neck.

"Good-bye, dear," she said. "Take care of yourself, and come back safe to me!"

"I'll come back," replied Roy stoutly, forgetting all about the twenty-three second lieutenants. He had no doubts about anything now. Then:

"Marjorie," he asked, "when will you marry me? As soon as the war is over?" He waited, expectant.

Marjorie's answer took the rather puzzling form of a little choking laugh, accompanied by two large tears.

"As soon as that?" she asked.

The young of the male species possesses no intuition.

"Yes," replied Roy earnestly, "just as soon! Or"—with the air of one conceding a point—"pretty soon after." He came closer. "Marjorie—will you?"

This time Marjorie smiled without any tears at all—a purely maternal smile.

"Leave it to me, little man!" she said.

Then she kissed him again, and sent him off to fight for her.

That night Joe Clegg crept downstairs, out of the house, and thence (per two-seater) to the railway junction twelve miles away. Here he caught the early morning train to London, where it was his intention to enlist. He was accompanied by his sister Marjorie, who, after a final and tempestuous debate with her father upon the subject of filial duty and feminine usefulness in war-time, had decided to burn her boats too, and enlist in the gallant sisterhood of those who were Really Trying to Help.

CHAPTER VI
SOLO

The lights sank low again, and a flickering announcement appeared upon the screen, to the effect that the next picture would be a further instalment of that absorbing serial, *The Marvels of Natural History*—upon this occasion, *Still Life in the Frog Pond*. The majority of the audience took the hint, rose to their feet, and shuffled out. But Marjorie stayed on. Some of us go to the pictures to see pictures, others to hold hands, others to sit down and rest. Marjorie belonged to the third class. Not even the prospect of a quarter-of-an-hour in a frog pond could induce her to concede to the management the chance of selling her seat once more before closing time. She sat on, in a tired reverie.

Marjorie had arrived in London three months ago, to find that overcrowded metropolis fairly evenly divided between two classes—the people who had taken up war work, and the people who were doing it. The chief difficulty of the latter was to push their way through the unyielding ranks of the former. Things righted themselves later, under the unsentimental *régime* of necessity; but in November, nineteen-fifteen, the road to victory was blocked with good intentions.

Having invaded London, Marjorie and Joe devoted two days to exploration. Marjorie had been in London twice before—going to and returning from school in Paris—her stay upon each occasion being limited to a single extremely domestic evening at Uncle Fred's house in Dulwich. This experience naturally qualified Marjorie (being Marjorie) for the role of guide and courier to that unsophisticated yokel, brother Joe. They put up at the Grand Hotel, because Marjorie considered Trafalgar Square a good *point d'appui*, and a difficult place to lose altogether even in the howling wilderness of Central London. They pooled their money. Marjorie had drawn the whole of the savings of her dress allowance—about one hundred pounds—from the custody of Mr. Gillespie shortly before the day of her departure, and Joe had a quarter's salary intact. They dined, went to the play, sat in the Park, lunched at the Carlton, and generally had their fling (but not of) a world composed entirely of elegantly dressed females and uniformed officers of every grade.

After keeping carnival for forty-eight hours, Marjorie conducted her brother to a recruiting office, where the authorities were unfeignedly glad to see him, business at that period being lamentably slack. There, having kissed him, she left him and returned to the Grand Hotel. At the end of half-an-hour she rose from her bed, dabbed her eyes with a cold sponge, sent for her bill, paid it with a bright smile, and removed herself and her effects to a self-contained flat near the Brompton Road. There she sat down to make a plan. She had several sketched out, but her choice depended, like so many other choices in this life, upon sordid financial considerations. If her allowance were continued, she could afford to do war work for love. If not, she must perforce do war work for money. So she wrote to her father, telling him frankly why she and Joe had left home, giving her new address, and concluding her letter:

So now you know where I am. If I don't hear from you I shall know that you don't intend to have anything more to do with me. But I hope I shall hear from you. Love. Marjorie.

Upon the question of her father's financial intentions she refrained from inquiry, for she knew full well what the result of such directness would be. Her intention was to hold on until the September quarter, and then try the experiment of a cheque to her own order on Mr. Gillespie's bank. Her hope was that the allowance would continue automatically, as it might not occur to her father to stop it—presuming he wished to do so.

"If he does," she said to herself, "I must just go and work in an ammunition factory, or something—that's all! Still, I don't believe he will. Father's a hard man, but he does try to be just. He can't punish me for simply wanting to work now, of all times!"

In this she did her father no less, and as it ultimately proved, no more than justice; for a *ballon d'essai* despatched northward to Mr. Gillespie at the end of September was received by him with the honour due to a credit balance.

But September was a long way off. Marjorie methodically reviewed all the avenues of occupation open to her. Nursing attracted her most; but she knew herself to be pathetically ignorant of the elements of the craft, and furthermore doubted (rightly) if her combative nature would endure the complete subservience to the professional element inevitable in the life of that plucky, much-enduring, self-effacing Cinderella, the V.A.D. Stenography and typewriting were unknown to her. Munition-making at this time was but an infant industry—as the occupants of the trenches had continuous occasion to note, with characteristic comment. There were a number of minor Red Cross activities open to her—bandage-rolling, parcel-packing, and the like—but these pursuits were too sedentary for ebullient Marjorie. Other forms of war activity, such as selling programmes at charity *matinées*, or pestering total strangers in 'buses and tube-trains to purchase flags to relieve the contingent wants of hypothetical Allied babies, were pushed contemptuously aside as war work *pour rire*. It was not too easy, either, to know where to apply, with adequate results. Upon the Olympus whence the country was being directed to victory, the Organisation of Womanhood still lay in the tray—much the biggest tray on Olympus—marked "Pending." Those quaint but proud expressions, "Wren," "Waac," and "Wraf" had not yet been added to the English language.

Marjorie finally decided to try canteen work. Vicarious service had no attraction for her; to get as close as possible to the human side of an enterprise was all her aim. At the canteen she would see and wait upon the most human member of the human family, one Thomas Atkins. A single fear made her hesitate. She wanted to spend herself utterly upon the Cause. Might not this canteen business prove just a little too trivial; a little too like playing at work?

She tried it for a week. After carrying tea-urns from the kitchen to the counter for eight consecutive hours she decided, without any hesitation whatever, that her apprehensions were groundless.

Month by month, Marjorie bent her giant's spirit and her straight young back to her task. The Canteen, near Waterloo Station, was never closed, and was full at practically every hour of the day and night. But, day-shift or night-shift, fair weather or foul, good news or bad, nothing made any difference to Marjorie. She was always on time, always cheerful, always perfectly ready to perform tasks left undone by the Undertakers of War Work. She set herself a standard of endurance and privation approximately as nearly as possible to that which she understood prevailed on the Western Front. This seemed to her the least that a stay-at-home person like herself could do, in consideration of the fact that no bodily risk attached to her duties. (As yet, Zeppelin frightfulness was merely one of London's gratuitous entertainments.)

Consequently, after six months' unceasing drudgery, Marjorie was beginning to feel very tired, and just a little despondent.

The spirit of despondency stalked abroad in those days: it was the natural reaction from the wave of enthusiasm which had carried the country so highheartedly through the anxieties and uncertainties of the first twelve months. It was becoming increasingly obvious that "K" was right; that the war was going to last for a term of years; and that the country could not reach the goal on its first wind. Pending the arrival of the second, a slump in martial enthusiasm was inevitable. Tubes and omnibuses no longer carried men in uniform for nothing. Civilians no longer offered their seats to soldiers and sailors. Patriotic flappers no longer presented white feathers to wounded officers in mufti. It was no longer considered *de rigueur* for the orchestra in public restaurants to bring a docile public to its feet by periodical excursions into patriotic melody. The Battle of Loos had demonstrated once more that the young British soldier never fights better than in his first battle; also, alas! that when a nation goes to war free from the taint of "militarism," soldiers must die that Staffs may learn. Gallipoli had been evacuated, when with a little luck and good management the evacuation might have taken place at the other end. Bulgaria had recently joined our enemies, and it was felt that with more skilful handling she would have come down upon our side of the hedge. Early in December figures to date of British casualties in all theatres of war were officially announced for the first time: they reached a total more than five times as great as the numbers of the original Expeditionary Force. A shortage of men was becoming apparent: although nearly four million had joined the Colours, the cry was still for more. The Voluntary system was at its last gasp. Despite the honest and ingenious Derby scheme for a more even distribution of the burden, it was plain that an intolerable and increasing weight was being borne by The Willing Horse. Conscription, long overdue, was clearly on the way, with the result that the voice of the Conscientious Objector was now heard in the land. On the top of all this the No-Treating Order had come into force, and another injustice was inflicted upon that section of the community which preferred that its refreshment should be paid for, as its battles were being fought, by some one else. Even Marjorie's spirits sagged a little during that black winter. Her sense of oppression was increased by two potent factors. In the first place, she was underfed. It was entirely her own fault, or, rather, that of her first parent, Eve. In their hearts, all women cherish a profound contempt for what men call good food. Formal meals, consumed at leisure and with comfortable ritual, are to them a mere pandering to gross male standards of self-indulgence. A woman hates sitting at a dinner-table through a meal of thoughtfully varied courses. To her the perfect repast is, was, and always will be an egg on a tray, on a chair, in any room but the dining-room.

Marjorie was not exempt from this failing. Too often her principal meal of the day was eaten in a tea-shop, and consisted of food that satisfied quickly and nourished not at all. The meals at Netherby had been irksome, but they were at least wholesome. Furthermore, in her desire to emulate the soldier's lot, she imposed upon herself a voluntary rationing scheme—which if applied in military circles would have undoubtedly produced a mutiny. She had the zealot spirit, too. After the twelfth of October, the day upon which Edith Cavell died, Marjorie ate neither butter nor jam for a fortnight. Less sincere tributes have been paid to our great dead.

But, above all, she was desperately lonely. If it is not good for man to be alone, it is far worse for woman. And Marjorie was very much alone. It is surprising what a small acquaintance most of us really possess. Such as are occupied every day in earning a living—and who is not in these times?—are almost entirely dependent for human companionship upon the people with whom they work and the people with whom they share a home. Of course, there is a certain type which makes sociability its life work; which is eternally busy with visiting-cards and engagement-book; scraping acquaintance here, exchanging addresses there—the type, in fact, which entertains a not altogether unreasonable dread of being left alone with itself. But if you possess neither the inclination nor the leisure for these amenities, and do not live at home, and do not happen to work in company with a throng of your fellow-creatures, you can be a very lonely individual indeed, especially in a great city.

Marjorie, fortunately, had the canteen. She formed acquaintanceships quickly, as all attractive people do. Some of these, owing to her natural discrimination, were short-lived, and none made an abiding impression. Marjorie was more interested in things than people in those days. But the soldiers appreciated her. Sometimes their appreciation took the form of tips. One Canadian presented her with half a crown, and commanded her to buy "candy" with it; but the majority of her patrons furtively thrust a penny or twopence—and twopence meant a good deal to Tommy in those shilling-a-day times—under the saucer, adjusted cap, and said awkwardly, "Well, so-long, miss!" hurrying out before the delinquency was discovered. Many of them sent her post cards, from Flanders, or Egypt, or India, addressed as often as not, if they had lacked the courage to ask her name beforehand, to the "Young Lady with the Tea Urns."

But Marjorie's leisure hours were not exhilarating. That moment at the end of the day's work, when every member of the human family ought to be provided by law with some one or something to go home to, was the worst. Still, it was all part of the game, and she played up sturdily. She invented amusements for herself—such as could be indulged in by one person, gifted with imagination and a sense of humour. London itself was her playground. Most of the picture galleries and museums were closed by this time; but London's real attractions are ever in the street. Walking home on a fine morning from night duty, Marjorie would frequently look in at St. James's Palace to see that the Guard was properly changed. Sometimes she trudged as far as Buckingham Palace with the relief. She bought a little book which dealt with London landmarks, and sought out for her own amusement the Old Curiosity Shop, London Wall, the site of Tyburn Tree, and the birthplaces of numerous historical celebrities. She acquired a store of useless but pleasant knowledge: for instance, that the wooden slab with iron legs, which stands by the railings of the Green Park in Piccadilly, was originally set up to enable ticket-porters to rest their bundles for a moment before breasting the gradient—more perceptible to a ticket-porter than a modern taxi—that leads to Hyde Park Corner.

The great railway stations were a perpetual feast to her, especially Victoria and Waterloo. Many an evening found her at the barrier at Victoria as the leave train drew up at the platform, to disgorge a wave of bronzed, boisterous, mud-caked, unshaven children into the arms of demonstrative relatives. Sometimes, too, in the early morning, she attended this same train's departure, upon the shortest run in the world—the run in the opposite direction was the longest—the journey between London and Folkestone. With swelling heart and tightening lips she watched the crowd of returners to duty—all curiously silent, and all smiling in the most unanimous and resolute manner for the benefit of those who had come to see them off. The silence and the resolution broke sometimes when the warning whistle sounded—perhaps for ten seconds. As soon as the train began to move, Marjorie always turned and walked rapidly away before the women came wandering aimlessly back from the empty platform. She could bear most things, but not that.

There were few amusements upon which she could afford to spend money. The theatre generally was beyond her reach, but the cinema was an abiding boon to herself and countless others—a fact to which the attention of intellectual despisers of common pleasures is respectfully directed. The cinema was always open; one could go in when one had time, and come out when one had had enough. One could go there alone without looking or feeling conspicuously alone, which is not possible in the ordinary theatre; there were no waits, and no noise; and the darkened auditorium, whether one regarded the screen or not, was a rest-cure in itself.

Then there was the recreation of correspondence. Marjorie wrote to Roy every day, and Joe once a week. She had received no letter from Netherby in answer to her own; so she decided to make no present attempt to repair the rupture of diplomatic relations in that quarter. Joe was now a private in the Royal Engineers, undergoing intensive training in the north of England. She had not seen him since his enlistment, nor expected to, for leave was difficult. Moreover, Joe referred frequently and appreciatively in his letters to local hospitality. Marjorie scented a romance, but Joe gave nothing away.

And there were Roy's letters. They arrived with amazing regularity—the postal service of the British Expeditionary Force was one of the unadvertised marvels of the war—written in pencil upon the thin blue-squared sheets of a field dispatch-book, with the censor's triangular stamp in one corner of the envelope and Roy's own name scribbled on the other. They contained little military information, and a surprising amount of irrelevant foolishness. Roy told Marjorie about life in billets. He reported upon his progress with the French tongue. He told her of Madame *la fermière*, in whose loft he slept, and with whom he practised elegant conversation, but who was unfortunately only intelligible upon Sunday, that being the one day in the week when her false teeth were in actual use. For the rest of the week they reposed thriftily in a drawer. He told her how he visited a French Field Hospital, and had committed the solecism of addressing the nurse—an elderly Sister of Charity—as "Mademoiselle Nourrice." He wrote, as a schoolboy might, of some extra good "blow-out" at an *estaminet*; of his small amusements; of his small grievances. He wrote, as a lover does, of his lady, and how much he loved and missed her, and how greatly the thought of her inspired him. But of tactical operations, or the joy of battle—and there is such a thing—or the privations and horrors of war, there was nothing. The whole aim of the man in the trenches at this time appears to have been to maintain the morale of the people at home. It was during this very month that Forain, the French cartoonist, epitomised the psychology of the entire war in a single drawing—two gaunt, mud-caked *poilus*, crouching waist-deep in the water of a devastated trench during an intensive bombardment, gasping anxiously to one another: "*Si les civils tiennent!*"

Of Roy's whereabouts Marjorie knew little. He had come safely through the Battle of Loos—more fortunate than the majority of his colleagues. He had served in Belgium for a space; after that the Division had been transferred to France again. He was fond of indicating his position on the map by cryptograms insoluble by friend or foe, or codes which not even their author could decipher the day after their invention. But occasionally he succeeded:

Of course we are not permitted to say where we are, but it would be harmful to blub about it.

The latter half of this sentence sounded so more than usually idiotic that Marjorie felt sure it conveyed some subtle message. But though she applied every solution known to the amateur detective, she could make nothing of it. It was not for many weeks that it occurred to her, during the night watches, to cease probing for key-words or transposing vowels, and to try paraphrasing the sense of the text. By this means she reached the conclusion that there was "harm in tears"—and a "buried town" immediately sprang to view. But more often she was trapped in the pitfalls of ambiguity.

"*This is a pleasant old-world spot,*" Roy had remarked in a recent letter. "*You would love the Vicar.*"

"The Vicar! The Vicar? The Vicar of what?" Marjorie spent half an hour poring over the *Daily Mail* map of the Western Front which decorated the greater part of her bedroom wall, in a vain search for a place called Wakefield, or anything like it. She wrote back:

By the way, the Vicar you are so enthusiastic about is an entire stranger to me.

To-night another letter had come, conveying enlightenment:

Sorry you don't like the Vicar. He used to be a good chap. An up-river man, and some singer in his day.

Two minutes later, Marjorie's pencil was on the map, underlining Bray-sur-Somme. Dear Roy! She leaned back in her cheap little stall in the darkness, and chuckled softly to herself. How wonderfully these foolish trifles lubricated the grinding wheels. But oh—!

Spots and splashes appeared upon the film, and it began to rain ink—an infallible sign in the world of moving-picture romance of the less expensive kind that the end of the tale is approaching. Marjorie rose to her feet, pulled on her hat, and felt her way out into the Earl's Court Road. She was sufficiently well known to the asthmatic Admiral of the Fleet—at least he looked like that—who guarded the portals of the Electric Palace to receive from him a gracious good night.

"O reevoyer, miss! I 'ope to see you on Thursday. We shall 'ave a fresh picture then—Charlie Chaplin, the new screen comedian. Everybody's talking about 'im. Very comical, 'e is!"

Not far from Earl's Court Station, in the obscurity of the discreetly darkened street, Marjorie came upon a motor-car. A girl chauffeur was endeavouring to jack up the off-hind wheel. Marjorie ranged up alongside at once.

"Let me help you," she said.

"Thanks," gasped the girl. Together they wrestled with the stiff jack.

"A puncture?" inquired Marjorie.

"Yes. Rotten luck! I am only a mile from home, and this old tyre has gone on the blink. I must put on the spare rim."

"I know this kind," said Marjorie, fired with characteristic enthusiasm at the prospect of a thoroughly irksome job. "Let me do it!"

"You're welcome!" said the girl, who was white with fatigue. "I don't mind the driving and the long hours," she continued sociably, settling down on the running board while Marjorie deftly removed the unserviceable rim; "but changing tyres, and oiling the engine, and filling up grease-cups, and all those messy things—that's what I can't stick!"

"Is this your—your work during the war?" asked Marjorie, suddenly interested.

"Yes—The Women's Legion. We haven't been started long. It's hard work in all weathers; but it's helping—a bit. I'm trying to keep my husband's job open for him."

Ten minutes later, utterly exhausted, Marjorie let herself into her tiny flat in a by-street off the Brompton Road. It was half-past nine. She set the alarm clock for half-past five, and went to bed with Roy's letter under her pillow. She dreamed that Roy had been promoted—suddenly, but not unexpectedly—to the rank of Commander-in-Chief, and that it was her privilege to drive him to battle every morning at five-thirty, in a motor-car with the off-hind tyre punctured.

CHAPTER VII
DUET
I

In one respect her dream came true.

Shortly after nine o'clock next morning, as the breakfast rush eased off, Marjorie was aware of the flushed features of the lady superintendent of the canteen, Miss Penny—"The Mouldy Old Copper," in the unregenerate language of the junior staff—angrily visible through a mephitic fog to which steaming tea, frying bacon, and moist humanity had all contributed. (Even in the crispest weather Tommy Atkins is a most hygroscopic individual.)

"We are for it, my dear!" announced The Mouldy Old Copper.

"What—Zeppelins?" inquired Marjorie, setting her tenth urn in position.

"Worse! Inspection! They are coming at twelve. The Government have suddenly decided to inquire into the feasibility of making the Canteen Service an official affair—a branch of the A.S.C., or the R.A.M.C., or the Q.M.G., or some other futility. So they are coming to inspect us, as 'a typical example of a canteen maintained by voluntary effort and service.' I got it over the telephone just now."

"It was decent of them to warn you," said Marjorie.

"That's just what they haven't done! I got the news by a side wind. It's to be a surprise inspection. They want to see what a show run by women is like when it's off its guard. I like their impudence! What do they expect to catch us doing, I wonder—arranging the tea-cups in the wrong formation; or not keeping accounts in triplicate; or flirting with the men; or what!" The Mouldy Old Copper turned a bright bronze colour. "I'll jolly well talk to them, if they start any of their old—!"

"Don't you think," suggested Marjorie, "that it would be a good plan to telephone round at once to make sure that there are enough waitresses? You know what a bear-garden this place is when the men can't get served."

Miss Penny considered.

"Yes, you are right," she said. "At least, we will warn some of them. Not all—oh dear no, not all! There are women connected with this place who haven't allowed their so-called work here to interfere with a single tea-fight or subaltern-hunt since they joined. Of course they would sell their souls to crush in to-day. Well, they shan't! They shall hear all about it to-morrow, instead! I shall love telling them—especially the Toplis girl, and Lady Adeline, and Mrs. Napoleon Jones—or whatever the name of that horror with the pekineses is! You run along, dear, and telephone to about a dozen of the decent ones, and tell them to be sure and turn up by ten-thirty."

The result was that at high noon, when the Olympians descended upon Waterloo Road, they found the canteen crowded with happy warriors partaking of nourishment from the hands of a bevy of attractive and competent Hebes. The Committee of Inspection consisted of a much-beribboned Major-General, two or three lesser luminaries proportionately decorated, and an elderly civilian in a shocking hat.

The Mouldy Old Copper conducted the procession round the canteen. Here and there a halt was called at a table, where the Major-General, having made the diners thoroughly comfortable by commanding them straitly to "sit at ease," inquired, in the voice of a Bengal tiger endeavouring to coo like a dove, whether there were "any complaints." There were none, which was most gratifying, but not altogether surprising.

Marjorie, greatly diverted by the *sotto voce* remarks which reached her from tables in her neighbourhood, rested her tired arms upon the speckless counter and looked demurely down her nose. Upon her ear fell a raven's croak:

"Very good—with such a short time for rehearsal! But these damsels must come here *every* day, you know! By the way, does he write to you regularly? I told him to."

Marjorie turned, and gaped in the most unladylike manner. The elderly civilian in the bad hat had strayed away from his escort, and now stood at her elbow—revealed as Lord Eskerley, to whom she had once been presented at a regimental gymkhana at Craigfoot. Apparently he was aware that the Olympian deputation were being treated to a display of "eyewash." Apparently, also; he knew Marjorie. Not only Marjorie, but Marjorie's most private affairs. Altogether, he seemed to know too much.

"By the way," continued his lordship characteristically, "how do you do? I forgot." They shook hands. "Lovely day, isn't it? You look overworked. What are your hours here?"

Marjorie told him.

"What is your particular *métier*?"

Marjorie introduced the tea-urns.

"No woman, however young or muscular, should carry heavy things about," said Lord Eskerley. "Razors to cut grindstones; as usual! Would you like a change of occupation?"

"Indeed I should," replied Marjorie—"so long as it was helping things along, you know."

"What can you do?"

Marjorie fingered the dimple on her chin dolefully.

"Not much, I'm afraid. I don't know anything about nursing, or shorthand, or anything useful."

"You can drive a car, though."

"How do you know that?"

"How does the trembling fawn know that the wolf is not a vegetarian?" The old gentleman glared at Marjorie over his spectacles.

"I expect its mother warns it," hazarded Marjorie, a little guiltily.

"Ah! Possibly. My mother, unfortunately, never saw you, though I am sure that if she had she would have warned me. But there are other ways—instinct, to a certain extent; also experience. You and your two-seater once missed me by inches in the Craigfoot road. You were on your way to keep an appointment, I thought: I forbore to speculate with whom. But never mind that. Now—my chauffeur very properly joined the army to-day. Would you care to step into his shoes? He wears large fourteens, and your appointment would probably wreck my prospects as an eligible widower; but I think those are the only two objections. Will you give me a trial? Thank you very much! Report this evening."

II

Marjorie's labours henceforth were as arduous as ever, but were mainly performed in the open air—which to her meant all the difference between work and play. Each morning she drew up before Lord Eskerley's gloomy mansion in that aristocratic slum, Curzon Street, at nine o'clock sharp, and conveyed her employer upon his daily round. First to the Ministry of Intelligence, an unobtrusive mansion in the purlieus of Whitehall Gardens. Then, about eleven, to Downing Street. Then back to the Ministry. About one, to Curzon Street, for a brief luncheon. In the afternoon Marjorie ran errands: that is to say, she conveyed visitors to the Ministry from all quarters of London—from other Ministries, from the House of Commons, or from remote private addresses. At seven she conveyed his lordship home to Curzon Street, where, day in, day out, in victory or defeat, he dined at seven forty-five precisely.

"Give your digestion fair play," he once suddenly advised his chauffeuse, as she tucked him into the car on a bitter January afternoon, "and the world is yours!"

Marjorie promised to do so.

"Have a clear understanding with your stomach in early life," his lordship resumed, the moment Marjorie reopened the door of the car twenty minutes later. "Remember he *rules* the rest of your internal economy. Socially, we never meet him, or speak of him; but he is the whole show! And—he is as sensitive as an upper servant! Give him the consideration due to his position; don't ask him to work at unusual times, or do things that are not part of his duty; and he will not only serve you for a lifetime, but will keep your heart up to its work, restrain your brain from more than usual foolishness, and put the fear of death into the organs below stairs! But treat him casually, or give him odd jobs to do—and he will let you down, as sure as fate! Call for me at the usual time, please."

Marjorie's duties did not end at dinner-time; for war knows nothing of the eight-hour day, or early closing, or Sabbath observance. Lord Eskerley frequently went out about nine in the evening—sometimes to Downing Street, occasionally to Buckingham Palace, not infrequently to an unpretentious house in Dulwich, where he found it convenient to interview persons whom it would have been undesirable to receive officially at the Ministry or Curzon Street. The house stood in the same road as Uncle Fred's. The fact gave Marjorie, gliding past in the wintry darkness, a pleasant sensation of escape from futility.

One bleak and muddy day in February she drove Lord Eskerley down to Bramshott Camp, to assist at a review of two new divisions. Somewhere outside Godalming the gears began to burr and slip. Finally, Marjorie pulled in at the side of the road and descended.

The window of the car was let down and Lord Eskerley's head appeared.

"How long will it take?" he inquired, avoiding superfluous questions, as usual.

"About ten minutes. The lever has worked loose; I can't get my gears in properly," replied Marjorie.

"Do you want any help? I have with me"—his lordship leaned back and exhibited his fellow-passengers—"General Brough-Brough; his A.D.C., Captain Sparkes; and Mr. Meadows. The General and Captain Sparkes, as you will observe, are all dressed up in review order, and I cannot have them tarnished or made muddy, or I should be bringing contempt and ridicule on the King's uniform; also rendering aid and comfort to the enemy, which is not allowed in war time. So that disposes of them. I shall not insult a lady of your capabilities by offering my assistance. That leaves Meadows. Do you want him?"

"No, thank you," said Marjorie, swiftly removing the floor boards above the gear box. The window was drawn up again, and Mr. Meadows, Lord Eskerley's private secretary, a young man debarred from warlike exercises by acute astigmatism and valvular murmurs, looked very much relieved.

Ten minutes later, Marjorie, somewhat flushed and not a little oily, resumed her place at the wheel, and deposited her passengers at the stroke of the appointed hour at Divisional Headquarters at Bramshott.

Her employer, stepping out of the car, surveyed her grimy features quizzically.

"Habakkuk!" he chuckled.

Six hours later, at the end of the return journey, he inquired:

"Do you read your Voltaire at all? Probably not: I'll send you his 'Life.'"

The volume reached her next morning. Therein Marjorie discovered a marked passage, in which it was recorded that Voltaire found Habakkuk "*capable de tout.*" Thereafter, Lord Eskerley habitually addressed her as Habakkuk.

III

Still, Marjorie was not entirely happy. As already stated, any form of outdoor occupation was, in her view, play; and the present was essentially a time for work. She belonged to that zealous breed which is never really contented unless it is uncomfortable—to whom congenial occupation is merely idleness under another name. She enjoyed her present employment so much that she felt ashamed: she felt that she was not pulling her weight in the war. Probably a short conversation with a sensible person would have cured her of these illusions; but Marjorie had no one with whom to converse. She might have confided in her employer; but she argued, with some reason, that he would merely make an apposite and caustic reference to the gentleman who is reputed to have painted himself black all over in order to play Othello. It did not occur to her to mention the matter to Roy in a letter. Roy, for the present, belonged to his country, and was not to be diverted from his duty by domestic or personal trifles. What Marjorie needed and longed for at this time was a confidant.

If we desire a thing urgently enough we usually get it. Sometimes we get more than we bargain for.

One day Lord Eskerley came down his front-door steps arm-in-arm with an officer in uniform. His lordship's *chauffeuse*, who prided herself upon her soldierly restraint, did not look round from her wheel as the pair entered the car, but she heard her employer say:

"You can drop me at the office, Eric, and the car will take you on to the club."

Eric Bethune's voice replied that this arrangement would suit its owner top-hole.

When Lord Eskerley alighted at Whitehall Gardens he turned and addressed Marjorie.

"Habakkuk," he announced, "inside the car I have left a D.S.O. on a fortnight's leave. Please deposit him at the Army and Navy Club in Pall Mall. He is a Scotsman, so there will be no gratuities."

"Very good, my lord," replied Marjorie, looking rigidly to her front. She and the old gentleman made quite a speciality of these solemn little pleasantries.

The portals of the Ministry had hardly closed upon the Minister when his guest emerged from within the interior of the car and climbed into the front seat beside Marjorie.

"May I come and sit here?" asked Eric, shaking hands. "I recognised your back view through the front window-glass."

"It's against regulations," replied Marjorie, smiling, "but I can't disobey a colonel. Besides, I want to hear all about the Western Front. How are the Royal Covenanters?"

"I am commanding the Second Battalion now," replied Eric. "I have been with them since October."

"Yes, I know," said Marjorie thoughtlessly.

"How did you know?" asked Eric, not altogether displeased.

Marjorie, carefully negotiating the cross-currents of Trafalgar Square, bit her lip. She was beginning to give herself away already. But she replied, looking steadily before her:

"I get letters sometimes."

"I hope your correspondents report favourably on me," said Eric lightly. "Do you know many of my officers?"

"Not many—now. Let me see." Marjorie decided swiftly not to be evasive, but to reply to Eric's naïve inquisitiveness as naturally as possible. "Major Laing—I have met him once or twice. Is he still with you?"

"'Old Leathery'? Yes. He goes on for ever. Who else?"

"One hardly likes to ask these days, for fear—you know?"

"Yes, I know. But we've been lucky lately. We are in a quiet sector of the line. We have had no officer casualties for two months. Wait while I touch wood!" He tapped the mahogany dashboard. "Do you know Kilbride, my adjutant?"

"I don't think so."

"He's a stout fellow. Let me see. Do you know young Birnie? He comes from your part of the world, and mine."

"Yes, I know him," said Marjorie. "Is he quite well?" For the life of her she could not help asking.

"Yes, he's all right." Eric gave Marjorie a sudden sidelong glance. He possessed the curiosity of a child, and not a little of a child's jealousy. He had certain things in mind—rumours, nods, innuendoes, elephantine jests in the mess. Marjorie's eyes were fixed steadily upon the road ahead of her, and her face expressed nothing more than polite interest. But if Eric had been a really observant person—a woman, for instance—he would have noticed that her hands were gripping the steering-wheel until the nails were white.

"Whom else do you know?" he continued. "Garry—Balfour—Carruthers—little Cowie?"

"No." Marjorie knew none of these. They were a later vintage.

"Laing and Birnie seem to be all of your friends that are left," said Eric. "Which of them is your correspondent? Not old Leathery, surely?"

"No; Mr. Birnie. We are quite old acquaintances," said Marjorie, thoroughly annoyed at the unfair tactics which had isolated Roy.

"Well, all that I can say is that I am thoroughly jealous of Master Birnie!" announced Eric, smiling. "Now tell me all about yourself. What are you doing here in London, driving a car?"

"Here is your club," said Marjorie, putting on her brake.

"Confound it!" Eric's annoyance was quite genuine. "We had so much to discuss. Can't you lunch with me somewhere?"

"I never know when I shall lunch. It depends on Lord Eskerley."

"Well, can you dine? Surely you don't work all night as well!"

Marjorie hesitated. As it happened, she was free that evening, for she knew that two cabinet ministers were dining and conferring with her employer. There was no reason whatever why she should not accept Eric's invitation. But for a moment some instinct held her back. Then she thought of the eternal solitude of the flat.

"Thank you very much," she said. "I will."

They dined together and went to a play. Eric made a charming host and a decorative escort. For the rest of the week—he was spending six days of his leave with Lord Eskerley—Marjorie saw him constantly. She drove him about London, and they went upon more than one exhilarating excursion together. By the time that Eric departed to Scotland to visit Buckholm she knew all about the regiment—its exploits, its smartness, even its private jokes. Her general impression was that the regiment had improved greatly since Colonel Bethune had taken command.

On the subject of Roy, both exhibited considerable reticence. When Eric mentioned his name, he did so in a manner which jarred—"Your little friend Birnie"; "Cowie, Douglas, Birnie, and other riff-raff of the mess." Colonel Bethune might almost have been trying to belittle Roy intentionally. So Marjorie, afraid of losing her temper and giving away the position, carefully avoided Roy as a topic—an omission which Eric may or may not have noted, but made no attempt to correct.

But the week was soon over, and Colonel Bethune and cheery nights out were no more. Marjorie fell back into the old routine with an inevitable sense of reaction. She realised next afternoon, as she sat waiting in the rain at her wheel in Curzon Street, how improvident it is to accept happiness or distraction from sources outside one's normal environment. She knew now that the only permanent happiness is the happiness that comes from common things. More than ever she yearned in her heart for a regular companion—a crony, a confidant, a pal—as lively and as "safe" as the companion she had just lost.

As noted above, it was raining—raining on a dismal afternoon in March. It had been an anxious and busy week, for the Boche had fallen like an avalanche upon Verdun, and the French resistance was in the preliminary and uncertain stages of what was to prove one of the most heroic defensive actions in history. Allied Councils of War had been frequent, and Lord Eskerley's department had been heavily engaged.

Word had just been sent out to Marjorie that his lordship would be detained another hour at least, and that Miss Clegg, if she pleased, was at liberty to take the car back to the garage. But Miss Clegg was pleased to remain where she was. She sat on, with the rain dripping off her peaked cap and down the bridge of her nose, sedulously nursing a theory that in so doing she was getting a little nearer to the Western Front.

It never rains but it pours. Suddenly, from round the corner of Queen Street, there came to Marjorie a new factor in her life—a humid but quite alluring vision of attenuated skirt, black silk stockings, and inadequate fur stole. The rain was working its will upon the vision: she had not even an umbrella. But she pattered bravely along upon her absurd heels, taking what shelter the lee of the houses afforded, and keeping her head well down—presumably for reasons connected with her dazzling complexion.

As she passed Marjorie she looked up, and Marjorie saw that she was little more than a child, and a not very robust child at that. With Marjorie, to think was to act.

"I say! Wait a minute!" she cried, and began to rummage under the cushion of her seat, extracting ultimately a spare raincoat of her own.

"You must put this on," she announced to the girl: "you are soaking." She bustled her new protégée into the garment without waiting for permission. Then another thought occurred to her.

"I have half an hour to spare," she said. "May I take you anywhere? Nobody"—indicating her employer's mausoleum-like residence—"will mind."

Appealing blue eyes looked up at her. An enormous but attractive mouth broke into a grateful smile.

"It's jolly decent of you," said a voice of incredible childishness. "Are you sure?"

"Rather!" said Marjorie. "Will you get inside, or sit by me?"

"By you, please."

"All right! Come along!"

Marjorie cranked her engine, and took her place at the wheel. Her new little friend snuggled down beside her.

"You *are* strong!" she said admiringly. "And yet you don't look very hefty. Your hands are lovely. How do you keep them so nice, doing this kind of work?"

"They are my vanity!" laughed Marjorie. "I sit up half the night trying to keep my nails in order. I wonder if it's worth while: I sometimes feel inclined to let them rip—for the duration! Where can I take you?"

"The Imperial Theatre, if you don't mind. I have a rehearsal at three, and it's after that now. I shall get a telling-off, as usual, I suppose. Well, I'm not worrying: such is life!"

"Are you on the stage?" asked Marjorie, genuinely thrilled.

"Yes. We open in about a month, with a new musical show."

"What's it called?"

"I never can remember: they change the title about once a day. Not that it really matters. 'Too Many Girls' is the latest; and pretty suitable, too! My dear, you simply can't get men for the theatre nowadays! The good ones have all joined up, and the rotters daren't walk on. You ought to see our chorus men! They are all about seventy, or else they have one lung, or one rib, or one ear, or something. Still, we carry on somehow. Are you driving a car for war work?"

"Yes. I don't really feel that I ought to be doing it; it's too much like fun. I was in a canteen at first, but I got rather run down and hard up, and I was offered this job as a chauffeur, so I took it. I think I should go back to the canteen if I could afford it. I never see any soldiers now. At the canteen one could do something for them, poor things."

"They're lambs!" agreed the passenger—"especially the young officers. Are you engaged?"

Marjorie, very much occupied in negotiating Piccadilly Circus, nodded.

"An officer?"

Marjorie nodded again.

"My boy's an officer, too. What's your name, by the way?"

"Marjorie Clegg."

"Mine's Liss Lyle. (It's Elizabeth Leek really, but in the profession one has to think of something better than that.) There's the Imperial there. Just shake me off at the front entrance, and I'll slip round to the stage door."

"Oh, but I want to drive you right up to the stage door!" said Marjorie frankly. "It will be wonderful!"

The little woman of the world at her side smiled indulgently.

"Very well then, dear, you shall! Round that corner, and then round again."

Marjorie set down her passenger with a genuine pang. She was certain now what was wrong in her life. She had no one to gossip with.

The two girls shook hands.

"Thanks awfully!" said Liss. "Also for Little Willie Waterproof." She took off the raincoat.

"Stick to it just now," said Marjorie: "it may be raining when you come out."

"Can I? I love you for that. I'll come round and leave it for you somewhere, shall I?"

Marjorie dived impulsively into the opening offered.

"Come to-night!" she said. "We might go and have some dinner somewhere. I can always get off for an hour—sometimes for the whole evening. I have a lot of evenings to myself," she added.

Ultimately the pair dined together, *chez* Lyons, and Marjorie spent her happiest hour since her invasion of London. She found her little friend a characteristic medley of childishness and maturity—featherheaded, affectionate, naïve, with far more worldly wisdom than herself, yet with all a child's dread of being laughed at for ignorance.

She came from Finchley—and apologised for doing so. She had no mother, and her father, overburdened, it seemed, with daughters, had raised no particular objection to Miss Elizabeth's theatrical predilections. She was at present living at a boarding-house near Paddington. Did not like it much. Said so—apparently to every one, including the other boarders. But nothing troubled her long. Her thoughts, birdlike, hopped to another twig, and her cheery little song of life was resumed. She was not deeply concerned with how and why. She pecked carelessly here and there at what fortune offered, without pausing to reason why or count the cost; but so far appeared instinctively to have avoided what was unwholesome. Her chief passions were dress, gossip, and expensive confectionery. Her conversation was a blend of theatrical shop and military slang—including many parrot-phrases which could have conveyed no meaning to her whatever—and was chiefly remarkable for a certain confiding frankness and a glorious contempt for what Mr. Mantalini would have called "demnition details."

"You must meet my boy," she said to Marjorie, as they walked homeward. "You'd love him. He's a *pukka sahib*!"

"What is his name?" asked Marjorie.

"I am not quite sure of his name," replied Miss Lyle, with characteristic candour; "but I think he's in the Yeomanry. His Christian name's Leonard. I met him with two other fellows at a party, and I got all their surnames mixed up—I always do—and I can never remember which of the three is his."

"You will find out before you marry him?" suggested Marjorie respectfully.

"Oh, rather! But there's plenty of time for that. Besides, he's going out soon, and then it won't matter."

"It won't *matter*?"

"No. We are not so potty about one another as all that. I could see the lad wanted to be engaged—after all, poor things, they can't afford to wait, these days—so I let him. He's nice, and clean, and it looks well to be called for after rehearsal. I shall miss him awfully when he goes. It's rotten to be by yourself in this world—isn't it?" A pair of pathetic eyes were upturned to Marjorie's.

Next moment Marjorie's arm was round the waif's shoulders.

"Liss, you shall come and live with me!" she said impulsively.

"Righto!" replied Liss. "I was dying to be asked, but it seemed too wonderful to be possible. I shall have to sponge on you for a bit, though. I haven't a bean until the show opens."

"That's all right," said Marjorie.

"Now, where shall we have our dug-out?" asked Liss, becoming terribly busy.

The pair spent a rapturous evening building castles in Kensington.

CHAPTER VIII
CHORUS
I

Finally they found an eyrie—a flat, somewhere in the sky at the back of Victoria Street, consisting of a big bedroom, a tiny sitting-room, a gas stove, and a surprisingly modern bath. They bought furniture at unpretentious establishments in Tottenham Court Road, laying their own carpets and hanging their own curtains. (The latter were the only really essential articles of domestic furniture in those days of aerial visitation.) Marjorie hung up a few reprints and photographs; Liss contributed a portrait of her nebulous and anonymous fiancé, together with seventeen picture post cards of stage celebrities; and the ideal home was opened.

Still, Marjorie's hunt for happiness was not yet complete. There were two crumpled rose-leaves. Firstly, her implacable conscience continued to inform her that her war work was too easy. Secondly, her evenings were as lonely as ever. As soon as rehearsals finished, and "Too Many Girls" started upon its nightly and tumultuous presentation, Liss disappeared regularly every evening about half-past six; to return, sometimes exhilarated, sometimes gloomy, sometimes affectionate, sometimes quarrelsome, but invariably hungry and inexorably talkative, about midnight. Supper was then served. The two ladies rarely ate at a table: as already noted, the keynote of a feminine meal is its passionate avoidance of anything in the shape of ceremonial routine. As often as not Marjorie would take her supper to bed with her, while Liss, munching and babbling, plied back and forth between the sitting-room and bedroom, in progressive stages of disrobement, bearing fresh supplies and relating the experiences of the day—continuing long after she had shed her flimsy garments over two rooms and a vestibule, arrayed herself in night attire, and crawled into bed.

"My dear, we had the most wonderful house to-night. Seven *legitimate* calls after the first act! What an audience these boys on leave make! (Here are a couple of sardines: the bloater paste is nah-poo.) They gave Phyllis Lane such a reception! She had to do the dance after 'Pull Up your Socks!' three times; (and if you want any more cocoa tell me, because I am going to turn out the gas-ring.) Her husband has been mentioned in dispatches. Leonard wasn't in front to-night—selfish pig! I'll tell him off for that, to-morrow. (Oh, you darling, did you put this hot-water-bottle in my bed? I must give you a kiss for that. There! No, it won't hurt you, it's only lip salve.) Mr. Lee came behind to-night, and spoke to us all. Said the show was a credit to everybody, and he was very pleased to hear how brave we all were during the raid the other night. Yes, he's the managing director. (Have you finished? Very well, then! Give me the tray. Here's a cigarette for you.) By the way, I was talking to Uncle Ga-Ga to-night. Oh, didn't I tell you about him? He's one of the chorus gentlemen—about a hundred years old, and simply mad to get into the war. But they won't take him. He keeps changing his name, and dyeing his hair a fresh colour, and trying again; but they turn him down every time. Seems queer, doesn't it, that when a man wants to go he can't, while there are so many who should and won't? (Can I use your cold cream, dear? I can't find mine.) Lee said they would probably put on a second edition about August: we start rehearsing the new numbers next week. Why don't you come and get a job in the chorus? It wouldn't interfere with your other work. There's two or three other girls doing the same as you, and Lee lets them off with one *matinée* a week. He's very patriotic. A-a-a-h! Oo-oo-oo! Ee-ee-ee! What a *lovely* warm bed! Well, as I was saying—Marjorie Clegg, what is the use of my wearing myself to a shadow waiting on you at supper and then the moment I get into bed and begin to chat for a couple of minutes before lights out you start snoring like a grampus? Very well, have it your own way. Live and let live, *I* say.... That's all.... As for that little toad Leonard—!..."

Miss Lyle's baby eyes closed, her small nose buried itself in the pillow, and her little tongue was still for several hours.

But Marjorie was not asleep. She lay awake thinking, while outside London, shrouded in the blackest obscurity, snatched such slumber as that endless, flaring, muttering line of outposts in Flanders could guarantee. For all her splendid vitality, Marjorie was a highly-strung girl—with a conscience. That morning Colonel Bethune, passing through London from Scotland on his way back to the Western Front, had invited her to a "farewell luncheon." She had accepted, gladly—and had repented ever since. For behold, over the coffee, Colonel Bethune had asked her to marry him!

He had asked her very charmingly, and with obvious confidence—a combination which made it an ungrateful and difficult business to say no without offence. At first Marjorie had been too taken back to say anything at all. When her answer came its sincerity was unmistakable; and poor, vain Eric was obviously and deeply mortified. With a vague idea of consoling him, she had mentioned that her affections were already engaged. He had asked her for no name, but she knew that it had been written in her face, and that Eric had read it there. Then a new and disappointing characteristic of the man had cropped out. He had turned and reproached her—had told her that she had flirted with him, and led him on—which was a base lie. But for all that, she was filled with remorse. In her selfish desire for a good time she had been thoughtlessly inconsiderate of Colonel Bethune, and almost disloyal to Roy.

She and her host had parted miserably ten minutes later, each having learned a bitter lesson—Eric, that in the field of love, especially under stress of war, callow youth can be more than a match for dazzling maturity; Marjorie, that where a pretty girl is concerned no man can be regarded as 'safe' until he is dead.

Well, she would expiate her fault in the only way she knew. This decided, she fell asleep.

II

Next morning Marjorie, depositing her noble employer upon the steps of the Ministry of Intelligence, inquired:

"May I speak to you for a moment, sometime, Lord Eskerley?"

"Twelve-twenty-five," was the prompt reply—"after Downing Street and before signatures. But I will not exert my influence to have him made Commander-in-Chief!"

At twelve-twenty Marjorie presented herself to Mr. Meadows, in the secretary's room, and was passed through double doors into the presence of the minister. His lordship looked up over his spectacles and indicated a chair.

"Habakkuk! Good! Sit down. Four-and-a-half minutes! Well?"

"I want to say," announced Marjorie, plunging head foremost into her confession, "that I can't stay here any longer."

"Why?"

"I am not happy in my mind. I must go away."

"Good gracious! Don't say Meadows has fallen in love with you! I will not permit my subordinates to encroach upon my prerogatives! No—not that? Proceed, then!"

"I think I ought to leave you," Marjorie continued, quite unmoved by her employer's senile quips, "because I am having too good a time. I have been feeling all along that I ought to be doing something else."

"So I have observed. Well?"

"The only trouble is that if I go back to the canteen work (where they want my help very badly), I shan't get paid for it; and I can't afford to work without pay of some kind. I have a small allowance from home, but it doesn't go far, and the girl I share a flat with was pretty hard up when I first picked—became acquainted with her."

"Oh! Ah! So you keep a foundling hospital, too?"

"Only one!" explained Marjorie. "She's a dear," she added warmly. "She's on the stage. She was badly in debt before the new piece started—they don't get paid during rehearsals, you see—and she is only just beginning to get on her feet again; so I can't afford to work for nothing during the day just now, unless—"

"Unless you go on the stage yourself at night? Is that it, O *Capable de tout*?"

"I was thinking of it," confessed Marjorie; "but I don't know how you guessed."

"It's the first thing every pretty girl thinks of when confronted with the necessity of earning a living. Go on."

"And I want to ask you: Is it playing the game to be on the stage *at all* in war time? I mean, ought the men to be encouraged to go to revues, and things like that, when they are on leave? Is it all wrong, and demoralising, and unpatriotic, as some people say?"

Lord Eskerley sat up, and took off his spectacles.

"Unpatriotic fiddlesticks!" he remarked with great vigour. "In war time there are just three things that matter. The first is morale. I have forgotten the other two. The maintenance of purely military morale can safely be left in military hands; but civilian morale—and that includes the morale of the men on leave of course, rests mainly on the triple foundation of the Church, the Press, and the Stage; and, as things are to-day, I am not sure that the Stage doesn't have the biggest say in the whole business. (Don't tell Doctor Chirnside I said that, will you?) So you are thinking of joining your foundling behind the footlights. Chorus, I presume?"

"Yes. They would give me three pounds a week."

"They would get you cheap! And you want me to satisfy your conscience that the life of a galley-slave in a vitiated atmosphere all day, followed by vocal and calisthenic exercises in an even more vitiated atmosphere for three hours every night, is a sufficiently close approach to hard work to exonerate you from all suspicion of lukewarmness with regard to the war?" The old man stood up and shook hands. "Donna Quixota Habakkuk, the certificate is granted! I suppose you will stay on for a week or two, until I find a successor—I won't say a substitute? Don't forget me, altogether. Come and see me sometimes. I am less busy, and more solitary, than you suppose. You know when to come: you are familiar with my goings out and comings in. And—good luck, my dear!"

III

Life behind the scenes, as usual, falsified expectation. Marjorie's first visit to the theatre was paid a few weeks after her interview with Lord Eskerley. They entered by the stage-door, Liss explaining to a taciturn but benevolently disposed person in a glass box, whose name appeared to be "Mac," that her companion had an appointment with Mr. Lee. Thereafter, Marjorie was conducted through an iron door, which commanded the thoughtless, by stencilled legend, to close it gently; through a mass of ghostly scenery, past whitewashed walls bearing notices extolling the virtues of Silence; and out through another iron door (marked, somewhat paradoxically, "*Not an exit*") into the auditorium, rendered dimly visible by the overflow of light from an economically-illuminated stage.

Liss turned back the holland covering from two stalls at the end of a retired row.

"Sit there, dear," she said. "I will grab hold of old Lee some time, and tell him you are here. I can sit with you for a bit. This rehearsal is for principals; the chorus aren't called until twelve."

The rehearsal of the principals consisted, for the moment, of an altercation between a fat man, standing in the middle of the stage, and the musical director, sitting at his desk in the orchestra. It was a most friendly—one might almost call it an affectionate—altercation. No epithet ever fell to a lower level of mutual esteem than "Old Boy!" or "Old Man!"—or, under extreme provocation, a "Dear Old Boy!" As is not unusual in these cases, it was difficult for the casual outsider to discover:

(*a*) What the argument was about.

(*b*) Which side of the argument was being sustained by whom.

In the front row of the stalls stood an ascetic-looking man in black tortoise-shell spectacles, apparently acting as umpire. Seated upon a partially dismantled throne beside a step-ladder, up stage, sat a pretty girl in a pink tam-o'-shanter, placidly perusing a crumpled brown-paper-covered manuscript. Other persons were dotted about the auditorium—fat men, cadaverous men; men with tortoise-shell spectacles, and men without; an occasional female. All were conferring in monotone. Round the bare walls of the stage, at present destitute of scenery, sat the ladies of the chorus, most of them wearing rehearsal dresses of unpretentious design—knitting socks of khaki, and occasionally exchanging a guarded confidence. Altogether the atmosphere struck Marjorie as more domestic than theatrical—almost ecclesiastical in its dullness and drowsiness.

"Who are these people sitting about in the stalls?" she asked Liss.

"Oh, just odds and ends! The author, and the lyric writers, and extra lyric writers, and costumiers, and photographers, and people like that—all waiting to catch Mr. Lee, and start an argument with him about something. That's Tubby Ames on the stage. He's having a row with Phil Kay; he has about two a week. I bet you he's trying to get Phyllis Lane's song cut. (That's her, in the pink tam; she's sweet.) It's been going too well lately. Tubby was kept waiting for his entrance in the Second Act last night while she did her third encore dance. Trust Tubby to step on other people's fat! Yes, I thought so."

The comedian's voice was heard again. The gist of the dispute was emerging from a cloud of verbiage.

"Phil, dear old man," he exclaimed earnestly, "I should be the last person in the world to interfere with a brother or sister artist; but really, I am only saying what every one feels. After all, we must all pull together in these days, and I feel instinctively that unless the way is kept *ab-so-lute-ly* clear for that entrance of mine, the action will drop—and flop goes your Second Act! And where are you then?" He leaned right over the footlights.

The conductor, apparently a man of peace, flinched visibly.

"Old boy," he began, "it's this way. I quite see your point—"

The comedian pressed his advantage swiftly.

"I thought you would," he said. "I have had a good many years' experience in this sort of work—more than you, perhaps. For instance, when I was with Charles Wyndham—"

"It's the Story of his Life!" whispered Liss despairingly. "We get it about every second rehearsal. He's out of pantomime, really. It's only because there's nobody else to be had that he's here at all. He has varicose veins, and—"

But the ascetic referee in the stalls broke in upon the autobiographist.

"Mr. Ames," he commanded—his voice was strong and harsh, and was obviously extensively employed in shouting down other discordant noises—"talk sense!"

"That's Mr. Lancaster," whispered Liss excitedly. "He's the producer. We are all frightened to death of him. He's a wonder!"

"Miss Lane's song cannot be cut," continued the wonder, "and it cannot be transferred elsewhere; so you must lump it! Now, Miss St. Leger, come on, please, and try your 'Plum and Apple' duet with Mr. Ames."

Miss St. Leger, the leading lady, was standing in the wings. Her face was round and childish; her eyes were brown and pathetic; her whole appearance suggested timidity and helplessness. Hearing her name called, she walked obediently down to the footlights, favoured the producer with a dazzling smile, and began:

"Say, listen, Mr. Lancaster! I got a kick coming too! That duet I am putting over with Mr. Ames in the Second Act of the present show is practically a solo! When we started in singing it, way back in last fall, it was a duet, I'll allow. But somehow I got a kind of crowded feeling, now. I don't seem to belong in that duet when Mr. Ames is around. And I want to say right here that I am not going to stand for that kind of rough stuff any more!"

By this time the languid chorus were sitting straight up on their chairs. The scattered figures in the auditorium had ceased their muttered incantations, and were leaning forward, all ears. The pacific Phil Kay was squirming in his seat. Marjorie and Liss gripped hands ecstatically; the ecclesiastical atmosphere had evaporated.

"I understand team work," continued the ethereal Miss St. Leger, "as well as any artist; and you won't ever find me stepping on any other folks' laughs or business. But one thing I will not do, and that is feed fat to a dub comedian all the time—especially a guy that's too fat already!"

There was a roar of laughter from stage and stalls. Even the austere Lancaster grinned sardonically. Mr. Tubby Ames, gaping like a stranded fish, surrendered abjectly, as was his invariable custom when firmly handled.

"All right," he said, with a pathetic smile. "Carry on! Nobody loves a fat man! Chord, please!"

Said an Apple to a Plum;—
"Seeing how this War has come,
Join me in the stew-pan, do!"

Miss St. Leger, flushed with victory, took her demoralised opponent in an affectionate embrace, and replied:

Said the Plum, "I guess I will!
I am fairly stony; still,
I will do my bit, like you!"

"There's Mr. Lee now," said Liss—"just by the stalls entrance. Let's catch him!"

Our two conspirators descended upon the great man. He proved to be much less formidable than Marjorie had feared.

"We can make room for you, girlie," he announced paternally, "and"—with a glance at Marjorie's face and figure—"a hundred more like you, *if* they can be found, which I doubt!" He patted her shoulder. "Now—where will you fit in? Let me think! You are too big to go prancing about the stage with Baby Lyle, and the other little people. Your life's work is to stand well down stage in a stunning frock, and fill the eye! Take her along to Mr. Lancaster, Baby, and say I sent you. I must be off."

"I ought to tell you," said Marjorie, "that I may find matinées a difficulty. I am working at a canteen. I have only one free afternoon a week."

"That will do," said Mr. Lee. "I believe in helping girls who are doing war work. I'm a special constable myself. Not bad for an old man of fifty-four, eh? But we all try to do something here. Now, run along to Lancaster, girls! I have to report for duty at Vine Street at three o'clock."

With a gracious smile, Mr. Lee disappeared through the stalls entrance. Liss squeezed Marjorie's hand excitedly.

"My dear, you have made a *tremendous* hit with him! He can be horribly grumpy when he likes. Come and be introduced to Lancaster."

The producer was found dismissing the rehearsal of principals. The plum and apple had become jam in the last verse, so both romance and patriotism were satisfied.

"Very good," he said. "It all goes all right now, except the dance. Mr. Kosky will take care of that." He raised his voice. "Principals, same time to-morrow! Good morning, Miss St. Leger! Good morning, Tubby, old man!" His voice boomed louder. "Now then, chorus ladies and chorus gentlemen, please!"

The damosels round the stage laid down their khaki socks, hitched up their own stockings, and gathered in groups in the wings. Simultaneously a procession of six gentlemen appeared from the direction of the stage-door, extinguishing cigarettes.

Liss hurriedly introduced Marjorie. Lancaster shook hands.

"I think we can find a place for you in the show," he said, regarding her with critical approval. "Can you sing?"

Marjorie, with a sudden and incongruous recollection of the harmonium at Netherby on Sunday afternoons, smiled, and replied that she could sing a little.

"Mr. Kay will try your voice after rehearsal. No previous experience, I suppose?"

"No."

"It doesn't matter. You had better sit and watch this rehearsal this morning, and try to learn our language. Baby, my dear, run along and get into your place."

Liss, who appeared to be the *enfant gâté* of the establishment, scampered away, and presently appeared among the chattering throng on the prompt side. Mr. Lancaster clapped his hands. There was silence.

"Now, ladies and gentlemen," he explained, "we are going to try the first new number in the Second Act—'Honolulu Lulu.' Places, please, and try to put some ginger in it this time! You come on laughing and chatting. Now—*commence*!" He clapped his hands again. "For pity's sake, everybody, *desist*! Gentlemen, gentlemen, remember that you are happy South Sea Islanders, without a care in the world—not welshers coming back from a dirty day at Kempton! Again, please! And ladies, don't come bolting on in that panic-stricken way. You aren't taking shelter from an air raid; you are young village belles, come to participate in the Annual Festival of the Sun! You are joyful! You are glad! You are going to sing about it! For the Lord's sake, *smile*! Phil, old man, the symphony once more, if you please! All come in at the end of six bars. La-la! La-la! La-la! *Now*, all together! No! no! no! *no*!" Mr. Lancaster clapped his hands and beat his breast alternately. "Ladies, ladies, *ladies*! Let me tell you, for the last time, that it is a human impossibility to sing with the mouth shut! It can't be done! For generations and centuries people have been trying to sing out of their noses, and their ears, and the back of their necks; but no one has ever succeeded yet. Open your little mouths! Open them wide! And *keep* them open, for the love of Mike!"

And so on, until a standard of approximate harmony was attained.

IV

Next day Marjorie walked on at her first rehearsal, and practised the new numbers with the rest. Mr. Lancaster's attitude towards her was the same as Mr. Lee's. That is to say, he addressed her much as an old gentleman of seventy might address a little girl of six.

"Now, dear, I know you are feeling nervous, and aren't going to do yourself justice, just at first—"

"I am not a bit nervous, thank you," said Marjorie.

"Oh, yes, you are," said Mr. Lancaster. "But remember that I understand about that, and am making allowances all the time. So don't be frightened; but keep your head up, and sing out, that's a good girl!"

"He's a hard nut," remarked her next-door neighbour into her ear—"but he never swears at you. At least, if he does, he always apologises afterwards. He's quite a gentleman."

In a few days Marjorie was admitted an accepted member of the choral sisterhood. She found her colleagues, for the most part, young, friendly, talkative, excitable, and as improvident as grasshoppers. Most of them possessed a "boy" of some kind—usually a callow subaltern of the one-star brand, with a vocabulary largely composed of the expressions "priceless" and "pathetic." Some of them were married. A few had husbands actually out in France, or farther afield. One or two had babies, and talked about them a good deal.

Of the principals, Miss St. Leger, with her magnetic personality and tough little Chicago voice, was a prime favourite with everybody. Her hold over the audience was wonderful: she could galvanise a Wednesday matinée into enthusiasm. Compared with her, the second girl, Phyllis Lane, was no more than an attractive amateur. But both were kind to their humbler sisters. Indeed, nearly everybody was kind to everybody in those days. The theatrical profession is conspicuous for its big generosities and petty jealousies. In August, nineteen-sixteen, the former had almost entirely obliterated the latter. A huge daily casualty-list is a very levelling—indeed, binding—influence, especially in such a community; there was not a girl in the chorus at the Imperial who had not an interest, actual or prospective, in that casualty-list.

The male members of the company, as was only natural at the time, were remarkable neither for their youth nor their physical fitness. In addition to the phlebitic Ames, there were—Jack Hopeleigh, a well-preserved hero with a light baritone—he was registered under the Derby Scheme in group forty-three; Hubert Hartshorn, a comic manservant, who owed his irresistible wheezy laugh to the fact that he had been badly gassed at Ypres more than twelve months previously, and was now discharged permanently unfit; and one Valentine Rigg, a stage lawyer, who for forty years had earned a modest but steady income by arriving in the Third Act with a black bag, and clearing up all misunderstandings just before the clock struck eleven.

To the student of humanity the chorus gentlemen were really more interesting than the principals. There was a dismal individual named Chivers, who now kept a stationer's shop in Brixton, but had once been in grand opera—Carl Rosa's chorus. He contributed a reedy tenor to the ensemble. There was a plump little man with a round face and little tufts of white whisker, invaluable in scenes of revelry where guests of the "jolly old uncle" type were required. This was his first theatrical engagement for fifteen years. In the interim he had supported life with invincible cheerfulness, as a bookmaker's clerk, a traveller in hymn-books, and head-waiter in an old-fashioned Brighton hotel. There was a discharged corporal of the Machine Gun Corps, with lungs of brass, the D.C.M. ribbon on his waistcoat, and twenty-seven fragments of German H.E. in his left leg. There was an unpleasant-looking youth named Mervyn, with bobbed hair and a patronising manner—debarred from volunteering his services to his country by reason of a susceptibility to chills upon the liver. Popular rumour located these elsewhere.

And there was Alf Spender—"Uncle Ga-Ga." His age was a mystery. His own estimate, for war purposes, was forty-one. The ladies of the chorus put it among themselves at a hundred and fifty. It was possibly fifty-four, or thereabouts. He was a frail creature, with a simple soul, and what Americans call a "single-track" mind. He had been a super or chorus man ever since he could remember; and until the year nineteen fourteen had never relinquished a humble ambition to achieve a speaking part. But now all that was cast to the winds. His single track was carrying other traffic. Somewhere within his ill-nourished frame burned the pure white flame of genuine patriotism. His one desire was to be admitted to the privilege of khaki, and to do his humble part in "teaching those dirty Germans a lesson." He never rested in his efforts to qualify. He dyed his scanty locks; he endeavoured, by daily study of a manual of Swedish exercises, to school his feeble limbs and sickly body to the requisite pitch of efficiency. He offered himself at every recruiting station in London, giving a different name at each. But all in vain; no one would accept him. He could pass no physical test; a big heart was not enough.

"Still, I haven't given up hope," he confided to Marjorie. "I have just discovered a really admirable hair-tonic; and there's a new strengthening-food come on the market, which may help. Of course, the chief difficulty is my teeth; an M.O. turns me down the moment he examines them! I haven't many, you see, and what I have don't fit together very well; and good dentistry runs into money—a fiver, at least. But I don't despair—not by any means. They will want me in time! It seems inhuman to say so, but I do trust this battle that's just started on the Somme won't finish the war right off. I couldn't bear to see the troops coming back victorious, and feel that I did nothing to help!"

Here was another Willing Horse. Marjorie's heart warmed to him; they became friends. They shared a newspaper at rehearsals, discussing Sir Douglas Haig's daily bulletin word by word. They read between the lines, and decided that, despite newspaper heroics to the contrary, the gigantic offensive of July the First had only been partially successful.

"We never got through on the left at all," said Alf. "Look at that place on the map—Thiepval. We were meant to carry that bang off, and we didn't! They don't say so, but we didn't! We have broken their line all right, but the trouble is that we have broken it on too narrow a front—and I think it's all because of that Thiepval place. We must widen the gap, or the attack fails. Shall I tell you what I would do if I were head of the Army Council?"

"Yes—do," said Marjorie, eagerly.

"I would secretly construct some sort of contrivance that would protect our troops as they dashed across No Man's Land. That's the most dangerous moment. I'm not worrying about artillery fire, mind you! You may dodge that, or you may not; anyhow, there's a sporting chance about it. It's those machine guns! The Germans have them fixed in such a way that when they are all fired at once there is not a yard of ground that isn't a running river of bullets. Now mark you, once we get across that bullet zone, we have the Hun at our mercy. We British"—Alf's emaciated frame stiffened exultantly—"can do *anything* with the bayonet! But we must get across first!"

"But how?" Marjorie sighed despairingly.

"I don't know: I haven't enough technical knowledge. But some sort of armour-plated motor 'bus would be the idea. I'll bet old Kitchener would have fixed it, if he'd been alive. Oh, dear!" (The *Hampshire* had gone down some six weeks previously.) "By the way, have you heard from Mr. Birnie of late?"

Then Marjorie would tell him all Roy's news. Naturally it contained little of military value, but our two enthusiasts read it—or rather, approved portions thereof—with all the solemn deference due to the Authority on the Spot.

"He may get home on leave some time soon," Marjorie said. "He went out last August, and it's July now. Leave is long over-due, but they stopped it all for weeks before the battle. His battalion was in the opening attack, I think, but they are out now, refitting."

"It must have been an anxious time for you while they were in," said Alf. "Did you know?"

"Yes—at least, I knew a few weeks before that they were at Bray-sur-Somme; so when the news of the attack came I felt pretty certain."

Alf's mild blue eyes flashed.

"I wish I had been with him," he said, "instead of"—he glanced disparagingly downstage, to where Phil Kay, entrenched in the orchestra, was resisting Tubby Ames's bi-weekly offensive—"*this*! It must be a grand moment, coming back to rest, right out of a battle—all mud-splashed, and exhausted, knowing you have made good! Did he give you any details when he wrote?"

"The only detail that mattered," said Marjorie with an unsteady little laugh, "was this!"

She produced a field post card—muddy, crumpled, evidently dispatched by the grimy hand of a stretcher-bearer or a ration orderly. On the back were printed certain alternative statements, familiar enough by this time, designed by the authorities to cover all the chances incident to the life of a soldier in the field. They were all deleted with a blunt pencil, save the first:

I am well.

"That was the nicest letter I ever had from him!" said Marjorie.

"And I bet that's saying a good deal!" replied Alf, with a stately little bow. "Now, touching this Delville Wood, on the right—"

But here the battle-call of Mr. Lancaster was heard in the stalls; and our strategists turned reluctantly from the prosecution of the military campaign to the maintenance of civilian morale.

V

The Second Edition was produced in due course, with the success inevitable in that enthusiastic, unsophisticated, *carpe diem* period. Marjorie appeared successively, and with distinction, as a Lady Guest at the reception of a most unconvincing Duchess, where she flourished an empty champagne glass painted yellow inside; as a Bird of Paradise in the chorus of an ornithological ditty entitled, "If my Girl was a Bird, I would Build Her a Nest," contributed by the well-preserved light baritone aforementioned; as a damsel of the South Sea Islands, participating, with somewhat improbable ritual, in the Annual Festival of the Sun; and in other less exacting roles. Her most distinguished appearance was in the Finale (in a tableau of the Allied Nations), as The Spirit of France. In this she was entrusted with a separate entrance, a solitary walk down stage, and the deliverance of a rhymed couplet of a patriotic nature, in which General Joffre suffered the indignity of rhyming with "Our hats we doff," "nasty cough." She was quite composed, and offered her outrageous contribution with such *aplomb* as to arouse frantic applause. Liss was a dancer, and her activities were mostly linked with those of seven other little creatures like herself. She was whole-heartedly delighted with her friend's successful graduation.

Next morning the company were called at eleven, to be photographed. The morning after, Marjorie reported for duty at the canteen, and was received with open arms by the Mouldy Old Copper. With renewed enthusiasm she settled down to the old drudgery. She was supporting herself; her long and dreary evenings were over; and, best of all, she was really Doing Something to Help.

VI

One morning a few weeks later Mrs. Clegg was deposited by the Rolls-Royce at the front door of Buckholm, and was ushered by Mr. Bates into the amber drawing-room. She entered with the uneasy self-consciousness of the visitor to a great house who has come, not to pay an intimate call, but to attend a committee meeting.

"The other ladies have not yet arrived, madam," announced Bates; and added, in stately reproof: "It is not quite eleven o'clock. Her ladyship will be down presently. Will you please to be seated?" He deposited the flustered and untimely caller upon a sofa, handed her a magazine, and left her alone.

Mrs. Clegg mechanically turned over the pages of the magazine. It was one of those periodicals which was doing its characteristic best at that time to compensate our warriors in the field for compulsory severance from domestic felicity by a weekly display, on a generous—nay, prodigal—scale, of the forms and features of loved ones far away—particularly of such as happened to be connected with the lighter walks of the lyric drama. Mrs. Clegg's eye was caught by a photograph on the middle page—of a tall, slender girl, draped from head to foot in what looked like a flag, with the Cap of Liberty perched upon her fair head. The face seemed familiar. Mrs. Clegg adjusted her tortoise-shell lorgnette—at home, when reading, she wore simple spectacles—and examined the photograph in greater detail. Then she perused the journalistic effusion underneath. It began:

One cannot have *Too Many Girls* of This Kind, Can one?...

Mrs. Clegg was a dutiful wife. On her way home she stopped at the railway station and bought a copy of the magazine at the book-stall. After dinner she showed the middle page to her husband. It was a courageous act, for no such literature had ever been introduced into Netherby before.

That night, when the household had retired to bed, Albert Clegg reopened the Family Bible, lying since prayers at the head of the dining-room table; turned to the Births, Marriages, and Deaths and sent his fountain-pen scouting down the first column. Presently he came to the name he wanted. He scored it out—scored it, and scored it, to complete obliteration. When he had finished, Marjorie had joined Aunt Eliza in the ranks of the Legion of the Lost.

CHAPTER IX
THE BOOK OF THE WORDS

We were due back in the line that night, and I was struggling, in company with one humid orderly-room sergeant and several hundred houseflies, to clean up the usual orderly-room mess—indents, returns, and other nuisances which, in the absence of the adjutant, usually fall upon the patient shoulders of that regimental tweeny, the second-in-command.

I was seated at the kitchen table of a farm-house in Picardy. The weather had been wet and misty for weeks—the weather at critical moments in this war was invariably pro-Boche—but this afternoon the sun had reappeared and summer had come back with a rush. Still, on the overworked highway outside mud still lay deep. At the farm-gate two transport men were admonishing two mules, in the only way they knew, for indicating reluctance (in the only way *they* knew) to hauling the headquarters company's field-kitchen out of the oozy ruts where it had reposed for ten days. Through the open door, looking east, I could descry the wrecked spire of Albert Church, with its golden Virgin and Child projecting horizontally from the summit, like the flame of a candle in a steady draught.

To my ears all the time, through the heavy summer air, came the incessant muffled thunder of guns, and guns, and more guns—British guns, new British guns; hundreds of them—informing Brother Boche that he, the originator of massed artillery tactics, was "for it" himself at last. The bombardment had begun systematically about the middle of the month, all up and down the Western Front. Last Saturday it had intensified in the neighbourhood of the Somme and Ancre Valleys; I had lain awake in my billet, listening, and recalling that summer afternoon, less than two years ago, when Lord Eskerley had gloomily explained to me that it took at least three years to make a British gunner. This afternoon the whole earth trembled; the final eruption could not be much longer delayed.

For Britain was ready to strike at last. True, she had struck before, both recently and frequently; but that had been mainly in self-defence, or for experiment, or to create a diversion. Now she was in a position to strike home. For nearly two years the Willing Horse had stood up indomitably under the strain, while a nation, mainly willing, but shamefully unready, was getting into condition. To-day that nation was ready; every man worth his salt was at last a trained soldier. Never before in our history had such an army been gathered, and never again would such an army be seen, as strained at the leash behind that twenty-five mile front on the thirtieth of June, nineteen sixteen. True, we launched greater armies, and won greater victories in the two years that followed; but—the very flower of a race can bloom but once in a generation. The flower of our generation bloomed and perished during the four months of the First Battle of the Somme. We shall not look upon their like again. It is to be doubted if any generation will—or any race.

Sometimes, in these later days of reaction and uncertainty, we are inclined to wonder whether that sacrifice was justified; whether it would not have been better to wait just a little longer. But in truth we had waited long enough. Strategy might advocate delay, but honour could not. For four months Verdun had stood up like a rock against the rolling tide of assault; it was time we took some weight off Verdun's shoulders. For two years the half-equipped armies of Russia had maintained a suicidal offensive on our account; even now fresh German divisions were streaming away from the Western Front to the Eastern. It was time we called them back. Strategy or no strategy, we meant to accomplish those two purposes. And we did—with something over. Perhaps the Flowers who sleep by the Somme to-day feel, on that account, that what they perished for was worth while. They kept the faith.

I had just dictated provisional Battalion Orders for the morrow; made the usual mistakes in the weekly Strength Return; and was wrestling with an incomprehensible document—highly prized by that section of the Round Games Department which sees to it that wherever the British soldier goes, whether singly or in battalions, his daily rations and weekly pay are diverted from their normal course to meet him—when there came a scuttering of hooves, and Master Roy Birnie, our esteemed sniping and intelligence officer, came flying round the corner on a borrowed horse (mine), as if all the Germans in Picardy were after him. However, this was merely Roy's exuberant way of coming home for his tea. He descended, hitched his steed to the farm-pump, and came striding into the kitchen with blood in his young eye. I dismissed the sergeant in quest of tea. Roy favoured me with a formal salute, then sat down, and began:

"Uncle Alan, I wonder why every battalion in the British Army (except ours) is entirely composed of damn fools!"

"I have heard that speculation so often upon the lips of members of other units of the British Army," I replied, "that I have given up trying to find the answer. Tell me your trouble."

Roy accepted the invitation at once.

"Well," he said, "I had a peach of an observation post up in the front line. It was an old derelict mill-wheel affair—one of those contraptions you see on the end wall of every farm-house in this country, with a poor brute of a mongrel dog inside, treadmilling away to work a churn, or play the pianola, or something. It lies out flat in front of C Company's sector, on top of a little rise, looking like nothing at all. You know it?"

"Yes," I said. "It has been there for months; it is one of the accepted features of the landscape by this time."

"That's right; the Boche has never suspected it. Well, I have been using it as an O. Pip for six weeks. There is a private covered sap leading out to it, and once you're inside you can stand in a pit, with your little circular peep-show all round you. Why, through one loophole I can see right away to Beaumont Hamel! Now, as you know, ten days ago we handed over to the Late and Dirties. This morning, when I went up into the line to see about taking over again to-morrow, what do you think I found—in my own special private O.P.?"

"I don't know," I said. "A hairpin?"

"Uncle Alan, for the Lord's sake don't play the fool! I'll *tell* you what I found; the whole floor of the post—*my* post, mind you—was covered with empty cartridge cases! Some Late-and-Dirty perisher had been in there with a rifle, firing volleys—no, *salvoes*—out of it! With an oily barrel, too, I'll bet! Of course the Boche has the place registered now; and next time there is any general unpleasantness brewing, up it will go! And I hope the Late-and-Dirty dog who gave it away will be inside, that's all!"

"It's rotten luck, I admit, boy. But in this case it doesn't particularly matter. In a day or two, we hope, your observation post will be far in rear of us. Perhaps some clerkly gentleman from the base will be making his nest therein."

Roy's face brightened suddenly.

"When do we push off?" he asked eagerly.

"That is a secret known only to the powers above. But I shouldn't be surprised if it were to-morrow, or the next day. The Colonel is away at a Brigade Conference now—the last, I dare say. He will probably call an officers' meeting when he comes back."

"Is Kilbride with him?" asked Roy quickly.

"Yes. Why?"

Roy smiled awkwardly.

"Well, *you* know!" he said. "Addressing you as Uncle Alan, and not as second-in-command, it's a little difficult sometimes for us Hoy Polloy to gather from the C.O.'s account of the proceedings what really *is* settled at these Brigade pow-wows. That is why we find it so useful to pump old Kilbride afterwards. The Colonel is such a fire-eater that he loathes all this chess-board warfare, as he calls it. His idea of fighting is to go over the parapet about a hundred yards ahead of his men, rush straight at the nearest German, and bite him to death. A pretty sound plan too, in many ways. The men would follow him anywhere."

"You are right, Roy—they would. And addressing you, not in your official capacity, but as my nephew, that's just what makes me anxious."

"You mean you are not sure where he *will* lead them?"

"I am not sure where he *won't* lead them! However, we must not criticise our superiors. Go and have your tea, you disrespectful young hound, and then come and help your uncle to wrestle with B.213. Hallo, here is the Colonel!"

There came a fresh sound of hooves; a neigh of welcome from the bored animal already tethered to the pump; and Eric Bethune and his adjutant rode into the yard.

Eric had been sent to us after Loos—our first commander, Douglas Ogilvy, having been killed in a bomb-fight near Hulluch. (I remember the day well. The Germans were furnished with bombs which exploded on impact; ours were of the Brock's Benefit type, and had to be lit with a match. Unfortunately, it was raining at the time.)

I need not say how joyfully the coming of Ogilvy's successor was greeted by the second-in-command. Eric came to us with a reputation. For nearly twelve months he had ruled an overcrowded and under-staffed depot at home, containing never less than two thousand turbulent ex-militiamen, and had licked into shape and self-respecting shape some of the toughest material that our country produces. After that, he had achieved his heart's desire and been sent out, to be second-in-command of our First Battalion. His first proceeding on arrival was to organise a successful attack upon a valuable sector of the line lost by another unit ten days previously. He led the attack in person, and was mentioned in Dispatches.

He came to us, inevitably, with a halo—or should it be nimbus?—and set to work to make us the smartest battalion on the Western Front. Physical fear appeared to be quite unknown to him. For my part, I confess quite frankly that I do not enjoy an intensive bombardment in the least. I really believe Eric did. So, I think, in soberer fashion, did his predecessor. But we were soon conscious of the change of regime in other directions. Where Eric differed from Douglas Ogilvy was in his passion for the spectacular side of soldiering—the pomp of ceremonial, the clockwork discipline, the perfectly wheeling line, the immaculate button in the midst of mud and blood. Eric was at last in a position to model a battalion on his own beliefs. The result had been an ecstasy of worship at the shrine of Spit and Polish.

"A dirty soldier," he was fond of telling his followers, "means a dirty rifle; and a dirty rifle means, in the long run, a dead soldier. Go and shave, and save your life!"

And there was no doubt that, within limits, he was right. That mysterious and impalpable entity, which we call morale, is apt to languish without the aid of soap and water, and a certain percentage of officially fostered *bravura*. The chief difficulty about this war was to prevent it from degenerating into a troglodytic game of stalemate. Everything that maintained morale and stimulated pride of Regiment was welcome.

But there are other things; and if these be lacking, look out for danger—especially under modern conditions. And it was this fear which possessed my slow-moving, uninspired mind as I took tea in that Picardy farm-house that hot and fateful afternoon with my superior officer and lifelong friend.

"Well," Eric began, filling his pipe, "we have had our last pow-wow, thank God! The Brigadier was in his element. He had the whole affair worked out in a little time-table—like a Jubilee Procession. Salute of twenty-one guns at dawn—procession to move off in an orderly manner at six a.m.—buffet luncheon at noon—carriages at five-forty-five, and everything!"

"Did old Kilbride take down a copy of the time-table?" I asked.

"I don't know. Probably he did: it's the sort of thing he would do. As for me, the whole business nearly made me weep. Why are we treated like children, or amateurs in charge of a Territorial Field Day? Don't these chuckle-headed Mandarins realise that we are fighting under conditions of actual warfare, when at any moment things may happen which no time-table can cover? Don't they understand that you *cannot* control the course of a battle by drawing up a niggling time-table any more than you can control the weather by buying a barometer? There are only two things that count in a soldier. The first is initiative in attack; the second is a complete understanding with his officers. Thank God, my men have both. Show them the objective; send them over the parapet; and they will see to the rest of the business without any time-table or book of the words whatever, thank you very much! Discipline! Discipline! Discipline! That's the only thing that matters!"

"Did you communicate your views to the meeting?" I asked.

"I took that liberty. In fact, I have been taking it for the last three weeks. I fancy I am getting slightly unpopular among the higher forms of animal life; but some one has to take the lead in these matters. Most of the men are too newly promoted—too recently gazetted, for that matter—to intrude their opinions. Good fellows, but amateurs—and diffident amateurs at that! Of course they regard everything the Brigadier says as gospel—and he did worry them so! He explained over and over again to each Battalion Commander the exact route by which he was to lead his men to their objective, and what he was to do when he got there. He was to dig in, and consolidate, and mop up, and re-establish communication—with Brigade Headquarters first and foremost, of *course*!—make arrangements for a ration dump—fancy *thinking* of food at such a moment—!"

"'An army fights on its stomach.' *N. Bonaparte*,' I observed.

"Trust you to remember yours, old man! Then he told us a lot more things, mainly about keeping touch with the Gunners, the Machine-Gunners, and the Signallers, and the R.E., and the Ammunition Column, and the Dry Canteen, and the Old Folks at Home—everybody, in fact, except the enemy. After that, a Gunner Brass-Hat stood up, and spoke *his* little piece. He rubbed in the time-table business; said we must adhere to its provisions *very* carefully; otherwise his guns would invariably be pooped off into the stern of the Brigade instead of the bows of the Boche. He didn't put it quite so baldly as that, but he waffled about the urgent necessity of observing the greatest exactitude, especially when the Gunners proceeded from bombardment to barrage. Then the Brigadier pronounced a sort of benediction, and asked, as a kind of after-thought, if there were any further points he could elucidate for us."

"That, no doubt, was where you put your little oar in!"

"It was. I asked him straight—and I could see half the fellows in the room agreed with me—if he had considered the effect of such paralysing exactitude upon *morale*? Our tradition—at least the tradition of my Regiment—was, and always had been, to seek out the enemy and destroy him. My men had not had a Staff College education; they did not understand or cotton on to this business of limited objectives, and working to a time-table. Their objective was Berlin, and their time-table was the limit of physical endurance; in other words, they were sufficiently disciplined to go until they dropped. Wasn't it rather a pity to cramp their style, and so on? I am afraid I rather riled the Brigadier; for the moment I forgot he had been through the Staff College himself."

"What did he say?"

"He mumbled something to the effect that my suggestions, if adopted, would involve a radical rearrangement of the plan of operations of an entire Army Corps; and that if my men didn't understand the tactical requirements of a modern battle it was my job to explain them to them. He said that—to *me*! Offensive old bounder! But of course, discipline is discipline, so I said no more. One cannot humiliate these old boys in the presence of long-eared subalterns; I remembered that."

"It's a pity you didn't remember it a bit sooner, old man!" It was a rash observation, but I was thoroughly alarmed.

Eric flushed a dusky red.

"Look here, Alan," he said, "I can't take criticism from any officer of mine, however old—"

"Sorry!" I replied. "But do be careful, Eric! You know what these people are. For God's sake, don't get sent home!"

Eric wheeled round upon me.

"What do you mean?" he snapped. "What gossip have you been listening to?"

I began to feel my own temper rising.

"I am not in the habit of listening to gossip," I said stiffly—"especially about my Commanding Officer. But the Brigade Major dropped me a pretty broad hint the other day, to the effect that your independent attitude was causing alarm and despondency among the Brass Hats; and—well, I think it's only fair to mention the fact to you."

But Eric was in no mood for sage counsel that day. He smelt battle; he was "up in the cloods."

"Pack of old women!" he exclaimed impatiently. "Wait till they see what we do in the show to-morrow, compared with the notebook wallahs!"

Then he glanced at my troubled face, and the old boyish smile came back—the smile which had held me captive for thirty years or more. He leaned over, and clapped me on the shoulder.

"Cheer up, Alan!" he said. "It was good of you to warn me; but I *must* use my own judgment in this matter—and I take full responsibility for doing so." He rose, and knocked out his pipe. "Now, I suppose I must have an officers' meeting, and let old Kilbride read to them the Brigadier's impression of how this picnic is to be conducted. They are a very earnest band. They will take it all down—they'd take down the multiplication table if you recited it to them—and read it to their N.C.O.'s; and the N.C.O.'s will misquote it to the men; and to-morrow I shall see my battalion, guide-book in hand, methodically advancing to victory, chanting elegant extracts from Orders, to encourage themselves and frighten the Germans! It's a mad war, this! Now, where is the orderly sergeant?"

"Sit down a minute," I said, "and listen to me." I was imperilling the foundations of an ancient friendship, but I could not leave matters like this. Eric dropped impatiently into his chair.

"Well, what about it?" he asked.

"Eric, old man," I began, "I was at Loos—the only show which we have put up in any way comparable with to-morrow's unpleasantness—and you were not; so I am going to improve the occasion. The great ones above us are quite rightly trying to fight this battle on the basis of the lessons taught us by Loos—and they were pretty considerable lessons. May I give you the experience of your own battalion?"

"Go ahead!" said Eric, resignedly filling his pipe again.

"We went off like a bull at a gate, and bundled the Boche out of his front and second lines in a few hours. I am only giving you our own experience, mind you. Other people weren't so well placed, and got practically wiped out crossing No Man's Land. On the other hand, a Division farther along on our right went slap through everything, up Hill Seventy and down the other side. (They say a platoon of Camerons penetrated right into Lens. Of course they never came out again.) Anyhow, by noon on the first day we were cock-a-hoop enough, right up in the air on perfectly open ground behind the Boche reserve line, without the foggiest notion where Brigade Headquarters was, where the next unit was—as a matter of fact, the people on our immediate left were farther ahead still, while the people on our right hadn't got up, and never did—where our artillery was, where our next meal was to come from, and what we were going to do now! We did all we could, which wasn't much. We tried to reverse the captured trenches, without tools. The Sappers turned up, as Sappers invariably do, just when they were wanted most, and performed marvels in the way of improvising defences; but we were still in a pretty precarious position. For the next twenty-four hours nothing in particular happened. Then the Boche, who had been regularly on the run, rallied, and came stealing back. He found our victorious line echeloned in the most ridiculous fashion all over the place, without any semblance of co-ordination, full of gaps you could march a battalion through. He made all the notes he wanted, called up his reserves, and delivered an extremely well thought-out counter-attack. Strung about as we were, he had us cold. We couldn't get up any ammunition or bombs. Special one-way communication trenches *had* been dug for the purpose, but they, of course, were jammed with traffic going the wrong way—stretcher-parties, prisoners, and details of every kind. (Fifty thousand wounded went back to Bethune in the first forty-eight hours.) We had nothing to hope for from the people farther back. Our gunners were there all right, ready and willing; but they didn't know where we were, and dare not fire for fear of hitting us. Whole Divisions of reinforcements were trying to get through, but the roads were packed with transport. In multiplying our artillery and machine guns we had overlooked the fact that for every gun you put into the line you add at least one limber or waggon to the general unwieldiness of the Divisional Ammunition Column. The country for miles behind the line was like Epsom Downs on Derby Day; nothing could get through at all. It was forty-eight hours before a really adequate scheme of reinforcement could be put into effect, and by that time we were practically back where we started. Up to a point, Loos was a well-conceived and splendidly executed operation; but after the first rush everything got out of gear. We had been told our final objective was Brussels! With a little luck and management we might have got Lille. As things turned out we got one pit-village. Luckily we got a lesson too; and to-morrow's show is going to be fought on that lesson. We are to advance to a fixed line and stay there, so as to eliminate gaps; we are to work to a time-table, to enable our gunners to fire with confidence; and we are to maintain communication from front to rear by a very carefully prepared scheme of one-way trenches and armoured telephone cables. Hence all the pow-wows and the little notebooks, Eric!"

But Eric was not convinced. He was in his most childish mood.

"It won't work! It won't work!" he reiterated. "It sounds all right at the pow-wows, and reads all right in the book of the words, but you can't perform these chess-board antics of peace-time under actual war conditions. There is only one way to win big battles, and that is by initiative, resting on perfect *discipline*—by having each separate unit disciplined and disciplined to such a pitch that its commander can handle a thousand rifles like a single pocket-pistol. I am vain enough to believe that my men are disciplined to that extent. Some of the other units are not; and not all the pow-wows and guide-books in the world will help them!"

He rose, and began to buckle on his equipment, whistling through his teeth. I knew that sound, and I dropped the subject.

"Is the kick-off hour fixed?" I asked.

"Yes. About three hours after dawn to-morrow; Kilbride has the details. We are going in from our present sector. I suppose the battalion are all ready to move?"

"Yes; they are parading now. They are timed to pass through Albert after dark, and take over from the Mid-Mudshires just before midnight."

"Good! They may as well know at once that they are going to attack, if they haven't guessed it already. I shall say a word to them before they move off. Are they all going together?"

"No. By companies, at twenty minutes interval."

"Well, let them parade together, anyhow. After I have spoken to them I shall go on with the leading company, and take Kilbride with me. I want you to stay here and clean up. Is another unit taking over this billet?"

"Yes—the Mid-Mudshires; we are simply changing places with them. I am expecting their advance-party at any moment."

"All right. When you have handed over, come along with the Orderly-room staff and join me. Have you much left to do here?"

I glanced round the littered table.

"A fair amount. You are taking Kilbride yourself?"

"Yes. Do you want help?"

"If you could spare me an odd subaltern—"

Eric glanced out of the window, to where the Headquarters Company were parading in the muddy road. His eye fell upon Master Roy, who, a little apart, was inspecting his own particular beloved command—a workmanlike squad of snipers. Eric swung round.

"If you want a really odd subaltern," he said, "take young Birnie! Appoint him Assistant Adjutant for the occasion, and tell him to send those pop-gun experts of his back to duty!"

I fairly gasped.

"You will break their hearts!" I said. "Can't you use them as scouts, or—"

Eric blazed right out this time.

"For God's sake, Laing, allow me to command my own battalion!" he cried. Then—characteristically— "I'm sorry, old boy! You mean well, I know; but really I must do things my own way. We don't require Bisley specialists in a hand-to-hand battle. As for Roy Birnie, a little less sniping and a little more intelligence won't do him any harm at all. Now I'm off to harangue the battalion. Sergeant, is my groom outside? I want my horse."

CHAPTER X
DISCIPLINE! DISCIPLINE! DISCIPLINE!

Exhortation before Action was a form of military ceremonial exactly to our commander's taste. I had heard him address his followers many a time. Nearly thirty years ago I had formed one of an audience of fourteen—shivering in shorts and jerseys in an east wind at the back of the school pavilion what time we were addressed by one Eric Bethune, about to lead us into a Final House Match which, owing to the size, speed and prestige of our opponents, could be regarded as little else than a forlorn hope. We won that Final House Match. I decided then, and have never departed from that belief, that no more gallant and inspiring leader of a forlorn hope than that same Eric could have been found among the manhood of our race. And here we were again, eight hundred strong this time, gathered in hollow square for the same purpose.

Eric spoke to us for perhaps five minutes, sitting his horse like a graven image, with the last rays of the setting sun glinting upon his burnished equipment. ("Protective dinginess" was anathema in Eric's battalion.) Around him, steel-helmeted, perfectly aligned, motionless, stood his men. It was characteristic of their commander that he did not preface his address with the order that they should stand at ease. All ranks remained rigidly at attention while he spoke.

I need not repeat his words. It is enough to say that, having heard them, I, for one, would willingly have followed the speaker anywhere he chose to lead me, without a thought (for all my fundamental convictions on the subject) of limited objectives, or artillery time-tables, or other mechanical hindrances to free fighting. He moved his men, too—representatives of the dourest and most undemonstrative element of the dourest and most undemonstrative nation in the world. I could see the effect of his words, in the glow of tanned faces, in the setting of square jaws, in the further stiffening of sturdy, rigid bodies. It was hard to decide which to be most proud of—the leader, or the men. I glowed inwardly as my eye ran down the motionless ranks. Great hearts! Great stuff! And, above all, representative stuff—truly representative, at last! They were not of the Regular Army type, nor the Territorial type, nor Kitchener's Army type. They were of the National Army—Britain in Arms—voluntary Arms—The Willing Horse, reinforced and multiplied to his most superlative degree.

Five minutes later A Company were streaming down the road in fours, Eric striding at their head with the company commander and adjutant. He had sent his horse back to the transport lines, and was "foot-slogging" exultantly with his men. I returned to the farm kitchen. I entered rather suddenly. Our newly-appointed assistant adjutant was sitting at the table, with his head buried in his arms. His back was to the door.

I tripped heavily upon the door-sill. Roy sat up hurriedly, and busied himself with the papers before him.

"Everything cleared up now?" I asked briskly, slipping off my heavy marching equipment.

"Yes, sir," replied a muffled voice—"very nearly."

"In that case," I continued, with great heartiness, "we can get away almost immediately. I am expecting our relief here in five minutes."

I babbled on a little longer, to give him time to recover. Presently he turned upon me, and spoke. His face was flushed—absurdly like his mother's when something had roused her chivalrous indignation.

"Uncle Alan, it's a rotten shame! I had a wonderful scheme all mapped out! It was in Orders, too! We had marked down all sorts of cushy spots for sniping Boche machine guns from. I had an aeroplane map of our sector, with Thiepval, and Beaumont Hamel, and everything! Now, my poor chaps are all sent back to their companies, where they will be treated like dirt; and—I am given a job as assistant office boy!"

It is impossible to furnish adequate comfort to a man who has been deprived unexpectedly of his first independent command. I merely patted Roy's shoulder, and said gruffly—

"Discipline, Discipline, Discipline, lad! That's the only thing that matters!"

Roy sat up at once. He was a soldier, through and through.

"I beg your pardon, sir," he said. "I am afraid I was mixing up Major Laing with Uncle Alan! That wasn't the game, was it? My error! It shan't occur again." He smiled resolutely. "I think everything is in order now. Shall I hand these files over to the Orderly-room sergeant?"

"Righto!" I said. "Was that a despatch rider I saw at the door just now?"

"Yes—from Brigade Headquarters. He left two messages."

"Did you give him a receipt for them?"

"No. He slung them in and bolted off. I expect Brigade Headquarters are on the move, and he didn't want to lose touch with them."

"Never mind! See what they are about."

Roy opened the first envelope, and extracted a field despatch-form. He glanced at it, and grinned.

"It's lucky we got this before going up into the line!" he observed; and read aloud:

The expression "Dud" must no longer be employed in Official Correspondence.

"It's a memo from Olympus," I explained: "They mean well, but their sense of proportion is not what it might be. And the next article?"

Roy did not reply. I looked up. His face was as white as chalk. He was breathing heavily through his nose, staring in a stupefied fashion at the flimsy pink slip in his hand.

"My God!" he muttered; "My God! It'll break his heart."

"What on earth's the matter, old man?" I leaned across the table. Roy thrust the despatch towards me.

"From Divisional Headquarters," he said, mechanically. "The Brigade Major has sent it on."

The message was quite brief:

Lt.-Col. E. F. B. Bethune, D.S.O., commanding Second Battalion, Royal Covenanters, will return home forthwith and report to War Office.

Pinned to the despatch was a hastily scrawled covering slip from the Brigade Major:

Passed to you, for immediate compliance, please.

The next thing that I remember was Roy's voice:

"They've done it on him! The dirty dogs! They're sending him home! Did you—know?"

"No! Yes! Well, I was half afraid of it. I knew the people higher up were getting a bit restive: in fact, I tried to warn him only this afternoon. But I never dreamed they would strike back at a moment like this. You are right, Roy—it will break his heart." (It was the second occasion upon which I had employed that phrase within the last hour.)

Another thought struck Roy.

"You are in command now!" he said.

"I suppose so; but not until this despatch is actually delivered to the Colonel."

We were silent again. We were both picturing the same scene, I fancy. Presently Roy said:

"If only it had been delayed in some way!"

I nodded.

"Even for a day!—"

"Even for an hour!—"

"Even for ten minutes! We should have been gone out of this place, and they would not have got us until the show was over!"

Our eyes met, then dropped hurriedly. We had read one another's thoughts. Discipline, Discipline, Discipline!

Roy picked up the two despatches, folded them, and put them mechanically into the pocket of his field despatch-book. Then he cleared his throat huskily. I found myself doing the same.

"Look here!—" we began both at once.

A cheery voice interrupted us:

"Good evening, sir. Is this Caterpillar Farm?"

We both jumped, like detected conspirators.

In the doorway stood a subaltern, saluting, with the totem of the Royal Mid-Mudshire Regiment stencilled upon his tin bowler.

"Come in," I said. "This is the place you want. I presume you have come to take over?"

About midnight, the Orderly-room Staff filed through the ghostly streets of Albert, to the music of innumerable big guns working up to their final spasm. At their head marched a silent major and a preoccupied assistant adjutant.

Next morning, just after dawn, the Second Royal Covenanters went raging to the opening attack of the greatest battle yet fought in the history of warfare. We were led into action by our Commanding Officer, Eric Bethune.

CHAPTER XI
ENFIN!

If those years brought unprecedented misery to the human family, they had their compensating moments—especially for those most deeply concerned. Lovers, for instance—true lovers. When two people really love one another, and are limited by inexorable circumstances to rare and brief periods of companionship, each one of which may be the very last—and each succeeding day of those four years saw some six hundred British soldiers of all ranks go back from Leave never to return—their love is lifted to heights, and breathes an atmosphere, of which ordinary workaday lovers can know nothing. Poor peace-time lovers—sitting holding hands in a conservatory, or spooning on a golf course—what do they know? Faced by a future all their own (and the enervating consciousness that there will probably be a good deal of it), what do they know? What do they know of the blind rapture of Six Days' Leave?

Roy's telegram preceded him by exactly one hour, so Marjorie had little time to get excited. She merely embraced Liss, changed her frock, embraced Liss again, changed her frock again, and dashed off to Victoria. After that her recollection of events went out of focus a little. She had watched the arrival of the Leave-train so often merely as a benevolent spectator, that sudden and personal participation in that function disarranged her perspectives.

She caught sight of Roy almost at once—singling out his glengarry from among the flat caps and steel helmets. He was politely resisting the importunity of an elderly gentleman in a grey uniform and a red brassard, bent on luring him to a free ride upon the Underground Railway. Next moment, Marjorie had slipped her arm through his. After that, neither of them remembered anything much until they found themselves sitting hand in hand in a taxi, gliding stealthily through the darkened streets of London, both feeling a little constrained and embarrassed. Re-united lovers, especially of our nation, do not always spark immediately on contact. We are a highly-insulated race.

"They keep this old place pretty dark," said Roy, peering out of the cab window. "Zeppelins, I suppose?"

"Yes. We had some last week."

"Have you ever seen one?"

"Rather!"

Roy laughed, constrainedly.

"It's funny you should have seen something in this war that I haven't," he said. "Where are we going?"

"To my flat."

Roy turned and surveyed Marjorie's profile in the dim light of the cab.

"I shall be able to see you properly then," he announced with satisfaction. "It's as dark as the inside of a cow here. Have you changed at all, I wonder?"

"You will find I am quite a big girl now," replied Marjorie, laughing constrainedly.

Roy laughed too, and his face came closer to hers. Her hair brushed his lips. Next moment their arms were about one another.

Five minutes later, they groped their way mechanically upstairs to Marjorie's landing, while a slightly incredulous taxi-driver, with one of the newly-invented pound notes in his oily palm, drove hurriedly away before somebody came out of the chloroform.

"You are thinner, dear, and older—much older," was Marjorie's verdict when they found themselves under the lamp by the sofa. "You look more like thirty than twenty. I expect things have been pretty awful sometimes, haven't they?"

Roy nodded. "Yes, sometimes," he said. "I'll tell you about it one day." Then, suddenly and boyishly: "Dearest, you look wonderful!"

It was no more than the truth. Marjorie had felt tired enough a couple of hours ago; but now her cheeks were pink, and her eyes glowed. Her hair had suddenly recovered its lustre. For the first time in six months she looked what she was—twenty. But she realised that the old Roy could never come back to her. Her smooth-cheeked schoolboy was gone, and in his place she had a man—thin as a lath, healthily bronzed, and curiously grave. The Western Front lost no time in making a man in those days—or breaking him.

They kissed again, with absolute lack of shyness this time. Suddenly a thought struck Marjorie.

"Good gracious!" she cried. "What time is it?"

"Seven o'clock. Why?"

"My dear—the theatre! I'd forgotten all about it. I am an honest working girl, and the curtain goes up at eight-thirty!"

"By gum!" said Roy, who of course knew all about "Too Many Girls." "*Absent from parade when warned for duty*, eh? That will never do. What about it? Can't you get a night off?"

"I might," said Marjorie doubtfully. "Most of the girls send a doctor's certificate. But I don't think it's the game. They overdo it so."

"Quite right!" said that young disciplinarian, Lieutenant Birnie. "But it's a bit rough, all the same."

A key rattled loudly and tactfully in the outer door, which then opened with mature deliberation, and Liss appeared.

"I hadn't meant to butt in," she explained, after introductions, "but I just want to say that I have seen Lancaster, and he says you can have the night off. I told him about you," she explained to Roy, "and he said you could have her this evening if you promised faithfully to send her back for to-morrow's show."

"I will bring her back myself," replied Roy, "and buy the whole front row to watch her from!"

"Righto! Good-bye, children! Enjoy yourselves!" said Liss, and vanished, like a diplomatic little wraith.

After that, Roy and Marjorie sat down to make plans.

"First of all," began Roy, "I must hop off to the club and order a bed and have a hot bath—a real hot bath! *Sah vah song dearie*, as we say at the Quai D'Orsay. My last one was in a little house somewhere behind Albert, in a sort of zinc coffin in front of the kitchen stove, with the family sitting tactfully in the scullery. But I am digressing: let us resume! After that, we will go and dine somewhere. By the way, I suppose there is still plenty of food to be had in these days?"

"There is a shortage of potatoes at present, I am sorry to say," replied Marjorie in her best canteen manner. "But—"

"We can worry along without potatoes," said Roy. "What I chiefly want is to dine off a table covered with a white cloth instead of a newspaper; and drink out of a glass instead of a tin cup. I think the Carlton will meet the case. Oh, my dear, my dear! I can't believe it all yet! Are you *really* here?" ...

At this rate of progress it was nine o'clock before they sat down to the feast, which was served to them by an obsequious neutral in a corner of the big restaurant. It was a luxurious dinner for war time, though bully beef and stewed tea would have served equally well. Reunited lovers are not, as a rule, fastidious.

They talked steadily now, unfolding reminiscence after reminiscence. Roy had most to tell; for Marjorie's adventures had been faithfully recorded in her daily letters, while Roy, as previously noted, had usually confined himself to breezy irrelevance.

"Uncle Alan is in command now," he said. "I suppose you heard that the Colonel had been knocked out?"

"Colonel Bethune? Yes, I saw it in the paper." To her own annoyance, Marjorie felt her colour rising. But Roy noticed nothing.

"Yes, he stopped a five-point-nine with his left arm on the second day of the Somme show, and went home without it. We were in a pretty tight place at the time, and it was a bit of a job getting him away. But I hear he's all right again now, though short of a fin. Have you seen him by any chance?"

"Not since April," said Marjorie. "He was in London then, on leave." She was feeling thoroughly self-conscious, and despised herself for it.

"They gave him a bar to his D.S.O.," continued Roy. "He deserved it too, for what he did."

"What did he do?" asked Marjorie jealously. She was a little critical of a system which gave a decoration to a man for getting wounded and coming home, and nothing to those who had to remain and carry on.

"We were right up in the air," explained Roy, "uncovered on both flanks. We did not know where we were; Brigade Headquarters didn't know where we were, so couldn't reinforce us; and the gunners didn't know where we were, so couldn't fire for fear of hitting us. The only person who really knew where we were was the Boche—a well-informed little fellow, the Boche!—and he gave it to us good and hard. But the Colonel was wonderful. We had no cover in particular, beyond a kneeling-trench which we had scooped out for ourselves. There was no room for any officer to pass up and down, so we all stayed where we found ourselves, as ordered, and controlled our fire as well as possible. But the Colonel came walking to us across the open from Battalion Headquarters—an old mine-crater about a hundred yards in rear of us—and strolled right along our whole front from end to end, with Boche snipers taking pot-shots at him all the time; looking as if he had just come out of his tailor's—he had *gloves* on!—stopping here and there to talk to the men, and telling them that no battalion of the Covenanters had ever been known to go back, and that reinforcements were coming up, and how pleased he was to see us so steady. (We weren't feeling a bit steady, really.) The trenches were full of wounded men whom we couldn't get away. He stopped and spoke to them all—by name!—and gave them cigarettes. The result was that when the Boche attacked, our fellows fought like tigers. It was after the attack got round our undefended flanks that the hard time began. Finally, their gunners got our range, and simply blew us out of the trench. Even then the C.O. wouldn't give in. He stood on the parapet, giving fire orders as cool as you please, and telling us how well we were doing. Finally he was hit. They carried him away on a blanket, insensible, and Uncle Alan took command. By this time we were surrounded on three sides—enfiladed, and everything. Uncle Alan passed word along that we were to fall back slowly to our proper place in the line."

"Your proper place?"

"Yes. I forgot to tell you about that. We had overrun our objective, it seemed. Everybody else in the brigade was snugly dug in about half a mile behind us, on a continuous line, except for a gap that we ought to have been filling. We got there at last, but it was a pretty awful walk. We got all our wounded away, though."

"Were there many?"

"A good lot. It was bad luck getting into that position at all. However, we got a tremendous pat on the back from the Divisional Commander afterwards. Apparently there had been some misunderstanding about orders. Now let us talk about something else."

And that was as much as was ever told of the story of how Eric Bethune's lofty contempt for the "book of the words" led a fine battalion into a skilfully baited death-trap.

After that they talked, as lovers will, of the present. They even spoke of the future—a subject upon which, in those days, few young people cared to hazard conjecture in cold blood. But to-night their blood ran hot and high. The world was theirs—for six days.

"To-morrow morning," continued Roy, with an air of immense authority, "I shall take you out and buy you an engagement ring. It is perfectly scandalous your going about with me in this way without one! (Still, I suppose you will have to wear it round your neck on a string, anyway!) After that, a little shopping! I suppose there will be no harm if I buy you some things—long gloves, and high-heel shoes, and silk stockings, and things like that? We'll throw in a nice sensible umbrella, as a chaperon! Then in the evening we will dine early, so as to give you plenty of time to get to your show."

Marjorie laid her slim fingers upon Roy's brown paw.

"Darling," she said firmly, "to-morrow morning I am going to take you to a railway station, and you are going to take the train to Scotland, to see your father!"

Roy's face fell ludicrously. Then the smile he had inherited from his mother came suddenly back. He was all contrition.

"Good Heavens! You had me there, dear. I own up! For the last twenty-four hours my noble parent has entirely escaped my memory. As soon as they told me that I could go on leave I simply grabbed my haversack, asked the Buzzers to send a wire, and then sprinted for the railhead. Poor old dad! Of course you're right. I haven't had a line from him for six weeks, by the way. I'll send a telegram to Baronrigg at once, and start to-morrow." Then he added anxiously:

"How long must I stay?"

Marjorie considered.

"Your father doesn't know anything about *me*, of course?" she said.

"No; nobody knows. It's our secret—ours, and no one else's!" The impulsive pair squeezed hands upon the secret, instantly revealing it to the obsequious neutral aforementioned. "Still, perhaps it would be as well if I told him, eh? Then he couldn't object to my coming back here pretty quick."

"Supposing he doesn't approve?" said Marjorie doubtfully. "He doesn't know me—nor my people, so far as I am aware. Or perhaps he does, which might be worse!"

"My old dad's a white man," said Roy stoutly. "He'd understand. He knows what it is for a fellow to have to go without. He once had to endure seeing his girl—my mother—engaged to another man for several months. He'll understand, all right!"

"I never knew that," said Marjorie. "Who was the other man?"

"Colonel Bethune. Of course he was only a subaltern then."

"*Who?*" Marjorie was fairly startled out of herself this time.

"Eric Bethune, our C.O. I thought that would surprise you! I never knew myself until a few months ago. Uncle Alan told me. The Colonel has always been rather heavily down on me—I never knew why—and one day when I was more than usually fed up with things in general, having just been informed by my commanding officer that I was not fit to hold the King's Commission, old Uncle Alan told me all about it. He explained that the Colonel didn't really think me a dud soldier; he was only peeved at not being my father. Fancy disliking a fellow for that! It's a queer world!"

Queer indeed! Marjorie, better informed than Roy, mused upon the diabolical trick of fate which had caused a man to be baulked of the only thing that really matters by two successive generations—first by the father, then by the son. For the first time she felt a genuine pang of pity for Eric Bethune. But it passed, in a flash. Eric was "heavily down on" Roy—her Roy! All her generous soul revolted at the pettiness of such a revenge.

"I often wondered," continued Roy, "why my mother broke it off. I don't believe Uncle Alan knew. Why was it, do you think?"

"I don't know," said Marjorie. But she did.

Five minutes later they arrived at the theatre where the musical comedy—or musical tragedy: you never know—of their choice was in progress. The vestibule was deserted, but Roy held open the swing door and ushered Marjorie into the darkened auditorium. A blast of hot air and a concerted feminine screech greeted them.

"The curtain's up," said Roy. "Come along! Our seats are in the back row, on the gangway. Rotten, but convenient!"

They slipped unostentatiously into their places. The company were massed upon the stage; the orchestra was in full cry; the young persons of the Chorus were in a state of unwonted animation. In the centre, a lady of ravishing beauty was melting into the arms of a distinguished-looking individual just over military age. Humourists supported either flank.

"This is going to be some show!" announced Roy, groping for Marjorie's hand, and surveying the chorus with all the appreciation of a Robinson Crusoe of six months' standing. "I shouldn't mind being Adjutant of *that* battalion! Not that any of them could walk down the same street with you! Hallo, hallo! What's all this? The interval! We must have come in late."

The curtain fell, and the audience, with one accord, rose to their feet and made for the doors. The band offered a hurried tribute to the Crown. Roy looked at his watch, and turned to Marjorie with a comical grimace.

"Eleven o'clock!" he announced. "We must have sat over dinner a bit longer than we thought. The show's over! Does it matter?"

"Nothing in the world matters—this week!" said Marjorie, taking his arm.

CHAPTER XII
TOM BIRNIE
I

Roy was duly despatched to Scotland the following morning.

"When does your leave end?" Marjorie asked, as they waited for the crowded train to start.

"Let me see—this is Friday. I go back by the leave-train next Wednesday afternoon—"

"Then travel back here on Sunday night," said Marjorie; "unless, of course, you can persuade your father to come back with you at once."

Roy pondered.

"I don't know," he said, "that it wouldn't be better to stick the week-end out at Baronrigg, and then come back alone, and have you all to myself."

Your true lover is an uncompromising egotist. Marjorie at once recognised the superiority of Roy's view.

"All right," she said. "There's the whistle! Get into the train, little man. Send me a telegram when you arrive."

She watched the long train crawl out of sight, and went back to the flat with a hungry heart. Six days! And she had to give him up for three of them! Still, it was the game.

But she had not to wait so long. Roy burst into the flat about noon the very next day—to the entire *bouleversement* of Liss, who was a dilatory dresser. Redirected by her (from behind the bathroom door) he sought Marjorie at the canteen, dragged her almost forcibly out to lunch, and communicated his news in a breath.

"Baronrigg is closed up tight! Has been for six weeks! Dad put all his affairs into order at the beginning of last month, and disappeared!"

"Disappeared? What do you mean?"

"Well, he simply shut up the house, gave what servants were left by the war a year's wages, walked to the station, and took the train for London. He hasn't been heard of since."

"But where has he gone?"

"Nobody knows!"

"Was he ill, or anything?"

"No. By all accounts he was as hard as nails and as fit as a fiddle."

"But didn't he leave any message?" asked Marjorie, bewildered.

"Yes," replied Roy, unbuttoning his tunic pocket, "he did. This letter, for me. I got it from old Gillespie at the Bank. I expect Dad knew I'd pop in there!"

"But doesn't it explain?" asked Marjorie.

"I don't know," said Roy calmly. "I haven't opened it yet."

"You have had it for a day and a night, and haven't opened it?"

"No. I wanted to wait until you and I could read it together."

"But weren't you dying of curiosity?"

"I was, rather. Still, I said to myself—"

Marjorie slipped her arm impulsively into his.

"Roy, dearest," she said, "*I* could never have done that!"

It was the first and last time Marjorie ever admitted to Roy that her sex was in any way inferior to his. They returned to the flat and read the letter together. That is to say, Roy read it aloud to Marjorie:

My dear Son,

You will remember that when the war broke out I was among those who thought it might have been avoided. I was also numbered among those who thought it would be a short war. I was wrong in both views.

My errors did not end there. I was not in favour of the raising of a great army. My opinion was that we should limit our efforts to the efficient policing of the seas, the supplying of munitions and equipment to France and Russia, and the enforcement of a great commercial blockade against the enemy. Neither honour nor interest, I said, demanded more of us. When our young men left all and followed the Colours without, as it seemed to me, pausing to reason why, I was inclined to regard them as hysterical Jingoes.

"I remember him saying that," observed Roy. "We had quite a battle before he would let me apply for a commission."

The war has now been in progress for two years. My first purpose in writing to you is to acknowledge to you that in your conception of national duty you, my son, were right and, I, your father, was wrong.

"It was decent of him to put in that," said Roy, looking up again.

I realise now that not only was the war inevitable, but that unless we make a superhuman effort as a nation we shall not win it. That realisation, unfortunately, is not universal in this district. Most of our people have done magnificently, and I shall always be proud to think that my only son was among the first and the youngest to volunteer.

"This," commented Roy, "is darned embarrassing to read aloud."

"Go on!" commanded Marjorie: "I love it!"

Indeed, the effort has been too great. Too high a tax has been levied on spontaneous loyalty. The general enthusiasm of the country has not been maintained. Consequently the best of our stock, both gentle and simple, is bearing the burden alone, at a cost which is ruining the future of the country.

That brings me to the second thing I have to say to you. In this very neighbourhood there are many blind optimists, many drifters, many irritating phrase-mongers, and a certain number of so-called Conscientious Objectors to warfare.

"He must have met Amos!" said Marjorie.

These latter are not dangerous: their very cowardice makes it easy to deal with them. Far more pernicious are the optimists, the drifters, and the phrase-mongers. Yesterday, at a meeting of the Territorial Association, I met a typical specimen—Mr. Sanders, of Braefoot. You may know him.

"I do," said Roy, grinning. "A celebrated captain of industry, now a county magnate—Nineteen-Thirteen vintage!"

This man said to me: "Sir Thomas, what I like about the situation is the way we are all doing our bit. I, for instance, have been working overtime on Government contracts for two years. I have bought nearly one hundred thousand pounds worth of War Bonds, and I have given seven nephews to the Army. Pretty good, eh?" By what authority, or with whose knowledge, he had presented other men's sons to the Army he did not explain.

Roy, I am ashamed of such people. But who am I to be ashamed of anyone but myself for not realising sooner—as soon as you—that in this sacred cause of ours there is only one thing that counts, and that is personal service? I am sound in wind and limb, and I have no helpless dependents. To-morrow I am going to London to join the Army. As an earnest of the fact that I do so in the spirit of humility and contrition, and not from any desire to pose or advertise, I shall communicate my intention to no one but yourself. I shall enlist as a private soldier, but in a unit where I am not likely to meet any one I know; and I pray God that he will enable me to serve my country as effectively as my own dear son.

Roy's voice shook a little. He had just made his father's acquaintance.

Should I not come back, you will find my affairs in perfect order, and Baronrigg waiting for you. Your trustees are Lord Eskerley and Alan Laing. Should neither of us come back—

"Don't read any more, dear," said Marjorie.

"All right!" replied Roy. "That's practically all now." He folded the letter and put it away in his tunic.

"I wish," he added thoughtfully—"I wish fathers and sons could get to know one another a bit better while they have the chance!" Then, "I wonder what regiment he enlisted in! I wonder if we shall ever meet out there! I'm sorry he didn't see you before he went. You'd have liked him, I think."

"I like him now," said Marjorie, with shining eyes. "I think he's splendid! And"—she broke into a happy laugh—"I like him particularly at this moment, because he has given you to me for four days more instead of two!"

"Let's go shopping!" said Roy, rising importantly.

II

After a gloriously deliberate start, the six days, as usual, gathered momentum. The last forty-eight hours whizzed by like an eighteen-pounder shell.

On Wednesday morning Roy, once more equipped in mud-stained khaki and bristling with portable property, appeared at the flat for breakfast at nine o'clock. Marjorie was ready for him. Liss joined the party a little later. For all her feather-head, she was no mean tactician. Having conscientiously effaced herself throughout the week, instinct now told her that her presence at the parting breakfast would be a good thing. So she uprooted herself from her beloved bed, and entered upon the task of distracting the lovers from the contemplation of the immediate future.

"I thought it was just time," she announced to Roy, "to bring myself to your notice a little. I am here, you know! I have been here most of the week, only I don't think you observed me very much."

"Oh, yes, I did," replied Roy gallantly. "Who could help it?"

"Well, you could—and did! I don't much like being in the same room with people who don't know I'm there. It's not safe. You walked straight through me the other afternoon, when you called to collect Marjorie. And the day before that, when I opened the door to you, you wiped your feet on me! I've had a wonderful week!"

With such blunt shafts of wit as these Miss Lyle ultimately provoked the lovers to a smile.

"That's better!" she said. "Now, next time you come home on leave, give us longer notice, and I will warn Leonard, or somebody, for duty. Then I shan't feel such an outsider."

Roy promised to do so.

"You will take care of Marjorie, won't you?" he added.

Miss Lyle favoured him with a gaze of withering wonder.

"You have been trying to take care of her yourself most of this week, haven't you?" she demanded.

"I have been doing my best," admitted Roy, cautiously.

"Very well, then! What happened? How did it end?"

"It ended, I think," confessed Roy, "in her taking care of me!"

Liss nodded her bobbed head triumphantly. "That's it," she said. "That's what always happens to people who try to take care of Marjie. She grabs them by the neck, puts them in her pocket, and keeps them there! That's what she'll do to me again, when you're gone. It's no good my pretending I ever do anything for her."

"Nonsense!" said Marjorie.

"But I'll tell you what," continued Liss: "I'll see she doesn't take care of anybody else while you're away—if I can. That's her trouble: she'd take care of the whole army, and navy, and munition people, and Red Cross, and everything, if she was let! But I'll watch her, and save the leavings for you!" She glanced at the clock, and rose. "Now, children, your Auntie Liss is going to leave you! Tactful—that's me! When is your train, General?"

"Two o'clock," said Roy. "I fancy we sail from Folkestone about six."

"Then," inquired Liss, playing a carefully hoarded ace of trumps, "why not go down to Folkestone *now*, both of you, by the morning train? That way you would have her until nearly six, instead of two. It's all right; don't thank me!" she concluded pathetically, as Marjorie, without a word, dived into the bedroom for her hat, and Roy began to struggle madly into his equipment.

III

They spent the bleak November afternoon on the Leas at Folkestone. At their feet lay the Straits of Dover, across whose waters British soldiers had come and gone for twenty-six months, and continued to come and go for twenty-five more, without the loss of a single soldier's life. But they could not see their feet that afternoon: their heads were in the clouds—private clouds, to which we will not presume to follow them.

As the autumn darkness fell, they took an early dinner in an almost empty hotel hard by the harbour, talking cheerfully of things that did not matter. Roy ordered champagne, and they drank a silent toast with a fleeting glance over the rims of their glasses.

"When does my train start?" asked Marjorie at length. "Don't forget that I have to be back for the evening performance."

Roy would inquire.

"Half-past five, from the Town station," he announced on returning. "That's some way from here. I have ordered a car, and if we start now I can go with you and see you off. That will give me just time to hop into the official leave-train coming down from London. It stops at Folkestone Town to turn round, and then backs right down to the boat."

Once more the parting was staved off. However, one cannot go on pilfering minutes eternally. This time it really was good-bye. It was half-past five; and they stood on the Town station platform.

"This is your train," said Roy, "standing here. Mine is due at the other platform now. There goes the signal! I must skip across the bridge. So—"

He drew Marjorie behind a friendly pile of luggage.

"It has been wonderful, Roy dear—wonderful!" For a moment she laid her head on Roy's breast. "But we did one stupid thing."

"What was that?"

"We ought to have got married!"

"I never thought of it," said Roy simply. "We were so happy, there didn't seem to be anything else."

"But we'll remember next time!" said Marjorie.

"I will give the matter my personal attention!" Roy assured her. "So-long, and take care of yourself!"

CHAPTER XIII
ALBERT CLEGG

In the early summer of Nineteen-Seventeen Uncle Fred paid a prolonged visit to Netherby—ostensibly to renew family ties, in reality for reasons not altogether unconnected with air-raids on London.

For the moment the fortunes of the war were back in the melting pot. The Battle of the Somme had bundled Brother Boche right back to the Siegfried Line, and enemy morale on the Western Front was low. The British army, fortified by twelve months of conscription, was blundering forward in characteristic fashion upon many fronts. The navy had swelled to a size undreamed of by any, and known only to few. Over the British coast alone nearly three thousand vessels of all sorts and conditions were keeping watch. The "Q" boat, too, with its crazy crew of immortals, was abroad upon the face of the waters, and the hunter had become the hunted.

But there was much to be set down upon the contra side. The spring offensive of the French army, after a brilliant beginning, had faltered, then halted. There had been recriminations, inquiries, resignations; and Pétain, the saviour of Verdun, had succeeded the gallant Nivelle. To keep the enemy from benefiting by the sudden relaxation of pressure on the Chemin des Dames the British army had flung itself into the premature Battle of Arras, and once more the casualty lists had shot up.

At home, the talk was mainly of Gothas—the Zeppelin was entirely *démodé*—and ration cards. The war was costing us six million pounds a day. Income tax at six shillings in the pound was teaching the man of moderate means the meaning of war; super-tax and excess profits tax were subjecting the capitalistic waistcoat to a not unsalutary reduction. Labour—or rather what was left, now that all that was best and soundest in Labour was away fighting—was going on strike periodically and with invariable success for more adequate recognition of its efforts to furnish the sinews of war to its wasteful and unproductive brothers in the trenches.

In Russia the Empire, battered from without and all corroded within, had collapsed upon itself; and an earnest but unpractical gentleman named Kerensky was rapidly undermining what was left of Russian staying-power, and, with the enthusiastic assistance of the German General Staff, paving the way for those great twin brethren, Lenin and Trotsky. One jaw of the vice which had been crushing the Hun to death was relaxed for good.

Still, there was no weakening on the Western Front. The Messines Ridge had recently "gone up," with a bang which had warmed the heart of every schoolboy in that schoolboy army, the British Expeditionary Force. The Salient of Ypres, that graveyard of British soldiers and German hopes, stood more inviolate than ever. Bagdad had been captured: Palestine was being freed. And in France, down in the Vosges, within the great quadrilateral formed by Chaumont, Toul, Vittel, and Ligny-en-Barrois, huge cantonments were being run up, and roads and railways laid down, by long-legged, slim-hipped, slow-speaking, workmanlike young men from a vast continent overseas—the forerunners of an army of indefinite millions which had pledged itself to come and redress the final balance at no very distant date.

But all this did not prevent London from being an extremely uncomfortable, not to say unsafe, place of residence for a high official of the noble army of Bomb-Dodgers. Finally, after a Gotha raid over London in broad daylight one bright morning in July, in which fifty-seven people were killed, Uncle Fred decided that it was no longer either just or prudent to risk a valuable life further, and went to Netherby, where he succeeded without any difficulty whatever in outstaying his welcome by a considerable margin.

Netherby itself was not over-cheerful, even though the master of the house was absent a good deal. Albert Clegg spent most of his time in those days on Tyneside, making himself liable to excess profits tax. Amos, his eldest son, who from early boyhood had cultivated the valuable habit of keeping one ear to the ground, was by this time in Glasgow, safely embedded in a convenient stronghold labelled "Civilian War Work of National Importance." Brother Joe was far away, as happy as a sandboy—and living like one—assisting General Allenby to construct a military railway from Beersheba to Dan. The younger members of the family were occupied in making unserviceable articles for the Red Cross, and complaining of the shortage of sugar. Mrs. Clegg faithfully attended committee meetings and gatherings where bandages were rolled and inside information imparted. Craigfoot lay remote from the tumult of war, though Edinburgh to the north, and Tynemouth to the south, had each been soundly bombed. Still, there was no lack of military atmosphere. Colonel Bethune himself—minus an arm, and with a bar to his D.S.O.—was back in command of the depot, an object of respectful worship to the entire community; and was always ready and willing to enlarge upon the situation, whether to an attentive mess or to a casually encountered ploughman. His august mother, Lady Christina, specialised upon the crimes of the Government, and had it on reliable authority that the counsels of the Cabinet were now entirely directed from Potsdam. Men on leave came and went, with tales of glory and gloom. Many of the girls were in London or in France; and there were countless letters to quote. Mrs. Clegg sat and listened to the babble of rumour and conjecture, shyly contributing here and there an excerpt from Palestine. Joe had never been home since his clandestine enlistment, but as the event had proved that conscription would have claimed him in any case, his father had decided to forgive him.

Marjorie's name was never mentioned at Netherby, by decree of the master of the house. With Mrs. Clegg—gentle, submissive, colourless—to yield in act was to yield in opinion. She possessed the faculty (recently enjoined, with indifferent success, upon an entire nation) of being "neutral even in thought." She accepted Marjorie's excommunication as she would have accepted her death, or any other form of irrevocability.

It was the last day of Uncle Fred's hegira. On the morrow he was to return, to face the dangers of Dulwich. Evening prayers had been concluded, and Albert Clegg was setting the markers in the Bible for to-morrow morning's exercises. Suddenly he looked up, and spoke:

"Fred!"

"Yes, Albert?"

"When you return to London I shall be obliged to you if you will make inquiries about my daughter."

Uncle Fred sat up—his back perfectly straight for the first time for many years. Mrs. Clegg's knitting dropped from her fingers. No one else was present. Only children remained at Netherby, and they had gone to bed.

"I have been thinking matters over," announced Albert, in measured tones. "I try to be a just man in all my dealings. It is one year to-day since the news came to me that my daughter had taken to—her present ways. By this time her punishment has possibly begun. It is not my intention to intervene between her and her Maker; but I have decided that there can be no harm in taking steps to ascertain what has become of her."

Mrs. Clegg caught her breath. Uncle Fred, utterly dazed, wagged his beard weakly.

"That's very handsome of you, Albert," he said respectfully.

"Handsomeness has nothing to do with it!" snapped Albert, among whose rare and austere amusements none was more prized than that of keeping his younger brother in his place. "I am simply doing what I consider to be right and just. Now, when you return to London I want you to institute inquiries as to where my daughter is to be found. If you are successful, I wish you to visit her. I should not like to think that she was actually destitute. Of course, she can never return here, but I can see that she is provided for."

There was silence. Then Uncle Fred inquired, after the fashion of all feeble folk:

"How should I set about finding her? London is a big place. I suppose the police—"

"I will not have the police brought into the matter until absolutely necessary," thundered Albert. "You must search the theatres!"

It was a magnificent suggestion, but too daring for Albert's audience—certainly for Uncle Fred.

"I have never been inside a theatre in my life," he objected.

"Neither have I. But you need not go inside. Enquire at the door whether my daughter is employed there. Demand to see the manager!"

"Do you think he will tell me?"

"Threaten him with the law if he won't. These fellows are usually under police observation, in any case. They won't dare to fight."

"Perhaps a word with the stage-door keeper—" suggested Mrs. Clegg timidly.

"There's no need for Fred to get mixed up with the dissolute crowd that hangs round stage-doors," was the stern reply. "He'll go in by the front!"

Uncle Fred, flattered on the whole at being still regarded as a potential profligate, hastened to associate himself with this sentiment. But at heart he felt a little ashamed. There were elements of the dare-devil about Uncle Fred. Still, he reflected, he could take his own line of action when he got back to London. He propounded another conundrum.

"Supposing she isn't in one of the theatres—what then? Would it be any good trying the churches? She may be attending some place of worship regularly."

"If she is, it is bound to be Church of England; and I don't intend to be beholden to that body for *any* help!" replied Albert firmly. "You might try the Salvation Army. Their rescue work brings them in contact with every walk of life—the West End restaurants and clubs, and haunts of that kind."

The implied spectacle of Uncle Fred, assisted by a contingent of Hallelujah Lasses, raiding the Athenæum or The Popular Café, for a lost niece was not without its humour; but the paths of humour and righteousness converge too seldom, to their mutual detriment.

"When you find her," concluded Albert, "ascertain quietly what her circumstances are, and report to me. I will then decide what it is best for me to do."

Uncle Fred, duly uplifted, wagged his head with increased solemnity.

"I must say, Albert," he announced, "even though it angers you, that you are acting in a very generous manner."

"Yes, father," added Mrs. Clegg wistfully.

In a watery way, her heart yearned over her daughter.

"Nothing of the kind!" said Clegg. "I am merely acting as my conscience directs me. These are demoralising times for the best of us"—perhaps Albert's excess profits were pricking him—"and we must make certain allowances. Of course, having acted the way she has, after her Christian upbringing, she can never expect forgiveness. But—well, I shall wait until I hear from you, Fred."

CHAPTER XIV
TWO SPARROWS

I

Marjorie was one of those who were "able to proceed to their own homes after receiving surgical aid." Others were not so fortunate. The Mouldy Old Copper—badly wounded by splinters of glass, and excoriating the entire Teutonic race with a failing tongue but unabated spirit—was borne off to St. Thomas's Hospital, followed by others. The canteen had been moderately full at the time, and more than one soldier home on leave had had his leave indefinitely prolonged by the visitation. Providentially, no one was killed; the bomb had fallen just too far down the street.

The raid took place on a Sunday evening, during Marjorie's one period of night duty in the week. (In this way, she gave herself one clear weekday for fresh air and exercise.) They kept her at the hospital until she had breakfasted, then dispatched her homeward, with instructions to return daily as an out-patient until further notice.

She walked across Westminster Bridge in the morning sunshine, feeling badly shaken, but not a little proud. Few of us ever outgrow a childish thrill at finding our arm in a sling. Not only was Marjorie's arm in a sling, but her right shoulder was bandaged. ("Just missed your carotid artery, my dear," had been the comment of the elderly house surgeon.) She felt gloriously conspicuous. A 'bus-load of convalescent soldiers in hospital blue recognised her as one of the elect, and inquired affectionately whether she had been out in a trench raid. She waved her sound arm in cordial acknowledgment of the pleasantry. Roy would be interested to hear about this. On second thoughts, no. Roy never told her when he had had an escape; she must maintain Roy's standard of reticence.

She walked jauntily into the flat, and sat down, a little suddenly, upon the feet of Miss Elizabeth Lyle, who, as already noted, was usually insensible until about eleven a.m. Liss rolled over with a resigned sigh, poked her *nez retroussé* out from under the sheet, and remarked meekly:

"All right! Give me just five minutes more, and I promise—My goodness gracious, Marjie, what *have* you been doing to yourself?"

Marjorie described the raid. She told the tale as lightly as she could, with humorous touches here and there; for she had seen human blood flow freely, and was feverishly conscious of a desire to get the picture out of her mind. Gradually the narrative became more frivolous, the touches more and more humorous. Finally, the narratress grew so amused with the recollection of her own experiences that she threw her head back and laughed loud and long.

Liss slipped hurriedly out of bed, put both arms round her uproarious friend, and laid her by main force in the place which she had just vacated.

"You stay there, dearie," she said. "They ought never to have let you out."

"The hospital was so full!" Marjorie was shivering all over now, and battling with an inclination to tears. "They said that they were very sorry—*very* sorry—very sorry indeed—but—"

"That's all right!" said little Liss soothingly, covering her up, and patting her undamaged arm. "I'll make you a good, strong cup of tea, and then you will have a nice sleep, and you'll wake up as right as ninepence! I'll slip round to the theatre and tell them they needn't expect to see you again for a week or two. The show is going to close soon, anyhow."

"I don't care if it does!" murmured Marjorie, her head on Liss's pillow. She did not even trouble to cross the room to her own bed. "I have learnt one thing in the last year, and that is that I am not cut out for the stage. It bores me. I was meant to stay at home, and look after little people like you—and Roy! *That's* what I—"

She settled down like a tired child, and fell sound asleep. Liss snatched some apparel from a chair, padded out of the room in her bare feet, and closed a door gently for about the first time in her life.

II

Marjorie woke up in the afternoon—herself again, but stiff and bruised. She rose, and entered the sitting-room. Liss was lying on the sofa, reading the *Daily Mirror* and smoking a cigarette. She sprang up on seeing Marjorie, and flew to her, stopping just in time.

"Sorry, duckie!" she said. "I must remember that arm of yours. Are you feeling all right again?"

"Splendid!" said Marjorie. "What time is it?"

"About four."

"Let us have some tea then, and I'll go round to the hospital and get my arm dressed again. Hallo, it's raining!"

"Yes; it has been pouring ever since eleven o'clock this morning," said Liss; and coughed.

Marjorie turned upon her sharply. Liss was one of those persons to whom coughing is a forbidden luxury.

"Liss," she cried, "you're soaking! Every rag you have on is sticking to you! What's the matter?" She began to fumble at the back of the child's blouse. "Here, undress yourself! I have only one hand."

"I got a bit wet when I went out to the theatre," said Liss airily.

"But why on earth didn't you—" Marjorie glanced towards the bedroom door, and stopped abruptly. She understood. "I see," she said, "you didn't want—? Was that it? How long have you been like this?"

"Oh, not long," Liss assured her; and coughed again.

III

Marjorie, returning from her alternative role of out-patient to resume that of head nurse, walked into the flat, and sat down heavily on Liss.

"How are you feeling this morning, Baby?" she inquired.

"Top-hole!" replied the invalid.

Three weeks had passed. Liss was now convalescent; but congestion of the lungs is not a malady to be taken lightly, especially by little wraiths with weak chests. Marjorie herself had nearly shaken off the shock-effect of the raid. Her arm was still lightly bandaged.

"It's a lovely day," she said. "I will take you for a bus ride this afternoon, if you're good. Meanwhile, I want to have a pow-wow with you." Marjorie had picked up this expression from Roy, and was rather proud of it.

"What about?"

"Well—have you any money?"

"I thought there'd be a catch about it," said Liss, reaching out to the little table beside her bed for the bag in which the young woman of to-day is reputed to keep everything but the kitchen stove. "Let me see!" she said. She laid out on the counterpane a cigarette-case bearing a regimental crest, a match-case bearing another, entirely different, a long cigarette-holder, a powder-puff box, a lip-stick, and a diminutive handkerchief. "Now we're getting down to business!" she announced encouragingly. "Here's a shilling—a threepenny bit—and four pennies. Wait a minute! Here's a crumpled up thing here that might be a Bradbury. No, it's a note from Reggie. I suppose I oughtn't to keep that now!"

Liss tore up the *billet-doux* with a sentimental sigh. It may be noted in passing that her engagement to Master Leonard had terminated some months previously by mutual and violent consent. A subsequent contract of eternal fidelity to a young gentleman in the Royal Flying Corps—one Reginald Bensham—had recently been dissolved, by unanimous vote. At present Miss Lyle's affections were disengaged.

"One and sevenpence!" she announced. "You can search me for more!"

"That's rather a blow," said Marjorie.

"Are we running short?" asked Liss. "Of course we must be, both having been out of a job for three weeks. But I thought—"

"So did I," replied Marjorie. "I thought we had a nest-egg in the bank at my home in Scotland. I haven't touched it for a year, because I wanted it to accumulate for a rainy day. On Monday I came to the conclusion that our present days were rainy enough—there's the doctor's bill, for one thing—so I wrote to Mr. Gillespie, the manager, and asked what my balance was. I got his answer this morning."

"I hate to ask—but what is the balance?"

Marjorie smiled dismally.

"That's just it! There isn't any balance at all! Just a few odd shillings. My father seems to have cut off my allowance about a year ago. I wonder why? At least, if he was going to do it at all I wonder why he didn't do it in the very beginning. However, we won't worry about that. The situation is, that you have one and sevenpence, and I have about two pounds ten."

"Two pounds ten, and one and sevenpence—that's about two pounds fifteen," announced Liss, after a brief calculation. "We can live for weeks on that. Before it's gone we shall be back in a job again."

"I shan't let you take a job again for a long time, my dear," said Marjorie. "They won't have much use for me, either; I can't lift my arm above my shoulder at present. How could I hold up the Torch of Liberty in the last act?"

"We'll rub along," announced the small optimist in the bed. "If the worst came to the worst, I could always get engaged again. There's a perfectly sweet boy in the Tanks—"

But Marjorie's hand was over Liss's mouth. "Baby, remember you don't get engaged again without my permission!"

"All right!" mumbled Liss. "Have it your own way! But what about your Roy? Can't you raise a small subscription out of him? That would be quite O.K., wouldn't it? You're going to marry—" Suddenly Liss sat up in bed, for she had caught sight of Marjorie's face. "Why, what's the matter, dear?" she asked.

"I haven't heard a word from him for five weeks," said Marjorie in a low voice. "I'm most awfully unhappy, Liss."

Liss forgot all about herself at once, and put both arms round her protector.

"Think what a lot of letters must be lying waiting for you somewhere," she said. "You'll get a whole bunch one morning. Now I'm going to get up, and we'll go on that bus ride."

They lunched frugally at an A.B.C. shop, and having boarded a Number Nine bus sped westward along Piccadilly. A communicative man with a broken nose, wearing the silver badge of a discharged soldier, leaned over their shoulders from the seat behind them.

"Sir Douglass 'as done it again, ladies!" he announced importantly, thrusting an evening paper before them. "Look! *Fifteen-mile front—twelve villages—five thousand prisoners*! That's the stuff to give 'em!"

The girls read the report eagerly. It described the opening British attack of the Third Battle of Ypres. (In the first two, the attack had come from the other side.) Woods and villages, long familiar in daily bulletins as German strongholds, were at last in British hands—Hollebeke, Sanctuary Wood, Saint Julien, Hooge—and the advance was still continuing. Marjorie's heart quickened—then faltered. Great victories mean big casualties—and she did not even know where Roy was. When last heard of she had gathered that he was in a rest-area somewhere behind Amiens. But that had been five weeks ago.

"Do you know that district?" Liss was asking.

"Know it? I should think I did, miss—like the back of me 'and! I copped a sweet one there in 'fifteen—near Cambray."

"But Cambrai is not in the Salient," observed Marjorie.

The communicative man conceded the point immediately.

"Neither it is, miss—not in that *Salient*. My error! They rushed us up and down that Western Front so fast, no wonder a feller gets mixed! I was hit in both places, though. Well, 'ere we are in good old 'Ammersmiff. This is where I 'ops off. Good-day, ladies! Keep the paper, and welcome."

"It's big news, isn't it?" said Liss, continuing to skim through the heavily leaded paragraph.

"I wonder why that man thought Cambrai was in the Salient," remarked Marjorie.

"Swank, I expect," said Liss. "Probably he hasn't been out at all—*or* wounded!"

"But he was wearing a silver badge," objected Marjorie, to whom all military geese were swans.

"Perhaps he pinched it," suggested Miss Lyle, who harboured few illusions concerning the male sex.

Her theory received entire corroboration a moment later. On folding up the newspaper before descending they discovered that Marjorie's vanity-bag, which was lying on the seat between them, had been neatly slit open and its entire contents extracted.

The pair turned and regarded one another silently. Liss was the first to speak.

"That brings us down to one and sevenpence," she remarked. "No wonder he didn't know where Cambrai was!"

IV

"Luncheon is served," announced Liss.

"What is there?" asked Marjorie.

"The same as breakfast, with Willie and John thrown in. Also the rest of the day before yesterday's loaf. Pull up your chair, dear."

As breakfast had consisted of nothing at all, the prodigality of this menu can be readily gauged. Willie and John, by the way, were the last two sardines in the tin.

"You take Willie," said Liss. "Here's your half of the bread. Oh my, but I'm hungry! Good-bye, John dear! Marjorie, what are we going to do next?"

Marjorie bent her brows judicially.

"Let me see," she said. "I've tried the theatre, and they don't begin rehearsing the new piece for a fortnight. It was no use trying the canteen, because it isn't there any more—at least, nothing worth considering. And as it happens, I don't know anyone else in any other canteen."

"We haven't got an account at any shop," continued Liss, "because we've always been to the cheap cash places. I don't know a living soul in London, except my family; and if I go back to Finchley I know I'll jolly well have to stay there for the duration."

"And I," supplemented Marjorie, "know no one except Uncle Fred, in Dulwich. And I'd rather die than ask *him* for help!"

"No one at all?" exclaimed Liss. "Do you and I mean to sit here and tell each other that we know no one in London, except the people at the theatre, and the people at your canteen, and one or two dud relations? Why not call on your old Lord Eskerley?"

Marjorie hesitated.

"I don't think I can," she said. "I have no particular claim—"

"No claim? Didn't you drive his silly old car in all weathers for nearly a year? Didn't he tell you to come back and see him whenever you had time? It's no use being modest when you're starving. If you don't go and see him, I shall."

"Then I may as well tell you, dear," announced Marjorie, "that I have been already."

"Why didn't you say so before?"

"I didn't want to disappoint you."

"Why? Were you chucked out?"

"No. He's away in Paris, on an indefinite mission. The butler was very nice about it, but he had no information as to when his lordship would be back. I hadn't been entirely forgotten, though. There was a message for me. It had been lying there for weeks."

"What did it say?"

"It was just a scribbled note in an envelope with my motor licence, which I had left behind in the garage." Marjorie crossed the room to her little bureau. "Here it is! It says:

My dear late lamented Habakkuk,—I enclose your licence, which you have inadvertently left on my premises. No doubt you will need it again some day.

With kind regards,

Yours sincerely—

There's a postscript," she added:

Apropos of motor licences, let me offer you a piece of advice. Always keep an adequate sum—say a pound or so—folded up and tucked away between the covers of the licence itself. This expedient, when you get held up in a police-trap, and the minion of the law examines your credentials, may obviate a public appearance before the local Beaks. Verb, sap.! Very useful. Don't say I told you.

Marjorie laid down this characteristic effusion, and laughed.

"I don't think we are likely to tie up any capital in that way at present!" she said, finishing the last crumb of her bread. "We are down to fourpence now. We had better keep that for to-morrow, and go without supper to-night. No, we'll spend threepence on biscuits, and have a biscuit apiece at bed-time!"

"By golly, we do go it, don't we!" Liss looked round the room hungrily. "Isn't there *anything* left that we can pop?"

"Nothing, I'm afraid. My jewellery is all at Netherby. I have my engagement-ring, of course—"

"That stays!" announced Liss firmly. "It was lucky," she went on with more cheerfulness, "that my little Leonard did not want his back! Not that we got much for it; I always *said* he bought it at a stationer's! Now, if it had only been the one Reggie gave me, that would have been a different story; his was a beauty. But the little beast practically grabbed it back from me. Marjie, I *really* think I'd better get engaged again. I could wire Toby, at—"

"You will do no such thing!" said Marjorie. "Besides, you can't send a wire for fourpence."

"I suppose," continued Liss (whose motto in life was "Anything Once!") "it wouldn't do to go and sit about in a restaurant somewhere, and get taken out to dinner by an Australian, or somebody? All right, I was only joking! Well, we must just hang on till Saturday; then there will be lots of our nice boy friends in town for the week-end, and we can make up for lost time. Meanwhile, let's go round and see if we can't get a job directing envelopes, or something. Carry on, partner!"

V

Towards evening our two hungry sparrows forgathered again, footsore and faint, but still smiling. Liss, who ought by rights to have been in bed consuming chicken-broth, was as white as wax.

"What luck?" she enquired.

"Nothing doing!" sighed Marjorie. "They will take me on at an office in Holborn as soon as my arm is well enough to write, but they wouldn't give me an advance of pay. They just told me to report at nine o'clock on Monday."

"And to-day's Thursday! Thank them for nothing!"

"Did you get anything?" asked Marjorie.

"No—except that I went round to the theatre again, and they are putting on the new show a little sooner. There's a call for rehearsal on Saturday. That doesn't mean any salary for a long while, but I ought to be able to borrow a shilling or two from the girls. Not that it will be easy: they all need the money themselves these days, poor things! I'm cold. Let's have our biscuit and go to bed."

"I wonder what time it is?" said Marjorie, getting up from her chair.

"About eight, I should say." (Watches had been hypothecated long since.) "It's a bit early."

"*Qui dort, dine,*" quoted Marjorie.

"What does that mean?"

"It's what Lord Eskerley used to say when he'd been to the House of Lords. Let's go to bed; I'm comfortably tired. London's a big place to get about in—when one hasn't a bus fare!"

They shared Marjorie's bed that night, for misery loves company.

"I say," suggested Liss suddenly, "couldn't we go round and get a meal from the Red Cross, or somebody?"

Marjorie, who was just dropping off to sleep, replied with great firmness:

"The Red Cross can only assist people who have been wounded in action. If they go beyond that, the Geneva Convention allows them to be fired on; and then Roy might—No, we *can't* ask the Red Cross—unless we get hit in another air-raid!" she added hopefully.

Having no more suggestions to offer, Liss dropped off to sleep in her favourite attitude—with her head under the pillow. Marjorie lay awake for a long time, pondering many things in her heart—speculating mainly as to whether she could last out until Baby's flock of plutocratic second lieutenants came to town on Saturday. She decided immediately that she could, adding a mental rider condemning persons who, like herself, worried about their own personal comforts when there was a war on. She also wondered, again and again, what had become of Roy. She wondered whether he were hungry too. Presumably not. He had assured her that the British Army on the Western Front were grossly overfed—in fact, the inevitability with which the Army Service Corps got the rations up and through bordered on the uncanny. No, she need not worry about Roy's diet. His safety was another matter. Five weeks! She dropped into a troubled sleep.

CHAPTER XV
THE EXPLORER

Meanwhile, in a crowded street just off the Strand, in the fading light of a July evening, an elderly gentleman with a goat's beard, spectacles on nose, was diligently examining the framed photographs exhibited outside a very popular theatre. His attention was particularly directed to a large chorus group—an ensemble of attractive young women in costumes attuned to the economical spirit of wartime.

Aware of a sudden interference with the not too abundant supply of light, the elderly investigator turned round, a little guiltily, to find that he was being assisted in his investigations by three hard-breathing members of His Majesty's Forces—an English Sapper, a Highlander, and a Canadian of enormous bulk.

"And very nice, too!" observed the Sapper. "But Grandpa, not at your time of life, you didn't ought to—reelly! 'Op it—there's a good boy!"

"Awa' hame!" added the Scot severely—"or I'll tell on ye tae Grandmaw!"

Bitterly ashamed at having his motives thus misconstrued, Uncle Fred hurried away. His course now took him westward along the Strand, which was packed from end to end with seekers after diversion—mostly soldiers and their adherents. He plodded steadily through the press, with the air of a man who has a definite goal before him. This was the second week of his search for Marjorie, but he had considerably modified the plan of action laid down for him by his elder brother. His attempts to call upon the theatrical managers of London, *seriatim*, for the purpose of compelling them to disgorge his niece, had resulted in a sequence of humiliating reverses at the hands of stunted but precocious children in the outer office. Uncle Fred had now evolved a plan of his own. He had observed that theatres were accustomed to stimulate the appetites of their patrons by displaying samples of their wares—in the form of large framed photographs—outside the entrance to the theatre. Good! He would resolve himself into an investigating committee of one, visit each theatre in turn, and examine photographs until he had located Marjorie. After that, the stronghold itself must be penetrated. A somewhat hazardous enterprise, he decided, but not without its romantic side. As already noted, there was the making of a man-about-town in Uncle Fred.

His self-imposed quest had been in progress for several evenings, and, as yet, had borne no fruit. Uncle Fred was not familiar with the life of the West End—his knowledge of social life in London, like that of too many Members of Parliament, was limited to the tea-room of the House of Commons—and he had wasted a good deal of time hunting for photographs outside establishments where chorus girls are not usually to be found—Maskelyne and Cook's, for instance, and the Polytechnic. Also, it required expert knowledge to distinguish the humble home of the Drama from the palace of the Movie Queen. But he was learning rapidly. Assisted by the advertisements in the daily press and a District Railway map of London, he had now charted out the whole of theatre-land, and had very nearly completed a most methodical survey thereof. He knew the name of every revue and musical comedy in London, and could have given points, in his familiarity with the features of professional beauty, to the average Flying Corps subaltern.

He crossed Trafalgar Square, and headed for the Shaftesbury Avenue district. A hurried reference to the map, in a quiet corner behind the National Gallery, confirmed him in his bearings. Presently he found himself before another theatre. It was nearly nine o'clock; but, thanks to the Summer Time Act, it was still daylight. The name of the current attraction of the house, as stated on the bill-boards outside, was *Too*

Many Girls. Diagonally across each bill-board was pasted a printed slip which said, a little ambiguously, "*Last Week*."

"That's a pity," mused Uncle Fred. "But I can slip inside and find out what they are doing this week and next. There's some sort of entertainment going on: I can hear it."

Thrusting his beard well forward, Uncle Fred marched boldly into the vestibule of the theatre. The framed photographs had been taken in for the night, and were ranged round the wall on easels. Uncle Fred set his spectacles in position, and began his usual methodical tour of inspection, at his regulation range of six inches.

A stout lady, confined in a gilded cage in one of the walls, engaged in counting change, suspended operations to watch him. She caught the eye of the commissionnaire who stood at the swing-door leading to the stalls, and coughed delicately. Certainly Uncle Fred, in his semi-ecclesiastical frock-coat and Heath Robinson tall hat, crouching astride his umbrella in a strained endeavour to scrutinise the very lowest row in a large photographic group of chorus girls, fairly invited comment.

"Boys will be boys!" observed the commissionnaire, to no one in particular; and the siren in the cage giggled.

Suddenly Uncle Fred came to a dead point opposite the very last photograph in the last row. Feverishly reinforcing his spectacles with a pair of eye-glasses, he made a confirmatory examination, and then rose to an upright position—looking as Stanley may have looked when he found Livingstone. Then, for the first time, he became aware that he was not alone.

"Naughty, naughty!" said a wheezy feminine voice.

"Haw, haw, haw!" roared the commissionnaire.

"I'm ashamed of you, little brighteyes!" declared the accusing angel in the cage.

"Outside!" added the commissionnaire, recalled to a sense of duty by the appearance at the swing-door of an authoritative-looking person in a dinner jacket.

Uncle Fred, shamefully misunderstood and deeply wounded, hurried out. In the street he hesitated.

"Those people might have given me some useful information," he reflected. "But I won't go back now, to be insulted! I think, after all, it would be best to see the caretaker at the stage door. I suppose that will be somewhere at the back."

A voyage of circumnavigation brought him to the dingy portal which early training and settled conviction had always represented to him as giving direct access to the Infernal Regions. With a guilty thrill he crossed the threshold, and found himself confronted by an unshaven man slumbering in a glass box. Uncle Fred coughed nervously. The man opened his eyes, and pushed open a glass shutter.

"Well?" he enquired.

"I want to ask a favour," began Uncle Fred. But the man cut him short.

"What is it? Temperance, or Christian Science? You can't put up no notices on our call-board. Management don't allow it."

"I have reason to believe," pursued Uncle Fred, with feeble dignity, "that a young woman is employed here—"

"We employ thirty-six of 'em," said the stage-door man.

"I have just seen her likeness—in a group—round there"—explained Uncle Fred, waving his umbrella vaguely towards the front of the house.

"It very often starts that way," remarked the stage-door man. "But why not pay for a seat, like a little gentleman, and go in front and see the gel?"

"She's my niece," explained Uncle Fred.

"They always are," said the stage-door man. "Or else cousins! Good night, Tirpitz!"

He shut the little glass shutter in the investigator's face, and recomposed his features to slumber. But Uncle Fred, though not a dashing person, possessed some elements of the dogged persistence of the Clegg family. He rapped on the window-pane. The stage-door man opened it again.

"Now, you run away!" he said. "'Op it! Sling yer 'ook, or I'll set the cat on you!"

"Is my niece here to-night?" asked Uncle Fred, employing the handle of his umbrella as a lever of the third order. "I am very anxious to have a few words with her, on a domestic matter. I see a notice outside, saying that the present entertainment concluded last week. But it has occurred to me that it is still possible—"

The stage-door man slid from his stool, came out of his den, and laid a heavy hand, not unkindly, on the orator's shoulder.

"What you want to do, ole friend," he said, "is to 'ire the Albert 'All, and make a night of it! That'll get it out of your system nicely. Good-bye!" He gently impelled his guest in the direction of the street.

"I want my niece's address," gasped Uncle Fred, clinging like a limpet to the door-post.

"Go along, you silly old sinner!" said the stage-door man, disengaging him. "I'm ashamed of you."

"I will pay you!" said Uncle Fred desperately.

The stage-door man relaxed at once.

"Now you're *talking*!" he announced.

Five minutes later, after a sordid commercial wrangle, Uncle Fred emerged from the stage door with a slip of paper in his hand. He walked straight into the arms of three members of His Majesty's Forces. They recognised him, and drew back in affected horror.

"What, again?" cried the Canadian. "My God, he's a Mormon! Come along, boys!"

CHAPTER XVI
THE GREAT PRETEND

"And the sweet?" enquired Marjorie, pencil poised.

"*Méringues!*" said Liss firmly.

"Well, I would say chocolate *soufflé* every time—with whipped cream, of course!" replied Marjorie. "But have it your own way. Now for the savoury!"

"We don't want a savoury," said Liss.

"Remember," Marjorie reminded her, "that there will be gentlemen present."

"I was forgetting the gentlemen. Well—what?"

"*My* gentleman friend," said Marjorie, "is very fond of angels-on-horseback."

"All right! You can put them down if you like; only don't ask me to eat them: I expect I shall be stodged by that time, anyhow. Oh Marjie, if only it were true!" Liss hugged her hungry little self, longingly.

"There, that's the complete *menu*," said Marjorie. She laid down her pencil, took up the writing pad, and began to read:

"*Oysters!*" She took up her pencil again. "By the way, we can't have oysters."

"Why not?"

"You can only have oysters when there's an R in the month."

"Well, it's August!" said Liss. "And as they aren't going to be there anyhow, they may as well stay in!"

"No," said Marjorie. "This dinner is going to be things we would order here and now—just supposing we could. So don't let us spoil it by putting down impossible things."

Liss at once recognised the logical consistency of this view.

"All right!" she said. "No oysters! *Hors d'oeuvres*, instead. Then nice hot soup!"

"Yes—*Potage à la reine*."

"It sounds a bit watery; but I don't mind, so long as it's hot. Oh, how *lovely* it would be!"

"*Sole meunière*. That's Roy's favourite."

"Oh—Roy's to be there? That's your pretend, is it?"

Marjorie nodded over her hypothetical menu.

"That's a good idea. Who shall I pretend my man is? Toby?"

"All right."

"In that case, we shall want more than one bottle of champagne. You know what that child is! But never mind that just now! Read out some more food."

"*Duckling*—"

"And green peas, of course?"

"Of course!"

"What then?"

"That brings us to the *méringues*."

"Good! That should be enough. We will have coffee and *crème de menthe* afterwards, of course?"

"We will have cognac as well. You see, Roy—Oh, Liss!" For a moment Marjorie's fortitude forsook her. Her face sank into her friend's fluffy hair.

"Liss, dear," she murmured, "if *only* I knew!"

"It's Friday afternoon now," said Liss cheerfully. "We'll get lots to eat to-morrow, when the boys come up to town."

"I wasn't thinking of food," said Marjorie—"just then!"

"Well, I was! Oh, my *dear*, I'm hungry! I didn't know it was possible to be so hungry. What time is it?"

"About five, I think."

"Well, let's have a nice drink of water, and eat a couple of biscuits, and go to bed. It's the best way."

"Very well," said Marjorie listlessly. She was the more exhausted of the two; for Liss was of the ethereal type that seems to thrive on a diet of next-to-nothing. Neither girl had touched food, except a few biscuits, since the previous evening. This afternoon they had endeavoured to maintain *morale* by indulging in one of the oldest pastimes known to children of the world—the game of "Let's pretend!"—sturdily endeavouring to hold a fire in their hands by thinking on the frosty Caucasus.

Suddenly there came a tapping on the outer door. Both girls started up.

"Who on earth can that be?" said Marjorie, hurrying automatically to the mirror above the mantelpiece.

"I wonder if it is anybody with any money!" remarked Liss, hastily removing herself from the couch, where she had been stifling the pangs of hunger by lying on her front.

"Go and see!" commanded Marjorie, busy at the mirror.

Liss went out into the little vestibule, and reappeared, followed by a visitor. Her face was a study.

"This gentleman wants to see you, dear," she said solemnly. "I will leave you together!"

Marjorie turned hastily round.

"No—stay!" she commanded. "How do you do, Uncle Fred?"

"I am very well, thank you," said Uncle Fred in a low voice. Apprehension was written upon his features, and his large, weak mouth trembled. This adventure was trying him high. To penetrate into the boudoir of an actress—two actresses, apparently—was practically equivalent to visiting a theatre dressing-room, which he knew to be the last station before perdition.

Marjorie shook hands.

"Sit down," she said. "I am afraid we are not quite dressed for callers. Do you mind?"

Uncle Fred shook his head feebly, guiltily conscious that he did not mind enough. His niece was dressed in a very simple blue serge frock, with touches of scarlet at her waist and wrists. She was thinner and paler than when he had last seen her. Late suppers, of course. She had done something theatrical but undeniably becoming to her hair, which, instead of being discreetly piled upon her head, framed her face in a sort of aureole. In order to shake hands with him she had deposited upon the mantelpiece, without any attempt at concealment, a small powder-puff, with which she had obviously been tampering with that infallible symbol of respectability, a shiny nose. She wore very thin black silk stockings and patent leather shoes, with dangerously high heels. One of the shoes had a hole in the sole, but Marjorie kept that sole glued to the floor throughout the interview. The silk stockings had lisle tops, but naturally Uncle Fred did not know this. Blinking feebly, he turned his attention to Marjorie's companion. In the obscurity of the vestibule he had not particularly noticed her. He did so now. His pale blue eyes bulged.

Before him he beheld a small, fluffy creature in a flimsy garment which she would have called a *negligée*, but which to Uncle Fred looked suspiciously like a nightgown. On her feet were padded pink satin bedroom slippers. Her lips were bright red, and were directing a dazzling smile upon him. There were dark hollows under her large grey eyes. Uncle Fred resolutely averted his gaze, and turned again to his niece.

"This is Miss Lyle," announced Marjorie. "We share the flat. Liss, dear, this is my uncle, Mr. Clegg. Well, Uncle Fred, how are you? I'm sorry we can't offer you tea, but we—we have practically all our meals at a restaurant. Don't we, Liss?"

"We simply live there!" affirmed Liss.

"Will you have a cigarette?" continued Marjorie, offering a box. "Don't mind about that being the last one! There are plenty more."

"I do not smoke," replied Uncle Fred coldly.

"Throw it to me, Marjorie!" chirped the vision in the *negligée*. A moment later, genuinely oblivious of the sensation she was causing, Liss was lying back in the arm-chair, blowing smoke rings up to the ceiling.

Marjorie proceeded to make conversation.

"Have you been at Netherby lately?" she asked. "I haven't heard a word from anybody there since I left. I wrote to father and mother, but neither of them answered, so I gave it up. I was sorry, all the same. I hear from Joe, of course. Have they conscripted Amos yet? How are the children?"

This was neither the tone nor the temper that Uncle Fred had anticipated from the prodigal. He had expected either flamboyant defiance or broken-hearted contrition—most probably the latter. This resolute, cheery, ladylike—yes, he had to admit it, ladylike—bonhomie was making his mission more difficult than he had anticipated. He cleared his throat.

"I was at Netherby during July," he began. "Your father and mother are well, though borne down with sorrow, over—over—"

"Over what?"

Uncle Fred, who had meant to improve the occasion, baulked at his first fence.

"Over this wicked war," he substituted.

"Well, they haven't much to worry about," said Marjorie composedly. "Joe tells me that he's in no particular danger, except from odd long-range shells. Amos—I suppose he has kept out of it all right?"

"Your brother is in Glasgow," said Uncle Fred, "doing civilian war work of national importance."

"I thought so," said Marjorie. "Trust Amos!"

"Your father," continued Uncle Fred, "commissioned me to ascertain your whereabouts in London—"

"How *did* you find us, by the way?" asked Marjorie. "It was rather clever of you."

"I set an investigation on foot," replied Uncle Fred with a not very successful assumption of grandeur.

"Quite a little Sherlock Holmes!" remarked an approving voice.

Despite himself, Uncle Fred looked round. The small siren in the arm-chair was regarding him with obvious interest. Doubtless she was taking his moral measure, with a view to ultimate conquest. As a matter of fact, Liss was wondering whether it would be feasible to borrow five shillings from him.

"How *did* you set about it?" Marjorie continued.

"I decided not to question the police. We were anxious to have as little scandal as possible—"

Marjorie rose with some deliberation, and took her stand upon the hearthrug exactly opposite her diplomatic relative.

"What did you do?" she asked.

"I began by instituting inquiries among the London theatrical managers."

"Then you knew I was working on the stage?"

"Yes. Your mother recognised your likeness in some periodical."

Marjorie nodded her head.

"So that was why father stopped my allowance!" she said. "I was wondering. Well, go on. Father has sent you to see me? What for?"

Uncle Fred had carefully rehearsed the little address which he proposed to deliver to his errant niece. Marjorie's point-blank query gave him as good an opening as he appeared likely to get.

"Your father," he began, settling down to work, "is a just man—"

"Yes; I think you're right there," agreed Marjorie. "He tries to be, anyhow; but he's too ignorant and narrow to succeed. That was why I left home. Go on!"

"Your father," reiterated Uncle Fred, who was of that brand of orator which finds it easier, when interrupted, to go right back to the beginning, "is a just man—"

"Yes; I know. You said that before," said Marjorie.

"*No Encores, by Request!*" added Liss.

"Your father suggested that when I returned to London I should institute inquiries as to your whereabouts. He was anxious to know if you had been spared during these years, and—"

"That was very kind of him," said Marjorie. "No!"—as Uncle Fred took another breath—"don't go back to the beginning again! 'If I had been spared'—yes?"

"And, if so, what your circumstances were."

"Why?"

"Your father said he would not like to feel that you were in actual destitution, and—"

"Oh! *And?*"

"I was to tell him if you were."

"And if I were?"

"He did not say; but he practically gave me to understand that if you would send him your assurance that you were truly and humbly repentant, and would endeavour in future, by Divine Grace, to raise yourself from your present condition"—Uncle Fred was settling comfortably down now to his pulpit manner—"he was prepared on his part, to temper justice with mercy. You would be provided for. Of course, you would never be permitted to return home. There are the children to think of—"

Next moment, Uncle Fred had the surprise of his blameless and dreary existence. A small figure in a tempestuous *negligée* whirled into his field of vision, and Liss—white-faced, stammering, passionate—stood over him.

"What do you mean?" she screamed. "You silly old blear-eyed devil, what do you mean by it? What do you mean by crowding into this flat where you weren't invited, and insulting my Marjie? How *dare* you! Get out before we throw you out—do you hear? You psalm-singing old nanny-goat, for two pins I'd pull your rotten little beard off!" She flew to Marjorie, and threw an arm round her shoulders. "And to think that real men are dying in this war every minute—and the finest women in the world killing themselves with overwork—just to keep insects like you *alive!* Why, I—*Oh!*" She choked.

Marjorie restored her small, hysterical, half-famished champion to the arm-chair.

"That's all right, Baby," she said placidly. "He means well, but he's had the same upbringing as father—poor old man! Sit down! Sit down too, Uncle Fred!" (The dazed ambassador was groping for the door.) "I want to talk to you."

The symposium resumed its session. Uncle Fred was so benumbed by his recent experience that when his late assailant deliberately renovated the scarlet of her lips in his presence he made no protest at all. How quickly a man can become a *roué*, even at fifty-nine!

"You can tell father," announced Marjorie, "that you gave me his message, and that I know him well enough to understand his point of view. In a way, there's something rather fine about it. I have seen enough of life in the last year or two to know that this world would be none the worse for a touch of good old-fashioned, Old Testament, discipline. Also, that many of my sex aren't to be trusted with a latch-key. But you can remind him, from me, that I am his daughter—and quite capable of taking care of myself!" She sat down again.

"Now, I will tell you exactly what I have been doing during the last two years. Like every decent, able-bodied person in this land, I have been doing what I could in the way of war work. I wasn't able to do as much as I wanted, because my education had been completely neglected; also, as most war work is unpaid, I had to work for my living at the same time. That was why I went on the stage. By working at night I had my days free to serve in a canteen. I have been in the canteen for more than a year now. I am not working at present, because I had a slight accident to my arm. I have also driven a motor-car, for a cabinet minister, liberating a man for active service. That was why I bobbed my hair, so that I could put my service-cap on and off my head easily. Most of us have done it; no one has time to waste over doing hair these days. We girl chauffeurs and munition makers have set quite a fashion. But, of course, you aren't interested in fashions. Besides, bobbed hair doesn't really prove anything. What you want is some direct evidence of what I have been doing." She thought for a moment. "I'll tell you what—I'll show you my motor-driver's licence. I know I put it away somewhere."

She crossed to the bureau, and took the licence out of a drawer.

"Here it is," she said, unfolding it. "You will notice it hasn't been renewed. That was because—"

Her voice died away. Liss glanced up, saw that her friend had turned white, and was swaying on her feet. She ran impulsively to her aid; but in a moment Marjorie had recovered herself, walked across to her flinching relative, and proffered the licence.

"There—you see!" she said. "I drove a car during all that time. It was war work, all right."

Uncle Fred examined the document mechanically, and handed it back.

"That seems quite in order," he muttered.

"Father is a business man, I know," continued Marjorie, with a cheery smile; "and I know business men like to see evidence in black and white. You can keep that licence, if you like, and send it to him from me, as a certificate of character, and tell him that I am very well—*and* busy—*and* happy—*and* respectable—and don't require providing for in any way whatever. And you can give my love to mother."

Uncle Fred rose to his feet, and held out his hand hesitatingly. Down in his puny soul he dimly felt himself in the presence of something rather unusually big.

"I will tell your father I have seen you," he said, "and what you have told me. And I'm—I'm sorry, if—"

Marjorie cut him short.

"That's all right!" she said, with great cheerfulness. "It was a difficult mission for you, I know, and I'm not surprised you made a mess of it. Now," she added briskly, "I feel terribly inhospitable at not having given you any tea. Liss and I are just going out to dinner. It's—it's—rather a special occasion with us, and we are going to have an extra good one. Won't you join us?"

She crossed to the bureau again, and picked up the writing-pad.

"We are going," she announced, resolutely avoiding the bulging eyes of Miss Elizabeth Lyle, "to have *Potage à la reine, Sole meunière, Duckling, Méringues*—"

But Uncle Fred was down and out.

"I can't accept," he replied, almost piteously. "I must be off to Dulwich. But thank you kindly!" He moved to the door. "I will write to your father. Good-bye, my girl!" He nodded nervously towards Liss. "Good-evening, all!"

Next moment the vestibule door had clicked behind him, and the girls were alone.

Liss threw her arms round Marjorie's neck.

"O magnificent, wonderful angel! How you stood up to that silly old Nosey Parker! How you put him in his place! How you bluffed him! But, darling, what a risk! Supposing he had accepted—what then?"

"What then?" Marjorie laughed unsteadily. "We would have taken him round the corner to Savroni's, and *given* him his dinner—every bit of it—that's all!"

Liss looked timidly up into her idol's face.

"Dearest," she enquired apprehensively, "are you feeling *funny*, at all? I don't like the way your fist is clenched. Relax!"

"I'm not feeling funny," Marjorie assured her, relaxing the fist in question. "Unless it's funny to be rich!" She held out her hand. "Look! Look what I found inside the pocket of my motor licence! I might have guessed, after that message. Dear, kind old man! I might have guessed—bless him!"

In her upturned palm lay a neatly folded bank-note.

Liss's eyes goggled.

"How much?" she whispered.

"We'll see." Marjorie unfolded the rustling treasure-trove. "Ten pounds! Now wasn't I right not to put down oysters? Oh, Baby, if only, only, only we had the guests!"

But Fortune, once she veers round, seldom does things by halves. There came a knock on the outer door.

"Hallo!" cried Liss. "Surely it's not that old Nanny back again?"

It was not. It was a soldier—or rather, an elderly civilian in uniform. He saluted, with all the elaboration of the newly initiated. Both girls surveyed him in perplexity. Then Liss screamed:

"It's Uncle Ga-Ga!" and embraced him forthwith.

Uncle Ga-Ga it was. With his hair dyed a new and awe-inspiring colour, and an almost convincing set of false teeth, he did not look a day over forty-five. He held his old head proudly erect, and offered a hand to each of the girls, with a gallant gesture.

"Yes, ladies," he said; "I have the great happiness to inform you that I have this day been accepted as a member of His Majesty's Forces. I wear the uniform of King George the Fifth." His right hand went to the salute. "The King—God bless him! I have only just put it on, and I came round here at once to show myself to you—my two kind friends and unfailing supporters! There were some of my colleagues"—his mild eyes flashed—"men who should have known better—who derided my pretensions—who said that the King had no need of my services! But not you, ladies! You knew the King better than they did! Now, behold me! It is a common triumph for us all!"

"And we are going to celebrate it!" announced Liss. "You are coming straight out to dinner with us—isn't he, Marjorie?"

"Most certainly he is!" said Marjorie.

"We are going," proclaimed Liss, "to have *Potage à la reine; Sole meunière*—"

Uncle Ga-Ga laid his hand upon his heart, and made a courtly bow.

"Ladies," he announced, "you overwhelm me! But before I accede to your most hospitable invitation, pray read this: it may affect your immediate plans. I found it lying thrust under your outer door."

He proffered an orange-coloured envelope. It was addressed to Marjorie.

Telegrams in war-time take tense priority over everything else. Marjorie seized the envelope, ripped open the flap with one feverish movement, took out the message, and carried it to the window to read. Then, very deliberately, for the first and only time in her life, she slid down upon the floor, with her head on the window-seat, in a dead faint."

"Oh, God!" cried Liss, running to her—"it must be something about Roy!"

They carried her to the sofa, and laid her down. Her eyes were closed, but began to flutter again almost immediately.

"The telegram—should we read it? Would it be right?" asked Uncle Ga-Ga.

"Oh, yes!" said Liss: "I'd forgotten about it." She turned back Marjorie's closed fingers, extracted the crumpled message, and smoothed it out. Then she gave a little sudden chuckling sob.

"Listen!" she said; and read the message aloud....

"Sent off from Folkestone," she added breathlessly, "at four-forty. What time is it now?"

"About half-past six, I think."

"Then he will be here any minute!" cried Liss, in sudden panic. "We must get her to for him," she added, in the mysterious syntax of her kind. "Help me, Uncle!"

"A lovely face!" observed Uncle Ga-Ga, respectfully, as he assisted Liss in administering to Marjorie what they both firmly believed to be First Aid—"but pale, and thin!" He sighed gently. "It is rather beautiful to think that people can still swoon for joy."

"Not joy," said Liss, panting—"starvation! But she'll have her guest at dinner, after all. (She's coming to now.) It's been a great pretend! (Darling, lean your head on me.) She'll be as right as rain to-morrow. In fact, she's jolly well got to be. It's her wedding day!"

CHAPTER XVII
THE UNDEFEATED

This morning I went to church, in a real church—the parish church of Craigfoot. After more than three years, I found myself once again in the Baronrigg gallery.

Of late, I have become accustomed to performing my religious exercises in the open air, in a boggy field of Flanders or Picardy, struggling, in company with a choir of some hundreds of devout, mud-splashed "Jocks," armed to the teeth and insufficiently supplied with hymn-books, to produce a respectable volume of psalmody; or listening resignedly, in an east wind, to a sermon replete with apposite references to the canker-wurrum and the pammer-wurrum, delivered with gusto by an untimely young chaplain newly out from home.

I shared the Baronrigg pew with the Matron of the Eskerley Auxiliary Military Hospital, and some half-dozen restive convalescents in hospital blue. It was January, and bitter cold, but no fire burned in old Neil Carrick's grate at the back of the gallery. The coal ration—like the thermometer—hovered near to zero in those days.

Of the rightful occupants of the pew there was no representative. The son of the house was commanding his company somewhere in the neighbourhood of La Bassée: at least, that was where I had left him last week. The master—well, there I was no wiser than the rest. All I knew was what I had read in the letter which he had written me at the time of his disappearance—a letter very similar in substance and temper to that received by his son.

My eyes wandered over the familiar scene below. Here, too, were changes: even the immutable ritual of a Scottish parish church had been affected by forty-one months of war. Doctor Chirnside was still in command. He was preaching the sermon now—on a text from his beloved Isaiah—more gaunt, more eagle-eyed, more uncompromising than ever. The parish, I knew, were of the opinion that "the auld man was failing." Still, there he was, sticking to his post.

"The most practical way," he had declared recently to a tactfully inquisitive Kirk Session, "to maintain national efficiency at a time of abnormal national wastage is for those of us who are spared to increase our output; to work longer hours—longer years, in my case—in order to make good the loss of those who have been called from our midst. So, though I have laboured long in the vineyard; though I have lingered long in the arena, and am now perhaps *dignus rude donari*, I shall remain at my post until God giveth the Victory. In other words, Gentlemen, you may whistle for my resignation!"

Still, the influences of the time seemed to have affected the Doctor like the rest of us. He was more human, less Olympian. The First Prayer—in which, it may be remembered, the Doctor was accustomed to commune with his Maker to the pointed exclusion of the congregation—was now much shorter. The Second Prayer—the Prayer of Intercession—was considerably longer, and very moving to hear. In that prayer, week by week, the progress of the Great War was reviewed—reviewed from the standpoint of an obscure but not altogether undutiful little parish in the Lowlands of Scotland. Not a boy from that parish, be he laird's son or herd laddie, fell in action on this front or that but the fact was duly noted, with sorrowful pride and amazing tenderness, in the Prayer of Intercession in the Parish Kirk of Craigfoot on the following Sabbath.

There were many such events to record. The Roll of Honour, fluttering in the draughty porch outside, bore witness to that fact. So did the composition of the congregation. Most of the men present were forty-five years old and upwards. Those below that age were mainly in khaki. But it was the women who told the most eloquent tale. The three tall daughters of Sir Alistair Graeme—The Three Grenadiers—still sat side by side in the Burling pew, to all appearances unchanged except for their V.A.D. uniforms. Yet I knew that each of those girls had been made a wife and widow within three short years. Mrs. Gillespie, the Bank Manager's wife, on the other hand, made no pretence of being the same woman: her son Robert, the Divinity student, had died of dysentery in Mesopotamia. Of the Misses Peabody, only the elder now sat in the pew. The younger was dead—dead of overwork as a ward-maid in a Base Hospital. None disputed her claim to be of the elect now. Little Mrs. Menzies, the wife of Lord Eskerley's late factor, was changed too—but only in name. She had done her bit—by becoming the widow of a D.S.O. and promptly marrying a C.M.G.

Looking further afield, I observed that old Couper and his wife were almost crowded out of their pew by a string of grandchildren, billeted upon Abbotrigg until such time as a newly-widowed daughter-in-law could adjust her compasses again. I missed the kindly vacant countenance of my friend Jamie Leslie, our organ-blower, which had usually been visible, on pre-war days, peering furtively round the red rep curtain which screened the organ-bellows from view. His place was now occupied by a bucolic young gentleman of thirteen. Subsequent inquiry on my part elicited the news that Jamie had at last achieved his heart's desire and been accepted for the Army, the authorities having very properly decided that what was sauce for the Staff was sauce for the rank-and-file.

In a back pew under the gallery I noticed old Mrs. Rorison, accompanied by her giant son, Jock, the Scots Guardsman—discharged, permanently unfit, with a crippled foot. I had met the pair in Main Street the day before.

"That's bad luck, Jock!" I had said, noting his crutches.

"It's naething of the kind!" replied Jock's mother, tartly. (She usually replied for Jock.) "See him, sir! Sax feet fower—and gets himsel' shot in the fit! I doot he was standing on his head in they trenches!" concluded the old lady bitterly. "Trust him!"

Eric was sitting in the Buckholm pew, with his lady mother: I was to lunch with them presently. I surveyed my friend's handsome profile, his empty sleeve, and the medal ribbons on his uniform. I thought of our regiment—which I now commanded and which he himself had led. I thought of the day, eighteen months since, when we had carried him away insensible, followed by what was left of our personnel, from that tight corner opposite Beaumont Hamel. Eric was home now with a decoration and a soft job—the idol and the oracle of the country-side. I had not been decorated, or even mentioned in Dispatches, but I had, so far, preserved a whole skin—which was far better—and been confirmed in my rank. Though lean and grizzled, I still felt fighting fit, and had no desire to change places with any one. I was staying at The Heughs—a sober household in those days, for my brother Walter had lost his eldest boy at Gallipoli. Of the other two, John was helping to navigate one of His Majesty's Destroyers, while the youngest, Alan, my namesake and particular crony, was consuming his impatient young soul—to his mother's private relief—at Sandhurst.

"*Finally, my brethren*"—began Doctor Chirnside; and I knew that we were within five minutes of the end of the sermon. The maimed men beside me wriggled in relieved anticipation, then settled down again; and I hastened to conclude my church inspection.

I glanced across to the Netherby pew. Mr. and Mrs. Clegg were both there, with the younger children. The two grown-up sons were absent: I remembered having heard vaguely that one of them had enlisted and that the other had secured a "cushie" job somewhere. The fair daughter was nowhere to be seen. I was sorry, because a thing of beauty is a joy for ever—especially during a long sermon. I wondered what had become of her—and Master Roy's infatuation. I had once or twice, during the early days in France, made playful allusion to the lady in Roy's presence, but my pleasantries had not been well received, and had been discontinued.

I gave a final glance round the church.

"*Plus ça change*—!" I said to myself.

But I was a little too quick in my judgment.

"*They that wait upon the Lord shall renew their strength; they shall mount up with wings as eagles; they shall run, and not be weary: they shall walk, and not faint.* May God sanctify to us this poor exposition of His Word; and to Him alone be the glory and the praise!"

The last sentence, at least, was familiar enough. It had rounded off every one of Doctor Chirnside's sermons, to my certain knowledge, for the last thirty-five years. The congregation came to life: the organ-bellows began to pump, almost automatically, for the last hymn. The elders of the kirk fumbled under their seats for the collection-bags.

We rose on a triumphant chord from the little organ, and sang the hymn—stoutly enough, and with that prickly sensation at the back of the nose which attacks undemonstrative people engaged in a slightly emotional exercise; for the hymn was "Onward, Christian Soldiers"! I learned afterwards that it had been sung (alternately with the hymn For Those at Sea), at the close of morning worship every single Sunday since the regular casualty lists had started. Then, in good Scottish fashion, we remained standing for Doctor Chirnside's patriarchal and impressive Benediction.

"*May the Peace of God, which Passeth All Understanding...*"

His old voice died away; and I was on the point of stooping down to grope for my glengarry, when I became conscious of a gradual stiffening in the attitude of the congregation. The organ began to rumble again. (I could see the young organ-blower working as if to crack every muscle in his back.) Then, suddenly, explosively, with every pedal and stop in action, it crashed into "God Save the King"!

Instinctively I came to attention. But though my head was immovable, I fear I allowed my eyes to stray downward to the scene below. Here was an unexpected test of war spirit.

Our National Anthem is a curious canticle; you never know what it will do with you. It may cause you to feel merely ridiculous—as when an orchestra of aliens in a restaurant drags you to your feet in the middle of your soup. Too often it elicits a purely perfunctory acknowledgment. But there are occasions when the sound of it grips the very heart of you; when you are conscious, deep down in your well-ordered British soul, of a sudden, tremendous, irresistible wave of passionate loyalty to the Sovereign who rules you and the thousand-year-old tradition for which he stands. Here was such an occasion. Here, in this little church, was our battle hymn being thundered forth, after more than three years of battle, to a community who had been paying the maximum price for their participation therein. How would they take it?

My field of vision was naturally constricted, but without moving my head I could command a fair view. Eric Bethune, of course, was standing as straight as a ramrod. So was the elder Miss Peabody—also the three poor Grenadiers. The wounded men beside me stiffened their twisted bodies proudly: evidently it was incumbent upon them to teach the rest of the congregation something.

Finally, my eyes fell upon the Abbotrigg pew. Old Couper and his wife were standing side by side, with bowed heads. I saw that they were holding hands. Beside them, in order of size, were ranged five small figures in black—three boys and two girls—the grandchildren whose father had fallen in action six days ago. They did not look too well-fed—milk and meat were not over plentiful in those days—but they stood shoulder to shoulder in a perfectly aligned row, emulating the soldiers in the gallery above. It was difficult to believe that they had not rehearsed the formation. (Probably they had, under the personal direction of a martinet home on leave.) Each small head was held resolutely up; each small chest—situated rather low down, as is usual when we are very young—was thrust resolutely forward; each small pair of arms pointed rigidly to the floor; and each pair of round eyes gazed fixedly and unblinkingly into space.

Suddenly, I saw nothing more. But I remember feeling reassured about things.

CHAPTER XVIII
THE OLD ORDER

After church I joined Lady Christina and Eric, and was conveyed in a very ancient victoria—her ladyship had "put down" the motor, owing to petrol difficulties—to Buckholm for luncheon. I noticed that my friend Bates no longer attended to the front door; he was now, I gathered, guarding our coast from invasion somewhere in Suffolk. His deputy was a grim-looking crone in a black skirt, silver-buttoned coat, and yellow waistcoat, which made her look something between a female impersonator and a prison wardress. I seemed to have encountered her in a previous existence hanging washing on a line on the drying-green behind the Buckholm orchard. She relieved me of my glengarry, gloves, and stick, and demanded my ration-book.

"There will be meat for dinner," she explained.

I handed over the emergency ration-book with which soldiers on leave were supplied in those days. It was returned to me when I left the house, lacking not only one full meat coupon, but all the butter and sugar coupons as well.

"Her leddyship said you would no be needing them," explained the wardress, and I meekly acquiesced. If Lady Christina said that I did not need a thing, who was I to say that I did? In any case I was due to rejoin the best-fed Army in the world in a few days' time.

The luncheon party consisted of Lady Christina, as bolt upright as ever, at the head of the table; Eric, at the foot; Lord Eskerley; and a weather-beaten Lieutenant-Commander of the Royal Naval Volunteer Reserve, named John Wickersham. Five years ago he had been mainly known to fame as a prominent King's Counsel, a superb bridge-player, and a fair-weather yachtsman. Now, for three years or more, his converted pleasure-craft, navigated by its owner and enrolled an original member of a certain silent, unadvertised brotherhood of the sea, had been keeping grim vigil over our island coast, with such effect that German submarine crews were breaking into open mutiny rather than face that flotilla of terror any longer. John Wickersham was ashore on long leave, for the first time for many months.

Doctor Chirnside, who seldom missed his Sunday luncheon at Buckholm, had been called away, to say what he could to a girl-wife who had just received a telegram from the War Office.

Having consumed its meat ration and sugarless apple tart, the company proceeded to mitigate the austerity of Lady Christina's war-time régime with a glass of port. Then, after a perfunctory and short-lived struggle, we yielded to the inevitable and settled down to the topic of the military situation. It was a curious experience for me, who had heard little round that peaceful table since boyhood but hunting shop and county gossip, to find myself involved in the same eternal debate as was exercising every mess, billet, and dug-out on the Western Front—a debate distinguished in both cases by extreme personal bias and entire ignorance of essential details. It is hardly necessary to mention that Lord Eskerley, the one person who could have enlightened us, offered no contribution.

Naturally we concentrated upon the rumours of the knock-out blow which Germany was preparing to deal her arch-enemy in the early spring—a blow which came near, in the actual event, to driving a wedge between the armies of France and Britain, and establishing a German base on the English Channel. But in January, nineteen-eighteen, when we had not lost a field-gun or a trench system since the First Battle of

Ypres, and had been steadily winning back the soil of France and accumulating German prisoners for more than three years, no one took such a possibility seriously. Eric was particularly sanguine.

"A good thing, too!" he said. "Let them come! Then we can sit well back, and make a clean job of the lot, instead of getting hot and dusty going to look for them! This war will end when we have killed enough Boches; and if the Boches will help us by coming along to get killed—and you know what the Boche can do in that way once he gives his mind to it—there will be no complaints on our side. I feel—"

This characteristic pronouncement was interrupted by Lord Eskerley.

"It's only human nature, you know," he said. "You can't blame them. Naturally they think of their own front first. Must!"

This did not seem to fit in well with the rest of the conversation—a not altogether unusual feature of his lordship's table-talk.

"Napoleon was right," he continued. "Or was it Hannibal? Said he would sooner fight two first-class generals collaborating than one single-handed second-rater. It works out this way. Tweedledum says to Tweedledee: 'You must take over more Front.' Tweedledee says to Tweedledum: 'It can't be done! Look at my casualty list for the last three months!' Tweedledum replies: 'But you are only holding about half as much line as I am.' Thereupon Tweedledee produces statistics to show that although he holds the shorter line he has sixty-seven and a half per cent. of the enemy massed against him. And so it goes on. The old game! I believe that in Bohemian circles it is known as 'Passing the Buck.' A colloquial but apposite expression! I picked it up from an American *attaché* in Paris. In due course we shall come to the only solution—a Supreme Commander, responsible for the safety of the whole line. But, as usual, we shall pay in advance—through the nose!"

The import of the old gentleman's ruminations was now tolerably apparent to all; that is, to all but our hostess.

"Eh, what? What's he talking about?" she inquired sharply of me. (Of late, Lady Christina's hearing has deteriorated a little.) "What's he talking about? Tell me; he mumbles so! What's all this nonsense about Tweedledee and Tweedledum? Who are Tweedledee and Tweedledum? They sound like people out of Punch—two of those wretches in the Government. In German pay, every man-jack of them! Do you know what Bessie Brickshire told me last week? She went to Downing Street—"

"Your leddyship's coffee is up the stair," announced the deep voice of the prison wardress; and a libellous and irrelevant anecdote was nipped in the bud.

Lady Christina rose, informed us that she proposed to take her coffee in her own room, and, with a passing admonition to her son to be sparing of the saccharine, left us to ours.

We lit cigars and stretched ourselves, like schoolboys relieved of the pedagogue's presence.

"How do they feel about things in general up at the top, Eskerley?" asked John Wickersham. "We never hear any news in our job. Are they all quite happy and comfortable?"

"Not at all!" replied his lordship brusquely.

"What's the trouble?"

"Not enough troops."

"How? The number of Divisions on the Western Front hasn't been reduced, has it?"

"Oh, dear, no. We are as strong as ever—on paper. But instead of going frankly to the Labour bosses and telling them that another half-million men must be released from civilian employment, our politicians have reduced the personnel of each Division from thirteen battalions to ten—nearly twenty-five per cent. It's an admirable scheme, because it satisfies so many people. It satisfies the politician, because it saves his face; it satisfies the slacker, because it saves his skin; and it satisfies the Boche, because it's going to save him a lot of trouble when he makes his spring offensive. The only people who are inclined to criticise it are the insignificant individuals who are responsible for the safety of the Western Front. In fact, they are crying out to Heaven for more men. But, of course, nobody takes any notice of recommendations from such a prejudiced person as a soldier. His turn will come later, when the scapegoats are being rounded up." The old gentleman sighed. "That's one of our worries. The other is that we have too many Allies."

"I see! Too many cooks—eh?"

"Precisely! I spend all my working hours nowadays propitiating plenipotentiaries from countries whose existence I had never heard of two years ago. By the time I have recognised the status of this Ally, and soothed the susceptibilities of that, the day is over and there's no time left to get on with the war. I sometimes sigh for the era when the French and ourselves muddled along by rule of thumb without having to expend any tact upon anybody, except a periodical slap on the back to Russia. *We few, we happy few, we band of brothers!*—and so on. Life was simple then. Now it is a perpetual Pentecost, without the feast. Give me a forlorn hope and a lone hand every time; that's an invincible combination—eh, Alan?"

"I agree," I said. "In the first year or so there was a sort of cheerful, simple, all-in-the-same-boat feeling about everything. The French liked us; there was not too many of us; and what there were were perfectly disciplined—old Regulars and the pick of 'K's' Army; or else Indian troops, with the manners of Hidalgoes. Now, the average French citizen never wants to see an ally again—"

Lord Eskerley nodded.

"Exactly!" he said. "And I can't say I blame him. I sometimes feel that way myself. We're a fairly promiscuous lot. We may be a host of modern crusaders, but we're a *crowd*! I feel like old McKechnie at the revivalist meeting here five years ago, who refused to stand up and be 'saved' with the rest because he objected to going to heaven 'with a d———d Cheap Trup!' Still, we mustn't be ungrateful. Our post entries may have complicated the machine, but they have made it a pretty reliable piece of mechanism."

"What I complain of," interposed Eric, "is that we, upon whom the whole burden fell at the start, are almost forgotten now. Most of us have ceased to exist, and the rest are lost in a mob of amateurs."

"The wrong attitude entirely!" announced Lord Eskerley promptly.

"What's the right attitude, then?" asked Eric, who hated correction almost as much as Lord Eskerley delighted to administer it to him.

"The right attitude," replied the old man, with sudden seriousness, "should be a feeling of pride that We were fortunate enough to find ourselves Original Members of the Brotherhood—to hold Founders' Shares. When the edifice is completed—and completed it will be—the world won't be able to see the foundations. But they will be there all right! And we shall know who laid them—the Old Order!"

"What do you mean by the Old Order?" asked Eric. "The landed gentry?"

"Far more than that. I mean the people to whom this country, as such, has always really meant something; I mean every mother's son who felt the ancient spirit of our race wake in him, perhaps for the first time, when the challenge came in Nineteen Fourteen. I don't care who he was—squire's son, parson's son, miner's son, poacher's son—it was all the same. If he was conscious then of that single blind impulse to get up and play the game, just because it was the game; just because it was impossible to do otherwise—without any dialectics about Freedom, or Altruism, or Democracy, or whether his job would be kept open for him or not; simply because the Blood told him to—then he belonged to the Old Order! He held a Founder's Share, all right!

"Of course," the old man continued presently, "the more one has to give the more one is expected to give, at a time like this. And as a rule it seems to be the best that is taken. '*This is the heir; come, let us kill him!*'—that has been the general attitude of the War Gods. Only the very best would suffice—only the very best!"

We sat silent again. Lord Eskerley himself had lost his two sons, and his only grandson. After him, what was to become of the ancient title—of the "Big Hoose" and its "policies"—of the family which had served the State for three hundred years? "*This is the heir!*" How true that was. I thought of my brother Walter's eldest son. Fortunately in this case there were two more. And Roy? What would become of Baronrigg, if—

But Lord Eskerley was speaking again—more to himself than to us.

"The Old Order! The Willing Horse! There's hardly an estate, or a farm, or an allotment, in this countryside, or in any part of Scotland or England, that has not changed hands, prospectively at least, during the last three years. And what with designedly disruptive death duties, and income tax on the same scale, levied on people who have no personal income—only a few precious, ancient, barren acres—the old estates are passing right away from the original owners—one half sold to pay the charges on the other half. It seems a queer way of rewarding people who have given everything—to sell them up because they have nothing more to give! Still, one has the supreme satisfaction of having played the game. Our record stands—" He broke off. "I apologise: I was sermonising! Bad habit!" He looked at his watch. "Three o'clock! I must go; a trunk call comes through from London every afternoon at four. Alan, I will give you a lift."

A few minutes later I found myself rolling home in an unaccustomed motor.

"I still get twenty gallons a month," explained Lord Eskerley. "Business of State, and so on. Going back soon?"

"Thursday," I said.

"Well, enjoy the war while you can. When it is over there will be no peace for anybody. After the Boche has given his last expiring kick we are going to sit down to a Peace Congress in comparison with which the Congress of Vienna will take rank as a model of sagacity and altruism. The Millennium that we are all composing cantatas about is not coming—yet."

"Are we going to have more wars, then?" I asked, gazing rather dejectedly at the red, wintry sunset.

"We are always going to have more wars," replied my companion testily—"and then more! (The final war will be between men and women. Even that won't really settle anything, because there will be too much rendering aid and comfort to the enemy going on.) By the way, how is Roy?"

I reported favourably upon my nephew's health and service record.

"I suppose you know," I remarked, "that Tom Birnie appointed yourself and myself Roy's trustees and executors?"

"Yes. Tom wrote me a letter to that effect before he enlisted."

"He did enlist, then?"

"I believe so."

I did not press for details. Lord Eskerley has means at his disposal of discovering most of the secrets of this world—which is not to say that he is accustomed to pass these on to third parties.

"Have you seen Roy," I continued, "or heard from him of late?"

"I have not seen him, and he has not favoured me with a single line since he went out for the first time. By the way, I observe she received a decoration the other day—for conspicuous bravery during an air-raid."

"Who?"

"Who? The girl!"

"The girl? You mean—the Netherby girl? Is that *affaire* still—?"

"Yes. Name of Clegg. You know what became of her, I suppose?"

"No. Roy has never been communicative on the subject, although I believe he used to maintain a correspondence with her. The junior members of the mess were quite intrigued about it. I had almost forgotten her existence. What became of her?"

"She couldn't stand Papa's peaceful principles, so ran away from home and came to London. I employed her to drive my car for some time; but she left me. Said the work wasn't hard enough. She now supports herself on the stage, so as to have her days free for some sort of drudgery in a canteen."

"And you think that she and Roy still—

"Married, last August!" replied his lordship simply.

"*What?*"

"On the quiet—registry office! Wonderful, heavenly secret, and all that! How the young love a clandestine romance! And some of us never grow up!" added the old man complacently.

CHAPTER XIX
THE LAST THROW

"I'm sorry, gentlemen," said the Divisional Commander, "but I can't possibly let any unit proceed to rest areas at present. Our orders are to stand by, day and night, and be ready to move in any direction at an hour's notice. By the way, this is quite an informal meeting, so ask any questions you like."

"What is the latest news of the tactical situation, sir?" inquired the senior Brigadier, articulating the question that was on every one's lips.

We were gathered together at a Commanding Officers' Meeting. The Division had just emerged from four months of winter trench-warfare in the north—only to be diverted from its search for well-earned repose by an urgent summons to repair southward without delay to its ancient stamping-ground behind Albert. We had marched all night, to be intercepted at dawn by orders to bivouac where we stood. I myself was summoned to the meeting, hastily convened in a village school five miles farther on.

"It's a pretty sticky business all round," said the General frankly. "The situation appears to be this. As you know, it has been obvious for months that the Boche has been meditating a tremendous offensive against some part of the British front. The Commander-in-Chief, not having sufficient troops to give adequate protection to the whole of his line—

"Why *hasn't* he sufficient troops?" inquired a voice—the voice of the C.R.A., a fiery old gentleman with a monocle. He was a coeval of the General's, so was qualified to act as cross-examiner for us lesser lights.

"It's not my business to explain, or ours to wonder. I can only give you the facts. Last year the British Army had, roughly speaking, one million casualties. This year the British Army is fighting in France, Belgium, Italy, Saloniki, Palestine, Mesopotamia, the Indian frontier, and East Africa; so you can imagine the clamour for reinforcements that is going on all over the globe. Thirdly, the French, not long ago, asked us to take over another twenty-eight miles of line. We did so; with the result that the C.-in-C. found himself in the position of having to decide, since he hadn't enough men to hold all the line securely, where he must hold on at all costs, and where he could afford to take chances. Obviously, he had to make the Straits of Dover impregnable; so the northern part of the line got the lion's share of troops. Down here, the Fifth Army were strung out to a beggarly bayonet per yard. North of them, the Third Army had about three bayonets to two yards. Opposite this line, during the past few weeks, the Boche was known to have accumulated a force averaging seven bayonets per yard—" A low murmur ran round the crowded little school-room. It was fully light now, and we could see one another's startled faces. "In other words, sixty or seventy divisions. Against that force we had available twenty-two divisions in the line, with twelve infantry divisions and three cavalry divisions in reserve. The attack opened six days ago. The Boches, as usual, had the Devil's own luck with the weather—thick mist—and were on us in a solid phalanx before we saw them at all. I may add that they were backed by the most terrific concentration of artillery fire on record, and raised unexpected Sheol in our back areas by a new very long range gas-shell. By all the rules they ought to have wiped us right out. But they didn't. We were bowled over again and again; but we always managed to re-form some sort of line—until the want of reserves began to tell, and brigades and divisions, thinned out to nothing, began to draw in upon themselves and leave gaps on their flanks. The cavalry worked like heroes to cover the intervals; but they couldn't be everywhere, and one position after another was outflanked and had to be given up. Noyon has gone; Péronne has gone; Monchy has gone; the whole Somme battle-field of Nineteen-Sixteen has gone. Even Albert"—there came a groan here from all of us who had fought in the Somme battle—"has fallen into Boche hands. Yes, I know! But things might be worse. Arras is holding fast; and the good old Vimy Ridge is still standing right up to them. It's tolerably certain now that the Boche was booked to get Amiens in three days. He hasn't got it; and if we can continue to make him pay his present price he will never get it at all."

There was small comfort in this. The very fact that Amiens had become a Boche possibility was a staggerer in itself. We thought of the Hôtel du Rhin, and other haunts of ancient peace, and sighed.

"How is morale?" asked the C.R.A.

The General held up a paper.

"Here is the Commander-in-Chief's latest dispatch," he said. "Listen to this, gentlemen!"

At no time was there anything approaching a breakdown of command or a failure of morale. Under conditions that made rest and sleep impossible for days together, officers and men remained undismayed, realising that for the time being they must play a waiting game, and determined to make the enemy pay the full price for the advantage which, for the moment, was his.

We broke into applause. We could not help it.

"Naturally," continued the General, "the strain has been awful, because we are employing tired men, fighting without reinforcements against ever fresh bodies of troops. However, more divisions are coming down from the north—you are one of the first arrivals—and Foch has taken supreme command, which means that hereafter the Allied forces will be more evenly distributed and the line stabilised. The long and short of it all is that the enemy has been frustrated, for the time being, in his amiable attempt to drive a wedge between the British and French armies."

"Still," said the voice of the C.R.A., "I suppose the situation is pretty critical?"

"Critical isn't the word! But the line is still intact, though badly bent, and we have beaten all our previous records for Boche-killing, which is saying something. And if they fail to break through—good-bye Germany! It's their last throw. A German who knows he cannot win is a German beaten. Now, gentlemen, you will understand why it is that you cannot go into retirement at present. That's all, I think! To your tents, O Israel—and breakfast! But be ready to move at an hour's notice."

Roy and I jogged wearily back across country to the field where the men were bivouacking. Roy was my senior company commander, and I had brought him to the meeting in preference to the adjutant, who was very young and already bowed down with regimental routine. Roy, a seasoned Ironside of twenty-two, with two-and-a-half years continuous active service to his record, was now my shield and buckler and right-hand man.

We had little to say to one another. We were both dog-tired, and were suffering in addition from that unpleasant form of reaction which comes from hope deferred. We were thinking, too, of the men. They had completed four months of exhausting and expensive trench duty, working by "internal reliefs," which really means no relief at all; each man staying his dour dogged heart with the only two consolations available in those days—the humdrum certainty of ultimate relief by another division, and the ever present possibility of a "Blighty" wound. And now, when they had actually packed up and removed out of the shell area, with a spell of rest and relaxation well within their grasp, they found themselves pulled back into the line. That sort of experience is a severer test of morale than an intensive bombardment. The danger was that they might go stale—just as I had once seen a highly-trained college crew go, when the races were postponed for a week owing to ice on the river.

"We will call a pow-wow when we get back," I said to Roy, "and tell the officers to explain matters to the men as well as they can. They must sing the usual song about our trusty old indispensable Division, the prop and stay of the weaker brethren, proudly filling the breach and saving the situation, and so forth."

"They'll respond all right," said Roy confidently. "They are a wonderful crowd."

"They certainly are; but it will break their hearts if they are shoved back for another spell of trench duty. Of course, if we go right into the scrap, with a fair chance to get above ground and grab the Boche by the ears, they won't mind at all—quite the reverse. It will be a perfect tonic."

"If half of what His Nibs said is true, they'll get all the tonic they want!" remarked my sage young companion. "We're for it, this time!"

He was right. Even at that moment our task had been assigned to us; for when we reached Battalion Headquarters—a G.S. waggon in the corner of a field, in the middle of which certain incurable greathearts were playing football—we found that the telephone had outstripped us, and that our orders were waiting.

We gobbled breakfast, with that curious mingling of sentiment and satisfaction which comes to men who are not sure if they will ever see a poached egg again. Then I summoned my officers. I passed on to them the substance of the General's statement, and spoke of the gaps that were being created in the line by lack of reinforcements.

"Such a gap," I explained, "has occurred almost directly in front of us, along the crest of a low ridge called Primrose Hill. (The Adjutant will give you the map reference in a minute.) The gap is being filled at present by a rather raw battalion of newly-arrived Territorials, rushed up from Corps Reserve. It is a very important point, and we are to go in and stiffen them. Written orders will be issued to you immediately; but it may save time if I mention that I propose to march the battalion direct to the back of Primrose Hill, deploy, and advance in lines of companies until we strike the trench system which the Royal Loyals are holding. In that way we ought to be able to plug any possible gap in the shortest possible time. We may have to advance through a barrage; but that, of course, is all in the day's work. Company commanders will take such precautions as are possible to ensure the safety of their men, but they must not waste time on this occasion looking for covered lines of advance. In other words, the situation is critical, and must be tackled bald-headed. The point of deployment, as at present fixed, is a blacksmith's forge on the road running direct from here to Primrose Hill. It is marked in the map, *Michelin Forge*; there's a big motor-tyre advertisement on the western gable, the Brigade Major tells me. I shall go there now myself, and establish temporary headquarters. Companies will move off independently in succession, A Company leading. Company commanders will report at Michelin Forge for further instructions. Later, after we have deployed and advanced up the reverse slope of Primrose Hill—it is a mere swelling in the ground, as a matter of fact—Battalion Headquarters will be established, if possible, in a *point d'appui* just behind the crest, called Fountain Keep. It is a ruined ornamental garden, I believe, with the wreck of a fountain in the middle. I hope you'll all arrive there in due course—and find me there! That's all! Good luck to you!"

My officers saluted in a manner that warmed my heart, and hurried off to their duties. I felt sorry I had not been able to give them a more stirring harangue: I felt sure that Eric would have done so. Still, harangue or no harangue, I knew they would lead their men to the crest of Primrose Hill. I looked after them affectionately. Most of them I never saw again from that hour. But I remember them all to-day—their faces, their voices, their characteristics. They were of many types—the variegated types of a whole nation at last in arms. There were Public School and Sandhurst products, like Roy; there were promoted rankers, with permanently squared shoulders and little waxed moustaches; there were professional and business men verging on middle-age, who had long shed their stomachs and acquired a genuine passion for army forms and regimental routine. The last two figures that caught my eye were those of my machine-gun officer, a Mathematical Fellow of an ancient Cambridge college, and Adams, second-in-command of B Company, who in a previous existence had officiated as under gate-porter in the same foundation. The British Army in those days was one great ladder, up which all men, gentle or simple, might climb if they had the character and the will. In that army at the end of the war there was a Divisional General who had been editor of a newspaper; there was a Brigadier-General who had been a taxi-cab driver; another who had been a schoolteacher. Numbered among that exclusive hierarchy, the General Staff, were an insurance clerk, an architect's assistant, and a college cook. A coal miner, a railway signalman, a market gardener, and countless promoted private soldiers commanded battalions.

A few minutes later I rode off with my adjutant, young Hume-Logan, in the direction of Michelin Forge. My faithful orderly—a gigantic, inarticulate Lowland hind named Herriott—jogged along in rear of us. It was a distressing ride. A badly mangled terrain, restored to France and cultivation by Hindenburg's operatic retirement to the Siegfried line, was being overrun once more: and the plucky, industrious peasant population, which had been so busily employed for the past twelve months in rebuilding their villages and re-ploughing their emancipated soil behind the traditionally sure shield of a British trench line, found itself uprooted and cast forth for the second time. The panic-stricken flood of refugees had now subsided; but along the road we encountered sights which wrung the heart and tweaked the conscience—here, a pitiful little cart loaded with worldly possessions which hardly seemed worth salving; there, a tired woman struggling along a muddy roadside with her children

Respiciens frustra rura laresque sua

—as Ovid used to say in the Repetition Book. I felt somehow, perhaps unjustifiably, but none the less poignantly, that for once the British Army had failed in a trust.

But presently I saw something which inspired me. Down the road came a big elderly peasant woman wheeling a barrow, piled high with household furniture. (You have to invade French peasant territory very suddenly and very early in the morning indeed, if you expect to find so much as an orange-box left to sit down upon.) We looked down on the barrow as it passed.

"She doesn't seem to have forgotten anything, sir," observed Master Hume-Logan.

I gave Madame a respectful salute as we rode past. Her hard features never relaxed. Instead, she set down her barrow by the roadside, turned round, and started back in the same direction as ourselves: in fact, she outstripped our two horses, which were walking delicately amid the puddles.

"She seems to have forgotten something, after all," I said.

But I was wrong. She had forgotten nothing. Two hundred yards along the road stood another wheelbarrow. In it—mute, helpless, patient—lay a very old man. The old woman seized the shafts of this barrow and began to wheel it after the first. In so doing she met us again—and again I saluted her. We turned in our saddles and looked after her. At her original halting-place she deposited the second barrow as close to the side of the road as possible, turned again to the first, and trundled it forward, without a moment's rest, another hundred yards or so. When last we saw her she was coming back—grim, resolute, invincible—for the old man. She *was* France—La Patrie, incarnate!

At last we penetrated beyond what we may call the refugee zone, and arrived at Michelin Forge. There was little of it left save the western gable, which was still decorated by a tattered presentment of two pre-war friends, the Bibendum Twins. The low ridge of Primrose Hill defined the horizon about a mile or two ahead of us. It was nothing of a hill; it looked no higher than its namesake in distant "N.W." A quarter-of-a-mile away from us enemy shells were falling with Teutonic regularity of interval into a group of poor houses, clustered round a cross-roads. Over the ridge itself shrapnel was bursting intermittently. Away to our left a large canteen hut was burning fiercely: probably it had been cleared and set alight to save it from falling into enemy hands. To the right of the forge a battery of our Four-point-Five Howitzers was firing salvoes—securely dug in, and screened from aeroplane view by nets interwoven with leaves and twigs. When, to the great content of our horses, this performance ceased, I rode over and sought out the young officer in command. He had not shaved for a week, and his quite creditable beard was encrusted with mud.

"Yes, sir," he said, "I can tell you a little. The enemy are in force just beyond that low ridge—Primrose Hill. We are strafing them now. Our F.O.O. is somewhere in Fountain Keep, which is a strong point just behind the crest, with one or two observation posts stretching over it. He has direct observation; his last telephone-message said that the enemy were massing again behind their own second line. I haven't heard from him since: that's why I stopped firing. Something gone wrong with the works, I expect."

"What's the distance from here to the ridge?" I asked.

"Well, we are firing at a range of four thousand three hundred; but that, of course, reaches Boche territory. The range to the crest is about three thousand five hundred."

"I see; a brisk country walk of about two miles? I shall deploy here. Has the Boche been shelling the reverse slope of the hill at all?"

"Not lately. But yesterday afternoon, during a big attack, he put down a heavy barrage from end to end of it."

"Hum! That means that when he attacks again he will put down another heavy barrage. The sooner we get to the crest of that hill the better."

I was turning away, when the gunner said:

"There's a sunken road over there, sir, behind that hedge. It runs straight towards Primrose Hill for nearly a mile, and ends where the gradient really begins. If you followed that you could get shelter for a bit, and need not take open order quite so soon."

"That's good advice," I said. "I will have a look at it. Is there much going on in the air at present?"

"They set one of our sausage-balloons on fire early this morning. The observer got down all right in his parachute; but I fancy the heavies behind us are a bit in the dark about things, in consequence."

"How are the gas-works?"

"They put mustard down with their last barrage."

"Any aeroplanes been over?"

"One Boche machine came over at dawn, but our Archies hunted him back. This battery hasn't been spotted so far; but I expect we shall have to limber up and do another Hindenburg act presently; we have been doing nothing else for a week. A fortnight ago we were in rest billets about here, running about and playing football and going to the pictures! It's a bit thick!" he grunted ruefully, through his mask of dirt.

"We are to go in and stiffen the line ahead of us," I said. "You stay where you are, and back us! Here's my leading company coming up now. Good-morning!"

"Good-morning, sir, and good luck!"

The gunner hurried back to his camouflaged emplacements, and I turned to find Roy at my elbow.

"A message came through from brigade, sir," he said, "just after you left, to say that the enemy were massing heavily opposite Primrose Hill, and that we were to get up as soon as possible."

"Right! Let us have a look at a covered approach I have just heard about."

We crossed a meadow and looked over a hedge. Sure enough, at our very feet lay a deep cutting, following the line of the hedge towards Primrose Hill.

"Bring your company over here," I said, "and start them up this thoroughfare for all they're worth. Have the signallers arrived?"

"Yes, sir; they came with me."

"Tell the signal sergeant to establish telephone communication with Brigade Headquarters as quickly as he can." I turned to that faithful shadow, my adjutant. "Notify the other companies as they arrive—to this effect." I scribbled an order. "Explain to Major Wylie"—Major Wylie was my second in command—"that I have gone ahead with A Company. He will take charge of affairs here and maintain communication as far as possible from front to rear. Is that quite clear?"

"Yes, sir."

"Good! Ah! here is Captain Birnie, with A Company. Now, Roy, young fellow-my-lad, what about it?"

Five minutes later Roy and I were heading up the sunken lane, followed by A Company, with steel helmets adjusted and gas-masks at the ready.

"By rights," I grunted, "I suppose I ought to be sitting in Michelin Forge maintaining touch with Brigade Headquarters. But I think this is going to be one of those occasions upon which a C.O. is justified in leading his regiment from the front. I am fed up with this Duke of Plaza Toro business."

Roy did not reply. He struck me as a little *distrait*, which did not altogether surprise me, considering that we were both going, in all probability, straight to an early demise. In fact, I was feeling a little *distrait* myself. But this was no time for preoccupation. Progress along the lane was not too easy. There was a good deal of traffic coming the other way—stragglers, stretcher-cases, walking wounded, and dispatch-riders urging their reluctant motor-cycles through a river of mud. Phlegmatic cave-dwellers in dug-outs in the banks of the lane, mainly signallers, looked out upon us, exchanging grisly jests with my followers. Sappers, imperturbable as ever, were running out wire across an open space to the right. A water-party met us, jangling empty petrol-cans. At one point we passed a row of our dead, awaiting removal. On nearly every sleeve I noticed one, two, or even three gold stripes. It seemed desperately hard that The Willing Horse, healed three times of his wounds, should have gone down for good so near the end—as the event proved it to be—when others had never left the stable.

Presently we overtook a slow-moving procession, advancing with that injured bearing and gait which mark Thomas Atkins when employed upon an uncongenial job. They were a fatigue party, carrying enormous trench-mortar bombs.

"We can never get past this crowd," I said to Roy. "We'll climb out here, and deploy to the left."

Roy gave the order, and soon A Company were advancing in extended formation with their faces set towards Fountain Keep. Roy and I tramped ahead of them: the ridge of Primrose Hill was barely a thousand yards away now. The morning mists had cleared away, and we could see it quite distinctly.

Suddenly Roy turned to me.

"Uncle Alan," he began—

But he got no further. There came a roar and a shock that shook the ground. Five hundred yards ahead of us the brown face of Primrose Hill broke into a spouting row of earth-fountains, intermingled with the smoke of shrapnel and whizz-bangs. The evening's barrage had begun. The line of men behind us recoiled for a moment, then pressed stolidly forward.

"We have got to get through that," I announced—a little superfluously.

Roy replied—somewhat unexpectedly—right in my left ear, at the top of his voice:

"Uncle Alan, I want to tell you that I am married!"

"So I have been given to understand!" I bellowed. The din was growing louder.

"Who told you? Old Eskerley?"

I nodded; halted; and sniffed the air,

"I thought so," I said. "Gas-masks, Roy—quick!"

Roy turned and waved an order to his company. In a few seconds we were advancing again: each man had transformed God's image into a goggled deformity, and was breathing God's air from a box of chemicals through a jointed tube.

Roy and I adjusted our masks last.

"Come along," I said, with a glance ahead of us: "the longer we look at it the less we shall like it!" I tried to fit my mask to my face, but found that Roy was shouting into my ear again.

"Uncle Alan—"

I inclined my head towards him.

"Well?"

"*I am a father!*"

I nodded my hideous head, and smiled congratulations as well as I could.

"I only got word this morning," I heard him bawl as his face disappeared into his mask. "BOY!" And with that he led his company into the barrage.

I felt convinced if we got through it Roy would tell the first German he met about the baby.

CHAPTER XX
FOUNTAIN KEEP

Of the next half-hour my recollection is mercifully blurred. All that I know is that most of us got through the barrage and foregathered at the back of Fountain Keep, which proved to be a circular *point d'appui* intersected and honeycombed with trenches, saps and tunnels.

"Carry right on with the company," I said to Roy. "I think you will find some hand-to-hand work going on just over the ridge; so your men will be welcome. I will try to find the Headquarters of the Royal Loyals. Take care of yourself, laddie!"

Our gas-masks were off again by this time, so we could smile at one another as we parted.

Ultimately Herriott and I discovered the Headquarters of the Fifth Royal Loyals—a dug-out at the back of the Keep, occupied by a slightly hysterical second lieutenant (apparently the adjutant) and a telephone orderly vainly trying to make connection with a Brigade Headquarters which we learned afterwards had been shelled out of existence twenty minutes before.

"The battalion are cut to pieces, sir," gasped the second lieutenant. "They are fighting more or less in the open.... There are hardly any trenches.... The C.O. was killed half an hour ago.... Most of the company commanders have been scuppered too. The line's broken in two or three places, and we are fighting in small groups.... They are putting up a wonderful kick.... But there's hardly anybody left ... no platoon commanders or anything. I seem to be in command of the battalion!" He giggled, foolishly. "I came back here to try and telephone for help.... All the numbers seem to be engaged, though!" He began to sob. He looked barely twenty.

"That's all right," I said. "I have sent a company of my Jocks to stiffen your front line, and three more are coming up. Here, take a pull at my flask, and then show me the way through this Keep of yours! Looks like the Maze at Hampton Court, doesn't it? We must hold on to it whatever happens: it's the key to the whole business. Who's in command up in front, by the way?"

"A corporal, I think."

"*A corporal*? Come along! The sooner we reinforce him the better."

But the boy was too badly shell-shocked to guide me, so Herriott and I went on alone. We plunged into the depths of the Keep, and followed its deep mazes as best we could. Here and there I noticed traces of the ornamental garden. We passed by the wrecked fountain, with a broken stucco figure lying across its basin. Once our road took us through an artificial rockery, reinforced with sandbags. The trenches were deep, and we could see nothing but the sky above our heads. Everywhere was the old familiar reek—humanity and chloride of lime. The noise was terrific now. Our own shells were whistling over our heads: evidently my grimy friend with the four-point-fives had got to work again. Enemy artillery was silent, probably through fear of hitting its own men; but bombs and trench-mortars were busy.

The windings of the Keep were tortuous, and we wandered more or less at random, stepping here and there over some obstruction—an abandoned case of ammunition, or a dead soldier. Suddenly we emerged into what was obviously a firing-trench. It was lined with men, mounted on the step and maintaining a steady fusillade. From their deliberate movements I saw that they were fighting well within themselves. Some were Roy's men, others members of that sturdy Territorial unit, the Fifth Royal Loyals. There were other details—cyclists, signallers, Labour Corps men—all contributing. Evidently some organising influence had been at work. A few yards along the trench to the right I observed a sort of projection, or bastion, in which a Lewis gun team were maintaining enfilade fire along the wire to their own right.

Realising that I had reached the forward edge of Fountain Keep, I was about to hoist myself on to the firing step in order to see what was happening on the other side of the parapet, when my attention was attracted to the man who appeared to be in general charge of the sector. It was difficult to discern his rank, for he was in his shirt sleeves, like many of his comrades. (Tommy Atkins has a passion for *déshabillé*.) Obviously he was not an officer, for he wore the unæsthetic boots and grey flannel shirt of the rank-and-file. His steel helmet had fallen off, and I could see that his hair was quite grey. His face, like those of most present, was framed in a six days' beard, with a top-dressing of dirt; but he was an undoubted leader of men. When first I saw him he was directing the Lewis gun team. Presently he came down the trench towards me, throwing up fresh clips of ammunition and shouting encouragement to the men on the firing-step—though in that hellish din I doubt if they heard much of what he said.

He passed the mouth of the communication trench in which I was standing without noticing me, and disappeared round a traverse on the left, evidently on his way to stiffen morale in the next bay. I found myself gazing after him with an interest for which I could not quite account. Probably he was the corporal of whom the shell-shocked boy behind us had spoken....

I became suddenly conscious that Herriott was stiffening to attention. This meant that Herriott desired permission to deliver himself of a remark.

"Well, Herriott?" I said.

"I beg your pardon, sirr—"

"Yes? What?"

"Yon, sirr, is—"

At that moment a German trench-mortar bomb came sailing over, and burst some thirty yards to our left. Fortunately our bay was screened from the effects by a stout island-traverse. However, I fear I missed the purport of Herriott's statement. In fact, I doubt if I heard it at all, for at that moment Roy appeared round the corner on the right, followed by an orderly.

He was bleeding from a scratch on the cheek, and held his Colt automatic in his hand.

"We have just pushed them back on the right, sir," he announced. His eyes were blazing. "They tried to rush a bad bit of our line about a hundred yards along; but our boys were splendid, and very few Boches got as far as the parapet. They simply withered up when they got to the wire."

I pointed to the bastion, where the Lewis gunners were recharging magazines.

"Those are the fellows you have to thank," I said. "How is the situation generally?"

"The Boche has gone back everywhere, for the moment," Roy replied. "I fancy he will give us a dose of trench-mortars and H.E., and then try again. I am going along the line now, to see if all the men are in place."

"You will find a very efficient understudy round that traverse," I said—"a corporal. I found him handling this bit of line like a field-marshal."

Again I was aware of the dour presence of Herriott at my elbow.

"I beg your pardon, sirr—" he began again.

Again the words were taken out of his mouth. Round the corner of the traverse to our left struggled a pitifully familiar group—two stooping men supporting a third between them. The wounded man held an arm resolutely round the neck of each supporter, but his feet dragged in the mud. It was the grey-headed corporal.

"Stretcher-bearers, there!" cried one of the men gruffly.

"How did they cop you, Corporal?" inquired a Royal Loyal, leaning down sympathetically from the firing-step.

"That last trench-mortar!" gasped the grey-haired man, as they set him down on the floor of the trench, just below the Lewis gun emplacement. He turned his head feebly in our direction, and our eyes met for the first time. At the same moment Roy gave a cry and started forward.

Then I understood what Herriott had been trying to tell me. Tom Birnie lay dying before our eyes—at the feet of his own son.

Roy, very white, dropped on his knees beside his father. A stretcher came, and we did what we could. Tom had a dreadful wound in his side; plainly it was only a matter of minutes. I remember seeing Roy unbuckle his own equipment, take off his tunic, and wrap it round his father's shoulders. Tom's eyes were closed; his breathing was laboured; he recognised no one.

For a moment the tempest of battle around us seemed to stand still. The crowded trench was silent; the men on the firing-step looked down curiously. Roy still knelt beside his father, motionless. Herriott, who had worked on the Baronrigg estate ever since he could walk, stood rigidly at attention at the foot of the Laird's stretcher, with tears trickling down his cheeks.

At last Tom's eyes opened. He smiled and said faintly:

"That you, Roy? Good boy! I was expecting you.... I carried on as well as I could, until you came to take over.... I knew you would come.... I knew! Give your father a kiss, old man."

Roy bowed his head....

Next moment, with the shriek of an express train emerging from a tunnel, a German shell whirled out of the blue and exploded against the traverse a few yards away.

When I came to myself I was being carried in Herriott's arms—and I weigh nearly fourteen stone—back through the mazes of Fountain Keep in the direction of the first aid post. After more than three years of continuous seeking I had achieved the soldier's ambition—a "blighty."

That night, as I passed on my jolting way to the base, with a smashed collar-bone and a damaged skull, my rambling dreams ran naturally on one subject—that strange meeting between father and son; and the spectacle of the one passing on to the other, as it were some precious inheritance, the safe custody of Fountain Keep.

CHAPTER XXI
IDENTITIES
I

Night had fallen on Fountain Keep; for the moment the guns were silent and the battle had died down. To-morrow the Boche would come again—and again. But he would get no farther. The high-water mark of the great spring offensive of Nineteen Eighteen had been reached—in this region at any rate, though none knew it. To the right the long, attenuated British line had been pressed back to the village of Villers Bretonneux, within sight of Amiens; the Australians were destined to do historic work here six weeks later, when the bundling-out process began. On the left, before Arras, despite massed attacks and reckless expenditure of German cannon-fodder, the line had held fast. On every side, for the moment, the enemy had sullenly withdrawn, to lick his wounds. He would try again later on further north, in the flat plain of the sluggish Lys—only to create a second spectacular and untenable salient in the British line, with the Vimy Ridge standing up invincibly between the two, like a great rock splitting the force of a spring spate.

Fountain Keep was very still and silent. It lay once more well within the British lines. It had been captured by the enemy in a massed attack at three o'clock that afternoon, despite the gallant defence put up by A Company and the great-hearted remnants of the Royal Loyals—to be recaptured in a most skilfully directed counter-attack just before nightfall by the three remaining companies of the Royal Covenanters. With the key position restored, a gallant rally had taken place all along the line, and once more the whole of Primrose Hill was in British hands.

Out in front weary men were consolidating the position—replacing sandbags and running out wire. Fountain Keep itself, lying snugly behind its restored trench-line, had resumed its proper function of *point d'appui* and battalion headquarters. But British prestige had been restored at the usual prodigal cost. Stretcher-bearers were everywhere, stumbling about in the darkness from shell-hole to shell-hole, where wounded men usually contrive to drag themselves. Many of those wounded had seen khaki puttees, then German field-boots, then khaki puttees pass over their heads that day.

They were nearly all collected by this time; our own particular Alan Laing had passed through the field dressing-station hours ago. Now the battle-ground was occupied by other search-parties, whose business lay with those who had been delivered for ever from the pain of wounds and the weariness of convalescence.

Such a party was at this moment employing itself in Fountain Keep, under the direction of a conscientious but not over-imaginative sergeant, named Busby.

"We'll go along the front parapet first," he announced; "that's where most of 'em are.... Yes, 'ere's one—a Jock; lance-corporal, by his stripe. Get his pay-book out of his pocket, 'Erb. Not got one? Well, he *ought* to 'ave, that's all; it's in Regulations. Look at his identity-disc, then. Read it out, and read it slow; my pencil's blunt. *Number Seven-Six-Five-Fower-Eight—Private J. Couper*—been promoted since he got that—*Second Royal Covenanters—Presbyterian*. Righto! Now, this one—No, never mind 'im, it's only a 'Un; no need to take *his* number! Pass along, boys! Get a move on; we've got a lot to do."

The little procession moved on, performing its grim duties with characteristic sang-froid, lightened by the incurable, untimely, invaluable flippancy of the British soldier. Presently they came to a place where a bastion of sandbags had been improvised as an emplacement for a Lewis gun. The gun itself lay twisted and earthy on a heap of burst sandbags; below the emplacement lay the gun's crew.

"One shell got the lot, I fancy," remarked Sergeant Busby. "Switch on your torch, Alf; there are four or five of 'em here. Lift them clear of one another, boys."

Four bodies were lifted, not irreverently, and laid side by side on the ground behind the emplacement, with sightless eyes upturned to the twinkling stars. One remained—a long-legged figure in shirt-sleeves, lying with face turned to the parapet.

"Help me to turn this feller over, 'Erb," commanded the sergeant. "Seems to have lost his toonic; Government property, too! Well, he can't be brought up for it now. Hallo! ... 'Strewth! ... Did you see that, 'Erb? It give me a turn for a minute. 'Alf a tick!" He bent down hurriedly, and listened. "He's breathing! There's a stretcher-party round that traverse; you, Richards, double off and bring them, quick!"

Five minutes later the insensible form of the man who had mislaid Government property was borne away, and Sergeant Busby proceeded with the identification of his less (or more) fortunate companions. 'Erb, the *littérateur* of the party, read off the identity-discs one by one.

"*Smith—Turner—'Opkins*," repeated the sergeant, labouring with the blunt pencil. "That's the first lot of Loyals we've struck. There must be a heap more somewhere; we'll find 'em presently. What's the name of this last one? Give us his number first. *Six-O-Four-O-Two; Private T. Birnie*—spelt with two I's—right! Royal Loyals, I suppose? *Religion*? Eh, what's the trouble now?"

"Sergeant," interposed 'Erb, in a puzzled voice, "look 'ere! This ain't no private; it's an orficer! Look at his tunic—three stars, and all!"

Sergeant Busby flashed his electric torch once more. It revealed a grey-haired man, with a captain's tunic wrapped round his shoulders, tied by the sleeves.

"Yes," he announced judicially, "he's an officer, all right; and what's more, he's an officer in a Jock regiment. I know a bit about uniforms, my lad; and no English officer wears a cutaway tunic like that, or his pips in that position. And there's his collar-badges! He's not a Loyal at all, this feller; he's a Covenanter."

"What about his identity-disc?" inquired 'Erb, respectfully. "That says 'Private.'"

The sapient Busby pondered. Then—

"He was a private once," he explained, "in the Loyals; then he got his commission and was gazetted to the Covenanters; but he never got himself issued with a new identity disc. Economical that's what he was. Real Scotch, I expect! Well, if he's an officer, we needn't worry with his regimental number; that goes out." The blunt pencil thudded. "I'll just put him down as *Captain Birnie, Royal Covenanters—Presbyterian*; that's enough. Carry on, boys!"

The heavy-footed procession filed away through the mud, round the traverse, and out of this narrative.

And that was how it came to pass that Sir Thomas Birnie, Baronet, of Baronrigg, who in the humility of his heart had enlisted as a private and died as a corporal, was buried next day, with absolute justice, as the officer and gentleman that he really was.

II

Meanwhile Roy, with his stout young skull almost riven by a glancing Boche nose-cap, lay tossing and muttering in a Base Hospital.

One dream beset and obsessed him for weeks. He, Roy Birnie—the soldierly, the punctilious, the immaculate—had been haled by an escort of overwhelming numbers and terrifying appearance before his commanding officer—Uncle Alan, swollen to enormous size and invested with Mephistophelean eyebrows—upon the charge of coming upon parade improperly dressed. It was not merely a question of an unbuttoned pocket, or a pair of badly-wound puttees; he had paraded in his shirt-sleeves—minus his tunic! And in his dream, try as he might, poor Roy could not for the life of him recall, in response to the nightmare cross-examination of his satanic superior and relative, what he had done with it.

All he could recollect was that he had wrapped it round someone—someone who appeared to have lost his own and to be badly in need of another; because he was lying on the ground in the mud. Roy had fitful glimpses of the face—the face of a man dying in great pain, but in great peace—a strangely familiar face. Roy had tried to converse with its owner; but in his dreams their intercourse was limited chiefly to intensely affectionate smiles. Then, suddenly, he had recognised the face, and was stooping, in an awkward, boyish fashion, to kiss it, when something happened, and he remembered no more.

III

Gradually these troubled visions faded, and with the steady healing of his wound came healthy sleep and tranquillity of mind. Finally he came to himself; and one bright morning in May was carried on board a hospital ship and transferred, across the most efficiently guarded strip of water in the world, to a convalescent hospital in a great country house in Kent.

That night he slept in a little room in a long passage full of doors, behind each of which lay a boy, seldom older than himself, who had squandered his youth, mayhap a limb, too often his whole constitution, in the service of his country.

Next morning, when he awoke, the sun was streaming down the passage. All the doors stood wide open, and the air was rent by a raucous and irregular chorus, proceeding from the doorways and beginning:

Nurse, Nurse, I'm feeling rather worse;
Come and kiss me on my little brow!

Words of rebuke were audible, and the riot died down. A majestic young woman, admirably composed, presented herself at Roy's door.

"Good morning, Captain Birnie. I hope you slept well."

"Thank you, I did," replied Roy. "Are you the Sister?"

Across the passage came a voice:

"Let me present you, sir, to Little Lily, our Cross Red nurse! She—"

The lady indicated whirled round upon the offender, whose grinning face, partially obscured by a patch over one eye, could be discerned upon the pillow of the bed in the room opposite.

"Mr. Abercrombie," she announced, "if you can't behave I shall report you to the Matron."

Mr. Abercrombie was all contrition at once.

"All right, Nurse!" he announced. "I apologise! I only want to warn you, sir," he added to Roy, "that she's married! But she never tells us that until it's too late! *Do* be careful!"

Little Lily, the Cross Red nurse—otherwise the Lady Hermione Mulready—turned an unruffled countenance to Roy. It was true that she was married; she possessed what Mr. Abercrombie would have called "a perfectly good husband of her own" in the Irish Guards. She had once possessed two brothers also, somewhat akin in appearance and disposition to the effervescent Abercrombie. Perhaps that was why she suffered his impertinences so readily.

"Here is your breakfast, Captain Birnie," she continued. "The Matron says you can't have bacon yet; but if you are good you may reach an ordinary diet next week."

Roy thanked her.

"After breakfast," he asked politely, "may I write a letter—just one? And see a paper? I'm a bit behind with the war, and—"

"You can have anything you want, in reason, so long as you lie still and don't fidget. We have enough babies in this place already!" announced Little Lily, with a withering glance in the direction of the room opposite where Master Abercrombie was acting foolishly.

"It's all right," Roy assured her. "You will have no trouble with me. I'm quite an old man, really: a kind husband, and an indulgent father, and all that," he added, with a curious little air of pomposity.

His nurse looked down upon him with quickened interest.

"Are you a father?" she asked.

"Yes. Only just, though! I—I—haven't seen It yet!" His voice quivered suddenly, to think how near he had gone to not seeing It at all.

"I am glad you came through," said Little Lily quietly; and handed him *The Times* to read with his breakfast.

Roy poured out his tea, stretched back luxuriously, and unfolded the paper. Like most of us in those days, he turned first to the casualty list. The names of the officers alone filled two columns.

"I wonder if my old cracked cranium has figured here yet," he ruminated. "What a nice little thrill if it's in to-day!"

He glanced down the long list of wounded.

"No, nothing doing! It has probably been in already." He turned in more leisurely fashion to the previous column, and began to read the names of the killed. But his eye got no further than the first name. There were no A's to-day: this began with B.

He laid the paper down, and grinned to himself.

"I'd rather read it than be it!" he reflected.

Then, suddenly, a blinding thought smote him.

Marjorie! What if she had seen it? He sat up excitedly, as a further probability occurred to him.

"She must have been notified privately by the War Office long ago. Then, of all times!" He was talking to himself now, in a low, agitated voice. "My God! I wonder where she is! The old man never told me when he wired; but he'll know." His voice rose. "Nurse! Nurse! Nurse!"

"Great Scott!" announced Mr. Abercrombie from the opposite room: "The lad has succumbed already! And I *warned* him!"

But already Lady Hermione's tall figure was framed in Roy's doorway.

"Here I am," she said. "Don't shout, please. You will find a bell-push under your pillow, if you look.... Why, my *dear*, what is it?"

Roy handed her the paper, pointing dumbly.

"My wife!" he whispered. "She'll think I'm— And I don't even know where she is—to contradict it! Have you a telephone here? Could you ring up Lord Eskerley's house in London? He'll know! He knows everything! He knows—"

Lady Hermione laid a cool hand upon his bandaged forehead.

"Don't get flustered!" she said. "Get up, and put on your dressing-gown. I will show you where the telephone is."

Next moment, with Roy swaying on her arm, she was sailing down the passage in the direction of the office in the front hall.

"They're keeping company already! Quick work! Quick work!" commented Master Abercrombie, admiringly.

CHAPTER XXII
THE MILLS OF GOD

"He must have left a will of some kind," said Lord Eskerley.

"He made one before he went to France," I replied; "but that has been invalidated by his marriage. It doesn't really matter; because everything—the baronetcy, Baronrigg, and so on—will pass automatically to the child."

"Still, you know what lawyers are when a man dies intestate! There will be nothing left worth scraping up if we don't provide something of a documentary nature for them to bite on. Didn't they find anything in his pockets, when they—found him?"

"Nothing but his cigarette-case, and Marjorie's last letter."

We were standing in the outer library of Lord Eskerley's great house in Curzon Street. It was a bright morning in May, and the sun, streaming between the heavy window-curtains, made the rest of the room look more than usually funereal by comparison. At one end, double doors opened into his lordship's *sanctum sanctorum*, where few but the faithful Meadows ever presumed to track him. At the other yawned a great empty fireplace, with a curiously carved mantelpiece, over which hung Millais' radiant portrait of Lady Eskerley as a bride.

Beside the fire-place stood the secretary's own particular writing-table. To the wall just above it was fixed an incongruously modern-looking telephone switch-board. Lord Eskerley's eye fell on this; and he was off in a moment down one of his usual by-paths.

"Private wire, and so on!" he explained. "Meadows had it put in. He just pushes a few buttons, and puts a plug in a hole; and I can telephone not only to the outside world but direct to the office, or the War Cabinet, or to my own bathroom. Wonderful invention! Wonderful fellow! It's the devil, though, when he goes out for a walk: I'm no good at it myself. I tried to ring up the P.M. the other day, and found myself breathing private and confidential war secrets to my own laundry-maid. By the way, have you looked through those things yet? You may find what you want there."

He pointed to the corner of the room, where a mud-stained, sun-bleached Wolseley valise of green Willesden canvas lay rolled and strapped. It had once been Roy's, and had arrived the previous day, forwarded to me as next-of-kin, bearing that pitiful designation: "*Deceased Officers Effects*."

"I will go through it this morning," I said, "and report. Eric is coming along; he'll help me. By the way, how is Marjorie to-day? Eric is sure to want to know."

"Why should he want to know—eh? Why this solicitude?"

"I don't know. He always does. Why shouldn't he take an interest in her, like the rest of us?"

But plainly my old friend was not quite satisfied.

"To take an interest in a beautiful young widow is right and proper," he said—"especially if you happen to be an eligible D.S.O. But not too premature an interest, please! Bethune is a gallant soldier; but fine feeling never was his *forte*." Suddenly the old man blazed up. "Good God! Has he realised that the poor child doesn't even know she is a widow?"

That Eric should be taking, or ever have taken, a more than fatherly interest in Marjorie was news to me. I am not very perceptive in these matters; but the possibility of such a thing explained a good deal to me—Eric's persistent dislike of Roy, for instance. Still, I had no desire to pursue the topic; and switched accordingly.

"I am afraid she will have to be told now," I said. "It's in the paper this morning. People will be writing to condole, and so on."

"I know," said Lord Eskerley. "I shall tell her myself—this afternoon." He shook his white head sorrowfully. "It will be pretty awful, though: a woman ought to do it really." He glanced up at the portrait of his long dead wife. "We will give her one more morning, poor little soul! Hark!"

The door into the hall stood open; so, apparently, did the door of Marjorie's room, on the first floor above us. As we stood, we could hear her voice uplifted in a somewhat exaggerated apostrophe to her own son; also that self-satisfied infant's gurgling reception of the same. Mother and son, by the way, had been in the house for more than three weeks, having been conveyed thither from a nursing home in Kensington, where, thanks to the timely warning of a flamboyant but attractive young person named Liss Lyle, we had been constrained to look for them. Miss Lyle was now our constant visitor, and had completely enmeshed the hitherto impregnable Meadows.

"Extraordinary gibberish, baby talk!" remarked Lord Eskerley. "Primeval, of course, and quite unaltered through the ages." Then, suddenly:

"Poor child, she's had a hard time! Three years of exhausting self-imposed drudgery—then maternity! And now she has to be told that she's a widow. My God, Alan, how I hate Wilhelm sometimes! And he once dined in this house!"

"What is the news, by the way?" I asked.

"Good, decidedly good! I think we have the Boche cold at last. Internally Germany is on her last legs. Only one thing could have braced her up—a spectacular success last March. As things turned out, that enterprise went off at half-cock—though it gave us a most salutary scare. Now our morale is returning: Foch has the situation well in hand. I fancy he will encourage the enemy to attack a little longer: then, when he has blown a few more swollen salients in our line, come right back at him and puncture them one by one. That and the arrival of the Americans—they are splendid troops, I hear, and are being rushed over at the rate of three hundred thousand a month now—should put the last nail into the Teutonic coffin." The old man paused, and sighed. "Not before it was time, though! Our casualties passed the three million mark the other day, Alan! Still, our tribulations of the past three months may have been worth while. They have taught us two things: firstly, that this blundering, flat-footed old country of ours retains its ancient staying-power; secondly, never to be too cocksure about winning until you have won! What time is he coming?"

"Eleven o'clock," I replied, concluding that this lightning reference was to Eric.

"Umph! I have to be at Downing Street at twelve. Meanwhile, I shall be in my own inner chamber if you want me. Good-bye! There are cigarettes in that box. Poor little girl!"

The double doors closed, and I was left alone.

I unstrapped Roy's valise without much difficulty—my comminuted collar-bone was mending nicely, though I had been warned that I might never be able to wield a salmon-rod again—and emptied out its jumbled contents on to the floor. At the same moment Eric was announced.

"Come along," I said, "and get that new tin arm of yours to work. Sort out everything in the shape of papers from that mess, and let us go through them."

"Are we looking for anything in particular?" asked Eric, reluctantly setting to work. He always hated drudgery.

"Roy's will."

Eric nodded; and laid a heap of documents on the table. There was a tattered sheaf of battalion orders; an old field dispatch book, a number of maps; and a bundle of letters.

"I fancy the letters are from Marjorie," I said. "We need not bother to read them."

"How is she, by the way?" asked Eric, looking up.

"Getting along, I believe."

"One would like to show her any little kindness that is possible," Eric continued. "One has sent her flowers, of course, and so on. Is there anything else? I wonder if she would like to see me? It would probably do her good."

It was the old touch. I smiled despite myself.

"I wouldn't suggest it at present, if I were you," I said. "She is to have some news broken to her this afternoon."

"You mean—?"

I nodded.

"It's in the paper this morning," I said. "The War Office telegram we could keep from her; but not that."

Eric was silent, and began to turn over the papers.

"These maps had better go back to Ordnance," he remarked. "They ought to have been taken out at Battalion Headquarters, by rights. Some of these old Orders are interesting: they have a musty flavour now. Listen to this":

The C.O. has observed that N.C.O.'s and Men are falling into the habit of washing their gas-helmets.

"Do you remember those noisome old flannel jelly-bags, Alan?"

"I do! They were abolished, as far as I can remember, about the middle of nineteen sixteen."

"Yes, that's right. They were about as much use as the sick headache which they produced."

Officers Commanding Companies will see that this practice is discontinued at once. Helmets so washed are entirely useless against a gas attack.

"Still," I commented, "if you wore them unwashed you died whether there was a gas attack on or not; so altogether, I don't blame the washers!"

"Hallo," continued Eric; "here's a *billet-doux* from Corps Headquarters."

"What is it?"

Eric grinned.

"*Mules, Brief Notes on the Treatment of.* They do manage to think of things on Olympus!..."

The mule is much more dainty about what he drinks than about what he eats.

"I think that's true: my last consignment ate seventeen nose-bags and three pack-saddles in a single night."

The mule is not really of a vicious disposition; he is only shy and nervous, and is very responsive to petting—

"So am I, for that matter! But let's get on, Eric. Here's a field despatch book. It has been lying in a puddle, I fancy: these carbon duplicates have run a bit. Never mind! I don't suppose there is anything of importance inside it."

"The only legible despatch is the last one," said Eric, turning over the pages. "A pretty stately epistle, too! Listen!"

To O.C. 7th Battalion, the Grampian Regiment.

Sir,—Reference your FZ/357, in which it is stated that the one hundred picks and shovels which this Battalion was directed to hand over to yours on the 16th inst. were handed over deficient five picks and four shovels; I am to inform you that an N.C.O. was duly sent in charge of the picks and shovels in a G.S. Waggon to Bluepoint Farm at seven a.m. on that date, and there handed over the full number of picks and shovels to an N.C.O. of your Battalion, who counted them and gave a receipt for same, a copy of which I now enclose.

Your obedient servant,
R. T. C. Birnie, Lieut.,
For Lt.-Col. Commanding
2nd Battalion, Royal Covenanters.

"That fairly puts it across the Grampian Regiment!" was Eric's verdict. "I congratulate you!"

"It was Roy who was responsible," I said. "He got me out of a nasty mess with the C.R.E. by producing that receipt. He was a grand adjutant, bless him!"

Eric continued to turn over the leaves of the despatch book.

"There is nothing in the shape of a will or testament here," he said at last. "No; wait a minute; there's something in the pocket of the flap."

He held the pocket open, and shook out its contents on to the table cloth—two faded slips of pinkish paper.

"These don't look very promising," he said. "Field telegraph despatches!"

He unfolded the first slip, smoothed it out, and read aloud:

The expression "Dud" will no longer be employed in Official Correspondence.

He laughed. "There's Staff work for you!"

"Eric—!" I began suddenly. Some inward monitor had jerked an alarm-cord in my brain. Where had I heard that message before? And in conjunction with what? I leaned across the table and stretched out my hand; but already Eric had unfolded the second despatch, and was smoothing it out with the wrist of his artificial arm. I noticed that a covering slip was pinned to the despatch.

Passed to you, read Eric—*for immediate compliance, please.—J. E. F.*

"That was old Forrester, the Brigade Major. It sounds quite urgent; I wonder what it is all about."

"Eric—!" I said again. Then, suddenly, I held my peace. Who was I, to interfere with God?

"Hallo," continued Eric—"here's my name!"

Lieutenant-Colonel E. F. B. Bethune, D.S.O., Commanding Second Battalion Royal Covenanters—

He stopped suddenly—as I knew he would. I looked up, and watched his face go white, as he read the message to the end. I saw him re-read it, again and again. Then he examined the date, and hour of despatch. Then came a long, deathly silence.

At last he lifted his face to me—the face of a man suddenly aged. He pushed the pink slip in my direction.

"Have you ever seen that before?" he asked, in a hoarse voice.

I read the message mechanically through, though I knew it by heart. It said:

Lt.-Col E. F. B. Bethune, D.S.O., Commanding Second Battalion, Royal Covenanters, will return home forthwith, and report to War Office.

CHAPTER XXIII
THE SOUL OF ERIC BETHUNE

How long we sat there I do not know. But at last I was conscious that Eric was speaking again.

"When did Roy Birnie get this?"

"Immediately after you had moved off with the battalion—that afternoon at Caterpillar Farm, before the Somme show. He and I stayed to clear up, you remember?"

"Yes, yes!" he muttered, staring at the paper. "I remember. But—but why didn't he give it to me? Didn't he realise what it meant?"

"Yes, he realised all right. That was why he didn't give it to you."

Eric took up the despatch in his shaking hand.

"Roy Birnie deliberately held that back?" he said.

I nodded.

"And you?"

"Don't ask me about it," I replied, lighting my pipe and feeling thoroughly uncomfortable. "It's no part of a second-in-command's duty to supervise the adjutant's correspondence."

"But—didn't he show it to you?"

"Now you ask me, he did."

"But—but—it would have put you in command of the battalion!"

"My dear sir," I explained gruffly, "a man can't take command of a battalion if the adjutant neglects to publish the order which appoints him." I felt horribly mean, but this seemed to me to be a case where the dead could most conveniently bear the responsibility.

Suddenly Eric rose to his feet. I glanced at him, and flinched, for I knew what was coming. The colour had come back to his face, and his blue eyes were aglow. He was "up in the cloods." He came round to my side of the table, and laid his hands on my shoulders. It was strange to feel the lifeless weight of his artificial arm. I flinched again, and made a testy reference to my comminuted collar-bone.

But Eric was not to be denied. He had been exposed to himself as an incompetent and a failure; but what mattered more—solely—to him was that the world did not know about it; Roy and I had saved him from that. All that was grateful in his nature had been roused by that infernal telegram. He sat down beside me and took my hand in his. I felt very ridiculous.

"My God, old man," he said, "you saved me! You two saved me from being broke! You, who might have commanded the battalion—and young Roy! Young Roy! After what I had done to him—and—tried to do to him!"

"Oh, come!" I said. "You were a bit of a martinet, sometimes—the heavy C.O., and all that—but there's no need to reproach yourself over Roy."

Eric let go my hand—greatly to my relief—and began to walk about the room. Suddenly he turned to me.

"Alan, old man," he said, "do you know exactly what I did to Roy? I tried to take his girl away from him!"

I looked up. Lord Eskerley had been right, as usual.

"You mean—Marjorie?"

"Yes—Marjorie! Not once—nor twice—not accidentally—nor casually; but deliberately and continuously! Listen!" He was in the flood-tide of confession now, and I knew that in that mood he was not apt to be reticent.

"I made love to her at Craigfoot—in a 'you're-a-nice-little-girl' sort of way—while Roy was at Sandhurst. I made love to her in London, when I was on leave and he was in France—took her out to dinner and lunch, and so on—"

"Why not? It was up to her to refuse."

"She didn't refuse."

"In that case, she must have found your society agreeable."

"No, she didn't! I am pretty vain about myself, Alan; but I could see she didn't!"

"Then why did she accept your invitations?"

"I fancy it was because it gave her a chance to talk about the regiment—which meant Roy. Not that she ever mentioned him; but—I see it now! My God, what a cad I was! I let her sit there, while I crabbed him—talked patronisingly of him—belittled the good work he had always done for me and my battalion. Ugh!"

"Did you really care for her?"

"I was fascinated by her for the time. She is a glorious creature!"

"She certainly is."

"But I think that in the main it was jealousy—jealousy of Roy's youth, and the fact that instead of being my son, as he might have been, he was my rival. It was a mad business altogether. Finally, I asked her to marry me."

"She turned you down?" It was an unnecessary remark.

"Of course she turned me down! But she did it very sweetly. She was rather apologetic about it; said she was engaged already, and perhaps she ought to have made that fact a little clearer to me from the start; only she never suspected, and so on."

"She didn't mention Roy's name, I suppose?"

"No! I half thought that she would, just to score me off. It would have been a real slap in the face for me, his Colonel, if she had. But she didn't: she just said she was very, very sorry, but that she was engaged to some one else!"

"Well, there was no great harm done," I said, wishing he would stop. But he had not finished yet.

"And then—oh Lord, Alan!—do you know what I did then? I turned round on her, like a spoiled child, and accused her of having flirted with me, and led me on! And, not content with that, I turned on the pathetic tap. I said something rotten about expecting a little more consideration from her, seeing that I was going back to the trenches to-morrow—and muck like that! And she just looked at me, and said, quite quietly: 'He is there, too—now!' As if I didn't know! Oh, what a miserable rotter I was—and am!"

He dropped into a chair, and buried his face in his arms. He was "doon in the midden" now. I puffed wretchedly at my pipe and longed, from the bottom of my heart, for an air raid. I found myself wondering whether Marjorie had ever told Roy of this incident. I decided that my Eve would not have done so; and therefore probably not Marjorie.

Presently Eric began to talk again, with his forehead still close to the table.

"And this very morning," he said bitterly—"with Roy's death hardly made public—I came to this house fooling round Roy's widow with flowers, and silly old man's messages! I believe I was actually jealous of the dead, Alan! Well, that's over now. I needn't insult her any more—or him!" He sat up again, and took the pink slip. "This has killed my conceit at last—and perhaps saved my soul. Thank God I came across it! It has brought me to myself. And thank *you*, old friend"—Eric turned swiftly to me, and his face broke into the smile that I loved—"for what you did for me! You saved me from being sent home! Yes, and you provided me with a far more creditable exit from my soldiering career than I ever deserved!"

"That's all right," I said. "Let's clear up these papers."

But Eric was not listening. He had fallen into a rare mood—gentle and frank. He talked on—more calmly now.

"Men are queer mixtures. And, oh Lord, how truly some women judge us! Marjorie saw through me from the start, I believe. So did Diana. Did you ever know why she broke off our engagement?"

I shook my head. I had not heard Eric mention Diana's name for twenty years.

"Eve and I never spoke of it," I said.

"No, of course; you two wouldn't—being you two. Well, Diana said to me, quite suddenly, one day: 'Eric, I want to tell you that I can't marry you after all.' Just that! Of course, I asked her why."

"That was probably a mistake."

"It was. She asked me not to press her; but, being me, that only made me more unreasonable. So finally she told me.

"'Eric,' she said, 'I am very fond of you; I always shall be—more than I care to think about. But you have one fault that I can't get over: you have a mean streak in you. I would take you with every other fault in the world—but not that! So—good-bye!' They were the last words she ever spoke to me. You know, she was like that. I took my medicine with a smiling face, as you may remember; but it hurt like hell—and it taught me nothing! Well"—he tapped the telegraph form—"here is my second dose! It has got home this time. I *have* a mean streak in me, and I know it at last! Still"—he rose to his feet and held up his right hand: he could never resist the dramatic touch—"it's not too late. I am still on the right side of fifty; and I am going to spend the rest of my life eradicating that yellow streak from my system. I think I can do it. A thing's never dangerous once you know it's there." Suddenly he leaned over towards me. "Alan, old boy, I'm not a *hopeless* outsider, am I? Tell me! You know me! What am I?"

"You are what I have always thought you," I said—"a very brave soldier, with a weakness for facing difficult situations with both eyes shut! Also, you are my oldest friend. Now, for goodness sake, let's clear up this mess, and report entire lack of progress to Eskerley!"

The telephone bell rang sharply.

CHAPTER XXIV
THROUGH

The double doors at the end of the room swung back, and Lord Eskerley appeared. The bell was still ringing. A tiny hinged metal flap on the switchboard had fallen open, revealing a white disc with a number on it. His Lordship gazed absently down upon the apparatus.

"The inestimable Meadows is still taking the air," he said, "so I must tackle this contraption myself. Let me think; what is the combination?"

He peered at the vibrating flap and the revealed number.

"Three!" he announced. "Aha! I haven't the faintest notion what that implies. Let us stop this noise, anyhow."

He pushed up the flap again, and the bell stopped ringing.

"Shall we retire?" I asked.

"No, no, no! If it's desperately confidential I will switch it through to the instrument in my room; but I don't expect"—he put the receiver to his ear—"Who wants me? What wants me? ... Caperton? Never heard of him! Oh, an exchange? A locality? A trunk call? Very well! *Rien ne m'étonne*! Carry on!"

Lord Eskerley's back was turned to us. Suddenly I saw his shoulders stiffen; he caught his breath sharply. As this was the first sign of emotion that he had betrayed, to my knowledge, for the last thirty years, I watched him with quickening interest.

"Yes!" he said ... "Yes, yes! This is Lord Eskerley ... Louder, please!" Then came a pause, while the receiver squeaked steadily. Then, a little unexpectedly: "Praise God from Whom all blessings flow!"

Eric was watching too, now. The old man steadied himself, grasping the end of the mantelpiece with his disengaged hand. Then he looked round over his shoulder at us, peering over his spectacles.

"A most interesting communication coming through here!" he announced. "Forgive my demeanour!" His voice was as harsh as ever, but there were tears in his old eyes. He turned to the instrument again.

"Yes," he said, "I concur. Such a rumour would be *most* prejudicial to your future career. Shall we contradict it? You are quite sure it's incorrect?" ... He chuckled; so did the receiver. Then he continued:

"Eh? ... Oh! Naturally! You would like to do that at once? ... Yes, I think I can put you in communication with the party in question.... When? Oh, within a fairly reasonable interval of time, I hope. Let us say next week—" He moved the receiver a few inches away from his ear. "I can hear you quite easily in your ordinary voice, thanks!"

He chuckled again, laid down the receiver, and brooded once more over the switchboard. Then, after a brief mental calculation, he selected a plug at the end of a wire, thrust it into a hole, and pressed a small ivory button.

A bell rang faintly upstairs, then ceased sharply. Our noble operator took up the receiver again.

"That you, Habakkuk?" he inquired.... "Good! Some mysterious individual in Kent wishes to speak to you on the telephone. Wonderful invention!"

The old gentleman made a final adjustment of the switches on the board, and spoke for the last time—apparently to the person in Kent:

"You still there?"

The telephone vibrated stormily.

"All right! You are through to her—dear boy!"

He hung up the receiver, and left them together.

A Safety Match

CHAPTER ONE.

HAPPY FAMILIES.

"Nicky, please, have you got Mr Pots the Painter?"

"No, Stiffy, but I'll trouble you for Mrs Bones the Butcher's Wife. *Thank* you. And Daph, have you got Master Bones the Butcher's Son? *Thank* you. Family! One to me!"

And Nicky, triumphantly plucking from her hand four pink-backed cards, slaps them down upon the table face upwards. They are apparently family portraits. The first—that of Bones *père*—depicts a smug gentleman, with appropriate mutton-chop whiskers, mutilating a fearsome joint upon a block; the second, Mrs Bones, an ample matron in apple-green, proffering to an unseen customer a haunch of what looks like anæmic cab-horse; the third, Miss Bones, engaged in extracting nourishment from a colossal bone shaped like a dumb-bell; the fourth, Master Bones (bearing a strong family likeness to his papa), creeping unwillingly upon an errand, clad in canary trousers and a blue jacket, with a sirloin of beef nestling against his right ear.

It was Saturday night at the Rectory, and the Vereker family—"those absurdly handsome Rectory children," as old Lady Curlew, of Hainings, invariably called them—sat round the dining-room table playing "Happy Families." The rules which govern this absorbing pastime are simple. The families are indeed happy. They contain no widows and no orphans, and each pair of parents possesses one son and one daughter—perhaps the perfect number, for the sides of the house are equally balanced both for purposes of companionship and in the event of sex-warfare. As for procedure, cards are dealt round, and each player endeavours, by requests based upon observation and deduction, to reunite within his own hand the members of an entire family,—an enterprise which, while it fosters in those who undertake it a reverence for the unities of home life, offers a more material and immediate reward in the shape of one point for each family collected. We will look over the shoulders of the players as they sit, and a brief consideration of each hand and of the tactics of its owner will possibly give us the key to the respective dispositions of the Vereker family, as well as a useful lesson in the art of acquiring that priceless possession, a Happy Family.

Before starting on our tour of the table we may note that one member of the company is otherwise engaged. This is Master Anthony Cuthbert Vereker, aged ten years—usually known as Tony. He is the youngest member of the family, and is one of those fortunate people who are never bored, and who rarely require either company or assistance in their amusements. He lives in a world of his own, peopled by folk of his own creation; and with the help of this unseen host, which he can multiply to an indefinite extent and transform into anything he pleases, he organises and carries out schemes of recreation beside which all the Happy Families in the world become humdrum and suburban in tone. He has just taken his seat upon a chair opposite to another chair, across the arms of which he has laid the lid of his big box of bricks, and is feeling in his pocket for an imaginary key, for he is about to give an organ recital in the Albert Hall (which he has never seen) in a style modelled upon that of the village organist, whom he studies through a chink in a curtain every Sunday.

Presently the lid is turned back, and the keyboard—a three-manual affair, ingeniously composed of tiers of wooden bricks—is exposed to view. The organist arranges unseen music and pulls out invisible stops. Then, having risen to set up on the mantelpiece hard by a square of cardboard bearing the figure 1, he resumes his seat, and embarks upon a rendering of Handel's "Largo in G," which its composer, to be just, would have experienced no difficulty in recognising, though he might have expressed some surprise that so large an instrument as the Albert Hall organ should produce so small a volume of sound. But then Handel never played his own Largo in a room full of elder brothers and sisters, immersed in the acquisition of Happy Families and impatient of distracting noises.

The Largo completed, its executant rises to his feet and bows again and again in the direction of the sideboard; and then (the applause apparently having subsided) solemnly turns round the cardboard square on the mantelpiece so as to display the figure 2, and sets to work upon "The Lost Chord."

Meanwhile the Happy Families are being rapidly united. The houses of Pots the Painter, Bun the Baker, and Dose the Doctor lie neatly piled at Nicky's right hand; and that Machiavellian damosel is now engaged in a businesslike quest for the only outstanding member of the family of Grits the Grocer.

Nicky—or Veronica Elizabeth Vereker—was in many respects the most remarkable of the Rectory children. She was thirteen years old, was the only dark-haired member of the family, and (as she was fond of explaining) was possessed of a devil. This remarkable attribute was sometimes adduced as a distinction and sometimes as an excuse,—the former when impressionable and nervous children came to tea, the latter when all other palliatives of crime had failed. Certainly she could lay claim to the brooding spirit, the entire absence of fear, the unlimited low cunning, and the love of sin for its own sake which go to make the master-criminal. At present she was enjoying herself in characteristic fashion. Her brother Stephen—known as "Stiffy"—Nicky's senior by one year, a transparently honest but somewhat limited youth, had for the greater part of the game been applying a slow-moving intellect to the acquisition of one complete Family. Higher he did not look. Nicky's habit was to allow Stiffy, with infinite labour, to collect the majority of the members of a Family in which she herself was interested, and then, at the eleventh hour, to swoop down and strip her unconscious collaborator of his hardly-earned collection.

Stiffy, sighing patiently, had just surrendered Mr, Mrs, and Miss Block (Hairdressers and Dealers in Toilet Requisites) to the depredatory hands of Nicky, and was debating in his mind whether he should endeavour when his next chance came to complete the genealogical tree of Mr Soot the Sweep or corner the clan of Bung the Brewer. Possessing two Bungs to one Soot, he decided on the latter alternative.

Presently he was asked by his elder sister, Cilly (Monica Cecilia), for a card which he did not possess, and this gave him the desired opening.

"I say, Nicky," he began deferentially, "have you got Master Bung?"

Nicky surveyed her hand for a moment, and then raised a pair of liquid-blue eyes and smiled seraphically.

"No, Stiffy, dear," she replied; "but I'll have Mr Bung and Mrs Bung."

Stiffy, resigned as ever, handed over the cards. Suddenly Sebastian Aloysius Vereker, the eldest son of the family (usually addressed as "Ally"), put down his cards and remarked, slowly and without heat—

"Cheating again! My word, Nicky, you are the absolute *edge*!"

"*Who* is cheating?" inquired Veronica in a shocked voice.

"You. Either you *must* have Master Bung, or else you are asking for Stiffy's cards without having any Bungs at all; because I've got Miss myself."

He laid the corybantic young lady in question upon the table to substantiate his statement.

Nicky remained entirely unruffled.

"Oh—*Bung*!" she exclaimed. "Sorry! I thought you said 'Bun,' Stiffy. You should spit out your G's a bit more, my lad. *Bung-gah*—like that! I really must speak to dad about your articulation."

In polite card-playing circles a lady's word is usually accepted as sufficient; but the ordinary courtesies of everyday life do not prevail in a family of six.

"Rot!" said Ally.

"Cheat!" said Cilly.

"Never mind!" said loyal and peaceable Stiffy. "I don't care, really. Let's go on."

"It's not fair," cried Cilly. "Poor Stiffy hasn't got a single Family yet. Give it to him, Nicky, you little beast! Daph, make her!"

Daphne was the eldest of the flock, and for want of a mother dispensed justice and equity to the rest of the family from the heights of nineteen. For the moment she was assisting the organist, who had inadvertently capsized a portion of his keyboard. Now she returned to the table.

"What is it, rabble?" she inquired maternally.

A full-throated chorus informed her, and the arbitress detached the threads of the dispute with effortless dexterity.

"You said you thought he was asking for Miss Bun and not Bung?" she remarked to the accused.

"Yes—that was all," began Nicky. "You see," she continued pathetically, "they're all so beastly unjust to me, and—"

Daphne picked up her small sister's pile of completed Families and turned them over.

"You couldn't have thought Stiffy wanted *Buns*," she said in measured tones, "because they're here. You collected them yourself. You've cheated again. Upstairs, and no jam till Wednesday!"

It is a tribute to Miss Vereker's disciplinary methods that the turbulent Nicky rose at once to her feet and, with a half-tearful, half-defiant reference to her Satanic inhabitant, left the room and departed upstairs, there to meditate on a Bun-strewn past and a jamless future.

Daphne Vereker was perhaps the most beautiful of an extraordinarily attractive family. Her full name was Daphne Margaret. Her parents, whether from inherent piety or on the *lucus a non lucendo* principle, had endowed their offspring with the names of early saints and martyrs. The pagan derivative Daphne was an exception. It had been the name of Brian Vereker's young bride, and had been bestowed, uncanonically, linked with that of a saint of blameless antecedents, upon the first baby which had arrived at the Rectory. Mrs Vereker had died eleven years later, two hours after the birth of that fertile genius Anthony Cuthbert, and Brian Vereker, left to wrestle with the upbringing of six children on an insufficient stipend in a remote country parish, had come to lean more and more, in the instinctive but exacting fashion of lonely man, upon the slim shoulders of his eldest daughter.

There are certain attributes of woman before which the male sex, whose sole knowledge of the ways of life is derived from that stern instructor Experience, can only stand and gape in reverent awe. When her mother died Daphne Vereker was a tow-headed, long-legged, irresponsible marauder of eleven. In six months she looked like a rather prim little nursery-governess: in two years she could have taken the chair at a Mother's meeting. Circumstance is a great forcing-house, especially where women are concerned. Her dreamy, unpractical, affectionate father, oblivious of the expectant presence in the offing of numerous female relatives-in-law, had remarked in sober earnest to his little daughter, walking erect by his side in her short black frock on the way home from the funeral:—"You and I will have to bring up the children between us now, Daphne;" and the child, with an odd thrill of pride at being thus promoted to woman's highest office at the age of eleven, had responded with the utmost gravity—

"You had better stick to the parish, dad, and I'll manage the kids."

And she had done it. As she presides at the table this Saturday evening, with her round chin resting on her hands, surveying the picturesque crew of ragamuffins before her, we cannot but congratulate her on the success of her methods, whatever those may be. On her right lolls the apple of her eye, the eldest son, Ally. He is a handsome boy, with a ready smile and a rather weak mouth. He is being educated—God knows by what anxious economies in other directions—at a great public school. When he leaves, which will be shortly, the money will go to educate Stiffy, who is rising fourteen.

Next to Ally sprawls Cilly, an amorphous schoolgirl with long rippling hair and great grey eyes that are alternately full of shy inquiry and hoydenish exuberance. Then comes the chair recently vacated by the Madonna-like Nicky; then the ruddy countenance and cheerful presence of the sunny-tempered Stiffy, completing the circle. In the corner Master Anthony Cuthbert, cherubic and rapturous, is engaged, with every finger and toe in action, upon the final frenzy of the "Hallelujah Chorus." The number 6 stands upon the mantelpiece, for the recital is drawing to a close.

To describe Daphne herself is not easy. One fact is obvious, and that is that she possesses an instinct for dress not as yet acquired by any of her brothers and sisters. Her hair is of a peculiarly radiant gold, reflecting high lights at every turn of her head. Her eyes are brown, of the hue of a Highland burn on a sunny afternoon, and her eyebrows are very level and serene. Her colouring is perfect, and when she smiles we understand why it is that her unregenerate brothers and sisters occasionally address her as "Odol." When her face is in repose—which, to be frank, is not often—there is a pathetic droop at the corners of her mouth, which is perhaps accounted for by the cares of premature responsibility. She is dressed in brown velvet, with a lace collar—evening dress does not prevail in a household which affects high tea, but Daphne always puts on her Sunday frock on Saturday evenings—and, having discovered that certain colours suit her better than others, she has threaded a pale blue ribbon through her hair.

Altogether she is a rather astonishing young person to find sitting contentedly resting her elbows upon a dingy tablecloth in an untidy dining-room which smells of American leather and fried eggs. It is as if one had discovered the Venus de Milo presiding at a Dorcas Society or Helen of Troy serving crumpets in an A.B.C. shop.

The "Hallelujah Chorus" has just stopped dead at that paralysing hiatus of two bars which immediately precedes the final crash, when the door opens and the Reverend Brian Vereker appears. A glance at his clear-cut aristocratic features goes a long way towards deciding the question of the origin of the good looks of "those Rectory children."

He is a tall man—six feet two,—and although he is barely fifty his hair is specklessly white. He looks more like a great prelate or statesman than a country parson. Perhaps he might have been one or the other, had he been born the eldest son of the eldest son of a peer, instead of the youngest son of the youngest. And again, perhaps not. The lines of his face indicate brain rather than character, and after all it is character that brings us out top in this world. There are furrows about his forehead that tell of much study; but about the corners of his mouth, where promptitude and decision usually set their seal, there is nothing—nothing but a smile of rare sweetness. His gentle blue eyes have the dreamy gaze that marks the saints and poets of this world: the steely glitter of the man of action is lacking. Altogether you would say that Brian Vereker would make a noble figurehead to any high enterprise; but you would add that if that enterprise was to succeed, the figurehead would require a good deal of imported driving-power behind it. And you would be right.

The Rector paused in the doorway and surveyed the lamp-lit room.

..."*Halle-lu-u-ja-ah!*" vociferated the Albert Hall organ with an air of triumphant finality. Brian Vereker turned to his youngest son with the ready sympathy of one child for another child's games.

"That's right, Tony! That's the stuff! Good old George Frederick! *He* knew the meaning of the word music—eh?"

"Yes—George Fwederick!" echoed the organist. "*And* Arthur Seymour, daddy! You've just missed 'The Lost Chord.'"

"Ah," said the Rector in a tone of genuine regret, "that's a pity. But we had the Seventy-Eighth Psalm to-night, and I'm later than usual."

"Quadruple chant?" inquired Tony professionally.

"Rather! But is your recital quite over, boyo?"

"Yes—bedtime!" replied the organist, with a reproachful glance in the direction of his eldest sister.

"Run along, dear!" was all the comfort he received from that inflexible despot.

"All right! I must lock up, though."

Master Tony removed the last number from the mantelpiece, disintegrated his keyboard and packed it up with the other bricks, and drawing aside the window-curtain remarked solemnly into the dark recess behind it—

"That will be all to-night, organ-blower. You can go home now."

To which a husky and ventriloquial voice replied—

"Thank you kindly, Mr Handel, sir. Good-night."

"Now," concluded Mr Handel, turning to his elders with the air of a martyr addressing a group of arena lions, "I'm ready!"

"Take him up, Cilly dear," said Daphne. "I must look after dad's supper."

"Come on, Tony," said Cilly, uncoiling her long legs from under her and rising from the hearthrug.

"Righto!" said Tony. "You be a cart-horse and I'll be a broken-down motor."

Monica Cecilia Vereker meekly complied, and departed upstairs, towing the inanimate mechanism of the inventive Anthony behind her bump by bump, utilising her sash, which she had removed for the purpose, as a tow-rope.

"Ally and Stiffy," commanded Daphne, turning to the two remaining members of the family, "you'd better go and pump the cistern full. Saturday night, you know, and the kids' baths have just been filled; so look sharp before the boiler bursts."

Stiffy, obliging as ever, rose at once; Ally, cumbered by that majesty which doth hedge a sixth-form boy and a member of the school Fifteen (especially when ordered about by a female), was more deliberate in his acquiescence. However, presently both the boys were gone, and five minutes later Daphne, with the assistance of the one little maid whom the establishment supported, had laid the Rector's supper. She installed her father in his seat on one side of the table, and took her own on the other, assisting the progress of the meal from time to time, but for the most part sitting with her chin resting upon her two fists, and contemplating the tired man before her with serious brown eyes. Twice she had to leave her seat, once to remove the butter from the vicinity of her parent's elbow, and once to frustrate an attempt on the part of that excellent but absent-minded man to sprinkle sugar over a lettuce.

"Well, my daughter," remarked the Rector presently, "what of the weekly report?"

Saturday night at the Rectory was reserved for a sort of domestic budget.

"Here are the books," said Daphne. "They're much as usual, except that I had to pay two bob on Wednesday for a bottle of embrocation for Ally. He is in training for the mile in the sports at the beginning of next term, and it does his muscles so much good."

"When I won the mile at Fenner's, Daphne," began the Reverend Brian, with a sudden glow of reminiscence in his dreamy eyes, "I did it without embrocation, or any other new-fashioned—"

"Yes, dear, but they have to run so much *faster* now than they did," explained Daphne soothingly. "Then, about the kitchen chimney—"

"But I only took four minutes, twenty-eight—"

"Yes, old man, and I'm *proud* of you!" said Daphne swiftly. "Well, the sweep is coming in on Wednesday, when you'll be away at Wilford, so *that's* all right." She was anxious to get away from the question of the embrocation. It had been a rank extravagance, and she knew it; but Ally was ever her weak spot. "Then, I've got three-and-nine in hand out of current expenses just now, and if I take two half-crowns out of the emergency bag and we go without a second joint this week, I can get Nicky a new pair of boots, if you don't mind. (Don't cut the cheese with a spoon, dear; take this knife.) Of course, we ought not to have to go to the emergency bag for boots at all. It's rather upsetting. To-day I find that a perfectly ducky pair of Sunday shoes, which I outgrew just before I stopped growing, and was keeping specially for that child, are too small for her by yards. (I had tried them on Cilly a year ago, but she simply couldn't get her toe in.) And now they'll be wasted, because there are no more of us girls. My feet are *most* exasperating."

"Your mother had tiny feet," said the Rector, half to himself.

He pushed away his plate, and gazed absently before him into that land where his son Tony still spent so much of his time, and whither Tony's young and pretty mother had been borne away eleven years before. Daphne permitted him a reverie of five minutes, while she puckered her brow over the account-books. Then she rose and took down a pipe from a rack on the mantelpiece. This she filled from a cracked jar thirty years old, adorned with the coat-of-arms of one of the three royal colleges of Cambridge, and laid it by her father's left hand.

"Then there's another thing," she continued, lighting a spill at the fire. "Isn't it time to enter Stiffy for school? Mr Allnutt asked us to say definitely by April whether he was coming to fill Ally's place after summer or not, otherwise he would be obliged to give the vacancy to some one else. It's the end of March now."

The Rector lit his pipe—his one luxury—in a meditative fashion, and then leaned back to contemplate his daughter, with her glinting hair and troubled little frown.

"Mr Allnutt? To be sure! Of course! A ripe scholar, Daphne, and a long-standing personal friend of my own. He took the Porson and Craven in successive years. His Iambics——"

All this was highly irrelevant, and exceedingly characteristic. Daphne waited patiently through a *résumé* of Mr Allnutt's achievements as a scholar and a divine, and continued:—

"Will you enter Stiffy at once, then? It would be a pity not to get him into Ally's old house."

Brian Vereker, suddenly recalled to business, laid down his pipe and sighed.

"Boys are terribly expensive things, little daughter," he said. "And we are so very very poor. I wonder if they are worth it."

"Of *course* they are, the dears!" said Daphne, up in arms at once.

"Of course, of course," agreed the Rector apologetically. "You are right, child; you are always right. It is ungrateful and un-Christian of me to give expression to such thoughts when God has granted me three good sons. Still, I admit it *was* a disappointment to me when Ally failed to gain a scholarship at Cambridge. He may have been right in his assertion that there were an exceptionally strong set of candidates up on that occasion, but it was unfortunate that he should have overslept himself on the morning of the Greek Prose Paper, even though, as he pointed out, Greek Prose is his weak subject. What a pity! Strange lodgings, probably! Still, his disappointment must be far greater than ours, so it would be ungenerous to dwell further on the matter. But I fail to see at present how he can be started in life now. If only one had a little money to spare! I have never felt the need of such a thing before."

"Yes, we could do with a touch of it," assented Miss Vereker elegantly. She began to tick off the family requirements on her fingers. "There's Ally to be started in life; and Cilly ought to be sent somewhere and finished—she's tragically gawky, and she'd be perfectly lovely if she was given half a chance; and Stiffy has to be sent to school; and the two kiddies are growing up, and this house is simply tumbling down for want of repairs; and it's really time you had a curate for long-distance visiting."

"Never!" said Brian Vereker firmly.

"All right. Never, if you like, but he'll have to come some day," said Daphne serenely. (The question of the curate cropped up almost as regularly as that of the second joint on Wednesdays.) "And all we've got to run the whole show on," she concluded, with a pathetic little frown which many a man would gladly have given his whole estate to smooth away, "is—two pounds seventeen and ninepence in the emergency bag! It's a bit thick, isn't it?"

Brian Vereker surveyed his daughter's troubled countenance with characteristic placidity. Simple faith—some called it unpractical optimism—was the main article of his creed.

"The Lord will provide, my daughter," he said.

At this moment the door opened with a flourish, and, the crimson and enraged countenance of Master Anthony Cuthbert Vereker having been thrust into the room, its owner inquired, in a voice rendered husky by indignation, how any one could be expected to impersonate a Dreadnought going into action in the bath, when the said bath was encumbered with the flotsam and jetsam of a previous occupant. In other words, was he to be bathed in the same water as Nicky?

It was an old grievance, arising from the insufficient nature of the Rectory water-supply (which had to be pumped up by hand from the garden) and the smallness of the kitchen boiler; and Daphne had perforce to go upstairs to adjust it. Consequently the sitting of the Committee of Ways and Means, with all its immediate necessities and problems for the future, was incontinently suspended.

CHAPTER TWO.

WANTED, A MAN.

Five gentlemen sat side by side along a baize-covered table in a dingy room in a dingier building not far from the principal pit-head of Mirkley Colliery. They were the representatives of the local Colliery Owners' Association, and they were assembled and met together for the purpose of receiving a deputation representing the united interests and collective wisdom of their *employés*.

It should be noted that although there were five gentlemen present, six chairs were set along the table.

Now a deputation may be defined as an instrument designed to extract from you something which you have not the slightest desire to give up. Consequently the reception of such, whether you be a damsel listening for the rat-a-tat of an undesired suitor who has written asking for an interview, or a dethroned Royal Family sitting in its deserted abode awaiting the irruption of a Committee of Public Safety composed of the greater part of its late loyal subjects armed with billhooks and asking for blood, is always an uncomfortable business at the best. Our five gentlemen do not appear to be enjoying their present position any more than the two examples cited above. In fact, they look so exceedingly averse to interviews or arguments of any description, that we will leave them for a moment and divert our attention to the deputation itself, which is delicately skirting puddles of coal-black water and heaps of pit refuse on its way from the boiler-house, where its members have assembled, to the office-buildings of the colliery.

They are six in number, and we will describe them *seriatim*.

Mr Tom Winch is a professional agitator, though he calls himself something else. He is loud-voiced, and ceaseless in argument of a sort. His notion of a typical member of the upper classes is a debilitated imbecile suffering from chronic alcoholism and various maladies incident on over-indulgence, who divides his time between gloating over money-bags and grinding the faces of the poor. He privately regards Trades Unions as an antiquated drag upon the wheels of that chariot at the tail of which he hopes one day to see Capital led captive, gentlemen like Mr Tom Winch handling the reins and plying the whip.

Mr Amos Entwistle is a working collier, and is rightly regarded by both parties as a safe man. He is habitually sober, scrupulously honest, and has worked at Belton Pit for nearly forty years. He looks upon Trades Unions as his father and mother.

Mr Jacob Entwistle is the Nestor of the party. (Amos is his son.) He is a patriarchal old gentleman, with a long white beard, the manner of an ambassador, the deafness of an adder, and the obstinacy of a mule. Altogether he is just the sort of man to prove a valuable asset to any properly constituted deputation. He is the senior member of the local branch of the *Employés'* Association. He regards himself as the father and mother of Trades Unions.

Mr Albert Brash is an expert in the art of what may be called Righteous Indignation. Never was there such an exploiter of grievances. Is short time declared? Mr Brash calls for an Act of Parliament. Is there an explosion of fire-damp? Mr Brash mutters darkly that one of these days a director must swing. Does a careless worker remove a pit-prop and bring down an avalanche of coal on himself? Mr Brash raises clenched hands to heaven and clamours for a revolution. So persistently and so methodically does Mr Brash lay upon the shoulders of Capital the responsibility for all the ills to which flesh is liable, from a hard winter to triplets, that he has ultimately (as is the way in this short-sighted world of ours) achieved the position of Sir Oracle. His deportment is that of a stage conspirator, and he rarely speaks above a hoarse and arresting whisper. He calls himself an Anarchist, but he quails at the passing of the most benevolent policeman. He regards Trades Unions as well-meaning institutions, with but little discrimination as to their choice of leaders.

Mr James Killick is a thoroughly honest, thoroughly muddle-headed Socialist of a rather common type. Like many a wiser and more observant man before him, he has realised something of the grinding misery and suffering of this world, and a great and vague desire to better things is surging inarticulately within him. He has come to the conclusion, as most half-educated philosophers usually do, that the simplest remedy would be to take from those who have and give the proceeds to those who have not. The fact that the world is divided into men to whose hands money sticks like glue and men through whose fingers it slips like water, and that consequently a Utopian re-distribution of property would have to be repeated at inconveniently frequent intervals in order to preserve the social balance, has not yet been borne in on him. He regards Trades Unionism as a broken reed.

Mr Adam Wilkie is a Scot of the dourest and most sepulchral appearance. Native reticence and an extremely cautious manner of expressing himself have invested him with that halo of business acumen which appears to be inevitable to the Scot as viewed by the Sassenach, and his very silence is regarded with respectful admiration by his more verbose colleagues. In reality, he is an intensely stupid, entirely placid individual. Still, he has kept himself by native thrift in tolerable comfort all his life without extraneous assistance, and he consequently regards Trades Unionism as an institution specially and mercifully introduced by Providence for the purpose of keeping the weak-kneed English out of the poorhouse.

"Who's to be there?" inquired Mr Brash of Mr Entwistle senior.

That patriarch, who was negotiating a mountainous waste-heap, made no reply.

"Who are we going to meet?" repeated Mr Brash in a louder tone.

"Eh?" inquires Mr Entwistle, giving his invariable answer to any sudden question.

"Who are we going to *meet*?" bawled Mr Winch.

Mr Entwistle, who was never at a loss a second time, smiled benignantly and replied—

"Ay, that's so. But maybe we can manage to dry 'em at the fire in the office."

"I expect there will be five of them, Mr Winch," interpolated Amos, coming to the rescue. "Kirkley, Thompson, Crisp, Aymer, Montague——"

There was a grunt of disapproval from Mr Wilkie as the last name was mentioned.

"Yon felly!" he observed darkly. "Aha! Mphm!"

Then he relapsed into silence. It was upon such safe utterances as these that Mr Wilkie's reputation for profound wisdom was based.

"Is that all?" said Winch. "Because if it is, I'll undertake to learn that lot right enough! Kirkley, of course, is just an empty-headed aristocrat: he don't count. Then that Crisp—he's too cautious to do anything. We can talk Thompson round all right: done it half a dozen times meself. Aymer never knows his own mind two minutes together, and Moses is a coward. But *is* that all? Ain't the big man going to be there? He's the lad that counts in that crowd."

"He was away in London yesterday," said Entwistle junior. "But you never know——"

"Wallowing in the vice and luxury of the metropolis!" chanted Mr Brash suddenly, as if from some internal missal. "The master absent, squandering his tainted millions, while we stay here and starve! If I was a Member o' Parliament——"

"Talk sense," said Amos Entwistle curtly. "He may be back for all we know. Anyway, they're certain to bring him up if they can, because they know they can't do without him. Mind that tank-engine, father."

He impelled his aged parent, who, oblivious to delirious whistling, was resolutely obstructing the progress of a diminutive locomotive hauling a string of trucks, on to safer ground.

"Well, we'll hope for the best," said Mr Winch piously. "It would be something if he was to come late, even. Give me twenty minutes with the rest before he can get his oar in, and I'll undertake to make them outvote him."

By this time the deputation had arrived at the managerial offices, and five minutes later they were admitted to the presence of the Board. They did not know that they had been immediately preceded by an orange-coloured envelope, which was eagerly torn open by Lord Kirkley, the deputy-chairman.

"Good egg!" observed his lordship, with a sigh of heartfelt relief. "Juggernaut's coming."

A gentle murmur of satisfaction was audible. Evidently the Board felt the need of a little stiffening. We may as well describe them.

The Marquis of Kirkley was more accustomed to exercising a kindly despotism over rustics who lived contentedly on fourteen shillings a-week than to splitting hairs with unbending mechanics earning four pounds, whose views on the relations between master and man were dictated by a cast-iron bureaucracy, and who regarded not the elastic laws of Give and Take. He was a handsome, breezy, kind-hearted patrician of thirty-four, and considered Trades Unions a damned interfering nuisance.

James Crisp was a solicitor, and represented the Dean and Chapter of Kilchester, beneath the very foundation of whose mighty cathedral ran a very profitable little seam of coal, which was chiefly responsible for making the bishopric of the diocese one of the richest ecclesiastical plums in England. He was a shrewd man of business, probably the best qualified of those present to take the lead in the present instance. Consequently he remained studiously in the background. He regarded Trades Unions as inevitable, but by no means invulnerable.

Sir Nigel Thompson had inherited great possessions, including a colliery, from his father. There was no vice in him, but he loved coal about as much as a schoolboy loves irregular verbs, and his only passions in life were old furniture and chemical research. He attended under compulsion, having torn himself from his comfortable house in London at the bidding of his manager, in whose hands he was reported (not altogether unjustly) to be as wax. He was full of theoretical enthusiasm for Trades Unions, which he identified in some mysterious way with the liberty of the individual; but wished mildly that people could contrive to settle their affairs without dragging him north. Altogether a pleasant but entirely useless member of the Board.

Mr Alfred Aymer was the owner of Cherry Hill Colliery. He was middle-aged, timorous, and precipitate. Left to himself, he would probably have been a kind and fair-dealing employer. But it was his misfortune to be so constituted that his opinions on any subject were invariably those of the last man with whom he had discussed it. Consequently his line of action in the affairs of life was something in the nature of an alternating electric current. After an interview with his manager he would issue a decree of unparalleled ferocity: after five minutes with a deputation of *employés* he would rescind all previous resolutions and promise a perfectly fabulous bonus next pay-day. In his present company he was an adamantine Capitalist, and regarded Trades Unions as the most pernicious of institutions.

Last of all came Mr Montague, whose surname at an earlier and less distinguished period in his history had probably rhymed with "noses." He came from London, where he earned a livelihood by acquiring the controlling interest in various commercial ventures, and making these pay cent per cent. He had recently become proprietor of Marbledown Colliery, and it was said that he was making a better thing out of it than his*employés*. He regarded Trade Unions as an impertinent infringement of the right of the upper classes to keep the lower classes in their proper place. From which the intelligent reader will have no difficulty in deciding to which class Mr Montague considered that he himself belonged.

The deputation was introduced with the usual formalities. Its object was to effect the reinstatement of two*employés* at Marbledown Colliery, an engineman and a hewer, who had been summarily dismissed from their positions for endeavouring, in a society whose relations had never been of the most cordial, to heighten dissension between master and man.

Mr Tom Winch's version of the case, delivered with great wealth of detail and a good deal of unnecessary shouting, was different. The men, it appeared, were models of what enginemen and hewers should be. Their sole offence consisted in having incurred the dislike of the mine-manager, Mr Dodd—whether through their own sturdy independence as true-born Englishmen (*applause from Mr Brash*), or the natural jealousy of an incompetent official towards two able and increasingly prominent subordinates, it was not for Mr Winch to say. Proceeding, the orator warmed to his work, and mentioned that one man was as good as another. Indeed, but for the merest accident of fortune, Lord Kirkley himself might be delving for coal in the bowels of the earth, what time Messrs Conlin and Murton, the dismissed *employés*, sate in the House of Lords smoking cigars and drinking champagne.

After this singularly convincing peroration Mr Winch fell back into line with his companions, amid the *sotto voce* commendations of Messrs Brash and Killick. Mr Aymer, who had been taking notes on a sheet of paper, tore it up with a resigned air of finality. The case was clear: these poor fellows must be reinstated.

The chairman conferred briefly with Mr Crisp.

"Would any other of you gentlemen like to say anything?" he inquired.

The question was communicated to Mr Entwistle senior, who stepped forward and delivered himself of a courtly but rambling discourse, consisting chiefly of reminiscences of something portentous but unintelligible which had happened forty years ago, and even to the most irrelevant mind presented no sort of bearing upon the case whatsoever.

After this Lord Kirkley replied. His remarks were not convincing, for he was hampered in dealing with the question by complete inability to understand where the men's grievance came in, and said so. The owners, he explained, tried to do the fair thing, and most of them did considerably more. Sick funds, pensions, benevolent schemes, and all that sort of thing, didn't they know? He quite admitted that an employer of labour had grave responsibilities and duties laid upon him, and he for one had always tried to live up to them. But hang it! surely an employer had the right to get rid of a couple of fellows who went about preaching anarchy and red revolution in all the public-houses in the district—what? He did not mind ordinary grousing. It did everybody good to blow off steam periodically: he did it himself. But there was grousing and grousing: and when it came to the sort of game that Messrs Conlin and Murton were playing, it was his lordship's opinion that a *ne plus ultra* of thickness had been attained.

The chairman concluded a somewhat colloquial address amid a deathly silence, and the deputation and the board glared uncomfortably at one another. An *impasse* had been reached, it was clear.

"It's all very well, gentlemen," broke in Killick suddenly, "for you aristocrats——"

Lord Kirkley, who was not without a certain sense of proportion, glanced involuntarily at Mr Montague and then at Mr Killick. Did this omniscient and self-opinionated son of toil really see no moral difference between a Peer of the realm, with centuries of clean-bred ancestry behind him, and a man who wore diamond rings and elastic-sided boots? Mr Montague looked up, and regarded Mr Killick with something akin to affection.

There was a sudden rumble underneath the windows, accompanied by the hoot of a motor-horn.

The drama having run itself to a deadlock, the *deus* had duly arrived—in his *machina*.

CHAPTER THREE.

THE WHEELS OF JUGGERNAUT.

There was a dead silence, unbroken until Juggernaut entered the room.

"Good-morning, gentlemen," he said briskly. "I am glad to see that the deputation has only just arrived."

He turned to the clerk who had shown him in.

"Andrews," he said, "bring chairs for these gentlemen, and then we can get to business."

Chairs were brought, and the deputation, which had been balancing itself on alternate legs for nearly half an hour, sat down with an enhanced sense of comfort and importance to what they realised at once was to be the interview proper.

Juggernaut took the seat at the middle of the table vacated by Lord Kirkley, and inquired—

"Has any one spoken yet?"

Progress was reported by Mr Crisp.

"I wonder if I might trouble the deputation again," said the chairman. "Not you, Mr Winch, thank you!" as that Demosthenes cleared his throat in a threatening manner. "In the first place, you don't represent the men in any sense. In fact, considering that you are engaged in no employment in this district, I think it would have been much wiser on the part of those responsible for this deputation to have left you out altogether. You are not even a properly accredited Trades Union official."

"Gentlemen of the Board," began Mr Winch portentously, "I appeal——"

"Don't trouble, really, Mr Winch," broke in Juggernaut with inflexible cheerfulness. "You see, I know exactly what you are going to say. I have heard it so often in other places where you have been kind enough to come forward and champion the cause—of—of—the oppressed millions of this country. That's right, isn't it?"

A muffled sound proceeded from the interior of Mr Wilkie—his first contribution to the debate—and the chairman proceeded.

"I wonder if Mr Entwistle junior would kindly give us the facts."

Amos Entwistle, rising from his seat, re-stated the case of the two men. They were competent and industrious workmen, he maintained, and so long as they gave satisfaction in their situations their private lives and leisure occupations were entirely their own concern. Possibly their views on the relations of Labour and Capital were extreme, but the speaker begged respectfully to point out that there were extremists on both sides; and since many employers might and did regard the men they paid as dirt beneath their feet, it seemed only natural that a section of the men should regard their employers as bullies and tyrants. Mr Entwistle followed up this undoubted home-thrust with a request for a categorical list of the offences alleged against the two men, and solemnly but respectfully warned the Board against risking a serious upheaval by endeavouring to stifle legitimate criticism of its actions. With apologies for plain-speaking he resumed his seat, and Mr Aymer tore up a sheet of paper upon which he had commenced operations on the arrival of the chairman.

"Would any other gentleman like to say anything?" inquired Juggernaut. "Mr Brash? Mr Wilkie?"

No, the gentlemen addressed had nothing to say. Their *forte* was plainly that of chorus.

"Very well," said Juggernaut. "In the first place, I am going to accede to Mr Entwistle's perfectly just request that a definite reason should be given for the dismissal of these men. I agree with him that it is a foolish thing to stifle legitimate criticism. Unfortunately, I don't agree with him that the criticisms of Messrs Conlin and Murton *are* legitimate. I have been making inquiries into the antecedents of these two. Murton is a paid agitator. He is not a local man. He came here less than a year ago, and has been making deliberate mischief ever since. He has money to spend: he backs his arguments with beer. I shouldn't be surprised if he drew his salary from the organisation which retains your services, Mr Winch."

Mr Winch's small eyes began to protrude. He did not relish this line of argument. In dealing with Boards and other representatives of bloated Capital he preferred to keep to the high moral and sentimental plane—the sufferings of the downtrodden sons of Labour, the equality of all men in the sight of God, and so on. Mundane personalities, coupled with the suggestion that he, a high priest of altruism, was making a good thing out of his exertions on behalf of his fellow-toilers, took him below the belt, he considered.

"Conlin," continued Juggernaut, disregarding the fermenting Mr Winch, "seems to be a comparatively sincere and honest grumbler. He has realised that this is an unjust world, and he wants to put it right by Act of Parliament. Consequently he goes about advocating certain special and particular forms of legislation which, if they came into being, would benefit about one member of the community in a hundred and be grossly unfair to the other ninety-nine. He has not yet discovered for himself that the aim of all legislation must be to benefit the type and not the individual. That is the rock upon which all your friends split, Mr Winch. You are always trying to legislate for special cases, and it can't be *done*. I quite agree with you that the conditions of labour in parts of this country are deplorable. We all want to put them right. But there are two things we cannot do. We can't cure them in a hurry, and we can't cure them by swallowing quack medicines. What we have to do is to set to work on systematic lines, and go on working, with patience and a sense of proportion, until our whole social fabric develops into a sounder and more healthy condition. That requires time, and time requires patience, and patience requires common-sense, and common-sense is a thing which is lamentably scarce in this world, Mr Winch. We are marching on to a better state of things every year; but every bit of unsound, panic-stricken, vote-catching legislation—Right-to-Work Bills, Unemployment Acts, and so on—throws us back a step, because its tendency is to remove the symptom instead of curing the disease. Now, symptoms are very valuable assets. They give us reliable and necessary information, which is more than can be said of most intelligence departments. If ever you have such a vulgar thing as a pain in your stomach, Mr Winch, that is a kindly hint from Nature that there is something wrong with the works. If you drink two of whisky hot the pain may cease, but it does not follow that the real cause of the trouble has been removed. In effect you have merely put back the danger-signal to safety without removing the danger. That is just what all this despicable, hand-to-mouth, time-serving legislation that you and your friends are trying to force upon a popularity-hunting Government is doing for the country to-day."

The speaker paused. The deputation wore a distinctly chastened appearance. Mr Aymer was engaged upon a third sheet of notes. Sir Nigel Thompson was working out a chemical formula on the back of an envelope.

"Let us get back to the point, sir," said Amos Entwistle doggedly. "I agree with a great deal of what you say——"

"Shame!" interpolated Mr Killick suddenly.

"But we came here to ask for the reinstatement of these two men, and not to discuss social problems."

"Granted all the time," said Juggernaut cheerfully. "I admit that I have not made Messrs Conlin and Murton my Alpha and Omega in these remarks of mine; but that is because I deliberately went back to first principles instead of cutting into the middle of things. Now for your request! You want an answer? Here it is. The two men cannot be reinstated under any circumstances whatsoever. I confess I am rather sorry for Conlin: he is in a different class from Murton. But he is tarred with the same brush, and he must go."

"Take care, Sir John," broke in Mr Winch, in the declamatory bray which he reserved for extreme crises. "Don't push us too hard! What if a strike was to be proclaimed at Marbledown Colliery? You wouldn't like that, Mr Montague! You have a bad enough name in the district as it is. You grind your 'eel——"

"Mr Winch," said Juggernaut in a voice of thunder, "I must ask you to address yourself to me. This matter has been taken out of Mr Montague's hands by the combined action of the Owners' Association; so if you have any strictures to offer they must be laid upon me as representing the Association collectively. As for striking—well, you struck before, you know. I don't think any of us have forgotten that winter—masters or men!"

"We nearly beat you then," said Killick hotly.

"That," retorted Mr Montague, suddenly breaking into the debate, "was because some sentimental fool sent food and necessaries to your wives."

"It's the women and children who pay for strikes, you know, Mr Winch," said Mr Crisp, speaking for the first time—"not you men. You can do without beer and baccy at a pinch, but your families must have groceries and fire. If they had not been kept going by that unknown benefactor the strike would have collapsed as soon as the Union funds gave out."

"Perhaps they will be kept going again," said Amos Entwistle quietly.

"They won't," said Juggernaut emphatically. "You can take my word for that, Mr Entwistle. I have seen to it. And I may add that if you consider it advisable to proclaim a sectional strike, the owners on their part might find it necessary to declare a lock-out at all the collieries in the district. If men can combine, so can masters."

There was a staggered silence. Even the Board were hardly prepared for this. Juggernaut had so dominated the situation since his arrival that one or two—Mr Montague in particular—were beginning to wonder rather peevishly why they had been admitted to the meeting. But Mr Crisp leaned back and took snuff contentedly. He appreciated strong measures, though he was averse to initiating them.

Still, the temper of the meeting was rising. Killick broke out furiously. It was a burning shame, a monstrous iniquity, he declared, that men who had never done an honest day's work in their lives should be enabled, simply because they had money in their pockets, to force humiliating conditions on a majority who had no alternative but to submit or starve. He spoke with all the conviction that absolute sincerity carries; but the effect of his philippic was not enhanced by the marginal comments of his colleague, Mr Brash, who kept up a running fire of *sotto voce* references to bloody-minded tyrants, champagne, ballet-girls, and other equally relevant topics with a persistence and enthusiasm which would have proved embarrassing to a more self-conscious and less frenzied rhetorician than Mr Killick.

When both solo and *obligato* had subsided, Juggernaut spoke again.

"It is one of the most common delusions of men of your way of thinking, Mr Killick, to imagine that the only kind of work worthy of the name is manual labour. Personally, I have tried both. For two years after I came down from the University I worked for experience's sake in a pit not far from here. I went down with my shift daily and worked full time; but I assure you that those two years were far from being the most laborious of my life."

"Your case was different, sir," said Amos Entwistle, with a practical man's quick perception of his opponent's weak points. "You were doing it for pleasure, to acquire experience—not to earn your bread. You could look forward to something better later on."

"And so can every man!" replied Juggernaut. "Each one of us is able if he likes to work his way up, and up, and up; and the lower he starts, the greater is his range of opportunity. The man at the bottom has the whole ladder to climb, instead of a few paltry rungs, as is the case of a man born near the top. Let him think of that, and be thankful!"

The chairman's sombre eyes glowed. His tone of raillery was gone: he was in sober earnest now. To him poverty and riches were nothing; he could have lived happily on a pound a-week: the salt of life lay in the overcoming of its difficulties.

But Amos Entwistle was a man of tough fibre—by far the strongest man, next to the chairman, in that assemblage.

"You can't deny, sir," he persisted doggedly, "that it is very difficult for a poor man to rise. His employers don't help him much. They are best satisfied with a man who keeps his proper station, as they call it."

"Tyrants!" interpolated Mr Winch hastily.

"Star Chamber!" added Mr Brash, *à propos de bottes*.

"Tyrants? Star Chamber?" Juggernaut surveyed the interrupter quizzically. "Here is a question for you, Mr Brash. Which is the worse—the tyranny of the harsh employer who gathers where he has not strawed, or the tyranny of a Trades Union which a man is forced to join, and which compels the best worker to slow down his pace to that of the worst, and frequently compels him to come out on strike over some question upon which he is perfectly satisfied? I won't attempt to place them in order of merit, but I should feel inclined to bracket—"

"Trades Unions," interrupted Mr Winch, who was beginning to feel himself unduly excluded from the present symposium, "are the first steps towards the complete emancipation of Labour"—he smacked his lips as over a savoury bakemeat—"from the degrading shackles of Capital. Every man his own master!"

Juggernaut nodded his head slowly.

"Ye-es," he said. "That sounds admirable. But what does it *mean* exactly? As far as I can see, it means that every one who is at present a labourer is ultimately going to become a capitalist. In that case it rather looks as if there would be a shortage of hands if there was work to be done. Your Utopia, Mr Winch, appears to me to resemble the Grand Army of Hayti, which consists of five hundred privates and eleven hundred Generals. No, no; you must bear in mind this fact, that ever since the world began mankind has been divided up into masters and men, and will continue to be so divided until the end of time. What we—you and I—have to do is to adjust the relations between the two in such a fashion as to make the conditions fair for both. I don't say that employers aren't frequently most high-handed and tyrannical, but I also say that *employés* are extraordinarily touchy and thin-skinned. I think it chiefly arises from a sort of distorted notion that there is something degrading and undignified in obeying an order. Why, man, obedience and discipline are the very life-blood of every institution worthy of the name. They are no class affair either. I have seen the captain of a company stand at attention without winking for ten minutes, and receive a damning from his colonel that no non-commissioned officer in the service would have dreamed of administering to a private of the line. Master and man each hold equally honourable positions; and what you must drum into the minds of your associates, gentlemen—I'm speaking to the Board as much as to the deputation—is the fact that the interests of both are *identical*, instead of being as far apart as the poles, which appears to be your present impression. Neither can exist without the other. So far you have imbibed only half of that truth. You reiterate with distressing frequency, Mr Winch, the fact that Capital cannot exist without Labour. Perfectly true. Now try to absorb into your system the fact—equally important to a hair's-breadth—that Labour cannot exist without Capital. Each depends upon the other for existence, and what we have to do is to balance and balance and balance, employing a sense of proportion, proportion, *proportion*!"

Juggernaut's fist descended with a crash upon the table, and for a minute he was silent—free-wheeling, so to speak, over the pulverised remains of Mr Winch. Presently he continued, with one of his rare smiles—

"A Frenchman once said that an Englishman begins by making a speech and ends by preaching a sermon. I am afraid I have justified the gibe, but it's a good thing to thrash these matters out. I don't deny that the average employer is in the habit of giving his *employés* their bare pound of flesh in the way of wages and no more. But I think the *employé* has himself to blame for that. If you invoke the assistance of the law against your neighbour, that neighbour will give you precisely as much as the law compels him to give. Well, that is what organised Labour has done. It has its Trades Union, its Workmen's Compensation and Employers' Liability, and so on; and lately it has gouged out of a myopic Government a scheme of Old Age Pensions, to be eligible for which a man must on no account have exercised any kind of thrift throughout his working life. If he has, he is disqualified. All this legislation enables you to get the half-nelson on your employer. Under the circumstances you can hardly expect him to throw in benevolence as well. You can't have your cake and eat it. The old personal relations between master and man are dead—dead as Queen Anne—and with them has died the master's sense of moral responsibility for the welfare of those dependent on him."

"Time, too! Degradation! Feudal system!" observed the ever-ready Mr Killick.

"Well, perhaps; but the Feudal System had its points, Mr Killick. It fostered one or two homely and healthy virtues like benevolence and loyalty and pride of race; and I don't think a man-at-arms ever lost his self-respect or felt degraded because he lived in time of peace under the protection of the Lord of the Manor whom he followed in time of war. Yes, I for one rather regret the passing of the old order. Listen, and I will tell you a story. Forty years ago Cherry Hill Pit was flooded—flooded for nearly three months during a bitter hard winter. Sir Nigel Thompson's father, the late baronet—"

Sir Nigel, who was puzzling out some specially complicated formula, suddenly looked up. He had an idea that his name had been mentioned; but as every one present appeared to be listening most intently to the chairman, he resumed his engrossing occupation with a sigh of relief.

"—paid full wages during the whole of that time; and as coal was naturally unobtainable in the village, he imported sufficient to supply the needs of the whole community. Not a house in the village lacked its kitchen fire or its Sunday dinner during all those weeks. That was before the days of the Employers' Liability, gentlemen! If a similar disaster were to occur to-day, I doubt if Sir Nigel here would feel morally bound to do anything for such an independent and self-sufficient community. The present state of things may safeguard you against the ungenerous employer, but it eliminates the milk of human kindness from our mutual transactions, and that is always a matter for regret. That is all, gentlemen. You have our last word in this matter. These two men must go. If you would like to withdraw to the next room for a few minutes and consider whether you have anything further to say, we shall be glad to wait your convenience here."

The deputation rose and filed solemnly from the room, and the Board were left alone.

Presently Mr Aymer observed timidly—

"Mr Chairman, don't you think we might let Conlin stay, and content ourselves with dismissing Murton?"

"Afraid not," said Juggernaut. "It's a bit hard on Conlin, but we have to consider the greatest good of the greatest number. He's a plague-spot, and if we don't eradicate him he'll spread. Do you agree, Kirkley?"

"Bad luck on the poor devil, but I think you are right," assented his lordship.

"Crisp?"

Mr Crisp nodded.

"Nigel?"

Sir Nigel Thompson looked up from his seventh envelope with a contented sigh.

"I have it at last," he said. "It's a perfectly-simple solution, really, but the obvious often escapes one's notice owing to its very proximity. The eye is looking further afield. Eh—what? My decision? I agree implicitly with you, Jack—that is, gentlemen, I support the chairman in his view of the case."

And this vigilant counsellor collected his envelopes and stuffed them into his pocket. The chairman continued—

"Montague?"

"Before I answer that question," began Mr Montague, "I should like to protetht—protest, I mean—against the arbitrary manner in which you have conducted this meeting, Mr Chairman. You have taken the case out of our hands in a manner which I consider most unwarrantable; and, speaking as the actual employer of the two men—"

Juggernaut swung rather deliberately round in his chair.

"Mr Montague," he said, "you got yourself into a hole, and you called—no, *howled*—for a meeting of directors to come and pull you out. These agitators settled down in your district because they knew that it was the most fertile district to work in. You are considered, rightly, the worst employer of labour here. You are greedy, unscrupulous, and tyrannical. It is men like you who discredit Capital in the eyes of Labour, and make conciliatory dealing between master and man almost an impossibility. We have bolstered you up through a very difficult crisis, sitting here and putting those poor fellows, five of whom are infinitely more honest than you are, quite undeservedly in the wrong, and imperilling our immortal souls by whitewashing such employers as you. Accept the situation and be thankful!"

It is said that hard words break no bones. Still, if you happen to be a member of a race which has endured hard words (to say nothing of broken bones) for twenty centuries, and when the hard words on this particular occasion are delivered by a large man with angry blue eyes and a tongue like a whip-lash, you may be forgiven for losing your nerve a little. Mr Montague lost his. He flapped his ringed hands feebly, mumbled incoherently, and was understood to withdraw his objections unconditionally.

"Mr Amos Entwistle," announced a clerk at the door.

Entwistle junior re-entered the room.

"I am commissioned to inform you, Mr Chairman," he said, "that we acquiesce in your decision; but under protest. I should like to add, gentlemen," he continued, less formally but none the less earnestly, "that the Committee are very much dissatisfied with the result of the interview. I am afraid you haven't heard the last of this trouble. Good-day, and thank you, gentlemen!"

"What does it all mean? Strike—eh?" inquired Lord Kirkley, as he and Juggernaut descended the stairs together five minutes later.

"Perhaps. If so, we'll fight."

"Righto—I'm on! I say, it was pretty smart of you finding out where those private supplies of theirs came from last time. We shall be able to put the lid on that sort of think in future—what?"

Juggernaut nodded, but said no more.

Mr Crisp, Sir Nigel Thompson, and Mr Aymer walked across to the latter's offices for luncheon. Mr Montague had gone home to lunch by himself. He usually did so.

"The chairman arrived at the meeting in the nick of time," said the lawyer. "Kirkley would have been no match for Winch."

"The chairman was very inflexible," sighed Mr Aymer, with all a weak man's passion for compromise. "He has a way of brushing aside obstacles which can only be described as Napoleonic. Is he always within his rights from a legal point of view?"

"From a legal point of view, practically never," said the lawyer simply. "From a common-sense point of view, practically always."

"He is a hard man—as hard as flint," mused Mr Aymer. "I wonder if he has a soft side to him *anywhere*. I wonder, for instance, how he would treat a woman."

"I wonder," said Mr Crisp.

CHAPTER FOUR.

THE DEVIL A MONK WOULD BE.

The first member of the Rectory household whose eyes opened on Sunday morning was the Rector himself, who promptly arose and repaired to the church, there to conduct the early morning service. The second was a certain Mr Dawks, who has not previously been mentioned in this narrative. He was a dog. The term may include almost anything, which is perhaps fortunate for Mr Dawks; otherwise it might have been necessary to class him under some more elastic heading. Of his ancestry nothing was known, though many conjectures could have been made, and most of them would have been correct. He had been found lying half-dead in a country lane by Daphne six years ago, and though mistaken at the time for a derelict monkey jettisoned from some migratory hurdy-gurdy, had subsequently proved to be a mongrel puppy of a few months old. Regular meals and ripening years had developed him into a sort of general epitome of all the dogs that ever existed. He possessed points which, exhibited individually, would have gained many marks at Cruft's Dog-Show. His tail would have increased the market value of a Chow fourfold; his shoulders and forelegs would have done credit to a prize bull-terrier; his ears would have inflated the self-esteem of the silkiest spaniel in existence; and his lower jaw would have been regarded as an asset by an alligator. His manners were without reproach, but were derived rather from mental vacuity than nobility of character; for with the deportment of an hidalgo he combined the intelligence of a permanent official.

His name, as already mentioned, was Mr Dawks, but he responded with equal amiability to "Angel Child" or "Beautiful One" (Daphne); "Flea-Club" (Ally); "Puss, puss!" (Nicky); and "Tank-Engine" (Stiffy), to whose mechanical mind bandy legs and laboured breathing suggested a short wheel-base and leaky outside-cylinders.

Mr Dawks, having arisen from his nightly resting-place outside Daphne Vereker's bedroom door, strolled downstairs to the study. The Rector was frequently to be found there early in the morning, and were he not too deeply absorbed in some dusty volume, there might be biscuits. But the room was empty. Mr Dawks laboriously remounted the staircase and scratched delicately at his mistress's bedroom door.

He was admitted, and found Daphne, in dressing-gown and slippers, preparing for her Sunday morning round, in which she doubled the parts of what is known in the North of England as a "knocker-up" and mistress of the wardrobe; for the week's clean garments were always distributed on these occasions. The pair set forth together.

After a tap at her father's door, answered by a melodious "Good-morning, daughter!" which showed that the Rector had returned from his ministrations, Daphne proceeded to the regions above. Here upon the landing she encountered her youngest sister, who ought properly to have been dressing in the bedroom which she shared with Cilly. Instead, she was sitting resignedly outside the door upon a bundle composed of her Sabbath garments. As she was obviously posing for the excitation of sympathy, Daphne ignored her and passed into the bedroom, where the window-blind was flapping in the breeze and Cilly lay in a condition of almost total eclipse (if we except a long tawny pig-tail) under the bed-clothes.

"Cilly," inquired Daphne, "what's Nicky doing outside?"

"I kicked her out," replied a muffled voice.

"Why?"

"Well"—Cilly poked her head, tortoise-fashion, from under its covering—"she cheeked me—about"—the head retired again—"something."

"Bobby Gill, I suppose," remarked Daphne calmly.

Cilly's countenance reappeared, rosily flushed with healthy sleep and maiden modesty.

"Yes."

"Well, you must take her in again," said Daphne. "She's only playing up for a cold, sitting out there, and it will be a score for her if she can sniff the house down to-morrow."

"All right," said Cilly resignedly. "I suppose I can pay her out some other way."

"I wouldn't, if I were you," advised the elder sister. "She'll only wait till she gets you and Bobby together, and then say something *awful*. It's your own fault, dear. You do ask for it, you know."

Cilly, whose flirtations were more numerous than discreet, sighed deeply, and rolled a pair of large and dreamy eyes upon her sister.

"Daph, don't you *ever* fall in love with men? Well—boys, if you like!" she continued, parrying an unspoken comment. "I know I do overdo it a bit; but you—well, you never do it at all. Don't you love to feel them edging up to you, and getting pink in the face, and trying to think of things to say to you, and offering to take you—"

"No," said Daphne decidedly; "they bore me. Barring Dad and Mr Dawks and the boys, I have no use for males. Besides, I'm always too busy to bother with them: they waste so much of your time. Now, my child, if you want any breakfast you had better get up. I must go and see the boys."

She departed, and with a passing admonition to Nicky to abandon her eleemosynary vigil and be sure to wash her neck, continued on her way, still accompanied by the faithful Dawks, to the chamber occupied by her two youngest brothers.

Here peace reigned. Stiffy, one of whose chief joys in life was the study of the British Railway System, from Automatic Couplings to Newspaper Specials, was sitting up in bed with an old *Bradshaw*, laboriously ascertaining by how many routes and with how few changes the ordinary railway maniac might travel from Merthyr-Tydvil to Stockton-on-Tees. At the other end of the room the ever-occupied Anthony, with his night-shirt for a surplice and a stocking for a stole, was standing by an open grave (the hearthrug) rehearsing the opening passages of the Service for the Burial of the Dead,—an exercise to which, in common with various other ecclesiastical offices, he was much addicted.

Daphne, having kissed Stiffy and gravely given her verdict upon a knotty point which was exercising that scrupulous youth's mind, namely, whether it was permissible by the rules of the game to include in his schedule of connections a train which ran on Thursdays Only, handed him his weekly dole of clean linen and turned to the youngest member of the family.

"Good-morning, Tony dear," she said cheerfully.

The celebrant, who, true artist that he was, disliked unnecessary abruptness in his transitions, stopped short in the Ninetieth Psalm.

"Dearly Beloved Brethren," he gabbled in an apologetic undertone, "I am called for a moment from the side of this the last resting-place of our lamented sister"—apparently it was a lady friend he was interring—"by other business; but I shall be back in a minute." Then, unwinding the stocking from about his neck—

"Daphne, those new vests are beastly scratchy. Must I wear them?"

"I know, old man," responded his sister sympathetically. "But they've been bought and paid for—horribly dear, too!—so you must lump it. Try wearing them inside out for a time. That takes the edge off a bit."

And thus, with sage counsel and practical suggestion (together with a brief whistle to Mr Dawks, who was moistening his internal clay at the water-jug), our young Minerva passed on to the sleeping-place of her beloved Ally.

Rather to her surprise, Mr Aloysius Vereker was awake and out of bed. The reason was plain. Before him upon the dressing-table lay a pot of shaving-soap of a widely advertised brand, a new shaving-brush, a sixpenny bottle of bay rum, and a lather dish of red indiarubber,—youthful extravagances to which the hardened shaver of twenty years' standing, who smears himself with ordinary Brown Windsor out of the soap-dish and wipes his razor on a piece of newspaper or the window-curtain, looks back with mingled amusement and regret. In his hand gleamed a new razor.

"Careful!" he gasped through a sea of lather. "Don't shake the room, kid!"

Daphne sat cautiously down upon the bed, and surveyed the operator with unfeigned pride and enthusiasm. She clasped her hands.

"Ally, how splendid! When did you begin doing it?"

Ally, weathering a hairless and slippery corner, replied—

"Third time. I'm doing it chiefly to make something *grow*. A man simply *has* to shave after he gets into the Fifteen: you look such a fool on Saturday nights if you don't. A chap in our house called Mallock, who has had his colours four years, has a beard about half-an-inch long by Friday. He's a gorgeous sight."

Daphne shuddered slightly.

Ally continued.

"I don't expect to rival him, of course, but I should like to have something to scrape off in the dormitory. My fag always grins so when he brings me my shaving-water—little tick!"

Daphne was too well versed in the eccentricities of the young of the male species to experience the slightest feeling of surprise at her brother's singular ambition. She merely wrapped a blanket round her shoulders and settled herself against the head of the bed, anxiously contemplating the progress of a sanguinary campaign in the region surrounding Ally's jugular vein.

Presently operations came to a conclusion; the traces of battle were obliterated with much sponging and spraying; and the pair sat and gossiped amicably while Ally stropped his razor and put studs in his Sunday shirt.

It was a full quarter of an hour before Daphne returned to her room, for her Sunday morning call upon Ally was always a protracted affair. But before she left she had, after the usual blandishments, exacted from him a promise that he would come to church. Their father never exercised any compulsion in this matter; but if any member of the family did stay at home on Sunday morning, the Rector's mute distress was such as to blight the spirits of the household for the rest of the day; and Daphne always exerted herself to the full to round up her entire flock in the Rectory pew at the appointed hour. The most recalcitrant members thereof were Ally and Nicky, but the former could usually be cajoled and the latter coerced.

After breakfast the Rector retired to his study to con his sermon; and not long afterwards was to be seen, key in hand, passing through the wicket-gate which led from the garden into the churchyard. Having tolled the church bell for five minutes, he busied himself at the altar, and then turned up the lessons at the lectern, marking these same in plain figures; for the Squire, who fulfilled the office of reader, required careful guidance in this respect. (He had been known to read the same lesson twice; also the Second Lesson before the First; and once he had turned over two pages together towards the end of a long chapter, and embarked with growing huskiness and visible indignation upon a supplementary voyage of forty-seven verses.)

Presently the Rector returned to the house for his surplice; and ten minutes later, a tall and saintly figure, followed his hobnailed and bullet-headed choristers into the chancel.

Snayling Church, though a diminutive building, was one of the oldest of its kind in England. The tower was square and stumpy, and had served as a haven of refuge more than once. A later generation, following the pious but unnecessary fashion of the day, had erected upon its summit a steeple of homely design, which indicated the route to heaven in an officious and altogether gratuitous manner. Inside the building itself the roof was supported by massive stone pillars and Norman arches. Beneath the floor lay folk long dead, their names, virtues, and destination set forth in many curious inscriptions in stone and brass, all greatly prized by the tourist with his tracing-paper and heel-ball. The chancel contained a real Crusader, who reclined, sword in hand and feet crossed, upon a massive sarcophagus, his good lady by his side. Tony Vereker had woven many a legend about *him*, you may be sure.

Each of the tiny transepts contained two square pews, decently veiled from the public gaze by red curtains. Those on the north side belonged respectively to the Squire, whose arrival in church with his wife and four daughters always served as an intimation to the organist—Mr Pack, the schoolmaster—that it was eleven o'clock and time to wind up the voluntary; and old Lady Curlew of Hainings, who invariably arrived five minutes before the hour, accompanied by her maid; who, having packed her mistress into a corner of the pew with cushions and hassocks, retired discreetly to the free seats by the door.

Of the pews in the south transept one was the property of the Lord of the Manor, the Marquis of Kirkley. It was seldom occupied, for his lordship suffered from the misfortune (which modern legislation is doing so much to alleviate) of possessing more residences than he could comfortably live in. His adjacent seat, Kirkley Abbey, was seldom open except for a few weeks during the pheasant season; and even the recurrence of that momentous period did not postulate undue congestion in the family pew.

The other pew was the Rector's, and here Daphne succeeded on this particular Sabbath morning in corralling the full strength of her troupe.

Non sine pulvere, however. Ally, as already related, had proved fairly tractable, but Nicky (who just at present stood badly in need of the services of a competent exorcist) had almost evaded ecclesiastical conscription by a new and ingenious device. At ten-fifteen precisely she had fallen heavily down a flight of two steps and sprained her ankle. Unsympathetic Daphne, experienced in the detection of every form of malingering, had despatched her upstairs with a bottle of Mr Elliman's strongest embrocation—the property of Ally—with instructions to anoint the injured member and report herself for duty at ten-forty-five prompt. At the appointed hour Nicky, limping painfully and smiling heroically, had joined the rest of the family in the hall.

Presently Ally remarked casually—

"Rotten stink here. Furniture polish, or something."

"Yes—filthy reek!" agreed Stiffy.

"It's turpentine," cried Cilly, crinkling her nose.

"It's Elliman," said Tony.

"It's *you*, Nicky!" said everybody at once.

Daphne, who was drawing on her gloves, peeled them off again with some deliberation, and took her youngest sister by the shoulders.

"Nicky," she inquired, "how much Elliman did you use?"

That infant martyr, wincing ostentatiously, delicately protruded a foot, and exhibited a long black leg heavily swathed from knee to instep under her stocking with a bandage of colossal dimensions.

"Not more than I could help, Daph," she said. "I found one or two other bruises on my—all over me, in fact: so I—I just put a little Elliman on each. I didn't want to be a trouble to any one, so—"

"Run upstairs, Stiffy," Daphne interpolated swiftly, "and see how much Elliman is left in the bottle."

By this time Cilly had thrown open the front door and staircase windows, and the remainder of the Vereker family were fanning themselves with their Sunday hats and ostentatiously fighting for breath—an exercise in which they persevered until Stiffy reappeared carrying an empty bottle.

"Two bobs' worth!" shouted Ally. "And I meant it to last for months! Nicky, you little *sweep*!"

Daphne glanced at the hall clock.

"Fourteen minutes!" she calculated frantically. "Yes, it can just be done. Nicky, my cherub, you shall come to church this morning if I have to *scrape* you. Go on, you others! I'll follow myself as quickly as I can."

The last sentence was delivered far up the staircase, which Miss Vereker was ascending with flying feet, a tearful and unwilling appendage trailing behind her. Next moment the bathroom door banged, and the departing worshippers heard both taps turned on.

At two minutes past eleven precisely Daphne and Nicky, the former cool, collected, and as prettily dressed as any woman in the congregation, the latter scarlet as if from recent parboiling, walked demurely down the aisle just as the choir entered the chancel, lustily bellowing a hymn which drew attention to the advantages accruing in the next world to that Servant of the Lord who should be found Waiting in his Office, in a Posture not specified—Tony used often to wonder what would happen if the Day of Judgment should fall upon a Bank holiday or Saturday afternoon—and joined the rest of the family in the Rectory pew.

A sermon, we all know, offers unique facilities for quiet reflection. As their father's silvery voice rose and fell in the cadences of his discourse—he had soared far above the heads of his bucolic audience, and was now disporting himself in a delectable but quite inaccessible æther of his own, where the worshippers (such of them as had not yielded to slothful repose) followed his evolutions with mystified and respectful awe, much as a crowd of citizens in a busy street gape upwards at the gambols of an aeroplane—the Rectory children wedged themselves into their own particular nooks of the pew, and prepared to get through the next twenty minutes in characteristic fashion.

Ally closed his eyes and assumed an attitude of slumber, as befitted his years and dignity. But he was not asleep. He did not look comfortable. Perhaps his breakfast had disagreed with him, or possibly he was contemplating within himself the vision of a receding University and an all-too-adjacent office-stool. Daphne, with her eyes fixed on the wall opposite and her brow puckered, was pondering some domestic problem—her own extravagantly small feet, mayhap, or Wednesday's hypothetical leg of mutton. Despite her burden of care, her face looked absurdly round and childish under her big beaver hat. One hand supported her chin in a characteristic pose, the other controlled the movements of the restless Anthony, who was impersonating something of a vibratory nature. Cilly, with glowing eyes and parted lips, was reading the Marriage Service in her Prayerbook. Nicky, whose recent ablutions had apparently purged her of outward sin only, had pulled forward two long wisps of black hair from behind her ears, and by crossing these under her nose had provided herself with a very realistic and terrifying pair of moustaches, by portentous twistings of which, assisted by the rolling of a frenzied eye, she was endeavouring to make poor Stiffy laugh. That right-minded youth, though hard pressed, had so far withstood temptation by resolutely reciting to himself a favourite excerpt from Bradshaw's Railway Guide, beginning "Brighton (Central), Preston Park, Burgess Hill, Hassocks" ... and ending with ... "Grosvenor Road, Victoria,"—a sedative exercise to which he was much addicted at moments of bodily anguish or mental stress; but it was plain that his defence was weakening.

Fortunately, the approaching explosion, which would have been of a cataclysmal nature,—Stiffy was not a boy to do things by halves,—was averted by a change of demeanour on the part of the temptress. Her quick ear had caught some unaccustomed sound behind her. Letting go her moustaches, which immediately assumed a more usual position, she squirmed round in her seat and gently parted the red rep curtains which separated the Rectory pew from that of Kirkley Abbey. An excited gurgle apprised her fellow-worshippers of the fact that some unusual sight had met her eyes.

What Nicky saw was this.

Immediately opposite to her improvised peep-hole sat a man—a large man with square shoulders and an immobile face. He was clean-shaven, with two strong lines running from his nostrils to the corners of his mouth—a mouth which even in repose looked determined and grim. He possessed a square jaw and rather craggy brows. It was difficult to decide if he were sleeping or no, for though his eyes were closed there was none of the abandon of slumber about his pose. His most noticeable feature was the set of his eyebrows, which, instead of being arched or level, ran upwards and outwards in a diagonal direction, and gave him a distinctly Satanic appearance—a circumstance which Nicky noted with sympathetic approval. He was dressed in the somewhat *dégagé* Sabbath attire affected by Englishmen spending the week-end in the country, and his feet were perched upon the seat opposite to him.

Presently, for some cause unknown—possibly Nicky's hard breathing—he opened his eyes.

Immediately in front of him the stranger beheld a small excited face, a pair of saucer-like blue eyes, and a wide but attractive mouth—the whole vision framed in dusty red rep. The face was flushed, the eyes glowed, and the mouth was wide open.

The picture, suddenly surprised in its inspection by a pair of the shrewdest and most penetrating eyes it had ever beheld, dropped hurriedly out of its frame and disappeared. If Nicky had waited a moment longer she would have received a less one-sided impression of the stranger, for almost simultaneously with the discovery of the apparition in the peep-hole the man smiled. Instantly his whole face changed. The outer corners of his eyebrows descended, the crease between them disappeared, and magnificent teeth gleamed for a moment in the dim religious light of the pew.

Nicky leaned across to her eldest sister and whispered huskily:—

"There's somebody in the other pew. I think it's the Devil. Look yourself!"

But Daphne, deep in domestic mental arithmetic, smiled and shook her head; and Nicky received little more encouragement from the rest of the family. The profession of scare-monger and exploiter of mares' nests, though enjoyable on the whole, has its drawbacks: if you get hold of a genuine scare or an authentic mare's nest, nobody believes you.

The sermon began to draw to a close, and a few minutes later the Rector descended from the clouds and gave out the final hymn, prefacing his announcement by an intimation that the offertory that day would be devoted to the needs of the Children's Cottage Hospital in the neighbouring county town. His appeal was characteristic.

"Money," he mused, "is the most hampering and perplexing thing in this life. It is so artificial and unnecessary. I often sigh for a world where all commerce will be in kind—where a cheque on the Bank of Gratitude will settle the weekly bills, and 'I thank you!' be regarded as legal tender up to any amount. But there is no give and take in these days. Everything, from Life and Love down to the raiment we wear, is duly appraised and ticketed, and if we stand in need of these things we must render a material tale of pounds and pence or go without. No wonder men call this the Iron Age! But, though money as a rule brings nothing in its train but disappointment and regret (and therefore it is better to have too little than too much), there are times and seasons when it is permitted to us to purchase happiness with it. To-day gives us one of these opportunities. Do not let that opportunity slip. *Post est Occasio calva.*" (Respectful intake of breath on the part of the congregation.) "I do not urge you to give on the plea put forward in a hymn that you will find in your books—a hymn written by a man who should have known better—a hymn which shall never, so long as I am Rector of this parish, emerge from the obscurity of the printed page—advocating generosity in almsgiving on the ground that contributions to the offertory on earth will be refunded at the rate of a hundred thousand per cent in heaven. I do not ask you to give either much or little. Very few of us here are over-burdened with this world's goods. Still, we can each afford to buy *some* happiness to-day, at a very low rate. And it will not be transitory or temporary happiness either; for every time hereafter that your daily task or a country walk takes you past the Children's Hospital at Tilney, that happiness will blossom again with ever-reviving fragrance in your hearts. Let us sing Hymn number three hundred and sixty-nine—

'Thine arm, O Lord, in days of old
Was strong to heal and save....'"

There was a general upheaval of the congregation and a clatter of rustic boots; the little organ gave a premonitory rumble, and the hymn began.

The hymn after the sermon is not, as a rule—to-day was an exception—an impressive canticle. *Imprimis*, it is of abnormal length and little coherence, having apparently been composed for the sole purpose of lasting out the collection of the offertory; *item*, the congregation is furtively engaged in retrieving umbrellas from under seats and gliding into overcoats. Hence it was always a pleasant diversion to the Rectory children to follow the movements of the two churchwardens as they ran their godly race up the aisle in the pursuit of alms and oblations. They even risked small sums on the result. When the Squire and Mr Murgatroyd (Stationer and Dealer in Fancy Goods) stepped majestically from their respective pews and set to work on this particular morning, Daphne produced five sixpences and handed them to her brothers and sisters. Nicky, in her anxiety to see what sum the stranger in the Kirkley Abbey pew would contribute to the total, received her own contribution with such nonchalance that the coin slipped from her hand, and was being hunted for among hassocks upon the floor at the moment when Mr Murgatroyd reached the stranger's pew.

Nicky found her sixpence, and resumed an upright attitude just in time to hear (in a pause between two verses) a faint papery rustle on the other side of the curtain.

A moment later Mr Murgatroyd opened the door of the Rectory pew, with his usual friendly air of dropping in for a cup of tea, and presented the bag. The children put in their sixpences one by one. Nicky's turn came last. She peered into the bag, and her sharp eyes caught sight of something white protruding from amid the silver and copper.

Taking the bag from Mr Murgatroyd's hands—she controlled that indulgent bachelor as she willed: he counted it a pleasure to turn his stock inside out on a Saturday afternoon whenever Miss Veronica came in with a penny to spend—Nicky deliberately drew out a piece of folded crinkly white paper. This, laying the offertory bag upon the baize-covered table in the middle of the pew, she carefully unfolded, and perused the staring black legend inscribed upon the flimsy white background. When she raised her eyes they were those of an owlet suffering from mental shock.

"Golly!" she observed in bell-like tones. "The Devil has put in a ten-pound note!"

CHAPTER FIVE.

A SABBATH-DAY'S JOURNEY.

The Rectory children, washed and combed for Sunday dinner, sat at ease in the old nursery—promoted to schoolroom since Tony went into knickerbockers—and discussed the munificent stranger of the morning.

Their interest in his movements and identity had been heightened by the fact that after service was over he had proceeded to the right instead of the left on leaving the Kirkley Abbey pew, and, turning his broad back upon an undisguisedly interested congregation, had stalked up the chancel and disappeared through the door leading to the vestry.

"I *wonder* what he went for," said Cilly for the third time.

"Perhaps he was going to give Dad more banknotes," suggested the optimistic Stiffy.

"More likely going to ask for change out of the first one," rejoined Ally, the cynic.

"I expect he was going to complain about you making faces at him through the curtain, Nicky," coldly observed Cilly, who had not yet forgiven her small sister's innuendoes on the subject of Mr Robert Gill.

"Rats!" demurred Nicky uneasily. "I didn't make faces. I expect he's only some tourist who wants to rub brasses, or sniff a vault, or something."

"He must be a friend of Lord Kirkley's," said Ally, "because—"

"*I'll* show you who he is," shrilled a voice from the depth of a cupboard under the window.

Tony, who had been grubbing among a heap of tattered and dusty literature in the bottom shelf, now rose to his feet and staggered across the room carrying an ancient but valuable copy of 'The Pilgrim's Progress,' embellished with steel engravings.

Having deposited the volume upon the hearthrug he proceeded to hunt through its pages. Presently, with a squeal of delight, he placed a stumpy fore-finger upon a full-page illustration, and announced triumphantly—

"That's him!"

The picture represented Christian's battle with Apollyon. Christian, hard pressed, had been beaten to his knees, and over him towered the figure of the Prince of Darkness, brandishing a sword and (in the most unsportsmanlike manner) emitting metallic-looking flames from his stomach. The children gathered round.

"You are right, Tony," said Cilly at length, "it *is* like him."

Certainly Apollyon bore a sort of far-away resemblance to the late occupant of the Kirkley Abbey pew.

"Look at his eyebrows," said Nicky, "they go straight up—"

The churchyard gate clicked, and voices were heard in conversation outside. Daphne sped to the window.

"Heavens!" she exclaimed in an agonised whisper, "Dad is bringing him in to lunch! Ally, take your boots off the mantelpiece! Nicky, pull up your stockings! Cilly, knock Dawks off the sofa! I must fly. I wonder if there's enough cream to make a trifle. Anyhow, the beef—"

And she sped away kitchenwards like an agitated butterfly.

A few minutes later the Rector appeared in the schoolroom, smiling joyously, with his hand resting lightly on the shoulder of the recently identified Apollyon. Tony was restoring 'The Pilgrim's Progress' to its shelf with the complacency of a second Bertillon.

"These are my flock, Jack," said Brian Vereker. "I wonder if any of you children can guess who this gentleman is? Would you think that he and I were at school together? Tony, I have often told you of little Jack Carr, who used to light my fire and cook my breakfast. And a shocking mess he used to make of it, eh? Didn't you, Jack? Do you remember the day you fried sausages in marmalade, because the label on the pot said marmalade would be found an excellent substitute for butter? Well, here he is, Tony. We have run together again after twenty-five years. Come and shake hands. These are my two younger girls, Jack, and these are my three boys. Where is Daphne, children?"

The Vereker family, drawn up in a self-conscious row, were understood to intimate that Daphne was downstairs. A move was therefore made in the direction of the dining-room, where Keziah, the little maid, was heatedly laying an extra place. Daphne joined the party a moment later, and welcomed Sir John Carr—such was his full title, it appeared—with prettiness and composure. But Cilly and Nicky noted that she had found time to rearrange her hair in honour of the occasion, and adorn herself with most of her slender stock of jewellery—two bangles and a thin gold chain.

Sunday dinner was something of a function at the Rectory. For one thing there was hot roast beef, which counts for much when you see the like only once in the week. The Rector carved and Stiffy handed round the plates, Keziah, whose Sunday-afternoon-out commenced technically the moment the sirloin was dished, being excused from further attendance. Daphne presided over the vegetable dishes and Ally cut bread at the sideboard. The office of butler was in abeyance, for the Vereker family drank only water from their highly polished christening-mugs. Nicky was responsible for the table-napkins, and Cilly mixed salads in season.

All these domestic details Daphne explained, with captivating friendliness and a freedom from self-consciousness that many a more matured hostess might have envied, to the silent man beside her.

"Sorry to have *all* the family pouring things over you," she said, as Stiffy with a plate of beef, Ally with a lump of bread impaled upon a fork, and Cilly with a bowl of lettuce, egg, and beetroot cunningly intermingled, converged simultaneously upon the guest; "but we have only one servant, and——"

Stephen Blasius Vereker, poised upon his toes and holding his breath, was leaning heavily over the guest's right shoulder, proffering a platter upon the edge of which a billow of gravy, piling itself up into a tidal wave, strove to overcome the restraining influence of surface tension. Apollyon, his features unrelaxed, gravely took the plate, and restoring it to a horizontal position, turned deferentially to resume his conversation with his young hostess.

——"And I like poor Keziah to have as long a Sunday out as possible," continued Daphne, entirely unruffled.

"Her young man waits for her at the stile down by Preston's farm," supplemented Nicky. "They go for a walk down Tinkler's Den, and never speak a *word* to each other."

——"So we wait on ourselves at this meal," concluded Daphne. "What will you drink, Sir John? Father is a teetotaller, and so are all of us; but if you are not, I've got some brandy upstairs in the nursery medicine cupboard."

"Thank you, I will drink water," said Sir John solemnly.

By this time the Vereker family had settled down to their own portions, and were babbling as cheerfully and unrestrainedly as usual. Shyness in the presence of strangers was not one of their weaknesses, and presently, taking advantage of Daphne's departure to the kitchen in quest of the second course, they engaged their guest in conversation, inviting his opinions on such widely different subjects as the quality of the salad (Cilly), the merits of the automatic vacuum railway brake as compared with those of the Westinghouse (Stiffy), and the prospects of Cambridge in the coming Boat Race (Ally). All of which queries were answered in a fashion which, while lacking in geniality and erring a little on the side of terseness, showed that the respondent knew what he was talking about.

The Rector, at the head of the table, smiled benignantly. To him this reticent man of over forty, with the deep-set eyes and square jaw, was the sturdy chubby boy who had cooked his breakfast and worshipped him from afar in the dim but joyous days when Brian Vereker was a giant of nineteen, with side whiskers, and Jacky Carr a humble fag of twelve. It was almost a shock to hear him offered spirits to drink.

Presently Daphne returned, and another general post ensued, at the end of which the beef and vegetables had disappeared, and a suet pudding (the standing Sabbath sweet at the Rectory), flanked by a dish of trifle of diminutive proportions, lay before the hostess. The Rector was confronted by a melon.

Taking advantage of a covering conversation between the guest and her eldest brother, Miss Vereker made a mysterious pass over the surface of the trifle with a spoon, while she murmured to such of the family as were within earshot the mystic formula, "F. H. B.!" Then she inquired aloud—

"Cilly, dear, which pudding will you have?"

"Baby Maud, please," replied Miss Cecilia promptly, indicating the stiff, pallid, and corpse-like cylinder of suet.

She was helped, and Nicky's choice was ascertained.

"I don't *think*," that damsel replied sedately, "that I'll have anything, thank you, Daphne. I'm not very hungry to-day."

Daphne, with a slight twitch at the corners of her mouth—she appreciated Nicky's crooked little ways, despite herself—turned to the guest.

"Will you have pudding or trifle, Sir John? Let me recommend the trifle."

"Thank you, I never eat sweets," was the reply.

An audible sigh of relief rose from the Messrs Vereker.

"Daph, dear," said Nicky before any one else could speak, "I think I'll change my mind and have some trifle."

And thus, by prompt generalship, Miss Veronica Vereker, while obeying to the letter the laws of hospitality and precedence, stole a march upon her slow-moving brethren and sisters and received the lion's share of the trifle, the balance going to Tony by virtue of juniority.

As Daphne handed her triumphant little sister her portion, she distinctly heard a muffled sound on her right.

"I like this man!" she said to herself.

"If you don't take sweets, Jack," observed the Rector from the other end of the table, "allow me to introduce you to this melon—a present from the Squire. Take the melon round to Sir John, Stiffy, and he shall cut in where he pleases; though, strictly speaking," he added, with simple enjoyment of his own joke, "it is hardly etiquette to cut anything you have been introduced to!"

There was a momentary stoppage in the general mastication of "Baby Maud," and the right hand of each Vereker present performed the same evolution. Next moment the repast was resumed, but the guest observed, not without surprise, that every christening-mug—even Daphne's—had a knife lying across its top.

"That is one of our customs," explained Cilly politely. "We do it whenever any one makes a stale joke."

"*Alice through the Looking-Glass*," corroborated Nicky, scooping up trifle with an air of severe reproof—"page two hundred and seven."

"You see my servile and dependent position in this house, Jack!" said the Rector, not altogether dejectedly.

"I perceive that I have dropped into a Republic," said Sir John Carr.

"Republic? A more absolute despotism never existed. Wait until you have transgressed one of the Laws of the Medes and Persians and been brought up for judgment before my eldest daughter? *We* know, don't we—eh, Nicky?"

Brian Vereker projected the furtive smile of a fellow-conspirator upon his youngest daughter, and then turned to gaze with unconcealed fondness and pride upon his eldest.

"I trust that when I transgress," said Sir John, "I shall get off under the First Offender's Act."

"You have broken that already," said Daphne readily; "but it's Dad's fault. It is twenty minutes to three, and you two ought to have been smoking in the study ten minutes ago instead of talking here. I want to get this room cleared for the children to learn their Catechism in."

At half-past three Brian Vereker summoned his eldest daughter to the study, and announced with frank delight that Sir John Carr had agreed to vacate the Kirkley Arms and accept the hospitality of the Rectory.

"I am going to walk down to the inn now," said Apollyon to Daphne, "to see about my luggage. Perhaps you will keep me company?"

"All right," said Daphne. "I'll bring Mr Dawks too. He wants a walk, I know."

Sir John made no comment, but gave no active support to the inclusion of Mr Dawks in the party. It may be noted, however, that when Daphne had at length achieved that feat which encroaches so heavily upon a woman's share of eternity—the putting on of her hat—and joined her guest in the garden accompanied by Mr Dawks in person, Apollyon greeted the owner of the name with far more cordiality than he had greeted the name itself. It is sometimes misleading to bestow Christian titles upon dumb animals.

Once away from the rest of the family, Daphne's maternal solemnity fell from her like a schoolmaster's cap and gown in holiday time. She chattered like a magpie, pointing out such objects of local interest as—

(1) Farmer Preston's prize bull;
(2) The residence of a reputed witch;
(3) A spinney, where a dog-fox had once gone to ground at one end of an earth and a laughing hyena (subsequently ascertained to be the lost property of that peripatetic nobleman Lord George Sanger) had emerged from the other, to the entire and instantaneous disintegration of a non-abstaining local Hunt.

"I say, where do you live?" she inquired suddenly, breaking off in the middle of a detailed history of Kirkley Abbey, whose *façade* could be discerned through the trees on their right—"London?"

"Yes."

"All the year round?"

"No. I spend a good deal of my time in the North."

"Oh. What do you do there? What *are* you, by the way?" Daphne looked up at her companion with bird-like inquisitiveness. She moved in a society familiar with the age, ancestry, profession, wardrobe, ailments, love affairs, and income of every one within a radius of five miles. Consequently she considered a new acquaintanceship incomplete in the last degree until she had acquired sufficient information on the subject in hand to supply, say, a tolerably intimate obituary notice.

"I suppose you are *something*," she continued. "I hope so, anyhow. An idle man is always so mopy."

"What would you put me down as?" asked Apollyon.

Daphne scrutinised him without fear or embarrassment.

"I'm not much of a judge," she said. "You see, we don't come across many men here, and we are so poor that we don't get away much."

"Don't you go up to London occasionally, to buy a new frock?" said Sir John, covertly regarding the trim figure by his side.

"Me—London? Not much. Dad has a lot of grand relations there, but I don't think he bothered much about them, or they about him, after he married. He was too much wrapped up in mother. So we never hear anything of them now. No, I have hardly ever been away from Snayling, and I'm a great deal too busy here to worry about London or any other such place. So I don't know much about men," she concluded simply—"except my own, of course."

"Your own?"

"Yes—Dad and the boys. And then I know all about the sort of man one meets round here. I can tell a ditcher from a ploughman; and if I meet a man in a dog-cart with cases at the back I know he's a commercial traveller, and if he has a red face I know he's a farmer, and if he hasn't I know he's a doctor; but I haven't had much other experience."

"Still, what am *I*?" reiterated Apollyon.

"Well—I suppose you are not a soldier, or you would have a moustache."

"No."

"You might be a lawyer, being clean-shaven. Are you?"

"No."

"Oh! That's rather disappointing. You would make a ripping judge, with a big wig on. Well, perhaps you write things. I know—you are an author or an editor?"

"No."

"Foiled again!" said Daphne cheerfully. "Let me see, what other professions are there? Are you a Don, by any chance? A fellow, or lecturer, or anything? We had a Fellow of All Souls down here once. He was a dear."

"No."

"You are a 'Varsity man, I suppose."

"Yes."

"Oxford or Cambridge?"

"Cambridge."

"I am glad. Dark blue is *so* dull, isn't it? Besides, Dad is a Cambridge man. He is an old Running Blue. He won—but of course you know all about that. It seems queer to think you knew him before I did! Well, I give you up. What *do* you do?"

Apollyon reflected.

"I sell coals," he replied at last, rather unexpectedly.

This announcement, and the manner in which it was made, momentarily deprived Miss Vereker of speech—a somewhat rare occurrence.

"I see," she said presently. "We get ours from the station-master," she added politely.

"I was not proposing to apply for your custom," said Apollyon meekly.

At this point they reached the Kirkley Arms, and in the effort involved in rousing that somnolent hostelry from its Sabbath coma and making arrangements for the sending up of Sir John Carr's luggage to the Rectory, the question of why he sold coals, and whether he hawked the same round in a barrow or delivered his wares through the medium of the Parcels Post, was lost sight of.

On the homeward walk conversation was maintained on much the same terms. Daphne held forth unweariedly, and Apollyon contented himself for the most part with answering her point-blank questions and putting a few—a very few—of his own. Certainly the man was a born listener, and amazingly magnetic. Tacitus himself could not have said less, and the greatest cross-examiner in the legal profession could not have extracted more. As they strolled side by side through the Kirkley woods, where the last of the daffodils were reluctantly making way for the first of the primroses, Daphne found herself reciting, as to a discreet and dependable father-confessor, a confidential but whole-hearted summary of the present state of domestic politics.

Ally's failure to secure a scholarship at the University was mentioned.

It was disgusting of him to miss the Greek Prose paper, Daphne considered. "He didn't oversleep at all, of course. I soon found *that* out. The real reason was that he had gone to some man's rooms the night before, and the silly brat must go and drink a whisky-and-soda and smoke a cigar. That did it! It was no use telling Dad, because he simply wouldn't believe such a story; and if he did, it would make him unhappy for weeks. Besides, who can blame the poor dear? You can't be surprised if a schoolboy kicks over the traces a bit the first time he finds himself out on his own—can you?"

"I thought," replied Sir John, finding that some answer was expected of him, "that you said you knew nothing of men?"

"I said I didn't know *many* men," corrected Daphne. "But those I do know I know pretty thoroughly. They're very easy to understand, dear things! You always know where you are with them. Now, girls are different. Did you notice that boy whom we passed just now, who went pink and took off his hat. That's Bobby Gill—a flame of Cilly's. I'm going to have a lot of trouble with Cilly's love-affairs, I can see. She falls down and worships every second man she meets. I believe she would start mooning round the place after *you* if you weren't so old," she added. "Cilly's a darling, but what she wants——"

She plunged, with puckered brow and tireless tongue, into a further tale of hopes and fears. Stiffy's schooling, Nicky's boots, the curate who *had* to come—all were laid upon the table. Even the Emergency Bag and Wednesday's joint crept in somehow.

They were almost home when she concluded.

Suddenly Apollyon inquired:

"Do you know the name of that little hollow on our right? Is it Tinkler's Den?"

"Yes; we often have picnics there. How did you know?"

"It is part of Lord Kirkley's estate, as you are probably aware; and his lordship, finding like most of us that he has not sufficient money for his needs, has asked me to come and have a look at the ground round Tinkler's Den on the off-chance of our finding coal there."

Daphne turned upon him, wide-eyed and horror-struck.

"You mean to say," she gasped, "that you are going to dig for coals in Tinkler's Den?"

"I can't tell you, until——"

Apollyon paused. A small hand was resting on his sleeve, and a very small voice said beseechingly—

"Don't—*please*!"

"Very well, then: I won't," he said, in a matter-of-fact fashion; and they resumed their walk.

"I hope you haven't been bored," said Daphne, the hostess in her rising to the surface as the shadow of the Rectory fell upon her once more. "Your ears must be simply aching, but it's such a treat to talk to any one who knows about things. I never get the chance to ask advice. I usually have to give it. Dad and the boys are so helpless, bless them!"

They were passing through the wicket-gate. Daphne suddenly paused, and looked up at her guest with more mischief in her eyes than her brothers and sisters would have given her credit for.

"It's queer," she mused, "that you should sell coals. *We* thought you *shovelled* them!"

"Explain, please!" said Sir John.

Daphne did so. "We *had* to call you something," she concluded apologetically. "Do you mind?"

"Not at all. I have been called a good many names in my time," said Sir John grimly.

"What do your friends call you?" asked Daphne—"your intimate friends."

"I am not sure that I have any."

Daphne surveyed him shrewdly, with her head a little on one side.

"No—I should think you *were* that sort," she said gravely. "Well, what do your—do other people call you?"

"Most of them, I believe," said Sir John, "call me 'Juggernaut Carr.'"

CHAPTER SIX.

DAPHNE AS MATCHMAKER.

Juggernaut's stay at the Rectory had been prolonged for more than three weeks, the business upon which he was engaged being as easily directed, so he said, from Brian Vereker's study as from his own London offices. An unprejudiced observer might have been forgiven for remarking that to all appearances it could have been directed with equal facility from the Two-penny Tube or the North Pole; for if we except a prolonged interview with Lord Kirkley's land agent on the second day after his arrival, Juggernaut's activities had been limited to meditative contemplation of the Rector's spring flowers and some rather silent country walks in company with the lady to whom the Rector was wont to refer to in his playful moments as "my elderly ugly daughter."

Whether Daphne's impulsive protest against the desecration of her beloved Tinkler's Den carried weight, or whether that sylvan spot was found wanting in combustible properties, will never be known; but it may be noted here that Lord Kirkley was advised that there was no money in his scheme, and Snayling remains an agricultural centre to this day.

However, if it be a fact that no fresh experience can be altogether valueless, Juggernaut's time was certainly not wasted. He was absorbed into the primitive civilisation of Snayling Rectory. He was initiated into tribal custom and usage, and became versed in a tribal language consisting chiefly of abbreviations and portmanteau words. He was instructed in the principles which underlie such things as precedence in the use of the bath and helpings at dinner. He also studied with interest the fundamental laws governing the inheritance of out-grown garments. Having been born without brothers and sisters, he found himself confronted for the first time with some of those stern realities and unavoidable hardships which prevail when domestic supply falls short of domestic demand. The mystic phrase "F. H. B.!" for instance, with which Daphne had laid inviolable taboo upon the trifle on the day of his arrival, he soon learned stood for "Family, hold back!"

Again, if Master Stephen Blasius Vereker suggested to Miss Veronica Elizabeth Vereker that a B. O. at the T. S. would be an L. B. of A. R.; to which the lady replied gently but insistently, "Is it E. P.?" Juggernaut was soon able to understand that in response to an intimation on the part of her brother that a Blow Out at the Tuck Shop would be a Little Bit of All Right, the cautious and mercenary damsel was inquiring whether her Expenses would be Paid at the forthcoming orgy. If Stiffy continued, "Up to 2 D.," and Nicky replied, "If you can't make it a tanner, Stiffy, darling, je pense *ne*!" the visitor gathered without much difficulty that in the opinion of Miss Veronica no gentleman worthy of the name should presume to undertake the entertainment of a lady under a minimum outlay of sixpence.

Juggernaut soon settled down to the ways of the establishment. He said little, but it was obvious, even to the boys, that he was taking a good deal in. He seldom asked questions, but he possessed an uncanny knack of interpreting for himself the most secret signs and cryptic expressions of the community. This established for him a claim to the family's respect, and in acknowledgment of the good impression he had created he was informally raised from the status of honoured guest to that of familiar friend. What the Associated Body of Colliery Owners would have thought if they could have seen their chairman meekly taking his seat at the breakfast-table, what time the family, accompanying themselves with teaspoons against teacups, chanted a brief but pointed ditty consisting entirely of the phrase "pom-pom!" repeated *con amore* and *sforzando* until breathlessness intervened—an ordeal known at the Rectory as "pom-pomming," and inflicted daily upon the last to appear at breakfast—is hard to say. Mr Montague for one would have enjoyed it.

Only once did this silent and saturnine man exhibit any flash of feeling. One morning before breakfast Daphne, busy in the knife-and-boot shed at the back of the house, heard a step on the gravel outside, and Juggernaut stood before her.

"Good-morning!" she said cheerfully. "Excuse my get-up. I expect I look rather a ticket."

Juggernaut surveyed her. She wore a large green baize apron. Her skirt was short and business-like, and her sleeves were rolled up above the elbow. Her hair was twisted into a knot at the back of her head. Plainly her toilet had only reached the stage of the *petit lever*. She was engaged in the healthful but unfashionable occupation of blacking boots; *per contra*, what Juggernaut chiefly noted was the whiteness of her arms. Finally his eye wandered to the boot in which her left hand was engulfed.

"Whose boot is that?" he asked.

"Yours, I should say. Dad's are square in the toes."

Next moment a large and sinewy hand gripped her by the wrist, and the boot was taken from her.

"Understand," said Apollyon, looking very like Apollyon indeed, "this must never occur again. I am angry with you."

He spoke quite quietly, but there was a vibrant note in his voice which Daphne had never heard before. Mr Tom Winch and Mr Montague would have recognised it. She looked up at him fearlessly, rather interested than otherwise in this new side of his character.

"I can't quite grasp why you *should* be angry," she said, "though I can see you are. Not being millionaires, we all clean our own boots—excepting Dad, of course. I always do his. You being a visitor, I threw yours in as a make-weight. It's all in the day's work."

But Juggernaut's fit had passed.

"I beg your pardon," he said. "I have no right to be angry with any one but myself. I am ashamed. I should have thought about this sooner, but I accepted your assurance that my visit would throw no extra burden upon the household rather too readily. Now, for the rest of the time I am here I propose, with your permission, to black my own boots. And as a sort of compensation for the trouble I have caused, I am going to black my hostess's as well."

"Do you know *how* to?" inquired the hostess, rather apprehensively.

For answer Juggernaut picked up a laced shoe from off the bench and set to work upon it.

"I once blacked my own boots every day for two years," he said, breathing heavily upon the shoe. "Now, if you want to go in and superintend the preparation of breakfast, you may leave me here, and I will undertake to produce the requisite standard of brilliancy." His face lit up with one of his rare and illuminating smiles, and he set grimly to work again.

Daphne hesitated for a moment, and surveyed her guest doubtfully. He was burnishing her shoe in a manner only to be expected of an intensely active man who has been utterly idle for a fortnight. His face was set in the lines which usually appeared when he was driving business through a refractory meeting. Daphne turned and left the boot-house, unpinning her apron and whistling softly.

Juggernaut finished off her shoes with meticulous care, and putting them back upon the bench turned his attention to his own boots. But his energy was plainly flagging. Several times his hand was stayed, and his eye wandered in the direction of his hostess's shoes. They were a remarkably neat pair. Daphne was proud of her feet—they were her only real vanity—and she spent more upon her boots and shoes than the extremely limited sum voted for the purpose by her conscience. More than once Juggernaut laid aside his own property and returned to the highly unnecessary task of painting the lily—if such a phrase can be applied to the efficient blacking of a shoe. Finally he picked up his boots and departed, to endure a pom-pomming of the most whole-hearted description on his appearance at the breakfast table.

But henceforth he found his way to the boot-house every morning at seven-thirty, where, despite his hostess's protests, he grimly carried out his expressed intention.

This was the only occasion, however, on which he asserted his will with Daphne. In all else she found him perfectly amenable. He permitted her without protest to overhaul his wardrobe, and submitted meekly to a scathing lecture upon the negligence apparent in the perforated condition of some of his garments and the extravagance evinced by the multiplicity of others. In short, Daphne adopted Juggernaut, as only a young and heart-whole girl can whose experience of men so far has been purely domestic. She felt like his mother. To her he was a child of the largest possible growth, who, not having enjoyed such advantages as she had all her life bestowed upon the rest of the flock, must needs be treated with twofold energy and special consideration. He was her Benjamin, she felt.

Juggernaut was to depart to-morrow. His socks were darned. Items of his wardrobe, hitherto anonymous, were neatly marked with his initials. His very pocket-handkerchiefs were numbered.

"You are sending me back to work thoroughly overhauled and refitted," he said to Daphne, as she displayed, not without pride, his renovated garments laid out upon the spare bed. "I feel like a cruiser coming out of dry dock."

"Well, don't get your things in that state again," said Daphne severely—"that's all! Who looks after them?"

"My man."

"He ought to be ashamed of himself, then. By the way, there is a dress waistcoat of yours with two buttons off. Can I *trust* you, now, to get them put on again, or had I better keep the waistcoat until I can get buttons to match?"

"You are very good," said Juggernaut, bowing before the storm.

"That's settled, then. Where shall I send it to?"

Juggernaut thought, and finally gave the address of a club in Pall Mall.

"Club—do you live in a *club*?" inquired Daphne, with a woman's instinctive dislike for such a monastic and impregnable type of domicile.

"Sometimes. It saves trouble, you see," said Juggernaut apologetically. "My house in town is shut at present. I spend a good deal of time in the north."

"Where do you live when you are in the north?" inquired Daphne, with the healthy curiosity of her age and sex.

"I have another house there," admitted Juggernaut reluctantly. "It is called Belton."

"How many houses have you got altogether?" asked Daphne, in the persuasive tones of a schoolmaster urging a reticent culprit to make a clean breast of it and get it over like a man.

"I have a little place in the Highlands," said Juggernaut humbly—

Daphne rolled her brown eyes up to the ceiling.

—"But it is the merest shooting-box," he added, as if pleading for a light sentence.

"Is that all?"

"Yes—on my honour!"

"And—you live in a *club*!"

Then came the verdict—the inevitable verdict.

"What you want," said Daphne, regarding the impassive features of the prisoner at the bar, "is a wife. It's not too late, really," she added, smiling kindly upon him. "Of course, you think now at your age that you could never get used to it, but you could."

"Do you think any girl would marry a man practically in his dotage?" inquired Juggernaut respectfully.

"Not a girl, perhaps," admitted Daphne, "but somebody sensible and good. I'll tell you what—don't you know any nice widows? A widow would suit you top-hole. She would be used to men already, which would help her a lot, poor thing! Then, she would probably let you down more easily than an old maid. She would know, for instance, that it's perfectly hopeless to get a man to keep his room tidy, or to stop leaving his slippers about on the dining-room hearthrug, or dropping matches and ash on the floor. Do marry a widow, Sir John! Don't you know of any?"

Sir John smiled grimly.

"I will consult my visiting-list," he said; "but I won't promise anything. In spite of the apparent docility of my character, there are just one or two things which I prefer to do in my own way."

"Still, I don't despair of you," said Daphne. "Old Martin down in the village married only the other day, and he was seventy-two. Nearly bedridden, in fact," she added encouragingly.

That evening after supper the Rectory children sat round the table engaged in card games of a heating and complicated nature, Miss Vereker as usual doubling the parts of croupier and referee. The guest and the Rector were smoking in the study.

Suddenly the door of the dining-room opened, and Brian Vereker appeared.

"Daphne, my daughter," he said, "can you leave these desperadoes for a while and join us in the study?"

"All right, Dad. Ally, you had better be dealer. Nicky, if you cheat while I am away you know the penalty! Come with me, Dawks. So long, everybody. Back directly!"

But she was wrong. Game succeeded game: the time slipped by unheeded by all except Nicky and Tony, who, because it was past their hour for going to bed, noted its flight with special and personal relish; and it was not until the almost tearful Cilly had been rendered an old maid for the fourth consecutive time that the family realised that it was nearly half-past ten and Daphne had not returned.

"Of course," said Nicky, wagging her head triumphantly, "we all know what *that* means!"

And for once in her small, scheming, prying life, she was right.

CHAPTER SEVEN.

THE MATCH IS STRUCK.

Daphne sat rather dizzily by her father's side, holding his hand tightly and gazing straight before her. A sudden turn, and lo! before her lay a great break in the road. She had arrived at one of life's jumping-off places. No wonder she gripped her father's hand.

Now, for a young girl to consent to a marriage with a man considerably older than herself, a man whom she hardly knows and does not love, is rightly regarded as a most unromantic proceeding; and since romance is the sugar of this rather acrid existence of ours, we are almost unanimous in discouraging such alliances. And yet there are two sides to the question. A loveless marriage may lead to the ruin of two lives: on the other hand, it introduces into the proceedings an element of business and common-sense all too rare in such enterprises. It is true that the newly united pair dream no dreams and see no visions. Each comes to the other devoid of glamour or false pretences. But if a couple find marriage feasible under such circumstances, the chances are that they are of a type which stands in no need of that highly intoxicating stimulant, Passion. They are simply people who realise at the outset, instead of later on, that life is a campaign and not a picnic; and each sees in the other not so much an idol or a plaything as a trusty ally. For such, mutual respect cannot but spring into being, and will in all likelihood grow into mutual love; and mutual love which matures from such beginnings as these is ten thousand times more to be desired than the frothy headachy stuff which we quaff in such reckless magnums in our thirsty youth.

On the other hand, marriages made on earth (as opposed to what are popularly regarded as the celestial variety) can and often do lead to shipwreck. Granted. Still, marriage is a leap in the dark in any case, and humdrum philosophers must at least be excused for suggesting that one may as well endeavour to illuminate this hazardous feat of agility by the help of the Torch of Reason as not. But of course no one ever agrees with such suggestions. Romance and Sentiment cry, "Never! Shame! Monstrous!" And most of us very humanly, naturally, and rightly associate ourselves in the most cordial manner with the opinions of this old-established and orthodox firm.

We left Daphne gazing into the study fire, with a silent man on either side of her and Mr Dawks' head upon her knee. She looked perfectly composed, but something was rocking and trembling within her.

It is certainly disconcerting, even for the most self-possessed of maidens, to realise, suddenly and without warning, that there are deeper things than the domestic affections. It is still more disconcerting when an individual whom Nature might with perfect propriety have appointed your father, and whom you with feminine perversity have adopted as a son, suddenly kicks over the traces and suggests as a compromise that he should occupy the intermediate position of husband.

Brian Vereker sat smiling, happy and confident. The fact that Sir John Carr was forty-two and Daphne barely twenty had not occurred to him. All he realised was that the little boy who had been his fag at school, who had lit his fire and made his toast in return for occasional help with cæsuras and quadratic equations, had grown up into a man, and desired to marry his daughter. The whole thing seemed so natural, so appropriate. He glowed with humble pride that Providence should so interest itself in his little household. He beamed upon the young people.

Suddenly Daphne turned to him, and released her hold on his hand.

"Dad, will you leave us for a little?" she said. "I want to talk to Sir John."

The Rector rose.

"By all means," he said. "Now I come to think of it, the presence of a third party is not essential to a proposal of marriage. I am *de trop*! I shall be upstairs."

He laughed boyishly, and left them.

When the door closed Daphne turned to her suitor.

"So you want me for your wife?" she said, with the air of one opening a debate.

"I do," said Juggernaut. It was the first time he had spoken since she entered the room.

"And you went and saw Dad about it," continued Daphne, rather unexpectedly.

"Yes. As I understood you were not of age, I asked his permission to speak to you. He rather took the words out of my mouth by calling you in and telling you himself."

"I'm glad to hear you say that," said Daphne. "I thought at first the thing was being arranged over my head, and that I wasn't to be consulted at all. But you *were* going to ask me properly, weren't you? We prefer that, you know." She spoke for her sex.

Juggernaut nodded.

"Only Dad rushed in and spoiled it—eh?"

"That is correct," said Juggernaut.

"Well, begin now," said Daphne calmly. "A girl doesn't like to be done out of a proposal. It would be something to tell the kids about afterwards, anyhow."

Juggernaut became conscious of a distinctly more lenient attitude towards the Rector's precipitancy.

"Now that you know," he began, "a formal proposal would sound rather dull and superfluous, wouldn't it?"

"Perhaps you are right," said Daphne, half regretfully. "Dad has spoiled it for me, after all!"

Presently—

"I wonder *why* you want to marry me," she mused, fondling Mr Dawks' ears. "I suppose you have come to the conclusion that it is time you had some one to look after all those houses and servants of yours. Is that it?"

Juggernaut regarded her curiously for a moment.

"Perhaps," he said.

"You are not in love with me, of course," continued the practical Miss Vereker, ticking off the unassailable features of the case. "At least, I suppose not—I don't see how you possibly could be. It's rather hard for me to tell, though, because I don't quite know the meaning of the word. I love Dad and the boys, and Cilly, and Nicky, and Mr Dawks—*don't* I, Dawks, dear?—and I would do *anything* to save them pain or unhappiness. But I suppose that's not the sort of love that people call love. It seems to have been left out of my composition, or perhaps it hasn't cropped up yet. Now Cilly—I am her exact opposite—Cilly is always in love with some man or other. By the way, she told me last night when I went to dry her hair that she had just fallen in love with you, so evidently you aren't too old after all! Would it do as well if you married Cilly?" Daphne inquired tentatively.

"I'm afraid not," said Juggernaut.

"Well, perhaps you are right. Cilly's a darling, but she is very young yet," agreed the time-worn Miss Vereker. "But"—she broke off short—"it seems to me that I am doing most of the talking. Would you care to address the meeting—say a few words? I think I should like to hear a bit of that proposal after all. So far, all I know is that you want to marry me. And *that* I got from Dad. Now—I'm listening!"

Daphne leaned back in her big chair and smiled upon her suitor quite maternally. There was something pathetic in her childish freedom from embarrassment or constraint under circumstances which usually test the *sang-froid* of man and maid alike. Perhaps Sir John was struck by this, for his eyes suddenly softened and the lines about his mouth relaxed.

"You needn't say you love me, or anything like that, if you don't," supplemented Daphne. "I shall understand."

Sir John's eyes resumed their normal appearance.

"As you seem to prefer to keep matters on a strictly business footing," he said, "I will come to the point at once. If you will marry me I think I can make you tolerably happy and comfortable. I am a prosperous man, I suppose, and as my wife you would find a certain social position awaiting you. Any desires of yours in the way of houses, clothes, jewels, and so on, you could always gratify, within limits, at will. I mention these things, not because I think they will influence your decision—I should not want you for a wife if I thought they would—but because I feel that every woman is entitled to a plain statement of fact about the man who wishes to marry her. Too often, under the delusion that the sheer romance of a love-affair wipes all mundane considerations off the slate, she puts up with the wildest of fictions. However, I may point out to you that acceptance of my worldly goods would enable you to carry out certain schemes that I know lie very near your heart. You could send Ally to the University. You could have Cilly finished, or whatever the expression is, and bring her out yourself. And you could pay for a curate for your father. You can have all the money you want for these enterprises by asking for it; or if you prefer something more definite I would settle an annual sum upon you—say a thousand a-year."

A thousand a-year! Daphne closed her eyes giddily. Before her arose a vision of a renovated Rectory—a sort of dimity Palace Beautiful—with an enlarged kitchen-boiler, new carpets, and an extra servant. She saw her father bending happily over his sermon while a muscular young Christian tramped round the parish. She saw Ally winning first classes at Cambridge, and Cilly taking London drawing-rooms by storm. Her pulse quickened. But Juggernaut was still speaking.

"On the other hand, I ought to warn you that I am a hard man—at least, I believe that is my reputation—with somewhat rigid notions on the subject of *quid* and *quo*. I would endeavour to supply my wife with every adjunct to her happiness; but—I should expect her in return to stand by my side and do her duty as my wife so long as we both lived. They say of me that I never make a mistake in choosing a lieutenant. Well, the instinct which has served me so often in that respect is prompting me now; and it is because I see in you a woman who would stand by her husband as a matter of duty alone, quite apart from"—he hesitated—"from inclination, that I ask you to marry me."

Daphne gazed at him. Her heart was bumping gently. There was something rather fine about this proposed bargain—a compact between a man and a woman to stand by one another through thick and thin, not because they liked doing so but because it was playing the game. Daphne felt proud, too, that this master of men should have adjudged her—a woman—to be of the true metal. But she was honest to the end.

"You would give all that to have me for your wife," she said.

Sir John bowed his head with grave courtesy.

"I would," he said simply.

"I'm not worth it," said Daphne earnestly. "I am only accustomed to looking after our little Rectory and the family. I might make a fearful mess of all your grand houses. Supposing I did? What if I wasn't up to your mark? How if your friends didn't like me? It would be too late to send me back," she pointed out, rather piteously.

Sir John's features did not relax.

"I am willing to take the risk," was all he said.

There was a long pause.

"Let me think," said Daphne suddenly and feverishly.

She slipped out of her chair on to the hearthrug, and lay before the twinkling fire with her arms clasped round the neck of the ever-faithful Mr Dawks and her face buried in his rough coat. There was a tense silence, accentuated by the amiable thumping of Dawks' tail. Sir John Carr sat in his chair like a graven image, looking down upon the slim lithe figure at his feet. Daphne just then was a sight to quicken the blood in a man's veins, but Juggernaut never moved. Perhaps he realised, for all his lack of lover's graces and his harsh methods of wooing, something of the solemnity of the moment. A child, without experience, with nothing but her own untutored instincts to guide her, was standing at her cross-roads. Would she go forward with the man whose path through life had so suddenly converged on hers, or fare on alone? And the man—what were his feelings? None could have told by outward view. He simply waited—sitting very still.

At last Daphne sat up, and shook back her hair from her eyes.

"We'll leave it to Mr Dawks," she said. "Dawks, old boy, shall we *do* it?"

The house waited in breathless silence for Mr Dawks' casting vote. That affectionate and responsive arbitrator, hearing himself addressed, raised his head, licked his mistress's hand, and belaboured the floor with his tail in a perfect ecstasy of cordiality.

Daphne turned to the man in the chair.

"All right!" she said. "It's a bargain. I'll marry you."

CHAPTER EIGHT.

"MORITURA TE SALUTAT."

On a bright spring afternoon three weeks later the Rectory children sat huddled together like a cluster of disconsolate starlings upon the five-barred gate leading into Farmer Preston's big pasture meadow.

It was the eve of Daphne's wedding-day.

To those readers of this narrative who feel inclined to dilate upon the impropriety of marrying in haste, it may be pointed out that the bride possessed no money and the bridegroom no relatives. Consequently there would be no presents, no *trousseau*. The principal incentives to what Miss Veronica Vereker pithily described as a "circus wedding" being thus eliminated, the pair were to be married quietly next day in the little church where Daphne had been christened and confirmed, and under the shadow of which she had lived all her short life.

As noted above, the bride had no *trousseau*, for her father could not afford one, and she flatly declined to take a penny from her *fiancé* until he became her husband. The little village dressmaker had turned out a wedding-dress over which Cilly hourly gloated, divided between ecstasy and envy; and this, together with an old lace veil in which her mother had been married, would serve Daphne's needs.

In truth, she had little time to think of herself. She was relinquishing a throne which she had occupied since she was eleven years old, and the instruction and admonition of her successor had occupied her attention ever since the date of her wedding had been fixed. Keys had to be handed over, recipes confided, and the mysteries of feminine book-keeping unfolded. There were good-byes to be said to bedridden old women and tearful cottage children. The bridegroom too, she felt, had a certain claim upon her attention. He had departed the morning after Daphne had accepted him, and was now very busy preparing his house in London for the reception of the future Lady Carr. But he had spent a good deal of time at the Rectory for all that, coming down for week-ends and the like; and Daphne, mindful of the duties of a *fiancée*, devoted herself conscientiously to his entertainment whenever he appeared.

But now the end of all things was imminent. To-morrow the management of the Rectory would pass into the hands of the dubious and inexperienced Cilly.

Meanwhile the Rectory children continued to sit disconsolately upon the gate. They were waiting for Daphne, who had promised to spend her last afternoon with them. Sir John, who was now staying at Kirkley Abbey,—to the mingled apprehension and exhilaration of the chief bridesmaid Lord Kirkley had offered to act as best man,—was to come over that afternoon, but only to see the Rector on matters connected with settlements and other unromantic adjuncts to the married state.

The gate proving unsuitable for prolonged session, the family abandoned their gregarious attitude and disposed of themselves in more comfortable fashion. Ally, home on two days' special leave from school, lay basking in the sun. Cilly sprawled on the grass with her back against a tree trunk, her brow puckered with the gradual realisation of coming responsibility. Stiffy, simple soul, with his knees clasped beneath his chin, sorrowfully contemplated to-morrow's bereavement. Master Anthony Cuthbert, perched on a log with a switch in his hand, was conducting an unseen orchestra. Nicky, soulless and flippant as ever, speculated at large upon her sister's future.

"It'll be pretty hot for Daph living down there at first," she mused. A joke lasted Nicky a long time: the humorous fiction that the bride-elect would to-morrow be carried off to reside permanently in the infernal regions was still as a savoury bakemeat to her palate. "Of course, Polly"—this was her abbreviation for Apollyon, adopted as soon as that gentleman had ascended from the grade of familiar friend to that of prospective relative—"will be glad to get back to his own fireside, but Daph will feel it a bit, I should think. Perhaps he will let her use a screen to begin with!... I wonder what housekeeping will be like. I suppose the cook will have horns and a tail, and all the food will be devilled. I should like to see Daph ordering dinner. 'Good morning, Diabolo!' 'Good morning, miss! What would you like for dinner to-night?' 'Well, Diabolo, what have you *got*?' 'There's a nice tender sinner came in this morning, miss. You might have a few of his ribs; or would you prefer him served up grilled, with brimstone sauce? And I suppose you would like devils-on-horseback for a savoury.' 'That will do *very* nicely, Diabolo. Oh, I forgot! It's possible that the Lucifers will drop in. Perhaps we'd better have yesterday's moneylender cold on the side-board in case there isn't enough to go round. And we must have something special to'—Ally, what do people drink in Hades?"

"Dunno," said Ally drowsily; "molten lead, I should think."

"Only the *lower* classes, dear," said Nicky witheringly. "I am talking about the best people."

"Sulphuric acid?" suggested Ally, who was beginning to study chemistry at school.

"That will do," said Nicky, and returned to her dialogue. "'Diabolo, will you tell the butler to put a barrel—no, a *vat*—of sulphuric acid on ice. You know what the Lucifers are, when'—hallo, here's Daph at last!"

The bride-elect approached, swinging her garden-hat in her hand, and followed by Mr Dawks.

"Well, family," she said, "I'm yours for the rest of the day. What shall we do?"

"Where is John?" inquired Ally. (John, it may be explained, was the name by which the family, with the exception of Nicky, had decided to address their future brother-in-law.)

"In the study with Dad."

"Has he arranged about having the five o'clock train stopped to-morrow afternoon?" inquired the careful Stiffy.

"No. We are going in a motor all the way to London," said Daphne. "Jack was keeping it as a surprise for me. It's a new one, a——"

"All the way to *where*?" inquired that economical humourist, Miss Veronica Vereker.

"London."

"H'm! Yes, I *have* heard it called that, now I come to think of it," conceded Nicky; "but it seems a waste of a good car, especially if it's a new one. Unless it's made of some special—Stiffy, what's the name of that stuff that won't burn?"

"Asbestos?"

"That's it—asbestos. I didn't expect to see you drive off down the road, somehow," continued Nicky in a somewhat injured voice, "just like an ordinary couple. I thought Polly would stamp his foot on the lawn, and a chasm would yawn at your feet, and in you'd both pop, and you would be gone for ever, like—Ally, who were those two people in the Latin book you had for a holiday task?"

"What you want, Nicky," responded Mr Aloysuis Vereker, "is chloroform. Do you mean Pluto and Proserpine?"

"That's it—Proserpine. Well, Proserpine, what are you going to do to entertain your little brothers and sisters this afternoon?"

"Anything you like," said Proserpine, endeavouring to balance herself on the top bar of the gate. "How about making toffee down in the Den?"

There was a chorus of approval. Nursery customs die hard. Even the magnificent Ally found it difficult to shake off the glamour of this youthful dissipation.

"I'll tell you what," continued Daphne, warming up to the occasion, "we'll have a regular farewell feast. We'll send down to the shop and get some buns and chocolates and gingerbeer, and—and——"

"Bananas," suggested Tony.

"Nuts," added Cilly.

"Cigarettes," said Ally.

"Who has got any money?" inquired Nicky.

The family fumbled in its pockets.

"Here's threepence—all I have," said Cilly at length.

"Twopence," said Ally, laying the sum on Cilly's threepenny bit.

"Awfully sorry," said Stiffy, "but I'm afraid I've only got a stamp. It's still quite gummy at the back, though," he added hopefully. "They'll take it."

Tony produced a halfpenny.

"You can search *me*, friends!" was Nick's despairing contribution.

"I have fourpence," said the bride—"not a penny more. I handed over all the spare housekeeping money to Dad this morning. That only makes tenpence-halfpenny, counting Stiffy's stamp." She sighed wistfully. "And I did so want to give you all a treat before I went! Well, we must do without the nuts and chocolates, and——"

Nicky rose to her feet, swelling with sudden inspiration.

"Daph, what's the matter with running along to this millionaire young man of yours and touching *him* for a trifle?" she inquired triumphantly.

Daphne hesitated. True, to-morrow she would be a rich man's wife, able to afford unlimited gingerbeer. But the idea of asking a man for money did not appeal to her. Pride of poverty and maidenly reserve make an obstinate mixture. Yet the flushed and eager faces of Nicky and Tony, the polite deprecations of the selfless Stiffy, and the studied indifference of Cilly and Ally, were hard to resist.

"I wonder if he would mind," she said doubtfully.

"Mind? Oh, no. Why should he?" urged the chorus respectfully.

"Have a dart for it, anyhow," said Nicky.

Daphne descended from the gate.

"Righto!" she said. "After all, it's our last afternoon together, and I *should* like to do you all proud. I'll chance it. The rest of you can start down to the Den and collect sticks, while I run along to the house and ask him. Nicky, you had better come with me to carry down saucepans and things. Come on—I'll race you!"

Three minutes later, Sir John Carr, smoking a meditative cigar upon the lawn, was aware of a sudden scurry and patter in the lane outside. Directly after this, with a triumphant shriek, the small figure of his future sister-in-law shot through the garden-gate, closely followed by that of his future wife. Mr Dawks, faint yet pursuing, brought up the rear.

The competitors flung themselves down on the grass at his feet, panting.

"We have been having a race," explained Daphne rather gratuitously.

"I won!" gasped Nicky. "Daph has the longest legs," she continued, "but I have the shortest skirts. Now, my children, I must leave you. Wire in!" she concluded, in a hoarse and penetrating whisper to Daphne.

Her short skirts flickered round the corner of the house, and she was gone. Daphne was left facing her *fiancé*.

"I say," she began rather constrainedly—"don't get up; I'm not going to stay—do you think you could lend me a little money? I—I'll pay you back in a day or two," she added with a disarming smile. "The fact is, we are going to make toffee down in the Den, and I wanted to get a few extra things, just to give them all a real treat to finish up with, you know. Will you—Jack?"

Juggernaut looked up at her with his slow scrutinising smile.

"What sort of extra things?" he inquired.

"Oh!"—Daphne closed her eyes and began to count on her fingers—"buns, and chocolates, and nuts, and gingerbeer. And I wanted to give Ally a packet of cigarettes. (After all, he's eighteen, and he does love them so, and they are only ten for threepence.) And if you could run to it, I should like to get a few bananas as well," she concluded with a rush, laying all her cards on the table at once.

Juggernaut leaned back in his chair and looked extremely judicial.

"What will all this cost?" he inquired.

"One and eleven," said Daphne. "Jack, you *dear*! We *shall* have a time!"

Juggernaut had taken a handful of change out of his pocket.

"One and eleven," he said; "I wonder, Daphne, if you will be able to purchase an afternoon of perfect happiness for that sum in a year's time."

He handed over the money.

"May I have a receipt?" he asked gravely.

Daphne took his meaning, and kissed him lightly. She lingered for a moment, anxious not to appear in a hurry to run away.

"Is there anything else?" inquired Sir John at length.

Daphne ran an inward eye over the possibilities of dissipation.

"No, I don't think so," she said. "Thanks ever so much! We shall be back about six. So long, old man. Don't go to sleep in this hot sun."

She flitted away across the lawn, jingling the money in her hand. At the gate she turned and waved her hand. Juggernaut's eyes were fixed upon her, but he did not appear to observe her salutation. Probably he was in a brown study about something.

Daphne was half-way down to the Den before it occurred to her that it would have been a graceful act—not to say the barest civility—to invite the donor of the feast to come and be present thereat. But she did not go back.

"It would bore him so, poor dear!" she said to herself; "and—and us, too!"

———

Next day they were married.

BOOK TWO.
FLICKERINGS.

CHAPTER NINE.

A HORSE TO THE WATER.

"And how is her ladyship?" inquired Mrs Carfrae.

"Her ladyship," replied Sir John Carr, "is enjoying life. What good bread-and-butter you always keep."

They were sitting in Mrs Carfrae's tiny drawing-room in Hill Street. Mrs Carfrae was a little old lady in a wheeled chair. Her face was comparatively youthful, but her hair was snowy white. She spoke with what

English people, to whom the pure Highland Scots of Inverness and the guttural raucousness of Glasgow are as one, term "a Scotch accent."

"I am glad you like my bread-and-butter," she said; "but I fancy you get as good at your wife's tea-table."

"I don't often see my wife's tea-table," confessed Juggernaut. "She is out a good deal, and as a rule it is more convenient for me to have my tea sent into my study."

"Where you grumble at it, I'll be bound. I ken husbands. So her ladyship is out a good deal? Well do I mind the first time I caught her in, the besom! That was nearly three years ago. I am not a payer of calls, as you know; but I felt that I must be the very first to greet your wife, Johnny boy. So the day after I knew you had settled in, I had myself bundled into the carriage, and off I went to Grosvenor Street. I told Maxwell to ring the bell and inquire if her ladyship was at home. The door was thrown open immediately—rather prematurely, in fact. I heard a sound like the cheep of a frightened mouse, and I saw a grand silk skirt and a pair of ankles scuttering up the staircase. I knew fine what had happened. I was her first caller: and though the child was sitting in her new drawing-room waiting for me and those like me, her courage had failed at the sound of the bell, and she was galloping up the stair out of the way when the man opened the door. Poor lassie! I did exactly the same thing at her age."

"Did you go in?"

"I did. I was determined to do it. I gripped my crutch and was out of the carriage and up the steps before the footman could answer Maxwell. I hobbled past the man—he just gaped at me like a puddock on a hot day—and got to the foot of the stair and looked up. As I expected, there was Madam, hanging over the banisters to see what sort of a caller she had hooked the first time. There was another creature beside her, with wild brown hair and eyes like saucers. They were clutching each other round the waist. When they saw me they gave a kind of horrified yelp. But I cried to them to come down, and in ten minutes we were the best of friends. They were terribly prim at first; but when they found out that I was just a clavering old wife and nothing more, they lost their grand manners. They overlaid me with questions about London, and while I was answering them the saucer-eyed one set to work cracking lumps of sugar with her teeth. The other—her ladyship—was eating jam out of an Apostle spoon. The spoon was in her mouth when a footman came in to mend the fire. She was fairly taken by surprise, and tried to push the whole concern into her mouth until the man should be gone. I thought at first she had swallowed it, but presently I saw the Apostle sticking out. And that was three years ago. Well, I have become less active since then, and I pay no more calls—wheel me a piece nearer the fire, Johnny—so I do not see so much of her ladyship as I did. Still, I am glad to hear she is enjoying life. And how is the baby?"

"The baby," replied its male parent, "looks and sounds extremely robust. He uttered several articulate words the other day, I am told."

"Can he walk?"

"He can lurch along in a slightly dissipated manner."

"Good! And how does your Daphne handle all these houses and servants of yours?"

Sir John smiled.

"She was a little out of her depth at first," he said. "She had not been accustomed to cater for a large household. The extravagance of ordering at least one fresh joint a-day appalled her, and it was a long time before the housekeeper could cure her of a passion for shepherd's pie. But she has a shrewd head. She soon discovered which items of domestic expenditure were reasonable and which were not. She has cut down the bills by a half, but I don't notice any corresponding falling off in the quality of the *menu*."

"And does she love fine clothes, and gaiety?"

"I think she found her maid rather a trial at first. She had been so accustomed not only to attiring herself but to going round and hooking up her sisters as well, that a woman who handled her like a baby rather paralysed her. She also exhibited a *penchant* for wearing her old clothes out—to rags, that is—in private. But I think she is getting over that now. I received her dressmaker's latest bill this morning. It reveals distinct signs of progress."

"And I hear she looks just beautiful."

"She does. I must admit that."

"*Then*," the old lady raised herself a little in her chair, and settled her spectacles with her unparalysed hand, "what is the trouble, Johnny Carr?"

Juggernaut laid down his tea-cup with a slight clatter.

"I was not aware," he said curtly, "that there was any trouble."

Mrs Carfrae surveyed him long and balefully over her spectacles.

"Johnny Carr," she observed dispassionately, "I have known you ever since you could roar for your bottle, and I have never had any patience with you either then or since. You are a dour, dreich, thrawn, camstearie creature. You have more money than you can spend, grand health, and a young and beautiful wife. But you are not happy. You come here to tell me so, and when I ask you to begin, you say there is nothing! Well, *I* will tell you what the matter is. There is some trouble between you and your Daphne."

Considerable courage is required to inform a man to his face that all is not well between him and his wife; but courage was a virtue that Elspeth Carfrae had never lacked. Juggernaut experienced no feeling of resentment or surprise that this old lady should have instantaneously sized up a situation which he himself had been investigating in a groping and uncertain fashion for nearly three years. Life is a big book of problems, and while man is content to work them out figure by figure, taking nothing for granted which cannot be approved by established formulæ, woman has an exasperating habit of skipping straight to the solution in a manner which causes the conscientious and methodical male to suspect her of peeping at the answers at the end of the book.

"Perhaps you had not realised that," pursued Mrs Carfrae. "Men are apt to be slow in the uptake," she added indulgently.

"I fail to see where you get your *data* from," replied Juggernaut. "I have not been particularly communicative on the subject. In fact, I don't remember telling you a single——"

Mrs Carfrae subjected him to a withering glare.

"If all that women knew," she observed frostily, "was what men had told them, I wonder how many of us would be able to spell our own names. No, laddie, you have told me nothing: that's true enough. But I know fine why you came here to-day. You are worried. You and Daphne are getting on splendidly. The match has been a great success. You have a son and heir. But—you are not happy; and it is about your Daphne that you are not happy."

Juggernaut gazed into the fire.

"You are right," he said. "I confess that my marriage has not been so uplifting as I had hoped. I daresay it is my own fault. As you point out, I am—well, all the Caledonian adjectives you heaped upon me just now: all that and a good deal more. I have the reputation of being a harsh man, and I hate it. I hoped, when I married that child, that she would pull me out of my rigid, undeviating way of life, and broaden my sympathies a little. I looked forward to a little domesticity." His dark face coloured slightly. "I may be an ogre, but I have my soft side, as you know."

"None better," said the old lady gently.

"Well, somehow," continued Juggernaut, "my marriage has not made the difference to me that I had hoped. We two have had our happy hours together, but we don't seem to progress beyond a certain point. We are amiability itself. If I ask Daphne to see to anything about the house, she sees to it; if she asks me to go with her to a tea-fight, I go. But that seems to be about the limit. I can't help thinking that marriage would not have survived so long as an institution if there had been no more behind it than that. I was under the impression that it made two one. At present we are still two—very decidedly two; and—and——"

"And being you, it just maddens you not to be able to get your money's worth," said Mrs Carfrae calmly. "Now, John Carr, just listen to me. First of all, have you had any trouble with her?"

"Trouble?"

"Yes. Any direct disagreement with her?"

"Never. Stop—we had one small breeze."

Mrs Carfrae wagged a forefinger.

"You have been bullying her, monster!"

"Heavens, no!"

"Well, tell me the story."

"Six months ago," said Juggernaut, "she came to me and asked for money—much as a child asks for toffee—with a seraphic smile and an ingratiating rub up against my chair. I asked her what it was for."

"Quite wrong!" said Mrs Carfrae promptly.

"But surely——" began Juggernaut, the man of business up in arms at once.

"You should have begun by taking out your cheque-book and saying, 'how much?'" continued his admonitress. "Then she would have called you a dear, or some such English term of affection, and recognising you as her natural confidant would have told you everything. After that you might have improved the occasion. As it was, you just put her back up, and she dithered."

"She did, so far as I understand the expression. But, finding that I was firm——"

"Oh, man, man, how can a great grown creature like you bear to be *firm—hard*, you mean, of course—with a wild unbroken lass like that? Well, go on. You were firm. And what did her poor ladyship say she wanted the money for?"

"For her young cub of a brother," said Juggernaut briefly.

"A wealthy young wife daring to want to help her own brother! Monstrous!" observed Mrs Carfrae.

"I think you are unjust to me in this matter. Listen! When I married Daphne I was aware that she would want to finance her entire family: in fact, it was one of the inducements to marrying me which I laid before her. For that purpose, to save her the embarrassment of constantly coming to me for supplies, I settled upon her a private allowance of—what do you think?"

"Out with it! No striving after effect with *me*, my man!" was the reply of his unimpressionable audience.

"I gave her a thousand a year," said Juggernaut.

"That should have been sufficient," said Mrs Carfrae composedly. "But do not be ostentatious about it. You could well afford the money."

"Well, she had spent most of that year's allowance in six months," continued Juggernaut, disregarding these gibes—"on her father's curate, the younger children's education, and so forth—and she wanted more."

"What age is this brother?"

"Twenty, I think. He is up at Cambridge, and wants to get into the Army as a University candidate. At present he appears to be filling in his time philandering with a tobacconist's daughter. The tobacconist's bill for moral and intellectual damage came to five hundred pounds. Before writing the cheque, I stipulated—"

"You would!" said the old lady grimly.

—"That I should be permitted to make a few investigations on my own behalf. Young Vereker is a handsome, fascinating rascal, with about as much moral fibre as a Yahoo. He was a good deal franker in his admissions to me than he had been to his sister—"

"Ay, I once heard you cross-examining a body," confirmed Mrs Carfrae.

—"And on the completion of my inquiries I paid the money down on the nail. It was the only thing to do."

"Did you tell Daphne the whole story?"

"No. I should hate to dispel her illusions. She loves her brothers and sisters."

"There is no need to excuse yourself, John Carr. I knew fine that you would not tell her. Instead, you glowered at her, and read her a lecture about extravagance and improvidence. She tried to look prim and penitent, but danced down the stair the moment she got the door shut behind her. Now, mannie, listen to me. This is no light charge you have taken on yourself—to rule a wild, shy, impulsive taupie like that. You cannot contain the like with bit and bridle, mind. I have been one myself, and I know. There is just one thing to do. She must learn to *love* you, or the lives of the pair of you will go stramash!"

Juggernaut's old friend concluded this homily with tremendous emphasis, and there was a long silence. Then the man drew his chair a little closer.

"How can I teach her?" he asked humbly. "I have no *finesse*, no attractiveness. Do you think I—I am too old for her?"

"Old? Toots! I was nineteen when I married on my Andy, and he was thirty-nine. For the first few years after we married I called him 'daddy' to his face. After that I found that I was really old enough to be the man's mother; so I called him 'sonny.' But that is a digression. I will tell you how to teach her. Do not be monotonous. It's no use just to be a good husband to her: any gowk can be that. Do not let your affection run on in a regular, dutiful stream: have a spate occasionally! Get whirled off your feet by her, and let her see it. Prepare some unexpected ploy for her. Rush her off to dine somewhere on the spur of the moment—just your two selves. Stop her suddenly on the staircase in a half-light, and give her a hug."

"She'd never stand it!" cried Juggernaut in dismay. "And I could never do it," he added apprehensively.

"You *do* it, my callant," said Mrs Carfrae with decision, "and she'll stand it right enough! She may tell you not to be foolish, but she will not make a point of coming down by the back stair in future for all that. And let her see that with you she comes *first* in everything. What a crow she will have to herself when she realises that a feckless unbusinesslike piece like herself has crept right into the inmost place in the heart of a man whose gods used to be hard work and hard words and hard knocks! She'll just glory in you!

"Lastly, do not be discouraged if you have no success to begin with. At all costs you must keep on smiling. A dour, bleak man is no fit companion for a young girl who has always lived a sheltered sunny life. He just withers her. She may last for a while, and do her duty by him, but in time he'll break her heart. Ay, keep on smiling, Johnny, even if she hurts you. She will hurt you often. Young girls are like that. It takes time for a woman to realise that a man is just about twice as sensitive as herself in certain matters, and she will not make allowances for him at first. But until she does—and she will, if you give her time—keep on smiling! If you keep on long enough you will get your reward. Make the effort, my man! I have had to make efforts in my time—"

"I know that," said Juggernaut.

—"And the efforts have been the making of *me*. For one thing, I have acquired a sense of proportion. When we are young and lusty our knowledge of perspective is so elementary that in our picture of life our own Ego fills the foreground to the exclusion of all else; with this result, that we get no view of the countless interesting and profitable things that lie behind. My Ego is kept in better order these days, I assure you. It gets just a good comfortable place in the picture and no more. If Elspeth Carfrae stirs from that, or comes creeping too far forward so as to block out other things, she hears from me!"

"Does she always obey you?" asked Juggernaut.

"She got far beyond my control once," admitted the old lady. "I mind when my Andy went from me she swelled and swelled until she blotted out everything—earth, sea, and sky. But she has been back in her place these twenty years, and there she shall bide. There is no great selfish Ego blocking the view now when I sit and look out upon my section of the world. You have no idea how interesting it is to study your friends' troubles instead of your own, John. The beauty of it is that you need not worry over them: you just watch them—unconcernedly."

The Scots have their own notion of what constitutes an excursion into the realms of humour, and Juggernaut, knowing this, made no attempt to controvert his hostess's last statement.

"Not that I grudged my Andy," continued the old lady presently. "No wife worthy of the name could grudge her man to his country when he died as Andy died. But my only son—that was my own fault, maybe. I would not put him into the Army like his father, thinking to keep him safer that way; and he died of pneumonia at seven-and-twenty, an East End curate. Then my Lintie. But I have no need to be talking of Lintie to you, John Carr. You mind her still, Daphne or no Daphne. Then"—she indicated her paralysed shoulder—"this! But I keep on smiling. Perhaps that is why people are so kind to me. Perhaps if I did not smile they would not seek my company so freely. I suppose they see something in me, that they come and listen to me havering. When I first settled down here by myself in this little house many kind people called. I never thought to see them twice; but they come again and again. Maybe it is because English people have a notion that the Scots tongue is 'so quaint!' They seem to find something exhilarating in hearing fish called fush. Not that I call it any such thing, but they think I do. Anyhow, they come. Some of them bring their troubles with them, and go away without them. When they do that I know that it was worth while to keep a smiling face all these years. So smile yourself, Johnny Carr! And some day, when your Daphne comes and puts her head on your shoulder and tells you all that is troubling her, you will know that you have won through. And when that happens come and call me. I like to hear when my methods succeed."

"I will remember," said Juggernaut gravely. "Good-bye."

Mrs Carfrae watched his broad back through the doorway.

"But I doubt you will both have to be worse before you are better," she added to herself.

An hour later Lady Carr, a radiant vision of glinting hair and rustling skirts, on her way upstairs to dress for dinner, encountered her husband coming down. There was a half light. Sir John paused.

"Are you dining anywhere to-night, Daphne?" he said.

Daphne, her youthful shrewdness uneradicated by three years of adult society, replied guardedly—

"Are you trying to pull my leg? If I say 'No,' will you tell me that in that case I shall be very hungry by bedtime, or something? I suppose that old chestnut has just got round to your club. Have you been electing Noah an honorary member?"

"I was about to suggest," said Juggernaut perseveringly, "that we should go and dine at the Savoy together."

Daphne dimpled into a delighted smile.

"You dear! And we might go on somewhere afterwards. What would you like me to wear?" She preened herself in anticipation.

"Oh, anything," said Juggernaut absently. He was regarding his wife in an uncertain and embarrassed fashion.

Suddenly he drew a deep breath, and took a step down towards her. Then, with equal suddenness, he turned on his heel and retired upstairs rather precipitately in the direction of his dressing-room.

It was as well that Mrs Carfrae was not present.

CHAPTER TEN.

A DAY IN THE LIFE OF A SOCIAL SUCCESS.

By nine o'clock next morning Lady Carr, becomingly arrayed, was sitting up in bed munching a hearty breakfast, and reflecting according to her habit upon yesterday's experiences and to-day's arrangements.

She had dined with her husband at the Savoy, but the meal had not been quite such a success as she had anticipated. Juggernaut had treated her with the restrained courtesy which was habitual to him; but ladies who are taken out to dinner at the Savoy, even by their husbands, usually expect something more than restrained courtesy. You must be animated on these occasions—unless of course you happen to be a newly-engaged couple, in which case the world benignantly washes its hands of you—or the evening writes itself down a failure. Juggernaut had not been animated. He had ordered a dinner which to Daphne's gratification and surprise—she had not credited him with so much observation—had consisted almost entirely of her favourite dishes. But he had not sparkled, and sparkle at the Savoy, as already intimated, is essential.

About ten o'clock he had been called away to an important division in the House, and Daphne had gone on to a party, escorted by her husband's secretary, factotum, and right-hand man, one Jim Carthew, who arrived from Grosvenor Street in answer to a telephone summons. Carthew was a new friend of Daphne's. She accumulated friends much as a honey-pot accumulates flies, but Jim Carthew counted for more than most. They had never met until five weeks ago, for Carthew had always been up north engaged on colliery business when Daphne was in London; and when Daphne was at Belton, her husband's old home near Kilchester, Carthew had been occupied by secretarial work in town. But they had known one another by name and fame ever since Daphne's marriage, and at last they had met. Daphne was not slow to understand why her husband, impatient of assistance as he usually was, had always appeared ready to heap labour and responsibility upon these youthful shoulders. Carthew was barely thirty, but he was perfectly capable of upholding and furthering his leader's interests in the great industrial north; while down south it was generally held that whenever he grew tired of devilling for Juggernaut the Party would find him a seat for the asking.

But so far Carthew seemed loth to forsake the man who had taught him all he knew. He cherished a theory, somewhat unusual in a rising man, that common decency requires of a pupil that he shall repay his master, at the end of the period of instruction, by a period of personal service.

He was a freckle-faced youth, with a frank smile of considerable latitude, and a boyish zeal for the healthy pursuits of life. He possessed brains and character, as any man must who served under Juggernaut; and like his master he was a shrewd judge of men. Of his capacity for dealing with women Daphne knew less; but she had already heard rumours—confidences exchanged over teacups and behind fans—of a certain Miss Nina Tallentyre, perhaps the acknowledged beauty of that season, at the flame of whose altar Jim Carthew was said to have singed his wings in a conspicuously reckless fashion. But all this was the merest hearsay, and Daphne was unacquainted with the lady into the bargain. Possibly it was with a view to remedying this deficiency in her circle of acquaintance that she kept Jim Carthew at her side for the space of half an hour after they reached Mrs Blankney-Pushkins' reception.

After a couple of waltzes Lady Carr expressed a desire to be fed with ices and cream buns.

Mr Carthew assented, but with less enthusiasm than before. Daphne noticed that his eye was beginning to wander.

"After that," she continued cheerfully, "we will find seats, and you shall tell me who everybody is. I am still rather a country mouse."

"I should think so!" said Carthew, reluctantly recalling his gaze from a distant corner of the refreshment-room. "I beg your pardon! You were saying?"

"Perhaps there is some one else whom you have promised to dance with, though," continued the country mouse demurely.

Carthew, whose eye had slid stealthily round once more in the direction of a supper-party in the corner, recovered himself resolutely, and made the only reply that gallantry permitted.

"That's all right, then," said Daphne. "Tell me who those people are, having supper over there. That man with the fierce black eyes—who is he? He looks wicked."

"As a matter of fact," said Carthew, resigning himself to his fate, "he is about the most commonplace bore in the room. If he takes a girl in to dinner he talks to her about the weather with the soup, the table decorations with the fish, and suffragettes with the *entrée*. About pudding-time he takes the bit between his teeth and launches out into a description of the last play he saw—usually *Charley's Aunt* or *East Lynne*. If he goes to a wedding he refers to the church as a 'sacred edifice,' and the bride and bridegroom as 'the happy couple.' When he unexpectedly encounters a friend at a sea-side watering-place, he observes that 'the world is a very small place.' At his own funeral (to which I shall send a wreath) he will sit up and thank the mourners for 'this personal tribute of affection and esteem.'"

Daphne sat regarding this exhibition of the art of conversation with some interest. She observed that Carthew's wits were wandering, and that with inherent politeness he was exercising a purely mechanical faculty to entertain her pending their return. Jim Carthew was a true Briton in that he hated revealing his deeper thoughts to the eyes of the world. But unlike the ordinary Briton who, when his feelings do get the better of him, finds himself reduced to silent and portentous gloom, he instinctively clothed his naked shrinking soul in a garment of irresponsible frivolity. The possession of this faculty is a doubtful blessing, for it deprives many a deserving sufferer of the sympathy which is his right, and which would be his could he but take the world into his confidence. But the world can never rid itself of the notion that only still waters run deep. Consequently Jim Carthew passed in the eyes of most of his friends as a kindly, light-hearted, rather soulless trifler. But Daphne was not altogether deceived. She took an instinctive interest in this young man. She interrupted his feverish monologue, and inquired—

"Tell me, who is that girl? The tall one, with fair hair and splendid black eyes."

"What is she dressed in?" asked Carthew, surveying the throng with studied diligence.

"Flame-coloured chiffon," said Daphne.

"That is a Miss Tallentyre," replied Carthew carelessly. "Do you think she is pretty?" he added, after a slightly strained pause.

"I think she is perfectly magnificent. Do you know her?"

"Er—yes."

"Will you introduce me?" asked Daphne. "I should like to know her. See, she has just sent away her partner. Take me over and leave me with her, and then you will be free to run off and find the charmer I can see you are so anxious about."

The hapless Carthew having asserted, this time with considerably more sincerity, that he had now no further thoughts of dancing, the introduction was effected. The sequel lay this morning upon Daphne's breakfast-tray, amid a heap of invitations—Daphne was in great request at present—in the form of a note, written upon thick blue paper, in a large and rather ostentatious feminine hand. It ran—

"DEAR LADY CARR,—Don't consider me a forward young person if I ask you to be an angel and come and lunch with me to-day. I know all sorts of ceremonies ought to be observed before such a climax is reached; but will you take them for granted and *come*? We had such a tiny talk last night, and I do so want to know you better. I have been dying to make your acquaintance ever since I first saw you.—Sincerely yours,

"NINA TALLENTYRE."

Daphne was not the sort of girl to take it amiss that she, a married woman of twenty-three, with a husband and baby of her own, should informally be bidden to a feast by a young person previously unknown to her, who possessed neither. In any case the last sentence would have been too much for her vanity. She scribbled a note of acceptance to Miss Tallentyre's invitation, and set about her morning toilet.

Once downstairs, she paid her regulation punctilious visit to the library, where her husband was usually to be found until twelve o'clock. She inquired in her breezy fashion after the health of the Mother of Parliaments, and expressed a hope that her spouse had come home at a reasonable hour and enjoyed a proper night's rest. She next proceeded to the orders of the day.

"Are you dining out to-night, dear?" she inquired.

"Yes, for my sins! A City dinner at six-thirty."

"You'll be bad the morn!" quoted Lady Carr.

"True for you, Daphne. Are you going anywhere?"

"No."

"Well, you had better have Carthew to dine with you, and then he can take you to the theatre afterwards. Sorry I can't manage it my—for our two selves," he added, guiltily conscious of Mrs Carfrae's recent homily.

But Daphne was quite satisfied with the arrangement, which she designated top-hole.

"Now I am off shopping," she announced. "After that I am lunching with a girl I met last night; then Hurlingham, with the Peabodys. If you are going gorging at six-thirty, I probably shan't see you again to-day; so I'll say good-night now. Pleasant dreams! I am off to play with Baby before I go out. So long!"

She presented her husband with his diurnal kiss, and departed in search of Master Brian Vereker Carr, whose domain was situated in the upper regions of the house. Here for a time the beautiful and stately consort of Sir John Carr merged into the Daphne of old—Daphne, the little mother of all the world, the inventor of new and delightful games and repairer of all damages incurred therein. Her son's rubicund and puckered countenance lightened at her approach. He permitted his latest tooth to be exhibited without remonstrance; he nodded affably, even encouragingly, over his mother's impersonation of a dying pig; and paid her the supreme compliment of howling lustily on her departure.

Master Carr never interviewed his parents simultaneously. His father's visits—not quite so constrained as one might imagine, once the supercilious nurse had been removed out of earshot—usually took place in the evening, just before dinner; but father and mother never came together. Had they done so, it is possible that this narrative might have followed a different course. A common interest, especially when it possesses its father's mouth and its mother's eyes, with a repertory of solemn but attractive tricks with its arms and legs thrown in, is apt to be a very uniting thing.

II.

Daphne duly lunched with Miss Tallentyre.

"May I call you Daphne?" the siren asked, in a voice which intimated that a request from some people is as good as a command from most. "I have taken a fancy to you; and when I do that to anybody—which isn't often—I say so. My dear, you are perfectly *lovely*! I wish I had your complexion. You don't put anything on it, do you?"

"Soap," said Daphne briefly. She was not of the sort which takes fancies readily.

Miss Tallentyre smiled lazily.

"I see you haven't got the hang of me yet," she drawled. "You are a little offended with me. Most people are at first, but they soon find that it's not really rudeness—only *me*!—and they come round. I don't go in for rouge either. Like you, I don't need it. But I have to touch up my eyebrows. They are quite tragically sandy, and my face looks perfectly insipid if I leave them as they are." She laughed again. "Have I shocked you? You see, I believe in being frank about things—don't you? Be natural—be yourself—say what you think! That is the only true motto in life, isn't it?"

Daphne agreed cautiously. She had not yet plumbed this rather peculiar young woman. It had never occurred to her, in the whole course of her frank ingenuous existence, to ask herself whether she was herself or not. Such things were too high for her. She began to feel that she had been somewhat remiss in the matter. Miss Tallentyre appeared to have made a speciality of it.

But as shrewd Daphne was soon to discern for herself, this was only pretty Nina's way. A more confirmed *poseuse* never angled for the indiscriminate admiration of mankind. Nina Tallentyre was no fool. Having observed that in order to become conspicuous in this world it is an advantage to possess marked individuality, and having none of her own beyond that conferred by her face and figure, she decided to manufacture an individuality for her herself. She accordingly selected what she considered the most suitable of the *rôles* at her disposal, rehearsed it to her satisfaction, assumed it permanently, and played it, it must be confessed, uncommonly well. Her pose was that of the blunt and candid child of nature, and her performances ranged from unblushing flattery towards those with whom she desired to stand well to undisguised rudeness towards those whom she disliked and did not think it necessary to conciliate.

Her method prospered. Whatever wise men may think or say of us, fools usually take us at our own valuation. Consequently Miss Tallentyre never lacked a majority of admirers. She set a very high price upon her friendship, too, conferring it only as an exceptional favour; and the public, which always buys on the rise, had long since rushed in and bulled Miss Tallentyre's stock—her beauty, her wit, her transparent honesty—sky high.

The luncheon was a *tête-à-tête* function, the parent-birds, as Miss Tallentyre termed them, being absent upon a country visit. Afterwards Russian cigarettes and liqueur brandy were served with the coffee. Daphne declined these manly luxuries, but her hostess took both.

"Not that I like them," she explained with a plaintive little sigh, "but it looks *chic*; and one must be *chic* or die. Besides, I am doing it to annoy one of my admirers—one of those simple-minded, early Victorian, John Bullish creatures who dislike seeing a girl smoke, or drink cognac, or go to the theatre without a chaperone. Here is his latest effusion; it will make you shriek."

She picked up a letter from a little table by her side and began to read aloud.

"'*Nina, dear child, I know you don't care for me any more*,'—

As a matter of fact I never cared for him at any time—

"'*but I can't help still taking an interest in you, and all that. I must say this. On Tuesday night I saw you sitting at supper with two men at the Vallambrosa, without anybody else to keep you in countenance, sipping liqueur brandy and smoking. Well, don't—there's a dear! You simply don't know what cruel things people say about a girl who does that sort of thing in public. Of course I know that you are absolutely——*'"

But Lady Carr was on her feet, slightly flushed.

"I think I must be going now," she said. "I had no idea it was so late. I have to meet some people at Hurlingham."

"Sorry you have to rush off," said Miss Tallentyre regretfully; "we were so cosy. Isn't this letter perfectly sweet?"

Daphne, who was glowing hotly, suddenly spoke her mind.

"If an honest man," she said, "wrote me a letter like that, I don't think I should read it aloud to total strangers, even if I was mortally offended by it. It doesn't seem to me cricket. Good-bye, and thank you so much for asking me to lunch."

"*Not* altogether a successful party," mused Daphne, as a taxi-cab conveyed her to Hurlingham. "What a hateful girl! And yet, at the back of all that affectation I believe there is something. I couldn't help liking her. She certainly is very lovely, and she must have been a darling before men got hold of her and spoiled her.... I wonder if that letter was from Jim Carthew. It sounded like his blunt blundering way of doing things. Well, he is well rid of her, anyhow. Hurrah! here is Hurlingham, and there are the Peabodys! How lovely to see the trees and grass again! And the *dear* ponies!"

The country-bred girl drew a long luxurious breath, and in the fulness of her heart grossly overpaid her charioteer on alighting. Then, forgetting Miss Tallentyre and her exotic atmosphere utterly and absolutely, she plunged with all the energy of her sunny soul into the sane delights and wholesome joys afforded by green trees, summer skies, and prancing polo-ponies.

III.

Daphne concluded her day, after a joyous drive home in the cool of the evening on the box-seat of a coach, by entertaining Jim Carthew to dinner. Afterwards he was to take her to *The Yeoman of the Guard*, which was running through a revival at the Savoy Theatre. Daphne was by no means a *blasée* Londoner as yet, for much of her short married life had been spent at Belton; and the theatre was still an abiding joy to her. On the way she rattled off a list of the pieces she had seen.

"And you have never been to a Gilbert and Sullivan opera?" asked Carthew incredulously.

"No—never."

"All I can say is—cheers!"

"Why?"

"Supposing you were a benevolent person about to introduce a small boy to his first plum-pudding, you would feel as I do," replied her companion. "But wait. Here is the theatre: we are in the fourth row of stalls."

Daphne sat raptly through the first act. Once or twice her laughter rang out suddenly and spontaneously like a child's, and indulgent persons turned and smiled sympathetically upon her; but for the most part she was still and silent, revelling in Sullivan's ever-limpid music and following the scenes that passed before her with breathless attention.

When the curtain fell slowly upon the finale of the first act—the suddenly deserted stage, the bewildered Fairfax holding his fainting bride in his arms, and the black motionless figure of the executioner towering over all—Daphne drew a long and tremulous breath, and turned to her companion.

"I understand now what you meant," she said softly. "How splendid to be able to bring some one here for the first time!"

"What surprises me," said Carthew, "is that Sir John hasn't brought you here already. I know he simply loves it."

"I am usually taken to places like the Gaiety," confessed Lady Carr. "Probably Jack considers them more suited to my intellect. Hallo, here are the orchestra-men crawling out of their holes again! Good!"

Presently the curtain went up on the last act, and Jack Point introduced a selection of the Merry Jests of Hugh Ambrose, to the audible joy of the fourth row of stalls. The Assistant Tormentor and his beloved were likewise warmly received; but presently Daphne's smiles faded. Poor Jack Point's tribulations were too much for her: during the final recurrence of *I Have a Song to Sing, O!* tears came, and as the curtain fell she dabbed her eyes hurriedly with an inadequate handkerchief.

"Awfully sorry!" she murmured apologetically. "Luckily you are not the sort to laugh at me."

Carthew silently placed her wrap round her shoulders.

"Mr Carthew," said Daphne suddenly, "will you take me somewhere gay for supper? It wouldn't be awfully improper, would it? I can't go home feeling as sad as this."

"Come along!" said Carthew.

He escorted her to an establishment where the electric lights blazed bravely, a band blared forth a cacophonous cake-walk entitled (apparently) "By Request," and the brightest and best of the *jeunesse dorée* of London mingled in sweet companionship with the haughty but hungry divinities of the musical comedy stage.

Carthew secured a table in a secluded corner, as far as possible from the band.

"Sorry to have given you the hump," he said, with his boyish smile. "Next week I will take you to *The Mikado*. No tears there! You will laugh till you cry. Rather a bull that—what?"

He persevered manfully in this strain in his endeavour to drive away impressionable Daphne's distress on Jack Point's behalf, and ultimately succeeded.

"I hope he was *dead*, not simply in a faint," was her final reference to the subject. Then she continued: "I shall take them *all* to see that lovely piece—separately. I am not sure about Nicky, though. She is just at the scoffing age just now, and I don't think I could bear it, if she——"

"Not long ago," said Carthew, "I took a girl—that sort of girl—to see *The Yeomen*."

Daphne regarded him covertly. She knew the girl.

"Well?" she said.

"I took her on purpose," continued Carthew—"to see how she——"

Daphne, deeply interested, nodded comprehendingly.

"I know," she said. "How did she take it?"

"She never stirred," said Carthew, "all through the last act. When the curtain fell, she sat on for a few moments without saying a word, and she never spoke all the time I was taking her home. When I said goodnight to her, she—she said something to me. It was not much, but it showed me that she *was* the right sort after all, in spite of what people said——"

He checked himself suddenly, as if conscious that his reminiscences were becoming somewhat intimate. But Daphne nodded a serious head.

"I'm glad," she said simply. "One likes to be right about one's friends."

Carthew shot a grateful glance at her; and presently they drifted into less personal topics, mutually conscious that here, if need be, was a friend—an understanding friend.

The evening had yet one more incident in store for Daphne.

Twelve-thirty, the *Ultima Thule* of statutory indulgence—the hour at which London, thirty minutes more fortunate than Cinderella, must perforce fly home from scenes of revelry and get ready to shake the mats—was fast approaching; and the management of the restaurant began, by a respectful but pertinacious process of light-extinguishing, to apprise patrons of the fact.

As Daphne and Carthew passed through the rapidly emptying vestibule to their cab, five flushed young gentlemen, of the *genus* undergraduate-on-the-spree, suddenly converged upon the scene from the direction of the bar, locked together in a promiscuous and not altogether unprofitable embrace. They were urged from the rear by polite but inflexible menials in brass buttons.

"What ho, Daph!"

The cry emanated from the gentleman who was acting for the moment as keystone of the arch. Daphne, stepping into the cab, looked back.

"Mr Carthew," she exclaimed, "it's Ally—my brother! He must have come up from Cambridge for the day. Do go and bring him here."

She took her seat in the hansom, and Carthew went back. Presently he returned.

"I would not advise an interview," he said drily. "Your brother—well, you know the effect of London air upon an undergraduate fresh from the country! Let him come round and see you in the morning."

He gave the cabman his orders, and their equipage drove off, just as Sebastian Aloysius Vereker, the nucleus of a gyrating mass of humanity (composed of himself and party, together with two stalwart myrmidons of the Hilarity Restaurant and a stray cab-tout), toppled heavily out of the portals of that celebrated house of refreshment into the arms of an indulgent policeman.

More life—real life! reflected Daphne, as she laid her head on her pillow, tired out and utterly contented. To-day had yielded its full share. That peculiar but interesting interview with Miss Tallentyre, that glorious carnival under the blue sky at Hurlingham, and that laughter-and-tear-compelling spectacle at the Savoy—

all had contributed to the total. Finally, that *tête-à-tête* supper with Jim Carthew—indubitably a dear—ending with the episode of Ally. A little disturbing, that last! Well, perhaps Ally was only trying to see life too, in his own way. Life! Daphne tingled as she felt her own leap in her veins. And to-morrow would bring more!

Then the sandman paid his visit, and she slept like the tired child that she was, having completed to her entire satisfaction another day of what, when you come to think of it, was nothing more or less than an utterly idle, selfish, unprofitable existence.

CHAPTER ELEVEN.

DIES IRAE.

At Belton, Daphne, like her Scriptural counterpart, came to herself. Attired in what she called "rags," she ran wild about the woods and plantations, accompanied by the faithful Mr Dawks, who found a green countryside (even when marred at intervals by a grimy pithead) infinitely preferable to Piccadilly, where the pavement is hot and steerage-way precarious.

They were to stay at Belton till Christmas, after which the house in Berkeley Square would be ready for her. Hitherto she had been well content with the little establishment in Grosvenor Street; but her ideas in certain directions, as her husband had observed to Mrs Carfrae, were developing in a very gratifying manner.

One hot morning Daphne arrived at breakfast half-an-hour late. To do her justice, this was an unusual fault; for in the country she would never have dreamed of indulging in such an urban luxury as breakfast in bed. Her unpunctuality was not due to sloth. She had already superintended the morning toilet of Master Brian Vereker Carr, and had even taken a constitutional with Mr Dawks along the road which ran over the shoulder of a green hill towards Belton Pit, two miles away. She knew that her husband had gone out at seven o'clock to interview the manager at the pithead, and she had reckoned on being picked up by the returning motor and brought home in time for nine o'clock breakfast. Unfortunately Juggernaut had changed his plans and gone to another pit in the opposite direction, with the result that Daphne, besides being compelled to walk twice as far as she intended, found an uncomfortable combination of cold food and chilly husband waiting for her when she reached home.

Juggernaut never called Daphne to book for her shortcomings now. It had become his custom of late, if he found anything amiss in the management of the establishment, to send a message to the housekeeper direct. He should have known better. Daphne, regarding such a proceeding as an imputation of incompetence on her part, boiled inwardly at the slight, though her innate sense of justice told her that it was not altogether undeserved. Being a great success is apt to be a slightly demoralising business, and Daphne herself was beginning dimly to realise the fact. There was no doubt, for instance, that she was not the housekeeper she had been. But what was the good? There had been some credit in feeding the boys and Dad on half nothing, and in conjuring that second weekly joint out of a housekeeping surplus that was a little financial triumph in itself. But now, who cared if a leg of mutton were saved or not? What did it matter if the cook sold the leavings and the butler opened more wine than he decanted? Her husband could afford it. And so on.

A discussion had arisen upon this subject the evening before; and the silent enigmatical man whom she had married, whom she understood so little, and who, from the fact that he treated her as something between an incompetent servant and a spoiled child, appeared to understand her even less, had spoken out more freely than usual, with not altogether happy results. Daphne above all loved openness and candour, and she could not endure to feel that her husband was exercising forbearance towards her, or making allowances, or talking down to her level. Consequently the laborious little lecture she had received, with its studied moderation of tone and its obvious desire to let her down gently, had had an unfortunate but not altogether unnatural result. Juggernaut would have done better to employ his big guns, such as he reserved for refractory public meetings. As it was, Daphne lost her temper.

"Jack," she blazed out suddenly, "I *know* I'm a failure, so why rub it in? I *know* you married me to keep house for you, so you have a perfect right to complain if I do it badly. Well, you have told me; now I know. Shall we drop the subject? I will endeavour to be more competent, honest, and obliging in future."

Juggernaut rose suddenly from the table—they were sitting over their dessert at the time—and walked to the mantelpiece, where he stood leaning his head upon his arms, in an apparent endeavour to mesmerise the fender. Daphne, cooling rapidly, wondered what he was thinking about. Was he angry, or bored, or indifferent?

Presently he turned round.

"I'm afraid I don't handle you as successfully as I handle some other problems, Daphne," he said reflectively. "Good-night!"

That was all. He left the room, and Daphne had not seen him since. Her anger was gone. By bedtime she was thoroughly ashamed of herself, and, being Daphne, no other course lay open to her than that of saying so. Hence her early rising next morning, and her effort to intercept the motor.

The failure of the latter enterprise made matters more difficult; for courage once screwed to the sticking-point and timed for a certain moment cannot as a rule outlast postponement.

Still, she walked into the breakfast-room bravely.

"Jack," she began, a little breathlessly, "I'm sorry I was cross last night."

Her husband was sitting with his back to the door. Possibly if he had seen her face—flushed and appealing under its soft hat of grey *suède*—he might have acted a little more helpfully than he did. He merely laid down his newspaper and remarked cheerfully—

"That is all right, dear. Let us say no more about it. Sit down to your breakfast before it gets colder. You must have been for a long walk. Fried sole or a sausage?"

He rose and helped her to food from the sideboard, as promptly and carefully as if she had been a newly arrived and important guest. It was something; but compared with what he might have done it was nothing. In effect, Daphne had asked for a kiss and had been given a sausage.

It was rather a miserable breakfast. Daphne had vowed to herself not to be angry again: consequently she could only mope. Juggernaut continued to read the newspaper. The political world was in a ferment at the moment. There was a promise for him in all this of work—trouble—the facing of difficulties—the overcoming of strenuous opposition—the joy of battle, in fact. Manlike, he overlooked the trouble that was brewing at his own fireside.

Presently he put down his newspaper and strolled to the open window.

"What a gorgeous day, Daphne. And I have to spend it in a committee-room at Kilchester!"

"Anything important?" asked Daphne, determined to be interested.

"Important? I should just think it was, only people refuse to realise the fact. It's a meeting of the County Territorial Association. What humbug the whole business is! They started the old Volunteers, coddled them, asked nothing of them but a few drills and an annual picnic in camp, and then laughed them out of existence for Saturday-afternoon soldiers. Now they start the Territorials and go to the other extreme. They require of a man that he shall attain, free gratis and for nothing, at the sacrifice of the few scanty weeks which he gets by way of holiday, to practically the same standard of efficiency as a regular soldier, who is paid for it and gets the whole year to do it in. And then they blame us, the County Associations, because we can't find recruits for them! Luckily, we shall have compulsory service soon, and that will end the farce once and for all."

Daphne liked to be talked to like this. In the first place, it removed the uncomfortable and humiliating sensation that she was a child in her husband's eyes; and in the second, it adjusted her sense of proportion as regards the male sex. Obviously, with all these dull but weighty matters to occupy him, a man could not be expected to set such store by conjugal unity as his wife, who had little else to think of.

"Perhaps I have been a little fool," she philosophised. "After all, a man doesn't in the least realise how a woman——"

"What are you going to do to-day?" asked her husband.

"This afternoon I am going over to Croxley Dene to play tennis."

"Anything this morning?"

"I am going to order the motor for twelve o'clock"—rather reluctantly. "I suppose Vick will be back from Kilchester."

"Oh, yes. Are you going out to lunch somewhere?"

"N-no."

"Just a drive?"

"Yes. The fact is," said poor Daphne, hating herself for feeling like a child detected in a fault, "I am going to try my hand at driving the motor myself."

There was a pause, and Juggernaut continued to gaze out of the window, while Daphne pleated the tablecloth.

Presently the hateful expected words came.

"I would rather you didn't."

Daphne rose suddenly to her feet. Her face was aflame, and all her good resolutions had vanished. She had always longed to drive the big car, her appetite having been whetted by occasional experiments upon the property—usually small, easily handled vehicles—of long-suffering friends. She had broached the subject more than once, but had found her husband curiously vague as regards permission. Usually it was "yes" or "no" with him. This morning, tired of the humiliation of constantly asking for leave, she had decided to give orders on her own account. And but for Juggernaut's unlucky question she would have achieved her purpose and settled accounts afterwards—a very different thing from asking leave first, as every child knows.

"And why?" she asked, with suspicious calmness.

"Well, for one thing, I don't think a lady should be seen driving a great covered-in limousine car. You wouldn't go out on the box seat of a brougham, would you? As a matter of fact, if you will have patience for a week or two——"

"Yes, I know!" broke in Daphne passionately. "If I have patience for a week or two, and am a good little girl, and order the meals punctually in the meanwhile, you will perhaps take me for a run one afternoon, and let me hold the wheel while you sit beside me with the second speed in. Thank you! *Good* morning!"

She pushed back her chair, whirled round with a vehement swirl of her tweed skirt, and left the room.

Juggernaut continued to finger a typewritten letter which he had just taken from his pocket. It bore the address of a firm of motor-makers, and said—

"Sir,—We beg to inform you that one of our Handy Runabout 10-12h-p. cars, for which we recently received your esteemed order, is now to hand from the varnishers', and will be delivered at Belton Hall on Tuesday next. As requested, we have given the clutch-pedal and brake a particularly easy spring, with a view to the car being driven by a lady.

"Thanking you for past favours, we are, sir yours faithfully,"

"The Diablement-Odorant
Motor Co., Ltd."

Juggernaut put the letter back into his pocket.

II.

In due course the Belton motor conveyed its owner to Kilchester and left him there.

"Shall I come back for you, sir?" inquired Mr Vick, the chauffeur. He was a kindly man, despite his exalted station.

"No, thanks—I'll take the train. But I believe Lady Carr wants you to take her over to Croxley Dene this afternoon."

"Her ladyship shall be took," said Mr Vick, with an indulgent smile—Lady Carr was a favourite of his—and forthwith returned to Belton.

On running the car into the yard he found the coachman, Mr Windebank, a sadly diminished luminary in these days, putting a polish upon an unappreciative quadruped.

"You and your machine, Mr Vick," announced Mr Windebank, "is wanted round at twelve sharp."

It was then eleven-fifteen.

"Ho!" replied the ruffled Mr Vick, feeling much as the Emperor Nero might have felt on being requested by the most recently immured early Christian to see that the arena lions were kept a bit quieter to-morrow night—"ho, indeed!"

"Them's your orders, Mr Vick," said Mr Windebank, resuming the peculiar dental *obligato* which seems to be the inseparable accompaniment of the toilet of a horse, temporarily suspended on this occasion to enable the performer to discharge his little broadside.

Mr Vick turned off various taps and switches on his dash-board, and the humming of the engine ceased.

"I take my orders," he proclaimed in majestic tones, "from the master and missus direct, and from nobody else."

Mr Windebank, after spending some moments in groping for a crushing rejoinder, replied—

"Well, you'd better go inside and get 'em. And you'd better 'ang a nosebag on your sparking-plug in the meanwhile," he added, with sudden and savage irrelevance.

Mr Vick adopted the former of these two suggestions, with the result that at the hour of noon the car slid submissively round to the front of the Hall. Presently Daphne appeared, and disregarding the door which

Mr Vick was holding open for her, stepped up into the driver's seat—the throne itself—and took the wheel in her vigorous little hands.

"I am going to drive, Vick," she observed cheerfully.

Mr Vick preserved his self-control and smiled faintly.

"I suppose you have a licence, my lady?" he inquired.

"Gracious, no! I am only just beginning," replied Daphne, who regarded a driver's licence as a sort of reward of merit. "I want you to teach me. Which of these things is the clutch-pedal?"

"The left, my lady. I am afraid," added Mr Vick, with the air of one who intends to stop this nonsense once and for all, "that you will find it very stiff."

"Thanks," said Daphne blandly. "And I suppose the other one is the brake."

"Yes, my lady; but——"

"Then we can start. How do I put in the first speed?"

Mr Vick, in what can only be described as a *moriturus-te-saluto!* voice, gave the required information; and the car, after a dislocating jerk, moved off at a stately four miles per hour. Presently, with much slipping of the clutch and buzzing of the gear-wheels, the second, and finally the third speed went in, and the car proceeded with all the exuberance of its forty-five horse-power down the long straight drive. Fortunately the lodge gates stood open, and the road outside was clear.

Certainly Mr Vick behaved very well. Although every wrench and jar to which his beloved engines were submitted appeared to react directly upon his own internal mechanism, he never winced. Occasionally a muffled groan or a muttered exclamation of "My tyres!" or "My differential!" burst from his overwrought lips; but for the most part he sat like a graven image, merely hoping that when the crash came it would be a good one—something about which it would be really grateful and comforting to say "I told you so!" He also cherished a strong hope that his name would appear in the newspapers.

But Daphne drove well. She had a good head and quick hands; and steering a middle course between the extreme caution of the beginner and the omniscient recklessness of the half-educated, she gave Mr Vick very little excuse for anything in the shape of a genuine shudder. She experienced a little difficulty in getting the clutch right out of action in changing gear; and once she stopped her engine through going round a corner with the brakes on—but that was all. Mr Vick began to feel distinctly aggrieved.

There was a spice of *abandon* in Daphne's present attitude. She had burned her boats; she had flown in the face of authority; and she intended to brazen it out. The breeze whistled in her ears; her eyes blazed; her cheeks glowed. She felt in good fighting trim.

Presently, fetching a compass, the car began to head towards Belton again, and having been directed in masterly fashion through the narrow gates by the back lodge, sped along the final stretch which led to home and luncheon, at a comfortable thirty miles an hour.

At the end of the dappled vista formed by the overarching trees of the avenue appeared a black object, which presently resolved itself into Mr Dawks, lolling comfortably in a patch of sunlight pending his mistress's return.

"Mind the dog, my lady!" cried Mr Vick suddenly.

Daphne had every intention of minding the dog; but desire and performance do not always coincide. Suddenly realizing that Mr Dawks, who was now sitting up expectantly in the middle distance, wagging his tail and extending a welcome as misplaced as that of Jephtha's daughter under somewhat similar circumstances, had no conception of the necessity for vacating his present position, Daphne put down both feet hard and endeavored to bring the car to a standstill. But thirty miles an hour is forty-four feet a second, and the momentum of a car weighing two tons is not lightly to be arrested by a brake constructed only to obey the pressure of a masculine boot. Next moment there was a pathetic little yelp. Daphne had a brief vision of an incredulous and reproachful doggy countenance; the car gave a slight lurch, and then came to full stop, as Mr Vick, having already snapped off the ignition switch on the dashboard, reached across behind Daphne's back and jammed on the side brake.

III.

It was Mr Dawks who really showed to the greatest advantage during the next half-hour. He assured his mistress by every means in his power that the whole thing was entirely his fault; and, like the courteous gentleman that he was, he begged her with faintly wagging tail and affectionate eyes not to distress herself unduly on his account. The thing was done; let there be no more talk about it. It was nothing! By way of showing that the cordiality of their relations was still unimpaired he endeavored to shake hands, first with one paw and then the other; but finding that both were broken he reluctantly desisted from his efforts.

They carried him—what was left of him—into the house, where Daphne, white-faced and tearless, hung in an agony of self-reproach over the friend of her youth—the last link with her girlhood. Dawks lay very still. Once, opening his eyes and evidently feeling that something was expected of him, he licked her hand. The tears came fast after that.

Presently Windebank arrived. He loved all dumb beasts, and was skilled in ministering to their ailments—wherein he transcended that highly educated automaton Mr Vick, to whom the acme of life was represented by a set of perfectly timed sparking-plugs—and he made poor mangled Dawks as comfortable as possible.

"Is he badly hurt, Windebank?" whispered Daphne.

"Yes, miss," said Windebank, touching his forelock. He was a man of few words in the presence of his superiors.

"Will he die?"

Windebank gazed down in an embarrassed fashion at the close coils of fair hair, bowed over the dog's rough coat. Then he stiffened himself defiantly.

"He'll get well right enough, miss," he said with great assurance. "Just wants taking care of, that's all."

It was a lie, and he knew it. But it was a kind lie. To such much is forgiven.

Daphne sat with her patient until three o'clock, and then, overcome with the restlessness of impotent anxiety, and stimulated by an urgent telephonic reminder, ordered out the horses—not the motor.

"Good-bye, old man," she said to Dawks, caressing the dog's long ears and unbecoming nose. "I'll be back in an hour or two. Lie quiet, and you'll soon be all right. Windebank says so."

Mr Dawks whined gently and flapped his tail upon the floor, further intimating by a faint tremor of his ungainly body that if circumstances had permitted he would certainly have made a point of rising and accompanying his mistress to the door and seeing her off the premises. As things were, he must beg to be excused.

Daphne drove to Croxley Dene, where for an hour or so she exchanged banalities with the rest of the county and played a set of tennis.

She drove home in the cool of the evening, more composed in mind. The fresh air and exercise had done her good. Windebank had said that the dog would live: that was everything. Less satisfactory to contemplate was the approaching interview with her husband in the matter of the car. Until now she had not thought of it.

On reaching home she hurried to the library, where she had left the invalid lying on a rug before the fire. Mr Dawks was not there.

"I wonder if Windebank has taken him to the stable," she said to herself. "I'll go and——"

She turned, and found herself face to face with her husband.

"Jack," she asked nervously, "do you know where Dawks is? I suppose you have heard——"

"Yes, I have heard."

Daphne shrank back at the sound of his voice. His face was like flint.

"Then—where is he?" she faltered. "Windebank said——"

"I had him shot."

Daphne stared at him incredulously.

"You had him *shot*?" she said slowly. "*My* Dawks?"

"Yes. It was rank cruelty on your part keeping the poor brute alive, after—after reducing him to that state."

The last half of the sentence may have been natural and justifiable, but no one could call it generous. It is not easy to be merciful when one is at white heat.

Daphne stood up, very slim and straight, gazing stonily into her husband's face.

"Have you buried him?"

"I told one of the gardeners to do so."

"Where?"

"I did not say, but we can——"

"I suppose you know," said Daphne with great deliberation, "that he was the only living creature in all this great house that loved me—really *loved* me?"

Verily, here was war. There was a tense silence for a moment, and an almost imperceptible flicker of some emotion passed over Juggernaut's face. Then he said, with equal deliberation—

"Without any exception?"

"Yes, without *any* exception!" cried poor Daphne, stabbing passionately in the dark. "And since he is dead," she added—"since you have killed him—I am going home to Dad and the boys! They love me!"

She stood before her husband with her head thrown back defiantly, white and trembling with passion.

"Very good. Perhaps that would be best," said Juggernaut quietly.

CHAPTER TWELVE.

CILLY; OR THE WORLD WELL LOST.

"Stiffy," bellowed the new curate ferociously, "what the—I mean, why on earth can't you keep that right foot steady? You edge off to leg every time. If you get a straight ball, stand up to it! If you get a leg-ball, turn round and have a slap at it! But for Heaven's sake don't go running *away*! Especially from things like pats of butter!"

"Awfully sorry, Mr Blunt!" gasped Stiffy abjectly, as another pat of butter sang past his ear. "It's the rotten way I've been brought up! I've never had any decent coaching before. Ough!... No, it didn't hurt a bit, really! I shall be all right in a minute." He hopped round in a constricted circle, apologetically caressing his stomach.

They were in the paddock behind the Rectory orchard. The Reverend Godfrey Blunt, a ruddy young man of cheerful countenance and ingenuous disposition, had rolled out an extremely fiery wicket; and within the encompassing net—Daphne's last birthday present—Stephen Blasius Vereker, impaled frog-wise upon the handle of his bat, and divided between a blind instinct of self-preservation and a desire not to appear ungrateful for favours received, was frantically endeavouring to dodge the deliveries of the church militant as they bumped past his head and ricochetted off his ribs.

"That's better," said Mr Blunt, as his pupil succeeded for the first time in arresting the course of a fast long-hop with his bat instead of his person. "But don't play back to yorkers."

"All right!" said Stiffy dutifully. "I didn't know," he added in all sincerity, "that it was a yorker, or I wouldn't have done it. Oh, I say, well bowled! I don't think anybody could have stopped that one. It never touched the ground at all!"

Stiffy turned round and surveyed his prostrate wickets admiringly. He was an encouraging person to bowl to.

"No, it was a pretty hot one," admitted the curate modestly. "I think I shall have to be going now," he added, mopping his brow. "Parish work, and a sermon to write, worse luck! I think I have just time for a short knock, though. Bowl away, Stiffy!"

He took his stand at the wicket, and after three blind and characteristic swipes succeeded in lifting a half-volley of Stiffy's into the adjacent orchard. When the bowler, deeply gratified with a performance of which he felt himself to be an unworthy but necessary adjunct, returned ten minutes later from a successful search for the ball, he found his hero hastily donning the old tweed jacket and speckled straw hat which he kept for wear with his cricket flannels.

"Hallo! Off?" cried Stiffy regretfully.

"Yes; I'm afraid so," replied Mr Blunt. He was gazing anxiously through a gap in the hedge which commanded the Rectory garden-gate. "This is my busy day. So long, old man!"

He vaulted the fence, and set off down the road at a vigorous and businesslike trot. But after a hundred yards or so he halted, and looked round him with an air which can only be described as furtive. Before him the road, white and dusty, continued officiously on its way to the village and duty. Along the right-hand side thereof ran a neat rail-fence, skirting the confines of Tinkler's Den. The landscape appeared deserted. All nature drowsed in the hot afternoon sun.

Mr Blunt, who was a muscular young Christian, took a running jump of some four feet six, cleared the topmost rail, and landed neatly on the grassy slope which ran down towards the Den.

"Now then, Sunny Jim!" remarked a reproving voice above his head, "*pas si beaucoup de cela!*"

However sound our nervous systems may be, we are all of us liable to be startled at times. Mr Blunt was undoubtedly startled on the occasion, and being young and only very recently ordained, signified the same in the usual manner.

When he looked up into the tree where Nicky was reclining, that virtuous damsel's fingers were in her ears.

"Mr Blunt," she remarked, "I am both surprised and shocked."

"Veronica Vereker," replied Mr Blunt, turning and shaking his fist as he retreated down the slope towards Tinkler's Den, "next time I get hold of you I will wring your little neck!"

Miss Veronica Vereker kissed the tips of her fingers to him.

"We will now join," she proclaimed, in a voice surprisingly reminiscent of the throaty tenor which Mr Blunt reserved for his ecclesiastical performances, "in singing Hymn number two hundred and thirty-three; during which those who desire to leave the church are recommended to do so, as it is *my—turn—to—preach—the—sermon*!"

But by this time the foe, running rapidly, was out of earshot.

Half-an-hour later Stiffy, who was a gregarious animal, went in search of his younger sister, whom he discovered, recently returned from her sylvan skirmish with the curate, laboriously climbing into a hammock in the orchard.

"Nicky, will you come and play cricket?" he asked politely.

"I suppose that means will I come and bowl to you?" replied Nicky.

"No. You can bat if you like."

"Well, I won't do either," said Nicky agreeably.

"What shall we do, then?" pursued Stiffy, with unimpaired *bonhomie*.

"Personally, I am going to remain in this hammock," replied the lady. "I recommend you, dear, to go and put your head in a bucket. *Good* afternoon! Sorry you can't stop."

"I wonder if Cilly would play," mused Stiffy.

"Cilly? I don't think! She is gloating over her clothes in her bedroom. If you and I, my lad," continued Veronica reflectively, "were going to be presented at Court next week, I wonder if we should make such unholy shows of ourselves for days beforehand."

"I know her boxes are all packed," pursued Stiffy hopefully, "because I went and sat on the lids myself after lunch. Perhaps she will come out for half-an-hour before tea. Dad and Tony won't be back from Tilney till seven, so they are no good."

"Well, run along, little man," said Nicky, closing her eyes. "I'm fed up with you."

Stiffy departed obediently, and for ten minutes his younger sister reclined in her hammock, her sinful little soul purged for the moment of evil intent against any man. When next she opened her eyes Stiffy was standing disconsolately before her.

"Go away," said Nicky faintly. "We have no empty bottles or rabbit-skins at present. If you call round about Monday we shall be emptying the dustbin——"

"Cilly's not there," said Stiffy. "Keziah thinks she has gone out for a walk. She saw her strolling down towards the Den half-an-hour ago."

"*The Den?*" Nicky's eyes suddenly unclosed to their full radius. "My che-ild! So *that's* the game! *That* was why the pale young curate was jumping fences. Ha, *ha*! Stiffy, would you like some fun?"

Stiffy, mystified but docile, assented.

"We are going," announced Nicky, rolling gracefully out of the hammock, "to stalk a brace of true lovers."

"What—Mr Blunt and Cilly? Do you mean——? Are they really keen on each other?" inquired the unobservant male amazedly.

"*Are* they? My lad, it has been written all over them for weeks! I'm not certain, though," continued the experienced Nicky, "that the poor dears are aware of it themselves yet. But to-day is Cilly's last for months, so——"

"Do you mean they are down in the Den together?" demanded Stiffy.

"I do."

"But—Mr Blunt has gone off to do parish work. He told me so himself."

"Parish work my foot!" commented Nicky simply. "Come on! Let's go and mark down their trail! We can pretend to be Red Indians, if you like," she added speciously.

But the sportsmanlike Stiffy hung back.

"Let's play cricket instead," he said hesitatingly.

"Not me! Come on!"

"Nicky," said Stiffy, searching his hand, so to speak, for trumps, "Preston is killing a pig this afternoon at four o'clock. I've just remembered. He promised not to begin till I came. We shall just be in time. Hurry up!"

"I am going," said Nicky firmly, "to stalk that couple. Are you coming?"

"No. It's not playing the game," said Stiffy bravely.

Nicky, uneasily conscious that he spoke the truth, smiled witheringly.

"All right, milksop!" she said. "I shall go by myself. You can go and hold the pig's hand."

So they departed on their several errands.

Meanwhile Cilly and the curate sat side by side beneath a gnarled and venerable oak in Tinkler's Den.

..."Then your name is called out," continued Cilly raptly, "and you give one last squiggle to your train and go forward and curtsey—to *all* the Royalties in turn, I think, but I'm not quite sure about that part yet—and then you pass along out of the way, and somebody picks up your train and throws it over your shoulder, and you find yourself in another room, and it's all over. Won't it be heavenly?"

"Splendid!" replied Mr Blunt, without enthusiasm.

"After that," continued Cilly, "my sister is going to take me simply everywhere. And I am to meet lots of nice people. It's too late for Henley and Ascot and that sort of thing this summer, but I am to have them all next year. Later on, we are going to Scotland. I'm not at all a lucky girl, am I?"

It was one of those questions to which, despite its form, an experienced Latin grammarian would have unhesitatingly prefixed the particle *nonne*. But the Reverend Godfrey Blunt merely replied in a hollow voice—

"What price me?"

Cilly, startled, turned and regarded his hot but honest face, and then lowered her gaze hastily to the region of her own toes.

The Reverend Godfrey was a fine upstanding young man, with merry grey eyes; and there was a cheerful and boisterous *bonhomie* about his conversation which the exigencies of his calling had not yet intoned out of him. No one had ever considered him brilliant, for his strength lay in character rather than intellect. He was a perfect specimen of that unromantic but priceless type with which our public schools and universities never fail to meet the insatiable demands of a voracious Empire. The assistant-commissioner, the company officer, the junior form-master, the slum-curate—these are they that propel the ship of State. Up above upon the quarter-deck, looking portentously wise and occasionally quarrelling for the possession of the helm, you may behold their superiors—the Cabinet Minister, the Prelate, the Generalissimo. But our friends remain below the water-line, unheeded, uncredited, and see to it that the wheels go round. They expect no thanks, and they are not disappointed. The ship goes forward, and that is all they care about. Of such is the British Empire.

The Reverend Godfrey Blunt was one of this nameless host. At school he had scraped into the Sixth by a hair's-breadth; at the University he had secured a degree of purely nominal value. He had been an unheroic member of his House eleven; thereafter he had excoriated his person uncomplainingly and unsuccessfully upon a fixed seat for the space of three years, not because he expected to make bumps or obtain his Blue, but because his College second crew had need of him. Since then he had worked for five years in a parish in Bermondsey, at a stipend of one hundred pounds a-year; and only the doctor's ultimatum had prevailed on him to try country work for a change. His spelling was shaky, his theology would have made Pusey turn in his grave, and his sermons would have bored his own mother. But he was a man.

Cilly, whom we left bashfully contemplating her shoe-buckles under an oak-tree, was conscious of a new, sudden, and disturbing thrill. Young girls are said seldom to reflect and never to reason. They have no need. They have methods of their own of arriving at the root of the matter. Cilly realised in a flash that if a proper man was the object of her proposed journey through the great and enticing world before her, she need never set out at all. Something answering to that description was sitting beside her, sighing like a furnace. Her face flamed.

"What did you say?" she inquired unsteadily.

"I said 'What price me?'" reiterated the curate mournfully.

"What do you mean?"

"I mean——" he spoke hesitatingly, like a man picking his words from an overwhelming crowd of applicants—"well, I mean this. You and I have seen a lot of each other since I came here. You have been awfully good to me, and I have got into the way of bringing you my little troubles, and turning to you generally if I felt dismal or humpy. (There *are* more joyful spots, you know, to spend one's leisure hours in than Mrs Tice's first-floor-front.) And now—now you are going away from me, to meet all sorts of attractive people and have the time of your life. You will have a fearful lot of attention paid to you. Nine out of ten men you meet will fall in love with you——"

"Oh! nonsense!" said Cilly feebly.

"But I *know* it," persisted Blunt. "I simply can't conceive any man being able to do anything else. Do you know——" the words stuck in his throat for a moment and then came with a rush—"do you know that you are the most adorable girl on God's earth? I love you! I love you! *There*—I've said it! I had meant to say a lot more first—work up to it by degrees, you know—but it has carried me away of its own accord. I love you—dear, *dear* Cilly!"

There was a long stillness. All nature seemed to be watching with bated breath for the next step. Only above their heads the branches of the oak-tree crackled gently. Cilly's head swam. Something new and tremulous was stirring within her. She closed her eyes, lest the spell should be broken by the sight of some mundane external object. A purely hypothetical fairy prince, composed of equal parts of Peer of the Realm, Lifeguardsman, Mr Sandow, Lord Byron, and the Bishop of London, whom she had cherished in the inmost sanctuary of her heart ever since she had reached the age at which a girl begins to dream about young men, suddenly rocked upon his pedestal. Then she opened her eyes again, and contemplated the homely features of the Reverend Godfrey Blunt.

Not that they appeared homely any longer. Never had a man's face undergone such a transformation in so short a time. To her shy eyes he had grown positively handsome. Cilly felt her whole being suddenly drawn towards this goodly youth. The composite paragon enshrined in her heart gave a final lurch and then fell headlong, to lie dismembered and disregarded, Dagon-like, at the foot of his own pedestal.

...Slowly their hands met, and they gazed upon one another long and rapturously. How long, they did not know. There was no need to take count of time. They seemed to be sitting together all alone on the edge of the universe, with eternity before them. The next step was obvious enough; they both realised what it must be: but they did not hurry. They sat on, this happy pair, waiting for inspiration.

It came—straight from above their heads.

"Kiss her, you fool!" commanded a hoarse and frenzied voice far up the tree.

Crackle! Crash! *Bump!*

And Nicky, overestimating in her enthusiasm the supporting power of an outlying branch, tumbled, headlong but undamaged, a medley of arms and legs and blue pinafore, right at their feet.

A few hours later Daphne, preceded by a rather incoherent telegram, drove up to the Rectory in the station fly.

She was met at the door by Cilly, and the two, as if by one impulse, fell into each other's arms.

"Daphne, *dear* Daph," murmured the impetuous Cilly, "I am the happiest girl in all the world."

"And I," said Daphne simply, "am the most miserable."

CHAPTER THIRTEEN.

THE COUNTERSTROKE.

The scene is the Restaurant International, a palatial house of refreshment in Regent Street; the time half-past one. At a table in the corner of the Grand Salle à Manger, set in a position calculated to extract full value from the efforts of a powerful orchestra, a waiter of majestic mien, with a powdered head, and a gold tassel on his left shoulder, stands towering over two recently arrived patrons with the *menu*.

The patrons, incredible as it may appear, are Stephen Blasius Vereker and Veronica Elizabeth Vereker. Stiffy, in the gala dress of a schoolboy of eighteen, is perspiring freely under the gaze of the overpowering menial at his elbow; Nicky, in a new hat of colossal but correct dimensions (the gift of her eldest sister), with her hair gathered into the usual *ne plus ultra* of the "flapper,"—a constricted pigtail tied with a large black bow of ribbon,—is entirely unruffled.

How they got there will appear presently.

"Will you lunch *à la carte* or *table d'hôte*, sir?" inquired the waiter, much as an executioner might say—"Will you be drawn or quartered?"

The flustered Stiffy gazed helplessly at his sister.

"He means, will you pay for what you eat or eat what you pay for, dear," explained that experienced and resourceful young person. "You must excuse him," she added, turning her round and trustful orbs upon the waiter. "He is not accustomed to being given a choice of dishes."

The waiter, realising that here was a worthy opponent, maintained a countenance of wood and repeated the question.

"You had better give *me* the *menu*," said Miss Vereker. "How much is the *table d'hôte* lunch?"

"Four shillings, madam."

Madam mused.

"Let me see," she said thoughtfully. "Can we run to it, dear?"

"Of course!" said Stiffy in an undertone, reddening with shame. "You know Daphne gave me——"

Nicky smiled joyfully.

"So she did. I had forgotten. Two and nine, wasn't it?"

Stiffy, with a five-pound-note crackling in his pocket, merely gaped.

"Then," continued Nicky, calculating on her fingers, "there is the three and a penny which we got out of the missionary-box. That makes five and tenpence. And there is that shilling that slipped down into your boot, Stiffy. You can easily get under the table and take it off. Six and tenpence. I have elevenpence in stamps, and that, with the threepenny-bit we picked up off the floor of the bus, makes eight shillings. We can just do it. Thank you," she intimated to the waiter with a seraphic smile—"we will take *table d'hôte*. I suppose," she added wistfully, "there would be no reduction if I took my little boy on my knee?"

"None, madam."

And the waiter, still unshaken, departed to bring the *hors d'œuvres*.

"Nicky, don't play the goat!" urged the respectable Stephen in a low and agitated voice. "That blighter really *believes* we are going to pay him in stamps. We shall get flung out, for a cert!"

"It's all right," said Nicky. "I am only going to try and make him laugh."

"You'll fail," said her brother with conviction.

At this moment a mighty tray, covered with such inducements to appetite as anchovies, sliced tomatoes, sardines, radishes, chopped celery, Strasburg sausage, *et hoc genus omne*—all equally superfluous in the case of a schoolboy up in town on an *exeat*—was laid before him with a stately flourish. Then the waiter came stiffly and grimly to attention, and stood obviously expectant. *Hors d'œuvres* are rather puzzling things. Here was a chance for the tyros before him to show their mettle.

They showed it.

"One gets tired of these everlasting things," mused Nicky wearily. "I'll just peck at one or two. You can fetch the soup, waiter: we shall be ready for it immediately."

"Thick or clear soup, madam?"

"We'll have thick to begin with, please: then clear," replied Nicky calmly. "Stiffy, I will take an anchovy."

The waiter was not more than two minutes absent, but ere he returned a lightning transformation scene had been enacted.

Certainly the Briton, with all his faults, surpasses the foreigner in the control of the emotions. What a Gaul or a Teuton would have done on witnessing the sight which met the eyes of the imperturbable Ganymede of the Restaurant International when he returned with the thick soup, it is difficult to say. The first would probably have wept, the second have sent for a policeman. For lo! the richly dight *hors d'œuvres* tray had become a solitude—the component parts thereof were duly discovered by the charwoman next morning amid the foliage of an adjacent palm—and the tail of the last radish was disappearing into Stiffy's mouth. Stiffy, once roused, made an excellent accomplice, though he had no initiative of his own.

The waiter's face twitched ever so slightly, and there was an undulating movement in the region of his scarlet waistcoat. But he recovered himself in time, and having served the thick soup, departed unbidden in search of the clear.

"Nicky," said Stiffy in a concerned voice, "are we really going to have everything on the *menu*?"

"You are, my son," replied Nicky. "I, being a lady, will make use of this palm-tub."

The waiter brought the clear soup, and asked for instructions with regard to the fish.

"What sort of fish have you?"

The man proffered the card.

"*Sole: Sauce Tartare*. That means sole with tartar sauce," Nicky translated glibly for the benefit of her untutored relative. "We had better not have that. Tartar sauce always makes him sick," she explained to the waiter, indicating the fermenting Stiffy. "What else is there? Let me see—ah! *Blanchailles!*—er—*Blanchailles!* A very delicate fish! Quite so. You may bring us"—her brain worked desperately behind a smiling face, but fruitlessly—"a *blanchaille*, waiter."

There was an ominous silence. Then the waiter asked, in a voice tinged with polite incredulity—

"A *whole* one each, madam?"

"Certainly," said madam in freezing tones.

The waiter bowed deferentially, and departed.

"Stiffy," inquired Nicky in agonised tones, "what *is a blanchaille?* Don't say it's a cod!"

Stiffy devoted three hours a-week to the study of Modern Languages, but so far no *blanchaille* has swum into his vocabulary.

"I've a notion," he said after a prolonged mental effort, "that it is a sturgeon."

"How big is a sturgeon?"

"It's about the size of a shark, I think."

"Mercy! And we have ordered a whole one each!"

But their capacity was not to be taxed after all. The waiter returned, and with the nonchalant demeanour of a hardened clubman playing out an unexpected ace of trumps, laid down two plates. In the centre of each reposed a single forlorn diminutive whitebait.

But it was here that Veronica Elizabeth Vereker rose to her greatest heights. She inspected her own portion and then her brother's.

"Waiter," she said at last, "will you kindly take away this young gentleman's fish and ask the cook to give you a rather longer one? About three-quarters of an inch, I should say. The child"—indicating her hirsute and crimson senior—"gets very peevish and fretful if his portion is smaller than any one else's."

Without a word the waiter picked up Stiffy's plate and bore it away. His broad back had become slightly bowed, and his finely chiselled legs had a warped and bandy appearance. The strain was telling.

Stiffy gazed upon his sister in rapt admiration.

"Nicky, you *ripper*!" he said.

After this it was mere child's play to request a stout gentleman with a chain round his neck to submit the wine list—an imposing volume of many pages—and after a heated and highly technical discussion on the respective merits of Pommery and Cliquot, to order one stone-ginger and two glasses.

Nicky next instructed the waiter to present her compliments to the leader of the band, and to request as a special favour that he and his colleagues would oblige with a rendering of *Shall We Gather at the River?* The waiter returned with a reply to the effect that the *chef d'orchestre* would be delighted. Unfortunately he had not the full score by him at the moment, but had sent along to the Café Royal to borrow a copy. Everything would be in readiness about tea-time. It was then a little after two, and it was admitted by both Nicky and Stiffy that honours on this occasion were divided.

So far both sides, as the umpires say on Territorial field-days, had acquitted themselves in a manner deserving great credit; but the waiter scored the odd and winning trick a little later, in a particularly subtle manner. Age and experience always tell. Nicky, unduly inflated by early success, insisted upon Stiffy ordering a liqueur with his coffee. Green Chartreuse was finally selected and brought.

"Shall I pour it into your coffee, sir?" asked the waiter respectfully.

"Please," said the unsuspecting Stiffy.

The man obeyed, and directly afterwards emitted a sound which caused both children to glance up suddenly. They glared suspiciously, first at one another, then at the back of the retreating foe.

"Do people drink Green Chartreuse *in* their coffee?" asked Nicky apprehensively.

"I don't know," said Stiffy. He tasted the compound. "No, I'm *blowed* if they do! Nicky, we've been had. He's one up!"

"It would score him off," replied the undefeated Nicky, "if you could manage to be sick."

But Stiffy held out no hope of this happy retaliation; and they ultimately produced the five-pound note and paid the score with somewhat chastened mien, adding a *douceur* which was as excessive as it was unnecessary. Waiters do not get much entertainment out of serving meals as a rule.

II.

"Now we must meet Daphne," said Stiffy, as they left the restaurant and hailed a cab.

They were in town for an all-too-brief sojourn of twenty-four hours, to assist at the inspection of Daphne's new house. It was now February, and Lady Carr had not seen her husband since the eruption at Belton last summer. Juggernaut had made no attempt to prevent her going home, and when she wrote later, requesting that Master Brian Vereker Carr might be sent to her, had despatched him without remonstrance. No one save Cilly and her beloved Godfrey—least of all the Rector—knew of the true state of affairs; and all during that autumn and winter Daphne was happier in a fashion than she had ever been. To a large extent she resumed command of the household, setting Cilly free for other very right and natural diversions; and a sort of *édition de luxe* of the old days came into being, with first-hand food at every meal and a boy to clean the boots and drive the pony.

Daphne was entirely impervious to the gravity of the situation. There are certain women who are curiously wanting in all sense of responsibility. They preserve the child's lack of perspective and proportion even after they grow up, and the consequences are sometimes disastrous. If love arrives upon the scene no further harm ensues, for the missing qualities spring up, with that Jonah's-gourd-like suddenness which characterises so many feminine developments, at the first touch of the great magician's wand. The retarded faculties achieve maturity in a flash, and their owner becomes maternal, solicitous, Martha-like; and all is well.

Daphne was one of these women; but so far, unfortunately, she had failed to fall in love. Her marriage had never really touched her. Her husband had vibrated many strings in her responsive impulsive young heart—gratitude, affection, admiration,—but the great harmonious combination, the master-chord, had yet to be struck. Consequently she saw nothing unusual in living apart from her husband, financing her family with his money, and enjoying herself with friends whom he did not know.

Early in the year, however, it occurred to her that it would be pleasant to go home again for a time. Her elastic nature had entirely recovered from the stress of last summer's crisis, and she was frankly consumed with curiosity on the subject of the new house in Berkeley Square—and said so. It was perhaps an unfortunate reason for a wife to give for wishing to return to her husband, but this did not occur to her at the time. She received a brief note in reply, saying that the furnishing and decorating were now practically completed, and the house was ready for her inspection any time she cared to come up to town. Hence this joyous expedition.

Daphne had half expected to find her husband waiting for her at the house, for the Parliamentary recess was over and she knew he was almost certain to be in town. Instead, she was received by an overwhelmingly polite individual named Hibbins, from the house-furnishers. Mr Hibbins' appearance and deportment proved a sore trial to the composure of Nicky, who exploded at frequent and unexpected intervals throughout the afternoon, lamely alleging the fantastic design of some very ordinary wallpaper or the shortness of Stiffy's Sunday trousers in excuse.

It was essentially a masculine house, furnished in accordance with the man's ideas of solidity and comfort. The high oak panelling and dark-green frieze in the dining-room pleased Daphne, who recognised that glass and silver, well-illuminated, would show up bravely in such a setting. The drawing-room was perhaps a little too severe in its scheme of decoration: Daphne would have preferred something more feminine. "But that comes," she reflected characteristically, "of leaving the declaration to your partner!" There was a billiard-room in which Nicky declared it would be a sin to place a billiard-table, so perfectly was it adapted for waltzing after dinner.

Opening out of the billiard-room was a plainly furnished but attractive little set of apartments—"the bachelor suite" Mr Hibbins designated it—consisting of a snug study with an apartment adjoining, containing a small camp-bed and a large bath. Daphne's own rooms consisted of a bedroom and boudoir on the first floor, with wide bow-windows.

The nursery came last. It was a large irregular-shaped room at the top of the house, full of unexpected corners and curious alcoves such as children love, affording convenient caves for robbers and eligible lairs for wild beasts, fabulous or authentic. In addition to the regulation nursery furniture there was a miniature set, in green-stained wood—a table barely eighteen inches high, a tiny arm-chair, and a pigmy sofa upon which Master Brian's friends might recline when they came to drink tea, or its equivalent. Round the whole room ran a brightly coloured dado covered with life-size figures of all the people we love when we are young—Jack the Giant-Killer, Old King Cole, Cinderella, and the Three Bears. Even Peter Pan, with residence and following, was there. The spectacle of Doctor Johnson taking a walk down Fleet Street would pale to insignificance compared with that of Master Brian Vereker Carr enjoying a constitutional along his own dado, encountering a new friend round every corner.

Daphne suddenly realised that here was yet another aspect of this strange, impenetrable husband of hers. The room in its way was a work of genius—the genius that understands children.

As they departed to catch the afternoon train to Snayling the obsequious Mr Hibbins produced a letter.

Sir John Carr, he explained, had called at the head office of their firm that morning—in *person*, Mr Hibbins added with a gratified smile—and requested that this letter should be handed to her ladyship in the afternoon. Sir John had also instructed Mr Hibbins to inform her ladyship that any improvements or alterations which she desired had only to be mentioned to be carried out.

Mr Hibbins having handed them into a cab and bidden them an unctuous farewell, they drove away to the station, Nicky atoning for previous aloofness by hanging out of the window and waving her handkerchief until they turned the corner.

III.

The journey from London to Snayling, involving as it does a run of forty miles by main line, a wait of indefinite duration at a junction furnished with no other facilities for recreation than a weighing-machine and a printed and detailed record of the fate which awaits persons who compass the awe-inspiring but cumbrous crime of travelling-by-a-class-superior-to-that-to-which-the-ticket-in-their-possession-entitles-them, and concluding with an interminable crawl along a branch line, is not at first sight an enterprise that promises much joyous adventure; but Nicky and Stiffy, who usually contrived to keep *ennui* at arm's-length, had a very tolerable time of it.

Their efforts at first were directed to securing an apartment to themselves—an achievement which, when you come to think of it, fairly epitomises the Englishman's outlook on life in general.

"Hang your face out of the window, Stiffy, my lad," commanded Nicky, returning from an unsuccessful attempt to wheedle the guard into labelling their carriage "engaged," "and play at Horatius Cocles till the train starts. That ought to do the trick."

But no. At the last moment a crusty-looking old gentleman wrenched the door open, nearly precipitating Horatius Cocles (and face) on to the platform, and sat down with great determination in the corner seat. He glared ferociously at the demure-looking pair before him, in a manner which intimated plainly that he was too old a customer to be kept out of his usual compartment by tricks of *that* kind. After this he produced *The Westminster Gazette* from a handbag and began to read it.

Nicky gave him five minutes. Then, turning to her brother and scrutinising his freckled countenance, she observed in clear and measured tones—

"I think they have let you out rather *soon*, John."

Stiffy, realising that he was the person addressed and that some fresh game was afoot, looked as intelligent as possible, and waited. Daphne, in the far corner of the carriage, hurriedly opened her husband's letter and began to read it.

"The marks aren't all gone yet," continued Nicky, inspecting her brother anxiously. "Are you still peeling?"

"Yes—I think so," said Stiffy, groping for his cue.

"Ah!" Nicky nodded her head judicially. "We must give you a carbolic bath when we get you home."

The Westminster Gazette emitted a perceptible crackle.

"It will never do," pursued Nicky, getting into her stride, "to have you disfigured for life."

Stiffy, who was impervious to all reflections upon his personal appearance, grinned faintly. Opposite, a scared and bulging eye slid cautiously round the edge of *The Westminster Gazette*, and embarked upon a minute and apprehensive inspection of the plague-stricken youth. Nicky saw, and thrilled with gratification. She was on the point of continuing when the train dived into a tunnel. Having no desire that her schemes should go awry in the din, she waited.

The train came to a sudden and unexplained stop. Deathlike silence reigned, broken only by murmurs of conversation from next door. Presently in the gross darkness Nicky's voice was once more uplifted.

"By the way, is it infectious, or merely *contagious*? I meant to ask when I called for you at the Institute"—she was rather proud of that inspiration: an Institute sounded more terrifying and mysterious than a Hospital—"but in the excitement of that last fainting-fit of yours I forgot. Which is it?"

"Both, I think," said Stiffy, anxious to help.

"Ah! I feared as much. Still, things might be worse," commented Nicky philosophically. "So many of these complaints are infectious in the early stages, when no one suspects any trouble. Mumps, for instance, or scarlet fever. But others, like yours, are only dangerous in the convalescent stage, and then of course one knows exactly where one is."

There was a crumpling of paper in the darkness, accompanied by a shuffling of feet and a vibratory motion of the seat-cushions—all indicative of the presence of one who knows exactly where *he* is, and regrets the fact exceedingly.

"The air is very close in here," resumed Nicky's voice. "I wonder——" she whispered a sentence into Stiffy's ear, the only distinguishable word in which was "germs." "Of course, I have *had* it—slightly," she added in a relieved tone.

Something moved again in the darkness opposite to them, and then came a sound as of a window being cautiously slid open.

"Still, I *think*," replied Stiffy solicitously—as usual he was warming up to the game slowly but surely—"that it would be wiser for you to keep your mouth closed and breathe through your nose. One cannot be too careful."

"All right," said Nicky.

Once again silence reigned. But presently there fell upon the ears of the conspirators, rendered almost incredulous by joy, an unmistakable and stertorous sound, as of some heavy and asthmatic body taking in air through unaccustomed channels.

Five minutes later the train, groaning arthritically, resumed its way and crawled out of the tunnel into a station. Nicky and Stiffy, blinking in the sudden daylight, beheld the reward of their labours. A corpulent and rapidly ageing citizen, shrinking apprehensively into a corner of the compartment and holding a small handbag upon his knees as if with a view to instant departure, sat glaring malignantly upon them. His face was mottled, his mouth was firmly closed, and he breathed perseveringly through his nostrils.

Next moment he had flung open the door and was out upon the platform, inhaling great gulps of vernal air and looking for the station-master.

"Stiffy, you darling! I'll never call you a fat-head again!" declared Nicky, enthusiastically embracing her complacent accomplice. "That notion of yours was simply *It!* Daph, wasn't it splen—Hallo! Bless me, Stiffy, if Daph isn't breathing through her nose too! Look!"

Certainly Daphne's lips were tightly compressed, but she turned to her companions and smiled faintly.

"It's all right, kids," she said; "I think this carriage is overheated or something. I shall be all right in a minute. Keep that window open, Stiffy dear."

She was very white, but on emphatically declining Nicky's offer of first aid she was left to herself, while her brother and sister discussed the course to be followed in the event of another invasion of the carriage. Like true artists, they scorned to achieve the same effect by the same means twice running.

Meanwhile Daphne re-read her husband's letter.

"... I have waited six months, and as you display no inclination to look facts in the face, I am compelled to take the initiative myself. As far as I can gather from your attitude, you seem to consider that things are very well as they are. On this point I beg to differ from you. The present situation must *end*. We must either come together again or part for good on some definitely arranged terms.

"... As you have exhibited no desire to reconcile yourself to me—your letter indicates that your sole object in returning home is to play with your latest toy, the new house—I conclude that you wish to remain your own mistress. I therefore place the new house entirely at your disposal. You can draw money as you require it from Coutts', and I will see to it that there is always an adequate balance. I think, if you have no objection, that it would be as well if I occasionally came to the house, and occupied the bachelor suite off the billiard-room; but I shall come and go without troubling you. We ought to make this concession to appearances.

"I should not like your father, for instance, to be made unhappy by the knowledge that his daughter and her husband found it better to go their several ways.

"... As for the custody of the boy——"

A long, slow shudder rippled down Daphne's spine. Custody! There was a horrible legal, end-of-all-things, divorce-court flavour about the word.

"I think it would be a good scheme, Stiffy dear," broke in Nicky's cheerful voice, "for you to pretend this time that you have just been discharged from an asylum. I will be taking you home, and ..." Her voice faded.

" ... You will naturally like to have him with you while he is a mere child. I will therefore leave him in your hands for the present. Later, when he goes to a public school and University, I think I should like him to be with me during his holidays. When he grows up altogether, he must please himself about——."

Public School! University! Daphne turned sick and faint. Were the provisions of this merciless letter to cover all eternity? What had she done to deserve this?

"It would be a bright thought," continued Nicky's voice, returning from a great distance, "to roll up your handkerchief into a ball and put it right into your mouth. Then do something to attract their attention, and when they are all looking, pull it right out with a jerk, and mop and mow. *Can* you mop and mow, Stiffy? Mop, anyhow! Just before a station, you know, so that they can get out. If that doesn't work, roll about on the cushions, and——."

Daphne detached her gaze from the flying landscape, and finished the letter.

"Forgive me if I appear to have resorted to extreme or harsh measures. I suppose I am a hard man: at any rate, I am not pliable. I dare say if I had been differently built I might have played the part of the modern husband with fair success, and you could have picked your companions at will. Unfortunately, I would rather die than permit you to impose such a *régime* upon me, as you seem prepared to do. The thing is degrading. To my mind there can be no compromise, no half-measures, between man and wife. It must be all in all, or not at all....

"Lastly, Daphne, let me say how sorry I am that things have come to this pass. I realise that it is my fault. I should not have asked a young and inexperienced girl to marry me. You could not be expected to know better: I might and should. And it is because I realise and admit that the fault is mine, that I refrain from "attaching any blame to you or uttering any reproaches. All I can do is to say that I am sorry, and make it possible for you to go your way, unhampered as far as may be by the ties of a marriage which should never have taken place.

"If I can at any time be of service to you, command me. I can never forget that we have had our happy hours together."

Daphne folded up the letter with mechanical deliberation. The first numbness was over. Her brain was clear again, and thoughts were crowding in upon her. But two things overtopped all the others for the moment.

The first was the realisation of the truth of her husband's words. The old situation *had* been impossible—as impossible as the new one was inevitable. She saw that—at last. "All in all, or not at all," he had said, and he was right.

The second was a sudden awakening to the knowledge that we never begin really to want a thing in this world until we find we cannot have it.

CHAPTER FOURTEEN.

INTERVENTION.

"Madame," announced the major-domo of the Hôtel Magnifique with a superb gesture, "the post from England!"

"Thank you, Thémistocle," said Mrs Carfrae. "But you are over-generous: one of these letters is not for me."

She handed back an envelope.

Thémistocle, needless to remark, was desolated at his own carelessness, and said so. But the old lady cut him short.

"Don't distress yourself unduly, Thémistocle. It is a mistake even an English body might have made. There is not much difference between Carfrae and Carthew."

The punctilious Thémistocle refused to be comforted.

"But no, madame," he persisted; "I should have observed that the letter addressed itself to a monsieur, and not a madame. Doubtless it is intended for one of the English party who arrive this afternoon."

"An English party? Is my seclusion to be disturbed by the disciples of the good Monsieur Cook?"

"Assuredly no, madame. These are English milords from Marseilles. The Riviera season has been a failure: the mistral blows eternally. Therefore the party abandons Cannes and telegraphs for apartments at the Hôtel Magnifique."

"Are they from London? Possibly I may be acquainted with some of them. What are their names?"

Thémistocle would inquire. He departed amid a whirlwind of bows, leaving Mrs Carfrae to continue her *déjeûner* in the sunny verandah of her sitting-room. She came to Algiers every spring, and she came unattended save for a grim-faced Scottish maid of her own age. It was Mrs Carfrae's habit to assume that she and her wheeled chair were a drag upon the world; and she systematically declined invitations to join friends upon the Riviera. People, she explained, who would otherwise have been playing tennis at the Beau Site or roulette at the Casino would feel bound to relinquish these pursuits and entertain her. So she came to Algiers by herself, this proud, lonely old lady.

"Carthew?" she mused. "That is the name of Johnny Carr's familiar spirit. And that letter was in Johnny's handwriting. Well, Thémistocle, who are—stand *still*, man!"

Thémistocle reluctantly curtailed an elaborate obeisance, and came to attention. The leader of the expedition, he announced, was Milord the Right Hon. Sir Hilton Bart., with Milady Hilton Bart. The names of the other guests were not known, but there were eleven of them.

They arrived on the steamer that afternoon, and drove in an imposing procession up the long and dusty hill that leads to Mustapha Supérieur, leaving Algiers—that curious combination of Mauretanian antiquity and second-rate French provincialism—baking peacefully in the hot sunshine below. As Thémistocle had predicted, they came unshepherded by the good Mr Cook. They were of the breed and caste that has always found its own way about the world.

There was Sir Arthur Hilton, a slow-moving Briton of few words, with a pretty wife of complementary volubility. There were one or two soldiers on leave; there was a Cambridge don; there were three grass widows. There were two newly emancipated schoolgirls, gobbling life in indigestible but heavenly lumps. There was a tall and beautiful damosel, with a demeanour which her admirers—and they were many—described as regal, and which her detractors—and their name was legion—described as affected; and whom her chaperon, Lady Hilton, addressed as "Nina, dearest." And there was a squarely built, freckle-faced young man with whom we are already acquainted. His name was Jim Carthew.

Altogether they were a clean-bred, self-contained, easy-going band, unostentatious but quietly exclusive—thoroughly representative of the sanest and most reputable section of that variegated cosmos which represents what Gallic students of British sociology term "Le Higlif." Very few of them possessed much money: theirs was a stratum of society to which money was no passport. You could have money if you liked, they conceded, but you must have a good many other things first. Hence the absence from their midst of Hoggenheimer and Aspasia.

Jim Carthew had not meant to come. Juggernaut had given him six weeks' leave, for there had been an Autumn Session in town and an industrial upheaval in the country, and the squire had worked early and late by his knight's side. Consequently when the spring came Carthew was summarily bidden to go to Scotland and fish. Without quite knowing why, he went to Cannes instead, where Nina Tallentyre, attended by a zealous but mutually-distrustful guard-of-honour, was enjoying herself after her fashion under the inadequate wing of Lady Hilton. When the exodus to Algiers was mooted, Carthew labelled his portmanteau London. But he ultimately crossed the Mediterranean with the rest. He had never seen Africa, he explained to himself.

Daphne was of the party too. (Possibly the reader has already identified her as one of the three grass widows.) She had despatched Master Brian Vereker Carr to Belton for a season, and joined the Hiltons' party four weeks ago. The great new house in town stood empty. After her husband's bombshell in February, she had felt bound to do something to show her spirit. Another strike was brewing in the north, so doubtless her lord and master would soon be congenially occupied in starving his dependents into submission. Meanwhile her duty was to herself. Domestic ties were at an end. She would enjoy life.

She experienced no difficulty in the execution of this project. Every one seemed anxious to assist her. Despite precautions, the fact that all was not well in the house of Juggernaut was public property; and the usual distorted rumours on the subject had set out upon their rounds, going from strength to strength in the process. Daphne was soon made conscious that people were sorry for her. Frivolous but warm-hearted women were openly sympathetic. Large, clumsy men indicated by various awkward and furtive acts of kindness that they too understood the situation, but were too tactful to betray the fact. Altogether Daphne was in a fair way to becoming spoiled. With all her faults no one had ever yet been able or inclined to call her anything but unaffected and natural; but about this time she began to assume the virtuous and long-suffering demeanour of a *femme incomprise*. She was only twenty-four, and few of us are able to refuse a martyr's crown when it is pressed upon us.

Only her monosyllabic host—"The Silent Knight," his friends called him, denying him his baronetcy in their zest for the nickname—was unable to appreciate the extreme delicacy of the situation. He was a plain man, Arthur Hilton, and hated mysteries.

"Why isn't that girl at home, lookin' after her husband, Ethel?" he inquired of his wife one morning.

"I think she is happier with us, dear," replied Lady Hilton with immense solemnity.

The Silent Knight emitted a subdued rumble, indicative of a desire to argue the point, and continued—

"Happier—eh? Hasn't she got a baby, or somethin', somewhere? What the dev——"

"Yes, dear, she *has* a baby," replied his wife, rolling up her fine eyes to the ceiling; "but I fear she has not been very fortunate in her marriage. She was the daughter of a country clergyman—*dreadfully* poor, I understand—and wanted to improve the family fortunes. There were eight or nine of them, so she took this old man."

The Silent Knight's engine fairly raced.

"Old man be damned!" he observed with sudden heat. "Sorry, my dear! But Jack Carr can't be more than forty-six. I'm forty-eight. I'm an old man, too, I suppose! Back number—eh? One foot in the grave! You lookin' about for my successor, Ethel—what?"

It was useless to explain to this obtuse and uxorious critic that a young and sensitive girl cannot be expected to dwell continuously beneath the roof of a husband whose tastes are not her tastes, who has merely married her to keep house for him, and who neglects her into the bargain. Not that this prevented Lady Hilton from endeavouring to do so. When she had finished, her husband knocked the ashes out of his pipe, and remarked—

"Can't make you women out. Here's old Juggernaut—best man *I* ever came across, and as kind as they make 'em—marries this little fool of a girl and gives her everything she wants; and she goes off and leaves him slavin' at his work, while she comes trapesin' about here with a collection of middle-aged baby-snatchers and knock-kneed loafers. Next thing, she'll start flirting; then she'll fall in love with some bounder, and then there'll be the devil of a mess. Rotten, I call it! Don't know what wives are comin' to nowadays. Have *you* goin' off next, Ethel—leavin' me and the kids, and becomin' a Suffragette—what?"

After this unusual outburst the Silent Knight throttled himself down and said no more, all efforts on his wife's part to lure him into ground less favourable to his point of view proving fruitless. He merely smoked his pipe and emitted an obstinate purr.

"But what else can one expect, dearest," Ethel Hilton confided to a friend afterwards, "if one marries an internal combustion engine?"

II.

Neither was Mrs Carfrae satisfied to find her beloved Johnny Carr's lawful wife disporting herself in her present company. One afternoon she heckled Jim Carthew upon the subject, to the extreme embarrassment of that loyal youth. The rest of the party had gone off to explore Algiers, and were safely occupied for the present with the contemplation of the passing show—ghostlike Moors in snowy burnouses, baggy-trousered members of that last resort of broken men, *La Légion Étrangère*, and spectacled French officials playing at colonies.

Mrs Carfrae's chair had been wheeled into a corner of the open courtyard which occupied the middle of the Hôtel Magnifique, as far as possible from the base of operations of a pseudo-Tzigane orchestra which discoursed languorous melody twice daily; and its occupant was dispensing to Carthew what Thémistocle was accustomed to describe as "some five o'clock."

"So you are leaving us, Mr Carthew," observed the hostess.

"Yes, the day after to-morrow. There is a boat then. I must go. There is trouble brewing in the colliery districts again, and Sir John wants me."

"And you will take Lady Carr with you?"

"Oh no," said Carthew, flushing. "We are not together. I mean, it is not on her account that I am here."

"So I have noticed," said Mrs Carfrae dryly.

"I was invited here by the Hiltons," explained Carthew, and plunged into a sea of unnecessary corroborative details. "I was quite surprised to find Lady Carr here," he colluded. "I thought she was in London."

"And why," inquired the old lady with sudden ferocity, "is she not at Belton, with her man?"

The faithful Carthew stiffened at once.

"I expect Sir John sent her out here to have a good time," he said. "He could not get away himself, so——"

Mrs Carfrae surveyed him for a moment over her glasses.

"You are a decent lad," she observed rather unexpectedly.

This testimonial had its desired effect of reducing Carthew to silence, and Mrs Carfrae continued—

"You have been with John Carr for some time now, have you not?"

"Yes; ever since I came down from Cambridge."

"How did you meet him? He does not take to young men readily as a rule, so I have heard."

"I had the luck," said Carthew, his eye kindling with historic reminiscence, "to meet him at dinner one night at the end of my third year, at my tutor's. Sir John was an old member of the College, staying there for the week-end. He told us at dinner that he had come up to find a good ignorant unlicked cub to help him with his work, who could be trusted to obey an order when he received one and act for himself when he did not. Those were his exact words, I remember."

"Ay, they would be. Go on."

"This unlicked cub was to come and be a sort of general factotum to him, and do his best to help him with his work, and so on. Marvyn (the tutor) and I sat trying to think of likely men, and finally we made a list of about six, whom Sir John said he would run his eye over next day. After that I went off to bed. I remember wishing to myself that I had taken a better degree and been a more prominent member of the College: then I might have had a shot for this berth, instead of going into a solicitor's office. But as things were, I hadn't the cheek. Well, do you know, Jug—Sir John came round to me next morning——"

"Before breakfast, I doubt."

"Yes, as a matter of fact I had just come in from a run and was sitting down to it. He asked if he might have some: and after that he offered me—*ME!*—this grand billet. Of course I jumped at it—who wouldn't, to be with a man like that?—and I have been with him ever since."

"Well," said Mrs Carfrae, "you should know more of the creature than most folk. What is your unbiassed opinion of him?"

"I think he is the greatest man that ever lived," said the boy simply.

"Hmph! As a matter of fact, he has less sense than anybody I ever knew," replied the old lady calmly. "Still, you are entitled to your opinion. I need not trouble you with an account of *my* first meeting with him: it occurred a long time ago. But—wheel me a little nearer the sun, laddie: this corner is a thing too shady—it may interest you to know that he would have been my son-in-law to-day, had it not been—" she paused for a moment, very slightly—"for the uncertainty of human life. And that is why I take something more than a passing interest in the doings of that slim-bodied, brown-eyed, tow-headed hempie that he married on. And that brings me to the point. Laddie, those two are getting over-far apart, and it must be *stopped*!"

"Yes, but how?" inquired Carthew dismally. "I understand that entering a lions' den just before dinner-time is wisdom itself compared with interfering between husband and wife."

A quiver passed through Elspeth Carfrae's frail body, and she straightened herself in her chair.

"I am a havering and doited old woman," she announced with great decision, "and no one takes any notice of what I say or do. But I tell you this. So long as my old heart beats and my old blood runs, I shall be perfectly willing to face every single lion in the Zoo, gin it will bring a moment's happiness to Johnny Carr. The lad deserves a good wife. Once he nearly got one—the best and fairest in all the world—but God decided otherwise. Now he has got another: I know her: she has the right stuff in her. And when I leave this hotel next week I am going to take her with me, in her right mind, and deliver her to her man!"

The old lady concluded her intimation with tremendous vigour. Carthew sat regarding her with a mixture of reverence and apprehension.

"You are going to—to speak to her about it?" he asked.

"I am," replied Mrs Carfrae, with vigour.

"I would do anything," said Carthew awkwardly, "to put things right between those two. But supposing you make your attempt, Mrs Carfrae, and—and fail, won't it make matters worse?"

"Much," said Mrs Carfrae calmly. "If I interfere, unsuccessfully, I doubt if either of them will ever speak to me again. That is the usual and proper fate of busybodies. But—I am going to risk it!... Run me back to my sitting-room now, and call Janet. I hear your friends yattering out there in the verandah. They will be through with Algiers."

CHAPTER FIFTEEN.

JIM CARTHEW.

But our two conspirators were fated, for all practical purposes, to exchange *rôles*.

The following evening Daphne and Carthew found themselves sitting together in the hotel garden after dinner. A great moon shone from a velvety African sky; the scented breeze rustled in the palms; and the music of the band drifted to their ears in intermittent waves.

It was one of those nights which touch the imagination and stir the emotions—a night upon which human nature expands to its utmost limits. A night upon which passion awakes, and long-cherished secrets are whispered into suddenly receptive ears. Also a night upon which the devil stalks abroad. Dido resided a few miles from this spot. It was probably a night like this that made the Fourth Book of the Æneid worth writing.

If Dido failed to resist such environment, what of Daphne? She was young; she was intensely susceptible to such things as moonshine and soft music; and, disguise the fact from herself as she might, she was lonely. It is not altogether surprising that, as she surveyed this silent comely youth who lolled beside her eyeing the glittering Mediterranean in stolid abstraction, she should unconsciously have acquiesced in the first of the dismal prognostications of that splenetic but clear-sighted baronet, Sir Arthur Hilton. Jim Carthew had occupied Daphne's thoughts a good deal of late, and to-night she felt suddenly conscious of a desire to flirt with him.

"Cigarette, please!" she commanded.

Carthew silently handed her his case, and allowed her to select and light her own cigarette—a prodigal waste of opportunity, as any professional philanderer could have told her.

"A penny for your thoughts!" continued Daphne pertly.

Carthew, struck by a peculiar note in her voice, turned and looked at her. He was met by a provocative glance. There was a brief silence. Then he said gravely—

"I don't think you are quite cut out for that sort of thing, Lady Carr."

Daphne, feeling as if she had received a whip-lash in the face, stared at him, white with anger. Then she rose stiffly from her seat and moved towards the hotel. Carthew did not stir.

"Don't go," he said. "We may as well have this out."

Daphne stood irresolute. Then curiosity got the better of virtuous indignation, and she sat down again.

"Will you kindly tell me," she said, "what you mean by talking in that way?"

Carthew's honest eyes lingered on her face in a manner which she could not fathom. Did the man love her, or was he pitying her, or was he merely indulging in sarcastic reflections at her expense? Whatever his motives, he had a knack of compelling attention.

Presently he began to speak.

"I wonder," he said, as if talking to himself, "why men and women are made as they are? Why does A love B, while B worships C, who cares for no one in the world but himself? And why does D insist on confusing things still further by not quite knowing what he—she—wants? I wonder! They say there is enough money spent in charity every year to supply the needs of every poor person living, but so much is misapplied that many have to go without. I think it is the same with human affection. There is so much true love going about in this world—enough to keep all of us well-nourished and contented. But what a lot of it goes to waste! There is so much overlapping! *Why*, I wonder? It is a difficult business, Life, Daphne."

He had never called her Daphne before, but neither of them seemed to notice the familiarity.

"We're a contrary crew, we mortals," he continued presently. "Here we are, you and I, sitting in the moonshine inaugurating a flirtation, though neither of us cares a snap for the other—in that way. Why, I wonder? I think it is partly due to pride—wounded pride. You are angry with your husband——"

Daphne, who was methodically picking her cigarette to pieces, looked up indignantly.

"I'm *not*!" she said hotly.

"Oh yes, you are," replied Carthew. "You think you are not, but you are. You try to believe that you are merely indifferent to him, but you are not. As for me, I am angry too—piqued—furious—jealous—raging—I admit it—with a girl whom I dislike intensely. The more I see of her the more selfish, affected, shallow, unwomanly I see her to be. And yet—I *love* her! Why? Why? Why? People tell me she is heartless, soulless, sordid, greedy, vulgar—everything, in fact. Sometimes I feel they are right. Still—" he dropped his head into his hands and continued doggedly—"what difference does that make to *me*? I love her!... She cared for me once, too. She told me so—and she meant it! Perhaps if I had been a little more patient with her I might have kept her, and—and helped her a bit. Perhaps that was what I was sent into the world for—to make things easier for Nina. I could have done so much for her, too. I could have made a woman of her. She has her soft side: I know: I have seen it. No other man can say that. Meanwhile," he continued with a whimsical smile, "I am trying to solace myself by allowing you to flirt with me——"

Daphne drew her breath sharply.

"And you are not very good at it," concluded Carthew unexpectedly.

"You are very candid," said Daphne frigidly.

"Yes, but I speak truth. You are not good at it. Flirtation is a crooked business, and you are straight, *mon amie*. But wounded pride is not the only thing that has drawn us here together. Something else is responsible. We are both craving for sympathy. 'A fellow-feeling,' you know! I know all about *you*," he continued quickly, as Daphne's lips parted. "You are by way of being a neglected wife; and since Nina has informed me that she has told you all about *me*, I suppose you regard me as a bit of a derelict too. Well, we have forgathered. What is going to happen next?"

Daphne was silent. She certainly did not know what was going to happen next. Her ideas on all subjects were a little jumbled at this moment. Presently Carthew continued—

"We came together," he said gently, "just when each of us required a little companionship and sympathy; and we got it. I think our chance encounter on the highway of life has been a very profitable one. But it has served its turn. Our roads diverge again. We must part company, little comrade."

"Why?"

Daphne spoke this time in a tremulous whisper. A great wave of loneliness was surging up towards her.

"Because," said Carthew's deep voice, "it is the only thing to do. Think what may happen if we travel on together too far. At present we are safe. I love some one else, and so do—and you are angry with some one else, let us say. Supposing, since the girl I love does not love me any more—supposing I ceased to love her? It seems hopeless, incredible, I admit; but it might conceivably happen. And supposing you gave up being angry with—some one else, and became indifferent to him, where might we not find ourselves? Our sheet-anchor—our platonic sheet-anchor—would be gone. And sooner than send you adrift among cross-currents, little Daphne, I prefer to forgo the only friendship in this world that I really value. You are too delicate and too fragrant to be tarnished by common gossip, so I am going away to-morrow. Let us say good-bye now—you beautiful thing!"

Daphne looked up at him in amazement. But there was no passion in his face—only an infinite tenderness. To him she was simply a woman—one of the rarest and fairest of her sex, perhaps, but still simply a woman—whom to succour, without expectation or desire of reward, was the merest courtesy on the part of any knight worthy of the name. This was a man! Daphne bowed her head, wondering dimly and scornfully at the insensate folly of Nina Tallentyre.

"Shall we go back to the hotel?" asked Carthew at length.

There was no reply. Turning to note the cause, he saw something bright and glistening fall upon his companion's hand—then another. With innate loyalty and delicacy he averted his gaze, and surveyed the distant seascape with laborious intentness.

Meanwhile Daphne sat on, her head still bowed. Through the night air, from the hotel verandah, there came the refrain of a waltz. It was called *Caressante*, she thought. Carthew knew it too, and dug his teeth into his lower lip. Waltzes have an unfortunate habit of reviving the memories of yester year.

"Don't go in," said Daphne at length. "Don't leave me—I can't bear it!" Her voice broke.

Suddenly Carthew turned to her.

"Daphne"—his voice was low, but he spoke with intense earnestness—"you are lonely, I know, and sad; and you are too proud to own it. Shall I tell you who is more lonely and more sad, and too proud to own it too?"

"Do you mean—" were Jim Carthew's good resolutions crumbling?—"yourself?"

"No, no,—nothing of the kind. I mean—your husband!" Then he continued hurriedly—

"Daphne, if I thought I was leaving you to real loneliness and inevitable wretchedness, I—well, perhaps I shouldn't go away at all. But I—I am not needed. Little friend, you have the finest husband in all the world, waiting for you. For all his domineering ways, he is shy, and wants knowing. You have never discovered that. I don't believe you know him a bit. It all comes of having begun wrong. Go back and study him. Give him a fair chance! Give yourself a fair chance! You and I have always been friends: will you promise me this? Go back, and give yourself and Jack Carr another chance."

Half an hour ago Daphne would have smiled sceptically and indulgently upon such a suggestion. But this lonely, loyal spirit had touched her. She felt she would like to please him.

"Very well," she said. "I promise. No, *I can't!*" The memory of some ancient wrong suddenly surged up in her, swamping the generous impulse. "*I can't!*"

"Why?"

"Jack is so hard," she said. "Look at the way he treats those in his power. His workpeople, his——"

Carthew laughed, positively boisterously.

"Hard? Jack Carr hard? Listen," he said, "and I will tell you a secret."

When he had finished Daphne stood up, white and gleaming in the moonlight, and gave him her hand.
"All right," she said softly—"it's a bargain. I go home to-morrow."

BOOK THREE.
THE LIGHTING OF THE CANDLE.

CHAPTER SIXTEEN.

SOME ONE TO CONFIDE IN.

Certainly matters were in a serious state in the Mirkley Colliery district. The whole industrial world was unsettled at the time. There had been trouble on the railways, and a great shipyard strike was threatening in Scotland. Most serious of all, the men were beginning to defy their own leaders. They had taken to organising little sectional revolts of their own, and Employers' Federations were beginning to ask how they could be expected to ratify treaties with Trades Union officials who were unable to hold their own followers to the terms of agreements concluded on their behalf.

The Mirkley district had caught the infection. The mischief had originated at Marbledown and Cherry Hill, the immediate cause of the trouble being a simple question of weights and measures.

The ordinary collier is paid by piecework—so much per ton for all the coal he hews. This coal is carefully weighed on coming to the surface, and to ensure fair play all round the weight is checked by the men's own representative at the pit-head. Now just as all is not gold that glitters, so all that comes to the surface of the earth from the interior of a coal-pit is not necessarily coal. A good deal of it is shale, stone, and the like—technically summarised as "dirt"—and has to be sorted out from the genuine article by a bevy of young ladies retained at some expense for the purpose. As colliers are paid for hewing coal and not dirt, the mine managers, reckoning one hundredweight as the average weight of dirt in a tub of coal, had been in the habit, when making out their pay-sheets, of deducting this amount from the total weight of each load brought to the surface. *Hinc lacrymæ*. The man in the pit claimed that he should be paid for all he sent up the shaft, alleging that it was impossible to separate coal from dirt at the face, and that dirt was quite as difficult to hew as coal. To this those in authority replied that a collier is a man who is employed to hew coal and not dirt, and that as such he should only be paid for the coal he hewed. It was a nice point, and so high did feeling run upon the subject, and so fierce was the demeanour of their *employés*, that pliable Mr Aymer and pusillanimous Mr Montague yielded to the extent of fifty-six pounds, and henceforth each toiler in Cherry Hill and Marbledown Colliery was debited with one half instead of one whole hundredweight of dirt per tub.

Encouraged by the success of their colleagues, the men employed at Sir John Carr's great pit at Belton proffered a similar request. But though the request was the same its recipient was different. Sir John greeted the deputation with disarming courtesy, and announced in a manner which precluded argument that on the question of the owners' right to deduct for dirt in each load he would not yield one inch. On this the deputation rashly changed their ground and alleged that the toll of one hundredweight per tub was excessive. Whereupon Juggernaut whisked them off without delay to the pit-head. Here a minute examination was made of the contents of the next ten tubs of coal which came to the surface, and it was found that, so far from defrauding his *employés*, Juggernaut was defrauding himself, for the average weight of dirt in each tub was not one hundred and twelve but one hundred and thirty pounds.

"You see, Mr Brash?" said Sir John cheerfully. "I am afraid you have all been in my debt to the extent of eighteen pounds of coal per tub for quite a considerable number of years. However, if you will be sensible and go back to work, we will call it a wash-out and say no more about it."

Then he departed to London.

But he had to return. The half-hundredweight of Cherry Hill and Marbledown outbalanced Belton's plain facts and ocular demonstrations. The Pit "came out" *en masse*, against the advice and without the authority of their Union officials; and for two or three weeks men loafed up and down the long and unlovely street which comprised Belton village, smoking their pipes and organising occasional whippet-races against the time when the despot who employed them should be pleased to open negotiations.

But the despot made no sign. Presently pipes were put away for want of tobacco, and whippet-racing ceased for want of stake-money. Then came a tightening of belts and a setting of teeth, and men took to sitting on their heels against walls and fences, punctuating recrimination by expectoration, through another four long and pitiful weeks.

Not so utterly pitiful though. For a wonderful thing happened. The unknown benefactor of the strike of seven years ago came to life again. Every morning the postman delivered to the wife of each man in Belton a packet containing a ration of tea, sugar, and (once a week) bacon. Coal, too, was distributed by a mysterious motor-lorry, bearing a London number-plate, and manned by two sardonic Titans, who deposited their sacks and answered no questions. So there was no actual destitution in the village. But there was no beer, and no tobacco, and no money. Women and children can live for an amazingly long time on tea and sugar eked out by a little bread, but man is the slave of an exacting stomach, and requires red meat for the upkeep of his larger frame. The whippets, too, had to be considered; and when, after an interval of seven weeks, a notice went up on the gates of the pit buildings, intimating that all who returned to work on the following Monday would be reinstated without question, Belton Colliery put its pride into its empty pocket and came back as one man.

But the danger was not over yet, as Juggernaut well knew. For the moment the men were subdued by sheer physical exhaustion. The first pay-day would fill their bellies and put some red blood into their passions. And it was certain information, received on this head at the Pit offices, that sent Sir John Carr home to Belton Hall with knitted brow and tight-set mouth one wintry Saturday afternoon in early April, a fortnight after the men had resumed work.

He stepped out of the big motor and walked into the cheerful fire-lit hall. He stood and gazed reflectively upon the crackling logs as the butler removed his heavy coat. But the removal of the coat seemed to take no weight from his shoulders. He felt utterly lonely and unhappy. Was he growing old, he wondered. He was not accustomed to feel like this. He did not usually shrink from responsibility, or desire a shoulder to lean upon, but at this moment he suddenly felt the want of some one to consult. No; consult was not the word! He could have consulted Carthew. In fact he had just done so, for Carthew had returned from his holiday two days before. What he wanted was some one to *confide* in. With a sudden tightening of the heart he thought of a confidante who might have been at his side then, had things been different—a confidante who would have sat upon the arm of his chair and bidden him play the man and fear nothing. Well, doubtless he would play the man and fear nothing, and doubtless he would win again as he had done before. But—*cui bono*? What doth it profit a man———?

He wondered where she was. Yachting on the Mediterranean, or frivolling on the Riviera. Or perhaps she was back in London by this time, ordering her spring clothes and preparing for another butterfly season. At any rate she was not at Belton Hall. Whose fault was that?...

Had he been lacking in patience with her? Had he treated her too much like a refractory board-meeting?... A little fool? Doubtless; but then, so were most women. And she was very young, after all....

"Will you take anything before dinner, sir?" inquired a respectful voice in his ear. "Tea? Whisky-and———"

"No, thank you, Graves. Is Master Brian in the nursery?"

"Yes, sir."

"I will go up shortly and say good-night to him. Meanwhile I shall be in the study if Mr Carthew or any one calls for me. But I don't want to be disturbed at present."

A minute later he opened the door of the apartment, half library, half smoking-room, which he called his study. It was in darkness, but for the cheerful glow of the fire.

As Juggernaut closed the door behind him and felt for the electric-light switch, there came a rustling from the depths of a great oak settle which formed a right-angle with the projecting mantelpiece; and a slim straight figure stood suddenly upright, silhouetted against the ruddy glare.

"Daphne!"

"Yes—me!" replied an extremely small voice.

CHAPTER SEVENTEEN.

THE CANDLE LIT.

There is no more disagreeable sensation in this world than that furnished by a sudden encounter with some one with whom we are on "awkward" terms. Most people know what it is to cross the street to avoid an old friend, or to dodge into a shop in order to escape the necessity of inflicting or receiving the cut direct. Very often the origin of the quarrel has been forgotten or ceased to be of real moment, but the awkwardness endures. Oftener still a reconciliation would be welcomed on both sides; but pride, pride, pride intervenes.

Now the best solvent of stubborn obstinacy is a sense of humour. As Juggernaut stood in the darkness, surveying the embarrassed little figure before him—in his eyes Daphne, five feet seven in her stockings, was always "little"—and feeling acutely conscious on his own part of an irresistible desire to shuffle with his feet, he suddenly and most providentially broke into one of his rare laughs—a laugh of quiet and unforced enjoyment.

Apparently this was not quite what Daphne expected.

"What is the matter?" she inquired. Her voice quavered pathetically, for she was highly wrought.

"I couldn't help thinking," said her husband, "of an episode in the history of two old friends of mine. They had been engaged for about three months, when they quarrelled—severely. They parted company for ever, and whenever he or she saw the other upon the horizon, he or she fled. However, after about six weeks of this sort of thing they were taken by surprise. One day the man saw the girl advancing straight upon him down the street, quite oblivious of his proximity. He dived into the nearest shop, which happened to be a baby-linen establishment—"

Daphne gave a sudden gurgle of laughter.

"—And when the girl walked in, two minutes later," concluded Juggernaut, "to match some silk, she found her late beloved diligently sampling Berlin wool. That did it! The sense of humour of that young couple came to their rescue, Daphne, and they walked out of the shop hand-in-hand, not caring a dump for anybody. To my knowledge they have never had a quarrel since. You see the reason why I laughed just now?"

Daphne sighed comfortably.

"Yes," she said. The tension of the situation was relaxed.

"I want to—to talk to you, Jack," she continued, considerably heartened.

"Certainly," replied Juggernaut, with a slight return of his board-room air. "I'll turn the light on."

"Please don't," said Daphne hastily. "I would rather talk in the dark. Will you sit down on the settle?"

Juggernaut obeyed silently. The firelight played upon his face, showing the clear-cut lines of his mouth and his tired eyes. Daphne stood erect before him, keeping her face in the shadow. She had removed her hat and furs, and her thick hair caught the light fantastically.

"Jack," she began, industriously scrutinising the vista of the room reflected by an ancient convex mirror hanging on the far wall, "I want to say something. I want to say that I am sorry. I have done you an injustice. I always thought you were a hard man, and I have discovered that you are not. In fact," she continued with a flicker of a smile, "I have found out that you are very much the other thing." She paused.

"May I ask for chapter and verse?" said Juggernaut.

"*Yes!*" The old Daphne flashed forth. "Here are you, fighting all these men with one hand, giving no quarter, and all that sort of thing—" Juggernaut stirred suddenly in his seat—"and feeding the women and children with the other! Aren't you, now?" She pointed an accusing finger.

"Since you tax me with it—yes," said her husband.

Daphne turned upon him impulsively, with the firelight full on her face.

"Jack," she said softly, "it was splendid of you!"

He looked up and saw that her eyes were glowing. She came a step nearer, and her head drooped prettily. "And I'm sorry if I have been unfair to you, Jack," she continued. "I—I thought you were just a feelingless sort of man, whose work was his world, and who cared for nothing but himself and what he had in view, and regarded women as merely useful things to keep house, and have babies, and so on. But now I *know* that I was wrong. There is more of you than that. Being me, I had to tell you."

She ended with a little catch in her voice. She had made her effort. She had humbled herself, and in so doing she had laid herself open to the cruellest of rebuffs. She waited tremulously. A hard word, a scornful smile, even silence now—and two lives would fall asunder for ever.

But the wheels of Juggernaut had never passed over a woman.

"Will you sit down?" said Sir John gently.

He made room for her, and she sank down beside him, leaning her head against the high back of the settle and gazing unwinkingly into the fire. She was conscious now that this man was overflowing with tenderness towards her, but she would not look him in the face yet.

"How did you find out about the rations to the women?" he enquired presently.

Daphne told him.

"But you mustn't blame Jim Carthew," she said in conclusion. "He simply *had* to tell me."

"Where did you see him?"

"Last week, in Algiers. In fact, he brought me home; but I made him promise not to tell you I was in London. He *is* a good sort!" she added irrelevantly.

"In what way?" asked her husband curiously.

Daphne turned and surveyed him.

"Would you be angry if I told you—jealous, I mean?"

"What right have I to be angry or jealous?" said Juggernaut simply. "In what way," he repeated, "has Carthew been showing that he is a good sort?"

"Well, in bringing me his troubles. That always makes a conquest of any woman, you know. And in letting me take my troubles to him. A woman always *has* to take a trouble to a man, Jack, when all is said and done—even if he is only the family solicitor!" she concluded hurriedly. She had suddenly skated on to thin ice, and she knew it. The man to whom she should have taken her troubles had not been there to receive them.

"So Jim Carthew has his troubles like the rest of us?" said Juggernaut.

"Yes, and I never suspected how he felt about them," said Daphne. "He is fearfully reserved about the things he really feels, although he babbles enough about the things he doesn't. So, when I was in trouble——"

"What was your trouble?"

"I was lonely," said the girl.

Juggernaut drew his breath sharply.

"I am glad you had some one to be kind to you," he said.

Then came a long pause—the sort of pause which either brings a discussion to an end or begets another, longer and more intimate. We all know them.

Finally Daphne braced herself.

"Jack," she said, "I want to say something more. I didn't mean to: I have said all I came here to say. But I must say this too—now or never. I—I—I was wrong to marry you, Jack. I didn't love you, but I thought it didn't matter. I felt how divine it would be to be able to help the boys and Dad. That was all I considered. Then, when I began to go about, and meet new people, and make comparisons, I—found myself criticising you! *Me—you!*"

"I wouldn't be too indignant about it if I were you," said her husband.

He reached out deliberately for her hand, and continued his contemplation of the fire.

"Go on," he said.

Daphne, foolishly uplifted, continued—

"I used to think you rough and hard and unsympathetic. I began to prefer the men who buzzed round and murmured things in my ear. And when people began to pity me as a neglected wife, I—I encouraged them. I let women say catty things about you, and I let men make love to me. That sort of thing has been going on ever since the time"—Daphne's grip of her husband's hand tightened—"when you and I decided—to go our own ways. I don't mind telling you now that it was a pill for me, Jack. My pride——"

"It was a brutal act on my part," blazed out Juggernaut with sudden passion.

"No it *wasn't*: it was what I deserved!" insisted Daphne, whose nature did not permit her to be repentant by halves. "Well, anyhow, I determined to flirt in real earnest now. So I began to carry on in an experimental fashion. But I can't say it was much fun. Finally I did fall in love with a man, in a sort of way—don't hurt my hand, dear; it was only in a sort of way—and I let him see it. Well, I got a facer over *him*. One night, under the moon, I tried to flirt with him; and he—well, Jack, he fairly put me in my place!"

"What did he do?"

"He made me feel ashamed of myself."

"What did he say?"

"Not much that we need talk of now, except one thing."

"What was that?"

"He told me to go back to you."

"Why?"

"Because he said"—Daphne's voice dropped low—"that you loved me."

There was a long silence, until a live coal subsided in the grate. Then Juggernaut said—

"It was Carthew, I suppose."

Daphne nodded.

"Jack," she said, "Jim Carthew is the best friend that you and I possess."

"I know it."

They were silent again, until irrelevant Daphne enquired suddenly—

"Jack, what made you do that unpractical thing? The tea and sugar, I mean. It was only prolonging the strike: even *I* can see that."

"It didn't prolong the strike to any particular extent," said Juggernaut with decision. "Not that I care," he added with unusual inconsequence, "if it did. It made things no easier for the men; and it is with the men that the decision lies in cases of this kind."

"But it was so *unlike* you," persisted Daphne.

Her husband turned and regarded her quizzically.

"Was it?" he said, smiling. "We all have our weaknesses," he added. "Mine are women and children. I think," he went on with great deliberation, "that there is only one woman in this wide world who has ever suffered ill at my hands."

"And she is——"

"My wife! Listen," he continued rapidly, "while I make confession. You have spoken your piece bravely, Daphne. Now hear me mine."

He rose in his turn, and stood before his wife.

"I never knew or cared very much about women," he said. "I do not remember my mother, and I had no sisters, which probably accounts for a good deal. Also, I was brought up by a man among men, and I learned to read men and handle men to the exclusion of all else. I was given to understand that women did not matter. I was trained to regard them as a sort of inferior and unreliable variety of the male sex. So I confined my dealings to men, and I found so much joy in handling and mastering men that my eyes became closed to the fact that life could offer me anything else."

"But didn't you miss female society? Most men can't get on without *some*," said experienced Daphne.

"You can't miss what you have never had, little girl. Perhaps if I had encountered female society early in life——"

"But didn't you sometimes instinctively long for a woman to come and take charge of you? Most men are so helpless and messy by themselves."

"Sometimes," admitted Juggernaut almost reluctantly, "I did. But I put the notion from me."

"Shall I tell you why?" said Daphne quietly.

"I suppose it was because I didn't want to yield to a weakness."

"It was nothing of the kind," said Daphne with immense decision. "It was because you were *afraid*!"

"Afraid?"

"Yes—afraid! You would have nothing to do with women, because you told yourself you despised them. We were a waste of time, you said—an encumbrance! The real reason was that you feared us. Yes—feared! Success was the breath of life to you. You had always had your own way wherever you went. You were the great Sir John Carr—the strong man—Juggernaut! You had never been beaten. Why? Because you had never had the pluck to try conclusions with a woman. Your excuse was that you were a woman-hater, when all the time you were a woman-lover. You have just admitted it, impostor! You were afraid that where every man had failed to turn you from your own hard selfish way of life, a woman might succeed. And so you ran away, and you have been running ever since. There, my strong man, there's the truth for you!"

For once in his life Sir John Carr, the terror of deputations, the scourge of unsound logicians, the respectfully avoided of hecklers, had no answer ready. The reason was obvious: no answer was possible. The victory lay with Daphne. She leaned back in the settle and looked fearlessly up into her husband's face. For the first time in her life she felt maternal towards this man—twenty-two years her senior—just as old Mrs Carfrae had predicted. She was utterly and absolutely happy, too, for she had just realised that she and her husband had come together at last. They were one flesh. The time for tactful diplomacy and mutual accommodation and making allowances was over-past. No need now to guard the flame from sudden gusts and cross-winds. The candle was safely lighted, and, please God, it should burn steadily to its socket. The Safety Match had accomplished its task after all.

Then she gave a happy little sigh, for her husband's great arm was around her shoulders.

"All my life, Daphne," said his deep voice, "I have thought that the sweetest thing in this world was victory. Now I have just received my first defeat—you routed me, hip and thigh—and I am happier than I have ever been. Why?"

"Think!" commanded a muffled voice in the neighbourhood of his waistcoat.

Juggernaut obeyed. Then he continued, and his grip round Daphne grew stronger—

"I think I see. I married you because I wanted some one to keep my house in order and bear me a son. (That point of view did not endure long, I may say, for I fell in love with you on our honeymoon, and I have loved you ever since; but it was my point of view when I asked you to marry me.) I thought then that it would be a fair bargain if I gave you money and position in return for these things. We could not help living contentedly together, I considered, under the terms of such a logical and business-like contract as that. Well, I did not know then, what I know now, that logic and business are utterly valueless as a foundation for any contract between a man and a woman. The only thing that is the slightest use for the purpose is the most illogical and unbusiness-like thing in the whole wide world. And"—his iron features relaxed into a smile of rare sweetness—"I believe, I believe, *cara mia*, that you and I have found that thing—together." His voice dropped lower. "Have we, Daphne—my wife?"

Daphne raised her head, and looked her man full in the face.

"We have found it, O my husband," she said gravely—"at last!"

The door flew open suddenly. There was a gleam of electric light. Graves, the imperturbable, inclined respectfully before them.

"You are wanted outside, sir," he said, "badly!"

CHAPTER EIGHTEEN.

ATHANASIUS CONTRA MUNDUM.

A confused medley of men and women—not to mention the inevitable small boy element—was pouring up the road from Belton Pit in the direction of the Hall, which lay beyond the brow of the hill in a green hollow as yet unsullied by winding-wheels and waste-heaps. People who have made up their minds to do evil are usually in a hurry to get it over. Consequently our friends were advancing at a high rate of speed, keeping up their courage by giving forth unmelodious noises.

Juggernaut's prophecy had come true. The rebellion had been damped down by sheer starvation; and now that starvation was over-past, the rebellion was flaming out again with tenfold vigour. That fine unreasoning human instinct which under a certain degree of pressure bids logic and argument go hang, and impels us to go forth and break some one else's windows, held the reins that evening. As the night-shift assembled at the pit-head, what time the day-shift was being disgorged, a cageful at a time, from the depths below, a great and magnificent project suddenly hatched itself in the fertile brain of Mr Tom Winch, who had been haunting the neighbourhood on business connected with the propaganda of his own particular revolutionary organisation for the past six weeks. Now was his chance. Evil passions, hitherto dimmed by hunger and privation, were reviving. The men were ripe for any mischief. What they were asking for, reflected Mr Winch, was blood, or its equivalent, and a man to lead them to it.

Mr Winch was, to do him justice, a master of his own furtive trade. In five minutes his project was circulating through the throng. In fifteen the crowd had pledged itself to do something really big; and in half an hour most of the windows of the pit offices had been broken as a guarantee of good faith.

Having whetted its appetite on this *hors-d'œuvre*, the mob listened readily to Mr Winch's suggestion of a brisk walk to Belton Hall and a personal interview with its proprietor. The notion ran through the excited mass of humanity like fire through dry grass; and presently, as if from one spontaneous impulse, the advance on Belton Hall began. No one quite knew what he proposed to do when he got there, but the possibilities of the expedition were great. It was a picturesque procession, for every man carried a safety-lamp in one hand and a missile in the other. It was probably owing to the multiplicity of the twinkling points of light thus produced that no one observed the flickering halo of a solitary bicycle-lamp, as the machine which bore it slipped out from the side-door of the pit offices and silently stole away through the darkness, carrying a frightened messenger over the hill to Belton Hall.

It may here be noted that Mr Tom Winch, having despatched his avenging host upon its way, remained behind at headquarters—doubtless to superintend the subsequent operations with that degree of perspective which is so necessary to a good general. Mr Killick, an old acquaintance of ours, supported by his friend Mr Brash, led the procession.

"Supposin' the lodge gates is locked—what then?" enquired Mr Brash—ever a better critic than creator of an enterprise—as they trudged along the muddy road.

"We shall trample them down," replied Mr Killick, ever contemptuous of irritating detail.

But the lodge gates stood hospitably open. The lodge itself was shuttered and silent; and the procession, pausing momentarily to deliver a hilarious and irregular volley of small coal, proceeded on its way.

Up the long avenue they tramped. There were electric lamps at intervals, intended for the guidance of strange coachmen on dinner-party nights. These were all ablaze. Evidently Juggernaut was expecting friends.

Five minutes later our glorious company of apostles rounded the last turn in the avenue, and the broad Elizabethan *façade* of Belton Hall loomed up before them. Every window was alight.

A flagged and balustraded terrace ran along the whole frontage of the Hall. In the middle of the balustrade was a gap, where a broad flight of shallow stone steps led down to a velvety lawn three hundred years old. Most of the crowd knew that lawn and terrace well. The grounds at Belton were constantly and freely granted for miners' *fêtes*, political demonstrations, and the like. On these occasions a band was nearly always playing upon the terrace, and not infrequently post-prandial orations were outpoured from the rostrum formed by the stone steps upon the heads of a gorged and tolerant audience on the grass below.

To-night no band was playing; but at the head of the steps—motionless, upright, inflexible—stood a solitary figure. It was the master of the house, waiting to receive his guests—one against four hundred.

But to one who knew, the odds were not overwhelming. In fact, provided that the crowd possessed no resolute leader, the chances were slightly in favour of the figure on the steps. One man with his wits about him has two great advantages over a crowd. In the first place, he knows exactly what he is going to do, and, in the second, he knows exactly what the crowd is going to do. The crowd knows neither. It is impossible to foretell how a single individual will behave upon emergency: the human temperament varies too widely. But there is nothing in the world so normal or conventional as a crowd. Mankind in the lump is a mere puppet in the hands of the law of averages. Given, as noted above, a resolute leader, the conditions are changed. The leader imbues the crowd with a portion of his own spirit, and creates an instinct of unanimity. Then the odds are once more in favour of the crowd; for now it is a resolute will, all alone, pitted against a resolute will with force behind it.

Sir John Carr knew all this. He had studied men all his life; and as he stood silent and observant, surveying the surging multitude at his feet—it had flowed to the base of the steps now—he noted that there was no leader in particular. The crowd were acting under the influence of blind impulse, and, if properly handled, could be swayed about and sent home.

Presently the hubbub ceased, and the men stood gazing upward, fingering lumps of coal and waiting for some one to fire the first shot.

"Good evening, ladies and gentlemen," observed Juggernaut. [The ladies, be it noted, constituted the front row of the assemblage, their cavaliers having modestly retired a few paces under their employer's passionless scrutiny.] "If you have come to serenade me, I shall have pleasure presently in sending you out some refreshment. If you have merely come to burn the house down, I strongly advise you to go home and think twice about it."

The recipients of this piece of advice were undoubtedly a little taken aback. Playful badinage was the last thing they had expected. They murmured uneasily one to another, debating suitable retorts. Presently a shrill female voice opened fire.

"Tyrant!"

"Money-grubber!" corroborated another voice.

"Who starves women and children?" shrieked a third.

"Yah! Booh!" roared the crowd, taking heart.

"Chuck some of his own coals at 'im!" was the frantic adjuration of a foolish virgin who had already expended all her ammunition against the shutters of the gate-lodge.

A lump of something black and crystalline sang past Juggernaut's head, and struck a richly glowing stained-glass window twenty feet behind him. There was a sharp crash and a silvery tinkle, followed by a little gasp from the crowd. The first shot had been fired. Juggernaut knew well that a broadside was imminent, and countered swiftly. In the startled silence which succeeded the destruction of the great window—it had lighted the staircase at Belton for generations—his voice rang out like a trumpet.

"Listen to me!" he cried. "You have a grievance. You have come up here to square accounts with me. You think you have right on your side: I think it is on mine. Both of us are spoiling for a fight. In our present frame of mind nothing else will satisfy us. Now here is a fair offer. Send up any two men you like out of that multitude down there, and I will take them on, both together or one after the other, as you please. I am rising forty-seven, but if I fail to drop either of your representatives over this balustrade, back where he came from, inside of five minutes, I promise to remit the dues on that odd hundredweight that you are making all this to do about. Is it a bargain, gentlemen?"

He had struck the right note. The low, angry murmuring suddenly ceased, and a great wave of Homeric laughter rolled over the crowd. The British collier has his faults, but within his limits he is a sportsman. He appreciates pluck.

"Good lad!" roared a voice out of the darkness. Then there fell another silence.

"I am waiting, gentlemen," said Juggernaut presently.

But he had to continue waiting. His audience, as previously noted, were sportsmen within limits. The limits, alas! in those soft days are too often the coursing of a half-blinded rabbit, or the backing of a horse in a race which will not be witnessed by the backer. It is always gratifying to be invited to participate in a sporting event, but there is a difference between a seat on the platform and a stance in the arena. Getting hurt gratuitously is slipping into the *index expurgatorius* of modern field sports.

Men began to look sheepishly at one another. One or two had started forward instinctively, but the impulse died away. A humourist was heard imploring his friends to hold him back. There was something unutterably grim about the towering figure up on the terrace. Democracy and the equality of mankind to the contrary, Jack usually recognises his master when it comes to a pinch. No Jack seemed to desire advancement on this occasion.

Juggernaut waited for another minute. He wanted the silence to sink in. He wanted the crowd to feel ridiculous. That object achieved, he proposed to turn his visitors to the right-about and send them home. He had been through this experience before, and felt comparatively sure of his ground.

Provided, that is, that one thing did not occur. There were women present.

Now women are exempt from the law of averages: the sex snaps its fingers at computations based upon laboriously compiled statistics. If the women—or more likely a woman—gave the men a lead, anything might happen. And just as Juggernaut uplifted his voice to pronounce a valediction, the disaster befel.

"Now go home," he began. "You are not yourselves to-night. Go home, and think things over. Consult the older men: I see none of them here. If you are of the same mind to-morrow, I promise to——"

"Call yourselves men? Cowards! cowards! cowards! One of *us* is worth the lot of you!"

A woman, with a shawl over her head and a child in her arms, had mounted half-way up the steps, and was addressing the mob below. Sir John recognised her as Mrs Brash, a quiet little person as a rule.

"Come up, chaps!" she shrieked. "Are you going to let him stamp on us *all*? Look at his fine house, and his electrics, and his marble steps and all!" [They were plain freestone, but let that pass.] "Where did he get 'em all? From *us*—us that he has starved and clemmed this last two months! Are you afraid of him—the lot of you? Great hulking cowards! I see you, Brash, hiding there! Isn't there *one* man here?"

"Yes—by *God* there is!"

With a bound, Killick, the brooding visionary, the Utopian Socialist, was at the top of the steps, brandishing a pit-prop and haranguing his comrades. There was no stopping him. Mrs Brash had fired the train and Killick was the explosion. His words gushed out—hot, passionate, delirious. The man's sense of proportion, always unstable, was gone entirely. He burned with the conviction of his own wrongs and those of his fellows. *Nobilis ira* gave him eloquence. He laid violent hands upon wealth and power and greed and tyranny, and flung them one by one down the steps on to the heads of his hearers. Most of what he said was entirely irrelevant; a great deal more was entirely untrue; but it served. For the moment Sir John Carr stood for all the injustice and cruelty that strength has ever inflicted upon weakness. Every word told. The mob was aflame at last. They hung upon Killick's fiery sentences, surging ever more closely round the steps. The next wave, Juggernaut saw, would bring them in a flood upon the terrace; and then—what? He thought coolly and rapidly. There was Daphne to consider—also little Brian. Daphne, he knew, was close by, standing with beating heart behind the curtains of the library window. He had forbidden her to come farther. Perhaps, though, she had been sensible, and taken the opportunity of this delay to slip away. Of course, of course.

There was a movement beside him, and he realised that his education in femininity still left something to be desired. A hand slid into his, and Daphne's voice whispered in his ear—

"Jack, I want to speak to them."

Her husband turned and smiled upon her curiously.

"What are you going to say?" he asked.

"I am going to tell them about—about the tea and sugar. It's the only thing to do," said Daphne eagerly.

"I would rather be knocked on the head by a pit-prop!" said Juggernaut. And he meant it. Some of us are terribly afraid of being exposed as sentimentalists.

Meanwhile the crowd had caught sight of Daphne. The men fell silent, as men are fain to do when a slim goddess, arrayed in black velvet, appears to them, silhouetted against a richly glowing window. But there was a vindictive shriek from the women.

"Get back at once, dear," said Juggernaut. "You are in great danger. Telephone to the police, and tell Graves to get the fire-hose out. It may be useful in two ways. I promise to come in if things get worse. Hallo! who is that?"

A burly man in a bowler hat, panting with the unwonted exertion of a two-mile run, was approaching him along the terrace. He had come up the drive unnoticed, and having skirted the edge of the crowd had gained access to the terrace from another flight of steps at the end. It was Mr Walker, the mine manager.

"I tried to get you on the telephone," he shouted in Juggernaut's ear; "but they have cut the wire."

"What is it?" asked Juggernaut.

Walker told him.

There was just time to act. The mob were pouring up the steps in response to Killick's final invitation. Juggernaut strode forward.

"Stop!" he cried in a voice of thunder. "Stop, and listen to what Mr Walker has to tell you!"

His great voice carried, and there was a moment's lull. Walker seized his opportunity.

"There has been an accident at the pit," he bellowed. "Some of your lads went down after you had left, to see what damage they could do to the plant. Some of the older men went down to stop them. Something happened. The roofs of the main road and intake have fallen in, and Number Three Working is cut off—with eight men in it!"

There was a stricken silence, and the wave rolled back from the steps. Presently a hoarse voice cried—

"Who are they?"

Mr Walker recited six names. Four of these belonged to young bloods who had been foremost in the riot at the pit-head. There were agonised cries from women in the crowd. All four men were married. The fifth name, that of Mr Adam Wilkie, who was a bachelor and a misogynist, passed without comment. The sixth was that of a pit-boy named Hopper.

Mr Walker paused.

"You said eight!" cried another woman's voice in an agony of suspense. "The other two—for the love of God!"

"Amos Entwistle," replied Mr Walker grimly—"and Mr Carthew."

CHAPTER NINETEEN.

LABORARE EST ORARE.

Six men sat upon six heaps of small coal in a long rectangular cavern five feet high and six feet broad. The roof was supported by props placed at distances specified by the Board of Trade. One side of the cavern was pierced at regular intervals by narrow openings which were in reality passages; the other was a blank wall of gleaming coal.

This was the "face"—that point in the seam of coal which marked the limits of progress of the ever-advancing line of picks and shovels.

The men were well over two hundred fathoms—roughly a quarter of a mile—below the surface of the earth, and they had been prisoners in Number Three Working ever since an explosion of fire-damp and coal-dust had cut them off from communication with the rest of Belton Pit six hours before.

The prisoners were Jim Carthew, Amos Entwistle, and Adam Wilkie, together with a hewer, a drawer, and a pit-boy, named Atkinson, Denton, and Hopper respectively. There had been two others, but they lay dead and buried beneath a tombstone twelve hundred feet high.

What had happened was this.

About four o'clock on that disastrous afternoon, Amos Entwistle was sitting despondently in his own kitchen. He was the oldest and most influential overman in Belton Pit, but his counsels of moderation had been swept aside by the floods of Mr Winch's oratory; and like the practical creature that he was he had returned home, to await the issue of the insurrection and establish an alibi in the event of police-court proceedings.

To him entered Mr Adam Wilkie, with the news that some of the more ardent iconoclasts of the day-shift had remained below in the pit, in order to break down the roofs of some of the galleries leading to the workings—an amiable and short-sighted enterprise which, though pleasantly irritating to their employer, must inevitably throw its promoters and most of their friends out of work for an indefinite period.

Here at least was an opportunity to act. Entwistle hastily repaired to the pit-offices, where he knew that Mr Carthew had been spending the afternoon; and the three, united for the moment by the bond of common-sense, if nothing else, dropped down the shaft with all speed. Fortunately the man in charge of the winding-engine was still at his post, and of an amenable disposition.

Arrived at the pit bottom, they hurried along the main road. The atmosphere was foul and close, for the ventilating machinery had ceased to work. There was a high percentage of fire-damp, too, as constant little explosions in their Davy lamps informed them.

Presently they overtook the enemy, who had done a good deal of mischief already; for they had set to work in the long tunnel known as the intake, down which fresh air was accustomed to flow to the distant workings; and at every blow of their picks, a pit-prop fell from its position and an overhead beam followed, bringing down with it a mingled shower of stone and rubbish.

There was no time to be lost, for the whole roof might fall at any moment. It was three against five; but authority is a great asset and conscience a great liability. By adopting a "hustling" policy of the most thorough description, Carthew, Entwistle, and Wilkie hounded their slightly demoralised opponents along the intake towards the face, intending to round up the gang in one of the passages leading back to the main road, and, having pursued the policy of peaceful dissuasion to its utmost limits, conduct their converts back to the shaft.

The tide of battle rolled out of the intake into the cavern formed by the face and its approaches. Master Hopper was the first to arrive, the toe of Mr Entwistle's boot making a good second.

"Now, you men," said Carthew, addressing the sullen, panting figures which crouched before him—the roof here was barely five feet above the floor—"we have had enough of this. Get out into the main road and back to the shaft. You are coming up topside of this pit with us—that's flat!"

But his opponents were greater strategists than he supposed.

"Keep them there, chaps!" cried a voice already far down one of the passages.

"Catch that man!" cried Carthew. "Let me go!"

Shaking off Atkinson, who in obedience to orders had made a half-hearted grab at him, he darted down the nearest passage. It led to the main road, but across the mouth hung a wet brattice-cloth. Delayed a moment, he hurried on towards the junction with the main road, just in time to descry two twinkling Davy lamps disappearing round the distant corner. They belonged to Davies and Renwick, the ringleaders of the gang. What their object might be he could not for the moment divine, but he could hear their voices re-echoing down the silent tunnel. Evidently they were making for the main road, perhaps to raid the engine-room or call up reserves. He must keep them in sight. Laboriously he hastened along the rough and narrow track.

Suddenly, far ahead in the darkness, he heard a crash, followed by a frightened shriek. Next moment there was a roar, which almost broke the drums of his ears, and the whole pit seemed to plunge and stagger. His lamp went out, and he lay upon the floor in the darkness—darkness that could be felt—waiting for the roof to fall in.

Renwick and Davies, it was discovered long afterwards, had reached the main road, running rapidly. Here one of them must have tripped over the slack-lying wire cable which drew the little tubs of coal up the incline from the lyes to the foot of the shaft. Two seconds later a tiny puddle of flaming oil from a broken lamp (which for once in a way had not been extinguished by its fall) had supplied the necessary ignition to the accumulated fire-damp and coal-dust of the unventilated pit. There was one tremendous explosion. Down came the roof of the main road for a distance of over half a mile, burying the authors of the catastrophe, Samson-like, in their own handiwork.

The survivors were sitting in the *cul-de-sac* formed by the face of the coal and its approaches, three-quarters of a mile from the shaft. No one had been injured by the explosion, though Carthew, being nearest, had lain half-stunned for a few minutes. Possibly the brattice-cloths hung at intervals across the ways to direct the air-currents had been instrumental in blanketing its force.

The party had just returned from an investigation of the possibilities of escape.

"Will you report, Mr Entwistle?" said Carthew, who found that the surviving mutineers appeared to regard him as the supreme head of the present enterprise and Entwistle as his chief adviser.

Amos Entwistle complied.

There were two ways, he explained in his broad north-country dialect, by which Number Three could be reached from the shaft. One was the intake, along which fresh air was conducted to the workings, and the other was the main road, which could be reached through any of the passages leading away from the face. The explosion in the main road had brought down the roof for a distance which might be almost anything.

The intake was blocked too. It was some way from the scene of the explosion, but the props were gone, and the roof had come down from end to end, for all he knew.

"Is there no other way out?" said Carthew.

"None, sir."

Carthew indicated the row of openings beside them.

"Don't any of these lead anywhere?"

"They all lead to the main road, except that one at the end, which leads to the intake. We have plenty of room to move about, and plenty of air; but we are shut in, and that's a fact, sir."

"Is that your opinion too, Mr Wilkie?"

"We canna get gettin' oot o' this, sir," replied the oracle with complacent finality.

There was a deathlike silence. Then Master Hopper began to cry softly. He was going to die, he reflected between his sobs, and he was very young to do so. It was hard luck his being there at all. He had only joined the riot from youthful exuberance and a desire to be "in the hearse," as an old Scottish lady once bitterly observed of a too pushful mourner at her husband's funeral. He entertained no personal animosity against the owner of the pit: in fact he had never set eyes on him. His desire had merely been to see the fun. Well, he was seeing it. He wept afresh.

Atkinson and Denton sat and gazed helplessly at Carthew. The part they had played in sealing up six souls in the bowels of the earth had faded from their minds: to be just, it had faded from the minds of their companions as well. The past lay buried with Renwick and Davies. The future occupied their entire attention.

There was another danger to be considered—the suffocating after-damp of the explosion. Carthew inquired about this. Entwistle considered that the risk was comparatively slight.

"The cloths hung across the approaches to the main road should keep it away," he said. "It's a heavy gas, and don't move about much, like. We shall be able to tell by the lamps, anyway."

"Then what had we better do?" said Carthew briskly. "Dig?"

One of the men—Atkinson—lifted his head from his hands.

"Ah were saaved by t' Salvationists once," he said hoarsely. "Ah could put up a prayer."

"I think we will try the effect of a little spade-work first," said Carthew. "*Laborare est orare*, just now!" he added to himself.

A few hours later they re-assembled. They had tapped, sounded, hewed, and shovelled at every potential avenue of escape, but to no purpose. The intake and main road appeared to be blocked from end to end. Six men were mewed up with no food, a very little water, twenty-four hours' light, and a limited quantity of oxygen; and they had no means of knowing how near or how far away help might be.

All they were certain of was that on the other side of the barrier which shut them in men were working furiously to reach them in time, and that up above women were praying to God that He would deliver them.

CHAPTER TWENTY.

BLACK SUNDAY.

The search party had concluded its investigations, and stood at the foot of the shaft, which fortunately had not been injured by the distant explosion, waiting for the cage.

A pit-bottom is an unexpectedly spacious place, more resembling the cellars of a ducal mansion, or a city station in the days of the old under-ground, than a burrow in the hidden places of the earth. Whitewashed brick archways open up long vistas, illuminated by electric lamps. Through an adjacent doorway streams the cheerful glow of the engine-room, from which the haulage of the trucks is controlled. Only in the "sump," below the level of the flooring at the foot of the shaft, the water gleams black and dismally.

"Is there any other road to explore, Mr Walker?" asked a huge man in blue overalls, with a patent breathing apparatus strapped upon his back.

"No, Sir John. All we can do at present is to get the ventilating gear going again, and then send down a double shift to get to work on the main road, in the hope of finding some one alive at the end of it. Meanwhile we will go up and look at the pit-plan."

"How long do you think it will take to get through? You know more of the geography of this pit than I do."

"It depends on how far the roof is down. It will be slow work, for we must re-prop as we go. Twenty yards an hour is about the best we can expect to do, working top-notch all the time. And if the road is blocked from end to end, as well it may be, it will be a question of days, Sir John."

"And in Number Three they have neither food nor drink?"

"Neither, to our knowledge. Probably they have a little water, though. We must get at them double quick. Here is the cage coming down."

The cage roared upwards between the wooden guides, black with long use and glistening with oil and water; and presently the party were back in the great shed which covered the pit-head, pushing their way through anxious inquirers to the office buildings.

Leaving the other members of the search party—an overman and two hewers—to report progress, Sir John and his manager shut themselves into the inner office. Here Walker unrolled the pit-plan, which, with its blocks and junctions and crossings, looked very like an ordinary street map.

"Here we are," he said. "We have been able to explore the whole pit except this part here"—he dug the point of his pencil into a distant corner—"and the reason is that the means of access to that particular level are blocked. Here is where the block begins." The pencil swiftly shaded in a section. "There is the intake, all blown to smithereens; that and the road to Number Three. But if there are men alive in the pit, Number Three is where we shall find them."

"Do you believe that they are alive?" asked Juggernaut.

"I do. It seems incredible that the whole roof should have come down. We must get the ventilating plant in order and dig them out; that's the only way. We should be able to start work immediately."

"Right!" said Juggernaut, bracing himself at the blessed thought of action once more. "I'll call for volunteers."

A minute later, appearing at a brilliantly lit window, he addressed the silent throng below him. To most of them this was the second speech that they had received from him in twelve hours.

"We have been down the pit," he said. "There has been a biggish explosion, and Number Three is cut off by a heavy fall. The air below will be breathable in less than an hour, and we are going to set to work right away, and clear, and clear, and clear until we find out whether there is any one left alive there. Now,"—his voice rang out in sudden and irresistible appeal—"we want *men*, and plenty of them. Short shifts and high pressure! Those poor fellows have very little water, no food, and a doubtful air supply. I ask for volunteers. Who will come down? Step forward—now!"

A gentle ripple passed over the sea of upturned faces. Then it died away. The distance between the speaker and his entire audience had diminished by one pace.

"Thank you!" said Juggernaut simply. "I knew I had only to ask. Mr Walker, will you call the overmen together and get going as soon as possible?"

A few hours earlier the men of Belton had failed in an enterprise for lack of a leader. Now they had found one.

Sir John Carr drove the first shovel into the mass which blocked the main road, and for the space of thirty minutes he set a standard of pace in the work of rescue which younger and more supple successors found it hard to maintain.

Shift followed shift.

Sunday morning dawned up above, and the sun swung into a cloudless April sky, but still the work below went on—grim, untiring, unprofitable work. Hope deferred succeeded to hope deferred.

Twenty-four hours of blind energy advanced the rescuers three or four hundred yards, but there seemed to be no end to the fall. Progress was growing slower too, for the excavated material had to be carried back farther every time. Once during the second night word was sent up the shaft that two men had been hurt through a fresh fall in the roof, over-eagerness being the cause. Still the work went on. And so Black Sunday drew to a close, to be succeeded by a Monday of a very similar hue.

CHAPTER TWENTY-ONE.

VEILLESSE SAIT.

Lady Carr was at the pit-head early on Monday morning. She had arrived in the Belton motor, just in time to provide for the conveyance of the two injured men to the county hospital, eleven miles away. She herself passed quietly in and out amid the anxious groups of men and women. She said little: it was not a time for words; but it was noted that she lingered for more than a few minutes in the company of Master Hopper's mother, and that her grave, slow smile appeared to hearten that broken widow mightily.

Presently she encountered her husband, whom she had not seen for two nights and a day.

"You here?" he said.

"Yes. I have sent those two poor men away to Kilchester in the car, and I am waiting for it to come back." Then a note of maternal severity intervened. "Have you been to bed at all since I last saw you?"

"Not much," admitted Juggernaut. "But I have a vague recollection of lying down somewhere for a few hours last night. It may have been on the office sofa or it may have been in the sump. What I am more certain of is that I have not washed for days. I feel like Othello. But what has brought you down to the pit?"

"I thought you would like to know," said Daphne, "that this affair is in the morning papers."

Othello looked, if possible, blacker than before.

"Have they got the names?"

"Yes, Jim Carthew's too. And what do you think the result has been, Jack? I have had a wire from—from—" for a moment Daphne's concern for the tragedy around her was swallowed up in the joy of the match-making sex over one sinner that repenteth—"whom do you think?"

"I don't know."

Daphne told him. "It was the first thing she heard when she landed in England. She is *frantic* about him, and is coming down here to-day. She has offered to sleep anywhere, do anything, if only she may come. Jack, isn't it too heavenly?" Daphne positively crowed.

Juggernaut's teeth flashed across his grimy countenance in a sympathetic smile.

"You women!" he said softly. "We must fish him out for her after this, Daphne. Well, Mrs Entwistle?"

A middle-aged woman with hungry eyes was at his elbow. She was Amos Entwistle's wife.

"Would you come and speak to old Mr Entwistle, sir?" she said—"my man's father. He is too rheumatic to move about easy, but he seems to have something on his mind about another way of getting at them."

Sir John Carr turned and followed her promptly.

"Shall I come too, dear?" said Daphne.

"Better not. Go and send Walker to me if you can find him."

Mrs Entwistle conducted Juggernaut to a sunny nook, sheltered from the keen breeze, against the brickwork of the power-house. Here sat Entwistle senior, stone-deaf, almost blind, but with his eighty-year-old wits still bright and birdlike.

He was no respecter of titles or employers, this old gentleman, and in high-pitched, senile tones he criticised the arrangements for rescue. The excavatory operations were a mistake. Time was being wasted. The poor lads inside had nobbut a little water to drink and nowt to eat. The air would be getting foul, too.

"You must get there *quick*, Sir John," he said, rising painfully from his seat. "See now."

He began to hobble laboriously away from the vicinity of the pit-head towards the rather grimy fields which lay to the north of the colliery. By this time Walker had arrived, bringing with him a burly, bearded pit-inspector, sent down by the Board of Trade.

Twenty minutes' laborious walking ended in a halt in the middle of a bleak pasture-field, from which a few unconcerned sheep were extracting some exceedingly dubious-looking nourishment. Mr Entwistle called a halt.

"Been thinking things over," said he, breathing stertorously. "Known this country-side, above and below, nigh seventy year. The lads, they go buzzing round the pit-head, but the old man"—as a matter of fact he said "t'owd mon," but it will be simpler to paraphrase his utterance—"sits at home and thinks things over. They has to come to him in the end!"

All this was highly irrelevant and proportionately exasperating; but old age has its privileges. Doubtless Agamemnon, Menelaus, and other eager stalwarts longed with all their hearts to tear Nestor limb from limb, what time that venerable bore delivered himself of fifty lines of autobiographical hexameters as a preliminary to coming to the point; yet they never did. Presently Mr Entwistle concluded his exordium and tapped upon the ground with his staff.

"We are standing," he announced, "right over the road to Number Three. Two hundred fathom down," he added, in case they should have overlooked this point.

This, at anyrate, was a statement of fact. Walker produced and consulted the pit-plan. "You are about right," he said. "Well?"

"How far along this road is the face?" inquired the old gentleman. "It's a tidy number of years since I———"

Walker told him, with the result that the excursion was resumed. Presently Mr Entwistle came to a halt again.

"We're over Number Three now," he said.

Walker again confirmed him, with the aid of a compass-bearing and the pit-plan.

"Well?" he said.

The old man pointed with his stick to some dismantled and abandoned pit buildings farther down the valley, a full mile away.

"The old Shawcliffe Pit," he croaked. "Worked out this forty year. But I knowed it well when I were a lad."

Juggernaut, suddenly seeing light, caught the old man by the arm.

"You mean," said he rapidly, "that the Shawcliffe workings run up this way———"

"No, no," said Walker, interrupting. "You are wrong, Mr Entwistle. The Shawcliffe workings all run down the other way, to the north."

"Nay," persisted the old gentleman—"not all. They thowt there were a seam this way, and they drove one road out here, if so be they might pick it up. They had got signs of it, boring. But it were a faulty seam. It weren't until Belton Pit were opened, thirty years later, that they struck it fair."

"And that road runs out this way, from Shawcliffe shaft?" asked the Inspector.

"Ay, and it must come very nigh to the Belton Workings now—nigh to Number Three. I reckon———"

"He is right!" said Walker excitedly. "It's a chance! I *have* heard of this road, now I think of it." He turned to Entwistle again. "How far out do you think it runs? Quick, man—tell us!"

For answer the veteran, much inflated, stumped off again in a northerly direction, with all the assurance of a water-diviner in full cry. After fifty yards or so he stopped.

"I should say it ended about here," he said. "You can trust the old man's memory. The youngsters———"

Another lengthy deliverance was plainly threatened, but this time our Nestor observed, not without justifiable chagrin, that the majority of his audience had disappeared. The symposium was suddenly reduced to himself and his daughter-in-law.

Testily curtailing his peroration, to the exclusion of severable valuable aphorisms upon the advantages of senile decay over youthful immaturity, the old gentleman resignedly took the arm of Mrs Amos, and permitted himself to be conducted back to his fireside.

But he had served his turn for all that.

The other three were hurrying back to Belton Pit talking eagerly, Juggernaut leading by half a pace.

"It's madness, of course," said Walker cheerfully. "This pit has been closed for forty years. The props will be down———"

"The air will be foul," said the Inspector thoughtfully.

"Or explosive," added Walker.

"And there will probably be water," continued both together.

"Is the shaft still open?" asked Juggernaut brusquely.

"I believe so," said Walker.

"I suppose it would be possible to rig a derrick and tackle over it?"

"Yes."

They strode on a dozen paces.

"I am going down," said Juggernaut.

"I am going with you," said Walker.

"And I," said the Inspector, "am coming too."

They broke into a trot.

CHAPTER TWENTY-TWO.

HOLD THE FORT!

The safety-lamps had burned themselves out hours ago, and the imprisoned party sat on in the dark. There was nothing else to do. Food they had none: their water was exhausted. They slept fitfully, but in the black darkness sleep seemed little removed from death, and time from eternity.

Jim Carthew lay with his head upon a friendly lump of coal, pondering with his accustomed detachment upon the sundry and manifold changes of this world. He thought of Death. Plainly he and his companions were about to solve the mystery of what lay hidden round that corner which our omniscience is pleased to consider the end of all things. What would they find there? Another life—a vista more glorious and sublime than man in his present state could conceive? Or just another long lane—just another highway of labour and love, of service and reward? Or—a *cul-de-sac*—an abyss—a jumping-off place? He wondered. Not the last alternative, he thought: more likely one of the other two. Anyhow, he would know soon, and it would be interesting. His one regret was that he would not be able to come back, even for five minutes, to tell his friends about it.

Friends!...

This brought a new train of reflection. He thought of Jack Carr and Jack Carr's wife. Would the latter keep her promise, and come back to her husband? He wondered. She should be in Belton this week, all being well—that is, if this was the week he thought it was. But time seemed rather a jumbled affair at present. Besides, he was so infernally hungry that he could not reason things out. Never mind!...

He thought of Nina Tallentyre. *That* difficulty had solved itself, anyhow. No need for further hopings or strivings: that was a relief! When their rupture occurred he had prayed to be excused from living further. He had even petitioned that the earth might open and swallow him up for ever. Well, the earth had done so, so he ought to be satisfied. He was gone down into silence, and Nina was rid of him—well rid of him! He was well rid of her, too. She had led him a dog's life the last few months. A *dog's* life. He repeated the fact to himself pertinaciously, but without any great feeling either of conviction or resentment.

He felt strangely contented and cheerful. His mind dwelt with persistence on the bright side of things. He thought of the day when she and he had first met, and Nina, in her superb, imperious manner, had desired him to take her out of "this rabble," and come and amuse her in a corner. He remembered subsequent meetings; various gracious acts of condescension on Nina's part; and finally one special evening on board a yacht in regatta-time, when they had sat together in a corner of the upper deck in the lee of the chart-house, with a perfectly preposterous moon egging them on, and the faint strains of *Caressante* pulsing across the silent water from the Commodore's yacht hard by; and Nina had nearly—almost—all-but—and then actually—capitulated.

She had gone back on her word three weeks later, it was true; but he drew consolation even now from the memory of something which had slipped through her long lashes and rolled down her cheek even as she dismissed him, a memory which had carried through many a black hour.

It was over episodes like this that his mind lingered. Other and less satisfactory items declined to come up for review. Perhaps, he reflected, dying men, provided they had lived clean and run straight, were always accorded this privilege. Only the credit side of the ledger accompanied them on their journey into the unknown. It was a comforting thought.

...He wondered what she would think when she heard about it. In a blue envelope at the bottom of his private strong-box they would find his will, a primitive document composed in secrecy, and endorsed: "To be opened when I have gone out for good." In this he had bequeathed all he possessed to "my friend Miss Nina Tallentyre," be she maid, wife, or widow at the moment. Carthew was not a man who loved by halves. All that he had was hers, whether she needed it or not. Of course she must not be made conspicuous in the matter; he had seen to that. The bequest was to be quite quiet and unostentatious. No probate, or notices in the papers, or rot of that kind. In the blue envelope was enclosed a private letter to his lawyers, dwelling on the importance of this point. They were decent old buffers, that firm, and would understand. They would square up any death-duties and other legal fakements that were necessary, and then pass on the balance to little Nina, to buy herself pretty things with. But no publicity! No embarrassment!

...He fell asleep, and dreamed, from the natural perversity of things, of roast beef and Yorkshire pudding.

When he awoke, low voices were conversing near him. Farther away he could hear the regular breathing of Master Hopper, who, with youth's ready amenability to Nature's own anodynes, was slumbering peacefully.

"I can weel understand, Mr Entwistle," observed Mr Wilkie in measured tones, "that no decent body would like to be seen entering yin o' they Episcopalian Kirks."

Amos Entwistle's heavy voice agreed. He commented with heat upon indulgence in vain repetitions and other heathen practices favoured by the Anglican community; and related with grim relish an anecdote of how his own daughter, lured from the Wesleyan fold by the external fascinations of the new curate, had once privily attended morning service at the parish church—to return, shocked to the foundations of her being, with horrific tales of candles burning on the altar in broad daylight and the Lord's Prayer repeated four times in the course of a single service.

"But what I couldna thole," continued Mr Wilkie, who had been characteristically pursuing his own line of thought in the meantime, "would be no tae belong tae the kirk of the *land*. A Chapel body! I could never endure the disgrace of it."

Entwistle demurred vigorously. It was no disgrace to be Chapel folks. Sturdy Independents were proud to be able to dispense with State-aided, spoon-fed religion. Disgrace, indeed! Were not Mr Wilkie's qualms on the subject of Dissent due rather to a hankering after the flesh-pots—the loaves and fishes—the——

"Well, perhaps no exactly a disgrace," continued Mr Wilkie, disregarding the latter innuendo, "but a kin' o' stigma, like. Man, it's an awful thing tae walk doon the street and meet the minister o' the pairish, and him pass by and tak' no more notice of ye than if ye were a Plymouth Brother or an Original Secessionist. I mind yince when I was in a Tynside pit, I sat under Mr Maconochie—him that gave up a grand kirk in Paisley tae tak a call tae oor wee bit Presbyterian contraption, Jarrow way. Now, although Mr Maconochie's kirk was my kirk and him oor minister, I used tae feel far more uplifted if I got a good-day frae the minister o' the English Kirk—Golightly, or some sic' name—an *Episcopalian*! I canna imagine why, but there it was. I doot it was just orthodoxy. He was the minister o' the kirk o' the land, and Mr Maconochie, being, for him, on the wrong side of the Border, was not. Gin I had met yon felly Golightly trapesing doon the High Street o' Jedburgh, things would hae been gey different; for then——"

The point at issue, Entwistle's deep patient voice asseverated, was this. Should a man who was an Independent allow himself or his bairns to have aught to do with Church folk on any pretence whatever?

He was answered in the darkness by a third voice. Denton, the hewer—Atkinson, the retired Salvationist, shovelled and wheeled away in a tub what Denton hewed—had awoken from an uneasy sleep, and was listening to the conversation. Of all that little band, probably he was the least prepared to die. He was a drunkard, a blasphemer, and an evil liver. But like the rest of us, he had his redeeming features. He had inspired and kept alive for a period of ten years the love of his wife—a feat which many an ex-sidesman, buried beneath a mountain of expensive masonry adorned by an epitaph beginning, "Well done, good and faithful servant!" has signally failed to accomplish. He sat up now.

"Ah niver 'ad nowt to do wi' churches or chapels," he began defiantly. "But ah knaws this. When my Maggie were lyin' badly four years agone, and us thought she was goin' to die, she asked me to go and fetch her pastor—dash;that's what she called him. Ah ran along to his house and begged him to come. He said"—the man's voice grew thick, and one could almost see his sombre eyes glow in the gross darkness—"he said he were busy! There was a swarry that neet that 'twas his duty to attend, and next day he was goin' off to a political meeting to protest against t' Education Bill, or summat. He said, too, that he had enough to do ministerin' to the wants o' them that deserved ministerin' to, wi'out comin' to the house o' the likes o' me. When had he last seen me in t' chapel, he would like to knaw? Yes, *that* was what he wanted to knaw! He wanted to stand and ask me questions like that when my Maggie——!... Ah cursed him, and his chapel, and his fat-bellied deacons till Ah were out o' puff with it: then Ah went off down the street half-crazed. There Ah runs straight into a young feller wi' a soft black hat and long legs. He was standing outside t' door of his lodgings, smoking a pipe in the dark. He was t' curate at t' parish church, and when he saw I wasn't in liquor, he asked me what was my trouble. I telled him. 'Is that all?' says he. 'Will I do? I've just come off my day's work, and I ain't got nothing to do but amuse myself now.' It were nigh ten o'clock. Well, he comes with me, and he sat by my Maggie all the neet through, and sent me with a note to a doctor that were a friend of his, and only went away himsel' at seven o'clock next morning, because he had to get shaved and take early service or summat. *That's* all your chapel folk ever done for me, Amos Entwistle."

"That was a special case, and proves no rules. Besides," said Entwistle soberly, "this is no time for religious differences. We are in God's hands now, and I doubt we shall all be in a place soon where there is neither Church nor Chapel."

"Would it no be best for us all tae keep silence for a matter o' ten minutes," suggested Wilkie, "and pit up a bit prayer each of his ain, we bein' no all of the same way of thinkin' in these matters? That gate, wi' so many prayers o' different denominations goin' up, yin at least should get gettin' through the roof of the pit. Are ye agreed, chaps?"

"Ay, ay!" said Entwistle.

The others all murmured assent, save Master Hopper, who shrieked out in sudden fear. The proximity of death had become instantly and dreadfully apparent to him on Mr Wilkie's suggestion. Carthew reached out and pulled him to his side.

"Come over here, by me," he said.

Master Hopper, greatly soothed, crept close, and settled down contentedly enough with an arm round Carthew's shoulders. Presently Carthew heard him repeating The Lord's Prayer to himself in a low and respectful whisper.

The silence lasted longer than ten minutes. For one thing, the supplicants were exhausted in body, soul, and spirit, and their orisons came slowly. For another, there was no need to hurry. For nearly an hour no one spoke.

At length some one sat up in the darkness, and the voice of Atkinson inquired—

"Mr Carthew, sir, I think a song of praise would hearten us all."

"I believe it would," said Carthew. He was not enamoured of the corybantic hymnology of the Salvation Army, but the horror of black darkness was beginning to eat into his soul, and he knew that the others were probably in a worse plight. "What shall we sing?"

"At the meeting where I were saved," said Atkinson deferentially, "we concluded worship by singing a hymn I have never forgotten since: *Hold the Fort!*"

"That sounds a good one," said Carthew, struggling with an unreasonable sensation of being in the chair at a smoking-concert. "Does any one else here know *Hold the Fort!*?"

Yes, Entwistle knew it. Master Hopper had heard it. Mr Wilkie had not. He did not hold with hymns: even paraphrases were not, in his opinion, altogether free from the taint of Popery. If it had been one of the Psalms of David, now! Still, he would join. Denton knew no hymns, but was willing to be instructed in this one.

Atkinson, trembling with gratification, slowly rehearsed the words, the others repeating them after him.

"We will sing it now," he said.

He raised the tune in a clear tenor. Most north-countrymen are musicians by instinct. In a few moments this grim prison was flooded by a wave of sonorous melody. The simple, vulgar, taking tune swelled up; the brave homely words rang out, putting new heart into every one. Each and all joyfully realised that there are worse ways of going to one's death than singing a battle-song composed by Moody and Sankey. With drawn white faces upturned to the heaven they could not see they sang on, flinging glorious defiance into the very teeth of Death—gentleman and pitman, Church and Chapel, zealot and infidel.

"Last verse again!" commanded Atkinson.

"Wait a moment!" cried Entwistle, starting up.

But no one heard him. The chorus was rolling out once more—

"*Hold the Fort, for I am coming*——"

Tap, tap, tap! Scrape, scrape, scrape! Hammer, hammer, hammer!

The hymn paused, wavered, and stopped dead on the final shout.

"By God!" screamed a voice—it was Denton's—"here they are!"

Carthew, with Hopper's arms tightening convulsively round him, started up.

"Is it true?" he asked hoarsely.

"Ay! Listen! They have found us. They are within a few yards of us," said Entwistle.

"*Praise God, from whom all blessings flow!*" sang Atkinson suddenly and exultantly, and the others joined him.

Entwistle was right. They were found. Reasoned calculation, dogged persistence, and blind indifference to their own safety had brought the search party triumphantly along the mouldering rickety passages of Shawcliffe Pit to the nearest point of contact with Number Three in Belton; and *Hold the Fort!* proceeding from a subterranean cave of harmony not many yards away, had done the rest.

CHAPTER TWENTY-THREE.

THE LAST TO LEAVE.

It was night once more, and the great arc lights snapped and sizzled above the waste-heaps and truck-lines surrounding the head of Belton Pit. But the scene was deserted. The centre of interest had shifted to Shawcliffe, a mile away. Here a vast silent throng of human beings stood expectantly in groups, their faces illuminated by the naphtha flares which had been erected here and there about the long-abandoned pithead.

There was news—tense, thrilling news—and the prospect of more. The ancient shaft had been opened and a bucket and tackle rigged—there was no time to ship a cage—and a search party had gone down at dusk. Word had shortly been sent up that the road to the south was still open, though the air was foul and the props rickety. Then came a frantic tug at the rope, and a messenger was hauled to the surface, crying aloud that men were alive in Belton Pit. It was hoped, he added, that the search party would reach them by midnight, for the dividing wall was surprisingly thin. Sir John Carr's order was that blankets and stretchers should be prepared; also food and medical comforts, for the prisoners had fasted for something like sixty hours. With that the messenger had dived below once more, and the game of patience was resumed.

It was past midnight now, and everything was in readiness. On the outskirts of the throng, at the side of the rough and lumpy road, stood a motor-car with two occupants—women. One of them was her ladyship; the other the spectators failed to recognise. But there were rumours about to the effect that she was a visitor to Belton recently arrived from London. Lady Carr had been seen meeting her at the station that afternoon.

The stranger's name, had it been told, would not have conveyed much information to the watchers. It was Nina Tallentyre.

There was a sudden swirl and heave in the crowd. The hand-turned windlass was at work again, and some one was being hauled slowly up the shaft. It was Mr Walker, the manager.

They made a lane for him, until he reached a convenient rostrum formed by an inverted and rusty truck. This he mounted and very briefly told them the news—news which made them laugh foolishly and sob by turns. There was no cheering: they were past that.

In the excitement the next man who followed him up the shaft passed unnoticed. It was Sir John Carr. He saw the hooded motor standing apart, Mr Vick sitting motionless at the wheel. Next moment he was in beside the two women, overalls and all, holding Daphne's hands in a single grimy fist and telling them what we know already.

"Is he *perfectly* safe?" asked Nina for the tenth time. She did not possess Daphne's aristocratic composure under critical circumstances.

"Yes—but very weak. I am sending him up second. The first is a pit-boy. When Carthew arrives you had better put him in the motor and take him straight home."

"Jack!" said Daphne.

She slipped out of the car and accompanied her husband into the darkness outside the radius of flaring lights.

"Are you going down again?" she asked.

"I am."

"And when are you coming up?" The unflinching courage which upholds so many women in the face of danger had never failed Daphne during those long days and nights. But now the courage was receding with the danger.

Juggernaut smiled.

"When would you have me come up?" he asked.

"Last," said Daphne, suddenly proud. "It is the only place for you. I will wait here. Nina can take her Jim home, and the car can come back later for you and me. Jack!"

Her husband turned and regarded her curiously. Their eyes met.

"Well?" he said.

"Jack," continued Daphne in a low voice, "is there much risk down there—for you, I mean?"

"There is always risk, of a sort, down a coal-pit," replied her husband pontifically. "A little explosive marsh-gas, or a handful of finely divided coal-dust lying in a cranny, might suddenly assert itself. Still, there are risks everywhere. One might be struck down by apoplexy at a vestry meeting."

Daphne gave his arm a squeeze, an ingratiating childish squeeze, suggestive of the Daphne of old negotiating for extension of dress allowance.

"Jack, stay up here! You have done enough."

"*Post me, Satanella!*" smiled her husband. Then, more seriously: "Daphne, if I came to you and asked for orders *now*, where would you send me, I being what I am—the proprietor of the pit—and you being what you are—the proprietress of my good name?"

Daphne's fit had passed.

"I should send you," she answered bravely, "down the shaft, with orders to stay there until every one else was safely out."

"I obey," said Juggernaut. "*Au revoir!*"

"Jack!" said Daphne faintly. Her face was uplifted.

"It will be a coaly one!" said her husband, complying. Then came an accusation.

"Daphne, you are trembling! This is not up to your usual standard."

"I can't help it," said Daphne miserably. "I am a coward. But I don't mind," she added more cheerfully, "so long as no one else knows. *You* won't give me away!"

At that Juggernaut held her to him a moment longer.

"Daphne, my wife," he whispered suddenly—"thank God for you—at last!"

Then they fell apart, and she ran lightly back to the motor and Nina.

Once she turned and looked over her shoulder, waving her hand prettily. Her face, framed in a motor bonnet and lit by the glare of a naphtha light, looked absurdly round and childish, just as it had done upon a dim and distant morning in Snayling Church.

It was the last time in his life that her man was ever to behold it.

Master Hopper, partially restored by brandy and meat juice, and feeling, on the whole, something of a hero, arrived at the pit-head an hour later, there to be claimed by his mother and hustled off, by more willing hands than he could comfortably accommodate, home to bed. The bucket, which provided standing-room for two passengers, then went down again.

This time it brought up Mr Walker, holding a supporting arm round Carthew—a sick man indeed. He was less hardened to subterranean existence than the rest. Sympathetic murmurs arose. The bucket was swung out from beneath the pulley and landed gently on the edge of the shaft. Carthew stepped out and stood swaying uncertainly.

A tall girl came suddenly forward.

"Jim, dear!" was all she said.

Carthew surveyed her, and smiled weakly.

"Hallo, Nina! That you?"

Miss Tallentyre took his arm.

"The car is waiting for you," she said. "Lean on me *hard*, old boy!"

And certainly no more desirable prop than this girl, with her splendid youth and glorious vitality, was ever offered to a weary mortal. Carthew, dazed but utterly content, put a feeble arm round the slim shoulders of the woman whose mere hand he had hitherto counted it heaven to touch, and the pair passed away together out of the crowd—and out of this narrative. Happiness has no history.

Others were coming up the shaft now. First Mr Wilkie, in a very fair state of preservation: then Denton, the reprobate, insensible—his hands were in tatters, so fiercely had he worked,—then Atkinson, still sheer drunk with the success of his own hymnology: then Amos Entwistle.

Denton's huge inanimate form was laid on a stretcher, to be carried home under the direction of his wife. (The wives of Renwick and Davis, poor souls, had gone home long ago.) But, the Belton Hall motor returning on that instant, Lady Carr insisted on carrying husband and wife home together. The rush through the night air brought Denton round, and he was able to walk into his own house, leaning undeservedly upon the proudest little woman in the north of England.

Daphne returned to the pit-head for the last time. The rescue work was completed. Surely she might claim him now!

No, the block and tackle were not working. No one else was coming up at present. Only round the shaft a knot of men conferred eagerly. She would wait in the car.

She lay back, wrapped in a rug—a cold dawn was breaking—and closed her eyes. The rush and excitement of the three days had told upon her. She had no clear recollection of having slept for any length of time or eaten at any definite period. She had done work among stricken wives and mothers that Belton village would never forget, but she had not realised this. All her head and heart were filled by the mighty knowledge that after five years of married life she and her husband had found one another.

Meanwhile there was silence round the pit-head.

"Vick," said Daphne, suddenly fearful, "go and find Mr Walker, or some one, and ask when Sir John will be up."

Mr Vick, who had been dozing comfortably at his wheel, clambered down into the muddy road and departed as bidden. Ten minutes later he returned falteringly.

"Mr Walker has just gone down the pit again, my lady," he said. "There has been a slight explosion of coal-dust, I was to tell you. Nothing serious—just a flash and a spit in a holler place in the roof, the message said."

"Is Sir John down there?" Cold fear gripped Daphne's heart.

"Yes, my lady."

"Is he safe, do you know?"

"I couldn't say, my lady," replied Vick doggedly. "I'll inquire."

He turned away, glad to escape, with the brisk demeanour of one anxious to investigate matters. But before he reached the pit-head the answer to all possible inquiries came to meet him, in the form of a slow-moving procession carrying something in its midst.

Very gently the bearers laid the stretcher on the grass by the roadside. Daphne, white, silent, but composed, stooped down and turned back the blanket which covered her husband's face. He lay very still. His head and eyes were roughly bandaged. Daphne whispered, so low that none other could hear.

"Jack—my Jack!"

His voice answered hers, from amid the bandages—faint, but imperturbable as ever.

"I'm all right, dear. Afraid it has got me in the eyes a bit, though. Take me home, wife of mine! You will have to lead me about with a string now!"

Daphne's head sank lower still, and she whispered, almost exultantly--

"At last I can really be of some use to you!"

CHAPTER TWENTY-FOUR.

ANOTHER ALIAS.

"Brian Vereker Carr," inquires a voice, "what time is it?"

"Half-past four, sir," replies the same voice respectfully. "In twenty minutes"—in a more truculent tone—"you will have to go upstairs and get ready for tea. You will have to wash your hands—and your face too, I expect," adds the voice bitterly.

Thus, at the age of eight, does Master Brian Vereker Carr commune with himself—a habit acquired during an infancy spent in a large nursery where there was no one else to talk to. The necessity for this form of duologue no longer exists, for now a sister shares the nursery with him—Brian lives in dread of the day when she shall discover that her manly brother not only owned but once rejoiced in the great doll's house in the corner by the fireplace—but the habit remains. Besides, Miss Carr is only four years old, and gentlemen who have worn knickerbockers for years find it difficult to unbend towards their extreme juniors to any great extent. Hence Mr Brian still confers aloofly with himself, even in the presence of adults. There are touches of Uncle Anthony Cuthbert about Brian.

At present he is inadequately filling a large arm-chair in front of the library fire at Belton. The fire is the sole illuminant of the room. The curtains are closely drawn, for it is a cold winter evening. Brian Vereker continues his observations, now approaching an artistic climax.

"If you go upstairs promptly *and* obediently, like a good boy, what do you think mother will give you?" inquires voice number one.

"Chocolates!" replies number two, with an inflection of tone which implies that it will be playing the game pretty low down if mother does not.

The owner of both voices then turns an appealing pair of brown eyes upon Daphne, who is sitting on the other side of the fireplace, engaged in the task of amusing her four-year-old daughter.

"We'll see," she replies after the immemorial practice of mothers.... "And suddenly," she continues to the impatient auditor on her lap, "his furry skin fell away, and his great teeth disappeared, and he stood up there straight and beautiful, in shining armour. He *was* a fairy prince, after all! Brian, dear, tumble out of that arm-chair. Here is dad."

Daphne must have quick ears, for a full half-minute elapses before the door opens and a figure appears in the dim light at the end of the room. Apparently the darkness does not trouble him, for he circumnavigates a round table and a revolving bookcase without hesitation, and finally drops into the arm-chair recently vacated by his son.

"Brian Vereker Carr," inquires a small and respectful voice at his elbow, "do you think dad will play with you to-night?"

"I am *sure* he will," comes a confident reply from the same quarter, "if you give him two minutes to light his pipe in, and refrain from unseemly demon—demonstrations of affection in the meanwhile."

"It's a hard world for parents," grumbles Juggernaut, getting up. "Where is my tobacco-pouch?"

His hand falls upon the corner of the mantelpiece, but encounters nothing there but a framed photograph of a sun-burned young man on a polo-pony—Uncle Ally, to be precise.

"Now where on *earth* is that pouch? I know I left it on the left-hand end of the mantelpiece after lunch."

There is a shriek of delight at this from Brian, in which Miss Carr joins, for the great daily joke of the Carr family is now being enacted.

"Where can it be?" wails Juggernaut. "Under the hearthrug, perhaps? No, not there! In the blotting-pad? No, not there! *I* know! I expect it is behind the coal-box."

Surprising as it may appear, his surmise proves to be correct; and the triumphant discovery of the missing property scores a dramatic success which no repetition seems able to stale. (This is about the fiftieth night of the run of the piece.)

Presently the pipe is filled and lit, Master Carr being permitted to kindle the match and Miss Carr to blow it out, the latter feat only being accomplished by much expenditure of breath and a surreptitious puff from behind her shoulder, contributed by an agency unknown.

"Now, Brian, young fellow," announces Juggernaut, "I will play for ten minutes. Let me speak to the sister first, though."

He lifts his daughter, whom he has never seen, from her mother's knee, and exchanges a few whole-hearted confidences with her upon the subject of her recreations, conduct, dolls, health, and outlook on life in general. Then he restores her, and shouts—

"Come on, Brian Boroo!"

There is a responsive shriek from his son, and the game begins. It is not every boy, Master Brian proudly reflects as he crawls on all fours beneath a writing-table, who can play at blind man's buff with a real blind man!

Daphne leans back in her chair and surveys her male belongings restfully. Time was when this husband of hers, at present eluding obstacles with uncanny facility and listening intently, with the youthful zest of a boy-scout, for the excited breathing of his quarry, found life a less hilarious business. There rises before her the picture of a man led from room to room, steered round corners, dressed like a child, fed like a baby—shattered, groping, gaunt, but pathetically and doggedly cheerful. Neither Daphne nor her husband ever speak of that time now. Not that she regrets it: woman-like, she sometimes feels sorry it is over and gone. She was of real use to her man in those days. Now he seems to be growing independent of her again. Then she smiles comfortably, for she knows that all fears on that score are groundless. He is hers, body and soul. And she——

A small, unclean, and insistent hand is tugging at her skirt, and Miss Carr, swaying unsteadily beneath the burden of a bulky and tattered volume, claims her attention.

"Show me pictures," she commands.

She and her tome are hoisted up, and the exposition begins.

"Where did you find this book, Beloved?" inquires Daphne. The book is an ancient copy of the 'Pilgrim's Progress,' and we have encountered it once before in this narrative.

"Over there," replies Beloved, indicating the bottom shelf of a bookcase with a pudgy thumb—"under ze 'Gwaphics.' What's ze name of that genelman?"

To Miss Carr distinctions of caste are as yet unknown. In her eyes every member of the opposite sex, from the alien who calls on Thursdays with a hurdy-gurdy to the knight-in-armour who keeps eternal vigil in the outer hall, is a "genelman." Even if you are emitting flames from your stomach, as in the present instance, you are not debarred from the title.

Daphne surveys the picture in a reminiscent fashion, and her thoughts go back to a distant Sunday morning at the Rectory, with her youngest brother kneeling on the floor, endeavouring to verify a pictorial reference in this very volume.

"What is he doin' to the other genelman?" continues the searcher after knowledge upon her knee, in a concerned voice.

"He is trying to hurt him, dear."

"What for?"

So the inexorable, immemorial catechism goes on, to be answered with infinite patience and surprising resource. Presently the cycle of inquiry completes itself, and the original question crops out once more.

"What did you say was ze name of that genelman?" with a puckered, frowning effort at remembrance.

"Apollyon, dear."

"Oh." Then the inquirer strikes a fresh note.

"Do you know him?"

"I used to," replies Daphne. "At least," she adds, "I used to know some one who I thought was like him. But his name turned out not to be Apollyon after all."

"What *was* his name, then—his pwoper name?" pursues Miss Carr, deeply intrigued.

Daphne turns to another illustration, coming much later in the book, and surveys it with shining eyes.

"His proper name, Beloved?" she asks.

"Yes. What *was* it?"

"Mr Greatheart," says Daphne softly.

Happy-go-lucky

CHAPTER I
A BRIEF INTRODUCTION

They--that is, the London-and-the-south-thereof contingent of the Hivite House at Grandwich--always celebrated the first morning of the holidays by breakfasting together at the Imperial Hotel at Oakleigh, as a preliminary to catching the nine-fifty-two.

A certain stateliness--not to say pomp--distinguished the function. Negotiations for the provision of the feast were opened at an early date--usually about half-term--the first step taking the form of a dignified but ungrammatical communication, cast in that most intricate and treacherous of moulds, the third person, to the proprietor of the hotel, intimating, after compliments, that *Mr. Rumbold* (*major*), *Hivite House, Grandwich School, would be much obliged if our party could be supplied with breakfast, and you usually do it for half-a-crown as there are a lot of us, and if you don't we shall probably go to the George, and as the party wishes to catch the train Mr. Rumbold would be obliged if you can give it to me punctually.*

To this mine host would reply with a most gratifying typewritten document addressed to--*Rumbold, Esq.,*--a form of address which never fails to please so long as your parents and other adult correspondents persist in designating you "Master,"--expressing the utmost willingness to provide breakfast for Mr. Rumbold's party at two-and-sixpence per head (which, by the way, was the normal charge), and concluding with a tactfully-worded request for information (inadvertently omitted from Mr. Rumbold's original communication) upon the following points:--

(1) The date of the feast.
(2) The number of young gentlemen likely to be present.
(3) The hour of the train which they propose to catch.

During the second half-term Mr. Rumbold's leisure would be pleasantly occupied in recruiting the breakfast-party and communicating its numbers and requirements, intermittently and piecemeal, together with searching enquiries re kidneys and ultimatums on the subject of scrambled eggs, to the rapidly ageing proprietor of the Imperial Hotel.

On the joyous morning of departure a dozen emancipated Helots, all glorious in bowler hats and coloured ties which atoned at a bound for thirteen weeks of statutory headgear and *subfusc.* haberdashery, descended upon the Imperial Hotel and sat down with intense but businesslike cheerfulness to the half-crown breakfast. On these occasions distinctions of caste were disregarded. Fag and prefect sat side by side. Brothers who had religiously cut one another throughout the term were reunited, even indulging in Christian names. Gentlemen who had fought to a finish behind the fives-court every alternate Wednesday afternoon since term began, took sweet counsel together upon the respective merits of Egyptian and Turkish cigarettes.

On the particular occasion with which we are concerned--a crisp morning in December--the party numbered twelve. It is not necessary to describe them in detail, for ten of them make their appearance, in this narrative, at any rate, for the first and last time. Let it suffice to say that Mr. Rumbold major sat at the head of the table and Mr. Rumbold minor at the foot, Mr. Rumbold tertius occupying a position about halfway down. Among others present might have been noticed (as the little society papers say) Mr. "Balmy" Coke, Mr. "Oaf" Sandiford, Mr. "Buggy" Reid, Mr. "Slimy" Green, Mr. "Lummy" Law, and Mr. "Adenoid" Smith. More notable figures were Messrs. "Spangle" Jerningham and "Tiny" Carmyle--lesser luminaries than Rumbold himself, but shining lights in the athletic firmament for all that.

One place only was vacant. The company, in accordance with what is probably the most rigorous social code in existence--schoolboy etiquette--had divided itself into two groups. The first, consisting of those whose right to a place at the head of the table was unquestioned, settled down at once with loud and confident anticipations of enjoyment. The remainder followed their example with more diffidence, beginning at the foot of the table and extending coyly upwards, those whose claim to a place above the salt was beginning to be more than considerable punctiliously taking the lowest places in order to escape the dread stigma of "side." Thus, by reason of the forces of mutual repulsion, a gap occurred in the very middle of the table, between a nervous little boy in spectacles, one Buggy Reid, and the magnificent Mr. Jerningham, Secretary of the Fifteen and the best racquets-player in the school.

"One short!" announced Rumbold. "Who is it?"

There was a general counting of heads. Mr. Reid timidly offered information.

"I think it is The Freak," he said.

There was a general laugh.

"Wonder what he's up to now," mused Mr. Jerningham. "You ought to know, Rummy. Your fag, is n't he?"

"I gave him the bag two terms ago," replied the great man contentedly. "Tiny has him now."

He turned to another of the seniors--a long-legged youth with a subdued manner.

"Still got him, Tiny?"

"Yes," said Mr. Carmyle gloomily, "I have still got him. It's a hard life, though."

"I know," said Rumbold sympathetically. "Does he cross-question you about the photographs on your mantelpiece?"

"Yes," said Carmyle. "He spoke very favourably of my youngest sister. Showed me a photograph of his own, and asked me to come and stay with them in the holidays. Said he thought I would have much in common with his father."

There was general merriment at this, for Mr. Carmyle was patriarchal, both in appearance and habits. But it did nothing to soothe the nerves of The Freak himself, who happened at the moment to be standing shyly upon one leg outside the door, endeavouring to summon up sufficient courage to walk in.

He was a small sandy-haired boy with shrewd blue eyes and a most disarming smile, and he belonged to a not uncommon and distinctly unlucky class. There are boys who are shy and who look shy. Such are usually left to themselves, and gradually attain to confidence. There are boys who are bumptious and behave bumptiously. Such are usually put through a brief disciplinary course by their friends, and ultimately achieve respectability. And there are boys who are shy, but who, through sheer self-consciousness and a desire to conceal their shyness, behave bumptiously. The way of such is hard. Public School disciplinary methods do not discriminate between the sheep and the goats. Variations from the normal, whether voluntary or involuntary, are all corrected by the same methods. Unconventionality of every kind is rebuked by stern moralists who have been through the mill themselves, and are convinced that it would be ungenerous to deprive the succeeding generation of the benefits which have produced such brilliant results in their own case.

The Freak--Master Richard Mainwaring--entered the school-world unfairly handicapped. He had never been from home before. He was an only son, and had had few companions but his parents. Consequently he was addicted to language and phraseology which, though meet and fitting upon the lips of elderly gentlemen, sounded ineffably pedantic upon those of an unkempt fag of fourteen. Finally, he was shy and sensitive, yet quite unable to indicate that characteristic by a retiring demeanour.

Life at school, then, did not begin too easily for him. He was naturally of a chirpy and confiding disposition, and the more nervous he felt the more chirpy and confiding he became. He had no instincts, either, upon the subject of caste. Instead of confining himself to his own impossible order of pariahs, he attempted to fraternise with any boy who interested him. He addressed great personages by their pet names; he invited high potentates to come and partake of refreshment at his expense. Now, promiscuous bonhomie in new boys is not usually encouraged in the great schools of England, and all the ponderous and relentless machinery available for the purpose was set in motion to impress this truth upon the over-demonstrative Freak. Most of us know this mighty engine. Under its operations many sensitive little boys crumple up into furtive and apathetic nonentities. Others grow into licensed buffoons, battening upon their own shame, cadging for cheap applause, thinking always of things to say and to do which will make fellows laugh. The Freak did neither. He remained obstinately and resolutely a Freak. If chidden for eccentricity he answered back, sometimes too effectively, and suffered. But he never gave in. At last, finding that he apparently feared no one,--though really this was far from being the case: his most audacious flights were as often as not inspired by sheer nervous excitement,--the world in which he moved decided to tolerate him, and finally ended by extending towards him a sort of amused respect.

All this time we have left our friend standing outside the door. Presently, drawing a deep breath, he entered, jauntily enough.

"Hallo, Freak, where have you been?" enquired Mr. Rumbold.

"I felt constrained," replied The Freak, as one old gentleman to another, "to return to the House upon an errand of reparation."

A full half of the company present were blankly ignorant as to the meaning of the word "reparation," so they giggled contentedly and decided that The Freak was in good form this morning.

"What was the trouble?" asked Jerningham.

"As I was counting my change in the cab," explained The Freak, "I found that I was a penny short. (I'll have fried sole, and then bacon-and-eggs, please. And chocolate.)"

"Shylock!" commented the humorous Mr. Jerningham.

The Freak hastened to explain.

"It was the only penny I had," he said: "that was why I missed it. The rest was silver. I saw what had happened: I had given a penny to Seagrave by mistake, instead of half-a-crown."

The thought of Mr. Seagrave, the stern and awful butler of the Hivite House, incredulously contemplating a solitary copper in his palm, what time the unconscious Freak drove away two-and-fivepence to the good, tickled the company greatly, and the narrator had made considerable inroads upon the fried sole before he was called upon to continue.

"What did you do?" asked Rumbold.

"I drove back and apologised, and gave him two-and-fivepence," said The Freak simply.

"Was he shirty about it?"

"No; he did n't seem at all surprised," was the rather naïve reply.

There was another laugh at this, and Jerningham observed:--

"Freak, you are the limit."

"I may be the limit," countered The Freak hotly,--ordinary chaff he could endure, but Mr. Jerningham had more than once exceeded the bounds of recognised fag-baiting that term,--"but I am wearing my own shirt, Jerningham, and not one of Carmyle's!"

There was a roar at this unexpected riposte, for Jerningham, though a dandy of the most ambitious type, was notoriously addicted to borrowed plumage, and the cubicle of the easy-going Carmyle was next his own.

"You will be booted for that afterwards, my lad," announced the discomfited wearer of Mr. Carmyle's shirt.

The Freak surveyed his tormentor thoughtfully. After all, he was safe from reprisals for nearly five weeks. He therefore replied, deliberately and pedantically:--

"I do not dispute the probability of the occurrence. But that won't prevent you," he added, reverting to the vernacular, "from feeling jolly well scored off, all the same. And"--after a brief interval to allow this psychological point full play--"mind you send the shirt back to Carmyle. I have enough trouble looking after his things as it is. Get it washed, and then carefully dis--"

"Carefully *what*?" enquired Mr. Jerningham, beginning to push back his chair.

The Freak, who had intended to say "disinfected," decided not to endanger his clean collar, carefully brushed hair, and other appurtenances of the homeward-bound.

--"And carefully despatched per Parcels Post," he concluded sweetly. "Hello, you fellows--finished?"

"Yes: buck up!" commanded Rumbold.

The feast ended in traditional fashion. No bill was ever asked for or presented upon these occasions. Rumbold major merely took the sugar-basin and, having emptied it of its contents, placed therein the sum of two-and-nine-pence--half-a-crown for his breakfast and threepence for the waiters. The bowl was then sent round the table in the manner of an offertory plate, and the resulting collection was handed without ceremony to the fat head-waiter, who received it with a stately bow and a few well-chosen and long-familiar phrases upon the subject of a good holiday and a Merry Christmas; after which the members of the party dispersed to the railway station and went their several ways.

It was characteristic of The Freak that he hung behind at the last moment, for the purpose of handing a furtive shilling to the inarticulate Teuton who had assisted in dispensing breakfast, and whose underfed appearance had roused beneath the comfortably distended waistcoat of our altruistic friend certain suspicions, not altogether unfounded, as to the principle upon which head-waiters share tips with their subordinates.

CHAPTER II
THE FIRST FREAK

My name is Carmyle. Possibly you may have noticed it in the previous chapter, among the list of those present at the breakfast at the Imperial. It was not a particularly hilarious meal for me, for I was leaving Grandwich for good that morning; and the schoolboy bids farewell to this, the first chapter of his life, with a ceremony--not to say solemnity--sadly at variance with the cheerfulness or indifference with which he sometimes turns the page at the close of later epochs.

I parted from the main body of Hivites at Peterborough, for they were bound for London, while I had to transfer my person and effects to the care of the Great Eastern Railway for conveyance to my home in Essex.

At Ely, a little tired of the company and conversation of five East Anglian farmers, who occupied more than their fair share of room and conducted an extremely dull technical conversation with quite surprising heat and vehemence over my head and across my waistcoat, I walked up the platform in search of a little more cubic space. At the very front of the train I found a third-class compartment containing only a single occupant.

"Hallo, Freak!" I said. "I thought you were bound for London."

"Your surmise," replied my late fag, "is correct. But there was a slight mishap at Peterborough."

"You got left behind?"

"Practically, yes. In point of fact, I was bunged out of the train by Spangle Jerningham."

"Why?"

"He bought some bananas, and I warned him not to. I said some people had been prosecuted only last week for eating fruit in a railway carriage."

"Silly young idiot!" I replied, falling into the trap, even as Jerningham had done. "Why--"

"But they *were*," persisted The Freak. "They were caught sucking dates--off their tickets! And as there was no train on for two hours," he concluded, neatly dodging "The Strand Magazine," "I decided to come round this way. We get to Liverpool Street by four. How far are you going?"

I told him, and the train resumed its journey through the fenland.

The next stop was Cambridge, where The Freak, suddenly remembering that the railway ticket in his possession was entirely useless for his present purpose, got out to buy another. I hung out of the carriage window, wondering which of the Colleges the tall yellow-brick building just outside the station might be, and gazing reverentially upon a group of three young men in tweed jackets and flannel trousers, who had temporarily torn themselves from the pursuit of knowledge for the purpose of bidding farewell to the members of a theatrical touring company.

Presently our engine and brake-van removed themselves to a place of refreshment down the line; whereupon a somnolent horse of mountainous aspect, which had been meekly standing by, attached by a trace to an empty third-class coach, took advantage of their absence to tow its burden to the front of our train and leave it there, like a foundling on a doorstep, subsequently departing in search of further practical jokes.

With that instinctive shrinking from publicity which marks the professions of literature, art, and the drama, each of the compartments of the third-class coach bore a label, printed in three colours, announcing that this accommodation was reserved for Mr. Wilton Spurge's Number One Company--I have always desired to meet a Number Two Company, but have never succeeded--in "The Sign of the Cross," proceeding from Cambridge to Liverpool Street, for Walthamstow.

The majority of Mr. Wilton Spurge's followers took their seats at once; but three young ladies, hugging boxes of chocolate, remained in affectionate conversation with the undergraduates upon the platform. Most of the gentlemen of the company still lingered in the refreshment-room. Suddenly there was a gentle tremor throughout the train, as the engine and brake-van reluctantly backed themselves into a position of contact. A whistle blew, and a white flag fluttered far down the platform.

"There's no hurry," observed The Freak, who had returned from the ticket office and was now surveying the passing show with his head thrust out of the window under my arm. "That white flag only means that the Westinghouse brake is working all right."

But the female mind takes no account of technical trifles, least of all upon a railway journey. To a woman flags and whistles all spell panic. At the first blast, a lady (whom I took to be the Empress Poppeia) hastily shepherded every one within reach into the train, and then directed a piercing summons in the direction of the refreshment-room. She was seconded by an irregular but impressive chorus of admonition upon the perils of delay, led by Mercia in person and supported by a bevy of Christian Martyrs and Roman Dancing-Girls.

The whistle sounded again, and a second flag fluttered--a green one this time. There was a concerted shriek from the locomotive and the ladies, followed by a commotion at the door of the refreshment-room, from which eftsoons the Emperor Nero, bearing a bag of buns and a copy of "The Era," shot hastily forth. He was closely followed by Marcus Superbus, running rapidly and carrying two bottles of stout. Three Roman Patricians with their mouths full, together with a Father of the Early Church clinging to a half-consumed pork-pie, brought up the rear.

Deeply interested in the progress of the race, and speculating eagerly as to whether Pagan or Christian would secure the corner-seats, The Freak and I failed for the moment to note that our own compartment was in danger of invasion. But resistance was vain. At the very last moment the door was wrenched open by the guard, and four human beings were projected into our company just as the train began to move. A handbag and two paper parcels hurtled through the air after them.

"Sorry to hurry you, Mr. Welwyn, sir," said the guard, standing on the footboard and addressing the leader of the party through the window, "but we are behind time as it is, with that theatrical lot."

"My fault entirely, guard," replied Mr. Welwyn graciously. He was a handsome scholarly man of about forty. I put him down as a University Don of the best type--possibly one of the Tutors of a great college. "We should have come earlier. And--er"--here followed the indeterminate mumble and sleight-of-hand performance which accompany the bestowal of the British tip--"thank you for your trouble."

"Thank you, sir," replied the gratified menial, and disappeared into space with half-a-crown in his palm. Evidently Mr. Welwyn was a man of substance as well as consequence.

"You did n't ought to have given him so much, father dear!"

This just but ungrammatical observation emanated from the female head of the party; and despite an innate disinclination to risk catching the eye of strangers in public, I turned and inspected the speaker. From her style of address it was plain that she was either wife or daughter to Mr. Welwyn. Daughter she probably was not, for she must have been quite thirty; and therefore by a process of exhaustion I was led to the reluctant conclusion that she was his wife. I say reluctant, for it seemed incredible that a suave polished academic gentleman could be mated with a lady:--

(1) Who would initiate a domestic discussion in the presence of strangers.

(2) Whose syntax was shaky.

(3) Who wore a crimson blouse, with vermilion feathers in her hat.

But it was so. Mr. Welwyn waved a hand deprecatingly.

"One has one's position to consider, dear," he said. "Besides, these poor fellows are not overpaid, I fear, by their employers."

At this, a grim contraction flitted for a moment over Mrs. Welwyn's florid good-tempered features, and I saw suitable retorts crowding to her lips. But that admirable and exceptional woman--as in later days she proved herself over and over again to be--said nothing. Instead, she smiled indulgently upon her extravagant husband, as upon a child of the largest possible growth, and accepted from him with nothing more than a comical little sigh two magazines which had cost sixpence each.

I now had time to inspect the other two members of the party. They were children. One was a little boy--a vulgar, overdressed, plebian, open-mouthed little boy--and I was not in the least surprised a moment later to hear his mother address him as "Percy." (It had to be either "Percy" or "Douglas.") He was dressed in a tight and rather dusty suit of velveteen, with a crumpled lace collar and a plush jockey-cap. He looked about seven years old, wore curls down to his shoulders, and extracted intermittent nourishment from a long and glutinous stick of licorice.

The other was a girl--one of the prettiest little girls I have ever seen. I was not--and am not--an expert on children's ages, but I put her down as four years old. She was a plump and well-proportioned child, with an abundance of brown hair, solemn grey eyes, and a friendly smile. She sat curled up on the seat, leaning her head against her mother's arm, an oasis of contentment and neatness in that dusty railway carriage; and I felt dimly conscious that in due time I should like to possess a little girl of my own like that.

At present she was engaged in industriously staring The Freak out of countenance.

The Freak, not at all embarrassed, smiled back at her. Miss Welwyn broke into an unmaidenly chuckle, and her father put down "The Morning Post."

"Why this hilarity, my daughter?" he enquired.

The little girl, who was apparently accustomed to academically long words, indicated The Freak with a little nod of her head.

"I like that boy," she said frankly. "Not the other. Too big!"

"Baby *dearie*, don't talk so!" exclaimed Mrs. Welwyn, highly scandalised.

"I apologise for my daughter's lack of reserve--and discrimination," said Mr. Welwyn to me, courteously. "She will not be so sincere and unaffected in twenty years' time, I am afraid. Are you gentlemen going home for the holidays?"

I entered into conversation with him, in the course of which I learned that he was a member of the University, off on vacation. He did not tell me his College.

"Do you get long holi--vacations, sir, at Cambridge?" I asked. "When do you have to be back?"

Youth is not usually observant, but on this occasion even my untutored faculties informed me that Mr. Welwyn was looking suddenly older.

"I am not going back," he said briefly. Then he smiled, a little mechanically, and initiated a discussion on compound locomotives.

Presently his attention was caught by some occurrence at the other end of the compartment. He laughed.

"My daughter appears to be pressing her companionship upon your friend with a distressing lack of modesty," he said.

I turned. The Freak had installed his admirer in the corner-seat beside him, and, having found paper and pencil, was engaged in turning out masterpieces of art at her behest. With a flat suitcase for a desk, he was executing--so far as the Great Eastern Railway would permit him--a portrait of Miss Welwyn herself; his model, pleasantly thrilled, affectionately clasping one of his arms in both of hers and breathing heavily through her small nose, which she held about six inches from the paper.

Finally the likeness was completed and presented.

"Now draw a cow," said Miss Welwyn immediately.

The Freak meekly set to work again.

Then came the inevitable question.

"What's her name?"

The artist considered.

"Sylvia," he said at length. Sylvia, I knew, was the name of his sister.

"Not like that name!" said the child, more prophetically than she knew.

The Freak apologised and suggested Mary Ann, which so pleased his patroness that she immediately lodged an order for twelve more cows. The artist executed the commission with unflagging zeal and care, Miss Welwyn following every stroke of the pencil with critical interest and numbering off the animals as they were created.

About this time Master Percy Welwyn, who had fallen into a fitful slumber, woke up and loudly expressed a desire for a commodity which he described as "kike." His mother supplied his needs from a string-bag. Refreshed and appeased, he slept anew.

Meanwhile the herd of cows had been completed, and The Freak was, immediately set to work to find names for each. The appellation Mary Ann had established a fatal precedent, for The Freak's employer ruthlessly demanded a double title for each of Mary Ann's successors. Appealed to for a personal contribution, she shook her small head firmly: to her, evidently, in common with the rest of her sex, destructive criticism of male endeavour was woman's true sphere in life. But when the despairing Freak, after submitting Mabel-Maud, Emily-Kate, Elizabeth-Jane, and Maria-Theresa, made a second pathetic appeal for assistance, the lady so far relented as to suggest "Seener Angler"--a form of address which, though neither bovine nor feminine, seemed to me to come naturally enough from the daughter of a Don, but caused Mr. and Mrs. Welwyn to exchange glances.

At last the tale was completed,--I think the last cow was christened "Bishop's Stortford," through which station we were passing at the moment,--and the exhausted Freak smilingly laid down his pencil. But no one who has ever embarked upon that most comprehensive and interminable of enterprises, the entertainment of a child, will be surprised to hear that Miss Welwyn now laid a pudgy fore-finger upon the first cow, and enquired:--

"Where *that* cow going?"

"Cambridge," answered The Freak after consideration.

"Next one?"

"London."

"Next one?"

Freak thought again.

"Grandwich," he said.

The round face puckered.

"Not like it. Anuvver place!"

"You think of one," said The Freak boldly.

The small despot promptly named a locality which sounded like "Tumpiton," and passed on pitilessly to the next cow.

"Where *that* one going?" she enquired.

"It is n't going: it's coming back," replied The Freak, rather ingeniously.

Strange to say, this answer appeared to satisfy the hitherto insatiable infant, and the game was abruptly abandoned. Picking up The Freak's pencil, Miss Welwyn projected a seraphic smile upon its owner.

"You give this to Tilly?" she enquired, in a voice which most men know.

"Rather."

"Tilly, ducky, don't act so greedy," came the inevitable maternal correction. "Give back the young gentleman--"

"It's all right," said The Freak awkwardly. "I don't want it, really."

"But--"

There came a shriek from the engine, and the train slowed down.

"Is this where they collect tickets, father?" enquired Mrs. Welwyn, breaking off suddenly.

Mr. Welwyn nodded, and his wife rather hurriedly plucked her daughter from her seat beside The Freak and transferred her to her own lap, to that damsel's unfeigned dolour.

"Sit on mother's knee just now, dearie," urged Mrs. Welwyn--"just for a minute or two!"

Miss Welwyn, who appeared to be a biddable infant, settled down without further objection. A moment later the train stopped and the carriage door was thrown open.

"Tickets, please!"

Mr. Welwyn and I sat next the door, and I accordingly submitted my ticket for inspection. It was approved and returned to me by the collector, an austere person with what Charles Surface once described as "a damned disinheriting countenance."

"Change next stop," he remarked. "Yours, sir?"

Mr. Welwyn handed him three tickets. The collector appeared to count them. Then his gloomy gaze fell upon the unconscious Miss Welwyn, who from the safe harbourage of her mother's arms was endeavouring to administer to him what is technically known, I believe, as The Glad Eye.

"Have you a ticket for that child, madam?" he enquired. "Too old to be carried."

Mrs. Welwyn looked helplessly at her husband, who replied for her.

"Yes, surely. Did n't I give it to you, my man?"

"No, sir," said the collector dryly; "you did not."

Mr. Welwyn began to feel in his pockets.

"That is uncommonly stupid of me," he said. "I must have it somewhere. I thought I put them all in one pocket."

He pursued his researches further, and the collector waited grimly. I looked at Mrs. Welwyn. She was an honest woman, and a fleeting glance at her face informed me that the search for this particular ticket was to be of a purely academic description.

"I must trouble you," began the man, "for--"

"It must be somewhere!" persisted Mr. Welwyn, with unruffled cheerfulness. "Perhaps I dropped it on the floor."

"Let *me* look!"

Next moment The Freak, who had been a silent spectator of the scene, dropped upon his knees and dived under the seat. The collector, obviously sceptical, fidgeted impatiently and stepped back on to the platform, as if to look for an inspector. I saw an appealing glance pass from Mrs. Welwyn to her husband. He smiled back airily, and I realised that probably this comedy had been played once or twice before.

The collector reappeared.

"The fare," he began briskly, "is--"

"Here's the ticket," announced a muffled voice from beneath the seat, and The Freak, crimson and dusty, emerged from the depths flourishing a green pasteboard slip.

The collector took it from his hand and examined it carefully.

"All right," he snapped. "Now your own, sir."

The Freak dutifully complied. At the sight of his ticket the collector's morose countenance lightened almost to the point of geniality. He was not to go empty away after all.

"Great Northern ticket. Not available on this linc," he announced.

"It's all right, old man," explained my fag affably. "I changed from the Great Northern at Peterborough. This line of yours is so much jollier," he added soothingly.

"Six-and-fourpence," said the collector.

The Freak, who was well endowed with pocket-money even at the end of term, complied with the utmost cheerfulness; asked for a receipt; expressed an earnest hope that the collector's real state of health belied his appearance; and resumed his corner-seat with a friendly nod of farewell.

Two minutes later this curious episode was at an end, and the train was swinging on its way to London. Mrs. Welwyn, looking puzzled and ashamed, sat silently in her corner; Mr. Welwyn, who was not the man to question the workings of Providence when Providence worked the right way, hummed a cheerful little tune in his. The deplorable child Percy slept. The Freak, with a scarlet face, industriously perused a newspaper.

As for Miss Tilly Welwyn, she sat happily upon a suitcase on the floor, still engaged in making unmaidenly eyes at the quixotic young gentleman who had just acted, not for the last time in his life, as her banker.

CHAPTER III
IO SATURNALIA!

I

Presently my turn came.

A small, spectacled, and entirely inarticulate gentleman in a very long gown, after a last glance to assure himself that my coat was sufficiently funereal and my trousers not turned up, took my hand in his; and we advanced mincingly, after the manner of partners in a country dance, over the tesselated pavement of the Senate House until we halted before the resplendent figure of the Vice-Chancellor.

Here my little companion delivered himself of a hurried and perfunctory harangue, in a language which I took to be Latin, but may for all I know have been Esperanto. The Vice-Chancellor muttered a response which I could not catch; impelled by an unseen power, I knelt before him and placed my two hands between his: an indistinct benediction fell from his lips, gently tickling my overheated scalp; and lo! the deed was done. I rose to my feet a Master of Arts of Cambridge University, at the trifling outlay of some twenty pounds odd.

Thereafter, by means of what the drill-book calls a "right-incline," I slunk unobtrusively past two sardonic-looking gentlemen in white bands, and escaped through the open north door into the cool solitude of Senate House Passage, and ultimately into Trinity Street.

I walked straight into the arms of my friend The Freak--The Freak in cap and gown, twenty-two years of age, and in his last year at the University.

"Hallo, Tiny!" was his joyous greeting. "This is topping!"

"Hallo, Freak!" I replied, shaking hands. "You got my wire, then?"

"Yes, what are you up for? I presume it is a case of one more shot at the General Examination for the B.A. Degree--what?"

I explained coldly that I had been receiving the Degree of Master of Arts.

"As a senior member of the University," I added severely, "I believe it is my duty to report you to the Proctors for smoking while in academic dress."

Freak's repartee was to offer me a cigarette.

"Let us take a walk down Trinity Street," he continued. "I have to go and see The Tut."

"Who?"

"My Tutor. Don't get fossilised all at once, old thing!"

I apologised.

"What are you going to see him about?" I enquired. "Been sent down?"

"No. I am going to get leave to hold a dinner-party consisting of more than four persons," replied my friend, quoting pedantically from the College Statute which seeks (vainly) to regulate the convivial tendencies of the undergraduate.

"Ah," I remarked airily--"quite so! For my part, such rules no longer apply to me."

Fatal vaunt! Next moment Dicky was frantically embracing me before all Trinity Street.

"Brave heart," he announced, "this is providential! You are a godsend--a *deus ex machina*--a little cherub sent from aloft! It never occurred to me: I need not go to The Tut for leave at all now! It would have been a forlorn hope in any case. But now all is well. *You* shall come to the dinner. In fact, you shall *give* it! Then no Tut in the world can interfere. Come along, host and honoured guest! Come and see Wicky about it!"

As The Freak hustled me down All Saints' Passage, I enquired plaintively who Mr. Wicky might be.

"Wickham is his name," replied The Freak. "He is nominally giving the dinner. We are going to--"

"Pardon me," I interposed. "How many people *are* nominally giving this dinner? So far, we have you, Wicky, and myself. I--"

"It's this way," explained my friend. "Wicky is nominally the host; he will do the honours. But I have dropped out. The dinner will be ordered in your name now. That's all."

"Why is Wicky nominally the host?" I enquired, still befogged.

"We are all giving the dinner--seven of us," explained The Freak; "all except yourself and The Jebber, in fact. Wicky has to be host because he is the only man who is not going to the dinner disguised as some one else. Now, do you understand?"

"There are one or two minor points," I remarked timidly, "which--"

"Go ahead!" sighed my friend.

"Who," I enquired, "is The Jebber? And why should he share with me the privilege of not paying for his dinner?"

The Freak became suddenly serious.

"The Jebber," he said, "is a poisonous growth called Jebson. He is in his first year. He owns bags of money, which he squanders in the wrong manner on every occasion. He runs after Blues and other celebrities, but has never caught one yet. On the other hand, he is rude to porters and bedmakers. He gathers unto himself bands of admiring smugs and tells them of the fast life he lives in town. He plays no games of any kind, except a little billiards with the marker, but he buttonholes you outside Hall in the evening and tells you how much he has won by backing the winner of the three o'clock race by wire. I think he has a kind of vague notion that he is sowing wild oats; but as he seems quite incapable of speaking the truth, I have no idea whether he is the vicious young mug he makes himself out to be or is merely endeavouring to impress us yokels. That is the sort of customer The Jebber is."

"And you have invited him to dinner?" I said.

"Yes; it's like this. We stood him as well as we could for quite a long while. Then, one evening, he turned up in my rooms when half a dozen of us were there--he is on my staircase, and I had rashly called upon him his first term--and after handing out a few fairy tales about his triumphs as a lady's man, he pulled a photograph from his pocket and passed it round. It was a girl--a jolly pretty girl, too! He said he was engaged to her. Said it as if--" The Freak's honest face grew suddenly hot, and his fingers bit ferociously into my arm. "Well, he began to talk about her. Said she was 'fearfully mashed on him!' That fairly turned our stomachs to begin with, but there was more to come. He confided to us that she was a dear little thing, but not quite up to his form; and he did n't intend to marry her until he had sown a few more of his rotten wild oats. And so on. That settled me, Tiny! So far I had not been so fierce about him as the other men. I had considered him just a harmless bounder, who would tone down when he got into the ways of the place. But a fellow who would talk like that before a roomful of men about a girl--his own girl--My God, Tiny! what would you do with such a thing?"

"Kill it," I said simply.

"That's what we nearly did, on the spot," said Dicky. "But--well--one feels a delicacy about even taking notice of that sort of stuff. You understand?"

I nodded. The reserve of the youthful male on affairs of the heart is much deeper than that of the female, though the female can never recognise the fact.

"So we simply sat still, feeling we should like to be sick. Then the man Jebson gave himself a respite and us an idea by going on to talk of his social ambitions. He confided to us that he had come up here to form influential friendships--with athletic bloods, future statesmen, sons of peers, and so forth. He explained that it was merely a matter of money. All he wanted was a start. As soon as the athletes and peers heard of him and his wealth, they would be only too pleased to hobnob with him. Suddenly old Wicky, who had been sitting in the corner absolutely mum, as usual, asked him straight off to come and dine with him, and said he would get a few of the most prominent men in the 'Varsity to come and meet him. We simply gaped at first, but presently we saw there was some game on; and when The Jebber had removed himself, Wicky explained what he wanted us to do. He's a silent bird, Wicky, but he thinks a lot. Here are his digs."

We had reached a house in Jesus Lane, which we now entered, ascending to the first floor.

Dicky rapidly introduced me to Mr. Wickham, who had just finished luncheon. He proved to be a young gentleman of diminutive stature and few words, in a Leander tie. He was, it appeared, a coxswain of high degree, and was only talkative when afloat. Then, one learned, he was a terror. It was credibly reported that on one occasion a freshman rowing bow in a trial eight, of a sensitive temperament and privately educated, had burst into tears and tried to throw away his oar after listening to Mr. Wickham's blistering comments upon the crew in general and himself in particular during a particularly unsteady half-minute round Grassy Corner.

He silently furnished us with cigarettes, and my somewhat unexpected inclusion in the coming revels was explained to him.

"Good egg!" he remarked, when Dicky had finished. "Go round to the kitchen presently. Have dinner in these rooms, Freak. May be awkward for the men to get into College all togged up."

"You see the idea now, Tiny?" said Dicky to me. "Wicky is going to be host, and the rest of us are going to dress up as influential young members of the University. We shall pull The Jebber's leg right off!"

"Do you think you will be able to keep up your assumed characters all dinner-time?" I asked. "You know what sometimes happens towards the end of--"

"That's all right," said The Freak. "We are n't going to keep it up right to the end. At a given signal we shall unveil."

"What then?" I enquired, not without concern.

"We shall hold a sort of court martial. After that I don't quite know what we will do, but we ought to be able to think of something pretty good by then," replied The Freak confidently.

Mr. Wickham summed up the situation.

"The man Jebson," he said briefly, "must die."

"What character are you going to assume?" I enquired of The Freak. "Athlete, politician, peer, scholar--?"

"I am the Marquis of Puddox," said my friend, with simple dignity.

"Only son," added Mr. Wickham, "of the Duke of Damsillie. Scotland for ever!"

"A Highlander?" I asked.

"Yes," said The Freak gleefully. "I am going to wear a red beard and talk Gaelic."

"Who are to be the other--inmates?" I asked.

"You'll see when the time comes," replied Dicky. "At present we have to decide on a part for you, my lad."

"I think I had better be Absent Friends," I said. "Then I need not come, but you can drink my health."

Mr. Wickham said nothing, but rose to his feet and crossed the room to the mantelpiece. On the corner of the mirror which surmounted it hung a red Turkish fez, with a long black tassel. This my host reached down and handed to me.

"Wear that," he said briefly--"with your ordinary evening things."

"What shall I be then?" I enquired meekly.

"Junior Egyptologist to the Fitzwilliam Museum," replied the fertile Mr. Wickham.

II

That shrinking but helpless puppet, the Junior Egyptologist to the Fitzwilliam Museum, duly presented himself at Mr. Wickham's at seven-thirty that evening, surmounted by the fez.

Here I was introduced to the guest of the evening, Mr. Jebson. He was a pasty-faced, pig-eyed youth of about four-and-twenty, in an extravagantly cut dress suit with a velvet collar. He wore a diamond ring and a soft shirt. He looked like an unsuccessful compromise between a billiard-marker and a casino croupier at a French watering-place. His right forefinger was firmly embedded in the buttonhole of a shaggy monster in a kilt, whom, from the fact that he spoke a language which I recognised as that of Mr. Harry Lauder, I took to be the heir of the Duke of Damsillie.

The Freak was certainly playing his part as though he enjoyed it, but the other celebrities, who stood conversing in a sheepish undertone in various corners, looked too like stage conspirators to be entirely convincing. However, Mr. Jebson appeared to harbour no suspicion as to the *bona fides* of the company in which he found himself, which was the main point.

I was now introduced to the President of the Cambridge University Boat Club, a magnificent personage in a made-up bow tie of light-blue satin; to the Sultan of Cholerabad, a coffee-coloured potentate in sweeping Oriental robes, in whom the dignity that doth hedge a king was less conspicuous than a thoroughly British giggle; and to the Senior Wrangler of the previous year, who wore a turn-down collar, trousers the bagginess of which a music-hall comedian would have envied, and blue spectacles.

Mesmerised by Mr. Wickham's cold eye and correct deportment, we greeted one another with stately courtesy: but the President of the Boat Club winked at me cheerfully; the Sultan of Cholerabad, scrutinising my fez, enquired in broken English the exact date of my escape from the cigarette factory; and the Senior Wrangler invited my opinion, *sotto voce*, upon the cut of his trousers.

In a distant corner of the room, which was very dimly lighted,--probably for purposes of theatrical effect,--I descried two more guests--uncanny figures both. One was a youth in semi-clerical attire, with short trousers and white cotton socks, diligently exercising what is best described as a Private Secretary voice upon his companion, a scarlet-faced gentleman in an exaggerated hunting-kit--horn and all. The latter I identified (rightly) as The Master of the University Bloodhounds, but I was at a loss to assign a character to The Private Secretary. I learned during the evening, from his own lips, that he was the Assistant Professor of Comparative Theology.

The party was completed by the arrival of a stout young gentleman with a strong German accent and fluffy hair. He was presented to us as The Baron Guldenschwein. (He actually was a Baron, as it turned out, but not a German. However, he possessed a strong sense of humour--a more priceless possession than sixty-four quarterings or a castle on the Rhine.)

Dinner was announced, and we took our places. Wickham sat at the head of the table, with Mr. Jebson on his right and the Marquis of Puddox on his left. I took the foot, supported on either hand by the President of the Boat Club and the Assistant Professor of Comparative Theology. The other four disposed themselves in the intervening places, the Sultan taking his seat upon Jebson's right, with the Baron opposite.

The dinner was served in the immaculate fashion customary at undergraduate feasts and other functions where long-suffering parents loom in the background with cheque-books. The table decorations had obviously been selected upon the principle that what is most expensive must be best, and each guest was confronted with a much beribboned menu with his title printed upon it. Champagne, at the covert but urgent representation of the Assistant Professor of Comparative Theology, was served with the *hors d'oeuvres*.

At first we hardly lived up to our costumes. A practical joke which begins upon an empty stomach does not usually speed from the mark. Fortunately The Freak, who was not as other men are in these matters, had entered upon his night's work at the very top of his form, and he gave us all an invaluable lead. The fish found him standing with one foot upon the table, pledging Mr. Jebson in language which may have been Gaelic, but more nearly resembled the baying of one of the University bloodhounds. This gave us courage, and presently the Assistant Theologian and the M.B.H. abandoned a furtive interchange of Rugby football "shop" and entered into a heated discussion with the Senior Wrangler upon certain drastic alterations which, apparently, the mathematical savants of the day contemplated making in the multiplication table.

I devoted my attention chiefly to observing the masterly fashion in which The Freak and the saturnine Mr. Wickham handled Jebson. The latter was without doubt a most unpleasant creature. The undergraduate tolerates and, too often, admires the vicious individual who is reputed to be a devil of a fellow. Still, that individual usually has some redeeming qualities. In the ordinary way of business he probably pulls an oar and shoves in the scrimmage as heartily as his neighbour: his recourses to riotous living are in the nature of reaction from these strenuous pursuits. They arise less from a desire to pose as a man of the world than from sheer weakness of the flesh. He is not in the least proud of them: indeed, like the rest of us, he is usually very repentant afterwards. And above all, he observes a decent reticence about his follies. He regards them as liabilities, not assets; and therein lies the difference between him and creatures of the Jebson type. Jebson took no part in clean open-air enthusiasms: he had few moments of reckless self-abandonment: to him the serious business of life was the methodical establishment of a reputation as a *viveur*. He sought to excite the admiration of his fellows by the recital of his exploits in what he called "the world." Such, naturally, were conspicuous neither for reticence nor truth. He was a pitiful transparent fraud, and I felt rather surprised, as I considered the elaborate nature of the present scheme for his discomfiture, that the tolerant easy-going crew who sat round the table should have thought the game worth the candle. I began to feel rather sorry for Jebson. After all, he was not the only noxious insect in the University. Then I remembered the story of the girl's photograph, and I understood. It was an ill day for The Jebber, I reflected, when he spoke lightly of his lady-love in the presence of Dicky Mainwaring.

The banquet ran its course. Presently dessert was placed upon the table and the waiters withdrew. The Sultan of Cholerabad, I noticed, had mastered the diffidence which had characterised his behaviour during the earlier stages of the proceedings, and was now joining freely in the conversation at the head of the table. I overheard Mr. Jebson extending to him a cordial invitation to come up with him to town at the end of the term and be introduced to a galaxy of music-hall stars, jockeys, and bookmakers--an invitation which had already been deferentially accepted by Mr. Wickham and the Marquis of Puddox. In return, the Sultan announced that the harem at Cholerabad was open to inspection by select parties of visitors on Tuesdays and Thursdays, on presentation of visiting-card.

The spirits of the party in general were now rising rapidly, and more than once the tranquillity of the proceedings was seriously imperilled. After the Baron Guldenschwein had been frustrated in an attempt to recite an ode in praise of the Master of the Bloodhounds (on the somewhat inadequate grounds that "I myself wear always bogskin boods"), our nominal host found himself compelled to cope with the Assistant Professor of Comparative Theology, who, rising unsteadily to his legs, proclaimed his intention of giving imitations of a few celebrated actors, beginning with Sir Henry Irving. The Theologian was in a condition which rendered censure and argument equally futile. He had consumed perhaps half a bottle of champagne and two glasses of port, so it was obvious that his present exalted condition was due not so much to the depths of his potations as to the shallowness of his accommodation for the same. I for one, having drunk at least as much as he and feeling painfully decorous, forbore to judge him. The rest of the company were sober enough, but leniently disposed, and our theological friend was allowed his way. He threw himself into a convulsive attitude, mouthed out an entirely unintelligible limerick about a young man from Patagonia, and sat down abruptly, well pleased with his performance.

Then came an ominous silence. The time for business was at hand. Mr. Jebson, still impervious to atmospheric influence, selected this moment for weaving his own shroud. He rose to his feet and made a speech. He addressed us as "fellow-sports"; he referred to Mr. Wickham as "our worthy Chair," and to myself as "our young friend Mr. Vice." The company as a whole he designated "hot stuff." After expressing, with evident sincerity, the pleasure with which he found himself in his present company, he revealed to us the true purport of his uprising, which was to propose the toast of "The Girls." Under the circumstances a more unfortunate selection of subject could not have been made. The speaker had barely concluded his opening sentence when the Marquis of Puddox, speaking in his natural tone of voice, rose to his feet and brought what promised to be a rather nauseous eulogy to a summary conclusion.

"Dry up," he rapped out, "and sit down at once. Clear the table, you fellows, and get the tablecloth off."

Without further ado the distinguished company present, with the exception of the Theologian, who had retired into a corner by himself to rehearse an imitation, obeyed Dicky's behest. The decanters and glasses were removed to the sideboard, and the cloth was whipped off.

"Take this loathsome sweep," continued the Marquis in the same dispassionate voice, indicating the guest of the evening, now as white as his own shirt-front, "and tie him up with table-napkins."

The dazed Jebson offered no resistance. Presently he found himself lying flat on his back upon the table, his arms and legs pinioned by Mr. Wickham's table-linen.

"Roll him up in the tablecloth," was The Freak's next order, "and set him on a chair."

This time Jebson found his tongue.

"Gentlemen all," he gasped between revolutions--the Master of the Bloodhounds and Baron Guldenschwein were swiftly converting him into a snowy cocoon--"a joke's all very well in its way between pals; but--"

"Put him on that chair," continued Dicky, taking not the slightest notice.

Willing hands dumped the mummified and inanimate form of Jebson into an armchair, and the unique collection of Sports sat round him in a ring.

Then suddenly Dicky laughed.

"That's all, Jebson," he said. "We are n't going to do anything else with you. You are not worth it."

Mr. Jebson, who had been expecting the Death by a Thousand Cuts at the very least, merely gaped like a stranded carp. He was utterly demoralised. To a coward, fear of pain is worse than pain itself.

Dicky continued:--

"We merely want to inform you that we think you are not suited to University life. The great world without is calling you. You are wasted here: in fact, you have been a bit of a failure. You mean well, but you are lacking in perception. There is too much Ego in your Cosmos. Napoleon, you will remember, suffered from the same infirmity. For nearly two terms you have deluded yourself into the belief that we think you a devil of a fellow. We have sat and listened politely to your reminiscences: we have permitted you to refer to all the Strand loafers that one has ever heard of by their pet names. And all the time you have entirely failed to realise that we see through you. For a while you rather amused us, but now we are fed up with you. You are getting the College a bad name, too. We are not a very big College, but we are a very old and very proud one, and we have always kept our end up against larger and less particular establishments. So I'm afraid we must part with you. You are too high for us. That is all, I think. Would any one else like to say anything?"

"Are n't we going to toy with him a little?" asked the Senior Wrangler. "We might bastinado him, or shave one side of his head."

But Dicky would have none of it.

"Too childish," he said. "We will just leave him as he is, and finish our evening. Then he can go home and pack his carpet-bag. But"--The Freak turned suddenly and savagely upon the gently perspiring Jebson--"let me give you one hint, my lad. Never again mention ladies' names before a roomful of men, or, by God, you'll get a lesson from some one some day that you will remember to the end of your life! That is all. I have finished. The Committee for Dealing with Public Nuisances is dissolved. Let us--"

"I will now," suddenly remarked a confidential but slightly vinous voice from the other end of the room, "have great pleasure in giving you an imitation of Mr. Beerbohm Tree."

And the Assistant Professor of Comparative Theology, who had been neglecting the rôle of avenging angel in order to prime himself at the sideboard for another excursion into the realms of mimetic art, struck exactly the same attitude as before, and began to mouth out, with precisely similar intonation and gesture, the limerick which had already done duty in the case of Sir Henry Irving.

After this the proceedings degenerated rapidly into a "rag" of the most ordinary and healthy type. The company, having dined, had ceased to feel vindictive, and The Freak's admirably appropriate handling of the situation met with their entire appreciation. With relief they proceeded from labour to recreation. Mr. Jebson was unceremoniously bundled into a corner; some one opened Mr. Wickham's piano, and in two minutes an impromptu dance was in full swing. I first found myself involved in an extravagant perversion of the Lancers, danced by the entire strength of the company with the exception of Baron Guldenschwein, who presided at the piano. After this the Theologian, amid prolonged cries of dissent, gave another imitation--I think it was of Sarah Bernhardt--which was terminated by a happy suggestion of Dicky's that the entertainer should be "forcibly fed"--an overripe banana being employed as the medium of nourishment. Then the Baron struck up "The Eton Boating Song." Next moment I found myself (under strict injunctions to remember that I was "lady") waltzing madly round in the embrace of the Senior Wrangler, dimly wondering whether the rôle of battering-ram which I found thrust upon me during the next ten minutes was an inevitable one for all female partners, and if so, why girls ever went to balls.

Presently my partner suggested a rest, and having propped me with exaggerated gallantry against the window-ledge, took off his dickey and fanned me with it.

After that we played "Nuts in May."

The fun grew more uproarious. Each man was enjoying himself with that priceless *abandon* which only youth can confer, little recking that with the passing of a very few years he would look back from the world-weary heights of, say, twenty-five, upon such a memory as this with pained and incredulous amazement. Later still, say at forty, he would look back again, and the retrospect would warm his heart. For the present, however, our warmth was of a purely material nature, and the only Master of Arts present mopped his streaming brow and felt glad that he was alive. To a man who has worked without a holiday for three years either in a drawing-office or an engineering-shop in South London, an undergraduate riot of the most primitive description is not without its points.

"The Eton Boating Song" is an infectious measure: in a short time we were all singing as well as dancing. The floor trembled: the chandelier rattled: the windows shook: Jesus Lane quaked.

"Swing, swing, together,"
we roared,
"With your bodies between your--"

Crash!

The flowing tartan plaid which adorned the shoulders of the scion of the house of Damsillie had spread itself abroad, and, encircling in a clinging embrace the trussed and pinioned form of the much-enduring Jebson, had whipped him from his stool of penance and caused him, from no volition of his own, to join the glad throng of waltzers, much as a derelict tree-trunk joins a whirlpool. In a trice the Assistant Professor of Comparative Theology and the President of the University Boat Club, who were performing an intricate reversing movement at the moment, tripped heavily backwards over his prostrate form, while the Most Noble the Marquis of Puddox (and lady), brought up in full career by the stoutly resisting plaid, fell side by side upon the field. The Senior Wrangler and the Junior Egyptologist, whirling like dervishes, topped the heap a moment later. The Baron Guldenschwein and the Master of the Bloodhounds leavened the whole lump.

My head struck the floor with a dull thud. Simultaneously some one (I think it was the Senior Wrangler) put his foot into my left ear. Even at this excruciating moment I remember reflecting that it would be a difficult matter, after this, to maintain a distant or stand-offish attitude towards the gentleman who at this moment was acting as the foundation-stone of our pyramid.

The music ceased, with a suddenness that suggested musical chairs, and I was aware of an ominous silence. Disengaging my neck from the embrace of a leg clad in a baggy silk trousering,--evidently it belonged to the Sultan: how he got into that galley I have no conception, for he had recently relieved the Baron at the piano,--I struggled to my hands and knees and crawled out of the turmoil upon the floor.

Set amid the constellation of stars which still danced round my ringing head, I beheld a sleek but burly gentleman in sober black, silk hat in hand, standing in the doorway. He was a University bull-dog. We were in the clutches of the Law.

"Proctor's compliments, gentlemen, and will the gentleman what these rooms belong to kindly step--"

It was a familiar formula. Wickham, who had struggled to his feet, answered at once:--

"All right; I'll come down. Wait till I put my collar on. Is the Proctor downstairs?"

"Yes, sir," said the man.

"Who is it?"

"Mr. Sandeman, sir."

"Sandy? Golly!" commented Mr. Wickham, swiftly correcting the disorder of his array. Several people whistled lugubriously. Wickham turned to Dicky.

"I'll go down," he said. "You sort out those chaps on the floor."

He disappeared with the bull-dog, leaving Dicky and myself to disintegrate the happy heap of arms and legs upon the carpet. Ultimately we uncovered our foundation-stone, black in the face, but resigned. We unrolled his winding-sheet, cut his bonds, and were administering first aid of a hearty but unscientific description when there was a cry from Dicky--

"Ducker, you young fool, where are you going to?"

Ducker, it appeared, was the real name of the Assistant Theologian. (As a matter of fact, it was Duckworth.) He was already at the door. Finding his exit detected, he drew himself up with an air of rather precarious dignity, and replied:--

"I am going to speak to Sandy."

"What for?"

"Sandy," explained Mr. Ducker rapidly, "has never seen my imitation of George Alexander as the Prisoner of Zenda. He has got to have it now!"

Next moment the persevering pantomimist had disappeared, and we heard him descending the stairs in a series of kangaroo-like leaps.

"Come on, Bill," said Dicky to me. "We must follow him quick, or there will be trouble."

We raced downstairs into the entrance-hall. The open doorway framed the dishevelled figure of Mr. Duckworth. He was calling aloud the name of one Sandy, beseeching him to behold George Alexander. Outside in the gloom of Jesus Lane we beheld Mr. Wickham arguing respectfully with a majestic figure in a black gown, white bands, and baleful spectacles. With a sinking heart I recognised one of the two saturnine clerical gentlemen in whose presence I had been presented for my M.A. degree only a few hours before.

"Sandy, old son," bellowed Mr. Duckworth perseveringly, "be a sportsman and look at me a minute!" He was now out upon the doorstep, posturing. "Flavia! Fla-a-a-via!" he yowled.

"It's no good our pulling him back into the house," said Dicky, "or Sandy will have him for certain. Let's rush him down the street, and hide somewhere."

Next moment, with a hand upon each of the histrionic Theologian's shoulders, we were flying down Jesus Lane. Behind us thundered the feet of one of the minions of the Reverend Hugo Sandeman. (The other had apparently been retained to guard the door.) Mr. Duckworth, suddenly awake to the reality of the situation and enjoying himself hugely, required no propulsion. In fact, he was soon towing us--so fast that Dicky, encumbered by his chieftain's costume, and I, who had not sprinted for three years, had much ado to hold on to him. The bull-dog, who was corpulent and more than middle-aged, presently fell behind.

It was raining slightly and there were not many people about, for it was close on ten o'clock. We emerged at the double from Jesus Lane into Sidney Street, and dashed down the first available opening. It brought us into a narrow alley--one of the innumerable "passages" with which Cambridge is honeycombed. Here we halted and listened intently.

III

Having now leisure to review the incredible sequence of events which had resulted in my being hounded through the streets of Cambridge by the University authorities,--when by University law I should have been one of the hounds,--in company with two undergraduates, one attired as a sort of burlesque Rob Roy and the other in a state of more than doubtful sobriety, I embarked upon a series of gloomy but useless reflections upon my imbecility. My only consolation was derived from the knowledge that I no longer wore the insignia of the Junior Egyptologist, having mislaid that accursed ornament in the course of the evening's revels.

My meditations were interrupted by the voice of The Freak.

"What shall we do next?" he enquired, with great gusto.

"Go home," said I, without hesitation.

"How?"

"Straight on: this passage must lead somewhere."

"Does it? Have you ever been down it before?"

"I can't remember; but--"

"Well, I have, and it does n't lead anywhere, young feller-my-lad. That's why that blamed bull-dog of Sandy's has n't followed us up harder. He knows he has got us on toast. I expect they 're all waiting for us at the mouth of this rat-hole now."

Certainly we were in a tight corner. But even now The Freak's amazing resource did not fail him. We were standing at the moment outside a building of rather forbidding aspect, which had the appearance of a parish institute. The windows of one of the rooms on the ground-floor were brightly lighted, and even as we looked a large podgy young man, of the Sunday-School superintendent type, appeared on the front steps. We feigned absorption in a large printed notice which stood outside the door.

The podgy man addressed us.

"Are you coming in, gentlemen? You'll find it worth your while. The professor is only just 'ere, 'avin' missed 'is train from King's Cross; so we are goin' to begin at once." He spoke in the honeyed--not to say oily--accents of a certain type of "townee" who sees a chance of making something out of a 'Varsity man, and his conversation was naturally addressed to me. My two companions kept modestly in the shadows.

"First lecture free to all," continued the podgy young man, smiling invitingly. "Members of the University specially welcomed."

At this moment The Freak emerged into the full glare of the electric light, and nudged me meaningly in the ribs.

"I have two friends with me," I said--"one from Scotland--er--the North of Scotland. I am taking them for an after-dinner stroll, to view the Colleges, and--er--so on."

"All are welcome," repeated the young man faintly, gazing in a dazed fashion at the Marquis of Puddox. "Step inside."

What we were in for we did not know. But it was a case of any port in a storm, and we all three allowed ourselves to be shepherded into a room containing some fifteen people, who, to judge by the state of the atmosphere, had been there some time. Our entrance caused an obvious flutter, and distracted the attention of the room from a diminutive foreigner in a frayed frock-coat, with a little pointed beard and pathetic brown eyes, who was sitting nervously on the edge of a chair, endeavouring to look collected under the blighting influence of a good honest British stare. The three newcomers at once retired to the only unoccupied corner of the room, where it was observed that the clerical member of the party immediately adopted a somewhat unconventional attitude and composed himself to slumber.

At this point the podgy young man, who appeared to be the secretary of the club,--some society for mutual improvement,--rose to his feet and announced that he had great pleasure in introducing "the professor" to the company. Apparently we were to have a French lesson. We had arrived just in time for the opening ceremony, which we might enjoy free gratis and for nothing; but if we desired to come again--a highly improbable contingency, I thought--we were at liberty to do so every Thursday evening throughout the quarter, at a fee of one guinea.

"I think, gentlemen," concluded the secretary, "that you will find your money 'as been well laid out. We 'ave very 'igh reports of the professor's abilities, and I am glad to see that the fame of 'is teaching 'as been sufficient to attract a member of the University here to-night."

At this he bowed deferentially in our direction, and there was some faint applause. To my horror Dicky promptly rose to his feet, and, returning the podgy young man's bow, delivered himself in a resonant Gaelic whinny of the following outrageous flight of fancy:--

"Hech-na hoch-na hoy ah hoo!"

As delivered, I am bound to admit that it sounded like a perfectly genuine expression of Celtic fervour. Dicky sat down, amid an interested murmur, and whispered hurriedly to me:--

"Interpret, old soul!"

I rose miserably to my feet.

"My friend," I announced, wondering dimly how long it would be before the podgy young man and his satellites uprose and cast us forth, "has replied to your very kind welcome by a quotation from one of his national poets,--er, Ossian,--which, roughly translated, means that, however uncouth his exterior may be, he never forgets a kindness!"

Which was rather good, I think.

There was more applause, which had the disastrous effect of rousing Mr. Duckworth from his slumbers. Finding that every one present was clapping his hands and looking in his direction, he struggled to his feet.

"Mr. Chairman, ladies and gentlemen," he began cheerfully, "in response to your most flattering encore I shall have great pleasure, with your attention and permission, in givin' you my celebrated imitation"--here he began to stiffen into the old familiar epileptic attitude--"of Sir George Irving--"

We drew him down, as gently as possible, into his seat, and the secretary, slightly disconcerted, called upon the lecturer to begin.

The professor rose, and having bowed gallantly to the secretary's wife, the only lady present,--a courtesy which was acknowledged by that young woman, with true British politeness, by a convulsive giggle,--proceeded, in language which betrayed the fact that although he might be able to teach French he could not pronounce English, to explain his *modus operandi*. He proposed, we discovered, to describe in his own tongue some familiar scene of everyday life, suiting his action to the word, and laying his hand, whenever possible, upon the objects mentioned in his discourse, in order to assist us in grasping his meaning.

"*Par exemple*," he explained, "if I touch ze 'at of madam, so"--here he darted across the room and laid a playful finger on the brim of Mrs. Secretary's rather flamboyant headgear, a familiarity which that paragon of British propriety greeted with an hysterical "Ow, George!"--"and say *chapeau*, den you vill onnerstan' vat I mean."

"I doubt it, old son," observed Mr. Duckworth gravely.

"To-night," continued the professor, who had fortunately been unable to understand this innuendo, "I vill describe a simple scene zat you all know--*n'est-ce pas?*"

Here he struck an attitude, as if to imply that they must be careful not to miss this bit, and declaimed:--

"*Ze postman, 'ow 'e brings ze letters.*"

This announcement was greeted with a stony silence.

"I tell you ze title," he added in warning tones, "but after now I spik no more Engleesh."

"Quite right; I would n't if I were you," remarked Mr. Duckworth approvingly.

The professor bowed politely at this commendation from such an exalted quarter, and plunged into his subject.

"*Le facteur, comment il apporte les lettres!*"

The audience, composed exclusively of podgy young men like the secretary, received this exordium with different degrees of self-consciousness, after the manner of the Englishman when a foreign language is spoken in his presence. Some looked extremely knowing, while others stirred uneasily in their seats, and regarded each other with shamefaced grins.

The professor meanwhile had advanced to the window, and was gazing excitedly out into the darkness.

"*Regardez le facteur qui s'approche!*" he cried, pointing with his finger in the direction where I calculated that the Reverend Hugo and his attendant fiends were probably still waiting for us; "*dans la rue, là-bas! Il m'apporte peut-être une lettre! Mais de qui? Ah, de--*" Here he clutched his heart convulsively, evidently bent upon a touch of humorous sentiment: but a glance at the adamantine countenances of his audience caused him to change his mind, and he continued, rather lamely:--

"*Je descendrai au rez-de-chaussée. Je m'approche à la porte*--pardon, m'sieur!"

The last remark was addressed to Mr. Duckworth, the professor having stumbled over his legs on his way to the door. The Theologian responded politely with an imitation of a man drawing a cork, and the demonstration proceeded.

"*Je saisis le bouton,*" continued our instructor, convulsively clutching the door-handle. "*Je tour-r-r-rne le bouton! J'ouvre la porte! Je m'éloigne dans le corridor*--Oh, pardon, m'sieur! Je vous--"

He had torn open the door with a flourish and hurled himself into the passage in faithful pursuance of his system, only to collide heavily and audibly with some unyielding body outside.

"Proctor's compliments, sir," said a deep voice, "but if you are in charge 'ere, will you kindly come and speak to 'im a minute?"

The Frenchman's answering flood of incomprehensible explanation was cut short by the secretary, who rose from his seat and hurried out. A few questions and answers passed between him and the bull-dog, and then we heard their footsteps dying away in the direction of the front door, where the Reverend Hugo was doubtless waiting.

Next moment the company in the room were surprised, and I firmly believe disappointed, when the three last-joined recruits, after a hurried glance round the walls as if for a humbler means of exit, rose and unostentatiously quitted the apartment by the door.

———

Once in the passage, we turned hastily and blindly to the left, leaving behind us the front door, which was blocked by an animated group composed of the secretary, the professor,--what he was doing there I do not know: perhaps he thought that three more pupils were applying for admission,--and the larger of the Reverend Hugo's two bull-dogs, while that avenging angel's voice could be heard uplifted in a stately harangue outside.

We scuttled up the passage and dived through the first door that presented itself, closing and locking it behind us. On turning up the electric light we found ourselves in a large deserted room, occupied by two bagatelle tables. It was unfortunately lighted from the roof, which put escape by the window out of the question. However, at the far end we spied another door. Through this we rushed, into what appeared to be a recreation-room, occupied solely by two spectacled gentlemen immersed in a game of chess. Their surprise when three total strangers, two in unusual dress and all in an obvious hurry, invaded the privacy of their apartment, only to make a hasty and undignified exit by the window, must have been considerable, but we did not stay to observe it.

IV

Three weeks later The Freak came up to town for his Easter vacation, and dined with me at my club, and I heard the end of the tale.

Nothing very dreadful had happened, it appeared. Mr. Wickham, having laconically accepted full responsibility for the riot in his rooms, had been gated at eight for the rest of the term. The fact that I had ordered the dinner was unknown to the Proctors, and the College cook had not enlightened them. The identity of the Marquis of Puddox, the Junior Egyptologist, and the Assistant Professor of Comparative Theology had never been discovered.

"So your guilty secret, old thing," concluded Dicky, "is safe. And now I want to invite you to another function."

"Thank you," I said gruffly, "but I think not. What sort of function is it this time?"

"A wedding," replied Dicky unexpectedly.

"Great Scott! Yours?"

"No--The Jebber's! He has grown quite a white man. The little homily which I took the liberty of delivering to him that evening, coupled with the very light sentence imposed, quite won his heart, it appears. He never leaves me now. Eats out of my hand. He is going down at the end of the May term like a sensible Jebber, and he is to be married to his girl in June."

"The girl of the photograph?"

"Yes. He has quite got over his wild-oats theories, and his girl now has him completely in hand. I have seen them together, and I know. They are very happy."

My romantic friend sighed comfortably, and concluded:--

"I have promised to be best man."

"You?"

"Yes; he asked me, and one can't decline. You are coming with me, fellow-sport, to represent the Senior Members of the University!"

I went. No one ever refuses anything to The Freak.

BOOK TWO
A BLIND ALLEY
CHAPTER IV
TRAVELS WITH A FIRST RESERVE

I arrived at Shotley Beauchamp (for Widgerley and the Sludyard Valley Branch) with my heart gradually settling into my boots.

Most of us--men, not women: a woman, I fancy, provided she knows that her hat is on straight, is prepared to look the whole world in the face at any moment--are familiar with the sinking sensation which accompanies us to the door of a house to which we have been bidden as a guest for the first time. We foresee ahead of us a long vista of explanations, and for the moment we hate explanations more than anything on earth.

First, we shall have to explain ourselves to the butler. Then, pending the tardy appearance of our host and hostess, we shall have to explain ourselves to uninterested fellow-guests. At tea, knowing no one, we shall stand miserably aloof, endeavouring *faute de mieux* to explain our presence to ourself, and wondering whether it would be decent to leave before breakfast next morning. After dressing for dinner we shall come down too early, and have to explain ourselves to an embarrassed governess and a critical little girl of twelve. There for the present our imagination boggles. Pondering these things, we enquire bitterly why we ever left the club, where, though life may be colourless, no questions are asked.

It is true that these illusions dispel themselves with the first grip of our host's hand, but they usually cling to us right up to the opening of the front door; and as I on this particular occasion had only got as far as the platform of the local station, my soul *adhæsit pavimento*.

After the habit of shy persons, I compiled a list of my own special handicaps as I sat in my solitary smoking-compartment. As far as I can remember they ran something like this:--

(1) I have been roaming about the waste places of the earth for more than ten years, and have entirely lost any social qualities that I ever possessed.

(2) For people who like that sort of thing, house-parties are well enough. But I do not understand the young man of the present day, and he apparently does not understand me. As for the modern young woman, I simply shrink from her in fear.

(3) I have never met my host and hostess in my life.

(4) It is quite possible that The Freak has forgotten to tell his parents that he has invited me.

(5) In any case I probably shall not be met at the station, and there are never any conveyances to be had at these places. Altogether--

At this moment the train drew up at Shotley Beauchamp, and a smiling groom opened the door and enquired if I were for The Towers. Item Number Five was accordingly deleted from my catalogue of woes. Two minutes later Items One to Four slipped silently away into the limbo of those things that do not matter. A girl was sitting in the brougham outside the station.

"Lady goin' up, too, sir," remarked the groom into my ear. "Her maid," he added, "is in the dogcart. You got a man, sir?"

"No."

The groom touched his hat and departed, doubtless to comfort the maid.

I paused at the carriage-door, and by means of a terrifying cough intimated that I, too, had been invited to The Towers, and, although a stranger and unintroduced, begged leave in the humblest manner possible to assert my right to a seat in the brougham.

I was greeted with a friendly smile.

"Come in! I expect you are Mr. Carmyle."

I admitted guardedly that this was so, and proceeded to install myself in that part of the brougham not already occupied by the lady's hat.

"My name is Constance Damer," said my companion, as the brougham started. "Perhaps you have heard of me?"

"No," I replied, "I have not."

"Not very well put!" said Miss Damer reprovingly.

"I have been abroad for several years," I murmured in extenuation.

"I know," said my companion, nodding her head. "You have been building a dam across something in Africa."

I accepted this precise summary of my professional career with becoming meekness. Miss Damer continued:--

"And I suppose you are feeling a little bit lost at present."

"Yes," I said heartily, "I am."

"You should have said 'Not *now*!'" explained my companion gently.

I apologised again.

"I shall make allowances for you until you find your feet," said Miss Damer kindly.

I thanked her, and asked whom I was likely to meet at The Towers.

Miss Damer ticked off the names of the party on her small gloved fingers. (Have I mentioned that she was *petite*?)

"Mr. Mainwaring and Lady Adela," she said. "You know *them*, of course?"

"No. I saw them once on Speech Day at school fifteen years ago. That is all."

"Well, they are your host and hostess."

"Thank you: I had gathered that," I replied deferentially.

"Then Dicky."

"Dicky? Who is-- Oh, The Frea-- Yes. Quite so! Proceed!"

"What did you call him?" asked Miss Damer, frankly curious.

"I--well--at school we used to call him The Freak," I explained. "Men very often never know the Christian names of their closest friends," I added feebly. "Who else?"

"There is Hilda Beverley, of course. You have heard of her?"

"N--no. Ought I to have done?"

Miss Damer's brown eyes grew quite circular with surprise.

"Do you mean to tell me," she asked incredulously, "that Dicky never informed you that he was engaged?"

"No. You see," I pointed out, anxious to clear my friend of all appearance of lukewarmness as a lover, "I only met him the other day for the first time in fifteen years, and we naturally had a good deal to tell one another; and so, as it happened--that is--" I tailed off miserably under Miss Damer's implacable eye.

"You are his greatest friend, aren't you?" she enquired.

On reflection I agreed that this was so, although I had never seriously considered the matter before. Women have a curious habit of cataloguing their friends into a sort of order of merit--"My greatest friend, my greatest friend but six," and so on. The more sensitive male shrinks from such an invidious undertaking. Dicky and I had corresponded with one another with comparative regularity ever since our University days; and when two Englishmen, one hopelessly casual and the other entirely immersed in his profession, achieve this feat, I suppose they rather lay themselves open to accusations of this sort.

"And he never told you he was engaged?"

I shook my head apologetically.

"Ah, well," said Miss Damer charitably, "I dare say he would have remembered later. One can't think of everything in a single conversation, can one?" she added with an indulgent smile.

I was still pondering a suitable and sprightly defence of masculine reserve where the heart is concerned, when the carriage swung round through lodge-gates, and the gravel of the drive crunched beneath our wheels.

"I hope the old Freak and his girl will be very happy together," I said, rather impulsively for me. "He deserves a real prize."

"You are right," said Miss Damer, "he does."

My heart warmed to this little lady. She knew a good man when she saw one.

"Have they been engaged long?" I asked.

"About a month."

"Where did he come across her?"

"He did not come across her," replied Miss Damer with gentle reproof, as a Mother Superior to a novice. "They were brought together."

"That means," I said, "that it is what is called an entirely suitable match?"

Miss Damer nodded her small wise head.

"From a parental point of view," I added.

"From Lady Adela's point of view," corrected Miss Damer. "Mr. Mainwaring, poor old dear, has not got one."

"But what about The Freak's point of view?" I enquired.

"I can hear you quite well in your ordinary tone of voice," Miss Damer assured me.

I apologised, and repeated the question.

The girl considered. Obviously, it was a delicate subject.

"He seems quite content," she said at last. "But then, he never could bear to disappoint any one who had taken the trouble to make arrangements for his happiness."

"Would you mind telling me," I said, "without any mental reservation whatsoever, whether you consider that this engagement is the right one for him?"

Miss Damer's eyes met mine with perfect frankness.

"No," she said, "I don't. What is more, the engagement is beginning to wear rather thin. In fact,"--her eyes twinkled,--"I believe that Lady Adela is thinking of calling out her First Reserve."

"You mean--"

"I mean," said Miss Damer, "that Lady Adela is thinking of calling out her First Reserve."

A natural but most impertinent query sprang to my lips, to be stifled just in time.

"You were going to say?" enquired Miss Damer.

"I was going to say what a pretty carriage drive this is," I replied rapidly. "You will be glad of a cup of tea, though?"

"Yes, indeed," replied my companion brightly; but her attitude said "Coward!" as plainly as could be.

Still, there are some questions which one can hardly ask a lady after an acquaintance of only ten minutes.

"There is the house," continued Miss Damer, as our conveyance weathered a great clump of rhododendrons. "Are n't you glad that this long and dusty journey is over?"

"Not *now*!" I replied.

My little preceptress turned and bestowed on me a beaming smile.

"That is *much* better!" she remarked approvingly.

CHAPTER V
VERY ODIOUS

I

We found the house-party at tea in the hall of The Towers. The Mainwaring parents proved to be a little old gentleman, with grey side-whiskers and a subdued manner, and an imposing matron of fifty, who deliberately filled the teapot to the brim with lukewarm water upon our approach and then gave me two fingers to shake. To Miss Damer was accorded a "Constance--dear child!" and a cold peck upon the right cheek.

After that I was introduced to Dicky's sister Sylvia--a tall and picturesque young woman, dressed in black velvet with a lace collar. She wore the air of a tragedy queen--not, it struck me, because she felt like a tragedy queen, but because she considered that the pose suited her.

The party was completed by a subaltern named Crick--a jovial youth with a *penchant* for comic songs, obviously attached to the person of Miss Sylvia Mainwaring--and of course, The Freak's lady-love, Miss Hilda Beverley, to whom I was shortly presented.

I am afraid our conversation was not a conspicuous success. Miss Beverley was tall, handsome, patrician, and cultivated, obviously well-off and an admirable talker. Still, it takes two to make a dialogue, and when one's own contributions to the same, however unprovocative, are taken up *seriatim*, analysed, turned inside out, and set aside with an amused smile by a lady who evidently regards a conversation with one of her *fiancé's* former associates as a chastening but beneficial form of intellectual discipline, a man may be excused for not sparkling.

Half an hour later, perspiring gently, I was rescued by The Freak and conducted to the smoking-room.

"You never told me you were engaged, old man," I said, as we settled down to a little much-needed refreshment.

"It's a fact, though," replied The Freak proudly. "*A marriage has been arranged*--and all that. Say when."

"*And will shortly take place*, I suppose?"

"No immediate hurry," said The Freak easily. "There are one or two things that Hilda wants to cure me of before we face the starter. This, for instance." He held up an extremely dilute whiskey-and-soda. "Between meals, that is. Likewise my--er--casual outlook on life in general."

"Miss Beverley will have her hands full," I observed.

"Think so? She will do it, though," replied my renegade friend confidently. "She is a very capable girl. Regards me as her mission in life. I feel jolly proud about it, I can tell you--like one of those reformed drunkards they stand up on the platform to tell people what a Nut he used to be in the old days, and look at him now! By the way, I promised Hilda I would n't use the word 'Nut' any more. Check me if I become too colloquial, old son. Hilda is rather down on what she calls my 'inability to express myself in rational English.'"

"Colloquialism was not formerly a failing of yours, Freak," I said. "As a small boy you were rather inclined the other way."

"As a small boy, yes," agreed The Freak. "But it is not easy to maintain the pedantic habit at a public school," he added feelingly.

"Do you remember once," I continued, "telling old Hanbury, when he dropped upon you for giggling in form, that your 'risible faculties had been unduly excited by the bovine immobility of Bailey minor'?"

"Yes, I remember. Hilda would have been proud of me that day," replied The Freak, sighing over his lost talent. "Now she thinks me too flippant and easy-going. Lacking in dignity, and so forth. But if you watch me carefully during your stay here you will find that I have very largely regained my old form. I am getting frightfully intellectual. You ought to see us reading Browning together before breakfast. It is a sublime spectacle. Talking of sublime spectacles, we are all going to Laxley Races on Tuesday, and I can give you an absolutely dead snip for the Cup."

The next ten minutes were devoted to a conversation which, from the point of view both of subject-matter and expression, must have undone the regenerative work of several weeks. Fortunately Miss Beverley was adorning herself for dinner at the time--the most austere feminine intellect goes into *mufti*, so to speak, between the hours of seven and eight P.M.--and we made our provisional selections for Tuesday's programme undisturbed.

The student of Browning finished scribbling down the names of horses on the back of an envelope.

"That is all right," he said. "Plumstone for the Shotley Stakes, Little Emily for the Maiden Plate, and Gigadibs or Jedfoot for the big race. The others can keep. Shall we go up and dress for dinner?"

I agreed, and we knocked out our pipes.

"What do you think, by the way," enquired The Freak casually, "of little Connie Damer?"

I told him.

We were late for dinner.

II

A shy but observant male, set down in an English country-house, soon realises, especially when he has been compelled for a period of years to rely for amusement almost entirely upon his own society, the truth of the saying that the proper study of mankind is Man--with which is incorporated Woman.

At The Towers I became an interested and uneasy spectator of the continued reformation of my friend Dicky Mainwaring. During the same period I had constant opportunities of comparing the characters and dispositions of his first and (presumably) second choices, Mesdames Beverley and Damer, and in a lesser degree of his sister Sylvia.

Further acquaintance with Miss Beverley confirmed my first impression of her. She struck me more and more as exactly the kind of girl whom a careful mother would select as a helpmeet for a somewhat erratic son. She was cool, aloof, capable, and decided, with very distinct ideas upon the subject of personal dignity and good form. She had already cured her fiancé of many regrettable habits. Dicky, I found, no longer greeted under-housemaids upon the stairs with "Hallo, Annie! How is your bad knee getting on?" Instead, he hurried past the expectant damsel with averted eyes. He no longer slipped warm shillings into the hands of beggar-women who assailed him with impossible tales of woe in the back drive: instead, he apologetically handed them tickets of introduction to the Charity Organisation Society, with a packet of which Miss Beverley had relentlessly provided him. He kept accounts. He answered letters by return of post. He perused closely printed volumes, and became enrolled in intellectual societies with mysterious aims and titles difficult to remember.

"Tiny, my bonny boy," he enquired of me one morning after breakfast, "do you happen to have any sort of notion what Eugenics is--or are?"

"I believe," I replied hazily, "that it is some sort of scheme for improving the physique of the race."

Dicky nodded appreciatively.

"I see," he said. "One of old Sandow's schemes. His name is Eugen. That is better than I thought. I was afraid it was going to be another kind of political economy. Hilda wants me to become a local vice-president of the Eugenic Society; and as it seems to be a less pois--complicated business than most of her enterprises, I think I will plank down five bob and win a good mark."

And off he went, money in hand, to gain an indulgent smile from his Minerva.

Of Sylvia Mainwaring I need only say at present that she was a pale shade of Miss Beverley.

Miss Constance Damer was the exact opposite of Miss Beverley, physically, mentally, and spiritually. Miss Beverley was tall, dark, and stately; Miss Damer small, fair, and vivacious. Miss Beverley was patronising and gracious in her manner; Miss Damer's prevailing note was unaffected bonhomie. But where Miss Beverley slew her thousands, Miss Damer slew her tens of thousands; for she possessed what the other did not, that supreme gift of the gods--charm--magnetism--personality--whatever you like to call it. In all my life I have never known a human being who attracted her fellow-creatures with so little effort and so little intention, and who inspired love and affection so readily and lastingly, as Constance Damer. She never angled for admiration; she bestowed no favours; she responded to no advances; but she drew all the world after her like Orpheus with his lute.

That is all I need say about Miss Damer. This narrative concerns itself with the career of my good friend The Freak, Dicky Mainwaring; and the persevering reader will ultimately discover (if he has not already guessed) that Fate had arranged The Freak's future on a basis which did not include the lady whom I have just described.

With masculine admiration Miss Damer did not concern herself overmuch. We all think lightly of what can be had in abundance. Not that she did not take a most healthy interest in noting what mankind thought of her; but her interest would undoubtedly have been heightened if she could have felt less certain what the verdict was going to be. I honestly believe she would have been thrilled and gratified if some one had passed an unfavourable opinion upon her. But no one ever did.

She had no sisters of her own, so large families of girls were an abiding joy to her. These received her with rapture--especially the shy and gawky members thereof--and made much of her, sunning themselves in the unaffected kindliness of her nature and gloating over her clothes for as long as they could keep her. She was greatly in request, too, among small boys, for purposes of football and the like; but her chief passion in life, as I discovered one afternoon when Dicky and I surprised her at tea with the coachman's family, was a fat, good-tempered, accommodating, responsive baby.

As for her character in general, I think its outstanding feature was a sort of fearless friendliness. (Miss Beverley may have been fearless, but she certainly was not friendly.) Constance Damer's was the absolute fearlessness of a child who has never yet encountered anything to be afraid of. It is given to few of us to walk through life without coming face to face at times with some of its ugliness. Apparently this had never happened to Miss Damer. I say "apparently," but such a wise and discerning young person as I ultimately found her to be could never really have been blind or indifferent to the sadder facts of this world of ours. Consequently I often found myself enquiring why her attitude towards her fellow-creatures as a whole was so entirely fearless and trustful, when she must have known that so many of them were to be feared and so few to be trusted. I fancy the reason must have been that she possessed the power of compelling every one--man, woman, child, horse, and dog--to turn only their best side towards her. Rough folk answered her gently, silent folk became chatty, surly folk smiled, fretful folk cheered up, awkward folk felt at home in her presence; children summed up the general attitude by clinging to her skirts and begging her to play with them. It was impossible to imagine any one being rude to her, and certainly I never knew any one who was--not even Miss Beverley.

But she never abused her power. She never domineered, never put on airs, never ordered us about, never revealed her consciousness that we were all her servants. That is true greatness.

―――

As you very properly observe, this is a book about Dicky Mainwaring. *Revenons à nos moutons*!

CHAPTER VI
FORBIDDEN FRUIT--A DIGRESSION

Lady Adela stood in the hall, engaged in her favourite pursuit of guest-dragooning.

"Mr. Mainwaring is not coming," she announced. "Dick, Hilda, Constance, Sylvia, and Mr. Crick will go in the motor. Mr. Carmyle, will you give me your company in the victoria?"

I smiled wanly and thanked her. Perhaps the punishment fitted the crime, but it was none the less a heavy one. Still, one should not seek out forbidden fruit, or tamper with First Reserves.

Briefly, the facts of the case were these.

After breakfast on the day of Laxley Races--a blazing August morning--Miss Constance Damer invited me to accompany her to the orchard to pick green apples.

"I have a clean white frock on," she explained, "or I would not trouble you."

I assured her that it was no trouble.

We duly reached the orchard, where Miss Damer ate three green apples and presented me with a fourth, which, fearing a fifth, I consumed as slowly as possible, hoping for the sake of our first parents that Eve's historic indiscretion took place in late September and not early August.

Presently we came to a red-brick wall with a south aspect, upon which the noonday sun beat warmly. High up upon its face grew plums, fat, ripe, and yellow.

Miss Damer threw away the core of an apple and turned to me.

"I should like a plum," she said, with a seraphic smile.

The wall was fifteen feet high, and the plums grew near the top.

"I will find a ladder," I replied obediently.

"That would be bothering you too much," said the considerate Miss Damer. "Can't you put your foot in that root and pull yourself up by the branches?"

The branches, be it said, were gnarled and fragile, and lay flat against the wall.

"I think the ladder would be better," I repeated. "My weight might pull the whole thing away from the wall, and then we should have a few observations from Lady Adela."

"You are right; that would never do," replied my right-minded companion gravely. "But I don't know where they keep the ladder, and in any case it would probably be locked up. What a pity I have this white skirt on!"

She turned away. A low tremulous sigh escaped her.

Next moment, feeling utterly and despicably weak-minded, I found myself ascending the wall, much as a blue-bottle ascends a window-pane. Miss Damer stood below with clasped hands.

"Do be careful, Mr. Carmyle," she besought me. "You might hurt yourself very seriously if you fell. I will have that big one, please, just above your head."

I secured the object indicated and threw it down to her. She caught it deftly.

"There is another one on your left," continued Eve. "Can you reach it?"

I could, and did.

"I will keep this one for you, Mr. Carmyle," said my thoughtful companion as she caught it. "I think I will have one more. There is a perfectly lovely one there, out to your right. You can just get it if you stretch. Throw it down."

The plum in question was a monster, and looked ripe to the moment. I straddled myself athwart the plum tree, much in the attitude of a man who is about to receive five hundred lashes, and reached far out to the right.

"Another two inches will do it," called out Miss Damer encouragingly.

She was right. I strained two inches further, and my fingers closed upon the fruit. Simultaneously the greater part of the plum tree abandoned its adherence to the wall, and in due course,--about four-fifths of a second, I should say,--I found myself lying on my back in a gooseberry-bush, clasping to my bosom the greater part of a valuable fruit tree, dimly conscious, from glimpses through the interstices of my leafy bower, of the presence of a towering and majestic figure upon the gravel walk beside Miss Damer.

It was Lady Adela Mainwaring, my hostess, armed *cap-à-pie* in gauntlets, green baize apron, and garden hat, for a murderous morning among the slugs.

I struggled to a sitting position, slightly dazed, and not a little apprehensive lest I should be mistaken for a slug.

Neither Miss Damer nor my hostess uttered a word, Lady Adela because her high breeding and immense self-control restrained her; Miss Damer, I shrewdly suspect, because she was engaged in bolting the last evidence of her complicity. But both ladies were regarding me with an expression of pained reproach.

I shook myself free from my arboreal surroundings, and smiled weakly.

"Have you hurt yourself, Mr. Carmyle?" enquired Lady Adela.

"No, thank you," I replied, wondering if I would have received a lighter sentence if I had said yes.

"If you should desire to eat fruit at any time," continued Lady Adela in a gentle voice, much as one might address an imbecile subject to sudden attacks of eccentric mania, "one of the gardeners will always be glad to get it for you. You had better go in now and dress, as we start for the races in half an hour. Constance, dearest, run and find Puttick, and ask him if anything can be done for this tree."

Miss Damer tripped obediently away in search of the head-gardener, and Lady Adela led me kindly but firmly past the gooseberry-bushes and other sources of temptation to the house.

I did not see Miss Damer again until I met her with the others in the hall half an hour later.

She projected a sad smile upon me through her motor-veil, and shook her head.

"I hope you did n't hurt yourself," she said softly.

"I hope the last plumstone did n't choke you!" I replied sternly.

At this moment Lady Adela joined the party, and pronounced sentence as recorded at the beginning of this chapter. The other five accordingly descended the steps and began to pack themselves into the motor.

"May I drive, Dicky?" enquired Miss Damer.

No one ever thought of refusing Miss Damer anything. Her request was evidently the merest matter of form, for she was at the wheel almost as soon as she made it. Even Lady Adela merely smiled indulgently.

"Constance, *dear child*!" she murmured.

Dicky carefully packed his *fiancée* into the back seat, where his sister had already taken her place.

"You had better sit between us, I think," said Miss Beverley.

"I am going to sit in front," said Dicky, "in case Connie does anything specially crack-brained with the car. Crick, old friend, just separate these two fair ladies, will you?"

Mr. Crick obeyed with alacrity. The Freak, heedless of a tiny cloud upon Miss Beverley's usually serene brow, stepped up beside Miss Damer. That lady released her clutch-pedal, and the car, spurting up gravel with its back wheels, shot convulsively forward and then began to crawl heavily on its way.

"We'll put something on for you if you aren't in time for the first race, Bill," called The Freak to me. "What do you want to back?"

I inflated my lungs, and replied *fortissimo*:--

"Plumstone!"

Miss Damer's small foot came heavily down upon the accelerator, and the car whizzed down the drive.

CHAPTER VII
UNEARNED INCREMENT

Lady Adela and I studiously avoided all reference to gardening or diet upon our six-mile drive to Laxley, and reached the course in a condition of comparative amicability.

We arrived just in time to hear the roar that greeted the result of the first race.

"I wonder what has won," I said, as the victoria bumped over the grass.

"I have never been greatly interested in racing," said Lady Adela majestically. "My father was devoted to it, and so is my brother Rumborough. But I never know one horse from another. For instance, I have not the faintest notion which of the two animals now drawing us is Romulus and which is Remus, although Dick says it is impossible to mistake them. But then Dick has a name for every animal in the estate. Ah! there is the motor, against the railings! That is rather a relief. Dear Constance is an excellent driver, Dick says, but she is inclined to be venturesome."

"Miss Damer appears to be a lady of exceptional talents," I observed.

"Yes, indeed!" agreed Lady Adela, with, for her, quite remarkable enthusiasm. "It is a pity she has no money."

I do not know whether the last remark was intended as a lamentation or an intimation. But I understood now why Miss Damer was only First Reserve.

I changed the subject.

"I suppose you do not bet, Lady Adela?"

"I make it a rule," replied my hostess precisely, "to put half-a-sovereign on any horse whose owner we happen to know. One should always support one's friends, should not one?"

I was still pondering in my heart Lady Adela's system of turf speculation, wondering whether if every animal in the race had belonged to a friend she would have backed it, and in any case what benefit or otherwise (beyond shortening the price) one confers upon an owner by backing his horses at all, when the victoria, rolling heavily, came to anchor astern of the motor, and Hilda Beverley, Sylvia, and Crick, who had been standing upon the seats to view the race, turned to greet us.

"I had no idea racing was so exciting, dear Lady Adela," exclaimed Miss Beverley. "I came armed with a copy of 'The Nation,' prepared to spend the afternoon in the back seat of the car, and here I am quite thrilled."

"I am so glad, dear Hilda," said Lady Adela graciously. "Dick would have been disappointed if you had not enjoyed yourself. Where is that boy, by the way?"

"He and Connie have gone to collect Mr. Carmyle's winnings," said Sylvia.

"Has--ha! h'm!--Plumstone won, then?" I enquired, timorously avoiding Lady Adela's eye.

"Yes, worse luck!" replied Mr. Crick lugubriously. "We were all on Mercutio. But Miss Damer stuck to it that Plumstone was the right horse, and made Dicky put on five shillings for her and five for you. They got three to one, I believe."

At this moment Dicky and Miss Damer returned from the ring, and I was duly presented with six half-crowns.

"Three-quarters of an hour till the next race," announced Dicky. "Better have lunch."

By this time the whole party had become infected with that fierce spirit of cupidity which assails respectable Britons when they find themselves in the neighbourhood of that singularly uncorrupt animal, the horse; and the succeeding half-hour was devoted by seven well-born and well-to-do persons to an elaborate consideration of the best means of depriving a hard-working and mainly deserving section of the community of as large a sum of money as possible.

Our symposium resulted in a far from unanimous decision. Lady Adela, having studied the list of owners' names upon the card, handed me a sovereign and instructed me to seek out a book-maker who should be both cheap and respectable, and back the Earl of Moddlewick's Extinguisher and Mr. Hector McCorquodale's Inverary. Mr. Crick, the expert of the party, let fall dark hints on the subject of a quadruped named The Chicken. Dicky and I decided to wait until the numbers went up.

"Dick, you must positively back a horse for me this time," announced Miss Beverley.

"You are getting on, Hilda!" replied The Freak, obviously pleased to find his beloved in sympathy with his simple pleasures.

Miss Beverley handed him five shillings.

"And if the horse does n't win I shall never speak to you again," she concluded; and from the tone of her voice I could not help feeling that she meant what she said.

"What is your selection this time, Connie?" asked Sylvia.

Miss Damer produced a dirty pink envelope and began to open it.

Dicky laughed.

"Connie has been patronising a tipster," he said.

"I got this," explained Miss Damer, "from a man on the course. His name was Lively. He was trying to earn an honest living, he said, by supplying reliable stable information to sportsmen; but he did n't seem to be getting on very well, poor thing! People were standing all round him in a ring, laughing, and nobody would buy any of his envelopes, although he had given lots of them the winner of the first race for nothing. Just then he caught sight of Dicky and me standing on the edge of the crowd. He pushed his way towards us, and said that if I bought one of his tips, he knew it would bring him luck. He said," Miss Damer added with a smile of genuine gratification, "that I was a beautiful young lady. So I bought one of his envelopes, and after that a lot of other people did, too."

Dicky grinned.

"Yes; that was the point at which we ought to have passed along quietly," he said.

"Did n't you?" I asked.

"Bless you, no! Connie had n't nearly finished. She and her friend were as thick as thieves by this time. The conversation was just beginning to interest them."

"What did you find to talk about, Miss Damer?" asked Hilda Beverley curiously.

"I could n't help wondering," Connie continued, "whether he had a wife and children to support; so I asked him if he was married. He said he was afraid he was, but if ever he became a widower he would let me know. We left after that."

"Constance, *dear* child!" began Lady Adela, amid unseemly laughter.

"It was all right, Lady Adela," Miss Damer assured her. "They were quite a nice crowd, and I had Dicky with me."

"You are a great deal better able to take care of yourself than I am, old lady," said The Freak admiringly.

I saw Miss Beverley's fine eyes rest disapprovingly for a moment upon her philogynistic swain. Then some one asked:--

"What is your tip, Connie?"

Miss Damer scanned her paper.

"It's not very well written," she said. "Perry--Perry--something."

"Periander?" I suggested. "He is on the card."

"Yes--Periander. I shall back him."

"Rank outsider," said Mr. Crick's warning voice.

"I shall back him all the same," persisted Miss Damer, with a little nod of finality. "It would n't be fair to Lively's luck if I did n't. Mr. Carmyle, will you come and find a bookmaker with me?"

We departed together, and pushed our way through the crowd to the ring. On our journey we passed Miss Damer's protégé, still dispensing reliable information in a costume composed of check trousers, an officer's scarlet mess-jacket, stained and bleached almost beyond recognition by the accidents of many race-courses, and a large bowler hat adorned with a peacock's feather. A broken nose made him conveniently recognisable by those (if such there were) who might desire to consult him a second time. Miss Damer, for whom castaways and lame dogs in general seemed to have a peculiar fascination, showed a disposition to linger again; but a timely reminder as to the necessity of getting our money on at once took us past the danger point and saved me from participating in a public appearance.

Presently we found ourselves amid the book-making fraternity. The numbers of the runners had gone up, and lungs of brass were proclaiming the odds in fierce competition.

"What does 'six to four the field' mean?" enquired Miss Damer. "I always forget."

I turned to answer the question, but found that it had not been addressed to me. My companion was now engaged in animated conversation with a total stranger, and for the next five minutes I stood respectfully aloof while the pair discussed *seriatim* the prospects of each horse upon the card.

"He says Periander is an outsider," Miss Damer informed me, as the man moved away, awkwardly raising his hat. "But I think I must back him. Cornucopia is a certainty for this race, he told me." ("A pinch" was what the gentleman had said: I overheard him.) "You had better put something on him."

I meekly assented, and after Miss Damer had found her bookmaker we adventured ten shillings upon Periander and Cornucopia respectively. Public estimation of the former animal's form was such as to secure odds of ten to one for Miss Damer. I was informed that the two steeds owned by the Earl of Moddlewick and Mr. Hector McCorquodale were not running, so a Diogenean search for Lady Adela's cheap and respectable bookmaker was not required of me.

Suddenly a bell rang.

"They're off!" exclaimed Miss Damer. "We can't cross the course now. Come on to this stand."

We raced up a flight of steps, and presently found ourselves on a long balcony in a position which commanded a view of the entire course.

"Your jockey," announced Miss Damer to me, "is pale blue with chocolate sleeves and cap. Mine is red, with white hoops. Can you see them anywhere?"

"I can see mine," I said. "He is having a chat with the starter at present, but I have no doubt he will tear himself away presently."

"But the others are halfway home!" cried Miss Damer in dismay.

"So I perceive."

"You poor man!"

"Never mind!" I replied quite cheerfully. There is something very comforting about being called a poor man by some people. "Where is your friend?"

"There, in that bunch of four. He is going well, is n't he? That's the favourite, Mustard Seed, lying back."

"I expect his jockey will let him out after he gets into the straight," I said.

"If he isn't very careful," observed Miss Damer with perfect truth, "he will get shut out altogether."

The horses swept round the last corner and headed up the final stretch in a thundering bunch. Suddenly Miss Damer turned to me.

"This is fearfully dull for you," she said.

"Not at all," I assured her. "My horse has just started."

"Come in with me on Periander," pleaded my companion. "You can only lose five shillings."

I closed with her offer by a nod. Some partnerships can be accepted without negotiation or guarantee.

Suddenly the crowd gave a roar. The favourite had bored his way through the ruck at last. He shot ahead. The noise became deafening.

"There goes our half-sovereign!" shrieked Miss Damer despairingly in my ear.

"Wait a minute!" I bellowed. "Periander is n't done for yet."

There came a yet mightier roar from the crowd, and as we leaned precariously over the balustrade and craned our necks up the course, we perceived that a horse whose jockey wore red and white hoops was matching the favourite stride for stride.

"Periander! Periander!" yelled those who stood to win at ten to one against.

"Mustard Seed!" howled those who stood to lose at six to four on.

But they howled in vain. The flail-like whips descended for the last time; there was a flash of red and white; and Periander was first past the post by a length.

We descended into the ring and sought out our bookmaker. There was no crowd round him: backers of Periander had not been numerous; and it was with a friendly and indulgent smile that he handed Miss Damer her half-sovereign and a five-pound note.

"Can you give me two-pounds-ten for this?" she asked, handing me the note.

It was useless to protest, so I humbly pocketed my unearned increment, and we left the ring in search of the rest of our party.

"I have never won gold before," announced the small capitalist beside me, slipping the coins into her chain-purse--"let alone paper." Her smiling face was flushed with triumph.

"I think I know who will rejoice at your victory to-morrow," I said, "and participate in the fruits thereof."

"Who?"

"The coachman's children, the gardener's children, the lodge-keeper's children--"

But Miss Damer was not listening.

"Poor Lively!" she said suddenly. "He gave me that tip, and yet he could n't afford to back the horse himself."

"Tipsters do not as a rule follow their own selections," I said. "I don't suppose, either, that Periander's was the only name contained in those pink envelopes of his. You really ought not--"

"Why, there he is!" exclaimed Miss Damer, upon whom, I fear, my little homily had been entirely thrown away.

We had made a detour to avoid the crowd on our way back to the carriage, and were now crossing an unfrequented part of the course. My companion pointed, and following the direction of her hand I beheld, projecting above a green hillock twenty yards away, a battered bowler hat, surmounted by a peacock's feather.

"Come this way," commanded Miss Damer.

I followed her round to the other side of the hillock. There lay the retailer of stable secrets, resting from his labours before the next race. Apparently business was not prospering. His dirty, villainous face looked unutterably pinched and woe-begone. His eyes were closed. Obviously he had not lunched. His broken nose appeared more concave than ever.

At our approach he raised his head listlessly.

"Go on, and wait for me, please," said Miss Damer in a low voice.

I obeyed. One always obeyed when Miss Damer spoke in that tone, and evidently some particularly private business was in hand. Already the child's impulsive fingers were fumbling with the catch of her chain purse.

I took up my stand a considerable distance away. I had no fears of Lively. One does not snatch at the purse of an angel from heaven. My only concern was that the angel's generosity might outrun her discretion.

I could hear her making a breathless little speech, but Lively said never a word. I was not altogether surprised. Probably he was afraid of waking up.

Presently she came back to me, smiling farewell at her pensioner over her shoulder.

"You'll give one of them to your wife, won't you?" was the last thing I heard her say.

Then she rejoined me, and we walked on.

"How much money," I enquired severely, "will you have left out of your winnings, after providing for me and your other friend and the families of the coachman and the gardener and the lodge-keeper?"

Again Miss Damer was not attending.

"Poor Lively!" she said softly.

There were tears in her eyes.

CHAPTER VIII
A RELAPSE

The most unpopular man in the group which we now rejoined was undoubtedly Mr. Crick, a blind faith in whose prescience had induced Miss Beverley and Sylvia Mainwaring to adventure an aggregate sum of ten shillings upon Mustard Seed. Ranking a good second in the order of odium came Dicky, who had executed the commission. The fact that he had done so under protest was deemed to have no bearing on the case.

Miss Damer said nothing about our little triumph, and I was well content. There is something very intimate and comfortable about a secret of this kind.

The great race of the day, the Laxley Cup, was now imminent, and, with the exception of Lady Adela, who issued to me from the depths of the victoria a distinctly somnolent injunction to persevere in my support of the property of the Earl of Moddlewick and Mr. Hector McCorquodale, we departed in a body to back our respective fancies.

"Miss Beverley seems a bit put out about something, my son Richard," I observed, as The Freak and I strolled along in the rear of the party.

Dicky nodded.

"Yes," he said, "she is. She is a dear, but she hates losing money worse than an eye-tooth. I must find a winner for her this time, or I shall have to listen to a song and chorus. You noticed it, too, then?"

"Yes. But it was before she lost money. Do you think she disapproves of--"

"Of the way I trot around after Connie--eh? No, to do her justice, I don't think she minds that a bit. She knows that Connie and I have been pals ever since we were quite small nippers. Besides," concluded my friend with an entirely gratuitous chuckle, "everybody trots around after Connie, don't they?"

I admitted briefly that this was so.

"No; it is the loss of cash chiefly that makes her fractious," continued Dicky. "That, and my want of dignity and repose on public occasions."

"What sort of exhibition have you been making of yourself this time?" I enquired gruffly. Dicky's last remark still rankled.

"Nothing to signify. Hilda and I were taking a stroll on the course together, before you arrived, and I stopped to have a brief chat with an aged Irish beggar-woman. The old dame had a shilling out of me in no time, and we departed under a perfect blizzard of benediction. Hilda seemed rather miffy about it: said I was making her and myself conspicuous. For the Lord's sake, put me on to a winner for her, old soul!"

"Ask Miss Damer," I said. "She is the member of this party who picks up reliable information."

But Miss Damer was nowhere to be seen.

"She is somewhere in that seething mob, backing horses on her own account," explained Sylvia later. "She said she was n't going to bother any of the men this time. Do you think it is quite safe?"

"Connie knows her way about," said Dicky. "But perhaps we had better go and have a look for her. Do you know which bookie she has been patronising, Tiny?"

"Yes; that gentleman by the railings, with the gamboge waistcoat," I replied. "But she is n't going to him any more. She has taken money off him twice, and considers it unfair to fleece him again. We shall find her looking for a man with a large bank-balance and no children."

"How will she be able to tell?" enquired that simple soul, Mr. Crick.

"From what I know of her," I said, "she will ask him."

Loaded with injunctions and commissions from the other two ladies, Dicky and I pushed our way once more into the crowd of speculators. Finding that the Earl of Moddlewick's Ginger Jim figured upon the programme and was actually proposing to run, I backed that animal on Lady Adela's behalf, blushing painfully before the thinly veiled amazement and compassion of the bookmaker and his clerk. Myself, I supported the favourite, for reasons of my own. Dicky moved feverishly up and down the line, putting money on horse after horse. Apparently Miss Beverley was to back a winner this time.

As I concluded my business, I caught sight of Miss Damer's lilac frock and big black hat in the paddock. She was engaged in an ardent conversation with a group of three--two girls and a man--and I remember wondering whether they were actual friends of hers or acquaintances of the moment, drawn unwittingly but perfectly willingly into the small siren's net. (As it turned out, they were old friends, but I think I may be excused for not feeling certain.) I was a little disappointed at her preoccupation, for I had been hoping for another deed of partnership.

But the starting-bell had rung, and people were clambering on to the stands.

"Which is my horse, Dick?" enquired Hilda Beverley, as we took our places.

This was an obvious poser for my friend.

"I'll tell you in a minute," he said, gazing diligently through his binoculars. "Yes, yes!" He coughed with intense heartiness. "It is doing very well--very well, indeed!"

"But which one is it?" asked Miss Beverley impatiently.

"The one in front," replied The Freak, with perfect truth.

The finish was imminent. A hundred yards from the post the favourite cracked, and his place was taken by a raking black horse with a pink jockey, which ultimately won the race with a length in hand.

The bulk of the crowd naturally received the defeat of the favourite without enthusiasm, but a small section near the judge's box raised a loud and continuous yell of jubilation. Evidently some particular stable had "known something" and kept it dark.

"What is the name of that black animal?" I enquired of Dicky.

"Malvolio."

"Did you back him?" I enquired loudly.

"Rather!" yelled Dicky. "Come with me and help me to collect Hilda's winnings for her. Back directly, dear!"

"How many horses did you back in that race?" I enquired, as we elbowed our way to the ring.

"Seven," said Dicky. "Expensive game, executing commissions for your best girl--what?"

"Let us hope this little victory will have the desired effect," I said piously.

"It will be cheap at the price," replied Dicky with fervour.

At the foot of the stand we found Miss Damer taking leave of her three friends. She joined us.

"Will you chaperon me into the ring, please?" she asked of me politely.

I stopped short and gazed at her.

"Do you mean to tell me," I said, "that you have won again?"

Miss Damer nodded brightly.

"Yes," she said.

"You backed Malvolio--that outsider?"

Miss Damer smiled seraphically. "Yes."

"And where did you get the tip this time?" I enquired.

"I asked the bookmaker," replied Miss Damer simply. "I thought he would know."

"And he gave you Malvolio?"

"Yes. I had thought of backing the favourite, but he would n't let me. He said Malvolio was 'a real snip,' but very few people knew about him. He was a kind man. Come and help me to find him."

We duly discovered her altruistic friend, who smiled at me over his client's head in a resigned and humorous fashion, as if to imply that there are occasions upon which Homer may be excused from nodding. "If this be Vanity," his expression seemed to ask, "who would be wise?" Who, indeed?

Of all Constance Damer's achievements in the matter of unduly influencing her fellow-creatures, I hold--and always have held--that this was the greatest. I have been present at many of her triumphs. I have seen her tackle a half-drunken ruffian who was ill-treating his wife, not merely subjugating him, but sending the pair away reconciled and arm-in-arm; I have seen her compel crusty and avaricious old gentlemen to pay not only largely, but cheerfully, for bazaar-goods for which they could have had no possible use, and the very purchase of which implicated them in the furtherance of a scheme of which they heartily disapproved; and I have seen her soothe a delirious child into peaceful slumber by the mere magic of her touch and voice. But to interrupt a hard-working, unsentimental, starting-price bookmaker at the busiest moment of his day, for the purpose of eliciting from him information as to the right horse to back, and to receive from him--a man whose very living depends upon your backing the wrong one--not merely reliable but exclusive information, strikes me as a record even for Miss Constance Damer.

Presently Dicky rejoined us.

"Collected your winnings?" I enquired.

"Yes--and handed them over. There are only two runners in the next race. Come and have a look at the merry-go-rounds. I know you love them, Connie."

Miss Damer admitted the correctness of this statement, but declined to come.

"I see Lady Adela over there," she said--"all alone. That's not fair. She has a new toque on, too, poor thing! I will go and take her for a walk round the enclosure. You two can come back presently and give us tea. If you discover anything really exciting in the way of side-shows I will come and see it before the last race."

She flitted away. Two minutes later we saw her, looking like a neat little yacht going for a walk with a Dreadnought, carefully convoying Lady Adela across the course into the enclosure.

"What about Miss Beverley and the others, Freak?" I asked, as we turned away.

"Oh, they are all right," said Dicky shortly. "Leave them alone for a bit longer."

From which I gathered that Miss Beverley was still suffering from what is known in nursery circles as "a little black dog on her back."

A large section of the crowd evidently shared our opinion that the next race would be a tame affair, for the merry-go-rounds and other appurtenances of the meeting were enjoying abundant patronage as we approached. We passed slowly along the fairway, where hoarse persons implored us, *inter alia*, to be photographed, win cocoanuts, and indulge in three rounds under Queensberry Rules with "The Houndsditch Terror."

Dicky, suddenly throwing off his low spirits, won two cocoanuts; insisted upon being photographed with me upon the beach of a *papier-mâché* ocean, and, although he drew the line at The Houndsditch Terror, submitted his palm to an unclean and voluble old lady who desired to tell his fortune.

He was cautioned by the beldame against a fair man with a black heart--"That's you, old son!" he remarked affectionately to me--and received warning of impending trouble with a dark lady. ("Thanks; I know all about that," he assured her feelingly.) On the other hand, he was promised two letters, a journey across the ocean, and a quantity of gold--precise amount not specified--within a short period of time.

"You have a very peculiar nature," was the next announcement. "You have paid attention to many ladies, but you have never really loved any of them. Your heart--"

"I beg your pardon; I have loved them all!" replied The Freak emphatically.

"Don't be angry with Gipsy, pretty gentleman!" pleaded the aged Sibyl. "Gipsy knows best. Gipsy only says what she reads in the hand. So--but what is this?" She bent closer. "Ah! Very soon, sir, you will meet the lady of your dreams, and you will love her as you have never loved before."

"No, really?" exclaimed Dicky, deeply interested. "Tell me, shall I marry her?"

"Many difficulties and obstacles will be placed in your path," chanted the prophetess. "You will be misunderstood; you will have to deal with peculiar people. Many times you will be tempted to give up in despair. But persevere, and you will triumph in the end. Now, gentleman, cross Gipsy's palm with silver--"

Here high prophetic frenzy tailed off into unabashed mendicancy, and the interview dropped to a purely commercial level. My attention wandered. Not far away a ring of people had collected round some fresh object of interest. I could hear the sound of a woman's voice singing, and the thrumming of a harp. I could even distinguish the air. A fresh number was just beginning. It was "Annie Laurie"--the most beautiful love-song, in my humble opinion, ever written.

"Maxwellton's braes are bonny,
Where early falls the dew--"

Then the voice quavered and ceased, and I found myself wondering what had happened.

"And now, would the other handsome gentleman like to show his palm to Gipsy?" enquired an ingratiating croak at my side.

Realising with difficulty that I was the individual referred to, I turned, to find that our aged friend, having satisfactorily arranged Dicky's future, was now soliciting my patronage.

"No, thanks," I replied. "Come and see what is going on over there, Freak."

"Ah, but Gipsy will tell the gentleman *all*," promised the old lady. "He has a wicked eye," she added, alluringly but incorrectly.

We escaped at last, at a price, and presently found ourselves upon the outskirts of the little crowd which I have already mentioned.

"What is going on inside here?" enquired Dicky of his nearest neighbour.

"Gel singin' to the 'arp," replied the gentleman addressed. He supplemented this information by adding that the lady was no class, and had a nasty cough.

He was right. As he spoke, the voice of the singer broke again, and we could hear the sound of a spasm of coughing.

We elbowed our way into the crowd, which had grown with the easy facility of all race-course crowds into quite an assemblage; and presently found ourselves in the inmost ring of spectators.

In the centre of the ring sat an old man on a camp-stool, cuddling a big battered harp to his shoulder. Beside him stood a tall tired-looking woman, very handsome in a tawdry fashion, of about thirty-five. She was dressed as a Pierrette. Her right hand rested upon the old man's shoulder, her left was pressed hard against her chest. She was coughing violently, and her accompanist's hands lay patiently idle in his lap until she should be ready to continue. On the grass beside the old man sat a hollow-eyed little boy, also in regulation Pierrot costume.

I heard Dicky draw his breath sharply. Don Quixote was astir again.

Presently the singer recovered, stood bravely erect, and prepared herself for another effort. The old man's hands swept over the strings, and the harp emitted a gentle arpeggio.

"Like dew on the gowans lying

Is the fall of her fairy feet,
And like winds in summer sighing
Her voice is low and sweet.
Her voice is low and sweet,
And she's all the world to me;
And for bonnie Annie Laurie--"

The song floated up into the blue summer sky, carrying me with it--possibly in pursuit of the fairy feet (for which I had already found an owner). Exposure, rough usage, mayhap gin-and-water--all these had robbed the singer's notes of something of their pristine freshness; but they rang out pure and limpid for all that. It was a trained voice, and must once have been a great voice. The crowd stood absolutely still. Never have I beheld a more attentive audience.

"Grand opera, once," said Dicky's voice softly in my ear. Then--"Oh, you poor thing!"

I recalled my thoughts from their sentimental journey, to realise that the verse had broken off before the end and that the woman was once more in the throes of another attack of coughing, the black pompoms on her little white clown cap vibrating with every spasm. Impatient spectators began to drift away.

I was conscious of a sudden movement beside me, and Dicky's voice exclaimed, in the hoarse whisper which I knew he reserved for conversations with himself:--

"Go on! Be a man!"

Next moment he had left my side and was standing in the centre of the ring, addressing the crowd. He was quite cool and self-possessed, but I saw his fingers curling and uncurling.

"Ladies and gentlemen!" he shouted.

"Git out of the ring, Elbert!" suggested a voice, not unkindly.

But The Freak continued:--

"I know we all sympathise with the plucky attempt this lady is making to entertain us under very difficult circumstances."

The crowd, suspicious of a hoax of some kind, surveyed him dumbly.

"I am sure," Dicky went on, "you will agree with me that with such a bad cough our entertainer has no right to be working so hard this afternoon; and I therefore propose, with your kind permission, in order that she may have a rest and get her voice back, to sing you one or two songs myself. I can't sing for toffee; but I will do my best, and I know that you, being sportsmen all, will assist me by singing the choruses!"

He took off his hat, bowed genially, and turned to the harpist. There was a buzz of appreciation and anticipation among the crowd. Evidently Dicky had touched the right note when he appealed to them as sportsmen.

"Can you vamp a few chords, do you think?" I heard him say to the accompanist.

"Yes, sir," replied the old man quickly. "Go on: I'll follow you."

The tired woman sank down upon the trampled grass beside the little boy; The Freak, hat in hand, struck an attitude; and the entertainment began.

I do not know how many songs he sang. He passed from one to another with amazing facility, discoursing between the verses upon topics well suited to the taste and comprehension of his audience. His songs were not new, and the tales that he told were neither true nor relevant; but they served their purpose. He uplifted his voice and carried us all off our feet. He conducted us over the whole of that field of Music Hall humour which is confined within the following limits:--

(1) Alcoholic excess.
(2) Personal deformity (e.g., Policemen's feet).
(3) Conjugal infelicity; with which is incorporated Mothers-in-law.
(4) Studies of insect life (e.g., Seaside lodgings).
(5) Exaggerated metaphor (e.g., "Giddy kipper").

He enlarged upon all these, and illuminated each. He was unspeakably vulgar, and irresistibly amusing. The crowd took him to their bosoms. They roared at his gags; they sang his choruses; they clamoured for more.

I shouted with the rest. This was the real Dicky Mainwaring--the unregenerate, unrestrained Freak of our undergraduate days--my friend given back to me in his right mind after a lamentable period of eclipse. My heart swelled foolishly.

"Chorus once more, please, gentlemen!" shouted Dicky. "Last time!"

"CHORUS ONCE MORE, PLEASE, GENTLEMEN!"

The refined and elevating pæan rolled forth, Dicky conducting:--
"Beer, Beer, glorious Beer!
Fill yourself right up to here!
(*Illustrative gesture.*)
Take a good deal of it,
Make a good meal of it--"

With head thrown back and mouth wide open, I shouted with the rest--and--caught the eye of Miss Hilda Beverley! She was standing exactly opposite to me on the other side of the circle. Next moment she was gone.

———

It was the accompanist who gave in first. For nearly half an hour his aged but nimble fingers had followed the singer's most extravagant flights, and he now began obviously to falter.

Dicky seized this opportunity to conclude his performance.

"That is all, gentlemen," he said, with a flourish of his hat. "I know no more. Thank you for your kind attention and assistance. But don't go away. I am going to ask the Colonel here to carry his hat round."

He signalled to the small pale-faced boy to take up a collection, but the child hung back shyly. Evidently he was not accustomed to enthusiastic audiences. Dicky accordingly borrowed his cone-shaped headpiece and set to work himself.

Touch your neighbour's heart, and his pocket is at your mercy. The bell was ringing for the last race, but not a man in that crowd stirred until he had contributed to Dicky's collection. Silver and copper rained into the cap. I saw one sturdy old farmer clap Dicky upon the shoulder with a "Good lad! good lad!" and drop in half-a-crown.

Then the audience melted away as suddenly as it had collected, and we five were left--Dicky, myself, the old man, his daughter, and the recently gazetted Colonel. The daughter still sat limply upon the grass. Dicky crossed over to her and emptied the collection into her lap.

"You had better tie that up in a handkerchief," he said. He spoke awkwardly. He was no longer an inspired comedian--only a shy and self-conscious schoolboy. My thoughts flew back to a somewhat similar scene in a third-class carriage on the Great Eastern Railway many years before.

The woman was crying softly. Her tears--those blessed faith-restoring tears that come to people who encounter kindness when they thought that the world held no more for them--dropped one by one upon the pile of coins in her lap. She caught Dicky's hand, and clung to it. The Freak cleared his throat in a distressing manner, but said nothing. Far away we could hear the roar of the crowd, watching the last race.

"I must be going now," said Dicky at length. "I hope you will soon get rid of your cough and have good luck again. We all get under the weather sometimes, don't we? Good-bye! Good-bye, Colonel!"

The officer addressed fixed round and wondering eyes upon the eccentric stranger, but made no remark.

"Good-bye, sir," said the woman. "God--"

Dicky released his hand gently and turned deferentially to the old gentleman, who was still sitting patiently at his harp.

"Thank you very much, sir," he said, speaking like a polite undergraduate to an aged don who has just entertained him to dinner, "for your splendid accompaniments. I can't imagine how you contrived to follow me as you did. I'm a pretty erratic performer, I'm afraid. Good-bye!"

He held out his hand.

The old man struggled to his feet, and gave a little old-fashioned bow, but disregarded Dicky's proffered hand.

"Good-bye, sir," he said, "and thank you kindly for what you have done for us."

"Would you mind putting your hand in his, sir?" said the woman to Dicky. "He can't see it. He's blind," she added apologetically.

Five minutes later we found ourselves back at the railings. The motor was already purring, and Romulus and Remus had been put into the victoria.

Miss Damer hastened up to us. Her brown eyes looked very soft.

"Dicky dear," she said tremulously, "we all saw you, and I think you are a brick. But keep away from Hilda for a bit."

CHAPTER IX
THE ONLY WAY OUT

The ladies, pleading fatigue after their long day, retired early, bringing a somewhat oppressive evening to a timely conclusion. Dinner had been a constrained function, for Miss Beverley's aloofness had cast a gloom upon the spirits of her *fiancé*, and the rest of us had joined with him in a sort of sympathetic melancholy. In the drawing-room afterwards Mr. Crick, whose ebullient soul chafed beneath what he termed "compulsory hump," sat down at the piano and treated us to a musical sketch,--something humorous but lingering. Whereupon Lady Adela awoke out of her sleep, and with a disregard for the performer's feeling that was almost indecent, cut short the entertainment and shepherded her flock to the upper regions.

The four gentlemen adjourned to the billiard-room. Here Mr. Mainwaring and Crick set about a game of billiards--fifty up--at which the latter, with a loftiness of spirit which his subsequent performance entirely failed to justify, insisted upon conceding his elderly opponent twenty-five points. Aided by this generous subsidy and by the fact that the scratch player, in bringing off some delicate long shots into the top pocket, more than once omitted the formality of glancing off one of the other balls on the way, our host made quite surprising progress. His own contributions to the score were mainly derived from a monotonous but profitable system of potting the white and leaving his opponent a double balk. Indeed, the old gentleman reached his points before Mr. Crick had accomplished a feat vaguely described by himself as "getting the strength of the table." Mr. Mainwaring then trotted happily upstairs to bed, followed very shortly afterwards by his highly incensed play-fellow.

As the door closed, Dicky put down his pipe and turned to me.

"Bill, old man," he said, "I don't often face facts; but this time I admit that I have fairly torn the end off things."

"You are in disgrace, my boy," I agreed. "What are you going to do about it?"

Dicky pondered, and finally summed up.

"The fact is," he said, "I am not up to Hilda's standard, and never shall be."

I rose, and took my stand upon that tribunal beloved of the Briton--the hearthrug--and looked down upon my friend's troubled countenance.

"Dicky," I began, having blown my nose nervously, "you and I don't usually go deeply into these matters together; but--do you love that girl?"

We two regarded one another deliberately for a minute, and then Dicky shook his head.

"I do not," he said at last. "Not more, that is, than I love half a dozen others. I suppose the truth is," he continued, relighting his pipe, "that I don't quite realise the meaning of the word--yet. Some day, perhaps, the big thing will come to me; but until it does and wipes out everything else, I shall go on imagining, as at present, that I am in love with every girl who happens to attract me or whom I happen to attract--if such a thing is possible. Nature, I suppose--just Nature! Just now I am making the instinctive involuntary experiments that every man must make, and go on making, until he encounters his right mate. Some men, I imagine, are luckier than others. They are not inflammable. They do not make false starts or get down blind alleys. I believe you are one, Tiny, but there are not many. With women, I believe, it is different. They have more intuition than men, and can tell almost immediately whether they have found the goods this time or not. But the average man must just go blundering on, making an ass of himself, and learning by experience. I fall into love readily enough, but have never been able to stay there. That is my trouble. I am therefore forced to the conclusion that I have never really been in love at all."

"That is because you have never met *the* girl, Freak."

"Possibly; but there is another explanation, and that is that I am incapable of a sustained affection under any circumstances whatever. However, you may take it from me that such is not the case. I *know* that. I can't explain it or prove it, but I know it. What I really want--but I have n't met one so far--is a girl who will fall in love with me, and *show* it--show that she is willing to burn her boats for me. A good many young women, estimable creatures, have indicated that they care for me a little, but not one has done it in the way I have described. I don't believe that I could ever really throw myself absolutely headlong into love with a girl unless I knew in my heart that she was prepared to do the same for me. They are all so cautious, so self-contained, so blooming independent, nowadays, that a man simply cannot let himself go on one of them for fear she should turn round and laugh at him. But if a girl once confided to me that she wanted to entrust herself to me--body and soul, for better, for worse, and so on--without any present-day stipulations about maintaining her independence and preserving her individuality, and stuff of that kind--well, good-bye to all indecision or uncertainty on my part! What man who called himself a man could resist such an appeal as that--a genuine whole-hearted appeal from weakness to strength? (Not that I am exactly a model of strength," he commented, with a disarming smile; "but I know I soon should be, if such an honour were done me.) Weakness to strength! That's what it comes to in the end, old man, whatever the modern advanced female may say. Male and female created He them--eh? When I do meet that girl--perhaps she is the girl the old gipsy foretold for me to-day--I shall love her, and slave for her, and fight for her, so long as we both live, just because she is so utterly dependent on me. That is what brings out the best in a man. Unfortunately, I have not yet met her. When I do you may take it from me that I shall cease to be a Freak. Amen! Here endeth the First Lesson. There will be no collection."

His discourse thus characteristically concluded, my friend sat silent and pensive.

This was quite a new Dicky to me.

"You appear to have studied the question deeply and scientifically," I said, frankly impressed.

"My lad," replied Dicky with feeling, "if you possessed a disposition as flighty as mine--"

"Quixotic," I amended.

"All right--as quixotic as mine, and were also blessed with a dear old mother who spent her life confronting you with attractive young women with a view to matrimony, you would begin to study the question deeply and scientifically too. I am only a Freak, and all that, but I don't want to make a mess of a girl's life if I can help it; and that, old friend, owing to my susceptible nature and gentle maternal pressure from the rear, is exactly what I am in great danger of doing. I have had to mark time pretty resolutely of late, I can tell you. And that brings us to the matter in hand. Hilda and I seem to have reached the end of our tether. Something has got to be done."

"It is just possible," I said, "that Miss Beverley has done it already."

"What?"

"It--the only thing that ought to be done."

"What do you mean?"

"When the others went upstairs to bed Miss Hilda retired into an inner drawing-room and sat down at a writing-table. There is no post out of here until lunch-time to-morrow. Therefore she was probably writing to some one in the house."

Dicky nodded comprehendingly.

"Proceed, Sherlock," he said.

"To whom was she writing?" I enquired.

Dicky thought.

"To me," he announced at length. "Economical hobby. No stamps required. Well?"

"Supposing," I continued, "that Miss Beverley has been writing to you to-night--what then?"

"I shall receive a letter from her in the morning," concluded Dicky. "Eh? Wrong answer? Sorry! What will happen, then?"

"You will get your letter to-night."

Dicky looked doubtful.

"Where? When?" he asked.

"That's it. Where and when?"

Dicky pondered.

"On my pin-cushion, when I go upstairs to bed," he said at last--"although it strikes me as a most unmaidenly action for Hilda."

"So unmaidenly," I replied, "that you will probably find the letter on the hall table by your candle. Come and see."

My faith in Miss Beverley's sense of propriety was fully justified, for we found the letter in the hall beside the candlesticks exactly as I had foretold. Probably it had not lain there more than five minutes.

"What do you think of that?" I enquired.

"By Heavens, Holmes," exclaimed Dicky, who after his late lofty flight had characteristically relapsed into one of his most imbecile moods, "this is wonderful!"

We bore the letter back to the billiard-room.

"Four sheets!" murmured The Freak dejectedly. "Well, the longer I look at them the less I shall like them. Here goes!"

He began to unfold the crackling document.

"What is that protuberance down there, between your finger and thumb?" I enquired. "It may epitomise the letter for you."

Dicky turned the envelope upside down, and shook it over the billiard-table. Something fell out, rolled a short distance, and lay sparkling and shimmering on the green cloth.

Dicky picked up the ring very slowly, and regarded it long and intently. Then he turned to me.

"Thank God!" he said, softly and quite reverently; and I knew he spoke less for himself than for a certain superior young woman upstairs, who considered him flippant, lacking in depth, and altogether unworthy of her.

CHAPTER X
STILL AT LARGE

I saw very little of The Freak the following winter. For one thing, I went abroad again. The Government of the Auricula Protectorate had decided to connect their capital with the sea by means of a canal. I happened to know the district, for I had been engaged eight years previously upon the great dam, thirty miles from Auricula, which now holds in beneficent restraint the turbid waters of the Rumbolo River. I accordingly applied for work in connection with the scheme. By the greatest luck in the world one Vandeleur, C.B., a magnate of no small standing in the Auricula district, happened to be home on leave. He had visited my dam in his official capacity, and had noted that it was still standing. He spoke the word, and I got my canal.

The next four months I spent upon the continent of Africa, sketching, surveying, and drawing up specifications. Then I came home to be married.

At the very first dinner-party to which we were bidden on our return from our honeymoon I encountered The Freak.

I saw him first, so to speak. Covers had been laid, as they say in country newspapers, for twenty-two persons. My wife, through the operation of an inscrutable but inexorable law, had been reft from my side, and was now periodically visible through a maze of table decorations, entertaining her host with what I could not help regarding as the most unfeeling vivacity and cheerfulness. I began to take an inventory of the company. We had been a little late in arriving--to be precise, the last--and I had had no opportunity of observing my fellow-guests. My own partner was a Mrs. Botley-Markham, an old acquaintance of mine. She combined short sight and an astonishingly treacherous memory for names and faces with a rooted conviction that the one infallible sign of good breeding is never to forget a name or a face. ("A truly *Royal* attribute," she had once announced in my presence.) I was therefore agreeably surprised to find that she remembered not merely my face, but my name and *métier*. After putting me at my ease with a few kindly and encouraging remarks upon the subject of canals, she turned to her other neighbour.

"Dear Sir Arthur," I heard her say, "this is indeed a pleasant surprise!"

"Dear lady," replied a hearty voice, "the pleasure is entirely mine."

I leaned carelessly forward to inspect the menu, and shot a sidelong glance in the direction of Sir Arthur. I was right. It was The Freak, in his most acquiescent mood. I wondered what his surname was, and whether he knew it.

"We had such a teeny talk last time we met," continued Mrs. Botley-Markham. "Now we can chat as long as we please."

Heaving a gentle sigh of relief, Mrs. Botley-Markham's rightful dinner-partner helped himself to a double portion of the *entrée* and set to work.

The chat commenced forthwith.

"And how is Gipsy?" enquired Mrs. Botley-Markham.

"Gipsy," replied Sir Arthur without hesitation, "is top-hole."

"How quaint and original you always are in your expressions!" cooed my neighbour. "But I am so glad to hear about Gipsy. Then the dear thing has quite recovered?"

"Absolutely," replied Dicky courageously.

Mrs. Botley-Markham cooed again. Then she enquired, confidentially:--

"Now tell me, what *was* it?"

"What *was* it?" echoed The Freak cautiously. "Ah!"

"Yes; what *was* it?" pursued his interlocutor, much intrigued. "Don't tell me they never found out!"

"Never. At least," admitted The Freak guardedly, "not for some time."

"Then they actually operated without being sure?" exclaimed Mrs. Botley-Markham, shuddering.

Dicky, making up his arrears with a portion of quail, inclined his head gravely, and the quail reached its destination.

"And when they did find out," pursued Mrs. Botley-Markham, clasping her hands--she had finished her quail--"what *was* it? Tell me, dear Sir Arthur!"

Sir Arthur cogitated for a moment, and then took the plunge.

"It was clavicle," he said solemnly.

Assuming that my friend was labouring under the same disadvantage as myself--namely, inability to decide whether Gipsy was a woman, child, horse, dog, cat, or monkey--to invent a mysterious and non-committal disease upon the spur of the moment struck me as quite a stroke of genius on Dicky's part. Connie would enjoy hearing about this.

"How truly terrible!" said Mrs. Botley-Markham, in an awe-struck voice. "Clam--clavicle is a very rare disease, is it not?"

"Rare and mysterious," replied my friend in the same tone. "In fact, the doctor--"

"You mean Sir Herbert?"

"No, the other blo--the other gentleman--the anæsthetist, you know! He told me that he had never encountered a case of it before."

"How truly terrible!" said Mrs. Botley-Markham again. "And all the time you suspected appendicitis."

The Freak acquiesced readily. Here was light. Gipsy apparently was human--not equine, canine, feline, or simian.

"And the little one?" enquired Mrs. Botley-Markham tenderly.

I held my breath. Sir Arthur had reached his second fence.

"The little one," he replied after consideration, "is doing nicely. Not so very little, though, when you come to think of it," he continued, boldly taking the initiative.

"Has she grown so big, then?" enquired Mrs. Botley-Markham, unconsciously giving away another point. The little one's sex was determined. Certainly it was an exhilarating game.

"Quite extraordinary," said Dicky. "How big," he continued cunningly, "would you imagine she was now?"

"Not as big as my Babs?" cried Mrs. Botley-Markham incredulously.

"That," replied The Freak, "is just exactly how big she is." There was the least tinge of disappointment in his voice. Evidently he had hoped for something more tangible. For purposes of mensuration Babs was useless to him.

"Why 'just exactly'?" enquired Mrs. Botley-Markham doubtfully. "You are very precise about it."

"We met Babs in the Park the other day," replied the audacious Dicky, "and compared them."

Mrs. Botley-Markham frankly gaped.

"But, dear Sir Arthur," she exclaimed--"How?"

"How does one compare--er--little ones?" was the evasive reply of Sir Arthur.

The outraged parent turned upon him.

"You mean to say you laid those two innocents side by side upon the wet grass," she gasped, "and--"

"It was nearly dry," said Dicky soothingly.

I choked noisily, for I was rapidly losing self-control; but neither of the performers in the duologue took the slightest notice of me.

"I shall speak to my nurse to-morrow morning," announced Mrs. Botley-Markham firmly. "I cannot imagine what she was thinking about."

"Don't be hard on her," begged Dicky. "It was my fault entirely."

"It certainly was *very* naughty of you," said Mrs. Botley-Markham, already relenting, "but I forgive you--there!" She tapped the eccentric Sir Arthur playfully upon the arm. "Tell me, though, what does Gwladys weigh? Mere bigness in children is so often deceptive."

Even assuming that Gwladys was also the Little One, it was obvious that Dicky had not yet cleared his second fence. I began vaguely to calculate what a healthy child should weigh. A thirty-pound salmon, for instance--how would that compare with a fat baby? But Dicky made a final and really brilliant effort.

"Fourteen point eight," he said promptly.

"I beg your pardon?" replied Mrs. Botley-Markham.

"Fourteen point eight cubic centimetres," repeated The Freak in a firm voice. "That is the metric system of weights and measures. It is the only accurate and scientific method. All the big doctors have taken to it, you will find. I never allow any other to be employed where Gwladys is concerned. I strongly advise you," he added earnestly, "to have Babs weighed in the same manner. Everybody's doing it now," he concluded lyrically.

Mrs. Botley-Markham quivered with pleasure. An opportunity of getting ahead of the fashion does not occur to us every day.

"I will certainly take your advice, dear Sir Arthur," she replied. "Tell me, where does one get it done?"

"At the British Museum, between seven and eight in the morning," replied The Freak, whose pheasant was growing cold. "And now, dear lady, tell me everything that you have been doing lately."

Mrs. Botley-Markham, being nothing loath, launched forth. She even found time to re-include me in the conversation, disturbing my meditations upon the strenuous awakening which awaited poor Babs upon the morrow with an enquiry as to whether my canal was to contain salt water or fresh. But she had not finished with Dicky yet. Suddenly she turned upon him, and remarked point-blank:--

"How pleased the Stantons will be!"

"Indeed, yes!" replied The Freak enthusiastically.

At the sound of his voice I trembled. We had reached the dessert, and with port in sight, so to speak, it was impossible to tell what foolishness he might not commit.

"In fact," he continued shamelessly, "I happen to know that they are not merely pleased but ecstatic. I saw them yesterday."

"Where?" asked Mrs. Botley-Markham.

"Dear lady," replied Dicky, smiling, "where does one invariably meet the Stantons?"

"You mean at the Archdeacon's?" said Mrs. Botley-Markham.

"I do," said my reprobate friend. "They had all been down the Str--I mean to the Pan-Mesopotamian Conference," he added quite gratuitously.

"Ah, of course; they would," assented Mrs. Botley-Markham hazily, evidently wondering whether she ought to have heard of the Pan-Mesopotamian Conference. "Were they all there?"

"All but the delicate one," replied The Freak, abandoning all restraint.

"Do you mean Isobel?"

"Yes," replied the graceless Richard--"I do. Poor Isobel!" he added gently.

"I am afraid they are not a strong family," said Mrs. Botley-Markham, with a sympathetic glance which rather alarmed me. I foresaw complications.

The Freak wagged his head gloomily.

"No; a weak strain, I fear."

"I hope--I *hope*," said Mrs. Botley-Markham, evidently choosing her words with care and tact, "that the weakness does not extend to Gipsy."

Then Gipsy was connected with the Stantons! Freak would have to walk warily. But at this moment his attention was wandering in the direction of our hostess, who was beginning to exhibit symptoms of upheaval with a view to withdrawal. He replied carelessly:--

"No. Why should it?"

Mrs. Botley-Markham, a little offended and flustered at being taken up so sharply, replied with exaggerated humility:--

"I only *meant*, dear Sir Arthur, that if one sister is delicate, possibly another may be slightly inclined--"

Then Isobel and Gipsy were sisters. I knew it!

At this moment the hostess gave the mystic sign, and the company rose. Freak turned a sad and slightly reproachful gaze upon Mrs. Botley-Markham.

"You are forgetting, dear lady," he said gently. "Isobel and Gipsy are not related. Isobel was the sister of my poor first wife."

He drew back Mrs. Botley-Markham's chair with grave courtesy, and that afflicted lady tottered down the room and out of the door, looking like the Leaning Tower of Pisa.

The Freak and I resumed our seats.

"Dear Sir Arthur," I said, "are you a knight or a baronet?"

Before this point of precedence could be settled, our host called to us to move up higher.

"I want to introduce you to Sir Arthur Twigg, Mainwaring," he said, indicating a pleasant-looking youth strongly resembling Dicky in appearance and bearing.

"Come to lunch with me to-morrow, Tiny," said Dicky hurriedly to me.

A few minutes later I heard him regretfully explaining to his host that an important legal consultation in his chambers at ten o'clock that evening would prevent him from joining the ladies afterwards in the drawing-room.

CHAPTER XI
THE FIRST TURNING TO THE RIGHT

Next day I lunched with The Freak in Hall in the Inner Temple, where I was introduced by my host to the surrounding company as a "distinguished engineer, who had dammed the Nile several times and was now prepared to speak disrespectfully of the Equator."

After luncheon Dicky suggested that I should walk round with him to his chambers in Bolton Street. It was a murky December afternoon. Christmas shopping had set in with its usual severity, and visitors from the country, armed with sharp-cornered parcels, surged tumultuously along the wrong side of every pavement, while the ordinary citizens of London trudged resignedly in the gutter.

Dicky, quite undisturbed by the press, continued the conversation.

"Yes, the family are all very fit," he said. "You must come and stay with us. I shall give myself a week's holiday at Christmas and take you and Connie down to Shotley Beauchamp, and we will have a pop at Ethelbert, our pheasant, and discuss the days that are no more."

"Talking of the days that are no more," I began, stepping aside to avoid a stout lady carrying an inverted baby under one arm and an imperfectly draped rocking-horse under the other, "what has become--"

"Hilda Beverley--eh?" replied Dicky cheerfully. "I'll tell you all about her. (Don't apologise, sir, really! After all, I still have an eye left, and you very nearly lost your umbrella.) She is engaged, if not married, to an Oxford Don. I believe they are very happy. They go out and sing an ode to Apollo every morning before breakfast, or something of that kind."

A wedge of excursionists clove its way between us, and it was with a voice unconsciously raised that I remarked from the gutter:--

"You had an escape that time, my lad."

"Not at all!" yelled Dicky loyally from the other side of the pavement. ("Mind that kiddie's balloon, old son!) No," he continued, as we converged once more, "I had a very profitable six months. Hilda took immense pains with me, and it was n't her fault that I turned out a failure."

Presently I asked a question which always rose to my lips when I met Dicky after any considerable interval.

"Have your family any fresh matrimonial irons in the fire for you at present?" I enquired.

"No," replied my friend, "I rejoice to say they have not. The market is utterly flat. The Hilda Beverley slump knocked the bottom out of everything, and for the last half-year I have been living a life of perfect peace. I am settling down to a contented spinsterhood," he added, to the obvious surprise and consternation of a grim-looking female in a blue mackintosh who had become wedged between us. "In a few years I shall get a tabby cat and a sampler, and retire to end my days in the close of some quiet cathedral city."

The female in the mackintosh, by dint of using her elbows as levers and our waistcoats as fulcrums, heaved herself convulsively out of our company and disappeared in the crowd, probably in search of police protection. Dicky and I came together again.

"Occasionally," he continued fraternally, "I shall come and stay with you and Connie, and give you advice as to--Bill! Tiny! My son William! Look at that girl's face! Did you catch her profile? Did you ever see anything so lovely in all your life?"

We had reached that spot in the narrowest part of Piccadilly where all the omnibuses in the world seem to stop to take up passengers. Dicky's fingers had closed round my left biceps muscle with a grip like iron. I turned and surveyed him. His cheery good-tempered face was transfigured: his eyes blazed.

"Look!" he said again, pointing. He was trembling like a nervous schoolgirl.

But I was just too late. All I saw was a trim lithe young figure--rather like Connie's, I thought--stepping on to an omnibus. (When I told the story at home I was at once asked how she was dressed, but naturally could not say.) I caught sight of a pair of slim square shoulders, a good deal of pretty brown hair, and finally a pair of neat black shoes, as their owner deftly mounted to the top of the swaying vehicle.

"I just missed her face, old man," I replied. "Was she pretty?"

Here I stopped. To address empty air in Piccadilly for any length of time causes one to incur the unworthy suspicions of the bystanders. It also causes a crowd to collect, which is an indictable offence.

For I was alone. Afar off, pursuing a motor-omnibus just getting into its top speed, I beheld the flying figure of my friend. Presently he overtook the unwieldy object of his pursuit, hopped on board, and proceeded to climb to the top.

At this moment the omnibus reached Bond Street--the first turning to the right--swung round the corner, and disappeared.

BOOK THREE
THE RIGHT ROAD
NOTE

The main idea of Book Three was suggested by a very minor episode in the closing chapters of 'A Man's Man.' The usual acknowledgments are therefore made to the author of that work.

CHAPTER XII
MICE AND MEN

"Sylvia, is your father in from his walk?"

Miss Sylvia Mainwaring, attired in a sage-green robe and distressingly rational boots, turned and surveyed her male parent's recumbent form upon the sofa.

"Yes, mother mine," she replied. (Sylvia was rather addicted to little preciosities of this kind.)

"Is he awake?"

"He is reading 'The Spectator,' Mother," was the somewhat Delphic response.

"Then ring for tea, dear."

It was a bleak Saturday afternoon in late February. Darkness was closing in, and the great fire in the hall at The Towers flickered lovingly upon our leading weekly review, which, temporarily diverted from its original purpose in order to serve as a supplementary waistcoat for Mr. Mainwaring, rose and fell with gentle regularity in the warm glow.

Mr. Mainwaring's daughter rang a bell and switched on the electric light with remorseless severity; his wife came rustling down the broad oak staircase; and Mr. Mainwaring himself, realising that a further folding of the hands to sleep was out of the question, peeled off "The Spectator" and sat up.

"Abel," observed Lady Adela--her husband's baptismal name was a perpetual thorn in her ample flesh, but she made a point of employing it on all occasions, as a sort of reducing exercise to her family pride--"tea will be here in a moment."

Mr. Mainwaring rose to his feet. He was an apologetic little gentleman, verging on sixty, with a few wisps of grey hair brushed carefully across his bald head. At present these were hanging down upon the wrong side, giving their owner a mildly leonine appearance. A kindly, shy, impulsive man, Abel Mainwaring was invariably mute and ill at ease beneath the eye of his wife and daughter. Their patrician calm oppressed him; and his genial expansive nature only blossomed in the presence of his erratic but affectionate son.

"Tea?" he exclaimed with mild alacrity--"Who said tea?"

"Abel," announced Lady Adela in tones which definitely vetoed any further conversational openings originating in tea, "I think it only right to tell you that a visitor may arrive at any moment; and your present appearance, to put it mildly, is hardly that of the master of a large household."

"My dear, I fly!" said Mr. Mainwaring hurriedly, and disappeared. At the same moment there was a tinkle in the back premises.

"There goes the front-door bell," said Sylvia. "I never heard the carriage. Can it be Connie already?"

"A caller, probably," sighed her mother. "How tiresome people are. See who it is, Milroy, and then bring tea."

The butler, who had entered from the dining-room, crossed the hall to the curtained alcove which screened the front door.

"Hardly a caller on an afternoon like this," said Sylvia, shivering delicately. "It is raining in sheets."

"My experience," replied Lady Adela peevishly, "has always been that when one's neighbours have made up their minds to be thoroughly annoying, no weather will stop them."

Simultaneously with this truthful but gloomy reflection Lady Adela composed her fine features into an hospitable smile of welcome and rose to her feet.

"Misterilands!" announced Milroy, drawing back the curtain of the outer hall.

Lady Adela, still smiling, rolled an enquiring eye in the direction of her daughter.

"New curate!" hissed Sylvia.

Through the curtained archway advanced a short, sturdy, spectacled young man, dumbly resisting Mr. Milroy's gracious efforts to relieve him of his hat and stick.

Lady Adela extended her hand.

"How do you do, Mr. Highlands?" she enquired, as the ruffled Milroy, shaken off like an importunate limpet, disappeared into the dining-room.

"My name," replied the visitor apologetically, "is Rylands--not Highlands."

"How stupid of me!" said Lady Adela condescendingly. "But my butler is a most inarticulate person, and in any case we give him the benefit of the doubt where H's are concerned."

"It's of no consequence," Mr. Rylands assured her. "Oh, I beg your pardon!"

He picked up his walking-stick, which had fallen upon the polished floor with a shattering crash, and continued breathlessly:--

"The fact is, Lady Adela, the Archdeacon asked me to come round this afternoon and warn Mr.--Mr.--" he was uncertain of Mr. Mainwaring's exact status and title, so decided to hedge--"your husband, about the First Lesson in to-morrow morning's service. The Arch-deacon--"

"Be seated, Mr. Rylands," said Lady Adela, in the voice which she reserved for golfers, politicians, and other people who attempted to talk shop in her presence. "My husband will be downstairs presently. This is my--"

"The Archdeacon," continued the conscientious Rylands, "thinks it would be better to substitute an alternative Lesson--"

At this point his walking-stick, which he had after several efforts succeeded in leaning against the corner of the mantelpiece, fell a second time upon the floor, and a further hail of apology followed.

"--An alternative Lesson to-morrow morning," he resumed pertinaciously, "in view of the fact that certain passages--"

"This is my daughter Sylvia," said Lady Adela coldly.

"Oh, I beg your pardon!" exclaimed the curate to Sylvia, starting up and dropping his hat. "I did n't see you. My glasses are rather dimmed by the rain. I have come here," he recommenced rapidly, evidently hoping for a more receptive auditor this time, "at the request of the Arch-deacon, to see Mr.--your father--about an alteration in the First Lesson to-morrow--"

"I don't think you need trouble, Mr. Rylands," replied the dutiful Sylvia. "My father will probably read the wrong Lesson in any case."

"Who is taking my name in vain?" enquired the playful voice of Mr. Mainwaring, as its owner, newly kempt, descended the stairs.

"This is Mr. Rylands, Abel, who has recently come among us," said Lady Adela. "To assist the Archdeacon," she added, with feeling.

Mr. Mainwaring shook hands with characteristic friendliness.

"Welcome to Shotley Beauchamp, Mr. Rylands!" he said warmly.

"Thank you, sir, very much," replied the curate, flushing with pleasure. "I have called," he continued with unabated enthusiasm--evidently he saw port ahead at last--"at the request of the Archdeacon, with reference to the First Lesson at Matins to-morrow. One of those rather characteristic Old Testament passages--"

"Mr. Rylands," interposed Lady Adela, with the air of one who cannot stand this sort of thing much longer, "how many lumps of sugar do you take?"

"Four, please," replied Mr. Rylands absently, with his finger in Mr. Mainwaring's buttonhole.

Lady Adela's eyebrows rose an eighth of an inch.

"Four, did you say?"

The curate came suddenly to himself.

"I beg your pardon," he said cringingly, "I meant none."

"Then why did you specify four, Mr. Rylands?" enquired Sylvia, who disliked what she called "vague" people.

"Well, the fact is," explained the curate, in a burst of shy confidence--"I always take four when I am alone in my lodgings. But when I go out to tea anywhere, four always seems such a fearful lot to ask for, that--oh, I beg your pardon!"

He had stepped heavily back into a cake-stand, and *patisserie* strewed the hearthrug.

But both crime and apology passed unnoticed, for at this moment Milroy, who had crossed the hall a minute previously, reappeared at the curtained entrance, and announced, in tones of intense personal satisfaction:--

"Mrs. Carmyle!"

Even the female Mainwarings had no eyes for any one else when Connie Carmyle entered a room.

During the mêlée of greetings and embraces which ensued, Mr. Rylands, blessing the small deity who had descended to his aid, found time to right a capsized plum-cake and restore four highly-speckled cylinders of bread and butter to the plate on the bottom storey of the cake-stand. He even succeeded in grinding a hopelessly leaky chocolate *éclair* into the woolly hearthrug with his heel. By the time that the Mainwarings had removed their visitor's furs and escorted her to the fireplace, no trace of the outrage remained. The undetected criminal sat nervously upon the edge of an *art nouveau* milking-stool in the chimney-corner, waiting to be introduced.

"This is Mr. Rylands, Connie," announced Lady Adela. "Mrs. Carmyle."

"How do you do, Mr. Rylands?" said Connie, holding out her hand with a friendly smile.

Mr. Rylands, with an overfull teacup in one hand and a tiny plate entirely obscured by an enormous bun in the other, rose cautiously to his feet, and bestowing a sickly smile upon Mrs. Carmyle, entered at once upon a series of perilous feats of legerdemain with a view to getting a hand free.

"Let me hold your cup for you," suggested Connie kindly. "That's better!"

The curate, gratefully adopting this expedient, ultimately succeeded in wringing his benefactress by the hand.

"What has the Archdeacon been up to lately?" enquired Connie, gently massaging her fingers.

The curate's face brightened.

"It is curious that you should mention the Archdeacon's name," he said. "The fact is, I have just come *from* the Arch--"

"Constance dear," enquired Lady Adela in trumpet tones, "did you see anything of Dick on your way down?"

"No, Lady Adela," said Connie, extending a slim foot towards the blazing logs. ("Mr. Rylands, would you mind bringing me one of those little cakes? No, not those--the indigestible-looking ones. Thank you so much!) Are you expecting him for the week-end?"

"Yes, but I am afraid there is a little disappointment in store for him. I invited Norah Puncheon down--a sweet girl, Constance!--but at the last moment she has had to go to bed with one of her throats."

"Poor thing!" murmured Mrs. Carmyle absently. The reason for her own invitation--by telegraph--had just been made apparent to her.

"So perhaps you would not mind keeping Dick amused," concluded Lady Adela. "You and he used to be such particular friends," she added archly.

"Bow-*wow*!" observed Mrs. Carmyle dreamily into Mr. Rylands's left ear.

The curate choked, then glowed with gentle gratification. He realised that he had come face to face at last with one of the Smart Set, of which one heard so much nowadays.

"The naughty boy," concluded the fond mother, "must have missed his train."

"The naughty boy," replied Mrs. Carmyle, "is probably coming down by the four-fifteen. It is a much better train. Mr. Rylands, will you please choose me a nice heavy crumpet?"

"In that case," said Lady Adela, "he will probably be here in about half an hour. Sylvia dear, will you go upstairs and see if Constance's room is ready? I forgot to give orders about a fire."

Sylvia obediently disappeared, and Lady Adela crossed the hall to a chair under a lamp, where her husband was furtively perusing the evening paper. Mr. Mainwaring was now favoured with a brief but masterly display of the fast dying art of pantomime, from which he gathered without any difficulty whatever that he was to remove himself and Mr. Rylands to another part of the house, and that right speedily.

Mr. Mainwaring coughed submissively, and rose.

"Mr. Rylands, will you come and smoke a cigarette with me?" he said.

"Second Chronicles?" remarked Connie's clear voice. "I shall look it up during the sermon to-morrow." The Archdeacon's emissary had unburdened his soul at last.

Lady Adela extended a stately hand. "Good-bye, Mr. Rylands," she said. "My husband insists on carrying you off to the smoking-room."

Mr. Rylands, by this time hopelessly enmeshed in Connie Carmyle's net, sprang guiltily to his feet.

"Oh, I beg your pardon!" he exclaimed. "Good-bye! Good-bye, Mrs. Carmyle!"

He shook hands, gathered together his impedimenta, and hurried blindly up the staircase.

"Remember I am coming to hear you preach to-morrow," Connie called after him, with a dazzling smile. "Morning or evening?"

The godly but mesmerised youth halted, and broke out afresh. "I am preaching at Evensong," he began, "but--"

"This way, Mr. Rylands," said Lady Adela patiently, indicating her husband, who was standing by a swing door at the opposite side of the hall.

Mr. Rylands, utterly confounded, pattered headlong downstairs again, and disappeared with Mr. Mainwaring, still apologising.

Lady Adela tapped Connie playfully but heavily upon the cheek. ("*Like being tickled by a mastodon*" wrote that lady to her husband a short time later.)

"Constance dear," she said, with a reproving smile, "you are incorrigible. Now let us sit down and have a cosy chat."

The incorrigible one sat submissively down upon the sofa and waited. She knew that her hostess had not rendered the hall a solitude for nothing.

Presently the cosy chat began. Not too suddenly, though. Lady Adela first enquired after the health of Mr. Carmyle, and expressed regret that he had been prevented from accompanying his wife to The Towers.

"He was sent for about his wretched canal," explained Connie. "But he saw me off at Waterloo, and promised to come down on Monday if he could get away."

"Is it the first time you have been parted?" asked Lady Adela.

"Yes," said Connie, in quite a small voice.

Her hostess, suddenly human, patted her hand.

"The time will soon pass, dear," she said. "You will find this house quiet but soothing. I like it much better than town myself. Mr. Mainwaring is no trouble, and things are so cheap. The only drawback is Sylvia. She dislikes the people about here."

"By the way," enquired Connie, recovering her spirits, "what is Sylvia's exact *line* just at present? Last year it was slumming; the year before it was poker-work, and the year before that it was Christian Science. What does that sage-green gown mean? Don't tell me she has become a Futurist, or a Post-Impressionist, or anything!"

"I never attempt," replied Lady Adela, closing her eyes resignedly, "to cope with Sylvia's hobbies. At present she is a Socialist of some kind. She is evolving a scheme, I believe, under which the masses and classes are to intermarry for the next twenty years. By that time, she considers, social distinctions will have ceased to exist, and consequently the social problem will have solved itself."

Mrs. Carmyle nodded her head comprehendingly.

"I see," she said, "it sounds a good idea. I shall start looking out in the 'Morning Post' for the announcement of Sylvia's engagement to a plumber. Just half a cup more, please."

Lady Adela now decided to begin the cosy chat. She accordingly discharged what is known on rifle-ranges as a sighting shot.

"By the way, dear Constance, have you and your husband seen much of Dick lately?"

"Oh, we meet him about occasionally," replied Connie, casting about for cover--"at parties, and so on."

"I fear," continued Lady Adela, with what the police call "intent," "that the poor boy is lonely."

"The last time I saw him," replied Connie, "he was entertaining five people to luncheon at the Trocadero. He did n't *look* lonely."

"There is a loneliness of spirit, dear," replied Lady Adela gently, "of which some of us know nothing. I think it shows that Dick *must* be feeling lonely if he requires no less than five people to cheer him up."

"I am sure you are right," said the obliging Mrs. Carmyle.

"Was Norah Puncheon of the party, by any chance?" enquired Lady Adela carelessly.

"No. I did n't know any of the people. Is Norah a friend of Dicky's?"

"They have seen a good deal of one another of late, I believe," replied the diplomatic Lady Adela, much as a motorist with his radiator full of feathers might admit having recently noticed a hen somewhere. "Constance dear," she continued, coming in her maternal solicitude quite prematurely to the point, "you are always so discreet. It is high time Dick was married, and this time I really do think--no, I *feel* it instinctively--that Norah Puncheon is the right woman for him."

"The right woman!" replied the late First Reserve pensively. "How awful that always sounds! The wrong one is always so much nicer!"

"My dear," exclaimed the horrified Lady Adela, "whoever put such a notion into your head?"

"Dicky. He told me so himself."

"Has Norah Puncheon much influence over him, do you know?" continued Lady Adela, falling back on to safer ground.

"Yes, lots," replied Connie, stifling the tiniest of yawns. "There goes your telephone."

"Milroy will attend to it, dear. Let me see," pursued Lady Adela, with studious vagueness--"what were we talking about?"

"Norah Puncheon's influence over Dicky," replied Connie, popping a lump of sugar into her mouth and crunching it with all the satisfaction of a child of six.

"You have noticed it yourself, then?"

Connie, quite speechless, nodded.

Lady Adela beamed. The scent was growing stronger.

"In what way, dear?" she asked, with unfeigned interest.

"Well," said Connie, after an interval of profound reflection, "Dicky wanted to back Prince Caramel for the St. Leger, and Norah would n't let him. He was so grateful to her afterwards!"

Lady Adela summoned up a lopsided smile--the smile of a tarpon-fisher who has pulled up a red herring.

"I think her influence goes deeper than that, dearest," she rejoined in patient reproof. "You, who only knew my son as a rather careless and light-hearted boy, would hardly credit--"

"A telephone message, my lady!" announced Milroy, appearing at the dining-room door.

Lady Adela, tripped up on her way to a striking passage, sighed with an air of pathetic endurance, and enquired:--

"From whom, Milroy?"

"From Mr. Richard, my lady."

"Mr. Richard? Where is he?"

"He has telephoned from Shotley Post-Office, my lady," replied Milroy, keenly appreciating the mild sensation he was about to create; "to say that he has arrived by the four-fifteen and is walking up."

"*Walking*--on a night like this?" cried Lady Adela, all the mother in her awake at once. "Tell him to wait, and I will send the motor."

"Mr. Richard said he preferred walking, my lady," rejoined Milroy, growing more wooden as he approached the *clou* of his narrative. "He said he would explain when he arrived. But the luggage-cart was to go down."

"For one portmanteau?"

"For the young lady's trunks, my lady."

"Young lady?" Lady Adela turned a puzzled countenance to her companion. "Constance, dear, was not your luggage sent up with you?"

"Yes," replied Connie, scenting fun; "it was. I fancy this must be some other lady."

Light broke in on Lady Adela.

"Norah Puncheon, after all!" she exclaimed joyfully. "Her throat must be better, and that headstrong son of mine has compelled her to come down by the four-fifteen."

"And walk up in the rain," supplemented Connie.

"The thoughtless boy!" wailed Lady Adela insincerely. "He will give her pneumonia."

"Perhaps it is n't Miss Puncheon," suggested Connie soothingly.

"But, my dear," said Lady Adela, refraining with great forbearance from slapping the small but discouraging counsellor by her side, "who else can it be?" She turned to Milroy.

"Did Mr. Richard mention if he was bringing the young lady up with him?" she asked.

"Yes, my lady," replied Milroy with unction--"he did."

"Did he mention her name, Milroy?" enquired Connie.

"No, Miss. He just said 'the young lady.' Will there be anything further, my lady?"

"No," snapped Lady Adela; and her aged retainer, as feverishly anxious beneath his perfectly schooled exterior to solve the mystery of his beloved Master Dick's latest escapade as his mistress, departed to lay another place for dinner.

In the hall there was a long silence. The wind roared round the house, and the rain drummed softly upon the diamond panes of the big oriel window.

"It might be some old friend of the family," said Lady Adela hopefully--"some one whom Dick has encountered unexpectedly and invited down. You know his impulsive, hospitable way! Aunt Fanny, perhaps."

"A *young* lady, I think Milroy said," replied the Job's comforter beside her.

"Perhaps," pursued Lady Adela, still endeavouring to keep her courage up, "it is only one of the foolish boy's practical jokes."

These speculations were cut short by the prolonged buzz of an electric bell, followed by the sound of a spirited tattoo executed upon the panels of the front door, apparently by a walking-stick. The Freak (and party) had arrived.

Lady Adela sat bolt upright, almost pale.

"Mercy! here they are!" she said.

Milroy, who had appeared from his lair with uncanny celerity, was already in the outer hall. There was the sound of a heavy door being opened; the curtains bulged out with the draught; and a voice was heard uplifted in cheery greeting.

Then the door banged, and Dicky Mainwaring appeared through the curtains.

He was alone, and very wet.

"What ho, Mum!" he observed, after the fashion of the present generation.

"My son!" exclaimed Lady Adela, advancing with outstretched arms.

Dicky, enduring a somewhat lengthy embrace, suddenly caught sight of a small alert figure on the sofa. Curtailing the maternal caress as gently as possible, he darted forward.

"Connie!" he cried enthusiastically. "What tremendous luck meeting you!" He shook his ancient ally by both hands.

"I want you more at this moment," he continued earnestly, "than at any other period of my life."

Connie Carmyle pointed an accusing finger at him.

"Dicky Mainwaring," she enquired sternly, "where is your lady friend?"

"I was just going to introduce her," replied Dicky, with a rapturous smile. "I wonder where she has got to, by the way. Found a mirror, I expect."

Then he raised his voice and cried:--

"Tilly!"

"Hallo!" replied an extremely small voice; and a shrinking figure appeared in the opening of the curtains.

CHAPTER XIII
LUCIDITY ITSELF

I

"This, Mum," announced Dicky in tones of immense pride, "is Tilly. Miss Welwyn, you know."

He advanced to the girl, who still stood hesitatingly in the opening of the curtains, and drew her forward by the hand.

"Come along, little thing," he said, in a voice which made Connie Carmyle's heart warm to him. "Don't be frightened. I present to you my lady mother. You will know one another intimately in no time," he added untruthfully.

Miss Tilly Welwyn advanced with faltering steps. It was seen now that she was *petite*, almost the same height and build as Connie Carmyle, with great grey eyes and a pretty mouth. She was wrapped in a man's Burberry coat, and wore a motor veil tied under her chin. Rain dripped from her in all directions. Timidly she extended a glistening and froggy paw in the direction of her hostess.

"How do you do, Miss Weller?" said Lady Adela, mystified but well-bred.

"Very well, thank you," replied the visitor in a frightened squeak.

Dicky cheerfully set his parent right upon the subject of Miss Welwyn's surname, and then introduced Mrs. Carmyle.

"Tilly," he said, "this is Connie--one of the very best that ever stepped! Don't forget that: you will never hear a truer word."

The two girls regarded one another for a moment, and then shook hands with instinctive friendliness. The small stranger's face cleared, and she smiled, first at Connie and then up at Dicky.

Thereafter came a pause. The atmosphere was tense with enquiry. One could almost feel the Marconigrams radiating from Lady Adela. But apparently The Freak's coherer was out of order. He merely turned towards the staircase, and exclaimed:--

"Hallo, here are Dad and Sylvia. These are the last two," he added in a reassuring undertone to Miss Welwyn. "Quite tame, both of them."

Mr. Mainwaring's face lit up joyfully at the sight of his son, and he hurried forward.

"Dick, my boy, you've arrived at last! Capital!" He clapped the prodigal on the shoulder.

"Yes, Dad," replied Dicky with equal zest; "we have arrived. This is Tilly!"

Mr. Mainwaring, entirely at sea but innately hospitable, greeted Tilly heartily. "You must be terribly cold," he said. "Come to the fire and let me take off that wet garment of yours."

He led the girl to the blaze, then turned to shoot a glance of respectful enquiry in the direction of his august spouse. It was ignored. Meanwhile Dicky had introduced the languid but far from indifferent Sylvia.

"Now you all know one another," he said. "Sylvia, be a dear old soul and take Miss Welwyn up to your room and give her some dry things, will you? She is soaking, and her luggage is n't here yet. You see," he added a little lamely--Sylvia's patrician calm had rather dashed him as usual--"we walked from the station-- did n't we, Tilly?"

Tilly nodded dutifully, eyeing Sylvia the while with some distrust.

"You will take care of her, won't you?" concluded the solicitous Dicky.

"Surely!" replied Sylvia, in her grandest manner. "This way, Miss Welwyn."

She swept across the hall and up the staircase, followed by the small, moist, and mysterious figure of the newcomer.

At the foot of the stair Tilly halted and looked back. Dicky, who had been following her with his eyes, was at her side in a moment.

"What is it?" he asked in a low voice.

The girl laid an appealing hand on his arm.

"Don't leave me, Dicky!" she whispered.

The Freak replied by tucking her arm under his own and propelling her vigorously up to the turn of the stair.

"Don't be a little juggins," he said affectionately. "*I* can't come and change your shoes and stockings for you, can I?"

Miss Welwyn, acquiescing in this eminently correct view of the matter, smiled submissively.

"All right," she said. "Au revoir!"

She ran lightly upstairs after the disappearing Sylvia, turning to wave her hand to Dicky before she disappeared.

Dicky, who had waited below for that purpose, acknowledged the salute, and turned to find Mrs. Carmyle at his elbow.

"Dicky," announced that small Samaritan, "I am going up, too. Sylvia might bite your ewe lamb."

The Freak smiled gratefully.

"The Lady and the Tiger--eh?" he said. "Connie, you are a brick! Be tender with her, won't you?" he added gently. "She's scared to death at present, and no wonder!"

Connie Carmyle, with a reassuring pat upon the anxious young man's arm, turned and sped upstairs. Dicky, hands in pockets and head in air, strolled happily back into the circle of firelight and took up his stand upon the hearthrug. Lady Adela, looking like a large volcano in the very last stages of self-suppression, sat simmering over the teacups.

The heir of the Mainwarings addressed his parents affectionately.

"Well, dear old things," he enquired, "how are we? So sorry to be late for tea, but it was an eventful and perilous journey."

The long-overdue eruption came at last.

"Dick," demanded Lady Adela explosively, "why have you brought that young person here?"

"Young per--oh, Tilly?" Dicky smiled ecstatically to himself at the very sound of Miss Welwyn's name. "Tilly? Well, I don't see what else I could have done with her, Mummie dear. I could n't leave her at the station, could I? But I must tell you about our adventures. First of all we lost Percy."

"Dick," repeated Lady Adela, "*who--is--*?"

"Who is Percy?" asked Dicky readily. "I forgot; I have n't told you about Percy. He is her brother. A most amazing fellow: knows everything. Can explain to you in two minutes all the things you have failed to understand for years. Teach you something you did n't know, I should n't wonder, Mother. He is going to introduce me to some of his friends, and put me up for his club."

"What club, my boy?" interposed Mr. Mainwaring, snatching at this gleam of light in the general murkiness.

"'The Crouch End Gladiators,' I think they 're called," said Dicky. "But I have n't met any of them yet."

"Where is Crouch End?" enquired Lady Adela. "And why should one have a club there?"

"It is a cycling club," explained Dicky. "You go out for spins in the country on Saturday afternoons. Topping! I'll bring them down here one day if you like! Each member is allowed to have one lady guest," he added, with a happy smile. "But to resume. We lost friend Percy at Waterloo. He went to get a bicycle ticket, or something, and was no more seen. The train started without him. Tilly was fearfully upset about it: said she thought it was n't quite proper for her to come down without a chaperon on her first visit."

"She proposes to come again, then?" said Lady Adela, with a short quavering laugh.

Dicky stopped short, and regarded his mother with unfeigned astonishment.

"Come again? I should think she was coming again! Anyhow, the poor little thing was quite distressed when we lost Perce."

"That, dear," remarked Lady Adela icily, "is what I should call straining at a gnat and swallowing a camel. And now, my boy, let me beg you to tell me--"

Dicky, who was too fully occupied with the recollections of his recent journey to be aware of the physical and mental strain to which he was subjecting his revered parents, suddenly started off down a fresh alley of irrelevant reminiscence.

"Talking of camels," he said, "there is the goat."

"Bless my soul, my dear lad!" exclaimed Mr. Mainwaring. "What goat?"

Dicky was perfectly ready to explain.

"When Tilly and I got out of the train at Shotley Beauchamp station," he began, "and found that you two absent-minded old dears had forgotten to send anything to meet us--"

"But Dick, my boy," interposed the old gentleman--Lady Adela was rapidly progressing beyond the stage of articulate remonstrance--"how could your mother be expected to divine your intentions with regard to trains, or to know that you were bringing down--er--a guest?"

"I wrote and told you," said Dicky.

"When, pray?" enquired Lady Adela, finding speech again.

"The day before yesterday," said Dicky positively; "breaking the news about Tilly, and when we were coming, and--"

"We received no letter from you," replied Lady Adela.

"But I wrote it, Mum!" cried Dicky. "I spent three hours over it. It was the most important letter I have ever written in my life! Is it likely a man could forget--"

"Feel in your pockets, my boy," suggested the experienced Mr. Mainwaring.

Dicky smiled indulgently upon his resourceful parent, and pulled out the contents of his breast-pocket--a handful of old letters and a cigarette case.

"Anything to oblige you, Dad," he ran on, scanning the addresses. "But I know I posted the thing. A man does not forget on such an oc-- No! you are right. I'm a liar. Here it is!"

He produced a fat envelope from the bunch, and threw it down upon the tea-table.

II

"I forgive you both," he said, smiling serenely, "for not sending to meet us. Well, to return to the goat--"

Veins began to stand out upon Lady Adela's patrician brow.

"Richard," she exclaimed, in a low and vibrant tone--"for the last time, *who is that young woman*?"

Dicky stared down upon his afflicted parent in unaffected surprise, and then dissolved into happy laughter.

"I must tell Tilly about this," he roared. "Of course, now I come to think of it, you don't know a thing about her. You never got my letter! Fancy you two poor old creatures sitting there as good as gold and wondering why I had brought her down here at all! Oh, my sainted Mother!"

"Who is she?" reiterated the sainted Mother, fighting for breath.

"She is my little girl," replied Dicky proudly. "We're engaged."

"I knew it," said Lady Adela, in a hollow voice.

"And I have brought her down here to make your acquaintance, that's all!" concluded the happy lover, apparently surprised that his relationship to Miss Welwyn should ever have been a matter of doubt to any one. "We met the goat outside the station--"

Lady Adela uttered a deep groan. Mr. Mainwaring rose from his seat and advanced upon his tall son, who still leaned easily against the mantel-piece, with his feet upon the hearthrug and his head above the clouds.

"My dearest boy," he said, patting Dicky affectionately and coaxingly upon the shoulder, "do you realise that you are our only son, and that as such we take a not unreasonable interest in your welfare? Would you mind postponing the goat for a moment and giving us a more explicit account of the young lady? I had only the merest glimpse of her just now," he concluded, doggedly avoiding his wife's eye, "but she struck me as charming--charming!"

Dicky's air of cheerful inanity fell from him like a cloak. Exultantly he took his father by the shoulders.

"Dad," he shouted, "she's the most blessed little darling that ever walked this earth! She's a princess! She's a fairy! She's a--"

The rhapsodist broke off short, and flushed red.

"Forgive me," he said, "for waffling like that, but I don't quite know what I'm doing just at present. Dad, I'm the happiest man that ever lived!"

"My boy, my boy," cried little Mr. Mainwaring, "I'm glad--I'm glad!"

And father and son, regardless of the feelings of the unfortunate lady upon the sofa, proceeded to shake one another violently and continuously by both hands.

At last they desisted, a little sheepishly.

"Abel," said a cold voice, "be seated. Dick, take that chair."

Both gentlemen complied meekly.

"I see," said Lady Adela, looking up from a rapid perusal of her son's letter, "that the girl's name is Tilly Welwyn. Tilly, I presume, is an abbreviation of Matilda?"

"I don't know," confessed Dicky. "But Tilly will," he added brightly. "She knows everything."

"I notice," continued the Counsel for the Prosecution, still skimming through the letter, "that you have known one another for a short time--"

"Seven weeks, five days, four hours, and a few odd minutes," confirmed the defendant, looking at his watch.

"--And you became engaged as recently as last Sunday." Lady Adela laid down the letter. "Where?"

"On the top of a 'bus."

"H'm!" said Mr. Mainwaring uneasily.

"A rather unusual place, was it not?" enquired Lady Adela coldly.

"Unusual," agreed Dicky readily, "but not irregular. Oh, no! Besides, Percy was there, three seats behind. Perfect dragon of a chaperon, old Perce! Yes, the proceedings were most correct, I promise you."

"I note," continued Lady Adela, taking up the letter again, "that you do not say where you made Miss Welwyn's acquaintance."

"That was on the top of another 'bus," explained Dicky, with a disarming smile.

"And was her brother," enquired Lady Adela, ominously calm, "present on *this* occasion?"

"Percy? Rather not! Otherwise I need not have interfered."

"Int--" began both Lady Adela and Mr. Mainwaring together.

"Yes," said Dicky glibly. "It was like this. The rain began to come down hard, and a rather poisonous-looking bounder sitting beside her offered her his umbrella."

"Any gentleman would have done the same, Dick," interposed Mr. Mainwaring quietly.

"Yes, Dad. But I don't think any gentleman would have insisted on paying a girl's fare for her; and I don't think any gentleman would have considered a half-share in a three-and-ninepenny brolly an excuse for putting his arm round a girl's waist," replied Dicky, with sudden passion.

"He did that?"

"Yes."

"What did you do?"

Dicky grinned cheerfully.

"I did a pretty bright thing," he said. "It was no business of mine, of course, and I naturally did n't want to start a brawl on the top of a Piccadilly omnibus--"

"Dick, what were you doing on the top of an omnibus at all?" demanded Lady Adela unexpectedly. "Such economies are a new feature of your character."

Dicky nodded his head sagely.

"Yes," he agreed, "that's a sound point--a sound point. What *was* I doing on the top of that omnibus at all? That's the mystery. I was extremely surprised myself. I have spent whole days since, wondering how I got there. I have come to the conclusion that it was Fate--just Fate! That's it--Fate!"

"My dear boy, don't talk nonsense," said Lady Adela impatiently.

"But I am quite serious, dear Mum," persisted Dicky. "I don't as a rule go following unprotected young females onto the summits of omnibuses--"

Lady Adela's fine eyes began to protrude, crabwise.

"You *followed* her?" she gasped.

"I did. What else was there to do?" said Dicky simply. "I might never have seen her again if I had n't. Fate does n't as a rule give a man two chances. I got this one, and I took it. One moment I was walking along Piccadilly, bucking about something to old Tiny Carmyle. Next moment there she was, stepping on to that Piccadilly 'bus. In about five seconds I found myself up on top, too, sitting on the seat behind her. I tell you, it must--"

"What became of Mr. Carmyle?" asked Lady Adela, ruthlessly interrupting another rhapsody.

Dicky smiled vaguely, and rubbed his head.

"Upon my soul, I don't know," he confessed. "It's the first time the matter has occurred to me. I expect he went home. He's a resourceful old creature."

"How did you dispose of the man with the umbrella, my boy?" enquired Mr. Mainwaring.

"Ah," said Dicky, abandoning Carmyle to his fate, "that was where I did the bright thing. The fellow looked as if he made rather a hobby of this sort of game, and that gave me an idea. When he started amusing himself, I tapped him on the shoulder and said, right in his ear: 'Look here, my man, do you remember what happened to you the last time you were rude to a lady when you thought no one was with her?"

Mr. Mainwaring rubbed his hands gently.

"Well?" he said.

"At that," continued The Freak with relish, "my sportsman went a sort of ripe gorgonzola colour, grabbed his filthy brolly, and slid heavily down the back stairs of the 'bus."

"And what did you do then?" enquired Lady Adela.

"I," replied Dicky triumphantly, "got up and took his seat and gave Tilly my umbrella!"

"Ha! ha! ha!" crowed Mr. Mainwaring delightedly. "H'm! h'm! h'm! Honk! honk! honk!" he concluded hurriedly, coughing laboriously and patting himself upon the chest, as his consort turned menacingly in his direction.

"And where did you part company?" asked Lady Adela.

"Well," explained the culprit, "I offered to see her home. She was rather shaken up by what had happened."

Lady Adela nodded her head as if she had expected this.

"I see. And what did the young woman--

"Don't you think, Mum dear, that you might start calling her 'lady' now?" suggested Dicky gently.

"--Say to that?" she enquired, without taking the slightest notice of the interruption.

"She said she was n't going home. She was out shopping, it seemed. In fact, she got down at a shop in Oxford Street. I insisted on her keeping the umbrella, though."

"As a gift?"

"No," said Dicky with a twinkle; "as a hostage."

"And you gave her your address?"

Dicky's radiant countenance clouded for a moment.

"Not quite," he said. "I meant to, of course; but I can't have been quite my own calm self; for instead of giving her my own address, I asked for hers."

"She gave it, I suppose?" said Lady Adela dryly.

"No. She hesitated badly. I ought to have realised at once that I was not quite playing the game; but I was so mad keen to see her again that the idea never occurred to me. I simply thought she had forgotten where she lived, or something, and waited."

"But finally," said Lady Adela, "the young--lady did confide her address to you?"

Dicky nodded, and his mother continued:--

"Where does she live?"

"Russell Square," said Dicky rapturously.

"Russell Square? Ah! I know it. One drives through it on the way to Euston. In Bloomsbury, I believe?" said Lady Adela.

Her infatuated son corrected her. "Not Bloomsbury," he said reverently; "Heaven."

"Quite so," agreed Lady Adela, entirely unmoved. "What number?"

"I have forgotten the number long ago," replied Dicky, "but I could find my way to the place blindfold by this time."

"Don't you ever write to her?" asked his mother curiously.

"Every day."

"Then you must know her postal address," was the crushing rejoinder.

Dicky merely shook his head, and smiled serenely.

"No, I don't," he said.

"Then where do you address her letters?"

"I walk round every night after bedtime, and drop the letter into her letter-box. Is it likely I would let a postman touch it? Anyhow, on this occasion Tilly told me that if I asked for my umbrella any time I was passing it would be handed out to me. Then she thanked me again, the darling, and went into the shop."

"Front entrance?" enquired Lady Adela swiftly.

"Was it?" said Dicky vaguely. "I don't remember. Yes, I do. She went round and in at the side somewhere. Why?"

"Nothing," said Lady Adela. "And did you call at Russell Square?"

"Rather! I went there next afternoon."

"Were you invited in?"

"As a matter of fact, I met her coming out, with her father. A splendid old chap! Apparently Tilly had told him the whole tale, and he had expressed a desire to make my acquaintance. A lucky desire for me, what? He took us both out to tea."

"Where?"

"Gunter's. Said he was sorry he could n't ask me into the house at present, as they had the paperhangers in. After that visitation was over, I was to come and make the acquaintance of the rest of the family."

"And did you?"

"Yes."

"What is the house like inside?" was the next inevitable feminine enquiry.

"To tell you the truth I have n't been inside yet, except the front hall. But I met the rest of the family at a very friendly little luncheon given in my honour at the Criterion on the following Saturday afternoon."

"And what are the rest of the family like?"

Dicky pondered.

"Now I come to think it over," he confessed at length, "I'm not very clear about the rest of the family. Collectively they struck me as being the most charming people I had ever met, but I don't seem to have noticed them individually, if you know what I mean. You see, Tilly was there."

"How many are there?" pursued his mother, with exemplary patience.

"Four or five, I should think, but I have never counted them," replied the exasperating Richard. "Tilly--"

Mr. Mainwaring came timidly to his wife's aid.

"Is there a mother, my boy?" he asked.

"Yes, there is a mother," replied Dicky hastily. "Oh, yes," he repeated with more confidence, "certainly there is a mother."

"Any sisters?"

"There is a small girl--a dear. And I have a kind of notion there are some twins somewhere. Tilly--"

"Any brothers?"

Dicky smiled, apparently at some amusing thought.

"Yes," he said, "there is Percy. A sterling fellow, Perce! I wonder where he is, by the way. If he were here he might be able to do something with the goat. Any one would respect Percy--even a goat."

Lady Adela sighed despairingly. Mr. Mainwaring, taking the goat by the horns, so to speak, asked his son to elucidate the mystery once and for all.

"Did n't I tell you about the goat?" asked Dick in surprise. "Well, it was like this. When Tilly and I were hunting for a cab in the rain at the station just now, we met a woman with a goat, in tears."

"The goat?" said Lady Adela incredulously.

"No, its mother--I mean, its proprietress. She had missed the market, or something, owing, to her pony breaking down, and she had come to the station as a forlorn hope, to see if she could catch a departing goat-merchant and unload Maximilian on him."

"Maximilian?" interjected Lady Adela giddily.

"Yes--the goat. We had to call him *something*, you know. Her husband was very ill in bed, and Maximilian had to be sold to defray expenses, it seemed."

"And so you--er--purchased Maximilian?" said Mr. Mainwaring.

"We did," replied The Freak gravely. "That was why we had to walk. The cabman would not allow us to take Maximilian inside with us, and Max absolutely declined to sit on the box beside the cabman--which did n't altogether surprise me--so we all three had to come here on our arched insteps. I wonder where Tilly is."

"Where is the animal now?" enquired Lady Adela apprehensively. She was quite prepared to hear that Maximilian was already in the best bedroom.

"We left him on the lawn, tethered to the rain-gauge," replied Dicky. "Ah, there she is!"

Forgetting the goat and all other impediments to the course of true love, he hurried to the foot of the staircase.

III

Miss Welwyn and Mrs. Carmyle descended the stairs together, Sylvia stalking majestically in the rear. Tilly wore a short navy-blue skirt and a soft silk shirt belonging to Connie--garments which, owing to the mysterious readiness with which the female form accommodates itself to the wardrobe of its neighbour, fitted her to perfection. In this case, however, the miracle was less noticeable than usual, for the two girls were of much the same height and build, their chief points of difference being their hair and eyes.

In reply to her swain's tender enquiries, Miss Welwyn intimated that she was now warm and dry.

"In that case," replied Dicky, "come and sit up to the tea-table and take some nourishment."

On her way to her tea Tilly was met by Mr. Mainwaring senior, with outstretched hands.

"My dear young lady," he said, with shy cordiality, "we owe you a most humble apology."

Tilly, flushing prettily, asked why.

"For our extremely vague greeting to you just now," explained her host. "You see"--he clapped Dicky fondly on the shoulder--"this intellectual son of ours forgot to post the letter announcing your--telling us about you. We have only just heard the news. Now that we have you, my dear"--the old gentleman's eyes beamed affectionately--"we are going to make much of you!"

"Oh, thank you! You *are* kind!" cried Tilly impulsively; and smiled gratefully upon her future father-in-law. His were the first official words of welcome that she had received.

"Good old Dad!" said Dicky.

Meanwhile Lady Adela had come to the conclusion that her male belongings were overdoing it.

"Do you take sugar, Miss Welwyn?" she enquired loudly.

"Yes, please," said Tilly, still engaged in smiling affectionately upon the Mainwarings, *père et fils*.

"I wonder now," continued Mr. Mainwaring, "if you are in any way related to an old friend of mine--or perhaps I should say acquaintance, for he moved on a higher plane than I--Lucius Welwyn? I was at school with him more than forty years ago, and also at Cambridge."

"Lucius Welwyn?" cried Tilly, her eyes glowing. "He is my Daddy--my father!"

"You don't say so? Capital!" Abel Mainwaring turned to his wife. "Adela, do you hear that? Miss Welwyn and I have established a bond of union already. Her father was actually at school with me."

Lady Adela flatly declined to join in the general enthusiasm.

"Are you sure, dear?" was all she said. "There might be two."

Mr. Mainwaring pointed out, with truth, that Lucius Welwyn was an uncommon name. "But we can easily make sure," he said. "The Lucius Welwyn whom I remember was a Fellow of his College. Did your father--"

"Yes, Dad was a Fellow of his College for some years," said Tilly. "I think I will come a little farther from the fire now, if you don't mind. I am quite warm."

"Come and sit here by me, dear Miss Welwyn," said Lady Adela with sudden affability. "I want to have a cosy little chat with you. Dick, you are very wet and muddy. Go and change."

"All right," said Dicky obediently.

As he left the hall he said something in a low voice to Mrs. Carmyle. That small champion of the oppressed nodded comprehendingly, and established herself at a writing-table under the curtained window.

"Abel," enquired Lady Adela, in pursuance of her policy of once more clearing the decks for action, "what have you done with Mr. Rylands?"

"I quite forgot him," confessed Mr. Mainwaring. "I was so much occupied with Miss Welwyn. I fear he is still in the smoking-room."

"Go and let him out--by the side door," commanded Lady Adela.

"Come on, Dad!" said Dicky.

Father and son disappeared, arm-in-arm; Lady Adela and Sylvia closed in upon the flinching Miss Welwyn; and Mrs. Carmyle, taking up her pen, addressed herself to the composition of an epistle to her lord and master.

Lady Adela looked round, and remarked in solicitous tones:--

"Constance, dear, you have chosen a very draughty corner for yourself."

"I have put fresh note-paper in your bedroom, Connie," added Sylvia cordially.

"I'm as right as rain, thanks," said Connie. "Just scribbling a line to Bill."

And she began:--

I have arrived quite safely, old man, and the most tremendously exciting things are happening here. Listen!

CHAPTER XIV
ANOTHER COSY CHAT, WITH AN INTERRUPTION
I

The victim, continued Connie presently, *is now upon the sofa, wedged in between the Chief Ogress and the Assistant Tormentor. She is scared out of her wits, poor thing, but has stood up to the pair of them splendidly so far.*

"It was good of you to come down to this poky little corner of the country, Miss Welwyn," Lady Adela was saying, handing Tilly a second cup of tea. "It is so nice when one's friends take one as they find one, is it not?"

Tilly, wide-eyed and quaking, was understood to assent to this proposition.

"You live in town, I understand?" continued Lady Adela cautiously.

Tilly took a deep breath, and began:--

"Yes--in Russell Square. The house," she continued rapidly, "is very old-fashioned. It belonged to my grandfather. My father inherited from him, and we have lived there ever since we left Cambridge. We have often talked of leaving, but Dad says he can't bear transplanting at his time of life. So," concluded Tilly, with an hysterical little gasp--Lady Adela and Sylvia were listening with the dispassionate immobility of a pair of well-nourished sphinxes--"we just stay on."

She has confessed that she lives in Bloomsbury, wrote Mrs. Carmyle. *The Inquisition are one up.*

"Russell Square!" cooed Lady Adela. "How charming and old-fashioned! So handy for the British Museum, too!"

"And Euston Road!" added Sylvia enthusiastically.

Cats! Cats!! Cats!!! recorded Connie furiously.

Lady Adela offered Tilly a bun, and resumed her long-distance fire.

"You are quite a small family, I imagine?"

"Well," began Tilly readily--they had reached a topic that lay very near her heart--"there are Father and Mother, of course, and my brother Percy, and my sister, and two quite tiny ones. My grandmother--"

"How nice," murmured Lady Adela indulgently, closing her eyes as if to mitigate the strain of this enumeration. "And what is your little sister's name?"

"Amelia."

"Amelia? Delightful! Perfect! It suits Russell Square exactly."

"One feels," corroborated Sylvia, "as if the Sedleys and the Osbornes and the Rawdon Crawleys all lived next door."

Why don't they smack people like Sylvia more in their youth? enquired Mrs. Carmyle's letter plaintively.

"I don't think we have met any of *them*," said Miss Welwyn doubtfully. "The Mossops live on one side of us and the Rosenbaums on the other. We don't call on them, of course," she added apprehensively. "And oh, Lady Adela, I have an invitation for you from my mother, to come and have tea with us."

"That is very kind of your mother," said Lady Adela graciously. "You shall give me the invitation when you have unpacked your boxes."

"It's--it's not a written invitation," said Tilly. "Mother just asked me to ask you, any day you happen to be coming into town. Then you would meet my father and the others."

"That will be charming," replied Lady Adela. "I think we have no engagement on Monday." (*Lady A. is simply bursting with curiosity about the girl's family*, observed Connie at this point.) "I will write a little note to your mother, and you shall take it back with you on Monday morning. Are you the eldest of the family?"

"No. Perce--Percy is the eldest. He is twenty-two."

"Is he at the University?"

Miss Welwyn shook her head.

"Not now," she said. She spoke with more freedom. The restraint of her surroundings was wearing off, and her courage, which was considerable, was beginning to assert itself. "He is in the City. He dislikes it very much, poor boy. He is so fond of open-air sports, and he finds an office very trying. My father was a great sportsman, too. He used to go racing a good deal at one time, but he has given it up now. He says he is on the shelf."

"And he was a Fellow of his College, I think you said?" remarked Lady Adela, a little bored with this prattle.

"Yes--Fellow and Tutor."

"But he is no longer in residence, you say?"

"No," said Tilly briefly.

There is something shady about the poor child's father, wrote Mrs. Carmyle, *but Lady A. has got no change out of her so far.*

"I am looking forward greatly to making your father's acquaintance, Miss Welwyn," said Lady Adela, with absolute sincerity. "Now, I wonder if I know any of your mother's people. I don't think you have mentioned her maiden name."

"She was a Banks," replied Miss Welwyn readily.

Bill, dear, this little girl is splendid! recorded Connie enthusiastically.

"I beg your pardon?" said Lady Adela.

"A Banks," repeated Tilly politely.

Lady Adela nodded her head intelligently.

"Ah, to be sure!" she said. "Let me see. Are they a Warwickshire family, now?"

"Or is it a Cornish name?" queried Sylvia, with an encouraging smile.

"No," said Tilly. "Mother came from Bedfordshire--or else Cambridgeshire," she added rather breathlessly, for the four eyes of the sphinxes were upon her once more.

"But, dear Miss Welwyn--" began Sylvia.

I can stand this no longer! scribbled Connie, and threw down her pen.

"Thank goodness, that's over!" she exclaimed, rising and coming over to the fire. "What a nuisance affectionate husbands are! Talking of husbands, Sylvia, I hear you are going to marry a plumber."

Lady Adela and Sylvia, taken in flank, both turned and eyed the frivolous interloper severely. Had they not done so, they would have noted that Miss Welwyn's teacup had almost leaped from its saucer.

"Dear Connie, you are priceless," commented Sylvia patronisingly. "I wonder where you got your quaint sense of humour."

"Lady Adela was my informant," said Connie, quite unruffled. She had drawn the enemy's fire upon herself, which was precisely what she had intended to do. "Jolly sensible of you, too! A plumber is a useful little thing to have about a house. My Bill is practically one, you know, although he calls himself something grander. Now, what about a four-handed game of billiards before dinner? Do you feel inclined to play, Miss Welwyn?"

"I am rather out of practice," said Tilly dubiously.

"Never mind!" said Connie. "You can play with Dicky against Mr. Mainwaring and me."

She walked to the foot of the staircase, and called up: "Mr. Richard, forward!"

"In one moment, Miss!" replied a voice far up the height. "I'm just attending to a lady at the ribbon counter. I'll step down directly." Then a stentorian bawl: "Sign, please!"

During this characteristic exchange of inanities an electric bell purred faintly in the distance, with the usual result that the dining-room door opened, to emit the jinnee-like presence of Mr. Milroy.

"What is it, Milroy?" enquired Lady Adela.

"Front door bell, my lady," replied Milroy, and disappeared like a corpulent wraith through the curtains.

"Heavens, not *another* caller!" exclaimed the overwrought mistress of the household.

"Probably Mr. Rylands come back for his goloshes," said Sylvia. At the same moment Dicky and his father appeared, descending the staircase together.

"*And* the next article, madam?" continued Dick lustily, addressing Mrs. Carmyle, who stood below.

He was answered, not by the lady to whom his query was addressed, but by Milroy, who appeared holding back one of the curtains which covered the entrance to the vestibule, to announce, in the resigned tones of a man for whom life holds no further surprises:--

"Mr. Percy Welwyn!"

II

Mr. Percy Welwyn entered. He was a slender young man with an insufficient chin and a small moustache. He looked like a shop assistant; and Dicky's last remark, still ringing through the hall, emphasised rather than suggested the comparison. His hair was brushed low down upon his forehead, with an elaborate curl over his right eyebrow. His eyes were bulgy. He wore a tight-fitting cycling suit, splashed with mud, and carried in his hand a small tweed cap bearing a metal badge. Altogether an impartial observer might have been excused for not feeling greatly surprised that Dicky and Tilly had mislaid him.

Mr. Welwyn advanced to the fire, with the easy grace of one who is habitually a success in whatever grade of society he finds himself, and remarked: "Good-evenin', all!"

For a moment there was a frozen silence. Then Dicky hurried forward.

"My dear Percy," he exclaimed, wringing the newcomer by the hand, "here you are, after all! Dear old soul! Let me present the rest of my family."

He linked his arm in that of the travel-stained cyclist, and led him towards the petrified Lady Adela.

"Mother," he announced, "this is my friend Percy Welwyn."

"Mr. Percy Welwyn," said a gentle voice in his ear.

"Sorry, old man!" said Dicky hastily.

"No offence taken," Mr. Welwyn assured him, "where none intended. This, I presume,"--he waved his dripping tweed cap in the face of the speechless matron before him,--"is your hostess."

"Yes," said Dicky. "My mother, Lady Adela Mainwaring."

Mr. Welwyn shook hands affably.

"How de do, your ladyship?" he said. "Very pleased to make your ladyship's acquaintance, I'm sure."

"And this," continued Dicky, swiftly wheeling his guest out of the danger zone, "is my old Dad."

"How do you do, Mr. Welwyn?" said Mr. Mainwaring, with a courteous little bow. "We make you welcome."

"How de do, your lordship?" replied Mr. Welwyn, repeating his hand-shaking performance. "Very pleased to make your lordship's acquaintance."

"That's an error on your part, Percy," said Dicky smoothly. "Dad's only a commoner. But we'll work it out afterwards. This is my little sister Sylvia."

Mr. Welwyn greeted the statuesque Miss Mainwaring as he had greeted her parents, throwing in an ingratiating ogle which plainly intimated that he intended to make an impression in this quarter.

"Very pleased to make *your* acquaintance, Miss," he said. "We shall be calling each other Perce and Sylvie in no time, I can see. And now," he continued, turning his back upon the quivering figure of his future playmate, "I should like to address a few observations to the happy couple. You're a nice pair of turtle-doves to come and play gooseberry to, I don't suppose! Here I give up a whole Saturday afternoon to come and chaperon our Tilly and her young gentleman down to his ancestral home; and the first thing I know is the pair of them give me the slip at Waterloo! Chronic, I call it!"

"What else did you expect, Mr. Welwyn?" interposed Connie, coming characteristically to the rescue, the majority of the Mainwaring family being in no condition to cope with Percy. "Have n't you ever been engaged yourself?"

Her unsolicited intrusion into the conversation was plainly a shock to Percy's sense of decorum. He coughed reprovingly behind his hand, and turning to Dicky, remarked:--

"Introdooce me!"

Dicky, humble and apologetic, complied. Mr. Welwyn went through his usual performance, and continued:--

"Engaged, Mrs. Carmyle? Not me! Not that I might n't have bin, mark you, if I had n't been born careful. Be born careful, and you need n't be born lucky. The Proverbs of Perce--Number one!" he added, in a humorous aside. "Well, to resume. Luckily I had the old push-bike with me, and I managed to find my way down here in a matter of an hour and a half or so. And then what happens? Just as I am doing a final spin up your kerridge-drive, your ladyship--*bing! bang!* and I get bowled over in the dark by a charging rhinoceros!"

Mr. Welwyn concluded this dramatic narrative with a few appropriate gestures, and paused to note its effect upon his auditors.

"That was Maximilian, I fancy," explained Dicky cheerfully. "The little fellow must have got loose. Did you notice which way he was going?"

"I did," replied Percy with feeling. "He was going the opposite way to me."

"In that case," replied Dicky reflectively, "he must be halfway back to mother by this time. Well, perhaps it is just as well. Did you happen to observe whether he had the rain-gauge with him?"

"All I remarked," replied Mr. Welwyn bitterly, "was about half a mudguard. But that," he continued, with a winning smile to the ladies, "is neither here nor there, is it? Seeing as you are safe, Tilly, old girl, I think I may now resign the post of chaperon into her ladyship's hands. And perhaps," he added with a graceful bow, "I may be permitted to remark that in my humble opinion a more capable pair of hands could not be found for the job."

Lady Adela had suffered severely that day, and her spirit for the time being was almost broken. She merely smiled weakly.

Mr. Welwyn, now at the very top of his form, struck an attitude.

"My trusty iron steed," he declaimed, "waits without the battlements--all but a few spokes, that is, accounted for by the aforesaid rhinoceros--and I must hence, to ketch the seven-fifteen back to Londinium."

"Does that mean he is going?" murmured Lady Adela to her daughter, with a flutter of hope upon her drawn features.

Sylvia was nodding reassuringly, when the tactless Dicky broke in:--

"Percy, old son, you really must stay for dinner, if not for the night."

"We can't send you away empty in weather like this, Mr. Welwyn," added Mr. Mainwaring hospitably. "My dear--"

He turned to his wife, but the words froze upon his lips, for Lady Adela presented an appearance that can only be described as terrible. But the impervious Percy noticed nothing.

"By my halidom," he exclaimed, highly gratified, "that was well spoken! Yet it cannot be. I thank you, ladies and gentles all, for your courtly hospitality; but, as the bard observes: 'I *must* get home to-night!'" (Here he broke into song, and indulged in what are known in theatrical circles as "a few steps.") "The club has an important run billed for to-morrow, and if little Percy is missing, there will be enquiries. Still, rather than disoblige, I'll split the difference. I will drain a stirrup-cup of foaming Bass with ye ere I depart. Then, forward across the drawbridge! Yoicks! Likewise Tally Ho! Which way, fair sir," concluded this high-spirited youth, turning to his host, "to the Saloon Bar?"

"Percy," remarked Dicky hurriedly, "you are immense! You ought to go on the Halls. Come along! This way!"

"I have bin approached, mind you," began the comedian, taking Dicky's arm, "but!"

"Are you coming too, Tilly?" asked Dicky, looking back.

Tilly, who had been apprehensively regarding the flinty countenances of her future relatives-in-law, assented hurriedly and gratefully.

"Yes, please," she said. "I will come and see Percy off."

She took Dicky's free arm.

"'T is meet and fitting," observed the ebullient Percy. "We will drain a tankard jointly. Right away! Pip, pip! Good-morrow, knights and ladies all!"

The trio disappeared into the dining-room, leaving a most uncanny silence behind them!

Mr. Mainwaring hastily picked up the evening paper and enshrouded himself in its folds. Lady Adela feebly signalled to Sylvia for the smelling-salts.

"A perfectly *appalling* young man!" she announced.

"And a perfectly sweet little girl!" quoth loyal Connie.

CHAPTER XV

A DAY OF CALM REFLECTION

I

At half-past eight next morning Connie Carmyle, wearing a tweed coat and skirt and neat brown brogues, came whistling downstairs, intent upon a constitutional before breakfast.

Upon the sofa in front of the hall-fire, self-consciously perusing a Sunday newspaper, sat a large man of slightly sheepish appearance. At the sight of Connie he rose guiltily to his feet. Mrs. Carmyle embraced him in a motherly fashion.

"And may I ask what you are doing here, my man?" she enquired.

"Finished things off last night after all," replied her husband; "so thought I might as well run down this morning and spend the day."

"Why?" asked Mrs. Carmyle wonderingly. She knew perfectly well; but being a woman and the possessor of an undemonstrative husband, it pleased her to spur him into making an exhibition of himself.

"Thought I should like a rest," said Mr. Carmyle gruffly. "Had a pretty tough week," he added, in a pusillanimous attempt to excite compassion.

"Is that the only reason?" persisted his heartless spouse.

"Having a wife, thought I might as well come and see her for an hour or two," conceded Carmyle grudgingly.

"You must put it better than that, darling," said Connie inexorably. "Now, be a little man! You came because--because--"

The sorely-harrassed husband, driven into a corner, turned a deep plum-colour.

"Because I love you!" he growled. "Now chuck it, Connie, for goodness' sake!"

He was rewarded by a radiant smile.

"That is much better," said Connie approvingly. "Now you shall have some breakfast. After that I have a great deal for you to do."

"What?"

"You can take us for a drive in the car."

"Us?"

"Yes--us. Me, Dicky, and his fiancée," answered Connie very distinctly.

"Righto!" replied this maddening man unconcernedly.

Connie heaved a patient little sigh, and repeated:--

"Me, Dicky, and--his fiancée."

This effort was more successful.

"Righto!" said Carmyle once more. "Freak engaged again?" he added as an afterthought.

Connie cast up her eyes in a piteous fashion, as if to imply that it is better to have a husband like this than none at all, and replied resignedly:--

"Yes. It's a long story. I wrote you a letter about it last night. Here it is in the post-basket. Read it now; while I run and break the news of your visitation to Lady Adela."

By the time that Connie returned, her taciturn but capable husband had mastered the contents of her letter--parentheses, italics, notes of exclamation, and all--and was ready to receive the orders of the day.

"Now, listen," commanded Connie swiftly. "At breakfast you will invite Dicky and Tilly to come for a run in the motor. I don't know anything about that girl, but I had a long talk with her last night when we were getting ready for bed, and she is the right sort. She seemed to like me, too. What did you say?"

"Nothing," replied the exasperating William. "Go on."

"Anyhow," continued Connie, ignoring a mysterious chuckle, "I am not going to have her pumped and bullied by Lady Adela and Sylvia before she has found her feet. Therefore we will take her and Dicky away for the day. Get your invitation off at breakfast, before Lady Adela begins organising a party for church. The young couple can have the back seat to themselves, and I will come in front with you."

"Anything you like," replied Carmyle cheerfully. He had been looking forward to an indolent morning with Connie in the smoking-room, for he really had had a hard week; but he never questioned the dispositions of the small goddess who controlled his movements. Whatever she ordained was right.

"Thank you, Bill darling! I love you very much."

Mrs. Carmyle stood upon tiptoe, and with an affectionate sigh endeavoured to lay her head upon her husband's left shoulder. Mr. Carmyle gave her no assistance. He merely removed his sovereign-purse with some ostentation from his left-hand waistcoat-pocket to his right.

II

"This is the first time that you and I have been out in a motor together, Tilly," remarked Dicky a few hours later, taking advantage of a jolt on the part of the car to annihilate a portion of the space which separated him from his beloved.

Tilly, availing herself of a margin which instinct and experience had taught her to provide for such contingencies as this, moved a corresponding number of inches farther away, and pointed out that they had enjoyed a motor-ride together only three days previously.

"On a motor-'bus," she explained.

"Motor-'bus? Not a bit. Fairy coach!" declared her highly imaginative swain.

"Fairy coaches don't as a rule carry eighteen inside and twenty-two outside, dear," replied the matter-of-fact Miss Welwyn.

"No, you are right," admitted Dicky. "Fairy coaches are invariably two-seaters. This one is n't a bad substitute, though--what?"

He lolled luxuriously, and turned to survey the profile beside him. Tilly was wearing a saxe-blue *suède* hat, secured to her head by a filmy motor-veil--both the property of the open-handed Mrs. Carmyle, who was sitting in front driving the car under the complacent contemplation of her husband. The fur rug which Tilly shared with Dicky enveloped her to the chin: her cheeks glowed; her lips were parted in a smile of utter content; and her eyes were closed. Dicky tried to count the long lashes that swept her cheek. She was his! His--to keep, to cherish, to protect, to pamper, to spoil! Something very tremendous stirred within him--something that had never found a place in that receptive and elastic organ, his heart, before. All the dormant tenderness and chivalry of his nature seemed to heap itself up into a mighty tidal wave, topple over, and inundate his very soul. Foolish tears came into his eyes. Very reverently he reached for Tilly's hand under the rug. She surrendered it, smiling lazily, without raising her lashes. Dicky wondered what she was thinking about.

Tilly, on her part, was trying to summon up courage to tell him.

By this time the car had cleared the village of Shotley Beauchamp, filled with parties of worshippers hastening in what Connie described as "rival directions," and was spinning along the open road bound for the Surrey hills. It was a crisp and sunny morning. There was a touch of spring in the air, quickening the pulse.

"I wonder," began Dicky, whose conversation at this period, like that of all healthy young men in a similar condition, wandered round in a clearly defined and most constricted circle, "if I had not had that row with the umbrella-merchant on the top of the Piccadilly 'bus, whether you and I would ever--"

Bang!

Mr. Carmyle said something distressingly audible. Mrs. Carmyle applied the brakes; and the car, bumping uncomfortably, came to a standstill at the side of the road, under the lee of a pine wood.

"Was that your collar-stud at last, Tiny, old man?" enquired The Freak anxiously.

"Back tyre," replied Mr. Carmyle shortly, disencumbering himself of his rug.

They stepped out upon the muddy road and examined the off-hind wheel. The tyre was flat, but apparently whole.

"It is the valve," announced Carmyle, after unscrewing the dust-cap. "Blown himself clean out of bed. That means a fresh inner tube. And I lent the Stepney wheel to a broken-down car coming along this morning!"

"Bad luck!" said Dicky speciously, glancing up at the pine wood. "Can Tilly and I help?"

"No, better run away and play."

Dicky and Tilly, without further insincerities, obeyed at once.

"I fear you will besmirch yourself, comrade," said Dicky over his shoulder, as they departed.

"Bet you half-a-crown I don't even dirty my gloves," replied Carmyle.

"No: you'll take them off," replied the astute Richard.

"No, kid!" persisted Carmyle. "I undertake to get a new inner tube put into this tyre without laying a finger on it. Is it a bet?"

"Is Connie going to do it?" asked Dicky incredulously.

"She is and she is n't. She won't lay a finger on the tyre either, though. Will you stake your half-crown like a man?"

"I suppose there is a catch about it somewhere," said The Freak resignedly. "Still, I fancy we must humour the young people, Tilly. All right, my lad."

Mr. Carmyle turned to his wife.

"Show them, Connie," he said.

His dutiful helpmeet selected a large tyre-lever, and sitting down in the midst of the King's highway upon the tool-box, in a position which combined the maximum of discomfort with the minimum of leverage, began to pick helplessly at the rim of the wheel. Occasionally she looked up and smiled pathetically.

"Will that do, Bill dear?" she enquired.

"Yes; but try and look a bit more of an idiot."

Mrs. Carmyle complied.

"Now you're overdoing it," said her stage-manager severely. "Don't loll your tongue out like a poodle's! *That's* better. Hallo, I believe I can hear a car already! Come on, you two--into this wood!"

Next moment Tilly, beginning dimly to comprehend, was propelled over a split-rail fence by two muscular gentlemen and bustled into the fastnesses of the pine wood. The Casabianca-like Connie remained in an attitude of appealing helplessness upon the tool-box.

The pine wood ran up the side of a hill. The trio climbed a short distance, and then turned to survey the scene below them. Round the bend of the road came a car--a bulky, heavy, opulent limousine, going thirty-five miles an hour, and carrying a cargo of fur coats and diamonds.

"Rolls-Royce. Something-in-the-City going down to lunch at Brighton," commented Dicky. "That's the wrong sort, anyhow."

"Connie will be run over," cried Tilly apprehensively.

"Not she," replied the callous Carmyle.

He was right. Connie, diagnosing the character of the approaching vehicle from afar, had already stepped round to the near side of her own, escaping a shower bath of mud and possibly a compound fracture.

"Do you always get your running repairs done this way, Tiny?" enquired Dicky of Carmyle.

"As a rule. Connie loves it. Gives her a chance of talking prettily to people and smiling upon them, and all that. She thinks her smile is her strong point."

"I should be afraid," said Tilly.

"Connie is afraid of nothing on earth," said Carmyle. "Why, she--" he flushed red and broke off, realizing that he had been guilty of the solecism of paying a public tribute to his own wife. "Here's another car coming," he said. "This looks more like what we want."

A long, lean, two-seated apparition, with a bonnet like the bow of a battleship, had swung round the bend, and was already slowing down at the spectacle of beauty in distress. It contained two goggled and recumbent figures. Presently it slid to a standstill beside the stranded car, and its occupants leaped eagerly forth.

"Metallurgique, twenty-forty," announced Dicky, with technical precision.

"Undergraduates--or subalterns," added Carmyle contentedly, beginning to fill his pipe. "That's all right. You two had better go for a little walk, while I stay here and keep an eye on the breakdown gang."

He produced from his greatcoat pocket a copy of "The Sunday Times," and having spread it on the ground at the foot of a convenient tree, sat down upon it with every appearance of cheerful anticipation, already intent upon the, to him, never-palling spectacle of his wife adding further scalps to her collection.

Dicky and Tilly, nothing loath, wandered farther along the hillside, under strict injunctions not to return for twenty minutes. It was the first time that they had found themselves alone since their arrival on the previous evening, and they had long arrears of sweet counsel to make up.

"Dicky," said Tilly, suddenly breaking one of those long silences that all lovers know, "have you ever--loved any one before me?"

Most men are asked this question at some time in their lives, and few there be that have ever answered it without some mental reservation. But The Freak merely looked surprised--almost hurt.

"Loved any one *before*? I should think I had!" he replied. "Who has n't?"

"I have not," said Tilly,

Dicky was quite prepared for this.

"I meant men--not girls," he said. "Girls are different. Not that some of them don't fall in and out of love rather easily, but they only do it as a sort of pleasant emotional exercise. The average male lover, however youthful, means business all the time. Quite right, too! It is a healthy masculine instinct for an Englishman to want to found a household of his own just as soon as he grows up. But it is this very instinct which often sends him after the wrong girl. He is full of natural affection and sentiment, and so on, and he wants some one to pour it out upon. So he picks out the first nice girl he meets, endows her in his mind with all the virtues, and tries to marry her. Usually it comes to nothing--the girl sees to that; for she is gifted by nature with a power of selection denied to men--and in any case it is hardly likely that he will meet the right girl straight off. So he goes on seeking for his mate, this child of nature, in a groping, instinctive sort of way, until at last he finds his pearl of great price. Then he sells all that he has, which being interpreted means that he straightway forgets all about every other girl he ever knew, and loves his Pearl forever and ever. Therefore, Tilly, if ever a man comes to you and tells you that you are the only girl he ever loved, trust him not. It is not likely. It is against nature."

"A girl likes to believe it, all the same, dear," answered Tilly, voicing an age-long truth.

"I don't see why she should," argued the ingenious Dicky. "It is no compliment to be loved by a man who has had no experience. Now *I* can love and appreciate you properly, because I am able to compare you with about"--he counted upon his fingers, finally having recourse to a supplementary estimate on his waistcoat-buttons--"with about fourteen other ladies, of all ages, whom I have admired at one time and another; and can unhesitatingly place you in Class One, Division One, all by your own dear self, so far as they are concerned. Is n't that something?"

But Tilly was not quite satisfied.

"I should like to feel," she said, instinctively giving utterance to that point of view which makes a woman's love such an intensely personal and jealously exacting thing in comparison with a man's, "that you could never have been happy with any woman in the world but me. Could you, Dicky?"

Dicky pondered.

"It depends," he said, "on what you mean by happy. Our measure of happiness, it seems to me, depends entirely on what we *have* compared with what we want. If I had never met you, I could never have missed you; and so I dare say I might have settled down happily enough--or what I considered happily enough--with some other girl. But that is impossible now. I have met you, you see. If I were to lose you"--Tilly caught her breath sharply--"no one else could ever take your place. Love like ours makes all substitutes tasteless and colourless, as they say in chemical laboratories. You have raised my standard of love so high that no one but yourself can ever attain to it. So," concluded the philosopher, with a smile which brought more happiness and reassurance into Tilly's heart than all the laborious logic-chopping in the world could have done, "though I don't know that I never *could* have been happy with any one but you, I can truly say this, that I never *can* be happy with any one but you. It's merely a matter of the difference between two conditional sentences, that's all."

But a girl talking with her lover is not interested in points of syntax.

"And will you go on loving me?" asked Tilly, putting a small but unerring finger upon the joint in Dicky's harness.

Dicky glanced down upon the eager, wistful face beside him, and smiled whimsically.

"Madam," he said, "your fears are groundless."

"How do you know?" enquired Madam, convinced in her heart, but anxious to be reassured.

"Because," said Dicky simply, "you love me. You have said it. Don't you see how that binds me to you? The mere fact of your love for me makes mine for you imperishable. The moment a man discovers that the woman he loves loves him in return, he is hers, body and soul. Previous to that something has held him back. Pride--reserve--caution--call it what you like--it *has* held him back. He has not let himself go *utterly*. After all, we can only give of our best once in this life, and usually some instinct inside us makes us refuse to surrender that best, however prodigal we may have been of the inferior article, until we know that we are going to get the best in return." Dicky was talking very earnestly now. "I have been keeping my best for you all these years, little maid, though neither of us knew it. Such as it is, you have it. That is why I *know* I can never go back on you. Besides, what man worthy of the name could let a girl down, once she had abandoned her reserve--her beautiful woman's reserve--and confessed her great secret to him? Why, I once nearly married a girl whom I could not stand at any price, just because the little idiot gave herself away one day when we were alone together."

"Why should you have married her," asked single-minded, feminine Tilly wonderingly, "if you did n't love her?"

"It seemed so mean not to," said Dicky.

Tilly nodded her head gravely.

"Yes," she said, "I think I understand." (As a matter of fact, she did not. To her, as to most women, such a quixotic piece of folly as that to which Dicky had just confessed was incomprehensible. But she desired to please her lover.) "It was like you to do it, but I hate the girl. I expect she was a designing minx. But go on, dear. Go on convincing me. I love it. Say it over and over again."

"Say what?" enquired Dicky, who was not aware that he had been saying anything unusual.

"Pearls, and things like that," replied Tilly shyly.

"Oh!" said Dicky dubiously, "that takes a bit of doing. Wait a minute!"

Tilly obediently refrained from speech while her beloved dredged his imagination for further metaphors. They were a curiously old-fashioned couple, these two. That uncanny blend of off-hand *camaraderie* and jealously guarded independence which constitutes a modern engagement meant nothing to them. They loved one another heart and soul, and were not in the least ashamed of saying so.

Presently Dicky took up his parable.

"Hearken, O my Daughter," he began characteristically, "to the words of the Prophet. Behold, I tell you an allegory! Do you know what riveting is?"

"No, dear. Women don't understand machinery," replied Tilly resignedly, in the tones of a young mother threatened with an exposition of the mechanism of her firstborn's clockwork engine.

"Well, a rivet," pursued the Prophet, "is a metal thing like a small mushroom. It is used for binding steel plates together, and requires two people to handle it properly. First of all the rivet is heated red-hot, and then a grimy man (called the holder-on) pops the stalk of the mushroom into a hole bored through two overlapping plates and keeps the little fellow in position with a sort of gripping-machine, while another grimy man (called the riveter) whangs his end of the stalk with a sledge-hammer. That punches the poor little rivet into the shape of a double mushroom, and the two plates are gripped together for good and all."

Tilly nodded her head. The allegory was beginning to emerge from a cloud of incorrect technical detail.

"Now it seems to me," continued Dicky, "that love is very like that. Men are the holders-on and women the riveters. I have occupied the position of holder-on several times in my life. I fancy most men do: it is their nature to experiment. (I have also had the post of riveter thrust upon me, but we need not talk about that. One tries to forget these things as soon as possible," he added, with a little wriggle.) "But the point which I want to bring out is this--a rivet can only be used *once*. It may be slipped through various plates by its holder-on in a happy-go-lucky sort of way over and over again; but once it meets the hammer fairly, good-bye to its career as a gallivanting, peripatetic little rivet! It is spread-eagled in a moment, Tilly--fixed, secured, and settled for life. And if it is the right stuff, sound metal all through, it will never wriggle or struggle or endeavour to back upon its appointed task of holding together its two steel plates. It won't *want* to. It will endure so long as the two plates endure. Nothing can shake him, that little rivet-- nothing! Poverty, sickness, misunderstanding, outside interference--nothing will have any effect. That is the allegory. The wanderings of Dicky Mainwaring are over. He has flitted about long enough, poking his inquisitive little head into places that were not intended for him; and he has come to the right place at last. One neat straight crack on his impressionable little cranium, and the deed is done! The Freak's place in life is fixed at last. Mutual love has double-ended him, and he is going to hold on now for keeps."

Dicky was silent for a moment, and then continued:--

"No one but you could have dealt that stroke, Tilly, or I should have been fixed up long ago. I could never have remained engaged to Hilda Beverley, for instance. She was a fine girl, but she did not happen to be my riveter or I her holder-on--that's all. I should have dropped out of my place at the first rattle. Lucky little rivet! Some poor beggars don't get off so cheap. They pop their impulsive little heads into the first opening, and never come out again. But Providence has been good to me, Freak though I am. I have come safe through, to the spot where the Only Possible Riveter in the World was waiting for me. Here we are together at last, settled for life. Launch the ship! *Ting-a-ling*! Full speed ahead! I have spoken! What are you trembling for, little thing?"

"I was only thinking," replied Miss Welwyn shakily, "how awful it would have been if one of the other girls had been a better riveter." Then she took a deep breath as of resolution.

"Dicky," she began, "I want to talk to you about something. I think I ought to tell you--"

But as she spoke, the figure of Mr. Carmyle, heralded by unnecessary but well-intentioned symptoms of what sounded like a deep-seated affection of the lungs, appeared among the trees, and announced:--

"Off directly, you two! Connie is just having a last farewell with her mechanics. She has collected quite a bunch of them by this time."

"They have n't taken long over the job," said Dicky, in a slightly injured tone.

Carmyle, who too had once dwelt in Arcady, smiled.

"An hour and ten minutes," he said concisely.

Dicky and Tilly said no more, but meekly uprose from the fallen tree upon which they had been sitting and accompanied their host to the road.

All signs of disaster had disappeared. The punctured back tyre stood up once more, fully inflated; the tool-box had been repacked and put away; and Connie, smiling indulgently, sat waiting at the wheel. Far away in the distance could be descried two other cars, rapidly receding from view. They contained in all five knights of the road--grotesquely attired and extremely muddy, but very perfect gentle knights after their kind--who were now endeavouring, in defiance of the laws of the land, to overtake the time lost by their recent excursion into the realms of romantic adventure; all wishing in their hearts, I dare swear, that life's highway contained a few more such halts as this.

"Connie is going to write a book one day," observed Mr. Carmyle, as they climbed into the car, "called 'Hims Who Have Helped Me.' All right behind there?"

The car set off once more.

III

The rest of the day passed uneventfully, and as it was spent *à quatre* need not be described at length.

They sped home in the gathering darkness of a frosty evening. Connie, who had relinquished the wheel to her husband, with instructions to get the car home as speedily as possible--she had not forgotten her promise to go and hear Mr. Rylands's evening sermon--now shared the back seat with Tilly; and the two ladies snuggled contentedly together under the warm rug, silently contemplating the outlines of their squires against the wintry sky.

The car swung in at the lodge gates and began to run along the crackling gravel of the drive. Presently, as they rounded a bend, the lights of the house sprang into view.

"Tea--and a big fire!" murmured Connie contentedly.

To Tilly the sight of the house suggested other thoughts. Suddenly she removed her gaze from Dicky's broad back and slipped a cold hand into Connie's.

"Will they try to take him from me?" she whispered passionately.

One of Connie Carmyle's many gifts was her ability to catch an allusion without tiresome explanations. Straightway she turned and looked deep into the appealing grey eyes beside her. Her own brown ones glowed indomitably.

"If they do, dear," she answered--"fight for him."

"I will," said Tilly, setting her teeth.

The two girls gripped hands in the darkness.

CHAPTER XVI
AN IMPOSSIBLE FAMILY

Amelia Welwyn, grievously overweighted by a tray containing her father's breakfast, tacked unsteadily across the floor of the drawing-room at Russell Square; and, having reached the door of her parent's bedroom, proceeded to arouse the attention of its occupant by permitting the teapot to toboggan heavily into one of the panels.

"Don't come in!" said a muffled voice.

"Half-past eleven, Daddy," announced Amelia cheerily. "Your breakfast!"

"In the fender, my child," replied the voice.

Amelia obediently put over her helm, and despite a heavy list to starboard induced by a sudden shifting of ballast (in the form of the hot-water jug) ultimately weathered the sofa and deposited the breakfast tray in the fender, without throwing overboard anything of greater moment than a piece of buttered toast.

By the fireside, in a very large armchair, sat a small, alert, wizened, and querulous old lady of eighty-one.

"Cup of tea, Grannie?" said Amelia.

"What's that?" enquired Mrs. Josiah Banks--late of Bedfordshire (or Cambridgeshire).

"Will you have a cup of tea?" repeated the child in a louder voice.

"No," replied her aged relative; "I won't."

"Very well, then," said Amelia good-temperedly. "Now you two, not so much of it, if you please!"

This warning was addressed to her younger brother and sister, who, together with herself, had joined the Welwyn family at a date subsequent to that upon which we first made its acquaintance. Amelia was twelve years of age, The Caution five, and The Cure some twenty minutes younger. At present the latter young lady, in the course of a life-and-death struggle for the possession of the jettisoned piece of buttered toast, had become involved in an embrace with her brother, so involved that it seemed as if no one unfamiliar with the use of letter-locks could ever unravel them. However, the experienced Amelia succeeded; and having shaken the skirts of The Cure a little lower and pulled the knicker-bockers of The Caution a little higher, dumped both combatants upon the sofa and divided the now hopelessly mangled booty between them.

"And don't let me catch you at it again," she added magisterially. "Only Monday morning, and your pinnies no more use than nothing! Come in!"

At the sight of the figure which appeared in the doorway in response to this invitation The Caution and The Cure set up a combined howl of apprehension, only to be quelled by a dole of lump-sugar--hush-money in the most literal sense of the word--supplied by the resourceful Amelia.

"Come in, Mr. Mehta Ram! What can we do for you this morning?" she enquired maternally. "Never mind those two"--indicating the quaking infants on the sofa. "It's their consciences, that's all. You see, I always threaten to give them to you when they are naughty, and now they think that you have really come for them. It's all right," she added, turning reassuringly to the culprits. "Mr. Ram won't eat you this time."

Benevolent Mr. Mehta Ram beamed upon the chubby buccaneers through his gold spectacles.

"Believe me, Miss Amelia," he replied, "I could cherish no cannibalistic designs upon such jolly kids. Is your excellent mother within her domicile, or has she gone for a tata?" (Mr. Ram prided himself upon his knowledge of colloquial English.)

"She is out--shopping. Tell me your trouble," said businesslike Amelia.

"I came here," began the Bengalee, "to address your mother in her offeecial capacity."

"I know," said Amelia swiftly. "It was that kipper you had for breakfast. I thought it was wearing a worried look while mother was cooking it. Well, you shan't be charged for it."

Mr. Mehta Ram waved a fat and deprecating hand.

"Far be it from me," he replied, "to reflect upon the culinary ability of your excellent mother Welwyn. I came about a very different pair of shoes."

Mr. Ram then proceeded, in the curious blend of Johnsonian English and street-boy slang which constitutes the vocabulary of that all-too-precocious linguist, the Babu, with all the forensic earnestness and technical verbiage of the student who has spent the past six months grappling with the intricacies of English Law, to bring a weighty indictment against the gentleman on the second-floor back.

"In brief," he concluded, "Mr. Pumpherston has impounded my sugar-basin."

"Broken it, you mean?"

"No, Miss Amelia. He has confiscated it--pinched it, in fact. And"--Mr. Ram swept onward to his peroration, his brown face glistening with mild indignation--"although I have assured him upon my word of honour that there will be father and mother of a row if same is not returned forthwith, he merely projects the sneer of scorn upon my humble petition."

"Oh, does he?" exclaimed Miss Amelia, with heat. "Mr. Pumpherston has been enquiring for trouble for a long while now, and this time he is going to get it. Mother"--as Mrs. Welwyn, humming a cheerful air, entered the room and began to deposit parcels upon the table, much as a mountain deposits an avalanche--"here is Mr. Ram says Mr. Pumpherston has sneaked his sugar-basin and won't give it back."

"What's that, Ducky?" enquired Mrs. Welwyn, breaking off her little tune. She was a large, still handsome, and most unsuitably attired matron of about forty-five. Her task (and be it added, her joy) in life was the support of a rather useless husband, of whom she was inordinately proud because he happened to have been born a gentleman; and all the energy and resource of her honest simple nature had been devoted to the single aim of raising her children to what she considered his level rather than permit them to remain upon her own. In the case of the girls she had been singularly successful. Percy was her failure, but fortunately she regarded him as her greatest triumph. (Providence is very merciful to mothers in this respect.) And her love had not been utterly vain, for although her taste in dress was disastrous and her control of the letter "h" uncertain, her family were devoted to her.

"You ask Mr. Mehta Ram all about it!" replied Amelia darkly.

"The aforesaid Pumpherston," resumed Mr. Ram at once, "has threatened me with personal violence--to wit, a damn good skelp in the eyeball. I quote his *ipsissima verba*."

"Oh, *has* he?" replied Mrs. Welwyn, with decision. "Well that puts the lid on Pumpherston, anyway. He's behind with his rent as it is; so the moment our Perce gets home to-night, up goes Perce to the second-floor back, and out goes my lord Pumpherston! I never could abide Scotchies, anyhow."

"Martha," enquired a piping but painfully distinct voice from the fireside, "what does that black 'eathen want in 'ere?"

"All right, Mother," replied Mrs. Welwyn. She turned soothingly to the Babu. "We'll put things straight for you, Mr. Ram," she said reassuringly. "You'll get justice in this country, never fear! Good-morning!"

Mr. Mehta Ram, inarticulate with gratitude, salaamed himself out of the room, to the manifest relief of The Caution and The Cure. Mrs. Welwyn followed him onto the landing.

"You'll get your sugar-basin back, double-quick!" she announced in a loud voice. "That'll frighten Pumpherston," she observed grimly, re-entering the room and shutting the double doors behind her.

"It's a pity losing a lodger, Mother," said Amelia.

"Yes, dearie, it is," agreed Mrs. Welwyn with a sigh. "But it can't be helped. I'll tell you what, though. Run after that blackamoor and ask him if he has n't got a friend wants a room--a nice peaceable creature like himself. The Museum Reading-Room is full of them, Father says. Tell him to pick us a good one. Take the children up with you. Father will be in here for his breakfast in a minute."

As the door closed upon Amelia and her charges, Mrs. Welwyn crossed the room to her surviving parent's side.

"Well, Mother," she enquired cheerily, arranging the old lady's shawl, "how goes it to-day? World a bit wrong?"

The genial Mrs. Banks did not answer immediately. Obviously she was meditating a suitable repartee. Presently it came.

"When is that good-for-nothing 'usband of yours going to get up?" she enquired.

Mrs. Welwyn flushed red, but patted her cantankerous parent good-humouredly on the shoulder.

"That's all right, Mother," she said. "You mind your business and I'll mind mine. Lucius sits up very late at night, working,--long after you and I have gone to bed,--so he's entitled to a good long lay in the morning."

"Pack o' nonsense!" observed Mr. Welwyn's mother-in-law. "I'd learn 'im!"

"Good-morning, good people!"

Lucius Welwyn strode into the room with all the buoyancy and cheerfulness of a successful man of forty. As a matter of fact he was a failure of fifty-nine, but he still posed to himself with fair success as a retired man of letters. His rôle was that of the philosophic onlooker, who prefers scholarly ease and detachment to the sordid strivings of a commercial age. In reality he was an idle, shiftless, slightly dissipated, but thoroughly charming humbug. He was genuinely attached to his wife, and in his more candid moments readily and bitterly acknowledged the magnitude and completeness of his debt to her. He possessed a quick smile and considerable charm of manner; and when he was attired, not as now in a dressing-gown and slippers, but in the garments of ceremony, he still looked what he undoubtedly was--a scholar and gentleman.

"Good-morning, Father. Your breakfast is all ready. Sit down, do, and take it while it's hot," Mrs. Welwyn besought him.

"Breakfast?" exclaimed Mr. Welwyn with infectious heartiness. "Capital!" He seated himself before the tray. "A good wife and a good breakfast--some men are born lucky!"

"Some men," remarked an acid voice, "are born a deal luckier than what they deserve to be."

Mr. Welwyn, who was sitting with his back to the oracle, did not turn round.

"That you, Grandma?" he said lightly, pouring out his tea. "You are in your usual beatific frame of mind, I am glad to note."

"None of your long words with me, Lucius Welwyn!" countered his aged relative with spirit. "I never 'ad no schooling, but I knows a waster when I sees 'un."

"Kidneys? Delicious!" remarked Mr. Welwyn, lifting the dish-cover. "Martha, you spoil me."

This pronouncement received such hearty endorsement from the fireside that Mrs. Welwyn crossed the room and laid a firm hand upon her sprightly parent's palsied shoulder.

"Now then, Mother," she said briskly, "you trot across the landing to your own room. I'm going to turn this one out presently. I've lit a fire for you."

Mrs. Banks, who knew full well that behind a smiling face her daughter masked a hopelessly partisan spirit, rose to her infirm feet and departed, grumbling. At the door she paused to glare malignantly upon the back of her well-connected son-in-law. But that unworthy favourite of fortune was helping himself to kidneys.

"Seems to me," remarked Mrs. Welwyn apologetically, as the door closed with a vicious snap, "that Mother got up on the wrong side of her bed this morning. You don't mind, do you, Father dear?"

"I? Not in the least," replied Mr. Welwyn with much cheerfulness. "I find your worthy mother, if anything, a tonic. You are a good soul, Martha. Sit down and have a cup of tea with me: it must be some time since you breakfasted. Take mine."

He pushed his brimming cup towards his wife.

"Oh, no, Father!" said Mrs. Welwyn, quite distressed. "I'll get one for myself."

She rose, and went to the sideboard.

"On consideration," interposed her husband, as if struck by a sudden idea, "I think--yes, I think--I should prefer a tumbler. I was working late last night; and possibly--I rather feel--You know what the doctor said. A man of letters--thank you, dearest. You anticipate every wish!"

The man of letters helped himself from the decanter and siphon which his prescient spouse had already laid beside the tray, and attacked the kidneys with renewed confidence.

"Father," observed Mrs. Welwyn presently, nervously sipping her second-hand cup of tea, "there's trouble among the lodgers again."

Mr. Welwyn gave her a reproving little glance.

"I think, dearest," he said gently, "that we agreed to call them paying guests."

"That," retorted Mrs. Welwyn with sudden indignation, "is just what they're not. Pumpherston has paid nothing for three weeks, and now he is threatening to murder poor old Mehta Ram."

"In my house?" exclaimed Mr. Welwyn grandly. "Impossible! This must stop. Where is Percy?"

"Percy," replied matter-of-fact Mrs. Welwyn, "is where you would expect him to be at this hour, you dear old silly--earning his living at Cratchett and Raikes's!"

"Talking of Cratchett and Raikes," said Mr. Welwyn, characteristically forgetting all about Mr. Pumpherston, "is there a letter this morning from Gandy and Cox?"

"No," said Mrs. Welwyn quickly. "Why?"

"Nothing, nothing," said Mr. Welwyn, rising to look for his cigarette-case. "They have been rather pressing over their little account lately. In fact, they have had the presumption to threaten me with distraint."

"How much was the bill, dear?" enquired Mrs. Welwyn, removing the breakfast-tray to the sideboard.

"A mere trifle," was the airy reply. "Seven pounds odd, I fancy, for a case of champagne which I had a year or two ago, when my heart was a little--you recollect? The doctor--"

"Yes, lovey," said Mrs. Welwyn. "It was an anxious time for all of us. But"--her brow puckered--"did n't you pay cash for it? I seem to remember giving you the money."

"Now you mention it," said Mr. Welwyn, lighting a cigarette, "I believe you did--ah--hand me the money. But I fear I was weak--quixotic, if you will. I gave it away." He raised a deprecating hand. "No! Please! I beg! Do not ask me more, dearest. It was one of those private disbursements for which a man with a weakness for his fellow-creatures often finds himself made liable. A little nameless charity. It will appear upon no subscription-list; no public acknowledgment will be made. But--I have my reward. Do not embarrass me, Martha, by alluding to the matter again."

Mr. Welwyn, quite affected by the memory of his own generosity, took his wife tenderly in his arms and kissed her upon the forehead. He then blew his nose violently, evidently ashamed of his own weakness, and sat down by the fire with the newspaper.

Mrs. Welwyn knew only too well what the little nameless charity had been; but, after all, seven pounds odd was a small price to pay for the affection of such a husband as hers. She accepted the embrace gratefully, sighed, and said:--

"Very well, dearie. It's a good thing," she added inconsequently, "that the house is our own and we don't have to bother about rent. Rates are bad enough. The butcher has been a bit crusty of late; and what with Pumpherston not paying for his room and Tilly giving up her blouse-designing, I don't believe there's change for a sovereign in the house."

Mr. Welwyn arose from his armchair, finished the refreshment contained in the tumbler (which he had placed conveniently upon the mantel-piece), and smiled indulgently upon his care-worn helpmeet.

"You women, you women!" he said, shaking his handsome head in playful reproach. "No breadth of view! No sense of proportion! Martha, dearest, how often have I begged you never to judge a situation by its momentary aspect? Cultivate a sense of perspective. Step back--"

Suiting the action to the word, Mr. Welwyn trod heavily upon the fire-irons in the fender. These resentfully retaliated, the knob of the shovel springing up and striking him a sharp rap upon the knuckles, while the tongs nipped him viciously in the ankle.

After the clatter had subsided and Mr. Welwyn had said what many a less distinguished man would have said under similar circumstances, his habitual placidity of temper returned, and he resumed his lecture where it had been interrupted.

"I was about to urge you, Martha," he continued, "to cast your mind *forward*--forward to the time when you will possess a wealthy son-in-law."

Mrs. Welwyn, who was endeavouring to remove from the sofa certain traces of its recent occupancy by the glutinous Caution and the adhesive Cure, turned suddenly and faced her husband.

"Lucius," she said gravely, "I have a feeling that there is going to be trouble over this business."

"Over what business?" enquired Mr. Welwyn.

"Over this son-in-law business," said Mrs. Welwyn doggedly. "Mr. Mainwaring--"

"Richard, dear--Richard!"

"All right--Richard! I don't think Richard will take very kindly to us when he sees us at home, and he'll have to see us here sometime, you know. Things look different in Russell Square from what they do at the Trocadero. And if he sheers off after all--well, it'll break our Tilly's heart."

At this moment the door burst open, to admit the sisters Welwyn, locked in an affectionate embrace and dancing a two-step to a whistled accompaniment. Tilly had returned.

CHAPTER XVII
THE WORD "SWANK"

"That's how it goes, 'Melia," panted Tilly, whirling her partner into an armchair. "It's quite easy, really; Dicky taught me in the billiard-room on Saturday night in ten minutes. Hallo, hallo, hallo! Here I am, everybody! Hallo, Mother darling!"

Mrs. Welwyn gently parried the approaching embrace.

"Here's your father, dear," she remarked, with the least tinge of reproof in her voice.

"Hallo, Dad! I did n't see you," exclaimed Tilly, kissing her male parent excitedly.

"Welcome home, my daughter!" said Mr. Welwyn. "Now kiss your mother."

Tilly had already begun to do so, and an eager conversation followed.

"Of course, we've heard a bit from Perce," began Mrs. Welwyn at once, drawing the pins out of her daughter's hat, "and my word! you seem to have got into the very thick of it this time, and no mistake!"

"I should just think so," gabbled Tilly. "Such a place, Mother! Billiard-rooms, and garages, and butlers, and a fire in your bedroom and a hot bottle in your bed, and a maid to put you into your clothes, and I don't know what all! And I was introduced to a lot of future relations. There was Lady Adela. She tried to patronise me, but was n't much good. Then Sylvia, the daughter. I hate her--she is a cat. And Connie Carmyle. She is no relation, but I love her. And Father Mainwaring, he is a dear. He says he was at Cambridge with you, Dad."

Mr. Welwyn put down the newspaper.

"What is that?" he enquired in a sharp voice. "Cambridge?"

"Yes. He does n't remember you at all distinctly," said Tilly, "but says he has an impression that you were the most brilliant man of your year."

"If that," remarked Mr. Welwyn, in a distinctly relieved tone, "is all that he recollects about me, I shall be pleased to meet him again."

"How is Dicky, Tilly?" enquired Amelia.

Tilly's merry face softened.

"Dicky," she said, half to herself, "is just Dicky. He brought me as far as the door, but I would n't let him come in."

"And are they all coming to tea?" enquired Mrs. Welwyn anxiously.

"Yes--the whole boiling of them, at five this afternoon--a state call!" replied Tilly. "By the way, Mother, that was a bloomer we made about the invitation. I knew at the time we talked about it that you ought to have written a note and chanced the spelling. Her ladyship made that *quite* plain to me."

"Oh dear!" said Mrs. Welwyn in distress. "What did she say?"

"She did n't say anything in particular," admitted Tilly, crinkling her brow. "Nothing one could take hold of, you know. Just--just--"

"Sort of snacks," suggested her mother sympathetically.

Tilly nodded her head.

"That's it," she said. "Anyhow, she has sent you a written reply. Here it is."

Mrs. Welwyn and Amelia breathed hard and respectfully at the sight of the large thin grey envelope, addressed by Lady Adela's own compelling hand.

"You read it, dearie," said Mrs. Welwyn.

"No; I'll tell you what," exclaimed Tilly. "We'll let little 'Melia read it. She does n't get much fun."

"Oh, Tilly!" cried Amelia gratefully.

She took the letter, opened it with an air, and began:--

"*My deah Mrs. Welwyn--haw!*"

There was great merriment at this, for in her own family circle Miss Amelia enjoyed a great reputation as a wit and mimic. The fact that neither she nor any of her audience, save Tilly, had ever beheld Lady Adela in the flesh detracted not a whit from their enjoyment of her performance.

"*It is really too good of you,*" continued Amelia, in the high-pitched and even tones of a lady of exceptional breeding, "*to invite us all--such a crowd of us--to come to tea on Monday. As it happens, we shall be in town that day, so Mr. Mainwaring and I propose to take you at your word, and shall be charmed to come with our son and daughter at five o'clock.*"

"That'll be four cups," murmured Mrs. Welwyn abstractedly. "We can get Mehta Ram's. Go on, Ducky."

"*After our recent experience of your daughter's society--*"

Here Amelia broke off, to observe that in her opinion the last phrase sounded tabbyish.

"Never mind! Go on!" urged Mrs. Welwyn.

"*--Daughter's society, we are naturally anxious to make the acquaintance of her forbears.*"

"Her four what?" asked Mrs. Welwyn in a dazed voice.

Amelia carefully examined the passage, and repeated:--

"It says 'four bears'--written as one word. Does that mean you and Dad and me and Perce?"

"If her ladyship," began Mrs. Welwyn warmly, "is going to start naming names from the Zoo--"

Tilly laid a quick hand upon her mother's arm and turned in the direction of the fireplace.

"Dad," she enquired, "what does 'forbears' mean?"

A chuckling voice from behind "The Daily Mail" enlightened her.

"The laugh is on your mother, children," said Mrs. Welwyn good-temperedly. "Finish it, 'Melia."

Amelia did so. "*What weather! Sincerely yours, Adela Mainwaring.* That's all."

"Quite enough, too!" commented Mrs. Welwyn, who still had her doubts about the four bears.

"Any way," remarked Tilly energetically, "they are coming; and we have till five o'clock to get ready for them. Hallo, Perce!"

To the company assembled entered Mr. Percy Welwyn, immaculate in frock coat, brown boots, and a rakish bowler hat.

"What oh, Sis!" he exclaimed, kissing Tilly affectionately. "Back again from the Moated Grange--eh? My dinner ready, Mother?"

"Wait a minute, Percy dear," said Tilly quickly. "I want to talk to you--all of you. Sit down, everybody. Father!"

"My daughter?"

"Come and sit here, please!"

"A round-table conference?" enquired Mr. Welwyn amiably. "Capital!"

Tilly upon her own quarter-deck was a very different being from the frightened little alien whom we saw at Shotley Beauchamp. In two minutes the Welwyn family had meekly packed themselves round the octagonal table. Tilly took the chair.

"Now, then, all of you," she began, with a suspicion of a high-strung quaver in her voice--"Father, Mother, Percy, and little 'Melia--listen to me! You know, no one better, that when I went down to Shotley Beauchamp on Saturday I meant to act perfectly square to Dicky's people--tell them who I was and what I was, and that I worked for my living and so on; and generally make sure that they did n't take me in on false pretences. Is that correct?"

"Yes--quite correct," chorused the family.

"Well," continued Tilly defiantly--"I have n't done it! I have n't said a word! There! I *couldn't*! I have seen Dicky's people, and their house, and their prosperity, and the way they look at things. They're a pretty tough proposition, the Mainwarings. They are no better born than we are; but they are rich, and stupid, and conceited, and purse-proud--"

"Tilly! Tilly!" said Mrs. Welwyn, scandalised to hear the gentry so miscalled.

"Yes, they *are*, Mother!" cried the girl passionately. "You don't know what I have had to put up with this week-end, when Dicky was n't by. Why--"

"Dicky," observed Mr. Welwyn dryly, "is also a Mainwaring, Tilly."

"Dicky," replied Tilly, with feminine contempt for the laws of heredity and environment, "may be a Mainwaring, but he does n't take after the rest of the family. But never mind Dicky for a moment. What I want to say is this. In dealing with people of this kind--people who regard those who have no money as so much dirt beneath their feet--there is only one thing that pays; and that thing," she concluded with intense conviction, "is--swank, swank, swank!"

"Good old Tilly!" shouted Percy enthusiastically; and the rest of the Welwyns, quite carried away by their small despot's earnestness, beat upon the table with their fists.

"The Mainwarings swanked for my benefit, I can tell you," continued Tilly, with cheeks glowing hotly. "They laid off to me about their town house and their country house and their shooting and their hunting and their grand relations; and they did their best--especially the daughter--to make me feel like a little dressmaker who has come in for the day."

"I bet you stood up to them, Sis," said the admiring Percy.

Tilly smiled in a dreamy, reminiscent fashion.

"I did," she said. "I matched them, brag for brag. They asked who you were, Mother. I said you were a Banks--one of *the* Bankses--of Bedfordshire!"

Unseemly but sympathetic laughter greeted this announcement, and Mrs. Welwyn was made the recipient of several congratulatory thumps from her son and younger daughter.

"I wasn't quite sure whether it was Bedfordshire or Cambridgeshire," continued Tilly. "Where is Hitchin, anyway?"

"Hertfordshire," replied Amelia, and every one laughed again. They had all things in common, the Welwyns, especially their jokes.

"Then," Tilly proceeded, "I told them a lovely fairy-tale about our old town house. Been in the family for generations, and so on."

"So it has," said Mr. Welwyn.

"And I also told them," continued the unfilial Tilly, "that Dad was a bit of an antique himself, and could n't bear to move. Has his roots in the cellar, so to speak. You don't mind, do you, dear?" she enquired eagerly.

"My child," replied Mr. Welwyn, "I feel proud to have figured as one of your assets."

"And finally," concluded Tilly, "as I began to warm up to my work a bit, I added a few things, looking as sweet as anything all the time--like this!" (Here she treated her enraptured audience to a very creditable reproduction of Sylvia Mainwaring's languid and superior smile.) "I chatted about our billiard-room, and our old family butler, and our motor, and so on. I am afraid I lost my head a bit. I have a notion that I gave them to understand that we went yachting in the summer!"

There was more laughter, but Mrs. Welwyn added anxiously:--

"You did n't mention anything about Southend, did you, dearie?"

"Not me!" said Tilly; "though I was feeling utterly reckless by that time. For two pins I would have told them that I had been presented at Court!"

She rose to her feet.

"That is all I have to say," she announced. "I just mention these little facts to you so that when the Mainwarings come to tea this afternoon you may know what to talk about. See?"

The other members of the conference, avoiding the eager eye of the chairwoman, began to regard one another uneasily. Then Percy said:--

"Tilly, old girl, you've landed us with a bit of a shipping order, ain't you?"

Tilly nodded. "You are right," she said. "But it will only be for an afternoon. We need not invite them again."

But Percy, who was an honest youth, although he wore a dickey, hesitated.

"How about the gallant Ricardo?" he enquired. "What's his position in this glee-party? Is he with us or them?"

"Oh--Dicky?" said Tilly, with less confidence. "I have been quite square with him. I have told him everything."

"Everything?" enquired several people at once.

"A good deal, anyhow," maintained Tilly. "I have warned him that I shan't have a penny to my name; and that I have had very few of the advantages that the ordinary girl gets; and that he must take me and my people as he finds us. And he says he prefers me that way. In fact"--Tilly's thoughts flew back to Sunday's idyll in the pine wood--"he has said a good deal more than that. And if I want him and he wants me," she added eagerly, like one anxious to struggle on to less debatable ground, "what does it matter what we say or do to his silly old mother and sister? I want my Dicky!" Her eyes shone. "He loves me and I love him, and that is all there is to be said about it. Father, Mother, Percy, 'Melia"--Tilly's hands went forth appealingly--"promise that you will stand by me and see me through!"

Eight impulsive Welwyn hands closed upon Tilly's two.

"We'll see you through, Sis," said Percy reassuringly. His eye swept round the board in presidential fashion. "Those in favour?"

Four hands flew up.

"Carried unanimously!" announced Percy; while Tilly, reassured, ran round the table showering promiscuous embraces upon her relatives.

"There's the front-door bell, 'Melia," said Mrs. Welwyn, whose provident instinct never deserted her in her most exalted moments. "It may be a new lodger. Run down and see."

Amelia obeyed, and the rest of the House of Welwyn went into Committee.

"I say," remarked the far-seeing Percy; "may I enquire who is going to open the front door to our guests this afternoon?"

The Committee surveyed one another in consternation.

"None of us can't do it, that's quite plain," said Mrs. Welwyn. "They would think we had n't got a servant."

"They would be right, first time," confirmed Percy.

"The old family butler must do it," said Mr. Welwyn with a dry chuckle.

"You certainly overreached yourself in the matter of the butler, Sis," observed Percy.

"We could get the charwoman, or borrow the girl from the Rosenbaums," suggested Mrs. Welwyn.

"But I said a *butler*, Mumsie," objected Tilly dismally.

"Oh, dear, so you did," sighed Mrs. Welwyn.

Tilly pondered.

"I know what we can do," she said. "Percy must meet them, quite casually, outside in the Square, on his way home from the City--"

"And let them in with my latch-key--eh?" cried Percy. "That's the ticket!"

Mrs. Welwyn, greatly relieved, smiled upon her fertile offspring. Mr. Welwyn coughed gently.

"The word 'swank,'" he observed, "is unfamiliar to me; but as we have decided to incorporate it in our plan of campaign, may I suggest, Percy, that you allow your guests to ring the front-door bell before overtaking them?"

"Righto, Dad," said Percy. "But why?"

"Well," continued Mr. Welwyn diffidently, "it has occurred to me that when you have ushered the party into the hall, you might call down the staircase into the basement, distinctly but not ostentatiously, to some one--James, or Thomas--you can address him by any name you please--that there is no need to come up. You see the idea?"

"Dad," declared Percy, shaking his parent affectionately by the hand, "you are a marvel! Why, 'Melia, what's the trouble?"

Amelia, wide-eyed and frightened, was standing in the doorway.

CHAPTER XVIII
DE L'AUDACE, ET ENCORE DE L'AUDACE, ET TOUJOURS DE L'AUDACE!

"Daddy," announced Amelia in a stage whisper, "there's a man downstairs."

"What sort of man?" enquired Mr. Welwyn, rising from his seat and edging carelessly in the direction of his bedroom door.

"A rough-looking man."

"Tell him," said Mr. Welwyn with his hand on the door-handle, "that I am not at home. Percy! Quick! Keep that fellow out!"

But it was too late. A stranger stood in the midst of the House of Welwyn.

He was an elderly, undersized, seedy-looking individual, with a blue chin, a red nose, and a faded theatrical manner. In his hand he held a blue-grey slip of paper. He smiled amiably upon the shrinking figure of the master of the house.

"Don't trouble to exit on my account, sir," he remarked wheezily.

"Who are you?" stammered Mr. Welwyn. "What is the meaning of this intrusion?"

"Name of Welwyn?" enquired the stranger briskly.

"Yes."

"Loosius?"

"Yes."

"Then," announced the stranger, proffering the blue paper, "I must arsk you for your hospitality for a short time--a mere matter o' *form*, of course--until this small account is settled. It's Gandy and Cox," he continued chattily: "seventeen-seventeen-six; and I 'm put in possession until it's settled. In other words, 'ere I am, and 'ere I stays until I gets what I came for."

Depositing his frayed headgear upon the piano, the emissary of Gandy and Cox was upon the point of selecting a chair, when he became conscious of a sudden pressure upon the nape of his neck.

"Outside!" intimated Percy's voice.

"Pardon me," replied the visitor without moving, "but you touch me at your own risk. I'm put in by the law."

There was a stifled cry from Mrs. Welwyn and the girls.

"The warrant was signed and 'anded to me this morning," continued the representative of Justice, "at ten-thirty exact. It is now in the 'ands of your Pa, young ladies--"

"Law be damned! Out you go!" shouted Percy, whirling the speaker round towards the door.

"Reflect!" urged the broker's man, gently resisting Percy's efforts to eject him by leaning back and digging his heels into the carpet. "What's the good? If you dot me one and fling me out, it merely means fourteen days without the option for assaulting a sheriff's officer in the execution of his duty, on top of the distraint. If you don't believe me," he added, clinging affectionately to the leg of the piano, which he was passing at the moment, "go and read the warrant."

"He is right, Percy," said Mr. Welwyn. "Leave him alone. A sheriff's officer!" he muttered brokenly to himself, as his son relinquished his endeavour to speed the parting guest. "And I was once Fellow and Tutor!"

"A broker's man!" wailed Mrs. Welwyn, putting an arm round each of her daughters. "And I brought you up respectable, dearies!"

"A broker's man!" echoed Tilly, "and Lady Adela coming here this afternoon!"

This was too much for that unpolished but chivalrous youth Percy. Something must be done, for Tilly's sake.

"Dad," he said desperately, laying a hand on his father's shoulder, "ain't you got no money nowhere?"

Mr. Welwyn shook his head helplessly.

"Mother?" said Percy.

"I've got about fifteen shillings," said Mrs. Welwyn, brightening up at the prospect of action. "How much did that insect"--she indicated the minion of the law, now warming himself at the fireplace--"say it was?"

"Seventeen-seventeen-six," replied the insect, with the air of one letting off a telling repartee.

"There is n't so much money in all the world!" whispered Amelia despairingly.

"I've got six-and-threepence," said Percy, diving into his pockets.

A thought occurred to Mrs. Welwyn.

"Father," she enquired of the motionless figure on the sofa, "did n't you tell me that Gandy and Cox's bill was only a matter of seven pounds?"

"It was, it was," said Mr. Welwyn, "but--I ordered a little more, to keep them quiet."

Mrs. Welwyn, admirable woman, wasted no time in useless reproaches. Instead, she turned once more upon the broker's man.

"Now, look here," she said; "I want to ask a favour of you. We're expecting company here this afternoon. Will you go away, and come back in the evening?"

"And find the front door bolted!" replied the broker's man affably. "No, I don't *think*! I prefer to remain. I've been in this profession for some time now--ever since I abandoned *the* profession, in fact--and I know a thing or two. I'm sorry," he added, "to disoblige a lady, and I hope you won't take offence where none was intended. Try to look on the bright side of things. I might 'ave been a auction."

Percy broke in upon these comfortable words.

"Look here," he said; "will you go away for a quid?"

"There is nothing," replied the visitor, "that I should like at this present moment better than a quid; but I'm afraid it's my duty to stay. I shan't do nobody any 'arm, beyond taking a inventory of the furniture. You'll find me quite a confidential family friend in a day or two, I should n't wonder. Oh, dear, 'ere's another of 'em coming to 'ave a go!"

He closed his eyes resignedly. Before him stood Tilly--small, slim, white to the lips, with all her world tottering on the brink of the abyss. In her hands she held a cigar-box.

"What is your name?" she asked.

"Surname," replied the broker's man pedantically, "Stillbottle. Christian ditto, Samuel. Net result, Samuel Stillbottle."

"Have a cigar, Mr. Stillbottle," said Tilly, with a ghost of a smile.

Mr. Stillbottle helped himself without comment. He was a man for whom life held few surprises. "Thank you. But I won't go, mind you," was all he said.

Next moment Tilly motioned him to a chair beside the table, and set the decanter and a glass beside him. "Have something to drink, Mr. Stillbottle," she said.

"I shall be pleased to do so," replied Mr. Stillbottle graciously. "Without prejudice, of course," he added, filling his glass.

By this time the others, astonished and interrogative, had gathered round Tilly.

"Tilly," burst out Percy, "what's the good? He won't go--don't you think it!"

"Young man," corroborated Mr. Stillbottle, "you are right. I won't. You 've done it in one."

Tilly took an arm of Percy and another of her mother and drew both in the direction of the sofa. Her breath came fast.

"Listen," she said rapidly--"you too, Dad! We *will* have our tea-party. We won't throw up a single item in the programme. We'll entertain the Mainwarings, and we'll show them that we know how to do things in proper style, and we'll make them all enjoy themselves--even Sylvia--and I'll get my Dicky yet!"

She paused, and surveyed her mystified audience with shining eyes.

"But, Sis," enquired the dubious Percy, indicating the fully occupied Mr. Stillbottle, "what about Rockefeller over there?"

The indomitable Tilly laughed.

"He is our old family butler!" she said simply.

CHAPTER XIX

SIDELIGHTS ON A PUBLIC CHARACTER

Mr. Samuel Stillbottle, notebook in hand, with a look of professional severity upon his pinched features, slowly circumnavigated the drawing-room, making an inventory of the furniture. He was followed, step for step, by the deeply interested Caution and Cure, who, finding the bonds of discipline unusually relaxed, owing to the preoccupation of their elders, had seized an early opportunity of escaping from the region belowstairs in which they were supposed to be enjoying their afternoon siesta, in order to pursue their acquaintance with the gentleman whom they had christened, on sight, "the funny man." They had encountered Mr. Stillbottle in the kitchen, and had conceived a liking for him at once. As appraisers of character their point of view was circumscribed and their judgment immature; but Mr. Stillbottle's performance at dinner had won their unqualified respect and admiration. They had accordingly decided to spend the rest of their lives in his company, and with that intent in view had laboriously scaled the staircase, and were now doing their best, by a series of ill-timed demonstrations of cordiality, to obstruct their new friend in the execution of his duty.

"Chesterfield sofa--two castors loose--one-fifteen," murmured Mr. Stillbottle, plying his pencil. ("Run away, that's good children.) Me'ogany whatnot"--he slipped his hand round behind the piece of furniture in question--"with deal back, two-ten. Armchair, with off 'ind leg cracked, twelve-and-six. (Run away, that's little dears. Run away and drown the kitten, or give the canary a shampoo; but don't stand there starin' at me like a pair of images. I don't like it, so don't do it.) Now for the 'arpsichord!"

The harassed Mr. Stillbottle began to examine the Welwyns' piano. The Cure turned to The Caution.

"Funny man!" she reiterated ecstatically.

"Yesh," assented The Caution, who suffered from a slight palatal affection. "Funny man! Lesh fight him a little bit!"

As an intimation that the approaching combat was to be of the friendliest description, he first smiled seraphically upon Mr. Stillbottle (who was looking the other way at the moment), and then dealt that gentleman a well-directed blow in the back of each knee simultaneously with his pudgy fists. Mr. Stillbottle, who, owing to his ignorance of infantile patois, was entirely unprepared for this onslaught, promptly fell head-first into the arm-chair with the damaged hind leg, reducing its value by a further one-and-ninepence. Before he could extricate himself his enraptured admirers had conceived and partially put into execution the happy design of tickling him to death.

"Now, look 'ere," he exclaimed indignantly, when he was sufficiently recovered from the suddenness of this outrage to resume an upright position, "you must drop it! Pop off! I won't 'ave it! If I ketch 'old of either of you--if I ketch--all right, say no more about it! I believe that little girl 'as got the evil eye," he muttered weakly to himself. Mr. Stillbottle's nerves were not in good order, and The Cure had regarded him with unwinking steadfastness for something like five minutes. "Go and play over there," he urged, almost piteously, "and let me do my job. Now, where was I? Ho, yes--the pianner."

He submitted that venerable instrument to a further scrutiny.

"*Collard and Collard*," he observed. ("A very appropriate title, too, for this 'ouse!) Date, about seventy-four or five, I should say." He lifted the lid and struck a few inharmonious chords. "Not been tooned since bought. Loud pedal broke, and ivories off three keys. Mouse-'ole in the back. Say thirty-five bob, or two p--Will you *drop* it?"

Mr. Stillbottle made this request from the floor, upon which he had suddenly adopted a recumbent attitude. The Caution and the Cure, having decided to initiate their idol into what they had always considered the most consummate jest in existence, had placed a heavy footstool close behind his heels; and Mr. Stillbottle, stepping back a pace in order to view the *tout ensemble* of the piano, had carried the joke to a successful and rapturous conclusion.

Amid appreciative shrieks of merriment from the twins, their fermenting playfellow rose solemnly to his feet, and was pausing dramatically for the double purpose of recovering his breath and deciding upon an effective scheme of reprisal, when he became aware that the door was open and that the master of the house was smilingly contemplating the entertainment.

"You three appear to be having a romp," said Mr. Welwyn genially. "You are evidently a lover of children, Mr. Stillbottle!"

Fortunately for the delicate ears of The Caution and The Cure, Mr. Stillbottle was still incapable of utterance. By the time that his two admirers had been escorted to the door by their progenitor and bidden to return to their own place, his power of speech had returned; but perceiving that the time for explanation was now past, the misjudged romper decided to postpone the refutation of the libel until some other occasion.

"Be seated, Mr. Stillbottle," said Mr. Welwyn politely.

Mr. Stillbottle selected the sofa, which it will be remembered had been marked as high as one pound fifteen.

"I hope you had a comfortable dinner," continued Mr. Welwyn.

"Thank you," replied Mr. Stillbottle briefly--"I 'ad."

Mr. Welwyn produced half-a-sovereign.

"I make a point of being punctilious over money matters," he said, handing the coin to the broker's man. "When our little--er--contract has been carried to a successful conclusion I shall be happy to hand you another."

Mr. Stillbottle pocketed the money.

"When may I expect the other?" he enquired.

"If all goes well, about six o'clock this evening."

"I see," said Mr. Stillbottle comprehendingly. "Carriages at five-forty-five--eh?"

"Precisely," said Mr. Welwyn. "You have hit off the situation to a nicety." He laughed, in high spirits. His resilient nature had entirely recovered from the humiliation of the morning. "Meanwhile"--he produced a sheet of note-paper--"I shall be obliged if you will kindly commit these notes to memory."

Mr. Stillbottle laboriously perused the document.

"Lord love a duck!" he observed in a dazed voice--"What's this?"

"A list of--let us say, your entrances and exits this afternoon," explained Mr. Welwyn smoothly. "You understand theatrical terms, I believe."

He had struck the right chord. Mr. Stillbottle's rheumy eye lit up.

"Entrances and ex-- oho! Now I begin to take you," he said. "We 're agoin' to do drawing-room theatricals, are we? Kind o' benefit matinée--eh?"

"In a sense, yes," replied Mr. Welwyn. "Are you endowed with the dramatic instinct?"

"Come again!" said Mr. Stillbottle politely.

"Could you play a part, do you think?"

"Could I play a part?" repeated Mr. Stillbottle witheringly. "Could a duck swim? Why, I was *in* the profession, off and on, for a matter of fourteen years."

"In what capacity?" asked Mr. Welwyn, much interested.

"Well, I've bin a good many things," said the versatile Stillbottle, putting his feet up on the sofa. "I've bin a guest in the palace of the Dook of Alsatia; I 've bin the middle bit of the sea-serpent--what you might call the prime cut--in a ballet of fish; and I was once the second wave on the O.P. side of the storm what wrecked Sinbad the Sailor."

Mr. Welwyn smiled sympathetically. Here was another rolling stone.

"What made you abandon such a promising career, Mr. Stillbottle?" he asked.

The late prime cut of the sea-serpent shook his head gloomily.

"The old story," he said--"professional jealousy. It started with my bein' cast for the front legs of a elephant in a pantomime. That was the stage-manager's bit of spite. My usual place is the 'ind legs--and that takes a bit of doing, I can tell you. (The 'ind legs 'as to wag the tail, you see.) If I was to tell you the number of 'ind legs I'd played, you'd be surprised," he continued, plunging into an orgy of irrelevant reminiscence. "Why, I recollect in eighty-four, at the Old Brit., 'Oxton way--"

"But what was the matter with the front legs you were speaking of?" enquired Mr. Welwyn opportunely.

"The matter," replied Mr. Stillbottle testily, "was that they was n't 'ind legs. Not bein' used to them, I stepped in wrong way round on the first night. We got shoved on the stage somehow, but every time we started to move I ran straight into the 'ind legs. In the end we broke the elephant's back between us. What was more, we spoiled the Principal Boy's best song. The audience was much too occupied watchin' a elephant givin' a imitation of a camel to listen to 'er. Besides, she was sittin' on the elephant 'erself at the time, and bein' rather stout, 'ad 'er work cut out to 'old on. She got me fired next day. Said I was n't sober."

"That was a libel, of course," said Mr. Welwyn soothingly.

"In a manner of speakin'," replied Mr. Stillbottle guardedly--"yes." He took up Mr. Welwyn's sheet of note-paper again.

"What is all this?" he enquired rather querulously. "Stage directions, or cues, or what?"

"Everything," said Mr. Welwyn. "Your lines and business, in fact."

Mr. Stillbottle nodded comprehendingly, and proceeded to read aloud:--

"*When front-door bell rings, answer door and show party up, asking their names and announcing them distinctly.*"

"You can do that?"

"I'll 'ave a dash for it, anyway. Then: *Bring in tea and put it on tea-table.*"

Mr. Stillbottle's unsteady gaze wandered round the apartment until it encountered the table.

"Tea-table, left centre," he remarked to himself. "*Then, at irregular intervals, come in and make the following remarks to me*:--that's you, I suppose?"

Mr. Welwyn nodded, and Mr. Stillbottle read the paper aloud to the end. Then he slowly folded it up, and remarked, not altogether unreasonably, that he was damned. He added a respectful rider in the French tongue, to the effect that Mr. Welwyn was *très moutarde*.

"You understand," said his employer with great seriousness--he had crossed the Rubicon now, and was determined to risk nothing by imperfect rehearsal--"you must use your own discretion as to when you come in with your messages. About once every ten minutes, I should say."

"Don't you think, governor," suggested Mr. Stillbottle, almost timidly, "that that last stretcher--the one about the shover--is just a bit *too* thick? Suppose your guests start askin' to see the car--what, then? You'll be in the cart, you know!"

"It is all right," said Mr. Welwyn. "I am giving the car up, on account of recent taxation, and so on. It is in the market now, and may be sold at any moment--to-day, perhaps."

"I beg pardon," said Mr. Stillbottle humbly. "I see I can teach you nothing." Then he added, conversationally: "Did you ever know a Captain Slingsby, by any chance?"

"No. Who was he?"

"Another of the lads, like yourself. I thought perhaps you might have been workin' with him at some time. I came acrost him once or twice. He was a pretty tough nut. His line was to dress up as a curate and get himself adopted by rich widders; but he was n't the artist you are, sir. He 'ad n't your education, I should say. Are the whole family in this, may I enquire?"

"Er--yes," replied Mr. Welwyn helplessly.

"Ah!" Mr. Stillbottle nodded his head. "I thought somehow that I had come on a happy visit to the Nut Family as soon as I got acquainted with your two youngest. Well, it's a pleasure to work with people at the top of their profession, and I'll see you through."

Mr. Welwyn thanked him, almost inaudibly.

"But when do you suppose," pursued Mr. Stillbottle, transferring his feet from the sofa to the floor, "that I shall get out of this Dramatic Academy of yours? I 'ave n't come 'ere for a *course*, you know. Are you going to touch the tea-party for the money, or let me distrain on the furniture, or what?"

"I can't tell you at present," said Mr. Welwyn; "but I will endeavour to arrange something by the evening."

"Well, let me know soon, ole sport," said Mr. Stillbottle--"that's all. I 'ave my arrangements to make, too, remember. My *word*, look at Mother!"

This interjection was occasioned by the entrance of Mrs. Welwyn and Amelia, dressed for the party. Mrs. Welwyn was arrayed in a quieter and more tasteful fashion than might have been expected. Her costume, which had been designed and constructed by her eldest daughter, would have struck an impartial critic as one which made the very best of her age and figure. Amelia wore a short white frock, with a blue sash. Her long coppery hair flowed to her waist, and her hazel eyes were aglow with excitement.

"Father dear, what do you think of the way Tilly has turned me out?" enquired Mrs. Welwyn gaily.

For the moment her troubles were behind her. For once she was suitably--and to the outward eye expensively--attired; and the knowledge of the fact had induced in her humble but feminine soul that degree of minor intoxication which the materially-minded male usually achieves, more grossly but less extravagantly, by means of a pint of champagne.

Slowly gyrating for the delectation of her husband, Mrs. Welwyn unexpectedly encountered the unsympathetic gaze of Mr. Stillbottle. She blushed red, and ceased to revolve.

"Oh, that you?" she exclaimed, in an embarrassed voice.

"Yes, it's me--what's left of me," replied Mr. Stillbottle lugubriously. "Wearing me out, this job is."

He displayed his paper of cues.

Mrs. Welwyn regarded him severely.

"It's time you dressed yourself," she said. "I have put my son's evening clothes out for you--in the bathroom," she added pointedly. "You had better go and put them on. He is bigger than you, but you'll manage."

Mr. Stillbottle acquiesced.

"Very good," he remarked graciously. "Wardrobe mistress must be obeyed, I suppose. I'm beginning to warm up to this part. I shall surprise you all yet."

"I hope not," murmured Mr. Welwyn devoutly.

"Did you tell him about the name, Father?" prompted Amelia.

"No, I forgot," said Mr. Welwyn. "Mr. Stillbottle, I think this afternoon that we had better address you by some other name than your own."

"What," enquired Mr. Stillbottle, with a touch of hauteur, "is the matter with me own little patteronymic?"

"Just to sustain the character, you know," urged Mr. Welwyn.

Mr. Stillbottle sighed, in humorous resignation.

"All right," he said. "Confer the title."

Mr. Welwyn turned to his wife.

"What do you say to 'Howard,' Mother?" he asked.

"Nothing with an H in front of it for *me*, dearie, if you please," announced Mrs. Welwyn firmly. "I can see enough rocks of that kind ahead of me this afternoon as it is."

"Why not 'Russell'?" suggested Amelia. "Russell Square, you know."

Mrs. Welwyn stroked her resourceful little daughter's hair gratefully.

"That will do finely," she said. "You are Russell," she announced briefly to Mr. Stillbottle.

The newly christened infant acquiesced listlessly, and rose from the sofa.

"Now I must tear myself away," he said, "to don me trunks and 'ose and get up this patter. I'm a slow study. No promptin', I presume?"

"No," said Mr. Welwyn.

"Gaggin' permitted?" enquired Mr. Stillbottle, without much hope.

"Certainly not."

"Very good. So long, everybody. *Exit Russell*, door in back."

With a theatrical gesture, the ci-devant impersonator of elephants' hind legs disappeared. The Welwyns regarded one another apprehensively.

"Oh, dear!" said Mrs. Welwyn.

"We must make the best of him, Martha," said her husband. "After all, we did not invite him here of our own accord: he *has* to be present in the house in some capacity. Still, I admit he is the weak spot in our enterprise--the heel of Achilles, so to speak."

But Mr. Welwyn was wrong.

CHAPTER XX
REHEARSED EFFECTS

"*H*as *H*erbert," enquired Mrs. Welwyn, taking a deep breath, "*h*urt *H*orace?" She choked. "Oh, dear!"

"Very good, Mumsie," said Amelia encouragingly. "Go on."

"But it puts me out of breath so, child, as soon as I begin to think of it," complained her pupil. "I shall never learn."

"Yes, you will," said Amelia confidently. "H's are just a matter of proper breathing, Daddy says. Now try the next sentence, and remember there's a trap in it!"

Miss Amelia seated herself upon the floor, clasping her long black legs with her arms and resting her chin on her knees.

"Now," she said, with a little nod.

Conscientious Mrs. Welwyn, having audibly recharged her lungs, now began to emit another heavily aspirated sentence.

"*H*ildebrand," she announced, "*h*as *h*it *H*enry *h*ard *h*intentionally. There, that's done it!" She sighed despairingly.

"And I warned you, Mother," said Amelia reproachfully. "That last word is put in on purpose to trip you up."

"Yes, I know," replied her mother with an apologetic smile. "And it always does. You can't teach an old dog new tricks, ducky, and that's a fact. I have always been common in my talk, and common in my talk I always will be. All I can promise is that I will do my best this afternoon; and I hope, for all of your sakes, that your old mother won't go and disgrace you."

Little 'Melia's reply to this humble aspiration was an embrace which entirely disorganised the hooks and eyes at the back of Martha Welwyn's festal garment. While the disaster was being repaired, Tilly entered briskly. In her hand she held a printed card, bearing the legend

APARTMENTS

in staring letters. This she dropped behind the piano.

"Hook me up behind, 'Melia, will you," she said, "when you have finished Mother? No, I'll do Mother and you do me. Your hair-ribbon is wrong. Let me get hold of it."

The Welwyns, *mère et filles*, formed themselves into a voluble equilateral triangle.

"I found that 'Apartments' card lying on the hall table," said Tilly with a shiver. "I suppose Russell took it out of the drawer when he was making his inventory. A nice thing if they had all marched in through the front door at that very moment! Still," she added cheerily, "there's no harm done. Am I all right, do you think?"

"Tilly, you look lovely," said Amelia.

"One thing about being a dress-designer," admitted Tilly, kissing her little sister, "is that you can design yourself a dress. 'Melia, you look a little duck. Mother, your hair is n't quite right. Let me pull it out a bit here."

She tweaked the coiffure of her much-enduring parent into position, whistling blithely. Her cheeks were pink, her eyes sparkled. She was determined to look her best for Dicky that day. And to do her justice, she did.

"Tilly dear," remarked Mrs. Welwyn dubiously, "can we all get round that table for tea?"

"Gracious!" cried Tilly, observing the heavily loaded table for the first time. "You are never going to plant everybody round *that*, like nursery tea?"

"Ain't we?" said Mrs. Welwyn blankly.

"Certainly not," replied Tilly.

Swiftly she sketched out the fundamentals of that meal which combines the maximum of discomfort with the minimum of nourishment--afternoon-tea as consumed by high society in the present period--and in three minutes the great round table, tipped onto its edge, was trundled rapidly into Mr. Welwyn's bedroom, to the surprise and discomfort of Mr. Welwyn, who was dressing at the time.

"Now a small tea-table," commanded Tilly.

"There is n't such a thing in the house, love," panted her overheated parent.

"Yes, there is," said little 'Melia, the ever-ready. "In Mr. Pumpherston's room. He keeps a text framed in fir-cones on it."

"You're right, dear; I had forgotten," admitted Mrs. Welwyn. "Well, Pumpherston is going to get bounced this evening anyway, so we might as well have his table now as then. Come with me and get it. He's out."

Left alone, Tilly flitted about the room, reviving its faded glories as far as she was able by deft touches here and there; straightening curtains, patting cushions, and confiding to various unresponsive articles of upholstery the information that her Love was like a Red, Red Rose.

"Tea-table here, I think," she said, pausing. "Probably Lady Adela would have hers nearer the fire; but then Lady Adela's drawing-room carpet has not got a hole in it. Come in!"

The door opened, and an eerie figure appeared. It was Mr. Russell--*né* Stillbottle--in his shirt-sleeves, wearing an insecurely fastened dickey. His black trousers, being much too long for him, presented a corrugated appearance. In his hand he carried a great bunch of pink carnations.

"These 'ave just been 'anded in, Miss," he announced. "No name, and"--with a slight note of congratulation in his voice--"nothing to pay."

Tilly thanked him, and, taking the flowers, buried her face in the heart of the bunch. When she withdrew it she found that Mr. Stillbottle was still present.

"If you could find him, Miss," he said deferentially, "I should like to 'ave a word with the Chief Nut."

"Who?"

"The old feller that's running this fake."

"Oh, my father?" said Tilly, biting her lip. "He is dressing, I think." She tucked three or four carnations into her belt and began to arrange the others in a bowl.

"Then, perhaps," said Mr. Russell, "you could advise me on a purely personal matter."

"Certainly," replied Tilly absently. Dicky's gift still claimed all her attention.

"It's these trousers, Miss," explained Russell confidentially. "They are the pair supplied by the management; and between ourselves I don't think they suit me. Brother Perce may 'ave a faithful 'eart, but 'e 's *built* all wrong. These trousers are six or eight inches too long in the leg. I feel as if I was wearin' a pair of concertinas. Now--"

This sartorial jeremiad was cut short by the entrance of Mrs. Welwyn, who, travelling full-speed astern and towing Amelia and the tea-table of Pumpherston in her wake, butted the double doors open, and backed heavily into the orator. Mr. Russell, looking deeply injured, retired to complete his toilet.

"That's better," said Tilly, when the small tea-table had been placed over the hole in the carpet, and the tea-tray had been placed over a hole in the tablecloth. "Is everything ready?"

"Yes," said Amelia.

"What about the babies?"

"I have washed and dressed them," said Mrs. Welwyn. "Melia will fetch them down for a few minutes about a quarter-to-six."

"That's all right," said Tilly approvingly. "They are darlings, both of them, and I should like to have them down all the time, but it's too risky. What time is it now?"

"Ten minutes to five," said Amelia.

"Mercy!" exclaimed Mrs. Welwyn, greatly agitated at the proximity of her hour. "Where shall I sit, Tilly dear?"

"On the sofa, Mumsie; and don't get hot, because you are looking very nice," said Tilly soothingly. "Hallo, Dad--just in time!"

Mr. Welwyn in a frock-coat, looking quite the scholar and gentleman, had entered from his bedroom.

"I perceive the feast is spread," he observed jauntily. "Mistress of Ceremonies, how do we dispose ourselves?"

"Mother here," replied meticulous Tilly--"on the sofa with the 'Morning Post.' I picked it up off the floor of the railway-carriage this morning. Don't read it; just be glancing at it carelessly. Father, sit by the fire with a book. Here's one. 'Melia, you had better be on a footstool at Mother's feet, with your head against her knee. Don't fall over her when you get up, Mother. And don't come forward more than three steps to meet Lady Adela: you 're as good as she is, remember. Say it's very sweet of her to come all this way. And if you call her 'your Ladyship,' I shall walk straight across the room and kill you--see?"

"Yes, lovey," sighed the flustered Mrs. Welwyn. "What *do* I call her?"

"Lady Adela--not Lady Mainwaring, mind!"

"It sounds so familiar, starting Christian names right off," objected Mrs. Welwyn feebly.

"Never mind; you've got to do it," said Tilly ruthlessly. "I shall be here by the tea-table, and if any of you get on to thin ice I shall drop a teaspoon. Do you all understand?"

"Yes, Tilly," replied a respectful chorus.

"Very well, then," replied the Mistress of Ceremonies. "Now let me see you all in your places. Attention!"

Tilly clapped her hands, and her well-drilled retinue froze into their appointed attitudes.

"Don't hold the 'Morning Post' as if you were trying to lick butter off it, Mother," said Tilly. "'Melia, pull up your stocking. Dad, you are splendid, but you are laughing. This is a serious business, remember. Now, all keep like that for two minutes, to see if--Mercy on us, here they are!"

But she was wrong.

The door creaked, and swung slowly open, to admit the attenuated figure of Grandma Banks, who in the most unconcerned fashion possible hobbled across the room to the fireplace and seated herself in the vacant armchair opposite to her son-in-law, with every appearance of having come to anchor for the evening.

———

Grandma's descendants gathered into a panic-stricken knot in the corner.

"She *can't* stay!" whispered Tilly frantically. "Mother, get her to bed."

"My dearie," responded Mrs. Welwyn helplessly, "you know what she is when she smells a rat!"

"Try, anyhow!" urged Tilly, glancing feverishly at the clock.

Mrs. Welwyn approached her aged parent much as a small boy approaches a reputed wasp's nest.

"Mother," she said nervously.

"Eh?" replied Mrs. Banks, looking up sharply and scrutinising her daughter over her glasses. "What 'ave you got them things on for? Goin' out somewhere? At your age, too!" she added irrelevantly.

"Yes--no--yes," stammered Martha Welwyn, who tampered with the truth with difficulty. "I've arranged for you to have your tea in your own room this afternoon, Mother."

"Why?" enquired Mrs. Banks at once.

"You are not looking very well," interposed Mr. Welwyn rashly.

"I'm eighty-one," retorted the old lady with great spirit, "and as 'earty as ever I was, Welwyn. I shall 'ave my tea in 'ere."

"We rather want this room this afternoon, dear," resumed Mrs. Welwyn gallantly. "Father has some people coming in on business."

"Is Father going to get a job of work to do?" riposted Grandma Banks, in tones of gratified surprise.

Mr. Welwyn blew his nose sheepishly, and the clock struck five. Tilly came forward and knelt by her grandmother's chair.

"It is very important for all of us, Granny," she pleaded, "that Father should have an undisturbed talk with these people; so we thought we would keep this room clear this afternoon. You don't want to be troubled with strangers, do you? Nasty, loud-voiced people."

"I likes people with loud voices," replied the old lady cantankerously. "I can 'ear what they says."

"But they're only going to talk business," urged Tilly. "Come along, there's a dear old Grandma. You'll be much more comfortable in your own room. There's a nice fire there, and I'll bring you in a lovely tea. Take my arm."

By this time Mrs. Banks had been raised to her feet, and now found herself being gently but inexorably propelled in the direction of the door.

"You don't *want* me, that's the truth," she observed, getting reluctantly under way. "You're ashamed of your old Grandma, that's what it is."

"Nonsense, darling," said Tilly. "You know how fond we all are of you. But you would only be tired out by a lot of people."

"No," persisted the old lady, "you don't want me."

She hobbled through the door on her grand-daughter's arm, still speaking the truth.

"Poor old Granny!" Tilly's voice said very gently. "I promise to make it all up to you some day."

The bedroom door on the other side of the landing was heard to open and shut, and there was momentary silence. Then the front-door bell emitted a majestic peal. The sound thrilled the Welwyns like a tocsin. Tilly darted in.

"Get to your places," she whispered.

The troupe hastily resumed their proper poses, and a tense silence ensued.

Mrs. Welwyn took a deep breath.

"*H*as *H*orace," she enquired in a hoarse and hysterical whisper, "*h*urt *H*erbert? No, but *H*ildebrand--"

"They are in the hall," hissed Amelia.

"They are coming up," said Mr. Welwyn calmly.

Suddenly Tilly's fortitude deserted her.

"I can't bear it!" she wailed, and bolted incontinently through the inner door into her father's room.

"Tilly darling, don't leave us!" was the agonised cry of Mrs. Welwyn and Amelia....

Next moment Mr. Welwyn, finding himself alone in his own drawing-room, rose to his feet and, as rapidly as was compatible with the dignity of a scholar and a gentleman, joined the panic-stricken mob in his bedroom.

Almost simultaneously the door onto the landing was thrown open, and Mr. Stillbottle's wheezy voice announced:--

"Lord Mainwaring, Lady Mainwaring, and party!" Then in a surprised and informal tone:--

"Hallo! Stage clear?"

CHAPTER XXI
UNREHEARSED

Mr. Mainwaring, Lady Adela, and party--the latter comprised Sylvia, Connie Carmyle, and Dicky--came to a standstill in the middle of the vast and empty drawing-room and looked enquiringly about them. Lady Adela, upon whom the labour of climbing the staircase had told heavily, first deleted from her features the stately smile which she had mechanically assumed before crossing the threshold, and then began to sit down upon the piece of furniture which Mr. Stillbottle had recently valued at twelve-and-six-pence.

"I would n't set in that chair, mum, not if I was you," remarked a husky voice in her ear. "The off 'hid leg is a trifle dicky."

Lady Adela, suspended in mid-air like Mahomet's coffin, started violently upwards into a vertical position, and then, having, on the advice of the officious Mr. Stillbottle, selected the sofa, took in the drawing-room with one comprehensive sweep of her lorgnette.

Mr. Stillbottle withdrew, doubtless to con his lines.

"H'm," remarked Lady Adela. "This is evidently not one of the rooms that has just been in the hands of the painters and decorators."

"Dick," enquired Sylvia, who had been superciliously inspecting the mahogany whatnot with the deal back, "who was that furtive Oriental person who slipped past us on the staircase? Not another future relative-in-law, I trust."

"The stout nigger gentleman, you mean?" said Dicky, with unimpaired good humour. "I fancy he must have been calling on Mr. Welwyn about his studies. I have a notion that London University is somewhere about here."

"What a jolly old-fashioned house this is," said Connie from the window-seat. "How nice and shady this big square must be in summer."

"It is a fairly shady locality all the year round, I fancy," observed Sylvia sweetly.

Kind-hearted Mr. Mainwaring coughed, and looked unhappily towards his son. But Dicky did not appear to have heard. He had just discovered his carnations.

415

Lady Adela took up the tale.

"There was a small but ferocious-looking creature with red whiskers," she announced, "hanging over the banisters on the top floor. Who would he be, now?"

"Don't ask me, Mum," said Dicky. "I've never been in the house before, remember, except downstairs. Probably a paper-hanger, or--"

He was interrupted by the entrance of a stately procession headed by Mrs. Welwyn, the rest following in single file.

Tilly effected the necessary introductions prettily and with perfect composure; and presently the company assorted itself into what we will call Tableau Number One. Mr. Welwyn led Lady Adela back to the seat which she had vacated.

"Most of the furniture in this mansion of ours is Early Victorian," he announced with a ready laugh; "but I think you will find this sofa comfortably Edwardian, Lady Adela."

Lady Adela, favourably impressed with her host's appearance and manner, smiled graciously and once more cautiously lowered herself onto the sofa. Here, in obedience to an almost imperceptible sign from her husband, the quaking Mrs. Welwyn joined her, and announced, in a voice which she entirely failed to recognise as her own, that it was very sweet of them all to come so far.

Amelia ran impulsively to Dicky and kissed him. Mrs. Carmyle, Sylvia, and Tilly fell into a chattering group round the tea-table. Mr. Welwyn and Mr. Mainwaring shook hands warmly and exchanged greetings. The tea-party was launched.

"How many years is it, Welwyn?" asked Mr. Mainwaring.

"Let us not rake up the past, my dear Mainwaring," said Mr. Welwyn. "More years than we care to count--eh? We'll leave it at that. But I am delighted to meet you again. I wonder how the old College prospers. Foster was your tutor, was n't he?"

"Yes," replied Mr. Mainwaring, pleasantly flattered to find that a man who had been two years senior to him should remember so much about him.

"Mine, too," mentioned Mr. Welwyn, as if determined to put his guest at his ease.

"He's a bishop now, I hear," said Mr. Mainwaring.

"*Eheu, fugaces*!" sighed Mr. Welwyn. "Come and sit by the fire."

"I think we had better have tea, Tilly," said Mrs. Welwyn, as per programme.

The Welwyn family, recognising a cue, began to bestir themselves for Tableau Number Two.

"I seem to hear it coming up, Mother," replied Tilly.

She was right. Portentous rattlings and puffings were now audible without. Next moment the doors were bumped open and Mr. Stillbottle appeared, carrying the tea-pot on a tray.

Apparently something was on his mind. His appearance was that of a righteous man deeply wronged. His was the demeanour of a British artisan compelled by forces which he cannot control to perform a task not included in his contract.

A moment later the situation explained itself. Behind Mr. Stillbottle, clinging affectionately to his flowing coat-tails, marched The Caution and The Cure. They were dressed in white, and looked exactly alike except that The Caution wore abbreviated white knickerbockers and The Cure a little white skirt. Their socks were white, their sashes and chubby legs were a radiant pink, and the angelic countenance of each was wreathed in smiles.

The procession drew up at the tea-table, where its leader proceeded to deposit the tea-pot. For a moment there was a pause in the conversation, while the hearts of the Welwyns stood still. The Twins, uncontrolled, sometimes erred on the side of originality.

"He's the Queen," explained The Cure, indicating the flinching figure of Mr. Stillbottle.

"Yesh; and we're holdin' up of his train," added The Caution.

Next moment Connie Carmyle had captured them both.

"You darlings!" she cried, and carried them off to the window-seat. The situation was saved.

"Little pets!" observed Lady Adela, smiling.

Even Sylvia forgot to pose for a moment. Tea was served amid a hum of cheerful conversation. The children had evoked the maternal instinct, and all was well.

Only Mr. Stillbottle remained cold.

"You oughter 'ave kep' them locked up somewhere," he announced severely to Tilly; and left the room.

"I don't see your son here, Mrs. Welwyn," said Lady Adela. "We had the pleasure of his company for a few minutes on Saturday."

"He will be here any minute, your--Lady Adela," replied Mrs. Welwyn with a jerk. "He is usually kept in the City till close on five, poor boy."

"That aged retainer of yours seems to be a bit of an autocrat, Tilly," said Dicky, taking Mrs. Carmyle's chair at the tea-table.

"Yes," agreed Tilly, feeling rather miserable at having to talk to Dicky in this strain; "but you know what old servants are. In their eyes we never grow up."

"Has he been with you for long, then?" enquired Sylvia, with a deep appearance of interest.

"How long has Russell been with us, Mother?" said Tilly, noting that Mrs. Welwyn's conversation with Lady Adela was beginning to flag.

"I can't remember, dear. It seems a long time, anyhow," replied Mrs. Welwyn with sincerity. "Ah, here is Percy. Come in, my boy. Just in time to hand round the cakes!"

"You can trust little Perce," observed that engaging youth, entirely at his ease, "to be on the spot at the right moment. How de do, Lady Adela? I hope this finds you as it leaves me."

He shook the very limp hand of Lady Adela, and having bestowed an ingratiating smile upon Sylvia, proceeded amid a slowly intensifying silence to offer a humorous greeting to Mr. Mainwaring. Finally he turned to Dicky, and slapped him boisterously upon the shoulder.

"Well, my brave Ricardo," he enquired, "how goes it?"

"Percy, dear old thing," responded Dicky promptly, with his most vacant laugh, "how splendid to see you again! Come and tell me all about your club run on Sunday."

He drew the flamboyant cyclist to a place of safety, and Tilly breathed again.

"There is sugar and cream in this cup, Lady Adela," said Amelia, with a neat bob-curtsey.

"Thank you, little girl," said Lady Adela, taking the cup and smiling indulgently. ("Like a Duchess out slumming," Amelia told Tilly afterwards.) "What pretty manners!" she continued, turning to Mrs. Welwyn. "Where do you send her to school? I used to find it so difficult--"

"She has left school," replied Mrs. Welwyn. "I suppose we ought to send her somewhere to get finished later on, but there--we can't do without her, and that's the truth. Can we, dear?"

Martha Welwyn put an arm round her little daughter. She was talking with greater freedom and confidence now, with her aspirates under perfect control.

"I can quite understand *that*," said Lady Adela affably. "I dare say you find her indispensable."

"I should think so," replied Mrs. Welwyn, lowering her guard. "What with all the staircases, and a basement kitchen, and separate meals--"

Tilly dropped a teaspoon with a clatter on to the tray.

"I'm so sorry, Sylvia," she said. "Did I make you jump?"

"No," responded Sylvia absently. "I was looking at your butler. He seems to have something on his mind."

Mr. Stillbottle, who had entered the room two minutes previously, and had been awaiting an opportunity of gaining the ear of the company, took advantage of the partial silence which now ensued.

"A person has called, sir," he announced to Mr. Welwyn, "for to iron the billiard table."

Mr. Welwyn broke off his conversation with Mr. Mainwaring.

"Thank you," he said in an undertone. "Let him do so by all means."

"Yes, sir," replied Mr. Stillbottle, turning to go.

"Tell him," added Percy, highly pleased with the manner in which the little comedy was unfolding itself, "to see if any of the cues want tips."

"Very good," said Mr. Stillbottle, in a voice which plainly asked why Percy should "gag," when he might not.

The door closed once more, and another hurdle was negotiated. The Welwyns heaved little sighs of relief: Russell's was an unnerving presence. But Tilly glanced at the honest, laughing face of the man who loved her, and felt suddenly ashamed.

"Quite a character, that old fellow," said Mr. Welwyn breezily. "Incorrigibly idle; painfully outspoken; a domestic tyrant of the most oppressive type; but honest as the day. I must get some one to put him in a book. Lady Adela, you have nothing to eat."

Mr. Welwyn deftly changed places with his wife, who gratefully engaged in a conversation with Mr. Mainwaring; and the rest of the company performed one of those complicated evolutions which children call a "general post," and which affords persons of mature years but intellectual poverty the inestimable boon of being able to employ the same topics of conversation several times over. Tableau Number Three was now set.

For a moment Dicky and Tilly found themselves together.

"Tea, old man?" asked Tilly, offering a cup.

"Thanks, little thing," replied Dicky, touching her hand under the saucer.

"Did you send these?" Tilly looked down at her pink carnations.

Dicky nodded, and his gaze became suddenly ecstatic.

"Tilly," he said in tones of exultant pride, "you are looking perfectly beautiful."

"This is a strictly business meeting," smiled Tilly; but her heart bumped foolishly. For a moment nothing seemed to matter save the knowledge that Dicky loved her and she loved Dicky.

The next event of any importance was the discovery that Mrs. Carmyle, engrossed with the twins, had had no tea. There were cries of contrition from the Welwyn family, and Connie was hurried to the tea-table, followed by the desolating howls of her youthful admirers--howls which increased to yells when Mrs. Welwyn announced that it was time for them to return whence they came. However, they were pacified by an offer from their new friend to accompany them part of the way; and after submitting with a sweetness as adorable as it was unexpected to an embrace from Lady Adela, they left the room clinging to Connie's skirts, having contributed to the programme the one unassailably successful item of the whole afternoon.

Amelia went with them, but returned almost immediately.

"Mrs. Carmyle is telling them a story in the dining-room," she said to her mother. "They are as good as gold with her."

"Dear Constance! She is a fairy godmother to all children," remarked Lady Adela, who was feeling quite remarkably beatific.

"Yes--children of all ages," corroborated Dicky, catching Tilly's eye.

"I declare," cried Mrs. Welwyn suddenly, as this pleasant episode terminated, "I had almost forgotten. Tilly dear, you had better take your grandmother's tea in to her."

"All right, Mother," assented Tilly blithely. The party was shaping into a success.

"I am so sorry, Lady Adela," said Mr. Welwyn, picking up the new topic with the readiness of a practised conversationalist, "that you will not meet my wife's mother this afternoon. She spends a good deal of her time with us. A dear old lady--quite of the Early Victorian school."

"She is not unwell, I hope," said Lady Adela politely.

"A slight chill--a mere nothing," Mr. Welwyn assured her; "but at that age one has to be careful. The doctor is keeping her in bed to-day. I regret it, because I think you would have enjoyed a conversation with her. She is a mistress of the rounded phrase and polished diction of two generations ago. So unlike the staccato stuff that passes for conversation nowadays."

"Too true, too true!" agreed Lady Adela, eagerly mounting one of her pet hobby-horses. "She sounds most stimulating. It is unfashionable to-day to be elderly. My daughter informs me that no one--not even a grandmother--should have any recollection of anything that happened previous to the period when people wore bustles. All time before that she sums up as the chignon age. No, there is no sense of perspective nowadays. We are all for the present."

"Admirably put, dear Lady Adela," cooed Mr. Welwyn. "I remember--"

What Mr. Welwyn remembered will never be known, for at that moment the door opened, slowly but inexorably, and Grandma Banks appeared. She advanced into the room with a few uncertain and tottering steps, peered round her, and nodded her head with great vigour.

"I thought so," she observed triumphantly. "Company! No wonder I were sent to bed."

There was a paralysed silence. Mr. Welwyn was the first to recover his presence of mind. He advanced upon his infirm but irrepressible relative shaking a playful finger.

"This is very, very naughty," he announced reproachfully. "What will the doctor say?"

"THIS IS VERY NAUGHTY," HE ANNOUNCED REPROACHFULLY

"Eh?" enquired Grandma.

"You were told to stay in bed, you know, dear," said Mrs. Welwyn, coming to her husband's assistance.

"I were n't never told no such thing by nobody," replied the old lady explicitly.

Tilly, avoiding Sylvia's eye, decided to make the best of the situation.

"Well, now you are here, Granny," she interposed brightly, "you must come and sit snugly by the fire and have some tea. 'Melia, bring that little three-legged table and put it by Granny's chair, and bring a footstool."

The Welwyns, swiftly taking their cue from Tilly, bestirred themselves in fulsome desperation, and in a few minutes Grandma Banks, a trifle flustered by her sudden and most unusual popularity, found herself tucked into her armchair by the assiduous efforts of the entire family.

"This is my grandmother, Mrs. Banks," said Tilly to Mr. Mainwaring, who happened to be sitting nearest.

"I trust, Mrs. Banks," began Mr. Mainwaring with a deferential bow, "that you are not allowing your sense of hospitality to overtax your strength."

"Eh?" enquired Mrs. Banks, as ever.

"She is rather deaf," explained Tilly in an undertone. "Don't strain your voice by talking to her too long."

"The gentleman," announced Grandma unexpectedly, "shall talk to me as long as he likes."

"Aha, Tilly, old lady! That's one for you," cried the watchful Percy, and the Welwyn family laughed, hurriedly and tumultuously. Grandma's octogenarian heart glowed. Social success had come to her at last. She began to enjoy herself hugely. Tilly cast an anxious glance round her. Grandma's entrance had sensibly lowered the temperature of the tea-party, and worse threatened. Already Lady Adela was exhibiting a tendency to edge towards the fireplace. It was only too plain that she contemplated yet another "cosy chat." Tilly decided to fall back upon the one trustworthy person in the room.

"Granny," she said, taking Dicky by the arm and leading him forward, "I want to introduce Mr. Dick Mainwaring. You have heard of him, have n't you?"

Mrs. Banks surveyed Dicky over her spectacles.

"Yes," replied Mrs. Banks with deliberation, "I 'ave 'eard of you. You and our Tilly are walking out."

Dicky assented with a happy laugh, and dropped into the only chair in Grandma's vicinity. Tilly breathed again: Lady Adela's further advance was checked. The party settled down once more, and talk broke out afresh.

Grandma Banks, whose conversational flights were not as a rule encouraged by her relatives, availed herself of her present emancipation to embark upon a brief homily to Dicky.

"I tells you this, young man," she said in a hectoring voice, "you've got a treasure in our Tilly. Don't you forget it."

"I made that discovery for myself a long time ago," said Dicky. He smiled up at his treasure, who was sitting upon the arm of his chair.

The treasure's grandmother, having in the mean time been supplied with refreshment by Amelia, took a piece of bread-and-butter and rolled it up into a convenient cylinder.

"Yes," she continued, dipping the end of the cylinder into her tea, "she takes after her mother, does Tilly. She may get some of her looks from her father's side, but when it comes to character, she's a Banks." Her aged voice rose higher. "Always been respectable, 'as the Bankses," she announced shrilly. "Very different from--"

At this point not less than three persons enquired of Lady Adela if she would not take another cup of tea; and in the hospitable mêlée which ensued Grandma's further utterances were obscured.

Percy was holding Lady Adela's cup, and Tilly was re-filling it, when the door opened and Mr. Stillbottle made his second entrance. As before, he came to a halt immediately on appearing, and coughed in a distressing fashion without making any attempt to deliver his lines.

"There is that quaint old retainer of yours again, Tilly," said Sylvia.

Tilly turned quickly.

"Well, Russell?" she asked.

Mr. Stillbottle, ignoring her entirely, addressed himself to the master of the house.

"A message has came through on the telephone, sir," he chanted, fixing his eyes upon an imaginary prompt-book on the opposite wall, "askin' for you to be so kind as to attend a meetin' of the Club C'mittee at three o'clock on Toosday next."

"I think I am engaged," replied Mr. Welwyn, with an anxious glance in the direction of his mother-in-law (who was fortunately busily occupied in masticating a cylinder); "but say I will let them know."

"Right," said Mr. Stillbottle, and departed.

The Welwyns, who during the time occupied by their butler's second "turn," had been inclining uneasy ears in the direction of the open doorway, surveyed one another in a frightened fashion. All was not well on the second floor: evidence to that effect was plainly audible.

"Great bore, these committee meetings," commented Mr. Welwyn. "I expect you have your fill of them, Mainwaring."

"Alas, yes!" said Mr. Mainwaring. "They are all the same. Everybody sits and looks portentously solemn--"

"All sorts of non-controversial business is brought forward as a matter of pressing importance--"

"Everybody disagrees with everybody else--"

"And ultimately everything is left to the Secretary, who arranges matters quite satisfactorily without any assistance whatsoever!"

The two elderly gentlemen laughed happily at their own spirited little dialogue, and Mr. Welwyn rose to lay down his cup. It was a tactical blunder of capital magnitude. Lady Adela, left momentarily unguarded, immediately slipped her moorings, rose to her feet, and sailed with great stateliness in the direction of the fireplace.

"I am going to have a chat with your dear mother," she observed graciously to Mrs. Welwyn in passing. "Dick dear, let me have your chair."

Dicky, feeling that it was not for him to participate in a battle of giants, obeyed, and Lady Adela sank down opposite Grandma Banks. Simultaneously sounds of further disturbances penetrated from the regions above, and a small lump of plaster fell from the ceiling. Grandma, still intent upon a hearty and unwholesome tea, made no acknowledgment of Lady Adela's presence until Mrs. Welwyn effected an introduction.

"Mother," she explained, "this is Lady Adela, Mr. Dick's mother."

Mrs. Banks nodded curtly.

"It is very kind of you, Mrs. Banks," intimated Lady Adela in the voice of one who meditates producing soup-tickets later on, "to make this special effort on our behalf. I hope we are not too much for you."

The relict of the departed Banks poured some tea from her cup into her saucer, took a hearty and sibilant sip, and replied:--

"Very few folks 'as ever bin too much for me. I 'ear as 'ow you have come on business."

"We told her," Mrs. Welwyn explained to Lady Adela, who was watching Grandma's performance with the saucer with hypnotic fascination, "that you and Mr. Mainwaring were coming to-day to have a talk about Tilly and Mr. Dick. That is what she meant by business, I expect."

But the explanation fell on inattentive ears.

Lady Adela's gaze had now risen from the saucer to the ceiling, which was vibrating madly, apparently under the repeated impact of one or more heavy bodies. The rest of the company had given up all pretence at conversation some time ago.

It was Dicky who supplied a line of explanation.

"Mrs. Welwyn," he said gravely, "your paper-hangers seem to be skylarking a little bit--what?"

"That's it," agreed Mrs. Welwyn, transparently grateful. "But what can one do?" she continued, speaking with pathetic solicitude in Lady Adela's direction. "You know what paperhangers are!"

"A playful race! A playful race!" cooed Mr. Welwyn helpfully.

There was another heavy bump overhead. The prism-decked chandelier rattled, and the ceiling shed another regretful flake.

"Sounds as if some one had tried to walk up the wall and failed," observed Percy, with that courageous facetiousness which comes proverbially to Britons at moments of great peril.

"How exasperating it must be for you all, Tilly," said Sylvia sympathetically. "I wonder you don't go and live somewhere else while it is going on."

Tilly, whose powers of endurance were fast coming to an end, made no reply. Kindly Mr. Mainwaring bridged the gulf of silence.

"It is extraordinary," he began chattily to the company at large, "how completely one is at the mercy of the British workman. Once you get him into your house he sticks. I suppose the title of arch-limpet must be awarded to the plumber; but I should think the paperhanger--"

He was interrupted by the querulous but arresting voice of Grandma Banks.

"What's that?" she enquired with ominous distinctness, "about plumbers?"

"I was awarding the palm for general iniquity, dear Mrs. Banks," explained Mr. Mainwaring smilingly, "to the plumbing fraternity. Plumbers--"

Mrs. Welwyn made a hasty movement, but it was too late. Grandma's bowed and shrivelled form suddenly swelled and stiffened.

"Ho, was you?" she enquired with rising indignation. "Then let me tell you that my late 'usband, Mr. Josiah Banks, what was very 'ighly respected in 'Itchin--"

Tilly dropped two teaspoons despairingly, and there was another and more timely bump overhead.

"Percy dear," interposed Mrs. Welwyn hastily, "don't you think you had better run up and see what those wretches are doing?"

"Righto, Mother," said Percy, rising with alacrity.

"My late 'usband--" resumed Mrs. Banks, *crescendo*.

"It certainly is an extraordinary noise," remarked Mr. Welwyn loudly. "They appear to be on the staircase now."

"Sliding down the banisters, no doubt," said Dicky. "Playful little fellows! Shall I come with you, Percy?"

Percy Welwyn paused, a little embarrassed.

"Don't trouble," he said. "You see--"

He paused again--fatally.

"My late 'usband," proclaimed Grandma Banks on the top note of her register, "was a plumber 'imself."

Next moment the double doors burst open, and Mr. Mehta Ram, frantic with terror, hurled himself into the room.

CHAPTER XXII
THE REAL TILLY

Mr. Mehta Ram promptly fell at the feet of Mr. Welwyn, and attempted, in true Old Testament fashion, to embrace that embarrassed scholar and gentleman by the knees.

"Keep him out!" he shrieked. "Great snakes, I implore you! Lock the door!"

In the absence of the snakes this office was performed by Percy and Dicky. Directly afterwards there was a rush of feet down the staircase, and a fusilade of blows began to rain upon the panels.

"Open the door!" commanded a voice, in a frenzied Paisley accent. "I'm wanting in! Tae break his neck," it added in explanation.

Dicky and Percy promptly put their backs against the door. Mrs. Welwyn crossed hastily to her husband's side.

"It's that Pumpherston," she announced in a low voice. "What are we to do?"

Mr. Welwyn addressed the suppliant at his feet.

"Come, Mr. Mehta Ram," he said, "don't be frightened. He can't get in. What is the trouble?"

Mr. Mehta Ram lifted his face from Mr. Welwyn's boots and addressed the company at large.

"Mr. Welwyn, Mrs. Welwyn, and general public," he began--the latter designation was apparently intended for the Mainwaring family, who, with the exception of Dicky, had ranged themselves into a compact group on the further side of the room--"I appeal to you as British subject--as a member of that great Empire upon which the sun never sits--"

"Sets, old comrade!" corrected Dicky from the door.

"Shed your tears!" commanded Mr. Ram, disregarding the interruption. "Give us a look in! I am in jeopardy--in a damtight place! My adversary knocks upon the door--the avenging Pumpherston! He arraigns me of petty larceny. He accuses me that I have confiscated his table. But I am innocent! I make my defence! I throw myself--Ah-a-a-a-a-h! Help!"

The other door--that leading into Mr. Welwyn's bedroom, which itself communicated with the landing outside--burst open, and a small, red-whiskered, and intensely ferocious gentleman bounded in. It was the avenging Pumpherston.

Mr. Ram bolted across the room like an obese rabbit, and took refuge behind the hostile but protective form of Lady Adela.

The avenger paused, obviously nonplussed by the size of the assembly.

"I beg your paurdon," he said awkwardly. "I wis not aware--"

He turned, to find Percy and Dicky standing beside him, one at each shoulder.

"We were half expecting you, Mr. Pumpherston," said Dicky, with a friendly smile. "But if you and this gentleman are playing hide-and-seek, the den is upstairs."

"I beg your paurdon," repeated Mr. Pumpherston, whose bellicosity was fast evaporating, "but yon fat heathen has robbed me. He has lifted a piece of furniture--Heh! Let me get at him!"

With a convulsive bound he wrenched himself free from his interlocutors and made a dash for the door. But he was too late. Mr. Mehta Ram, keeping under the lee of Lady Adela and the furniture, had made use of the brief respite afforded by the recital of his assailant's grievances to effect an unostentatious departure, and was now halfway up the staircase again. The baffled Pumpherston followed him with a long-drawn howl.

"Come on, Percy!" said Dicky.

The pair raced out in pursuit, banging the door behind them. Presently from abovestairs came the sound of renewed conflict; a few dull thuds and muffled crashes; and then--silence.

―――

Lady Adela rose to her feet in awful majesty, and addressed the stunned and demoralised remnants of the tea-party.

"Is this a private asylum," she enquired in trumpet tones, "or is it not?"

Grandma Banks was the only member of her audience who replied.

"My late 'usband," she whimpered--"my late 'usband, Mr. Josiah Banks! Greatly respected in 'Itchin--greatly respec--"

Tears coursed slowly down her furrowed cheeks.

In a moment Tilly was kneeling beside her, with her arms round the frail old body, whispering gently and caressingly into her ear. There was a long silence, and Sylvia began to pull on her gloves.

"I think we had better be going," said Lady Adela.

"I suppose so," said Mrs. Welwyn helplessly.

But Lucius Welwyn made a last effort. All seemed lost, yet his inherent polish and *savoir faire* rebelled against such an inglorious and ignominious end as this.

"I must apologise most sincerely for this *contretemps*, Lady Adela," he said with a ready smile. "Those fellows are two disciples of mine. Law students--British Museum--and so on. They come here periodically to receive instruction from me in my library upstairs"--Lady Adela looked up and regarded him steadily, but he continued with perfect coolness--"but I fear that on this occasion racial animosity has proved stronger than academic unity of purpose. You will understand, I am sure."

"Perfectly," replied Lady Adela. "Come, Sylvia."

Sylvia was quite ready, but at this moment the door flew open once more, and Dicky and Percy reappeared, flushed, panting, but triumphant.

"It's all right, Mrs. Welwyn," announced Dicky reassuringly. "The brunette gentleman has bolted himself into the bathroom, and we have locked up the blonde in a broom-cupboard. Hallo, Mum--going?"

"Yes. Come, Sylvia."

"Certainly, Mother," said Sylvia.

Dicky's ear caught the danger-note in his sister's voice. He stood transfixed, with dismay written across his frank but heated features.

"I say," he stammered. "Mum--Sylvia--what does all this mean?"

"Good-bye, Mrs. Welwyn," said Lady Adela calmly. "Thank you for--ah--entertaining us. I suppose one can get a cab here?"

She shook Mrs. Welwyn's nerveless hand and turned to Mr. Mainwaring, who stood awkwardly smoothing his hat.

"Are you ready, Abel?" she enquired.

Suddenly Tilly Welwyn rose from her knees by her grandmother's side, and, to employ a dramatic expression, took the centre of the stage. She stood face to face with her departing guests, her head thrown back and her hands clenched--a very slim, very upright, very dignified little figure.

"Sit down, please, everybody, if you will be so kind," she said quietly. "I shan't keep you long."

Lady Adela, looking like a boa-constrictor which has been challenged to mortal combat by a small and inexperienced chicken, stood stockstill, with her head oscillating from side to side in a slightly uncertain fashion. Then, recovering herself, she fell back in good order upon her supporters.

The Welwyns, closing loyally upon their small champion, spoke in anxious undertones.

"Don't chuck up the sponge, Sis," whispered Percy encouragingly. "We'll pull you through."

"Don't lose your head, my child," counselled her father. "You may make things worse."

"Tilly, dearie, can you ever forgive me?" was all Mrs. Welwyn said. She forgot, in her selfless grief for the destruction of her daughter's castle-in-the-air, that she herself had predicted its fall.

Little 'Melia said nothing, but passionately squeezed her sister's hand.

"You are all dears," said Tilly in a clear voice, "and I love you for the way you have stood by me to-day; but I want to speak to the others just now."

She took a step forward towards the Mainwarings, who were grouped beside the tea-table. But before she could speak, Dicky, who had been hovering silently on the outer wing of his own party, crossed the floor and joined her.

"I'll come and stand over here, Tilly," he said, "if you don't mind. There's a nasty draught in that corner."

Tilly smiled faintly.

"I would rather you did n't," she said, with the suspicion of a tremor in her voice. "Please go over there."

Dicky responded by standing-at-ease, military fashion.

"Carry on," he said briefly.

"Please, Dicky!" urged Tilly, "It only makes it harder for me."

Dicky glanced at her white face, and retired one pace backward.

"That is my limit," he said.

Meanwhile Lady Adela had come to the conclusion that all this was very emotional and undignified.

"Miss Welwyn," she enquired, "what does this mean?"

"I will tell you," said Tilly. "But first of all I must say one thing. I did not try to trap your son, as you seem to think. We fell--we came to care for one another quite naturally. I made no attempt to catch him. I knew nothing whatever about him. It--it just happened." She turned wistfully to Dicky. "Did n't it?" she asked.

Dicky nodded his head gravely.

"It just happened," he said.

"And since we cared for one another--or thought we did"--continued Tilly with a little choke, "it never came into my head that anything else could matter. But last Saturday, when I went to stay at your house, and saw your grand ways and your grand servants, and all the commotion you made about Members of Parliament, and county families, and all that--well, I began to see rocks ahead. I felt common. My courage began to fail. I began to be afraid that you would not take kindly to the Family--"

"It was n't you that was afraid, dearie," said a respectful voice behind her. "It was the Family."

"I saw, too, Lady Adela," continued Tilly, "that *you* were against me--dead against me--and that as soon as you got hold of a decent-excuse I should be bundled out of your son's life, like--like an entanglement. That put my back up. I had meant to be perfectly straight and unpretentious with you, but when I saw what you were after, I determined to fight. So I have deceived you."

"We all have," murmured a loyal chorus.

"You have been *done*!" proclaimed Tilly defiantly. She was fast losing control of herself. She felt dimly that she was behaving in an hysterical and theatrical manner; but when one's world is tumbling about one's ears, one may be excused for stating the truth rather more explicitly than is usual. "Yes--*done*!" she repeated. "I will tell you just exactly who we are and what we are. Father is a gentleman, right enough"--her voice rang out proudly--"as well-born a gentleman as any of the land; but he has followed no regular profession for twenty years, and he lives on Mother. Mother keeps lodgings. This house is a lodging-house, and those two men you saw were lodgers. Percy works in a wholesale haberdasher's in Holborn. I do a little dress-designing. 'Melia helps Mother with the lodgers. So you see you have been imposed on: we work for a living! But you must n't blame the Family for what has happened. It was my idea from start to finish: the Family only backed me up. And they did back me up! No girl ever had such a splendid father or mother, or brother or sister." Tilly stepped back into the heart of her bodyguard, feeling for friendly hands. "I 'm proud of them," she cried passionately, "proud to belong to them! I'm proud that my name is Tilly Welwyn, and I never wish to change it for any other. We Welwyns may be nobodies but we stick together. There! You may go now."

The drawing-room door creaked and opened, but no one noticed.

"I have told you everything, I think," said Tilly, more calmly. "I know now that I should have told you in any case. That's all.... No, it's not."

She swung round towards the doorway, and pointed to the grotesque figure of that earnest student of the drama, Samuel Stillbottle, who was myopically deciphering a small but tattered document, all but concealed in the palm of his hand.

"We're paupers!" she cried. "We're in debt! We're broke! There's a distraint on the furniture; and that creature"--Mr. Stillbottle, hazily conscious that a cue was coming, furtively thrust his manuscript into his waistcoat pocket--"that creature is a broker's man! Oh, Mother, Mother, Mother!"

In an instant Martha Welwyn's arms closed round her daughter.

"There, there!" she crooned. "My lamb, my pretty, my precious, my dearie--don't you cry!"

There was a deathlike stillness, broken only by Tilly's sobs. The Mainwarings stood like statues. Mr. Welwyn sat on the sofa, his head bowed between his hands. Grandma Banks slumbered peacefully. The bewildered but conscientious Stillbottle seized his opportunity, and cleared his throat.

"The shover, sir," he announced huskily, "is below, a-waitin' for--"

Next moment a hand like a vice closed upon the herald's collar, and Dicky Mainwaring's voice remarked concisely into his ear:--

"Go to the devil."

Mr. Stillbottle, utterly dazed, raised his head and surveyed the company. Then he smiled apologetically.

"Wrong entrance," he observed. "My error! *Exit hastily!*"

He turned, and shuffled out.

CHAPTER XXIII
THE REAL MR. WELWYN

"*There is an evenin' paper--*"
quavered Mr. Stillbottle blithely, with his feet upon the kitchen hob,--
--"*which is published in the mornin'!*
Twinkle, twinkle, twinkle, little Star!"

He unfolded the early edition of the organ in question and devoted himself to a laboured perusal of the list of probable starters for the Lincolnshire Handicap, now looming in the immediate future; for he was anxious to ascertain whether his premonitions as to the identity of the winner coincided with those of the prophet retained by the management. Apparently they did; for presently the paper was laid aside with a contented sigh, and the student of form resumed the hoary lay which anxiety connected with the investment of his newly acquired capital had caused him momentarily to abandon.

"*Twinkle, Star!*
Tiddley Wink!
Twinkle on till you dunno where you are!
Oh, we 'll make things warm for 'Arcourt,
*If 'e ever comes down our court!**
Twinkle, twinkle, twinkle, little St--"

Conscious of a draught upon the back of his neck, the vocalist turned uneasily in the direction of the door. It had opened some six inches, revealing to view a pair of cherubic heads, set one above the other. Each head was furnished with a pair of quite circular blue eyes, which surveyed Mr. Stillbottle, with unwinking and unnerving ecstasy.

"The Funny Man!" proclaimed The Cure joyously.

"Yesh," agreed The Caution. "Lesh box him."

The pair entered the room hand in hand, and advanced grimly to the attack.

Mr. Stillbottle hastily removed his feet from the hob.

"You two," he announced, "can get on out of this. I ain't never done you no 'arm, 'ave I?" he added appealingly; "so why---"

At this point The Caution dealt him a playful but disabling blow in the waistcoat. The Cure, with a shriek of rapture, seized Mr. Stillbottle's frayed coat by the tails and whirled its owner round three times upon his axis.

"Now catch me!" she shrieked.

"If I *do*--" gasped Mr. Stillbottle, clutching dizzily at the mantelpiece. Further words failed him, and entrenching himself behind a table, he waited like a hunted animal for the further assaults of his enemies.

He was not kept long in suspense. Having armed themselves with the fire-irons, the two affectionate but boisterous infants were upon the point of inaugurating a game of what they called "beat-the-carpet"--it is hardly necessary to specify the rôle assigned to Mr. Stillbottle--when the door opened, revealing the welcome figure of Dicky Mainwaring.

Straightway weapons were thrown down, and the newcomer found himself the centre of a cloud of embraces. Dicky was a prime favourite with children and dogs--no bad test of character, either.

Presently, having shaken himself free from the unmaidenly caresses of the youngest Miss Welwyn, Dicky became aware of the pathetic presence of Mr. Stillbottle.

"Good-morning, Mr. Russell," he said. "You are just the man I want to see."

"You can see me as often and as long as you like, sir," replied the afflicted Russell fervently, "if only you'll put those two imps on the other side of that door."

"Certainly," said Dicky. "Now you two, skedaddle!"

To the amazement and admiration of their late victim the two freebooters departed immediately, merely pausing to receive a valedictory salute from their evictor. Dicky closed the door upon them, and motioning the broker's man to a chair, enquired:--

"Where is everybody this morning, Mr. Russell?"

"My name, in mufti, to my friends," replied the grateful Russell, "is Stillbottle. But you was asking about 'everybody.' Meanin' the Barcelona Troupe of Performing Nuts?"

Dicky nodded.

"Upstairs, most of 'em," said Stillbottle. "All but your little bit. She 'as gone out."

Dicky looked up sharply.

"For long?" he asked.

"I could n't say," replied the broker's man. "Perce has gone to the City. Mother and the little 'un are a-makin' of the beds. The Principal Filbert is still between the sheets. I'm the only member of the cast visible at present. But as you say it's me you came to see, perhaps you'll kindly state your business."

Dicky did so.

A quarter of an hour later he ascended to the drawing-room, restored to its usual aspect of dingy propriety after yesterday's junketings. He noticed that his carnations had disappeared.

Mr. Welwyn was just entering from his bedroom. At the sight of Dicky he started, but recovering himself with his usual readiness, shook hands.

"Good-morning, Mr. Mainwaring," he said. "Be seated."

Dicky complied. "You seem surprised to see me, sir," he said.

"Frankly," replied Mr. Welwyn, "I am. After our treatment of you yesterday I hardly expected you to return. I can only extenuate our performance by assuring you that what looked like a carefully graduated series of insults was nothing more than the logical, if unforeseen, development of a somewhat childish attempt upon our part to delude your family into the impression that our circumstances were not so straitened as, in point of fact, they are. We meant well, but--"

Mr. Welwyn concluded this explanation with a rather helpless gesture. It was an awkward and difficult moment. With all his faults he was a man of feeling, with a gentleman's inherent distaste for anything savouring of sharp practice; and he knew that the boy before him felt the situation as acutely as himself. There are few sadder sights than that of an old man eating humble pie to a young man.

But Dicky, The Freak, was equal to the occasion. He answered gravely:--

"The point of view which I prefer to take, Mr. Welwyn, is this--that you were all trying to do a good turn to Tilly."

"Thank you, Dick," said Mr. Welwyn simply. "Still, there was a second reason which I thought might perhaps keep you away."

"What was that?"

"Well--the presence in one's abode of a sheriff's officer is apt to exercise a dispersive influence upon one's calling acquaintance."

"On this occasion, however," replied Dicky serenely, "you will find that a calling acquaintance has dispersed the sheriff's officer."

Mr. Welwyn, who had been perambulating the room, stopped dead.

"You don't mean to tell me," he exclaimed, "that the fellow is gone?"

Dicky nodded. "Five minutes ago," he said.

"But--I don't understand," muttered the elder man. "Did you *kick* him out? If so, the fat is in the fire with a--"

"He left this behind him," interposed Dicky awkwardly. "Under the circumstances--I took the liberty."

Mr. Welwyn gazed long and silently at the stamped document which lay beneath his eyes. Then he looked up at Dicky and made a movement as if to shake hands; then drew back and bowed, not without dignity.

"Mr. Mainwaring," he said, "I thank you. I will leave it at that. If I possessed a less intimate knowledge of my own character, I should hasten to give utterance to the sentiment which at this moment dominates my mind--namely, a sincere determination never to rest until I have repaid you this sum. But I have not arrived at my present estate without learning that any such impulse on my part would be entirely transitory. From the age of five I can never recollect having formed a single resolution that I was able to keep. I therefore accept your very generous aid without protest or false pride. My wife, of course, would not approve. She comes of a class whose sole criterion of respectability is a laborious solvency during life and an expensive funeral after death. Do not imagine that I am belittling her. She is the one sound investment I ever made. I need not trouble you with the facts of our courtship and marriage; but I will tell you this, my boy, that if a man had real cause to be grateful for and proud of his wife, that man is Lucius Welwyn. And the extraordinary part of it all is that she is proud of me--*me*! Instead of acting like a sensible woman and deploring me as a commercial and domestic liability, she persists in exalting me into a social asset of the first water. I do not attempt to dispel these illusions of hers. In a woman's hands an illusion, after she has fashioned it to the shape that pleases her, hardens into a solid, enduring, and comforting fact. Perhaps, then, things are best as they are. But I cherish no illusions about myself. I know my limits. I am a considerate husband and an affectionate father. My temper, except at times of the severest domestic stringency, is irreproachable; and I find myself generally regarded as good company by my friends. But I am not a worldly success. I take life too easily, perhaps. I allow others to step over my head. I am too ready to stand by and watch the passing show, rather than plunge in and take my part."

The speaker paused, and for a moment his glance rested upon the honest, rather puzzled, but deeply interested eyes of the young man upon the sofa. Suddenly an exposition of candour came upon Mr. Welwyn.

"There was a time," he said in a less buoyant tone, "when these propensities of mine used to distress me. The day I was deprived of my Fellowship, for instance--"

His voice shook suddenly.

"Don't tell me about it, sir, if you would rather not," said Dicky quietly.

"For drunkenness, Mr. Mainwaring--for drunkenness!" burst out Mr. Welwyn. "Not for chronic, sordid soaking--that has never been a foible of mine--but for characteristic inability to do things in their right order. Take warning by me, Dick, and never put the cart before the horse. I had been invited to lecture to a very learned body upon a very special occasion. A successful appearance would have gained me my F.R.S. The natural and proper course for me to pursue was to deliver the lecture first and treat myself to a magnum of champagne afterwards. What I actually did was to treat myself to the magnum of champagne and then deliver the lecture. I may say with all modesty that that lecture caused a profound sensation. It is still quoted--but not in textbooks; and it ended my University career. My life since has been a series of similar incidents--disaster arising from my inherent inability to distinguish between the time to be merry and the time to sing psalms. Still, I keep on smiling. Fortune has not touched me for many years now. Fortune likes fresh blood: once you get used to her she leaves you alone. You see the manner of man I now am--a seasoned philosopher--a man who takes life as it comes--a man who never meets trouble halfway--a man unburdened by the sentimental craving, so prevalent in this hysterical age, to confer unsolicited benefits upon his fellows--a man unhampered at the same time by narrow scruples about accepting, in the spirit in which it is offered, the occasional assistance of his friends. In short, a sane, dispassionate, evenly balanced man of the world, insured against sudden upheaval by a sense of proportion, and against depression of spirits by a sense of humour."

Mr. Welwyn paused again, and there was another silence, punctuated by the rattle of traffic outside. Presently he continued, in yet another mood:--

"Sometimes my point of view changes. I look at myself, and what do I see? An elderly, shabby-genteel inhabitant of Bloomsbury, with not a single memory of the past to fall back on, save that of a youth utterly wasted--a youth hung about with golden opportunities, each and all successively disregarded from a fatuous, childish belief that the supply was inexhaustible--and with nothing to look forward to but a further period of dependence upon a wife who is as much my moral superior as she is my social inferior. An earner of casual guineas--a picker-up of stray newspapers--the recipient of refreshment respectfully proffered by unintellectual but infinitely more worthy associates in bar parlours. A loafer--a waster--a *failure*! That, Mr. Mainwaring, is the father of the girl whom you desire to marry.... I am not what you would call religious, but sometimes the impulse comes upon me--and I obey it forthwith--to go down upon my knees and thank God from the bottom of my heart that my children take after their mother."

The broken scholar dropped wearily into his chair.

"Youth! Youth! Youth! Youth!" he murmured. "Rejoice, O young man, in thy youth!"

His head slipped down between his hands.

Dicky, curiously stirred, attempted to say some word, but nothing came.

Suddenly Mr. Welwyn sprang to his feet. The cloud had lifted, or else pride had come to the rescue. It is often difficult to tell which.

"Dick," he said, "I perceive from your attitude that you are about to be sympathetic. Don't! Sympathy is wasted on me. In five minutes from now this mood will have passed. In half an hour I shall be as happy as an ostrich with its head in the sand. That has been my lifelong posture, and a very comfortable posture, too, once you get used to it! It is only when one comes up to breathe that things hurt a bit. Now, if you will excuse me, I must go out. I have had a letter this morning offering me some exceedingly welcome and possibly permanent work. I do not know where Tilly is, but she should be in presently. I do not ask what your business with her may be. I have no right--and no need."

The two men shook hands.

"Good-bye, dear Dick," said Mr. Welwyn, "and thank you for the very unobtrusive manner in which you have helped a lame dog over a stile."

Next moment the door closed, and he was gone.

"We are queer mixtures," mused philosophic Dicky.... "I wonder where Tilly is!"

———

Five minutes later the drawing-room door opened again, this time to admit little 'Melia. She paused and drew back, at the spectacle of her late ally sprawling at ease before the scanty fire.

"Hallo, 'Melia!" said Dicky cheerfully.

"Hallo!" replied Amelia cautiously. "Have you come to--see mother?"

"Not to-day, thank you," said Dicky. He regarded the little girl curiously. "I say, 'Melia, have I offended you in any way?"

"You? Me? No!" replied Amelia, in wide-eyed surprise. "Why?"

Dicky smiled coyly.

"There used to be a pleasant little form of greeting," he intimated.

"You still want to?" cried 'Melia in a flutter.

"Please."

Next moment Miss Amelia Welwyn, feeling that the bottom had not dropped out of the universe after all, was giving Mr. Richard Mainwaring a kiss.

"Where is Tilly this morning?" asked Dicky carelessly.

"Gone out," said Amelia--"to look for a job. She gave up the other one when she got--engaged."

"I see," said Dicky, nodding his head.

"I suppose you have come to break it off," continued the experienced Amelia. "They all said last night you were bound to do it, after what had happened."

"That sort of thing," explained Dicky, "is done for one by one's parents, I believe. I am rather young, you see," he added apologetically.

He rose, gently displacing his small admirer from his knee.

"Now I must be off," he said. "Give this to Tilly for me, will you?"

Amelia was still twisting and turning the letter in her hands when the bang of the front door signalled Dicky's departure.

"If his parents are going to break it off for him," said Amelia to herself in a puzzled whisper, "what does he want to go writing to her for?"

CHAPTER XXIV
A GARDEN PLOT IN RUSSELL SQUARE

Outside, leaning contentedly against the railings of the garden opposite to the Maison Welwyn, and enjoying the spring sunshine, Dicky encountered the Carmyles.

"Hallo, you two!" he said. "What are you doing here? Liable to get run in for loitering, hanging about like this."

"We have followed you, Dicky," began Connie rapidly, "to tell you that your mother is coming up to town, and--"

"Mother--already?"

Connie nodded.

"Fourth speed in," confirmed Mr. Carmyle. "Live axle--direct drive--open exhaust."

"Trailing your father behind her," added Connie. "I understand you had an interview with them this morning."

The Freak gave a wry smile.

"I did," he said. "It was rather a heated interview, I'm afraid. Words passed. But we can't stand here dodging taxis. Come into the garden, Maud!"

"Don't we require a key?" enquired the re-christened Connie, surveying the iron railings which enclosed the Bloomsbury Eden.

"I have one," said Dicky. "It belongs to the Welwyns. Tilly and I used to use it a good deal," he explained, in a subdued voice.

He led the way into the dingy but romantic pleasance which had sheltered himself and his beloved, and the trio sat down upon a damp seat. Mrs. Carmyle, looking rather like one of the sparrows which hopped inquisitively about her daintily shod feet, established herself between her two large companions. Her husband, who was a creature of homely instincts, hung his silk hat upon an adjacent bough with a sigh of content, and began to fill a large briar pipe. Dicky, a prey to melancholy, kicked the grass with his heels.

"Where is Tilly this morning?" asked Connie.

"Gone out--to look for a job!" replied Dicky through his clenched teeth. "Just as if a snug home and the life of a lady were things she had never dreamed of!" His eyes blazed. "Great Heavens, Connie--the pluck of the child! What a brute it makes me feel!"

Connie patted his hand maternally, but said nothing. There was nothing to say. Presently Dicky continued, in a more even voice:--

"So my mother is coming up this morning--to strike while the iron is hot--eh?"

"'To make a direct appeal to Miss Welwyn's better nature,' was what she *said*," replied Mrs. Carmyle cautiously.

"I am afraid there will be a bit of a scrap," said Dicky thoughtfully. "My dear mother's normal attitude towards her fellow-creatures is that of a righteous person compelled to travel third-class with a first-class ticket; but when she goes on the warpath into the bargain--well, that is where I take cover."

"She'll roll the Welwyns out flat," observed Mr. Carmyle, with that conviction which only painful experience can instill.

"She won't roll Tilly out flat," said Dicky.

"Nor Mrs. Welwyn either," added Connie; "so kindly refrain from putting in your oar, Bill! We are n't all terrified of Lady Adela. *Cowardy, cowardy, cus--*"

Mr. Carmyle, flushing with shame, abruptly invited his small oppressor to switch off; and Dicky proceeded to review the situation.

"I don't think my dear parent will get much change out of any of the Welwyns," he said. "They are a fairly competent lot. Moreover, they have burned their boats and have nothing to lose; so I expect there will be some very pretty work. My lady mother is an undoubted champion in her class, I admit, but she has got a bit out of condition lately. Managing Dad and harrying the County are n't really sufficient to keep a woman of her fighting-weight up to the mark. Still, I don't particularly want her big guns let loose on Tilly."

"Tilly has gone out for the day, I suppose?" said Connie.

"So I was told. But how did you guess?"

Connie Carmyle flapped her small hands despairingly.

"Oh, what creatures!" she cried, apparently apostrophising the male sex in general. "Can't you understand anything or anybody--not even the girl you love? Of course, she is out for the day; and if you go there to-morrow she will be out for the day, too!"

"Why?" asked Dicky blankly.

"Yes--why?" echoed that sympathetic but obtuse Philistine, Bill Carmyle.

His wife turned upon him like lightning.

"Bill," she said, "keep perfectly quiet, or I shall send you off to meet Lady Adela's train at Waterloo! I want to talk to Dicky. Now, Dicky, listen to me. That little girl"--Connie's eyes grew suddenly tender, for she loved her sex--"cares for you, old man--quite a lot. Quite enough, in fact, to draw back if she thinks she is going to stand in your way during life. That pathetic little fraud of a tea-party yesterday has set her thinking. She has suddenly realised that although she might *get* you by false pretences, she could not *keep* you by false pretences--nor want to. She has also realised that her Family are impossible. That means that she will have to give up either you or the Family. And you are the one she will give up, Dicky. She loves you too much to pull you down to their level. She won't give that as her reason--women are built like that--but she will give you up, all the same."

The usually placid Dicky had grown excessively agitated during this homily.

"Connie," he burst out, "for goodness' sake don't try to frighten me like that! Tilly's Family are not impossible. They 're only a bit improbable. And besides, talking of impossible families, look at mine! Do you know who my grandfather was? He was a Lancashire cotton operative--a hand in a mill. He invented something--a shuttle, or a bobbin, or something of that kind--and made a fortune out of it. He ultimately died worth a hundred thousand pounds; but to the end of his days he dined without his coat, and, if he could possibly escape detection, without his collar either. I never saw him, but my Dad says he was a dear old chap, and I can quite believe it. As a father-in-law he was a sore trial to my poor mother, whose ancestors had worn their collars at meals for quite a considerable period; but the hundred thousand overcame her susceptibilities in the end, and she and Dad have lived happily ever since."

Dicky rose restlessly to his feet, and continued his address standing.

"Now I think," he said, "that we can set my grandfather, cotton operative, against the late lamented Banks, plumber and gas-fitter. Banks, of course, was the bigger man socially--you know how plumbers get asked simply *everywhere*--but Mainwaring's son married the daughter of an Earl; so we will call them quits. Anyway, Tilly is quite as good as I am--miles better, in fact."

"Dear Dicky!" murmured Connie approvingly. Here was a lover of the right metal.

"What about friend Perce?" enquired a gruff voice.

It was a telling question. If Dicky could clothe such an uncompromising fact as Percy Welwyn in a garment of romance, he was capable of making a success of any marriage. Mr. Carmyle waited grimly for his answer.

"Ah--Percy!" replied Dicky thoughtfully. "Yes, Tiny, old soul, that's a sound question. Well, Percy is n't exactly polished--in fact, one might almost be forgiven for describing him as a holy terror--"

"He wants losing," said Carmyle with conviction.

"But listen," pursued Dicky. "Percy may be all we say, but he cheerfully hands over half his weekly screw, which is n't a fabulous one, to the common fund of the Family. It is not every young man who would do that, especially such a social success as Percy. Oh, yes, Connie, he is a social success; so don't look incredulous. I tell you he is a regular Apollo at shilling hops. He took me to one a few weeks ago."

"Where?" asked Connie.

"Somewhere near Kennington Oval. The girls simply swarmed over him. But he is not in the least stuck up about it; and--well, he is kind to Tilly. I am, therefore," concluded Dicky stoutly, "an upholder of Percy."

Mr. Carmyle, encouraged by the silence of his wife, felt emboldened to continue his cross-examination.

"What about mother-in-law?" he queried.

It was a foolish question.

"She is a woman in a thousand," said Dicky promptly, and Mrs. Carmyle, with a withering side-glance at her unfortunate lord, nodded her head vigorously in affirmation.

"Mrs. Welwyn is not what we call a lady," proceeded Dicky, "but she is the right stuff all through. I admit that she has not been quite successful in her efforts to polish Percy, but look at the others! The little sister, 'Melia, is a dear. The twins are rippers. Old Welwyn--well, he's a rotter, but he's a gentlemanly rotter; which pretty well describes the majority of my friends, now I come to think of it. And he is no hypocrite: he is quite frank about his weaknesses. Now, to sum up. On her father's side Tilly is a lady; on her mother's side she is a brick. That's a pretty good combination. Anyhow, it's good enough for me; and if she'll have me I'm going to marry her."

Dicky concluded the unburdening of his soul with a shout and a wave of his hat, and all the sparrows flew away.

"Now," said Connie, patting the seat in a soothing fashion, "sit down and tell me how you are going to do it."

Dicky resumed his place beside her and said meekly:--

"I'm looking to you to tell me that, Connie."

Apparently he had made the remark that was expected of him, for Connie immediately assumed a little air of profound wisdom, and her unregenerate husband emitted an unseemly gurgle.

"Your first difficulty, of course," she said to Dicky, ignoring her wretched and ill-controlled spouse, "will be to see Tilly. After the humiliation of yesterday her only instinct will be to hide herself. She will be not-at-home to you every time you call; and of course, it is n't fair that you should hang about in the hopes of catching her outside."

"No," agreed Dicky. "Not the game."

"You have written to her, I suppose?" said Connie.

"Yes. Left a note this morning," replied Dicky, brightening up.

"Well, of course, that is no use. It will make her happier, poor little soul, but it won't change her decision. Letters never do. You've simply got to see her, Dicky! Bill, run away for a minute, there's a dear. Go and think about a cantilever, or something, over there."

Mr. Carmyle, puffing smoke, obediently withdrew to the other side of a clump of sooty rhododendrons. Connie turned eagerly to Dicky. Her face was flushed and eager, like a child's.

"Dicky," she whispered earnestly, "*see* her! *See* her! See her alone! Take her in your arms and tell her that you will never, never, never let her go! She will struggle and try to break away; but hold on. Hold on tight! Go on telling her that you love her and will never leave her. When she sees that you mean it, she will give in. I know. I'm a woman, and I know!" Connie squeezed Dicky's arm violently. "I *know*!" she repeated.... "You can come back now, Bill dear."

"Nice goings-on, I don't think," observed Mr. Carmyle severely, reappearing round the rhododendron. "Shouting all over the garden--what?"

But the two conspirators, still in the clouds together, took no notice of him. Instead, Connie rose to her feet and began to walk towards the nearest gate. The two men followed.

"Connie, how am I going to do it?" asked Dicky deferentially.

"I have a plan," replied Connie, with portentous solemnity. She was launched on an enterprise after her own heart. "Listen! Have you a portmanteau?"

"Yes, at my rooms."

"Well, go there and pack it."

"Why?" asked Dicky in a dazed voice.

Mrs. Carmyle replied by quoting a famous and oracular phrase which had lately fallen from the lips of a prominent statesman, and the party reached the railings.

"Hallo, there's a taxi at the Welwyns' door," said Carmyle. "I wonder--oh, Lord!"

He fell hastily to the rear, his knees knocking together. Two figures were ascending the steps of the house. One was majestic and purposeful; the other small and reluctant. The front door opened and closed upon them.

"My mother--already!" exclaimed Dicky in dismay.

That burned child, William Carmyle, broke into a gentle perspiration.

"Never mind," said Connie reassuringly. "She was bound to come. She can't do any harm."

"Supposing she gets Tilly to agree never to see me again?" said Dicky feverishly. "Supposing she insults her with money?" He ground his teeth, and Carmyle groaned sympathetically.

Connie patted his arm soothingly.

"The last word is the only thing that matters in this case," she said with great confidence; "and you are going to have that, Dicky, my friend. Now, run away and pack your portmanteau. Then come and lunch with us at Prince's. I must fly. I have an appointment with a gentleman at Russell Square Tube Station at twelve-thirty. It is after that now."

Dicky glanced at Bill Carmyle for an explanation of this mysterious assignation, but that gentleman merely shook his head in a bewildered fashion.

"Don't ask me, old man," he said.

"Who is the gentleman, Connie?" Dicky enquired.

"An admirer of mine," replied Mrs. Carmyle, with a gratified smile. "I met him in the train this morning."

"For the first time?"

"No--second. When I saw him I had an idea, so we arranged to meet again at twelve-thirty. He has another engagement, but he said it did n't matter when I asked him. After he has done what I want, he is coming to lunch, too. Now run and pack. Au revoir!"

Revelling in every turn of the highly complicated plot which she was weaving, little Mrs. Carmyle, followed by her inarticulate but inflated husband, pattered swiftly away round the corner--and incidentally out of this narrative--turning to wave a reassuring hand to her client before disappearing.

The Freak, puzzled but confident, went home to pack his portmanteau.

CHAPTER XXV
PURELY COMMERCIAL

I

"Well," said Mrs. Welwyn, taking off her apron, "the beds are done, anyway. One less to make," she added philosophically, "now that Pumpherston has hopped it. That's something."

"We could do with the rent of his room for all that, Mother," commented practical Amelia.

"That's true, dearie," sighed Mrs. Welwyn. "Well, perhaps we shall get another lodger. Where's your father, by the way?"

"He went out half an hour ago. I expect he's at the Museum."

"Did Mr. Dick see him?"

"I don't know."

"And Mr. Dick said he did n't want to see me?" Mrs. Welwyn spoke rather wistfully.

"That was what he said," admitted 'Melia in a respectful tone.

"I don't suppose he's very anxious to see any of us much," said Mrs. Welwyn candidly. "We must just get the idea out of our heads, that's all. Forget it! Then, there's that broker's insect. We are going to get *him* paid off double-quick, or I 'm a Dutchman. I don't know how it's going to be done. Still, we have got round worse corners than this, have n't we, duckie?"

"Yes, Mother," said Amelia bravely.

Martha Welwyn suddenly flung her arms round her little daughter.

"My precious," she whispered impulsively, "I would n't mind if it was n't for you children." Her voice broke. "God pity women!"

"Mother, Mother!" cried little 'Melia reprovingly. "That's not like you!" And she hugged her tearful but contrite parent back to cheerfulness again.

A door banged downstairs, and the two fell apart guiltily.

"That's Tilly," said Mrs. Welwyn. "We must n't be downhearted, or she'll scold us. Bustle about!"

With great vigour and presence of mind this excellent woman snatched the cloth off the table and shook it severely. Amelia, having hastily removed a tear from her mother's cheek with a duster, opened the piano and began to wipe down the keys, to the accompaniment of an inharmonious chromatic scale.

The door flew open and Tilly marched in, humming a cheerful air.

"Such luck, Mother!" she cried.

For a moment Martha Welwyn was deceived. She whirled round excitedly.

"What do you mean, dearie?" she exclaimed.

"I've got a berth--with Madame Amelie--old Mrs. Crump, you know--in Earl's Court Road. One of her girls is leaving--"

"Got the sack?" enquired Mrs. Welwyn, rearranging the tablecloth.

"No. She's only"--Tilly's voice quavered ever so slightly--"going to be married. I've got her place, and I 'm once more an independent lady."

"That's capital news, Tilly," said Mrs. Welwyn heartily. At any rate, her daughter would have something to occupy her mind.

"Now the next thing to do," proceeded Tilly with great animation, "is to get rid of the broker's man. We ought to be able to raise the money all right. I'm at work again. Dad has had an offer of newspaper articles; and if only we can get Mr. Pumpherston's room let--"

"The broker's man has gone, Sis," said Amelia.

"Gone?" cried Tilly and Mrs. Welwyn in a breath.

"Well, gone out, anyhow. I saw him shuffling across the Square half an hour ago."

"My lord will find the chain up when he comes back," said Mrs. Welwyn grimly.

"Still, we must find the money," persisted Tilly. "We have never been in debt yet, and we are never going to be." Her slight figure stiffened proudly. "Independence! That's the only thing worth having in this world. Be independent! Owe nothing to nobody!"

Certainly, whether she derived it from her father's ancestry or her mother's solid worth, Tilly Welwyn was composed of good fibre. With flushed cheeks and unnaturally bright eyes she turned to the mirror over the drawing-room mantelpiece and began to take off her hat.

"It's a mystery to me," ruminated the puzzled Mrs. Welwyn, "why that creature went out. He must have known we would n't let him in again."

"Perhaps Dicky kicked him out," suggested that small hero-worshipper, Amelia, with relish.

Tilly turned sharply.

"Who?" she asked. A hatpin tinkled into the fender.

Little 'Melia bit her lip, and turned scarlet.

"Mr. Dick, dearie," said Mrs. Welwyn, coming to the rescue. "He looked in this morning."

"What for?" asked Tilly, groping for the hatpin.

"I don't know. I did n't see him," admitted her mother reluctantly.

"I do," said 'Melia, having decided to get things over at once. "He left a letter for you, Sis."

Tilly rose to her feet again, keeping her back to her audience.

"Where is it?" she enquired unsteadily.

"Here," said Amelia, with a hand in the pocket of her pinafore.

"Put it on the table," said Tilly, standing on tiptoe while she patted her brown hair into position before the glass. "I'll read it presently."

"There's the front-door bell!" said Mrs. Welwyn nervously. "What are we to do if it's Russell again?"

"Lock the door," said Amelia promptly.

"I don't know, I'm sure," said Mrs. Welwyn doubtfully. "I wonder what the law is. I wish Daddy was in." She considered, perplexed. "Anyhow, I'll go down and see. Come with me, 'Melia," she added tactfully.

The pair slipped out of the room and went downstairs, leaving Tilly alone with her letter.

"Supposing he rushes in the moment we open the door?" whispered Amelia, as they consulted on the mat. "What then?"

"We'll put the chain up first, and then open the door a crack," said Mrs. Welwyn.

This procedure was adopted, with the result that Mr. Mainwaring and Lady Adela, waiting patiently upon the steps outside, were eventually confronted, after certain mysterious clankings had taken place within, with a vision of two apprehensive countenances, one childish and the other middle-aged, set one upon another against a black background in a frame eight feet high and three inches wide. It was but a glimpse, for the vision was hardly embodied when it faded from view with uncanny suddenness: and after a further fantasia upon the chain, the door was tugged open, to reveal the shrinking figures of Mrs. Welwyn and Amelia.

"Good-morning, Mrs. Welwyn," said Lady Adela. "I hope you will forgive this early call, but we are anxious to have a talk with--er--Miss Welwyn."

Miss Welwyn's agitated parent ushered the visitors into the dining-room, bidding Amelia run upstairs and give warning of the coming interview. Resistance did not occur to her.

Amelia found her sister sitting motionless on the edge of a chair, with her arms upon the table. In her hands she held an open letter, which she was not reading. Her grey eyes, wide open, unblinking, were fixed on vacancy. Her lips moved, as if repeating some formula.

Amelia touched her softly on the arm.

"Tilly," she whispered, "they want to see you."

Tilly roused herself.

"Who?" she asked dreamily.

The question was answered by the appearance in the doorway of Lady Adela, followed by her husband. Tilly rose, thrust the letter into her belt, and greeted her visitors.

"How do you do?" she said mechanically. "Won't you sit down?"

Lady Adela, singling out that well-tried friend of yesterday, the sofa, sank down upon it. Mr. Mainwaring remained standing behind. Little 'Melia, after one sympathetic glance in the direction of her sister, gently closed the door and joined her mother on the landing outside.

"'Melia," announced that harassed châtelaine, "there's the front door again! It must be Stillbottle this time. Supposing he meets *them*?"

"It don't signify if he does," replied her shrewd little daughter. "They have met once already. Still, we may as well keep him out."

Mother and daughter accordingly proceeded to a repetition of their previous performance with the door-chain. As before, the front door was ultimately flung open with abject expressions of regret.

On the steps stood a small, sturdy, spectacled young clergyman.

"Oh, good-morning," he exclaimed. "I am so sorry to trouble you, but I have been asked by a friend to look at your vacant room. Might I do it now?"

This was familiar ground, and Mrs. Welwyn escorted the stranger upstairs with a sigh of relief.

"My friend proposes to move in almost immediately," explained Mr. Rylands, mounting at a distressingly rapid pace, "if they are satisfactory. That is--of course"--he added in a panic--"I am sure they will be satisfactory. But my friend proposes to move in at once."

His approval of the late lair of the bellicose Pumpherston when--almost before--the panting Mrs. Welwyn had pulled up the blind and unveiled its glories, erred on the side of the ecstatic. The terms asked for the dingy but speckless apartment were not excessive, and Mr. Rylands agreed to them at once.

"May I ask, sir," enquired Mrs. Welwyn, as they descended the staircase--"did some one recommend us? We like to know who our friends are."

Mr. Rylands was quite prepared for this question.

"As a matter of fact," he explained volubly, "I believe the gentleman saw the card in the window; and being particularly fond of Russell Square, and--and its associations, and so on, he decided to come and reside here. He will send his luggage round this afternoon."

By this time they had passed the closed drawing-room door and were in the hall again.

"Will you give me the gentleman's name, sir, please?" asked Mrs. Welwyn, in obedience to a reminding gleam in the eye of her small daughter, who was standing full in the open doorway, apparently with the intention of collaring Mr. Rylands low. "I suppose he can give a reference, or pay a week in advance? That's our usual--"

"Certainly, by all means," said Rylands hurriedly. Like most men, he found it almost as delicate and embarrassing an undertaking to discuss money matters with a woman as to make love to her. "In point of fact," he continued, searching furtively in his pocket, "my friend would like to pay a month in advance. He is anxious to make quite sure of the rooms, so--oh, I beg your pardon!" (This to little 'Melia, into whom he had cannoned heavily in a misguided but characteristic attempt to walk out of the house backwards.) "*Good*-morning!"

And the Reverend Godfrey Rylands, thrusting a warm bank-note into Mrs. Welwyn's palm, stumbled down the steps into the Square, and set off at a most unclerical pace in the direction of Piccadilly. He was going to lunch, it will be remembered, with Connie Carmyle.

"He never left the new lodger's name," recollected Mrs. Welwyn, too late.

"No, but he left a five-pound note," said practical Amelia.

II

Meanwhile, upstairs, Lady Adela was concluding a stately and well-balanced harangue. Of her two auditors Mr. Mainwaring appeared to be paying more attention. He looked supremely unhappy.

Tilly sat bolt upright on a hard chair, staring straight through Lady Adela at the opposite wall. Occasionally her hand stole to her belt. It is regrettable to have to add, in the interests of strict veracity, that the greater part of Lady Adela's carefully reasoned and studiously moderate address was flowing in at one ear and out at the other. Tilly had no clear idea that she was being spoken to; she was only vaguely conscious that any one was speaking at all. All her thoughts were concentrated on the last page of Dicky's letter--all she had read so far. She sat quite still, occasionally nodding intelligently to put her visitors at their ease. Once or twice her lips moved, as if repeating some formula.

"Do not imagine, Miss Welwyn," Lady Adela was saying, "that we are in any way angry or resentful at what has occurred. We are merely grieved, but at the same time *relieved*. So far from wishing you ill in consequence of this attempt upon your part to--to better yourself, my husband and I are here to offer to do something for you. You must not think that we want to be unkind or harsh. This is a difficult and painful interview for both of us--"

"For all of us, Miss Welwyn," murmured Mr. Mainwaring.

"You appreciate that fact, I hope, Miss Welwyn," said Lady Adela in a slightly louder tone; for the girl made no sign.

Tilly nodded her head absently.

"He loves me! He loves me!" she murmured to herself. "He loves me still!"

Lady Adela ploughed on. She was a kindly woman, and in her heart she felt sorry for Tilly. Not that this fact assisted her to understand Tilly's point of view, or to remember what Dicky had never forgotten, namely, that the girl before her was a lady. She laboured, too, under a grievous disadvantage. Deep feeling was to her a thing unknown. She had never thrilled with tremulous rapture. The sighing of a wounded spirit had no meaning for her. Her heart was a well-regulated and rhythmatic organ, and had always beaten in accordance with the laws of what its owner called common sense. It had never fluttered or stood still.

Lady Adela had married her husband because he was rich and she was the youngest daughter of a great but impoverished house; and after the singular but ineradicable habit of her sex, she had founded her entire conception of life upon her own experience of it. To her, marriage was a matter neither of romance nor affinity. It was a contract: a sacred contract, perhaps,--in her own case it had even been fully choral,--but a mere matter of business for all that. To her, her son's ideal bride was a well-bred young woman with the same tastes and social circle as himself, and possibly a little money of her own. It had never occurred to her that Love contained any other elements. Accordingly she ploughed on; trying to be fair; quite prepared to be generous. She offered to "advance" Tilly in life. She talked vaguely of setting her up "in a little business." She remarked several times that she was anxious to do the right thing, adding as in duty bound that certain conditions would be attached to any arrangement which might be made, "the nature of which you can probably imagine for yourself, my dear." She begged Tilly to think things over, and assured her that no reasonable request would be refused. Altogether Lady Adela's was a very conciliatory and well-balanced proposition. Had it been made by an encroaching railway company to a landed proprietor in compensation for compulsory ejection from his property, or by a repentant motorist to an irate henwife, it might fairly have been regarded as a model of justice and equity. As a scheme for snatching an amiable but weak-minded young man from the clutches of a designing harpy, it erred if anything on the side of generosity. But as a tactful attempt to convey to a young girl the information that she could never marry the man she loved, it was a piece of gross brutality. But Lady Adela did not know this.

Fortunately Tilly heard little or nothing. Occasionally a stray sentence focused itself on her mind. "My husband and I communicated our views to our son this morning," was one. "Impart our decision *ourselves* ... avoid the necessity of a painful interview ... unnecessary correspondence," and the like--the disconnected phrases fell upon her ears; but throughout it all the girl sat with her head in the clouds, fingering her letter and hugging her secret. Once Lady Adela, in a flight of oratory, half-rose from her seat. Tilly, with a vague hope that the call was over, put out a hand, which was ignored.

But the interview came to an end at last; and Lady Adela, conscious of a difficult task adequately and tactfully performed, but secretly troubled by Tilly's continuous apathy, rose to her feet. Tilly mechanically stood up, too.

"Good-morning, Miss Welwyn," said Lady Adela, offering her hand. "We have to thank you for a patient hearing."

Tilly smiled politely, shook hands, but said nothing. Mr. Mainwaring, his heart sore for the girl, timidly signalled to his wife to leave her in peace.

"Do not trouble to show us out," said Lady Adela; and departed imposingly through the door.

With a long sigh of relief Tilly dropped back into her seat. Suddenly she was aware that she was not yet alone. Mr. Mainwaring had lingered in the room. He came forward now, and took the girl's hand in both of his.

"My dear, my dear!" he said quickly. "I wish you were my daughter. God give you a good husband!"

There was an ominous cough upon the landing outside; and the old gentleman, recalled to a sense of duty, trotted obediently out of the room, closing the door behind him.

Tilly snatched the letter from her belt.

"He loves me!" she murmured. "He loves me! He loves me still!"

She was not referring to Mr. Mainwaring senior.

CHAPTER XXVI
THE FINAL FREAK

Tilly finished writing her letter, signed and addressed it, and leaned back in her chair.

She had just declined to marry Dicky Mainwaring.

"That's done, anyhow," she said to herself, with the instinctive cheerfulness of those who are born plucky. "Now I'll go out and post it before the Family come home, and then perhaps a little walk round Bloomsbury will give me an appetite for tea." But as Tilly rose briskly to her feet her eye fell upon the letter from Dicky, lying beside the answer to it which she had just written. For the tenth time she picked it up and re-read certain passages.

I don't think I ever loved you as I did yesterday afternoon. As I watched you fighting that brave, uphill battle of yours in the face of the most awful odds--Mother and Sylvia are awfully odd, you know--I suddenly realised how utterly and entirely I had become part of you--or you of me, if you like. I was on your side in that plucky, preposterous, transparent little conspiracy from start to finish, and when the crash came I think I was harder hit than anybody. The only complaint I have to make is that you did not take me into your confidence. I could have put you up to one or two tips which might have made all the difference--you see, I have known Mother and Sylvia longer than you have--and we could have enjoyed the fruits of victory together. Still, I forgive you for your obstinacy in trying to put the enterprise through single-handed. It was very characteristic of you, and anything that is characteristic of you is naturally extra precious to me. So don't imagine that yesterday's little interparental unpleasantness is going to make any difference to you and me--to You and Me!

"To You--and Me!" echoed Tilly softly.

... You will probably receive a call from my esteemed parents. They mean well, but I mistrust their judgment. They will probably intimate that we must never see one another again, or something of that kind. I am afraid it is just possible that my dear old mother will offer you compensation, of a sort. If she does, try to forgive her. She does not understand. Not at present, that is. One day she will laugh at herself--which will establish a record--and apologise to you for having entertained the idea.

"No, she won't!" observed Tilly at this point.

... It seems ridiculous, does n't it, that any one should seriously set out to appeal to you to "abandon your demands" upon me? As if things were not entirely the other way. It is I who am making demands upon you, dearest. The idea! To lecture you as if you were some designing little adventuress, instead of the most wonderful worker of miracles that ever lived--the girl who made bricks without straw--the girl who made a man of Dicky Mainwaring!

... So do not be afraid with any amazement--do you know where that quotation comes from?--at anything my mother may say. She will probably pile on the agony a bit about the various kinds of trouble that await a couple who marry out of different social circles, and punk of that kind. She is a dear thing, my old mother, but very feminine. When she wants to argue about anything she always begins by begging the question. Besides, our love is big enough to square any circle, social or otherwise. So don't you worry, little girl. Leave things to me, and--

Tilly read more slowly and yet more slowly, and then stopped reading altogether. Then she rose slowly to her feet, crossed the room, and stood gazing into the fire. She did not know what begging the question meant, but she had other food for reflection. Connie Carmyle was right. When it comes to a pinch, letters are useless things, and being useless are, more often than not, dangerous.

On the mantelpiece stood two framed photographs--one of Tilly, the other of Dicky. The original of the first addressed the second.

"I wish you had n't put in that last bit, Dicky dear ... 'Abandon my demands' ... 'A little adventuress.' ... That's what I am, when all is said and done. A little adventuress, trying to better herself! Lady Adela is right and we were wrong. What else could you think of me, Dicky, once you married me and found me out--a silly, hysterical, common little chit? ... There's your letter, dear. I dare say I could have got quite a lot for it in a court of law; but some adventuresses are n't up to sample. They have no spirit."

Dicky's much-read epistle dropped into the flames, and Tilly turned with sudden briskness from her lover's photograph to her own.

"As for you, Tilly Welwyn," she observed severely, "just remember that you are only an ordinary, hard-working, matter-of-fact little London work-girl. You can put all fancy notions about fairy princes and happy-ever-after out of your head. You are getting a big girl now, you know. You must live your life and go your own way; and sometimes--only sometimes, mind!--when you are feeling downhearted and up against it, I'll allow you to let your thoughts go back to the best man that ever walked; and although you may cry a bit, you will thank God you did not spoil his life by marrying him."

The doors leading onto the landing creaked, and Amelia peeped cautiously in. Tilly started guiltily. None of us like to be caught talking to ourselves. The habit savours of exclusiveness--and other things.

"Tilly dear," said little 'Melia listlessly, "the new lodger has come with his luggage. Could you give him a hand with it? Everybody is out, and it's rather heavy for me."

"All right," said Tilly readily. "I'll be down in half a minute."

Amelia disappeared, leaving the doors open; and Tilly hastily assumed a business-like yet hospitable expression, suitable for the welcoming of a second-floor.

"One thing more, though, my girl," she remarked sternly, releasing her features for a moment in order to address her own reflection in the overmantle mirror. "Just remember that this will require a real *effort*. It's all very well to feel heroic just now, and talk about giving him up, and living your own life, and so on; but it won't be easy. You will have to put your back into it. Supposing you meet him in the street one day? What then? Can you walk past him? You know you are as weak as water where he is concerned. What are you going to do about it?"

Tilly met her own eyes in the glass, and looked very determined. The eyes in the glass responded by filling with tears. Tilly turned away impatiently from this disloyal exhibition.

"Very well, then," she said. "If you are as weak as that about it, you must just make up your mind to *avoid* him--that's all. There's nothing else for it. You must never see him again.... And I love him so!" she added inconsequently.... "Poor Tilly!"

Little 'Melia appeared in the doorway again.

"He's bringing up his portmanteau," she announced breathlessly, and vanished.

Tilly turned towards the door. Laborious steps were audible upon the staircase, as of one ascending with a heavy load. Presently a man in a great-coat passed the open doorway. On his left shoulder he carried a large portmanteau, which hid his face. He passed up the second-floor staircase and out of sight.

Tilly, hot and cold by turns, stood shaking in the middle of the floor.

There was a bump overhead. Then steps descending, slowly. He was coming back.

Tilly shut her eyes tight for a full half-minute; then opened them and tottered forward with a cry.

In the doorway--laughing, joyous, open-armed--stood The Freak.

"You foolish, foolish Tilly!" he said; and caught her as she fell.

The Right Stuff, Some Episodes in the Career of a North Briton

CHAPTER ONE.
OATMEAL AND THE SHORTER CATECHISM.

The first and most-serious-but-one ordeal in the life of Robert Chalmers Fordyce—so Robert Chalmers himself informed me years afterwards—was the examination for the Bursary which he gained at Edinburgh University. A bursary is what an English undergraduate would call a "Schol." (Imagine a Scottish student talking about a "Burse"!)

Robert Chalmers Fordyce arrived in Edinburgh pretty evenly divided between helpless stupefaction at the sight of a great city and stern determination not to be imposed upon by the inhabitants thereof. His fears were not as deep-seated as those of Tom Pinch on a similar occasion,—he, it will be remembered, suffered severe qualms from his familiarity with certain rural traditions concerning the composition of London pies,—but he was far from happy. He had never slept away from his native hillside before; he had never seen a town possessing more than three thousand inhabitants; and he had only once travelled in a train.

Moreover, he was proceeding to an inquisition which would decide once and for all whether he was to go forth and conquer the world with a university education behind him, or go back to the plough and sup porridge for the rest of his life. To-morrow he was to have his opportunity, and the consideration of how that opportunity could best be gripped and brought to the ground blinded Robin even to the wonders of the Forth Bridge.

He sat in the corner of the railway carriage, passing in review the means of conquest at his disposal. His actual stock of scholarship, he knew, was well up to the required standard: he was as letter perfect in Latin, Greek, Mathematics, and Literature as hard study and remorseless coaching could make him. Everything needful was in his head—but could he get it out again? That was the question. The roaring world in which he would find himself, the strange examination-room, the quizzing professors—would these combine with his native shyness to seal the lips and cramp the pen of Robert Chalmers Fordyce? No—a thousand times no! He would win through! Robert set his teeth, braced himself, and kicked the man opposite.

He apologised, attributing the discourtesy to the length of his legs—he stood about six feet three—and smiled so largely and benignantly, that the Man Opposite, who had intended to be thoroughly disagreeable, melted at once, and said it was the fault of the Company for providing such restricted accommodation, and gave Robert *The Scotsman* to read.

Robert thanked him, and, effacing himself behind *The Scotsman*,—though, for all the instruction or edification that his present frame of mind permitted him to extract from that coping-stone of Scottish journalism, he might as well have been reading the Koran,—returned to his thoughts. He collated in his mind the pieces of advice which had been bestowed upon him by his elders and betters before his departure. In brief, their collective wisdom came to this:—

His father had bidden him—

- (a) To address all professors with whom he might come in contact as "Sir";
- (b) To arrive at the Examination each morning at least five minutes before the advertised time;
- (c) To refrain from lending money to, or otherwise countenancing the advances of, persons of insinuating address who would doubtless accost him in the streets of Edinburgh.

The Dominie had said—

"When in doubt, mind that practically everything in an examination governs the subjunctive.

"If there is a *viva voce*, be sure and speak up and give your answers as though you were sure of them. They may be wrong, but on the other hand they may be right. Anyway, the one thing the examiners will not thole is a body that dithers.

"Take a last keek at that Proposition—they *may* call them Theorems, though—about the Square on the Hypotenuse. It hasn't been set for four years.

"If you are given a piece of Greek Testament to translate, for mercy's sake do not be too glib. Dinna translate a thing until you are sure it is there. They have an unholy habit of leaving out a couple of verses some place in the middle, and you're just the one to tumble head-first into the *lacuna*. (I ken ye, Robbie!)

"And whatever ye do, just bear in mind it's your only chance, and *grup* on tae it! *Post est occasio calva*, laddie! And dinna disappoint an auld man that has taught ye all he kens himsel'!"

Much of his mother's advice was of a kind that could not be expressed so concisely, but two salient items remained fixed in Robert's mind:—

"If ye canna think o' the right word, pit up a bit prayer.

"For ony sake see that your collar is speckless a' the time."

Robert's first impressions of Edinburgh were disappointing. Though extensive enough, the city was not so great or so imposing as he had expected. It was entirely roofed with glass,—a provision which, though doubtless advantageous in wet weather, militated against an adequate supply of sunlight and fresh air. The shops, of which Robin had heard so much, were few in number; and the goods displayed therein (mainly food and drink, newspapers and tobacco) compared unfavourably in point of variety with those in the window of Malcolm M'Whiston, the "merchant" at home. The inhabitants all appeared to be in a desperate hurry, and the noise of the trains, which blocked every thoroughfare, was deafening. Robert Chalmers was just beginning to feel thoroughly disappointed with the Scottish capital, when it occurred to him to mount a flight of stairs which presented itself to his view and gave promise of a second storey at least. When he reached the top he found he had judged Edinburgh too hastily. There was some more of it.

His horizon thus suddenly enlarged, Robert Chalmers Fordyce began to take in his surroundings. He now found himself in a great street, with imposing buildings on one side and a green valley on the other. On the far side of the valley the ground ran steeply upward to an eminence crowded thickly with houses and topped by a mighty castle.

The street was alive with all sorts of absorbingly interesting traffic; but for the present Robert was chiefly concerned with the Cable Cars. It was upon one of these majestic vehicles, which moved down the street unassisted by any apparent human or equine agency, that he had been bidden to ride to his destination. He was not to take the first that came along, nor yet the second—they went to various places, it seemed; and if you were taken to the wrong one you had to pay just the same—but was to scan them until he espied one marked "Gorgie." This would carry him down the Dalry Road, and would ultimately pass the residence of Elspeth M'Kerrow, a decent widow woman, whose late husband's brother had "married on" a connection of Robert's mother. Here he was to lodge.

At first sight the cars appeared to be labelled with nothing but Cocoa and Whisky and Empire Palaces of Varieties Open Every Evening; but a little perseverance discovered a narrow strip of valuable information painted along the side of each car. The first that caught our friend's eye was "Pilrig and Braid Hills Road." That would not do. Then came another—"Murrayfield, Haymarket, and Nether Liberton." Another blank! Then, "Marchmont Road and Churchill." Foiled again, Robert was beginning to feel a little sceptical as to the actual existence of the Dalry Road, when a car drew up opposite to him labelled "Pilrig and Gorgie." It was going in the right direction too, for his father had warned him that his destination lay to the west of the town; and you can trust a Scotsman to know the points of the compass with his eyes shut. (They even talk of a man sitting on the north or south side of his own fireplace.)

Robert clambered on to the top of this car, and presently found himself confronted by a gentleman—splendid in appearance but of homely speech—who waved bundles of tickets in his face, and inquired tersely—

"Penny or tippeny? or transfair?"

"I am seeking the Dalry Road," said Robert cautiously.

"Which end o't?"

"I couldna say."

"Ca' it a penny," said the conductor.

Robert, with the air of a man who has beaten down his opponent to the lowest possible figure, produced the coin from his pocket. (It was just as well that the man had not demanded a larger sum, for Robert's more precious currency was concealed in a place only accessible to partial disrobement.) The gorgeous man carelessly snapped a ticket out of one of the bundles, and having first punched a hole in it with an ingenious instrument that gave forth sounds of music, handed it to Robert in exchange for the penny. He was a saturnine man, but he smiled a little later when Robert, mindful of the fate of his railway-ticket at the last station but one, airily attempted to give up his car-ticket in similar fashion on alighting at the end of the journey.

The greater part of the next four days was spent by our friend in an examination-room, into which we, more fortunate, need not attempt to follow him. Robert diligently answered every question, writing at the foot of each sheet of his neat manuscript, "More on the next page," in case the examiner should be a careless fellow and imagine that Robert had finished when he had not. Robert was not the man to leave anything to chance, or to such unsafe abbreviations as P.T.O.

Outside the examination-room he devoted most of the time that he could spare from preparation for the next paper to a systematic exploration of Edinburgh. He did the thing as thoroughly as possible, for he knew well that he might never spend four days in a large town again.

He began by climbing the Calton Hill. He remained at the summit quite a long time, constructing a rough bird's-eye plan of the streets and buildings below him; and having descended to earth, proceeded on a series of voyages of discovery.

He regarded the exterior of Parliament House with intense interest, for he was a debater by instinct and upbringing. St Giles' he passed by without enthusiasm—he was a member of the Free Kirk—and St Mary's Cathedral struck him as being unduly magnificent to be the property of such a small and pernicious sect as the Episcopalians. The Post Office and other great buildings struck him dumb; and he hastened past the theatres with averted eyes, for he had it upon unimpeachable authority that the devil resided there.

He knew no one in Edinburgh save Elspeth M'Kerrow. However, he made another friend—to wit, one Hector MacPherson, a gigantic Highland policeman, who controlled the traffic with incredible skill at a place where several ways met. The said Hector stood beneath the shadow of a great lamp-post, and whenever a vehicle drove past one side of him, Hector relentlessly called it back and made it go on the other. Their acquaintance began with the entire effacement of Robert's features by the palm of Hector's hand, which was suddenly extended across the thoroughfare for traffic-regulating purposes, with the result that Robert, who was plunged in thought at the time, ran his nose right into the centre of it. The ejaculation to which each gave vent at the moment of impact revealed to both that they were from the same part of the country, and thereafter Hector MacPherson became Robert's adviser-in-chief throughout his stay in Edinburgh. Indeed, Robert used Hector as the starting-point for all his excursions, and whenever he became hopelessly lost in the wilds of the Grassmarket or the purlieus of Morningside, he used to ask his way back to his mentor's pitch and make a fresh start. We shall hear of Hector again.

The foolhardy feat of entering a shop Robert did not attempt until his very last day in Edinburgh, and then only because he was absolutely compelled to do so by the necessity of executing a commission for his sister Margaret—the purchase of half a yard of ribbon.

It is true that the same ribbon could have been obtained at home from Malcolm M'Whiston or a travelling packman, but Margaret was determined to have it from Edinburgh; and she was particularly emphatic in her injunctions to Robert to see that the folk in the shop stuck a label on the parcel, "with their name printed on, and a picture of the shop and a'."

On Saturday morning, then, Robert approached the establishment which he had chosen for the purpose. After a careful reconnaissance he discovered that it possessed several doors. Here was a poser. Which would be the ribbon door? Supposing he entered the wrong one and found himself compelled to purchase a roll of muslin or a wash-hand-stand? With natural acumen he finally selected a door flanked by windows containing lace and ribbon; and waiting for a moment when the surging crowd was thickest, attempted to slip in with them. He got safely past a hero in a medal-sown uniform, but immediately after this encountered an imposing gentleman in a frock-coat, who asked his pleasure. Robert inquired respectfully if the gentleman kept ribbon. The gentleman said "Surely, surely!" and Robert's modest requirements were thereupon sent ringing from a throat of brass into the uttermost recesses of the establishment, and he himself was passed, hot-faced, along the fairway until he reached the right department. Here his tongue clove to the roof of his mouth, and the siren behind the counter, with difficulty stifling her amusement, was reduced to discovering his needs by a process of elimination.

"What will I show you?"

No answer.

"Ladies' gloves?"

A shake of the head.

"Handkerchiefs?"

Another shake.

"Stockings?"

Another shake, accompanied by a deepening of complexion.

"Well—ribbon?"

"Aye, that's it," replied Robert, suddenly finding his voice (which, by the way, rather resembled the Last Trump). "Hauf a yaird—one inch wide—satin—cream!" he roared mechanically.

He received the small parcel, and furtively fingering the money in his pocket, asked the price.

"Two-three, please," replied the damsel briskly.

How Robert thanked his stars that he had some cash in hand! But what a price! All that for a scrap of ribbon! It seemed sinful; but he laid two shillings and threepence on the counter. Greatly to his alarm, the young woman behind it, who up to this point had kept her feelings under commendable control, suddenly collapsed like a punctured balloon on to the shoulder of her nearest neighbour—there being no shop-walkers about—and expressed a wish that she might be taken home and buried. Finally she recovered sufficiently to push Robert's two shillings back across the counter and to place his threepence in a mysterious receptacle which she thrust into a hole in the wall, from which it was ejected with much clatter a minute later; and on being opened proved to contain what the dazed Robert at first took for a half-sovereign, but which he ultimately discovered, when he had abandoned the still giggling maiden and groped his way out into the street, to be a bright new farthing.

The same day he returned to his home; but he did not reach it without one more adventure, a slight one, it is true, but not without its effect upon his future.

The train was over-full, and Robert ultimately found himself travelling in company with nine other passengers, seven of whom were suffering from that infirmity once poetically described by an expert in such diagnoses as "a wee bit drappie in their een." The exception was a gentleman in the far corner, accompanied by a most lovely young lady, upon whom Robert gazed continuously with an admiration so absorbing and profound that it took him some little time to realise, shortly after the commencement of the journey, that the rest of the company were indulging in a free fight all over the compartment, and that the lady was clinging in terror to her escort. Robert was of considerable service in restoring order, and found his reward in the eyes of the lady, who thanked him very prettily. Her husband had the sense not to offer Robert money, but gave him his card, and said in a curious, stiff, English way that he hoped he might be of service to him some day. They got out at Perth, and Robert travelled on alone.

Hours later he was met by his brother David at a little wayside station, and driven over fifteen miles of hilly road to the farm where he had been born and brought up.

Next morning he was up at daybreak, and set to work at his usual tasks about the yard, well knowing that such would be his lot to the end of his life if the examination list did not show his name at the top.

Some days had to elapse before the result could be known; but Robert Chalmers Fordyce—by the way, I think we know him well enough now to call him Robin, which was the name his mother had given him on his third birthday—and his household, being Scottish and undemonstrative, made little or no reference to the subject.

Robin was the scholar of his family. He was the second son, David being four years older. But in accordance with that simple, grand, and patriarchal law of Scottish peasant life, which decrees that every lad of parts shall be given his chance to bring credit on the family, even though his parents have to pinch and save and his brothers bide at the plough-tail all their lives in consequence—a law whose chief merit lies in the splendid sacrifices which its faithful fulfilment involves, and whose vital principle well-meaning but misguided philanthropy is now endeavouring to dole out of existence—he had been sent to Edinburgh to make the most of this, his one chance in life.

Still, though the credit of the family hung upon the result of the examination,—if he won the Bursary, the money, together with the precious hoard which his father and mother had been accumulating for him for ten years, would just suffice to keep him at the University,—no one discussed the matter. It was in the hands of God, and prognostication could only be vain and unprofitable. His mother and sister, indeed, questioned him covertly when his father and brother were out of hearing; but that was chiefly about Edinburgh, and the shops, and the splendours of the Dalry Road. The Bursary was never mentioned.

On the day on which the result was to be announced their father took Robin and David away to a distant hillside to assist at the sheep-dipping. The news would come by letter, which might or might not get as far as Strathmyrtle Post Office, seven miles away, that very afternoon. In the morning it would be delivered by the postman.

But there are limits to human endurance, none the less definite because that endurance appears illimitable. When father and sons tramped back to the farm that evening, just in time for supper, it was discovered that Margaret was absent. John Fordyce, grim old martinet that he was, looked round the table inquiringly; but a glance at his wife's face caused him to go on with his meal.

At nine o'clock precisely the table was cleared. The herdman and two farm lasses came into the kitchen from their final tasks in the yard, and the great Bible was put down on the table for evening "worship."

John Fordyce, having looked up the "portion" which he proposed to read, then turned to the Metrical Psalms. These were sung night by night in unswerving rotation throughout the year, a custom which, while it offered the pleasing prospect of variety, occasionally left something to be desired on the score of appropriateness.

All being seated, the old man, after a final fleeting glance at his daughter's empty chair, gave out the Psalm.

"Let us worship God," he said, "by singing to His praise in the Hundred and Twenty-first Psalm. Psalm a Hundred and Twenty-one—

'I to the hills will lift mine eyes,
From whence doth come——'"

The door opened, and Margaret entered. She was dusty and tired, for she had walked fourteen miles since milking-time; but in her hand she held a letter.

She glanced timidly at the clock, and was for slipping quietly into her seat; but her father said—

"You had best give it to him now. A man cannot worship God while his mind is distracted with other things."

Robin took the letter, and after a glance in the direction of his father and the waiting Bible, opened and read it amidst a tense silence. Finally he looked up.

"Well?" said the old man.

"They have given me the First Bursary, father," said Robin.

No one spoke, but Robin saw tears running down his mother's face. John Fordyce deliberately turned back several pages of the Bible.

"We will sing," he said in a clear voice, "in the Twenty-third Psalm—the whole of it!—

'The Lord's my Shepherd, I'll not want——'"

The Psalms of David, as rendered into English verse by Nahum Tate and others, are not remarkable for poetic merit; neither does the old Scottish fashion of singing the same, seated and without accompaniment, conduce to a concord of sweet sounds. But there are no tunes like old tunes, and there are no hearts like full hearts. If ever a song went straight up to heaven, the Twenty-third Psalm, borne up on the wings of "Martyrdom," did so that night.

CHAPTER TWO.
INTRODUCES A PILLAR OF STATE AND THE APPURTENANCES THEREOF.

The time had undoubtedly arrived when I must have a Private Secretary.

Kitty, for one, insisted on it. She said that I was ruining my health in the service of an ungrateful country, and added that she, personally, declined to be left a widow at twenty-eight-and-a-half to oblige anybody.

"It is exactly the wrong age," she said. "If it had happened four or five years ago, I could have done pretty well for myself. Now, I should be out of the running among the *débutantes*, and a little too young and flighty to suit a middle-aged bachelor."

I may add that my wife does not often talk in this unfeeling manner. But she suffers at times from a desire to live up to a sort of honorary reputation for sprightly humour, conferred upon her by undiscriminating admirers in the days before she became engaged to me. As a matter of fact, her solicitude on my behalf was largely due to an ambition to see a little paragraph in the newspapers, announcing that "Mr Adrian Inglethwaite, M.P., Director of the Sub-Tropical and Arctic Department at the Foreign Office, has appointed Mr Blankley Dash to be his Private Secretary."

Dolly and Dilly seconded the motion. They had not the effrontery to wrap up their motives in specious expressions of concern for my health, but stated their point of view with brutal frankness, as is their wont. I was an old dear, they conceded, and of course Kitty was Kitty; but a sister and brother-in-law were, to put it quite plainly, a hopelessly dull couple to live with: and the visits of Mesdames Dolly and Dilly to our roof-tree would, it was hinted, be more frequent and enduring if the establishment was strengthened by the addition of a presentable young man.

I consented. It was three to one. To any one acquainted with the trio of sisters arrayed against me, it will at once be apparent that "these odds" (as the halfpenny papers say) "but faintly represent the superiority of the winning side."

Having thus dragged the reader without apology into the most intimate regions of my family circle, I had perhaps better introduce myself and my *entourage* a little more formally.

My name is Samuel Adrian Inglethwaite. Why I was called Samuel I do not know. Possibly my parents did. Samuel may have been a baptismal sprat set to catch a testamentary whale, but if this was so no legacy ever came my way. Personally, I am rather attached to the name, as I was called nothing else until I encountered the lady who ultimately consented to become Mrs Inglethwaite. Since that epoch in my career I have been S. Adrian Inglethwaite.

I am thirty-six years of age, and hold an appointment under Government, which, while it does not carry with it Cabinet rank—though Kitty cannot see why—is sufficiently important to make the daily papers keep my obituary notice handily pigeon-holed, in case I fall over the Thames Embankment, get run over by a motor-bus, or otherwise contravene the by-laws of the London County Council.

As no man can possibly give an unbiassed opinion of his own wife, I shall not attempt to describe mine at this juncture, except to mention that she is a woman with no fault that I can for the moment recall, beyond a predilection for belonging to societies which are better known for their aims than for their achievements, are perennially short of funds, and seem to possess no place of meeting except my drawing-room.

Dolly and Dilly are Kitty's sisters. They are twins, and there present age is, I think, nineteen. Though I say it who should not, they are both astonishingly attractive young persons, and the more I see of them the more the fact is borne in upon me. Indeed, a casual remark of mine to that effect, uttered to my wife, by an unfortunate coincidence, on the very morning upon which one of the numerous Deceased Wife's Sister's Bills passed its Second Reading in the House, gave rise to a coldness of demeanour on her part which was only dispelled by an abject apology and a dinner for two at the Savoy on mine.

To return to Dolly and Dilly. I never know them apart, and I do not think Kitty does either. Both are divinely tall and divinely fair; they are exactly like each other in form, voice, and feature; and they possess the irritating habit, not uncommon with twins, of endeavouring to exaggerate their natural resemblance by various puzzling and, I consider, unsportsmanlike devices. They wear each other's clothes indiscriminately, and are not above taking turn and turn about with the affections of unsuspecting young men, of whom they possess a considerable following. They attract admiration without effort, and, I honestly believe, without intention. Of the meaning of love they know nothing,—they are female Peter Pans, and resolutely refuse to grow up, except outwardly,—and the intrusion of that passion into their dealings with persons of the male gender is regarded by them at present as a contingency to be discouraged at all costs. The conditions under which they admit their admirers to their friendship are commendably simple and perfectly definite. If a man is adjudged by them to have attained all the complicated and inexplicable standards by which women judge the opposite sex, he is admitted into the ranks of the Good Sorts; and as such, provided that he keeps his head, has an extremely pleasant time of it. If, however, any obtuse and amorous youth persists in mistaking what Nanki-Poo once described as "customary expressions of affability" for an indication that his infatuation is reciprocated, the Twins act promptly. They have "no use" for such creatures, they once explained to me; and they proceed to rid themselves of the incubus in a fashion entirely their own.

As soon as the pressure of the *affaire* rises to danger-point—*i.e.*, when the youth begins to pay markedly more attention to one Twin than the other—he is asked, say, to lunch. Here he is made much of by the object of his affections, who looks radiant in, let us say, white *batiste*; while the unemployed Twin, in (possibly) blue poplin, holds discreetly aloof. After lunch the Twins, leaving their victim to smoke a cigar, retire swiftly to their room, where they exchange costumes, and descend again to the drawing-room. There

Dolly, now arrayed in white *batiste*, enters upon the path of dalliance where Dilly left off; and Dilly, relieved from duty, crochets in a window-recess, and silently enjoys her sister's impersonation.

One of two things happens. Romeo either does not notice the difference, or else he does. If he does not, he continues to flounder heavily along in pursuit of the well-beloved, oblivious of the fact that he is wasting his efforts on an understudy. After an appropriate interval the cold truth is revealed to him in a hysterical duet, and he goes home, glaring defiantly, but feeling an entire and unmitigated ass.

Or he may actually recognise that Dilly has been replaced by Dolly,—this is what happens when the case is a really serious one,—and if this occurs he is more sorrowful than angry, poor fellow, for he sees that he is being trifled with; and your true lover is the most desperately earnest person in the world. In either case the *affaire* terminates then and there. And that is how my sisters-in-law, with adroitness and despatch, return immature and undesirable suitors to their native element. The whole proceeding reminds me irresistibly of the Undersized Fish Bill, a measure whose progress I once assisted in its course through a Committee of the House.

However, having been bidden to procure a Private Secretary, I meekly set about looking for one. One night at dinner we held a symposium on the subject, and endeavoured to evolve an outline of the kind of gentleman who was likely to suit us. The following is a *précis* of the result. I leave the intelligent reader to trace each item to its author; also the various parenthetical comments on the same:—

- (a) He must be a 'Varsity man.
- (b) He must be able to keep accounts, and transact business generally.
- (c) He must be content with a salary of two hundred a-year, with board and residence in the house. ("He can have that little room off the library for a sitting-room, dear, and sleep in the old night-nursery.")
- (d) He must not wear celluloid collars or made-up ties. ("But he'll *have* to, poor dear, if the Infant Samuel only gives him two hundred a-year.")
- (e) He must be prepared to run through my speeches before I deliver them. ("I suppose that means *write* them!"), look up my subject-matter, verify my references, and so on. ("That *will* be an improvement. But what will the halfpenny papers do then, poor things?")
- (f) He must be the sort of man that one can have in to a dinner-party without any fear of accidents. ("Yes. He *must* be all right about peas, asparagus, and liqueurs. *And* finger-bowls, dearest. You remember the man who drank out of his at that queer political dinner to the constituents?")
- (g) He must be nice to my Philly.
- (h) He must be dark. ("Pshaw!")
- (i) He must be fair. ("Ugh!")
- (j) He must be able to waltz and play bridge.

At this point I suggested that a prepaid telegram to the Celestial Regions would alone procure the article we required. However, we ultimately descended to an advertisement in the *Morning Post*, and in due course I obtained a secretary. In fact, I obtained several. We had them *seriatim*, and none stayed longer than a month. I do not propose to write a detailed history of the dynasty which I now found it my privilege to support. A brief *résumé* of each will suffice.

Number One.—Cambridge Football Blue. Big and breezy. Spelling entirely phonetic. Spent most of his time smoking in the drawing-room, and laboured under the delusion that, as my amanuensis, he was at liberty to forge my signature to all documents, including cheques. He used my official note-paper to back horses on, and was finally requested to leave, after an unseemly brawl with a book-maker's tout on my doorstep.

Number Two.—Oxford: a First in Greats. A heavy manner, usually beginning his observations with "Wherewithal" or "Peradventure." The Twins suffered severely from suppressed giggles in his presence. Regarded my superficial ideas of statesmanship with profound contempt, but left after a fortnight, having allowed a highly confidential and extremely personal pencil note, written in the margin of a despatch by the Premier himself, to blossom forth in large type in the text of a Blue Book.

Number Three.—Rather elderly for the post—nearer forty than thirty—but highly recommended. Reduced my chaotic papers to order in twenty-four hours, charmed my wife and her sisters, drafted a speech which won me quite a little ovation in the House, suggested several notable improvements in the "Importation of Mad Dogs Bill," with which I was to be entrusted next session—and was found lying dead drunk in his bedroom, at eleven o'clock in the morning, on the second Sunday after his arrival. Half a dozen empty brandy bottles were afterwards discovered on the top of his wardrobe. Poor devil!

Number Four.—(Subsequently handed down to posterity as "The Limit"). Small, spectacled, and nervous. Came from a Welsh University, and was strong on "the methodical filing of State and other documents." He stayed two days. On the first night (after inquiring whether we were expecting guests that evening, and receiving an answer in the negative) he came down to dinner in a sort of alpaca smoking-jacket and a tartan tie. On the second, having evidently decided to treat us to all the resources of his wardrobe as soon as possible, he appeared in more or less ordinary evening attire. He wore a small white satin bow-tie, attached to his collar-stud by a brass clip. The tie fell off the stud into his soup almost immediately, and its owner, after furtively chasing it round the plate with his forefinger, finally fished it out with the aid of a fork; and, having squeezed as much soup as possible back into the plate, put the bow into his waistcoat pocket and resumed his meal with every appearance of enjoyment.

He left next morning. As the Twins pathetically observed: "It had to be him or us!" I was sorry, for he was a tidy little creature away from table.

After that I did a rash thing. I engaged a Private Secretary on the spur of the moment and without consulting my household.

One morning I had occasion to visit the British Museum. That mausoleum of learning is not an habitual resort of mine, but on this occasion I had found it necessary to refresh my memory on the subject of a small principality situated somewhere in the Pacific, and reported to be in a state of considerable unrest, concerning which the member for Upper Gumbtree, an unpleasantly omniscient young man with a truculent manner, had been asking questions in the House. It seemed that British interests in that quarter were not being adequately protected by our Department, and this extremely pushing gentleman was now gaining much cheap applause in the columns of those low-priced organs which make a living by deriding his Majesty's Ministers, by bombarding us with fatuous inquiries on the subject. My Chief had only the most hazy notion about the place—as a matter of fact I do not believe that either he or any of the permanent officials had ever heard of it—and I was in a precisely similar condition. I was accordingly bidden to get up the subject, and accumulate a mass of information thereon which would not only satiate the appetite of the honourable member, but choke him off for all time.

Finding myself in want of a particular Gazetteer which was not to be found in the office, and being in no mood to take a clerk, however uncritical, into my confidence, I called a hansom and drove straight to the Museum; where, having ensconced myself in the reading-room with the work in question, I prepared to devote a dusty and laborious morning to the service of State.

Immediately opposite me sat a gigantic young man of a slightly threadbare appearance, who was copying some screed out of a bulky tome before him. I regarded him in a reminiscent sort of way for a few minutes, and presently found that my scrutiny was being returned fourfold. Next came an enormous hand that was suddenly thrust across the table towards me, and I remembered him.

We had met six years ago in a railway train, under circumstances which made me extremely glad to make his acquaintance at any price. Kitty and I were on our honeymoon, and happened to be travelling on a Saturday afternoon from Edinburgh to Perth in a train packed to suffocation with the supporters of a football team of the baser sort. We were bound for Inchellan, the Scottish residence of my Chief, who was sending to meet us at Perth.

As the first-class carriages were all occupied by gentlemen with third-class tickets, we travelled third with a company who did not seem to possess any tickets at all. Just before the train started the door was thrown open and two inebriated Scots, several degrees further gone than the rest of the company—which is saying a good deal—were hurled in. If the assemblage had all been of one way of thinking we might have reached Perth with nothing worse than bad headaches, but unfortunately some supporters of the other team were present, and in the midst of a heated and alcoholic debate on the rights and wrongs of the last free kick, two rival orators suddenly arose, clinched, and continued their argument at close grips on the floor. In a moment the party divided itself into two camps, and the conflict became general. As there were ten people in the compartment, of whom seven were engaged in a life-and-death struggle, the movements of the non-combatants—Kitty, myself, and a gigantic youth of gawky appearance—were, to put it mildly, somewhat restricted. Kitty became thoroughly frightened, and hampered my preparations for battle by clinging to my arm. The gigantic youth, seeing this, suddenly took command of the situation.

"Watch you the young leddy!" he bellowed in my ear, "and I'll sort them."

With that he hurled himself into the tumult. The exact details of his performance I could not see, the scientific dusting of railway cushions not having penetrated any further north of the Forth than it has south of the Thames; but the net result was that each combatant was pulled off, picked up, shaken until his teeth rattled, and banged down on to his seat with a brief admonition to mind his manners, until seven bewildered, partially sobered, and thoroughly demoralised patrons of sport sat round about in various attitudes of limp dejection, leaning against one another like dissipated marionettes; while our rustic Hector, bestriding the compartment like a Colossus, dared them to move a finger under penalty of being "skelped."

He bundled them all out at the next stopping-place, without inquiring whether they desired to alight there or no, and I am bound to say that they all seemed as anxious to leave the carriage as he was to expel them. He then shut the door, pulled up the window, and turned to my wife with a reassuring smile.

"Yon was just a storrm in a teapot," he remarked affably.

He accepted my thanks with indifference, but blushed in a gratified manner when Kitty addressed him. He was her bond-slave by the time that we bade him farewell at Perth. I presented him with my card, which he carefully placed inside the lining of his hat; but he forbore, either from native caution or excessive shyness, to furnish us with any information as to his own identity.

Well, here he was, sitting opposite to me in the Reading Room of the British Museum, and seemingly none too prosperous. Six years ago he had looked like a young and healthy farm lad. Now, fourth-rate journalism was stamped all over him.

CHAPTER THREE.
"ANENT."

We conversed awhile in whispers to avoid disturbing the other worshippers—I always feel like that in the British Museum—and finally abandoned our respective tasks and issued forth together. With a little persuasion I prevailed upon my companion to come and lunch with me, and we repaired to a rather old-fashioned and thoroughly British establishment close by, where the fare is solid and the "portions" generous.

My guest, after a brief effort at self-repression, fell upon the food in a fashion that told me a far more vivid tale of his present circumstances than the most lengthy explanation could have done. When he was full I gave him a cigar, and he leaned back in his padded arm-chair and surveyed me with the nearest approach to emotion that I have ever observed in the countenance of a Scot.

"I was wanting that," he remarked frankly, and he smiled largely upon me. He was looking less gaunt now, and the rugged lines of his face were tinged with a more healthy colour. He was a handsome youth, I noticed, with shrewd grey eyes and a chin that stood out like the ram of a battle-ship.

He told me all about himself, some of which has been set down here already. He had done well at Edinburgh University, and, having obtained his Arts degree, was on the point of settling down to study for the ministry—the be-all and end-all of the hope of a humble Scottish household—when disaster came tumbling upon his family. His brother David fell sick in his lungs, and the doctor prescribed a sojourn in a drier climate for at least a year.

The next part of the narrative was rather elliptical; but from the fact that money was immediately forthcoming to send David abroad, and that Robin had simultaneously given up his work in Edinburgh and returned home to help his father about the farm, I gathered that a life's ambition had been voluntarily sacrificed on the altar of family duty. Anyhow, when David returned, marvellously and mercifully restored to health, setting his younger brother free once more, two precious years had flown; so that Robin now found himself, at the age of twenty-three, faced with the alternative of making a fresh start in life or remaining on the farm at home, that most pathetic and forlorn of failures, a "stickit minister." The family exchequer had been depleted by David's illness, and Robin, rather than draw any further on the vanishing little store of pound-notes in the cupboard behind the kitchen chimney, determined to go to London and turn his education to some account.

He had arrived three years ago, with a barrel of salt herrings and a bag of meal; and from that time he had earned his own living—if it could be called a living.

"Once or twice," he said, "I have had an article taken by one of the big reviews; sometimes I get some odd reporting to do; and whiles I just have to write chatty paragraphs about celebrities for the snippety papers."

"Uphill work that, I should think."

"Uphill? Downhill! Man, it's degrading. Do you know what I was doing in that Museum this morning?"

"What?"

"Have you heard tell of a man they call Dean Ramsay?"

"Let me see—yes. He was a sort of Scottish Sidney Smith, wasn't he?"

"That is the man. Well, he collected most of the good stories in Scotland and put them in a book. I was copying a few of them out; and I shall father them on to folk that the public wants to hear about. I get a guinea a column for that."

"I know the sort of thing," I said. "*'A good story is at present going the round of the clubs, concerning——'*"

"Not 'concerning'—'anent'!"

"I beg your pardon—'anent a certain well-known but absent-minded Peer of the Realm.'"

"That's the stuff. You have the trick of it. Then sometimes I do bits of general information—computations as to the height of a column of the picture postcards sold in London in a year, and all that. Nobody can check figures of that kind, so the work is easy—and correspondingly ill-paid!" (I cannot reproduce the number of contemptuous *r*'s that Robin threw into the adverb.)

"It's a fine useful place the Museum," he continued reflectively. "You were busy there this morning yourself. You would be collecting *data* anent—I mean *about*—the Island of Caerulea."

I sat up in surprise at this.

"How on earth——?" I began.

"Oh, I just jal—guessed it. You being the only member of his Majesty's Government in whom I have any personal interest, I have always followed your career closely. (You gave me your card, you'll mind.) Well, I saw you were having trouble with yon havering body Wuddiford—I once reported at one of his meetings: he's just a sweetie-wife in *pince-nez*—and when I saw you busy with an atlas and gazetteer I said to myself:—'He'll be getting up a few salient facts about the place, in order to appease the honourable member's insatiable thirst for knowledge—Toots, there I go again! Man, the journalese fairly soaks into the system. I doubt now if I could write out twenty lines of 'Paradise Lost' without cross-heading them!"

We finished our cigar over talk like this, and finally rose to go. Robin lingered upon the steps of the restaurant. I realised that he, being a Scotsman, was endeavouring to pump up the emotional gratitude which he felt sure that I, as an Englishman, would expect from a starving pauper who had lunched at my expense.

"I must thank you," he said at last, rather awkwardly, "for a most pleasant luncheon. And I should like fine," he added suddenly and impetuously, "to make out a *précis* for you on the subject of Caerulea. Never heed it yourself! Away home, and I'll send it to you to-morrow!"

An idea which had been maturing in my slow-moving brain for some time suddenly took a definite shape.

"It is extremely kind of you," I said. "I shall be delighted to leave the matter in your hands. But when you have made the *précis*, I wonder if you would be so good as to bring it to my house instead of sending it?"

I gave him my address, and we parted.

Robert Chalmers Fordyce arrived at my house next morning. He brought with him a budget of condensed but exhaustive information on the subject of Caerulea, the assimilation and ultimate discharge of which enabled me to score a signal victory over Mr Wuddiford of Upper Gumbtree, relegating that champion exploiter of mare's nests to a sphere of comparative inoffensiveness for quite a considerable time.

After reading the *précis*, I offered Robin the position of my Private Secretary, which he accepted politely but without servility or effusiveness. I handed him a quarter's salary in advance, gave him two days' holiday wherein to "make his arrangements"—*Anglicè*, to replenish his wardrobe—and we sealed the bargain with a glass of sherry and a biscuit apiece.

As he rose to go, Robin took from his pocket a folded manuscript.

"I see you have a good fire there," he said.

He stepped across to the hearth-rug and pitched the document into the heart of the flames, which began to lick it caressingly.

Presently the heat caused the crackling paper to unfold itself, and some of the writing became visible. Robert pointed, and I read—

"Pars about Personalities. A capital story is at present going the round of the clubs, anent——"

Here the flimsy manuscript burst into flame, and shot with a roar up the chimney.

I looked at Robert Chalmers Fordyce, and his face was the face of a man who has gone through deep waters, but feels the good solid rock beneath his feet at last.

He turned dumbly to me, and held out his hand.

The worst of these inarticulate and undemonstrative people is that they hurt you so.

CHAPTER FOUR.
A TRIAL TRIP.

Three days later I introduced Robert Chalmers Fordyce into the bosom of my family. I had declined to give them any previous information about him, beyond a brief warning that they would find him "rather Scotch."

I have always found it utterly impossible to foretell from a man's behaviour towards his own sex how he will comport himself in the presence of females. I have known a raw youth, hitherto regarded as the hobbledehoy of the shooting-party and the pariah of the smoking-room, lord it among the ladies like a very lion; and I have seen the hero of a hundred fights, the master of men, the essence of intrepid resolution, stand quaking outside a drawing-room door. The *début* of Robin, then, I awaited with considerable interest. I expected on the whole to see him tongue-tied, especially before Dolly and Dilly. On the other hand he might be aggressively assertive.

He was neither. He proved to be that rarest of types—the man who has no fear of his fellow-creatures, male or female, singly or in battalions. Our sex is so accustomed to squaring its shoulders, pulling down its waistcoat, and assuming an engaging expression as a preliminary to an encounter with the fair, that the spectacle of a man who enters a strange drawing-room and shakes hands quietly and naturally all round, without twisting his features into an agreeable smile and mumbling entirely inarticulate words of rapture, always arouses in me feelings of envy and respect.

We found Kitty and the Twins picturesquely grouped upon the drawing-room hearth-rug, waiting for the luncheon gong.

I introduced Robin to my wife, in the indistinct and throaty tones which always obtrude themselves into an Englishman's utterance when he is called upon to say something formal but graceful. Kitty greeted the guest with a smile with which I am well acquainted (and which I can guarantee from personal experience to be absolutely irresistible on one's first experience of it), and welcomed him to the house very prettily.

"You are very kind, Mrs Inglethwaite," said Robin, shaking hands. "But I am not quite a stranger to you. Do you mind my face?"

Kitty turned scarlet.

"Mind your——? Not in the—I mean—I am sure we are de——" She floundered hopelessly.

Robin laughed pleasantly.

"There is my Scots tongue running away with me already," he said. "I should have asked rather if you*remembered* my face."

This time Kitty ceased to look confused, but still retained a puzzled frown.

"No," she said slowly; "I don't *think*——"

"No wonder!" said Robin. "We met once, in a railway carriage, six years ago. Between Edinburgh and Perth—on a Saturday afternoon," he added expressively.

Light broke in upon Kitty. "Of course!" she said. "Now I remember. That dreadful journey! You were the gentleman who was so kind and helpful. How nice and romantic meeting again! Adrian, you silly old creature, why didn't you tell me? Now, Mr Fordyce, let me introduce you to my sisters."

She wheeled him round and presented him to the Twins.

That pair of beauties, I saw at a glance, were out after scalps. They stood up side by side on the hearth-rug, absolutely and weirdly alike, and arrayed on this occasion in garments of identical hue and cut. This was a favourite device of theirs when about to meet a new young man; it usually startled him considerably. If he was not a person of sound nerve and abstemious habits, it not infrequently evoked from him some enjoyably regrettable expression of surprise and alarm. I knew all the tricks in their *répertoire*, and waited interestedly to see the effect of this series.

On being presented, both smiled shyly and modestly, and each simultaneously proffered a timid hand. The average young man, already a little rattled by the duplicate vision of loveliness before him, could never make up his mind which hand to shake first; and by the time he had collected his faculties sufficiently to make an uncertain grab at one, both would be swiftly and simultaneously withdrawn.

Robin, however, immediately shook hands with Dilly, who stood nearest to Kitty, and then with Dolly. After that he stepped back a pace and surveyed the pair with unconcealed interest.

Then he turned to my wife.

"A truly remarkable resemblance!" he observed benignantly. ("Just as if we had been two babies in a bassinette!" as Dolly afterwards remarked.)

Then he resumed his inspection. The Twins, who were entirely unused to this sort of thing, were too taken aback to proceed to their second move—the utterance of some trivial and artless remark, delivered by both simultaneously, and thereby calculated to throw the victim into a state of uncertainty as to which he should answer first. Instead, they stood wide-eyed and tongue-tied before him.

"I must certainly discover some point of difference between these ladies," continued Robin with an air of determination, "or I shall always be in difficulties. Do not tell me the secret, Mrs Inglethwaite. Perhaps I can find out for myself."

He concluded a minute inspection of the indignant Dilly, and turned his unruffled gaze on Dolly.

"Yes," he said, "I have it! You" (triumphantly to Dolly) "have a tiny brown spot in the blue of your left eye, while your sister has none."

It was quite true: she had. But it was a fact which most young men only discovered after many furtive and sidelong glances. This imperturbable creature had taken it all in in one resolute scrutiny; and Dolly, blushing like Aurora—an infirmity to which I may say neither she nor her sister are particularly subject—dropped her long lashes over the orbs in question and looked uncommonly foolish.

The tension of the situation was relieved by the announcement of luncheon, and Robin was called upon to accompany Kitty downstairs; while I, putting a consoling arm round the waist of each of my fermenting sisters-in-law, marched them down to further experiences in the dining-room.

The Twins rapidly recovered their equanimity at lunch. They sat, as they always did, together on one side of the table, opposite to Robin. The latter conversed easily and pleasantly, though his discourse was dotted with homely phrases and curious little biblical turns of speech.

"Have you been in London long, Mr Fordyce?" inquired Kitty as we settled down.

"Three years," said Robin.

"I suppose you have lots of friends by this time."

"I have a good many acquaintances, but my friends in London are just three, all told," said Robin, in what Dilly afterwards described as "a disgustingly pawky manner."

"You must be very exclusive, Mr Fordyce," chirrupped Dolly.

"Far from it," said Robin; "as you will admit when I say that my three friends are a policeman, a surgeon, and a minister."

"How quaint of you!" said Dilly.

But Robin did not seem to think it quaint. He told us about the policeman first—a Highlander. Robin had made his acquaintance in Edinburgh, apparently about the same time that he made ours, and had renewed it some years later outside the House of Commons, when a rapturous mutual recognition had taken place. The policeman's name was Hector MacPherson.

"And the surgeon?" inquired Kitty, with a certain friendly assumption of interest which announces (to me) that she is getting a little bored.

"He is just my uncle. I go and see him, whi—now and then. He is a busy man."

"And the—er—minister?"

"He is Dr Strang. He has the Presbyterian Church in Howard Street. I have sat under him every Sabbath since I came to London."

"Wh—what for?" asked Kitty involuntarily, and in a rather awestruck voice. Her acquaintance with the ritual of the Church of Scotland was hazy, and she was evidently determined to-day to be surprised at nothing; but evidently this mysterious reference could not be allowed to pass without some explanation. The Twins convulsively gripped each other's hands under the table. (They are of course perfectly bred girls—indeed, their self-possession at trying moments has often surprised me—but, like all the young of the human species, there are times when their feelings become too much for them. Then, if the occasion is too formal for unrestrained shrieks, they silently interdigitate.)

"That is a Scottish expression," said Robin, smiling upon us. "You must pardon me, Mrs Inglethwaite. I should perhaps have said that I was an adherent of Dr Strang's church—or rather," he added with a curious little touch of pride, "I am a communicant now. I was just an adherent at first."

We assented to this, politely but dizzily.

Scratch a Scot and you will find a theologian. Robin was fairly started now; and he proceeded to enlarge upon various points of interest in the parallel histories (given in full) of some three or four Scottish denominations, interwoven with extracts from his own family archives. His grand-uncle, it appeared, had been a minister himself, and had performed the feat—to which I have occasionally heard other perfervid Scots refer, and never without a kindling eye—known as "coming out in the Forty-three."

"That," added Robin in parenthesis, "is why my second name is Chalmers—after the great Doctor. You will have heard of him?"

(Polite but insincere chorus of pleased recognition.)

We were then treated to a brief *résumé* of the events leading up to a religious controversy of colossal dimensions which was at that moment threatening to engulf Scotland. Robin was deeply interested in the matter, and gave us his reasons for being so. He passed some scathing comments on the contumacy and narrow-mindedness of the sect who had the misfortune to be his opponents; and after that he proceeded to say a few words about Free Will and Predestination.

By this time lunch was over, but we sat on. I nodded gravely over my coffee, saying "Quite so" when occasion seemed to demand it. Kitty was completely out of her depth, but still maintained a brave appearance of interest. It was the Twins who brought the *séance* to a close. Placing their hands before their mouths, they with difficulty stifled a pair of cavernous yawns.

Next moment they were sorry. Robin stopped dead, flushed up, and said—

"Mrs Inglethwaite, I am sorry. I have been most inconsiderate and rude. I have wearied you all. The truth is," he continued quite simply, "it is so long since I sat at meat with friends, that I have lost the art of conversation. I just run on, like—like a leading article. I have not conversed with a woman, except once or twice across a counter, for nearly three years."

There was a rather tense pause. Then Dolly said—

"We're awfully sorry, Mr Fordyce. It was very rude of us. We quite understand now, don't we, Dilly?"

"Rather," said Dilly. "It was horrible of us, Mr Fordyce. But we thought you were just an ordinary bore."

"Children!" said Kitty.

"But what you have told us makes things quite different, doesn't it, Dolly?" continued Dilly.

"Quite—absolutely," said Dolly.

And they smiled upon him, quite maternally. And so the incident passed.

"How queer, not talking to a woman for three years!" continued Dolly reflectively.

"How *awful* it would be not to talk to a man for three years!" said Dilly, with obvious sincerity.

"There is little opportunity for social intercourse," said Robin, "to a man who comes to London to sink or swim."

The conversation was again taking a slightly sombre turn, and I struck in—

"Well, I hope, Mr Fordyce, that a few weeks' experience of my establishment won't have the effect of making you regret your previous celibate existence."

Dolly and Dilly looked at each other.

"Dolly," said Dilly, "is that an insult?"

"I think so."

"Insulting enough to be punishable?"

"Rather."

"All right. Come on!"

They fell upon me, and the next few minutes were devoted to what I believe is known in pantomime circles as a Grand Rally, which necessitated my going upstairs afterwards and changing my collar.

Robin was not present at tea, and my household took advantage of his absence to run over his points.

Considering that a woman—especially a young woman—judges a man almost entirely by his manner and appearance, and dislikes him exceedingly if he proceeds to dominate the situation to her exclusion—unless, by the way, he has her permission and authority so to do, in which case he cannot do so too much—the verdict delivered upon my absent secretary was not by any means unfavourable, though, of course, there was much to criticise.

"He'll do," said Dilly; "but you must get his hair cut, Adrian."

"And tell him about not wearing that sort of tie, dear," said Dolly.

"I suppose he can't help his accent," sighs Kitty.

But their criticisms were limited to such trifles as these, and I felt that Robin had done me credit.

Dilly summed up the situation.

"I think on the whole that he is rather a pet," she said.

A more thoroughly unsuitable description could not have been imagined, but Dolly agreed.

"He has nice eyes, too," she added.

"He was perfectly sweet with Phillis after lunch," said Kitty. "Took her on his knee at once, and talked to her just as if we weren't there. That's a good test of a man, if you like!"

"True for you," I agreed. "I could not do it with other people's children to save my life."

"Oh, you are hopeless," said Dilly. "*Far* too self-conscious and dignified to climb down to the level of children, isn't he, Dolly?" She crinkled her nose.

Dolly for once was not listening.

"What was that weird stuff the Secretary Bird spouted when you showed Phillis to him, Kit? About her being forward, or coy, or something. It sounded rather cheek, to me."

"Yes, I remember," said Dilly. "Can you do the way he said it? 'Sometimes forrrwarrrd, sometimes coy, she neverrr fails to pullllease!' Like that! Gracious, how it hurts to talk Scotch!"

"I don't know, dear," said my wife thoughtfully. "It sounded rather quaint. But I daresay all Scotch people are like that," she added charitably.

"Perhaps it was a quotation," I observed mildly.

"Of course, that would be it. What is it out of?"

"A song called 'Phillis is my only Joy,' I think."

"Ah, then you may depend upon it," said Kitty, with the air of one solving a mystery, "that is what the man was doing—*quoting*! Burns, probably, or Scott, perhaps. How clever of him to think of it! And do you know," she continued, "he said such a nice thing to me. While you were bear-fighting with the Twins after lunch, Adrian, I said to him: 'Pity me, Mr Fordyce! My husband never ceases to express to me his regret that he did not marry one of my sisters.' And he answered at once, quite seriously, without stopping to think it out or anything:—'I am sure, Mrs Inglethwaite, that his regret must be shared by countless old admirers of yours!' Wasn't it rather sweet of him?"

Further conversation was prevented by the opening of the drawing-room door, where the butler appeared and announced "Mr Dubberley."

Dubberley is a pillar of our party. I can best describe him by saying that although I hold office under a Conservative Government, ten minutes' conversation with Dubberley leaves me a confirmed Radical, and anything like a protracted interview with him converts me into a Socialist for the next twenty-four hours. A week-end in his society, and I should probably buy a red shirt and send out for bombs. He is a good fellow at bottom, and of immense service to the party; but he is the most blatant ass I have ever met. There are Dubberleys on both sides of the House, however, which is a comfort.

Robin joined us almost directly after Dubberley's entrance, just in time to hear that great man conclude the preamble of his discourse for the afternoon.

There had been a good deal of talk in the papers of late about improving the means of transport throughout the country; and the nationalisation of railways and other semi-socialistic schemes had filled the air. Dubberley, it appeared, had out of his own gigantic intellect evolved a panacea for congestion of traffic, highness of rates, and railway mortality.

He was well launched in his subject when Robin entered and was introduced.

"As I was saying," he continued, waving an emphatic teaspoon in the direction of the sofa where the ladies sat, smiling but limp,—even the Twins knew it was useless to stem this tide,—"as I was saying, the solution of the problem lies in the revival of our far-reaching but sadly neglected system of *canals*. Yes! If we go to the very root of the matter"—Dubberley is one of those fortunate persons who never has to dig far in his researches—"we find that our whole hope of regeneration lies in the single, simple, homely word—Canals! Revive your canals, send your goods by canal, travel yourself by——"

"How long, Mr Dubberley," interpolated Robin, leaning forward—"how long do you consider one would take to travel, say, a hundred miles by canal?"

"Under our present antiquated system, sir,"—Dubberley rather prides himself on preserving the courtly fashions of address of a bygone age,—"an impossibly long time. The average speed of a canal-boat at the present day under the ministrations of that overburdened and inadequate quadruped, the—er—horse, is three miles per hour. Indeed—one moment!"

Dubberley fished a sheaf of documents out of his pocket—he is the sort of man who habitually secrets statistics and blue-books about his person—and after stertorously perusing them closed his eyes for a moment, as if to work out a sum upon an internal blackboard, and said—

"I see no reason why swift canal-boats should not be constructed to run fifteen, twenty, or even twenty-five miles per hour. Indeed, in these days of turbines——"

Robin put down his cup rather emphatically, and said—

"Mphm."

(It is quite impossible to reproduce this extraordinary Caledonian expletive in writing, but that is as near to it as I can get.) Then he continued urbanely—

"Then you would organise a service of fast turbine steamers running all over the canal systems of the country?"

"Exactly. Or let us say—er—launches," said Dubberley. "I must not overstate my case."

"Travelling twenty miles an hour?"

"Say fifteen, sir," said Dubberley magnanimously.

"Mr Dubberley," said Robin, in a voice which made us all jump, "have you a bathroom in your house?"

Even the Twins, who were growing a trifle lethargic under the technicalities of the subject, roused themselves at this fresh turn of the conversation.

"Ah—eh—I beg your pardon?" said Dubberley, a trifle disconcerted.

"A bathroom," repeated Robin—"with a good long bath in it?"

"Er—yes."

"Well, Mr Dubberley, when you go home this afternoon, go upstairs and fill the bath with water. Then take a large bath-sponge—something nearly as broad as the bath—and sweep it along from end to end, about a foot below the surface, at a speed of fifteen miles per hour—that will be twenty-two feet per second—and see what happens!"

Robin had unconsciously dropped into what I may call his debating-society manner. His chin stuck out, and his large chest heaved, and he scooped the air, as if it had been the water of Dubberley's bath, with one of Kitty's priceless Worcester teacups.

Dubberley sat completely demoralised, palpitating like a stranded frog.

"Then," continued Robin, "you would observe the result of placing a partly submerged and rapidly moving body in a shallow and restricted waterway. You would kick half the water right out of the canal to begin with, and the other half would pile itself up into a wave under your bow big enough to offer an almost immovable resistance to the progress of your vessel."

He leaned back and surveyed the bemused Dubberley with complete and obvious satisfaction. We all sat round breathless, feeling much as Sidney Smith must have felt when some one spoke disrespectfully of the Equator. Great was the fall of Dubberley. He moved, perhaps instinctively, in a society where he was seldom contradicted and never argued with. One does not argue with a gramophone. And here this raw Scottish youth, with the awful thoroughness and relentless common-sense of his race, had taken the very words out of his mouth, torn them to shreds, and thrust them down his throat.

I am afraid I chuckled. The Twins sat hand in hand, with dreamy eyes staring straight before them. They were conjuring up a joyous vision of Dubberley, in his shirt-sleeves, meekly refuting one of his own theories by means of a childish and sloppy experiment in practical hydrodynamics in his own bathroom.

I give this incident as a fair example of Robin's point of view and methods of action on questions which I for one would never dream of debating. He was entirely lacking in an art which I am told I possess to perfection—that of suffering fools gladly. Its possession has raised me to an Under-Secretaryship. People who should know tell me that it will also prevent my ever rising to anything higher.

"We had a taste of our friend's quality this afternoon," I remarked to my household when we met for dinner that evening. "He is a thorough-going warrior. Fancy any man taking all that trouble to lay out old Dubberley!"

"Poor Mr Dubberley!" said tender-hearted Kitty.

"Do him good!" said Dilly, in whose recollection Dubberley's past enormities loomed large. "I shall be nice to the Secretary Bird now."

Dolly said nothing, which was unusual. Perhaps the brown spot still rankled.

CHAPTER FIVE.
ROBIN ON DUTY.

Beyond the fact that they are all desperately in earnest, all know each other, and occupy all the most responsible and lucrative posts on the face of the earth, Scotsmen are a class with whose characteristics I am not well acquainted. But I learned a great deal from my new secretary.

Robin soon settled down to work. He not only performed his duties with zeal and discretion, but he kept me up to mine. He hounded me through the routine work of my Department; he verified my references; he managed my correspondence; and he frequently drafted my speeches. He even prepared some of my impromptus. Indeed, my—or rather his—description of a certain member of the other side, a lesser light of the last Government, a worthy man, always put up to explain matters when his leader had decided that honesty on this occasion was the best policy, as "a political niblick, always employed to get his party out of bad lies," won me more applause and popularity in a House of enthusiastic golfers than endless weeks of honest toil behind the scenes had ever done.

But I learned more from Robin than that. I suppose I am a typical specimen of Conservative officialdom. Until Robin came into my house it had never occurred to me to ask myself why I was a Conservative: I had been born one, and it was difficult for me to understand how any man of ordinary intelligence could be anything else.

My father and grandfather were Conservative members before me, and I come of a line which has always feared God, honoured the King, paid its tithes, and tried to do something for the poor; and which regards Radicals, Socialists, Nonconformists, and criminal lunatics as much the same class of person. The only difference between myself and my forebears is that I am much too pacific (or lazy) to cherish any animosity against people whose views differ from my own. This fact, coupled with certain family traditions, has brought me to my present position in life; and, as I have already indicated, it will probably keep me there. At least, so Kitty says.

"You must *assert* yourself, dear," she declares. "Be *rude* to people, and go on being rude! Then they will take notice of you and give you nice big posts to keep you quiet. Do you know what the Premier said about you the other night at dinner, to Lady Bindle? (She told Dicky Lever, and he told the Twins.) 'Inglethwaite? A dear fellow, a sound party man, and runs his Department admirably. But—he strikes only on the box!' Pig!"

It was about this time that Robin became a member of our establishment. I had no idea what his political views were—it was just like me not to have asked him, Kitty said—but felt confident that whatever side he supported he would do so hot and strong.

But at first he gave no indication of his leanings. It was not until we sat one night over our wine, in company with John Champion (member for a big northern constituency, and regarded by many, notwithstanding various eccentricities, as the coming man of the party) that he first gave definite utterance to his views.

The cigars had gone round, and we had just performed that mysterious national rite which, whether it owes its existence to economy or politeness, invariably ends in several people burning their fingers with the same match.

"I suppose, Mr Fordyce," said Champion, who had not met Robin before, but obviously liked him, "that in common with all Scotsmen you are at heart a Radical."

"Am I?" said Robin, with native caution.

"Most of your countrymen are," said Champion, with a sigh. "'They think too much'—you know the rest of the quotation, I expect."

Robin nodded.

I was a little scandalised at this flagrant tribute to the enemy, and said so.

Champion laughed.

"You are a whole-hearted old war-horse, Adrian. I envy you. Sometimes, I wish that I——"

"For mercy's sake don't go and say that you are a Radical at heart too," I cried.

"N-n-o. But isn't it rot, the whole business?"

"What whole business?"

"Ask Mr Fordyce there. He will tell you. I see it in his eye."

"What is rot, Robin?" I asked. "Party government?"

"Yes," said Robin, quite explosively for him. "It is such a scandalous waste of power and material." He laid down his cigar. "Man, it's just pitiful. Consider! A party is returned to office. With great care and discrimination a Cabinet is chosen. It is composed of men who are mainly honest and patriotic. They are not necessarily men of genius, but they are all men of undoubted ability, and they are genuinely anxious to do their duty by the country. Now observe." (As a matter of fact he said "obsairrve.") "How is this energy and ability expended? About half of it—fifty per cent—goes in devising means to baffle the assaults of the Opposition and so retain a precarious hold on office. Sir, it's just ludicrous! Instead of concentrating their efforts upon—upon—I want a metaphor, Mr Champion."

"Upon steering the ship of State," said Champion, with a twinkle in his eye.

"That'll do, fine.—Upon steering the ship of State, they have to devote half their time and energy to dodging the missiles of their shipmates. That is what I mean when I say the thing is pitiful. What should we think of the sanity of an ordinary ship's company, if the man at the wheel had to spend half his time up in the rigging because a minority of his messmates wanted to throw him overboard?"

"I think you are putting the case too strongly," I said. "The criticism of a healthy public opinion is no bad thing. Besides, your Cabinet still have fifty per cent of their energy left. What do they do with that?"

"Of that," said Champion, joining in, "about forty per cent is wasted on mere parade—dummy legislation—bills that never will be passed, and which no sensible man has any desire should be passed, except in a mutilated and useless condition; bills merely brought forward by the Government as a sop to the extreme wing of their own party. It doesn't matter which side is in power. If they are Liberals, they have to propose a few socialistic and iconoclastic measures, secretly thanking God for the House of Lords all the while. If they are Conservatives, they propitiate the Landlords and the Church by putting forward some outrageously retrograde proposal or other, secure in the knowledge that it will be knocked on the head by the halfpenny papers. Of the remaining ten per cent——"

"About nine," resumed Robin, "is appropriated automatically to absolutely essential routine business, like the Budget and Supply——"

"And the remaining one per cent," struck in Champion, "is devoted to real live Legislation."

Then they both looked at me, this pair of carping pessimists, rather furtively, like two fags who have allowed their tongues to wag over freely in the presence of a monitor. It was a curious tribute to the power of officialdom, for they were both far bigger men, in every sense, than I. Finally Champion laughed.

"Don't look so horrified, Adrian," he said. "Mr Fordyce and I croak too much. Still, you will find a grain or two of sense among the chaff, as Jack Point says."

But I was not to be smoothed down so easily.

"According to you fellows," I grumbled, as I passed the port, "there is practically no difference between one political party and another."

"None whatever," said Champion cheerfully—"not between the *backbones* of the parties, that is. Of course excrescences don't count. Tell me, Adrian, what bill, barring one or two contentious semi-religious measures, has ultimately reached the Statute Book during the last twenty years that might not have been put there by either party without any violent departure from its principles? Not one! Foreign policy, again. Does it make any difference to our position in the world which party is in office nowadays? Not a scrap. The difference between the two sides is immaterial. There is often a far deeper line of cleavage between two sections of the same party than between party and party. We make faces at each other, it is true; and one side plumes itself on the moral support of Royalty and the aristocracy, while the other always bawls out that it has the inviolable will of the people at its back,—I daresay one assertion is about as true as the other—but I don't think there is a pennyworth of difference, really. There used to be a lot, mind you, when the Plebs were really struggling for a footing in the scheme of things; but bless you! we are all more or less in the same crowd now. Just a difference of label, that's all."

"There was a story my dominie used to tell," said Robin, who had been listening to this diatribe with rapt attention, "about a visitor to a seaside hotel, who ordered a bottle of wine. The boy brought up the wrong kind, so the visitor sent for the landlord and pointed out the mistake, adducing the label on the bottle as evidence. 'I'm very sorry, sir, I'm sure,' said the landlord, 'but I'll soon put it right. Boy, bring another label!' An old story, I am afraid, but it seems to me to put Party goverment into a nutshell."

I rose, and began to replace the stoppers in the decanters. I was feeling rather cross. I hate having my settled convictions tampered with. They are not elastic, and this makes them brittle, and I always feel nervous about their stability when the intellectual pressure of an argument grows intense.

"When you two have abolished the British Constitution," I remarked tartly, "what do you propose to substitute for the present *régime*?"

"'There,'" said Champion, "as the charwoman replied when asked for a character, 'you *'ave* me.' Let us join the ladies."

But I was still angry.

"It always seems best to me," I persisted doggedly, "to take up a good sound line of action and stick to it, and to choose a good sound party and stick to that. Half a glass of sherry before we go upstairs?"

"No, thanks. That is why I envy you, Adrian," said Champion. "It's a wearing business for us, being so—so—what shall we call it, Mr Fordyce?"

"Detached?" suggested Robin.

"That's it."

"Two-faced would be a better word," I growled.

Champion clapped me on the shoulder.

"Adrian," said he, "in time of peace there is always a large, critical, neutral, and infernally irritating party, for ever philandering betwixt and between two extremes of opinion. But when war is declared and it comes to a fight, the ranks close up. There is no room for detachment, and there are no neutrals. When occasion calls, you'll find all your friends—your half-hearted, carping, Erastian friends—ranged up tight beside you. Shall we be trapesing about in Tom Tiddler's ground when the pinch comes, Mr Fordyce—eh?"

"Never fear!" said Robin.

And I am bound to say that we all of us lived to see John Champion's assertion made good.

CHAPTER SIX.
ROBIN OFF DUTY.

I have yet to introduce to the indulgent reader two more members of the family into which I have married.

The first of these is my daughter Phillis, of whom I have already made passing mention. She is six years old, and appears to be compounded of about equal parts of angelic innocence and original sin. In her dealings with her fellow-creatures she exhibits all the *sangfroid* and self-possession that mark the modern child. She will be a "handful" some day, the Twins tell me, and they ought to know. However, pending the arrival of the time when she will begin to rend the hearts of young men, she contents herself for the present with practising that accomplishment with complete and lamentable success upon her own garments.

She is the possessor of a vivid imagination, which she certainly does not inherit from me, and is fond of impersonating other people, either characters of her own creation or interesting figures from story-books. Consequently it is never safe to address her too suddenly. She may be a fairy, or a bear, or a locomotive at the moment, and will resent having to return to her proper self, even for a brief space, merely to listen to some stupid and irrelevant remark—usually something about bed-time or an open door—from an unintelligent adult.

Kitty says that I spoil her, but that is only because Kitty is quicker at saying a thing than I am. She is our only child; and I sometimes wonder, at moments of acute mental introspection (say, in the night watches after an indigestible supper), what we should do without her.

The other character waiting for introduction is my brother-in-law, Master Gerald Rubislaw. He is the solitary male member of the family of which my wife and the Twins form the female side. He is, I think, fourteen years of age, and he is at present a member of what he considers—very rightly, I think; and I should know, for I was there myself—the finest public school in the world. Having no parents, he resides at my house during his holidays, and refreshes me exceedingly.

He is a sturdy but rather diminutive youth, with a loud voice. (He always addresses me as if I were standing on a distant hill-top.) He bears a resemblance to his sisters of which he is heartily and frankly ashamed, and which he endeavours at times to nullify as far as possible by a degree of personal uncleanliness which would be alarming to me, were it not that the traditions of my own extreme youth have not yet been entirely obliterated from my memory.

His health is excellent, and his intellect is in that condition euphemistically described in house-master's reports as "unformed." He is always noisy, constitutionally lazy, and hopelessly casual. But he possesses the supreme merit of being absolutely and transparently honest. I have never known him tell a lie or do a mean thing. To such much is forgiven.

At present he appears to possess only two ambitions in life; one, to gain a place in his Junior House Fifteen, and the other, to score some signal and lasting victory over his form-master, a Mr Sydney Mellar, with whom he appears to wage a sort of perpetual guerilla warfare. Every vacation brings him home with a fresh tale of base subterfuges, petty tyrannies, and childish exhibitions of spite on the part of the infamous Mellar, all duly frustrated, crushed, and made ridiculous by the ingenuity, resource, and audacity of the intrepid Rubislaw. I have never met Mr Mellar in the flesh, but I am conscious, as time goes on and my young relative's reminiscences on the subject accumulate, of an increasing feeling of admiration and respect for him.

"He's a rotten brute," observed Gerald one day. "Do you know what he had the cheek to do last term?"

"What?"

"Well, there was a clinking new desk put into our form-room, at the back. I sit there," he added rather *naïvely*. "As soon as I saw it, of course I got out my knife and started to carve my name. I made good big letters, as I wanted to do the thing properly on a fine new desk like that."

"Was this during school hours?" I ventured to inquire.

"Of course it was. Do you think a chap would be such a silly ass as to want to come in specially to carve his name during play-hours, when he's got the whole of his school-time to do it in?"

"I had not thought of that," I said apologetically.

"And don't go putting on side of that sort, Adrian, old man," roared Gerald, in what a stranger would have regarded as a most threatening voice, though I knew it was merely the one he keeps for moments of playful badinage. "I saw *your* name carved in letters about four inches high in the Fifth Form room only the other day. I don't see how you can jaw a man for doing a thing you used to do yourself thirty or forty years ago."

I allowed this reflection on my appearance to pass without protest, and Gerald resumed his story.

"Well, I did a first-class G to begin with, and was well on with the Rubislaw—all in capitals: I thought it would look best that way—when suddenly a great hand reached over my shoulder and grabbed my knife. It was Stinker, of course."

"St——"

"Oh, I forgot to tell you that. We call him 'Stinker' now. You see, his name is S. Mellar, and if you say it quickly it sounds like 'Smeller.' So we call him 'Stinker.' It was a kid called Lane thought of it. Pretty smart—eh? Oh, he's a clever chap, I can tell you," yelled Gerald, with sincere enthusiasm.

"He must be a youth of gigantic intellect," I said.

"Oh, come off the roof! Well, Stinker grabbed my knife, and said, 'Hallo, young man, what's all this? Handing down your name to posterity—eh?' with a silly grin on his face.

"I said I was just carving my name.

"'I see you have just finished it,' he said.

"I didn't quite tumble to his meaning at first, because I had only got as far as G. RUB,—and then I saw that the whole thing as it stood spelled 'GRUB.' Lord, how the swine laughed! He told the form all about it, and of course they all laughed too, the sniggering, grovelling sweeps!

"Then Stinker said: 'A happy thought has just occurred to me. I shall not have your name obliterated in the usual manner'—they cut it out and put in a fresh bit of wood, and charge you a bob—' this time. I have thought of a more excellent way.' (He always talks like that, in a sort of slow drawl.) 'We will leave your name exactly as you have carved it. But remember, young man, not another letter do you add to that name so long as you are a member of this school. A Grub you are,—a nasty little destructive Grub,—and a Grub you shall remain, so far as that desk is concerned, for all time. And if ever in future years you come down here as a distinguished Old Boy—say a K.C.B. or an Alderman,—remember to bring your numerous progeny'—oh, he's a sarcastic devil!—'to this room, and show them what their papa once was!'

"Of course all the chaps roared again, at the idea of me with a lot of kids. But that wasn't all. He switched off *that* tap quite suddenly, and said—

"'Seriously, though, I am not pleased about this. Carving your name on a desk is not one of the seven deadly sins, but doing so when I have told you not to *is*. This silly street-boy business has been getting too prevalent lately: we shall have you chalking things up on the walls next. I particularly gave out last week, when this new desk was put in, that no one was to touch it. Come to me at twelve, and I will cane you.' And he *did*," concluded Gerald, with feeling.

"What a shame!" said Dilly, who was sitting by. "All for carving a silly old desk."

"He was perfectly right," said Gerald, his innate sense of justice rising to the surface at once. "I wasn't lammed for cutting the desk at all: it was for doing it after I had been told not to."

"It's the same thing," said Dilly, with feminine disregard for legal niceties.

"Same thing? Rot! Fat lot you know about it, Dilly. It's a rum thing," he added to me in a reflective bawl, "but women never can understand the rules of any game. Stinker is a bargee, but he was quite right to lam me. It was for disobedience; and disobedience is cheek; and no master worth his salt will stand cheek. So Stinker says, and he is right for once."

Gerald is the possessor of a bosom friend, an excessively silent and rather saturnine youth of about his own age. His name is Donkin, and he regards Gerald, so far as I can see, with a grim mixture of amusement and compassion. He pays frequent visits to my house, as his father is a soldier in India; and he is much employed by the Twins for corroborating or refuting the more improbable of their brother's reminiscences.

Robin soon made friends with the boys. Like most of their kind, their tests of human probity were few and simple: and having discovered that Robin not only played Rugby football, but had on several occasions represented Edinburgh University thereat, they straightway wrote him down a "decent chap" and took the rest of his virtues for granted.

It came upon them—and me too, as a matter of fact—as rather a shock one evening, when Robin, during the course of a desultory conversation on education in general, suddenly launched forth *more suo* into a diatribe against the English Public School system.

English boys, he pointed out, were passed through a great machine, which ground up the individual at one end and disgorged a mere type at the other—("Pretty good type too, Robin," from me),—they were taught to worship bodily strength—("Quite right too!" said my herculean brother-in-law),—they were herded together under a monastic system; they were removed from the refining influence of female society—(even the imperturable Donkin snorted at this),—and worst of all, little or nothing was done to eradicate from their minds the youthful idea that it is unmanly to read seriously or think deeply.

I might have said a good deal in reply. I might have dwelt upon the fact that the English Public School system is not so hard upon the stupid boy—which means the average boy—as that of more strenuous forcing-houses of intellect abroad. I might have spoken of one or two moral agents which prevent our schools from being altogether despicable: unquestioning obedience to authority, for instance, or loyalty to tradition. I might have told of characters moulded and fibres stiffened by responsibility—our race bears more responsibility on its shoulders than all the rest of the world put together—or of minds trained to interpret laws and balance justice in the small but exacting world of the prefects' meeting and the games' committee. But it was Gerald, who is no moralist, but a youth of sound common-sense, who closed the argument.

"Mr Fordyce," he said, "it's no use *my* jawing to you, because you can knock me flat at that game; and of course old Moke there"—this was Master Donkin's unhappy but inevitable designation among his friends—"is too thick to argue with a stuffed rabbit; but you had better come down some time and see the place—that's all."

Robin promised to suspend judgment pending a personal investigation, and the incident closed.

Gerald's verdict on Robin's views, communicated to me privately afterwards, was characteristic but not unfavourable.

"He seems to have perfectly putrid notions about some things, but he's a pretty sound chap on the whole—the best secretary you have had, anyhow, old man. Have you seen him do a straight-arm balance on the billiard-table?"

But I did not fully realise how completely Robin had settled down as an accepted member of my household until one afternoon towards the end of the Christmas holidays.

There is a small but snug apartment opening out of my library, through an arched and curtained doorway. The library is regarded as my workroom—impregnable, inviolable; not to be rudely attempted by devastating housemaids. There is a sort of tacit agreement between Kitty and myself as regards this apartment. Fatima-like, she may do what she pleases with the rest of the house. She may indulge her passion for drawing-room meetings to its fullest extent. She may intertain missionaries in the attics and hold meetings of the Dorcas Society in the basement. She may give reformed burglars the run of the silver-closet, and allow curates and chorus-girls to mingle in sweet companionship on the staircase. But she must leave the library alone, and neither she nor her following must overflow through its double doors during what I call business hours.

On this particular afternoon I had been engaged upon the draft of a small bill with which I had been entrusted—we will call it the "Importation of Mad Dogs Bill,"—and about four o'clock I handed it to Robin with instructions to write out a fair copy. Robin retired into his inner chamber, and I sat down in an arm-chair with *Punch*. (It was a Wednesday, the Parliamentary half-holiday of those days, and still, happily, the *Punch*-day of these.)

Kitty was holding a Drawing-room Meeting upstairs. I forget what description of body she was entertaining: it was either a Society for the Propagation of something which could never, in the nature of things, come to birth; or else an Association for the Prevention of something that was bound to go on so long as the world endured. I had been mercifully absolved from attending, and my tea had been sent in to me. I was enjoying an excellent caricature of my Chief in the minor cartoon of *Punch*, when I heard the door of the inner room open and the voice of my daughter inquire—

"Are you *dreful* busy, Uncle Robin?" (My secretary had been elevated to avuncular rank after a probation of just three hours.)

There was a sound as of a chair being pushed back, and a rustle which suggested the hasty laying aside of a manuscript, and Robin's voice said—

"Come away, Philly!" (This is a favourite Scoticism of Robin's, and appears to be a term denoting hearty welcome.)

There was a delighted squeal and the sound of pattering feet. Next ensued a period of rather audible osculation, and then there was silence. Presently Phillis said—

"What shall we do? Shall I sing you a hymn?"

Evidently the revels were about to commence.

"I have just learned a new one," she continued. "I heared it in Church yesterday afternoon, so I brought it home and changed it a bit. It's called 'Onward, Chwistian Sailors!'"

"'*Soldiers*,' isn't it?"

"No—'*Sailors*.' It *was* 'Soldiers,' but I like sailors much better than soldiers, so I changed it. I'll sing it now."

"Wait till Sunday," said Robin, with much presence of mind. "Will you not tell me a story?"

This idea appeared so good that Phillis began forthwith.

"Once there were three horses what lived in a stable. Two was wise and one was just a foolish young horse. There was some wolves what lived quite near the stable——"

"Wolves?" said my secretary, in tones of mild surprise.

"The stable," explained Phillis, "stood in the midst of the snowy plains of Muscovy. I should have telled you that before."

"Just so," said Robin gravely. "Go on."

"Well, one day," continued the narratress's voice through the curtains—I knew the story by heart, so I was able to fill up the gaps for myself when she dropped to a confidential whisper—"one cold, windy, berleak day, the old wolves said to the young ones, 'How about a meal of meat?' and all the young one's said, 'Oh, *let's*!'

"That very morning," continued Phillis in the impressive bass which she reserves for the most exciting parts of her narrative, "that *very* morning the foolish young horse said to the old horses, 'Who is for a scamper to-day?' Then he began to wiggle and wiggle at his halter. The old horses said, 'There is wolves outside, and our master says that they eat all sheep an' cattle an' horses,' But the young horse just wiggled and wiggled,"—I could hear my daughter suiting the action to the word upon her audience's knee,—"and pwesently his halter was off! Then out he rushed, kicking up the nimble snow with his feathery heels, and—what?"

Robin, who was automatically murmuring something about transferred epithets, apologised for this pedantic lapse, and the tale proceeded.

"Well, just as he was goin' to have one more scamper, he felt a growl—a awful, fearful, deep *growl*,"—Phillis's voice sank to a bloodcurdling and continuous gurgle—"and he terrembled, like this! I'll show you——"

She slipped off Robin's knee, and I knew that she was now on the hearth-rug, simulating acute palsy for his benefit.

"Then he felt somefing on his back, then somefing further up his back, then a bite at his neck; and then he felt his head bitten off, and he died. Now you tell me one."

"Which?"

Phillis considered.

"The one about the Kelpie and the Wee Bit Lassie."

Robin obliged. At first he stumbled a little, and had to be prompted in hoarse whispers by Phillis (who apparently had heard the story several times before); but as the narrative progressed and the adventures of the wee bit lassie grew more enthralling and the Kelpie more terrifying, he became almost as immersed as his audience. When I peeped through the curtain they were both sitting on the hearth-rug pressed close together, Phillis gripping one of Robin's enormous hands in a pleasurable condition of terrified interest. The fair copy of the "Importation of Mad Dogs Bill," I regret to say, lay on the floor under the table. I retired to my arm-chair.

"The Kelpie," Robin continued, "came closer and closer behind her. Already she could feel a hot breath on her neck." (So could Robin on his, for that matter.) "But she did not give in. She ran faster and faster until——"

"You've forgotten to say she could hear its webbed feet going *pad pad* over the slippery stanes," interpolated Phillis anxiously.

"So I did. I'm sorry. She could hear its webbed feet going *pad pad* over the slippery stanes. Presently though, she came to a wee bit housie on the moor. It was empty, but she slippit through the yard-gate and flew along the path and in at the door. The Kelpie came flying through the gate——"

"No, no—it loupit ower the dyke!" screamed Phillis, who would countenance no tamperings with the original text.

"Oh, yes. It loupit ower the dyke, but the wee lassie just slammed the door in its face, and turned the key. Then she felt round in the dark and keeked about, wondering what kind of place she was in. And at that very moment, through a bit window in the wall——"

"She went ben first."

"Oh, yes. She went ben; and at that very moment, through the bit window in the back-end of the house, there came a ray of light. The sun——"

"The sun had risen," declaimed Phillis, triumphantly taking up the tale; "and with one wild sheriek of disappointed rage the Kelpie vanished away, and the wee lassie was *saved*!"

There was a rapt pause after this exciting anecdote. Then Phillis remarked—

"Uncle Robin, let's write that story down, and then I can get people to read it to me."

"Why not write it down for yourself?"

"I can't write—much; and it ought to be writed in ink, and I—I am only allowed to use pencil," explained my daughter, not without a certain bitterness. "But I put the lead in my mouf," she added defiantly.

At this moment the door of my apartment was hurled open, and Gerald projected himself into the room. It was the evening before his return to school, and there was a predatory look in his eye. He was accompanied by his speechless friend.

"Adrian, old son," he began, in such tones as an orator might address to a refractory mob, "Moke and I are going to have a study next term, and we want some furniture."

I mildly remarked that in my day furniture was supplied by the school authorities.

"Yes, but I mean pictures and things. Can you give us one? We shall want something to go on that wall opposite the window, shan't we, Moke? The place where young Lee missed your head with the red-ink bottle. *Have* you got a picture handy, Adrian?"

I replied in the negative.

Gerald took not the slightest notice.

"It will have to be a pretty big one," he continued. "There is a good lot of red ink to cover. I have been taking a look round the house, and I must say the pictures you've got are a fairly mangy lot—aren't they, Moke?"

The gentleman addressed coughed deprecatingly, and looked at me as much as to say that, whatever he thought of my taste in art, he had eaten my salt and would refrain from criticism.

"There's one that might do, though," continued Gerald. "It's hanging in the billiard-room—a big steamer in a storm."

By this time Phillis and Robin had joined the conclave.

"I know," said Phillis, nodding her head; "a great beautiful boat in some waves. I should fink it was a friend of the *Great Eastern's*," she added, referring to an antiquated print of the early Victorian leviathan which hung in the nursery.

"We could take it for a term or two, anyhow," continued Gerald, "until we get something better. I'm expecting some really decent ones after summer. Ainslie *major* is leaving then, and he has promised to let me have some of his cheap. Then you can have yours back, Adrian. That's the scheme! Come on, Moke, we'll go and take it down now. Thanks very much, old chap" (to me). "I'll tell Kitty that you've let us. We can jab it off its hook with a billiard-cue, I should think, Moke. Come too, will you, Mr Fordyce? You can stand underneath and catch it, in case it comes down with a run. So long, Adrian!"

The whole pack of them swept from the room, leaving the door open.

When I looked in at the billiard-room on my way up to dress for dinner an hour later, nothing remained to mark the spot hitherto occupied by a signed and numbered proof of *An Ocean Greyhound*, by Michael Angelo Mahlstaff, A.R.A. (a wedding gift to my wife and myself from the artist), but the imprints of several hot hands on the wall, together with a series of parallel perpendicular scars, apparently inflicted by a full-sized harrow.

From which two chapters it will be gathered that Robert Chalmers Fordyce was a man capable, in his ordinary working-day, of playing many parts.

CHAPTER SEVEN.
A DISSOLUTION OF PARTNERSHIP.

I.

My wife and I would have been more than human if we had not occasionally cast a curious eye upon the relations of Robin and the Twins.

Of Robin's attitude towards that pair of charmers Kitty could make little and I nothing. He kept his place and went his own way—rather ostentatiously, I thought—and appeared if anything to avoid them. If he found himself in their company he treated them with a certain grave reticence—he soon grew out of his fondness for addressing us like a public meeting—and made little attempt to bestow upon them the attentions which young maidens are accustomed to receive from young men.

There was no mystery about the Twins' attitude towards Robin. "Here," said they in effect, "is a fine upstanding young man, full of promise, but hampered in every direction by abysmal ignorance on matters of vital importance. His instincts are sound, but at present he is quite impossible. What he wants is mothering."

And so they mothered him, most maternally. They exerted themselves quite strenuously to instil into him the fundamental principles of life—the correct method of tying a dress tie; the intricate ritual which governs such things as visiting-cards and asparagus; the exact limit of the domains of brown boots and dinner-jackets; the utter criminality of dickeys, turn-down collars, and side-whiskers; and the superiority of dialogue to monologue as a concomitant to afternoon tea.

In many respects, they discovered with pleased surprise, their pupil required no instruction or surveillance. For instance, he could always be trusted to enter or leave a room without awkwardness, and his manner of address was perfect. He was neither servile nor familiar, and the only people to whom I ever saw him pay marked deference were the members of what is after all the only real and natural aristocracy in the world—that of old age.

All their ministrations Robin received with grave wonder—he was not of the sort that can easily magnify a fetish into a deity—but, evidently struck by the intense importance attached by the Twins to their own doctrines, he showed himself a most amenable pupil. Probably he realised, in spite of hereditary preference for inward worth as opposed to outward show, that though a coat cannot make a man, a good man in a good coat often has the advantage of a good man in a bad coat. So he allowed the Twins to round off his corners; and, without losing any of his original ruggedness of character or toughness of fibre, he soon developed into a well-groomed and sufficiently presentable adjunct—quite distinguished-looking, Dilly said, when she met us one day on our way down to the House—to a lady's morning walk.

What he really thought of it all I do not know. I have a kind of suspicion that deep down in his heart every Scot entertains a contempt for the volatile and frivolous English which is only equalled by that of the English for the nation to whom I once heard a Highland minister refer as "the giddy and godless French"; but Robin was not given to the revelation of his private thoughts. He seldom spoke of the Twins to me—he was a discusser of manners rather than men—but he once remarked that they were girls of widely different character. He entered into no further details, but I remember being struck by the observation at the time; for I had always regarded my sisters-in-law as being as identical in disposition as they were in appearance.

Still it was pretty to see Robin unbending to please the two girls, and to hear him say "No, really?" or "My word, what rot!" when you knew that his tongue was itching to cry, "Is that a fact?" or "Hoots!" or "Havers!" as the occasion demanded.

He also possessed the great and unique merit of not being ashamed to ask for guidance in a difficulty. I have known him pause before an unfamiliar dish at table and ask one of his preceptresses, in the frankest manner possible, whether the exigencies of the situation called for a spoon or a fork: and out of doors it was a perpetual joy to hear him whisper, on the approach of some one whom he thought might be a friend of ours, "Will I lift my hat?"

All that year Robin was my right hand. It was a long session; and as my Chief sat in the Upper House, much work in the way of answering questions and making statements fell upon me. We had a good working majority, but the Opposition were a united and well-organised body that year, and we had to rise early and go to bed late to keep their assaults at bay while proceeding with the programme of the session. Every afternoon, before I entered the House to take my place at question-time, my secretary insisted on taking me through the answers which he had prepared for my recitation; and we also discussed the line of action to be pursued if I were cornered by questions of the "arising-out-of-that-answer" order.

Personally, I loathed this part of the work—I am a departmentalist pure and simple—but Robin's eye used to glow with the light of battle as he rehearsed me in the undoubtedly telling counters with which I was to pulverise the foe.

"I would like fine," he once said to me, "to stand up in your place and answer these questions for you."

"I wish you could, Robin," I sighed. "And," I added, "I believe you will some day."

Robin turned pink, for the first time in our acquaintance, and I heard his teeth click suddenly together.

So the wind lay that way!

II.

During the next year my household was furnished with three surprises, Dilly contributing one and Robin two.

Robin's came first. One was his uncle, the other his book.

One night it fell to my lot to dine in the City, as the guest of the Honourable Company of Tile-Glazers and Mortar-Mixers. As I swam forlornly through a turgid ocean of turtle-soup and clarified punch towards an unyielding continent of fish, irrigated by brown sherry, mechanically rehearsing to myself the series of sparkling yet statesmanlike epigrams with which I proposed to reply to the toast of his Majesty's Ministers I became aware that the gentleman on my left was addressing me in a voice that seemed vaguely familiar.

"And how is my brother's second boy doing with you, Mr Inglethwaite?"

I must have looked a trifle blank, for he added—

"My nephew, Robin."

I glanced obliquely at the card which marked his place at table, and read—

Sir James Fordyce.

Then I began to grasp the situation, and I realised that this great man, whose name was honourably known wherever the ills of childhood are combated, was Robin's uncle, the "doctor" to whom my secretary had casually referred, and whom he occasionally went to visit on Sunday afternoons. I had pictured an overdriven G.P., living in Bloomsbury or Balham, with a black bag, and a bulge in his hat where he kept his stethoscope. A man sufficiently distinguished to represent his profession at a public banquet was more than I had bargained for.

We became friends at once, and supported each other, so to speak, amid the multitude of dinners and dishes, our respective neighbours proving but broken reeds so far as social intercourse was concerned. On Sir James's left, I remember, sat a plethoric gentleman whose burnished countenance gave him the appearance of a sort of incarnate Glazed Tile; while my right-hand neighbour, from the manner in which he manipulated the food upon his plate, I put down without hesitation as a Mortar Mixer of high standing.

The old gentleman gave me a good deal of information about Robin.

"He had a hard fight his first year or two in London," he said. "I could see by the way he fell upon his dinner when he came to my house that his meat and drink were not easily come by. Still, now that he has won through, he will not regret the experience. I had it myself. It is the finest training that a young man can receive. Hard, terribly hard, but invaluable! You will not have seen his father yet—my brother John?"

I told him no.

"Well, try and meet him. You, as an Englishman, would perhaps call him hard and narrow,—after forty years of London I sometimes find him so myself,—but he is a fine man, and he has a good wife. So have you," he added unexpectedly—"Robin has told me that."

I laughed, in what the Twins call the "silly little gratified way" which obtrudes itself into my demeanour when any one praises Kitty.

"I hope you are in the same happy situation," I said.

"No, I am a bachelor. My brother John has not achieved a K.C.B., but he is a more fortunate man than I."

The conversation dropped here, but I repeated it to my wife afterwards.

"Of course, the whole thing is as clear as daylight," she said. "These two brothers both wanted to marry the same girl. She took the farmer one, so the other, poor thing, went off to London and became a famous doctor instead. That's all. He might have been Robin's father, but he's only his uncle."

Happy the mind which can reconstruct a romance out of such scanty material.

Sir James ultimately dined at my house, and became a firm friend of all that dwelt therein, especially Phillis.

Then came Robin's second surprise—his book. It was a novel, and a very good novel too. He had been at it for some time, he told me, but it was only recently that he had contrived to finish it off. Being distrustful of its merits, he had decided to offer it to just one good publisher, who could take it or leave it. If he took it, well and good. But if the publisher (and possibly just one other) exhibited an attitude of aloofness, Robin had fully decided not to hawk his bantling about among other less reputable and more amenable firms, but to consign it to his bedroom fire.

However, this inhuman but only-too-unusual sacrifice of the parental instinct was averted by the one good publisher, who accepted the book, and introduced Robin to the public.

Either through shyness or indifference Robin had told us nothing of the approaching interesting event, and it was not until one morning in October, when a parcel of complimentary copies arrived from the publisher's, that we were apprised of the fact that we had been cherishing an author in our midst. Robin solemnly presented us with a copy apiece (which I thought handsome but extravagant), and also sent one to his parents, who, though I think they rather doubted the propriety of possessing a son who wrote novels at all, wrote back comparing it very favourably with *The Pilgrim's Progress*, the only other work of fiction with which they were acquainted.

The book itself dealt with matters rather than men, and with men rather than women; which was characteristic of its author, but rather irritating for the Twins. It had a good deal to say about the under-side of journalism,—graphic and convincing, all this,—and contained a rather technical but absorbingly interesting account of some most exciting financial operations, winding up with a great description of a panic on the Stock Exchange. But there were few light and no tender passages, from which it will be seen that Robin as an author appealed to the male rather than the female intellect.

The Twins, I think, were secretly rather disappointed with the book, less from any particular fondness for the perusal of love-passages than from a truly human desire to note how Robin would have handled them; for it is always interesting to see to what extent our friends will give themselves away when they commit the indiscretion of a book. On this occasion Robin had been exasperatingly self-contained.

But life is full of compensations. There was a dedication. It read:—

THIS BOOK

OWES ITS INCEPTION,

AND IS THEREFORE

DEDICATED,

TO

A CIRCUMSTANCE

OVER

WHOM

I HAVE NO CONTROL.

R. C. F.

Now it is obvious that in nine cases out of ten there is only one circumstance over whom a vigorous young man has no control, and this circumstance wears petticoats. Hitherto I had not seriously connected Robin with the tender passion, and this sudden intimation that the most serious-minded and ambitious of young men is not immune from the same rather startled me.

The female members of my establishment were pleasantly fluttered, though they were concerned less with the lady's existence than with her identity.

"Who do you think she is?" inquired Kitty of me, the first time the subject cropped up between us.

"Don't know, I'm sure," I murmured. I was smoking my post-prandial cigar at the time, at peace with all the world. "Never had the privilege of seeing his visiting-list."

"I wonder who she can be," continued my wife. "He—he hasn't said anything to you, has he, dear?" she inquired, in a tentative voice.

I slowly opened one of my hitherto closed eyes, and cocked it suspiciously at the diplomatist sitting opposite to me. (The Twins and Robin were out at the theatre.) Then, observing that she was stealthily regarding me through her eyelashes—a detestable trick which some women have—I solemnly agitated my eyelid some three or four times and gently closed it again.

"Has he confided any of his love affairs to you, I mean?" continued Kitty, quite unabashed.

"If you eat any more chocolates you will make yourself sick," I observed.

"Yes, dear," said my wife submissively, pushing away the bon-bon dish. "But has he?"

"Are you trying to pump me?"

"Oh, gracious, no! What would be the good? I only asked a plain question. You men are such creatures for screening each other, though, that it's never any use asking a man anything about another man."

"True for you. As a matter of fact, Robin has hardly said a word to me on the subject of women since first I met him."

Kitty thoughtfully cracked a filbert with her teeth—an unladylike habit about which I have often spoken to her—and said—

"What exciting chats you must have!" Then she added reflectively—

"I expect it's a girl in Scotland. A sort of Highland lassie, in a kilt, or whatever female Highlanders wear."

"Why should a novel about the Stock Exchange 'owe its inception' to a Highland lassie?"

Kitty took another filbert.

"That's 'vurry bright' of you, Adrian, as that American girl used to say. There's something in that. (Yes, I know you don't like it, dear, but I love doing it. I'll pour you out another glass of port. There!) But any idiotic excuse is good enough for a man in love. Has he ever been sentimental with you—quoted poetry, or anything?"

"N-no. Stop, though! He did once quote Burns to me, but that was *à propos* of poetry in general, not of love-making."

I remembered the incident well. Robin had picked up at a bookstall a copy of an early and quite valuable edition of Burns' poems. He had sat smoking with me in the library late the same night, turning over the pages of the tattered volume, and quoting bits, in broad vernacular, from "Tam o' Shanter" and "The Cottar's Saturday Night." Suddenly he began, almost to himself—

"O, my love is like a red, red rose,
That's newly sprung in June;
My love is like a melody
That's sweetly played in tune.
As fair art thou, my bonnie lass,
So deep in love am I——"

He broke off for a moment, and I remembered how he glowered ecstatically into the fire. Then he concluded—

"And I will love thee still, my dear,
Till a' the seas gang dry."

"Man," he said, "that's fine! That's poetry. That's the real thing!"

I had agreed. It is no use arguing with a Scot about Burns. (I remember once being nearly dirked at a Caledonian Dinner because I ventured to remark that "before ye" was not in my opinion a good rhyme to "Loch Lomond.")

However, Kitty and I were unable to decide whether Robin's "bonnie lass" on that occasion had been a personality or an abstraction.

"Mightn't it be one of the Twins?" I remarked.

"Well, it *might* be," admitted Kitty judicially, "but he has kept it very close if it is. No," she continued more decidedly, "I don't think it can be. They are quite out of his line. Besides—it would be too absurd!"

It was not one Twin at any rate, for a fortnight later Dilly sprung upon us the third surprise of the series I have mentioned. She announced that she had decided to marry Dicky Lever.

There was, I suppose, nothing very surprising in that. Dicky had been in constant attendance upon the Twins for nearly two years, and had long since graduated into the ranks of the Good Sorts. The surprise to us—rather unreasonably, perhaps—lay in the fact of—

- 1. Dicky having definitely fixed upon a particular Twin to propose to;
- 2. That Twin having definitely selected Dicky out of the assortment at her command.

I was so accustomed to seeing my sisters-in-law compassed about by a cloud of young men who appeared to admire them both equally, and to whom they appeared to apportion their favours with indiscriminate *camaraderie*, that the idea of one admirer stealing a march on all the others seemed a little unfair, somehow.

As Dolly remarked, it would break up the firm horribly.

"You see," she confided to me rather plaintively, "Dilly will have no use for them now, and they'll have still less use for her—an engaged girl beside other girls is about as exciting as a tapioca-pudding at a Lord Mayor's Banquet—and they will only have me. That won't be half the fun."

"I should have thought that your fun would have been exactly doubled," I said.

"Not a bit. How like a man! Don't you see, the fun used to be in playing them backwards and forwards between our two selves—like ping-pong, you know! It was clinking!"

She sighed regretfully.

"Now I shall either have to avoid men or marry them," she concluded, vaguely but regretfully. "Before, if they got in the way, I could always volley them back to Dilly. Now—one *can't* play ping-pong all by oneself!"

III.

Dilly's engagement, as is usual under such circumstances, afforded my household many opportunities for airy badinage and innocent merriment.

Dolly always heralded her coming into the billiard-room, where the affianced pair had staked out a claim, by a cough of penetrating severity, and usually entered the room with her features obscured by an open umbrella. On several occasions, too, she impersonated her sister; and once, when Dicky was spending a week-end in the house, was only prevented by the fraction of a second from robbing that incensed damosel of her morning salute.

My share in the proceedings was limited to a single constrained interview with Dicky, at which, feeling extremely rude and inquisitive, I asked him the usual stereotyped questions about his income, prospects, and habits (most of which I knew only too well already), which, being satisfactorily answered, I rang the bell for the Tantalus, and thanked heaven that the Twins were not Triplets. I had indeed suggested that Dilly's nearest and most natural protector was her brother, Master Gerald, and that Dicky should apply not for my consent but his. This motion, however, was negatived without a division. I was sorry, for I think my brother-in-law would have shown himself worthy of the occasion.

My wife received the news of the engagement with all the enthusiasm usually exhibited by a Salvation lassie when a fresh convert is hustled forward to the "saved" bench, and henceforth divided her time between ordering Dilly's trousseau and giving tea-parties, at which the prospective bridegroom was produced and passed round, "as if," to use his own expression, "he were the newest thing in accordion-pleating."

As regards Robin's share in the event, I can only recall one incident. He had been away at Stoneleigh, the largest town in my constituency, on some party business, and when he returned home the engagement had been announced for nearly a week.

"I must go and offer my good wishes to Miss Dilly," he said, after hearing the news. "Do you know where she is, Mrs Inglethwaite?"

"I saw her upstairs a few minutes ago," said Kitty. "Come up, and we'll find her."

We were in the library at the time, and Kitty and Robin left the room together. The rest of the story my wife told me later.

"We went up," she said, "and looked into the drawing-room, where I had last seen Dilly. The room was nearly dark, but she was there, sitting curled up in front of the fire.

"'There she is,' I said. 'Go and say something nice.'

"Well, dear,"—Kitty's face assumed an air of impressive solemnity which makes her absurdly like her daughter—"he stood hesitating a moment, and then walked straight up to her and said—

"'Good afternoon! Can you tell me where your sister is? I want to offer her my good wishes on the great event.'

"It wasn't Dilly at all. It was Dolly! And he was able to distinguish between the two in that dim room. And *I* couldn't!"

"Oh," said I carelessly, "I expect he noticed she wasn't wearing an engagement-ring."

My wife looked at me and sighed, as over one who would spoil a romance for want of a ha'porth of sentiment. And yet I know she would have been quite scandalised if any one had hinted at tender passages between her sister and my secretary. Women are curious creatures.

CHAPTER EIGHT.
OF A PIT THAT WAS DIGGED, AND WHO FELL INTO IT.

Dicky Lever was a hearty and not particularly intellectual youth of the What ho! type (if you know what I mean). He was employed in some capacity in a Government office, but his livelihood was not entirely dependent on his exertions therein—which was, perhaps, fortunate, as his sole claim to distinction in his Department lay in the fact of his holding the record for the highest score at small cricket in the Junior Secretaries' room. He was a member of the Leander Club, a more than usually capable amateur actor, and a very good fellow all round.

The engagement was announced at the end of July, which is a busy time for this country's legislators. The session was drawing to a close, and we were passing Bills with a prodigality and despatch which provoked many not altogether undeserved gibes from a reptile Opposition Press concerning the devotion of his Majesty's Government to the worship of Saint Grouse.

One night I brought Champion home to dinner between the afternoon and evening sittings. At the latter he was to move the second reading of his "Municipal Co-ordination Bill," a measure which was intended to grapple with the chaos arising from the multitude of opposing or overlapping interests that controlled the domestic arrangements of the Londoner. An effort was to be made to bring all the Gas, Electricity, Water, Paving, and other corporations into some sort of line, and prevent them from getting into each other's way and adding to the expenses and inconvenience of the much-enduring ratepayer. It was a useful little Bill; but though everybody approved of it on principle, various powerful interests were at work against it, and its prospects of getting through Committee hung in the balance.

"Now, Mr Champion," said Dilly, who knew that a man always likes to be questioned about his work, especially by a pretty girl, "what will your Bill do for *us*? I have asked this person here,"—indicating her *fiancé*,—"but he says parish-pump politics aren't in his department. He licks stamps at the Foreign Office," she added in explanation.

"Tell her, Champion," said Dicky. "Out of my line altogether. Takes me all my time to keep an eye on those Johnnies in the Concert of Europe."

"I will tell you one thing the Bill will do, Miss Dilly," said Champion, a little heavily. (Dolly once said of him, "He's awfully clever and able and all that, but he hasn't got a light hand for conversational pastry.") "How many times have you noticed the streets up about here this year?"

"Heaps," said Dilly.

"They have hardly ever been down," corroborated Dolly.

"Let me see," continued Dilly. "Our side of the Square was repaved in January. Directly after that they took it up again and did something to the drains."

"In March they opened it again to lay down an electric light main," said I.

"In April something burst," said Dolly, "and that meant more men with wigwams and braziers."

"And last month," concluded Dilly, "they took away the wood pavement and relaid the whole Square with some new patent asphalte, which smelt simply, oh——"

"Rotten!" supplied Gerald. (Have I mentioned that he had just arrived home for his summer holiday?)

"Well," said Champion, "the Bill would regulate that sort of thing. It would protect the streets from being torn up at will by any Company who happened to have business underneath them. As things are, practically any one may come along and hew holes anywhere he pleases."

"The police ought to stop it," said Kitty, who has a profound belief in the Force. (I am convinced that if Beelzebub himself were to enter the house at any time during my absence, Kitty would lure him into the dining-room with the sherry, and then telephone for a constable.)

"The police have no right," said Champion. "If a gas company choose to give notice that they intend on a certain day to come and burrow in a road, all the police can do is to divert the traffic, and make the gas company as comfortable as possible."

I was not following this conversation with any particular interest. Being expected to speak in favour of the Bill that night, I was undergoing the preliminary anguish which invariably attends my higher oratorical efforts. But I remember now that about this time Dilly suddenly turned to Dicky and whispered something in his ear. Then they both looked across the dinner-table at Robin, who nodded, as who should say, "I know fine what you whispered then." After that they all three laughed and looked down the table at Champion, who was still expatiating on the merits of his Bill.

I suppose anybody else would have divined what was in the wind, but I did not.

A week later we were treated to an all-night sitting. The Irishmen had been quiescent of late, but on this occasion they made amends for their temporary relaxation of patriotism by resolutely obstructing an Appropriation Bill, which had to pass through Committee that night (if John Bull was to have any ready cash at all during the next few months), and kept us replying to amendments and trotting through division-lobbies until six o'clock next morning.

Robin stayed on in attendance at the House most of the night, but about three o'clock I sent him home, with instructions to stay in bed till tea-time if he pleased. He had had a hard time lately.

I was walking homeward in the early sunshine, marvelling, as people who accidentally find themselves up early pharisaically do, at the fatuity of those who waste the best hours of the whole day in bed, and revelling in the near prospect of a bath and my breakfast, when on turning a corner I walked into a hand-cart which was standing across the pavement. It contained workmen's tools—picks, shovels, and the like. On the near side of the roadway a man was erecting one of those curious wigwam arrangements which screen the operations of electricians and other subterranean burrowers from the public gaze. A dirty-faced small boy in corduroys was tending a brazier of live coals, upon which some breakfast cans were steaming. Between the wigwam and the pavement a gigantic navvy was hewing wooden paving-blocks out of the roadway.

The spectacle did not attract my interest specially, as this particular piece of street had been eviscerated so often that I had grown callous to its sufferings. But I paused for a moment to survey the big navvy's muscles, and to wonder how early in the morning it would be necessary to rise in order to catch a small boy with a clean face. The navvy was a fine specimen of humanity, with a complexion tanned a dusky coffee colour.

I was reflecting on the joys of the simple life and the futility of politics and other indoor pastimes in general, when the big man rose from his stooping posture and caught my eye. He appeared a little disconcerted by my scrutiny, and turned his back and renewed his exertions with increased vigour, favouring me hereafter with what architects call a "south elevation" of himself.

I went home to breakfast, wondering where I had seen the big navvy's back before. I mentioned casually to Kitty and the Twins that Goring Street was up again. They wondered how the management of the Goring Hotel liked it, with that mess under their very windows, and agreed with me that it was high time Champion's Bill, due for its Third Reading to-morrow, became law.

I stayed in bed till lunch-time, and then, rather late in the afternoon, set out for the House, which I knew I should find in an extremely limp condition after its previous night's dissipation. On the way I called in at the Goring Hotel in Goring Street, where Champion lived when in town. I found him in his room on the first floor, gazing out of the window into the street.

I looked out too, to see what was interesting him. Directly below us lay the encampment of the workmen whom I had seen in the morning. They had hewed up a few yards of the wood pavement, and the smaller of the two men was now immersed up to his waist in a hole, working rather laboriously in the restricted space at his command with a pick-axe. The boy was piling wooden blocks into a neat heap, and the big man, whose form was only partially visible, was doing something inside the wigwam.

The roadway was more than half blocked, and cabs and omnibuses, in charge of overheated and eloquent drivers, were being filtered through the narrow space left at their disposal by a phlegmatic policeman.

"Look here," said Champion.

I looked.

"What on *earth* are those fellows doing?" he continued.

"Re-laying the road, perhaps."

"One doesn't re-lay a road by making a deep hole in it."

"Well—gas!"

"Gas and electric light mains in this street are all led along a special conduit reached by manholes every eighty yards," said Champion. "There's no need to dig."

"Well—drains!" said I vaguely. But I was a mere child in the hands of this expert.

"The drains, as you call them," he said testily, "consist of a great sewer away in the depths, accessible from various appointed places. Besides, nobody in his senses tries to lift earth out of a hole with a pick-axe."

"Perhaps the solution of the mystery lies inside the wigwam," I said.

"No. That is just what complicates matters. When a shaft leading down to the electric light mains is opened, one of those canvas shelters is put over the top. Now there is nothing under that shelter—nothing but the bit of road it covers. The thing seems to be simply a stage accessory, planted there to give the encampment an aspect of reality. Ah, look at that!"

"That" was a small piece of paving-wood, dexterously hurled by the dirty-faced boy, who seemed to be finding time hang rather heavily on his hands. It took a passing citizen in the small of the back, but when he swung round to detect the source of the missile the boy was on his knees again industriously blowing up the brazier.

With an indignant snort the citizen passed on his way, doubtless adding the outrage, in his mind, to the long list of unsolved London crimes. But retribution awaited the youthful miscreant. The phlegmatic policeman who was regulating the traffic on the single-line system happened to notice the deed. He walked majestically across from the far side of the street towards our excavating friends.

"Come on!" said Champion to me. "There's going to be some fun."

We stepped out through one of the windows, which possessed a broad balcony, and took our stand behind some laurels in tubs which lined the balustrade. The street was comparatively quiet at the time, and we were able to hear most of the dialogue that ensued.

"'Ere, mate," began the traffic-expert to the smaller of the two navvies, "just ketch that boy of yours a clip on the side of the 'ead, will you?"

The smaller man desisted from his labours in the hole.

"Wotsye, ole sport?" he inquired cheerily.

The policeman was a little ruffled by this familiarity.

"I'll trouble *you*," he repeated with some hauteur, "to ketch that boy of yours a clip on the side of the 'ead. If not, I shall 'ave to do my duty, according——"

Here the roar of a passing dray drowned his utterance.

The smaller man clambered nimbly out of the hole and proceeded to grab his young friend by the scruff of the neck.

"Billy," he remarked dispassionately, "this gentleman says as 'ow I'm to give you a clip on the side of the 'ead."

"Woffor," inquired Billy, simulating extreme terror.

The man passed the question on to the policeman, who explained the nature of the offence. His statement was voluntarily corroborated by several members of an audience which seemed to have materialised from nowhere, and now formed a ring round the encampment.

"Righto!" said the man with cheery acquiescence. "Billy, my lad, you've got to 'ave it."

"Tha's right, ole son! You give 'im socks," remarked a hoarse and rather indistinct voice of the gin-and-fog variety, from among the spectators.

Simultaneously its owner lurched his way to the front rank, the others making room for him with that respectful sympathy, not unmixed with envy, which is always accorded to a true-born Briton in his condition. He was obviously a member of some profession connected with coal-dust, and it was plain that he had been celebrating the conclusion of his day's labours.

The smaller navvy, thus exhorted, administered the desired clip. It was not a particularly severe one, but it drew from its recipient the somewhat unexpected expostulation—

"You silly ass! Not so hard!"

Where had I heard that stentorian but childish voice before? Who was this road-breaker's acolyte, with his brazier, his dirty face, and—a public-school accent?

I leaned over the balustrade and surveyed him and his two companions. Then I drew my breath sharply.

Merciful heavens!

The dirty-faced boy was my brother-in-law, Master Gerald Rubislaw, the clip-administerer was Dicky Lever, and the gigantic and taciturn navvy was—my Secretary!

Having witnessed the carrying-out of the sentence, the policeman returned to his duties; none too soon; for a furniture van and a butcher's cart, locked in an inextricable embrace, the subject of a sulphurous duet between their respective proprietors, called loudly for his attention.

Meanwhile Coaldust, who had been inspecting the result of our friends' united labours with some interest, suddenly echoed the question which had first exercised Champion's logical mind by inquiring what the blank dash the two adjectival criminals and the qualified nipper thought they were doing to the asterisked road.

He received no encouragement. Robin was now engaged with a hammer and chisel in cutting a sort of touch-line all round the encampment, while Dicky did not cease manfully to delve with the pick-axe in the pit which he had digged for himself. For a long time they turned a deaf ear to the anxious inquiries of their interlocutor.

But there are limits to long-suffering. Coaldust's witticisms increased with his audience, and at last Dicky turned to Robin and cried, with a really admirable maintenance of character and accent—

"'Ere, Scotty, come and give this bloke one in the neck. 'E's askin' for it!"

Robin deliberately suspended operations, rose heavily to his feet, and cleared his throat. Then he turned upon the alcoholic Coaldust. I strained my ears. Surely *he* was not going to talk Cockney!

Far from it. He stuck to his last.

"See here, ma man," he roared, in a voice that made the crowd jump, "are ye for a ding on the side o' the heid?"

Coaldust capitulated with alacrity.

"No offence, 'Orace!" he remarked genially. "You an' me was always pals. Put it there!" He extended an ebony hand, which Robin solemnly shook and returned to his work.

Whatever my three friends were up to, it is possible that they might now have been left in peace for some time; for the crowd, seeing no chance of further sport from Coaldust, began to melt away. But a fresh character entered the scene to keep alive the nagging interest of the drama.

My first intimation that something new was afoot came from an errand-boy on the edge of the crowd, who, addressing a lady or ladies unseen, suddenly expressed a desire to be chased.

All heads were now turned down the street, and there, approaching with rather faltering steps, carrying a red cotton bundle and a tea-can, I beheld—one of my sisters-in-law!

Postulating Dicky, I presumed it was Dilly, and I began to piece together in my mind the plot of this elaborate comedy. Evidently Dicky, Robin, and Gerald had decided—for a bet, or because they were dared, or possibly with a view to giving Champion's Bill a leg-up by a practical demonstration of the crying need for it—to dress themselves up as workmen and come and "do a turn," as they say in the music halls, to the discomfort of his Majesty's lieges and the congestion of traffic, upon some sufficiently busy thoroughfare for a stated period of time.

Certainly they were doing it rather well. They were admirably made up,—Dicky was a past-master at that sort of thing,—and their operations so far had been sufficiently like the genuine article to impose upon the public in general,—if we except Champion and Coaldust,—even to the point of securing the assistance of the traffic-directing policeman.

But alas! with that one step further, which is so often fatal to great enterprises, they had sought to add a finishing touch of realism to their impersonation by the inclusion of a little feminine interest; and to that end Dilly had been added to the cast—or more likely had added herself—in the *rôle* of a young person of humble station bringing her affianced his tea.

And, not for the first time in the history of man, it was the woman who opened the door to disaster.

Dilly wore a natty print dress—probably my housemaid's—with a tartan shawl over her head. She had on her thickest shoes, but they were woefully smart and thin for a girl of her class. Moreover, her hair was beautifully arranged under the shawl, and her hands—though she had had the sense to discard her ruby and sapphire engagement-ring—were too white and her face was too clean to lend conviction to her impersonation. In short, in her desire to present a pleasing *tout ensemble*—an object in which I must say she had succeeded to perfection—Dilly had utterly neglected detail and histrionic accuracy.

Evidently she was not expecting a gallery. Two highly-interested concentric circles—one of people and one of dogs—round her *fiancé's* encampment was rather more than she had bargained for. She had emerged quite suddenly from a side street (which I knew led to a shortcut from home) and now paused irresolutely a few yards away, crimson to the roots of her hair, what time the errand-boy, with looks of undisguised admiration, continued to reiterate his desire to be pursued.

The crowd all turned and stared at poor Dilly. Obviously they did not know what to make of her. Possibly she was some one from the chorus of a musical comedy going to be photographed, possibly she was merely "a bit balmy," or possibly she was an advertisement for something, and would begin to distribute hand-bills presently. So far, she merely looked as if she wanted to cry.

It was Robin who saw her first. He immediately stepped over his newly-completed touch-line, and taking the spotted bundle and the tea-can from her hands, conducted her ceremoniously within the magic circle, saying, in a voice much more like his own than before—

"Come away, lassie!"

Dicky looked up from his labours at this, and beheld his *fiancée* for the first time. All he said was—

"By gad, you've done it after all! Bravo!"

But Dilly did not appear to be at all gratified She merely sat on Gerald's little mountain of paving-blocks, looking as if she could not decide whether to throw her apron over her face and scream, or take a header into the wigwam. My heart bled for her in spite of her folly. The crowd, deeply interested and breathing hard, stood round waiting for the performance to begin.

It was Coaldust who took the lead.

"Tip us a song and dance, Clara," he said encouragingly.

Robin, who had been making a show of unfastening the bundle, suddenly rose to his feet. Coaldust saw him.

"All right, Carnegie," he remarked hurriedly. "No offence, ole pal!"

But Robin turned to Dicky, and the two held a hasty conversation, whose nature I could guess. Dilly could not be exposed to this sort of thing any longer. They began to put on their coats.

"They are going to give it up," I said, not without relief. "About time, isn't it? Do you recognise them, Champion?"

But Champion, I found, was gone—probably to establish an *alibi*. Perhaps he was right. Questions might be asked in the House about this.

When I turned again to the scene below I found that the crowd had thickened considerably, and that the policeman had once more left the traffic to congest itself, and joined in the game.

"You must tell that young woman to move on," he said to Dicky, not unkindly. "She's causin' a crowd to collect, and that's a thing she can be give in charge for."

"All right," said Dicky hurriedly, "we're all going."

The policeman, struck by this sudden anxiety to oblige, became suspicious.

"All of you?" he said. "'Ow about this mess in the road?"

Robin came to the rescue.

"We'll be back presently and sort it," he said reassuringly.

"Of course," said Dicky, pulling himself together. "Back in 'arf a tick, governor!"

"Don't you go callin' me names," said the policeman, as the spectators indulged in happy laughter.

"Sorry!—I mean, certainly!" said Dicky, getting flustered. (I could see Robin glowering at him.) "We are just going down the street a minute. This—er—girl has brought us a bit of bad news. There's been an accident happened—er——"

"To her puir old mither," put in Robin, whom I began to suspect of rather enjoying this entertainment for its own sake.

This heartrending piece of intelligence touched the crowd, and Coaldust was instantly forward in proposing an informal vote of condolence, which was seconded by a bare-armed lady in a deerstalker cap. But the policeman, evidently roused by our friends' ill-judged and precipitate attempt to strike camp, suddenly produced a pocket-book from his tunic, and said—

"It is my duty to take your names and addresses, together with the name of the firm employing you."

This announcement obviously disconcerted Dicky and Robin; for it is one thing to take part in a masquerade, and another to get out of the consequences thereof by cold-drawn lying.

However, the policeman was sucking his pencil and waiting, so Dicky said—

"You can get all the information you want from the Borough Surveyor."

It was a bold effort, but the policeman merely said—

"Your name, please!"

Dicky, fairly cornered, replied—

"Er—Samuel"—I thought at first he was going to say "Inglethwaite," and was prepared to drop a flower-pot on his head if he did; but he continued, with the air of one offering a real bargain at the price—"Phillipps."

"Two P's?" inquired the constable.

"Three," said Dicky.

The policeman rolled a threatening eye upon him.

"Be careful!" he said in an awful voice.

"One of them comes at the beginning," said Dicky meekly.

"Haw, haw!" roared several people in the crowd, which was unfortunate for Dicky. He was one of those people who would risk a kingdom to raise a laugh.

"Address?" continued the policeman.

"Buck'nam Pallis!" shouted Coaldust, before any one else in the crowd could say it.

The policeman turned and directed upon him a look that would have entirely obfuscated a soberer man.

"I'll attend to you presently," he said in the exact tones which my dentist employs when he shuts me into the waiting-room. "Now then, your address? Come along!"

Dicky gave some address which I did not catch, and the representative of the law turned to Robin. The latter evidently saw rocks ahead if the inquisition was to be extended to the whole party. He said—

"Surely there is no need to take any more names."

"I'll be responsible for the lot," added Dicky eagerly—too eagerly. "Now let's be off! Come along Di—Liza!"

He took Dilly by the arm, and, preceded by Gerald, began to press through the crowd, which by this time extended almost right across the street.

But the now thoroughly aroused guardian of the peace, determined not to be rushed like this, broke away from Robin, who was engaging him in pleasant conversation, and, hastening after the retreating group, laid a detaining and imperious hand on Dilly's arm.

What happened next I was not quick enough to see. But there was a swirl and a heave in the crowd, and presently Dicky became visible, standing in a very heroic attitude with his arm round Dilly; while the policeman, with an awe-inspiring deliberateness which implied "Now you *have* gone and done it!" extricated himself majestically but painfully from the chasm in the road which had recently been occupying Dicky's attention, and into which Dicky in defence of his beloved had apparently pushed him.

Picking up his pocket-book and putting it back into his chest, and uttering the single and awful word "*Assault!*" the policeman produced a whistle and blew it.

Things were certainly getting serious, and I had just decided to send out the hotel porter to the policeman to tell him to bring his captives inside out of the way of the crowd, when I noticed that Robin was ploughing his way towards the outskirts of the throng, waving his arm as he went. Then I saw that his objective was another policeman—an Inspector this time. He was a gigantic creature, and Robin and he, slowly forging towards each other through the surrounding sea of faces, looked like two liners in a tideway.

Robin's conduct in deliberately attracting the notice of yet another representative of law and order appeared eccentric on the face of it, but his subsequent behaviour was more peculiar still.

He seized the newly-arrived giant by the arm, and drew him apart from the crowd, where he told him something which appeared to amuse them both considerably.

"Yewmorous dialogue," announced Coaldust to his neighbours, "between Cleopartrer's Needle and the Moniment!"

But it was more than that,—it was deep calling to deep. Presently the explanation, or the joke, or whatever it was, came to an end, and the Inspector advanced threateningly upon the crowd.

"Pass along, there, pass along!" he cried with a devastating sweep of his arm. He spoke with a Highland accent, and I realised yet once more the ubiquity of that great Mutual Benefit Society which has its headquarters north of the Tweed.

The crowd politely receded about six inches, and through them, accompanied by Robin, the Inspector clove his way to the encampment, where Dicky, who seemed to be rapidly losing his head, was delivering a sort of recitative to every one in general, accompanied by the policeman on the whistle.

What the Inspector said to his subordinate I do not know, but the net result was that in a very short time the former was escorting the entire party of excavators down the street, attended by a retinue of small boys (who were evidently determined to see if it was going to turn out a hanging matter); while the latter, to whom the clearing of the "house" had evidently been deputed, set about that task with a vigour and ferocity which plainly indicated a well-meaning and zealous mind tingling under an entirely undeserved official snub.

They told me all about it in the smoking-room that night.

"The idea," began Dicky, "was——"

"Whose idea was it?" I inquired sternly "It was all of our idea," replied my future relative by marriage lucidly.

"But who worked it out?" I asked,—"the plot, the business, the 'props'? It was a most elaborate production."

"Never you mind that, old man," said Dicky lightly. (But I saw that Robin was laboriously relighting his pipe and surrounding himself with an impenetrable cloud of smoke.) "Listen to the yarn. The idea was to stake out a claim in some fairly busy road and stay there for a given time—say, six o'clock till tea-time—and kid the passing citizens that we were duly authorised to get in the way and mess up the traffic generally. If we succeeded we were going to write to *The Times* or some such paper and tell what we had done—anonymously, of course—just to show how necessary Champion's Bill is."

"Have you written the letter?"

"Yes."

"I wouldn't send it if I were you."

"Well, that's what Robin here has been saying."

"Putrid rot if we don't!" remarked Gerald, who had by this time washed his face, but ought to have been in bed for all that.

"We can't do it," said Robin. "For one thing, we have attracted quite enough public attention already,—it's bound to be in the papers anyhow, now, and that will probably give the Bill all the advertisement it needs,—and if we give the authorities any more clues our names may come out. For another thing, it wouldn't be fair to Hector MacPherson."

"Who is he?"

"That Inspector who came up at the critical moment. He was one of my first friends in London."

"I remember. Go on."

"I was thankful to see him, I can tell you. Well, he undertook to square that poor bewildered bobby, and to take steps to get the road cleared and the hole filled up."

"How?"

"There is a street being mended just round the corner, and he said he would get the foreman of the gang, who is a relation of his wife's, to send a couple of men to put things right immediately. It's probably done by now."

"Then I suppose we may regard the incident as closed."

"Yes, I suppose so."

There was a silence.

"It was a bit of a failure at the finish," said Dicky meditatively, "but it was a success on the whole—what?"

"Rather!" said his fellow-conspirators.

"Our chief difficulty," continued Dicky, "was to decide on the exact type of drama to present. I was all for our dressing up as foreigners, and relaying an asphalte street. It would have been top-hole to trot about in list slippers and pat the hot asphalte down with those things they use. And think of the make-up!—curly moustaches and earrings! And we could have jabbered spoof Italian. But then old Robin here, who I must say has a headpiece on him, pointed out that the scenery and props would be much too expensive. We should want a cart with a bonfire in it and a sort of witches' cauldron on top, and all kinds of sticky stuff; so we gave up that scheme. We did not feel inclined to mess with gas-pipes or electric wires either, in case we burst ourselves up; so we finally decided to select some street with a wooden pavement, and maul it about generally for as long as we could. If we got interfered with by anybody official, we meant to talk some rot about the Borough Surveyor, and skedaddle if necessary. But it all worked beautifully!"

"Where did you get your tools and tent?"

"Robin managed that," said Dicky admiringly.

Robin looked extremely dour, and I refrained from further inquiry.

"Robin's got some rum pals, I *don't* think!" observed Gerald pertinently.

"Didn't I make these chaps up well?" continued Dicky enthusiastically. "We roared when you passed us at breakfast-time without spotting us."

"Very creditable impersonation," I replied, getting up and knocking my pipe out. "I only hope I shan't have to resign my seat over it. If I may venture to offer a criticism, the weak spot in the enterprise was the idea of inviting your lady friends to come and take tea with you."

"Just what I said all along, my boy," remarked the experienced Gerald, wagging his head sagely. "That was what mucked up the show. Wherever there's a petticoat there's trouble. Oh, I *warned* them!"

On my way up to bed I flushed Dilly from a window-seat on the staircase, where she had evidently been lingering on the off-chance of a supplementary good-night from Dicky.

"Well?" I said severely.

"Well?"

"Do you know what time it is?"

"I expect your wife will tell you that when you get upstairs," said Dilly.

I tried a fresh line.

"After the labours of to-day, I should have thought you would have been glad to go to bed," I said. "You imp!" And I laughed. There is something very disarming about the Twins' misdemeanours.

We turned and walked upstairs together, and paused outside Dilly's door.

"Good-night, Dilly," I said. "I admired your pluck."

"It wasn't me," said Dilly, in a very small voice.

"Not you?"

"N-no. I said I would come, because Dicky said I daren't, and at the last moment I funked it. (Adrian, I simply couldn't!) So Dolly went instead."

"Then that was Dolly all the time?"

"Yes."

"And she went, just to—to——"

"To save my face. She's a brick," said Dilly.

This, by the way, was the first occasion on which I realised the truth of Robin's dictum that Dilly and Dolly were girls of widely different character.

"And didn't the others recognise her?"

"No. That's the best of it!"

"Not Dicky?"

"No."

"Not even Robin? He is pretty hard to deceive, you know."

"No, not even Robin. *None* of them know Good-night!"

But she was wrong.

CHAPTER NINE.
THE POLICY OF THE CLOSED DOOR.

Dilly's wedding took place the following summer, just before Parliament rose, and the resources of our establishment were strained to the uttermost to give her a fitting send-off.

It is true that a noble relative, the head of my wife's family, offered his house for the reception, but Dilly emphatically declined to be married from any but mine, saying prettily that she would not leave the roof under which she had lived so happily until the last possible moment.

Accordingly we made immense preparations. The drawing-room on the first floor, accustomed though it was to accommodate congested and half-stifled throngs of human beings, was deemed too small for the mob of wedding-guests whom Kitty expected.

"You see, dear," she explained, "we can squash up *good* people as much as we like, because their clothes don't matter; but women in wedding-frocks will be furious if they don't get enough elbow-room to show themselves."

Accordingly a marquee was erected in the garden at the back of the house, opening into the dining-room through the French windows, and it was arranged that Dicky and Dilly were to take their stand in the middle of the same, what time the guests, having lubricated their utterance at the *buffet* in the dining-room *en route*, filed past and delivered their congratulations. After that the company was to overflow into the garden, there to be moved by a concord of sweet sounds emanating from a band of assassins in pseudo-Hungarian uniforms.

"And if it rains," concluded Kitty desperately, "they must have an overflow meeting in the basement—that's all!"

My library, as I had feared, was appropriated for the presents, and for several days I transacted the business of State at the wash-hand-stand in my dressing-room, while a stream of callers, ranging from the members of a Working Men's Club in which Dilly was fitfully interested, down to an organisation of Kitty's whose exact title I can never recall (but which Dicky, on first seeing them, immediately summed up as "The Hundred Worst Women"), filed solemnly past rows of filigree coffee-services, silver-backed hair-brushes, and art pen-wipers.

Of the bride-elect I saw little, and when I did, she was usually standing, in a state of considerable *déshabille*, amid a kneeling group of myrmidons, who, with mouths filled with pins and brows seamed with anxiety, were remorselessly building her into some edifice of shimmering silk and filmy lace, oblivious of their victim's plaintive intimations that she was fit to drop.

Dicky invited Robin to be his best man, a proceeding which, while it roused some surprise among those who were expecting him to fix upon a friend of longer standing and greater distinction, showed his good sense, for my secretary proved himself a model of organisation and helpfulness. Although born and reared up in the straitest sect of some Scottish denomination, about which I am unable to particularise beyond the fact that they regarded the use of harmoniums in churches as "the worship of men's feet," he betrayed a surprising knowledge of Anglican ritual and stage effect.

On the wedding morning, having left the bridegroom securely tucked up in bed, under strict orders not to get up till he was called, Robin personally conducted a select party of those interested—Dolly, Dilly, another bridesmaid, and myself—to the church, where he showed us the exact positions of our entrances and exits; and then proceeded, with the assistance of Dolly, to plant hassocks about the chancel in such a manner as to leave us no doubts as to the whereabouts of our moorings (or "stances," as he called them) at the actual ceremony.

The party was reinforced at this point by the arrival of no less a person than the bridegroom, who, having risen from his slumbers in defiance of Robin's injunctions, was now proceeding to infringe the laws of propriety by coming in search of his beloved four hours before he was entitled to do so.

However, as Dilly rather pessimistically pointed out, it was probably the last time she would ever get a kind word out of him, so we gave them ten minutes together in the porch, while Robin interviewed vergers and Dolly intimidated perspiring persons with red carpets and evergreens.

On our return home Dilly was snatched away by a cloud of attendant sprites, and we saw her no more until the time came for me to drive her to the church. We heard of her, though; for as we sat at luncheon, plying the bridegroom (who had collapsed after the complete and inevitable fashion of his kind about twelve o'clock) with raw brandy, a message came down from the upper regions, to the effect that Miss Dilly would take a couple of veal cutlets and a glass of Burgundy, as she wasn't going to be a pale bride if she could help it!

However, this half-hysterical gaiety came to an end in the face of reality, and in the carriage on the way to church poor Dilly wept unrestrainedly on my shoulder. I mopped her up to the best of my ability, but she was still sobbing when we reached the church door, to find the six bridesmaids, together with Phillis (inordinately proud of her office of train-bearer), preening themselves in the porch.

It had been arranged that the organ should break into "The March of the Priests," from 'Athalie'—Dicky's petition in favour of an ecclesiastical rendering of "The Eton Boating Song" had been thrown out with ignominy—as the bridal procession entered the nave. Unfortunately the organ-loft was out of sight of the west door, by which we were to enter, and the conveyance of the starting-signal to the proper quarter at exactly the right moment was a matter of some difficulty. However, Robin's gift for stage-management was sufficient to meet the emergency. When all was ready Dolly calmly mounting the steps of the font to an eminence which commanded a precarious but sufficient view of the body of the church, briefly fluttered a scrap of lace handkerchief, and then stepped demurely down into her place at the head of the bridesmaids. Simultaneously the organ burst into the opening strains of Mendelsohn's march—I suppose Robin had been waiting at some point of vantage to pass the signal on—and we advanced up the aisle, amid a general turning of heads and flutter of excitement.

The church was packed. In the back pew I remember noticing three young men with pads of flimsy paper and well-sucked pencils. I distinctly caught sight of the words "Sacred edifice" in the nearest MS., and I have no doubt the others contained it as well.

But Dilly was still quaking on my arm, and the only other spectacle which attracted my attention on the way up the aisle was that of my wife (looking very like a bride herself, I thought), sitting in a front pew with Master Gerald, that infant phenomenon shining resplendently in a white waistcoat and a "buttonhole" which almost entirely obscured his features. Then I caught sight of Robin's towering shoulders and the pale face and glassy eye of the bridegroom, and I knew that we had brought our horses to the water at last, and all that now remained to do was to make them drink.

The rest of the ceremony passed off with due impressiveness, if we except a slight *contretemps* arising from the behaviour of my daughter, who, suddenly remembering that the junior bridesmaid but one had not yet passed any opinion on her new shoes, suddenly sat down on the bride's train, and, thrusting the shoes into unmaidenly prominence, audibly invited that giggling damsel's approbation of the same. However, the ever-ready organ drowned her utterance with a timely Amen, and Dicky and Dilly completed the plighting of their troth with becoming shyness but obvious sincerity.

Then came the inevitable orgy of osculation in the vestry, from which I escaped with nothing worse, so to speak, than a few scratches, despite an unprovoked and unexpected flank attack (when I was signing the register) from an elderly female in bugles, whom I at first took to be a rather giddy pew-opener, but who ultimately proved to be a maiden aunt of the bridegroom's.

After Dicky and Dilly—the latter miraculously restored to high spirits and looking radiant—had passed smiling and blushing down the aisle, to be received outside with breathless stares by a large assemblage of that peculiar class of people—chiefly females of a certain age—who seem to spend their lives in attending the weddings of total strangers, we all got home, where there was much champagne, and cake-cutting, and bride-kissing, and melody from the aforementioned musicians in the garden.

The presents—guarded with an air of studied aloofness by a wooden-jointed detective, clad in garments of such festal splendour as to delude several short-sighted old gentlemen into an impression that he was the bridegroom—played their usual invaluable part in promoting circulation among the guests, and supplying a topic for conversation. They certainly sparkled and glittered bravely in the library, where the blinds were drawn and the electric lamps turned on. (Kitty had seen to that. Silver looks so well by artificial light, and so, by a happy and unpremeditated coincidence, does the female sex.)

The bride and bridegroom departed at last, amid a shower of rice, with that emblem of conjugal felicity, the satin slipper, firmly adhering to the back of the brougham. (Master Gerald had seen to *that*.) Then the guests began to make their adieux and melt away, and presently we found ourselves alone in the marquee, a prey to that swift and penetrating melancholy that descends upon those who begin to be festive too early in the day, and find themselves unable to keep it up till bed-time.

However, there was a recrudescence of activity and brightness in the evening, as the idea of a small dance had been proposed and carried, and the invitations issued and accepted, during the five minutes which witnessed the departure of the more intimate section of the guests.

When I returned from the House about midnight—I had gone there chiefly to dine, as lobster claws and melted ices appeared to be the only fare in prospect at home—tired to death, and conscious of an incipient cold in the head, arising from forced residence in a house in which hardly a door had been on its hinges for three days, I became aware that I was once again the lessee of a cave of harmony.

The pseudo-Hungarian assassins were pounding out the latest waltz, with a disregard for time and tune which I at first attributed to champagne, but which a closer survey proved to be due to the fact that the band was being conducted, surprising as it may seem, by my brother-in-law, who had kindly undertaken to wield the *bâton*, while the Chief Tormentor (or whatever his proper title may have been) charged himself anew at the refreshment counter. A popping of corks in the supper-room apprised me of the fact that my guests were doing their best, at my expense, to make the Excise Returns a more cheerful feature of next year's Budget.

I went upstairs in search of a white waistcoat and one or two other necessary contributions to the festivity of the evening, picking my way with the utmost care among the greatly-engrossed couples who impeded every step; and finally arrived at my dressing-room, to find that that hallowed apartment had been turned into a ladies' cloak-room, and that every available article of furniture stood elbow-deep under some attractive combination of furs and feathers.

I unearthed the things I required, but lacked the courage to stay and put them on. At any moment I might be invaded by a damsel who had met with some mishap in the heat of the fray, and was now desirous, as they say in the navy, of "executing repairs while under steam." I accordingly left the room and mounted towards the top of the house. I had in my mind's eye a snug little apartment, situated somewhere in the attics, devoted chiefly to dressmaking operations, where I knew there was a mirror, and I might complete my toilet in peace.

With becoming modesty I penetrated to this haven by the back-stairs. I had just reached the top, which was opposite the door in question, when I heard voices. Evidently some one was coming up to this same landing by the front stair.

A man does not look his best when found creeping up his own back-stairs with a white waistcoat in one hand and a pair of pumps in the other, and I confess I retreated downwards and backwards a couple of paces. The stair on which I stood was unlighted, and I had a good view of the landing.

The voices came nearer, and I could now hear the rustling of silks and laces. Presently I recognised the voices, and immediately after this their owners came into view, with their backs almost towards me.

"This is the room I mean," said the man, indicating my goal.

"That! All right! Only I don't see why you should drag me all the way up here," said the girl. "There are much nicer sitting-out places downstairs. Still, anything for a rest. Come on!"

She entered the room, followed by her partner. I saw his broad back for a moment as it filled the doorway. Then he turned in my direction with his hand on the handle, and it seemed to me that he hesitated a moment.

Finally he shut the door firmly, and—I distinctly heard the key turned in the lock.

I went downstairs again.

It was four o'clock in the morning. The last guest had gone, the domestics had retired to their subterranean retreat, and the musicians had all been booked through to Saffron Hill in one cab.

The dawn was just breaking over the house-tops on the other side of the square, and the sky was bathed in a curious heather-coloured light—a sure sign of a wet day to come, said hill-bred Robin. We stood out on the steps,—Kitty, Dolly, Robin, and I,—and Kitty put her arm round her sister's waist. I knew she was thinking of the absent Dilly.

Behind us, in the hall, Master Gerald, completely surfeited with about sixteen crowded hours of glorious life, lay fast asleep on a settee.

I looked curiously at Dolly as she leaned on her sister's shoulder. She was half a head taller than Kitty, and as she stood there, rosily flushed, in the dawn of her splendid womanhood, she might have stood for the very goddess whose first rays were now falling on her upturned face and glinting hair.

Then I looked at Robin, towering beside her, and suddenly I felt a little ashamed of myself.

For to tell the truth I had been very unhappy that evening, and I had been looking forward in a few minutes' time to unburdening myself to Kitty about recent events. But as I surveyed Dolly and Robin, curiously alike in their upright carriage and steady gaze, I suddenly realised that such a pair could safely be trusted to steer their own course; and I decided there and then not to communicate even to Kitty—my wife and Dolly's sister—the knowledge of what I had seen that night.

Kitty turned impulsively to her sister.

"After all, I've still got *you*, Dolly," she said.

I took a furtive glance at Robin's inscrutable countenance.

"I—*wonder*!" I said to myself.

"What, dear?" said Kitty.

"Nothing. I must carry this young ruffian up to bed, I suppose."

Curiosity has been most unfairly ear-marked as the exclusive monopoly of the female sex. But as I stumbled upstairs that night, bearing in my arms the limp but stertorous carcase of my esteemed relative by marriage, I could not help wondering (despite my efforts to put away from me a matter which I had decided was not my business) exactly what Robin *had* said to Dolly behind that locked door.

CHAPTER TEN.
ROBIN'S WAY OF DOING IT.

What happened when Robin locked the door on himself and Dolly is now set down here. Strictly speaking it ought to come later, but there is no need to make a mystery about it. I have taken the account of the proceedings mainly from the letter which Dolly wrote to Dilly three days later.

It would be useless to reproduce that document in full. In the first place, it contains a good deal that is not only irrelevant but absolutely incomprehensible. There is one mysterious passage, for instance, occurring right in the middle of the letter, beginning, *To turn the heel, knit to three beyond the seam-stitch, knit two together, purl one, turn: then knit ten, knit two together, knit one, purl one ...* introduced by an airy, "By the way, dear, before I forget"——which appears to have no bearing on the context whatever.

In the second place, Dolly's literary style is as breathlessly devoid of punctuation as that of most of her sex. Commas and notes of interrogation form her chief stock-in-trade, though underlining is freely employed. There is not a single full-stop from start to finish. The extracts from the letter here reproduced have been edited by me. Other details of the incident have been tactfully extracted by Kitty and myself—chiefly Kitty, I must confess—from the principals themselves, and the whole is now offered to the public, unabridged, with marginal comments, for the first time.

On entering the little room on the landing Dolly dropped on to a shabby but comfortable old sofa behind the door, and said, with a contented sigh—

"I'm so tired, Robin. Aren't you? Let's sit down and not talk till it's time to go downstairs again. It's—Robin, what *are* you doing?"

Robin was locking the door.

That operation completed, he turned and looked round the little room. There was an arm-chair in the corner, but he came and sat down on the sofa beside Dolly. Dolly gazed at him dumbly.

"He looked so utterly grim and determined" [says the letter], "that my heart began to bump in a perfectly fatuous way. I felt like a woman who is going to be murdered in a railway tunnel.

"He sat down, and one of his huge hands was suddenly stretched towards me, and I thought at first he was trying to grab one of mine. I did my best to edge away along the sofa, but I was up against the end already.

"Then his hand opened, and something dropped into my lap. It was the key of the door.

"'I have locked it,' he said, 'not with any intention of keeping you in, but in the hope of keeping other people out. You are perfectly free to get up and go whenever you please, if you don't wish to listen to what I have to say.'

"Well, dear, I suppose I ought to have risen to my full height, and, with a few superb gestures of haughty contempt, have swept majestically from the room. But—I didn't! I saw I was in for another proposal, and as the man couldn't eat me I decided to let him do his worst.

"It was a weird proposal, though." [*Spelt 'wierd.'*] "It wasn't exactly what he said, because one is never surprised at anything a man may say when he is proposing; but the way he said it. All men say pretty much the same thing in the end, but most of them are so *horribly* nervous that they simply don't know what they're talking about for the first five minutes or so. (Do you remember poor little Algy Brock? He was nearly *crying* all the time. At least he was with me, and I suppose he was with you too.) But Robin might have been having a chat with his solicitor the way he behaved. I'll tell you ..."

Robin apparently began by telling Dolly, quite simply and plainly, that he loved her. Then he gave a brief outline of the history of his affection. It had begun at the very beginning of things, he said, almost as soon as he discovered that he could distinguish Dolly from Dilly without the aid of the brown spot. "And that was after I had been in the house just three days," he added.

For some time, it appeared, he had been content to be pleasantly in love. He enjoyed Dolly's society when it came his way, but with native caution he had taken care to avoid seeking too much of it in case he should gradually find himself unable to do without it.

"I saw from the first," he said, "that you were entirely unconscious of my feelings towards you; and I would not have had it otherwise. If I was to succeed at all it must be as an acquired taste; and acquired tastes, as you know, are best formed unconsciously."

Dolly nodded to show her detached appreciation of the soundness of this point.

"I permitted myself one indulgence," Robin continued. "I dedicated a book to you."

"O-oh!" said Dolly, genuinely interested. "Was that me? Dilly and I thought it must be a girl in Scotland."

Then she realised that this was a step down from her pedestal of aloofness, and was silent again. Robin went on—

"Yes, it was you. It was a sentimental thing to do, but it afforded me immense pleasure. Love lives more on the homage it pays than that which it receives. Have you noticed that?"

"I have never thought about it," said Dolly distantly.

"I thought not," replied Robin; "because it shows, what I have always been tolerably certain of, that you have never been in love. However, to resume." [*"Like a lecture on Greek Roots, or something equally fusty,"* observes Dolly at this point.] "The time came, as it was bound to come, when I realised that I must tell you I loved you"——

"I rather like the way he always said *'love'* straight out," comments Dolly: "most men are so frightened of it. They say 'am fond of' or 'care for' or something feeble like that. All except the curate with pink eyes. (You remember him? Dora Claverton took him afterwards on the rebound.) He said 'esteem highly' I think."

——"or leave this house altogether. But before doing that I had to decide two things: firstly, whether I was good enough for you, and secondly, if not now, whether I ever should be."

Dolly's half-closed eyes opened a trifle wider. This was certainly a methodically-minded young man.

"It was difficult to decide the first question in practice," continued Robin. "In theory, of course, any man who is a *man*—honest, clean, and kind—is a fitting mate for any woman. Don't you think so?"

"No," said Dolly.

"I see," said Robin gently. "The theoretical is mainly the man's point of view: woman looks straight to practical results. She is rather inclined to take the virtues I have mentioned for granted, or do without them; and she founds her opinion of a man almost solely upon his capacity for boring her or stimulating her. In other words, she is guided by her instinct. Isn't she?"

"Is she?" said Dolly, determined this time to maintain her attitude of indifference.

"I think so," said Robin. "However, knowing how impossible it is for one sex to look at a matter from the point of view of another, I decided to stick to my own methods. So I made a summary of my points, good and bad. They are these: I am strong and healthy; I possess an appetite for hard work; I was born with brains; I have considerable capacity for organisation——"

"Some people have a good conceit of themselves!" said Dolly.

"*Every* one should have," replied Robin with conviction. "And," he added, "most of us have. *I* have—*you* have!"

"Oh!" said Dolly indignantly.

"But a man may have a good conceit of himself," Robin continued soothingly, "without being what the world calls conceited. Modesty consists not in taking a low estimate of one's own worth, but in refraining from the expectation that the world will take a high one."

Dolly nodded gravely.

"I see," she said. "I didn't know you meant that. Yes, there is something in what you say."

"I thank you," said Robin. "It is very helpful to me to get this courteous hearing from you; for to tell you the truth," he added rather explosively, "I find it a very, very great effort to speak to you like this at all. You see, I am talking of things that go right to the centre of the human heart—things that a man never speaks of to a man, and only once to a woman. It has to be done, but it is hard, hard!"

He drew a long breath, in a manner which made the sofa tremble; and Dolly suddenly realised the height and depth of the barrier of reserve and pride that this grave and undemonstrative man had had to break down before he could offer her the view of his inmost soul to which he considered that she was entitled. She felt a sudden pang of awe, mingled with compassionate sympathy. She was not given to wearing her heart on her sleeve herself.

"Well," continued Robin, evidently relieved by this little confession, "those are my assets. On the other hand, I have no money, no position—I will not say no birth, for I come of good, honest stock—and my prospects are at present in the clouds. But to one type of wife all that would not matter a scrap. There are two types, you know—two types of *good* wife, that is."

"I would have given worlds," says Dolly here, "just to have said 'Oh!' or something; but for the life of me I couldn't help asking what the two types were."

"The first," said Robin, "is the wife who loves her husband because she is proud of him, because he is successful and powerful, and people admire him; and not because she has any conception of or sympathy with the qualities which have made him what he is. To such a one the husband must come with his reputation ready made, and they will enjoy it together. The other type loves her husband because she sees through him, yet believes in him and sympathises with his aims, and intends to make a success of him. And she usually does."

"And which am I?" inquired Dolly.

"The latter, undoubtedly—the higher type. And therefore, if there had been nothing else in the way, I think I should have given myself the benefit of the doubt. But——"

"He turned and looked at me here," writes Dolly, and said—

"'But your feminine instinct is chafing against all this laborious weighing of pros and cons. In your own mind you summed up the situation ten minutes ago. I am—"impossible." Isn't that it?'

"My *dear*, I nearly *screamed*, for of course that is just what was in my mind. But I couldn't very well say so, so I just sat there and looked rather idiotic and he went on—

"'In other words, I am not quite a gentleman.'

"Then I said quite suddenly—

"'Robin, whatever else you may be, you *are* a gentleman.'

"He got quite pink. 'Thank you,' he said. 'But for all that, I am too rough a suitor for such a polished little aristocrat as yourself.' (Rather cheek, that! After all, Dilly, we're five feet seven.) 'We live in an artificial sort of world; and a man, in order not to jar on those around him, requires certain social accomplishments. I have few—at present. You have taught me a great deal, but I should still rather discredit you as a husband. My want of polish would 'affront' you, as we say in Scotland. I am a better beater than shot; I can break a horse better than I can ride it; and I dance a reel better than I waltz. I have strength, but no grace; ability, but no distinction. Of course, if you and I really loved each other—you being of Type Two—none of these things would matter. But for all that, it would hurt you to see people smiling at your husband's little *gaucheries*, wouldn't it?'

"I didn't answer, and he got up and went and leaned against the mantelpiece.

"'Listen,' he said, 'and I will tell you what I have decided to do. I have made up my mind not to have a try for you—badly though I want it—till I consider that I have reached your standard. I fixed that standard myself, so it is a very, very high one, I have been schooling myself and shaping myself to attain it ever since I met you. But I have not quite reached it yet, and therefore I have nothing to ask of you now.'"

"Then what on earth have you brought me here for?" inquired Dolly, feeling vaguely aggrieved.

Robin surveyed her rather wistfully, and then smiled in a disarming fashion.

"That was weakness," he said, "sheer weakness. But I think it was pardonable. I saw, now that your sister was married, that the days of your old irresponsible flirtations were over, and that you would henceforth regard proposals of marriage as much more serious things than hitherto. Consequently you might marry any day, without ever knowing that a little later on you would have received an offer from me. I have brought you here, then, to tell you that I am a prospective candidate, but that I do not feel qualified to put down my name at present. Ideally speaking, I ought to have kept silence until the moment when I considered that I was ready for you; but—well, there are limits to self-repression, and I have allowed myself this one little outbreak. All I ask, then, is that in considering other offers you will bear somewhere in the back of your mind the remembrance that you will, if you desire it, one day have the refusal of me. I admit that the possibility of your being influenced by the recollection is very remote, but I am going to leave nothing undone that *can* be done to get you."

"By this time," Dolly continues elegantly, "I was getting considerably flummoxed. The whole business was very absurd and uncomfortable, but I couldn't help feeling rather complimented at the way he evidently regarded me—as a sort of little tin goddess on a pedestal out of reach, being asked to be so good as to stand still a moment while Robin went to hunt for the steps—and I also felt a little bit afraid of him. He was so quiet and determined over it all. He seemed to have it all mapped out in a kind of time-table inside him. However, I pulled myself together and decided to contribute my share to the conversation. I hadn't had much of a look in, so far.

"So I settled down to talk to him like a mother. I began by saying that I was very much obliged and honoured, and all that, but that he had better put the idea out of his head once and for all. I liked him very much, and had always regarded him as a great friend, quite one of the family—you know the sort of stuff—but——

"It was no good. He held up his hand like a policeman at a crossing, and said—

"'Please say nothing. I have asked you no question of any kind, so no answer is required. All that I have said to-night has been in the nature of an *intimation*.' (O-h! how like church!)

"Then he sat down on the sofa beside me, very gently, and said—

"'The intimation in brief is this. I love you; and some day, please God, I shall ask you to marry me. But not until I feel that you would lose nothing by doing so.'

"We both sat very still for a few minutes after that. I fancy we were both doing a little thinking. My chief reflection was that Robin had had rather the better of the interview, because he had made me listen to him when I was determined not to. Suddenly Robin said—

"'Now that the business part of this conversation is over, I am going to allow myself a luxury. I have been talking most of the time about myself. For just five minutes I shall talk about you. I will tell you what I think of you.'

"He looked at his watch and began. Dilly, I had no idea I had so many good points! He put them better than any man has ever done before. But then the other men were always so jumbled up, and this creature was as cool and collected as if he were reading a Stores Catalogue.

"But he let himself go at last. It was my fault, though. I was in rather a twitter by this time, for although the whole thing was simply absurd—of course one couldn't marry a wild untamed creature like that, *could* one, Dilly?—I couldn't help seeing what a man he was, and feeling sorry that things couldn't have been a bit different, if only for his sake. So I gave him my hand" [I can see her do it] "and said: 'Poor old Robin!'

"He *seized* it—my child, it has waggled like a blanc-mange ever since!—and kissed it. Then, quite suddenly, he broke out into a sort of rhapsody—like '*The Song of Solomon,*' only nicer—with his head bowed over my hands. (He had got hold of the other one too, by this time.) I felt perfectly helpless, so I let him run on. I shan't tell you what he said, dear, because it wouldn't be cricket. Anyhow, a perfectly idiotic tear suddenly rolled down my nose—after all, I had had a *fearfully* long day—and I tried to pull my hands away. Robin let them go at once.

"'You are right. The time for such things is not yet,' he said, in a queer Biblical sort of way. 'It was a sudden weakness on my part. I had not meant it, you may be sure.'

"The only thing I *am* sure about," I said, feeling thoroughly vexed about the tear, "is that we have been in this room nearly an hour. Please unlock the door.

"Then we went downstairs."

After that follow one or two postscripts of a reflective nature, the general trend of which seems to indicate that Robin is rather a dear, but quite impossible.

"A flippant and unfeeling letter," you say, sir? Perhaps. But there is often no reserve so deep or so delicate as that which is veiled by a frivolous exterior and a mocking attitude towards sentiment in general.

Some sensitive people are so afraid of having their hearts dragged to light that, to escape inquisition, they pretend they do not possess any. Moreover, I know Dolly well enough to be certain that she was not quite so brutally unkind to Robin during this interview as she would have us believe.

"The blundering creature! He went about it in *quite* the wrong way," you say, madam? Very likely. But if a woman only took a man when he went about it in exactly the right way, how very few marriages there would be!

BOOK TWO.
THE FINISHED ARTICLE

CHAPTER ELEVEN.
A MISFIRE.

I.

There is an undefinable character and distinctiveness about Sunday morning which is not possessed by any other day of the week.

Not that the remaining six are lacking in individuality. Monday is a depressed and reluctant individual; Tuesday is a full-blooded and energetic citizen; Wednesday a cheerful and contented gentleman who does not intend to overwork himself to-day,—this is probably due to the fact that we used to have a half-holiday on Wednesdays at school; and when I got into Parliament I found that the same rule held there; Thursday I regard as one who ploughs steadily on his way, lacking enthusiasm but comfortably conscious of a second wind; Friday is a debilitated but hopeful toiler, whose sole joy in his work lies in anticipating its speedy conclusion; and Saturday is a radiant fellow with a straw hat and a week-end bag.

Still, one week-day is very like another at waking time. My mental vision, never pellucid, is in its most opaque condition in the early grey of the morning; and at Oxford, I remember, I found it necessary to instruct my scout to rouse me from slumber in some such fashion as this: "Eight o'clock on Thursday mornin', sir!" (as if I had slept since Monday at least), or "'Alf-past nine, slight rain, and a Toosday, sir!"

However, no one was ever yet needed to inform me that it was Sunday morning. This is perhaps natural enough in town, where the silence of the streets and the sound of bells proclaim the day; but why the same phenomenon should occur in the middle of a Highland moor, where every day is one glorious open-air Sabbath, passes my comprehension.

I discussed the problem after breakfast as I sat and smoked my pipe in the heathery garden of Strathmyrtle, a shooting-lodge at which we were being hospitably entertained by Kitty's uncle, Sir John Rubislaw, a retired Admiral of the Fleet, whose forty years' official connection with Britannia's realm betrayed itself in a nautical roll, syncopated by gout, and what I may describe as a hurricane-deck voice. My three companions in the debate were my host, Master Gerald, and another guest in the house, one Dermott, an officer in a Highland regiment.

The Admiral ascribed my Sabbath intuition to the working of some inward and automatic monitor; while Dermott, among whose many sterling qualities delicate fancy was not included, put it down to the smell of some special dish indigenous to Sunday breakfast. My brother-in-law's contribution to the debate was an unseemly and irreverent parallel between Saturday night potations and Sunday morning "heads."

To us entered Dolly and Phillis.

Our hostess, together with Kitty and the other girl of the party—an American young lady of considerable personal attractions—had driven off to church in what is locally called a "machine." The duties of escort had been voluntarily undertaken by an undergraduate named Standish, who was the latest recruit to the American young lady's army of worshippers. The rest of us had stayed at home—the Admiral because he not infrequently did so; I because I was expecting Robin back by the "machine" (which was to pick him up at a wayside station, where he had been sitting on his portmanteau ever since six o'clock that morning, having been dropped there by the night mail from London), and was anticipating two or three hours' solid work with him; Gerald because he had succeeded in evading his eldest sister's eye during the search for church recruits; Dolly to look after Phillis; and Captain Dermott for reasons not unconnected with Dolly.

It was Phillis's birthday, but out of consideration for Scottish views on Sabbath observance the festivities in connection with that anniversary had been postponed until the morrow. However, this did not prevent my daughter from demanding (and obtaining) various special privileges of an unofficial character this hot Sunday morning. Consequently a spiritually willing but carnally incompetent band, consisting of one jovial but arthritic baronet, one docile but self-conscious warrior, one indulgent but overheated parent, and Dolly—Gerald stood scornfully aloof—were compelled to devote the next two hours to a series of games, stage-plays, and allegories of an innocuous but exhausting description.

We began by joining hands and walking in a circle, solemnly chanting a ditty of the "I-saw-a-ship-a-sailing" variety, which culminated in the following verse—

"Then three times round went that gallant ship,
Then three times round went she;
Then three times round went that gallant ship—

(Here we were commanded by the mistress of the revels, in a hoarse and hurried stage whisper, to be ready to fall down)

—And sank to the bottom—of—the—sea!"

"Now all fall down!" screamed Phillis.

We did so, and lay on the grass in serried heaps. The remark which the Admiral made when my left elbow descended upon his goutiest foot was fortunately obscured by the fact that his face was inside his hat at the moment.

After that we performed the "most lamentable comedy" of "The Three Bears." Phillis assigned the parts, reserving for herself the *rôle* of Curly Locks and Stage Manager. Dolly was cast for Mother Bear, Captain Dermott for Father Bear, and I for Baby Bear. The Admiral, at his own urgent request, was allotted the comparatively unimportant part of Baby Bear's bed, and sat nursing his foot and observing with keen relish the preparations of the Bear family for their morning walk. We set out at last, all three on our hands and knees, Dolly and Dermott crawling amicably side by side, heroically regardless of white skirt and Sunday sporran; I, as befitted my youth and station, bringing up the rear.

The Bears having vacated their domicile (the grass plot), Curly Locks, after much furtive peeping round bushes, entered and advanced to the rustic table, where she proceeded to test the contents of the various porridge-bowls (represented by two tobacco-pouches and an ash-tray respectively).

"Too hot!" she said, after sampling the first bowl.

"Too cold!" she continued, trying the next.

"A-a-ah!" she cried, coming to the third; and swallowed its contents (some heather-tops) with every appearance of enjoyment.

After that came the inspection of the beds (two sofa-cushions and the Admiral), and finally Curly Locks retired to rest on her grand-uncle's knee.

Then the Three Bears came painfully back from the shrubbery, and Curly Locks' acts of spoliation were revealed one by one. My assumption of grief on the discovery of my empty porridge-bowl was so realistic that the Stage Manager sat up in bed and commended me for it. Finally we went the round of the furniture; Curly Locks was duly discovered; and I was engaged in a life-and-death struggle for her shrieking person with the bed itself, when there was a crunching of gravel, and the "machine" drove up with Robin inside it.

After my secretary had greeted those of us whom he knew, and been interrupted in the middle of a rapturous embrace from Phillis to be introduced to those whom he did not, I took him off indoors for a meal, through the breakfast-room window, and opened the portfolio of correspondence which he had brought me from London.

"Hallo! Here is a letter for Dermott," I said. "I'll take it to him."

I stepped through the window and handed the letter to Dermott, who was falling into line for a fresh game just outside.

"That envelope looks terribly official," said Dolly. "What does it all mean?"

"I expect it means Aldershot," said Dermott ruefully. "However, I shan't open it till lunch-time." And he stuffed the offending epistle into his pocket, and returned to the game in hand with a zest and abandon that betrayed ulterior motives in every antic.

We had seen a good deal of Captain Dermott that summer. Somehow he had been in nearly every house we had visited; and his laborious expressions of pleased surprise at meeting us there had now given way to specious and transparent explanations of his own presence. The experts at countless tea-tables and shooting-lunches were practically unanimous in the opinion that Dolly could land her fish when she chose now; and as the fish was a good fellow, and could offer her three thousand a-year and the reflected glory of a D.S.O., it was generally conceded that my youngest sister-in-law—have I ever mentioned that Dolly was the junior Twin?—was about to do extremely well for herself.

I sat by Robin as he consumed his breakfast, and waded through my correspondence. There was a good deal to sign and a good deal to digest, and a good deal that was of no importance whatsoever. But the *clou* of the whole budget was contained in a private letter from my Chief. I read it.

"My word, Robin!" I said. "There's to be a Dissolution in January."

There was no answer, and I looked up.

Robin was not listening. His attention had wandered to the game in progress on the lawn. This was one of Phillis' most cherished pastimes, and was called "Beckoning." The players, except the person who for the time being filled the *rôle* of "It," stood patiently in a row, until "It," after mature consideration, beckoned invitingly to one of them to approach. This invitation might or might not be a genuine one, for sometimes the player on responding was received by the beckoner with hisses and other symptoms of distaste, and fell back ignominiously on the main body. But if you were the *real* object of the beckoner's affections, you were greeted with embraces and a cry of "I choose you!" and succeeded to the proud post of "It."

It was a simple but embarrassing game, calling for the exercise of considerable tact when played by adults. At the present moment Phillis was beckoner, while Dolly, Dermott, and the Admiral stood meekly in line awaiting selection. Dolly and the Admiral were each called without being chosen, and Phillis's final selection proved to be Dermott, who, having received an enthusiastic salute from the retiring president, now stood sheepishly on one leg surveying the expectant trio before him.

He began by beckoning to his host; and, having relieved that gentleman's apprehensions by sibilant noises, waggled a nervous finger at Dolly. Dolly advanced obediently.

"Choose her, if you like," said Phillis magnanimously.

Dermott's martial eye kindled, but he made no sign, and the game faltered in its stride for a moment.

"Say," interpolated the prompter, "'I choose you!' and then k——"

But Dermott, hastily emitting a hiss which must have cost him a heartrending effort, relegated the greatly relieved Dolly to the ranks, and smoothed over the situation by "choosing" my daughter, to that young person's undisguised gratification.

It was at this phase in the proceedings that Robin's attention began to wander from the affairs of State, and I had to repeat my news of the impending Dissolution to him twice before he grasped its full significance. Even then he displayed about one-tenth of the excitement I should have expected of him; and finally he admitted that he was somewhat *dérangé* after his night journey, and suggested a postponement of business in favour of a little recreation on the lawn.

We accordingly added ourselves to the party, just in time to join the cast of Phillis' next production. This was an ambitious but complicated drama of an allegorical type, in which Robin appeared—not for the first time, evidently—as a boy called Henry, and Phillis doubled the parts of Henry's mother and a fairy. These two *rôles* absorbed practically the whole of what is professionally known as "the fat" of the piece, and the other members of the company were relegated—to their ill-disguised relief—to parts of purely nominal importance.

The curtain rose (if I may use the expression) upon Henry's humble home, where Henry was discovered partaking of breakfast (fir-cones). He complained bitterly to his mother of the hardship of *(a)* early rising, *(b)* going to school, and *(c)* enduring chastisement when he got there. The next scene revealed him in class, where the schoolmaster (Dolly, assiduously prompted by Phillis) asked him a series of questions, which he answered so incorrectly as to incur the extreme penalty of "the muckle tawse." (Here what textual critics term "internal evidence of a later hand" peeped out unmistakably.) The punishment having been duly inflicted by Dolly with a rug-strap, Henry retired, suffused with tears, to "a mountain-top," where he gave vent to a series of bitter reflections on the hardness of his lot and the hollowness of life in general.

He must have "gagged" unduly here, for presently he was cut short by a stern admonition to "wish for a fairy."

"I wish for a fairy," said Henry dutifully.

Phillis, given her cue at last, pirouetted before him with outstretched skirts.

"Go on!" she whispered excitedly. "Say, 'I wish that all Pain was Pleasure and all Pleasure Pain.'"

"Oh, sorry!" said Henry. "I wish that all Pain was Pleasure and Pleasure Pain."

"Have then thy wish!" announced the fairy solemnly, and fluttered away.

The drama thereafter pursued a remorselessly logical and improving course. Having got his wish, the luckless Henry found that his only moments of pleasure were those during which he was enduring the tawse, getting out of bed on a cold morning, or doing something equally unpleasant. On the other hand, his comfortable bed had become so painful that he could only obtain rest by filling it with stones; and his matutinal porridge was only made palatable by the addition of a handful of gravel.

After a fruitless interview with the family physician (Captain Dermott), in which the patient's mother set forth her offspring's symptoms with embarrassing frankness, Henry was compelled, as a last resort, to pay one more visit to the mountain-top. The indulgent fairy kindly agreed to put things right, but only under penalty of an improving homily on contentment with one's lot and the fatuity of asking for what you do not really want. This was only half finished when the party returned from church, and Phillis, realising that the absolute despotism of the last few hours would now be watered down by an unsentimental mother into a limited monarchy at the best, retired within her shell and declared the revels at an end.

II.

"What was the church like?" I inquired at lunch.

"I have witnessed more snappy entertainments," remarked Miss Buncle, the American girl, through her pretty nose. "Still, we smiled some. Mr Standish here got quite delirious when the minister prayed for 'the adjacent country of England, which, as Thou knowest, O Lord, lies some twa hundred miles to the sooth of us,'—I'm sorry I can't talk Scotch, Mr Fordyce,—as if he was afraid that Providence might mail the blessing to the wrong address and Iceland would get it."

Kitty broke in upon Miss Buncle's reminiscences.

"Who do you think we saw in church?" she said. "I nearly forgot to tell you. Your uncle, Robin—Sir James Fordyce!"

Robin nodded his head in a confirmatory way.

"He is often up here at this time of year," he said.

"He has friends here, perhaps?" said I.

"Oh yes; he has friends."

I could tell from Robin's voice that he was nursing some immense joke, but he betrayed no inclination to share it with us. Kitty went on.

"He was sitting in a pew with some farmery-looking people. There was a patriarchal old man, very stately and imposing, rather like—like——"

"Moses?" I suggested.

"No. I don't *think* Moses was like that."

I had got as far as 'Aar'—when Lady Rubislaw said—

"Elijah?"

"That's it," replied Kitty. "*Just* like Elijah." (All things considered, I cannot imagine why Moses would not have done as well.) "Then beside him was a perfectly dear old lady. Not so very old either; say sixty. Of course they may not have belonged to Sir James at all: he may just have been put in their pew. Still, they kept handing him Bibles, and looking up places for him at singing time."

"That means nothing," said I. "It's the merest courtesy here."

"True," said our hostess. "I was having a most lovely little doze during the Second Lesson, or whatever they call it, when a most officious young woman three or four pews away took up an enormous Bible, found the place, squeaked down the aisle, and thrust it under my nose. I had to hold it up for fifty-seven verses," she concluded pathetically.

"Did you go and speak to Sir James after the service?" I inquired.

"No. That was *this* child's fault," said Kitty, indicating Miss Buncle.

"How?"

"Well, there was a rather gorgeous-looking chieftain sort of person sitting in a front pew, and I saw Maimie twisting her head all during the service to look at him."

"Yes," admitted the culprit frankly. "Put me in the neighbourhood of a kilt, and I'm a common rubberneck straight away, Mr Inglethwaite. I'm just mad to know all those cunning tartans by heart."

"The moment the service was over," continued my wife severely, "I saw her edging through the crowd in the churchyard towards the chieftain. For a moment I thought she was going to ask him his name."

"I *wasn't*!" declared Miss Buncle indignantly.

"No, you did worse. She got close to the unfortunate man," continued my wife to us, "and suddenly I noticed that she had in her hand one of those little books you buy at railway book-stalls in the Highlands, with patterns of all the tartans in them and the name of the clan underneath. By the time I got up to her she had found the right tartan in the book, and was matching it up against the back of the poor unconscious creature's kilt. Then she turned to me in a triumphant sort of way and simply *bellowed*—'M'Farlane!'"

"We shall probably be hauled up before the Kirk-session," said the Admiral. "But I wonder who Sir James Fordyce's friends can be. I know most of the people who have shootings about here, but none of them are friends of his that I can think of. We must get him to come and shoot here one day. Rather late for to-morrow's drive, but there will be another on Thursday. I wonder who his host is, though?"

"I might help you," said Robin. "An old man, you said, with his wife?"

"Yes—oldish," said Kitty.

"Was there a son with them?"

"N-no."

"No? Well, he would be away at the lamb-sales, perhaps," said Robin reflectively. "Was there a daughter?"

"Now you mention it," said Kitty, "there was. A nice, bonny-looking girl. Twenty-four, I should say."

"Twenty-three," said Robin.

We all turned on him.

"Now then, what is all the mystery? Out with it! Who is the girl—eh?"

"She would be my sister," said Robin calmly. "And the others were my father and mother."

There was a little gasp of surprise all round the table. Robin went on—

"My home is just seven miles from here. This is the first time I have got near my folk for six years. To-morrow I mean to go and see them. And they would like fine, I know," he added a little shyly, "if some of you would come with me."

"I'll come," said Kitty promptly. "I should love to meet your mother, Robin."

"May *I* come, Uncle Robin?" piped Phillis. "For a birfday treat," she added, in extenuation.

Applications for an invitation rained in. Apart from a desire to please a man whom we all respected—and our ready offers undoubtedly did please him—I think we were all a little curious to view the mould which had turned Robin out.

"You can't *all* go," said the Admiral at last. "There's the grouse-drive to-morrow, and eight butts to fill; not to mention the need of female society at lunch."

Finally it was arranged that Robin should take Kitty and Phillis over on a sort of preliminary call, and they could arrange for the establishment of more substantial relations.

But that evening, as the ladies were having their candles lit at the foot of the staircase, I heard Robin say to Dolly—

"Will you come with us to-morrow?"

Dolly seemed to consider, and was about to reply, when Dermott, who never seemed very far away now, cut in.

"Too late, Fordyce! Miss Rubislaw has promised to come and load for me in my butt to-morrow afternoon."

"No, I'm afraid it can't be managed this time, Robin," said Dolly. "But I am coming with you later in the week, if you'll take me."

Robin said nothing.

Now Dolly, I knew, did not approve of the inclusion of females in the business part of a day's shooting; and she regarded Miss Buncle and her twenty-eight bore with pious horror. The fact that she had consented to come and hold Dermott's second gun to-morrow seemed to indicate that that gallant sportsman had accomplished a feat which had already proved too much for several highly deserving young men—I was not quite sure that Robin was not one of them; and there seemed to be every reason to anticipate (especially since he was due to start for Aldershot to-morrow night) that when the Captain returned from the chase to-morrow afternoon, his bag would include one head of game of an interesting and unusual variety.

III.

At ten o'clock next morning we met the keepers, dogs, and beaters not far from the first line of butts on the moor. There was a hot sun, and the bees were bumbling in the heather. Somehow Whitehall seemed a long way off.

The number of guns had been brought up to seven by the inclusion of a neighbouring laird—one Gilmerton of Nethercraigs—and his son.

"All the same, we are still a man short," complained the Admiral, to whom a house-party was a ship's company, and a day's shooting a sort of terrestrial naval manoeuvre. "However, we will cut out the end butt in each drive and put a stop there to turn the birds farther in. Now we'll draw for places. Each man to take the butt whose number he draws, counting from the right and moving up one place after each drive. And Heaven help the man who draws number four now, for it means number seven and a climb up The Pimple for him directly after lunch!"

There was a general laugh at this, which swelled to an unseemly roar when I drew the fatal number.

However, after lunch was a long way off, and I trotted contentedly to number four and settled down to a pipe, while the head-keeper led off his mixed multitude of assistants, dogs, boys, and red flags to make a *détour* and work the game up towards us.

The first drive was simple. We were in a long and rather shallow glen, across which ran a low ridge, dividing it into two almost equal sections. The butts were placed along this ridge; and after the birds had been sent over us the beaters would work round to the other end of the glen and drive them back again. The shooting would be easy, for the ground lay flat and open in either direction.

I found myself between Standish and Gerald; the former on my right, and the latter, together with the young keeper to whom his shooting education had been entrusted, in the butt on my left. Beyond Standish was Dermott, the crack shot of the party, and beyond Dermott, in number one butt, was the Admiral. The Gilmertons, *père et fils*, occupied the butts on the extreme left.

The drive was moderately successful. At first the birds came along singly, mostly on the right, and fell an easy prey to Dermott and the Admiral. But presently a great pack got up comparatively near the butts, and fairly "rushed" us. I brought off an easy right and left straight in front of me, and then, snapping out my cartridges and slipping another in, I swung round and just managed to bring down a third bird with a "stern chaser"—a feat which I regretted to observe no one else noticed, for there was a perfect fusilade all along the line at the moment. Master Gerald, who had discharged his first barrel straight into the "brown," succeeded, in obedience to his mentor's admonitions, in covering an old cock-grouse with his second, and carefully following that flustered fowl's course with the point of his gun, pulled the trigger just as it skimmed, low down, with an agitated squawk, between his butt and mine. I heard the shot rattle through the heather, and two pellets hit on my left boot.

The congenial task of telling Gerald, in a low but penetrating voice, exactly what I thought of him, occupied my attention so fully for the next minute that I failed to observe a blackcock which suddenly swung up into view and whizzed straight past my head, to the audible annoyance of the distant Admiral and the undisguised joy of my unrepentant relative.

No more birds came after that, and presently, the line of beaters having advanced within range, we put down our guns and collected the slain. We had not done badly, considering the fact that the main body of the birds had swerved away to our left over the unoccupied butt, despite the valiant efforts of an urchin with a red flag to turn them. Dermott headed the list with four and a half brace, and Gerald brought up the rear with a mangled corpse which had received the contents of his first barrel point-blank at a distance of about six feet. The laird of Nethercraigs (a cautious and economical sportsman, who was reputed never to loose off his gun at anything which did not come and perch on his butt) had fired just three cartridges and killed just three birds, but his son had seven. The Admiral and Standish had also had average luck, and altogether we had fourteen and a half brace to show for our exertions.

Off went the beaters again, and we changed butts and waited. The second drive gave us fewer birds but better sport. There were no great packs, but we got plenty to do in the way of sharp-shooting, and Gerald's keeper—a singularly ambiguous title in this case—succeeded by increased vigilance in preserving me from being further sniped by my enterprising brother-in-law.

We totalled up twelve brace this time, and then made ready for a tramp to the next line of butts, away round the shoulder of a fairly distant hill.

"We may as well spread out and walk 'em up this bit," said our host. "We can't have the dogs, though, as the keepers and beaters are going a different way; and each man will have to carry what he shoots. In that case we'll leave rabbits alone. Gerald, you had better get to the extreme left of the line. That will limit the risk to one man!"

"I'll carry home your bag if you'll carry mine, Gerald," cried Standish facetiously, as my brother-in-law, a trifle offended at the Admiral's last pleasantry, proceeded with much dignity to his allotted place.

Gerald was almost out of earshot, but he waved a defiant acquiescence.

We tramped round the shoulder of the hill, keeping our distance as well as we could on the steep slope, and occasionally putting up something to shoot at. My bag this time made no great demands on my powers of porterage, consisting as it did of a solitary snipe. However, when nearly an hour later we gathered at the foot of the next line of butts—the last before lunch—most of us were carrying something. Standish gleefully displayed two hares and a brace of grouse.

"There is something for Master Gerald to carry back to the luncheon-cart," he said. "I wonder what he has got for me. Where is he?"

"I don't quite know," said Dermott, who had been Gerald's nearest neighbour. "He was so offended by our gibes about the danger of his society that he walked rather wide of me. He kept down at the very foot of the hill most of the time, almost out of sight."

"I hope he hasn't shot himself," said the Admiral rather anxiously.

"Never fear!" said I. "That will not be his end. Here he is."

Sure enough, Gerald appeared at this moment. He was empty-handed.

Simple and primitive jests greeted him.

"Hallo, old man, what have you shot—eh? Where is your little lot?"

Gerald smiled seraphically.

"You'll find it down there," he said—"in that patch of bracken, Standish. I left it for you to bring up. Rather heavy for me."

"What on earth have you shot?" we cried involuntarily.

"A sheep," said Gerald calmly.

Great heavens!

We rushed down the hill as one man—and came up again looking not a little hot and uncommonly foolish. The sheep was there, it is true, stiff and stark in the bracken; but more senses than one apprised us of the fact that it had been dead for considerably more than five minutes. Gerald had stumbled on to the corpse, and had turned his discovery, we afterwards admitted, to remarkably good advantage. It was "Mr Standish's turn," as Miss Buncle, in the picturesque but mysterious vernacular of her race, remarked at luncheon, "to hold the baby this time."

After the third drive we gladly put up our guns and tramped down the hillside to the road below, where the ladies were waiting and the feast was spread. After we had disposed of grouse sandwiches, whisky-and-water, and jammy scones, and were devoting our post-prandial leisure to repose or dalliance with the fair—according as we were married or single—Lady Rubislaw inquired—

"Where are you shooting this afternoon, John?"

"The Neb, first," replied the Admiral. "And that reminds me, the man who drew the top butt had better start now, or he'll be late."

With many groans, and followed by the mingled derision and sympathy of the company, I picked up my *impedimenta* and started, leaving the others to decide who, if any, of the shooters was to have the honour of entertaining a lady in his butt.

The Neb was a great mountain spur, whose base ran to within two or three hundred yards of our resting-place. In appearance it roughly resembled a mighty Napoleonic nose. The butts ran right up the ridge of that organ; and nine hundred feet above where we sat, just below an excrescence locally known as "The Pimple," lay mine.

I reached my eyrie at last, and having laid my flask, tobacco-pouch, and twelve loose cartridges where I could reach them most handily on projecting shelves of peat inside the butt—I love neatness and method: Kitty says that when (if ever) I get to heaven I will decline to enter until I have wiped my boots,—settled down to enjoy a superb view and take note of the not altogether uninteresting manner in which the other members of the party were disposing themselves for the drive.

Just below me were Standish and Miss Buncle, the lady a conspicuous mark for all men (and grouse) to behold by reason of a red tam o'shanter, the sight of which made me regret that its wearer was not employed as a beater. In the butt below were Dermott and Dolly—both very workmanlike and inconspicuous. Below them came the Admiral, with his wife (she always came and sat behind him, like a remarkably smart little powder-monkey, during the afternoon drive): below them, the Gilmertons; and last of all, thank Heaven! Gerald.

The shooting on this beat would not be easy, though birds were always plentiful. They came round the face of the hill at very short range and express speed. My particular butt was notoriously difficult to score from. There was an awkward hummock in front of it, and driven birds swinging into view round this were practically right over the butt before its occupant could get his gun up.

It was a rather sleepy afternoon. Far away I could hear the sound of the advancing beaters—the cries of the boys, the occasional barking of a dog, and the shrill piping of the headkeeper's whistle. Suddenly three birds swung into view round the face of the hill, and made straight for the line of butts. They were just below me, nearer to Standish's butt than mine, but I put up my gun and picked off the nearest. The other two, instead of keeping on their course over Standish's head, suddenly swerved round to the left, almost at right angles—I think they had seen Miss Buncle's tam o' shanter and simultaneously decided that there are worse things than death—and flew straight down the line, followed by an ineffectual volley from the twelve and twenty-eight bores respectively.

"Now, Dermott, my boy!" I ejaculated, as the birds skimmed past the third butt. "There's a chance for a really pretty right and left."

But no sound—no movement even—came from our crack's lair. The birds flew by unharmed, only to fall later on, one to the Admiral, and one to young Gilmerton.

"*Dormitat Homerus*," I murmured, gazing curiously towards Dermott's butt. "I wonder if—Jove, there they go! What a pack! Well done, Gerald! Oh, Gilmerton, you old *sweep*! Fire, man, *fire*! Good old Admiral! Dermott, man, what the devil—— Have *at* them!"

I fairly danced in the heather. A perfect cloud of birds was pouring over the lower part of the line. The Admiral, the Gilmertons, and Gerald were firing fast and furiously,—even the laird of Nethercraigs loosed off at birds that were neither running nor sitting,—and when the beaters appeared in sight five minutes later, and the drive came to an end, the four lower butts totalled twelve brace among them.

I humbly proffered my solitary contribution.

"Twelve and a half," said the Admiral. "Now, Standish?"

"N.E. this time," remarked that youth philosophically.

The Admiral said nothing, but I saw his choleric blue eyes slide round in the direction of Miss Buncle's headgear. He turned to Dermott.

"How many, old man?"

"Blob!"

That Dermott should return empty-handed from any kind of chase was so surprising that we all turned round for the explanation. Dermott was looking very dejected. This was evidently a blow to his professional pride.

"Didn't any of that great pack come near you?" asked the Admiral sympathetically.

"No—don't think so," said Dermott shortly.

I had counted eight birds flying straight over his butt myself, but I said nothing. I was beginning to comprehend. *Et ego in Arcadia vixi.*

But the obtuse master-mariner persisted.

"How about that brace that flew right down the line? You must have seen 'em coming all the way. You didn't even try a shot at them, man!"

Dermott, who was fastening up his gaiter, answered rather listlessly—

"Sorry! It was—a misfire, I think."

"What?" cried the outraged Admiral. "A *misfire*? Both barrels—of both guns?"

I did not hear the answer to this. I was looking at Dolly. Her face could not be seen, for she was kneeling down a little distance away, assiduously fondling the silky ears of a highly-gratified red setter. And I realised then that some expressions are capable of a metaphorical as well as a literal interpretation.

IV.

My wife and daughter returned home in the "machine" in time for dinner, without Robin.

"His mother kept him," Kitty explained. She was favouring me with a summary of her day's adventures, in the garden after dinner. "Such an old dear, Adrian! And his father is a grand old man. Very solemn and scriptural-looking and all that, but so courtly and simple when once he gets over his shyness. (He tried to come in to tea in his shirt-sleeves, but his wife hustled him out of the kitchen just in time.) Sir James Fordyce was a shock, though. When we arrived he was chopping turnips in a machine, dressed in clothes like any farm-labourer's. He said it was fine to get back to his own people again. To look at him you would never guess that he was one of the best known men in London, and a favourite at Court, and *such* an old dandy in Bond Street. The rest of the household didn't seem to set any particular store by him. They took him quite as a matter of course."

"What a pity English people can't do the same," I mused. "If they do possess a distinguished relative they brag about him, and he usually responds by avoiding them. If he does honour them with a visit, they try to live up to him, and put on unnecessary frills, and summon all the neighbourhood to come and inspect him."

"There's nothing of that kind about the Fordyces," said Kitty. "Sir James was just one of themselves; he even spoke like them. It was, 'Aye, Jeems!' and 'Aye, John!' all the time."

"How about the rest of the family?" I inquired.

"The mother was immensely pleased to have Robin with her again, I could see," said Kitty. "She made no particular fuss over him, but I'm sure she simply hugged him as soon as we were gone. She had a talk with me about him when we were alone. She seems to regard him as the least successful member of the family, although he has been a good son to them. (Do you know, Adrian, he has sent them something like two hundred pounds during the time he has been with us? And that must have left him little enough to go on with, goodness knows!) But I don't think they consider him a patch on the eldest son, who is a great silent man with a beard—a sort of Scotch John Ridd. He looks years older than Robin, though of course he isn't. He is a splendid farmer, his mother tells me, and greatly "respeckit" in the district. But the poor dear was so frightened of me that he simply bolted from the house the moment he had finished his tea. The sister is pretty, and nice too, but shy. I'm afraid she found my clothes rather overpowering, though I'd only a coat and skirt on. But we got on splendidly after that. She is going to be married next month, to the minister, which is considered an immense triumph for her by the whole community. We must send them a present. By the way, what's the matter with Dolly?"

"What's the matter with poor old Dermott?" I retorted.

At this moment the much-enduring "machine" jingled up to the door, and Captain Dermott's luggage, together with his gun-cases and a generous bundle of game for the mess-table at Aldershot, was piled in at the back. Their owner followed after, and seeing the glowing end of my cigar in the dark, advanced to say good-bye.

Kitty uttered some pretty expression of regret at his departure, and flitted into the house. Dermott and I surveyed each other silently through the darkness.

"Is it any use asking you to come and look us up in town?" I said at last rather lamely.

He laughed through set teeth—not a pretty sound.

"I think I'll—avoid your household for a bit, Adrian," he answered.

I nodded gravely.

"I see," I said. "I—I'm sorry, old man!"

"I'm going to India, if I can get away," he continued, after a pause.

"Good scheme!" I replied. "We shall think of you most kindly—er, *all* of us."

He said nothing, but shook hands in a grateful sort of fashion, and turned away.

I suppose there is a reason for everything in this world. Still, the spectacle of a good man fighting dumbly with a cruel disappointment—and disappointment is perhaps the bitterest pill in all the pharmacopeia of life—is certainly a severe test of one's convictions on the subject.

At this moment the rest of the party—*minus* Dolly—flowed out on to the doorstep to say farewell; and two minutes later Captain Dermott drove heavily away—back to his day's work.

Well, thank God there is always that!

"I thought she was going to take him," said Kitty in her subsequent summing-up. "It was far and away the best offer she has ever had. And he is such a dear, too! What does the child want, I wonder! A coronet?"

"'A dinner of herbs,' perhaps," said I.

Kitty eyed me thoughtfully, and gave a wise little nod.

"Yes—Dolly is just that sort," she agreed. "But what makes you think that?"

"Oh—nothing," I said.

There are certain matters upon which it is almost an impertinence for a man to offer an opinion to a woman, and I rather shrank from rushing in where my wife had evidently not thought it worth while to tread. Still, I could not help wondering in my heart whether the arrival of one gentleman on Sunday may not sometimes have something to do, however indirectly, with the abrupt departure of another gentleman on Monday.

CHAPTER TWELVE.
THE COMPLEAT ANGLER.

The Division of Stoneleigh, which had hitherto done me the honour of returning me as its Member of Parliament, is a triangular tract of country in the north of England.

At the apex of the triangle lies Stoneleigh itself, a township whose chief assets are an ancient cathedral at one end, and a flourishing industry, proclaiming to the heavens its dependence upon Hides and Tallow, at the other. The base of the triangle runs along the sea-coast, and is dotted with fishing villages. Most of the intervening area is under cultivation.

It will be seen, then, that the character of my constituency varied in a perplexing manner, and while I could usually depend upon what I may call the Turnip interest, I could not always count with absolute certainty on the whole-hearted support of the Fish or Hides-and-Tallow.

To this delectable microcosm my household and I migrated one bleak day in February, to commence what promised to be an arduous and thoroughly uncomfortable electoral campaign.

The Government had gone out at last, more from inanition than over any definite question of policy; and we were going to the country to face what is paradoxically termed "the music." It would be a General Election in every sense of the word, for there was no particular question of the hour—this was before the days of Passive Resistance and Tariff Reform—and our chief bar to success would undoubtedly be our old and inveterate enemy, "the pendulum." Of course we were distributing leaflets galore, and blazoning panegyrics on our own legislative achievements over every hoarding in the country—especially where our opponents had already posted up scathing denunciations of the same—and of course we declared that we were going to come again, like King Arthur; but I think most of us realised in our hearts that the great British Public, having decided in its ponderous but not altogether unreasonable way that any change of government must be for the better, was now going to pull us down from the eminence to which we had been precariously clinging for five years, and set up another row of legislative Aunt Sallies in our stead.

However, we were far from admitting this. We wore our favours, waved our hats, and celebrated our approaching triumph with as great an appearance of optimism as the loss of seven consecutive by-elections would permit.

Our party—Kitty, Phillis, Dolly, and myself: Dilly and Dicky were to follow, and Robin had preceded us by two days—was met at the station by an informal but influential little deputation, consisting of Mr Cash, my agent, a single-minded creature who would cheerfully have done his best to get Mephistopheles returned as member if he had been officially appointed to further that gentleman's interests; old Colonel Vincey, who would as cheerfully have voted for the same candidate provided he wore Conservative colours; Mr Bugsley, a leading linen-draper and ex-Mayor of the town, vice-chairman of our local organisation; Mr Winch—locally known as Beery Bill—the accredited mouthpiece of the Stoneleigh liquor interest; and the Dean, who came, I was uncharitable enough to suspect even as he wrung my hand, on business not unconnected with the unfortunate deficit in the fund for the restoration of the North Transept. There were also present one or two reporters, and a *posse* of the offscourings of Stoneleigh small-boydom.

We drove in state to the hotel. Previous to this I shook hands warmly with the Station-master, who scowled at me—he was a Home-Ruler and a Baptist—and gave four porters half-a-crown apiece for lifting our luggage on to the roof of a cab. I also handed a newsboy sixpence for a copy of the local bi-weekly organ which supported our cause, and tendered half-a-sovereign in payment for a bunch of violets and primroses—our party colours in this district were purple and gold—which were proffered me outside the station by an ancient flower-selling dame who, Cash hissed into my ear, happened to be the mother of four strapping and fully-enfranchised sons; and presented an unwashed stranger who was holding open the cab door for us with a token of affection and esteem which could readily be commuted into several hours' beer.

On arriving at the hotel I handed the cabman a fare roughly equivalent to the cash value of the cab, and then proceeded to distribute largesse to a crowd of menials who kindly undertook the task of lifting the luggage from the roof and conveying it to our rooms. The horse, having no vote, received no pecuniary return for its labours, but was rewarded for its devotion to Conservative principles by a lump of sugar, which Phillis had been tightly holding in a moist hand ever since Cash had handed it to her at the station—a pretty and thoughtful act of disinterested kindness which was duly noted in the *Stoneleigh Herald* next morning, and effectually secured the votes of several elusive but sentimental wobblers on polling day.

After this unostentatious entry into my constituency I duly established myself in my apartments, where I spent most of the afternoon writing cheques. The restoration of the North Transept proved to be in an even more deplorable state of backwardness than I had feared; but the Dean ultimately left me with the utmost expressions of goodwill, promising to reassure the most exacting spirits in Cathedral society as to my soundness on the questions of (1) Disestablishment and (2) Secular Education in Elementary Schools.

Thereafter I received the captain of the local football team, who begged to remind me that my subscription of five guineas, as Honorary Vice-President of the club, was now due, and further requested that I would do himself and colleagues the honour of kicking-off in the match against the Scrappington Hotstuffs on Saturday week. (Saturday next, I heard afterwards, had been reserved for my rival.) He finally departed with my cheque in his pocket, and, I expect, his tongue in his cheek.

Robin next let in upon me a sub-section of the General Purposes Committee of the Municipal Library, who begged that I would kindly consent to open the new wing thereof, jointly with the rival Candidate, at three o'clock next Wednesday; and intimated as an afterthought that the oak bookcase in the eastern alcove was still unpaid for. They departed calling down blessings upon my head. (Five pounds ten.)

Next, after a brief call from a gentleman in a blue ribbon, who came to solicit a guinea for the Band of Hope, and who left in exchange one hundred copies of a picture of the interior of a drunkard's stomach, executed in three colours, came Beery Bill, to whom the reader has already been introduced. He had not come to talk Politics, he said, but just to have a quiet chat with one whom he hoped he could regard as a personal friend. (I got out my fountain pen.) The chat materialised presently into an intimation that the Licensed Victuallers Benevolent Something-or-Other was short of cash; and my visitor suggested that a trifle in support of the charities of that most deserving institution would come gracefully from my pocket. On handing me the receipt he informed me that the brewing trade was in a bad way, and that he looked to me to do something for it if he used his influence on my behalf at the Election.

The next visitor was an eccentric but harmless old gentleman who eked out a precarious livelihood as a Herbalist—whatever that may be—in the most plebeian quarter of the town. He inhabited a small and stuffy shop up a discreet alley, suffered much from small boys, sold curious drugs and potions of his own composition, and prescribed for persons whose means or modesty precluded them from consulting an orthodox practitioner.

He was threatened, it appeared, with the penalties of the law. He had sold a "love-philtre" (pronounced infallible for recalling errant *fiancés* to a sense of duty) to an amorous kitchen-maid who was seeking to rekindle the sacred flame in the bosom of an unresponsive policeman. The damozel had mingled the potion in a plate of beefsteak pudding, and had handed the same out of the scullery window to her peripatetic swain; with the sole result that that limb of the law had been immediately and violently sick, and, the moment he felt sufficiently recovered to do so, had declared the already debilitated match at an end. The kitchen-maid, rendered desperate, had told him the whole truth; and consequently my esteemed caller was now wanted by the police.

The catastrophe of the pie, he explained, was in no way to be attributed to the love-philtre (which was composed of sifted sugar and cinnamon), but was due to the fact that instead of the philtre he had inadvertently handed his fair client a packet out of the next drawer, which contained ready-made-up doses of tartaric acid for immediate use in the case of small boys who had swallowed sixpences. *Hinc lacrymcoe.* In spite of his complete consciousness of his own innocence, he now found himself compelled in a few days' time to defend his conduct in a court of law. The proceedings would cost money, of which he of course possessed little or none. He had called, he said, confident in the hope that I would assist him to defray the expense of vindicating his integrity as a high-class Herbalist by purchasing six bottles of his world-renowned specific for neuralgia, from which dread malady he had been informed—quite incorrectly, by the way—that I occasionally suffered. The thirty shillings thus subscribed, together with a few odd coins which he himself had contrived to scrape together during a long life of thrift, would secure the services of a skilled advocate, who would doubtless be able to prove to the satisfaction of justice that no high-class Herbalist would ever dream, save in the way of kindness, of putting tartaric acid into a policeman's beefsteak pudding.

He added, rather inconsequently, that he had voted Conservative at the last three elections, and had moreover persuaded all the other members of the Royal and Ancient Brotherhood of High-class Herbalists to do the same. (One pound ten.)

My last visitor was a seedy individual in corduroys, who asked for a private interview with the Candidate, and, on this favour being granted, informed me in a confidential and husky whisper that he knew of ten good men and true, fully qualified voters, who were prepared to go to the poll on my behalf for the trifling fee of two pound ten a-head and no questions asked. He was politely but firmly shown into the street. One has to be on the look-out against persons of this type.

I concluded the afternoon by a rather unsatisfactory interview with Mr Cash. He was by nature a boisterous and optimistic person, but on this occasion I found him inclined to be reticent and gloomy. He announced with a shake of the head that my rival was a very strong candidate; and finally, after a certain amount of pressing, admitted that I was not altogether as universally acceptable to my own side as I might have been.

"You are not violent enough, Mr Inglethwaite," he said. "You sympathise too much with the point of view of the opposite side. That's fatal."

I turned to Robin.

"You hear that?" I said. "Don't you ever call me a prejudiced old Tory again, Robin."

"Then," continued the dolorous Cash, "you are too squeamish. Those posters that you wouldn't allow to be put up—that was simply throwing away good votes. Politics in this part of the country can't be played with kid gloves. Then there are the meetings. You don't let the other side have it hot enough. Call 'em robbers and liars! That's what wins an election!"

"I suppose it is," I said mournfully. "Robin, we must put our opinions in our pockets and beat the party drum. Come on, let us go to the Committee Rooms!"

For the next fortnight we worked like galley-slaves. Each morning Kitty and I drove round the town in an open carriage-and-pair decorated with our colours, bowing to such of our constituents as would look at us, and punctiliously returning any salutes we received. Occasionally whole-hearted supporters would give us a cheer, and occasionally—rather more frequently, it seemed to me—disagreeable persons booed at us. Once we were held up outside a hide-and-tallow work by a gang of workmen who wished to address a few questions to the Candidate. We came well out of that ordeal, for both Kitty and Dolly happened to be in the carriage that day, and they so completely captivated the spokesman of the deputation—no wonder! a pretty woman never looks so attractive as in furs—that that gentleman concluded a catechism of unpremeditated brevity and incoherence by proposing a vote of confidence in, coupled with three cheers for, Mr Inglethwaite and his young ladies!

On another occasion a gnarled and fervent Radical of the bootmaking persuasion hobbled to the door of his establishment, and waving clenched and uplifted fists, called down upon us and our retreating equipage all the curses at the command of a rather extensive vocabulary until we were out of earshot.

Occasionally little girls threw posies into the carriage: little boys, not to be outdone in politeness, threw stones: and altogether I felt very much as the Honourable Samuel Slumkey must have done upon the historic occasion on which he solicited the votes of the electors of the borough of Eatanswill.

Talking of Eatanswill, I had already made the acquaintance of Mr Horatio Fizkin in the person of my opponent, Mr Alderman Stridge, Wholesale Provision Merchant and Italian Warehouseman. His selection as Liberal Candidate was a blow to us: we had hoped for nothing worse than a briefless carpet-bagger from the Temple, as on previous occasions. However, the Alderman on our introduction was extremely affable, and expressed a hope, with the air of one discovering the sentiment for the first time, that the best man might win; to which I, as in duty bound, replied that I hoped not; and we parted with mutual expressions of goodwill and esteem, to deride each other's politics and bespatter each other's characters on countless platforms and doorsteps until we should meet again, after the fray, at the counting of the votes.

On returning from our morning drive (which usually included an open-air meeting) we took luncheon, generally in the presence of various anæmic young men who represented local organs of public opinion, and who expected the long-suffering candidate to set forth his views between mouthfuls of chop and sips of sherry. I usually turned these over to Robin, who understood their ways; and he charmed them so wisely that even the relentless Cash was compelled to admit that our press notices might have been worse.

Robin was a tower of strength. Indeed he and Dolly were my two chief lieutenants; Dilly and Dicky, as became a pair who had only been married a few months, proving but broken reeds. A week's electioneering proved sufficient for their requirements; and, declining flatly to "grin like a dog and run about the city"—Dilly's pithy summary of the art of canvassing—any longer, they left us ten days before polling-day to pay a country-house visit. But Robin was everywhere. He answered my letters and he interviewed reporters. He could keep a meeting in hand (pending my arrival from another) with such success that when I finally appeared upon the platform to take up the wondrous tale of my party's perfections, the audience were loth to let Robin go. In six days he acquired a knowledge of the wants, peculiarities, weaknesses, and traditions of my constituents which had occupied all my powers of concentration and absorption for six arduous years. He used to drop into his speeches little topical allusions and local "gags" which, though Greek to the uninitiated, never failed to produce a roar: and a political speaker who can unfailingly make his audience laugh with him—not at him—has gone far on the road to success.

Once, at a meeting, when I was half-way through a speech to an unmistakably bored and rather hostile audience, Robin, who was sitting beside me, slipped a sheet of paper on to my table. The message on the paper, written large for me to read, said—*Compare Stridge to the Old Lady of Dippleton*. What the lady had done I did not know, neither had I time to inquire; but I took my secretary's advice, and, after pausing for a brief drink of water, concluded my sentence—

"—and I maintain, gentlemen, that my opponent, in advocating such a policy as that which he has had the—the—yes, the *effrontery* to lay before a clear-thinking and broad-minded Stoneleigh audience last night, has shown himself to be no wiser in his generation, no better or more statesmanlike in character, than—than—what shall we say? than"—I glanced at the paper on the table—"the Old Lady of Dippleton!"

There was a great roar of laughter, and I sat down. I was ultimately awarded a vote of thanks, which should by rights have been given to the heroine of my closing allusion. I may mention here that no subsequent inquiry of mine ever elicited from Robin or any one else what the Old Lady of Dippleton *had* done. Probably it was one of those things that no real lady ever ought to do, and I discreetly left it at that.

Dolly, too, proved a treasure. Her strong line was canvassing. She could ingratiate herself with short-tempered and over-driven wives apparently without effort; surly husbands melted before her smile; sheepish young men forgot the encumbering existence of their hands and feet in her presence; and she was absolutely infallible with babies. Her methods were entirely her own, and gratifyingly free from the superior and patronising airs usually adopted by fine ladies when they go to solicit the votes of that variegated and much-graded community which they cheerfully and indiscriminately sum up as "the lower classes."

Let us follow her as she flits on her way to pay a morning call upon Mr Noah Gulching of Jackson's Row.

Mr Gulching, she finds, is absent in search of a job, while Mrs Gulching, thoroughly cross and worried, is doing the housework with one hand and dangling a fractious teething baby from the other. The rest of the family are engaged in playing games of skill and chance (on the win, tie, or wrangle principle), in the middle of the street outside; and piercing screams testify to the fact that John William Gulching, aged two, had just been uprooted by Mary Kate Gulching, who wants to lay out a new Hop-Scotch court, from the flagstone upon which he has been seated for the last half hour and dumped down upon another, the warming of which, even his untutored sensations inform him, will be a matter of some time and trouble.

Dolly, not a whit dismayed by a thoroughly ungracious reception, tucks up her skirt, rolls up her sleeves, finishes washing-up, makes a bed, and peels some potatoes. Then she takes the baby and attends to its more conspicuous wants, what time Mrs Gulching, thoroughly mollified,—she had thought at first that Dolly was "a person with tracks,"—goes round the corner to the "Drop Inn," at which hostelry the work of which her spouse is habitually in pursuit invariably goes to ground, and brings that gentleman home with her, to find Dolly playing with a spotless infant whom she gradually recognises as her own offspring.

Dolly begins at once.

"Good morning, Mr Gulching! I expect you think I am one of those horrid canvassers."

Mr Gulching, a little taken aback, admits that such was his impression.

"Well, I'm not," says Dolly. (*Oh, Dolly!*) "I suppose there may be some excuse for canvassing among people who do not take much interest in politics,—though *I* shouldn't like to do it,—but it would be rather a waste of time for me or any one else to come and try on that sort of thing with *you*, wouldn't it, Mr Gulching?"

Mr Gulching, outwardly frigid but inwardly liquescent, agrees that this is so; and adds in a truculent growl that he would like to see 'em try it on.

"What I really want," continues Dolly, "is your *advice*. I am told that you are so respected here, and have such a knowledge of the requirements of the neighbourhood, that you might be inclined to give us a little help in a scheme which Mr Inglethwaite has in hand. Schemes for the improvement of some of the houses—not snug little cribs like this, but the homes of people who are not so clever and able to take care of themselves as you—and the supplying of more amusements in the evenings; entertainments, lectures——"

"Teetotal?" inquires Mr Gulching hoarsely.

"Oh dear, no. I am sure Mr Inglethwaite would not wish to deprive any one of his glass of beer. He quite agrees with your views about moderate drinking." (This, I may mention, is a slanderous libel on me, but it sounds all right as Dolly says it.) "But he knows that the success of his efforts will depend entirely upon whether he has the support of such men as yourself—men who know what they want and will see that they get it. We can't do without you, you see," she adds, with a bewitching little smile.

Visible swelling on the part of Mr Gulching. Dolly gets up.

"Well, I know you are a busy man, Mr Gulching, so I mustn't keep you listening to a woman's chatter any more. I'm afraid I haven't explained things very deeply, but then you men are such creatures for wanting to get to the root of the matter, aren't they, Mrs Gulching? However, Mr Inglethwaite will call shortly and discuss things with you. I know he wants your advice. Meanwhile, perhaps you will mention the matter to any friends of yours whom you think would be likely to help us, won't you? Good morning, and thank you so much for granting me this—er—interview. An Englishman's house is his castle, isn't it? That is why it was so good of you to let me come in. Good-bye, Mrs Gulching. He's a perfectly sweet little chap, and I must come and see him again, if I may." (The last remark is a little ambiguous, but probably refers to the baby.)

And Dolly, with a friendly nod to the rest of the family (who are by this time drawn up *en échelon* at the street door, under the personal direction of Violet Amelia Gulching), sails out, followed by a gratified leer from the greatly inflated Mr Gulching, having secured that free and independent elector's vote without even having asked for it. And yet some women are crying out for the right to control elections!

At the street corner, with a persuasive finger in the buttonhole of an unconvinced Socialist (and a vigilant eye straining down the long and unlovely vista of Jackson's Row), Dolly usually encounters Robert Chalmers Fordyce.

CHAPTER THIRTEEN.
A HOSTAGE TO FORTUNE.

Nomination day came, and I was duly entered by my proprietors for the Election Stakes, though I was painfully aware that my selection as Candidate was not universally popular.

However, as Cash remarked, "It is canvassing from door to door that does the trick, and there you have the bulge on Stridge. He's not a bad old buffer himself, but they hate his wife like poison. She drives up to their doors in a silver-plated brougham with a double-breasted coachman, and tells 'em to vote for Stridge, not because he used to live in a one-roomed house himself—which he did, and her too—but because he's a local god-on-wheels. Of course they won't stick that."

I also continued to address meetings, receive deputations, and generally solicit patronage in a way that would have made a cab-tout blush for shame. As a recreation I kicked off at football matches and laid foundation-stones. The most important function in which I took part was the opening of the new wing of the Municipal Library. The ceremony, which was by way of being a non-party affair, took place on a blustering February afternoon. The *élite* of Stoneleigh were picturesquely grouped upon the steps of the main entrance of the Library, from the topmost of which the Mayor, the Dean, and the Candidates addressed a shivering and apathetic audience below.

Fortunately, the company were too exclusively occupied in holding on their hats and blowing their blue noses to pay much attention to the improving harangues of Mr Stridge and myself; which was perhaps just as well, for men who have three or four highly critical and possibly hostile meetings to address later in the day are not likely to waste good things upon an assembly who probably cannot hear them, and will only say "Hear, hear!" in sepulchral tones if they do.

The actual opening of the wing was accomplished quite informally (and I may say unexpectedly) by Kitty and Mrs Stridge—a fearsome matron, who looked like a sort of Nonconformist Boadicea—who were huddling together for warmth in the recess of the doorway. On a pedestal before them lay two small gold keys, with which they were presently to unlock the door itself, what time I, in trumpet tones, declared the Library open. Whether through natural modesty or a desire to escape the assaults of the wind, the two ladies shrank back so closely into the door that that accommodating portal, evidently deeming it ungallant to wait even for a golden key under such circumstances, incontinently flew open, and Mesdames Inglethwaite and Stridge subsided gracefully into the arms of a spectacled and embarrassed Librarian, who was formally waiting inside to receive the company at the proper moment.

After that, the proceedings, which so far had been almost as bleak as the weather, went with a roar to the finish.

But events like these were mere oases in a desert of ceaseless drudgery. The fight grew sterner and stiffer, and, as always happens on these occasions, the neutral and the apathetic began to bestir themselves and take sides. A week before the election there was not an impartial or unbiassed person left in Stoneleigh. Collisions between supporters of either party became frequent and serious. On the first occasion, when a Conservative sought to punctuate an argument by discharging a small gin-and-ginger into the face of his Liberal opponent, and the Liberal retaliated by felling the Conservative to the earth with a pint-pot, Stridge and I wrote quite effusively to one another apologising for the exuberance of our friends. A week later, when certain upholders of my cause bombarded Stridge's emporium with an assortment of Stridge's own eggs, hitting one of Mr Stridge's white-jacketed assistants in the eye, and severely damaging the frontage of Mr Stridge's Italian warehouse—whereupon local and immediate supporters of the cause of Stridge squared matters by putting three bombardiers into a horse-trough—Mr Stridge and I expressed no sort of regret to one another whatsoever, but referred scathingly, amid rapturous cheers, at our next meetings to the blackguardly policy of intimidation and hooliganism by which the other side found it necessary to bolster up a barren cause and hopeless future; all of which shows that things were tuning up to concert pitch.

Results of other elections were coming in every day, and they were not by any means favourable to our side. Still, we kept on smiling, and talked largely about the swing of the pendulum—almost as useful a phrase as "Mesopotamia" of blessed memory—and other phenomena of reaction, and hoped for the best. Champion, who had been returned for his constituency by a thumping majority, had promised to come down and speak for me at a great meeting two nights before the election; and Dubberley, who had lost his seat, threatened to come and help me to lose mine.

With the exception of Robin, who appeared to be made of some material *ære perennius*, we were all getting the least bit "tucked up," from my humble self down to Phillis, who appeared at breakfast one morning looking flushed and rather too bright-eyed.

"Electioneering seems to be telling on you, old lady," I remarked. "Feeling quite well—eh?"

"Just a *teeny* headache, daddy. But"—hastily—"I can come with you to the meeting in the theatre to-morrow night, can't I? it will be such fun!"

"Meeting? My little girl, it does not begin till an hour after your bed-time."

"That's why I want to go," said my daughter frankly. "Besides, I do *love* pantomimes—especially the clowns!" She wriggled ecstatically.

Even the revelation of the plain truth—that the pantomime would be called by another name and the clowns would appear in mufti—failed to assuage Phillis's thirst for the dramatic sensation promised by a meeting in a theatre. I was, as usual, wax in her small hands; and, man-like, I threw the *onus negandi* upon Eve's shoulders.

"Ask your mother," I said; and flew to my day's work.

Thank goodness, it was almost the last. To-morrow would be the eve of the poll, and at night we were to hold our monster meeting. Three thousand people would be present; a local magnate, Sir Thomas Wurzel (of Heycocks), would occupy the chair; what one of our local reporters insisted on calling "the *élite* of the *bon ton*" would be ranged upon the platform; and the meeting would be addressed by John Champion, Robin,—they always wanted him now,—and the much-enduring Candidate. The audience would, further, be made the recipients of a few remarks from the Chair and (unless something providential happened) from Dubberley, who was to second a vote of thanks to somebody—a performance which might take anything up to fifty minutes. Altogether a feast of oratory, and a further proof, if any were needed, that the English are a hardy race.

Phillis was decidedly unwell next morning, and Kitty prescribed bed. I am inclined to be an anxious parent, but there was little time for the exercise of any natural instincts on this occasion. Hounded on by the relentless Cash, I spent the day in a final house-to-house canvass, being fortunate enough to find at home several gentlemen who had been out on previous occasions, and who now graciously permitted Kitty to present them with a resplendent portrait of what at first sight appeared to be a hairdresser's assistant in gala costume, but which an obtrusive inscription below proclaimed to be "Inglethwaite! The Man You Know, and Who Knows You!"

After a hasty round of the Committee Rooms I returned to our hostelry, the Cathedral Arms, where, after disposing of two reporters who wanted an advance copy of my evening's speech, and having effusively thanked a pompous individual for a sheaf of statistics on a subject which I cannot recall, but in which no one outside an asylum could have reasonably been expected to take any interest whatever, and which I was at liberty to quote (with due acknowledgments) to any extent I pleased, I sat down with Champion and Robin, faint yet pursuing, to fortify myself with roast-beef and whisky for the labours of the evening.

Presently Kitty entered, with Dolly.

"*Who* do you think has just arrived?" she said.

"I don't know. Not a deputation, I hope!"

"No. Gerald—from school."

"Great Scott! Expelled?"

"Oh no. It's his half-term *exeat*. I had forgotten all about it. As it just falls in with the Election, he has come to see you through, he says."

"Right! Give him some food and a bed, and we'll send him round with one of the brakes to-morrow, to bring people up to the poll. He has a gentle compelling way about him that should be useful to us. Has he brought his inarticulate friend?"

"Yes."

"Well, tell them to ask at the office for bedrooms."

"They have done that already," said Dolly. "They are down in the kitchen now, ordering dinner. They don't propose to go to the meeting. 'Better fun outside,' they say."

"Lucky little devils!" remarked the Candidate, with feeling.

"And, Adrian," said Kitty, "I don't think I'll come either. I'm rather bothered about Philly."

I laid down my knife and fork.

"What do you mean? Is she really ill?"

"N-no. I don't think so, but she is very feverish and wretched, poor kiddy. I tried to get hold of Dr Martin this afternoon, but he was miles away on an urgent case, and won't be back till to-morrow. But I got Dr Farquharson——"

"Roaring Radical!" said I in horror-struck tones.

—"Yes, dear, but such a nice old thing; and Scotch too, Robin——"

"Aberdonian," said Robin dubiously.

"Well," continued my wife, "he said she would need care, and must stay in bed. He was in a tearing hurry, as he had to go on to one of Stridge's meetings—horrid creature!—but he promised to come again on his way home. Do you think it very important that I should come with you?"

I turned to my secretary.

"What's your opinion, Robin?"

"I think Mrs Inglethwaite should come. They like to see her on the platform, I know."

"If the Candidate's wife does not appear, people say she is too grand for them," put in Champion.

"I'll stay with Philly, Kit," said Dolly.

"Will you? You dear! But I know you want to come yourself."

"Never mind. It doesn't matter."

And so it was arranged.

We found the theatre packed to suffocation. A heated band of musicians (whose degrees must have been conferred *honoris causa*) had just concluded a set of airs whose sole excuse for existence was their patriotic character, and Sir Thomas Wurzel (of Heycocks) was rising to his feet, when our party appeared on the platform. Election fever was running high by this time; the critical spirit was almost entirely obliterated by a truly human desire to cut the preliminaries and hit somebody in the eye; and we were greeted with deafening cheers.

Presently Champion was introduced and called upon to speak. He was personally unknown to the crowd before him, although his name was familiar to them. But in five minutes he had the entire audience in his grip. He made them laugh, and he made them cheer; he made them breathe hard, and he made them chuckle. There were moments when the vast throng sat in death-like silence, while Champion, with his voice dropped almost to a whisper, cajoled them as a woman cajoles a man. Then suddenly he would blare out another battle-call, and provoke a great storm of cheering. He made little use of gesture—occasionally he punctuated a remark with an impressive forefinger, but he had the most wonderful voice I have ever heard. I sat and watched him with whole-hearted admiration. It is true that he was not doing our cause any particular good. He had forgotten that he was there to make a party speech, to decry his opponents, and crack up his friends. He was soaring away into other regions, and—most wonderful of all—he was taking his audience with him. He besought them to be men, to play the game, to think straight, to awaken to a sense of responsibility, and to remember the magnitude and responsibility of their task as controllers of an Empire. He breathed into them for a moment a portion of his own great spirit; and many a small tradesman and dull-souled artisan realised that night, for the first (and possibly the last) time, that the summit of the Universe is not composed of hides and tallow, and that there are higher things than the loaves and fishes of party politics and the petty triumphs of a contested election.

From a strictly tactical point of view all this was useless, and therefore dangerous. But for a brief twenty minutes we were gods, Utopians, Olympians, joyously planning out a scheme of things as they should be, to the entire oblivion of things as they are. That is always worth something.

Then he sat down, and we came to earth again with a bump, recollecting guiltily the cause for which we were assembled and met together—namely, the overwhelming of an Italian warehouseman and the retention of a parliamentary seat in an unimportant provincial district.

Once only have I heard that speech bettered, and that was in the House of Commons on a night in June fifteen years later, when a Prime Minister started up from the Treasury Bench to defend a colleague whose Bill—since recognised as one of the most statesmanlike measures of our generation—was being submitted to the narrowest and meanest canons of party criticism. It was another appeal for fair-play, unbiassed judgment, and breadth of view, and it took a hostile and captious House, Government and Opposition alike, by storm. The name of the Prime Minister on that occasion was John Champion, and the colleague whom he defended was Robert Chalmers Fordyce.

After Champion had sat down—nominally his speech was a vote of confidence in my unworthy self—Robin rose to second the motion. I did not envy him his task. It is an ungrateful business at the best, firing off squibs directly after a shower of meteors. Even a second shower of meteors would be rather a failure under the circumstances. Robin realised this. He put something into his pocket and told his audience a couple of stories—dry, pawky, Scottish yarns—which he admitted were not new, not true, and not particularly relevant. The first was a scurrilous anecdote concerning a man from Paisley,—which illustrious township, by the way, appears to be the target of practically all Scottish humour,—and the other treated of a Highland minister who was delivering to a long-suffering congregation a discourse upon the Minor Prophets. Robin told us how the preacher worked through Obadiah, Ezekiel, Nahum, Malachi, "and many others whose names are doubtless equally familiar to you, gentlemen," he added amid chuckles, "placing them in a kind of ecclesiastical order of merit as he proceeded; and finally he came to Habakkuk.

"'What place, my friends, what place will we assign to Habakkuk?' he roared.

"That, gentlemen," said Robin, "proved to be the last straw. A man rose up under the gallery.

"'Ye can pit him doon here in my seat,' he roared. 'I'm awa' hame!'

"Gentlemen," added Robin, as the shout of laughter subsided, "I fear that one of you will be for offering *his* seat to Habakkuk if I go on any longer, so I will just second the motion and sit down."

After that I rose to my weary feet and offered my contribution. I have no intention of giving a *précis* of my speech here. It was exactly the same as all the speeches ever delivered on such occasions. Thucydides could have written it down word for word without ever having heard me deliver it. It was not in the least a good speech, but it was the sort of speech they expected, and, better still, it was the sort of speech they wanted. Everybody was too excited to be critical, and I sat down, perspiring and thankful, amid enthusiasm.

Then came the most trying ordeal of all—questions.

I am no hand at repartee; but practice had sharpened my faculties in this direction, and I had, moreover, become fairly conversant with the type of query to which the seeker after knowledge on these occasions usually confines himself. The great secret is to bear in mind the fact that what people want in one's reply is not accurate information—unless, of course, you are standing for a Scottish constituency, and then Heaven help you!—but something smart. If you can answer the question, do so; but in any case answer it in such a way as to make the questioner feel small. Then you will have your audience with you.

To prevent unseemly shouting (and, *entre nous*, to give the Candidate a little more time to polish up his impromptus), the questions were handed up on slips of paper and read aloud, and answered *seriatim*. They were sorted and arranged for me by Robin, and I not infrequently found, among the various slips, a question usually coming directly after a regular poser, in Robin's handwriting, with a brilliant and telling reply thoughtfully appended.

This evening as usual Robin collected the slips from the stewards, and ultimately laid them on the table before me. I rose, and started on the heap. The first was a typewritten document which had been handed up by a thoughtful-looking gentleman in the front row. It contained a single line—

Are you a Liberal or a Conservative?

This was a trifle hard, I thought, coming directly after my speech; but fortunately the audience considered it merely funny, and roared when I remarked pathetically, "This gentleman is evidently deaf."

Then came the question—

Are you in favour of Woman's Suffrage?

This was no novelty, and was fortunately regarded by the gallant electors present as a form of comic relief. I adopted my usual plan under the circumstances, and said—

"I am in favour, sir, of giving a woman whatever she wants. It is always well to make a virtue of necessity."

This homely and non-committal gibe satisfied most of the audience, and I was about to proceed to the next question when my interlocutor, a litigious-looking man with blue spectacles, rose in the circle and cried—

"You are evading the question, sir! Give me an answer. Are you in favour of Woman's Suffrage or not?"

"That's fair! Give him his answer!" came the cry from the fickle audience.

I was quite prepared for this. I went through an oft-rehearsed and not uneffective piece of pantomime with Kitty, and replied—

"Well, sir, I have just inquired of my wife, who is by my side——"

I paused expectantly. I was not disappointed. There were loud cheers, during which I seized the opportunity to glance through the next few questions. Then, as I was not quite ready—

"—As she has *always* been, all through this arduous campaign——"

Terrific enthusiasm, while Kitty blushes and bows very prettily; after which the conversation proceeds on the following lines:—

Myself. And she tells me that she does not want any Suffrage of any kind whatsoever!

"*Hear, hear!*" *But some cries of disapproval.*

Myself. I therefore recommend you, sir, to go home and follow my example——

(Perfect tornado of laughter. Apparently I have made a home-thrust.)

—And after that, if you will come back to me and report the result of your—er—investigations—*(yells)*—I shall be happy to go into the matter with you more fully.

Triumphant cheers, and the blue-spectacled man collapses.

The unfortunate espouser of the cause of the fair having thus been derided out of court, I took up the next question. It concerned a long-standing dispute as to the rights of the clergy of various denominations to enter the local Board Schools,—this was in the days far preceding the present educational deadlock,—and I felt that I must walk warily. I talked at large about liberty of conscience and religious toleration, but realised as I rambled on that my moderate views and want of bigotry in one direction or the other were pleasing no one. John Bull is a curious creature. You may get drunk and beat your wife, and he will tolerate you; you may run amok through most of the Decalogue, and he will still be your friend; but venture to worship your Maker in a fashion which differs one tittle from his own, and he will put down his pint-pot or desist from sanding the sugar and fell you to the earth. I was glad to get away from this subject, leaving the audience far from satisfied, and turn to the next question. It said—

Is the Candidate aware that the important township of Spratling is entirely without a pier or jetty of any description?

"Certainly I am aware of it," I replied, trying hard to remember where the place was. The audience began to titter, and I felt uneasy.

My questioner, a saturnine gentleman in the pit, rose to his feet and continued—

"And if returned to Parliament, will you exert your influence to see that a jetty is constructed there at the earliest opportunity?"

"Cer——" There was a very slight movement beside me. Robin was leaning back unconcernedly in his chair, but on the table under my nose lay a sheet of paper bearing these words in large printed capitals—

SPRATLING IS TEN MILES FROM THE SEA!

It had been a near thing.

"Certainly," I continued. "On one condition only," I added at the top of my voice, above the rising tide of mocking laughter,—"on condition that you, sir, will personally guarantee a continuous and efficient service of fast steamers between Spratling and—the sea-coast!"

It was not a brilliant effort. I think I could have made more of it if I had had more time. But it served. How they laughed!

But there were breakers ahead. The next question asked if I was in favour of compulsory land purchase and small holdings. Of course I was not; but if I said so I knew I should rouse a dangerous storm, for the community were much bitten at the time with the "Vine and Fig-tree Fetish," as some one had happily described it. If, on the other hand, I said Yes, I should, besides telling a lie,—though, as Cash once remarked to me, "You can't strain at gnats on polling-day,"—be committing myself to a scheme, which I knew Stridge had been strongly urging, for dividing up some of the estate of the Lord of the Manor, the Earl of Carbolton (whom I knew personally for one of the wisest and most considerate landlords in the country) into allotments for the benefit of an industrial population who probably thought that turnips grew on trees. It would have been easy to make some easily broken promise, but I have my poor pride, and I never offer the most academic blessing to a measure that I am not prepared to go into a Lobby for. I wanted time to think. Perhaps Robin would slip something on to the table. I accordingly played my usual card, and said—

"Now this, gentleman, is an important question, and I am very glad it has been asked." (Oh, Adrian, my *boy*!) "And when I am faced with such a question, I always ask myself, 'What, under the circumstances, would be the course of action of—our great leader?'"

The device succeeded, and the theatre resounded with frenzied cheers. I turned to Robin. He was not there.

I swung round in Kitty's direction. She had left her chair, and was hurriedly making her way through the group of important nobodies behind me in the direction of the wings. Robin was there already, in earnest conversation with a girl.

It was Dolly.

Phillis?

CHAPTER FOURTEEN.
"TO DIE—WILL BE AN *AWFULLY* BIG ADVENTURE!"
—*Peter Pan.*

Two minutes later we were driving back to the Cathedral Arms. It was snowing heavily, but I never noticed the fact. Neither did I realise that I had abandoned my post at a critical and dangerous moment, and left my friends on the platform to explain to a puzzled and angry audience why the Candidate had run away without answering their questions. But there are deeper things than politics.

Phillis, we learned from Dolly, had been attacked by violent pains early in the evening; and about nine o'clock there had been a sudden rise of temperature, with slight delirium, followed by a complete and alarming collapse. Dr Farquharson had been sent for, hot-foot, from Stridge's platform, and his first proceeding had been to summon me from mine.

He was waiting for us in the hall of the hotel when we arrived, and Kitty and I took him into our sitting-room and, parent-like, begged to be told "the worst."

The doctor—a dour and deliberate Scot—declined to be positive, but "doubted" it might be perityphlitis. "Appendicitis is a more fashionable term," he added. The child had rallied, but was very ill, and nothing more could be done at present except keep her warm and afford relief by means of poultices and fomentations until the malady should take a definite turn for the better or the worse.

"In either case we shall know what to do then," he said; "but for the present the bairn must just fight her own battle. Has she good health, as a rule?"

Yes, thank God! she had. Physically she was frail enough, but she possessed a tough little constitution. After I had taken a peep into the room where the poor child, a vision of tumbled hair and wide bright eyes, lay moaning and tossing, I left Kitty and Dolly and the doctor to do what they could for her, and went downstairs to take counsel with my friends.

Now that the first shock was past, my head was clear again, and my course lay plain before me. Downstairs I found Robin, Champion, and Cash silently taking supper.

"Now, gentlemen," I said, when I had answered Robin's anxious inquiries—I believe he loved the child almost as much as I did—"this misfortune has come at a bad time; but one thing is quite plain, and that is that I must go through with the election. I quite see that I am not my own master at present."

Cash looked immensely relieved. Evidently he had been afraid that I would throw up the sponge. Robin and Champion nodded a grave assent, and the latter said—

"You are right, Adrian. It's the only thing to do."

"That's true," said Cash. "I am sure you have our deepest sympathy, Mr Inglethwaite, but we can't possibly let you off on any account."

It was not a very happy way of putting it, but Cash was an election agent first and a man afterwards.

"It was bad enough your running away from the meeting to-night," he continued, in tones which he tried vainly to keep from sounding reproachful. "They'd have torn the benches up if Mr Fordyce hadn't let 'em have it straight. I'm afraid it will cost us votes to-morrow."

All this grated a good deal. I could hear Robin begin to breathe through his nose, and I knew that sign. I broke in—

"What did you say to them, Robin?"

"Say? I don't really know. I assured them that you must have some good reason for leaving in such a hurry, and persuaded them to keep quiet for a bit in case you came back. We put up a few more speakers, but the people got more and more out of hand; and finally, after about five minutes of Dubberley, they grew so riotous that we ended the meeting."

"They had every excuse," said I. "They considered themselves defrauded."

"So they were," said Cash.

"Of course, if they had *known*," said Champion, "they would have gone home like lambs."

"Somehow," said Robin, "I wish they could have been told, Adrian. I should have liked fine to explain to them that you didn't leave the meeting just because you couldn't answer that last question."

"By gum!" Cash had been striving to deliver himself for some time. "Mr Inglethwaite," he said excitedly, "they must be told at once! We can get more good out of your little girl's illness than fifty meetings would do us. You know what the British public are! I'll circulate the real reason of your departure from the meeting first thing to-morrow morning, and half the wobblers in the place will vote for you out of sheer kind-heartedness. I know 'em!"

The exemplary creature almost smacked his lips.

There was a tense silence all round the table. Then I said, with some heat—

"Mr Cash, I have delivered myself into your hands, body and soul, ever since Nomination Day, and I have obeyed you to the letter all through this campaign. But—I am not going to allow a sick child's sufferings to be employed as a political asset to-morrow."

There was a sympathetic growl from the other two.

"Oh, we shouldn't do it as publicly as all that," said the unabashed Cash. "Trust me! No ostentation; just an explanatory report circulated in a subdued sort of way—and perhaps a strip of tan-bark down on the road outside the hotel—eh? *I* know how to do it. It'll pay, I tell you. And there'll be no publicity——"

I laid my head upon the table and groaned. For three weeks I had had perhaps four hours' sleep a-night, and I had been worked down to my last reserve of energy, keeping in hand just enough to meet all the probable contingencies of to-morrow's election. Dialectics with Cash as to the market value of a little girl's illness had not been included in the estimate. I groaned.

Champion answered for me.

"Mr Cash, don't you see how painful these proposals are to Mr Inglethwaite? Put such ideas out of your head once and for all. No man worthy of the name would accept votes won in such a way."

There was a confirmatory rumble from Robin.

"We can't have *ad misericordiam* appeals here, Mr Cash," he said.

Champion continued briskly—

"Now, Mr Cash, we will get Mr Inglethwaite a drink and send him to bed. He has not had a decent night's rest for a fortnight. We trust to you not to talk of the child's illness to anybody,—that is the *only* way to avoid making capital of it,—and if you will call here to-morrow after breakfast I will guarantee that your Candidate will be fit and ready to go round the polling-booths with you, and"—he put his hand on my shoulder—"set an example to all of us."

Cash, completely pulverised, departed as bidden, desolated over this renunciation of eleemosynary votes; and Robin, Champion, and I finished our supper in peace,—if one can call it peace when there is no peace.

Champion was leaving by the night mail, for he had promised to address a meeting two hundred miles away next day. His cab was already at the door, and we said good-bye to him on the hotel steps.

He shook hands with me in silence, and turned to Robin.

"Three fingers, and not too much soda, and then put him straight to bed," he commanded.

Then he turned to me again.

"Don't sit up and worry, old man," he said. "Go to bed, anyhow. The doctor and your womenfolk will do all that can be done. Your duties commence to-morrow. Keep your tail up, and face it out. *Noblesse oblige*, you know. Good-night."

He drove away, and Robin and I returned to the sitting-room.

Robin mixed me a stiff whisky-and-soda.

"Champion's prescription," he said. "Down with it!"

I obeyed listlessly.

"Now come along upstairs with me. You are going to bed. I want to turn you out a first-class Candidate in the morning—not a boiled owl."

His cheery masterfulness had its effect, and I suddenly felt a man again.

"Never fear!" I said. "I shall go through with it right enough—the whole business—unless—unless—Robin, old man, supposing—supposing——"

"Blethers!" said Robin hastily. "She'll be much better in the morning. Here's your room. Good-night!"

He shepherded me into my bedroom, shut the door on me, and tiptoed away.

I really made a determined effort to go to bed. I actually lay down and covered myself up, but sleep I could not. After an hour of conscientious endeavour I rose, inspired with a new idea.

The doctor had straitly forbidden me to enter Phillis's room; but opening out of it was the apartment that was used as her nursery. There would be a fire there: I would spend the rest of the night on a sofa in front of it.

I looked at my watch. It was one o'clock. I took a candle, walked softly down the passage, and let myself quietly into the nursery. The door leading into Phillis's room was ajar, and a slight smell of some drug or disinfectant assailed my sharpened senses.

The room was in darkness, except that a good fire burned in the grate. A silent figure rose up from before it at my entrance.

It was Robin. Somehow I was not in the least surprised to see him there.

"Come along," he said softly. "I was expecting you."

We sat there for the rest of the long night. The house was very still, but every quarter of an hour the Cathedral chimes across the Close—our rooms lay in a quiet wing of the hotel, which formed a hollow square with the Cathedral, Chapter-house, and Canonries—furnished a musical break in the silence. So tensely mechanical does one's brain become under such circumstances, that presently I found myself anticipating the exact moment when the next quarter would strike; and I remember feeling quite disappointed and irritable if, when I said to myself *"Now!"* the chime did not ring out for another fifteen seconds or so. Truly, at three o'clock on a sleepless morning the grasshopper is a burden.

Once Robin rose softly to his feet and turned towards the door of Phillis's room. I had not heard any one move there, but when I looked round Dolly was standing on the threshold. She was wrapped in a kimono,—I remember its exact colour and pattern to this day, and the curious manner in which the heraldic-looking animals embroidered upon it winked at me in the firelight,—and she held an incongruous-looking coal-scuttle in her hand. It was not by any means empty, but she handed it to Robin with a little nod of authority and vanished again.

I looked listlessly at Robin, wondering what he was to do with the coal-scuttle. He began to cut a newspaper into strips, after which he picked suitable lumps of coal out of the scuttle and tied them up into neat little paper packets, half a dozen of which he presently handed through the door to Dolly. I suppose she placed them noiselessly on the fire in Phillis's room, but we heard no sound.

It was a bitterly cold night, and outside the snow was lying thick; so Robin busied himself with preparing other little packets of coal, and at intervals throughout the long night he passed them through the door to the tireless Dolly.

Various sounds came from within. Occasionally the child suffered spasms of pain, and we could hear her crying. Then all-wise Nature would grant the sorely tried little body a rest at the expense of the mind that ruled it, and poor Phillis would drop into a sort of rambling delirium, through which we perforce accompanied her. At one time she would be wandering through some Elysian field of her own; we heard her calling her mates and proposing all manner of attractive games. (Even "Beckoning" was included. Once I distinctly heard her "choose" me.) But more often she was in deadly fear. Her solitary little spirit was too plainly beset by those nameless ghosts that haunt the borderland separating the realms of Death from those of his brother Sleep. Once her voice rose to a scream.

"Uncle Robin! It's the Kelpie! Stop it! It's coming—it's breaving on me! Uncle *Robin*! oh——!"

I looked at Robin. He was sitting gripping the arms of his chair, with every muscle in his body rigid; and I knew that he, like myself, was praying God to strike down the cowardly devil that would torment a child.

Then I heard, for the first time that night, the soothing murmur of Kitty's voice.

"It's all right, dearie. Mother is holding you fast. It shan't hurt you. There, it's running away now, isn't it? See!"

Kitty's tones would have lightened the torments of the Pit, and Phillis's cries presently died down to an uneasy whisper. After a sudden and curiously pathetic little outburst of singing,—chiefly a jumble of scraps from such old favourites as "Onward, Christian *Sailors*!"—there was silence again, and the Cathedral chimed out half-past four.

Shortly after this the doctor came out of the room with a message from Kitty that I ought to be in bed. Evidently Dolly had told her about me.

"How is she now, doctor?" I whispered, disregarding the command.

"Up and down, up and down. She is making a brave fight of it, poor lassie, but we can do little at present except stand by and give relief when the bad fits come."

"May I go in and see her?"

"No, no! You could do no good, and she might be frightened if she caught sight of a large dim figure in the dark. Leave it to the women, and thank God for them. Hark!"

Phillis was back in Elysium again.

"Who's been eating my porridge?" said a gruff little voice. Then came a rapturous shriek. Evidently the Little Bear had caught Curly Locks in his bed. We sat listening, while the game ended and another followed in its place. Suddenly she began to sing again—

"Then three times round went that gallant ship,
And three times round went she;
Then three times round went that gallant ship,
And—sank—to the—bottom of the sea—ea—ee—"

There was a little wailing *rallentando*, and silence.

"Philly, Philly, *don't*!" It was the only time that night that Kitty gave any sign of breaking down. The doctor hurried back into the room. The clock struck five.

After that there was a very long silence. It must have lasted nearly an hour. Then Dolly tiptoed out to us. "She's asleep," she whispered. "He says she's a shade better. I want another coal-packet."

She took what Robin gave her, and faded away.

After that I think we dozed in our chairs. The next thing I remember was a knock at the outer door. I opened my heavy eyes and stirred my stiff joints. The Boots put his head in, and I realised it was daylight.

"Half-past eight, sir. Mr Cash is waiting downstairs. Poll's been open half an hour, he says."

CHAPTER FIFTEEN.
TWO BATTLES.

Before I left the hotel I struck a bargain with Cash. I would go anywhere and do anything, but he was to give me a written itinerary of my movements for the day, clearly stating where I should be at various times. This document I left in the hands of Dolly, who promised faithfully to send for me, if—if necessary.

Then, putting my paternal instincts into my pocket, I braced myself up and plunged into the vortex of polling-day.

Truly, if Time is the healer, Work is the anesthetic. In the turmoil of the crowded streets and polling-booths, I found myself almost as enthusiastic and whole-hearted as if no little girl of mine were fighting for life in a darkened room not many streets away. I shook hands with countless folk, I addressed meetings of the unwashed at street corners, and received the plaudits or execrations of the multitude with equal serenity.

Robin hastened away to the Hide-and-Tallow Works, whence, during the dinner-hour, he charmed many an oleaginous elector to come and plump for Inglethwaite, the Man Whom He Knew and Who Knew Him. Gerald and Donkin, smothered in violets and primroses, were personally conducting a sort of tumbril, which dashed across my field of vision from time to time, sometimes full, sometimes empty, but always at full gallop.

Election "incidents" were plentiful. I was standing in the principal polling-station at one time, when a gentleman called Hoppett, a cobbler by persuasion—I think I have already mentioned him as the benignant individual who used to come to the door of his establishment and pursue me with curses down the street— came out from recording his vote. He did not see me, but caught sight of Robin, who had just arrived with a *posse* of electors, and was standing by the Returning Officer's table. Hobbling up, the cobbler shook a gnarled fist under my secretary's nose.

"I've voted against your man," he shouted. "We're goin' to be rid of the lot of you this time. Set of reskils!... I've put my mark against Stridge, I have; and against Inglethwaite's name I've put a picture of a big boot—one of my own making, too! The big boot!" he screamed ecstatically—"that's what your man is a-going to get to-day. Set of——"

Robin smiled benignantly upon him, and glanced at the Returning Officer.

"You hear what this gentleman says?" he remarked.

"I do," replied the official.

"Is it not a fact that he has annulled his vote by making unnecessary marks on his voting-paper?" continued Robin solemnly.

"That is so," assented the Returning Officer. "I'm afraid your vote won't count this time, Mr Hoppett. Good morning!"

There was a roar of delighted laughter from friend and foe, and the fermenting Hoppett was cast forth.

I succeeded in getting back to the hotel for ten minutes at luncheon-time. Dolly met me—pale, sleepless, but unbeaten.

"The doctor is with her just now," she said. "She has been in fearful pain, poor kiddy; but he has given her a drug of some sort, and she is easier now."

"Couldn't I see her, just a moment?" I said wistfully.

"The answer to that question, sir," replied Dolly, "is in the negative."

We both smiled resolutely at this familiar tag, and Dolly concluded—

"Kitty is lying down. I made her. But she is going to get up when they—I mean——"

I detected a curious confusion in her voice.

"When what?" I asked.

"Nothing."

I surveyed my sister-in-law uneasily

"Are they expecting—a crisis, then?"

"Yes—a sort of a one."

"When?"

Dolly seemed to consider.

"About five," she said.

"Hadn't I better be near, in case——?"

"Where are you to be this afternoon?"

"Hunnable."

Dolly nodded her head reflectively.

"When can you be back?" she asked.

"I can do it by five, I should think."

"That will be soon enough. The doctor said that if—you were wanted, it would be about then. Good-bye, old gentleman!"

"Good-bye, Dolly! Mind you go to bed." (We seem to have spent a large portion of that twenty-four hours urging each other to go to bed.)

Then I went back to work.

Polling had been brisk during the dinner-hour, and both Cash and Robin considered that we were doing fairly well. Things would be slack at Stoneleigh itself during the afternoon, and the obvious and politic course now was to drive over to the fishing village of Hunnable—I had only time for one, and this was the most considerable—and catch my marine constituents as they emerged from the ocean, Proteus-like, between three and four o'clock.

I did so, and for the space of an hour and a half I solicited the patronage of innumerable tarry mariners, until their horny hands had filled up the voting-papers and my own smelt to heaven of fish. It was a quarter to five, and dark, before I escaped from the attentions of a small but pertinacious group of inquirers who wanted to understand my exact attitude on the question of trawling within the three-mile limit, and proceeded at a hand-gallop back to Stoneleigh. (That odoriferous but popular vehicle, the motor-car, was still in the preceded-by-a-man-ten-yards-in-front-bearing-a-red-flag stage in those days, and we had to rely on that antiquated but much more reliable medium of transport, the horse.) The snow lay very heavily in places, and our progress was not over-rapid. Moreover, passing the central Committee Rooms on my way to the hotel, I was stopped and haled within to conciliate various wobblers, and another twenty minutes of precious time sped. But I stuck to my determination to let nothing interfere with duty that day, and I argued with free-thinkers and pump-handled bemused supporters until all was settled and Cash said I might go.

Still, it was nearer six than five when my panting horses drew up at the Cathedral Arms.

There was no Dolly to receive me this time, but at the top of the stairs leading to our rooms I met the doctor. He was accompanied by a grey-haired, kind-eyed old gentleman in a frock-coat, with "London Specialist" written all over him. It was Sir James Fordyce.

"Well?" I asked feverishly as I shook hands.

The two men motioned me into the sitting-room, and Farquharson said, in a curiously uncertain fashion—

"Mr Inglethwaite, we have done a thing which should not, properly, have been done without your consent. Your secretary suggested the idea, and I agreed. Mrs Inglethwaite made a point of our saying nothing to you, and volunteered to take all responsibility on herself. She said you were not to be worried. So I wired for Sir James——"

"I see," I said, "and he operated?"

"Yes, at three o'clock this afternoon. Indeed, your sister-in-law, I think, purposely concealed from you——"

"She did." That, then, was the "crisis" that Dolly had in her mind, and that, too, was why she had told me to come back at five—when everything would be well over!

I continued—

"And how have you—I mean—is she——?"

"The operation," said the old man, "was entirely successful, and, as it turned out, most necessary. But of course for so young a patient the strain was terrible."

"How is she?"

"She came through finely, but I do not conceal from you the fact that her life hangs by a thread."

I had a premonition that something was going to be "broken" to me. I dropped into a chair, and waited dully. Then I felt a hand on my shoulder, and Sir James continued—

"Just weakness, you understand! Her exhaustion when she came out of the chloroform was extreme, but every moment now is in our favour. Children have such extraordinary recuperative power."

He was speaking in the usual cheery tones of the bedside optimist. I raised my head.

"Tell me straight, Sir James—will the child live?"

The old man's grip on my shoulder tightened just for a moment, and when he spoke it was in an entirely unprofessional voice.

"Thanks to two of the bravest and most devoted of women," he said, "I think she will."

I dropped my head into my hands.

"Please God!" I murmured brokenly.

"Of course," he continued, "anything may happen yet. But the way in which she has been cared for by my good friend here——"

"No, no," said Farquharson. "Give the credit to those that deserve it. I just afforded ordinary professional assistance. It was your wife and her sister, Mr Inglethwaite, that pulled the child through. She has had tight hold of a hand of one of them ever since ten o'clock last night."

"Yes," said Sir James; "I think it will be found that their nursing has just made the difference. You had better give him something, Farquharson."

In truth I needed something, though up to this point I had not realised the fact. Farquharson gave me a draught out of a little glass, which sent a steadying glow all through me, and presently I was able to shake hands, dumbly and mechanically, with the great surgeon, who, I found, was bidding me good-bye; for the world is full of sick folk, and their champion may not stay to see the issue of one battle before he must hurry off to fight another.

They left me to myself, while Farquharson went down to the door with Sir James. Presently he returned.

"I must be getting back to the patient shortly," he said. "The next hour or so will be very critical. The nurse is here, and I have sent the ladies to bed. But you may go in for a look, if you like. I am going out for exactly ten minutes."

"I see—a breather. You deserve it."

"Not exactly. I'm going to vote—for Stridge!"

He chuckled in a marvellously cheering way, and left me.

As I approached Phillis's room the door opened, and I was confronted with that most soothing and comforting of sights to a sick man—a nurse's uniform. She was a pleasant-faced girl, I remember, and she was carrying a basin full of sponges and water, cruelly tinged.

"Just a peep!" she said, with that little air of motherly sternness which all women, however young, adopt towards fractious children and helpless males.

She closed the door very softly upon me, and left me alone.

For a moment I stood uncertain in the shadow of the screen that guarded the door. There was a whiff of chloroform in the air, and through the doorway leading to the room where we had sat throughout the previous night I could see the end of a white-covered table. Thank God, that part of the business was over!

A shaded lamp burned at Phillis's bedside. She lay deathly still, an attenuated little derelict amid an ocean of white bed-clothes.

At first I thought I was alone with the child, and was moving softly forward when I became suddenly aware that some one was kneeling at the far side of the bed. It was Kitty. Evidently she had not obeyed the doctor's orders about going to bed.

A single ray from the lamp fell upon her face. Her eyes were wide open, and she seemed to be looking straight at me. Her lips were moving, and I became aware that she was speaking, very earnestly and almost inaudibly.

I stood still to hear her. Then I realised that her words were not addressed to me. Very carefully I stepped back to the door-handle, turned it, and slipped out.

CHAPTER SIXTEEN.
"QUI PERD, GAGNE."

Once more I was back in the thick of it all, and till the closing of the poll at eight o'clock I strove, in company with Cash, Robin, and others, to direct the inclinations of my constituents into the proper channels.

The tumult increased as the evening advanced. More snow had fallen during the afternoon, and outlying electors were being conveyed to the scene of action with the utmost difficulty. People were voting at seven o'clock who had intended to get it done and be home by six; and as time wore on it was seen that there would be a desperate rush of business right up till closing time.

Every one was in high spirits. That potent factor in British politics, the electioneering egg, had been entirely superseded by the snowball, and the youth of Stoneleigh, massed in the public square outside the Town Hall, were engaged, with a lofty indifference to party distinctions that would have been sublime if it had not been so painful, in an untrammelled bombardment of all who crossed their path.

At length the Cathedral chimed out the hour of eight, and the poll closed. Cash hurried up to me.

"It's going to be a desperately close thing," he said. "The counting will begin at once, in the Mayor's room on the first floor of the Town Hall. The outlying boxes should be in by half-past nine at the latest, and the result should be out by about eleven. You'll come and watch the counting, I suppose."

But there are limits to human endurance.

"Mr Cash," I said, buttoning my overcoat up to my ears as a preliminary to an encounter with the budding statesmen outside, "I think I have got to the end of my day's work. Nothing can affect the result now, and I'm going home—that's flat. Good-night!"

"Surely you're coming to hear the result announced," wailed Cash. "There's the vote of thanks to the Returning Officer. You'll have to propose that—or second it," he added grimly.

"Well, I'll see. But I think, now that the poll is closed, that my duty lies elsewhere," I said. "If I am really wanted, send word by Mr Fordyce."

Five minutes later, and I was once more at the Cathedral Arms. The ground floor of that hostelry hummed like a hive, and the bar and smoking-room were filled to overflowing with supporters of both sides, who were prudently avoiding all risk of disappointment by celebrating the result of the election in advance.

I pushed my way through a group of enthusiastic patriots—many of them in that condition once described to me by a sporting curate as "holding two or three firkins apiece"—who crowded round me, fired with a desire to drink success to the British Constitution—a rash shibboleth, by the way, for gentlemen in their situation to attempt to enunciate at all—at my expense, and hastened upstairs to our wing.

In the passage I met the nurse. She greeted me with a little smile; but I was mistrustful of professional cheerfulness that night.

"Will you tell Mrs Inglethwaite or Miss Rubislaw that I have come in, please?" I said, and turned into the sitting-room.

The sight of a snug room or a bright fire or a colossal arm-chair is always comforting to a weary man, even though his thoughts admit of little rest. I sank down amid these comforts, and closed my eyes. Now that my long day's play-acting was over, and nothing mattered any more, I began to realise how great the strain had been. I was utterly done. I had no clear recollection of having tasted food since breakfast, but I was not hungry. All I wanted was to be left in peace. Even the sickening anxiety about Phillis had died down to a sort of dull ache. In a few minutes a too-wakeful mind struggled with an exhausted body. I wondered dimly when somebody would come and tell me how Philly was. Perhaps——

I fell asleep.

I was awakened by the consciousness of a second presence in my arm-chair, which was a roomy one of the saddle-bag variety. It was Kitty. Presently I became aware that she was crying, softly, as women usually do,—men gulp noisily, because they have lost control of themselves, and children wail, chiefly to attract attention,—but so softly on this occasion that I knew she was trying to avoid disturbing me.

It had happened, then.

Well, obviously, this was one of the rare occasions upon which a husband can be of some use to his wife. I sat up, and made a clumsy effort at a caress.

"We've still got each other," I said, rather brokenly.

Kitty positively laughed.

"Adrian, you don't understand. Philly roused up for a few minutes about eight o'clock,—very *piano*, poor mite, but almost herself,—and then dropped off into a beautiful sleep, bless her! The doctor has gone home and left the nurse in charge. He says things should be all right now. Oh, Adrian, Adrian!"

And my wife sobbed afresh.

"Then what the—what on earth are you crying for?" I demanded.

"I don't know, dear," said Kitty, without making any attempt to stop. "I'm so happy!"

Really, women are the most extraordinary creatures. Here was I, after the labour and anxiety of the last twenty-four hours, ready to shout for joy. I was no longer tired: I felt as if my day's work had never been. I wanted to sing—to dance—to give three cheers in a whisper. And my wife, after giving me a very bad fright, was sitting celebrating our victory by a flood of tears and other phenomena usually attributed by the masculine mind to unfathomable woe. It was all very perplexing, and I felt a trifle ill-used; but I suppose it was one of the things that mark the difference between a man and a woman.

After that we sat long and comfortably. Our conversation need not be set down here, for it has no bearing on this chronicle.

Finally we looked at the clock, and then at each other.

"We must have been sitting here a long time," I said. "I wonder where the others are."

"By the way," said Kitty, "Dilly and Dicky have arrived. Robin and Dolly wired for them this morning. They may be upstairs any moment. They were having supper in the coffee-room when last I saw them." She patted her hair. "Do I look an awful fright?"

I turned in the restricted space at my command and surveyed her.

"Do my eyes look wet?" she inquired, feeling in my pocket for my handkerchief.

Kitty has large grey eyes. Once, during the most desperate period of our courtship, I referred to them as "twin lakes"—an indiscretion which their owner, in her less generous moments, still casts up to me. But to-night the territory surrounding them presented a distinct appearance of inundation. I continued to gaze. I thought of last night's ceaseless vigil and to-day's long-drawn battle. My wife had borne the brunt of all, and I had grudged her a few tears! My heart smote me.

"Kit!" I said suddenly; "poor Kit!"...

We were interrupted by the opening of the door and the entrance of what I at first took to be a chimney-sweep's apprentice, but which proved to be my brother-in-law, with evidence of electoral strenuousness written thick upon him.

"Hallo, you two!" he remarked genially. Then, noticing our unconventional economy of sitting-space—"Sorry! I didn't know. I thought you'd given up that sort of thing years ago!"

I rose and shook myself.

"Come in, my son," I said.

"Righto!" replied Gerald. Then he addressed himself to a figure which, with true delicacy of feeling, had shrunk back into the passage outside.

"Come in, Moke, old man. I've got them separated now!"

The discreet Master Donkin sidled respectfully in at the door, and Gerald continued.

"Moke and I would like to say how pleased we are to hear about Phillis," he said, rather awkwardly for him. "We have just got to hear how really bad she's been."

The resolution was seconded by a confirmatory mumble from Master Donkin.

"We met the nurse just now," continued Gerald, "and she told us about the operation, and all that. It must have been a pretty thick day for you, Adrian. And you're looking pretty rotten, too, Kitty," he added with brotherly directness. "But do you people know what time it is? Half-past eleven, nearly. The result should be out any minute. Aren't you coming to the Town Hall? They'll want you to make a speech, or get egged, or something."

I looked at my watch.

"Well, there's no particular reason why I shouldn't go—*now*," I said. "What do you say, Kitty? Hark! What's that?"

"That's the result, I expect," said my brother-in-law.

We drew up the blind and opened the window. The moon was shining brightly, and threw the monstrous shadow of the Cathedral very blackly upon the untrodden snow of the peaceful Close. Through the clear night air came the sound of frenzied cheering.

"That's it, right enough," said Gerald. "I wonder if you've got the chuck, my bonny boy."

"Ugh! It is cold! Come in," said Kitty.

We shut the window, drew down the blind, returned to the fire, and waited. Dolly joined us now, and Kitty vanished to sit by Phillis. We waited on. Somehow it never occurred to us to send downstairs for news. I suppose there are times when the human craving for sensation is sated. We sat and waited.

At last the door opened, and, as I expected, Robin entered. He looked like a man who has not been to bed for a week. He shut the door softly behind him—evidently he feared he might be entering a house of mourning—and surveyed us for a moment without speaking. I knew what was in his mind. Then he said—

"We have lost."

I stood up.

"On the contrary," I replied, "we have won."

In a bound Robin was on the hearth-rug, gripping my hand with his. (His other had somehow got hold of one of Dolly's, and I remember wondering if he was hurting her as much as me.)

"You mean it?" he roared.

"I do. She is sleeping like a lamb."

"Oh, man, I'm just glad! What does *anything* matter after that?"

Then we sat down and smiled upon each other largely and vacuously. We were all a little unstrung that night, I think. After all, it seems rather unreasonable to lavish one's time, labour, and money on an electoral contest, and then laugh when you lose, and say it doesn't matter, just because a child isn't going to die. Oh, I am glad Mr Cash was not there!

"But I must tell you what happened when the result was read out," said Robin. "It was a near thing—a majority of twenty-seven. (I don't think it is worth while to ask for a recount: everything was done very carefully.) When the figures went up there was the usual hullabaloo———"

"We heard it, thanks," said Gerald.

"And presently Stridge stepped out on to the balcony and bowed his acknowledgments. There was a lot more yelling and horn-blowing, and then they began to cry out for Inglethwaite."

"Naturally. Yes?"

"They were quiet at last, and Stridge got his speech in. He talked the usual blethers about having struck a blow that night that would ring through England,—just what *you* would have had to say if you had got in, in fact,—and *then* he went on, the old sumph, to say that for reasons best known to himself his *honourable* opponent had seen fit to withhold his presence from them that night, and he begged leave to add that he considered that a man, even though he knew he was going to be beaten, ought to have the pluck to come and face the music."

"Mangy bounder!" remarked my brother-in-law dispassionately.

"Oh, I was just raging!" continued Robin. "The people of course yelled themselves hoarse; and Stridge was going on to rub it into you, when I stepped on to the balcony beside him—I had been standing just inside the window—and I put my hand on Stridge's fat shoulder and I pulled him back a wee thing, and I roared—

"'Gentlemen, will you not let me say a word for Mr Inglethwaite?'"

Dolly's eyes began to blaze, and I saw her lips part in anticipation.

"There was a tremendous uproar then," Robin went on with relish. "The folk howled to Stridge to put me over the balcony———"

"I wish he had tried!" said Gerald with simple fervour.

"And other folk cried to me to go on. They knew there must be some explanation of your absence. I just stood there and let them roar. Inside the room there was a fine commotion; and with the tail of my eye I could see Cash hurrying round explaining to them what I wanted to say. (He has his points, Cash!) Then at last, as the noise got worse and worse, I put my mouth to Stridge's ear and bellowed that he would regret it all his life if he didn't let me say what I had to say, and that he would be grateful to me afterwards, and all that. He is a decent old buffer, really, and he was evidently impressed with what I said———"

"I should like to know exactly what you did say, Robin," I interpolated.

"Never mind just now. Anyhow, he turned and clambered back into the room, and left me with the crowd. They were soon quiet, and I just told them."

Robin leaned back in his chair.

"Told them *what*?" came from all parts of the room.

But Robin had become suddenly and maddeningly Caledonian again.

"I just told them about Philly," he said. "What else could I do? It wasn't like telling them during the election. That would have been an appeal to the gallery for votes. This was just common justice to you. Anyhow, they quite quietened down after that."

And that was all the report that its author ever gave us of a speech which, in the space of four minutes, turned a half-maddened election mob into a silent, a sympathetic, and (I heard afterwards) a deeply moved body of sober human beings.

"What happened next?" asked Kitty, who had rejoined us. (Phillis was still sleeping sweetly, she said.)

"After that I hauled old Stridge on to the balcony again and gave him a congratulatory hand-shake, *coram populo*, on your behalf. Then I retired and slipped out by a back way and came here. Stridge was in full eruption again when I left——"

Dolly held up her hand.

"What is that curious noise?" she said.

"It's outside," said Kitty.

Gerald went to the window and lifted the blind. Then he turned to us.

"I say," he said in an unusual voice, "come here a minute."

We drew up the blind and surveyed the scene before us.

Two minutes before the moon had shone upon an untrodden expanse of snow. Now the Close was black with people. There must have been two or three thousand. They stood there in the gleaming moonlight, silent, motionless, like an army of phantoms. At their head and forefront—I could see the moonlight glitter on his watch-chain, which lay in a most favourable position for lunar reflection—stood the newly elected Member for Stoneleigh, Mr Alderman Stridge.

Simultaneously there was a knock at the door, and the hall-porter of the hotel appeared.

"Mr Stridge's compliments, sir, and he would like to have a word with you."

"Go down quickly, Adrian," said Kitty anxiously. "They'll wake Philly!"

I descended without a word, and passed out into the Close from a French window on the ground floor.

I glanced up in the direction of our rooms and noticed that my party were standing on the balcony outside the sitting-room. I could see Kitty's anxious face. But she need have had no fear.

Mr Stridge advanced towards me, silk hat in hand. Behind him stood a variety of Stoneleigh worthies, and I had time to notice that the group was composed of an indiscriminate mixture of friends and foes.

"Mr Inglethwaite, sir," said Stridge, "I should like to shake you by the hand."

He did so, as did a few of those immediately around us, in perfect silence. I wondered what was coming.

"That is all, sir," said Stridge simply, and not without a certain dignity. "We shall move off now. We did you a wrong to-night, and we all of us"—he indicated the motionless multitude with a sweep of his hand—"agreed to come here in silence, just for a moment, as an indication of our sympathy and—respect."

I was unable to speak, which was not altogether surprising. There was something overwhelming about the dumb kindness of it all,—three thousand excited folk holding themselves in for fear of disturbing a sick child,—and I merely shook Stridge's hand again.

However, I found my voice at last.

"Mr Stridge," I said, "there is only one thing I will say in response to your kindness, but I think it is the one thing most calculated to reward you all for it. To-night my little girl's illness took a favourable turn. She is now fast asleep, and practically out of danger."

I saw a great ripple pass over the crowd, like a breeze over a cornfield, as the news sped from mouth to mouth. Both Stridge's great hands were on my shoulders.

"Good lad!" he said. "Good lad!"

He patted my shoulders again, and then, as if struck by a sudden idea, he turned and whispered a direction to his lieutenants. I overheard the words "Market Square," and "A good half mile away." Once more the wave passed over the cornfield, and without a sound the great concourse turned to the left and streamed away over the trampled snow, leaving me standing bareheaded on the steps of the French window, almost directly below the spot where the unconscious little object of all this consideration lay fast asleep.

I returned to the group on the balcony. They had heard most of the conversation, and Kitty was unaffectedly dabbing her eyes.

"Well, let us get in out of the cold," I said, suddenly cheerful and brisk. "I want my supper."

"Wait a moment," said Robin, "I don't think everything is quite over yet. What is that? Listen!"

From the direction of the Market Square came the shouts of a great multitude. Cheer upon cheer floated up to the starry heavens. The roars that had greeted the declaration of the poll were nothing to these. There was a united ring about them that had been lacking in the others. It was like one whole-hearted many-headed giant letting off steam.

"A-a-h!" said Kitty.

CHAPTER SEVENTEEN.
IN WHICH ALL'S RIGHT WITH THE WORLD.

After that we became suddenly conscious of our bodily wants, and clamoured for supper.

It was long after midnight, and most of the hotel servants had gone to bed. But one waiter of political leanings, who had been an enthusiastic witness of the proceedings in the Close, stood by us nobly. He laid a table in the sitting-room. He materialised a cold turkey, a brown loaf, and some tomatoes; and he even achieved table-napkins. Gerald and Donkin on their part disappeared into the nether regions, and returned bearing mince-pies and cider. Some one else found champagne and opened it; and in a quarter of an hour we were left to ourselves by the benignant waiter round a comfortably loaded table, in a snug room with the fire burning and the curtains drawn.

It was an eccentric kind of meal, for every one was overflowing with a sort of reactionary hilarity; and everybody called everybody else "old man" or "my dear," and I was compelled to manipulate my food with my left hand owing to the fact that my wife insisted on clinging tightly to my right. The only times I got a really satisfactory mouthful were when she slipped out of the room to see how her daughter was sleeping.

As the meal progressed, I began to note the exceedingly domestic and intimate manner in which we were seated round the table, which was small and circular. Kitty and I sat together; then, on our right, came Dicky and Dilly, then Gerald and Donkin, each partially obscured from view by a bottle of cider about the size of an Indian club; and Dolly and Robin completed the circle.

The party comported themselves variously. Kitty and I said little. We were utterly tired and dumbly thankful, and had no desire to contribute greatly to the conversation; but we turned and looked at one another in a contented sort of way at times. Dicky and Dilly were still sufficiently newly married to be more or less independent of other people's society, and they kept up a continuous undercurrent of lover-like confidences and playful nothings all the time. Gerald, upon whom solid food seemed to have the effect that undiluted alcohol has upon ordinary folk, was stentoriously engaged with Mr Donkin in what a student of *Paley's Evidences* would have described as "A Contest of Opposite Improbabilities" concerning his election experiences.

Lastly, I turned to Dolly and Robin. Dolly's splendid vitality has stood her in good stead during the last twenty-four hours, and this, combined with the present flood-tide of joyous relief, made it hard to believe that she had spent a day and a night of labour and anxiety. She was much more silent than usual, but her face was flushed and happy, and somehow I was reminded of the time when I had watched her greeting the dawn on the morning after Dilly's wedding. Robin, with the look of a man who has a hard day's work behind him, a full meal inside him, and a sound night's sleep before him—and what three greater blessings could a man ask for himself?—sat beside her, smiling largely and restfully on the company around him.

Suddenly Dicky made an announcement.

"There is one more bottle," he said. "Come on, let's buzz it!"

He opened the champagne in a highly professional manner and filled up our glasses. Gerald and Donkin declined, but helped themselves to fresh jorums of cider.

Then there was a little pause, and we all felt that some one ought to make a speech or propose a toast.

"Shall we drink some healths?" proposed Dilly.

There was a chorus of assent.

"We will each propose one," I said, "right round the table in turn. Ladies first! Yours, Kitty? I suppose it will be Philly—eh?"

Kitty nodded.

"Ladies and gentlemen," I announced, "you are asked to drink to the speedy recovery of Miss Phillis Inglethwaite. This toast is proposed by her mother, and seconded by her father."

The toast was drunk with all sincerity, but soberly, as befitted.

"Now, Dilly," I said, when we were ready again.

Dilly whispered something to her husband, which was received by that gentleman with a modest and deprecatory cough, coupled with an urgent request that his wife would chuck it.

"He won't announce my toast for me," explained Dilly, turning to us—"he's too shy, poor dear!—so I'll do it myself. Ladies and gentlemen, the toast is—Dicky!"

Dicky's health was drunk with cheers and laughter, and Dilly completed its subject's confusion by kissing him.

"Now, Dolly!" said every one.

"Not yet!" said Dolly. "Gerald and Moke are the next pair. Gerald must act lady, and think of a toast."

Master Gerald, hastily bolting a solid mass of mince-pie—one could almost follow the course of its descent—cheerfully complied.

"All right," he said; "I think I'll drink the health of old Moke himself. He's not much to look at, but he's a good sort. I shan't kiss him, though, Dilly. And," he added, "I think he had better drink mine too. He looks thirsty. Come on, sonny—no heeltaps!"

He elaborately linked arms with the now comatose Donkin, and each thereupon absorbed, without drawing breath, about a pint of cider apiece. After that, with a passing admonition to his friend not to burst, my brother-in-law returned to his repast.

So far, the toasts had all been of a most conventional and inevitable character. Now, automatically but a little tactlessly, we all turned to see what Dolly and Robin were going to do. From the standpoint of the last two toasts they were certainly in a rather delicate position.

"Come on, you two!" commanded Gerald. "Do something! Make a spring!"

Robin took up his glass of champagne and turned rather inquiringly to Dolly.

Without a word she linked her arm in his, and they drank together.

"Oh, come, I say, that's not fair! Whose health were you drinking, Robin, old man?" inquired the tactless Dicky.

"I was drinking to the future Mrs Fordyce—whoever she may be!" said Robin, obviously apologetic at being unable to think of anything more sparkling.

"Whose health were *you* drinking, Dolly?" yelled Gerald, with much enjoyment.

Then Dolly did a startling thing.

Robin's hand lay resting on the table beside her. Into it she deliberately slipped, her own; and then gazed—flushed and defiant, but proud and smiling—round a circle composed entirely of faces belonging to people suffering from the gapes.

I glanced at Robin. He looked perfectly dumfounded, but I saw his hand close automatically round Dolly's fingers, and I saw, too, her pink nails go white under the pressure.

But Dolly seemed to feel no pain. On the contrary, she continued to smile upon us. Then, bowing her head quickly, before any of us realised what she would be at, she lightly kissed the great hand which imprisoned her own. Then she looked up again, with glistening eyes.

"There!" she said. "*Now* you know!"

Our breath came back, and the spellbound silence was broken.

"*Dolly*!" said Kitty.

"My *dear*!" said Dilly.

"What—*ho*!" drawled Dicky.

But it was Gerald who rounded off the situation. He was standing on the table by this time.

"Three cheers for Dolly and Robin!" he roared.

We gave them, with full throats. (Fortunately we were a long way from Phillis's room.)

After that we all sat down again, feeling a little awkward, as people do when they have taken the lid off their private feelings for a moment. Finally Kitty led off with—

"But, Dolly, dear, why didn't you tell us? When was it?"

"I didn't tell you before," said Dolly composedly, "because it has only just happened—this moment."

"Only this moment? But——"

"Do you mean to say he hasn't *asked* you? Oh——"

"Are you asking *him*?"

The questions came simultaneously from all parts of the table; horribly inquisitive, some of them; but then the thing had been so frankly and deliberately done, that we knew Dolly wanted to explain everything to us there and then.

"I'll tell you," said Dolly, after silence had been restored by the fact that Gerald had shouted us all down and then stopped himself. "Robin told me—well—something, six months ago, the night after Dilly's wedding, at the dance——"

"That *was* why you locked the door, then," I said involuntarily.

Both Robin and Dolly turned upon me in real amazement. But I saw that this side-issue would interrupt the story.

"Never mind!" I said. "Go on! I'll explain afterwards."

"Well," continued Dolly, "he said to me—may I tell them, Robin?" She turned to the man beside her with a pretty air of deference. Robin, who up to this point had sat like a graven image, inclined his head, and Dolly proceeded—

"I have never told anybody about this—except Dilly, of course."

"I've got the letter still," said Dilly.

"Robin told me," Dolly went on, "that he wasn't going to ask me to marry him at present, because he had some childish idea—it is perfectly *idiotic* to think of; but—he thought he wasn't quite—well, *good* enough for me!"

"What rot!" said Dicky.

"Muck!" observed Gerald.

"But he said that he would ask me properly later on, as soon as he considered that he was good enough," continued Dolly. "And as he still seems to think," she concluded with more animation, "that he is not quite up to standard, it occurred to me to-night, as we were all here in a jolly little party, to notify him that he is. So I did. That's all. Robin, you are hurting my hand!"

Robin relaxed his grip at last, and remorsefully surveyed the bloodless fingers that lay in his palm. Then, with a rather shamefaced look all round the table, as much as to say—"I should like fine to restrain myself from doing this before you all, but I *can't*!"—he bent his head and kissed them in his turn.

And that was how Robin and Dolly plighted their troth at last—openly, without shame, and for all to see.

Robin and I lingered at the turning of a passage, lit only by our two flickering bedroom candles.

"Well, we can't complain of having had an uneventful day," I said.

"I'm sorry we didn't scrape other twenty-eight votes," said Robin characteristically.

"Never mind!" I said. "I shall be none the worse of a holiday for a year or two. If you will kindly take Dolly off our hands as quickly as possible"—he caught his breath at that—"Kitty and I and Phillis will go a trip round the world together. Then I'll come home and fight a by-election, perhaps."

"Meanwhile," said Robin, "you will be having no further need of a private secretary."

"I'm afraid not," I said. The fact had been tugging at my conscience for the last two hours. "And that raises another question. What are you two going to live on?"

"Champion wants me," said Robin. "He has offered me the post of Secretary to that Royal Commission of which he has been appointed Chairman. It is a fine opening."

"I should think it was!" I said with whole-hearted joy. "Good luck to you, Robin!"

"Thank you!" said Robin. "Still," he added, as he turned to go, "I wish I could have found you twenty-eight more votes."

"Between ourselves," I said, "I don't mind very much. I am not the right man for this constituency. It has outgrown me. I have not the knack of handling a big crowd. What I want is a fine old crusted unprogressive seat, where I shan't constantly be compelled to drop my departmental work and rush down to propitiate my supporters with untruthful harangues. I'm a square peg here. Now, if they had wanted a really fit and proper candidate for this Parliamentary Division, Robin, they ought to have approached *you*."

"Och!" said Robin carelessly, "they did—a month ago! Good night!"

CHAPTER EIGHTEEN.
A PROPHET IN HIS OWN COUNTRY.

An old woman in a white mutch stands at the door of a farmhouse in a Scottish glen. Her face is wrinkled, and her dim eyes are peering down the track which leads from the steading to the pasture. Being apparently unable to focus what she wants to see she adjusts a pair of spectacles.

This action brings into her range of vision a distant figure which is engaged in shepherding a herd of passive but resisting cows through a gap in the dyke. It is a slow business, but the procession gradually nears home; and when the man at the helm succeeds in steering his sauntering charges safely between the Scylla of a hay-rick and the Charybdis of the burn, the old lady takes off her spectacles and relaxes her vigilance.

When she looks again, though, she breaks into an exclamation of dismay. The leaders of the straggling procession have safely reached the door of the byre close by; but one frisky young cow, suddenly swerving through an open gate, breaks away down a sloping field of turnips at a lumbering gallop. The herdsman is out of sight round a bend in the road.

"The feckless body!" observes the old lady bitterly. Then she raises her voice.

"Elspeth!"

A reply comes from within the dairy.

"Ay, mem?"

"You'll need tae leave the butter and help Master Robert. He's no hand with the kye. He's let Heatherbell intill the neeps. And the maister is away at——"

With a muffled "Maircy me!" a heated young woman shoots out of a side door and proceeds at the double to the assistance of the incompetent cow-herd.

At length the animals are rounded up into the byre, and Elspeth proceeds with the milking.

Meanwhile Master Robert, "the feckless body," stands in a rather apprehensive attitude before the old lady. He is a huge man of about forty-five. He is clean-shaven, and he has humorous grey eyes and dark hair. Despite his homespun attire, he looks more like a leader of men than a driver of cattle.

"Robin Fordyce," says the old lady severely, "what garred ye loose Heatherbell in among the neeps.

"I'm sorry, mother. But I met Jean M'Taggart in the road, and—we stopped for a bit crack."

The old lady surveys her son witheringly over her glasses.

"Dandering wi' Jean M'Taggart at your time of life! I'll sort Jean M'Taggart when I see her. It's jist like her tae try and draw a lad from his duty. And you! A married man these fifteen years! 'Deed, and it's time yon lady wife of yours cam' here from London, tae pit a hand on you."

The big man's penitent face lights up with sudden enthusiasm.

"She is coming to-morrow!" he roars exultantly.

"Aye, you may pretend tae be glad! But she shall hear aboot Jean M'Taggart all the same," replies the old lady.

This, of course, is a tremendous joke, and the inquisition is suspended while mother and son chuckle deeply at the idea of Dolly's desperate jealousy. Suddenly Mrs Fordyce breaks off to ask a question.

"Did ye mind tae shut the gate of the west field?"

Robin thinks, and then raises clenched hands to heaven in an agony of remorse.

His mother groans in a resigned sort of way.

"Run!" she says, "or ye'll hae all the sheep oot in the road! Get them back, and I'll no' tell David on ye!"

Her son bounds away down the slope, but a further command pursues him.

"An' come back soon! I'll no' be getting you tae myself over much after—to-morrow!"

She sits down again in her chair outside the door in the afternoon sun; for she is getting infirm now, and cannot stand up for long. With an indulgent sigh she surveys the flying figure of the Right Honourable Sir Robert Chalmers Fordyce, Privy Councillor and Secretary of State, as he frantically endeavours to overtake and head off three staid ewes, who, having strayed through the open gate, have just decided upon a walking excursion to London.

"A good lad!" she murmurs contentedly. "A good lad, and a good son; and dae'n' weel. But—he's no' just David. It was always David that had the heid on him."

A prophet, we know, has no honour in his own country. Fortunately some prophets prefer that this should be the case.

Getting Together

CHAPTER ONE

For several months it has been the pleasant duty of the writer of the following deliverance to travel around the United States, lecturing upon sundry War topics to indulgent American audiences. No one—least of all a parochial Briton—can engage upon such an enterprise for long without beginning to realize and admire the average American's amazing instinct for public affairs, and the quickness and vitality with which he fastens on and investigates every topic of live interest.

Naturally, the overshadowing subject of discussion to-day is the War, and all the appurtenances thereof. The opening question is always the same. It lies about your path by day in the form of a newspaper man, or about your bed by night in the form of telephone call, and is simply:

"When is the War going to end?"

(One is glad to note that no one ever asks *how* it is going to end: that seems to be settled.)

The simplest way of answering this question is to inform your inquisitor that so far as Great Britain is concerned the War has only just begun—began, in fact, on the first of July, 1916; when the British Army, equipped at last, after stupendous exertions, for a grand and prolonged offensive, went over the parapet, shoulder to shoulder with the soldiers of France, and captured the hitherto impregnable chain of fortresses which crowned the ridge overlooking the Somme Valley, with results now set down in the pages of history.

Having weathered this conversational opening, the stranger from Britain finds himself, as the days of his sojourn increase in number, swept gently but irresistibly into an ocean of talk—an ocean complicated by eddies, cross-currents, and sudden shoals—upon the subject of Anglo-American relations over the War. Here is the substance of some of the questions which confront the perplexed wayfarer:—

1. "Do your people at home appreciate the fact that we are thoroughly pro-Ally over here?"
2. "How about that Blockade? What are you opening our mails for—eh?"
3. "Would you welcome American intervention?"
4. "What do you propose to do about the submarine menace?"
5. "You don't *really* think we are too proud to fight, do you?"
6. "Are you in favour of National Training for Americans?"
7. "Do you expect to win outright, or are both sides going to fight themselves to a standstill?"

And

8. "Why can't you Britishers be a bit kinder in your attitude to us?"

CHAPTER TWO

Let us take this welter of interrogation categorically, and endeavour to frame such answers as would occur to the average Briton to-day.

But first of all, let it be remembered that the average Briton of to-day is not the average Briton of yesterday. Three years ago he was a prosperous, comfortable, thoroughly insular Philistine. He took a proprietary interest in the British Empire, and paid a munificent salary to the Army and Navy for looking after it. There his Imperial responsibilities ceased. As for other nations, he recognized their existence; but that was all. In their daily life, or national ideals, or habit of mind, he took not the slightest interest, and said so, especially to foreigners.

"I'm English," he would explain, with a certain proud humility. "That's good enough for yours truly!"

This sort of thing rather perplexed the American people, who take a keen and intelligent interest in the affairs of other nations.

But to-day the average Briton would not speak like that. He will never speak like that again. He has been outside his own island: he has made a number of new acquaintances. He has been fighting alongside of the French, and has made the discovery that they do not subsist entirely upon frogs. He has encountered real Germans, at sufficiently close quarters to realize that the "German Menace" at which his party leaders encouraged him to scoff in a bygone age was no such phantom after all. Altogether he is a very different person from the complacent, parochial exponent of the tight-little-island theories of yester-year. He has encountered things at home and abroad which have purged his very soul. Abroad, he has seen the whole of Belgium and some of the fairest provinces of France subjected to the grossest and most bestial barbarity. At home, he has seen inoffensive watering places bombarded by pirate craft which came up out of the sea like malignant wraiths and then fled away like panic-stricken window-smashers. He has seen Zeppelins hovering over close-packed working-class districts in industrial towns, raining indiscriminate destruction upon men, women, and children. In fact, he has seen things and suffered things that he never even dreamed of, and they have broadened his mind considerably.

Last year, under stress of these circumstances, the average Briton relinquished his age-long propensity to "let George do it," and evolved a sudden and rather inspiring sense of personal responsibility for the safety and welfare of his country. He no longer limited his patriotism to the roaring of truculent choruses at music-halls, or the decorating of his bicycle with the flags of the Allies. He went and enlisted instead. Now he has faced Death in person—and outfaced him. He has ceased to attach an exaggerated value to his own life. Life, he realizes, like Peace, is only worth retaining on certain terms, the first of which is Honour, and the second Honour, and the third Honour.

Finally, he regards the present War as a Holy War—a Crusade, in fact. He went into it with no ulterior motives: his sole impulse was to stand by his friends, France and Belgium, in the face of the monstrous outrage that was being forced upon them. He is out, in fact, to save civilization and human decency. Consequently he finds it just a little difficult to understand how a warm-hearted and high-spirited nation can be expected to remain "neutral even in thought."

With this much introduction to the man and his point of view, we will allow him to speak for himself.

CHAPTER THREE

"Do I realize that you are pro-Ally over here? Well, somehow I have always felt it, but now I know it. When I get home I shall rub that fact into everyone I meet. What our people at home don't grasp is the fact that America is inhabited by two distinct races—Americans, and others. The others appear to me—mind you, I'm only giving you a personal impression—to consist either of alien immigrants who have not yet absorbed their new nationality, or professional anti-Ally propagandists, or people of mixed nationality with strong commercial interests in Germany, whose heart is where their treasure is. These make a surprising amount of noise, and attract a disproportionate amount of attention: but I know, and I intend the people at home to know, that the genuine American is with us in this business heart and soul.

"What's that? The Blockade? Yes, I want to talk to you about that. I take it you will admit that a blockade is a justifiable expedient of war. There have been one or two of them in history. In the American Civil War, for instance, the North established a pretty successful blockade against the Southern ports. British cotton ships were everlastingly trying to run through that cordon. In fact, I rather think we exchanged a few cousinly notes on the subject. Of course blockades are irksome and irritating to neutrals. But we look to you here to endure the inconvenience, not merely as one of the chances of war, but rather to show us that you in this country do recognize and indorse the ideal for which we are fighting. We *are* fighting for an ideal, you know: I think the way the old country came into this war, all unprepared and spontaneously, just because she felt she *must* stand by her friends, was the finest thing she has ever done. Of course no sane person expected America to saddle herself gratuitously with a European War—without good and sufficient reason, that is—but we in England would like to feel that your acquiescence in the inconveniences caused by our blockade is your contribution to the cause—your slap on the back, signifying:—Go in and win!

"Open your mails? Yes, I'm afraid we do. And we find a good lot inside them! Do you know, there is a great warehouse in London filled from top to bottom with rubber, and nickel, and other commodities for which the Hun longs, disguised as all sorts of things—rubber fruit, for instance—taken from the most innocent-looking parcels—all dispatched from the United States to neutral countries in touch with Germany? But we are most punctilious about it all. Every single article retains its original address-label, and will be forwarded direct to its proper consignee, directly the war is over. Can you beat that?

"Would we welcome Intervention? My dear sir, is it likely? Supposing *you* had been caught entirely unprepared, and had been sticking your toes in for two years—fighting for time and playing a poor hand pretty well—and were at last ready to hit back, and hit back, until you had rendered your opponent incapable of further outrage, and were in a fair way to fix this war so that it never could happen again— would you welcome Mediation, or offers of Mediation? I think not.

"Submarines? We aren't attaching *too* much importance to submarine frightfulness. It is true we have lost a number of merchant ships, and that a number of innocent lives have been sacrificed. But let us put our hearts in the background for the present and look at the matter from the economic and military point of view. We have lost, in twenty-seven months, about one tenth of our original merchant fleet. Against that you have to set the fact that we have been steadily building new merchant ships during the same period. The dead loss of merchandise involved amounts to about one half per cent. of the total value—ten shillings in every hundred pounds; or fifty cents per hundred dollars. That won't starve us into submission.

"But the Germans will build more and more submarines? Very probably. Still, I think we can leave it to the British and French navies to prevent undue exuberance in that direction. Our sailors have not been exactly garrulous during this war, but I think we may take it that they have not been entirely idle. Has it ever occurred to you that although there are hundreds of Allied warships patrolling the ocean to-day, you hardly ever hear of one being torpedoed by a submarine? Passenger ships and freight ships suffer to the extent I have quoted, but not the warships. Why is that? Don't ask me: ask Jellicoe! But it rather looks as if the submarine, as an instrument of naval warfare—as opposed to a baby-killing machine—had rather failed to deliver the goods.

"The Deutschland? I take off my hat to Captain Koenig: he is a plucky fellow. The *U 53*? I have no remarks to offer, except to repeat my previous reference to baby-killing machines. As for the presence of these two vessels in American waters—in American ports—I won't presume to offer an opinion. Still, not long ago the U 53 sank six British or neutral vessels off the American coast, just outside territorial waters. Fortunately for the passengers, an American cruiser was in the neighbourhood, to guard against violation of American waters, and picked them up. But the whole incident looks to me like a deliberate German plan to jockey an American cruiser into becoming a German submarine tender.

"Let me see—what else? Too proud to fight? Not much! We know the American people too well. Besides, we suffer from politicians ourselves, and know what political catch-phrases are. So don't let that worry you.

"National Training for America? There I am neither qualified nor entitled to offer advice. I know the difficulties with which the true American has to contend in this matter. I know that this vast country of yours is more of a continent than a country, and that so long as your enormous tide of immigration continues, it will be a matter of immense difficulty developing a national sense of personal responsibility. I also know that your Middle West is inhabited by people, many of whom have never even seen the sea, who are rendered incapable, by their very environment, of realizing the immensity of the external dangers which threaten their country. These must see things differently from the more exposed section of the community, and I see how dangerous it would be to enforce upon them a measure which they regard as ridiculous. But on this great subject of Preparedness, I can refer you to the case of my own country—not as an example, but as a warning. *We* were caught unprepared. In consequence, we had to sacrifice our best, our very best, the kind that can never be replaced in any country, just because they hurried to the rescue and allowed themselves to be wiped out, while the country behind them was being aroused and prepared. That is the price that we have paid, and no ultimate victory, however glorious, can recompense us for that criminal waste of the flower and pride of our youth and manhood at the outset.

"Do we expect to win the war outright? Yes, we do."

It is true that the Central Powers have recently succeeded in devastating another little country, though they have not destroyed its army. On the other hand, during the past few months the Allied gains on the Somme have included, among other items, a chain of fortresses hitherto considered impregnable, four or five hundred pieces of artillery, fourteen hundred machine-guns, and about ninety-five thousand unwounded German prisoners. Moreover, the French at Verdun have regained in a few weeks all the ground that the Crown Prince wrested from them, at the price of half a million German casualties, in the spring. German colonies have ceased to exist; German foreign trade is dead; the German navy is cooped up in Kiel harbour; and Germany is so short of men that she has resorted to outrageous deportations from Belgium in order to obtain industrial labour. On the other hand, our supply of munitions now, at the opening of 1917, is double what it was six months ago, and our new armies are not yet all in the field. The British Navy, despite all losses, has increased enormously both in tonnage and personnel. So I don't think we are fought to a standstill yet.

"Yes, you are right. All this bloodshed is dreadful. But responsibility for bloodshed rests not with the people who end a war but with the people who began it. As for discussing terms of peace now, what terms *could* be arranged which Germany could be relied upon to observe a moment longer than suited her? Have you forgotten the way the War was forced on the world by Prussian militarism? The trick played on Russia over mobilization? The violation of Belgian neutrality? Malines, Termonde, Louvain? The official raping in the market-place at Liége? The *Lusitania*? Edith Cavell? The Zeppelin murders? Chlorine gas? The deportations from Belgium and Lille? Wittenburg typhus camp, where men were left to rot, without doctors, or medicine, or bedding? How can one talk of "honourable peace" with such a gang of criminal lunatics? Ask yourself who would be such a fool as to propose to end a war upon terms which left the safety of the world exposed to the prospect of another outbreak from the same source?

"You, sir? *Why can't you people in England be a bit kinder in their tone to us here in America?* Ah, now you are talking! Let us get away from this crowd and go into the matter—get together, as you say."

CHAPTER FOUR

So the average Briton and the average American retire to a secluded spot, and "get together." The American repeats his question:

"Why can't your people over there be a bit kinder? Why can't you consider our feelings a bit more? You haven't been over and above polite to us of late—or indeed at any time."

"No," admits the Briton thoughtfully, "I suppose we have not. Politeness is not exactly our strong suit. In my country we are not even polite to one another!" (Try as he will, he cannot help saying this with just the least air of pride and satisfaction.) "But I admit that that is no reason why we should be impolite to other nations. The fact is, being almost impervious to criticism ourselves, we naturally find it difficult to avoid wounding the feelings of a people which is particularly sensitive in that respect."

"Very well," replies the American. "Now, we want to put this right, don't we?"

"We do," replies the other, with quite un-British enthusiasm. "No one who has spent any time as a visitor to this country could help——"

"Why then, tell me," interpolates the other, "what is at the back of your country's present resentful attitude toward America?"

The Briton ponders.

"Didn't someone once say," he replies at last, "that 'he that is not for us is against us?' That seems to sum up the situation. We on our side are engaged in a life-and-death struggle for the freedom of the world. We know that you are not against us; still, considering the sacredness of our cause, and the monstrous means by which the Boche is seeking to further his, we feel that you have not stood for us so out and out as you might. Only the other day your Government announced that in their opinion it was time that both sides stated plainly what they were fighting for! Now——"

The other checks him.

"Don't you go mixing up the officially neutral American Government," he says, "with the American people, or the American people with the inhabitants of America. In many districts of America, the balance of power lies with people who have only recently entered the country, and who have not yet become absorbed into the American people. As for our present Government, it was put into power mainly by the people of the West—people to whom the War has not come home in any way—and the Government, having to consider the wishes of the majority, naturally carries out the instructions on its ticket. That is how I, as an average American, sense the situation. However, that is not the point. Listen!

"You say that America has not helped you very much? Let us consider the ways in which America *could* have helped. Military aid? Well, of course that is out of the question so long as we remain neutral, as we agreed just now we certainly ought to remain. Still, there are more than twenty-five thousand American citizens serving in the Allied Armies to-day. Did you realize that?"

"I did not," says the Briton, interested.

"Well, it is true. There are battalions in the Canadian Army composed almost entirely of men from the United States. Others are serving in the French and British Armies. Then there is the American Flying Corps in France."

"Yes, I have heard of them. Who has not? Proceed!"

"Industrial help, again. We are making munitions for you, night and day. It is true that we are being paid for our trouble; but the cost of living has risen almost as much here as in your own country. Also let me tell you that we are making no munitions for Germany, and would not do so, money or no. The same with financial help. Loan after loan has been floated in this country for the Allied benefit. How many loans have been raised for Germany? Not one! That is not because German credit is so bad, but because no true American will consent to lend his money to such a cause. Believe me, the attempt has been made, and strong influence brought to bear, more than once, but the result has been failure every time.

"Red Cross Work, again. There are hundreds of Americans driving ambulances in the Allied lines to-day, and hundreds of American women working in Allied hospitals. There are complete hospital units over there, equipped and maintained by American money and American service. Have you ever heard of the Harvard Unit, for instance?"

"Vaguely. Tell me about it."

"Well, I mention the Harvard Unit because it was about the first; but others are doing nobly too. Let Harvard serve as a sample. At the outbreak of the War, Harvard put down ten thousand dollars to equip and staff the American Ambulance Hospital in Paris. Then, in June, 1915, Harvard took over one of your British Base Hospitals, with thirty-two surgeons and seventy-five nurses. That hospital has been maintained by Harvard folk ever since; they go out and serve for three months at a time. Harvard also sent an expedition to fight typhus in Serbia. Harvard's casualty list, in consequence, has grown pretty long. Not a bad record for one neutral University, eh? I don't seem to remember your Oxford or Cambridge sending out a medical unit to help us, when we were fighting for a moral issue too, away back in the 'sixties under Lincoln."

"I knew nothing of all this. People at home must be told," says the Briton, earnestly.

"Or," continues the American, we can take the work of the American Ambulance Field service. The American Ambulance Field Service with the Armies of France has carried over seven hundred thousand wounded since the beginning of the war; their sections and section leaders have been sixteen times cited for valuable and efficient work; fifty-four of their men have been given the Croix de Guerre for bravery, and two the Médaille Militaire. Three have been killed. The Society has at present over two hundred ambulances at the front, besides staff and other cars attached to different sections. This Service, which, at the beginning of the war, was a subsidiary part of the American Ambulance Hospital at Neuilly has for the past year been self-supporting, and although still co-operative with the Hospital, has its own administration and headquarters, and its own maintenance fund. If you require any further information on the subject, read 'Friends of France,'[1] or 'Ambulance No. 10,'[2] both of which books will stir you not a little.

"Talking of books, if you want to read a genuine American's opinion of the Allies and their cause, read 'Their Spirit,'[3] by Judge Robert Grant. And if you want to know what another prominent American, who formerly admired and revered Germany, thinks of Germany now, read Owen Wister's 'Pentecost of

Calamity.'[4] Or, if you want a complete exposure of German aims and methods in this war, read James M. Beck's 'The Evidence in the Case'.[5]

"Now a word concerning War Relief Societies in general. (There's more to hear than you thought, isn't there?) I cannot possibly give you details about them all, because their name is legion. For instance, this printed list contains the names of a hundred and ten such societies; and there are others. As you see, it covers Armenian, Belgian, British, French, Italian, Lithuanian, Persian, Polish, and Russian Relief enterprises of every kind. German Relief Societies? Yes, throughout the United States there are eleven German and Austrian Societies altogether; but they are all under purely Teutonic management, as a glance at the names of their supporters will show. America, as such, stands aloof from them.

"Let us have a look at the purely British Relief Societies, which naturally will interest you most. There is The American Women's War Hospital at Paignton, Devonshire, directed by Lady Paget, herself an American, and supported by American contributions. It is a far cry from America to Australia, but there is an Australian War Relief Fund in America. Then take the British War Relief Association of America. This Association occupies an entire floor in a lofty building on the busiest stretch of Fifth Avenue. All day and every day they work away, cutting surgical dressings at the rate of nine thousand yards a week. They also collect and despatch comforts of every kind, from motor ambulances to antiseptic pads. The rent of their premises is eight thousand dollars a year; but they get the whole place free. Their landlord, an American citizen, has given them that floor for the duration of the war, as his contribution to the fund. Isn't that pretty fine? Again, there is an American branch of your own Prince of Wales' fund. There is a United States Guild for British Soldiers' Comforts; there is an Indian Soldiers' Fund Committee, and many others. These, as you see, are purely pro-British organizations, but naturally your country also benefits under all general schemes of Allied Relief. Last summer, for instance a great bazaar was held in New York in aid of Allied War Charities, and over half a million dollars were cleared. Another bazaar, held more recently in Boston, raised over four hundred thousand dollars. Another, in Chicago, was equally successful. And so the tale goes on. France and Belgium, of course, receive the lion's share of American sympathy, as being invaded countries, but I have told you enough to show what we are trying to do for Great Britain too. We are somewhat handicapped, however, by the fact, firstly, that Great Britain is not exactly what one would call a gracious receiver of benefits, and secondly, that the man in the street over here regards your country as too fabulously rich to require relief of any kind. But after all, it is the spirit of good will which counts, and you have all ours.

"Well, the list which I have shown you will give you some idea of the big forces which are working for you over on this side. But big forces are made up of little forces. As we say in this country, it is the little things that tell. All over America I could show you little sewing meetings and social gatherings which have got together for the purpose of preparing clothing and medical comforts for the Allies. Even in cities like Milwaukee and Cincinnati, which have the reputation of being overwhelmingly Teutonic, there exist very efficient and plucky Allied Relief Societies which are carrying on in the face of open hostility. There is hardly a village or township that does not possess such a society. You have a song in England about 'Sister Susie Sewing Shirts for Soldiers.' Well, over here in the States, your cousin Susie is doing precisely the same thing. She is doing it so extensively that it has been found necessary to establish a great clearing house in New York to deal with the gifts as they come in, sort them out, and forward them to their destinations. The Clearing House also knows where to stretch out its hand for particular commodities. For instance, if there is a shortage of absorbent cotton, the Clearing House sends an appeal to Virginia for somemore, and Virginia sends it. Here is a copy of the monthly bulletin. They appear to have been busy. You notice that during one period of seven days last month, this Clearing House handled over a thousand cases of material a day.

"Yes, a clearing-house like this calls for some organization and labour. Who supply that? A number of American business men, each of whom has decided to run his business with his left hand for the present, leaving his right hand free for War Relief.

"Besides gifts in kind, these same organizations send gifts in money. Between seventy and eighty of the leading clubs in America have formulated a scheme under which members who feel so disposed may have five dollars or so debited to their monthly bill, to be devoted to Allied Relief work. During the last three months about eighty thousand dollars has been raised and distributed by the Clearing House from this source.

"Our Relief work is both collective and individual. At one end of the scale you find a scheme for raising a hundred million dollars to maintain and educate Belgian and French orphans. At the other, I could show you a poor woman in Boston who is living on a mere pittance, because she gives every cent that she can possibly spare to Allied Relief. I know many American business men who cross the Atlantic several times a year: on these occasions they seldom fail to take with them, as part of their personal baggage, a trunk stuffed with surgical dressings, rare drugs, and the like. Again, do you know who presented to your nation St. Dunstan's, the great institution for blinded soldiers in Regent's Park, London? An American citizen. So you see, here we are, the American people, the greatest race of advertisers in the world, doing all this good work, and saying nothing whatever about it. Doesn't that strike you as significant?"

"It strikes me as magnificent," says the Briton.

"Well," rejoins the other, I don't allow that it is magnificent, but it is pretty good. We might do more—ten times more. For instance, all our contributions to Belgian relief don't amount to more than the merest fraction of what France and Great Britain, in the midst of all the agony and impoverishment of their own people, have contrived to give. Still, I think I have said enough to show you that we are doing something. You'll tell the folks at home, won't you? It hurts us badly to be regarded as cold blooded opportunists."

"Trust me; I'll tell them!" says the Briton warmly.

And the Get-Together ends.

FOOTNOTES:

[1] Friends of France: The Field Service of the American Ambulance described by its members. (Houghton Mifflin Co., $2.00. Limited Edition, $10.00)

[2] Ambulance No. 10. By A. Buswell. (Houghton Mifflin Co., $1.00)

[3] Their Spirit: Some impressions of the English and French during the Summer of 1916. By Robert Grant. (Houghton Muffin Co., 50c.)

[4] Pentecost of Calamity. By Owen Wister (Macmillan Co., 50c.)

[5] The Evidence in the Case. By James M. Beck. (Putnam, $1.00).

CHAPTER FIVE

The only fact of importance which fails to emerge with sufficient clearness from the foregoing conversation is the fact—possibly the courteous American suppressed it from motives of delicacy—that America is by comparison more pro-Ally than pro-British. The fact is, the American is on the side of right and justice in this War, and earnestly desires to see the Allied cause prevail; but he has a sub-conscious aversion to seeing slow-witted, self-satisfied John Bull collect yet another scalp. American relations with France, too, have always been of the most cordial nature; while America's very existence as a separate nation to-day is the fruit of a quarrel with England.

In this regard it may be noted that American school history books are accustomed to paint the England of 1776 in unnecessarily lurid colours. The young Republic is depicted emerging, after a heroic struggle, from the clutches of a tyranny such as that wielded by the nobility of France in the pre-Revolution days. In sober fact, the secession of the American Colonies was brought about by a series of colossal blunders and impositions on the part of the most muddle-headed ministry that ever mismanaged the affairs of Great Britain—which is saying a good deal. It is probable that if the elder Pitt had lived a few years longer, the secession would never have occurred. It was only with the utmost reluctance that Washington appealed to a decision by battle. In any case the fact remains, that while in an American school-book the war of 1776 is given first place, correctly enough, as marking the establishment of American nationality, it figures in the English school-book, with equal correctness, as a single regrettable incident in England's long and variegated Colonial history. It is well to bear these two points of view in mind. Naturally all this makes for degrees of comparison in America's attitude toward the Allies. One might extend the comparison to Russia, and more especially to Japan; but that, mercifully, is outside the scope of our present inquiry.

To America, friendship with France is an historic tradition, as the Statue of Liberty attests, and rests upon the solid foundation of a common ideal—Republicanism. The tie between America and Great Britain is the tie of a common (but rapidly diminishing) blood-relationship; and, as every large family knows, blood-relationship carries with it the right to speak one's mind with refreshing freedom whenever differences of opinion arise within the family circle. But our idealists have persistently overlooked this handicap. They cling tenaciously to the notion that it is easier to be friendly with your relations than with your friends; and that in dealing with your own kin, tact may be economized. "Blood is thicker than water," we proclaim to one another across the sea; "and we can therefore afford to be as rude to one another as we please." This principle suits the Briton admirably, because he belongs to the elder and more thick-skinned branch of the clan. But it bears hardly upon a young, self-conscious, and adolescent nation, which has not yet "found" itself as a whole; and which, though its native genius and genuine promise carry it far, still experiences a certain youthfuldiffidence under the supercilious condescension of the Old World.

Our mutual relations are further complicated by the possession of a common language.

In theory, a common tongue should be a bond of union between nations—a channel for the interchange of great thoughts and friendly sentiments. In practice, what is it?

Let us take a concrete example. Supposing an American woman and a Dutch woman live next door to one another in a New York suburb. As a rule they maintain friendly relations; but if at any time these relations become strained—say, over the encroachments of depredatory chickens, or the obstruction of someone's ancient lights by the over-exuberance of some one else's laundry—the two ladies are enabled to say the most dreadful things to one another without any one being a penny the worse. *They do not understand one another's language.* But if they speak a common tongue, the words which pass when the most ephemeral squabble arises stick and rankle.

Again, for many years the people of Great Britain were extremely critical of Russia. Well-meaning stay-at-home gentlemen constantly rose to their feet in the House of Commons and made withering remarks on the subject of knouts, and Cossacks, and vodka. But they did no harm. The Russian people do not understand English. In the same way, Russians were probably accustomed to utter equally reliable criticisms of the home-life of Great Britain—land-grabbing, and hypocrisy, and whiskey, and so on. But we knew nothing of all this, and all was well. There was not the slightest difficulty, when the great world-crash came, in forming the warmest alliance with Russia.

But as between the two great English-speaking nations of the world, it is in the power of the most foolish politician or the most irresponsible sub-editor, on either side of the Atlantic, to create an international complication with a single spoken phrase or stroke of the pen. And as both countries appear to be inhabited very largely by persons who regard newspapers as Bibles and foolish politicians as inspired prophets, it seems advisable to take steps to regulate the matter.

This brings us to another matter—the attitude of the American Press toward the War. A certain section thereof, which need not be particularized further, has never ceased, probably under the combined influences of bias and subsidy, to abuse the Allies, particularly the British, and misrepresent their motives and ideals. This sort of journalism "cuts no ice" in the United States. It is just "yellow journalism." *Voilà tout!* Why take it seriously? But the British people do not know this; and as the British half-penny Press, when it does quote the American Press, rarely quotes anything but the most virulent extracts from this particular class of newspaper, one is reduced yet again to wondering whence the blessings of a common language are to be derived.

But taking them all round, the newspapers of America have handled the questions of the War with conspicuous fairness and ability. They are all fundamentally pro-Ally; and the only criticism which can be directed at them from an Allied quarter is that in their anxiety to give both sides a hearing, they have been a little too indulgent to Germany's claims to moral consideration, and have been a little over-inclined to accept the German Chancellor's pious manifestoes at their face value. But generally speaking it may be said that the greater the newspaper, the firmer the stand that it has taken for the Allied cause. The New York *Times*, the weightiest and most authoritative newspaper in America, has been both pro-Ally and pro-British throughout the War, and has never shrunk from the delicate task of interpreting satisfactorily to the British people the attitude of the President.

Journalistic criticism of Great Britain in America is frequently extremely candid, and not altogether unmerited. Occasionally it goes too far; but the occasion usually arises from ignorance of the situation, or the desire to score an epigrammatic point. For instance, during the struggle for Verdun in the spring, a New York newspaper, sufficiently well-conducted to have known better, published a cartoon representing John

Bull as standing aloof, but encouraging the French to persevere in their efforts by parodying Nelson's phrase:—"England expects that every Frenchman will do his duty." The truth of course was that Sir Douglas Haig had offered General Joffre all the British help that might be required. The offer was accepted to this extent, that the British took over forty additional miles of trenches from the French, thus setting free many divisions of French soldiers to participate in a glorious and purely French victory.

But this sort of foolish calumny dies hard, together with such phrases as:—"England is prepared to hold on, to the last Frenchman!" While not strictly relevant to our present discussion, the following figures may be of interest. In August 1914 the British Regular Army consisted of about a hundred and fifty thousand men. To-day, British troops in France number two million; in Salonica, a hundred and forty thousand; in Egypt, a hundred and eighty thousand; in Mesopotamia, a hundred and twenty thousand. The Navy absorbs another four hundred thousand, while a full million are occupied in purely naval construction and repair. And at home again enormous masses of new troops are undergoing training. This seems to dispose of the suggestion that Great Britain is winning the War by proxy.

And for the upkeep of this mighty host, and for this general comforting of the Allies, the British taxpayer is now paying cheerfully and willingly, in addition to such trifling impositions as a 60 per cent tax on his commercial profits, income tax at the rate of twenty-five cents in the dollar.

On the other side of the account, *Life*, the American equivalent of *Punch*, (if it is possible for the humour of a particular nation to find its equivalent in any other nation), published not long ago a special "John Bull" number, which will for ever remain a monument of journalistic generosity and international courtesy. *Life's* good deed was gracefully acknowledged by *Punch* and *The Spectator*.

But in spite of *Life's* good example, enough has been said under this head to illuminate the fact that a common language is a doubtful blessing. The joint possession of the tongue that Shakespeare and Milton and Longfellow and Abraham Lincoln spoke has bestowed little upon our two nations but a convenient medium, too often, for shrewish altercation, coupled with the profound conviction of either side that the other side is unable to speak correct English.

Well, this nonsense must stop.

CHAPTER SIX

Therefore, whenever a true American and a true Briton get together, let them hold an international symposium of their own. If it were not for the unfortunate interposition of the Atlantic Ocean, this interview would be extended, with proportional profit, to the greatest symposium the world has ever seen. Meanwhile, we will make shift with a company of two.

The following counsel is respectfully offered to the participants in the debate.

Let the Briton remember:—

1. Remember you are talking to a *friend*.
2. Remember you are talking to a man who regards his nation as the greatest nation in the world. He will probably tell you this.
3. Remember you are talking to a man whose country has made an enormous contribution to your cause in men, material, and money, besides putting up with a good deal of inconvenience and irksome supervision at your hands. Remember, too, that your own country has made little or no acknowledgement of its indebtedness in this matter.
4. Remember you are talking to a man who believes in "publicity," and who believes further, that if you do not advertise the fact, you cannot possibly be in possession of "the goods." So for any sake open up a little, and tell him all you can about what the British Nation is doing to-day for Humanity and Civilization—in other words, for America.

5. Remember this man is not so impervious to criticism as you are. Don't over-criticize his apparent attitude to the War. Remember you are talking to a man whose patience under such outrages as the sinking of the *Lusitania* has been strained to the uttermost; so don't ask him whether he is too proud to fight, or he may offer you convincing proof to the contrary.

6. Remember you are talking to a man whose business has been considerably interfered with by the stringency of the Allied blockade. So don't invite him to wax enthusiastic over the vigilance of the British Navy or the promptness of the Censor in putting the mails through.

7. And do try to disabuse the man's mind of the preposterous, Germany-fostered notion that your country regards this war merely as a vehicle for commercial aggrandizement, or that the British Foreign Office proposes to maintain the Black List and other bugbears after the War. It seems absurd that you should have to give such an assurance, but doubts upon the subject certainly exist in certain quarters in America to-day.

Let the American remember:

1. Remember you are talking to a *friend*.

2. Remember you are talking to a man who regards his nation as the greatest in the world. He will not tell you this, because he takes it for granted that you know already.

3. Remember you are talking to a man who is a member of a traditionally reticent and unexpansive race; who says about one third of what he feels; who is obsessed by a mania for understating his country's case, exaggerating its weaknesses, and belittling its efforts; who is secretly shy, so covers up his shyness with a cloak of aggressiveness which is offensive to those who are not prepared for it. Remember that this attitude is not specially assumed for *you*: as often as not the man employs it toward his own wife, who rather enjoys it, because she regards it as a symptom of affection.

4. Remember you are talking to a man who is fighting for his life. To-day his face is turned toward Central Europe, and his back to the United States. Do not expect him to display an intimate or sympathetic understanding of America's true attitude to the War. He is conducting the War according to his lights, and is prepared to abide by the consequences of what he does. So he is apt to be resentful of criticism. Bear with him, for he is having a tough time of it.

5. Enemy propaganda to the contrary, remember that this man is not a hypocrite. He is occasionally stupid; he is at times obstinate; he is frequently high-handed; and often he would rather be misunderstood than explain. But he is neither tyrannical nor corrupt. He went into this War because he felt it his duty to do so, and not because he coveted any Teutonic vineyard.

6. Remember that your nation has done a great deal for this man's nation during the War. Tell him all about it: it will interest him, *because he did not know.*

CHAPTER SEVEN

Practically every one in this world improves on closer acquaintance. The people with whom we utterly fail to agree are those with whom we never get into close touch.

Individual Americans and Britons, when they get together in one country or the other, usually develope a genuine mutual liking. As nations, however, their attitude to one another is too often a distant attitude—a distance of some three thousand miles, or the exact width of the Atlantic Ocean—and ranges from a lofty tolerance in good times to unreserved bickering in bad. Why? Because they are geographically too far apart. But with the shrinkage of the earth's surface produced by the effects of electricity and steam, that geographical abyss yawns much less widely than it did. So let us get together, whether in couples or in millions. The thing has to be done. No rearrangement of the world's affairs after the War can be either just or equitable or permanent which does not find Great Britain and the United States of America upon the same side. What we want is common ground, and a sound basis of understanding. Our present basis—the

"Hands-across-the-Sea, Blood-is-thicker-than-Water" basis—is sloppy and unstable. Besides, it profoundly irritates that not inconsiderable section of the American people which does not happen to be of British descent.

We can find a better basis than that. What shall it be? Well, we have certain common ideals which rest upon no sentimental foundations, but upon the bedrock of truth and justice. We both believe in God; in personal liberty; in a Law which shall be inflexibly just to rich and poor alike. We both hate tyranny and oppression and intrigue; and we both love things which are clean, and wholesome, and of good report. Let us take one common stand upon these.

We must take certain precautions. We must bear andforbear. We must forget a good deal that is past. We must make allowances for point of view and differences of temperament. And we must mutually and heroically refrain from utilizing the unrivalled opportunities for repartee and pettiness afforded by the possession of a common tongue.

Of course, we must not expect or attempt to work together in unison. National differences of character and standpoint forbid. And no bad thing either. Unison is a cramping and irksome business. Let us work in harmony instead, which is far better. And so—to paraphrase the deathless words of the greatest of Americans:—With charity toward all, with malice toward none, with mutual understanding and confidence, we shall go forward together, to bind up the wounds of the world, and prevent for all time a repetition of the outrage which inflicted them.

Printed in Great Britain
by Amazon